Towards a European Civil Code

Third Fully Revised and Expanded Edition

Towards a European Civil Code

Third Fully Revised and Expanded Edition

EDITORS

Arthur Hartkamp
Martijn Hesselink
Ewoud Hondius
Carla Joustra
Edgar du Perron
Muriel Veldman

AUTHORS

Ewoud Hondius - Reinhard Zimmermann - Klaus Peter Berger
Richard Hyland - Peter-Christian Müller-Graff - Walter van Gerven
Arthur Hartkamp - Konstantinos D. Kerameus - Christian Joerges
Horatia Muir Watt - Vincenzo Zeno-Zencovich - Noah Vardi
James Gordley - Christina Ramberg - Pierre Legrand
Brigitta Lurger - Ugo Mattei - Dieter Martiny
Alain Verbeke - Yves-Henri Leleu - Rodolfo Sacco - Sjef van Erp
Michael Joachim Bonell - Muriel Fabre-Magnan - Ruth Sefton-Green
Hector MacQueen - Thomas Wilhelmsson - Claus-Wilhelm Canaris
Hans Christoph Grigoleit - Martijn W. Hesselink - Denis Tallon - Ole Lando
Michael Joachim Bonell - Viola Heutger - Christoph Jeloschek
Jürgen Basedow - Marco B.M. Loos - Eric Clive
David Howarth - Geraint Howells - Michael Faure
Gerrit Betlem - Mauro Bussani - Vernon Valentine Palmer - Ulrich Drobnig
Roy Goode - Hans G. Wehrens - Michel Grimaldi - François Barrière
Peter Hommelhoff - Christoph Teichmann - Carl-Heinz Witt

2004
Ars Aequi Libri – Nijmegen
Kluwer Law International

From the Preface to the First Edition

In 1989 the European Parliament called for the elaboration of a European civil code (*Official Journal of the European Communities* 1989, No. C 158/400). Although the European Commission has not yet shown much enthusiasm for this idea, many legal academics see it as a great challenge.

In September 1991 we decided to ask some distinguished European legal scholars to take up this challenge and write a chapter on the desirability and possible content of a European Civil Code. This book is the result of their enthusiastic efforts.

The book is divided into two parts. The first part examines the general issues which concern the unification of those areas of private law that we considered to be appropriate for a unification on a European level.

The Hague/Utrecht, April 1994

Arthur Hartkamp
Martijn Hesselink
Ewoud Hondius
Edgar du Perron
Jan Vranken

From the Preface to the Second Edition

When Towards a European Civil Code appeared in 1994, it was one of the first publications on European private law. After its publication a great number of major events took place. To mention only a few: both the UNIDROIT and the Lando Commission published their principles; Markesinis published a book on the gradual convergence of common law and civil law in Europe, Kötz published the first book on European Contract Law, and Von Bar did so on European Tort Law; the Trento Project on The Common Core of Private Law in Europe was commenced by Mattei and Bussani; and an international conference was held in The Hague under the very title Towards a European Civil Code. These events, and indeed many others, convinced us that the idea of a possible common code for Europe is not as bold as it might have seemed when we started preparations for the first edition of this book in 1991. European private law has become an established field of research in which many eminent scholars from all over Europe got involved. Courses on European private law are taught in several European universities.

All these events – and the commercial success of the first edition – called for a second edition. This second edition differs from the first in several respects. First, we have added several new subjects which have increased the number of chapters from 22 to 36. Secondly, we no longer asked the contributors to discuss the feasibility of a European common law – except for a few chapters which deal with completely new topics – but instead to directly address the possible content of common rules. Thirdly, we are glad to welcome some new authors for some of the subjects already included in the first edition. Finally, all the chapters have been updated.

Utrecht, April 1998

Arthur Hartkamp
Martijn Hesselink
Ewoud Hondius
Carla Joustra
Edgar du Perron

Preface to the Third Edition

Since its original publication ten years ago, *Towards a European Civil Code* has become an international classic. Important new developments such as the European Commission's 2003 *Action Plan* on European contract law called for a new edition. Moreover, we saw new grounds for further expanding the scope of this book.

This third, fully revised and expanded edition includes new contributions on such important matters as constitutionalisation; social concerns; economic analysis; e-commerce; and sales, service and insurance contracts. In addition, it now also contains a chapter with a forceful plea against a European Civil Code. All forty four chapters have been brought up to date with European and national developments. However, it should be pointed out here that unfortunately, as a result of the slow production process, some contributions today are no longer completely up to date.

All editors are fully responsible for this new edition. However, we would like to point out that Muriel Veldman has done the bulk of the work, and the others would like to thank her for her extraordinary dedication.

Finally, we would like to express our gratitude to Ms. Janneke de Klerk, Ms. Carolijn Kuipers and Rob Wouters for having assisted us in preparing this edition and for having prepared the Index.

Amsterdam, July 2004

Arthur S. Hartkamp
Martijn W. Hesselink
Ewoud H. Hondius
Carla A. Joustra
C. Edgar du Perron
Muriel Veldman

Contents

B - Contract law – General issues

C - Contract law – Specific contracts

D - Restitution

E - Tort

F - Property

G - Trust

H - Company law

Abbreviations

AC	The Law Reports (Appeal Cases, House of Lords)
AcP	Archiv für die civilistische Praxis
All ER	The All England Law Reports
AJCL	The American Journal of Comparative Law
AP	*Tribunal de Apelacíon* [Court of Appeal] (Spain)
App.	*Corte d'Appello* [Court of Appeal] (Italy)
Arm.	Armenopoulos miniaia nomiki epitheorisis
Art.	Article
A&V	Aansprakelijkheid en Verzekering
BAG	*Bundesarbeitsgericht* [Federal Labour Court] (Germany)
BAGS	*Entscheidungen des Bundesarbeitsgericht* [Decisions of the Federal Labour Court]
BB	Der Betriebs-Berater
BGB	*Bürgerliches Gesetzbuch* [Civil Code] (Germany)
BG	*Bundesgericht* [Supreme Court] (Switzerland)
BGE	*Entscheidungen des Schweizerischen Bundesgericht*
BGHZ	*Amtliche Sammlung der Entscheidungen des Bundesgerichtshofes in Zivilsachen* [Decisions of the German Federal Court in civil matters]
BolMinJust	*Boletim do Ministério da Justiça* [Bulletin of the Ministry of Justice] (Portugal)
Bull.civ.	*Bulletin des arrêts de la Cour de Cassation rendus en matière civile* [Bulletin of the decisions of the Court of Cassation in civil matters] (France)
CA	Court of Appeal
Cass.	*Cour de Cassation* (France, Belgium); *Corte di Cassazione*
Cass.ass.plen.	*Cour de cassation, Assemblée plénière* (France)
Cass.civ.	*Cour de cassation, Chambre civile* (France)
Cass. crim.	*Cour de cassation, Chambre criminelle* (France)
Cass. req.	*Cour de cassation, Chambre des requêtes* (abolished) (France)
Cass.sez.pen.	*Corte di Cassazione, sezione penale* (Italy)
CFI	Court of First Instance
CJ	Colectânea de Jurisprudência (Portugal)
CLJ	The Cambridge Law Journal
D.	Recueil de jurisprudence Dalloz
EllDik	Elliniki Dikeosini (Greece)
ER	The English Reports
ERPL	European Review of Private Law

Foro it.	Il Foro italiano: raccolta di giurisprudenza civile, commerciale, penale, amministrativa
Gaz. Pal.	Gazette du Palais
Giur. it.	Giurisprudenza italiana
Giust. civ. Mass.	Giustizia civile. Massimario annotato della cassazione
HD	Højesteretsdom (Denmark); Høyesterettsdom (Norway); Högsta domstolens domar (Sweden, Finland) [Judgment of the Supreme Court]
HL	House of Lords (England)
HR	*Hoge Raad* [Supreme Court] (Netherlands)
i.e.	id est (that is to say)
ICLQ	International and Comparative Law Quarterly
ILRM	Irish Law Reports Monthly
Int.Bus.Lawyer	International Business Lawyer
IR	The Irish Reports
IRLR.	Industrial Relations Law Reports
J.	Judge
JBl	Juristische Blätter
JCP	Juris-Classeur Périodique La semaine juridique
J. de Paix	*Justice de Paix* (Luxembourg); *Justice de Paix* [Vredegerecht] [Justice of the Peace] (Belgium)
JT	Journal des Tribunaux (Brussels)
Jurid.Rev.	The Juridical Review
Ius	Juristische Schulung
JZ	Juristenzeitung
KB	The Law Reports. King's Bench Division
KF	Karlsruher Forum, supplement to VersR
La Ley	Revista jurídica española de doctrina, jurisprudencia y bibliografía
LJ	Lord Justice
Lloyd's Rep.	Lloyd's Law Reports
LM	Lindenmaier-Möhring, Nachschlagwerk des Bundesgerichtshofs
L.Q.Rev.	Law Quarterly Review
MLR	Modern Law Review
MR	Master of the Rolls
M&W	Meeson and Welsby's Reports, Exchequer
n., n°	number
NJ	Nederlandse jurisprudentie
NJA	Nytt juridiskt arkiv
NJB	Nederlands Juristenblad
NJW	Neue Juristische Wochenschrift
NJW-RR	NJW-Rechtsprechungsreport
no(s).	number(s)
NoB	Nomiko Bima; miniaion nomikon periodikon
OLD	*Østre Landsrets Dom* [Judgments of the Eastern High Court] (Denmark)

OGH	*Oberster Gerichtshof* [Supreme Court] (Austria)
OLG	*Oberlandesgericht* [Court of Appeal]
p(p).	page(s)
paras.	paragraphs
Pas. belge	Pasicrisie belge
Pasin. belge	Pasinomie belge
Pas. luxemb.	Pasicrisie luxembourgeoise
QB	The Law Reports. Queen's Bench Division
RAJ	Repertorio Aranzadi de Jurisprudencia (Spain)
Rb.	*Arrondissementsrechtbank* [District Court] (Netherlands)
RC	*Relação* [Court of Appeal] de Coimbra (Portugal)
RDAI	Revue de droit des affaires international
Rep. gen.	Repertorio generate della Giurisprudenza italiana
Resp.civ. et assur.	Responsabilité civile et assurances
Rev.dr.int.dr.comp.	Revue de droit international et de droit comparé
Rev. int.dr.comp.	Revue internationale de droit comparé
Rev.jur.pol.Ind. Coop.	Revue juridique et politique, Indépendance et Coopération
Rev.trim.dr.civ.	Revue trimestrielle de droit civil
RG	*Reichsgericht* [Supreme Court of the German Reich]
RGAR	Révue générale des assurances et des responsabilités
RGZ	Amtliche Sammlung der Entscheidungen des Reichsgerichtes in Zivilsachen [Decisions of the German Imperial Court in civil matters]
RL	*Relação* [Court of Appeal] de Lisboa (Portugal)
RP	*Relação* [Court of Appeal] do Porto (Portugal)
RW	Rechtskundig Weekblad
Sem.Jur.	La Semaine Juridique, Edition Générale
SHD	*Sø- og Handelsretsdom* (Judgement of the Maritime and Commercial Court Copenhagen)
SJT	*Svensk Juristtidning* (Sweden)
SLT (Rep.)	*The Scots Law Times*
STJ	*Supremo Tribunal de Justiça* [Supreme Court] (Portugal)
Sup.Ct.	Supreme Court (Eire)
SZ	*Entscheidungen des österreichischen Obersten Gerichtshofs in Zivilsachen*
TLR	Annual Digest of the Times Law Reports
Trib.	*Tribunale* [Court of First Instance] (Italy)
TS	*Tribunal Supremo* [Supreme Court] (Spain)
UfR	*Ugeskrift for Retsvæsen* (Denmark)
v.	versus
VersR	Versicherungsrecht (Juristische Rundschau für die Individual versicherung)
VLD	*Vestre Landsrets dom* [Judgments of Western High Court] (Denmark)
WLR	The Weekly Law Reports
WM	Wertpapiermitteilungen

WPNR	Weekblad voor Privaatrecht, Notariaat en Registratie
ZEPR	Zeitschrift für Europaisches Privatrecht
ZIP	Zeitschrift für Wirtschaftsrecht and Insolvenzpraxis
ZVglRWiss	Zeitschrift für vergleichende Rechtswissenschaft
ZVR	Zeitschrift für Verkehrsrecht

Part 1 – General Issues

CHAPTER 1

Towards a European Civil Code

Ewoud Hondius*

1   Introduction

This book concerns the development of European private law. In the past two decades, EC directives have led to the introduction of some unified, or at least harmonised, private law at a European level. A directive on product liability, which extends to the very core of tort law, has been implemented in all Member States[1] and in some other states, including a number of non-European countries,[2] as well. A directive on unfair contract terms, which goes to the heart of contract law, has likewise been transposed.[3] A regulation on the European Company will shortly enter into force.[4] These are but three of the best known objects of EC initiatives in the area of private law. A list of relevant regulations and directives is reproduced in Chapter 5 by Müller-Graff.

The introduction of these instruments has not always been uncontroversial. At the time, the constitutionality of the directive on product liability was doubted by some politicians.[5] The Single Act and especially the Treaty of Maastricht have put an end to such doubts,[6] but Maastricht has introduced a new theme: is civil law not something to be left to Member States under the principle of subsidiarity?[7] There are other criticisms as well. Not everyone, even when convinced of their constitutionality, is attracted by the quality of EC directives. A draft directive on liability for services was criticised in this respect from all sides, academics,[8] producers and consumers[9]

---

* Professor of Law, University of Utrecht; Editor-in-Chief of the European Review of Private Law. The first edition of this Chapter was written when he was Leverhulme Visiting Professor at Queen Mary and Westfield College of the University of London. Field of Specialisation: Consumer Law, Contract Law, Tort Law. Correspondence Address: Molengraaff Instituut voor Privaatrecht, Nobelstraat 2A, 3512 EN Utrecht, The Netherlands, E-mail: e.hondius@law.uu.nl.
1   See Chapter 35 by Howells.
2   See M. Reimann, Product Liability in a global context: the hollow victory of the European model, *ERPL* 2003, pp. 128-154.
3   See Chapter 24 by Wilhelmsson.
4   See Chapter 44 by Hommelhoff, Teichmann and Witt.
5   In Chapter 36 of this book, M. Faure suggests that the harmonisation of marketing conditions was probably only the formal goal to give Europe competence in this area. See also Geraint Howells, *Comparative Product Liability* (1993), pp. 20.
6   G. Betlem, E. Hondius, European Private Law after the Treaty of Amsterdam, *European Review of Private Law* 2001, pp. 3-20.
7   See in this book Legrand in Chapter 14 and Faure in Chapter 36.
8   E. Deutsch and J. Taupitz (eds.), *Haftung der Dienstleistungsberufe – natürliche Vielfalt und europäische Vereinheitlichung* (1993); S. Littbarski (ed.), *Entwurf einer Richtlinie über die Haftung bei Dienstleistungen* (1992).
9   For instance, the European Consumer Law Group, a network of consumer advocates, was highly critical of the draft.

alike. These questions raise the issue of whether or not the EC should contemplate the gradual build up of a corpus of private law. Until recently, the emphasis has rather been on social and economic law, but several of the prerequisites for a European private law do exist. The European Court of Justice has shown itself highly competent in this respect. In the past, the Court has brought into operation, really from scratch, a European administrative law, which in turn has influenced the development of national law.[10] More recently, the Court has created a private law caseload.[11] There is a European bar. What is lacking is consensus over the direction which this development should take. Should consensus not be arrived at as to the framework in which future directives and regulations in the area of civil law should find a place? Such framework might eventually be provided by a European Civil Code. It is this issue which in 2001 was firmly placed on the political agenda, when the European Commission issued its Communication on Contract Law.[12] The Communication has rightly been described as an academic green paper.[13] It has more recently been followed by the 2003 Action plan.[14]

The debate raises several questions. First, there is the question already referred to above: is there a constitutional basis for a European Civil Code in the Treaty of Rome, as amended by the Treaty of Maastricht? At a conference on European private law organised by the Dutch government in 1997 in Scheveningen, the seaside resort of The Hague, even those speakers who saw a constitutional basis for such a Code in the Treaty thought that the Comity principle should prevent the European Union from forcing a Code down 'an unwilling Member State's throat'.[15] Second, is codification of the law, more specifically of the civil or private law, a worthwhile idea, or is the common law system of precedents a better system to deal with changing situations? Or is a Restatement perhaps a compromise?[16] And, finally, is the harmonisation of private law feasible on a European level? This book basically aims to answer only the last question: whether or not the various domestic legal systems in Europe are not too far apart to even contemplate unification or harmonisation.

This Chapter, unlike the Introductory Chapter in the two previous editions of this Book, will argue that at present they are no longer too far apart. In ten years time, they may even be ready for a Restatement of Private Law. Substantive law, especially now, is closer than it has been during the last century. The difficulty seems to be that the legal cultures,[17] the ways of finding the law,[18] the role accorded to prece-

---

10 Two examples are the development of the law of legitimate expectations and the reception of the idea of proportionality into English law – see J. Schwarze, *European Administrative Law* (1992), pp. 869-870. This reception has met with scepticism from some authors who simply believe that proportionality as such is non-transplantable – see S. Boyron, Proportionality in English Administrative Law: A Faulty Translation?, (1992) 12 *Oxford Journal of Legal Studies* 237-264.

11 See Chapters 6 by Van Gerven and 9 by Joerges.

12 See for an analysis C. von Bar and O. Lando, *European Review of Private Law* 2002, pp. 183-248 and the comments of this response by Legrand in Chapter 14, as well as Mattei in Chapter 16.

13 S. Grundmann, J. Stuyck (Eds.), *An Academic Green Paper on European Contract Law* (2002).

14 See D. Staudenmayer, The Commission Action Plan on European Contract Law, *ERPL* 2003, pp. 113-127.

15 European Civil Code, *ERPL* 1997, pp. 455-547.

16 See Chapter 4 by Hyland.

17 See Legrand in Chapter 14.

18 See my paper 'Finding the law in Europe', in: *Mélanges Tallon* (2000), pp. 93-117. But see also for

4

dents,[19] procedural enforcement,[20] etc. are still very much apart. Not in all geographical areas is this the case. The Common law jurisdictions, England and Wales, and Ireland, are close. The same applies to the civil law countries of France, Belgium and Luxembourg, and to Denmark, Finland, Sweden and the European Economic Space State Norway. As between civil law and common law countries, England and Scotland are an example of close cooperation. As these examples show,[21] a common language or linguistic heritage and a common legal culture are often the basis for such cooperation.

A common language – Latin – and a common heritage – Roman law – did of course once exist in Europe. Although the present situation bears little resemblance to pre-XIXth century Europe, and therefore a 'return' to that period is highly unlikely, the present interest in a new European civil law is still a fascinating challenge to legal historians. This is set out below in Chapter 2 by Zimmermann.[22]

Is all this academic speculation designed to upgrade the profile of the law curriculum? A brief look at what the 'actors of the law' are doing shows us that the interest in the development of a European (civil) law is very real. Attorneys all over Europe have set up alliances. Judges have joined their efforts in setting up European courses for their continuing education. The most important event is that future attorneys and judges, the law students of today, are very much affected. Many present-day students are participating in various exchange programmes, of which Erasmus and Socrates are the most successful, and a common legal education is being prepared or is already in existence in various member states.[23]

Two groups of actors are still missing. First, politicians and public servants were until recently unaffected by the idea of harmonising private law. This has changed with the 2001 Communication on Contract Law, mentioned above. Second, business circles have been rather hostile towards harmonisation efforts. A similar experience has been noted with regard to the Convention on the International Sale of Goods

---

a less gloomy analysis S. Vogenauer, *Die Auslegung von Gesetzen in England und auf dem Kontinent* (2001).

19 See my paper 'Precedent: something of the past?', in: *Mélanges offerts à Marcel Fontaine* (2003), pp. 415-423.

20 See Basedow in Chapter 31.

21 Other examples include both North America – the harmonisation achieved by the Uniform Commercial Code and the Restatements is well-known – and Latin America. As to the latter see A.M. Garro, *Armonización y Unificación del derecho privado en América Latina: esfuerzos, tendencias y realidades* (1992); by the same author, Unification and Harmonization of Private Law in Latin America, 40 *American Journal of Comparative Law* 587-616 (1992).

22 As another German author, R. Schulze, European Legal History – A New Field of Research in Germany, 13 *Journal of Legal History* 270-295 (1992) has observed: 'The present and the past are linked in the concepts of European legal culture and European legal history in two ways: the awakening of interest in research into European legal history is prompted by the experience of the present, namely the present-day efforts towards the development of a body of common European law. The resulting research can in turn influence present-day thinking in that, contrary to another tradition and present-day experience, namely the legal thinking moulded by the nation-state, it contributes from a historical standpoint to a consciousness of a shared European identity. The concept of European legal culture is thus directed at the definition of an identity for the present based on the past whilst research in European legal history is both defined by and directed towards the present'.

23 See M. Faure, J. Smits, H. Schneider (Eds.), *Towards a European Ius Commune in Legal Education and Research* (2002).

(CISG). On 1 January 1991, the CISG entered into force and, as of 2004, it is in force in a large number of countries, including most EU Member States. This success seems to turn once hostile entrepreneurs into – possibly lukewarm – supporters of the CISG. Meanwhile, the CISG points to something else. If it has been possible to bring about this worldwide harmonisation, why could it not be achieved for the whole of private law?

Before embarking upon our exercise, I shall first have to limit the scope of this chapter in section 2.

2 Subject-Matter of this Book

The subject-matter of this book is what continental Europeans call private law. This includes contract, tort and restitution, sometimes brought together under the heading 'law of obligations'. It also means property (and trust), company law, succession and family law. There is little doubt that a future European Civil Code should also encompass what is now dealt with in Europe's Commercial Codes. Is it not so that Europe's impact on private law began with the company law directives? Yet, for practical reasons, this book will only touch upon commercial matters to a limited extent. The same is true for family law and succession law, which in recent years have become promising areas for research into the harmonisation option.

Most of the following Chapters deal with substantive law. Procedural law, on the other hand, was considered sufficiently important to invite a proceduralist – Marcel Storme for the first two editions of this book, Kerameus for the present edition – to write a Chapter (8) on this subject. A similar case has been made for private international law, which is therefore also covered, in Chapter 10, by Muir Watt. Private international law and the harmonisation of private law have sometimes been considered rivals in achieving legal certainty for cross-border transactions. The rivalry between the Hague Sales Conventions and the Hague Treaty on Private International Law relating to the Sale of Goods is an example. Yet, at present, both are rather considered to be allied forces.[24] The unification of European private international law, as for instance in the Brussels Convention and the Rome Treaty, is an important step forward.

An interesting issue is whether only transnational law should be dealt with or also domestic law. A case for the former is made in Chapter 42 on the *Eurohypotheque* by Wehrens and Van Velten. A drawback of this approach is the disintegration of domestic law through partial harmonisation,[25] which has even been called a threat to legal security.[26] But most authors in this book prefer a solution whereby crossborder

---

24 H.U. Jessurun d'Oliveira, Towards a 'European' Private International Law, in: B. de Witte, C. Forder (eds.), *The common law of Europe and the future of legal education* (1992), p. 265, 282 sees Private International Law from a Community point of view as a halfway house to harmonisation and approximation of the national laws of the Member States.

25 See Ch.E. Hauschka, Grundprobleme der Privatrechtsfortbildung durch die Europäische Wirtschaftsgemeinschaft, *Juristen Zeitung* 1990, pp. 290-299.

26 The President of the Belgian *Cour de cassation*, I. Verougstraete, puts it this way: 'Les cinq dernières années ont été caractérisées par l'effondrement de la sécurité juridique' (p. 3). He attributes this to the 'prolifération de législateurs (...): droit national, droit européen et droit international s'entre-croisent et s'entre-choquent'. The loss of legal security is also due to the proliferation of courts, such

rules would apply to domestic situations as well – see for instance Basedow in Chapter 31.

A comparison of legal developments in Europe is often facilitated by the common heritage of Roman and canon law.[27] This common heritage is also a subject-matter for this book. The common heritage does sometimes extend to America; witness the influence of American developments on European law.[28] It therefore seems appropriate occasionally at least to allude to – some – American developments. Nor should the European offspring be forgotten; recent examples are the Australian and Japanese adoption of product liability legislation after the model of the EC directive.[29]

Community law, as we have just seen, is rapidly gaining ground in the area of civil law. Yet EC law still covers only a fraction of the civil law. It is therefore natural that the law of individual European countries will be discussed. This raises the question of which jurisdictions are to be covered. It will be obvious that these jurisdictions should include not only the Member States of the EC, but also the Member States of the European Economic Space which – including Switzerland – have accepted the 'acquis communautaire' for introduction into their law. Because of the now imminent extension of the EU towards Central, Eastern and Southern Europe, an extension which has already taken place within the Council of Europe, it is also of interest to look east and south and to devote attention to developments in the new Member States.[30] At the present time of the recodification of Central and East European law, civil law has been in such turmoil there that, for practical reasons, it is hardly dealt with in this book. In years to come, however, there will be much to learn from Central and East European experiences when the work on a future European Civil Code will be in full swing.[31] These experiences will be especially fruitful when it comes to the question whether or not consumer protection should be integrated within civil law.[32]

3   Constitutionality

Does the European Community have the competence to adopt a European Civil Code? This book will not provide an indepth analysis of this interesting question. However, some attention to this issue is given in Chapter 11 by Zeno-Zencovich and in Betlem's Chapter 37 on Environmental law. Many protagonists of a European

---

as the highest civil court, a constitutional court, the European Court of Justice and the European Court for the Protection of Human Rights – I. Verougstraete, in: *Imperat Lex/Liber Amicorum Pierre Marchal* (2003), pp. 1-12.

27 See R.C. van Caenegem, *European Law in the Past and the Future/Unity and Diversity over Two Millennia* (2002).

28 W. Wiegand, The Reception of American Law in Europe, 39 *American Journal of Comparative Law* 229-248 (1991) and Chapter 4 by Hyland.

29 M. Reimann, Product Liability in a global context: the hollow victory of the European model, *ERPL* 2003, pp. 128-154.

30 For a more thorough survey of national interest in European private law see my Chronicles in *ERPL* 2000, pp. 385-416, and 2002, pp. 865-900.

31 See A. Harmathy and A. Németh (Eds.), *Questions of civil law codification* (1990).

32 This question is discussed by Lurger in Chapter 15.

Code point to a resolution of the European Parliament. Article 1 of this 'Resolution on action to bring into line the private law of the Member States' reads:

'Requests that a start be made on the necessary preparatory work on drawing up a common European Code of Private Law, the Member States being invited, having deliberated the matter, to state whether they wish to be involved in the planned unification'.[33]

There is no doubt that this is an interesting opinion. For a Dutch lawyer, the fact that the recodification of Dutch civil law also began with what seemed an innocuous parliamentary question springs to mind.[34]

4 Codification

Ever since the famous debate between Thibaut and Savigny in early XIXth century Germany, the following question has remained on the civil lawyer's agenda: to (re)codify the law or not.

Germany eventually obtained its codification, after Belgium, France, Luxembourg, the Netherlands, Portugal and Spain had preceded it. Poland (1936) and Greece (1940/1946) were still to come, while Italy (1942), Portugal (1966), East Germany (1975) and the Netherlands (1992) recodified their civil law. The most recent codifications have come from Central and Eastern Europe, where the former socialist states have all adopted new Civil Codes or are in the course of doing so. It should also not be overlooked that in the shadow of large-scale recodification, updating projects on a far smaller scale have brought most other codes into line with modern times. One cannot therefore really say that the codification idea is dead.

On the other hand, what about the common law – or mixed – jurisdictions: Cyprus, England and Wales, Ireland, Malta and Scotland, one may object. What about Denmark, Finland and Sweden? Are the common law countries not especially radically opposed to any codification whatsoever? In Chapter 20, Van Erp indeed argues that the adoption of a European *Code* is not possible for England and Wales. Yet, one should not forget that as recently as the 1950s, with the establishment of its Law Commissions, the United Kingdom did contemplate the adoption of a codification of at least its law of contract.[35]

Thus, the codification idea does have some chances of being adopted within Europe. This does not mean that such a codification should necessarily be European, but by all means regional efforts of harmonisation now seem to have better prospects than global efforts.[36]

Should it be along the traditional division of the law in private and public law, in substantive and procedural law, that European law should be codified? So far, codification along socio-economic lines seems to have been a better way. However, with

---

33 *Official Journal of the European Communities* 1989, No C 158/400.
34 See E.O.H.P. Florijn, *Ontstaan en ontwikkeling van het nieuwe Burgerlijk Wetboek* (1994).
35 The publication of the McGregor draft – H. McGregor, *Contract code drawn up on behalf of the English Law Commission* (1993) – has been one of the highlights of the Gandolfi project.
36 This idea is not shared by Berger in Chapter 3.

the advent of more harmonised private law, it is important to preserve the rich European tradition in this area and this can best be done by keeping traditional divisions intact, even though in most countries these are not as sharp as they may once have been. The one exception is the division of private law in civil and commercial law. As the Italian and the Dutch examples show, this distinction is no longer warranted.

Yet, the practical difficulties of codification, even along traditional lines, seem to be great. With the Italian author Mengoni one is apt to

'riconoscere che "un codice per l'Europa" non è un'alternativa realistica'.[37]

It is therefore worthwhile to consider alternatives to codification. Such alternatives are set out in Chapter 5 by Müller-Graff. One such alternative may be the elaboration of a Restatement based on Principles of European Contract Law, Tort Law, Procedure, etc., as set out in Chapter 7 by Hartkamp.

How does one proceed, once regulation – be it in the form of a codification, restatement or otherwise – has been opted for? Some advocate the use of a single text as a point of departure. Several authors, mostly Italians, have argued that the Italian Civil Code is best equipped to serve as a model for a European Code on Contract Law. For what reason?

'Pour deux raisons fondamentales: tout d'abord pour la position intermédiaire qu'il revêt par rapport non seulement aux deux principaux courants juridique français et allemand (...) mais par rapport aussi au droit anglais; ensuite pour sa modernité intrinseque, une modernité – diraisje – raisonnablement prononcée, exempte des exces qui ont amené certains pays a faire en toute hâte marche arriere'.[38]

In the practice of the Commission on European Contract Law (the Lando Commission), the text of the Dutch and Québec Civil Codes were also often consulted. There is a growing body of literature by those engaged in the various harmonisation commissions who write on their experiences,[39] which may well serve to indicate how future codificatory or regulatory work can be organised.

5   Is it Feasible?

'let contract flowers bloom rather than allow the tort elephant to trample them down'.[40]

Having seen that a European Civil Code, although raising serious constitutional issues, is not constitutionally impossible, we now turn to the main question raised in this book. Is a European Civil Code feasible? We shall look at this issue with respect to each of the eight main Parts, on Family law, Contract law in general, Specific contracts, Restitution, Tort, Property, Trust, and Company law separately.

---

37 Luigi Mengoni, *L'Europa dei codici o un codice per l'Europa?* (1993), p. 3.
38 G. Gandolfi, Pour un code européen des contrats, *Revue trimestrielle de droit civil* 1992, pp. 707, 726.
39 See the publications listed in the Bibliography.
40 H. Kötz, 10 *Tel Aviv University Studies in Law* 195, 212 (1990).

5.1 Family Law

Beginning with Family law, we should perhaps express our surprise at the rapid development of academic discussion as to its harmonisation on a European level. In 2002, the Commission on European Family Law held its opening conference in Utrecht[41] and, meanwhile, the first volumes of its work have already appeared in print.[42] Martiny in Chapter 17, however, warns us against too much optimism: 'In spite of an intensifying debate on a "Europeanisation of family law" and an increasing number of calls for a "European solution", a comprehensive concept is still not in sight and not to be expected in the near future'. Verbeke and Leleu in Chapter 18, on the other hand, consider the adoption of a uniform act on succession to be feasible.

5.2 Contract Law in General

With regard to the law of contract, three different strands may be discerned. First, there are some authors who think that a European Civil Code is quite feasible with regard to their subject-matter. A second group consists of those authors who have great reservations about a Code, but see the adoption of Eurowide Principles as feasible. A third group sees no possibilities of harmonisation whatsoever.

First the optimists. Sacco in Chapter 19 clearly takes as a point of departure that for the formation of contracts a Code is feasible. A strikingly optimistic note is struck by Bonell in Chapter 21, who considers the prospects – two decades after the adoption of the Geneva Convention – of bringing about greater uniformity in the law governing agency relationships of an international character to be greater than ever. In Chapter 24, Wilhelmsson arrives at the conclusion that the rules on standard form contracts in the various European countries are relatively similar, especially after the adoption of the Unfair Contract Terms Directive. In Chapter 25 Canaris and Grigoleit are of the opinion that the rules of interpretation in the different European legal systems largely overlap. Likewise, Hesselink in Chapter 26 concludes that the concept of good faith in itself should not keep common law and civil law divided. The solution should preferably be that a European code or restatement will not incorporate a general good faith clause. In a similar vein, Gordley in Chapter 12 argues against the recognition of the foreseeability rule in a future European Code. In Chapter 27, Tallon warns us of the difficulties in drafting a whole Civil Code, when the preparation of common rules on isolated topics of contract law already provokes so many problems. And yet, this author equally warns us against an excessive pessimism, which breeds resignation or despondency. He rather offers some good advice: agree upon the basic concepts and tackle the question of languages.[43] Lando, on the basis of his practical experience, concludes in Chapter 28 that it is possible to establish a system for nonperformance and a terminology accompanying this system. The price to be paid is that it has not been possible to provide general rules on performance and remedies which have any great precision.

---

41 See the conference proceedings in K. Boele-Woelki (Ed.), *Perspectives for the Unification and Harmonisation of Family Law in Europe* (2003).

42 C. Jeppesen and I. Sumner, *European Review of Private Law* 2003, pp. 269-272.

43 This linguistic preoccupation is also apparent in Chapter 22 by Tallon's compatriot Fabre-Magnan.

Then there is a second group. Van Erp in Chapter 20 on the pre-contractual stage is sympathetic to harmonising the rules on formation, but – as he already set out in the previous edition of this book – he sees no possibility for this to be attained by way of codification. Van Erp discerns a growing divergence between English and continental law, as is demonstrated by the case of *Walford* v. *Miles*.[44] In this case, the House of Lords determined the following: 'A duty to negotiate in good faith is as unworkable in practice as it is inherently inconsistent with the position of a negotiating party'. A European *Code*, which would point in a different direction, would be totally unacceptable to the United Kingdom according to the author. Van Erp sees no problem with the adoption of Principles of Contract Law, since such principles leave more freedom than rules. Fabre-Magnan in Chapter 22 is also more cautious:

> 'Contrary to what is usually suggested, it is not possible to achieve a European Civil Code, particularly on the question of defects, by looking for a mythical hard core of law which would 'naturally' be common to all European countries since, as already seen, the underlying values of the different countries are in reality very different'.

MacQueen in Chapter 23 advocates what he calls a 'structured discretion' approach, which he opposes to the Gandolfi proposals for a solution which is more in line with traditional civil codes.

Finally, in a third group, one might expect authors to take issue with the idea of harmonisation. These, however, with the exception of Legrand in Chapter 14, seem to be absent in this volume. The conclusion must be clear: contract law is ready for codification, or at least a Restatement.

5.3 Specific Contracts

Work on a European Civil Code is already well under way. As the heir apparent to the Commission on European Contract Law (Lando Commission), a Study Group on a European Civil Code, chaired by C. von Bar, started work in 1999. Several of the working teams present their progress in this Part. First, in Chapter 30, Heutger and Jeloschek analyse the need for a European Sales Law. The question of feasibility is here approached from a different angle than in other Chapters: it is rather whether or not – in the presence of the Convention on the International Sale of Goods and the European Directive on Consumer Sales – there is still a need for such a text. The question is rather different where services are concerned. With regard to these contracts, Loos in Chapter 32 gives an overview of the revolutionary views of the Study Group resulting in a wholly new set of rules for service contracts. In between, Basedow in Chapter 31 also sees a Restatement of European Insurance Contract Law as a real option.

Two other Chapters of this book also closely deal with the proceedings of the Study Group: they are Chapters 13 by Ramberg and 33 by Clive. Ramberg concludes that a European Civil Code is a good start for dealing with electronic contracts.

---

44 [1992] 2 *WLR* 174.

5.4 Restitution

In the first edition of this book, Clive concluded that the English law of restitution had a long way to go before any attempt at codification could be made. And even if the English law were to be sufficiently developed so as to be susceptible to codification, the author considered it doubtful whether any assimilation of the common law and the civil law could be made in this area. Then in the second edition, as he now does in the present Chapter 33, Clive informs us about his experience in drafting provisions on unjustified enrichment for the Study Group on a European Civil Code, and, in contrast, he is now absolutely positive about the feasibility of doing so.

5.5 Tort

In Chapter 34, Howarth does not argue in favour of uniform tort law, but rather for some degree of approximation, with room for experimentation and diversity. In Chapter 35, Howells is in the enviable position that Product liability has already been harmonised to some extent by the EC Directive of 1985. The lessons to be drawn from the ensuing implementation process are that national legal traditions are difficult to overcome, that formally harmonised laws may yet differ in their application and that the limited utility of harmonisation, if not all aspects, are harmonised. Faure in Chapter 36 informs us of the lessons we can draw from a law and economics perspective. In Chapter 37 on Environmental liability, Betlem demonstrates that he is an ardent supporter of an Environmental Liability Regulation, which in his view could easily be inserted into a European Civil Code. This author also writes about two aspects which are not taken up by most other authors. First, he sets out the constitutional basis for the Regulation which he advocates. Second, he puts Europe itself in perspective, seeing it not so much as something far larger than what we usually deal with, but rather as part of the world as a whole.

Compensation for pure economic loss is a subject-matter where European jurisdictions still vary widely, as is shown by Bussani and Palmer in Chapter 38. Their research, conducted under the auspices of the Trento project, reveals that four principal methodologies dominate the European landscape. Perhaps even more revealing is that in some member states, the whole notion of pure economic loss is unknown.

5.6 Property

Now turning to Property law, Drobnig in Chapter 39 on Transfer of property in corporeal movables sets out the profound differences between the various European countries. For once the English Channel does not seem to be the major divide, but rather an Anglo-French conglomerate versus Germany, Greece and the Netherlands. Yet this author does see a possibility of drafting a European Civil Code, provided that this will take into account two basic rules. An important point which the author makes, is that the rules on obligations and property are interdependent to such a degree that an isolated unification of rules of central importance is not advisable. In Chapter 40 Drobnig turns to security rights created by contract. He considers the development of a common regime possible. This should integrate the present two heterogeneous regimes into a modernised pledge law, and require registration.

In Chapter 41 Goode shows that property law can be harmonised. His paper deals with a global rather than a European project.

Then, in Chapter 42 Wehrens and Van Velten argue for the development of a *Euro-hypothèque* (mortgage), to be used in the case of transfrontier credit transactions as an alternative to the domestic mortgage. The authors raise two issues which are also discussed in some other chapters. First, does private international law provide a solution for transfrontier credit transactions under mortgage? They answer the question in the negative. A second issue is whether a European regulation should only deal with transfrontier mortgage transactions or should cover all such transactions, even domestic ones.[45] The major differences between the various mortgage institutions in the European countries turn the latter solution into a highly unrealistic and perhaps also an undesirable one.

5.7 Trust

In Chapter 43, Grimaldi and Barrière argue that the notion of trust is incompatible with continental law and the incorporation of the trust device throughout Europe is not feasible. They do see a possibility, however, for the creation of an analogous institution, the *fiducie*.

5.8 Company Law

Company law has been the subject of a fair number of harmonisation directives, as is demonstrated in Chapter 44 by Hommelhoff, Teichmann and Witt. Some of the these initiatives have failed, but others have proved to be a success, so harmonisation of company law is certainly feasible. The authors correctly point out that this success is also dependent upon adjacent legislation, such as that on capital markets, tax and merger control law.

6   How to Proceed

From the following Chapters the conclusion may be drawn that a European Civil Code may still lie a long way ahead, but that its imminent adoption is not to be excluded. It therefore seems appropriate to contemplate the elaboration of a code or restatement, which may at least provide a framework. Such a 'pre-code' – or a 'common frame of reference', as the Action Plan calls it – may for instance serve to make directives compatible with one another. Perhaps even more important is the contribution which an exchange of ideas may make towards elaborating a new international framework of civil law concepts and norms. The necessity for this has been underlined by several authors.[46] It is eloquently stated by H. Kötz, who suggests that

---

45 This was also a point of discussion within the Lando Commission – see Chapter 23 by MacQueen.

46 In this sense see for instance, O. Remien, Europäische Rechtswissenschaft – Voraussetzung oder Folge europäischer Rechtsangleichung, in: K.J. Hopt (ed.), *Europäische Integration als Herausforderung des Rechts: Mehr Marktrecht – weniger Einzelsetze* (1990), p. 124, at 131.

'auch die Grundlagen des Zivilrechts in den Prozess der Rechtsvergleichung einzube-
ziehen, also einen Bestand allgemeiner Regeln des Vertrags- und Deliktsrechts
herauszuarbeiten, der auf einen internationalen Konsens rechnen und dazu beitragen
kann, der Rechtsprechung die Anwendung des geltenden Einheitsrechts zu erleich-
tern, die geschilderten Auslegungsdivergenzen zu vermeiden und den Boden für
künftige Vorhaben der Rechtsvereinheitlichung vorzubereiten'.[47]

All of this requires what Sacco has called the circulation of legal ideas. In this respect, several international academic projects may be mentioned. One particular
project, which is strongly represented in this volume, is the Study Group on a European Civil Code, which is referred to in Chapters 13 (Ramberg), 31 (Heutger/
Jeloschek), 32 (Loos) and 33 (Clive). Perhaps it should be mentioned here that the
Study Group is not the only group of academics who are actively promoting the
harmonisation of European private law – or at least carrying research in this field.
First, there is the Lando Commission's main competitor, Gandolfi's *Académie des
privatistes*, which published a Draft Code ('avant-projet') in 2002.[48] One of the more
active private groups which are engaged in the development of 'Principles' of European Private Law is the Spier/Koziol group, based in the Netherlands and Austria.
Before publishing a set of Principles,[49] the group has set out to discover any common
ground between the various jurisdictions. The questionnaire method used is much
akin to that of the Trento Common Core project, discussed below. It is highly commendable that the group does not keep the results of the questionnaire approach to
itself, but is willing to share its findings with others through publication.[50] Another
private project is that of the Trento Common Core of European Private Law, directed
by Bussani and Mattei. The project is based on the ideas of the 'two Rudi's': Rodolfo
Sacco and the late Rudi Schlesinger. Every annual meeting begins with a plenary session,[51] but then it is back to the core business: the development of a common core of
private law. Three volumes have so far been published, on good faith,[52] the enforceability of promises[53] and pure economic loss.[54] Van Gerven has inspired a number of

---

47 Neue Aufgaben der Rechtsvergleichung, *Juristische Blätter* 1982, pp. 355, 361. In his paper on
   'Legal education in the future: Towards a European Law School?', in: B. De Witte and C. Forder
   (Eds.), *The common law of Europe and the future of legal education/Le droit commun de l'Europe
   et l'avenir de l'enseignement juridique* (1992), pp. 31, 41, Kötz argues that '[t]he aim of finding a
   European common core of legal principles (...) is simply to mark out areas of agreement and disagreement, to construct a European legal *lingua franca* that has concepts large enough to embrace legal
   institutions which are functionally comparable, to develop a truly common European legal literature
   and the beginnings of a European law school curriculum, and thus to lay the basis for a free and
   unrestricted flow of ideas among European lawyers that is perhaps more central to the idea of a
   common law than that of identity on points of substance'.
48 G. Gandolfi (Ed.), *Code européen des contrats/Avant-projet, Livre premier* (2001).
49 A first draft has been published in H. Koziol, B.C. Steininger (Eds.), *European Tort Law 2002*, Tort
   and Insurance Law Yearbook (2003), pp. 562-571.
50 So far, some twelve volumes have already been published, some of which are mentioned in the
   Bibliography.
51 See the collection of papers delivered at plenary sessions in M. Bussani, U. Mattei (Eds.), *The
   Common Core of European Private Law* (2002).
52 R. Zimmermann, S. Whittaker, *Good Faith in European Contract Law* (2000).
53 J. Gordley (Ed.), *The Enforceability of Promises in European Contract Law* (2001).
54 M. Bussani, V.V. Palmer (Eds.), *Pure Economic Loss in Europe* (2003).

European casebooks, the first three of which are Tort Law,[55] Contract Law[56] and Unjustified enrichment.[57] Perhaps in no legal system is there such a great impact being exerted by casebooks such as those by Van Gerven and Markesinis,[58] than in Great Britain, where the House of Lords is increasingly making use of comparative law. It is through the English translations of foreign case-law that the Lords have access to those cases. A case which can demonstrate this influence concerns the joint liability of sequential employers of an employee who contracted mesothelioma in one of their asbestos factories.[59] Van Gerven is not the only Editor of casebooks. The Münster-based 'acquis communautaire' group has published a 'Casebook Europäisches Privatrecht'[60] and a 'Casebook Europäisches Verbraucherrecht'.[61]

European regulations and directives may now be easily downloaded free of charge. Still, it can be useful to have them on paper, preferably in various linguistic versions. In Germany, both Basedow[62] and Magnus[63] and Schulze/Zimmermann[64] have edited readers with the most important Eurorules. In Italy, Benacchio and Simoni have edited a similar Italian-language reader, which has the added value of containing references to the case law of the European Court and to legal literature.[65] In the Netherlands, a Dutch-language source book has been published.[66] International instruments other than European law have been collected by Wiggers.[67] This brings us to domestic law. Domestic law should be given a much wider audience than only the citizens of the state concerned. Smaller nations, especially, should make an effort to 'export' their law. Most Nordic countries already have a tradition of providing government reports with English-language summaries. Countries such as Greece, the Netherlands and Portugal would be well advised to adopt this tradition. The Netherlands does have a long-standing tradition of supplementing doctoral theses with foreign-language summaries. Likewise, some countries publish annual translations or adaptations of major law review articles in English. The *Scandinavian Studies in Law* are perhaps the best known example, but this is not confined to smaller states. Of the larger European countries, Italy has also adopted this system. Law reviews such as the trilingual *European Review of Private Law*, *Europa e Diritto Privato* and the *Zeitschrift für Europäisches Recht* are also of assistance in disseminating legal ideas.

---

55 W. Van Gerven, J. Lever, P. Larouche (Eds.), *Tort Law* (2000).
56 H. Beale, A. Hartkamp, H. Kötz, D. Tallon (Eds.), *Contract Law* (2002).
57 Jack Beatson, Eltjo Schrage (Eds.), *Cases, Materials and Texts on Unjustified Enrichment* (2003).
58 B.S. Markesinis, H. Unberath, *The German Law of Torts* (4th ed., 2002).
59 Fairchild v Glenhaven Funeral Services, [2002] 3 *Weekly Law Reports* 89.
60 R. Schulze, A. Engel, J. Jones (Eds.), *Casebook Europäisches Privatrecht* (2000).
61 H. Schulte-Nölke, R. Schulze, J. Jones (Eds.), *A Casebook on European Consumer Law* (2000).
62 J. Basedow (Ed.), *Europäisches Privatrecht -Quellen*, 2 vols. (2000).
63 U. Magnus (Ed.), *Europäisches Schuldrecht Verordnungen und Richtlinien – European Law of Obligations Regulations and Directives – Droit Européen des Obligations Règlements et Directives*, Berlin: Sellier, 2002, 850 pp.
64 R. Schulze, R. Zimmermann (Eds.), *Basistexte zum Europäischen Privatrecht – Textsammlung*, 2d ed. (2002); an English language version has been edited by O. Radley-Gardner, H. Beale, R. Zimmermann, R. Schulze (Eds.), *Fundamental texts on European Private Law* (2003).
65 G. Benacchio, V. Simoni (Eds.), *Repertorio di diritto comunitario civile e commerciale (legislazione – dottrina – giurisprudenza)* (2001).
66 J.H.M. van Erp, J.M. Smits (Eds.), *Bronnen Europees privaatrecht* (2001).
67 W.J.H. Wiggers, *International Commercial Law/Source Materials* (2001).

Although for practical purposes, the number of languages used in Europe presents some obvious problems, I do not support the idea that in the future there should be a single European language. The diversity of languages, like that of cultures, seems to give Europe its distinct flavour. On a more abstract level, a case may well be made that the coexistence of several languages may contribute towards a higher quality of legal texts.[68]

7   Conclusion

The impact of European law on the development of private law has become more and more important in the recent past and is bound to become even more so in the imminent future. A number of directives have already forced Member States to harmonise part of their contract and tort law. Other areas of private law have also been the subject of harmonising efforts. The European Union not only uses directives as its sole instrument. The instrument of the regulation is becoming increasingly popular. Treaties and private self-regulation are other instruments.

What is needed at present is a framework within which all these efforts can be placed. Such a *framework* can be established by a European Civil Code or a European Restatement. The time has now come to adopt such a Code. As the following Chapters will demonstrate, the concepts and the practical solutions found within Europe are still diverse and in some areas, such as the formation of contracts, they are diverging rather than converging. However, if a Code emerges which only aspires to serve as a set of Principles of Civil Law, some practical difficulties seem to diminish. Such a set of Principles may also serve as a source of inspiration for both judges and academics alike.[69] Judges should play an important role, since it is only through case-law that major areas of civil law, such as that of corporeal securities, are formed. Academics are also important, since they will have to contribute towards the circulation of ideas with regard to this development.[70] A similar conclusion is reached by Manfred Wolf with regard to the necessity of the unification of civil procedure.[71] The new European challenge to lawyers in Europe seems to have been taken up with enthusiasm in a number of countries. This book is one of the fruits of that enthusiasm.

BIBLIOGRAPHY: G. Alpa, E.N. Buccico (Eds.), *La riforma dei codici in Europa e il progetto di codice civile europeo*/Materiali dei seminari 2001 (2002); H.D. Assmann, G. Brüggemeier, R. Sethe (Eds.), *Unterschiedliche Rechtskulturen – Konvergenz des Rechtsdenkens/Different Le-*

---

68 O. Remien, Rechtseinheit ohne Einheitsgesetze?, *RabelsZ* 1992, pp. 300, 307.

69 W. Van Gerven, 'Court decisions, general principles and legal concepts: ingredients of a common law of Europe, in: B. De Witte and C. Forder (Eds.), *The common law of Europe and the future of legal education/Le droit commun de l'Europe et l'avenir de l'enseignement juridique* (1992), pp. 339, 348. See also his Chapter 6 in this volume.

70 Such a circulation of ideas should in itself, apart from developments at a Community level, make a contribution towards the development of domestic private law. This has always been one of the main functions of comparative law.

71 M. Wolf, Abbau prozessualer Schranken im europäischen Binnenmarkt, in: *Wege zu einem europäischen Zivilrecht/Tübinger Symposium zum 80. Geburtstag von Fritz Baur* (1992), pp. 35, 67.

gal Cultures – Convergence of Legal Reasoning (2001); S. Banakas, 'European Tort Law: is it Possible?', *European Review of Private Law* 2002, pp. 363-375; C. von Bar, Die Study Group on a European Civil Code, in: *Festschrift Dieter Henrich* (2000), pp. 1-12; G. Barrett, L. Bernardeau (Eds.), *Towards a European Civil Code/Reflections on the Codification of Civil Law in Europe* (2002); J. Basedow, Codification of Private Law in the European Union: the making of a Hybrid, *European Review of Private Law* 2000, pp. 35-49; J. Basedow (Ed.), *Europäisches Privatrecht -Quellen*, 2 vols. (2000); H. Beale, A. Hartkamp, H. Kötz, D. Tallon (Eds.), *Contract Law* (2002); G. Benacchio, V. Simoni (Eds.), *Repertorio di diritto comunitario civile e commerciale (legislazione – dottrina – giurisprudenza)* (2001); G. Benacchio, *Diritto privato della Communità Europea/Fonti, modelli, regole,* (2d., 2001); K.P. Berger, Europäisches Gemeinrecht der Methode, *Zeitschrift für Europäisches Privatrecht* 2001, pp. 4-29; K.P. Berger, *Transnational Commercial Law in the Age of Globalization* (2001); U. Bernitz, Mot en europeisk civillag?, *Europarättslig Tidsskrift* 2001, pp. 469-474; G. Betlem, E.H.P. Brans, The Future Role of Civil Liability for Environmental Damage in the EU, 2 *Yearbook of European Environmental Law* 183-221 (2002); P. Biavati, Diritto comunitario e diritto processuale civile italiano fra attrazione, autonomia e resistenza, *Il Diritto dell'Unione Europea* 2001, pp. 717-748; H. Bocken *et al.*, *De invloed van het Europees recht op het Belgisch recht* (2003); K. Boele-Woelki (Ed.), *Perspectives for the Unification and Harmonisation of Family Law in Europe* (2003); D. Busch, *De middellijke vertegenwoordiging in Europa* (2002); M. Bussani, U. Mattei (Eds.), *The Common Core pf European Private Law* (2002); M. Bussani, V.V. Palmer (Eds.), *Pure Economic Loss in Europe* (2003); R.C. van Caenegem, *European Law in the Past and the Future/Unity and Diversity over Two Millennia* (2002); F. Cafaggi, *Quale armonizzazione per il diritto europeo dei contratti?* (2003); G.P. Calliess, Reflexive Transnational Law/The Privatisation of Civil Law and the Civilisation of Private Law, *Zeitschrift für Rechtssoziologie* 2002, pp. 185-216; S. Cámara Lapuente (Ed.), *Derecho Privado Europeo* (2003); C.W. Canaris, A. Zaccaria (Eds.), *Die Umsetzung von Zivilrechtlichen Richtlinien der Europäischen Gemeinschaft in Italien und Deutschland* (2002); C. Cauffmann, De Principles of European Contract Law, *Tijdschrift voor Privaatrecht* 2001, pp. 1231-1309; A. Chamboredon, C. Schmid, Pour la création d'un 'Institut européen du droit'/Entre une unification législative ou non législative, l'emergence d'une science juridique transnationale en Europe, *Revue internationale de droit comparé* 2001, pp. 685-708; Conference 'European contract law – the Action plan 2003, *ERA Forum* 2003, pp. 39-145; Conférence des notaires de l'Union européenne, *L'Europe du droit* (2002); I. Davies, Retention of Title Clauses and Non-Possessory Security Interests: A Secured Credit Regime within the European Union?, in: I. Davies (Ed.), *Security Interests in Mobile Equipment* (2002), pp. 335-373; J. De Mot, G. De Geest, De toekomst van het Europees privaatrecht na het Groenboek, *Nederlands Juristenblad* 2002, pp. 881-890; É. Descheemaeker, Fautil codifier le droit privé européen des contrats?, *McGill Law Journal* 2002, pp. 791-853; B. De Witte and C. Forder (Eds.), *The common law of Europe and the future of legal education/Le droit commun de l'Europe et l'avenir de l'enseignement juridique* (1992); L. Díez-Picazo, E. Roca Trias, A.M. Morales, *Los Principios del Derecho Europeo de Contratos* (2000); J.H.M. van Erp, *European Union Case Law as a Source of European Private Law/A Comparison with American Federal Common Law* (2001); J.H.M. van Erp, J.M. Smits (Eds.), *Bronnen Europees privaatrecht* (2001); S. Espiau Espiau, A. Vaquer Aloy (Eds.), *Bases de un derecho contractual europeo/Bases of a European Contract Law* (2003); M. Faure, J. Smits, H. Schneider (Eds.), *Towards a European Ius Commune in Legal Education and Research* (2002); B. Fauvarque-Cosson, D. Mazeaud (Eds.), *Pensée juridique française et harmonisation européenne du droit* (2003); M. Fontaine (Ed.), *Le processus de formation du contrat/ Contributions comparatives et interdisciplinaires à l'harmonisation du droit européen* (2002); J.G. Frick, Die UNIDROIT-Prinzipien für internationale Handelsverträge, *Recht der interna-*

tionalen Wirtschaft 2001, pp. 416-422; A. Furrer, *Zivilrecht im gemeinschaftsrechtlichen Kontext/Das Europäische Kollisionsrecht als Koordinierungsinstrument für die Entbindung des Zivilrechts in das europäische Wirtschaftsrecht* (2002); G. Gandolfi (Ed.), *Code européen des contrats/Avantprojet, Livre premier* (2001); K. Geist, *Die Rechtslage bei Zusendung unbestellter Waren nach Umsetzung der Fernabsatzrichtlinie/Eine rechtsvergleichende Untersuchung unter Berücksichtigung des deutschen, schweizerischen, österreichischen und englischen Rechts* (2002); R. Goode, *Contract and Commercial Law: the Logic and Limits of Harmonisation* (2003); J. Gordley, Ed., *The Enforceability of Promises in European Contract Law* (2001); I. Großkinsky, *Außervertragliche Produkt- und Umwelthaftpflicht – Paralellität oder Autonomie?* (2002); S. Grundmann, 'Verbraucherrecht, Unternehmensrecht, Privatrecht – warum sind sich UN-Kaufrecht und EU-Kaufrechts-Richtlinie so ähnlich?', *Archiv für die civilistische Praxis* 2002, pp. 40-71; S. Grundmann, C.M. Bianca (Eds.), *EU-Kaufrechts-Richtlinie/Kommentar* (2002); S. Grundmann, J. Stuyck (Eds.), *An Academic Green Paper on European Contract Law* (2002); W. Hakenberg, Gemeinschaftsrecht und Privatrecht/Zur Rechtsprechung des EuGH im Jahre 2001, *Zeitschrift für Europäisches Privatrecht* 2002, pp. 754-781; A. Herwig, *Der Gestaltungsspielraum des nationalen Gesetzgebers bei der Umsetzung von europäischen Richtlinien zum Verbrauchervertragsrecht* (2002); M.W. Hesselink, *The New European Legal Culture* (2001); M.W. Hesselink, G.J.P. de Vries, *Principles of European Contract Law* (2001); M. Hesselink and others, *European Review of Private Law* 2002/1, pp. 1-151; M.W. Hesselink, *The New European Private Law/Essays on the Future of Private Law in Europe* (2002); B. Heß, Aktuelle Perspektiven der europäischen Prozessrechtsangleichung, *Juristen-Zeitung* 2001, pp. 573-583; E.H. Hondius, A.W. Jongbloed, R.Ch. Verschuur (Eds.), *Van Nederlands naar Europees procesrecht?!/Liber amicorum Paul Meijknecht* (2000); E.H. Hondius, *Nieuwe methoden van privaatrechtelijke rechtsvinding en rechtsvorming in een Verenigd Europa* (2001); E. Hondius, A. Wieworowska-Domagalska, Europejski kodeks cywilny (Analiza prac Grupy Stuyjnej), *Panstwo i Prawo* 2002, pp. 27-36; Chr. Jamin, D. Mazeaud (Eds.), *L'harmonisation du droit des contrats en Europe* (2001); N. Jansen, *Die Struktur des Haftungsrecht* (2003); N. Jansen, Binnenmarkt, *Privatrecht und europäische Identität* (2003); D. Johnston, R. Zimmermann (Eds.), *Unjustified Enrichment/Key Issues in Comparative Perspective* (2002); K.D. Kerameus, Angleichung des Zivilprozeßrechts in Europa/Einige grundlegende Aspekte, *RabelsZ* 2002, pp. 1-17; E.M. Kieninger, *Wettbewerb der Privatrechtsordnungen im Europäischen Binnenmarkt/Studien zur Privatrechtskoordinierung in der Europäischen Union auf den Gebieten des Gesellschafts- und Vertragsrechts* (2002); B.A. Koch, H. Koziol (Eds.), *Unification of Tort Law: Strict Liability* (2002); H.J. van Kooten, *Restitutierechtelijke gevolgen van ongeoorloofde overeenkomsten/Een rechtsvergelijkende studie naar Nederlands, Duits en Engels recht* (2002); H. Koziol, B.C. Steininger (Eds.), *European Tort Law 2002*, Tort and Insurance Law Yearbook (2003); J. Laffineur, L'évolution du droit communautaire relatif aux contrats de consommation, *Revue européenne de droit de la consommation* 2001/3, pp. 19-42; O. Lando, My life as a lawyer, *Zeitschrift für Europäisches Privatrecht* 2002, pp. 508-522; O. Lando and others (Eds.), *Principles of European Contract Law*, Part III (2003); F. Lehmann, *Die Rezeption des europäischen Verbraucherschutzes im österreichischen Recht* (2002); M.B.M. Loos, Towards a European Law of Servcie Contracts, *European Review of Private Law* 2001, pp. 565-574; B. Lurger, *Grundfragen der Vereinheitlichung des Vertragsrechts in der Europäischen Union* (2002); H.L. MacQueen, A. Vaquer, S. Espiau Espiau, *Regional private laws and codification in Europe* (2003); U. Magnus (Ed.), *Europäisches Schuldrecht Verordnungen und Richtlinien – European Law of Obligations Regulations and Directives – Droit Européen des Obligations Règlements et Directives* (2002); U. Magnus, J. Spier (Eds.), *European Tort Law/Liber amicorum for Helmut Koziol*, (2000); A. Marciano, J.M. Josselin, *The Economics of Harmonising European Law* (2002);

B.S. Markesinis, *The Coming Together of the Common Law and the Civil Law/The Clifford Chance Millennium Lectures,* (2000); B.S. Markesinis, H. Unberath, *The German Law of Torts* (4th ed., 2002); M. Martín Casals, El Codi Civil de Catalunya en la cruïlla del Dret Privat Europeu, *Revista jurídica de Catalunya* 3/2002, pp. 9-38; J.M. Milo and others, Special Series on Trust, *European Review of Private Law* 2000/3, pp. 421-544; H. Nijs, *Patiënt in Europa* (2000); C. Ott, H.B. Schäfer (Eds.), *Vereinheitlichung und Diversität des Zivilrechts un transnationalen Wirtschaftsräumen* (2002); G. Palao Moreno, L. Prats Albentosa, M.J. Reyes López (Eds.), *Derecho Patrimonial Europeo* (2003); P. Pichonnaz, *La compensation* (2001); A. Pinna, Drafting a civil code for Europe – aims and methods, *Tilburg Foreign Law Review* 2002/4, pp. 337-357; J.M. Rainer (Ed.), *Europäisches Privatrecht/Die Rechtsvergleichung* (2002); F. Ranieri, *Europäisches Obligationenrecht,* 2d ed. (2003); N. Reich, H.W. Micklitz, *Europäisches Verbraucherrecht* (4th ed., 2003); M. Reimann, Product Liability in a global context: the hollow victory of the European model, *ERPL* 2003, pp. 128-154; P. Rémy-Corlay, *Les concepts contractuels français à l'heure des Principes de droit européen des contrats* (2003); W.H. Roth, Transposing 'Pointillist' EC Guidelines into Systematic National Codes – Problems and Consequences, *European Review of Private Law* 2002, pp. 761-776; I. Saenger, R. Schulze (Eds.), *Der Ausgleichsanspruch des Handelsvertreters/Beispiel für die Fortentwicklung angeglichenen europäischen Rechts* (2000); S.A. Sánchez Lorenzo, *Derecho privado europeo* (2002); H.N. Schelhaas (general ed.), *The Principles of European Contract Law and Dutch Law/A Commentary* (2002); J.N. Schlotter, *Erbrechtliche Probleme in der Société Privée Européenne* (2001); C. Schmid, Legitimitätsbedingungen eines Europäischen Zivilgesetzbuchs, *Juristen-Zeitung* 2001, pp. 674-683; M. Schmidt-Kessel, Auf dem Weg zu einem Europäischen Vertragsrecht/Zur Einordnung des Aktionsplans der Kommission, *Recht der Internationalen Wirtschaft* 2003, pp. 481-489; E.J.H. Schrage (Ed.), *Unjust Enrichment and the Law of Contract* (2001); H. Schulte-Nölke, R. Schulze, J. Jones (Eds.), *A Casebook on European Consumer Law* (2000); R. Schulze, A. Engel, J. Jones (Eds.), *Casebook Europäisches Privatrecht,* (2000); R. Schulze, R. Zimmermann (Eds.), *Basistexte zum Europäischen Privatrecht – Textsammlung,* 2d ed. (2002); R. Schulze, M. Ebers, H.C. Grigoleit (Eds.), *Informationspflichten und Vertrags-schluss im Acquis communautaire* (2003); R. Schulze, U. Seit (Eds.), *Richterrecht und Rechtsfortbildung in der Europäischen Rechtsgemeinschaft* (2003); K. Siegel, *Produkthaftung im polnischen, tschechischen und slowenischen Recht* (2002); L.D. Smith (Ed.), *Restitution* (2001); J.M. Smits, *The Good Samaritan in European Private Law/On the Perils of Principles without a Programme and a Programme for the Future* (2000); J. Smits (Ed.), *The Contribution of Mixed Legal Systems to European Private Law* (2001); J. Smits, *The Making of European Private Law/Toward a Ius Commune Europaeum as a Mixed Legal System* (2002); W. Snijders, *Building a European Contract Law; five Fallacies and two Castles in Spain* (2003); J. Spier (Ed.), *Principles of European Tort Law: Causation* (2000); J. Spier (Ed.), *Unification of Tort Law: Causation* (2000); D. Staudenmayer, The Commission Action Plan on European Contract Law, *European Review of Private Law* 2003, pp. 113-127; V. Trstenjak, Evropski Civilni Zakonik – Moznost, nujnost ali utopija?, *Pravnik, Ljubljana,* let. 56 (2001), 11-12, pp. 675-700; Um Código civil para a Europa, *Boletim da Faculdade de Direito, Universidade de Coïmbra* (2002); M. Van Hoeke and F. Ost (Eds.), *The Harmonisation of European Private Law* (2000); S. Vogenauer, *Die Auslegung von Gesetzen in England und auf dem Kontinent* (2001); G.J.P. de Vries, *Remedies op grond van niet-nakoming van internationale contracten in het licht van de PECL* (2002); S. Weatherill, The European Commission's Green Paper on European Contract Law: Context, Content and Constitutionality, *Journal of Consumer Policy* 2001, pp. 339-399; S. Weatherill, Can there be common interpretation of European private law?, 31 *Georgia Journal of International & Comparative Law* 139-166 (2002); J.C. Wichard, Europäisches Markenrecht zwischen Territorialität und Binnenmarkt, *Zeitschrift für*

Europäisches Privatrecht 2002, pp. 23-57; W.J.H. Wiggers, *International Commercial Law/ Source Materials* (2001); V. Zeno-Zencovich, Le basi costituzionali di un diritto privato europeo, *Europa e diritto privato* 2003, pp. 19-31; R. Zimmermann, *Roman Law, Contemporary Law, European Law/The Civilian Tradition Today* (2001); R. Zimmermann, S. Whittaker, *Good Faith in European Contract Law* (2000); R. Zimmermann, *Comparative Foundations of a European Law of Set-Off and Prescription* (2002).

CHAPTER 2

Roman Law and the Harmonisation of Private Law in Europe

Reinhard Zimmermann*

1 Harmonisation of Private Law in Europe

It is a self-evident characteristic of most disciplines taught at a modern university that they are international in substance, approach and outlook: this holds true from archaeology to medicine, and from philosophy to chemistry. But it cannot be said of legal scholarship. For more than 100 years there have been, in principle, as many legal systems in Europe as there are national states. To a large extent, the boundaries of legal scholarship have become identical with the political borders. German lawyers apply the *Bürgerliches Gesetzbuch,* while French lawyers use the *Code civil.* In England, the 'good old' common law still prevails. As a result, the doctrines of modern private law, the subject-matter of law courses, examination requirements and prerequisites for entry into the legal profession differ from country to country. In Germany, scores of legal writers continue their stern and unrelenting endeavours to beat a path through the dreaded third-party enrichment jungle;[1] to penetrate the mysteries of the so-called *Eigentümer-Besitzer-Verhältnis*[2] and to draw ever finer distinctions as to when a delictual action should be made available (in addition to a contractual claim for damages!), if an object that was sold has been destroyed as the result of a defect in an individual and identifiable part of it.[3] To an English lawyer this all seems as confusing and exotic as the abracadabra of conditions, warranties and intermediate terms, or the niceties of the so-called doctrine of consideration appear to us. Foreign literature is only rarely consulted in judicial decisions,[4] academic posts in universities are occupied almost without exception by local lawyers; and be-

---

* Professor of Law and Director of the *Max Planck Institut für Ausländisches und Internationales Privatrecht,* Hamburg, Germany.

1 The leading textbook in the field acknowledges that, even in simple cases, students tend to get caught up hopelessly in the maze of theories; and it therefore advises them, for purposes of their own discussions of the topic, pragmatically to disregard the more subtle doctrinal nuances: Karl Larenz, Claus-Wilhelm Canaris, *Lehrbuch des Schuldrechts,* vol. II/2, 13th ed., 1994, pp. 252 ff.

2 As far as compensation for improvements are concerned, the topic has now been subjected to critical analysis from an historical and European perspective by Dirk Verse, *Verwendungen im Eigentümer-Besitzer-Verhältnis,* 1999; for a summary of Verse's views, see Reinhard Zimmermann, *Roman Law, Contemporary Law, European Law: The Civilian Tradition Today,* 2001, pp. 115 ff.

3 The question becomes relevant as a result of differences in the periods of prescription; see Reinhard Zimmermann, 'Extinctive Prescription in German Law', in: Erik Jayme (ed.), *German National Reports in Civil Law Matters for the XIVth Congress of Comparative Law in Athens 1994,* 1994, pp. 164 ff. It has not been solved by the reform of the German law of obligations of 1 January 2002; see Dieter Medicus, 'Die Leistungsstörungen im neuen Schuldrecht' 2003 *Juristische Schulung* 529.

4 See, most recently, Hein Kötz, 'Der Bundesgerichtshof und die Rechtsvergleichung', in: *50 Jahre Bundesgerichtshof: Festgabe der Wissenschaft,* 2000, vol. II, pp. 825 ff.

cause the regulations for legal education are still predominantly oriented towards the law of the respective country, this particularisation of legal scholarship threatens to imprint itself also on the next generation of lawyers.[5] Even in his day and age, Rudolf von Jhering, who died in 1892, more than one hundred years ago, found this situation humiliating and undignified.[6] Today, it is also anachronistic. For in recent years, in the context of the European Community, we have experienced a process of legal unification which has increasingly affected even the classical core areas of private law.[7] In Germany, for instance, a person injured by the explosion of a defective washing machine can take legal recourse by way of the *Produkthaftungsgesetz* (Product Liability Act) of 15 December 1989. Whoever, in the course of a promotional leisure-time excursion, gets talked into buying the Encyclopaedia Britannica, may revoke the contract within two weeks in terms of § 312 read in conjunction with § 355 BGB.[8] Where someone purchases a new car by way of an instalment sale financed by a third party, he may raise as a defence even against the third party's claim for repayment of the instalments, that the accelerator is defective; this is provided for in § 359 read in conjunction with § 491 BGB.[9] A provision contained in a standard contract form excluding the liability of a seller can be invalid under § 309, no 7 BGB. All these rules concerning transactions and liability situations of everyday life are now based upon, and thus have to be interpreted in the light of, directives enacted by the European Union.[10] The consumer sales directive of 25 May 1999 has even triggered the most comprehensive reform of the BGB since its enactment on 1 January 1900.[11]

The disadvantages and dangers resulting from the selective and uncoordinated character of the uniform law emanating from the European Union are very evident today. The directives have tended to create 'islands of uniform law in a sea of national law but, apart from that, also wide areas with regard to which it is often difficult to determine whether they form part of the coast or the open sea, i.e. whether they are subject to the uniform law or the national law'.[12] On the level of the national legal systems, they have added another level of complexity. It is hardly surprising,

---

5 See, for Germany, Hein Kötz, 'Europäische Juristenausbildung', (1993) 1 *Zeitschrift für Europäisches Privatrecht* 268 ff.; Axel Flessner, 'Deutsche Juristenausbildung', 1996 *Juristenzeitung* 689 ff.

6 Rudolf von Jhering, *Geist des römischen Rechts auf den verschiedenen Stufen seiner Entwicklung*, vol. I, 8th ed., 1924, p. 15.

7 See, e.g., Martin Gebauer, *Grundfragen der Europäisierung des Privatrechts*, 1998; Peter-Christian Müller-Graff (ed.), *Gemeinsames Privatrecht in der Europäischen Gemeinschaft*, 2nd ed, 1999; Stefan Grundmann (ed.), *Systembildung und Systemlücken in Kerngebieten des Europäischen Privatrechts*, 2000.

8 Previously: *Haustürwiderrufsgesetz* (Cancellation of Front-Door Contracts Act) of 16 January 1986.

9 Previously: *Verbraucherkreditgesetz* (Consumer Credit Act) of 17 December 1990.

10 For a collection of all directives affecting the traditional core areas of private law, see Reiner Schulze, Reinhard Zimmermann, *Basistexte zum Europäischen Privatrecht*, 2nd ed., 2002, sub I (English edition by Oliver Radley-Gardner and Hugh Beale, 2003).

11 On that reform, and its background, see Reinhard Zimmermann, 'Modernising the German Law of Obligations?', in: Peter Birks, Arianna Pretto (eds.), *Themes in Comparative Law in Honour of Bernard Rudden*, 2002, pp. 265 ff.

12 Hein Kötz, 'Rechtsvergleichung und gemeineuropäisches Privatrecht', in: Peter-Christian Müller-Graff (ed.), *Gemeinsames Privatrecht in der Europäischen Gemeinschaft*, 2nd ed., 1999, p. 151.

therefore, that the codification of European private law has been suggested as a more coherent and systematic alternative. The European Parliament has been an early protagonist of this idea which is now widely debated.[13] As a precursor various sets of 'Principles' of specific areas of European private law have been published or are in the process of preparation.[14] An international 'Study Group on a European Civil Code' has even established itself.[15] But a European Civil Code will have to be preceded, inspired, and sustained, by a European (as opposed to merely national) scholarship of which, so far, we only see the first beginnings.[16] The discussion today has obvious parallels[17] to the great codification debate at the beginning of the 19th century in Germany when A.F.J. Thibaut argued that a General German Civil Code, modelled on the French *Code civil*, would facilitate the emergence of an undivided German nation. This idea was decisively rejected by Friedrich Carl von Savigny who insisted on the necessity of establishing 'an organically progressive legal scholarship which may be common to the whole nation'.[18] Savigny's Historical School led to German legal unification on a scholarly level and, eventually, even to the drafting of a Civil Code – a code, however which, rather than constituting a watershed in German legal development, bore certain characteristics of a restatement;[19] and which was described by one of its principal architects, Bernhard Windscheid, as 'merely a ripple in the stream'[20] within the development of the law by the community of courts and legal scholars.[21] In a similar vein, I think, that one of the great challenges with which we are faced today is to advance and accelerate the establishment of a legal scholarship 'which may be common to the whole of Europe': a scholarship which may,

---

13 See, for example, Winfried Tilmann, 'Zweiter Kodifikationsbeschluss des Europäischen Parlaments', (1995) 3 *Zeitschrift für Europäisches Privatrecht* 534 ff.; Jürgen Basedow, 'Das BGB im künftigen europäischen Privatrecht' (2000) 200 *Archiv für die civilistische Praxis* 445 ff.; Christian von Bar, 'Die Mitteilung der Europäischen Kommission zum Europäischen Vertragsrecht', (2001) 9 *Zeitschrift für Europäisches Privatrecht* 799 ff.; Herbert Kronke, *Brauchen wir ein europäisches Zivilgesetzbuch?*, 2002; Gavin Barrett, Ludovic Bernadeau (eds.), *Towards a European Civil Code*, 2002.

14 The most advanced project concerns the area of contract law: Ole Lando, Hugh Beale (eds.), *Principles of European Contract Law, Parts I and II*, 2000; Ole Lando, Eric Clive, André Prüm, Reinhard Zimmermann (eds.), *Principles of European Contract Law, Part III*, 2003.

15 Christian von Bar, 'Die Study Group on a European Civil Code', in: *Festschrift für Dieter Henrich*, 2000, pp. 1 ff.

16 See, e.g., Hein Kötz, *Europäisches Vertragsrecht*, vol. I, 1996 (English translation by Tony Weir, *European Contract Law*, 1997); Christian von Bar, *Gemeineuropäisches Deliktsrecht*, vol. I, 1996; vol. II, 1999 (English translation: *The Common European Law of Torts*, vol. I, 1999; vol. II, 2000); Filippo Ranieri, *Europäisches Obligationenrecht*, 1999.

17 See, for example, Ole Lando, 'The Principles of European Contract Law after Year 2000', in: Franz Werro (Hg.), *New Perspectives on European Private Law*, 1998, pp. 59 ff.

18 Friedrich Carl von Savigny, 'Vom Beruf unserer Zeit für Gesetzgebung und Rechtswissenschaft', easily accessible today in Hans Hattenhauer (ed.), *Thibaut und Savigny: Ihre programmatischen Schriften*, 2nd ed., 2002, p. 126.

19 See, in particular, Horst Heinrich Jakobs, *Wissenschaft und Gesetzgebung im bürgerlichen Recht nach der Rechtsquellenlehre des 19. Jahrhunderts*, 1983, e.g. pp. 120, 160.

20 Bernhard Windscheid, 'Die geschichtliche Schule in der Rechtswissenschaft', in: *idem, Gesammelte Reden und Abhandlungen* (ed. by Paul Oertmann, 1904), p. 76.

21 Reinhard Zimmermann, 'Das Bürgerliche Gesetzbuch und die Entwicklung des Bürgerlichen Rechts', in: Joachim Rückert, Mathias Schmoeckel, Reinhard Zimmermann (eds.), *Historisch-kritischer Kommentar zum BGB*, vol. I, 2003, Vor § 1.

eventually, pave the way for a codification of European private law which would also not disrupt the continuity of legal development and which would be as widely accepted as the *Code civil* in France or the BGB in Germany.[22]

2 The Re-Europeanisation of Legal Scholarship

This, of course, merely constitutes the roughest survey of the first aspect of my topic: harmonisation of private law in Europe. What does Roman law have to do with it? One might be inclined to answer: nothing. For it is just about out of the question that the officials and politicians in Brussels, in the course of drafting their Directives, have drawn their inspiration from Julian or Papinian, from Labeo or from Quintus Mucius Scaevola.[23] Were this indeed the case, they would not, for example, rely so heavily upon legislation as the high road towards establishing European legal unity. Case law and legal scholarship are among the alternatives to legislative unification,[24] and they have been important not only in the history of German private law but are characteristic for the development of Western legal tradition in general. Once again, today, they offer the promise of a more organic point of departure for transcending the national fragmentation of European private law. Furthermore, the reference to case law and legal scholarship reminds us that instead of 'Europeanisation', we might as well speak of a process of 'Re-Europeanisation' of private law. For a common European legal culture, centred around a legal scholarship and legal practice that were informed by the same sources, did once exist. Even today, the common tradition on which the modern national legal systems are based, constitutes a unifying force of great potential; and anyone aiming to found a renewed European legal culture should use it to his advantage.

This 'old' European law, to which the rest of this paper will be devoted, is known as the Roman-canon *ius commune*.[25] It came into being as part of a dramatic and far-reaching cultural upheaval: the so-called Renaissance of the 12th century.[26] First in

---

22 Reinhard Zimmermann, 'Savigny's Legacy: Legal History, Comparative Law and the Emergence of a European Legal Science', (1996) 112 *Law Quarterly Review* 576 ff.

23 But see, concerning the courts of the European Community, Rolf Knütel, '*Ius commune* und Römisches Recht vor Gerichten der Europäischen Union', 1996 *Juristische Schulung* 768 ff.

24 On non-legislative forms of legal unification, see the contributions in (1992) 56 *Rabels Zeitschrift für ausländisches und internationales Privatrecht* 215 ff.; to Mauro Bussani, Ugo Mattei (eds.), *Making European Law: Essays on the 'Common Core' Project*, 2000; and to Michael Faure, Jan Smits, Hildegard Schneider (eds.), *Towards a European Ius Commune in Legal Education and Research*, 2002. Of particular significance within the European Union is the European Court of Justice in Luxembourg; cf. Ulrich Everling, 'Rechtsvereinheitlichung durch Richterrecht in der Europäischen Gemeinschaft', (1986) 50 *Rabels Zeitschrift für ausländisches und internationales Privatrecht* 193 ff.; Martin Franzen, 'Privatrechtsangleichung durch die Europäische Gemeinschaft', 1999, pp. 291 ff.

25 Cf., in particular, Helmut Coing, *Die ursprüngliche Einheit der europäischen Rechtswissenschaft*, 1968; and see various other publications by the same author, e.g. Helmut Coing, *Europäische Grundlagen des modernen Privatrechts*, 1986. Cf. also Reinhard Zimmermann, 'Das römisch-kanonische *ius commune* als Grundlage europäischer Rechtseinheit', 1992 *Juristenzeitung* 10 ff.; Manlio Bellomo, *The Common Legal Past of Europe 1000-1800*, 1995, pp. 55 ff.

26 Cf., in particular, Harold J. Berman, *Law and Revolution: The Formation of the Western Legal Tradition*, 1983; Ennio Cortese, *Il Rinascimento giuridico medievale*, 1992.

Bologna, then also at other universities founded on the same model, lawyers began systematically, using the scholastic method, to penetrate the most important body of Roman sources, the Digest (which had only recently been rediscovered) and to make it intellectually accessible. This was necessary, above all, because the Digest is not a systematically-structured piece of legislation or a textbook in the modern sense of the word, but a compilation of fragments from classical Roman legal writings, put together under Justinian in the 6th century AD. These writings themselves were full of controversy; furthermore, they originated from different stages of the legal development. None the less, the legal wisdom handed down in the Digest, i.e. the concepts, legal rules and maxims, systematic discoveries and models of argumentation from Roman law proved superior to the contemporary customary laws. Thus the rationalisation of the law meant, to a significant degree, its Romanisation; and over the following centuries Roman law, in the form imparted by Justinian and turned into a 'legal science' (*Rechtswissenschaft*) by the lawyers of Bologna, conquered Europe. We call this process 'Reception'.[27] Three characteristic aspects should be emphasised.

3 The *Ius Commune*: A European Tradition

The first aspect is the truly European character of the tradition that was thus founded. Up until the time of the so-called *usus modernus pandectarum* in the 17th and 18th centuries, the whole of educated Europe formed a cultural unit; and law was a constitutent part of that European culture.[28] Lawyers who had received their education in one country could occupy a chair in another. The great French scholar Donellus, for example, was a professor at Heidelberg, Leiden and Altdorf; the Italian Alberico Gentili taught at Oxford, the German Natural lawyer Samuel Pufendorf at Lund, the Spaniard Antonius Perezius at Leuven.[29] By the end of the 17th century, Hugo Grotius' work *De jure belli ac pacis* had seen 40 editions in Germany, Holland, Italy and Switzerland;[30] apart from that, there had been ten French, seven English and six German translations, as well as one into Italian. Heineccius' *Elementa iuris civilis* was used as a textbook at universities such as Halle, Pavia, Bologna, Cracow and Oxford. Altogether, it appeared in 75 editions in Germany, Italy, Switzerland, Austria, Belgium, France and Spain. In his *Commentarius ad Pandectas,* Johannes Voet,[31] as

27 The standard account is by Franz Wieacker, *Privatrechtsgeschichte der Neuzeit,* 2nd ed., 1967, pp. 45 ff., 97 ff. (English translation by Tony Weir, *A History of Private Law in Europe,* 1995). For the significance of Roman law for European legal culture, see Paul Koschaker, *Europa und das römische Recht,* 4th ed., 1966. For an analysis of early modern German court practice, see Peter Oestmann, *Rechtsvielfalt vor Gericht,* 2002.

28 This is the point of departure for Helmut Coing's *opus magnum, Europäisches Privatrecht,* vol. I, 1985.

29 Specifically on the Dutch professors of the 17th century cf. Reinhard Zimmermann, 'Roman-Dutch Jurisprudence and its Contribution to European Private Law', (1992) 66 *Tulane Law Review* 1715 ff.

30 These and the following figures are to be found in Coing, *Einheit* (n. 25) 160 ff.

31 On whom see Robert Feenstra and C.J.D. Waal, *Seventeenth-Century Leyden Law Professors and their Influence on the Development of the Civil Law,* 1975, pp. 35 ff., 69 ff.; Reinhard Zimmermann, 'Römisch-holländisches Recht – ein Überblick', in: Robert Feenstra, Reinhard Zimmermann (eds.),

a matter of course, cited authors from Spain, Italy, France and Germany, from back in the 14th century up until his own time. German students came on their *peregrinatio academica* to Italy or France in the same way as Scottish students to Leiden or Utrecht. Law was not conceived of as a system of rules enacted for, and exclusively applicable in, a specific territory; it was recognised and applied on an international scale. Of course, this did not mean that the outcome of disputes would everywhere necessarily be the same.[32] Whether an error of law, for instance, excludes the possibility of reclaiming what had been delivered without legal ground was (owing to the fact that the sources are unclear on this point) answered differently by different lawyers at different times and in different parts of Europe.[33] Yet, all over Europe use was made of the same legal 'grammar': the dichotomy, in our example above, between *error iuris* and *error facti;* the system of the Roman *condictiones* which, over the centuries, formed the basis for the discussion of contested issues in enrichment law; and the prerequisites, generally agreed upon in principle, for the application of that most central of these enrichment actions, the *condictio indebiti*.[34] Moving with the same cultural tides running through Europe,[35] and moored to a common educational and intellectual tradition,[36] as well as to a common language,[37] European legal scholarship, in spite of many differences in detail, remained a unified intellectual world; the international *communis opinio doctorum* was authoritative for its application and development.[38]

Das römisch-holländische Recht: Fortschritte des Zivilrechts im 17. und 18. Jahrhundert, 1992, pp. 9 ff.

32 The civilian tradition is characterised by a considerable diversity; it is, however, a diversity within a fundamental intellectual unity. The theme is developed in an article entitled 'The Civil Law in European Codes', in: David L. Carey Miller, Reinhard Zimmermann (eds.), *The Civilian Tradition and Scots Law: Aberdeen Quincentenary Essays,* 1997.

33 For details see Reinhard Zimmermann, *The Law of Obligations: Roman Foundations of the Civilian Tradition,* 1990, paperback edition 1996, pp. 849 ff., 868 ff.

34 For details, see my article 'Unjustified Enrichment: The Modern Civilian Approach', (1995) 3 *Oxford Journal of Legal Studies* 403 ff.

35 See Helmut Coing, 'Die europäische Privatrechtsgeschichte der neueren Zeit als einheitliches Forschungsgebiet', (1967) 1 *Ius Commune* 17 ff.

36 This perspective has repeatedly been emphasised by Filippo Ranieri; see, e.g., 'Der Europäische Jurist: Rechtshistorisches Forschungsthema und rechtspolitische Aufgabe', (1990) 17 *Ius Commune* 9 ff.

37 On the relationship between law and language, see Bernhard Großfeld, 'Sprache und Recht', 1984 *Juristenzeitung* 1 ff.; Andreas Wacke, 'Lateinisch und Deutsch als Rechtssprachen in Mitteleuropa', 1990 *Neue Juristische Wochenschrift* 877 ff.; Jörn Eckert, Hans Hattenhauer (eds.) *Sprache – Recht – Geschichte,* 1991; Tony Weir, 'Die Sprachen des europäischen Rechts: Eine skeptische Betrachtung', (1995) 3 *Zeitschrift für Europäisches Privatrecht* 368 ff.

38 See Gino Gorla, 'La "communis opinio totius orbis" et la réception jurisprudentielle du droit au cours des XVIe, XVIIe et XVIIIe siècles dans la "civil law" et la "common law"', in: Mauro Cappelletti (ed.), *New Perspectives for a Common Law of Europe,* 1978, pp. 54 ff. and Coing, *Europäisches Privatrecht* (n. 28) 124 ff.

4   'Pure Roman Law' and *Usus Modernus*

The second aspect is Roman law's inherent flexibility and capability for development. What became the basis of the European common law was by no means pure Roman law, was not the law of Quintus Mucius or Papinian. Indeed, the mere mention of these names should remind us that any reference to 'pure Roman law' would be a fiction. Quintus Mucius Scaevola, one of the central figures of the most creative period in Roman jurisprudence, lived around the turn of the first century BC; Aemilius Papinianus, the most brilliant representative of the late classical period,[39] was *praefectus praetorio* under the Emperor Septimius Severus. Separating these two is a time-span of more than three hundred years, and if account is also taken of the time when the foundations of the Roman *ius civile,* the XII Tables, were established, we are dealing with a period of about 700 years, in the course of which the law was subjected to fundamental changes. In addition, the most important sources of this entire period were handed down to us in the form of a compilation, the above-mentioned Digest, which itself dates from the 6th century AD. At that stage, Rome was already in the hands of the Ostrogoths, while Constantinople was the new capital of the Empire. The Digest became the central component of a Byzantine law book, the *Corpus Juris Civilis* (as it was later called); and it was this work that was to determine the later view of Roman law and to become the basis of the common European legal scholarship. The Digest itself can be described as a gigantic torso of Roman law, which contains a colourful mixture of case decisions, legal opinions and rules, commentary, disputes, and excerpts from textbooks and monographs. Altogether it includes fragments from about two thousand works. The overall character of the Digest is casuistic. Much of it reflects the contemporary position at the various stages of Roman legal history; other parts were altered to suit the requirements of the 6th century; and some parts simply contradict each other. A further 600 years later, the scholars in Bologna transplanted this complex body of sources into their society, and sought in it answers to the legal problems of their time;[40] they were followed by the Italian Commentators and the subsequent law schools, down to the representatives of the *usus modernus pandectarum.* The latter designation – taken from an influential contemporary work[41] – shows clearly what had happened in the meantime: a contemporary practice of Roman law had been developed, taking into account the changed requirements and value systems of the day. This practice is documented in works such as Johannes Voet's great Commentary on the Digest or in Simon van Groenewegen's *Tractatus de legibus abrogatis et inusitatis* which lists all changes in the law in great detail. Thus, a great feat of integration, begun by Commentators such as Bartolus and Baldus, had been achieved. The law that was actually practised, and

---

39   On whom see Hans Ankum, 'Papinian, ein dunkler Jurist', (1996) 2 *Orbis Iuris Romani* 5 ff.; Okko Behrends, 'Papinians Verweigerung oder die Moral des Juristen', in Ulrich Mölk (ed.), *Literatur and Recht: Literarische Rechtsfälle von der Antike bis in die Gegenwart,* 1996, pp. 243 ff.

40   Hermann Lange, *Römisches Recht im Mittelalter,* vol. I, 1997.

41   Samuel Stryk, *Specimen usus moderni pandectarum,* first published between 1690 and 1712 in several volumes; see Klaus Luig, 'Samuel Stryk (1640–1710) und der *"usus modernus pandectarum"*', in: *Die Bedeutung der Wörter, Festschrift für Sten Gagnér,* 1991, pp. 219 ff.; *idem,* Usus modernus, in: *Handwörterbuch zur deutschen Rechtsgeschichte,* vol. V, 1998, cols. 628 ff.

that met the demands of the day (the *consuetudines hodiernae*), had not become barren under a one-and-a-half millenium-old layer of law, but had rather, by way of Romanistic conceptualisation and erudition, been made intellectually fertile. How was that possible?

5   An Example: The General Concept of a Contract

Let us take, as an example, the law of contract. In the Rome of the Republic and Principate, its cornerstones were, on the one hand, the stipulation, an oral promise which was applicable in every situation but which was tied to specific formal requirements, and, on the other hand, the consensual contracts, which were not subject to any formality but only available in a limited number.[42] But even in the *Corpus Juris,* the conversion of the stipulation from a *contractus verbis* to a promise in writing was widely documented. This development continued during the Middle Ages. The 'writing obligatory' which was common in medieval commercial practice appears to have been a degenerate descendant of the stipulation. Ultimately, however, the history of the stipulation ended in a cul-de-sac, for the application of contractual formalities had rapidly become an arcanum of notarial practice.[43] Instead of the stipulation, it was the informal *pactum* that was destined to become the root of modern contract doctrine. A *pactum* had only been actionable in Roman law if it could be classified as one of the four consensual contracts; otherwise the rule was: *nuda pactio obligationem non parit*[44] – a naked pact begets no right of action. However, even in the post-classical period, one freezing *pactum* after another received a garment – though sometimes rather makeshift, and cut to many different patterns.[45] Thus, there were the 'innominate' contracts (innominate even though some of them had actually acquired individual names). Furthermore, consensual agreements were enforceable if they had been attached to one of the recognised contracts and had been concluded at the same time as the main contract (*pacta in continenti adiecta*). Then, again, there were two groups of agreements which were not classified as contracts, but which were nevertheless enforceable: the so-called *pacta praetoria* and *pacta legitima*. Other informal arrangements, that did not fall into one of these categories, could be raised by way of defence. The *Corpus Juris* thus presented, in this as in many other areas, a somewhat patchy picture, marked by haphazard distinctions and internal inconsistencies. However a trend had become apparent, that was to set the tone for the ever-increasing erosion, and ultimate abandonment, of the principle *ex nudo pacto non oritur actio.*[46]

---

42 For details see *Law of Obligations* (n. 33) 68 ff. (stipulation), 230 ff. (consensual contracts).

43 *Law of Obligations* (n. 33) 546 ff.

44 Ulp. D. 2, 14, 7, 4. See further Ulp. D. 2, 14, 7, 5; Ulp. D. 19, 5, 15; Paul. Sent. II, XIV, 1; C. 2, 3, 10 (Alex.) and Bruno Schmidlin, *Die römischen Rechtsregeln: Versuch einer Typologie,* 1970, pp. 97 ff. This rule was later formulated somewhat differently: *ex nudo pacto non oritur actio.*

45 See for details *Law of Obligations* (n. 33) 508 ff.

46 See Klaus-Peter Nanz, *Die Entstehung des allgemeinen Vertragsbegriffs im 16. bis 18. Jahrhundert,* 1985; Coing, *Europäisches Privatrecht* (n. 28) 398 ff.; *Law of Obligations* (n. 33) 537 ff.; John Barton (ed.), *Towards a General Law of Contract,* 1990; Robert Feenstra, 'Die Klagbarkeit der *pacta nuda*', in: Robert Feenstra, Reinhard Zimmermann (eds.), *Das römisch-holländische Recht: Fortschritte des Zivilrechts im 17. und 18. Jahrhundert,* 1992, pp. 123 ff.

This development was propelled, in the first place, by the Canon lawyers who had charitably, as could be expected of them, taken pity on the poor and naked pacts; and thus we find in the Decretals of Pope Gregory IX a sentence which was to have far-reaching consequences: *pacta quantumcunque nuda servanda sunt* – the direct root of our expression *pacta sunt servanda*.[47] But international commercial practice also played its role in the development; and many an author took his inspiration from the supposedly Germanic[48] concept of good faith on which Tacitus had mused without much appreciation. Thereafter, from the 17th century onwards, the Natural lawyers made it their business to fashion a single dress pattern for all pacts. The binding nature of all agreements was, for them, an essential tool for the regulation of human affairs;[49] all the more so since even God would be acting against his nature were he not to keep his word.[50] At the same time the lawyers of the *usus modernus* finally overcame, for all practical purposes, the dogma of the non-actionability of the naked pact.

That binding contracts are based, in principle, on formless consent is recognised today in all Western European legal systems. It is one of the latent principles underlying, and constituting, European contract law.[51] And this principle, like many others, is in characteristic fashion Roman and non-Roman at the same time: it is Roman law in modern clothing, no longer in a toga or a medieval coat of mail.

6   *Ius Civile in Iure Canonico*

One a word must be added, in this context, on the role of the church. We have already referred to the Roman-Canon *ius commune* as the foundation of European legal unity,[52] for what was taught at the medieval universities was not only Roman law, but also Canon law – hence the term *ius utrumque* for the subject-matter of contemporary legal scholarship. Canon law is based upon a second large and also essentially casuistic legal compilation, the *Corpus Juris Canonici*. Its roots lie in the so-called *Decretum Gratiani,* which, not at all coincidentally, had also become the subject of scholarly attention in 12th century Bologna. Roman law and Canon law, however, were by no means unrelated to each other. As the great English legal historian

---

47 Lib. I, Tit. XXXV, Cap. I of the *Liber Extra* of the *Corpus Juris Canonici*. For all details, see Peter Landau, 'Pacta sunt servanda: Zu den kanonistischen Grundlagen der Privatautonomie', in: *'Ins Wasser geworfen und Ozeane durchquert': Festschrift für Knut Wolfgang Nörr*, 2003, pp. 457 ff.

48 *Germania* XXIV, 3 and 4; cf., e.g., Hugo Grotius, *Inleiding tot de Hollandsche Rechtsgeleertheyd*, 1631, III, I, 52.

49 See Samuel Pufendorf, *De jure naturae et gentium libri octo,* Francofurti ad Moenum, 1694, Lib. III, Cap. IV, § 2.

50 Hugo Grotius, *De jure belli ac pacis libri tres,* Amsterdami, 1631, Lib. II, Cap. IV, § 2.

51 See, for example, Art. 2:101 PECL.

52 Generally on the significance of Canon law cf. Peter Landau, 'Der Einfluß des kanonischen Rechts auf die europäische Rechtskultur', in: Reiner Schulze (ed.), *Europäische Rechts- und Verfassungsgeschichte: Ergebnisse und Perspektiven der Forschung,* 1991, pp. 39 ff.; Heinrich Scholler (ed.), *Die Bedeutung des kanonischen Rechts für die Entwicklung einheitlicher Rechtsprinzipien,* 1996; Hans-Jürgen Becker, 'Spuren des kanonischen Rechts im Bürgerlichen Gesetzbuch', in: Reinhard Zimmermann, Rolf Knütel, Jens Peter Meincke (eds.), *Rechtsgeschichte und Privatrechtsdogmatik,* 2000, pp. 159 ff.

Frederic William Maitland once put it: 'The imperial mother and her papal daughter were fairly good friends.'[53] The Popes could not, and did not want to, develop an intellectually independent legal system. Instead they relied to a large extent on Roman legal rules and concepts which thus, in a chasuble so to speak, not infrequently managed to influence the development of European law. Contract doctrine provides a good example. *Pacta quantumcunque nuda servanda sunt:* this seminal sentence from the *Corpus Juris Canonici* (quoted above) did not only find its pivotal point in the Roman concept of *pactum;* it also unmistakably alludes to the distinction, drawn by the Glossators, between naked pacts and those vested (or 'clothed') with actionability; and it subtly evokes the Roman praetor's promise contained in D. 2, 14, 7, 7: *pacta conventa servabo.*[54] Furthermore, the Canonists smoothed the transition from the Roman rule of *nuda pactio obligationem non parit* to the counter-rule of *ex nudo pacto oritur actio* by granting actionability only to those *pacta* which had been entered into by the parties *serio animo et deliberate.* This made it necessary to develop a criterion according to which serious agreements could be distinguished from those not seriously entered into. By using building stones hewn from the quarry of the Digest[55] and adding generous quantities of scholastic mortar,[56] a suitable doctrine could be built up relatively quickly: only those agreements which rested upon a lawful *causa*[57] were actionable. This *causa* doctrine can still be found today, for example, in Article 1131 of the French *Code civil*, though 'it is clear that it means quite different things in different contexts and that in many cases it is perfectly dispensable and contributes nothing to the proper resolution of the conflict of interests involved'.[58]

7   The Civilian Tradition Today

We may now turn our attention to the third important aspect: the characteristic – and thus fundamentally uniform – imprint which even our modern national legal systems have received from the tradition of the Roman-Canon *ius commune.* Of course, this is particularly conspicuous where the continuity of the development has not been disrupted, or obscured, by the intervention of the legislature. South Africa provides, perhaps, the best example in the modern world. Here the Roman-Dutch law, as imported by the settlers of the Dutch East India Company in the middle of the 17th century, i.e.

---

53 Sir Frederick Pollock, Frederic William Maitland, *The History of the English Law Before the Time of Edward I*, 2nd ed., vol I, 1898, p. 116. On the topic of 'The Learned Laws in "Pollock and Maitland"', see Richard H. Helmholz, (1996) 89 *Proceedings of the British Academy* 145 ff.
54 See Law of Obligations (n. 33) 508 ff.
55 In particular Aristo/Ulp. D. 2, 14, 7, 2; Ulp. D. 2, 14, 7, 4; Ulp. D. 44, 4, 2, 3; further details in *Law of Obligations* (n. 33) 549 ff.
56 On the scholastic *causa*-doctrine see Alfred Söllner, 'Die causa im Kondiktionen- and Vertragsrecht des Mittelalters bei den Glossatoren, Kommentatoren and Kanonisten', (1960) 77 *Zeitschrift der Savigny-Stiftung für Rechtsgeschichte, Romanistische Abteilung* 183 ff.; more recently, see the contributions in Letizio Vacca (ed.), *Causa e contratto nella prospettiva storico-comparatistica*, 1997.
57 On the development of this doctrine, see *Law of Obligations* (n. 33) 551 ff.
58 Kötz/Weir (n. 16) 55. The position is thus very similar to the one encountered with regard to its functional equivalent in England and the United States: the doctrine of consideration. On its breakdown in modern American law, see Ferdinand Fromholzer, *Consideration*, 1997.

the Roman-canon *ius commune* in its specifically Dutch variant, still applies today.[59] By that time, the United Netherlands had reached a pinnacle of political power, economic wealth and cultural ascendancy in Europe, and Dutch lawyers, too, had become the leading exponents of the civilian tradition.[60] Thus, even today, the courts in Cape Town, Bloemfontein and Pretoria rely on authors such as Voet and Vinnius, Van Bynkershoek and Van Leeuwen, Grotius and Ulrich Huber; and, when required, they also venture back directly to the Roman sources.[61] A decision on the extent of a contractual exemption from warranty claims for latent defects in an object sold, to mention one entirely arbitrary example, cites a string of fragments from title 21, 1 of the Digest *(de aedilicio edicto et redhibitione et quanti minoris)* and then includes, *inter alia,* an almost three-page-long analysis of a passage from Johannes Voet's Commentary on the Digest.[62] The position is similar in the neighbouring Roman-Dutch jurisdictions. In 1990 the Zimbabwe Supreme Court declared the Roman *praetor's edictum de nautis, cauponis et stabulariis* to be applicable *per analogiam* to land transport.[63] And in the September edition (1992) of the South African Law Reports there appears a decision of the Namibia Supreme Court, which deals with the permissibility of *pacta commissoria* in the law of pledge.[64] Southern Africa is far away from us. Geographically closer is Scotland, where the courts also still occasionally fall back on Roman law. For in spite of the Union of Crowns and Parliaments, Scotland has retained an independent legal system which owes its civilian flavour mainly to the Institutional Writers of the 17th and 18th centuries, among them, most prominently, Sir James Dalrymple, Viscount of Stair.[65] As a result of also having come under the influence of English law, Scots law today presents the picture of a

---

59 Reinhard Zimmermann, *Das römisch-holländische Recht in Südafrika,* 1983. On the beginning disintegration of the *ius commune* into Roman-Dutch, Roman-Scots, Roman-Hispanic law, etc. at the time of the *usus modernus,* see Klaus Luig, 'The Institutes of National Law in the Seventeenth and Eighteenth Centuries', 1972 *Juridical Review* 193 ff.

60 For a detailed exposition on the development of private law in the Netherlands during the 17th and 18th centuries, see Feenstra/Zimmermann (n. 31).

61 For details, see Reinhard Zimmermann, 'Roman Law in a Mixed Legal System: The South African Experience', in: Robin Evans-Jones (ed.), *The Civil Law Tradition in Scotland,* 1995, pp. 41 ff. In the course of the 19th century, due to the then prevailing English influence, South African law has become a mixed jurisdiction. The composite character of South African law is analysed, and its development has been traced, by the contributions in: Reinhard Zimmermann, Daniel Visser (eds.), *Southern Cross: Civil Law and Common Law in South Africa,* 1996; see also Reinhard Zimmermann, 'Gemeines Recht heute: Das Kreuz des Südens, in: Jörn Eckert (ed.), *Der praktische Nutzen der Rechtsgeschichte, Festschrift für Hans Hattenhauer,* 2003, pp. 601 ff.

62 *Van der Merwe v. Meades,* (1991) 2 SA 1 (A).

63 See Reinhard Zimmermann, 'Das römisch-holländische Recht in Zimbabwe', (1991) 55 *Rabels Zeitschrift für ausländisches und internationales Privatrecht* 505 ff.; see also Basedow/Zimmermann, (1997) 1 *Zeitschrift für Europäisches Privatrecht* 221 ff.

64 *Meyer v. Hessling,* 1992 (3) SA 851 (Nm SC) 851.

65 On the reception of Roman law in Scotland, see Peter Stein, 'The Influence of Roman Law on the Law of Scotland', 1963 *Juridical Review* 205 ff.; John W. Cairns, 'Historical Introduction', in: Kenneth Reid, Reinhard Zimmermann (eds.), *A History of Private Law in Scotland,* vol. I, 2000, pp. 45 ff., 64 ff.; and see the contributions to the volumes edited by Evans-Jones (n. 61) and Carey Miller/Zimmermann (n. 32). On the contribution of mixed legal systems to European private law, see Jan Smits, *Europees Privaatrecht in wording – Naar een Ius Commune Europaeum als gemengd rechtsstelsel,* 1999; *idem, The Contribution of Mixed Legal Systems to European Private Law,* 2001.

mixed jurisdiction;[66] together with South African law, it is the main exponent of this phenomenon in the modern world that has remained uncodified.[67]

Less obvious is the continuity of legal development in the modern codified legal systems. 'I simply do not believe that contemporary law has really grown from the old law, but I regard it as something new, created by the need of the present day and the sovereign will of the modern legislature', as the ideology prevailing among early 20th century German textbook-writers was expressed by one of them.[68] Since the codification, so it was assumed, contained a comprehensive and closed system of legal rules, it constituted an autonomous interpretational space. Thus, 'the recollection of pandectist scholarship, one of the supreme achievements of the German legal mind',[69] faded remarkably quickly; Savigny, Dernburg, Jhering and Windscheid were hardly cited any longer, not to mention the earlier literature of the *ius commune* and the Roman sources themselves. If, therefore, the BGB was supposed to have ended the 'second life' of Roman law, Roman lawyers, in turn, devoted their attention to greener pastures. They were now free to study their subject 'unaffected by the overwhelming weight of having to consider how Roman law might still be applied'[70] and could thus become legal historians in the proper sense of the word. A process was started which was pointedly described as an 'emancipation ... by thinking apart Roman law and modern law'.[71] This very pronounced historicisation of Roman law, however, with all the magnificent discoveries to which it led, was bought at a cost. For German legal scholarship ceased to be a historical scholarship.[72] As a result, the sense of continuity of the development of private law was lost.

In reality, the BGB has not been a radical turning point in German legal history.[73] For those who drafted the code did not intend it to constitute, on a doctrinal level, a fresh start, a break with the past. On the contrary: they largely aimed at setting out, incorporating, and consolidating 'the legal achievements of centuries',[74] as they had been processed and refined by pandectist legal learning.[75] The BGB was designed to

---

66 The historical development is traced by the contributions in Kenneth Reid, Reinhard Zimmermann (eds.), *A History of Private Law in Scotland*, vol. I and II, 2000.

67 In San Marino the *ius commune* still applies in its pure form, i.e. unaffected by a reception of English legal rules and doctrines. Professors from Italian faculties of law, appointed as judges of appeal, still today base their decisions ultimately on the *Corpus Juris Civilis*; see Michaela Reinkenhof, *Die Anwendung des ius commune in San Marino*, 1997.

68 Konrad Cosack, in: Hans Planitz (ed.), *Die Rechtswissenschaft der Gegenwart in Selbstdarstellungen*, vol. 1, 1924, p. 16.

69 Koschaker (n. 27) 190.

70 Ernst Landsberg, *Geschichte der deutschen Rechtswissenschaft*, vol. III/2, 1919, p. 850.

71 Ernst Immanuel Bekker, *Die Aktionen des römischen Privatrechts*, vol. I, 1871, p. 2; see the analysis by Maximiliane Kriechbaum, *Dogmatik und Rechtsgeschichte bei Ernst Immanuel Bekker*, 1984, pp. 30 ff.

72 The development is described in Zimmermann, (n. 2) 6 ff.

73 *Supra*, n. 20.

74 Windscheid (n. 20) 75.

75 For details, see Max Kaser, 'Der römische Anteil am deutschen bürgerlichen Recht' 1967 *Juristische Schulung* 337 ff.; Heinrich Honsell 'Das rechtshistorische Argument in der modernen Zivilrechtsdogmatik', in: Dieter Simon (ed.), *Akten des 26. Deutschen Rechtshistorikertages*, 1987, pp. 301 ff.; Rolf Knütel, 'Römisches Recht und deutsches Bürgerliches Recht', in: Walter Ludwig (ed.), *Die Antike in der europäischen Gegenwart*, 1993, pp. 43 ff.; Reinhard Zimmermann, 'Civil

provide a framework for Savigny's 'organically progressive scholarship',[76] which was itself an organic product of the civilian tradition.[77] It was in this spirit that the Imperial Court (*Reichsgericht*) started to interpret the BGB. It continued to apply the *exceptio doli* in the tradition of the *ius commune*.[78] It began, from a number of different starting points, to turn the decision of the draftsmen of the code not to recognize a general doctrine of *culpa in contrahendo*[79] and of *clausula rebus sic stantibus*[80] on its head; it granted claims arising from positive malperformance (*positive Forderungsverletzung*) of contracts of sale based on § 276 I 1 BGB in exactly the same way as it had previously done on the basis of the *actio empti* of the *ius commune*;[81] it recognised a right to terminate a contract even in these cases of positive malperformance;[82] and it was, in its approach to the interpretation of contracts, not irritated, in the least, by the enactment of §§ 133, 157 BGB.[83] Many other examples could be given.[84] Where the *Reichsgericht* developed the law, there are usually either covert lines of continuity linking the new law to the old either because the judges simply perpetuated their earlier case law, or because they extended a line of development which had its origin in the 19th century.

8 The European Character of English Law (1)

One other point should be mentioned as it is generally considered to be of vital importance for European legal unity today. It has to do with the position of the English common law, which Continental jurists have always regarded as particularly strange and awkward. "'What have we here? Who is that savage?' a foreign jurist would ask, with no small wonder, if the writings of Sir Edward Coke, for example, were laid before him. 'Whence comes this wild man; naked; tattooed, painted ..., with rings and fantastic toys in his ears and nostrils, – from what island of the South Sea, or from

---

Code and Civil Law', (1994/95) 1 *Columbia Law Journal of European Law* 91 ff.

76 *Supra* n. 18.

77 In the areas of application of the great codifications of Natural law, we can even study the surprising phenomenon of a third renaissance of Roman law on both a theoretical and practical level (which, in this case, was in stark contrast to the expectations and intentions of the draftsmen of the code; see Zimmermann (n. 2) 1 ff.). On the continuity between the *ius commune* and the French *Code civil*, see James Gordley, 'Myths of the French Civil Code', (1994) 42 *American Journal of Comparative Law* 459 ff.

78 Hans-Peter Haferkamp: 'Die exceptio doli generalis in der Rechtsprechung des Reichsgerichts vor 1914', in: Ulrich Falk, Heinz Mohnhaupt (eds.), *Das bürgerliche Recht und seine Richter*, 2000, pp. 1 ff.

79 Tomasz Giaro, '*Culpa in contrahendo*: eine Geschichte der Wiederentdeckungen' in: Falk/Mohnhaupt (n. 78) 113 ff.

80 Klaus Luig, 'Die Kontinuität allgemeiner Rechtsgrundsätze: Das Beispiel der *clausula rebus sic stantibus*', in: Reinhard Zimmermann, Rolf Knütel, Jens Peter Meincke (eds.), *Rechtsgeschichte und Privatrechtsdogmatik*, 2000, pp. 171 ff.

81 Hans Peter Glöckner, 'Die positive Vertragsverletzung', in: Falk/Mohnhaupt (n. 78) 155 ff.

82 Glöckner (n. 81) 167 ff.

83 Stefan Vogenauer, §§ 133, 157, in: Mathias Schmoeckel, Joachim Rückert, Reinhard Zimmermann (eds.) *Historisch-kritischer Kommentar zum BGB*, vol. I, 2003.

84 Zimmermann (n. 2) 53 ff.

what trackless forest? It cannot be that he was the Attorney-General of the King of England in an age of refinement – the contemporary of Cujacius ...""".[85] This is how many German lawyers essentially still think today when they are confronted with the casuistic nature of the English law, with its bizarre traditionalism, or with the peculiar interlocking of common law and Equity. Indeed, the English themselves sometimes like to cultivate the myth of their law as constituting an autochthonous national achievement. So, for example, in the third edition of the leading textbook on English legal history, we can still read the clear and pithy words: 'And so English law flourished in noble isolation from Europe.'[86]

However, as has just been said, this is a myth.[87] For in reality England was never totally cut off from Continental legal culture. Over the centuries, since the Norman conquest, there has been ongoing intellectual contact, which has left a definitive and characteristic mark on the English law. This becomes obvious wherever one chooses to look.[88] The agents of this continuous process of reception and adaptation of civilian ideas were, of course, the influential authors from Bracton in the 13th century[89] to Blackstone in the 18th[90] and Birks in the 20th century.[91] Particularly instructive in this context were the 'treatise writers' of the late 18th and 19th centuries.[92] This was the spirit with which they tackled their task (and I quote from the foreword to Sir

---

85 Thomas J. Hogg, *An Introductory Lecture on the Study of the Civil Law* (1831), printed in: Michael H. Hoeflich, *The Gladsome Light of Jurisprudence*, 1988, pp. 99 ff.

86 J. H. Baker, *An Introduction to English Legal History*, 3rd ed., 1990, p. 35. For an emphatic assertion of an irreducible *summa differentia*, on an epistemological level, between civil law and common law, see Pierre Legrand, 'Legal Traditions in Western Europe: The Limits on Commonality', in: R. Jagtenberg, E. Örücü, A. J. de Roo (eds.), *Transfrontier Mobility of Law*, 1995, pp. 63 ff., pp. 232 ff. Concerning the notion of (national) legal culture which is central to Pierre Legrand's argument see the critical remarks by Jürgen Basedow, 'Rechtskultur – zwischen nationalem Mythos und europäischem Ideal', (1996) 3 *Zeitschrift für Europäisches Privatrecht* 379 ff.

87 For a more detailed discussion of what follows, see Reinhard Zimmermann, 'Der europäische Charakter des englischen Rechts: Historische Verbindungen zwischen civil law and common law', (1993) 1 *Zeitschrift für Europäisches Privatrecht* 4 ff. From the point of view of modern comparative law, see James Gordley, 'Common law and civil law: eine überholte Unterscheidung', (1993) 2 *Zeitschrift für Europäisches Privatrecht* 498 ff.; Basil S. Markesinis (ed.), The *Gradual Convergence: Foreign Ideas, Foreign Influences and English Law on the Eve of the 21st Century*, 1994.

88 See, as far as the most basic statement of English customary law and constitutional principle is concerned: Richard Helmholz, '*Magna Charta* and the *Ius commune*', (1999) 66 *University of Chicago Law Review* 197 ff.

89 Cf. Carl Güterbock, *Bracton and his Relation to Roman Law* (English translation by Brinton Coxe, 1866; reprinted in 1979); further Samuel E. Thorne (ed., transl., comm.), *Bracton on the Laws and Customs of England*, 1968, e.g. pp. XXXIII, XXXVI.

90 On the systematic aspects of Blackstone's Commentaries on the Laws of England cf., in particular, John W. Cairns, 'Blackstone, An English Institutist: Legal Literature and the Rise of the Nation State', (1984) 4 *Oxford Journal of Legal Studies* 339 ff.; Alan Watson, 'The Impact of Justinian's Institutes on Academic Treatises: Blackstone's Commentaries', in: idem, *Roman Law and Comparative Law*, 1991, pp. 186 ff.

91 See, e.g., Peter Birks, 'Definition and Division: A Meditation on Institutes 3.13', in: idem (ed.), *The Classification of Obligations*, 1997, pp. 1 ff.; idem, 'More Logic and Less Experience: The Difference between Scots Law and English Law', in: David L. Carey Miller, Reinhard Zimmermann (eds.), *The Civilian Tradition and Scots Law: Aberdeen Quincentenary Essays*, 1997, pp. 167 ff.

92 A.W.B. Simpson, 'The Rise and Fall of the Legal Treatise: Legal Principles and the Forms of Legal Literature', (1981) 48 *University of Chicago Law Review* 632 ff.

William Jones' *An Essay on the Law of Bailments,* 1781): 'I propose to begin with treating the subject analytically, and, having traced every part of it up to the first principles of natural reason, shall proceed historically, to show with what perfect harmony these principles are recognised and established by other nations, especially the Romans, as well as by our English courts, when their decisions are properly understood and clearly distinguished.'[93] Also, the leading works of the continental Natural law movement had, since the 18th century, been available in English translations. Pufendorf's *De jure naturae et gentium* (together with Barbeyrac's gloss) had appeared, by 1730, in four editions;[94] by 1750, Grotius' *De jure belli ac pacis* had been published six times in English.[95] Particularly important is the influence which the translations of Pothier's most important *Traités* had on the development of English contract law.[96] Pothier's contract doctrine was held to be 'law at Westminster as well as at Orléans';[97] indeed, it enjoyed an authority which is 'as high as can be had, next to a decision of a Court of Justice in this country'.[98] Moreover, from about the middle of the 19th century, the views of the 'Historical School' gained currency in England,[99] particularly through translations of works by Thibaut, Savigny and Mackeldey. And John Austin discovered the model for his 'universal jurisprudence' in German pandectist law.[100] But whoever traces the influence in England of the continental civil law, will also very soon encounter a considerable number of distinguished judges in English legal history: Lord Holt, Sir Matthew Hale and Lord Mansfield number amongst the most prominent examples.[101]

The Ecclesiastical Courts, too, were important bearers of the reception of Roman law.[102] Up to the time of the Reformation they had exercised an extensive jurisdic-

---

93 On Sir William Jones, see David Ibbetson, 'Sir William Jones as Comparative Lawyer', in: Alexander Murray (ed.), *Sir William Jones 1746-1794: A Commemoration,* 1998, pp. 19 ff.
94 Sir William Holdsworth, *A History of English Law,* vol. XII, 1936, reprinted in 1966, p. 637.
95 Peter Stein, in: A.W.B. Simpson (ed.), *Biographical Dictionary of the Common Law,* 1984, p. 219.
96 Generally on Pothier and on his influence on English law see (1985) 102 *Zeitschrift der Savigny-Stiftung für Rechtsgeschichte, Germanistische Abteilung* 168 ff., 176 ff., 178 ff., 188 ff., 201 ff.
97 Sir William Jones, *An Essay on the Law of Bailments,* 1781, p. 29.
98 *Cox v. Troy,* (1822) 5 B & Ald 474 (480).
99 See Peter Stein, 'Continental Influences on English Legal Thought, 1600 – 1900', in: *idem, The Character and Influence of the Civil Law,* 1988, pp. 224 ff. Savigny's works "were amongst the most frequently translated into English": Michael H. Hoeflich, 'Savigny and his Anglo-American Disciples', (1989) 37 *American Journal of Comparative Law* 19. Cf. also Michele Graziadei, 'Changing Images of the Law in XIX Century English Legal Thought (The Continental Impulse)', in: Mathias Reimann (ed.), *The Reception of Continental Ideas in the Common Law World 1820-1920,* 1993, pp. 115 ff., pp. 165 ff.
100 See Andreas B. Schwarz, 'John Austin und die deutsche Rechtswissenschaft seiner Zeit', in: *idem, Rechtsgeschichte und Gegenwart,* 1960, pp. 73 ff.; Stein (n. 99) 223 ff.; Michael H. Hoeflich, 'John Austin and Joseph Story: Two Nineteenth Century Perspectives on the Utility of the Civil Law for the Common Lawyer', (1985) 29 *American Journal of Legal History* 36 ff.
101 Cf. the overview by Daniel R. Coquillette, *The Civilian Writers of Doctors' Commons, London,* 1988, pp. 215 ff.
102 See, in particular, Richard H. Helmholz, *Roman Canon Law in Reformation England,* 1990, and *Canon Law und the Law of England,* 1987; *idem,* 'Canon Law as a Means of Legal Integration in the Development of English Law', in: Heinrich Scholler, *Die Bedeutung des kanonischen Rechts für die Entwicklung einheitlicher Rechtsprinzipien,* 1996, pp. 49 ff.; *idem, The ius commune in England: Four Studies,* 2001.

tion. It reached far into the affairs of every layman, for it stretched from the law of marriage to succession, from matters of defamation to breach of contract *(laesio fidei)*. The Canon law was just as binding on the English ecclesiastical courts as it was on the Church Courts on the Continent; and, as has been mentioned, the connection between Roman and Canon Law was very close. Thus, also in England, the ecclesiastical courts paved the way for the actionability of informal *pacta*, a principle which was then also quickly received by the common law courts.[103] The Court of Chancery, the source of that second layer of English law known as Equity, must also be mentioned as an influential channel for Continental legal thought; after all, the Lord Chancellors serving in this court up to the time of Henry VIII were clergymen, usually well-versed in Canon law and Roman law. They had studied, predominantly, at Oxford University.[104] Up until the 19th century, Oxford and Cambridge remained the only English universities and their law faculties followed the Continental model.[105] Although the teaching of Canon law was suppressed after the beginnings of the Reformation, the study of Roman Law has remained firmly entrenched at both universities. In a society known as 'Doctors Commons', their graduates, the English 'civilians', kept the tradition of the learned laws alive.[106] They produced a rich literature, which corresponded to a great degree with the continental tradition.[107] The career opportunities of these learned jurists were by no means insignificant;[108] they monopolised legal practice before a number of specialised courts of law, from comparatively insignificant ones such as the High Court of Chivalry, dealing mainly with disputes over armorial bearings, to practically very important ones, such as the Court of Admiralty and the Ecclesiastical Courts. Moreover, they took up positions in the church administration, became bearers of clerical offices and benefices, served as judges in the courts which operated according to Roman-Canon procedure, and took posts in the diplomatic service and the government administration.

The Court of Admiralty,[109] which was responsible primarily for maritime disputes but also, at one stage, for all commercial contracts with a foreign connection, reminds us of a further source of modernisation of English law in a European spirit: the *lex mercatoria*,[110] anglicised as Law Merchant. This is the term for the customs and

---

103 See Richard H. Helmholz, '*Assumpsit* and *fidei laesio*', in: *idem, Canon Law and the Law of England*, 1987, pp. 270 ff.; *idem*, 'Contract and the Canon Law', in: John Barton (ed.), *Towards a General Law of Contract*, 1990, 59 ff.

104 Cf., e.g., Helmut Coing, 'English Equity and the Denunciatio Evangelica of the Canon Law', (1955) 71 *Law Quarterly Review* 238 ff.; Baker (n. 86) 47, 115.

105 On the early history of legal development in Oxford cf., e.g., the contributions of Southern, Barton and Boyle, in: J.I. Catto (ed.), *The History of the University of Oxford*, vol. I, 1984.

106 Cf., e.g., Coquillette (n. 101) 22 ff.

107 Helmut Coing, 'Das Schrifttum der englischen Civilians und die kontinentale Rechtsliteratur in der Zeit zwischen 1550 und 1800', (1975) 5 *Ius Commune* 16 ff.

108 See Brian P. Levack, *The Civil Lawyers in England 1603-1641*, 1973, pp. 21 ff.; *idem*, 'The English Civilians, 1500-1700', in: Wilfred Prest, *Lawyers in Early Modern Europe and America*, 1981, pp. 108 ff.

109 See, in summary, Sir William Holdsworth, *A History of English Law*, vol. I, 7th ed., 1956, pp. 544 ff.; William Senior, *Doctors' Commons and the Court of Admiralty*, 1922, pp. 14 ff., pp. 84 ff.; Baker (n. 86) 141 ff.

110 On which, see generally, Coing, *Europäisches Privatrecht* (n. 28) 519 ff.; Berman (n. 26) 333 ff.; Rudolf Meyer, *Bona fides und lex mercatoria in der europäischen Rechtstradition*, 1994; but see

rules, predominantly unwritten, but also partly laid down in statutes or legal compilations, which had developed since about the 12th century in connection with the blossoming trade around the Mediterranean, on the Atlantic coast and the Baltic Sea. Although these rules and customs, especially applicable to merchants, constituted largely 'new' law, there were at least parts of it which took their inspiration from Roman law: the general average (derived from the *lex Rhodia de iactu)* or the bottomry loan (based on the *foenus nauticum),*[111] to mention two examples. Also in this respect, England belonged to Europe. England's economy was integrated into the European trade system, and the development of its law merchant followed essentially the same pattern as in the rest of Europe. What had emerged in the Middle Ages as customary commercial law and was applied by special merchants' courts became, from about the 16th century, increasingly the subject of scholarly examination.[112] This classical period of a European scholarship of commercial law was followed from around the middle of the 17th century by the incorporation of that body of law into the developing national legal systems. The above-mentioned Lord Mansfield, a judge of Scottish descent who had, moreover, studied Roman Law at Oxford, was of paramount importance in this respect.[113] 'The law of nations', he declared,[114] 'in its full extent [is] part of the law of England, ... [and is] to be collected from the practice of different nations, and the authority of writers'; this explains the hundreds of quotations from Continental legal records and legislation, as well as from treatises on the *lex mercatoria,* on Natural law, Roman law and its *usus modernus,* which are to be found in Mansfield's judgments.[115]

9   The European Character of English Law (2)

In view of these (and many other) centuries-old connections, it is hardly surprising that large areas of English law (in particular the law of contract)[116] were inspired,

---

also Karl Otto Scherner, 'Lex mercatoria – Realität, Geschichtsbild oder Vision?', (2001) 118 *Zeitschrift der Savigny-Stiftung für Rechtsgeschichte, Germanistische Abteilung* 148 ff.

111 For a general overview, see Coing, *Europäisches Privatrecht* (n. 28) 519 ff.; on *lex Rhodia de iactu* and *foenus nauticum,* see *Law of Obligations* (n. 33) 406 ff., 181 ff.

112 See Coquillette (n. 101) *passim.*

113 See Sir William Holdsworth, *A History of English Law,* vol. XII, 1938, pp. 464 ff., pp. 493 ff., pp. 524 ff.; Stein (n. 99) 220 ff.; also, more recently, Christopher P. Rodgers, 'Continental Literature and the Development of the Common Law by the King's Bench, c. 1750-1800', in: Vito Piergiovanni (ed.), *The Courts and the Development of Commercial Law,* 1987, pp. 161 ff.; Michael Lobban, *The Common Law and English Jurisprudence 1760-1850,* 1991, pp. 98 ff.; and see James Oldham, *The Mansfield Manuscripts and the Growth of English Law in the Eighteenth Century,* 1992.

114 *Triquet v. Bath,* (1764) 3 *Burrow's Reports* 1478 (1481).

115 For details, see Rodgers (n. 113) 166 ff.

116 See, as far as the 19th century is concerned, A.W.B. Simpson, 'Innovation in Nineteenth Century Contract Law', (1975) 91 *Law Quarterly Review* 247 ff.; P.S. Atiyah, *The Rise and Fall of the Freedom of Contract,* 1979, pp. 139 ff., 405 ff.; Philip Hamburger, 'The Development of the Nineteenth Century Consensus Theory of Contract', (1989) 7 *Law and History Review* 241 ff.; James Gordley, *The Philosophical Origins of Modern Contract Doctrine,* 1991, pp. 134 ff.; generally, see David Ibbetson, *A Historical Introduction to the Law of Obligations,* 1999 (who commences his

characterised or at least influenced by the ideas and concepts, the rules and institutions as well as the general intellectual undercurrents of the European *ius commune*. This is sometimes even true of doctrines which we generally regard as typically English. The doctrine of consideration (which states that promises are binding and enforceable only if they are made in view of counterperformance of some sort by the promisee) provides an example: for it appears to be the specifically English variant of the medieval *causa*-doctrine.[117] The same is true of the trust (which was conceptualised as such only in the course of the 19th century). Most of the trust-like devices that existed for so long in England and on the Continent depended to some extent on Roman law. Roman law had itself not developed the trust as an abstract fiduciary concept, but it had known a fiduciary institution (the *fideicommissum*) and a fiduciary office (the *tutor*). It thus provided impulses towards, and examples of, the workings of the trust and the role of the trustee and stimulated the later legal development on both sides of the Channel.[118] Often, of course, the Roman impulses led to rather un-Roman results.[119] A classical Roman lawyer would be very surprised by the doctrine of vicarious liability which has been created on extremely slender Roman foundations in England as well as in continental jurisprudence but which has, none the less, managed to become one of the basic structural features of European private law.[120] The most famous of the so-called 'coronation cases' may be mentioned as another example: 'The real question in this case is the extent of the application in English law of the principle of the Roman law which has been adopted and acted on in many English decisions'.[121] This principle, which provided the point of departure, is the civilian rule *debitor speciei liberatur casuali interitu rei*:[122] the debtor is relieved of his duty to deliver the object if it has been destroyed through no fault of his own. In about the middle of the 19th century, English judges began to read this rule into the parties' agreement.[123] For this purpose they availed themselves of a construction which also originated in Roman law: the introduction of a (tacit) resolutive condition.[124] As a consequence, however, the entire contract had to be taken to have been

---

work by stating that "[t]he Common law of obligations grew out of the intermingling of native ideas and sophisticated Roman learning": p. 1).

117 See the overview in *Law of Obligations* (n. 33) 549 ff. and the references provided in (1993) 1 *Zeitschrift für Europäisches Privatrecht* 27, n. 141.

118 See the contributions in Richard Helmholz, Reinhard Zimmermann (eds.), *Itinera Fiduciae: Trust and Treuhand in Historical Perspective*, 1998.

119 This is also emphasised by Richard H. Helmholz, 'Continental Law and Common Law: Historical Strangers or Companions?', 1990 *Duke Law Journal* 1207 ff., 1218.

120 Hartmut Wicke, *Respondeat Superior: Haftung für Verrichtungsgehilfen im römischen, römisch-holländischen, englischen und südafrikanischen Recht*, 2000; Zimmermann (n. 2) 123 ff.

121 Cf. *Krell v. Henry* [1903] 2 KB 740 (CA), at 747 f. See, e.g., R.G. McElroy & Glanville Williams, 'The Coronation Cases', (1940) 4 *Modern Law Review* 241 ff.; (1941) 5 *Modern Law Review* 1 ff.

122 On which see Herman Dilcher, *Die Theorie der Leistungsstörungen bei Glossatoren, Kommentatoren and Kanonisten*, 1960, pp. 185 ff.

123 *Taylor v. Caldwell* (1863) 3 B & S 826 ff.; on which see Max Rheinstein, *Die Struktur des vertraglichen Schuldverhältnisses im anglo-amerikanischen Recht*, 1932, pp. 173 ff.; Barry Nicholas, 'Rules and Terms – Civil Law and Common Law', (1974) 48 *Tulane Law Review* 965 f.; G.H. Treitel, *Unmöglichkeit, 'Impracticability' and 'Frustration' im anglo-amerikanischen Recht*, 1991.

124 For a more detailed exposition of this topic, see Reinhard Zimmermann, "Heard melodies are sweet, but those unheard are sweeter ...'. Conditio tacita, implied condition und die Fortbildung des

dissolved in the event of fulfilment of the condition (i.e. when the object of the contract was destroyed). This principle was then carried over to cases in which the performance was not impossible, but in which merely the purpose for which the parties had entered into the contract had been frustrated. This occurred in the case of that faithful royalist who had hired an apartment situated on the route of the planned coronation procession of King Edward VII. But then the procession had to be cancelled because the monarch had contracted peritonitis. Did the rental have to be paid none the less? Vaughan Williams, L.J., relying on Roman law, answered this question in the negative. We refer today to the 'doctrine of frustration of contract'. It corresponds functionally to the civilian doctrine of *clausula rebus sic stantibus*[125] which had likewise been constructed of Roman building stones, even though as such it was also unknown to Roman law: a contract need not be performed if there has been a fundamental change of those circumstances which were decisive for its conclusion.

Statutory interpretation is another topic on which the English and the continental approaches are usually taken to be fundamentally different: an unimaginative and pedantic cult of a strict literalism prevailing in England is unfavourably contrasted with the more mature methods of interpretation focusing on the purpose of the statute in countries such as France or Germany. This view is, however, based on a skewed perspective in that it takes individual phases in the development of legal methodology to represent the whole.[126] This development has been characterised, for many centuries, by a liberal and flexible approach that was distinguished by an interplay of legal maxims (*regulae iuris*), that aimed at 'grasping the force and tendency of a statute rather than sticking to its words'[127] and that was based, ultimately, on *aequitas* and *publica utilitas*.[128] This is true not only for continental jurisprudence but also for England, where the period from the Middle Ages until the first third of the 19th century may be described as the age of equitable interpretation.[129] The courts availed themselves of a wide range of legal maxims, they aimed at finding 'the internal sense' of the law, and they were guided by the 'equity of the statute' that could prevail even against its words. This was the civilian approach. *Cessante ratione legis cessat lex ipsa; odiosa sunt restringenda; summum ius summa iniuria; ut res magis valeat*

---

europäischen Vertragsrechts', (1993) 193 *Archiv für die civilistische Praxis* 121 ff. On implied terms in modern English contract law, see Wolfgang Grobecker, *Implied Terms und Treu und Glauben: Vertragsergänzung im englischen Recht in rechtsvergleichender Perspektive*, 1999.

125 On which see *Law of Obligations* (n. 33) 579 ff.; since then Ralf Köbler, *Die 'clausula rebus sic stantibus' als allgemeiner Rechtsgrundsatz*, 1991, pp. 23 ff.; Michael Rummel, *Die 'clausula rebus sic stantibus'*, 1991.

126 See James Gordley, 'Legal Reasoning: Some Parallels in Common Law and Civil Law', in: Heinz-Dieter Assmann, Gert Brüggemeier, Rolf Sethe (eds.), *Unterschiedliche Rechtskulturen – Konvergenz des Rechtsdenkens*, 2001, pp. 31 ff.

127 'Scire leges non hoc est verba earum tenere, sed vim ac potestatem': Cels. D. 1, 3, 17; on which see *Law of Obligations* (n. 33) 702 ff.

128 For a detailed analysis, see Stefan Vogenauer, *Die Auslegung von Gesetzen in England und auf dem Kontinent*, 2001, pp. 430 ff.; Jan Schröder, *Recht als Wissenschaft*, 2001, pp. 48 ff., 130 ff.

129 Hans W. Baade, 'The Casus Omissus: A Pre-History of Statutory Analogy', (1994) 20 *Syracuse Journal of International Law and Commerce* 45 ff.; Pierre André Côté, 'L'interprétation de la loi en droit civil et en droit statutaire: Communauté de langue et différences d'accents', (1997) 31 *Thémis* 45 ff.; Vogenauer (n. 128) 669 ff.

quam pereat; optimus legum interpres consuetudo; exempla illustrant non restrin-gunt legem; talis interpretatio in ambiguis semper fienda est, ut evitetur inconveniens et absurdum; expressio unius est exclusio alterius: all these and many other maxims were taken from the civilian literature.[130] *Statuta sunt stricte interpretanda* (or: *sunt stricti iuris*) was applied in England to statutes derogating from the common law in the same way as it was applied in medieval Italy or early modern Germany to statutes contrary to the *ius commune*.[131] The metaphors of the body and the soul, or the shell and the kernel, used by Edmund Plowden to describe the relationship between the let-ter of the law and its sense and reason,[132] had been exploited again and again in con-tinental legal literature since the days of the *Decretum Gratiani*.[133] The 'equity of the statute' derives from the medieval notion of *aequitas* which, in turn, was ultimately based on Aristotle's Nicomachean Ethics.[134] Blackstone in his Commentaries pre-sents a summary of the chapter on the interpretation of statutes in a contemporary translation of Pufendorf's *De jure naturae et gentium*.[135] Even civilian doctrines such as the distinction between *interpretatio extensiva, restrictiva*, and *declarativa* were received in England. Thus, it is no exaggeration to state that, as far as statutory inter-pretation is concerned, England was for many centuries a province of the *ius com-mune*.[136] In Germany, the age of equitable interpretation was followed by an era of strict literalism. The famous prohibitions against interpreting, developing, and com-menting upon the codes of the age of Enlightenment enacted in the course of the 18th century remain the ultimate monuments to an ideology attempting completely to emasculate judges (as well as academic lawyers).[137] The same change occurred in England, though about fifty years later.[138] Judges now started to see themselves as 'philologists of the highest order'[139] and preferred to be 'accused of a narrow preju-dice for the letter of the law, than set up or sanction vague claims to discard it in favour of some higher interpretation'.[140] It was mirrored by the rise of the doctrine of *stare decisis* (also much less deeply entrenched, historically, in England than is com-monly assumed)[141] and rooted in the same ideological soil. Today, however, the

---

130 For references, see Baade, (1994) 20 *Syracuse Journal of International Law and Commerce* 65 ff.; Vogenauer (n. 127) 759 ff.
131 Willem Zwalve, 'Interpretatieproblemen voor de codificatie', in: *Liber Mémorialis François Laurent*, 1989, pp. 447 ff. ; Reinhard Zimmermann, 'Statuta Sunt Stricte Interpretanda ? Statutes and the Common Law : A Continental Perspective', (1997) 56 *Cambridge Law Journal* 315 ff.
132 Eyston v. Studd (1547) 2 Plowd 459 (465) (CP).
133 For references, see Vogenauer (n. 128) 465 ff.
134 Baker (n. 86) 240; generally on the notion of *aequitas canonica* in English law see, most recently, Javier Martinez-Torron, *Anglo-American Law and Canon Law: Canonical Roots of the Common Law Tradition*, 1998, pp. 70 ff.
135 Pufendorf (n. 49) Lib. V, Cap. XII; cf. William Blackstone, *Commentaries on the Laws of England*, vol. I, 11th ed., 1791, pp. 58 ff.
136 Vogenauer (n. 128) 1323 ff.; along the same lines Côté, (1997) 31 *Thémis* 45.
137 See Hans-Jürgen Becker, 'Kommentier- und Auslegungsverbot', in: *Handwörterbuch zur deutschen Rechtsgeschichte*, vol. II, 1978, cols. 963 ff.
138 Vogenauer (n. 128) 780 ff.
139 *Ex parte* Davis (1857) 5 WR 552 (523) (*per* Pollock, CB; Ex.).
140 Attorney-General v. Sillem (1863) 2 H & C 431 (437) (*per* Bramwell, B; Ex.).
141 See Baker (n. 86) 225 ff.; Zimmermann, *Roman Law* (n. 2) 178 ff.

courts in England have turned over a new leaf.[142] Since about the middle of the century there has been a move away from the purely literal towards a purposive construction of statutory provisions. The same methodological shift had occurred in Germany around the turn of the century. Thus, we see a remarkable rapprochment of thinking patterns:[143] a rapprochment, however, which merely re-establishes an intellectual unity based on a common legal tradition.

10   The New *Ius Commune*

We are living in an age of post-positivism.[144] The narrowness, but also the security, of a national codification, or common law, is increasingly left behind and we are moving towards a new *ius commune*. This new *ius commune* will have to be built around shared values and generally recognised legal methods as well as common principles and guiding maxims, and it will have to be shaped by judges, legislators, and professors, acting in cooperation with each other.[145] But since, as Savigny has put it, there is no autonomous human existence entirely isolated from the past, we cannot freely fashion our own existence, including our laws: we always, and necessarily, do it 'in indissoluble community with the entire past';[146] and unless we want unconsciously to be governed by the past[147] we should explore it in order to understand how we got to where we are. Historical scholarship (which will itself have to abandon its focus on national legal history)[148] may thus enable us to take stock of our present legal condition. It may help us to map out, and to become aware of, the common ground still existing between our national legal systems as a result of a common tradition, of independent but parallel developments, and of instances of intellectual stimulation or the reception of legal rules or concepts. At the same time, it will be able to explain discrepancies on the level of specific result, general approach, and doctrinal nuance. It is this kind of comprenhesion that paves the way for rational criticism and organic development of the law.[149] The past, of course, does not justify

---

142   Konrad Zweigert, Hein Kötz, *An Introduction to Comparative Law*, English translation by Tony Weir, 3rd ed., 1998, pp. 265 ff.; Vogenauer (n. 128) 963 ff.

143   Cf. also Ernst Kramer, 'Konvergenz und Internationalisierung der juristischen Methode', in: Assmann/Brüggemeier/Sethe (n. 126) 31 ff.

144   See Eugen Bucher, 'Recht – Geschichtlichkeit – Europa', in: Bruno Schmidlin (ed.), *Vers un droit privé européen commun? Skizzen zum gemeineuropäischen Privatrecht*, 1994, p. 23; Jürgen Basedow, 'Rechtssicherheit im europäischen Wettbewerbsrecht: Ein allgemeiner Rechtsgrundsatz im Lichte der wettbewerbsrechtlichen Rechtsprechung', (1996) 4 *Zeitschrift für Europäisches Privatrecht* 570 ff.

145   See the classic study of these protagonists of legal development in Europe by R.C. van Caenegem, *Judges, Legislators and Professors*, 1987.

146   'Über den Zweck dieser Zeitschrift', (1815) 1 *Zeitschrift für geschichtliche Rechtswissenschaft* 1 ff.; cf. also Maximiliane Kriechbaum, 'Römisches Recht und neuere Privatrechtsgeschichte in Savignys Auffassung von Rechtsgeschichte und Rechtswissenschaft', in: Reinhard Zimmermann, Rolf Knütel, Jens Peter Meincke (eds.), *Rechtsgeschichte und Privatrechtsdogmatik*, 2000, pp. 41 ff.

147   Friedrich Carl von Savigny, *System des heutigen römischen Rechts*, 1840, vol. I, pp. xv f.

148   Berman (n. 26) 17.

149   For individual examples of this approach, see the studies by Verse (n. 2), Wicke (n. 120), Vogenauer (n. 128), Martin Bauer, *Periculum Emptoris: Eine dogmengeschichtliche Untersuchung zur Gefahr-*

itself; nor does it necessarily contain the solutions for present-day problems.[150] But an understanding of the past is the first and essential prerequisite for devising appropriate solutions for the present day. This is as true within a given national legal system as it is for the formation of a European law. And just as legal history informs the development of private law doctrine in the one case, so it constitutes the basis for comparative scholarship on the other.[151]

The specific significance of Roman law in Europe consisted in the fact that it became the intellectual basis for a largely homogeneous legal culture. The *Corpus Juris Civilis* provided an essential point of departure for a common European scholarship of private law. It became a cornerstone of the civilian tradition. The modern national codifications are as much an emanation of this tradition as the attempted 'restatements' of various areas of private law, such as the Principles of European Contract Law.[152] We cannot return the oak tree to the acorn from whence it has sprung. Nor would we want to. 'The historical approach to legal scholarship', in the words of Savigny,[153] 'is completely misunderstood and distorted, if it is often presumed that the legal entities emanating from the past are posited as something which is in the highest degree exemplary and which has to retain its rule, in an unchanged form, over both the present time and the future. On the contrary, the essence of the historical approach consists in the dispassionate recognition of the value and individuality of every age. What that approach, however, emphatically insists upon, is recognition of the vital connection that ties the present to the past. For without such recognition we shall only be able to observe the outward form of our legal condition, not to grasp its inner substance'. Even if only for this reason, the study of Roman law remains indispensable in modern Europe.[154]

---

tragung beim Kauf, 1998; Sonja Meier, *Irrtum und Zweckverfehlung*, 1999; Andreas Richter, *Rechtsfähige Stiftung und Charitable Corporation: Überlegungen zur Reform des deutschen Stiftungsrechts auf der Grundlage einer historisch-rechtsvergleichenden Untersuchung der Entstehung des modernen deutschen und amerikanischen Stiftungsmodells*, 2001; Pascal Pichonnaz, *La compensation: Analyse historique et comparative des modes de compenser non conventionels*, 2001; Nicole Schneider, *Uberrima Fides: Treu und Glauben und vorvertragliche Aufklärungspflichten im englischen Recht*, 2003; Nils Jansen, *Die Struktur des Haftungsrechts: Geschichte, Theorie und Dogmatik außervertraglicher Ansprüche auf Schadensersatz*, 2003.

150 Alfred Cockrell, 'Studying Legal History in South Africa: The Lesson of Lot's Wife', (1997) 5 *Zeitschrift für Europäisches Privatrecht* 438.

151 See also Hein Kötz, 'Was erwartet die Rechtsvergleichung von der Rechtsgeschichte?', 1992 *Juristenzeitung* 20 ff.; Klaus Luig, 'The History of Roman Private Law and the Unification of European Law', (1997) 5 *Zeitschrift für Europäisches Privatrecht* 405 ff.; David Johnston, 'The Renewal of the Old', (1997) 56 *Cambridge LJ* 80 ff.; Axel Flessner, 'Die Rechtsvergleichung als Kundin der Rechtsgeschichte', (1999) 7 *Zeitschrift für Europäisches Privatrecht* 513 ff.; Eugen Bucher, 'Rechtsüberlieferung und heutiges Recht', (2000) 8 *Zeitschrift für Europäisches Privatrecht* 394 ff.; James Gordley, 'Why Look Backward', (2002) 50 *American Journal of Comparative Law* 657 ff.

152 I have attempted to substantiate this point in a lecture presented at the meeting of German teachers of private law: 'Europa und das römische Recht', (2002) 202 *Archiv für die civilistische Praxis* 243 ff. As far as the Principles of European Contract Law are concerned, see Reinhard Zimmermann, 'Konturen eines Europäischen Vertragsrechts', 1995 *Juristenzeitung* 477 ff.; and, for two specific topics, *idem, Comparative Foundations of a European Law of Set-Off and Prescription*, 2002.

153 Savigny, *System* (n. 147) xiv f.

154 The same point has recently been emphasised by Alfons Bürge, 'Das römische Recht als Grundlage für das Zivilrecht im künftigen Europa', in: Filippo Ranieri (ed.), *Die Europäisierung der Rechtswissenschaft*, 2002, pp. 19 ff.

CHAPTER 3

European Private Law, *Lex Mercatoria* and Globalisation

Klaus Peter Berger[*]

1 Introduction

The notions of "European private law", "*lex mercatoria*" and "globalisation" are closely connected and intertwined. Europe, the European Single Market and the economic forces behind these institutions are strong factors in the process of globalisation. The evolution of a global market place is the driving force in the evolution of transnational commercial law, the new *lex mercatoria*.[1] Conversely, the new *lex mercatoria* as a non-national based legal system in the making serves as a role model for the emerging European private law. Art. 1.101 (3) (a) of the Principles of European Contract Law (PECL) drafted by the *Lando* Commission states that the PECL may be applied to a contract "when the parties have agreed that their contract is to be governed by...the *lex mercatoria*...". With this statement the PECL claim that they are a "modern European *lex mercatoria*".[2] At the same time, the PECL are themselves generally regarded as a precursor of a European Civil Code.[3] It becomes clear therefore that the *lex mercatoria* plays an important role within the current debate about the evolution of European private law. A closer look at the economic and theoretical status quo of the modern *lex mercatoria* reveals that the progress which the development of transnational commercial law has made in the past years is an indication of an important change of paradigm in the discussion of transnational law. This turning point may best be characterised as the "new pragmatism"[4] in legal thinking. It has redirected the views of scholars, practitioners and policy makers from the theoretical basis of the theory of the new *lex mercatoria* to the content of its constituent rules and principles and to the way in which this content may be "codified". It will be demonstrated in this chapter that this is true not only for the global market place but also for the EU Single Market.

2 The Economic Basis of the "New Pragmatism"

While it is true that the notion of 'globalisation' of the world economy has become a *cliché* rather than a term with substantive content[5], it may help to explain the reasons

---

* Professor Dr. Klaus Peter Berger, LL.M., Center for Transnational Law (CENTRAL), University of Cologne, Germany.
1 See Berger, The New Law Merchant (2001), pp. 14 *et seq.*
2 Lando/Beale, p. XXIV; see also Hesselink, in: Hesselink/de Vries, p. 25.
3 See Lando, in: Weyers, p. 101; Lando (2002), p. 10; Lando (2003), p. 2; Blase (1999), p. 12.
4 Berger, The New Law Merchant (2001), pp. 3 *et seq.*
5 See generally Delbrück, pp. 9 *et seq.*; Walker/Fox, pp. 379 *et seq.*; Luhmann, pp. 571 *et seq.*

for the pragmatic redirection of the discussion on the new law merchant. At the same time, the look to the global phenomenon reveals striking parallels with the developments on the European, i.e. "regional", scale.

Basically, there are three reasons why globalisation has fostered the transnationalisation of commercial law. First, the transaction costs involved in the application of domestic laws to transnational commercial transactions tend to hamper the development towards globalised markets. Foreign law is generally regarded as the „globalisation trap".[6] Similarly, European scholars have always argued that the diversity between systems of private law constitute a major obstacle to the proper functioning of the EU Common Market and that this situation should be remedied through the development of a genuine European private law.[7] In fact, this was one of the major reasons for drafting the PECL.[8] This view is confirmed by one of the most recent branches of international economics, the "New International Economics of International Transactions". This theory takes a transaction-oriented approach to international business and deals with the territorial limitations of lawmaking and law enforcement and the resulting problems, e.g. with respect to coordination of economic behaviour, the increase of transaction costs arising out of this phenomenon for the property rights exchanged in international trade.[9] Secondly, globalisation tends to overcome state sovereignty. State sovereignty, however, was one of the major stumbling blocks towards a modern law merchant. In this context, the situation is even more advanced in the EU where the Member States have long since transferred sovereign rights to the EU institutions. Thirdly, the fathers of the *lex mercatoria* doctrine have always emphasised that economic factors – and above all the striving for enhanced productivity, for rationalisation of production and for the reduction of transaction costs as well as the development from domestic and regional to world markets that goes along with these developments – have a significant impact on the evolution of a transnational system of law.[10] The proponents of transnational commercial law regard themselves as "chroniclers of the development of international commerce and the conditions of its legal framework, drawing their legal conclusions from the observance of real-life phenomena".[11] The dramatic economic transformations of the world economy that have taken place and are taking place today at an enormous pace

---

6 Lando (1985), p. 748; Stein, pp. 16 *et seq.*; Park, p. 151: 'No one opts to lose a dispute because of an unfair application of legal 'technicalities'''; Delaume, p. IX: 'The legal context in which transnational contracts are negotiated and implemented is in the process of rapid evolution. The time is no longer where such contracts fitted into well established categories of transactions between commercial men, subject to private law, or between subjects of international law conducting business *inter se*. Today, a number of contractual relationships involve both subjects of private and public international law, and, with increasing frequency, a plurality of parties whose combined efforts are required for the carrying out of a single venture. Neither traditional domestic law rules nor, to the extent that they can be identified with sufficient precision, international law norms necessarily provide adequate answers to problems that they were not designed to meet in the first place.'

7 See, e.g., Hesselink, A New European Legal Culture (2001), p. 57.

8 Lando/Beale, p. XXI.

9 See Schmidtchen, pp. 62 *et seq.*

10 Goldstajn (1961), p. 13; Kahn (1964), p. 365.

11 Stein, p. 13.

relate directly to the social and economic processes "at the periphery" of the legal process. They serve as the laboratory for the creation of transnational legal structures. It is obvious that this applies with even more force for the economic developments within the highly integrated European Single Market.

It becomes clear from this look at the economic foundations of the transnationalisation process that both on the worldwide level and within the EU, there are both economic factors and legal developments which should be taken into account in evaluating the current climate for the transnationalisation of commercial law. This broad view also clarifies that today, the existence of the *lex mercatoria* as an autonomous legal order cannot be explained with a single factual or legal argument such as the proliferation of general contract conditions or the normative value of trade usages. In view of the dramatic changes to the economic and geopolitical conditions it requires a comprehensive view, taking into account all aspects of the modern economy. All of these factors have four common denominators: 1. the trend towards a *"global civil society"*;[12] 2. the erosion and irrelevance of national boundaries in markets which can truly be described as global and the decreasing significance of sovereignty in this area;[13] 3. the relative decline of state power to influence or steer national or international economic developments and 4. the strong trend towards informal approaches to international rule- and decision-making.

3 The New *Lex Mercatoria* as a "Pluralistic" Legal System

3.1 The End of Sovereignty

Based on these economic developments, a non-positivist notion of the law has emerged over the past years.[14] Since the law has to take account of the complexities of society,[15] it is not the public reason represented by the state or by inter-governmental organisations *alone* but also the power for self-regulation and coordination of the individual and of private "non-governmental" organisations and federations which justifies normative force. The traditional theory of legal sources which was centered around the notion of sovereignty[16] is being replaced by a legal pluralism which accepts that society's ability for self-organisation and coordination is more than a mere factual pattern without independent legal significance. Today, it assumes a normative quality of its own. The central instrument of self-organisation for the players on the global market place is the contract itself.[17] Concluded by businessmen

---

12 See generally Böhm, in: Mestmäcker, pp. 105 *et seq.*; see also the vision of a 'general global legal society' of v. Savigny, p. 30 *et seq.*

13 Walker/Fox, p. 380.

14 Canaris, pp. 10 *et seq.*

15 See for the 'normative force of fact' Jellinek, p. 338.

16 Jhering, p. 249: 'Only those rules imposed by society deserve the name of law which have behind them the force of the law or...the force of the sovereign state, meaning that only those rules adopt the quality of legal norms that have been vested with this effect by the sovereign state or that the state is the only source of the law.' (translation by the author).

17 See Zumbansen pp. 35 *et seq.*; Kolo/Wälde, p. 50.

for the purpose of bringing about that particular transaction, the morality and mutual trust ("my word is my bond") of international business turn the contractual promise into a categorical imperative.[18] The presumed rationality of *standard contracts* and general contract conditions[19], the idea of the increased professional competence and responsibility of international businessmen[20], the compliance control through international arbitral tribunals which, just as the contractual agreement itself, derive their authority from the will of the parties, the fine-tuning of comparative law into a "transnational rules method"[21] and the rule-making by international formulating agencies[22] and private working groups all contribute to a comprehensive legal process which ultimately results in the normative force of the principles and rules which result from it.[23] Within this "privatised" and highly deregulated commercial system which is centered around the contract and characterised by supranational governance structures, the role of states is reduced from that of an active participant in the economic field to that of a "facilitator" whose main role is to create a level playing field for private entrepreneurs.[24] On the EU level, this task is performed by the EU Commission by issuing harmonising directives. However, due to the omnipresent policy of consumer protection harmonisation and protective regulation go hand in hand and add a particular coloration to the Commission's task of creating a level playing field for EU commerce.

3.2 The Convergence of Legal Systems and the End of the Localisation Doctrine

The normative force of the contract has removed the two major obstacles which have hitherto stood in the way of the development of a transnational understanding of international business law. First, the evolution of autonomous legal rules of international trade bridges the gap between the various legal families in that it focuses on the function rather than on the dogmatic origin or legal tradition of a certain rule or principle, thereby detaching it from the constraints of domestic dogmatism which has long since prevented a transnational understanding of the law:

---

18 See Hyland, p. 545; see also for the 'family, friendship, firms' phenomenon in international trade which serves as a stabilising factor for long-term 'relational' contractual relationships Schmidtchen, p. 103.

19 See Goldstajn, in: Fabricius, p. 179: '...it is a fact that Standard Contracts and the General Conditions have often been corrected through competition and therefore constitute rational solutions'.

20 See Berman/Dasser, p. 54: 'As a general rule, merchants trading across national boundaries are deemed to have equal bargaining power and to know best what suits them. Kahn (1993), p. 242: 'On constatera que l'introduction de la notion de professionnalisme donne une coloration spécifique à la règle générale que le contrat tienne lieu de loi aux parties. see generally for the practical application of this principle by international arbitrators ICC Award No. 1990, Clunet 1974, p. 897; No. 1512, Clunet 1974, p. 905; No. 2291, Clunet 1976, p. 989; No. 2438, Clunet 1976, p. 969 with Note Derains, *id.*, p. 971; No. 3130, Clunet 1981, p. 932; No. 3380, Clunet 1981, p. 927; No. 5364, Clunet 1991, p. 1059.

21 See Gaillard, in: van den Berg, pp. 570 *et seq.*

22 See Pfund, in: Carbonneau, pp. 205 *et seq.*

23 See Braeckmans, p. 16; Stein, pp. 148 *et seq.;* Teubner, pp. 273 *et seq.*; Schmidtchen, pp. 101 *et seq.*; Galgano, p. 102; Gandolfi, p. 710; Berman/Dasser, pp. 54 *et seq.*; Ladeur, pp. 98 *et seq.*

24 Kolo/Wälde, p. 49; Fitzgerald, p. 739.

"The confluence of civil law, common law, and Shari'a is not only imaginable, in light of the ultimate origins of these systems; it is inevitable, in view of globalisation. The reemergence of the *lex mercatoria* and the publishing of the Unidroit Principles evidence the commonality."[25]

Secondly, the transnational quality of this lawmaking process does away with the natural territorial view of the law adopted by traditional conflict of laws doctrine which, since the days of *Voet*, *Story*, *Waechter* and *Savigny* has been devoted solely to the localisation, i.e. the search of the proper "seat", of a given case in a certain domestic legal system. Consequently, the microcosm of formal *conflict rules* developed over the past decades remains blind to the substantive law results it creates. Here lies the origin of Leo Raape's famous critique of conflict of laws as an unpredictable "jump in the dark".[26] Today this view is beginning to erode and some conflicts lawyers admit that "the elaboration of a supranational substantive law is preferable to relying on traditional private international law rules" in order to "promote... commonsensical solutions to the legal problems of a world in which transactions fail to respect state and national frontiers".[27]

Thus, the new pragmatism has finally helped to overcome one of the most basic assumptions of traditional legal theory: that every law outside the realm of public international has some territorial basis. In the age of pragmatism, functionality prevails over tradition.[28] The autonomous law of international trade has no national basis, but it has the principal qualities which *Benson* has defined as the "desirable characteristics" of the *new law merchant*: 1) universal character, 2) flexibility and dynamic ability to grow, 3) informality and speed, 4) reliance on commercial custom and practice.[29]

4 The New Problem: In Search of "Marketing Strategies" and "Codification Techniques"

The new pragmatism with its economic and legal implications described above has also created a new problem, or may be even a new opportunity. The discussion about the contents of transnational commercial law which has evolved out of the new pragmatism requires that all those who participate in these debates share the same degree of knowledge about the rules and principles which are alleged to form part of transnational commercial law. One may even go further and claim that a new "codification" technique is needed to shape the new *lex mercatoria* into a useable form.

---

25 Molineaux, Journal of World Investment (2000), p. 135; Zimmermann, p. 51; Gordley, pp. 498 *et seq.*; Kötz, pp. 497 *et seq.*

26 Raape, p. 90.

27 Juenger (2000), pp. 1133, 1149; see also Juenger, in: Berger, p. 88; Juenger, in: Carbonneau, p. 276; Juenger (1999), pp. 29 *et seq.*: 'Why, then, do we cling to the conventional wisdom, the idea that national law must govern international transactions and that all national laws are of equal value? Among the reasons that come to my mind there are, first and foremost, the force of habit and the hesitation to deviate from the trodden path.' see also Boutin, pp. 662 *et seq.*

28 See Zumbansen, p. 41.

29 Benson, p. 654.

Thus, the new pragmatism and the striving for commonsensical solutions has lead to the search for practicability and thus to the final acceptance of the theory of transnational commercial law:

"More than any other factor, the difficulty in determining the content of transnational law has typically stood in the way of a serious discussion concerning the practical usefulness of the *lex mercatoria*. Practicability – or its lack – is the watchword. Recent initiatives and new approaches evidence not only a resurgence of interest in the issue, but may in fact go a long way toward providing international practitioners with the workable tools they claim are lacking. At their core, these initiatives share certain defining traits: informality and pragmatism, rather than an insistence on overly formal and dogmatic methodology or result."[30]

Again, this development on the transnational plane finds its parallels in the EU where a forceful quest is made for spreading knowledge about the PECL and providing a structure to the rule making "from the bottom up" in order to preserve the advantages of this informal and decentralised method of rule making.[31]

4.1 The "Creeping Codification"-Technique

One possible way of tackling this problem is the concept of the "*Creeping Codification*"[32] of transnational commercial law. In view of the striking parallels between the economic conditions on the "global market place" and on the EU Single Market,[33] this concept can be used as a basis for a "bottom-up" codification process also on the EU level.[34] It rests on three basic premises.[35]

First, the *lex mercatoria*, which is characterised by openness, flexibility and informality, requires a codification technique which reflects its inherent characteristics.

Secondly, transnational commercial law is a worldwide phenomenon and requires a method of codification which allows instant and easy access to its contents at any time and everywhere over the world.

Thirdly, the method of codification has to include recourse to the extensive case law of international arbitral tribunals and to international drafting practice as the "social engineers" of the *lex mercatoria*.[36] This emphasis on arbitral case law distinguishes the list from the *UNIDROIT Principles*, for in the work of the UNIDROIT Working Group, awards of international arbitral tribunals played only a subordinate role. Even though they provide a clear, detailed and analytical picture of the present state of international commercial contract law, the UNIDROIT Principles are charac-

---

30 Fortier, p. 124.

31 Blase (1999), pp. 13 *et seq.*

32 See for the introduction of this terminology Berger, International Economic Arbitration (1993), p. 543; Berger, *American Review of International Arbitration* (1993), p. 29.

33 See *supra* note 2.

34 See Lando, The Harmonisation of European Contract Law (1997), p. 20; Berger, *European Review of Private Law* (2001), pp. 23 *et seq.*

35 See Berger (1999), pp. 210 *et seq.*

36 Schmitthoff, No. 71: 'Substantive law is often born in the womb of procedure. In keeping with their international character, the law which these international arbitral bodies create is transnational. It is the new *lex mercatoria.*'

terised by a certain degree of "analytical indifference" resulting from the fact that the international business community and its dispute settlement techniques were not a major focus of the research.

4.2   The "List-Procedure"

4.2.1   The Purpose of the List

The concept of the Creeping Codification is based on an open list of principles, rules and standards of the *lex mercatoria*.[37] The list reproduces as black-letter-law all those rules and principles of the *lex mercatoria* which have been accepted in international arbitral and contractual practice together with comprehensive comparative references. The list unifies the various sources that have fostered the evolution of a transnational commercial legal system[38] into a single, open-ended set of rules and principles: the reception of general principles of law, the codification of international trade law by "formulating agencies", the case law of international arbitral tribunals, the law-making forces of international model contract forms and general conditions of trade, and finally the analysis of comparative legal science.

Contrary to the UNIDROIT Principles of International Commercial Contracts (UPICC) and the PECL, the list is not limited to the field of international commercial *contract* law. Rather, the list follows the decision-making practice of international arbitration and, therefore, contains legal principles that are related to those fields of law which play a predominant role in international arbitral case law, such as international company law, conflict of laws, rules of evidence, the international law of expropriation and general arbitration law. At the same time, the idea of an open-ended list shows that the Creeping Codification of the *lex mercatoria* through the drafting of lists of rules and principles of transnational commercial law may not be substituted by the publication of Restatements of international contract law. Both projects have different objectives. The Restatements only provide valuable incentives and starting points for the extension and evolution of the list.

4.2.2   The List as a "Codification"-Technique

The idea to draft lists of general principles and rules of transnational law has a certain tradition in the context of the discussion on the modern law merchant.[39] However, the far-reaching consequences of this procedure for the concept of transnational law have never been realised. In almost all of these cases, the lists merely served as a means to

---

37 The idea was first introduced in Berger, Formalisierte oder „schleichende" Kodifizierung (1996), pp. 144 *et seq.*; a first list appeared in Berger, Internationale Wirtschaftsschiedsgerichtsbarkeit (1992), pp. 374 *et seq.*; Berger, International Economic Arbitration (1993), pp. 544 *et seq.*

38 See Gaillard, in: Berger, p. 65: '...if not a genuine legal order, transnational rules do perform, in actual practice, a function strikingly similar to that of a genuine legal system.'

39 See, e.g., the lists published by Paulsson, pp. 82 *et seq.*; Blessing, in: Böckstiegel, pp. 68 *et seq.*; see also the list published by the Cairo Regional Centre for International Commercial Arbitration (CRCICA), pp. 2 *et seq.*; cf. also the list reproduced in ICC Award No. 8365, Clunet 1997, pp. 1078, 1079 *et seq.*

prove that the *lex mercatoria* is not devoid of all content.[40] In one case, the reproduction of a list even served the purpose of showing the stealth of the *lex mercatoria*.[41]

Consequently, a codifying effect of these lists was never discussed and no attempts were ever made to develop these list procedures into an independent and autonomous codifying technique for transnational commercial law. In fact, international legal practice has criticised the fact that the existing lists were not found in the normal places to which judges and arbitrators (and lawyers) turn: "[t]he occasional law review article is no substitute for a code or, in common law jurisdictions, line of judicial opinions."[42] Likewise, international arbitrators have complained that "as far as general principles of international business [law] are concerned, their list cannot be found in a single textbook."[43] Today, the list-approach has been recognised as a viable means for the codification of transnational commercial law.

"...it is evident that the idea of 'the list'...is as close as we've come, in recent generations, to tackling the lex and wrestling it into usable shape."[44]

4.2.3   The Open-end Character of the List

Even though the lists perform an important function as "codifying focal point"[45] this should not be confused with a definite manifestation and petrifaction of transnational commercial law.

It is one of the main tasks of scientific and practical research in the field of the *lex mercatoria* to avoid the creation of an inflexible, rigid and predetermined system that leaves no or only little room for the further development of this doctrine. This leads to a constant process of cross-fertilisation between the decision-making work of international arbitral tribunals and the list. The list derives a substantial input from the case load of international arbitration, while international arbitrators may use the list and the comparative references contained therein to develop or 'discover' new rules or principles of this transnational commercial legal system. This means, that the lists are never "completed" or "closed". Although in its initial form, a list may not contain the solution to a certain legal issue of transnational law, a later version may very well include a principle or rule that has been acknowledged in international arbitral or contract drafting practice.[46] Here lies the decisive advantage of this non-formalised codification procedure when compared to the formalised approaches taken by the UNIDROIT Working Group when drafting the UPICC and by the *Lando*-Commis-

---

40 *Cf.* Bonell (1978), p. 498, n. 41; Bucher, in: Schwind, pp. 15 *et seq.*
41 The list published by Mustill, pp. 110 *et seq.* was not intended to furnish proof of the richness of the *lex mercatoria*, but to provide the basis for a critical appraisal of that concept, see footnote 81a, *id.*
42 Selden, p. 119.
43 ICC Award No. 5953, Clunet 1990, p. 1056, 1059.
44 Fortier, p. 127; see also Molineaux, *Journal of International Arbitration* (2000), p. 150: "... the list looks forward and provides an incentive for the future evolution of transnational commercial law as an open legal system. There can be no doubt that this is a list which will become a *sine qua non* reference....'
45 Cf. Schmidt, p. 60 for the judiciary of the state.
46 Cf. Goldman, p. 249 for the principles of defective contract formation, representation and form, which he initially did not consider to form part of the *lex mercatoria*.

sion. The work of these groups had to be "finished" at some point in time. Amending and updating the UPICC and PECL[47] always requires initiation of a new formalised codification procedure. The updating of the lists, however, does not require a formalised procedure of that kind and can therefore be effected through a constant dialogue between arbitral practice, legal science and the academic institution that is responsible for the list. It is for this reason, that the list contains a "more or less complete collection of principles" which reflect "the *lex mercatoria in its present form*".[48] The progressing quality of comparative science necessarily leads to an increase in the sophistication of existing lists. As a consequence of this dialectical process between comparative science and (arbitral) practice[49], new principles will be added to the list and existing ones will be refined or even substituted by others. In spite of the uncertainty that is necessarily connected with the drafting of the lists as a process of the constant evolution and change, they still provide the necessary prerequisite for the practical acceptance of the *lex mercatoria*: They create "a certain degree of predictability"[50] for the resolution of legal conflicts, thereby guaranteeing more legal certainty in transnational dispute resolution. This provides parties to international contracts with a certain basis for "conflict avoidance" through planning and drafting techniques, thereby depriving the *lex mercatoria* of the aura of a "*laissez faire*-doctrine".

At the same time, the goal to achieve legal certainty is not seen as an end on its own. Rather, the list technique leaves enough room for a teleological evolution of the *lex mercatoria*. Therefore, the application of the *lex mercatoria* in practice always oscillates between two extreme positions without ever reaching one or the other: a decision in equity on one side and a decision according to codified written law on the other.[51] Both aspects influence the doctrine of a transnational autonomous law, but taken alone, they would mean the failure of the *lex mercatoria*-doctrine.

4.2.4   WWW.TLDB.de: An Online Codification-Technique

The lists, which have been published so far, have been criticised for their lack of structure and difficulty of orientation.[52] The problem with this perfectly legitimate concern is that every attempt to "structure" or "formalize" the list runs counter to its informal character. The growth of the lists in the past years has, however, made it necessary to adopt a technique which ensures their practicability and accessibility while at the same time preserving a maximum degree of openness and flexibility. The Center for Transnational Law (CENTRAL) at Cologne University[53] operates the first

---

47 See for the current activities of the UNIDROIT Working Group and Lando Commission in this direction Lando (2002), pp. 2 *et seq.*
48 Mustill, p. 110; cf. also Stein, p. 161, speaking of a "necessarily limited snap shot'.
49 Cf. for domestic law Schmidt, pp. 75 *et seq.*
50 Langen, part I, Nos. 11 *et seq.*; Samuel, p. 248 mentions as one of the basic arguments against the *lex mercatoria*-doctrine the lack of predictability of decision-making.
51 Esser, p. 343: "Instead of the primitive "either-or" of domestic law and equity, a universal practice of general principles of law in the sense of Art. 38 No. 3 of the ICJ Statutes is more and more required.' (translation by the author).
52 See Basedow, p. 558.
53 See for more information www.transnational-law.de.

online database on transnational law ("*Transnational Law Database*", TLDB) on the internet at www.tldb.de. Making the list accessible through an online database on the World Wide Web combines these two basic prerequisites in an ideal way. Using the World Wide Web as a global archive of transnational commercial law makes it possible to keep pace with the ever-changing world of international commerce while at the same time structuring the list within a flexible and easy-to-use electronic framework.[54] A major purpose of the TLDB is to spread knowledge about the contents of transnational commercial law around the globe. Recent empirical studies have revealed that international practitioners hesitate to make use of this concept, not because they have doubts about the methodical basis of the concept, but simply because they lack knowledge about transnational law and do not want to use standard business negotiations as a laboratory for "innovative" solutions:

> "When a legal relationship between the parties may be perfectly framed in a set of (specific, well-known and complete) rules of transnational law, I would agree that the advantages that would arise from the knowledge of both parties of the applicable rules would be large."[55]

It is a complaint often heard from international practitioners that "information on transnational law (such as reference books, court decisions and arbitration awards in prior cases etc.) is not available."[56] At the same time, practitioners agree that "knowledge about transnational law belongs to the arsenal of every internationally oriented lawyer".[57]

The second task of the TLDB is to provide a means for the "codification" of transnational commercial law. The *lex mercatoria* as "law in action" requires a degree of codifying flexibility and subtlety that goes far beyond that which any code, model law, convention or restatement can provide. Thus, in the context of the *lex mercatoria*, the term "codification" assumes a new meaning. CENTRAL is not the legislature of the *lex mercatoria*. In fact, there is no single "legislature", since the *lex mercatoria* as reflexive law reflects the conduct, customs and habits of the community of merchants. "Codification", therefore in this context means that the TLDB puts the various principles and rules of the *lex mercatoria* into a readable form and, by reproducing the comparative references for each of those principles and rules, allows the user to make his own judgment on the "comparative persuasiveness" of these sources. This individual judgment is always necessary, since the TLDB merely establishes a presumption that the principles and rules reproduced in it form part of this evolving legal system.

---

54 The Tldb thus provides the answer to concerns raised by Fortier, p. 126: "One may legitimately ask whether *any* institutional framework is able to maintain the degree of openness and flexibility required to keep pace with the world of international commerce – particularly the world of e-commerce.'

55 Statement of a practitioner as response to the CENTRAL Enquiry on the Practice of Transnational Law, see Berger/Dubberstein/Petzold/Lehmann, in: Berger, p. 111; another practitioner responded: 'I want to see how it operates in practice first,' see *id.*

56 Berger/Dubberstein/Lehmann/Petzold, *id.*

57 Berger/Dubberstein/Lehmann/Petzold, *id.*, p. 113.

5 The Paradox of Pragmatism: From Informality to Formal Lawmaking?

Paradoxically, the new pragmatism has paved the way for formality. Both on the worldwide level and in the EU the search for informality in lawmaking has resulted in the resort to formal codification techniques. On the EU level, it is envisaged that the various forms of informal and decentralised rule making creating the amorphous body of European private law will, in the long run, end up in a formal process, the enactment of a European Civil Code.[58] For the global markets of the world, the UPICC provide the "*ratio scripta*" of international contract law. Also, the internet provides an ideal "virtual" framework for the codification of the *lex mercatoria* as an extremely flexible, ever changing and highly decentralised law in action. The TLDB provides an example of how an, albeit highly informal, online codification system, an online code for transnational law, can work. Some want to go farther and suggest a much more formal approach: the drafting of a "Global Commercial Code" for international transactions, possibly under the auspices of an international formulating agency such as the United Nations Commission on International Trade Law (UNCITRAL).[59] This idea revives proposals by *René David* and *Clive Schmitthoff* for the drafting of a convention on the "ius commune of international trade law" made in the late 1960s.[60] It is suggested that the Code should be somehow interlinked with the UPICC. Some think that in that case, the UPICC should be lifted from their present status as soft law to rules of law which are binding upon the courts.[61]

On the EU level, the creation of a European Civil Code makes sense since it does justice to the legitimate expectations of its main addressees: the consumers in the EU Single Market.[62] In that context, the notion of freedom of contract is replaced or at least overshadowed by the idea of contractual justice. It requires that the weaker party (the consumer) should be more strongly protected, that the non-consumer party should be obliged to be more considerate of the other side's interests, and that the very concept of contract should be reformulated and turned into a legal relationship with obligations to inform, to co-operate, and to show an enhanced degree of solidarity with the concerns and needs of the consumer-party.[63] The situation is totally different, however, on the worldwide level. The new *lex mercatoria* is the law of b2b transactions. It has nothing to do with consumer protection. It was for that very reason that transnational commercial law could free itself from the constraints of traditional dogmatism and the theory of legal sources. Also, the deficiencies of formal law making were at the heart of the new pragmatism. One should therefore be very careful with any attempt to convert the new pragmatism into a vehicle for universal for-

---

58 See most recently Blase (2002), p. 491; see also Blase (2001), p. 310.
59 See Bonell (2000), pp. 469 *et seq.*; Herrmann, p. 35; Lando (2002), pp. 12 *et seq.*
60 Cf. Draft basic convention establishing a common body of international trade law: proposal by the French delegation, UNCITRAL Yearbook 1968-1970, pp. 288 *et seq.*; the text of the *Draft Convention* together with a the official commentary is reprinted in UNCITRAL Yearbook 1971, pp. 139, 140; David (1987), pp. 66 *et seq.*; Schmitthoff, UNIDROIT Annuaire 1967-1968, vol. II., p. 115.
61 Lando (2002), p. 13.
62 Staudenmayer, pp. 63 *et seq.*
63 See, e.g., Kötz/Flessner, p. 12.

mal law making. While it is true that *David's* and *Schmitthoff's* progressive proposals made in the 1960s failed due to the strong position of state sovereignty in those days[64], today's decline of state sovereignty must be seen in the context of the globalisation phenomenon, the very essence of which is its search for decentralised and privatised rulemaking and informality. Moreover, reintroducing formal codification techniques both on the worldwide and the EU level brings with it the age old problems that come along with any codification process. This is exemplified by *Lando's* considerations about the exact delimitation of the scope of application of the Global Code and the European Civil Code, even though the scope of both instruments has not yet been determined, let alone defined.[65]

6   Conclusion

The new *lex mercatoria* has come a long way from the fierce trench fighting over its existence in the late 1960s to the development of online codification techniques at the beginning of the 21st century. Today, it is the new pragmatism which is the driving force behind the development of a modern new *lex mercatoria*. The evolution of transnational business law, of a system of private governance of international business and trade, is based on a marked change in the legal culture of global business transactions.[66] Today, *Ole Lando's* suggestion ventured in 1997[67] that not only international arbitrators but also domestic courts should be allowed to apply the *lex mercatoria* is close to reality. A remarkable shift from form to substance is also recognizable on the EU level. In November 2000, the Committee for Legal Affairs and Common Market Policy of the European Parliament has urged that there be a discussion on the issue of a European Civil Code „in a pragmatic fashion and freed from dogmatic constraints".[68] Even the domestic judiciary, which hitherto was not known for a proactive approach towards comparative or even transnational decision making, is adopting a much more progressive view towards this subject:

> „One effect of 25 years' involvement in the European Union has been to give to English common law Judges and European civil law Judges a much greater understanding of the strengths and weaknesses of each other's system of law... As the world gets smaller, and communications between lawyers and judges from different legal systems become easier, there is everything to be said for a common approach to the solutions of problems [...] unless principle or precedent stand irremovably in the path of progress."[69]

---

64   See Berger (1999), p. 138; David, in: UNIDROIT (1977), p. 10.
65   Lando (2002), p. 13.
66   See Appelbaum/Felstiner/Gessner, pp. 15 *et seq.*
67   Lando, in: Frändberg, p. 579.
68   See Working Paper on the Approximation of the Civil and Commercial Laws of the Member States of the Committee for Legal Affairs and Common Market Policy of the European Parliament of 6 November 2000, at 5.
69   See the statement of Judge Brook in *Laceys Footwear (Wholesale) Limited v. Bowler International Freight Limited & Another* [1997] 2 Lloyd's L. Rep. 369, 385; see generally Berger, *International and Comparative Law Quarterly* (2001), pp. 877 *et seq.*

In fact, comparative law plays an important catalytic role in bridging the gap between transnational legal thinking and the domestic judiciary.[70] In line with this development, it is recommended that domestic European courts seek guidance in their decision-making from the UPICC and PECL.[71] Generally speaking, European legal culture is undergoing a radical change from an overly formalistic tradition to a culture that is significantly less formal, less dogmatic and less positivistic than national legal cultures in Europe have been.[72] These parallel developments in Europe and on the globalised markets of the world provide the ideal breeding ground for informal, pragmatic rule making "from the bottom up".

However, two issues must always be kept in mind, by academics and rule makers alike. First, the new *lex mercatoria* is highly informal. Any attempt to "codify" this law in action must take account of this inherent specificity of transnational commercial law. Secondly, there is no such thing as a "European" *lex mercatoria*! Transnational commercial law has developed and is continuously developing on a worldwide level and Europe is part of the worldwide globalised markets. But it would mean the death of the *lex mercatoria* were one to start to dissect this ever growing global body of legal principles and rules into sectoral, i.e. regional "leges mercatoriae".[73] While the transnational commercial law provides an important impetus for the further evolution of a European private law, it is and remains, by its very nature, a worldwide phenomenon. The *lex mercatoria* is not a regional but a truly global law.

BIBLIOGRAPHY: Appelbaum/Felstiner/Gessner, The Legal Culture of Global Business Transactions, in: Appelbaum/Felstiner/Gessner, eds., *The Legal Culture of Global Business Transactions* (Oxford 2001), pp. 1-36; Basedow, Book Review, *RabelsZ* 62 (1998), pp. 555-558; Benson, The Spontaneous Evolution of Commercial Law, *Southern Economic Journal* (1989), pp. 644-662; Berger, Internationale Wirtschaftsschiedsgerichtsbarkeit (Berlin/New York 1992); Berger, International Economic Arbitration (Deventer/Boston 1993); Berger, Party Autonomy in International Economic Arbitration: A Reappraisal, *American Review of International Arbitration* (1993), pp. 1-36; Berger, Formalisierte oder „schleichende" Kodifizierung des Transnationalen Wirtschaftsrechts (München 1996); Berger, The Creeping Codification of the *Lex mercatoria* (The Hague/London/Boston 1999); Berger, Vom praktischen Nutzen der Rechtsvergleichung, in: Berger *et al.*, eds., *Festschrift für Otto Sandrock* (Heidelberg 2000), pp. 49-64; Berger, Harmonisation of European Contract Law, *International and Comparative Law Quarterly* (2001), pp. 877-900; Berger, The New Law Merchant and the Global Market Place, in: Berger, ed., *The Practice of Transnational Law* (The Hague/London/Boston 2001), pp. 1-22; Berger, The Principles of European Private Law, *European Review of Private Law* (2001), pp. 21-34; Berger, Transnationalisation of International Investment Contracts with Particular Reference to the Natural Resources Industry, *Journal of Energy & Natural Resources Law* (2004), pp. 51-58; Berger/Dubberstein/Petzold/Lehmann, The CENTRAL Enquiry on the use of Transnational Law in International Contract Law and Arbitration, in: Berger, ed., *The Practice of Transnational Law* (The Hague/London/Boston 2001), pp. 91-113; Berman/Dasser, The New Law Merchant and the Old: Sources, Content and Legitimacy,

---

70 See Lord Goff of Chieveley, p. 748: "Comparative law may have been the hobby of yesterday, but it is destined to become the science of tomorrow. Merryman, pp. 771 *et seq.*
71 See, e.g., for Danish law Lookofsky, p. 504; see generally Berger, *International and Comparative Law Quarterly* (2001), pp. 891 *et seq.*; Blase (2002), pp. 309 *et seq.*
72 Hesselink, A New European Legal Culture (2001), p. 72.
73 See Herrmann, p. 35.

in: Carbonneau, ed., *Lex Mercatoria and Arbitration*, 2nd ed. (The Hague/London/Boston 1997), pp. 53-69; Blase, Leaving the Shadow for the Test of Practice – On the Future of the Principles of European Contract Law, *Vindobona Journal* (1999), pp. 3-14; Blase, Die Grundregeln des Europäischen Vertragsrechts als Recht grenzüberschreitender Verträge (Münster 2001); Blase, A European Uniform Law of Contracts – Why and how?, *Columbia Journal of European Law* (2002), pp. 487-491; Blessing, Das neue internationale Schiedsrecht der Schweiz – Ein Fortschritt oder ein Rückschritt?, in: Böckstiegel, ed., *Die internationale Schiedsgerichtsbarkeit in der Schweiz (II)* (Cologne et al. 1989), pp. 13-97; Böhm, Privatrechtsgesellschaft und Marktwirtschaft, in: Mestmäcker, ed., *Freiheit und Ordnung in der Marktwirtschaft* (Baden-Baden 1980), pp. 105-168; Bonell, Das autonome Recht des Welthandels – Rechtsdogmatische und rechtsphilosophische Aspekte, *RabelsZ* 42 (1978), pp. 485-506; Bonell, Do We Need a Global Commercial Code?, *Uniform Law Review* (2000), pp. 469-481; Boutin, Derecho Internacional Privado (Panamá 2002); Braeckmans, Paralegale Normen en *Lex mercatoria*, *Tijdschrift voor Privaatrecht* (1986), pp. 1-35; Bucher, Transnationales Recht im IPR, in: Schwind, ed., *Aktuelle Fragen zum Europarecht aus der Sicht in- und ausländischer Gelehrter* (Wien 1986), pp. 11-24; Cairo Regional Centre for International Commercial Arbitration (CRCICA), in: CRCICA, ed., *A Newsletter of CRCICA* (Cairo January 1997), pp. 2-4; Canaris, Die Stellung der "UNIDROIT-Principles" und der "Principles of European Contract Law" im System der Rechtsquellen, in: Basedow, ed., *Europäische Vertragsrechtsvereinheitlichung und deutsches Recht* (Tübingen 2000), pp. 5-31; Dasser, Internationale Schiedsgerichte und *Lex mercatoria* (Zurich 1989); David, in: UNIDROIT (ed.), *New Directions in International Trade Law* (Dobbs Ferry 1977), pp. 5-23; David, Le Droit du Commerce International (Paris 1987); Delaume, Law and Practice of Transnational Contracts (Dobbs Ferry 1988); Delbrück, Globalisation of Law, Politics, and Markets – Implications for Domestic Law – A European Perspective, *Indiana Journal of Global Legal Studies* (1993), pp. 9-36; De Ly, De *Lex mercatoria* (Antwerp 1989); Esser, Grundsatz und Norm in der richterlichen Fortbildung des Privatrechts, 4th ed., (Tübingen 1990); Fitzgerald, Harnessing the Potential of Globalisation for the Consumer and the Citizen, *International Affairs* (1997), pp. 739-746; Fortier, The New, New *lex mercatoria* or, Back to the Future, *Arbitration International* (2001), pp. 121-128; Gaillard, Thirty Years of *Lex mercatoria*: Towards the Discriminating Application of Transnational Rules, in: van den Berg, ed., *Efficient Arbitration Proceedings: The Law Applicable in International Arbitration*, ICCA Congress ser. No. 7 (The Hague/London/Boston 1989), pp. 570-590; Gaillard, Transnational Law: A Legal System or a Method of Decision-Making? in: Berger, ed., *The Practice of Transnational Law* (The Hague/London/Boston 2001), pp. 53-65; Galgano, The New *Lex mercatoria*, *Annual Survey of International & Comparative Law* (1995), pp. 99-109; Gandolfi, Pour un Code Européen des Contrats, *Revue Trimestrielle de Droit Civil* (1992), pp. 707-716; Goldman, Nouvelles Réflexions sur la *Lex mercatoria*, in: Dominicé, ed., *Mélanges en l'Honneur de Pierre Lalive* (Basle/Franfurt a.M 1993), pp. 241-255; Goldstajn, The New Law Merchant, *Journal of Business Law* (1961), pp. 12-18; Goldstajn, The New Law Merchant Reconsidered, in: Fabricius, ed., *Festschrift für Clive M. Schmitthoff*, (Frankfurt a.M. 1973), pp. 171-185; Gordley, Common Law und Civil Law: eine überholte Unterscheidung, *Zeitschrift für Europäisches Privatrecht* (1993), pp. 498-518; Herrmann, The Role of UNCITRAL, in: Fletcher/Mistelis/Cremona, eds., *Foundations and Perspectives of International Trade Law* (London 2001), pp. 28-36; Hesselink, A New European Legal Culture (Deventer 2001); Hesselink, The Principles of European Contract Law: Some Choices Made by the Lando Commission, in: Hesselink/de Vries, eds., *Principles of European Contract Law* (Deventer 2001), pp. 8-103; Hyland, On Setting forth the Law of Contract: A Foreword, *American Journal of Comparative Law* (1992), pp. 541-550; Jellinek, Allgemeine Staatslehre, 3rd ed. (Berlin 1929); Jhering, Der Zweck im Recht, vol. 1, 6th-8th ed. (Leipzig 1923); Juenger, The *Lex mercatoria* and the Conflict of Laws, in: Carbonneau, ed., *Lex mercatoria and Arbitration*,

2nd ed. (The Hague/London/Boston 1997), pp. 265-277; Juenger, The Problem with Private International Law, in: Basedow *et al.*, eds., *Private Law in the International Arena* (The Hague 1999), pp. 289-309; Juenger, Conflict of Laws, Comparative Law and Civil Law: The *Lex mercatoria* and Private International Law, *Louisiana Law Review* (2000), pp. 1133-1150; Juenger, Some Random Remarks from Overseas, in: Berger, ed., *The Practice of Transnational Law* (The Hague/London/Boston 2001), pp. 81-89; Kahn, La Vente Commerciale Internationale (Paris 1964); Kahn, Conclusion, in: Gaillard, ed., *Transnational Rules in International Commercial Arbitration* (Paris 1993), pp. 235-243; Kötz, Europäisches Vertragsrecht, vol. I (Tübingen 1996); Kötz, Abschied von der Rechtskreislehre?, *Zeitschrift für Europäisches Privatrecht* (1998), pp. 493-505 *Kötz/Flessner*, European Contract Law, vol. 1, (Oxford 1997); *Kolo/Wälde*, Renegotiation and Contract Adaptation in International Investment Projects, *Journal of World Investment* (2000), pp. 5-58; Kronke, International Uniform Law Conventions: Advantages, Disadvantages, Criteria for Choice, *Uniform Law Review* (2000), pp. 13-21; Ladeur, Die rechtswissenschaftliche Methodendiskussion und die Bewältigung des gesellschaftlichen Wandels, *RabelsZ* 64 (2000), pp. 61, 103; Lando, The *Lex mercatoria* in International Commercial Arbitration, *International and Comparative Law Quarterly* (1985), pp. 747-768; Lando, European Contract Law, in: Weyers, ed., *Europäisches Vertragsrecht* (Baden-Baden 1997), pp. 81-101; Lando, The Harmonisation of European Contract Law through a Restatement of Principles (Oxford 1997); Lando, *Lex mercatoria* 1985-1996, in: Frändberg, ed., *Festskrift Till Stig Strömholm* (Stockholm 1997), pp. 567-584; Lando, Some Features of the Law of Contract in the Third Millennium, *Scandinavian Studies in Law* (2000), pp. 343-402; Lando, Principles of European Contract Law and Unidroit Principles: Similarities, Differences and Perspectives (Oxford 2002); Lando, Does the European Union need a Civil Code?, *Recht der Internationalen Wirtschaft* (2003), pp. 1-2; Lando/Beale, Principles of European Contract Law, Parts I and II (The Hague/London/Boston 2000); Langen, Transnationales Recht (Heidelberg 1981); Lookofsky, The Limits of Commercial Contract Freedom: Under the UNIDROIT "Restatement" and Danish Law, *American Journal of Comparative Law* (1998), pp. 485-508; Lord Goff of Chieveley, The Wilberforce Lecture 1997: The Future of the Common Law, *International and Comparative Law Quarterly* (1997), pp. 745-760; Luhmann, Das Recht der Gesellschaft (Frankfurt a.M. 1993); Malynes, Consuetudo Vel *Lex mercatoria* Or The Ancient Law-Merchant (1622); Merryman, Comparative Law Scholarship, *Hastings International and Comparative Law Review* (1998), pp. 771-792; Molineaux, Applicable Law in Arbitration, *Journal of World Investment* No.1 (2000), pp. 127-135; Molineaux, Book Review, *Journal of International Arbitration* No. 1 (2000), pp. 147-150; Mustill, The New *Lex mercatoria*: The First Twenty-five Years, *Arbitration International* (1988), pp. 86-119; Park, Control Mechanisms in the Development of a Modern *Lex mercatoria*, in: Carbonneau, ed., *Lex mercatoria and Arbitration*, 2nd ed. (The Hague/London/Boston 1997), pp. 143-172; Paulsson, La *Lex mercatoria* dans l'Arbitrage C.C.I., *Revue de l'Arbitrage* (1990), pp. 55-100; Pfund, United States Participation in Transnational Lawmaking, in: Carbonneau, ed., *Lex mercatoria and Arbitration*, 2nd ed. (The Hague/London/Boston 1997), pp. 203-218; Raape, Internationales Privatrecht, 5th ed. (Berlin *et al.*1961); Samuel, Jurisdictional Problems (Zurich 1989); Sandrock, How Much Freedom Should an International Arbitrator Enjoy? – The Desire for Freedom From Law v. The Promotion of International Arbitration, *American Review of International Arbitration* (1992), pp. 30-34; Savigny, System des heutigen Römischen Rechts, vol. VIII (Berlin 1849); Schlesinger, ed., Formation of Contracts, A Study of the Common Core of Legal (Dobbs Ferry 1968); Schmidt, Die Zukunft der Kodifikationsidee (Heidelberg 1985); Schmidtchen, Territorialität des Rechts, internationales Privatrecht und die privatautonome Regelung internationaler Sachverhalte, *RabelsZ* 59 (1995), pp. 56-112; Schmitthoff, International Trade Usages (Paris 1987); Selden, Lex Mercatoria in European and U.S. Trade Practice: Time to Take a Closer Look, *Annual Survey of International and Comparative Law* (1995), pp. 111-12; Spickhoff, Internationales Handelsrecht vor

Schiedsgerichten und staatlichen Gerichten, *RabelsZ* 56 (1992), pp. 116-141; Staudenmayer, Die Richtlinien des Verbraucherprivatrechts – Bausteine für ein europäisches Privatrecht?, in: Schulte-Nölke/Schulze, eds., *Europäische Rechtsangleichung und nationale Privatrechte* (Baden-Baden 1999), pp. 63-78; Stein, *Lex mercatoria*, Realität und Theorie (Frankfurt a.M. 1995); Teubner, Globale Bukovina, *Rechtshistorisches Journal* (1996), pp. 273-303; Toope, Mixed International Arbitration (Cambridge 1990); Triebel/Petzold, Grenzen der *lex mercatoria* in der internationalen Schiedsgerichtsbarkeit, *Recht des Internationalen Wirtschaft* (1988), pp. 247-250; Walker/Fox, Globalisation: An Analytical Framework, *Global Legal Studies Journal* (1996), pp. 375-411; Wallace, International Agencies for the Formulation of Transnational Economic Law: A Comment about Methods and Techniques, in: Horn/Schmitthoff, eds., *The Transnational Law of International Commercial Tranactions*, pp. 81-85; Zimmermann, Der europäische Charakter des englischen Rechts – Historische Verbindungen zwischen civil law and common law, *Zeitschrift für Europäisches Privatrecht (1993)*, pp. 4-51; Zumbansen, Piercing the Legal Veil: Commercial Arbitration and Transnational Law, in: European University Institute, Florence, Department of Law (ed.), *EUI Working Papers Law No. 2002/ 11* (Badia Fiesolana 2002).

CHAPTER 4

The American Experience: Restatements, the UCC, Uniform Laws, and Transnational Coordination

Richard Hyland*

1   Introduction

European lawyers have long been familiar with two unique products of American law – the Restatements and the Uniform Commercial Code (the 'UCC' or the 'Code'). Together, these two American legal institutions have contributed a harmonising influence in fields that had long been characterised by diversity. Over the past several years, American collaboration with foreign jurists has produced additional models of coordination and cooperation. From the point of view of the emerging European civil code, these American developments suggest that a European codification may already be possible.

My discussion proceeds as follows. After presenting the Restatements, the UCC, American uniform laws, and recent American collaboration with foreign jurists, I explore why American law has resisted codification in the European manner. I suggest that the lack of complete convergence among the European civil laws does not necessarily present a barrier to European codification. To test the relevance of my hypothesis, I consider the problem of bridging the gap between the common law consideration doctrine and the civilian notion of *pacta sunt servanda*.

2   American Contributions to Coordination Among Different Systems

2.1   The Restatements

The Restatements of the Law strive to present the basic principles of American law in systematic fashion. They are the work of one of the most distinguished associations in American law, the American Law Institute (the "ALI" or the "Institute"), which includes as its members the most eminent lawyers, judges, and law professors in America, as well as a selection of important foreign jurists. The Restatements are concerned chiefly with areas of the private law that, though generally codified in civilian systems, continue to be governed largely by case law in America. These areas include agency, the conflict of laws, contracts, property (both real property and some questions regarding chattels), restitution, suretyship, torts, and trusts. The ALI has also completed a Restatement-like project in the field of corporate governance. Restatements are also devoted to fields not directly relevant to private law codification,

---

*   Distinguished Professor, Rutgers University Law School, Camden NJ, USA

such as judgments, the law of foreign relations, and the law governing lawyers.[1] There is a separate Restatement for each of these fields.

The Restatements are not designed for legislative enactment. Instead, they are meant to influence judicial decision-making, which they do in two ways. First, they operate as persuasive authority for the rule or principle that, according to the Institute, best responds to the aspirations of the American legal system. For that reason, lawyers frequently cite to the Restatements in their briefs, and courts often include those citations in their opinions. Second, a state high court may adopt a particular Restatement section as the common law rule of the jurisdiction.[2]

Whether or not a Restatement provision is officially adopted, the common law evolution continues. After a generation or so, the decisions usually overtake even the most visionary Restatement provisions, and revision is then required. Work on the original Restatements began at the founding of the ALI in 1923. The Restatement of Contracts, the first to be completed, was published in 1932. Work on the second edition, the Restatement (Second), began in 1951. Most of the Restatements are now in a second edition, while for some a third edition, the Restatement (Third), has recently been concluded or is currently in progress.

Though the Restatements attempt to provide a reliable statement of generally accepted legal principles, they do not simply synthesise the case law. Instead, the drafting and revision of a Restatement may require as much as a decade of intensive reflection by a Reporter and an Advisory Committee of experts selected by the Institute. They meet several times a year during the drafting process. The evolving drafts are presented at regular intervals to the Council, the ALI's governing board, and approved at annual meetings of the Institute's more than two thousand members.

The Restatements each consist of one or more hard-bound volumes containing several hundred 'black-letter' provisions – rules or principles often formulated in a lapidary fashion and printed in bold type. The format for the text that accompanies the black-letter provisions has evolved over time. In the original Restatements, the black letter was followed by two or three short hypothetical cases – called illustrations – often together with a short paragraph of commentary. Though the original Reporters prepared extensive notes and included those notes in the tentative drafts, there was no citation to authority in the final text. The Restatements (Second) were more elaborate. New illustrations were added, as was a lengthier commentary to each section. Moreover, the Reporters Notes in many of the volumes provided case authority for the black letter and illustrations. This development has continued in the Restatement (Third), which now provides a treatise-like expository commentary, numerous illustrations, and, in the Reporter's Notes, an exhaustive survey of the relevant case law. Companion volumes, known today as the Appendix, provide summaries of the cases that have cited or relied on the Restatements.

---

1 For a complete list of the Restatements, together with all other ALI projects, past and present, see the ALI Annual Report, available online at http://www.ali.org/.

2 See, e.g., Cuker v. Mikalauskas, 692 A.2d 1042, 1049 (Pa. 1997) (adopting the procedure for shareholder derivative actions from the ALI Principles of Corporate Governance (1994)). The Supreme Court of Arizona has announced that it will follow the Restatements except when Restatement provisions contradict prior precedent or legislative enactment. See Byrne (1973). The legislature of the Virgin Islands has enacted the same principle into statute. See Virgin Islands Code, title 1, § 4.

2.2 The Uniform Commercial Code

The UCC is a uniform law drafted under the joint sponsorship of the ALI and the National Conference of Commissioners of Uniform State Laws ('NCCUSL').[3] The Code is divided into eleven substantive articles, each of which represents the equivalent of a separate topic in a European civil code. Article 1 is in the nature of a general part, providing definitions that are used throughout the Code. The following ten articles govern the sale and lease of goods, negotiable instruments and the bank collection of checks, funds transfers, letters of credit, bulk sales, documents of title (bills of lading and warehouse receipts), investment securities, and secured transactions in personal property. Each article consists of several dozen black-letter provisions. They are followed by extensive official comments, which, though designed to be authoritative, are not adopted as law. The UCC revision process is similar to that of the Restatements, though the evolving drafts are not accepted into the Code until approved by NCCUSL's annual meeting as well. A Permanent Editorial Board issues supplementary commentary to resolve issues of Code interpretation that arise in the case law.

The UCC is drafted for enactment by the legislatures of the individual states, the District of Columbia, the Virgin Islands, and Puerto Rico. Though the federal government would have the constitutional authority to enact a federal code governing commercial transactions, it has not done so, largely because such matters are believed to rest within the competence of the individual states.[4] The Code was not widely adopted throughout the United States until the 1960s. Revisions began to be made to some of the articles in the 1960s and have continued to the present. The articles dealing with the lease of goods and electronic funds transfers were added in the 1980s. At the moment, the Code is undergoing its first thorough-going redrafting, with revisions to most of the substantive articles either recently completed, currently in progress, or under study.

The UCC's title is misleading. Though it has been enacted in each of the American states – even the civilian jurisdiction of Louisiana has adopted most of the articles – it is far from uniform. There are several reasons for the lack of uniformity. First is the text of the Code itself. Several of its sections provide different alternatives available for adoption by the enacting legislatures.[5] The Code also frequently makes room for lesser variations, including optional bracketed language and blanks where state legislatures are to enter monetary amounts, time periods, or citations to local statutes. Second, since many states have not adopted the more recent revisions, different versions of several of the articles are currently in force. Finally, many states have adopted non-uniform amendments.[6] The UCC is also not – at least not in civilian understand-

---

3 NCCUSL is a law-reform organisation which comprises more than 300 lawyers, judges, and law professors appointed by state governors, as well as representatives of the District of Columbia, Puerto Rico, and the US Virgin Islands.

4 Nonetheless, federal law increasingly governs questions of consumer protection, check collection, electronic funds transfer, and bills of lading. Moreover, federal bankruptcy law limits the rights the Code provides to secured parties.

5 For example, UCC § 2-318, which concerns third-party beneficiaries of the seller's warranty liability, provides three alternatives. The 1987 Official Text of Art. 6 (Bulk Sales) provides both a revised version and the alternative of repeal.

6 For example, before the recent revisions, there were 1,482 local variations to the 55 sections in the text of Art. 9 (Secured Transactions).

ing – a commercial code. First, it governs many topics that, in civilian parlance, are considered in the special part of the law of obligations. Commercial codes in civil law systems typically provide special rules to govern transactions among merchants. In this sense, the UCC could be considered to govern both civil and commercial transactions – a number of provisions provide special rules when one or both parties to the transactions are merchants[7] – and revised Article 2, which governs the sale of goods, also includes numerous consumer protection measures. Finally, the UCC is not a code in the civilian sense.[8] A civil law code generally contains a comprehensive regime for a particular area of law. The UCC, on the other hand, is a 'common law code' – the general principles of law and equity continue to apply unless specifically displaced by the Code's provisions.[9]

2.3 Uniform Laws

Over the course of its 112 year history, NCCUSL has drafted uniform acts and model laws in many legal fields for which national uniformity is thought desirable and practicable. The organisation also works toward legislative enactment of its products. NCCUSL has completed nearly a hundred uniform laws, including acts in the fields of adoption, child custody, condominiums, declaratory judgments, electronic transactions, enforcement of foreign judgments, fraudulent transfers, guardianship, notarial acts, partnership, trade secrets, and victims of crime.[10] An important project on the law governing software licensing and the transfer of data bases was initially drafted as a new Article for the UCC. When it failed to secure the ALI's endorsement, it was instead approved by NCCUSL as a uniform law.[11]

Like the UCC, NCCUSL's uniform acts are drafted for adoption by state legislatures. The extent national uniformity is achieved therefore depends on the degree of acceptance each act receives during the approval process. Some of these laws have been adopted by many states. Others have exerted considerable influence on reform of state laws without being adopted. Since the drafting techniques of these statues varies, and their success differs, few generalisations apply to them all. From the perspective of codification in Europe, it is enough to note that even in fields in which uniformity is considered desirable, the subject matter has not been federalised. Instead, NCCUSL has assumed the task of reconciling the differing interests. The uniform law approval process provides each legislature a separate opportunity to debate the proposals.

---

7 See, e.g. UCC §§ 2-201(2) (statute of frauds), 2-205 (firm offers), 2-207(2) (Battle of the forms), 2-209(2) (modification).
8 Kripke (1962), pp. 331-32.
9 See UCC § 1-103 (supplementary general principles of law applicable).
10 A complete list of uniform laws completed by NCCUSSL is available at http://www.law.upenn.edu/bll/ulc/ulc_frame.htm. Current drafts of NCCUSL projects, including the succession of drafts for the current revisions of the UCC are available at the same URL.
11 The Uniform Computer Information Transactions Act ("UCITA"), available on the NCCUSL website indicated at note 10, *supra*.

2.4   Transnational Coordination

Over the past several years, the ALI has collaborated with foreign jurists to harmonise law across national boundaries. The projects have created new methods of transnational cooperation, produced comparative studies of great insight, and formulated norms available for adoption both by courts and by legislatures.

The Transnational Insolvency Project was the first of the ALI's international efforts. Its goal was to increase the ability of national courts in Canada, Mexico, and the United States (the three members of the North American Free Trade Agreement ("NAFTA")) to cooperate in insolvencies having contacts with more than one of these jurisdictions. Some of the leading bankruptcy authorities in each of the three countries collaborated on the project. They proceeded on the assumption that substantive harmonisation of bankruptcy laws was not achievable in the near term, and that priority should be accorded mechanisms that could be adopted by the parties and the courts without need of legislative enactment.[12]

In the first phase of the project, the national reporters produced detailed summaries of the substantive and procedural law of bankruptcy in force in their countries. The studies provide a subtle analysis of the theoretical differences and case-law holdings among the three legal systems. These monographs, initially drafted in English, will be translated into Spanish and French as sources for foreign courts. The project's final phase produced three further documents – general principles of bankruptcy law accepted in all three legal systems, procedural principles that can generally be put into effect under existing law, and recommendations for legislative enactment or international agreement.[13]

The ALI is also currently cooperating with UNIDROIT in drafting Principles and Rules of Transnational Civil Procedure, norms of civil procedure for transnational commercial disputes. A continually expanding group of international consultants participates in the project. In order to synthesise the civil and common law perspectives, the drafters have produced both general principles and more concrete rules. Though the precise relationship between the two sets of norms remains unclear, the principles are designed to accommodate the civilian preference for norms of interpretation, while the rules fulfill the common law inclination for more concrete formulation. The rules may be treated as a model for implementation of the principles, suitable for adoption or adaptation in local jurisdictions.

These two transnational projects have proceeded with even greater caution than NCCUSL's efforts at harmonisation of law among the different American states. The international projects begin with a detailed evaluation of the similarities and differences among the national laws involved. The second phase attempts to create a set of norms that may be adopted by the parties and the courts without recourse to national legislation or international agreement. The projects' authority derives principally from their persuasive power.

---

12 See Introduction, ALI Transnational Insolvency Project: International Statement of United States Bankruptcy Law (Tent. Draft Apr. 15, 1997), pp. 1-6.

13 For a comparison of the ALI Transnational Insolvency Project with the UNCITRAL Model Law and the EU Insolvency Regulation, see Westbrook (2002).

3   The American Understanding of Restatement and Codification

Despite the esteem in which the ALI is held, both the Restatements and the UCC, as well as the process by which they are drafted, have faced frequent – and increasing – scholarly criticism. Albert Ehrenzweig argued that the Restatements combine the rigidity of the civilian codes with the lack of systematicity of the common law.[14] Some believe that ALI projects merely present the privately-held views of a handful of American jurists and do not represent the law either as it is or as it ought to be.[15] Others have pointed out that the Restatements offer an over-simplified reading of the cases and therefore rarely influence the decisions.[16] Yet others claim that the drafting process is sometimes captured by special interests, particularly the banks.[17] Moreover, the very nature of the Restatements seems to argue against seeking in them inspiration for a European civil code – since they are not designed to be enacted into law, they seem to represent a form of systemisation suitable only to fields of the law governed by judicial precedent.

Nonetheless, I would like to suggest that one feature of the Restatements and the UCC – namely, their dialogic structure – should interest those considering a European codification, since it may provide a means to overcome the difficulties involved in reconciling the diverse legal norms currently in force in the different nations of Europe.

At the outset an explanation is needed for why the American common law has not been codified. The notion of codification is not foreign to American law. Most states have a code of civil procedure, a penal code, and an evidence code. The federal government has codified tax law and has promulgated a Bankruptcy Code. Moreover, private-law codification was on the American legal agenda throughout the 19th century. Louisiana adopted a civil code in the French tradition. The Field Code – the civil code drafted by David Dudley Field – was adopted in California and four other Western states and was also twice approved by the New York legislature, only to be vetoed each time by the Governor.[18] In contrast to civilian jurisdictions, however, American courts tend to consider codes as formulating a momentary pause in the case-law evolution rather than as definitive resolutions of the issues involved.[19]

---

14 Ehrenzweig (1969), pp. 343-344.
15 Keyes (1985); Ehrenzweig (1965). For a response to the arguments presented by Keyes, see Wade (1985). A former Director of the ALI has responded to this criticism by suggesting that the attempt to decide what the law should be plays an important role in determining what it is. See Wechsler (1968), p. 189.
16 Milner (1959); Clark (1933), pp. 646, 661-662.
17 'Art. 4 on Bank Deposits and Collections is an unfair piece of class legislation maneuvered through the American Law Institute and the Commission on Uniform Laws by pressure groups favoring the bankers over their customers.' Beutel (1952). See also Rubin (1993); Schwartz & Scott (1995). Others have defended the process, arguing that it provides a forum for the compromises that are required before the projects can be enacted into law. See Warren (1993).
18 See Friedman (1985), pp. 403-07; Reppy (1949), pp. 46-48.
19 '[I]t was not the intention of the Legislature in enacting Section 1714 of the Civil Code, as well as other sections of that code declarative of the common law, to insulate the matters therein expressed from further judicial development; rather it was the intention of the Legislature to announce and

One possible explanation for the historical reluctance of American law to enact a civilian-style codification is the dichotomous structure of the common law.[20] The common law combines two distinct legal traditions, each of which provides different – and often contradictory – answers to the same legal questions. The two traditions were once separate judicial institutions known as 'law' and 'equity'. Since the procedural merger of the two systems, both legal and equitable matters are generally heard by the same courts, though differences remain in terms of the remedies and defenses available, as well as the fact that the right to a jury trial is generally not available in equity.[21] In what follows, I focus on law and equity as references to two differing perspectives on the role of the state in the resolution of private law disputes.

The tradition known as 'law' is heir to the forms of action, the writ system, which structured the common law well into the 19th century.[22] A plaintiff could invoke the jurisdiction of the royal courts only if the cause of action fit within one of the narrowly drawn writs. Since the common law courts were courts of limited jurisdiction, they were always concerned with jurisdictional questions. Over time, those questions tended to be resolved by considering whether it was appropriate for the royal courts to intervene in the particular dispute at hand. This tradition produced a restrictive understanding of the role of the state in dispute resolution, which even today remains the foundation of the common law. Its central insight is that courts should not intervene in private disputes unless there is good reason to do so. The tradition was reformulated during the last century by Oliver Wendell Holmes,[23] and in a different way in this century by the school of law and economics.[24]

The role of equity, on the other hand, has traditionally been to remedy the injustice that inevitably is produced by a restrictive understanding of the jurisdiction of the common law courts. Initially, the role of the Chancellor was to provide flexibility to the writ system – by issuing writs when injustice would otherwise result. Eventually equity became as rigid as the original writ system.[25] The tradition of doing equity then resurfaced at law. From the perspective of equity, the courts should intervene whenever necessary to prevent injustice. This understanding has also been developed by a prestigious modern tradition. Equity's broad understanding of the purpose of adjudication found a brilliant proponent in the law courts in Justice Benjamin Cardozo. Arthur Corbin, the great contracts scholar, drew this lesson from Cardozo's opinions.[26] Karl Llewellyn, Corbin's student, reconceived American law in the same terms.[27] Legal Realism and Critical Legal Studies continue this tradition.

The common law has resisted codification because of this fundamental tension be-

---

formulate existing common law principles and definition for purposes of orderly and concise presentation and with a distinct view toward continuing judicial evolution.' Li v. Yellow Cab Co., 532 P.2d 1226, 1233 (Cal. 1975) (*en banc*).

20 See Hyland (1995), pp. 215-217.
21 See generally Dobbs (1993), vol. 1, pp. 55-276.
22 For a short history of the writ system, see Maitland (1936).
23 See Holmes (1897); Holmes (1963).
24 See Posner (1992).
25 See Pound (1905).
26 See Gilmore (1964), p.217.
27 See Llewellyn (1930).

tween law and equity. These two contrary views – the restrictive understanding of the role of the courts at law and the more expansive vision derived from equity – cannot be reduced to a single system. In fact, they are perennially at odds.[28] The highly productive debate between these two visions made of American law one of the most creative legal systems of the 20th century, but, at the same time, has prevented it from achieving a tranquil synthesis.

Each of the Restatement's three editions offers a different perspective on the dialogue between the traditions that make up the common law. The original Restatements were designed as a new starting point. They were drafted by the leading authorities in the fields. Partially as a result of the influence of Wesley Hohfeld's analytical jurisprudence, the original Restatements paid great attention to maintaining uniform legal terminology – not only across all American common-law jurisdictions but throughout the various fields of the law as well.[29] In the tradition of Blackstone, Kent, and Langdell, who believed that the common law could be understood as a consistent whole, the drafters of the first Restatements made a careful selection from the proliferating case law and honed their statements of the norms to produce a coherent system.[30] Their goal was to render it unnecessary for either lawyers or the courts to look behind the Restatement provisions to the preceding case law. Though the drafters wished to restate the case law accurately, they also wished to reduce the same complexity. As a result the final product made selections from the different positions and often camouflaged the controversies.[31] This masking of difficulty provoked criticism: 'Judges and professors . . . took fields of living law, scalded their flesh, drained off their blood, and reduced them to bones. The bones were arrangements of principles and rules (the black-letter law), followed by a somewhat barren commentary'.[32]

The courts did not cooperate. Instead of abandoning their prior case law, they considered the Restatements as yet another source for legal argument.[33] Moreover, just as the original Restatements were being completed, Legal Realism began to transform the way American jurists think about law. The Realists demonstrated not only that good legal arguments can be made on both sides of every case, but also that none of those arguments is capable of clinching the decision. Only recourse to the logic of the real world situation can point the way to a meaningful resolution.

The Restatement (Second) is a product of the Realist revolution. Its drafters no longer believed that they could reduce the mass of case law to a coherent system. Though they continued to select – and at times invent – the norms they thought most appropriate, they also understood additional techniques would be required to restate American law accurately. Three of those techniques are especially relevant here.

First, the relative importance of the rules and the commentary was reversed in the

---

28 'Law and equity cannot be blended or homogenised for they are antithesis. The one strives for predictability and treats cases as belonging to a generalised type, the other strives for individual justice and treats cases as being unique.' Emmerglick (1945), p. 248.

29 See Lewis (1932), pp. xii-xiv.

30 White (1997), pp. 15-16.

31 See Clark (1933), pp. 656-657.

32 Friedman (1985), p. 676.

33 Yntema (1936), p. 466.

Restatement (Second). The black letter operated chiefly as an index to the comments, which in turn examined the various positions in the debate and attempted to determine the appropriate limits to the conflicting principles.[34] Second, the drafters of the Restatement (Second) did not hesitate to restate contradictory ideas, which they juxtaposed without reconciling. The experience with the original Restatements taught them that a Restatement's refusal to cognise an argument does not cause it to disappear. The drafters knew that the courts would determine the proper domain for each of the competing ideas. In many cases, these conflicting thoughts descended from the rival traditions of law and equity. One striking example occurs in the Restatement (Second) of Contracts. In its discussion of formation questions, the Restatement announces the consideration doctrine[35] – a promise is enforceable at law only if it is part of a bargain – and examines the concept of bargain in detail.[36] The sections that immediately follow the consideration doctrine are entitled 'Contracts without Consideration'. In those sections, the Restatement (Second) presents the rules from equity that permit promises to be enforced even when no bargain – no offer, no acceptance, no consideration – is present.[37]

As a third technique, the Restatement (Second) provided flexibility by means of open-textured concepts. In the Restatement (Second) of Conflict of Laws, for example, the drafters generally provided that an issue is to be governed by the law that has the most significant relationship to that issue or the transaction as a whole. Instead of providing a preference for a particular result, the Restatement (Second) enumerated a series of factors especially relevant to an examination of the facts.

The UCC was drafted somewhat contemporaneously with the Restatement (Second). Its Chief Reporter, Karl Llewellyn, was one of the founders and chief proponents of the Realist movement. The Code adopted strategies similar to those of the Restatement (Second) in order to encourage dialogue between the two traditions. First, the principles of law and equity survive the codification – even in a case governed by the Code, the statutory provision may be circumvented in favor of a more equitable approach.[38] More importantly, the Code, and especially its Sales article, one of the great achievements of American codification, often refuses to answer questions specifically. At times, instead, the Code responds with another question – it asks the courts to determine what would be reasonable in the circumstances.[39] For example, when Article 2 is interrogated as to the seller's obligations under a typical shipment contract, the Code responds that the seller must 'put the goods in the possession of such a carrier and make such a contract for their transportation as may be

---

34 See Clark (1933), p. 664, where this change was suggested.
35 Restatement (Second) of Contracts (1981) § 17 (1).
36 Id. §§ 71-81.
37 Id. §§ 82-94. Some of the rules involve what would be considered to be an *obligatio naturalis* in civilian parlance (promises to pay debts discharged in bankruptcy or those on which the statute of limitations has run). Other sections rely on the doctrines of promissory estoppel and detrimental reliance.
38 The notion of the equitable lien in the law of secured transactions is a good example. '[I]f the equitable lien ... had not existed, it would have been necessary to invent it; if the Code in some sense abolishes the equitable lien, it will have to be invented all over again.' Gilmore (1965), p. 336.
39 See Danzig (1975), pp. 626-627.

reasonable having regard to the nature of the goods and other circumstances of the case . . . '.[40]

In sum, the dichotomous structure of the common law convinced the drafters of the Restatement (Second) and the UCC to prefer a dialogic form for its systemisation. Both are flexible and open-textured. Neither truly resolves the difficult questions – they seem rather to suggest that no final resolution will ever be achieved. They attempt instead to provide the long-term discussion with a workable conceptual framework.

Since the drafters are currently at work both on a Restatement (Third) and on a complete revision of the UCC, a word regarding current trends may be in order. Though the project is massive, diverse, and still largely incomplete, some factors influence many aspects of the current revision process. Perhaps most important is the critique of Legal Realism that has emerged since the completion of the Restatement (Second). In one form or another the Realist premise has been accepted in American law – since a good argument usually can be made on both sides of any legal dispute, disputes cannot be resolved solely by reference to the resources available within the law. However, American legal thought no longer believes that there is a unique logic to a real world situation that can resolve the disputes. There are only positions, arguments, points of view.

To provide some consistency and determinacy, a variety of solutions have been attempted. The Restatement (Third) of Torts is currently one of the ALI's most controversial undertakings.[41] The Institute decided against a complete revision of the Restatement (Second). Instead, only those topics are to be revised that are particularly in need of being updated and for which a suitable reporter can be found. The mushrooming law of products liability became the first candidate for such a reformulation. However, the field was caught in a firestorm of political difference. To resolve the most intractable issue, namely the definition of design defects, the reporters took the unusual step of retreating to a politically conservative position that, they believed, accurately summarised the current state of the case law. When they were challenged, they produced a document unique in the Restatement literature, a Reporters' Note that runs to over fifty pages and that catalogues the law of virtually every American jurisdiction and all of the major voices in the law-review literature.[42]

The Institute decided that the basic tort principles governing physical harm were also due for restatement. In this case, intense doctrinal controversies since the Restatement (Second) left little possibility for an easy synthesis.[43] Again the reporters resorted to an unusual method. They restated the norms at a high level of abstraction and provided each question with the monographic treatment necessary to define the concepts employed in the black letter. This topic of the Restatement (Third) now re-

---

40 UCC § 2-504(a).

41 See Sorenson (2003). A Restatement (Third) of Contracts would probably be even more controversial, but no such project is currently in the works, and Grant Gilmore has prophesied that no such a project will ever be undertaken.

42 See Restatement (Third) of Torts: Products Liability § 2 Reporters' Note at 51-106 (Proposed Final Draft 1997).

43 One scholar, dissatisfied with the Restatement (Third), has already made suggestions for a Restatement (Fourth). See Sugarman (2002).

sembles an civilian treatise – particularly reminiscent of Dean Carbonnier's volumes on French civil law, which include not only a black-letter statement and commentary, but a canvas of relevant theoretical and historical questions as well.[44]

The UCC revisions have faced similar controversies. Article 2, for example, the article governing the sale of goods, was subjected to a minutiose revision process for over a decade before the proposed final draft was rejected by NCCUSL, and new reporters were chosen. Part of the difficulty with those initial revisions seems to have been the resort to what might be called the strategy of momentary compromise. Though guided by a Reporter and an Advisory Committee, representatives from the areas of practical activity that will be affected by the rules were also included in the discussions. Only a minority of those who attended the meetings of the Sales Article's Drafting Committee were members of that committee. Representatives of trade associations, manufacturers, lenders, and consumers' representatives also sat around the large table, participated in the discussions, and, in many cases, in the voting. At the end of the day, a compromise was reached – which most accepted, even if none enthusiastically. As a result, the provisions were lengthy and technocratic, and a lengthy commentary was needed to explain the reasons for black-letter language that would otherwise remain incomprehensible to those who were not present the day it was agreed to.[45]

The new reporters adopted a more circumspect strategy, choosing to revise only the most problematic provisions. They have resuscitated Llewellyn's method, but not for Llewellyn's reasons. Instead they decided to leave to judicial determination those political issues they could not resolve, as well as those technical issues in need of additional consideration. Despite this technique, the new draft has not escaped controversy. The scope of the Sales Article has been in dispute for over a year, and particularly the question of the extent to which goods that incorporate computer software are to be governed by Article 2.

A special word might be added about the recently enacted revisions to the UCC's Article 9, which governs secured transactions in personal property. Half a century ago, the article's original drafters created the field by unifying a number of security devices that were each treated differently at common law. The field became one of the Code's principal triumphs, but, by leaving open a number of difficult questions, became increasingly problematic as the field became more technical. Though this subject matter too is rife with political dispute, and the revisions required collaboration between lenders and consumer representatives, the reporters resolved the difficulties by muscular new conceptualisations. They reimagined the field and fearlessly accepted the challenge to provide precise formulations to resolve complex issues. Article 9 has now replaced Article 2 as the Code's pivotal achievement, largely because it demonstrates that many legal issues can better be resolved by the creative use of the conceptual imagination than by momentary political compromise.

---

44 See Restatement (Third) of Torts: Liability for Physical Harm (Basic Principles), Tent. Draft No. 1 (2001). The Reporters' Notes explain, among other things, that there are 4.7 million dog bites in the United States each year at an estimated economic cost in excess of $1 billion, and that 18th century treatises suggested that corporations could not be sued in trespass.

45 See Hyland (1997).

4   European Codification on an American Model

European legal scholars have concluded that the domestic European legal systems currently diverge too greatly for the civil law to be successfully codified at the European level.[46] The American experience, however, suggests that the principal obstacle to European codification may be nothing more than an overly rigid understanding of what codification requires.

The European tradition has tended to assume that the principal purpose of codification is to integrate the rules in a particular field of the law into a systematic structure.[47] It has seemed obvious that systemisation requires the selection of the most appropriate rule from among various suggested alternatives – and a rejection of those remaining. If this is truly what codification requires, then it probably must be agreed that the domestic laws of Europe are not yet ripe for codification. If, on the other hand, codification is understood, as it is in the American experience, as the creation of a common vocabulary for further discussion, then a European codification may prove not only possible but fruitful. A codification of the American variety would emphasise the creative diversity that exists within the context of the European Union. It would suggest that Europe can advance not only when there is agreement but also, perhaps even more so, when there is dialogue. Both the Restatements and the UCC provide a framework for a continuing dialogue among divergent visions of the law. The American experience demonstrates that difficult legal issues do not need to be resolved before they can be codified.

The question that remains is whether diversity of the type present in the European civil laws could be accommodated in a structure such as that of the Restatements or the UCC. There is some evidence that it could be. For the civilian systems are also affected by a dichotomy between competing visions of the law – a bipolar structure related to, though not identical with, the division between law and equity. The civilian codes, on the one hand, encourage precise constructions and yet, on the other, they include general clauses that supplement or even supplant the logic-driven results – the principles of good faith and abuse of right being perhaps the most common.[48]

The understanding of a civil code as a coherent system masks the tension between analytical structures found in the civil law's substantive provisions and the commitment to fairness anchored in its general clauses. Since this tension is found in most civilian systems, the only prerequisite for a successful European civil law codifica-

---

46   'But the political social and cultural conditions in which the great codifications of the past century – which crowned the formation of the national states – were completed cannot be duplicated at the European level. In addition to the 'formidable obstacle' of the diversity of languages, there are difficulties that derive from the diversity of techniques and styles of the various legal systems – which were greatly accentuated by Great Britain's entry into the Community.' L. Mengoni (1993), p. 13 (my translation). The authors of the second edition of *Towards a European Civil Code* were also largely agreed that a European codification would today be premature. See Hondius (1998).

47   See Stoljar (1977), pp. 9-10.

48   '[O]ne cannot avoid the impression that those scholars who advocated an abandonment of most concrete legal provisions in favour of § 242 BGB have already succeeded, for one can find a court decision or a scholarly theory applying the provision [of good faith] to almost every situation governed by the Civil Code, and in addition very often overriding the text and the meaning of special provisions.' Schlechtriem (1997), pp. 7-8. See also Larenz (1989), 1 IV a, p. 25.

tion is the creation of the vocabulary and structure through which this discussion can be continued across national borders.

Some of the essential work has already been accomplished. At least in the field of contract law, the UNIDROIT Principles and the Principles of European Contract Law have artfully formulated a system-bridging conceptual vocabulary that renders a trans-European discussion possible. One example is the new concept of 'hardship', which mediates among the legal institutions of impracticability, frustration of purpose, *l'imprévision,* and *Wegfall der Geschäftsgrundlage.*[49] In fact, the process by which the two sets of Principles were developed very much resembles the conceptual clarification involved in the original Restatements. In both cases, the drafters were a small group of the most highly respected authorities in the field. The drafting groups examined the wide diversity of rules and principles that had developed in the jurisdictions for which they were writing, selected from the plentiful offering the best norms available, and then honed them into a workable system.[50] Similar efforts toward the creation of a common vocabulary are currently being undertaken in other fields of European private law.[51] The recent American experience of transnational harmonisation demonstrates that such efforts can be successful, even across diverse languages and legal systems.

Open-ended and flexible drafting would encourage colloquy among the national courts of the Member States. If the European civil code were to be drafted by nongovernmental working groups, in the tradition of the two sets of Principles, in collaboration with representatives from the central administration of the European Union, there would be significant scholarly discussion as well. One might imagine drafting the European code as a uniform act, which would be debated and enacted by the legislatures of each of the member states. A decentralised legislative mechanism would preserve what is considered one of the strengths of the UCC, namely that it is 'flexible enough to achieve uniformity in basic structural issues while permitting local variations to address different and changing circumstances'.[52]

In sum, nothing prevents the initiation of codification in the field of European civil law – as long as there is no objection to the dialogic model employed by the Restatements and the UCC.

5   Consideration and *Pacta Sunt Servanda:* An Example

My hypothesis is that the American experience suggests that a European civil code is already possible. In this section, I propose to test this hypothesis by proposing a

---

49   See UNIDROIT Principles of International Commercial Contracts Arts. 6.2.1 to 6.2.3. See generally Hyland (1992), pp. 549-550.

50   One of the architects of the UNIDROIT *Principles* has described the drafting process by borrowing words from a description of the procedure by which the original Restatement of Contracts was drafted. See Bonell (1994), p. 451 (quoting from E.W. Patterson, The Restatement of the Law of Contracts, 33 *Colum. L. Rev.*(1933), pp. 397 ff., at p. 399).

51   See, e.g., von Bar (1996).

52   Hisert (1994), p. 232. The American scholarly consensus seems to be that a commercial code enacted under the uniform law approach, which involves adoption by the legislatures of each of the American states, is preferable to a commercial code enacted by the federal government. See Cohen & Zaretsky (1993).

codical solution to the seemingly intractable difficulties posed by the differences between the common-law consideration doctrine, on the one hand, and the civilian commitment to the maxim *pacta sunt servanda*, on the other.

The consideration doctrine often serves to symbolise the difference between the
common and civil law systems. One practical consequence of the consideration doctrine is that gratuitous promises are generally unenforceable at law, as are a surprising number of agreements frequent in business, such as the promise to keep an offer
open for a designated period and certain modifications to on-going contractual relations. However, both the Restatements and the UCC frequently provide for the enforcement of some of these promises.[53]

To some American scholars, the consideration doctrine is an unfortunate remnant
of the writ system, an incoherent jumble of reasons for enforcing promises representing originally only the legal conclusion that the conditions were present at common
law to invoke the writs of assumpsit, debt, or covenant.[54] Arthur Corbin argued that
there never was such a thing as the consideration doctrine, since common law courts
have enforced promises when consideration in the traditional sense was lacking.[55]

Despite the criticism, the consideration doctrine fulfils a purpose for which some
rule would be required even if the consideration doctrine were abolished. Since no
legal system enforces all promises, some principle is needed to determine which
promises will be judicially enforced. The advantage of the consideration doctrine is
that it points to a truism – outside the social and family context, promises that are part
of a bargain are almost universally considered to be legally binding. It also points to
another almost universally held view, namely that promises outside of the bargain
context generally are not enforced unless there is serious societal interest in doing so.
In other words, the consideration doctrine stands for the restrictive view of the role of
private law in dispute resolution.

The civil law counterpart to the consideration doctrine is the maxim *pacta sunt
servanda*. The maxim reflects a more expansive vision of the role of the law in the
enforcement of promises.[56] In general, it mandates that courts should enforce a promise when the evidence strongly suggests that the promise was in fact made – and
meant. Thus, in German law, for example, a promise to make a gift is judicially enforceable, provided that the promise has been accepted and the prescribed formalities
are present.[57] The purpose of the form requirement – documentation of the promise
by a notary public (*notarielle Beurkundung*) – is to provide a mechanism by which
the donor may be cautioned against overly hasty commitment.

Despite the more friendly attitude in the civil law to the judicial enforcement of
promises, not all civilian systems enforce gift promises. French and Belgian civil
laws, for example, refuse to enforce gratuitous promises so that the rigorous formali-

---

53 See, e.g., Restatement (Second) of Contracts § 81 (1)(a) (binding offer), § 88 (promise to act as a
surety), § 89 (modification of an executory contract), and § 90 (promise reasonably inducing action
of forbearance); UCC §§ 2-205 (firm offers), 2-209(1) (modification).
54 See Restatement (Second) of Contracts § 71 comment a.
55 See Corbin (1963), vol. 1, § 109 at p. 487.
56 See Hyland (1994).
57 § 518 I BGB.

ties required to conclude a valid gift transaction might fully protect the donors' consent.[58]

These differences, not only between common and civil law systems, but among civilian systems themselves, seem at first glance to defy codification – unless codification involves a random choice among alternatives. Yet, at a different level, there are grounds for a productive discussion. To begin with, each of these legal systems enforces promises that have been bargained for and given in exchange for a *quid pro quo*. Moreover, each of the systems also expresses some suspicion with regard to gratuitous promises. Between these two poles are promises that are enforced to different degrees in each of the systems – such as promises to keep an offer open or agreements to modify an on-going contract.

As long as codification is understood as the creation of a framework for discussion, many criteria are available for determining when a promise is legally binding. One might imagine, for example, a provision such as the following:

ART. 1. ENFORCEMENT OF PROMISES

A promise is legally enforceable if it is made:
(1)   as part of a contractual bargain;
(2)   in the context of a business transaction;
(3)   after an opportunity for reflection commensurate with the extent of the promise and with the intent of creating a legally binding obligation; or
(4)   under other circumstances indicating that enforcement is appropriate.

This sample provision is constructed in concentric circles. At the center are the promises that create a contractual bargain. They are generally enforced in every modern legal system. Since there is slightly less consensus on other promises made in a transactional context – firm offers and modifications, for example – the language of the second subsection is slightly more flexible. The third provision, relating principally to gratuitous promises, is open-textured enough to permit the courts to elaborate the appropriate criteria – and also to encourage them to discuss the opinions of other courts. The final subsection provides each court with the opportunity to suggest its own grounds for enforcement – detrimental reliance, good faith, abuse of right, or some other doctrine. In the end, the precise wording of the individual provisions is less important than is the suggestion that the judges not only apply the norms but also are engaged in their creation.

It might be objected that, under such a code, the outcome of any particular case would be unpredictable. And that may be the result in the short term. However, after a couple decades of judicial dialogue, the positions of the individual courts would have become clear, and there may well have been more convergence than if the discussion had never begun.

---

58   See de Page (1962), no. 369 at p. 449.

6 Conclusion

The American experience with the Restatements and the Uniform Commercial Code provides two principal lessons. First, a European codification may already be possible, even without awaiting greater uniformity, provided that codification is understood as a framework within which diverse views may continue to flourish. Second, the American experience teaches that differences disappear very slowly if at all. If they are suppressed in one domain, they resurface elsewhere. The only question is how best to take advantage of them.

BIBLIOGRAPHY: C. von Bar, *Gemeineuropäisches Deliktsrecht: Lehr- und Handbuch zum Deliktsrecht in den Staaten der Europäischen Union,* vol. 1 (1996); F.K. Beutel, The Proposed Uniform [?] Commercial Code Should Not Be Adopted, 61 *Yale Law Journal* (1952), pp. 334-363; M.J. Bonell, *An International Restatement of Contract Law: The UNIDROIT Principles of International Commercial Contracts* (1994); J.F. Byrne, Jr., Reevaluation of the Restatement as a Source of Law in Arizona, 15 *Arizona Law Review* (1973), pp. 1021-1030; C. Clark, The Restatement of the Law of Contracts, 42 *Yale Law Journal* (1933), pp. 643-667; N.B. Cohen & B.L. Zaretsky, Drafting Commercial Law for the New Millennium: Will the Current Process Suffice?, 26 *Loyola of Los Angeles Law Review* (1993), pp. 551-562; A. Corbin, *Contracts* (1963); R. Danzig, A Comment on the Jurisprudence of the Uniform Commercial Code, 27 *Stanford Law Review* (1975), pp. 621-635; D.B. Dobbs, *Law of Remedies* (2nd ed. 1993); A. Ehrenzweig, The Second Conflict Restatement: A Last Appeal for Its Withdrawal, 113 *Univ. of Pennsylvania Law Review* (1965), pp. 1230-1244; A. Ehrenzweig, Das Desperanto des zweiten 'Restatement of Conflict of Laws,' in: E. von Caemmerer, *et al.,* eds., *Ius Privatum Gentium (Festschrift Rheinstein)* vol. 1 (1969), pp. 343-362; L.J. Emmerglick, A Century of the New Equity, 23 *Texas Law Review* (1945), pp. 244-256; L. Friedman, *A History of American Law* (2nd ed. 1985); G. Gilmore, the Assignee of Contract Rights and His Precarious Security, 74 *Yale Law Journal* (1964), pp. 217-261; G. Gilmore, *Security Interests in Personal Property* (1965); G.A. Hisert, Uniform Commercial Code: Does One Size Fit All?, 28 *Loyola of Los Angeles Law Review* (1994), pp. 219-233; O.W. Holmes, The Path of the Law, 10 *Harvard Law Review* (1897), pp. 457-478; O.W. Holmes, *The Common Law* (M.D. Howe ed. 1963); E. Hondius, Towards a European Civil Code, in: Arthur Hartkamp, *et al.,* eds., *Towards a European Civil Code* (2nd ed. 1998), pp. 3-19; R. Hyland, On Setting Forth the Law of Contract: A Foreword, 40 *American Journal of Comparative Law* (1992), pp. 541-550; R. Hyland, *Pacta Sunt Servanda*: A Meditation, 34 *Virginia Journal of International Law* (1994), pp. 405-433; R. Hyland, Life, Death, and Contract, 90 *Northwestern Univ. Law Review* (1995), pp. 204-218; R. Hyland, Draft, 97 *Columbia Law Review* (1997), pp. 1343-62; W.N. Keyes, The Restatement (Second): Its Misleading Quality and a Proposal for Its Amelioration, 13 *Pepperdine Law Review* (1985), pp. 23-57; H. Kripke, The Principles Underlying the Drafting of the Uniform Commercial Code, *Univ. of Illinois Law Forum* (1962), pp. 321-332; K. Larenz, *Allgemeiner Teil des deutschen bürgerlichen Rechts* (7th ed. 1989); W.D. Lewis, Introduction, in: *Restatement of Contracts* vol. 1 (1932), pp. vii-xv; K.N. Llewellyn, *The Bramble Bush: On Our Law and Its Study* (1930); F. Maitland, *The Forms of Action at Common Law* (1936); L. Mengoni, *L'Europa dei codici o un codice per l'Europa?* (1993); A. Milner, Restatement: The Failure of a Legal Experiment, 20 *Univ. of Pittsburgh Law Review* (1959), pp. 795-826; H. de Page, *Traité élémentaire de droit civil beige,* tome 8, vol. 1 (2nd ed. 1962); R.A. Posner, *Economic Analysis of Law* (4th ed. 1992); R. Pound, The Decadence of Equity, 5 *Columbia Law Review* 20-35 (1905); A. Reppy, The Field Codification Concept, in: A. Reppy, ed., *David Dudley Field: Centenary Essays* (1949), pp. 17-54; E. Rubin, Thinking Like a Lawyer, Acting Like a Lobbyist: Some Notes on the Process of Revising UCC Articles 3 and 4, 25 *Loyola of Los Angeles Law Review* (1993), pp. 743-788; P. Schlectriem, *Good Faith in German Law and in International Uniform Laws* (1997); A. Schwartz & R. Scott, The Political Economy of Private Legislatures, 143 *Univ. of Pennsylvania Law Review* (1995), pp. 595-654; S.R. Sorenson, A Reasonable Alternative? Should Wyoming Adopt the Restatement (Third) of Torts: Products Liability?, 3 *Wyoming Law Review* (2003), pp. 257-293; S. Stoljar, Codification and the Common Law, in: S.J. Stoljar, ed., *Problems of Codification* (1977), pp. 1-15; S. Sugarman, Rethinking Tort Doctrine: Visions of a Restatement (Fourth) of Torts, 50 *UCLA Law Review* (2002), pp. 585-619; J.W. Wade, The Restatement (Second): A Tribute to its Increasingly Advantageous Quality, and an Encouragement to Continue the Trend, 13 *Pepperdine Law Review* (1985), pp. 59-86; W.D. Warren, UCC Drafting: Method and Message, 26 *Loyola of Los Angeles Law Review* (1993), pp. 811-822; H. Wechsler, Restatements and Legal Change: Problems of Policy in the Restatement Work of the American Law Institute, 13 *St. Louis Univ. Law Journal* (1968), pp. 185-194; J.L. Westbrook, Multinational Enterprises in General Default: Chapter 15, the ALI Principles, and the EU Insolvency Regulation, 76 *American Bankruptcy Law Journal* (2002), pp. 1-41; G.E. White, The American Law Institute and the Triumph of Modernist Jurisprudence, 15 *Law and History Review* (1997), pp. 1-47; H. Yntema, What Should the American Law Institute Do?, 34 *Michigan Law Review* (1936), pp. 461-473.

CHAPTER 5

EC Directives as a Means of Private Law Unification

Peter-Christian Müller-Graff*

1 Introduction

EC directives as a means of private law unification is part of the more general question of private law unification in Europe by means other than of enacting a European Civil Code. It focuses attention on the alternatives to a codification[1] of the substantial rules of private law, as far as economic matters are concerned, in the European Union. The value of these alternatives depends upon the definition of the aim of private law unification in the European Union.[2] If the aim is to be the establishment of a coherent set of directly applicable uniform private law rules in all Member States, the question may fairly be raised whether there is any reasonable alternative to a codification at all. If, however, the aim is to be the establishment of a workable degree of compatibility and conformity of national private law rules for border-crossing activities, or of an advanced degree of common elements in private law inside the European Community, alternatives might be worthy of discussion. At least four of the most prominent fields of alternative development towards a higher degree of common private law rules in the Union can be distinguished: European Community Directives, treaties between Member States of the Union, 'restatements' like the General Principles of Contract Law as worked out by the Commission on European Contract Law[3] and the efforts of UNIDROIT.

This article is devoted to the most prominent and important alternative of a legally binding means, namely the harmonisation of private law by directives of the European Community. As a matter of fact, the demand for more common private law rules in the Community seems to increase as the scope of the freedom to conclude border-crossing contracts is extended in consequence of the basic freedoms of the EC-Treaty.[4] The continuous enactment of directives seems to meet these needs. Despite the actual deliberations on a European Civil Code, especially pushed forward by the European Commission's Communication on European Contract Law[5] the release of directives stays intense. Hence attention will be directed to the method (1), the potential topical scope (2), the legal effects (3), the fields covered (4), the potential for the private law system (5) and merits and problems (6).

---

* Universität Heidelberg
1 For the aim of a codification of private law see Resolution of the European Parliament, *OJ* 1981, C 158/400.
2 For harmonisation of private law in general see Müller-Graff (1998; 1999-I).
3 See Lando/Beale (1995); see also Kötz (1996).
4 For this effect see Müller-Graff (1991), pp. 17-18.
5 COM (2001) 398 final.

2   The Method

In its resolution of 16 March 2000[6] concerning the Commission's work program 2000, the European parliament stated "that greater harmonisation of civil law has become essential in the internal market" and thereby accelerated the discussion about a possible harmonisation of civil law. With its communication on European Contract Law of 11 July 2001,[7] the Commission managed to draw attention to the possibility of a codification of contract law and lanced it in the centre of the political agenda.[8] However, at present directives of the EC still seem to constitute the most realistic and preferred way of achieving a higher degree of common private law elements in the Member States of the European Community. They are based on the method of fixing binding 'master rules' for the national legal systems. Being legal measures of the Community by their very nature, directives are binding, as to the result to be achieved, upon each Member State to which they are addressed (Art. 249 para. 3 EC-Treaty). If the result to be achieved is defined in terms of certain precise private law notions or rules, a substantial choice is excluded for national authorities concerning the implementation.

However, in principle, directly applicable private law rules remain national in their legal character. As a consequence the European Court of Justice has no power to interpret the harmonised national rules directly. Hence the result of a directive is harmonisation of national laws rather than supranational unification. However, the Court's competence to interpret the provisions of the directives guides national courts in their interpretation of the national law in the area covered topically by the directive as far as national courts are bound by Community law to interpret the relevant national law in conformity with the directive.[9] Despite the distinction between national law and Community law it is this bridge that offers a potential for a lasting substantial unification of private law rules in the Union by means of EC directives.

3   The Potential Topical Scope

The potential topical scope of harmonisation of private law by means of directives depends upon the empowerments given to the Community to enact directives that concern private law issues. In the present state of development of primary Community law no express power is vested in the Community to issue a directive that would oblige the Member States to adapt a Civil Code or a coherent net of rules which constitute the core and system of private law. However, the EC-Treaty contains specific and general 'functional' empowerments for the Community that can be used and are in fact used in order to harmonize those national rules that are deemed to be necessary or required for the establishment and functioning of the internal market (e.g. Art. 94, 95, 44 par 2 letter g EC-Treaty) or for the achievement of the objectives of the

---

6   *OJ* C-377/2000, p. 323, 326 at 28.
7   COM (2001) 398 final.
8   Ein Bürgerliches Gesetzbuch für Europa, FAZ 6.11.2001, p. 31; Grundmann, NJW 2002, p. 393.
9   See, for example, the case 14/83 v. *Colson and Kamann* (1984) *ECR* 1891.

EC-Treaty (Art. 308 EC-Treaty). The identification of the measures that are necessary is conferred to the competent political institutions of the Community and depends upon their political assessments which may develop or change. These functional empowerments are highly disputed in the context of the present discussion on a "European constitution". While most scholars of European Community law wish to maintain these functionally defined competences,[10] others speak in favour of a catalogue of well-defined competences in the field of private law in order to guarantee the sovereignity of the Member States and even call for the elimination of Articles 95 and 308 EC-Treaty.[11] Although the political assessments can be procedurally subjected to judicial review by the European Court of Justice (in particular according to the procedures of Article 230 EC-Treaty or Article 234 EC-Treaty)[12] a basic power of discretion rests with the political institutions.

On the legal level a discussion has developed whether the principle of subsidiarity as laid down in Article 5 paragraph 2 EC-Treaty is applicable to the powers of the Community to approximate the provisions which have as their object the establishment and functioning of the internal market.[13] This is due to the fact that the applicability of Article 5 paragraph 2 EC-Treaty is restricted to areas which do not fall within the exclusive competence of the Community. However the first and more relevant question as to the power to adopt directives in this area is different. Since the Community is authorised to act on the basis, e.g., of Articles 44 paragraph 2 letter g, 94, 95 or 308 EC-Treaty only if a 'necessity' exists, the basic problem is posed by the question if a competence of the Community to adopt a specific directive exists at all (art. 5 para. 1 EC-Treaty). If this question is denied in a given case the question of applicability of Article 5 paragraph 2 EC-Treaty cannot arise. If, however, on the opposite the competence exists in a given case then this definition of the necessities of the internal market should be considered to fall within the exclusive competence of the Community and Article 5 paragraph 2 EC-Treaty should be considered to be not applicable.[14]

4   The Legal Effects

The basic legal effect of an EC directive is laid down in Article 249 paragraph 3 EC-Treaty. As mentioned already the directive is binding, as to the result to be achieved, upon each Member State to which it is addressed. The scope of the result (or objectives) has to be assessed separately for every single directive. In this respect the for-

---

10 See, e.g., Müller-Graff (2000), p. 164.

11 See, e.g., Lopez-Pina (2001), p. 11.

12 See, e.g., ECJ Case 376/98 Promotion of tobacco products (2000) *ECR* I-2247.

13 See Müller-Graff (1995), p. 34.

14 This opinion is equally voiced by Advocate General Fennelly in his conclusion delivered on June 15th 2000 on the Case C-376/98 (*Federal Republic of Germany* v. *European Parliament and the Council of the European Union*) (2000) *ECR* I-2247 and the Case C-74/99 (*the Queen* v. *Secretary of State for Health and Others, ex parte* Imperial tobacco Ltd and Others, para. 131) (2000) *ECR* I-8599: "The coordination or approximation of national rules which affect economic activity is the very essence of these competences... It is clear that only the Community can adopt measures which satisfy these requirements."

mulation can vary significantly from directive to directive. While the objective is sometimes only laid down in rather vague provisions, often the result to be achieved is defined by a set of precise provisions in private law directives.

As far as the obligation of Article 249 paragraph 3 EC-Treaty extends in a given directive, the Member States are bound to adjust their national law not later than the deadline fixed by the directive. In addition the obligation entails that a Member State does not subsequently change its law in contradiction to the directive. Moreover national courts are bound by virtue of their character as national public authorities to interpret national law in the light of the objectives and the wording of a directive,[15] as far as national law allows such an interpretation.[16]

Eventually the Court of Justice has held that provisions of a directive are directly applicable if certain requirements are met: firstly the fruitless lapse of the deadline for implementation and secondly a clear and unconditioned right of an individual in relation to the Member State.[17] Hence, e.g., the employee of a British Health Authority could rely directly on the provision of a directive which grants equal treatment.[18] However, until now, the Court of Justice denies, in principle, the right of an individual to rely directly on a directive in a dispute with another individual.[19] This general denial of a 'direct horizontal effect' of a directive remains doubtful for several reasons (e.g.: different treatment of employees in public and private service; obligation of national courts to contribute to the result to be achieved[20]) and may be softened in practice by a rather broad understanding of the obligation to interpret national law in the light of the objectives and text of the directive.[21]

5   The Fields Covered

Several fields of private law have been affected by Community directives to date thereby contributing to the appearance of a certain level of Community private law ('Gemeinschaftsprivatrecht').[22] This is especially true for *contract law*[23] where, for example, contracts negotiated away from business premises,[24] consumer credit contracts,[25] package travel contracts,[26] unfair terms in so-called 'consumer contracts',[27] contracts relating to the purchase of the right to use immovable properties on a time-

---

15 See case 14/83 v. *Colson and Kamann* (1984) *ECR* 1891.
16 See Müller-Graff (1996-II), 259 and 305.
17 See cases 9/70 Grad (1970) *ECR* 825; 148/78 Ratti (1979) *ECR* 1629.
18 See case 152/84 Marshall (1986) *ECR* 723.
19 See cases C-91/92 Faccini Dori (1994) *ECR* I-3356; C-192/94 El Corte Inglés (1996) *ECR* I-1281.
20 See, for example, Müller-Graff (1993), p. 13; see also Müller-Graff (1996-II), pp. 259 and 305.
21 See case C-106/89 Marleasing (1990) *ECR* 4135.
22 See Müller-Graff (1991), pp. 27-42; for the development of Community private law see also: Gebauer (1998); Klauer (1998); Franzen (1999); Müller-Graff (1999-I).
23 See Müller-Graff (1999-II), pp. 28 ff., 84 ff.; Joerges/Brüggemeier (1993), pp. 301 ff., 312 ff.
24 *OJ* 1985, L 372/31.
25 *OJ* 1987, L 42/48.
26 *OJ* 1990, L 158/59.
27 *OJ* 1993, L 95/29.

share basis,[28] the contractual relationship of self-employed commercial agents,[29] distance selling contracts[30] and the sale of consumer goods and associated guarantees[31] have been subjected to 'master rules' laid down in directives. The law of *liability for damages*[32] is dealt with in directives, too, especially the rules of liability for defective products,[33] and in cases of violations of the principle of equal treatment of men and women.[34] Proposals for two new Council directives have been put forward by the Commission: one concerning the liability of suppliers of services,[35] the other the civil liability for damages caused by waste.[36] *Property law*[37] has been part of directives only in the indirect way that conditions of the use of private property are embodied in legal rules in general and in provisions concerning industrial and commercial property in particular. *Labour law*[38] is the subject of directives to an increasing degree, for example, in the areas of equal treatment of men and women in labour relations,[39] collective redundancies,[40] the protection of workers in the event of the sale of an undertaking,[41] the insolvency of the employer[42] and the posting of workers.[43] Also certain fields of *commercial law* have been affected by directives such as commercial register publicity,[44] the rules pertaining to annual accounts[45] and the law of commercial agents.[46] *Company law*[47] particularly has been subjected to 'master rules' laid down in directives on the basis of Article 44 paragraph 2 letter g EC-Treaty.[48] In this context a variety of problems has already been covered including: capital, balance, qualification of auditors, commercial register publicity, one-man-companies, partition of enterprises, mergers of companies[49] and takeover bids,[50] etc. Somewhat surprisingly no equivalent development has taken place in the *law against unfair competition*.[51] Until now only a directive on misleading advertising[52] and another on comparative advertising[53] have been issued despite the projects and hopes for far-reaching ap-

---

28 *OJ* 1994, L 280/83.
29 *OJ* 1986, L 382/17.
30 *OJ* 1997, L 144/19.
31 *OJ* 1999, L 171/12.
32 See Müller-Graff (1999-II), pp. 34 ff., 84 ff.; Joerges/Brüggemeier (1993), pp. 301 ff., 329 ff.
33 *OJ* 1985, L 210/29.
34 *OJ* 1976, L 39/40.
35 *OJ* 1990, C 12/08 (withdrawn).
36 *OJ* 1989, C 251/03; amended proposal *OJ* 1991, C 192.
37 See Müller-Graff (1999-II), pp. 36 ff.
38 *Id.*, pp. 23 ff., 39 ff., Birk (1999), pp. 385 ff.
39 *OJ* 1975, L 45/19; *OJ* 1976, L 39/40.
40 *OJ* 1998, L 225/16.
41 *OJ* 2001, L 82/16.
42 *OJ* 1980, L 283/23.
43 *OJ* 1997, L 18/1.
44 *OJ* 1968, L 65/8.
45 *OJ* 1978, L 222/11; *OJ* 1983, L 193/1; *OJ* 1986, L 372/1.
46 *OJ* 1986, L 382/17.
47 See Lutter (1996); Müller-Graff (1999-II), pp. 40 ff., 89 ff.; Hommelhoff (1999), pp. 287 ff.
48 See Annex; see as a comprehensive survey and analysis Lutter (1996), pp. 36 ff., 101 ff.
49 See proposal – COM (1984) 727 final.
50 *OJ* 2004, L 142/12.
51 See Jacobs (1997), pp. 268 ff.; Ullrich (1999), pp. 403 ff., 420 ff., 445.
52 *OJ* 1984, L 250/17.
53 *OJ* 1997, L 290/18.

proximation in this area in the early times of integration.[54] No urgent need has emerged to lay down 'master rules' for national *anti-trust law* until now,[55] most probably as a result of the existence of a large set of directly applicable uniform Community laws against restrictions, preventions and distortions of competition within the common market[56] (Art. 81 ff. EC-Treaty, EC-regulations, Art. 65, 66 ECSC-Treaty) and also as a consequence of a gradual autonomous self-approximation of national anti-trust law in several states.[57] However, in the field of the *protection of industrial and commercial property* and *copyright*[58] some directives have already been issued concerning, in particular, trade mark law,[59] semiconductor protection,[60] the protection of computer software,[61] legal protection of designs[62] and biotechnological inventions.[63]

6   The Potential for the Private Law System

The development of the EC directives which contain rules for the conduct between individuals has not so far been guided by a coherent concept of private law codification.[64] This can be explained as a consequence of the functional orientation of the specific empowerments laid down in the EC-Treaty and their piece-by-piece use by the Community. The adoption of a directive is usually inspired and spurred by single problem areas like, for example, the consumer credit contracts or product liability.

However, most legal solutions of a conflict are usually based on many implicit and invisible normative premises. In this way EC directives that contain rules for the conduct between individuals usually mirror, though often vaguely, a widely accepted common core of basic assumptions of private law in the Member States of the Union. In addition it can be said that some specific substantial contributions towards the development of private law in the European Union become visible in the directives[65] such as the idea of a special private law of the consumer, the concept of increased protection of workers in private labour relations, the strengthening of the idea of equal treatment of men and women in private relations, the tendencies towards strict liability as well as specific limitations and expansions of the principles of private autonomy and responsibility. Those principles can lead to the development of general principles, such as mentioned in the communication of the Commission on European contract law.[66]

---

54   See as a comprehensive comparative analysis Ulmer (1965).
55   See as suggestions, for example, Rittner (1983), pp. 31 ff.; FIW (1991).
56   As a survey see Müller-Graff (1990); Ullrich (1999), pp. 412 ff.
57   See for examples Ehlermann (1992), pp. 5 ff.; Müller-Graff (1992-III), p. 8.
58   See Ullrich (1999), pp. 425 ff.
59   *OJ* 1989, L 40/1.
60   *OJ* 1987, L 24/36.
61   *OJ* 1991, L 122/42.
62   *OJ* 1998, L 289/28.
63   *OJ* 1998, L 213/13.
64   See Müller-Graff (1999-II), pp. 9 ff.
65   See Müller-Graff (1996-III).
66   COM (2001) 389 final, p. 17 para. 52.

7 Merits and Problems

7.1 Merits

The method of achieving a higher degree of common private law elements in the Member States of the European Community by way of directives undoubtedly has its advantages.

1. First of all it combines the creation of Community-wide conceived 'master rules' on a Community level with the competence and responsibility of the Member States to enact the concrete and directly applicable national rules that are deemed to be adequate to the specific legal system (statutory order, case law) and terminology of every State adressed. This method thereby implies the opportunity to add national authority and legitimation to the rules in question and to respect national sovereignty at the same time as far as the form and methods of implementation are concerned. In short, approximation by directives seems to be a way of combining the necessities for uniform Community standards on the one hand and the possibility to tolerate national individualities on the other.

2. Moreover, directives show several advantages when compared with private law harmonisation by means of treaties ('Europäisches Konventionsprivatrecht') and by means of so-called 'Restatements', in the tradition of the idea of pre-existing common private law rules in Europe ('Gemeineuropäisches Privatrecht').

   a. The conclusion of *treaties* between States containing the obligation to establish certain private law rules in the legal order of the contracting parties can be called the *traditional* method of achieving a higher degree of common private law elements ('Konventionsprivatrecht'). Such treaties can have different origins, having been prepared either by intergovernmental commissions or by specialised institutions like UNIDROIT,[67] the Council of Europe, the OECD, the United Nations (UNCITRAL[68]) or other organisations.[69]

   Common elements of private law based on international agreements of this kind are present in very different *fields* of private law and they often concern rather specific topics. Among the fields affected in a more comprehensive way rank especially the law of international sales[70] or the law of bills of exchange and cheque law.[71] Specific questions are not only covered, for example, in the areas of securities,[72] liability of inn-keepers,[73] liability for damages caused by nuclear activities[74] and transporta-

---

67 According to the original statute of UNIDROIT, its object is "(de) préparer graduellement l'adaption par les divers Etats d'une législation de droit privé uniforme." See, for example, Bonell (1978).
68 See General Assembly Resolution 2205 (XXI) of December 17, 1966.
69 For a survey on the status of uniform private law see Kegel (2000), pp. 69-111.
70 UN-convention of April 11, 1980; see Schlechtriem (1981), pp. 118-161.
71 As reference for the agreements see Kegel (2000), pp. 71-72.
72 Convention of May 28, 1970 (Council of Europe).
73 Convention of December 17, 1962.
74 OECD-Convention of July 29, 1960.

tion law,[75] but also in family law,[76] the law of inheritance,[77] industrial and commercial property rights and copyright.[78]

This traditional method of achieving a higher degree of common private law elements has some *advantages*. First of all it does not – outside of Article 293 EC-Treaty and Article 34 para. 2 letter d TEU[79] – require identity between participation and membership in the European Community. This method is not therefore restricted to Member States nor is it only applicable if at least all Member States become contracting parties. Moreover the subjects to be harmonised can be chosen more freely than in the context of Community law since the question is not put and does not have to be answered whether the Community has a positive competence to act. However, relevant Community law has to be respected to the extent that Member States incur international obligations. A particular advantage of the creation of common private law by treaties can be seen in the opportunity of this method to lead to voluntary acceptance of the involved rules by more States later on. Treaties may also show fields of possible approximation by measures of the Community, since at least some States have already seen and acknowledged the necessity to agree on common principles and rules in the affected matters. There can also be the possibility to transform the content of a Treaty into a Community regulation, as happened in case of the "Council Regulation (EC) No 44/2001 of 22 December 2000 on jurisdiction and the recognition of judgments in civil and commercial matters"[80] after the Community was granted the new power of Articles 65 and 67 EC-Treaty.

The *problems*, however, of achieving a higher degree of common private law elements in the Member States of the European Community by treaties are evident when compared to legislation by EC directives or EC regulations. This can be seen clearly in an analysis of the disadvantages of conventions worked out by Ivo Schwartz some years ago.[81] The most important problems arise in the enactment and interpretation. As far as the enactment of a uniform statute is concerned, there is no basic obligation of any State to take part in any treaty-project to harmonise the national private law with a model set of rules. In consequence, the composition of the group of participating States may vary from convention to convention, thereby creating a complex and badly arranged private law situation when looked upon from the viewpoint of a common private law in the Community. Moreover, as far as the interpretation of rules based on an international agreement is concerned, usually no mandatory judicial procedure is provided to guarantee a uniform interpretation and application of the principles and rules agreed upon in the treaty.[82]

---

75 See for references in detail Kegel (2000), pp. 86-93.
76 For references *id.*, pp. 94-95.
77 For references *id.*, pp. 95-97.
78 For references *id.*, pp. 81-85.
79 For the third original pillar of the European Union see Müller-Graff (1996-I).
80 *OJ* 2001, L 12/1 and Corrigendum *OJ* 2001, L 307/28.
81 See Schwartz (1978), pp. 1067 ff.
82 For this problem see already Riese (1961), pp. 604 ff. However, a mandatory judicial procedure was provided for in the Brussels convention of September 27, 1966 and in the Luxemburg convention of December 15, 1975.

b.   *Restatements* are a method and phenomenon developed in the USA by the American Law Institute, which was organised in 1923. Restatements were originally conceived to show, in a systematic and statute-like way, the rules of a certain field of law as applied by the courts.[83] In a different and developed sense this method may also be used to formulate common legal rules for a certain field of law as found in statutes and court judgments of the different Member States in the European Community. The underlying idea of this approach is the assumption that a common core can be found or proposed in certain areas of the different national legal orders ('Gemeineuropäisches Privatrecht'[84]), at least in the way that a rule can be considered to be the most common or advanced rule for a defined socio-economic problem, and that a different solution of the said problem in one state can be shown as a national particularity or deviation from this rule.

The developed 'restatement' method can be applied to comparative work in all *fields* of civil law, though the chances of finding or proposing a most common or advanced rule will vary considerably with the problem in question, for example in the field of the formation of contracts as opposed to the law of inheritance. In the United States, nine fields of law in which case law was dominant (agency, conflict of laws, contracts, judgments, property, restitution, security, torts, trusts) have become the subject of restatements[85] (in the classical sense). In Europe, the Commission on European Contract Law has dealt with 'contract law'.[86]

The classical American restatement method was supposed to gain its *merits* in a different area than that of the achievement of a higher degree of common private law elements in the legislation of the different states. The idea behind this endeavour was to repair two chief defects in American law as diagnosed by the American Law Institute: uncertainty and complexity.[87] Therefore restatements of law were conceived to create 'authoritative sources, making it unnecessary for each individual researcher to induce a rule from the increasingly unwieldy mass of case material'.[88] Obviously this would not be a proper objective in continental European States despite the increasing impact of court judgments on the development of law. In Europe, as it was said above, a developed 'restatement' method could rather serve the purpose of discovering and developing common rules in the different national legal systems than to overcome uncertainty or complexity caused by court decisions. At least one similar effect has been observed in the United States in so far as the reporter 'could resolve many of the conflicts only by making a choice between the various rules the courts had adopted',[89] thereby even creating rules and contributing to harmonisation.

As Whitmore Gray noted, while the codes of the last century could well be viewed as being in some way the spiritual background of the restatements in the United

---

83   For that "unique effort at systematisation of case law which culminated in the Restatement of the Law" see as a survey Farnsworth (1963), pp. 84-86.
84   For this idea see Kötz (1981), pp. 481 ff.; same (1999), pp. 149 ff.
85   Farnsworth (1963), p. 85.
86   See Lando/Beale (1995); Lando (1992), pp. 261, 273.
87   Report of the Committee on the Establishment of a Paramount Organisation for the Improvement of the Law Proposing the Establishment of an American Law Institute, Am. L. Inst. Proc. 1 (1923) I 6.
88   Gray (1986).
89   *Id.*

States, there was no intention of the restatements being adopted by legislatures.[90] In this respect the classical restatement method also differs from the idea of model uniform codes created by the American Bar Association.[91] Thus the importance of the American restatements has to be seen in their persuasive authority for the courts as illustrated in the development of the doctrine of promissory estoppel.[92] In the continental Member States of the European Community the situation is fundamentally *different*. Wherever courts are bound by codes and statutes they can not decide against explicit provisions by simply referring to the 'persuasive authority' of a deviating rule contained in a 'restatement'. This would amount to violation of the principles of separation of public powers in general and the prerogative of the legislative in particular. Thus in such a constitutional context a 'restatement' designed by scholars or institutes could only exert legitimate harmonising effects on different national jurisdictions in the frame of statutory general clauses that permit such an interpretation or by persuading national legislatures. In short, the developed 'restatement' method seems to be a very speculative way of achieving a higher degree of common private law elements in the reality of the different national legal systems in the European Community.

7.2 Problems

Hence, in general, EC directives seem to be a promising means and contribution for the development of a common private law in Europe. However, when looking more closely at the requirements as well as into the practice of private law approximation several problems become visible and have to be kept in mind.

1. Traditionally, private law mainly consists of very precise rules, so consequently the method of approximation by directives and national implementation can easily become a dilemma. It tends to either miss the objective of harmonisation or to restrict the leeway of national adaptation considerably.

The latter situation occurs in all cases in which the purpose of private law approximation is to overcome restrictions of trade or distortions of competition in consequence of differences in precise private law rules (e.g., requirements for the validity of consumer credit contracts). Here, even the 'result to be achieved' (e.g., the abolition of certain restrictions or distortions as a result of specific legal differences) requires precise definition. Therefore detailed rules nearly inevitably become part of the result to be achieved in the sense of Article 249 paragraph 3 EC-Treaty.[93] In fact, directives for the approximation of private law contain closely knit provisions which can be seen, for example, in the directives concerning product liability or consumer credit contracts. Directives may then partially approach the linguistic structure of regulations in the sense of Article 249 paragraph 2 EC-Treaty. Nevertheless, the necessity of national implementation remains and this again implies, among other

---

90 *Id.*, p. 120.
91 As a survey of the record of passage of uniform and model acts, as of September 1, 1985 see
    Appendix *id.*, pp. 160-165; particularly for the U.C.C. see Braucher (1958), p. 798.
92 See Hoffmann v. Red Owl Stores, Inc., 26 Wis. 2d 683, 133 N.W. 2d 267, 274 (1965).
93 See Müller-Graff (1993), p. 13.

problems, the risks of delay and of wrongful implementation[94] as well as difficulties of interpretation as a result of the need to interpret national provisions in the light of the relevant directive.[95] Moreover, the harmonisation by directives requires constant control of the actual implementation in the different Member States by the Commission.

If, however, provisions in private law directives are not formulated in a precise, but in a rather vague way to grant more leeway to the Member States, they are in danger of missing the objective of approximation and of being enacted without the necessary competence to harmonise. The Commission, too, takes into consideration this deficiency in its Communication on European contract law when searching for the best means of transposition of European contract law. One of the main problems in this context is the large discretion of the Member States in the transposition process which could endanger the functionality of the International Market.[96]

2. Another problem of the method of approximation by directives is rooted in the requirement that directives can be based only on certain provisions of the EC-Treaty.[97] As these provisions contain certain prerequisites, it is possible that a particular question may be subjected to a directive, but not some inter-locking questions in the same area.[98] Additionally, legislation by directives implies a certain danger of discharging the directive-issuing institutions of their responsibility to define coherent and applicable rules. Since the directly applicable version of a provision has to be formulated by the respective Member State, the wording of a directive may turn out to be less precise than it might be to useful for the result to be achieved. A last problem to be mentioned is the rather scattered appearance of the measures taken, both in regard to the areas covered and to the rules created. Coming from an institution that is composed of members of national governments, the directives show a feeling for actualities, but no coherent concept of legislation in private law (except in company law) so far. Thus the experience gained with the directive-method suggests conceiving a more coherent, systematic and possibly codification-oriented approach and prefering the adoption of regulations based on Article 95 or 308 EC-Treaty rather than the enactment of directives.

8   Conclusion

If the political will strives for a common private law in the European Community – and the actual work on European contract law seems to be a step into this direction – directives are only second-best to coherent codification-like regulations, voluntary treaties no preferable alternative to Community law, and 'restatements' as well as proposals of model statutes and recommendations of uniform rules no convincing substitute to binding law. Nevertheless, recommendations of uniform rules, proposals

---

94   See Müller-Graff (1992-II), p. 249.
95   For this need see the cases 14/83 *v. Colson and Kamann* (1984) *ECR* 1891; 79/83 *Harz* (1984) *ECR* 1921; 80/86 *Kolpinghuis* (1987) *ECR* 3969; 177/88 *Dekker* (1990) *ECR* I 3941 at p. 3976.
96   See COM (2001) 398 final, at 63.
97   E.g., Art. 44 paragraph 3 letter g, 94, 95 EC-Treaty.
98   For this problem see Müller-Graff (1992-I), p. 330.

of model statutes, 'restatements', voluntary treaties and in particular directives constitute valuable elements for the development of a higher degree of common private law in the European Community.

BIBLIOGRAPHY: J. F. Baur/P.-C. Müller-Graff/M. Zuleeg, eds., *Europarecht – Energierecht – Wirtschaftsrecht, Festschrift für Bodo Börner* (1992); R. Birk, Elemente eines Gemeinschaftsrechts der Arbeitsbeziehungen, in P.-C. Müller-Graff, ed., *Gemeinsames Privatrecht in der Europäischen Gemeinschaft*, 2nd ed. (1999), pp. 385-401; M. J. Bonell, The Unidroit Initiative for the Progressive Codification of International Trade Law, 27 *ICLQ* 1978, p. 413; Braucher, The Legislative History of the Uniforum Commercial Code, 58 *Colum. L. Rev.* 1958, p. 798; C.-D. Ehlermann, Der Beitrag der Wettbewerbspolitik zum Europäischen Binnenmarkt, *Wirtschaft und Wettbewerb* 1992, pp. 5 ff.; E.A. Farnsworth, *An Introduction to the Legal System of the United States* (1963); FIW, ed., *Harmonisierungsbedürfnis zwischen dem Wettbewerbsrecht der EG und der Mitgliedstaaten?* (1991); M. Franzen, *Privatrechtsangleichung durch die Europäische Gemeinschaft* (1999); M. Gebauer, *Grundfragen der Europäisierung des Privatrechts* (1998); U. Goll, M. Kentner, Brauchen wir ein europäisches Kompetenzgericht?, *Europäische Zeitschrift für Wirtschaftsrecht* 2002, p. 101, p. 103; Gray, E pluribus unum? A Bicentennial Report on Unification of Law in the United States, 50 *RabelsZ* 1986, p. 119; P. Hommelhoff, Konturen eines gemeinschaftsrechtlichen Unternehmensrechts, in P.-C. Müller-Graff, ed., *Gemeinsames Privatrecht in der Europäischen Gemeinschaft*, 2nd ed. (1999), pp. 361-384; R. Jacobs, EG-Harmonisierung, in W. Gloy, ed., *Handbuch des Wettbewerbsrechts* 2nd ed. (1997), pp. 268-296; C. Joerges/G. Brüggemeier, Europäisierung des Vertragsrechts und Haftungsrechts, in P.-C. Müller-Graff, ed., *Gemeinsames Privatrecht in der Europäischen Gemeinschaft*, 2nd ed. (1999), pp. 301-360; G. Kegel/K. Schurig, *Internationales Privatrecht*, 8th ed. (2000); I. Klauer, *Die Europäisierung des Privatrechts* (1998); H. Kötz, *Europäisches Vertragsrecht* (1996); H. Kötz, Gemeineuropäisches Zivilrecht, in *Festschrift für Konrad Zweigert* (1981), pp. 481 ff.; H. Kötz, Rechtsvergleichung und gemeineuropäisches Privatrecht, in P.-C. Müller-Graff, ed., *Gemeinsames Privatrecht in der Europäischen Gemeinschaft*, 2nd ed. (1999), pp. 149-162; Lando, Principles of European Contract Law, 56 *RabelsZ* 1992, p. 261; O. Lando/H. Beale, eds., *The Principles of European Contract Law, Part I* (1995); M. Lutter, *Europäisches Unternehmensrecht*, 4th ed. (1996); P.-C. Müller-Graff, *Privatrecht und Europäisches Gemeinschaftsrecht – Gemeinschaftsprivatrecht*, 2nd ed. (1991); P.-C. Müller-Graff, *Wettbewerbsregeln des gemeinschaftseuropäischen Binnenmarktes* (1990); P.-C. Müller-Graff, ed., *Gemeinsames Privatrecht in der Europäischen Gemeinschaft*, 2nd ed. (1999) (referred to as Müller-Graff (1999-I)); P.-C. Müller-Graff, ed., *Europäische Zusammenarbeit in den Bereichen Justiz und Inneres* (1996) (referred to as Müller-Graff (1996-I)); P.-C. Müller-Graff, Gemeinsames Privatrecht in der Europäischen Gemeinschaft, in P.-C. Müller-Graff, ed., *Gemeinsames Privatrecht in der Europäischen Gemeinschaft*, 2nd ed. (1999), pp. 9-100 (referred to as Müller-Graff (1999-II); P.-C. Müller-Graff, Gemeinsames Privatrecht in der Europäischen Gemeinschaft: Ebenen und gemeinschaftsrechtliche Grundfragen, in J.F. Baur/P.-Ch. Müller-Graff/M. Zuleeg, eds., *Europarecht – Energierecht – Wirtschaftsrecht, Festschrift für Bodo Börner* (1992), pp. 330 (referred to as Müller-Graff (1992-I)); P.-C. Müller-Graff, Common Private Law in the European Community, in B. de Witte/C. Forder, eds., *The common law of Europe an the future of legal education* (1992), p. 249 (referred to as Müller-Graff (1992-II)); P.-C. Müller-Graff, Die Freistellung vom Kartellverbot, *Europarecht* 1992, p. 8 (referred to as Müller-Graff (1992-III)); P.-C. Müller-Graff, Europäisches Gemeinschaftsrecht und Privatrecht – Das Privatrecht in der europäischen Integration, 46 *Neue Juristische Wochenschrift* 1993, p. 13 (referred to as Müller-Graff (1993)); P.-C. Müller-Graff, Binnenmarktauftrag und Subsidiaritätsprinzip?, 159 *Zeitschrift für das gesamte Handelsrecht* 1995, p. 34; P.-C. Müller-Graff, Europäische Normgebung und ihre judikative Umsetzung in nationales Recht, *Deutsche Richterzeitung* 1996, pp. 259 and 305 (referred to as Müller-Graff (1996-II)); P.-C. Müller-Graff, Diritto Privato Comunitario – Realtá in Germania e Prospettive per Europa, *Rassegna di Diritto Civile* (1996) (referred to as Müller-Graff (1996-III)); P.-C. Müller-Graff, Rechtsangleichung im Privatrecht durch die EG, in N. Horn/J. F. Baur/K. Stern, eds., *40 Jahre Römische Verträge* – Von der Europäischen Wirtschaftsgemeinschaft zur Europäischen Union (1998), pp. 107-150; P.-C. Müller-Graff, Europäische Föderation als Revolutionskonzept im Europäischen Verfassungsraum?, *integration* 2000, pp. 157 ff. (referred to as Müller-Graff (2000-I)); P.-C. Müller-Graff, Die Europäische Privatrechtsgesellschaft, in P.-C. Müller-Graff/H. Roth, eds., *Recht und Rechtswissenschaft* (2000), pp. 271 ff. (referred to as Müller-Graff (2000-II)); P.C. Müller-Graff, Extending Private Autonomy Across Border, in S. Grundmann, W. Kerber, S. Weatherill, eds., Party Autonomy and the Role of Information in the Internal Market (2001), pp. 133 ff.; F. Rittner, in FIW, ed., *Integration oder Desintegration der europäischen Wettbewerbsordnung?* (1983), pp. 31 ff.; Riese, Einheitliche Gerichtsbarkeit für vereinheitlichtes Recht, 26 *RabelsZ* 1961, pp. 604 ff.; pp. Schlechtriem, *Einheitliches UN-Kaufrecht* (1981); I.E. Schwartz, Wege zur EG-Rechtsvereinheitlichung: Verordnungen der Europäischen Gemeinschaft oder Übereinkommen unter den Mitgliedstaaten?, in *Festschrift für Ernst von Caemmerer* (1978), pp. 1067 ff.; H. Ullrich, Die gemeinschaftsrechtliche Gestaltung des Wettbewerbsrechts und des Rechts des geistigen Eigentums – Eine Skizze, in P.-C. Müller-Graff, ed., *Gemeinsames Privatrecht in der Europäischen Gemeinschaft*, 2nd ed. (1999), pp. 403-456; E. Ulmer, ed., *Das Recht des unlauteren Wettbewerbs in den Mitgliedstaaten der Europäischen Wirtschaftsgemeinschaft* (1965); B. de Witte/C. Forder, eds., *The common law of Europe an the future of legal education* (1992).

ANNEX

EC Directives

I Private Law in general

Council Directive 86/653/EEC of 18 December 1986 on the coordination of the laws of the Member States relating to self-employed commercial agents; *Official Journal* L 382, 31/12/1986 PP. 0017 – 0021

Council Directive 85/374/EEC of 25 July 1985 on the approximation of the laws, regulations and administrative provisions of the Member States concerning liability for defective products; *Official Journal* L 210, 07/08/1985 PP. 0029 – 0033

Directive 99/34/EC of the European Parliament and Council of 10 May 1999 amending Council Directive 85/374/EEC of 25 July 1985 on the approximation of the laws, regulations and administrative provisions of the Member States concerning liability for defective products; *Official Journal* L 141, 04/06/1999 PP. 0020 – 0021

Council Directive 92/59/EEC of 29 June 1992 on general product safety; *Official Journal* L 228, 11/08/1992 PP. 0024 – 0032

Council Directive 85/577/EEC of 20 December 1985 to protect the consumer in respect of contracts negotiated away from business premises; *Official Journal* L 372, 31/12/1985 PP. 0031 – 0033

Council Directive 87/102/EEC of 22 December 1986 for the approximation of the laws, regulations and administrative provisions of the Member States concerning consumer credit; *Official Journal* L 042, 12/02/1987 PP. 0048 – 0053

Directive 98/7/EC of the European Parliament and Council Directive of 16 February 1998 amending Directives 87/102 (as amended by Directive 90/88) for the approximation of the laws, regulations and administrative provisions of the Member States concerning consumer credit; *Official Journal* L101, 01/04/1998 PP. 0017 – 0023

Council Directive 90/314/EEC of 13 June 1990 on package travel, package holidays and package tours; *Official Journal* L 158, 23/06/1990 PP. 0059 – 0064

Proposal for a Council Directive on the liability of suppliers of services; /* COM/90/482 final – SYN 308 */, *Official Journal* C 012, 18/01/1991 P. 0008, withdrawal by Commission

Council Directive 93/13/EEC of 5 April 1993 on unfair terms in consumer contracts; *Official Journal* L 095, 21/04/1993 PP. 0029 – 0034

Directive 1999/44/EC of the European Parliament and of the Council of 25 May 1999 on certain aspects of the sale of consumer goods and associated guarantees; *Official Journal* L 171, 07/07/1999 PP. 0012 – 0016

Directive 97/7/EC of the European Parliament and of the Council of 20 May 1997 on the protection of consumers in respect of distance contracts – Statement by the Council and the Parliament re Article 6 (1) – Statement by the Commission re Article 3 (1), first indent; *Official Journal* L 144, 04/06/1997 PP. 0019 – 0027

Directive 98/27/EC of the European Parliament and of the Council of 19 May 1998 on injunctions for the protection of consumers' interests; *Official Journal* L 166, 11/06/1998 PP. 0051 – 0055

Directive 2002/65/EC of the European Parliament and of the Council of 23 September 2002 concerning the distance marketing of consumer financial services and amending Council Directive 90/619/EEC and Directives 97/7/EC and 98/27/EC; 271, 09/10/2002 PP. 0016 – 0024

Directive 94/47/EC of the European Parliament and the Council of 26 October 1994 on the protection of purchasers in respect of certain aspects of contracts relating to the purchase of the right to use immovable properties on a timeshare basis; *Official Journal* L 280, 29/10/1994 PP. 0083 – 0087

Proposal for a Council Directive on civil liability for damage caused by waste /* COM/89/282 final */, *Official Journal* C 251, 04/10/1989 P. 0003, withdrawal by Commission

Amended proposal for a Council Directive on civil liability for damage caused by waste /* COM/91/219 final – SYN 217 */, *Official Journal* C 192, 23/07/1991 P. 0006

Directive 2001/95/EC of the European Parliament and of the Council of 3 December 2001 on general product safety; *Official Journal* L 011, 15/01/2002 PP. 0004 – 0017

Directive 98/6/EC of the European Parliament and of the Council of 16 February 1998 on consumer protection in the indication of the prices of products offered to consumers; *Official Journal* L 080, 18/03/1998 pp. 0027 – 0031

II Law against Unfair Competition

Council Directive 84/450/EEC of 10 September 1984 relating to the approximation of the laws, regulations and administrative provisions of the Member States concerning misleading advertising; *Official Journal* L 250, 19/09/1984 PP. 0017 – 0020

Directive 97/55/EC of European Parliament and of the Council of 6 October 1997 amending Directive 84/450/EEC concerning misleading advertising so as to include comparative advertising; *Official Journal* L 290, 23/10/1997 PP. 0018 – 0023

Council Directive 89/552/EEC of 3 October 1989 on the coordination of certain provisions laid down by Law, Regulation or Administrative Action in Member States concerning the pursuit of television broadcasting activities; *Official Journal* L 298, 17/10/1989 PP. 0023 – 0030

Directive 97/36/EC of the European Parliament and of the Council of 30 June 1997 amending Council Directive 89/552/EEC on the coordination of certain provisions laid down by law, regulation or administrative action in Member States concerning the pursuit of television broadcasting activities; *Official Journal* L 202, 30/07/1997 PP. 0060 – 0070

Directive 98/6/EC of the European Parliament and of the Council of 16 February 1998 on consumer protection in the indication of the prices of products offered to consumers; *Official Journal* L 080, 18/03/1998 PP. 0027 – 0031

Directive 2000/13/EC of the European Parliament and of the Council of 20 March 2000 on the approximation of the laws of the Member States relating to the labelling, presentation and advertising of foodstuffs; *Official Journal* L 109, 06/05/2000 PP. 0029 – 0042

Official Journal Directive 2003/89/EC of the European Parliament and of the Council of 10 November 2003 amending Directive 2000/13/EC as regards indication of the ingredients present in foodstuffs *Official Journal* L 308, 25/11/2003 pp. 0015 – 0018

Council Directive 89/109/EEC of 21 December 1988 on the approximation of the laws of the Member States relating to materials and articles intended to come into contact with foodstuffs; *Official Journal* L 040, 11/02/1989 PP. 0038 – 0044

Council Directive 2001/114/EC of 20 December 2001 relating to certain partly or wholly dehydrated preserved milk for human consumption; *Official Journal* L 015, 17/01/2002 PP. 0019 – 0023

Directive 2003/33/EC of the European Parliament and of the Council of 26 May 2003 on the approximation of the laws, regulations and administrative provisions of the Member States relating to the advertising and sponsorship of tobacco products (presented by the Commission pursuant to Articles 47(2), 55 and 95 of the EC Treaty); *Official Journal* L 152, 20/06/2003 PP. 0016 – 0019

Directive 2002/46/EC of the European Parliament and of the Council of June 2002 on the approximation of the laws of the member states relating to food supplements; *Official Journal* L183, 12/07/2002 PP. 0051– 0057

Directive 2000/31/EC of the European Parliament and of the Council of 8 June 2000 on certain legal aspects of information society services, in particular electronic commerce, in the Internal Market ('Directive on electronic commerce'); *Official Journal* L 178, 17/07/2000 PP. 0001 – 0016

Directive 1999/41/EC of the European Parliament and of the Council of 7 June 1999 amending Directive 89/398/EEC on the approximation of the laws of the Member States relating to foodstuffs intended for particular nutritional uses; *Official Journal* L 172, 08/07/1999 PP. 0038 – 0039

Directive 98/6/EC of the European Parliament and of the Council of 16 February 1998 on consumer protection in the indication of the prices of products offered to consumers; *Official Journal* L 080, 18/03/1998 PP. 0027 – 0031

III Protection of Industrial and Commercial Property

Council Directive 87/54/EEC of 16 December 1986 on the legal protection of topographies of semiconductor products; *Official Journal* L 024, 27/01/1987 PP. 0036 – 0040

Council Directive 91/250/EEC of 14 May 1991 on the legal protection of computer programs; *Official Journal* L 122, 17/05/1991 PP. 0042 – 0046

Directive 96/9/EC of the European Parliament and of the Council of 11 March 1996 on the legal protection of databases; *Official Journal* L 077, 27/03/1996 PP. 0020 – 0028

Directive 98/71/EC of the European Parliament and of the Council of 13 October 1998 on the legal protection of designs; *Official Journal* L 289, 28/10/1998 PP. 0028 – 0035

First Council Directive 89/104/EEC of 21 December 1988 to approximate the laws of the Member States relating to trade marks; *Official Journal* L 040, 11/02/1989 PP. 0001 – 0007

Council Directive 92/100/EEC of 19 November 1992 on rental right and lending right and on certain rights related to copyright in the field of intellectual property; *Official Journal* L 346, 27/11/1992 PP. 0061 – 0066

Dirctive 2001/29/EC of the European Parliament and Council of 22 May 2001 on the harmonisation of certain aspects of copyright and related rights in the Information Society; *Official Journal* L 167, 22/06/2001 PP. 0010 – 0019

Council Directive 93/98/EEC of 29 October 1993 harmonising the term of protection of copyright and certain related rights; *Official Journal* L 290, 24/11/1993 PP. 0009 – 0013

Council Directive 93/83/EEC of 27 September 1993 on the coordination of certain rules concerning copyright and rights related to copyright applicable to satellite broadcasting and cable retransmission; *Official Journal* L 248, 06/10/1993 PP. 0015 – 0021

Directive 98/44/EC of the European Parliament and of the Council of 6 July 1998 on the legal protection of biotechnological inventions; *Official Journal* L 213, 30/07/1998 PP. 0013 – 0021

Directive 2001/84/EC of the European Parliament and of the Council of 27 September 2001 on the resale right for the benefit of the author of an original work of art; *Official Journal* L 272, 13/10/2001 PP. 0032 – 0036

Directive 2001/37/EC of the European Parliament and of the Council of 5 June 2001 on the approximation of the laws, regulations and administrative provisions of the Member States concerning the manufacture, presentation and sale of tobacco products; *Official Journal* L 194, 18/07/2001 PP. 0026 – 0035

Directive 2001/29/EC of the European Parliament and of the Council of 22 May 2001 on the harmonisation of certain aspects of copyright and related rights in the information society; *Official Journal* L 167, 22/06/2001 PP. 0010 – 0019

Directive 2002/19/EC of the European Parliament and of the Council of 7 March 2002 on access to, and interconnection of, electronic communications networks and associated facilities; *Official Journal* L 108, 24/04/2001 PP. 0007 – 0020

Amended proposal for a European Parliament and Council Directive approximating the legal arrangements for the protection of inventions by utility model /* COM/99/0309 final – COD 97/0356 */, *Official Journal* C 248 E, 29/08/2000 P. 0056 – 0068
Directive 98/84/EC of the European Parliament and of the Council of 20 November 1998 on the legal protection of services based on, or consisting of, conditional access; *Official Journal* L 320, 28/11/1998 PP. 0054 – 0057

IV Company Law

First Council Directive 68/151/EEC of 9 March 1968 on co-ordination of safeguards which, for the protection of the interests of members and others, are required by Member States of companies within the meaning of the second paragraph of Article 58 of the Treaty, with a view to making such safeguards equivalent throughout the Community; *Official Journal* L 065, 14/03/1968 PP. 0008 – 0012
Second Council Directive 77/91/EEC of 13 December 1976 on coordination of safeguards which, for the protection of the interests of members and others, are required by Member States of companies within the meaning of the second paragraph of Article 58 of the Treaty, in respect of the formation of public limited liability companies and the maintenance and alteration of their capital, with a view to making such safeguards equivalent; *Official Journal* L 026, 31/01/1977 PP. 0001 – 0013
Council Directive 92/101/EEC of 23 November 1992 amending Directive 77/91/EEC on the formation of public limited- liability companies and the maintenance and alteration of their capital; *Official Journal* L 347, 28/11/1992 PP. 0064 – 0066
Third Council Directive 78/855/EEC of 9 October 1978 based on Article 54 (3) (g) of the Treaty concerning mergers of public limited liability companies; *Official Journal* L 295, 20/10/1978 PP. 0036 – 0043
Fourth Council Directive 78/660/EEC of 25 July 1978 based on Article 54 (3) (g) of the Treaty on the annual accounts of certain types of companies; *Official Journal* L 222, 14/08/1978 PP. 0011 – 0031
Council Directive 84/569/EEC of 27 November 1984 revising the amounts expressed in ECU in Directive 78/660/EEC; *Official Journal* L 314, 04/12/1984 PP. 0028 – 0028
Council Directive 94/8/EC of 21 March 1994 amending Directive 78/660/EEC as regards the revision of amounts expressed in ecus; *Official Journal* L 082, 25/03/1994 PP. 0033 – 0034
Council Directive 90/605/EEC of 8 November 1990 amending Directive 78/660/EEC on annual accounts and Directive 83/349/EEC on consolidated accounts as regards the scope of those Directives; *Official Journal* L 317, 16/11/1990 PP. 0060 – 0062
Amended Proposal for a Fifth Directive founded on Article 54 (3) (g) of the EEC Treaty concerning the structure of public limited companies and the powers and obligations of their organs (submitted by the Commission persuant to Article 149 (2) of the EEC Treaty on 19 August 1983); COM (83) 185 final SYN 3 *Official Journal* C 240, 09/09/1983 P. 0002
Second Amendment for the Proposal for a Fifth Council Directive (91/C7/05) based on Article 54 of the EEC Treaty concerning the structure of public limited companies and the powers and obligations of their organs (submitted by the Commission pursuant to Article 149 (3) of the EEC Treaty on 20 December 1990); COM (90) 629 final SYN 3 *Official Journal* C 7, 11/01/1991 P. 0004

Sixth Council Directive 82/891/EEC of 17 December 1982 based on Article 54 (3) (g) of the Treaty, concerning the division of public limited liability companies; *Official Journal* L 378, 31/12/1982 PP. 0047 – 0054
Seventh Council Directive 83/349/EEC of 13 June 1983 based on the Article 54 (3) (g) of the Treaty on consolidated accounts; *Official Journal* L 193, 18/07/1983 PP. 0001 – 0017

Council Directive 90/605/EEC of 8 November 1990 amending Directive 78/660/EEC on annual accounts and Directive 83/349/EEC on consolidated accounts as regards the scope of those Directives; *Official Journal* L 317, 16/11/1990 PP. 0060 – 0062

Council Directive 90/604/EEC of 8 November 1990 amending Directive 78/660/EEC on annual accounts and Directive 83/349/EEC on consolidated accounts as concerns the exemptions for small and medium-sised companies and the publication of accounts in ecus; *Official Journal* L 317, 16/11/1990 PP. 0057 – 0059

Directive 2001/65/EC of the European Parliament and of the Council of 27 September 2001 amending Directives 78/660/EEC, 83/349/EEC and 86/635/EEC as regards the valuation rules for the annual and consolidated accounts of certain types of companies as well as of banks and other financial institutions; *Official Journal* L 283, 27/10/2001 PP. 0028 – 0032

Eighth Council Directive 84/253/EEC of 10 April 1984 based on Article 54 (3) (g) of the Treaty on the approval of persons responsible for carrying out the statutory audits of accounting documents; *Official Journal* L 126, 12/05/1984 PP. 0020 – 0026

Proposal for a tenth Directive of the Council based on Article 54 (3) (g) of the Treaty concerning cross-border mergers of public limited companies; /* COM/84/727 final – SYN 38 */, *Official Journal* C 023, 25/01/1985 P. 0011, withdrawal by Commission

Eleventh Council Directive 89/666/EEC of 21 December 1989 concerning disclosure requirements in respect of branches opened in a Member State by certain types of company governed by the law of another State; *Official Journal* L 395, 30/12/1989 PP. 0036 – 0039

Twelfth Council Company Law Directive 89/667/EEC of 21 December 1989 on single-member private limited-liability companies; *Official Journal* L 395, 30/12/1989 PP. 0040 – 0042

Thirteenth Directive 2004/25/EC of the European Parliament and of the Council of 21 April 2004 on company law, concerning takeover bids; *Official Journal* L142, 30/04/2004 PP. 0012 – 0023

Council Directive 2001/86/EC of 8 October 2001 supplementing the Statute for a European company with regard to the involvement of employees; *Official Journal* L 294 10.11.2001 PP. 0022 – 0032

Directive 2000/12/EC of the European Parliament and of the Council of 20 March 2000 relating to the taking up and pursuit of the business of credit institutions; *Official Journal* L 126, 26/05/2000 PP. 0001 – 0059

V Stock Market Law

Council Directive (89/298/EEC) of 17 April 1989 coordinating the requirements for the drawing-up, scrutiny and distribution of the prospectus to be published when transferable securities are offered to the public; *Official Journal* L 124, 05/05/1989 PP. 0008 – 0015

Directive (94/18/EC) of the European Parliament and of the Council of 30 May 1994 amending Directive 80/390/EEC coordinating the requirements for the drawing up, scrutiny and distribution of the listing of particulars to be published for the admission of securities to official stock-exchange listing, with regard to the obligation to publishing listing particulars; *Official Journal* L 135, 31/05/1994 PP. 0001 – 0004

Council Directive 89/592/EEC of 13 November 1989 coordinating regulations on insider dealing; *Official Journal* L 334, 18/11/1989 PP. 0030 – 0032

Directive 2001/34/EC of the European Parliament and of the Council of 28 May 2001 on the admission of securities to official stock exchange listing and on information to be published on those securities; *Official Journal* L 184, 06/07/2001, PP. 0001 – 0066

VI Banking Law

Council Directive 89/117/EEC of 13 February 1989 on the obligations of branches in a Member State of credit institutions and financial institutions having their head office outside that

Member State regarding the publication of annual accounting documents; *Official Journal* L 044, 16/02/1989 PP. 0040 – 0042

Council Directive 92/16/EEC of 16 March 1992 amending Directive 89/299/EEC on the credit institution's own funds; *Official Journal* L 075, 21/03/1992 PP. 0048 – 0050

Amended Proposal for a Council Directive 89/C 36/01 concerning the reorganisation and the winding-up of credit institutions and deposit guarantee schemes (submitted by the Commission on 11 January 1988); COM (88) 4 final *Official Journal* C 036, 04/01/1988

Directive 94/19/EC of the European Parliament and of the Council of 30 May 1994 on deposit-guarantee schemes; *Official Journal* L 135, 31/05/1994 PP. 0005 – 0014

Council Directive 85/611/EEC of 20 December 1985 on the coordination of laws, regulations and administrative provisions relating to undertaking for collective investment in transferable securities (UCITS); *Offical Journal* L 375, 31/12/1985 PP. 0003 – 0018

Council Directive 88/220/EEC of 22 March 1988 amending, as regards the investment policies of certain UCITS, Directive 85/611/EEC on the coordination of laws, regulations and administrative provisions relating to undertakings for collective investments in transferable securities (UCITS); *Official Journal* L 100, 19/04/1988 PP. 0031 – 0032

Amended Proposal for a Council Directive 87/C 161/04 on the freedom of establishment and the free supply of services in the field of mortgage credits (submitted by the Commission on 22 May 1987); COM (87) 255 final *Official Journal* L 161, 19/06/1987 p. 0004, withdrawal by commission

Council Directive 93/6/EEC of 15 March 1993 on the capital adequacy of investment firms and credit institutions; *Official Journal* L 141, 11/06/1993 PP. 0001 – 0026

Council Directive 91/308/EEC of 10 June 1991 on prevention of the use of the financial system for the purpose of money laundring; *Official Journal* L 166, 28/06/1991 PP. 0077 – 0083

Directive 94/19/EC of the European Parliament and of the Council of 30 May 1994 on deposit-guarantee schemes; *Official Journal* L 135, 31/05/1994 PP. 0005 – 0014

Directive 97/5/EC of the European Parliament and of the Council of 27 January 1997 on cross-border credit transfers; *Official Journal* L 043, 14/02/1997, PP. 0025 – 0030

Directive 97/7/EC of the European Parliament and of the Council of 20 May 1997 on the protection of costumers in respect to distance contracts – statement by the Council and the Parliament re Article 6 (1) – statement by the Council re Article 3 (1), first indent; *Official Journal* L 144, 04/06/1997 PP. 0019 – 0027

Directive 97/9/EC of the European Parliament and of the Council of 3 March 1997 on investor-compensation schemes; *Official Journal* L 084, 26/03/1997 PP. 0022 – 0031

Directive 98/31/EC of the European Parliament and of the Council of 22 June 1998 amending Council Directive 93/6/EEC on the capital of adequacy of investment firms and credit institutions; *Offical Journal* L 204, 21/07/1998 PP. 0013 – 0025

Directive 2000/12/EC of the European Parliament and of the Council of 20 March 2000 relating to the taking up and pursuit of the business of credit institutions; *Official Journal* L 126, 26/05/2000 PP. 0001 – 0059

Directive 2000/28/EC of the European Parliament and of the Council of 18 September 2000 amending Directive 2000/12/EC relating to the taking up and pursuit of the business of credit institutions; *Official Journal* L 275, 27/10/2000 PP. 0037 – 0038

Directive 2001/24/EC of the European Parliament and of the Council of 4 April 2001 on the reorganisation and winding up of credit institutions; *Offical Journal* L 125, 05/05/2001 PP. 0015 – 0023

Directive 2001/65/EC of the European Parliament and the Council of 27 September 2001 amending Directives 78/660/EEC, 83/349/EEC and 86/635/EEC as regards to the valuation on rules for the annual and consolidated accounts of certain types of companies as well as of banks and other financial institutions; *Official Journal* L 283, 27/10/2001 PP. 0028 – 0032

Directive 2001/97/EC of the European Parliament and of the Council of 4 December 2001 amending Council Directive 91/308/EEC on prevention of the use of the financial system for the purpose of money laundering; *Official Journal* L 344, 28/12/2001 PP. 0076 – 0082

Directive 2001/107/EC of the European Parliament and the Council of 21 January 2002 amending Council Directive 85/611/EEC on the coordination of laws, regulations and administrative provisions relating to undertakings for collective investment in transferable securities (UCITS) with a view tot regulating management companies and simplified prospectusus; *Official Journal* L 041, 13/02/2002 PP. 0020 – 0034

VII Insurance Law

First Council Directive 73/239/EEC of 24 July 1973 on the coordination of the laws, regulations and administrative provisions relating to the taking up and pursuit of direct insurance other than life insurance; *Official Journal* L 228, 16/08/1973 PP. 0003 – 0019

Council Directive 76/580/EEC of 29 June 1976 amending Directive 73/239/EEC on the coordination of the laws, regulations and administrative provisions relating to the taking up and pursuit of direct insurance other than life insurance; *Official Journal* L 189, 13/07/1976, PP. 0013 – 0014

Second Council Directive 88/357/EEC of 22 June 1988 on the coordination of the laws, regulations and administrative provisions relating to direct insurance other than life insurance and laying down provisions to facilitate the effective exercise of freedom to provide services and amending Directive 73/239/EEC; *Official Journal* L 172, 04/07/1988 PP. 0001 – 0014

Council Directive 72/166/EEC of 24 April 1972 on the approximation of the laws of the Member States relating to insurance against civil liability in respect of the use of motor vehicles and to the enforcement of the obligation to insure against such liability; *Official Journal* L 103, 02/05/1972 PP. 0001 – 0004

Second Council Directive 84/5/EEC of 30 December 1983 on the approximation of the laws of the Member States relating to insurance against civil liability in respect of the use of motor vehicles; *Official Journal* L 008, 11/01/1984 PP. 0017 – 0020

Third Council Directive 90/232/EEC of 14 May 1990 on the approximation of the laws of the Member States relating to insurance against civil liability in respect of the use of motor vehicles; *Official Journal* L 129, 19/05/1990 PP. 0033 – 0035

Council Directive 90/618/EEC of 8 November 1990 amending, particularly as regards motor vehicle liability insurance, Directive 73/239/EEC and Directive 88/357/EEC which concern the coordination of the laws, regulations and administrative provisions relating to direct insurance other than life assurance; *Official Journal* L 330, 29/11/1990 PP. 0044 – 0049

– incorporated by the Agreement on the European Economic Area – Annex IX – Financial Services List provided for in Article 36 (2); *Official Journal* L 001, 03/01/1994 PP. 0403 – 0416

Council Directive 84/641/EEC of 10 December 1984 amending, particularly as regards tourist assistance, First Directive 73/239/EEC on the coordination of the laws, regulations and administrative provisions relating to the taking up and pursuit of business of direct insurance other than life assurance; *Offical Journal* L 339, 27/12/1984 PP. 0021 – 0025

– incorporated by the Agreement on the European Economic Area – Annex IX – Financial Services List provided for in Article 36 (2); *Official Journal* L 001, 03/01/1994 PP. 0403 – 0416

Council Directive 87/344/EEC of 22 June 1987 on the coordination of laws, regulations and administrative provisions relating to legal expenses insurance; *Official Journal* L 185, 04/07/1987 PP. 0070 – 0080

– incorporated by the Agreement on the European Economic Area – Annex IX – Financial Services List provided for in Article 36 (2); *Official Journal* L 001, 03/01/1994 PP. 0403 – 0416

Council Directive 87/343/EEC of 22 June 1987 amending, as regards credit insurance and suretyship insurance, First Directive 73/239/EEC on the coordination of the laws, regulations and administrative provisions relating to the taking up and pursuit of business of direct insurance other than life assurance; *Official Journal* L 185, 04/07/1987 PP. 0072 – 0076
– incorporated by the Agreement on the European Economic Area – Annex IX – Financial Services List provided for in Article 36 (2); *Official Journal* L 001, 03/01/1994 PP. 0403 – 0416
First Council Directive 79/267/EEC of 5 March 1979 on the coordination of laws, regulations and administrative provisions relating to the taking up and pursuit of the business of direct life assurance; *Official Journal* L 63, 13/03/1979 PP. 0001 – 0018
– incorporated by the Agreement on the European Economic Area – Annex IX – Financial Services List provided for in Article 36 (2); *Official Journal* L 001, 03/01/1994 PP. 0403 – 0416
Council Directive 90/619/EEC of 8 November 1990 on the coordination of laws, regulations and administrative provisions relating to direct life assurance, laying down provisions to facilitate the effective exercise of freedom to provide services and amending Directive 79/267/EEC; *Official Journal* L 330, 29/11/1990 PP. 0050 – 0061 no longer in force
– incorporated by the Agreement on the European Economic Area – Annex IX – Financial Services List provided for in Article 36 (2); *Official Journal* J L 001, 03/01/1994 PP. 0403 – 0416
Council Directive 92/96/EEC of 10 November 1992 on the coordination of laws, regulations and administrative provisions relating to direct life assurance and amending Directives 79/267/EEC and 90/619/EEC (third life assurance Directive); *Official Journal* L 360, 09/12/1992 PP. 0001 – 0027 no longer in force
Council Directive 2001/17/EC of 12 March 2001 on the coordination of laws, regulations and administrative provisions relating to the compulsory winding-up of direct insurance undertakings (submitted by the Commission on 23 January 1987); *Official Journal* L 110, 20/04/2001 PP. 0028 – 0039
Amended Proposal for a Council Directive on the coordination of laws, regulations and administrative provisions relating to the compulsory winding-up of direct insurance undertakings (submitted by the Commission on 18 December 1989); COM (89) 394 final SYN 80 *Official Journal* L 253, 06/10/1989 p. 0003
Council Directive 91/674/EEC of 19 December 1991 on the annual account and consolidated accounts of insurance undertakings; *Official Journal* L 374, 31/12/1991 PP. 0007 – 0031
Council Directive 78/473/EEC of 30 May 1978 on the coordination of laws, regulations and administrative provisions relating to community co-insurance; *Official Journal* L151,07/06/1978 PP. 0025 – 0027
Council Directive 64/225/EEC of 25 February 1964 on the abolition of restrictions on freedom of establishment and freedom to provide services in respect of insurance and retrosession; *Official Journal* 1964 p 56, 04/04/1964 PP. 0878 – 0883
Council Directive 77/92/EEC of 13 December 1976 on measures to facilitate the effective exercise of freedom of establishment and freedom to provide services in respect of the activities of insurance agents and brokers (ex ISIC Group 630) and, in particular, transnational measures in respect of those activities; *Official Journal* L 026, 31/01/1977 PP. 0014 – 0019
Directive 95/26/EC of the European Parliament and of the Council of 29 June 1995 amending Directives 77/780/EEC and 89/646/EEC in the field of credit institutions, Directives 73/239/EEC and 92/49/EEC in the field of non-life insurance, Directives 79/267/EEC and 92/49/EEC in the field of investment firms and Directive 85/611/EEC in the field of undertakings for collective investment in transferable securities (UCITS) with view to reinforcing prudential supervision; *Official Journal* L 168, 18/07/1995 PP. 0007 – 0013
Directive 98/78/EC of the European Parliament and of the Council of 27 Oktober 1998 on the

97

supplementary supervision of insurance undertakings in an insurance group; *Official Journal* L 330, 05/12/1998 PP. 0001 – 0012

Directive 2000/12/EC of the European Parliament and of the Council of 20 March 2000 relating to the taking up and pursuit of the business of credit institutions; *Official Journal* L 126, 26/05/2000 PP. 0001 – 0059

Directive 2000/28/EC of the European Parliament and of the Council of 18 September 2000 amending Directive 2000/12/EC relating to the taking up and pursuit of the business of credit institutions; *Official Journal* L 275, 27/10/2000 PP. 0037 – 0038

Directive 2000/64/EC of the European Parliament and of the Council of 7 November 2000 amending Council Directives 85/611/EEC, 92/49/EEC, 92/96/EEC and 93/22/EEC as regards exchange of information with third countries; *Official Journal* L 290, 17/11/2000 PP. 0027 – 0028

Directive 2001/17/EC of the European Parliament and of the Council of 19 March 2001 on the reorganisation and winding-up of insurance undertakings; *Official Journal* L 110, 20/04/2001, PP. 0028 – 0039

VIII Telecommunications

Council Directive 90/387/EEC of 28 June 1990 on the establishment of the internal market for telecommunications services through the implementation of open network provisions; *Official Journal* L 192, 24/07/1990 PP. 0001 – 0009, no longer in force.

Commission Directive 88/301/EEC of 16 May 1988 on competition in the markets in telecommunications terminal equipment; *Official Journal* L 131, 27/05/1988 PP. 0073 – 0077

Commission Directive 90/388/EEC of 28 June 1990 on competition in the markets for telecommunications services; *Official Journal* L 192, 24/07/1990 PP. 0010 – 0016, no longer in force.

Commission Directive 96/2/EC of 16 January 1996 amending Directive 90/388/EEC with regard to mobile and personal communications; *Official Journal* L 020, 26/01/1996 PP. 0059 – 0066, no longer in force.

Commission Directive 94/46/EC of 13 October 1994 amending Directive 88/301/EEC and Directive 90/388/EEC in particular with regard to satellite communications; *Official Journal* L 268, 19/10/1994 PP. 0015 – 0021

Directive 95/5/EC of the European Parliament and of the Council of 9 March 1999 on radio equipment and telecommunications terminal equipments and the mutual recognition of their conformity; *Official Journal* L 091, 07/04/1999 PP. 0010 – 0028

Commission Directive 9/51/EC of 18 October 1995 amending Directive 90/388/EEC with regard to the abolition of the restrictions on the use of cable television networks for the provision of already liberalised telecommunications services; *Official Journal* L 256, 26/10/1995 PP. 0049 – 0054, no longer in force.

Commission Directive 96/19/EC of 13 March 1996 amending Directive 90/388/EEC with regard to the implementation of full competition in telecommunications markets; *Official Journal* L 074, 22/03/1996 PP. 0013 – 0024, no longer in force.

Directive 97/51/EC of the European Parliament and of the Council of 6 October 1997 amending Council Directives 90/387/EEC and 92/441/EEC for the purpose of adaptation to a competitive environment in telecommunications; *Official Journal* L 295, 29/10/1997 PP. 0023 – 0034

Draft Commission Directive amending Directive 90/388/EEC in order to ensure that telecommunications networks and cable TV networks owned by a single operator are separate legal entities; *Official Journal* C 0071, 07/03/1998 PP. 0023 – 0026

Directive 99/93/EC of the European Parliament and of the Council of 13 December 1999 on a community framework of electronic signatures; *Official Journal* L 013, 19/01/2000 PP. 0012 – 0020

Directive 2000/31/EC of the European Parliament and of the Council of 8 June 2000 on certain legal aspects of information society services, in particular electronic commerce, in the Internal Market ('Directive on electronic commerce'); *Official Journal* L 178, 17/07/2000 PP. 0001 – 0016

Directive 2001/29/EC of the European Parliament and of the Council of 22 May 2001 on the harmonisation of certain aspects of copyright and related rights in the information society; *Official Journal* L 167, 22/06/2001 PP. 0010-0019

IX Labour Law

Directive 2002/74/EC of 23 September 2002 of the European Parliament and of the Council amending Council Directive 80/987/EEC on the approximation of the laws of the Member States relating to the protection of employees in the event of the insolvency of their employer; *Official Journal* L 270, 08/10/2002 PP. 0010 – 0013

Directive 2003/41/EC of 3 June 2003 of the European Parliament and of the Council on the activities of institutions for occupational retirement provision; *Official Journal* L 235, 23/09/2001 PP. 0010 – 0021

Council Directive 2000/78/EC of 27 November 2000 establishing a general framework for equal treatment in employment and occupation; *Official Journal* L 303, 02/12/2000 PP. 0016 – 0022

Council Directive 2000/43/EC of 29 June 2000 implementing the principle of equal treatment between persons irrespective of racial or ethnic origin; *Official Journal* L 180, 19/07/2000 PP. 0022 – 0026

Council Directive 2000/78/EC of 27 November 2000 establishing a general framework for equal treatment in employment and occupation; *Official Journal* L 303, 02/12/2000 PP. 0016 – 0022

Council Directive 1999/70/EC of 28 June 1999 concerning the framework agreement on fixed-term work concluded by ETUC, UNICE and CEEP; *Official Journal* L 175, 10/07/1999 PP. 0043 – 0048

Council Directive 2000/34/EC of 22 June 2000 amending Directive 93/104/EC of 23 November 1993 concerning certain aspects of the organisation of working time to cover sectors and activities excluded from that Directive; *Official Journal* L 195, 01/08/2000 PP. 0041 – 0045

Proposal for a Directive of the European Parliament and of the Council on the posting of workers who are third-country nationals for the provision of cross-border services; /* COM/ 99/0003 final – COD 99/0012 */, *Official Journal* C 067, 10/03/1999 P. 0012

Council Directive 2002/14/EC of 11 March 2002 establishing a general framework for informing and consulting employees in the European Community; *Official Journal* L 80, 23/03/2002 PP. 0029 – 0034

Council Directive 2001/23/EC of 12 March 2001 on the approximation of the laws of the Member States relating to the safeguarding of employees' rights in the event of transfers of undertakings, businesses or parts of undertakings or businesses; *Official Journal* L 082, 22/03/2001 PP. 0016 – 0020

Council Directive 98/49/EC of 29 June 1998 on safeguarding the supplementary pension rights of employed and self-employed persons moving within the Community; *Official Journal* L 209, 25/07/1998 PP. 0046 – 0049

Council Directive 98/59/EC of 20 July 1998 on the approximation of the laws of the Member States relating to collective redundancies; *Official Journal* L 225, 12/08/1998 PP. 0016 – 0021

Council Directive 97/81/EC of 15 December 1997 concerning the Framework Agreement on part-time work concluded by UNICE, CEEP and the ETUC – Annex: Framework agreement on part-time work; *Official Journal* L 014, 20/01/1998 PP. 0009 – 0014

Council Directive 97/80/EC of 15 December 1997 on the burden of proof in cases of discrimination based on sex; *Official Journal* L 014, 20/01/1998 PP. 0006 – 0008

Directive 96/71/EC of the European Parliament and of the Council of 16 December 1996 concerning the posting of workers in the framework of the provision of services; *Official Journal* L 018, 21/01/1997 PP. 0001 – 0006

Council Directive 96/34/EC of 3 June 1996 on the framework agreement on parental leave concluded by UNICE, CEEP and the ETUC; *Official Journal* L 145, 19/06/1996 PP. 0004 – 0009

Proposal for a Council Directive amending Directive 76/207/EEC on the implementation of the principle of equal treatment for men and women as regards access to employment, vocational training and promotion, and working conditions; /* COM/96/0093 final – CNS 96/0095 */, *Official Journal* C 179, 22/06/1996 P. 0008, withdrawal by Commission

CHAPTER 6

The ECJ Case-Law as a Means of Unification of Private Law?

Walter van Gerven*

As requested by the editors, I will not focus herein on the feasibility of a European Civil Code but rather address myself to questions of substance relating to the law of obligations, that is the law of contract and tort, leaving aside the law of property,[1] as well as family law. I must nevertheless point out that I do not myself believe in the feasibility, or even desirability, of a uniform Civil Code for Europe and that, instead of using the technique of legislation to bring about uniformity, I am more in favour of finding common solutions, if not general principles, in the legal systems of Europe. Such common solutions, or general principles, can be derived from statute law and, just as important, from case-law prevailing in the major legal systems, including case-law from the European Community and the European Convention of Human Rights judiciary.[2] Nor do I believe, coming closer to my subject, that the case-law of the Community courts, namely the ECJ and the CFI,[3] will result in the *unification* of national private laws. Just like the impact of EC-Directives on private law – the subject of Prof. Müller-Graff's contribution to this book – the impact of ECJ and CFI case-law on private law will only lead to piece-meal *harmonisation*, that is harmonisation in those limited fields of private law over which the Community has jurisdiction. To be sure, such harmonisation will cause the Member State legal systems to converge in those limited fields – which is the bright side of harmonisation –, but it will also, within each national legal system, have the effect that a unity which previously existed, is disrupted and replaced by different sets of rules, one set for areas covered by Community law, and another for areas not affected by Community law. This is the dark side of harmonisation.[4] The only way to avoid that situation,

---

* Professor of Law, K.U. Leuven and University of Maastricht; formerly Advocate General at the European Court of Justice in Luxemburg (1988-1994).

1 That the Community has jurisdiction, in spite of (a possible restrictive interpretation of) Art. 222 EC, to promulgate substantive law provisions relating to (in that case: industrial) property law, has been confirmed by the ECJ in its Judgment of 13 July 1995, case C-350/92, *Spain* v. *Council*, [1995] *ECR* I-1985. Whether that includes the competence for the Community to change national property laws drastically is in my view unlikely. See also the article written before the abovementioned judgment by S. Bartels, 'Europees privaatrecht: over de bevoegdheidsverdeling tussen Unie en Lid-Staat met betrekking tot het eigendomsrecht', *Ars Aequi*, (1995), 244.

2 See also W. van Gerven, 'Codifying European private law? Yes, if ...!,' *European Law Review*, (2002) 156-176, at 174-176; also *id.*, 'The case-law of the European Court of Justice and National courts as a contribution to the Europeanisation of Private law', *European Review of Private law*, (1995) 367, at 375 *et seq.*

3 ECJ is the abbreviation used for the Court of Justice referred to in Arts. 221-223 EC, CFI is used for the European Court of First Instance referred to in Art. 224-225 EC. Both courts are, together, referred to as 'the Community courts'. EC refers to the European Community Treaty, and TEU refers to the Treaty on European Union, of which the EC is the first pillar.

4 See further W.van Gerven, 'Comparative Law in a Texture of Communitarisation of National Laws

would be to enact comprehensive codification, for, for instance, the whole field of contract law, but that is not something for the Community institutions, which have no jurisdiction to do so.[5] Such codification can only be achieved by means of parallel agreements concluded between all or some Member States.[6]

1 The ECJ's Role in the Interpretation of Community Law

Before assessing the impact of the ECJ case-law on contract and tort laws, it may be useful to briefly describe the role which the ECJ (not the CFI, as yet) plays, in cooperation with national courts, within the framework of the preliminary ruling procedure provided for in Article 234 EC. That role is mainly to interpret primary and secondary Community law. Insofar as the Court's interpretation bears on Treaty provisions and regulations, that is on provisions which are fully binding and uniform in all Member States, the Court's case law assures uniformity in the application of such rules throughout the Community. However, where interpretation bears on provisions of *directives* which are only binding for the Member States as to the result pursued by the directive but not in respect of the form and methods to be used by the Member States (Art. 249, paragraph 3, EC), the Court's case law will only bring about uniformity in the interpretation of the concepts and principles contained in the directive, and will eventually be taken over literally in the implementing national legislation. It will not be able to ensure uniformity in the interpretation of the implementing national rules themselves, as those remain within the jurisdiction of the Member States (subject, however, to the requirement of interpretation in conformity with the directive, as, mentioned below).[7]

---

and Europeanisation of Community Law" in *Judicial Review in European Union Law* (ed. David O'Keeffe) Liber Amicorum in honour of Lord Slynn of Hadley, Kluwer, 2000, 433-445, at 435-40.

5   That has become clear with the ECJ's judgment in Case C-376/98, *Germany* v. *Parliament and Council* [2000] *ECR* I-8419, para. 83 where the Court held that a mere finding of disparities between national rules and the abstract risk of obstacles to the exercise of fundamental [economic] freedoms or of distortions liable to result there from, [is not] sufficient to justify the choice of Art. [95] as a legal basis ... " When a Community measure does *genuinely* have as its objective the improvement of the conditions for the functioning of the internal market, then Art. 95 EC does offer a legal basis: see ECJ, Case C-491/01, British American Tobacco, [2002] *ECR* I-11453, and the Opinion of Advocate General Geelhoed. That, however, is obviously not the case for the enactment of contract law in general.

6   On this, see B. De Witte, "Chameleonic Member States: Differentiation by means of partial and parallel international agreements," *The Many Faces of Differentiation in EU Law* (eds. B. De Witte, D. Hanf and E.Vos), Intersentia, Antwerp, 2001, 231-267, at 255-6 and 260-66. An important restriction of this method of unification is that the agreements cannot grant jurisdiction to the ECJ when they fall completely outside the scope of EC or EU competence: see De Witte, at 261-3.

7   The preliminary ruling procedure has been subjected in recent years to important changes. Firstly, Art. 225 (3) EC, as amended by the Treaty of Nice, has opened the possibility, not yet used, to allow the CFI to hear references. Secondly, the Rules of Procedure of the ECJ have provided a simplified procedure permitting the Court to deal with a case by Order before the written procedure has begun, when a question may be clearly deduced from existing case-law, or where the answer to the question admits of no reasonable doubt (a procedure which the Court has since frequently used). Thirdly, the Court has been empowered to ask questions of the referring court. And, fourthly, the Court has become less tolerant in accepting references; thus, in *Bacardi-Martini* v. *Newcastle United,* Case C-

Having said that, it should be pointed out that the ECJ's case-law concerning the interpretation of provisions of directives (and of regulations) is often of a more limited nature than the ECJ's case-law concerning Treaty provisions and general principles – which include the general principles on (vertical) direct effect of directives, interpretation of national laws in conformance with directives and liability for non-implementation of directives.[8] Whereas the ECJ's interpretation of Treaty provisions and, even more so, of the underlying general principles is frequently bold, or even audacious, that is normally not the case as regards the ECJ's interpretation of specific directive provisions. This is, more often than not (but see *infra*, under 4.4), of a rather textual nature, relating, as it usually does, to precise and often technical expressions.[9]

An example of such textual interpretation is the one which the ECJ has given, in its *Panagis Pafitis* judgment of 12 March 1996,[10] to Article 25 of the Second Company directive.[11] In that decision the Court held that Article 25 "precludes national legislation under which the capital of a bank constituted in the form of a public limited liability company [which, as a result of its debt burden, is in exceptional circumstances] may be increased by an administrative measure, without a resolution of the general meeting".[12] By doing so, the Court gave absolute *precedence* to the provisions of the Second Company directive which require the approval of the shareholders meeting for an increase of capital, *over* the objective of reorganising a bank, which is in financial trouble, in favour of the bank's creditors, i.e. mainly small depositors. Indeed, if the increase of capital imposed by the national banking supervisory authority (in that case the Bank of Greece) in accordance with domestic law, has to be approved by the old shareholders (who objected to the allotment of the new shares to the new shareholders), chances may well be that no reorganisation will take place or, if it does, that it will come too late. The Court based its decision on a textual interpretation of the Second Company directive and on its previous case-law, setting

---

318/00, [2003] *ECR* I-905) where the Court refused a reference from the English High Court because it was not made clear by that court that it needed the answer to the preliminary question to give judgment in the case before it. The question related to an interesting issue of contract law (damage claimed for interference in the performance of a contract); see also *infra* under 4.4. For a recent discussion of the preliminary ruling procedure, see T.Tridimas, "Knocking on heaven's door: Fragmentation, efficiency and defiance in the preliminary reference procedure," *Common Market Law Review* (2003), 9-50.

8   Thus, for example, in the field of the direct effect of directive provisions, the judgment in *Marshall I*, case 152/84 [1986] *ECR* 723, in the field of interpretation in conformance with the directive, the judgment in *Marleasing*, case C-106/89 [1990] *ECR* I-1439, also mentioned below under 4.4, and, obviously, in the field of State liability the *Francovich* judgment, joined cases C-6/90 and C-9/90 [1991] *ECR* I-5391, discussed below under 3.

9   There are situations in which the ECJ displays bold interpretation techniques also in regard to directive provisions, namely when those are, as in the field of equal treatment of men and women in the social field, based on fundamental Community concepts or freedoms. See for example in respect of social security W. van Gerven, W. Devroe and J. Wouters, Current Issues of Community Law concerning Equality of treatment between Women and Men in Social Security, in C. McCrudden (ed.) *Equality of treatment between Women and Men in Social Security* (1994) at pp. 7 *et seq.* For an example, see P.V.S and Cornwall County Council, case C-13/94 [1994] *ECR* I-2143.

10   Case C-441/93 [1996] *ECR* I-1347.

11   Directive 77/91 EEC of 13 December 1976 (*OJ* 1977 L 26, p. 1) concerning the formation of public limited liability companies, and the maintenance and alteration of their capital.

12   The square brackets have been added to make the quotation more intelligible.

aside arguments drawn from existing, or proposed, Community legislation in respect of credit institutions,[13] as well as on arguments relating to the cohesion of the national banking supervisory systems, which contain a closed system of provisions designed to preserve public confidence in the financial structure and to protect depositors. The Court did not even try, as it might have done when dealing with the interpretation of Treaty provisions, to weigh the underlying and conflicting interests of shareholders and depositors against each other.[14] Whatever the merit of the solution retained by the Court, the method of text adhering interpretation followed by the Court in that case seems typical for the Court's attitude when it is asked to interpret precise wording in directives or regulations. It is in sharp contrast to some of the Court's case-law relating to the interpretation of basic Treaty provisions and of general principles which the Court reads into, or deduces from, the general structure and features of the Community legal order.[15]

An example of the latter is the ECJ's judgment of 9 March 1999 in *Centros*,[16] where the Court interpreted Articles 52 [now 43] and 58 [now 48] EC as prohibiting a refusal of the Danish authorities to register, in Denmark, a branch of a company formed in the UK – even although the two Danish nationals having formed the UK company had acted with a view of escaping the more cumbersome Danish legislation governing the formation of companies. Indeed, the Danish administration's refusal was based on the consideration that the UK company would carry out none of its business in the UK, but all of it in Denmark through its Danish branch, and that, accordingly, it was set up intentionally to avoid Danish law. In its judgment, the Court first referred to the text of Articles 52 and 58 but then relied on the objectives of these Treaty provisions to distinguish between two kinds of evasion: on the one hand, evasion of company rules in one Member State by opting for the rules in another Member State – which is permissible, as it is inherent in the exercise of the freedom of establishment laid down in Article 52; and, on the other hand, evasion of rules concerning the carrying on of certain trades, professions and business, and/or concerning the protection of private or public creditors. In accordance with well-established case law of the Court, evasions of the latter kind can be relied on by a Member State, within certain conditions, to prevent private parties from using their freedom of establishment. The judgment is one in a long row of judgments giving a broad interpretation to the economic freedoms embodied in the EC Treaty, but at the same time offsetting, in a series of exceptions, that broad interpretation, thus trying to find a correct balance between the Community interest in a well-functioning internal market

---

13 Para. 27 *et seq.* of the judgment.
14 Para. 46 *et seq.* of the judgment. The defendants in the national proceedings specifically relied, as reported in para. 47, on the Court's judgments in Case C-204/90, *Bachmann* v. *Belgium* [1992] *ECR* I-249 and Case C-300/90, *Commission* v. *Belgium* [1992] *ECR* I-305 where the Court, dealing with the interpretation of fundamental EC Treaty provisions, has acknowledged the need to recognise the cohesion of a closed system of national rules in the field of taxation.
15 See further, W. van Gerven, "Community and National Legislators, Regulators, Judges, Academics and Practitioners: Living together apart" in *Law Making, Law Finding, and Law Shaping* (ed. Basil S. Markesinis), Oxford University Press, (1997), 13-41, at 21-32.
16 Case C-212/97,[1999] *ECR* I-1459. For a comment, see Pedro Cabral and Patrícia Cunha, "'Presumed innocent: companies and the exercise of the right of establishment under Community law," *European Law Review* (2000) 157-164.

(including the right for individuals to choose the Member State legislation that best suits their interests), and the interest of Member States to pursue legitimate interests through own legislation. At first sight the *Centros* judgment may look like an example of simple 'law-interpretation,' but that is only so because it built further on jurisprudence of the Court which itself constitutes evidence of the ECJ's creative reasoning.[17]

2 The Harmonising Effect of the ECJ Case-Law in the Field of Legal Remedies: Interim Relief in Factortame-I as an Example

An area of Community law where the ECJ has traditionally displayed a great deal of creativity concerns the requirement of effective judicial protection, and the remedies which must be made available by Member State courts to enable private plaintiffs to secure their Community rights. As a result of decisions of the Community courts, private plaintiffs now possess a number of remedies which they can bring before national courts. The most general one is, for a domestic court, to set aside national rules, whatever their nature or importance, if they are inconsistent with Community law and affect the rights which an individual derives from Community law. Other more specific remedies are the remedies of restitution, interim relief and compensation. I have described those remedies, and the impact they have on the national legal systems, on another occasion,[18] and will limit myself here to two well-known examples, of how decisions of the Community courts make significant inroads in the national laws of the Member States, one relating to interim relief and the other to compensation.

The first example concerns the *Factortame-I* judgement. In that decision the ECJ, replying to a preliminary question submitted by the House of Lords, ruled that the English courts were obliged to grant *interim relief* in a suit initiated by Spanish fishermen. The Spanish plaintiffs claimed that their Community rights were infringed by an Act of the UK Parliament which prohibited vessels, owned by non-British nationals, to fish in British waters.[19] Examining the claim, the English courts, including the House of Lords, found that under English law the plaintiffs could not obtain suspension of the Act, because of "the old common law rule that an interim injunction may not be granted against the Crown, that is to say against the government, in conjunction with the presumption that an Act of Parliament is in conformity with Community law until such time as a decision on its compatibility with the law has been given."[20] Once the House of Lord had obtained the ECJ's ruling, it immediately granted interim relief, pending the judgment of the ECJ as to substance, that is as to whether the British Act was inconsistent with the Spanish fishermen's right of establishment

---

17 On this long evolution, see P. Craig & De Bùrca, *EU Law*, third ed., Oxford University Press (2003) 765-824.

18 W. van Gerven "Of Rights, Remedies and Procedures, *Common Market Law Review* (2000) 501-536."

19 Case C-213/89, *Factortame* [1990] *ECR* I-2433.

20 Para. 23 of the judgment.

laid down in Art. 52 (now 43) EC. In *Factortame-II*,[21] the ECJ ruled that this was indeed the case, which led the Spanish fishermen to initiate claims in damages, again before the English courts, to obtain compensation from the UK government for injury sustained during the period between the enactment of the British Act and the grant of interim relief by the House of Lords (see *infra*, under 3.1).

In *Factortame I*, the legislation held to be inconsistent with Community law was *national legislation*. In a later judgment, *Zuckerfabrik*,[22] the ECJ was asked by a German court whether the remedy of interim relief should also be made available in a situation where a national administrative measure implementing a Community regulation was challenged before a national court, on the ground that the *Community regulation* itself was invalid for being in conflict with general principles of Community law. The Court held in that judgment that "the interim legal protection which Community law ensures for individuals before national courts must remain the same, irrespective of whether they contest the compatibility of national legal provisions with Community law or the validity of secondary Community law, in view of the fact that the dispute in both cases is based on Community law itself."[23] The ECJ did not, however, stop there: observing that the national legal orders grant interim relief under differing conditions, the Court underlines the need for securing the *uniform application* of Community law which is "a fundamental requirement of the Community legal order". Following that remark, the Court set out to describe the substantive conditions for granting interim relief which, in its view, must be equally applicable in all Member States, and thus be equally applied by all Member State courts. To do that, it took as a starting point the criteria which the Court itself uses when asked to suspend contested Community acts under Article 185 (now 242) EC, that is "if it considers that circumstances so require."[24] Taking that position, the Court was able to harmonise the two sets of Community based legal rules on interim relief: those governing interim relief before national courts (in matters involving Community law), and those governing interim relief before the Community courts themselves.

As mentioned, after *Factortame-I*, the *House of Lords* immediately ordered the effect of the contested Act of Parliament to be suspended.[25] The consequence of that jurisprudence was, however, that individuals deriving rights from Community law were, in the UK, better protected than individuals deriving rights from national law. Indeed, by virtue of Community law, an interim injunction could be granted, even against the Crown, when Community rights of individuals were in danger but not in

---

21 Case 221/89, *Factortame*, [1991] *ECR* I-3905. See also Case 246/89, *Commission v. UK*, [1991] *ECR* I-4585.

22 Joined cases C-143/88 and C-92/89, *Zuckerfabrik*, [1991] *ECR* I-415.

23 At para. 20. In the following paragraphs the Court pointed out that suspension may only be ordered if the national court is persuaded that "serious doubts exist as to the validity of the Community regulation" and provided that the suspension retains the character of an interim measure, meaning that it may apply "only until such time as the Court has delivered its ruling on the question of validity" (paragraphs 23 and 24).

24 The *Zuckerfabrik* ruling was confirmed by the ECJ in its *Atlanta* judgment, case C-465/93 [1995] *ECR* I-3761, where the Court indicated that measures of interim relief may also include positive action.

25 *Factortame v. Secretary of State* [1990] 3 CMLR 375 (HL, 11 October 1990).

purely national law matters, although in such cases the rights of individuals might be impaired as much. To remedy that "unhappy situation", in Lord Woolf's qualification, the *House of Lords*, in a later judgment, granted interim relief against the Crown also in purely English situations.[26] This is an interesting illustration of how the application of Community law may *spill over* to areas of national law not falling within the scope of Community law.

The foregoing shows: (i) that Community law may have the effect that crucial national rules which hinder the legal protection that individuals are entitled to under Community law must be disregarded by the national courts; (ii) that the ECJ may, in order to secure the uniform application of Community law, circumscribe the conditions under which a specific remedy, in that case interim relief, must be applied by the national courts; and (iii) that, for reasons of consistency, legal protection given to individuals by virtue of Community law, may be extended by the national courts to encompass infringements of individual rights in purely national situations.

3 The harmonisation of tort laws: Francovich and Brasserie jurisprudence; Courage and Crehan following Banks; the ECJ and the Product liability Directive

3.1 The Francovich and Brasserie Jurisprudence

A second, and even more important, application of the Community law requirement of effective judicial protection, concerns the remedy of compensation for harm caused to individuals by Member States infringing Community law. The *first* crucial step in that direction was taken by the ECJ in *Francovich* on 19 November 1991.[27] In that judgment, the Court recognised the principle of liability in tort against a Member State whose authorities had not implemented a directive *at all* – provided that the directive was intended to grant rights to individuals, that the contents of such rights could be determined on the basis of the directive, and that there was a causal link between the harm sustained by the plaintiff and the breach . In later judgments, the principle was confirmed, and applied to situations of directives being incompletely or incorrectly implemented in Member State legislation.[28]

A *second,* equally important, step was taken in *Brasserie and Factortame-III,*[29] in which two (joined) cases were decided in a preliminary ruling procedure. One case concerned claims for damage brought by French importers of beer before a German court, and the other concerned the Spanish fishermen's damage claims in the litigation, before the English courts, referred to in the preceding section. In its judgment the Court re-confirmed the principle of State liability, now however in the context of

---

26 In re *M.* v. *Home Office* [1993] 3 All ER 537.
27 Joined cases C-6/90 and 9/90 [1991] *ECR* I-5357.
28 Case C-334/92, *Wagner Miret* [1993] *ECR* I-6911; Case C-392/93, *British Telecommunications* [1996] *ECR* I-1631; Joined cases C-178/94, C-179/94, C-188/94, C-189/94 and C-190/94, *Dillenkofer* [1996] *ECR* I- 4845; Case C-127/95, *Norbrook Laboratories* [1998] *ECR* I- 1531.
29 Joined cases C-46/93 and C-48/93 [1996] *ECR* I-1029.

breaches of directly effective *Treaty* provisions, which had been committed by the legislature proper of a Member State. It also took the occasion to redefine the three substantive conditions for State liability to arise: (i) the Community rule of law infringed must be intended to confer rights on individuals, (ii) the breach must be sufficiently serious ('suffisamment caractérisée' in the French version), and (iii) there must be a causal link between the breach and the damage sustained by the injured parties.[30] Furthermore, the Court tried to flesh out these conditions, particularly the second one, with the help of rules which it found in its own case-law relating to Article 215 (now 288), paragraph 2, EC, concerning damage caused to individuals by Community institutions acting in breach of superior Community law. The case law in which the Court was interested, was that on the exercise of competences by the Council or the Commission involving choices of economic policy, that is in a context characterised by the exercise of wide discretion, which it now applied to the exercise of discretion by Member State authorities. As a result, the Court was here also in a position to harmonise the two Community extra-contractual liability regimes: the one for breaches committed by Community institutions, governed by Article 288, second paragraph, EC, and the one for breaches committed by national legislatures and authorities, governed by the 'Francovich' principle. Both regimes were subjected by the ECJ to the same rules – however, "in the absence of particular justification."[31] These are the rules which the ECJ is commissioned, by Art. 288, second paragraph EC, to find itself in the "general principles common to the laws of the Member States." In a more recent judgment in *Bergaderm*,[32] the ECJ has explicitly confirmed that development, in that case in the reverse situation, i.e. by using 'Francovich' case-law to flesh out 'Article 288' liability.

As a *third* step, the foregoing case law has been further elaborated in several judgments concentrating on such issues as the condition of causation and the scope of discretion left to the Members States to apply State liability, two issues which, in previous case law, had remained in the dark.[33] As for the first, the Court indicated that causality must be direct, and that liability of the State cannot be precluded by 'causality breaking' factors, such as the imprudent conduct of a third party against whose conduct the breached rule was intended to protect consumers, or the occurrence of exceptional and unforeseeable events. As for the second issue, the Court de-

---

30 Paragraphs 51-66.

21 *Brasserie/Factortame III, supra*, n. 27, paragraph 42.

32 Case C-352/98P [2000] *ECR* I-5291, paragraphs 39-44. On all of the foregoing, see further W. van Gerven, "The emergence of a common European law in the area of tort law: the EU contribution" in *Tort Liability of Public Authorities in comparative Perspective* (ed. Duncan Fairgrieve, Mads Andenas and John Bell), The British Institute of International and Comparative Law, 2002, 125-147.

33 Judgments relating to the first issue are: Case C-319/96 *Brinkmann Tabakfabriken* GmbH *v. Skatteministeriet* [1998] *ECR* I-5255, and Case C-140/97 *Rechberger and Griendl v. Austria* [1999] *ECR* I-3499. Judgments relating to the second issue are: Case C-302/97 *Konle v. Austria* [1999] *ECR* I-3099, and Case C-424/97 *Haim II* [2000] *ECR* I-5123. On all these judgments, and other issues, see Takis Tridimas, "Liability for Breach of Community law: Growing up and Mellowing down?", in *Tort Liability of Public Authorities in comparative Perspective, supra*, n. 32, 149-181, at 153-169. The last mentioned case concerns liability arising from acts of the administration where discretion is normally reduced or absent; see in that respect the earlier judgment in Case C-5/94, *Hedley Lomas* [1996] *ECR* I-2553.

cided that it is, in principle, for the national courts to apply the conditions under which State liability could arise, within, however, certain guidelines supplied by the Court, mainly with regard to the seriousness of the breach, and under the condition that the existence and the scope of discretion left to Member State authorities must be determined by reference to Community law, and not to national law.

The foregoing shows: (i) that national courts must disregard national rules which are incompatible with the conditions laid down by the ECJ for State liability to arise; (ii) that, accordingly, national rules which, in many Member States, make it impossible to institute an action in damages against the legislature proper, or which, in some countries, make adequate compensation of pure economic loss impossible, or difficult, will have to be set aside by the national courts; and (iii) that, depending on the willingness of the Community courts to spell out the substantive (State) liability conditions in a more detailed manner,[34] this case law may lead, in the field of tort liability of public authorities, to a growing degree of uniformity of Member State laws.[35]

3.2 *Courage* v. *Crehan*, (finally) Following Banks

All of the foregoing relates to the non-contractual liability of Member States under 'Francovich' and, in conjunction therewith, of Community institutions, under 'Article 288 EC. The question, essential for our subject of private law, has long been whether the ECJ would also regard it as an obligation for the Member States,[36] to make a remedy in compensation available to private parties for injury sustained as a consequence of breaches of Community law *committed by other private parties*. Obviously, that can only occur when breaches are involved of Community law provisions which impose directly enforceable obligations upon the latter The classical example thereof are obligations imposed by Articles 81 and 82 (ex 85 and 86) EC which prohibit enterprises from concluding cartel agreements, or abusing a dominant economic position. As described in the previous version of this contribution, the question came before the ECJ in *Banks* v. *British Coal Corporation* but was, for reasons particular to that case, not answered by the Court in its judgment of 13 April 1994.[37] If the question had then been answered in the affirmative, as the Advocate General (as I then

---

34 The expression 'substantive conditions' (as opposed to 'procedural conditions') which the Court uses, e.g. in *Francovich* in paragraph 43, relates, it would seem, to both the conditions imposed by the Court for liability to arise (cf. paragraph 40) and those for determining the (extent and kind of) reparation of loss and damage (cf. paragraph 43).

35 See further my article quoted *supra*, n. 32, at 134-140 with regard to the possibility of uncovering general principles which Member State laws have in common, and, with regard to the concept of serious breach, my earlier article on "Bridging the unbridgeable: Community and national tort laws after *Francovich* and *Brasserie*," *International and Comparative Law Quarterly* (1996), 520-544.

36 An obligation that is not just a possibility, to the extent that the applicable national tort rules would allow such liability.

37 Case C-128/92 [1994] *ECR* I-1209. The reason why the ECJ did not answer the question then, is because the case related to the competition Arts. 65 and 66 of the European Coal and Steel Community Treaty (which, concluded for 50 years, has in the meantime expired) and because the ECJ was of the opinion that those articles were not directly applicable, contrary to the corresponding Arts. 85 and 86 EC.

was) encouraged the Court to do,[38] the ECJ would also have been brought, in the absence of Community legislation, to lay down, as it has done for State liability, the substantive law conditions for liability to arise between private parties. That would have meant that harmonisation of the Member States' private tort laws would have started then.

It was only in a judgment of 20 September 2001 that the ECJ had to tackle the question again, that is in *Courage* v. *Crehan,* a case relating to an exclusive dealing agreement between a pub tenant and a brewer.[39] In that case (relating to a contractual arrangement), Advocate General Mischo expressed the opinion that the direct effect of Article 81 EC in relations between private persons is "to include (…) the right, for individuals, to be protected from the harmful effects which an agreement which is automatically void may create", adding – putting the case in a broader (also extra-contractual) context – that "(T)he individuals who can benefit from such protection are, of course, primarily third parties, that is to say consumers and competitors who are adversely affected by a prohibited agreement".[40] The Court came to the same conclusion: recalling that Article 81 EC, like Article 82 EC, constitutes a fundamental provision for the functioning of the internal market, and that it produces direct effects in relations between individuals and creates rights for individuals which national courts must safeguard, it concludes, as regards the principle of liability, that "(t)he full effectiveness of Article 8[1] of the Treaty and, in particular, the practical effect of the prohibition laid down [in the first paragraph thereof] would be put at risk if it were not open to any individual to claim damages for loss caused to him by contract or by conduct liable to restrict or distort competition".[41]

The judgment is of crucial importance for the development of common principles of both contractual and non-contractual liability between private persons. Indeed, in subsequent decisions the Court will undoubtedly be required to flesh out the principle of "private law" liability, as has already happened to some extent in *Courage* v. *Crehan* itself. Asked by the referral court (the English Court of Appeal) concerning the possibility *for a contracting party* to the prohibited agreement to ask for damages, the ECJ answered that there should not "be any absolute bar to such an action,"[42] thus obliging the UK, and by the same token other Member States, to provide a remedy for compensation, in contract or in tort, between the contracting parties. That does not mean that the remedy must be identical in all Member States. Indeed, as the Court added, its ruling should not prevent a national legal system, subject to the principles of equivalence (between Community and national claims) and of effectiveness (not making claims practically impossible or excessively difficult), "from taking steps that the protection of the rights guaranteed by Community law does not entail the unjust enrichment of those who enjoy them."[43] Nor does it preclude national law "from de-

---

38 See the Opinion in *Banks*, *ECR* I-1212, paragraphs 43 ff.
39 Case C-453/99, [2001] *ECR* I- 6297. For a comment, see A.P. Komninos, "New Prospects for private enforcement of EC Competition law: Courage v. Crehan and the Community right to damages," *Common Market Law Review* (2002), 447-487.
40 Opinion at [2001] *ECR* I-6300, para. 37 and 38.
41 Para. 26 of the judgment.
42 Para. 28 of the judgment.
43 Para. 29 and 30.

nying a party who is found to bear responsibility for the distortion of competition the right to obtain damages from the other contracting party" for which the Court refers to "a principle which is recognised in most of the legal systems of the Member States and which the Court has applied in the past," according to which "a litigant should not profit from his own unlawful conduct, where this is proven."[44] In other words, Member States may, within the limits of the principles of equivalence and minimal effectiveness, frame the remedy differently, taking account of their own legal system's general principles. Nevertheless, even then the Court (as is did in State liability case law) offers, in the following paragraphs, some precise guidelines as to which elements a national court should take into consideration to apply the aforementioned principles in line with the ECJ's understanding of Community law.[45]

When asked in later decisions to flesh out the principle of liability of private parties for breaches of Community law, it is not at all unlikely that the Court will, at least in instances of non-contractual liability, that is when an infringement is complained of by a *third party*, e.g. a competitor[46] – draw inspiration from its earlier case law concerning State and Community institutions liability (ie. 'Francovich' and 'Article 288, para. 2, EC' case law). Actually, in *Courage* v. *Crehan,* the Court referred to its earlier case law, with regard to the aforementioned principles of unjust enrichment, and of not letting a defendant draw profit from his/her own unlawful conduct.[47] Obviously, for some issues such inspiration will come more easily than for others. For example, with regard to the condition of 'sufficiently serious breach', the case law with regard to public authorities possessing wide discretion will hardly be appropriate to serve as a model for assessing breaches of Articles 81 and 82 EC. Indeed, those are Treaty provisions which contain precise prohibitions and, in light of extensive case law of both Community courts, leave almost no discretion (other than 'interpretative' discretion) to undertakings participating in anti-competitive conduct.[48] In other words, in such a situation, the (particularly) 'Article 288' case law dealing with large policy discretion, cannot be used as a source of inspiration. In such a situation, it will be sufficient for liability to arise, that three conditions are fulfilled: (i) unlawful conduct existing in a breach of Article 81 or 82 EC;[49] (ii) the existence of actual damage sustained by the plaintiff, whether a contracting party or a third party; and (iii) a direct causation between the illegality and the damage. Contrariwise, with

---

44 Para. 30-31.
45 Para. 33-35.
46 It is clear from para. 26 of the judgment, as quoted above in the text accompanying n. 77, that "any individual" may claim in damages.
47 See the quotations to, *inter alia.*, Case 238/78 *Ireks-Arkady* [1979] *ECR* 2955, para. 14 (first principle named in the text, referring to Art. 288 (ex 215)) and Case 39/72 *Commission/Italy* [1973] *ECR* 101, para. 10 (second principle, referring to Art. 226 (ex 169) EC).
48 The Courage/Crehan judgment relates to a breach of Art. 81 EC. It is not unlikely, and on the contrary very probable, that in later cases breaches will concern other EC Treaty provisions which the ECJ has held also have *horizontal* direct effect (e.g. Art. 39 (ex 48) EC on free movement of workers: see case C-281/98, *Angonese,* [2000] *ECR* I-4139). Also in such instances Treaty provisions are concerned which have been so often interpreted in earlier case law that little scope for interpretation is left to the persons obliged to comply.
49 In para. 35 of the *Courage* v. *Crehan* judgment the ECJ points out that the conditions for application of Art. 81 (or 82) must not necessarily be the same as for certain civil law consequences to apply.

regard to the concepts of causation and damages, and the duty of reparation, guidance can surely be drawn from the ECJ's case law on liability of public authorities, since these concepts will tend to work out the same way in public and in private tort matters.[50]

3.3 Case Law Relating to the Product Liability Directive

So far we have discussed the impact of ECJ case-law on national tort law (mainly), as a result of judge-made liability rules for breaches of Community legal rules by Member States ('Francovich'-liability), Community Institutions (Art. 288, paragraph 2, EC), and their civil servants, or private parties ('Courage/Crehan' liability). As indicated above (*supra*, under 1), the Court's boldness in interpreting Treaty provisions and general principles when judicial protection of individuals is at stake, is in stark contrast to the Court's more cautious approach when it comes to the interpretation of provisions of directives, at least those which do not implement fundamental Community law concepts (but see *infra*, under 4.4). It is therefore interesting to see which role the ECJ plays in the interpretation of directive provisions in liability matters, such as Council Directive 85/374 EEC of 25 July 1985 on product liability.

It has taken some time before litigation concerning the Product Liability Directive came before the Court. Even now, the number of cases decided by the Court remains limited.[51] One important judgment related to the so-called 'product liability risk defence'-clause laid down in Article 7(e). That clause allows the producer to escape liability if "the state of scientific and technical knowledge at the time when he put the product into circulation, was not such as to enable the existence of the defect to be discovered."[52] The Court interpreted the provision to refer to general knowledge at the most advanced level, to be understood in an objective way, that is knowledge of which the producer is presumed to have been informed, provided it was accessible at the time the product was put into circulation. Another judgment[53] concerned the interpretation of Article 7 (a) and (c) and related to the question whether using a defective perfusion fluid prepared in a municipal hospital, and used in another in the course of a kidney transplantation, must be regarded as "a product put into circulation;" and whether, taking into account that both hospitals were entirely financed from public funds, the product was distributed "for economic purpose" and "in the course of ... business." The Court answered both questions in the affirmative. In the same judgment, the Court also interpreted the notion 'damage' in Article 9 of the Directive in a rather ambiguous way. To be sure, all of these are sensible interpretations of directive provisions, but, because of the technicality of the provisions, are not 'breath-taking' ones seen from a viewpoint of European private law in the making. In other words, they have not much in common with the principled approach of the ECJ in *Factortame* or *Francovich*. Moreover, as I have pointed out elsewhere, the neces-

---

50 See further my article referred to *supra*, n. 32, at 143-144.
51 On the Directive, *OJ* No. L 210/29 of 7 August 1985, and the case law relating thereto, see Geraint Howells contribution to this book.
52 See Case C-300/95, *Commission v. UK* [1997] *ECR* I-2649 concerning the alleged defective implementation of Art. 7 (e) of the Directive by the UK (allegation denied).
53 Case C-203/99, *Henning Veedfald* [2001] *ECR* I-3569.

sity for Member States, and their courts, to transpose the directive in their national law, contains the risk of 're-nationalisation' of the directive, rather than to promote the effectiveness of Community law, as those other cases do.[54]

4   The Harmonisation of Contract Laws: Mainly Through 'Directive-Related' Case-Law of the Court

4.1   Reasons for a Lesser Impact of ECJ Case Law on Contract Law than on Tort Law

In the earlier version of this article, I suggested two reasons why the impact of the case-law of the ECJ on contract law would be less than its impact on tort law. The *first* was, and remains, that the Court is not commissioned by the Community treaties, as it is in respect of non-contractual liability of Community institutions (and their civil servants), to develop rules on contractual liability "in accordance with the general principles common to the laws of the Member States" (art. 288, paragraph 2, EC). On the contrary, matters of contractual liability of the Community – for which the ECJ may have jurisdiction "pursuant to (an) arbitration clause ..."(Art. 238 EC) – "shall be governed by the law applicable to the contract in question" (Art. 288, paragraph 1, EC). Obviously, the Commission, which is normally the contracting party on behalf of the Community, could have tried to agree with the other contracting parties to designate general principles of *contract* law "common to the laws of the Member States" as the applicable law, leaving it to the ECJ to find these principles. It has been its practice, instead, to designate the national law of the Member State where the contract is concluded.

The *second* reason mentioned in the previous edition of this book, was that, at first sight, it is hard to visualise a situation that would have led the ECJ to define a general principle of *contractual* liability for reasons of legal protection of Community rights, as the Court has done in its 'Francovich' jurisprudence with regard to the non-contractual (State) liability. For the Court to do that, it should have been confronted with a situation where a remedy was needed to secure contractual rights which a private party would derive from Community law against a Member State, or public authority. That would suppose a situation where a Member State would, for example, have failed to perform under a contract which that Member State had concluded with an individual by virtue of Community law, and to which Community principles (instead of national law) would have been applicable, a situation which is not easy to imagine. However, as explained above, after *Courage* v. *Crehan*, the situation has changed insofar as that now, by virtue of Community law, Member States must make available a remedy in compensation in private relations, that is, between contracting parties, and on behalf of third parties, who have sustained damage as a result of breaches of Community law provisions which impose direct obligations upon a private party. The obvious example is a breach of Article 81 EC, as in *Cour-*

---

54 On this point, and on others, see further my article, referred to *supra* n. 32, with further references.

age v. *Crehan*, or for that matter Article 82, but the same may hold true with regard to Treaty provisions, such as Articles 49 (free services) or 141 (equal pay for men and women) EC, which the Court has recognised as having direct horizontal effect, *and* with regard to regulations (not directives, which so far lack horizontal direct effect) imposing direct obligations upon individuals, and granting corresponding rights to other individuals.

The upshot of the judgment may therefore be that, in subsequent case law, the Court would spell out rules, or give guidelines to national courts, for the uniform application in the Member States of such remedy of compensation, in contract and/or in tort. And, of course, situations may present themselves where other remedies are involved, such as restitution, or interim relief, besides rules regarding nullity, inapplicability or ineffectiveness of contractual provisions (see *infra*, 4.4) that are inconsistent with Community law. The most appropriate way to provide such remedies would obviously be, as I have suggested elsewhere in connection with the application of Articles 81 and 82 EC, that the Community legislature takes the initiative to lay down uniform 'remedial' and 'procedural' rules, but it is unlikely that this would occur in the near future – the Member States seemingly not being ready for it.[55]

4.2 Incremental Nature of Court Interferences with National Contract Law

When one looks through the registers of the ECJ's case-law, references to contractual principles do not seem to be absent. Thus, for example, the duty to cooperate, the principles of legal certainty and of legitimate expectations, the concepts of *force majeure*, legitimate defence and reasonableness, the maxim *nemo auditur*, and even abuse of rights can be found. Looking up the relevant judgments one finds, however, that these principles either relate to international obligations of the Community, or to institutional obligations between Member States or Community institutions, or to principles of administrative law applicable to the dealings of Community institutions with individual enterprises or citisens.[56]

That does not mean that private law concepts never arise in Community law, but when they do it is in a particular context. An example is where, in Article 81 EC the term 'agreement' is used – in the sense of a private law contract concluded between undertakings – within the framework of the prohibition on cartels, in combination with the terms "decisions by associations of undertakings and concerted practices". There is, indeed, a substantial body of case-law of the ECJ, and the CFI, defining the notion of agreement (or contract), mainly in an effort to delineate the scope of the prohibition of Article 81, and to distinguish between 'agreements' and 'concerted

---

55 See W. van Gerven, "Substantive remedies for the private Enforcement of EC Antitrust Rules before National Courts" in *European Competition Law Annual 2001, Effective Private Enforcement of EC Antitrust Law* (ed. C.D. Ehlermann and I. Atanasiu), Hart Publishing (2002), –. Also published in *Modernisation of European Competition Law* (ed. J. Stuyck and H. Gilliams), Intersentia (2002), 93-136. In annex to the article, I added a proposed draft regulation.

56 See, however, for an exception, the *Pafitis* judgment quoted *supra*, n. 10, where the notion of abuse of rights is considered by the ECJ, at the request of the referring Greek court, in a private law context (paragraphs 67-70).

practices'. The issues resolved therein concern the question of which forms of consent between the contracting parties are deemed to be agreements (rather than, perhaps, concerted practices), raising questions such as, whether exchanges of letters, circular letters, general conditions, so-called 'gentlemen's agreements", verbal agreements, unilateral acts taken within the framework of an agreement, are 'agreements' in the sense of Article 81 EC.[57] The problem with these court interpretations is that they are given, as they should be, in a context of determining whether the agreement is restrictive of competition. In other words, the interpretation is made with regard to the aim which Article 81 pursues in the context of the EC-Treaty provisions on the establishment and functioning of a genuine common market. Being a 'functional' interpretation, it cannot serve as a model when it comes to define the concepts in the context of contract law in general.[58]

Apart from Article 81 case law, and leaving aside for the moment decisions relating to specific consumer contracts, the impact of ECJ case law is limited to specific interferences with national contract law, on the basis of one or another general principle of Community law. A few examples are as follows. First, a judgment, *Dekker* v. *Stichting voor Jong Volwassenen,* in which the Court ruled that an employer's *refusal to employ* a woman on grounds of her pregnancy, constituted unlawful sex discrimination, in the sense of the Equal Treatment Directive 76/207.[59] Article 6 of that Directive requires Member States to introduce measures allowing a person who is the victim of unequal treatment, to pursue his/her claim by judicial process. Although each Member States has the freedom to choose the sanction to penalise an infringement, it may, where it opts for a sanction forming part of the rules on civil liability, not apply those rules to the extent that they make the victim's claim subject to a requirement of fault, or to a defence of justification, on the part of the defendant, as a result of which no full redress is guaranteed to the plaintiff. Whilst the former judgment concerns the freedom to contract, the second, *Marleasing SA* v. *La Commercial Internacionale de Alimentacion SA,* concerns the *conditions required to conclude* a valid contract.[60] The decision is well known: it related to the interpretation of the first Company law Directive which did not include 'lack of cause' as a ground of nullity of a company. The Court was asked by a Spanish Court whether the defendant company could nevertheless be declared null and void on the basis of provisions of the

---

57 See further P. Craig and De Bùrca, *EU Law,* third. ed. (2003), 940-943.
58 The same holds true for the concept of contract or agreement used in European private international law as laid down in the Brussels Convention on Jurisdiction and the Recognition and Enforcement of Judgments, now replaced by Council Regulation 44/2001, and in the Rome Convention on the law applicable to contractual obligations. See further Hans-W. Micklitz, "Der Vertragsbegriff in den Übereinkommen von Brüssel und Rom" in *Europäisches Vertragsrecht im Gemeinschaftsrecht* (eds H. Schulte-Nölke & R. Schulze), Band 22, Schriftenreihe ERA Trier, Bundesanzeiger (2002), 39-94. To give one example only, see the judgment in Case C-26/91, *Jakob Handle* v. *TMCS* [1992] *ECR* I-3967 where the Court held that the concept of obligations resulting from a contract in Art. 5 (1) of the Brussels Convention must construed as an autonomous concept in light of the system and the objectives of the Convention, that is as an exception to the general rule laid down in Art. 2 (1). On the basis thereof the Court decided that proceedings by a sub-purchaser of goods against the manufacturer may not be regarded as contractual.
59 Case C-177/88 [1990] *ECR* I-3941.
60 Case C-106/89, [1990] *ECR* I- 4135.

Spanish Civil code invalidating contracts that have an illicit cause. The Court answered the question in the negative, holding that the national court was obliged to interpret national law, even when predating the directive, as far as possible in light of the wording and the purpose of the directive. Since the directive enumerates the grounds of nullity of companies falling under it in a limitative way, the 'illicit cause' provision of the Civil Code was, if at all possible, to be construed accordingly.

In yet another judgment, *Unilever Italia SpA* v. *Central Food SpA*,[61] the ECJ held that Italian food labelling rules which had not been notified to the Commission in accordance with Directive 83/189, although they were of a nature to hinder interstate trade in a product, could not be applied by the Italian court, because violation of the notification requirement had made the Italian rules ineffective. As a result, the refusal on the part of the purchaser to accept and pay goods not labelled in accordance with the Italian rules, must normally be dismissed by the national court. It appears from this that, although horizontal direct effect of directives is not recognised by the ECJ, failure of a State not to comply with a directive may nevertheless have an impact on the national rules relating to *performance of contracts* between individuals.[62] In another case, *Bacardi-Martini*, a question of a third party *interfering with a contract* between others was brought before the Court (but was not decided by it because the preliminary reference was held inadmissible).[63] The case concerned a contract between Newcastle United and Dorna pursuant to which Dorna was appointed to sell and display advertisements at football matches. Dorna had agreed to sell advertising space to Bacardi-Martini but, when Newcastle found out that the match would be broadcast in France where such advertising was prohibited, it requested Dorna to remove the advertisement. Bacardi-Martini brought an action for damages against Newcastle claiming that Newcastle's interference with the contract could not be justified on the basis of French legislation which, in its view, was incompatible with Article 49 EC (freedom of services). Unfortunately, since the Court declined to answer the preliminary question, the issue remained unresolved. If the Court had decided the case either way, its decision would obviously have had an impact on the application of contract law.

The foregoing judgments show the incremental impact of ECJ case law on contract law. They indicate that one should not expect too much from the ECJ for the harmonisation of that branch of the law. The situation may be different for consumer law; however, not because of the ECJ but because of the large number of legislative acts that have been enacted in that area which, if viewed as a whole, would offer a comprehensive body of legislation that can give rise to 'cross-directive' interpretation on the part of the ECJ.[64]

---

61 Case C-443/98 [2000] *ECR* I-7535.

62 See Stephen Weatherill, "Breach of directives and breach of contract," *European Law Review* (2001), 177-186.

63 *Supra*, n. 7.

64 For a coherent overview, see the book referred to *supra*, n. 58 on *Europäisches Vertragsrecht im Gemeinschaftsrecht* where various directives are grouped, and discussed, under headings of contract law, by a group of expert authors.

4.3 'Cross-Directive' Interpretation of Consumer Law?

Re-arranging, improving and completing Community consumer law is the aim under-lying the Commission's *Green Paper on Consumer Protection* published in October 2001.[65] It is a well structured document which describes the present state of protection, outlines alternatives for the future direction and the issues involved, and analyses the methods of enforcement. Its general purpose is to examine how consumer regulation can facilitate easy access of consumers to goods and services promoted, offered and sold across the borders. (2.1) It observes that present Community legislation contains only a few generally applicable directives, in addition to numerous directives containing rules for specific sectors or selling methods. Accordingly, in important areas where no Community regulation exists so far – notably in the areas of marketing practices, contract related practices, payment and after-sales services (2.2) – only national regulation applies, with considerable differences in substance and application from Member State to Member State. To be sure, many Member States have a general legal principle, sometimes supported by specific laws, for regulating business-consumer commercial practices. (2.3) But in that respect also there are important differences which tend to become even more important with the growth of 'new economy' commercial practices which are unforeseen by existing specific rules but already caught by general principles and treated in different ways (*ibid*). As for the *future* direction that consumer law should take, and in line with the "away from detail and over-regulatory" approach – that is, in line with the 'mutual recognition' approach as applied to goods since the late 1980s – the Commission now favours a so-called 'mixed approach' of comprehensive (not piecemeal) regulation laid down in a framework directive,[66] supplemented by targeted directives where necessary, and leaving room for "formal stakeholder participation in the regulatory process." (3.4) The general framework directive would be based on a general clause drawing on existing legal models based on 'fair commercial practices' or 'good market behaviour' (4.1) or, in a more limited version, on a concept of 'misleading and deceptive practices.' (4.2)

It is not the place here to discuss this issue any further. It may suffice to say that improving the 'acquis communautaire' in the area of consumer law, and in other areas of Community law relating to contract law,[67] is a much desirable enterprise, as it would complement the abstract formulation of (binding, or not binding) general principles, by applying them to concrete areas where value judgments have to be made between the freedom to contract and the protection of weaker parties. However, to make the undertaking compatible with codification from a general viewpoint of comparative law, as a restatement of general principles aims to be, it should be under-

---

65 COM (2001) 531 final. See further in this book, the contribution of Carla Joustra.
66 The "mutual recognition approach" is typical for goods and relates more particularly to technical standards. It is based on the recognition of the rules in the country of origin of the goods. As such it cannot be applied to contract law where, according to a general principle of private international law, the contracting parties are free to choose their own law with regard to non-mandatory rules whereas for mandatory consumer contract rules the law of the country of the consumer's domicile is normally applicable. This is why the Commission opts for a so-called 'mixed approach.'
67 See in this book the list of legislation in attach to Peter-Christian Müller-Graff's contribution.

taken in a broader perspective than promoting the internal market – that is, without subjecting consumer protection, from the very outset, to a an 'external' objective. It would, moreover, also be desirable to include in the operation not only the 'acquis communautaire' of existing directives (and regulations), but also the 'acquis communautaire' of national rules which, over the years, have implemented the directives in the Member States The latter would, however, make the undertaking too difficult to succeed, and may, unfortunately enough, therefore have to be omitted.[68]

Having said all this, and returning to the subject of this contribution, ECJ case law would surely be more effective, from a viewpoint of coherent and uniform application, if the Court were to take the habit of dealing with consumer law litigation from a more comprehensive viewpoint, that is viewing any specific directive within the broader context of consumer legislation as a whole. That would enable the Court to use a less textual and more teleological method of interpretation – where its strength lies. A case in point could have been the Court's judgment in *Océano Grupo Editorial SA* dealing with the interpretation of Article 3, paragraphs 1 and 3, and Article 6, paragraph 1, of Council Directive 93/13/EEC of 5 April 1993.[69]

The issue turned around a contract for the purchase by instalments of an encyclopaedia for personal use. The contract contained a term conferring jurisdiction on the courts in Barcelona – a city in which none of the Spanish purchasers were domiciled but where the seller had its principal place of business. The purchasers did not pay the sums due on the agreed dates, and actions were brought against them in Barcelona. The court in Barcelona asked the ECJ whether the exclusive jurisdiction clause, "included in a contract without having been individually negotiated," must be regarded as unfair within the meaning of Article 3 of the Directive. The ECJ answered in the affirmative, adding, in conformity with its *Marleasing* judgment (*supra*, under 4.2), that the national court was obliged, when it applies national law provisions predating or postdating the Directive, to interpret those provisions so far as possible in the light of the wording and purpose of the Directive. According to the ECJ, that meant in the concrete case that the national court needed to "favour the interpretation that would allow it to decline of its own motion the jurisdiction conferred on it by virtue of an unfair term."[70] The case could have offered the ECJ an opportunity to resolve a question of general interest for consumer law, as I will try to point out below.

4.4 Boldness of Purpose Re-Discovered?

In the earlier version of this article, I have taken Article 3, paragraph 1, of the Directive as an example to support my opinion that, if the ECJ were called upon to interpret that provision, it would not go beyond the text of the provision. I expressed the opinion, more particularly, that the Court would not rely on some analysis of the con-

---

68 On all these points, see my article referred to *supra*, n. 2.
69 On unfair terms in consumer contracts, *OJ* 1993 L 95/29. The judgment was rendered on 27 June 2000 in Joined Cases C-240/98 to C-244/98 [2000] *ECR* I-4941.
70 Dispositivum under 2.

cept of *good faith* referred to in Article 3, and elaborated in the preamble to the Directive. Article 3, paragraph 1, treats a not individually negotiated contractual term as unfair "if, contrary to the requirement of good faith, it causes a significant imbalance in the parties' rights and obligations arising under the contract, to the detriment of the consumer."[71] From the wording of the article, it is not clear whether the requirement of good faith constitutes a condition which comes in addition to that of significant imbalance, or whether it aims only at putting the latter condition in a wider perspective. In the earlier version of this article, I opted for the latter, taking into account the preamble, where the requirement of good faith is stated to amount to "an overall evaluation of the interests involved," and where it is specified that "in making an assessment of good faith, particular regard shall be had to the strength of the bargaining position of the parties, whether the consumer had an inducement to agree to the term and whether the goods or services were sold or supplied to the special order of the consumer." All these are factors which do no more than explain whether, in a concrete case, a contract may have given rise to, in the wording of Article 3, paragraph 1, "a significant imbalance ... to the detriment of the consumer." They are not of a nature to turn the reference to good faith into an independent criterion, as is also made clear by the following statement in the preamble: "whereas the requirement of good faith *may* (sic) be satisfied by the seller or supplier where he deals fairly and equitably with the other party whose legitimate interests he has to take into account." To be sure, dealing fairly and equitably is the correct benchmark, but it does not add much from a conceptual viewpoint.

In this article's earlier version, I expressed the opinion that the ECJ, or its Advocate-General, having read Article 3 and the preamble, would probably not go much further, for example by requesting the Court's research department to prepare a comparative study on the 'good faith' requirement in the Member State legal systems. Such a study would certainly have been helpful, as it is sufficiently well known that the meaning which legal systems attach to good faith vary from one extreme to another,[72] and that it could help the Court, if a case were brought before it, to find a common denominator. Now that Article 3, paragraph 1, has come before the Court, my 'prophecy' became true: neither Advocate General Saggio nor the Court devoted, in *Océano,* any attention to the concept of good faith, and limited themselves to recalling the wording of the Directive provision. Both accepted, though, that the exclusive jurisdiction clause is unfair because of the imbalance between, on the one hand, the inconvenience which the clause entails for the purchasers whose presence in court

---

71 In the Annex to the Directive there is a list of examples of unfair contract terms which, however, are not binding. They are an illustration of the unwillingness of the Council to move towards a greater harmonisation of contract law, even in the field of consumer contracts, particularly when compared with the earlier drafts of the directive: see T. Wilhelmsson, *Social Contract law and European Integration*, 1994, at pp. 93 *et seq.*

72 Under Dutch and Belgian law three different functions are assigned to the concept of good faith in relation to the text of a contract: the interpretative, the supplementing and the derogating function. Under English and Scandinavian law, the requirement of good faith is said not to be part of contract law. For English law, see J. Beatson and D. Friedmann, "Introduction: 'From 'Classical' to Modern Contract law' in Beatson and Friedmann, ed., *Good Faith and Fault in Contract Law* (1995) pp. 14-15 from which it appears that English law nevertheless offers specific solutions based on a concept of unfairness.

may be rendered too onerous, due to geographic distance, especially in litigation involving small claims, and, on the other hand, the advantage which the clause represents for the seller who can concentrate all claims before the same court.[73] I do not take issue with the Court on this point: 'good faith' is a useful concept as long as it remains sufficiently flexible,[74] and the conclusion which the Court and its Advocate General reach, that is. that the clause is unfair, would seem to be correct.

I have more difficulty, however, with the Court's line of reasoning on the issue of whether a national judge may decline the unfair jurisdiction clause of its *own motion*. On this matter, the ECJ is much more forthcoming (as is its Advocate General), in that the Court bases its reasoning on the *aim* of Article 6, paragraph 1, of the Directive. That provision requires Member States to lay down that unfair terms "are not binding on the consumers" adding, however, that the contract will remain binding "between the parties ... if it can subsist without the unfair terms." The Court is of the opinion that such aim would not be achieved if the consumers were themselves "obliged to raise the unfair nature of such terms. In disputes where the amounts involved are often limited, the lawyers' fees may be higher that the amount at stake, which may deter the consumer from contesting the application of an unfair term."[75] Moreover, the Court adds in the following sentence, that although the procedural law of a number of Member States allows parties to defend themselves in litigation involving small amounts of money, the risk exists that the consumer, because of ignorance, would not raise the unfairness of the clause. It follows, in the opinion of the Court, that "effective protection of the consumer may be attained only if the national court acknowledges that it has the power to evaluate terms of this kind of its own motion."[76]

In its reasoning, the Court seems to have re-discovered, in matters dealt with in directives, the boldness of interpretation which has been its trademark in landmark cases such as the ones discussed previously (*supra*, 2 and 3). What gives me difficulty is not in the first place that boldness but, with due respect, the weakness of the Court's reasoning. Indeed, for the Court to base its reasoning on precise (and undocumented) considerations relating to the amount of lawyers' fees, is not a particularly strong argument. Nor is it a strong argument to refer to the risk of the consumer's presumed reluctance to raise the unfairness argument – as if that is not the first thing a defendant consumer will think of, particularly when he or she, in the (also presumed) absence of a lawyer, is asked appropriate questions by the judge (which is not the same as raising the defence *motu proprio*).

However, the weakest point in the Court's reasoning in my opinion is its failure to base its decision on firmer conceptual ground. This would be to not make any attempt to contrast, or to compare, the 'non binding' sanction which the Directive requires the Member States to impose, with the nullity sanction provided for in Article 81 (2) EC,

---

73 Paragraphs 22-24 of the judgment.
74 See in the same sense Fernando Martinez Sanz, "Good faith of the parties" in the book referred to *supra*, n. 58, at 127-138.
75 Paragraph 26, with additional arguments in the same paragraph and in the following paragraphs 27-28.
76 Paragraph 29.

of which the Court has stated, in *Eco Swiss*,[77] that a national court can apply it of its own motion. In that case the Court justified its ruling, however, by referring to the fundamental character of the provision of Article 81 which is *essential* for the functioning of the internal market (see also *Courage/Crehan, supra* 3.2) – which is surely in the first place a more fundamental objective, in the hierarchy of the EC Treaty, than "to promote the interests of consumers and to ensure a high level of consumer protection," however important, that is. As appears from Article 153 (1) EC, "[t]he Community shall contribute" to consumer protection (*ibid.*, at (3)), but does not bear prime responsibility for it (which remains with the Member States), as it does for the maintenance of a system of undistorted competition.

At first sight, this comparison could have led to a rejection of the 'own motion' character of the 'non-binding' sanction of the Directive, which means that the ECJ should, at least, have better justified why the sanction – which is to protect private parties' interests, rather than public policy[78] – can nevertheless be invoked by the judge at his own motion, for which the Court could have resorted to the 'balancing test' underlying its judgment in *Van Schijndel*.[79] In other words, the issue deserved a better treatment in the Court's judgment, and could have given rise to a discussion of private law sanctions in a broader perspective of consumer and competition law.[80] Such a broader analysis was also commendable for other reasons: first, because the 'non binding' sanction is also used in other directives thus in Article 7(1) of the important Sale of Consumer Goods and Associated Guarantees Directive 1999/44,[81] and, second, because there is a risk that the sanction be interpreted in the Member States in very different ways, at the expense of the requirement of uniform interpretation in an area as important as private enforcement.[82]

5   To Conclude

Harmonisation by means of Community law, through legislation or case law, has a bright side (convergence between Member State laws in certain limited areas) and a dark side (disruption, within each Member State, of areas of the law which were previously united). That is so because the European Community (or Union for that matter), and their institutions, have only limited powers in certain areas of the law, mainly for interstate, or cross-border, matters. Harmonisation through legislation of the Community legislature, or case law of the ECJ, occurs therefore in a piecemeal manner. In matters of private law, tort rules have been more affected than any others by case law of the ECJ and the CFI law. The reason for that is, that it is mainly

---

77 Case C-126/97 [1999] *ECR* I-3055, paragraph 36.

78 But see A.G.Saggio's Opinion, at paragraph 25.

79 See my contribution referred to in n. 18.

80 For a discussion of the non-binding sanction, see M.Teneiro, "The Community 0-283.directive on unfair terms and national legal systems; Principle of good faith and Remedies for unfair terms," *European Review of Private Law* (1995), 273 ff. at 282.

81 *OJ* 1999 L 171/12. For a comment of Art. 7, see W.van Gerven and S. Stijns in *EU Sales Directive, Commentary* (eds. Massimo Bianca and S. Grundmann), 235-266.

82 See in that regard also AG Saggio's Opinion, at paragaph 25, n. 11.

through tort law, that Community rights of individuals have been protected as a result of the remedy to claim compensation from Community or Member State authorities that have breached Community law and, in the process, have caused damage to individuals. Consequently, there is a large body of ECJ (and CFI) case law laying down the conditions of non-contractual liability under either Article 288 (2) EC, or the *Francovich* doctrine, and, in connection with that, following *Factortame*, there is also case law providing in a remedy of interim relief against public authorities threatening to violate individual Community rights. Moreover, in a more recent decision, that is in *Courage v. Crehan*, the ECJ has also recognised the liability of private parties, contractually or non-contractually, for (in that case, restitutionary) damages caused as a result of infringements of Community law. This applies, however, only when provisions are at issue which impose direct legal obligations upon private defendants, as in the case of Articles 81 and 82 EC.

In all those matters – which normally come before the ECJ through references by national courts under Article 234 EC – the ECJ has used its judicial power in a creative way. But that is not true, or less so, in contractual matters because, with the exception so far of contractual liability as in *Courage/Crehan*, Community law does not require national courts to provide remedies of compensation or interim relief for the performance of contractual obligations with public authorities or private parties. That does not mean that contract law is not affected at all by Community law: it is so, but mainly incrementally, that is when contracting parties, often public authorities, have violated a directly applicable principle of Community "public policy", such as for instance the principle of equal treatment of men and women in matters of employment, or one of the basic "internal market" economic freedoms, or the principle of undistorted competition. In such cases, Community law requires the national courts to set aside legal or contractual provisions, and to declare them null and void, or otherwise ineffective, in accordance with primary (Treaty), or secondary (regulations or directives), Community law.

Apart from *Courage/Crehan*, and beyond the incremental interference of Community law with contractual situations because of inconsistency with Community public policy, convergence of law in the area of contract law through judgements of the ECJ, may only have an opportunity to occur when the ECJ takes a more global view of directive law in areas such as consumer law (but also in other fields of protective private law, such as banking law, or corporate law). That would mean that the Court, when asked to interpret a specific directive provision, would be prepared to situate its ruling in a broader perspective of consumer contract law as a whole – in other words, would be prepared to promote coherence between directives in which similar provisions appear, even before the Community legislature itself has taken on that task (as suggested in the Commission's Green Paper). A case in point where that could have happened, is the ECJ's *Océano Grupo* judgment where the Court held that national courts can, of their own motion, declare unfair terms in a consumer contract "non binding." Even although the Court applied a more teleological approach, it missed an opportunity as regards that point of law to clarify the enforcement of 'public policy' versus (merely private interests) 'protective' Community law provisions, through private law sanctions, such as being 'null and void' as compared with 'non-binding.'

One last remark. Those who are familiar with the "casebook for a common law"-project, know that the author of this contribution is a strong believer in case law of

Community and national courts, that is, in convergence which grows 'bottom-up.' That is not only so for a purely legal reason which is that there is no legal basis for comprehensive 'top-down' legislation in the European Union Treaty as it now stands (and will remain so after adoption of the European Constitutional Treaty in the form approved in July 2003 in Thessaloniki). It is also because this author strongly believes that convergence of the minds of practitioners, judges, professors and future lawyers is at least as important as convergence of laws. Learning about each other's legal mentalities, and ways of solving concrete legal problems, is therefore of crucial importance – which means that it is also of the utmost importance to make available teaching materials for lawyers, young and old, who want to familiarise themselves with growing convergence between the EU Member States' legal systems.[83]

---

83 For a discussion of those 'flanking measures' see further my article, *supra* n. 2, at 174-176.

CHAPTER 7

Principles of Contract Law

Arthur S. Hartkamp[*]

1   Introduction

Uniform law presents itself in numerous manifestations. There are the well known international Conventions, prepared by an international organisation, adopted at a diplomatic conference and afterwards hopefully ratified by a significant number of states. There are model laws, drafted with a view to being adopted by national legislators. Furthermore, there are legal guides, destined for use by private or public operators in the field of international trade. The next category are standard terms (general conditions), drafted either by an organisation of interested business people or by an international intergovernmental organisation, which only become law between the parties after having been adopted by parties to an individual contract. Again, within international organisations there may exist a particular type of machinery devised to produce other variants of law binding upon the Member States or private actors (enterprises or individuals), such as the directives, regulations or court decisions within the framework of the European Union. All these types of international instruments present their proper advantages and disadvantages on which I do not have to dwell here since other contributions in this volume will elaborate them.[1]

This article is concerned with yet another type of uniform law: the UNIDROIT Principles for International Commercial Contracts and the Principles of European Contract Law. Attention will be paid to the history of the activities and to the commissions that carry them out. After a discussion of the nature of the Principles and of their possible functions I will give a brief survey of their contents. I will conclude with some comparative remarks on the work of both groups and some suggestions for future work.

2   The Work on the Principles

2.1   UNIDROIT

It is fair to start with the UNIDROIT Principles, since work on them has begun first and their international scope is wider.[2]

---

[*]   Procureur-Général at the Supreme Court of the Netherlands; Professor of Private Law, University of Amsterdam

[1]   See Kropholler (1975), pp. 93 ff., Trompenaars (1989), pp. 55 ff.

[2]   The UNIDROIT project has been described in several articles and books by its chairman Michael Joachim Bonell, professor at Rome University "La Sapienza" and legal adviser of the Institute. See

UNIDROIT (Institut International pour l'Unification du Droit) was founded in 1926 under the aegis of the League of Nations to promote the unification of private law. The Institute has its seat in Rome and counts at present 67 Member States, including many European States as well as the United States of America, the Russian Federation and the People's Republic of China. The activities of the Institute are directed by a Governing Council consisting of 25 eminent lawyers from different Member States (mostly academics, some state officials) who are elected by the General Assembly every five years.

Until recently, the Institute directed its activities exclusively towards international conventions, its most renowned success being the 1964 Hague Uniform Laws on the International Sale of Goods which subsequently served as a key source of inspiration for the 1980 UN-Convention on the International Sale of Goods (CISG), already ratified by more than 30 states. As early as 1971 the Governing Council decided to embark upon the project of the "Progressive Codification of International Commercial Law"; however, it soon became apparent that the project's title could give rise to misunderstandings (no decision had been taken as to the kind of instrument the Institute would eventually produce and, moreover, from the outset it was improbable that the outcome would be a codification in the proper sense of the word). As a result, the project was rebaptised as the Principles for International Commercial Contracts.

Preparatory work was carried out by three well known comparatists representing three major legal systems (David from Aix/Marseille, Schmithoff from Kent and Popescu from Bucharest) and at the end of the 1970s a working group was formed. The group eventually consisted of 17 members originating from various European civil law countries and, in accordance with the universal vocation of the Institute, other countries, including Great Britain, USA, Canada, Australia, Russia, Japan, China and Ghana. Preliminary drafts for the separate chapters or sections were produced by members of the group and were then discussed by the group as a whole; each chapter or section underwent at least two readings (one reading normally taking

---

e.g. Das UNIDROIT-Projekt für die Ausarbeitung von Regeln für internationale Handelsverträge, *RabelsZ* 56 (1992) pp. 274-289; Unification of Law by Non-Legislative Means: The UNIDROIT Draft Principles for International Commercial Contracts, *AJCL* 1992, pp. 617-634; The Unidroit Principles of International Commercial Contracts: Why? What? How?, *Tulane Law Review*, Vol. 69, 1995, pp. 1121-1148; An International Restatement of Contract Law, Transnational Publishers Inc., 2nd ed., 1997; the UNIDROIT Principles and Transnational Law, *ULR* 2000, pp. 199-218. See also (among others) M. Fontaine, Les principes pour les contrats commerciaux internationaux élaborés par UNIDROIT, *Rev.dr.int.comp.* 1991, pp. 25-40; J.M. Perillo, UNIDROIT Principles of International Commercial Contracts: the black letter text and a review, *Fordham Law Review* 1994, pp. 281-344. Several issues presented by the Principles are discussed in *AJCL* 1992, pp. 635-682 by U. Drobnig (Substantive Validity), Marcel Fontaine (Content and Performance), Dietrich Maskow (Hardship and Force Majeur), M.P. Furmston (Breach of Contract) and Denis Tallon (Damages, Exemption Clauses, and Penalties). At the XVth International Congress of Comparative Law held in Bristol 1998 the UNIDROIT Principles were the subject of a special session; see M.J.Bonell (ed.), A new approach to international commercial contracts: The UNIDROIT Principles of International Commercial Contracts (containing national reports and a general report). Literature on the Principles since 1994 is reported in the Bibliographies in the Uniform Law Review; in M.J.Bonell (ed.), The UNIDROIT Principles in Practice. Caselaw and Bibliography on the Principles of Commercial Contracts, Transnational Publishers Inc. (2002); and on the internet at http://www.unidroit.org/english/principles/pr-bib.htm.

a session of a week's length). Decisions normally were made by consensus, but sometimes, in exeptionally arduous cases, after long discussions this consensus was brought about by abiding to the outcome of an indicative vote.

The Principles are drafted as articles and are accompanied by comments, which include illustrations wherever deemed useful to illustrate their content and scope, and references to other pertinent international instruments of unified law. The comments do not refer to national legal systems, unless a specific rule or institution is borrowed from a national source and it is felt useful to indicate such origin; or, conversely, unless a rule intends – without expressly saying so – to exclude the application of a national rule, a notable example being the rule excluding any prerequisite for the conclusion of a contract like consideration or cause (see below, Section 4.1.3).

It will be clear from what has been said, that the editorial presentation of the Principles to a certain extent resembles the American Restatements of law. The main difference is that, whereas the latter in principle purports to set forth the existing law of the States of the Union as laid down by the courts, based on the common law, the Principles (and this is also true for the European Principles) cannot do so because of the divergencies in the laws of the nations even within the European Union itself.

Since 1980 the working group has met once or twice a year for a one week session. In 1994 the group finished the first part of its work and in the same year the Governing Council of UNIDROIT – which in the preceding years had already discussed a number of controversial questions – approved the work of the working group and consented to the publication of the Principles.[3]

The UNIDROIT Governing Council at its 1996 meeting decided to reconvene the working group in order to continue its work on other topics. This second phase of the group's activity was finished in 2003. The enlarged version of the Principles will be pubished in 2004.

2.2 The Commission on European Contract Law

Much of what has been said above equally applies *mutatis mutandis* to the Commission on European Contract Law (Lando Commission).[4] The Commission consisted in

---

3   UNIDROIT Principles of International Commercial Contracts, UNIDROIT 1994. Since 1994 a number of translations has appeared e.g. in Spanish, German, Dutch, Italian, Chinese and Arabic.

4   Here, too, various publications by the chairman of the group, Ole Lando, professor emeritus at the Institute of European Market law, Copenhagen, may be mentioned: European Contract Law, *AJCL* 1983, pp. 653-659; A Contract Law for Europe, *Int. Bus. Lawyer* 1985, pp. 17-21; Principles of European Contract Law, *Liber memorialis Laurent* 1989, pp. 555-568; Principles of European Contract Law. An Alternative or a Precursor of European Legislation, *RabelsZ 56* (1992) pp. 261-273; Teaching a European Code of Contracts, in De Witte/Forder (1992), pp. 223-237; Principles of European Contract Law: An Alternative to or a Precursor of European Legislation?, *AJCL* 1992, pp. 573-586; Die Regeln des Europäischen Vertragsrechts, in Müller-Graf (ed.), Gemeinsames Privatrecht in der Europäischen Gemeinschaft (1993), pp. 473 e.v.; A Short Introduction to the Principles of European Contract Law, in Gavin Barrett/Ludovic Bernardeau (eds.), Towards a European Civil Code. Reflections on the Codification of Civil Law in Europe (2002), ERA 2000, pp. 57-67. See also, e.g., O. Remien, Ansätze für ein Europäisches Vertragsrecht, *ZVglRWiss* 87 (1988) pp. 105-122, at pp. 117ff; F.J.A. van der Velden, Europa 1992 en het eenvormig privaatrecht, *Molengrafica* 1990, pp. 3-28, at pp. 19ff; U. Drobnig, Ein Vertragsrecht für Europa, *Festschrift Steindorff* 1990, pp. 1141-1154, at pp. 1149ff; R. Zimmermann, Konturen eines europäischen Vertragsrechts, *JZ* 1995, pp. 477-492; M.W. Hesselink and G.J.P. de Vries, Principles of European

its various compositions of 20-25 members recruited from all the Member States of the European Union, although the members were not selected by their governments and they do not represent their countries in an official capacity. They were mostly academics or practicing lawyers (or both) who were free to make up their minds independently and without any governmental instruction. Expenses were met partly by the European Commission, partly by other sources. The group started its work about 1980. The activities of the UNIDROIT working group and the Lando Commission were influenced reciprocally as some of the scholars are involved in both projects.

Like the UNIDROIT Principles, also the European Principles are drafted as articles and are accompanied by comments, which include illustrations wherever deemed useful to illustrate their content and scope, and references to other pertinent international instruments of unified law. Moreover, the comments are followed by notes containing brief references to the national legal systems of the European Union.

The European Principles were published for the first time in 1995.[5] That first part contained only a part of the subject-matter of the UNIDROIT working group. Afterwards the Lando Commission has proceeded to elaborate a second part (which was published in 2000 in a consolidated version with the first part)[6] and a third part, which was published in 2003.[7]

3   The Nature and Possible Functions of the Principles

The UNIDROIT Principles are not meant to become binding law. It would be unrealistic to hope for a codification of the general part of contract law on a world scale to be brought about by an international convention within the foreseeable future. Not even the success of the UN Convention on the International Sale of Goods, which contains a number of rules which undoubtedly may be considered as such general rules, has brought such a codification within reach.[8] On a European scale the idea of such a codification, be it only of contract law, is less unrealistic but still not very probable, strange though this may seem taking into account the official goals of an internal market unhampered by national economic or legal barriers.[9] Private law is merely dealt with on a piecemeal basis, although it is notable that the pieces (product liability, general conditions, sale of consumer goods and associated guarantees) have

---

Contract Law (Kluwer 2001); Busch/Hondius *et al.* (eds.), The Principles of European Contract Law and Dutch law (Ars Aequi/Kluwer 2002).

5   Ole Lando and Hugh Beale (eds.), Principles of European Contract Law, Part I: Performance, Non-performance and Remedies, Martinus Nijhoff Publishers 1995.

6   Ole Lando and Hugh Beale (eds.), Principles of European Contract Law, Parts I and II Combined and Revised, Kluwer Law International 2000.

7   Ole Lando, Eric Clive, André Prüm and Reinhard Zimmermann (eds.), Principles of European Contract Law, Part III, Kluwer Law International 2003.

8   See for a recent survey of the present state of affairs the papers delivered at the 2002 UNIDROIT Conference "Worldwide Harmonisation of Private Law and Regional Economic Integration."

9   See ERPL 1997, pp. 455-547; Gavin Barrett/Ludovic Bernardeau (eds.), Towards a European Civil Code. Reflections on the Codification of Civil Law in Europe (2002), ERA 2000; Special Issue European Contract Law, ERA-Forum 2-2002.

a tendency to increase in importance. What then are the functions that the Principles are meant to achieve? Those functions could be the following:

1. Since codification of private law, be it on a world or a European scale, is fragmentary, it is important to dispose of a general set of principles from which inspiration may be derived by national and international courts to interpret the provisions of the existing uniform law, to fill the gaps which it presents and to offer a background, however informal, for new law to be created. The need for such general principles is particularly manifest within the European Union. Incidentally, it is striking to note that not only on a national scale but also internationally, the part of the law most difficult to (re)form and therefore most commonly neglected by the legislature is the general part of private law.[10]

2. The Principles may serve as a model law that could inspire legislators who strive for law reform. In this respect, not only legislators in developing countries or in countries in transition may find them relevant, but also states trying to modernise existing legislation and seeking inspiration from common international standards as they have recently emerged. It is clear that the 1964 Hague Uniform Laws and CISG have exerted such an influence on states with a codified system. The Principles may assume a comparable function in areas not covered by CISG.

3. The Principles (and their accompanying comments) may serve to enlighten parties negotiating a contract in order to identify the problems to be resolved in their contract and, possibly, to find suitable rules to settle them. Parties may even decide to incorporate the Principles in part or as a whole in their contract. In this respect, the Principles could have the same function as for example the various legal guides drafted by UNCITRAL.[11]

4. Parties to an international contract could chose the Principles as the law applicable to their contract. Since it is rather uncertain whether a choice of law for the Principles could be upheld in proceedings before a state court,[12] parties are well advised to combine such a clause with an arbitration clause;[13] and even then they must take into account whether the law governing the arbitration (and preferably the law of the state where the arbitral award will probably be executed) will permit such a reference.[14] Even in the absence of an express reference arbitrators authorised to apply

---

10 Comp. H. Kötz, Gemeineuropäisches Zivilrecht, *Festschrift Zweigert* 1981, pp. 481-500, at p. 483.

11 United Nations Commission on International Trade Law.

12 See A.S. Hartkamp, The Use of the UNIDROIT Principles of International Commercial Contracts by National and Supranational Courts, in UNIDROIT Principles for International Commercial Contracts: A New Lex Mercatoria?, ICC/Dossier of the Institute of International Business Law and Practice 1995, pp. 253-262; A.S. Hartkamp, Modernisation and harmonisation of Contract Law: Objectives, Methods and Scope, Uniform Law Review 2003, pp. 81-90. See (on this problem and more in general about the Principles and private international law) K. Boele-Woelki, Principles and ipr, Inaugural lecture Utrecht University 1995; J. Wichard, Die Anwendung der UNIDROIT-Prinzipien für internationale Handelsverträge durch Schiedsgerichte und staatliche Gerichte, RabelsZ 1996, pp. 269-302; U. Drobnig, The Unidroit Principles in the Conflict of Laws, *ULR* 1998, pp. 385-395; F. Juenger, The *lex mercatoria* and private international law, *ULR* 2000, pp. 171-187.

13 See for examples Ulrich Drobnig, General Principles of European Contract Law, in Sarcevic/Volen (ed.), *International Sale of Goods* (Dubrovnik Lectures), 1985, pp. 305-333, at p. 309.

14 See Article 28 of the UNCITRAL Model Law on Commercial Arbitration: "The arbitral tribunal shall

such notions like the general rules of law, equity or the *lex mercatoria*, may resort to the Principles to find suitable solutions to the dispute at hand.[15]

5. The Principles will certainly have an important scholarly and educational value.[16] Concerning the European legal scene, they will encourage the emerging trend to find the common denominator of the different private law systems in Europe in order to construct a new *ius commune Europae*.[17] Moreover, the Principles will make it more attractive to introduce in law schools new curricula teaching European side by side with the national laws of their respective countries of residence. In the long run, this seems to be the most promising way to attain such a new ius commune.[18]

---

decide the dispute in accordance with such rules of law as are chosen by the parties as applicable to the substance of the dispute [..] Failing any designation by the parties, the arbitral tribunal shall apply the the law determinded by the conflict of law rules which it considers applicable [...]" Also e.g. Art. 42 of the 1965 Convention on the Settlement of Investment Disputes between States and Nationals of other States (ICSID Convention), Art. 1496 of the French Code de Proc. Civ. (enacted in 1981) and Art. 1054 of the Dutch Code of Civil Procedure (enacted in 1986).

15 See e.g. O. Lando, The Lex Mercatoria in International Commercial Arbitration, 34 *ICLQ* 1985, pp. 752-768; Y. Derains, L'ordre public et le droit applicable au fond du litige dans l'arbitrage international, *Revue de l'Arbitrage* 1986, pp. 375-413; A. Spickhoff, Internationales handelsrecht vor Schiedsgerichten und staatlichen Gerichten, *RabelsZ* 56 (1992), pp. 116-141. For some examples of decisions of national courts upholding such an approach by the arbitrators, see M.J. Bonell, Das UNIDROIT-Projekt für die Ausarbeitung von Regeln für internationale Handelsverträge, *RabelsZ 56* (1992) p. 287 Fn. 55 and Id., The UNIDROIT principles and Transnational Law, *ULR* 2000, pp. 199-218.

16 It must be pointed out that in this respect they not not stand alone anymore. In the second half of the 1990s other scholarly projects in the field of European Private law have come into being and started to flourish, such as the European Civil Code project, the Common Core of European Private Law (Trento Project) and the Ius Commune Casebooks for the Common Law of Europe. See on these (and still other) projects A.S. Hartkamp, in Mauro Bussani/Ugo Mattei (eds.), Making European Law. Essays on the 'Common Core' Project, *Quaderni del dipartimento di scienze giuridiche dell'Università degli studi di Trento*, No. 24, 2000 (pp. 39-60) (also in *WPNR* 6401 (2000)).

17 See for a short survey U. Drobnig, General Principles of European Contract Law, in Sarcevic/Volen (1985), pp. 305-333. The concept of a European *ius commune* in a broader sense is discussed by Thijmen Koopmans, Towards a new "ius commune", in De Witte/Forder (1992), pp. 43-51 and in many publications by Reinhard Zimmermann (also in this volume).

18 This idea seems to be popular especially among scholars from Germany and the Benelux Countries. See e.g. H. Coing, European Common Law: Historical Foundations, in Cappelletti (ed.), *New Perspectives for a Common Law of Europe*, 1978, pp. 31-44, at p. 44; R. Sacco, Droit commun de l'Europe, et Composantes du Droit, in Cappelletti (1978), pp. 95 ff., at p. 108; H. Kötz, Gemeineuropäisches Zivilrecht, *Festschrift Zweigert* 1981, pp. 481-500; Ewoud Hondius, *NJB* 1985, p. 1343; Ost/Van Hoecke, *RW* 1989-1990, pp. 1001-1002; Versteген, RW 1989-1990, pp. 657 ff.; H. Coing, Europäisierung der Rechtswissenschaft, *NJW* 1990, pp. 937-941; A.S. Hartkamp, Wetsuitleg en rechtstoepassing na de invoering van het nieuwe burgerlijk wetboek (1992), pp. 18 ff.; P. Ulmer, Vom deutschen zum europäischen Privatrecht?, *JZ* 1992, pp. 1-8, at p. 7; A. Flessner, Rechtsvereinheitlichung durch Rechtswissenschaft und Juristenausbildung, *RabelsZ* 56 (1992), pp. 243-260; H. Kötz, A Common Private Law for Europe: Perspectives for the Reform of European Legal Education, in De Witte/Forder (1992), pp. 31-41; P.-C. Müller-Graff, Common Private Law in the European Community, in De Witte/Forder (1992), pp. 239-254, at p. 252; B.S. Markesinis, Why a code is not the best way to advance the cause of European legal unity, *ERPL* 1997, pp. 519 ff.; M.A. Eisenberg, The Unification of Law, in Mauro Bussani/Ugo Mattei (eds.), *Making European Law. Essays on the 'common Core' Project* (2000), pp. 15 e.v.

6. Finally, the Principles will, by the sheer fact of their existence, prove that a reasonable compromise between the various legal systems of Europe and beyond, can be reached. It seems probable that this will add weight to the voices of those who advocate the preparation of a European Civil Code.[19] Until recently, on the official European level those voices had only received support from the European Parliament, which on 26 May 1989 passed a resolution requesting the Member States to commence the necessary prepatory work for the drawing up of a European Code of Private Law.[20] Afterwards resolutions to the same effect have been passed in 1994 and in 2000,[21] and recently the European Commission, in response to the Presidency Conclusions No. 39 of the Tampere European Council, has published its Communication on European Contract Law,[22] which was followed by the important Commission's Action Plan on 'A More Coherent European Contract law'.[23] Therefore, chances are increasing that the Principles may end up, probably in a revised form – taking into account scholarly criticisms, practical experiences and political negotiations – in the (partial) codification the absence of which has led to their coming into existence.[24] Until then, like the old *ius commune*, they may only aspire to be applied not *ratione imperii*, but *imperio rationis*.[25]

---

19 See e.g. (apart from the authors cited in the previous footnote), among others, R. Houin, Pour une codification européenne du droit des contrats et des obligations, *Etudes juridiques offertes à Léon Julliot de la Morandière* (1964), pp. 223-231; R. David, Le droit continental, la common law et les perspectives d'un ius commune Européen, in Cappelletti (1978), pp. 113-135; W. Tilmann, Zur Entwicklung eines europäischen Zivilrechts, *Festschrift W. Oppenhoff* 1985, pp. 495-507; G.J.W.Steenhoff, Naar een Europees Privaatrecht? Impulsen vanuit de rechtsvergelijking, in *Recht als norm en als aspiratie* (1986), pp. 85-101; P. Mansell, Rechtsvergleichung und europäische Rechtseinheit, *JZ* 1991, pp. 529-534; P. Hommelhoff, Zivilrecht unter dem Einfluss europäischer Rechtsangleichung, *AcP* 192 (1992), pp. 71-107; O. Lando, Why codify the European Law of Contract?, *ERPL* 1997, pp. 525-535 and *Id.*, The Future Development of the Principles of European Contract Law and a European Civil Code, in *Gavin Barrett/Ludovic Bernardeau (eds.), Towards a European Civil Code. Reflections on the Codification of Civil Law in Europe (2002)*, pp. 40-46.

20 In the preamble to the resolution it is said (sub E) that unification should be envisaged in branches of private law which are highly important for the development of the single market, such as contract law. See *OJ* EC C 158/401 of 26 June 1989.

21 *OJ* C 205/518 of 6 May 1994 and *OJ* C 377/323 of 16 March 2000.

22 *OJ* C 255/1 (2001).

23 *OJ* C 255 of 15 March 2003.

24 There are also other possibilities. In the discussion on the European Civil Code it has been suggested that a Restatement on Contract Law be given effect as European Law applicable to legal relations between parties to govern their contracts where these raise an EU internal 'foreign' element and the parties have not chosen another governing law. In relation to contracts, this would partially supersede the inevitably intricate regime provided for in Art. 4 of the Rome Convention to establish the most appropriate law to govern the transaction from among the various national systems (see Communication on European Contract Law. Joint Response of the Commission on European Contract Law and the Study Group on a European Civil Code, No. 91, stage 3). In a further stage, the applicability could perhaps be extended to contracts without a a cross-border aspect. Another possibility is that the Restatement could be chosen by the parties as the law applicable to their contract. In the Action Plan of the European Commission, mentioned above, this idea of an 'optional instrument' has been taken up (No. 89 ff.). See Staudinger, Ein optionelles Instrument im Europäischen Vertragsrecht?, ZEUP 2003, pp. 828 e.v.

25 The phenomenon that legal texts drawn up in the form of draft articles have a greater persuasive force

4 The Contents of the Principles

4.1 The UNIDROIT Principles

The UNIDROIT Principles consist of a preamble and 10 Chapters: general provisions, formation and authority of agents, validity, interpretation, content and third party rights, performance, non-performance, set-off, assignment of rights and limitation periods.[26] All together, these Chapters contain 184 articles, ranging from statements of principle and flexible standards to more (but never very) detailed provisions.[27] Some remarks about each chapter will be made.

4.1.1 Preamble and General Provisions

The Principles open with the statement (preamble, al. 1) that they set forth general rules for international commercial contracts. These concepts are not defined. However, the comments indicate that "commercial" is not to be understood in the sense of those legal systems whose codified law distinguishes between civil and commercial law, but is meant – following the example of CISG – to exclude the so called consumer contracts for which many states have specially legislated rules of a protective and mandatory character. On the other hand, this does not mean that according to the Principles in commercial contracts the principle of freedom of contract prevails without any restriction at all.[28] I refer to the provisions on general conditions and on gross disparity in the Chapter on Formation, to the rules on hardship in the Chapter on Performance, and to the rules on exemption clauses and on liquidated damages in the Chapter on Non-performance, which will be discussed presently.

The rest of the preamble lays out some of the functions discussed above in section 3.

Chapter 1 formulates some general principles, including the principle of freedom of contract, the binding character of contract, the extent to which parties are bound to usages and the principle of paramount importance in international trade: good faith.[29] In fact, Article 1.8 lays down that each party must act in accordance with good faith

---

and tend to exert a stronger influence on courts and arbitrators than a discussion of legal principles in a text book, however clear that may be, can also be observed on a national scale. I refer to the gradual law reform by the Dutch Supreme Court between 1965 and 1992 effected through the so called "anticipatory interpretation", *viz.* the interpretation of the existing texts of the old Civil Code on the basis of the drafts for the new Code. This was first noted by G.J. Scholten, Anticiperende interpretatie: een nieuwe interpretatiemethode?, *WPNR* 5031 (1969), p. 111.

26 The articles on authority of agents, third party rights, set-off, assignment of rights and limitation periods were elaborated by the second working group. As this book went to the press (December 2003) the text of these additions was not yet published.

27 Especially at the international level Kötz' precept (Taking Civil Codes Less Seriously, *MLR* 50 (1987), pp. 1-15, at p. 9) is valuable: "[...] the draftsman [...] must steer the best course available by finding language that strikes an apt balance between certainty and flexibility and facilitates the orderly development of the law without unduly fettering judicial creativity."

28 Comp. the warning of H. Kötz, Gemeineuropäisches Zivilrecht, *Festschrift Zweigert* 1981, pp. 481-500, at p. 494.

29 According to D. Tallon, Imprévision revisited: some remarks on the consequences of a change of

and fair dealing in international trade and that parties may not exclude or limit this duty. Throughout the Principles rules may be found containing express or implicit elaborations of the principle of good faith. To my mind, the rule of Article 1.8 constitutes a marked improvement to Article 7 CISG which mentions "the observance of good faith in international trade" merely as one of the factors to which regard is to be had in the interpretation of the Convention.

4.1.2 Formation and Authority of Agents

In the first section (formation) some ten articles on offer and acceptance closely follow the pattern offered by CISG. The other articles contain innovations, including confirmation in writing, contracts with terms deliberately left open, negotiations in bad faith (a party who has negotiated or broken off negotiations in bad faith is liable for losses caused to the other party), and the duty of confidentiality. Finally, there are several provisions on standard terms or general conditions, including a definition, a rule on the problem of the battle of the forms (standard terms not agreed upon bind the parties in so far as they are common in substance) and on surprising conditions (which shall not be effective unless expressly accepted by the other party).

The second section (authority of agents) governs the 'external aspect' of agency: the authority of a person, the agent, to affect the legal relations of another person, the principal, by a contract with a third party. Where the third party knew or ought to have known that the agent was acting as an agent (and the agent acts within the scope of its authority) there will be a contract between the principal and the third party. Where an agent acts without authority, the third party is protected if the principal caused the third party reasonably to believe that the agent has authority.

The problem of 'undisclosed agency' is solved in the following way. Where the third party neither knew nor ought to have known that the agent was acting as an agent (and the agent acts within the scope of its authority) the agent binds himself; but where the agent, when contracting with the third party on behalf of a business, represents itself to be the owner of that business, the third party, upon discovery of the real owner of the business, may exercise also against the latter the rights it has against the agent.

---

circumstances on contracts, in Attila Harmathy (ed), *Binding force of contract*, Budapest 1991, pp. 107-112, at p. 111 good faith "may be the only undisputed rule of the evanescent lex mercatoria". See also E.A. Farnsworth, Duties of Good Faith and Fair Dealing under the Unidroit Principles. Relevant International Conventions, and National Laws, *Tulane Journal of International and Comparative Law*, Vol. 3 (1995), pp. 47-63; A.S. Hartkamp, The Concept of "Good Faith" in the UNIDROIT Principles for International Commercial Contracts, *Tulane Journal of International and Comparative Law*, Vol. 3 (1995), pp. 65-71; and Juenger, Listening to Law Professors Talk about Good faith: Some Afterthoughts, *Tulane Law Review*, Vol. 69, 1995, pp. 1253-1257. See also several volumes in the Saggi, conferenze e seminari of the Centro di studi e ricerche di diritto comparato e straniero (diretto da M.J. Bonell): R. Goode, The Concept of 'Good Faith' in English law (No. 2, 1992); A.E. Farnsworth, The Concept of Good Faith in American Law (No. 10, 1993); D. Tallon, Le concept de bonne foi en droit français du contrat (No. 15, 1994); P. Schlechtriem, Good Faith in German Law and in International Conventions (No. 24, 1997).

4.1.3   Validity

The chapter on validity (which is clearly inspired by the 1972 UNIDROIT Convention for the Unification of Certain Rules relating to the Validity of Contracts of International Sale)[30] deals with a subject-matter which is nearly entirely excluded from the scope of CISG. Article 4 of that Convention states that it is not concerned with the validity of the contract or of any of its provisions.

Article 3.2 lays down the important rule that a contract is concluded, modified or terminated by the mere agreement of the parties, without any further requirement. The main purpose of this Article is to do away with the civil law doctrine of cause and with the common law doctrine of consideration.

The rest of this Chapter is devoted to the so called defects of consent. Mistake, fraud and threat are dealt with, as well as "gross disparity", namely the situation where either the contract or an individual term unjustifiably gives a party an excessive advantage over the other party.

In the cases mentioned above, the contract may be avoided by the disadvantaged party by a notice to the other party which must be given within a reasonable time after the avoiding party either knew or could not have been unaware of the relevant facts and became capable of acting freely. Avoidance may be partial and it has retroactive effect. The party who is entitled to avoid the contract may also claim damages (so as to put it into the same position it would have been in, if it had not concluded the contract) if the other party knew or ought to have known the ground for avoidance. In the cases of mistake and of gross disparity, it is possible for the other party to prevent the avoidance of the contract by a reasonable offer to modify the contract.

4.1.4   Interpretation

Chapter 4 deals with the interpretation of the contract, with reference to contractual terms, statements and other conduct. A contract shall be interpreted according to the common intention of the parties and if such an intention cannot be established, according to the meaning which reasonable persons would give to it in the circumstances. Moreover, there are articles on the interpretation of unclear terms, on the *contra proferentem* rule and on supplying an omitted term.

4.1.5   Content and Third Party Rights

Chapters 5 and 6 were for a long time combined under the heading of Performance. Eventually, however, the chapter was split in two and now Chapter 5, first section, contains some provisions which were considered to touch on the content rather than on the performance of contracts. The Articles 5.1 and 5.2 elucidate the distinction between express and implied obligations. Article 5.3 requires each party to cooperate with the other party when such cooperation may reasonably be expected. The Articles 5.4 and 5.5 describe the distinction between duties to achieve a specific result and du-

---

30 *Uniform Law Review* 1973, p. 60; also in *UNCITRAL Yearbook* VIII (1977), p. 104.

ties of best efforts (while recognising that an obligation may present the characteristics of both kinds), and specify a number of factors to which regard shall be had in determining the nature of a given obligation. Article 5.7 on price determination ensures that a contract will not be invalid where there is no fixed price or provision for determining the price: in that case a reasonable price will have to be paid. The same is true if the price is to be determined by one party whose determination is manifestly unreasonable.

Section 2 (third party rights) is devoted to contracts in favour of third parties.

4.1.6   Performance

This Chapter contains two sections, *Performance in general* and *Hardship*.

The first section is devoted to many problems that are well known to lawyers familiar with a codification of private law: time of performance, order of performance, place of performance, payment by cheque or other instrument (a subject which as yet has found its way only into some national codes), currency of payment, imputation of payments and the like. A new topic is dealt with in Articles 6.1.14 ff., which are concerned with national public permission requirements affecting the validity of the contract or making its performance impossible. The rules state which party shall take the measures necessary to obtain permission, and the position of the parties where permission is either refused or neither granted nor refused.

The section on hardship begins by stating that if the performance of a contract becomes more onerous for one of the parties, that party is nevertheless bound to perform his obligations. However, Article 6.2.2 allows for an exception in the case of hardship, described as the situation where the occurrence of events (specified in litt. a-d) fundamentally alters the equilibrium of the contract either because the cost of a party's performance has increased or because the value of the received performance has diminished. In the case of hardship the disadvantaged party is entitled to request renegotiations and upon failure to reach agreement the court may, if reasonable, either terminate the contract at a date and on terms to be fixed or adapt the contract with a view to restoring its equilibrium.

4.1.7   Non-Performance

The chapter is divided in 4 sections: general provisions, right to performance, termination, damages and exemption clauses.

Following the CISG-approach the Principles have adopted a unitary concept of "non-performance" (Article 7.1.1): the term denotes any failure of a party to effect due performance, including late performance and defective performance.[31] The term has been preferred to the term "breach" used in CISG, since the breach in the common law is restricted to non-performance which gives the other party the right to claim damages, whereas non-performance may also lead to the use of other remedies, such as termination of the contract and withholding performance, for which there is

---

31   See for a comparative survey O. Lando, Harmonisation of the rules on remedies for non-performance of contracts, in Attila Harmathy (1991), pp. 69-79.

no requirement that the non-performing party must be liable in damages. This can be illustrated by the operation of the rule which relates to *force majeure*, where a party proves that the non-performance was due to an impediment beyond its control and that it could not reasonably have been expected to have taken the impediment into account at the time of the conclusion of the contract or to have avoided or overcome it or its consequences (Article 7.1.7). Although the remedy of damages is not available the other party is not precluded from exercising the remedies mentioned above.

Section 2 relates to the right to claim specific performance. Not only the obligee of a monetary obligation disposes of that right, but also the obligee of a non-monetary obligation, unless one of the specific exceptions spelled out in Article 7.2.2 litt. a-e occurs. To this innovation (a compromise between the civil law and the common law systems) another is added in Article 7.2.4, whereby a court ordering a defaulting party to perform is authorised to award a penalty in the event of non-compliance with the order; and that this penalty be paid to the aggrieved party unless mandatory provisions of the law of the forum provide otherwise.

Section 3 deals with the right to terminate the contract in the case of a fundamental non-performance; this concept is described in Article 7.3.1 para. 2 in a more elaborate manner than in Article 25 of CISG. Similar to 'avoidance' in Chapter 3, the right to terminate[32] is exercised by a notice to the other party within a reasonable time. This Section also addresses issues of anticipatory non-performance, the effects of termination (which does not preclude a claim for non-performance) and, very briefly, restitution.

Finally, the right to damages is set out in Section 4: the principle of full compensation (including compensation for non-pecuniary harm), certainty of harm, foreseeability of harm, mitigation of harm, the right to interest in case of failure to pay a sum of money.

The chapter contains two modern rules restricting the freedom of the stronger party to impose unfair contract clauses on the other party. According to art. 7.1.6., exemption clauses may not be invoked if it would be grossly unfair to do so, having regard to the purpose of the contract. According to Article 7.4.14 a contractually specified sum to be paid in the case of non-performance may be reduced to a reasonable amount where it is grossly excessive in relation to the non-performance and the other circumstances.

4.1.8   Set-Off

The important policy choices in this chapter are the following. The right of set-off is exercised by notice to the other party. Set-off takes effect as from the time of notice.

4.1.9   Assignment of Rights, Transfer of Obligations, Assignment of Contracts

This a lengthy chapter, containing 30 articles, of which 15 (section 1) on assignment of rights. A right is assigned by mere agreement between assignor and assignee, with-

---

32   It should be noted that in CISG the term 'avoidance' is used in the sense in which 'termination' is used in the Principles.

out notice to the obligor. Articles 9.1.5 and 9.1.6 allow for the assignment of future rights and of rights without individual specification. Non-assignment clauses are to a large extent deprived of their effect (see Article 9.1.9). Until receiving a notice of assignment the obligor is discharged by paying the assignor. In case of successive assignments the obligor is discharged by paying according to the order in which the notices were received.

4.1.10 Limitation Periods

The general limitation period is three years after the day the obligee knows or ought to have known the facts as a result of which the obligee's rights can be exercised. The maximum limitation period is ten years beginning on the day after the day the right can be exercised. The running of the limitation period is suspended in case of judicial or arbitral proceedings, in case of alternative dispute resolution and in case of force majeure. The parties may modify the limitation periods within the limits indicated in Article 10.3.

4.2 The European Principles

The European Principles as published in 1995 consisted of four chapters: general provisions, terms and performance of the contract, non-performance and remedies in general, and particular remedies for non-performance. In the second part chapters were added on formation, authority of agents, validity and interpretation. Moreover, instead of the chapter on terms and performance of the contract there are two new chapters on contents and effects and on performance. In the third part chapters were added on plurality of parties, assignment of claims, substitution of new debtor and transfer of contract, set-off, prescription, illegality, conditions and capitalisation of interests.

Together there are now 17 chapters containing 198 articles, which like the UNIDROIT Principles, range from general statements and flexible standards to more detailed provisions. The survey of the chapters can be shorter than that of the UNIDROIT Principles, since there are many similarities between the two documents.[33] However, in the final version the European Principles comprise some subjects not covered by the UNIDROIT Principles: plurality of parties, illegality, conditions and capitalisation of interests.

4.2.1 General Provisions

Article 1:101 para. 1 states that the Principles are intended to be applied as general rules of contract law in the European Communities. This goes further than the

---

33 See for a comparison of the two instruments A.S. Hartkamp, The UNIDROIT Principles for International Commercial Contracts and the Principles of European Contract Law, *ERPL* 1994, pp. 341-357; M.J. Bonell, The UNIDROIT Principles of International Contracts and the Principles of European Contract Law: Similar Rules for the Same Purposes?, *ULR* 1996, pp. 229-246; R. Goode, International Restatements of Contract Law and English Contract Law, *ULR* 1997, pp. 231-248.

UNIDROIT Principles, as the European Principles are not confined to international commercial contracts. The chapter enumerates general principles, such as some rules on interpretation, the principle of good faith and fair dealing, the duty to cooperate, the concept of reasonableness and the extent to which parties are bound to usages (a slightly more liberal rule than that in the UNIDROIT Principles).

4.2.2 Formation

As in the UNIDROIT principles there is a series of articles on offer and acceptance closely following the pattern offered by CISG. Other subjects include standard terms (which may only be invoked against a party unaware of them if reasonable steps have been taken to bring them to that party's attention), merger clauses, conflicting general conditions and liability for negotiations conducted or broken off in a manner contrary to good faith. The rules of this chapter apply with appropriate modifications to contracts where the process of formation cannot be analysed into offer and acceptance (Article 2:211) and to promises which are intended to be binding without acceptance (Article 2:107).

4.2.3 Authority of Agents

Chapter 3 deals with the authority of agents. The chapter is only concerned with the ('external') relationship between principal and agent on the one hand and the third party on the other hand, not with the ('internal') relationship between principal and agent. After some general provisions there are two sections on Direct Representation and on Indirect Representation.

Direct representation presupposes that an agent acts in the name of the principal. If the agent acts within his authority (either real authority granted to him by the principal or apparent authority due to the principal's conduct which has induced the third party to belief that authority has been granted), his acts bind the principal and the third party directly. Furthermore, there are rules on the unidentified principal, on ratification of acts which the agent has committed without (or outside the scope of his) authority, conflict of interests and subagency.

Indirect representation is the situation where an intermediary acts (a) on instructions and on behalf of, but not in the name of, a principal, or (b) on instructions from a principal but the third party does not know and has no reason to know this. In these cases, the intermediary and the third party are bound to each other. However, the principal and the third party become bound to each other under the conditions set out in Articles 3:302 to 304. These articles are inspired by the 1983 UNIDROIT Convention on Agency in the International Sale of Goods. If the intermediary becomes insolvent, or if he commits a fundamental non-performance to the principal, the principal has the right to be informed as to the name and address of the third party and to exercise against the third party the rights acquired on the principal's behalf by the intermediary. *Mutatis mutandis*, the third party may exercise the intermediary's rights against the principal.[34]

---

34 See on this section A.S. Hartkamp, Indirect Representation according to the Principles of European

4.2.4   Validity

Chapter 4 covers the same ground as the Chapter on validity in the UNIDROIT Principles (see Section 4.1.3), but there are some additions and differences. Article 4:106 deals with liability for incorrect information even if the information does not give rise to a fundamental mistake. Article 4:109 allows avoidance for 'abuse of circumstances' if the other party "took advantage of the first party's situation in a way which was grossly unfair or took an excessive benefit". Article 4:110 (following the European Directive on unfair terms in consumer contracts) allows avoidance of standard terms which contrary to the requirements of good faith and fair dealing cause a significant imbalance in a party's rights and obligations arising under the contract to the detriment of that party. Whereas the UNIDROIT Principles prohibit a party from using a remedy on the basis of mistake if there is a remedy for non-performance (Article 3.7), the European Principles allows that party to pursue either remedy (Article 4:119).

4.2.5   Interpretation

The seven articles of Chapter 5 deal with the interpretation of the contract with reference to contractual terms, statements and other conduct. As in the UNIDROIT Principles a contract shall be interpreted according to the common intention of the parties and if such an intention cannot be established, according to the meaning which reasonable persons would give to it in the circumstances. Moreover, there are articles on relevant circumstances, the *contra proferentem* rule, preference to negotiated terms and linguistic discrepancies.

4.2.6   Content and Effects; Performance

These two chapters correspond to the subject-matter of Chapters 5 and 6 of the UNIDROIT Principles. They, too, contain provisions on the determination of price (compare section 4.1.5), quality of performance, place of performance, time of performance, form of payment (including payment by cheque or other negotiable instrument), currency of payment, imputation of payments and change of circumstances (comparable to the hardship provisions, see 4.1.6). Moreover, there are provisions on *mora creditoris* (the creditor not accepting the property or the money due to him), contracts in favour of a third party and performance by a third party.

4.2.7   Non-Performance and Remedies in General

The European Principles have adopted the same unitary approach as the UNIDROIT Principles; the general concept here being called 'failure to perform' (Article 8:101). The concept of fundamental non-performance is defined in Article 8.103; and is more

---

Contract Law, the Unidroit Agency Convention and the Dutch Civil Code, *Festschrift Drobnig* (1998), pp. 45-56 and D. Busch, Middellijke vertegenwoordiging in het Europese contractenrecht (Kluwer 2002).

detailed than Article 25 CISG, but less elaborate than Article 7.3.1 of the UNIDROIT Principles. Article 8:104 gives the defaulting party the right to cure by offering a new tender conforming to the contract, provided that the time for performance has not yet arrived or the delay would not be such as to constitute a fundamental non-performance. For reasons which cannot be explained here, this rule is less favourable towards the the defaulting party than Article 7.1.4 of the UNIDROIT Principles. The Chapter also contains provisions on *force majeure* and on clauses excluding or limiting liability which may not be invoked where the non-performance is intentional or grossly negligent.

4.2.8 Particular Remedies for Non-Performance

Chapter 9 is divided in five sections: right to performance, right to withhold performance, termination of the contract, price reduction, damages and interests.

Section 1. Article 9:101 contains a rule on specific performance of non-monetary obligations which is nearly identical to Article 7.2.2 of the UNIDROIT Principles.

Section 2. The same is true for Article 9:201 relating to the right to withhold performance; compare Article 7.1.3 of the UNIDROIT Principles.

Section 3. Also the rules on termination are comparable, but the European Principles contain a more elaborated set of rules on restitution (Articles 9.306-309).

Section 4. Art. 9:401 grants the party who accepts a tender of performance not conforming to the contract the right to reduce the price proportionally.

Section 5 on damages is comparable to Chapter 7, Section 4 of the UNIDROIT Principles. It also contains an Article (9:508) on liquidated damages and penalties that may be reduced when grossly excessive. Moreover this Article states that the aggrieved party is not limited to the specified sum where the non-performance by the other party is intentional or grossly negligent.

4.2.9 Plurality of Parties

Chapter 10 distinguishes between solidary, separate and communal obligations. Solidary obligations arise where several debtors are bound to render one and the same performance under the same contract or are liable for the same damage. The chapter lays down rules on recourse between solidary debtors and on the effects which events such as performance and set-off between one of the debtors and the creditor have on the liability of the other debtors.

4.2.10 Assignment of Claims

A right is assigned by mere agreement between assignor and assignee, without notice to the obligor. The chapter allows for the assignment of future rights and of rights without individual specification. Non-assignment clauses are to a large extent deprived of their effect (see Article 11:301). Until receiving a notice of assignment the obligor is discharged by paying the assignor, provided that he does not have knowledge of the assignment. In case of successive assignments the assignee whose assignment is first notified to the debtor has priority over any earlier assignee if at the time of the later assignment the assignee under that assignment neither knew nor ought to have known of the earlier assignment.

4.2.11 Set-Off

The important policy choices in this chapter are the following. The right of set-off is exercised by notice to the other party. Set-off takes effect as from the time of notice.

4.2.12 Prescription

The general perod of prescription is three years running from the time when the debtor has to effect performance or in the case of a right to damages, from the time of the act which gives right to the claim. The running of the period is suspended as long as the creditor does not know of, and could not reasonably know of the identity of the debtor or the facts giving rise to the claim including, in the case of a right to damages, the type of damage. It is also suspended in the case of proceedings and in case of force majeure and it is postponed in case of negotiations, death and incapacity. The period cannot be extended, by suspension (subject to suspension in case of proceedings) or postponement, to more than ten years or, in case of damages for personal injuries, to more than thirty years. The parties may modify the limitation periods within the limits indicated in Article 14:601.

4.2.13 Illegality

A contract is of no effect to the extent that it is contrary to principles recognised as fundamental in the laws of the Member States of the European Union. Where a contract infringes a mandatory law which does not expressly prescribe the effects of the infringement, the contract may be declared to have full effect, to have no effect, or to be subject to modification. This decision must be an appropriate and proportional response to the infringement, having regard to all relevant circumstances, including the circumstances enumerated in Article 15:102 para. 3. These factors are also relevant where restitution and damages are concerned.

4.2.14 Conditions

Chapter 16 contains some basic rules on conditions.

5 Concluding Remarks

Comparing the two sets of principles it is striking to note the extent to which they resemble each other, not merely in the editorial form in which they (and the accompanying commments) are presented, but also in substance. Most topics have been treated in both documents, the key exceptions being the chapters mentioned in section 4.2 *in fine* (plurality of parties, illegality and conditions) and moreover the protection against unreasonable standard terms (Article 4:110 European Principles), the rule on price reduction (Article 4.401 European Principles) and the duty to achieve a specific result versus the duty of best efforts (Articles 5.4 and 5.5 UNIDROIT Principles). In the chapters on assignment and prescription some different policy choices may be found. Generally, however, the two sets of Principles have adopted similar solutions. Indeed, it is difficult to find any significant differences caused by the fact that the UNIDROIT group consisted of members recruited from countries all over the world, including countries with developing economies and former socialist countries, whereas the European group was confined to representatives from the European Union Member States. Even taking into account the difference in the scope of the proposed rules (the UNIDROIT Principles being restricted to international commercial contracts, whereas the European Principles also propose to govern contracts on a national scale), such a result is remarkable and suggests that an international unification of the general part of contract law is not as unfeasable a prospect as many until recently have considered it to be. It goes without saying that this is even more so when we limit our view to the European scene.

A second observation relates to the connection between the two sets of Principles on the one hand and CISG on the other. It is clear that the solutions adopted by CISG have been followed by both groups of drafters to a large extent, and in particular where the rules on formation and on non-performance are concerned. However there are also marked differences. The Principles have not only broken new ground especially in the Chapters which deal with the validity of contracts, they also depart in respect of the subject-matter governed by CISG. New rules have been elaborated in both sets of Principles, including the rules on good faith, general conditions, hardship, specific performance, exemption clauses and liquidated damages. Occasionally, more liberal rules have been adopted, for instance with regard to a contract coming into existence without the price having been determined (see Articles 14 para. 1 and 55 CISG). Sometimes conceptual improvements have been achieved, such as the definition of the concept of fundamental breach. CISG offers an invaluable set of unified contract rules (it is to be hoped that this international character will be observed by the national courts when called upon to interprete the Convention!), but they are not perfect. Of course, we already knew this but now they are being challenged on a comparative international level for the first time.[35]

The UNIDROIT Principles have produced remarkable results, especially in the field of international commercial arbitration.[36] Now that the study group also has finished the second part of its work, an interesting option would be to resume and continue the work in UNCITRAL with a view to preparing an international convention on the general part of the law of contracts. The success of CISG, also in a sense a combined effort of both organisations, should provide inspiration and courage to un-

---

35 See for a comparison of CISG and the UNIDROIT Principles: A.S. Hartkamp, The UNIDROIT Principles for International Commercial Contracts and the United Nations Convention on the International Sale of Goods, in *Comparability and Evaluation, Essays on Comparative Law, Private International Law and International Commercial Arbitration in Honour of Dimitra Kokkinilatridou*, 1994, pp. 85-98, and Bonell, The UNIDROIT Principles of International Contracts and CISG – Alternatives or Complementary Instruments?, *ULR* 1996, pp. 26-39.

36 See M.J. Bonell, the UNIDROIT Principles in Practice: the Experience of the First Two Years, *ULR* 1997, partijen. 34-45; M.J. Bonell (ed.), The UNIDROIT Principles in Practice. Caselaw and Bibliography on the Principles of Commercial Contracts, Transnational Publishers Inc. (2002).

dertake such a momentous, albeit arduous, enterprise. However, it is not realistic to expect such a development to take place. Even if a 'Global Commercial Code' as advocated by some eminent figures in the unification of law were to materialise, such a Code most probably would weld together and systematise a number of existing instruments of international trade law and not create a general part of contract law.[37] The Principles could find a place in such a global instrument.[38]

The European Principles in their final stage will certainly have a strong influence on scholarly and educational developments in Europe in the years to come. However, even on the limited scale of the European Union it is by no means certain that a comprehensive codification of contract law will be a practicable solution.[39]

As a kind of successor to the Lando Commission, the Study Group on a European Civil Code[40] has taken up a number of other subjects of which a harmonised treatment will be indispensable in a future European legal framework. I think particularly of the law of securities on movable objects and claims, which is an important corollary to contract law. The same is true for tort law, since a unification of the rules on non-performance is only partially successful if for instance the producer or the seller of goods may be held liable in tort in a way which differs from country to country. As it is well known, the EC Directive on Product Liability does not infringe upon the national rules relating to the general part of the law of torts. Contract certainly is not dead, but it is equally certain that tort law flourishes, and this should also be reflected in the efforts directed towards the unification of the law in Europe.

---

37 G. Herrmann, The Role of Uncitral, in Fletcher/ Mistelis/Cremona (eds.), Foudations and Perspectives of International Trade Law (2001), pp. 28 ff. at p. 35; *Id.*, The Future of Trade Law Unification, *Internationales Handelsrecht (IHR)* 1-2001, pp. 6-12, at. p. 12; M.J. Bonell, Do We Need a Global Commercial Code?, *Dickinson Law Review* Vol. 106, 2001, pp. 87 ff. at p. 98 [also in *ULR* 2000, pp. 469 ff.]

38 See A.S.Hartkamp, Modernisation and harmonisation of Contract Law: Objectives, Methods and Scope, *ULR* 2003, pp. 81-90 with further references.

39 But see section 3 under 6 and footnote 24.

40 Already mentioned in footnote 16. See C. von Bar, The Study Group on a European Civil Code, in Alpa/Buccico (*eds.*), Il Codice Civile Europeo (Giuffrè 2001), pp. 20-33.

CHAPTER 8

Procedural Implications of Civil Law Unification

Konstantinos D. Kerameus*

1 Introduction

1.1. In the first edition of this book[1] Marcel Storme offered an overall picture of both worldwide trends to procedural approximation and European Community law requirements to this effect.[2] With regard to the latter aspect, he indicated some conspicuous discrepancies among national procedural rules in Europe on certain issues[3] and stressed the very function of internal market as a reason or, indeed, a mandate leading to some degree of procedural approximation.[4] He also referred briefly[5] to the outline of the work done, under his chairmanship, by the European Commission on Civil Procedure[6] and concluded by describing some methods of effecting the desired result.[7]

I had in 1990 the opportunity to present some considerations on types, conditions, and limits to procedural unification.[8] Based on an elaboration of the distinction between legal unification in general and procedural unification in particular,[9] that essay dealt with international, as opposed to internal procedural unification in a federal state, with derivative, as opposed to autonomous, procedural unification, and with partial, as opposed to global, procedural unification.[10] In this respect, a procedural unification may be called derivative to the extent that it tries not to endanger otherwise existing substantive uniformity: as did the old Italian Code of Civil Procedure of 1865, which paved the way not only to legal uniformity across the board in that country but also to national unity. In contrast, any procedural unification that is pursued regardless of substantive uniformity may be described as autonomous: for instance, both the 1958 New York Convention on recognition and enforcement of foreign arbitral awards and the 1968/1978/1982/1989/1996 Brussels Convention on jurisdiction and the enforcement of judgments in civil and commercial matters, since neither was

---

* Professor of Civil Procedure at the Faculty of Law, University of Athens; Director of the Hellenic Institute of International and Foreign Law; President of the International Academy of Comparative Law.

1 Hartkamp, Hessenlink, Hondius, du Perron, Vranken (1994).
2 Storme (1994), pp. 83-95.
3 *Ibid.*, p. 88.
4 *Ibid.*, pp. 86-89.
5 *Ibid.*, p. 94.
6 Storme, ed. (1994).
7 Storme, *supra* note 2, p. 95.
8 Kerameus (1995), pp. 21-46.
9 *Ibid.*, pp. 49-52.
10 *Ibid.*, pp. 52-55.

based on any preceding substantive unification.[11] The essay tried to explain why any meaningful procedural unification requires both a certain degree of convergence among the rules considered for unification and a somehow homogeneous constituency.[12] Finally, important limits to procedural unification were located in judicial organisation, in the diversity of functions attributed to the same procedural institution by various legal systems, and in the scope of unification along the line of distinction between international and purely domestic cases.[13]

1.2. The question to be answered here refers to the procedural implications of European civil law codification. An answer to that question was articulated in my essay included in the second revised and expanded edition of this book in 1998.[14] Now, five years later, I am trying to adapt that essay to the changes which have taken place in between. Now, as well as then, attention should be paid to the procedural unification which may prove to be necessary in order to implement, or at least not to jeopardise, the expected uniform body of substantive law. The procedural unification we are talking about is then, in view of the types just mentioned, clearly derivative. As far as the other pairs of unification are concerned (international – internal, global – partial), the appropriate qualification may raise some doubts. It is true that all legal unification within the European Union is inspired by the desire to promote the functioning of the single internal market. State borders, however, have not been eliminated, and the European Union is not, at least for the time being, a federal state. Accordingly, still in the 1990's, legal approximation used to be brought about by conventions or directives rather than by regulations; this meant, among other things, that the active cooperation of the member states was required. After the Treaty of Amsterdam the allocation of normative power within the European Union has changed. The transfer of justice and internal affairs from the third to the first pillar created the bundle of five procedural regulations which, within the short period of two years, changed the legal climate of the European Union.[15]

Finally a cautious position should be taken with regard to the global or partial scope of unification. A complete European civil code is not yet in close sight. Even if the general part of a civil code and the law of obligations might be apt for unification, no relevant work has been done, and presumably is not yet feasible, with regard to property, family and succession law. Besides, no overall uniform codification is envisaged for other parts of private law, like commercial or labour law, although they

---

11 The Lugano Convention of 16 September 1988 on jurisdiction and the enforcement of judgments in civil and commercial matters belongs to the same group.
12 Kerameus, *supra*, note 8, pp. 56-59.
13 *Ibid.*, pp. 61-65.
14 Kerameus (1998), pp. 121-132.
15 Council Regulation (EC) No 1346/2000 of 29 May 2000 on insolvency proceedings, OJ L 160/ 30.06.2000, pp. 1-18; Council Regulation (EC) No 1347/2000 of 29 May 2000 on jurisdiction and the recognition and enforcement of judgments in matrimonial matters and in matters of parental responsibility for children of both spouses, OJ L 160/30.06.2000, pp. 19-36; Council Regulation (EC) No 1348/2000 of 29 May 2000 on the service in the Member States of judicial and extrajudicial documents in civil or commercial matters, OJ L 160/30.06.2000, pp. 37-52; Council Regulation (EC) No 44/2001 of 22 December 2000 on jurisdiction and the recognition and enforcement of judgments in civil and commercial matters, OJ L 012/16.01.2001, pp. 1-23; Council Regulation (EC) No 1206/ 2001 of 28 May 2001 on cooperation between the courts of Member States in the taking of evidence in civil or commercial matters, OJ L 174/27.06.2001, pp. 1-24.

have been partly unified since the 1930s through international conventions. We are thus left with the prospect of a partial codification on the substantive level which cannot be exceeded in terms of coverage on the procedural one. Even in the areas of actual substantive law unification, the limitations to procedural unification[16] may well lead to a convergence of procedural norms which is narrower in scope than the substantive one; for instance, judicial organisation and all that flows therefrom, such as existence and scope of methods of appeal, is hardly suitable for unification.

1.3. There remains, then, on the table the prospect of a procedural unification which is derivative, partial, and midway between internal and international. Its derivative character calls, however, for a clarification. What is, undoubtedly, meant is that procedural unification becomes necessary to the extent that the operation of the unified substantive rules might otherwise be hampered or even frustrated. In this obvious respect the terms of reference of procedural unification are delivered by the correlative substantive unification. Nevertheless, one may think of somewhat broader terms of reference as well. Three important instruments of overall European integration come to mind: the European Convention on Human Rights (1950), the Treaty of Rome (1957) in its present shape after the Treaty of Amsterdam (1997), and the Brussels Convention (1968/1978/1982/1989/1996) on jurisdiction and the enforcement of judgments in civil and commercial matters. Since Marcel Storme already dealt with the impact of the Treaty of Rome, and particularly its rules on free movement and the internal market, on procedural unification,[17] I will limit myself, in the second part of this essay, to the other two parameters.

2 Safeguarding the Civil Law Unification

2.1 Substantive Rules Referring to the Commencement of Procedure

Several substantive rules, mainly in the area of obligations, explicitly or implicitly refer to the time of bringing a suit or of commencement of proceedings in order for some substantive consequences to take effect. For instance, as from the time of bringing a suit, the defendant's liability with regard to safekeeping the thing vindicated may increase; interest on a money claim may start running in any event, that is regardless of the defendant's culpability in defaulting; the running of the statute of limitations is interrupted;[18] the litigation is deemed to be pending *(lis pendens)* in all respects.[19] The examples indicated show that the operation of several substantive

---

16 Kerameus, *supra,* note 8, pp. 61-65.

17 Storme, *supra* note 2, pp. 87-90; see also *idem* (1992).

18 The characterisation of prescription as a substantive or procedural institution has deeply separated the civil from the common law world, although the traditional procedural qualification under common law seems now to be on the verge of vanishing; see the volume edited by Hondius (1995), pp. 23-24 (Hondius), pp. 95-96 (Des Rosiers), pp. 149-151 (Bandrac), pp. 209-210 (Gilead). Wengler (1981) I pp. 374-375, II p. 902 n. 188, offered a convincing explanation why the common law regards prescription as procedural, by conceiving it in terms of time limits to the jurisdiction of the courts: 'Man könnte hier von einer zeitlichen Beschränkung der Zuständigkeit des Gerichts sprechen'.

19 *Lis pendens* as such may serve both procedural and substantive functions. See Pälsson (1970) 59.

rules turns on a procedural phenomenon,[20] which is undoubtedly the bringing of a suit. In order to produce uniform results any substantive law unification which wishes to avoid becoming dead letter, has either to deal with the matter itself or else to be joined by a concomitant procedural unification. Since, for systematic reasons, the former alternative would rarely be followed, the second one must, as a rule, be chosen. According to this point of view, procedural unification becomes a corollary to the substantive one, providing it with the necessary tools for meaningful implementation. By the same token, the coherence of the legal system is stressed, as, in particular, no gaps between substance and procedure are allowed or left over. Thus, the first area of procedural unification, being implied or even compelled by a substantive one, lies where rules of substance, in order to become operative, require by their very wording some procedural underground.

Now Council Regulation (EC) No 44/2001 on jurisdiction and the recognition and enforcement of judgments in civil and commercial matters (Brussels I) gives, after the reticence of the Court of Justice of the European Communities,[21] a detailed answer as to the relevant time of seising a court (Art. 30):

> "For the purposes of this Section, a court shall be deemed to be seised:
> 1. at the time when the document instituting the proceedings or an equivalent document is lodged with the court, provided that the plaintiff has not subsequently failed to take the steps he was required to take to have service effected on the defendant, or
> 2. if the document has to be served before being lodged with the court, at the time when it is received by the authority responsible for service, provided that the plaintiff has not subsequently failed to take the steps he was required to take to have the document lodged with the court".

In substance, the new rule focuses on the first leg within the procedure of seising a court, *i.e.* either the lodging of the introductory document with the court or the delivery of the same document to the authority responsible for service. However, the unifying effect of the new rule is limited by two caveats. First, in both of the above instances, reliance on the first leg also imposes "that the plaintiff has not subsequently failed to take the steps he was required to take" in order for him to complete the second leg as well. While this second leg is clearly identified, it remains to be seen whether there might be any maximum time limit between the two legs. The second caveat refers to the starting sentence of Article 30 limiting its applicability [to] "[f]or the purposes of this Section", which is section 9 of chapter II: "Lis pendens-related actions". Such self-limitation probably leaves out substantive consequences of seising a court and, therefore, frustrates any beneficial effect of procedural unification upon substantive issues.

2.2 Substantive Rules on the Borderline with Procedural Rules

The second area does not include any reference to procedure but consists of rules that, in many legal systems, move on the borderline between substance and proce-

---

20 *Tatbestandsmerkmal*, in the German terminology.
21 Case 129/83, *Zelger* v. *Salinitri*, judgment of 7 June 1984, ECJ Reports 1984, p. 2397.

dure. To the extent that such rules, explicitly or implicitly, have been unified in a civil law codification, it is advisable that no inconsistent rules continue to exist on the procedural side. Otherwise, the substantive unification is going to be thwarted in this respect.

For instance, Article 2.101 (ex Art. 5. 101), as drafted by the Second Lando Commission on the formation of contracts, reads under the heading 'Conditions for the Conclusion of a Contract' as follows:

> "(1) A contract is concluded if:
>   (a)   the parties intend to be legally bound, and
>   (b)   they reach a sufficient agreement, without any further requirement.
> (2) These Principles do not require a contract to be concluded or evidenced in writing or to be subject to any other requirement as to form. The contract may be proved by any means, including witnesses."[22]

Obviously, the purpose of the second paragraph, already announced by the last words of the first paragraph ('without any further requirement'), is to depart from a well known rule in the Romanistic legal family which generally requires documentary evidence in all contracts beyond a specified monetary value, in other words, not by witnesses.[23] It is disputed whether such rule delineates the admissibility of methods of proof and therefore belongs to procedure or rather, at least indirectly, points to the form of concluding a contract and therefore is to be located on the substantive level. This debate is also reflected in, or animated through, its wavering position between civil codes and codes of civil procedure, and has a clear impact on private international law as far as the problem of qualification is concerned.[24] In any event, if a substantive law unification takes up the matter and regulates it, then – regardless of the content of the rule – the very idea and purpose of such unification demands that all national rules pertaining to the same matter, concurring and opposite alike, and regardless of their position in a code of civil procedure or a civil code, be eliminated. So far, substantive law unification may pre-empt rules of procedure.

The same is true with regard to the burden of proof. Here again, the respective rules may be classified as procedural or substantive. Actually, explicit rules on burden of proof are rare. In most cases they limit themselves to some very broad principles enunciated in codes of civil procedure, and for the rest the allocation of the burden of proof is derived from the way each substantive rule is drafted. That is, whether the requirements for a legal consequence to take effect are worded as conditions for the creation of a claim or as exceptions to be pleaded and proved by the defendant; in the first instance the burden of proof lies with the obligee, in the second with the obligor. In this respect, several rules of the first part of European Contract Law Principles (on the performance of contractual obligations) contain indeed, in

---

22   Lando/Beale (2000), pp. 138, 142-143.
23   See art. 1341 of the French Code Civil; arts. 393-394 of the Greek Code of Civil Procedure. Now Kötz/Flessner (1998), pp. 78-96; Beale/Hartkamp/Kötz/Tallon (2002), pp. 154-175.
24   See, for instance, Batiffol/Lagarde (1983), no. 600 ; Wengler (1981), I pp. 361-364 ; Kegel/Schurig (2000), pp. 553-554.

their very wording, an implied allocation of burden of proof.[25] Here again there will be a pre-emption vis-à-vis national rules, including procedural ones, on the same matters.

2.3 Procedural Rules which Support Substantive Rules

The third group of eventual procedural implications through a civil law unification goes further, presenting a lower degree of connection. In fact, we are not talking here about the direct implications of a civil law unification but rather about some procedural adaptations and improvements which may, or should, be envisaged as the opportunity for a comprehensive overhaul of the substantive law structure arises. The underlying consideration is the idea that substantive law does not exist in a vacuum but aspires to be complied with and, if need be, implemented by adjudication and enforcement. The possibility of adjudication, however remote, forms part of the system of functional coordinates that bear upon both the drafting and the interpretation of substantive norms. Substantive law is neither an abstract conglomeration of mandates nor a scholarly exercise; it is a system in operation. This is why modern trends in legal doctrine highlight with growing intensity the unavoidable coherence between rules of substance and rules of procedure, even in systems which have lived for a long time under a strong separation of the two branches of law.[26] That is also why any important substantive law codification has to take care of some not inconsistent procedural framework; and any important substantive law unification needs a minimum amount of common, or at least approximated, procedural instruments so that the purpose of substantive unification is not to be defeated from the very beginning.

In today's European legal reality, two such procedural instruments, which require a considerable degree of unification and deserve high priority, seem to be the provisional remedies and the order for payment of money claims. It is true that both – the second stronger than the first one – pertain more to the commercial and business activity than to other parts of classical private law, such as family and succession law. But, on the other hand, both, and particularly the provisional remedies, are often resorted to in all areas of private law, including its most personal, as opposed to transactional, parts. In addition, contemporary European integration as promoted by the European Union aspires in the first place to a single internal market rather than to a single society. This is, by the way, the leading reason why present attempts at civil law unification are mainly directed to the general part of a civil code and to the law of obligations. Lastly, a common and grave weakness of the administration of justice across the European board is located in the towering delays rather than in the quality of justice itself, once delivered. Consequently, the European Commission on Civil Procedure put both items on the first list of its agenda. One has to acknowledge that even a unified European civil law on the formation of contracts and the performance of obligations will not have in practice the same contents, and certainly not the same

---

25 This is called by Hartwieg, in a comparative paper presented to the common study programme of German and Greek Law Faculties, 'autonome Beweislast' in the framework of the 1980 Vienna Convention on Contracts for the International Sale of Goods.

26 Characteristically, for Germany, Blomeyer (1955), pp. 51 *et seq.*; Zeuner (1959); Henckel (1970).

effect, so long as the methods of its implementation will rely on largely divergent accessibility to, and operation of, provisional remedies and orders for payment. Nevertheless, substantive law unification may be slow to show an impact in this area. Europe has lived for about seventy years under uniform rules on commercial paper but without any common rules on orders for payment.

There remains, of course, the question of how the unified rules on these two procedural institutions should look like. In this respect no valuable assistance may be obtained from the civil law unification, except for the proposition that provisional remedies and orders for payment should be provided for, and they should be speedy and effective means of judicial protection. The fact, however, that the contents of these two procedural instruments are not pre-empted by the unified substantive rules does not negate the idea that there may well be some procedural implications of substantive law unification. Reciprocal influence between substance and procedure may indeed be value-empty. It often requires only the existence and operation of instruments, any instruments, that are fit to expediently serve the purposes set by the other branch of law. This is true, for instance, even as far as the first example in our discussion is concerned: substantive law unification requires a single procedural rule about the time of bringing a suit but does not impose or expect the determination of a particular time. What is needed is a common rule regardless of its content. Of course, the second set of our examples, namely the need for consistent rules in ambivalent areas, such as the form and proof of contracts or the allocation of the burden of proof, are value-oriented, in the sense that the functional coherence of substance and procedure requires in this case a common approach. But this is an exception within the whole spectrum of coexistence between substantive and procedural law. This exception is dictated by the fact that what is at stake here is to adopt a common approach over issues that are vindicated and addressed by both branches of law. For the rest, an explicit or implied reference from one branch to the other is satisfied as soon as the latter sets up a common instrument, regardless of its content. Commonality rather that quality is here what is asked for.

2.4 Technical Procedural Rules

The final ring in this chain of possible implications is made out of some purely technical procedural rules, which do not have any specific connection to substantive law but may well serve its purposes and operation. They generally include rules on the computation of time and the notification of documents. Both issues are traditionally considered as procedural but may become relevant within a purely substantive law context, for instance in order to calculate time provided for in a contract, or to serve extra-judicial declarations. Thus, an eventual unification on these points would reach a wider audience covering, as it were, both branches of law.

In national legal systems the notification of documents is usually dealt with in codes of civil procedure, and civil codes silently refer to them. As far as the computation of time is concerned, there is in the former not only an implicit[27] but in some instances an express[28] reference to the latter. Other countries prefer an autonomous

---

27 Cf. Art. 155(2) of the Italian Code of Civil Procedure.
28 Art. 185(1) of the Spanish Ley orgánica del poder judicial; para. 222(1) of the German ZPO.

regulation of the matter in their respective codes of civil procedure.[29] A similar position is taken in England through Rules 2.8-2.11 of the Civil Procedure Rules 1999. The modern tendency clearly goes in favour of laying down rules on computation of time for procedural purposes, regardless of whether similar or different rules exist in the various countries for substantive purposes.

However, the location of the rules is here irrelevant since the interests to be accommodated are identical, wherever the rules are to be found. The only thing that matters is that common rules should exist with respect both to substance and procedure. The starting point of unification is only a matter of convenience and expediency. The European Commission of Civil Procedure presented rules on computation of time and envisaged their extension to substantive law as well.[30] Should, however, the unification in the substantive law area take the lead, the new unified rules should have a wide scope of application and cover the issues addressed in all respects. By the same token, some additional procedural issues that display purely technical aspects and are devoid of intrinsic values other than order and integrity, such as procedural nullities or disqualification of judges, may be tackled as well.

3   External parameters

We have examined so far the procedural implications to be expected from an eventual substantive law unification in Europe. We have, however, indicated that, beside the civil law rules to be potentially unified, there already exist at least two other parameters which have an impact upon procedural unification, namely the Brussels Convention on jurisdiction and enforcement and the European Convention on Human Rights. Some reflections have to be devoted to them, starting from the former which, although considerably later as to the time of adoption, has exercised an earlier and more compact influence.

3.1 The Brussels Convention

A permanent problem with regard to the Brussels Convention has always been the distinction between autonomous and non-autonomous interpretation. This distinction pervades the case law of the Court of Justice of the European Communities. In fact, the procedural unification brought about by the Brussels Convention is qualified as partial, international and autonomous, the last qualification meaning that the Convention was not based on any preceding substantive unification but had rather to proceed on its own, setting purely procedural standards and goals. Thus the Court identified the place where the harmful event occurred;[31] determined the law under which the

---

29 For instance, Austrian ZPO paras. 123-129, 140-143; Belgian Code judiciaire arts. 48-57; French C.C.Proc. arts. 640-647, and Décret no. 72-788 of 28 August 1972 art. 192; Greek C.C.Proc. arts. 144-158; Portuguese C.C.Proc. arts. 143-148, 153; nowadays also the new Spanish LEC (law 1/2000) arts. 130-136.

30 Cf. Kerameus (1993), p. 241, 244.

31 Case 21/76, *Bier* v. *Mines de potasse d'Alsace*, judgment of 30 November 1976, ECJ Reports 1976,

place of performance of a contractual obligation had to be established;[32] decided which proceedings may have as their object rights *in rem* in immovable property, considering in effect the essence of the Roman-law originated *actio pauliana*;[33] or ruled on the same cause of action as a condition to *lis pendens*.[34] If, however, the Convention failed to rest on a body of unified substantive law to be served by the Convention, it did build upon existing national rules on international jurisdiction and enforcement. And since only a partial procedural unification has thus been achieved, the recurring question has arisen as to whether interpretation has to be made by reason of the Convention *per se,* as an autonomous set of rules, or rather by reference to the national procedural rules otherwise applicable.. The former alternative is called autonomous, the latter non-autonomous interpretation. One may discern that the adjective 'autonomous' is used here in a slightly different sense from the qualification of procedural unification as 'autonomous'. The difference lies in the terms of reference. They address in the former case national rules of procedure, while in the latter a unified body of substantive law. Nevertheless, in both instances 'autonomous' implies a self-contained search for values and interpretative guidance without outside control.

Against this background, my proposition is that the European Court of Justice, regardless of whether it adopts in a particular case an autonomous or non-autonomous interpretation of the Brussels Convention, contributes equally to an indirect procedural unification, albeit in different ways. The first case is almost obvious. Autonomous interpretation pretends to be uniquely derived from the system and the purpose of the Convention but in fact draws heavily on a comparative review of national legal systems. In the very first case in which autonomous interpretation was applied,[35] the Court, under Article 5 point 3 of the Convention, held that the place where the harmful event occurred includes both the place of event and the place of result, having ascertained that most legal systems of the member states adhere to such a twofold foundation of the *forum delicti.* Autonomous interpretation is, then, not solely limited to the body of the Convention but seems to extend beyond it, by reference to the common denominator of European procedural systems rather than by delegation to one system only. By doing so, it identifies the line of convergence among rules of procedure in the various European systems. It equally shows possibilities and contents of procedural unification.

It is surprising, but no less true, that even a non-autonomous stance taken by the Court may also pave the way to procedural unification. A telling example is offered by the second *Zelger/Salinitri* case[36] where, under Article 21 of the Convention, the

---

p. 1735; case C-364/93, *Marinari* v. *Lloyd's Bank*, judgment of 19 February 1995, ECJ Reports 1995, p. I-2719.

32 Case 12/76, *Tessili* v. *Dunlop*, judgment of 6 October 1976, ECJ Reports 1976, p. 1473; case 56/79, *Zelger* v. *Salinitri*, judgment of 17 January 1980, ECJ Reports 1980, p. 89; case C-32/88, *Six Constructions Ltd.* v. *Humbert*, judgment of 15 February 1989, ECJ Reports 1989, p. 341.

33 Case 115/88, *Reichert I* v. *Dresdner Bank*, judgment of 10 January 1990, ECJ Reports 1990, p. I-27.

34 Case 114/86, *Gubish* v. *Palumbo*, judgment of 8 December 1987, ECJ Reports 1987, p. 4861.

35 Case 21/76, *supra* note 31.

36 Case 129/83, *supra* note 21.

question when an action became definitively pending was explicitly referred to the national law of each court concerned. The Court did so once the comparative review of the laws of the six original member states failed to procure a conclusive answer.[37] It cannot be denied, however, that without a uniform determination of the issue when *lis pendens* is born, Article 21 of the Brussels Convention remains a *torso* and may well lead to inconsistent results.[38] This is why Council Regulation (EC) No 44/2001 attempted to provide a partly uniform answer, with the deficiencies and weak points explained above.[39]

In sum, the Brussels Convention and its detailed, refined and complex elaboration by the European Court of Justice have contributed, both positively and negatively, to procedural unification in Europe. Certainly, the Convention mainly addresses technical aspects of civil procedure. But technicality is more open to unification.[40] The Europe-wide elaboration on the Brussels Convention over the last thirty years has provided us with valuable tools for our profession.[41] What has been offered is no less than the grammar and the syntax of European civil procedure. Of course, this structural and conceptual framework needs to be fleshed out. But the basis is there. It extends an open invitation to balanced and considered additions. This tendency can only be strengthened by the substitution of Council Regulation (EC) No 44/2001 to the Brussels Convention. The very change from an international convention to a regulation will integrate the system of international jurisdiction and enforcement deeper into the Community structure and under the control of the Treaty of Amsterdam. On the other hand, a diverging approach to this Community instrument and the Lugano Convention cannot be ruled out.

3.2 The European Convention of Human Rights

A powerful response has been coming in recent years from the case law of the European Commission and the European Court of Human Rights under Article 6 of the Rome Convention. Certainly the Rome Convention is eighteen years older than the Brussels one. For almost three decades, however, only scarce attention was paid both by applicants as well as by the Strasbourg organs to the guarantee of a fair trial under Article 6(1)1. In contrast, the situation has been strikingly reversed in the 1980s and 1990s. It seems that no other provision of the Convention enjoys such a large number of applications[42] and such a close network of implementation – and indeed at an accelerated pace. One can only speculate about possible reasons for the reorientation of focus. Perhaps the more traditional human rights have by now more or less saturated the European continent, so that space has now become available for the consideration of such rights which, although not necessarily younger in origin,[43] nevertheless re-

---

37 *Ibid.*, points 11-12.
38 Cf. Kerameus/Kremlis/Tagaras (1989), Art. 21 no. 10, pp. 189-190.
39 See the text *supra* under 2.1.
40 See Kerameus, *supra* note 8, pp. 60-61.
41 In another context, Fasching (1984), p. 236, talks about 'Bauelemente des Verfahrens'.
42 In 1995 alone the Court dealt with 25 cases on Art. 6(1) of the Convention; JDI 1996, pp. 203-204.
43 The right to a fair trial, as described in Art. 6 ECHR, constitutes the second part of the due process of law, the first being the right to be protected against arbitrary arrest and detention (Art. 5 ECHR);

quire finer tuning to advanced needs; in the European reality of a generation ago the right to judicial protection might have been something hardly short of *luxuria immoderata*. Perhaps the increasingly crowded dockets of many courts and the corresponding delays in adjudication aroused the European sensibility vis-à-vis a potential control of judicial sloppiness. Maybe also legal circles around Europe had simply not been aware of the very existence and the hidden explosiveness of Article 6, due to deficient information or lack of precedents.

In any event, abundant case law is now flowing from Strasbourg under Article 6(1)1 with regard to three principal issues: the conclusion of litigation within a reasonable time; the right of all parties to a full and appropriate hearing; the adoption of safeguards of judicial impartiality and fair trial. Thus, in the case of *Allenet de Ribemont* v. *France*,[44] the Court held that the period of eleven years and eight months during which the French authorities debated the issue of whether or not to adjudicate compensation for the false incrimination of the petitioner was unreasonable, especially since it combined delays both before the administration and the courts. In the case of *Fischer* v. *Austria*,[45] the Court found that the judicial review of administrative action constitutes a manifestation of the right to a fair hearing and thus held that the applicant was denied access to a court of law. In the case of *Diennet* v. *France*,[46] the impartiality of a professional disciplinary body was questioned as some of its members had already sat during the examination of the same case in the first instance, while in the case of *Procola* v. *Luxembourg* it was the impartiality of the Conseil d'État, acting with the same membership in both its judicial and its administrative capacity, that was considered reprehensible.[47] The European Commission and the European Court of Human Rights have both developed an advanced ramification and specification of these three principles and evaluated against them several rules and practices of the national judiciaries.[48] In June 1996 Fritz Juenger stated at the Florence meeting on civil procedure (organised by the New York University School of Law) that, by having Article 6 of the Rome Convention and by handling it as it does, Europe has effectively acquired the due process clause of the Fifth and the Fourteenth Amendments to the Constitution of the United States – both in scope and in severity of implementation.

We have, thus, in Article 6 and its judicial elaboration a further important parameter of European procedural unification. If the Brussels Convention delivers the grammar and the syntax of European civil procedure, the Rome Convention provides, to a certain extent, some of its general principles and ideology. It is, however, an ideology transformed into practice, moulded closely to the facts and shaped through

---

see Roucounas (1995) no. 126 p. 84. Although the right to due process makes a first tentative appearance in Art. 7 of the Déclaration universelle des droits de l'homme et du citoyen (1789) and is guaranteed by the American Constitution (Fifth Amendment: 1791, and Fourteenth Amendment: 1868), it was effectively implemented in Europe only with Art. 6 ECHR (1950) while, on the global plane, it had to wait until Art. 14 of the 1966 International Covenant on Civil and Political Rights.

44 Series A, no. 308, judgment of 10 February 1995; see also JDI 1996, pp. 211-213.
45 Series A, no. 312, judgment of 26 April 1995; see also JDI 1996, pp. 216-218.
46 Series A, no. 325-A, judgment of 26 September 1995; see also JDI 1996, pp. 247-249.
47 Series A, no. 326, judgment of 28 September 1995, JDI 1996, p. 253-255.
48 See Henckel (1993), pp. 185-196; Matscher (1995); Rechberger and Oberhammer (1993).

their combinations and requirements. The future legislator of European civil procedure could well treat the case law produced under Article 6 of the Rome Convention in the same way the drafters of the law of obligations in the German Civil Code of 1896, about one century ago, treated the *Pandektenrecht*.

4 Conclusion

The three parameters examined in this essay concur to procedural unification in Europe from different starting points and in different ways. The civil law unification expects procedural instruments fit to promote the unified substantive rules, or at least not inconsistent with them. Such instruments can be meaningfully created at the level of the European Union. The Regulation No 44/2001 on jurisdiction and the enforcement of judgments addresses some elementary issues in any procedural system and refers for their elaboration to the innovative wisdom of the Court of Justice of the European Communities. Finally, the European Convention on Human Rights considers the fair administration of justice as an enforceable right of any citizen against the state in its capacity as a dispenser of judicial protection and asks, in the first place, the European Court of Human Rights to specify and develop this right.

The divergent approach implies that varying procedural issues are envisaged, depending on the starting point and the purpose of each unification factor. It also implies that piecemeal, rather than systematic, coverage is attempted. As far as the Brussels and the Rome conventions are concerned, the enunciation of procedural principles by the respective high courts comes almost at random, relying heavily on propensity to, and perseverance in, litigation.[49] But this drawback, if drawback be, is inherent in any system built on case law. What underlies all three parameters is their partial character. Consequently, unified procedural rules will have to coexist, for a considerable period of time, with national rules. But such partial coexistence and reciprocal cooperation is also characteristic of the actual relationship between Community law and national law. At the end of the day, procedural unification can hardly go beyond the constraints and limitations that accompany European integration as a whole.

Bibliography

BIBLIOGRAPHY: Henri Batiffol/Paul Lagarde, *Droit international privé*, 7ᵗʰ edition, II (1983); H. Beale/A. Hartkamp/H. Kötz/D. Tallon, *European Contract Law* (2002); A. Blomeyer, Beiträge zur Lehre vom Streitgegenstand, in *Festschrift der Juristischen Fakultät der Freien Universität Berlin zum 41. DJT in Berlin 1955* (1955), pp. 51-77; H. Fasching, *Lehrbuch des österreichischen Zivilprozeßrechts* (1984); A.S. Hartkamp, M.W. Hessenlink, E.H. Hondius, C.E. du Perron, J.B.M. Vranken, eds., *Towards a European Civil Code* (Nijmegen, Dordrecht/Boston/London, 1994); A.S. Hartkamp, M.W. Hessenlink, E.H. Hondius, C.E. du Perron, C. Joustra, eds., *Towards a European Civil Code*, Second Revised and Ex-

---

49 One is reminded here of Lord Devlin's thought, albeit expressed in a different context: 'Where injustice is to be found is not so much in the cases that come to court, but in those that are never brought there. The main field of injustice is not litigation but non-litigation', as quoted by Storme, *supra* note 2, p. 92 *in fine*.

panded Edition (Nijmegen, The Hague/Boston/London, 1998); Wolfram Henckel, *Prozeßrecht und materielles Recht* (1970); Wolfram Henckel, Das Recht auf Entscheidung in angemessener Frist und der Anspruch auf rechtliches Gehör – Art. 6 Abs. 1 Satz 1 EMRK und das deutsche zivilgerichtliche Verfahren, in Oskar J. Ballon and Johann J. Hagen, eds., *Festschrift Franz Matscher zum 65. Geburtstag* (Vienna, 1993); E. Hondius, *Modern Developments in Extinctive Prescription. Limitation of Actions* (Reports to the XIVth International Congress of Comparative Law in Athens, 1995), pp. 89-121; Gerhard Kegel/Klaus Schurig, *Internationales Privatrecht*, 8th edition (Munich, 2000); K.D. Kerameus, Procedural Implications of Civil Law Unification in A.S. Hartkamp, M.W. Hessenlink, E.H. Hondius, C.E. du Perron, C. Joustra, eds., *Towards a European Civil Code,* Second Revised and Expanded Edition (Nijmegen, The Hague/Boston/London, 1998), pp. 121-132; K.D. Kerameus, Procedural Unification: The Need and the Limitations, in I.R. Scott, ed., *International Perspectives on Civil Justice. Essays in honour of Sir Jack I.H. Jacob, Q.C.* (1990), pp. 47-66, reproduced in K.D. Kerameus, *Studia iuridica* III (1995); K.D. Kerameus, Relevance and Computation of Time in Civil Procedure, in Oskar J. Ballon and Johann J. Hagen, eds., *Festschrift Franz Matscher zum 65. Geburtstag* (Vienna, 1993), pp. 241-250; K.D. Kerameus/G. Kremlis/H. Tagaras, *The Brussels Convention on Jurisdiction and the Enforcement of Judgments. An Article-by-Article Commentary* (Athens-Komotini, 1989) [in Greek]; H. Kötz/A. Flessner, *European Contract Law* I (translated by T. Weir, 1998); O. Lando/H. Beale eds., *Principles of European Contract Law,* Parts I and II Combined and Revised (The Hague/London/Boston, 2000); Franz Matscher, Der Einfluß der EMRK auf den Zivilprozeß, in Walter Gerhardt, Uwe Diederichsen, Bruno Rimmelspacher, Jürgen Costede, eds., *Festschrift für Wolfram Henckel zum 70. Geburtstag am 21. April 1995* (Walter de Gruyter, Berlin/New York 1995), pp. 593-614; Pälsson, The Institute of *Lis Pendens* in International Civil Procedure, *Scandinavian Studies in Law*, 14 (1970); Walter H. Rechtberger and Paul Oberhammer, Das Recht auf Mitwirkung im österreichischen Zivilverfahren im Lichte von Art. 6 EMRK, ZZP 106 (1993), pp. 347-370; E. Roucounas, *International Protection of Human Rights* (Athens, 1995) [in Greek]; Marcel Storme, ed., *Approximation of Judiciary Law in the European Union* (1994); Marcel Storme, Procedural Consequences of a Common Private Law for Europe in A.S. Hartkamp, M.W. Hessenlink, E.H. Hondius, C.E. du Perron, J.B.M. Vranken, eds., *Towards a European Civil Code* (Nijmegen, Dordrecht/Boston/London, 1994) pp. 83-95; Marcel Storme, Rechtsvereinheitlichung in Europa. Ein Plädoyer für ein einheitliches europäisches Prozeßrecht, RabelsZ 56 (1992), pp. 290-298; Wilhelm Wengler, *Internationales Privatrecht* I-II (1981); Albrecht Zeuner, *Die objektiven Grenzen der Rechtskraft im Rahmen rechtlicher Sinnzusammenhänge. Zur Lehre über das Verhältnis von Rechtskraft und Entscheidungsgründen im Zivilprozeß* (1959).

On the Legitimacy of Europeanising Private Law: Considerations on a Law of Justi(ce)-fication (*Justum Facere*) for the EU Multi-Level System*

Christian Joerges**

1 Introduction

The Europeanisation of private law is very much a topical theme. And although this theme is no longer very new, it has, in the last three years, developed a new dynamic. Anyone taking it up with the intention or hope of keeping up with the pace of legal policy development and remaining on top of the current stage of the academic debate is letting themselves in for a race in which he will inevitably feel like the unfortunate hare which, despite all its efforts, kept on arriving too late: something else will have changed or articles whose relevance has to be assessed first will have appeared. Anyone seeking to dodge such a race by specialising in the general is not necessarily any better off. Hasn't everything already been said? Is it enough to add, as Karl Valentin did in a ceremonial address, "Quite so, but not by everyone"?

Surveys of the development of the law, legal policy and the academic debate remain meaningful if and because every new systematisation of the material takes some constructive steps. Admittedly, the more immense the material appears, the more time consuming it becomes to sift through it. In the present context, I have to have recourse to a form of reconstruction of the factual position that lets me refer to previous work,[1] which I now sharpen so as to relate the debates on the Europeanisation of

---

*   A preliminary German version of the essay was presented at a Workshop on private law theory organised in co-operation with Gunther Teubner (Frankfurt a.M.) at the European University Institute in April 2002. That text was rewritten for the *Ius Commune* Conference in Amsterdam on 28-29 November 2002 and subsequently again revised. I would like to thank many participants of the Amsterdam conference and the contributors to the workshop in Florence for their comments and suggestions. I am in particular indebted to Christoph Schmid (Florence/Munich), much more than the references to his work in my footnotes can indicate. – The artifially created term in the subtitle is a translation of the Geman construct "Recht-Fertigungs-Recht", a notion used by Rudolf Wiethölter in a recent essay: "Recht-Fertigungen eines Gesellschafts-Rechts", Frankfurt a.M. 2001. Iain F. Fraser's suggests the translation "Justifications of a Law of Society", adding that the German *Rechtfertigung* can be etymologised as making/manufacturing law/right. "Justi(ce)-fication" or "justice-making law" may retain a touch more of the German term's message. But it needed a *connaisseur* of Roman law, namely Wolfgang Ernst, Bonn/Cambridge, to remind me that *justum facere* is the common root of Recht-Fertigung and justification.

** Professor of Economic Law at the European University Institute, Florence, Italy; Formerly at the Centre for European Law and Politics at the University of Bremen.

1   Esp. Ch. Joerges/G. Brüggemeier, Europäisierung des Vertrags- und Haftungsrechts, in: P.-Ch. Müller-Graff (ed.), *Gemeinsames Privatrecht in der Europäischen Gemeinschaft*, 2nd ed. Baden-Baden: Nomos 1999, 301 ff.; Ch. Joerges, The Impact of European Integration on Private Law: Reductionist Perceptions, True Conflicts and a New Constitutionalist Perspective, *European Law Journal* 3 (1997), 378 ff.

private law to the basic problem of the legitimation of law production in the EU (2). I distinguish between the three strategies of legitimation and, in the next section (3), go on to test and to query their viability on the basis of three sets of examples. These theses and antitheses are intended to pave the synthesis in the closing section (4), intended as an outline of the constructive answer to the principal question of the legitimacy conditions of the Europeanisation process.

2 Three Competing Patterns of Legitimation

Europe expects much of the law, exposing it to changes from top to bottom – and it has to justify these challenges itself. This is a requirement that may sound like a matter of course, which, indeed, is really a claim raised in the Treaties and Treaty amendments, but is, in reality, in need of clarification and hard to meet. Why? The process of European integration has been seen as forming and formatting a "sovereignty association of a special nature" [*Herrschaftsverband eigener Prägung*] as M. Rainer Lepsius[2] puts it – a happy formulation, since, by simply using the Weberian category of *Herrschaft* (domination/sovereignty) it designates a continuing key problem in the European project. This *Herrschaftsverband* is dependent on recognition by its subjects – and this *de facto* dependency has continued to become visible and perceptible.[3] Social scientists ought not, and we lawyers may not, satisfy ourselves with an empirical concept of legitimacy: are Europe's sovereignty claims so justifiable as to deserve our recognition, too? This is a question which we have to ask ourselves, irrespective of whether we bring in Jürgen Habermas[4] for the purpose or not.

And, in fact, legal science did ask the question of the basis of the validity of European law "from the outset", namely, in the very stage of the establishment of the EEC. It is my impression that this happened more fundamentally in Germany than elsewhere – not necessarily for good reasons, but certainly for compelling ones: the Federal Republic was still a very young democracy at that time and did not need to call this achievement into question. At the same time, it was dependent on being included in Europe. The basic law had emerged with foresight and consistency, and had made both aspects into positive law: the inviolability of democracy (in Article 79 III) and its openness to integration (in Article 23). Is this a paradox which is an example

---

2   For this German term, see M Rainer Lepsius, Die Europäische Union als Herrschaftsverband eigener Prägung (The European Union as a Sovereignty Association of a Special Nature), in: Ch. Joerges/Y. Mény/J.H.H. Weiler (eds.), *What Kind of Constitution for What Kind of Polity? Responses to Joschka Fischer*, Europäisches Hochschulinstitut, Florenz/Harvard Law School, 2000, 203 ff. (213 ff.); http://www.iue.it/RSC/symposium/.

3   This has now been given thorough treatment by the explanatory disciplines, most recently in K.J. Alter, *Establishing the Supremacy of European Law: the making of an international rule of law in Europe*, Oxford/New York: Oxford University Press 2001; A. Wiener, They Just Don't Understand! Finality and Compliance: Opposing Rationales in the European Constitutional Debate, Ms. Belfast 2002.

4   For a very pointed treatment, see, once again, J. Habermas, Remarks on Legitimation through Human Rights, in *id.*, *The Postnational Constellation*, Cambridge: Polity 2001, 113 ff., 113.

of the intrinsic contradictoriness of all law? It is, at any rate, a challenge around which all European law to date must turn and which keeps its interpreters so restless I wish to distinguish between three sets of attempts to find fixed points here and give the European process a firm normative basis.

2.1 Market Rationality as a Principle of (Constitutional) Law

The first, *"ordo*-liberalism" (a German version of neo-liberalism), was ready even before the EEC existed. It had been developed in the confusion of the Weimar Republic, and posited that a free order for economic life must be legally shaped ("constituted") so as to be protected from the opportunistic, discretionary encroachments of politics.[5] This tradition survived the "Third Reich", and marked the Federal Republic's sensibility in relation to economic policy as *Ordnungspolitik*.** In the course of European integration, *ordo*-liberalism became the German "dominant theory", with a peculiar double meaning for both the components of the term: it "dominated" among professors of economic law and in many unofficial and officious policy statements; but the practice of law and of politics looked different.[6] The same holds true for the Community and its law: The "four freedoms" guaranteed in the EEC Treaty, the opening up of the national economies, the bans on discrimination and the competition rules, were understood as a "decision" in favour of an economic constitution which met the conceptions of the *ordo*-liberal school with regard to the framework conditions for a competitive market system.[7] And the very fact that Europe was set in motion as a mere economic community conferred plausibility on the *ordo*-liberal argument: through the interpretation of the economic law provisions in the EEC Treaty as a legally established order committed to guaranteeing economic freedoms, the Community gained a legitimacy of its own, which was independent of the institutions of the democratic constitutional state, and from which legally binding

---

5   Cf., on this tradition D.J. Gerber, Constitutionalising the Economy: German Neo-liberalism, Competition Law and the "New" Europe, *American Journal of Comparative Law* 42 (1994), 25 ff.; W. Sauter, *Competition Law and Industrial Policy in the EU*, 1997, 26 ff.; oddly (and significantly), this tradition hardly appears in political science and sociology. A remarkable exception is Ph. Manow, *Modell Deutschland* as an interdenominational Compromise. Program for the Study of Germany and Europe, Working Paper No. 00.3. Center for European Studies, Harvard University, Cambridge, MA, 2000.

** Again (see note * above) a notion which tends to lose its meaning in translation. "Economic governance", the term used in pertinent documents of the European Convention website (http://european-convention.eu.int) has little in common with "Ordnungspolitik".

6   Cf., for example, Ch. Joerges, The Market without a State? States without Markets? Two Essays on the Law of the European Economy, EUI Working Paper Law 1/96, San Domenico di Fiesole 1996 (http://eiop.or.at/eiop/texte/1997-019 and -020.htm); "Good Governance" in the European Internal Market: Two Competing Legal Conceptualisation of European Integration and their Synthesis, in: A. v. Bogdandy/P.C. Mavroides/Y. Mény (eds.), *European Integration and International Co-ordination. Studies in Transnational Economic Law in Honour of Claus-Dieter Ehlermann*, Den Haag-London-New York: Kluwer Law International 2002, 219 ff.

7   Admittedly, the many exclases from *Ordnungspolitik* in the EEC Treaties where then to be understood as mere exceptions; and one has to be willing to overlook the "original sin" of the agricultural policies.

policy commitments of this Community followed.[8] This was a framework which left room for alternatives. For many years, in fact, until the internal market programmes of 1985 and the Single European Act of 1987, private law was left to itself.[9] In the course of these initiatives, the legal principle of mutual recognition was discovered for private law, thus establishing the hope that the mechanisms of regulatory competition would promote an "economic" rationalisation of private law in Europe.[10] At any rate, a European code of private law was also envisaged in the early 90's.[11] The newest version of this idea is now, however, called the "privatisation of private law".[12]

2.2 Integration Functionalism

The reference to market rationality was not, however, enough to allow European law to establish supranational validity claims. In international law, constitutional law and law of the state [*Staatsrecht*], – and it was in the categories of these disciplines that Europe was probed in legal terms – the concept of a supranational legal order binding on constitutional states was hard to follow.[13] However, since no constitutional justification, i.e., one based on a parliamentary majority, for supranational political governance was available, the Community's possibilities of action had to be limited by restrictions on both its powers and its future positions in favour of the "masters of the treaties". Admittedly, it was to be foreseen that these restrictions would constrain the

---

8   Particularly significant, here, is A. Müller-Armack, Die Wirtschaftsordnung des Gemeinsamen Marktes, in *idem, Wirtschaftsordnung und Wirtschaftspolitik*, Freiburg i.Br.: Rombach 1966, 401 ff.

9   Or more or less decisively preserved itself against relevant early "special statutory private law" [*sonderprivatrechtliche*] projects, which existed from the mid-seventies onward (and fit in with the picture sketched out here; cf., Ch. Joerges, Zielsetzungen und Instrumentarien der Europäischen Verbraucherrechtspolitik: Eine Analyse von Entwicklungen im Bereich des Zivilrechts, *Zeitschrift für Verbraucherpolitik* 3 (1979), 213 ff.; cf. B. Börner, Die Produkthaftung oder das vergessene Gemeinschaftsrecht, in: W.G. Grewe (ed.), *Europäische Gerichtsbarkeit und nationale Verfassungsgerichtsbarkeit. Festschrift zum 70. Geburtstag von Hans Kutscher*, Baden-Baden 1981, 43 ff.

10 For an official position, see Wissenschaftlicher Beirat beim Bundesministerium für Wirtschaft, *Stellungnahme zum Weißbuch der EG-Kommission über den Binnenmarkt* (Schriften-Reihe 51), Bonn 1986.

11 Cf., in particular, E.-J. Mestmäcker Die Wiederkehr der bürgerlichen Gesellschaft und ihres Rechts, *Rechtshistorisches Journal* 10 (1991), 177 ff., 190 ff.; W. Tilmann, Eine Privatrechtskodifikation für die Europäische Gemeinschaft, in P.-H. Müller-Graff (ed.), *Gemeinsames Privatrecht in der Europäischen Gemeinschaft*, Baden-Baden: Nomos 1993, 485 ff.

12 See the programmatic title of the September 2002 Heidelberg conference of the German Association of young teachers of civil law, http://www.junge.zivilrechtswissenschaftler.de/ – Another school of thought, represented first and foremost by Reinhard Zimmermann, conceptualises private law as an autonomous body of law freeing itself from national ties (and finding the way back to the *ius commune europaeum*); cf. R. Zimmermann, Das Römisch-Kanonische Ius commune als Grundlage europäischer Rechtseinheit, *Juristen Zeitung* 1992, 8 ff.; Der Europäische Charakter des englischen Rechts – Historische Verbindungen zwischen civil law und common law, *Zeitschrift für Europäisches Privatrecht* 1993, 4 ff. [reprinted in P.-Ch. Müller-Graff (ed.), *Gemeinsames Privatrecht in der Europäischen Gemeinschaft*, 2nd ed., Baden-Baden: Nomos 1999, 103 ff.]; see, also, *idem*, Roman Law and European Legal Unity, in A.S. Hartkamp/M.W. Hesselink/E. Hondius/C. Joustra/E. du Perron (eds.), *Towards a European Civil Code*, 2nd ed., Nijmwegen-Den Haag: Kluwer 1998, 21 ff.

13 For a instructive account of the legal history, see Ch. Tietje, *Internationalisiertes Verwatungshandeln*, Berlin: Duncker & Humblot 2001, 50 ff., 86 ff., 155 ff.

integration project too much and therefore endanger it. For this very reason, the need was to find an alternative basis for legitimising supranational governance. Hans Peter Ipsen very soon succeeded in this, with his description of the (then) three European Communities as "special purpose associations for functional integration" [*Zweckverbände funktioneller Integration*].[14] The term "special purpose association" denoted areas not foreseen in the *ordo*-liberal concepts – without, however, exposing Community law to democratic requirements. As a special purpose association, Europe was supposed to deal with questions of "technical realisation", i.e., administrative tasks that could – and had to – be conveyed to a supranational bureaucracy.[15]

That all this has to do with private law may seem an assertion which is far-fetched, but it will, perhaps, become easier to see if one bears in mind that Ipsen's functionalism was a continuation at European level of the second tradition in German economic law that K.W. Nörr[16] has called the concept of the "organised economy". This tradition is indifferent as to the *ordo* in its economic policy; or to put this in a constitutionally positive way, it leaves the ordering of the economy to the democratically certified legislator. But, once again, the question arose of how politics is to be legitimised if it outgrows this framework without being able to find a basis in international law? Ipsen's ingenious answer: Europe should be understood as institutionalising technocratic, functionalist rationality as the basis of and contents of its law. And this seemed, for a considerable period of time, to be an adequate cause for what integration policy was actually doing. However, this ceased to be the case when the internal market programme mentioned set to work, leading to regulatory strategies that Giandomenico Majone saw as copies of the American "economic and social regulation".[17] Europe was a "regulatory state", whose main task was to correct the manifestations of market failure, and it should be interested to quote non-majoritarian institutions.[18]

From such perspectives, "private law proper" continued to be marginal. Both European lawyers and private lawyers shared this view: the former were participating in renewing the whole regulatory framework for Europe's economy; the latter – most especially, Germany's academic community – complained about distortions of private law by European statutes but emphasised that the core areas of private law continued to be in national hands: the logic of integration policy and the logic of the development of private law were, seemingly, operating autonomously.[19]

---

14 H.P. Ipsen, Der deutsche Jurist und das Europäische Gemeinschaftsrecht, *Verhandlungen des 43. Deutschen Juristentages*, München: C.H. Beck 1964, Bd. 2 L 14 ff.

15 H.P. Ipsen, *Europäisches Gemeinschaftsrecht*, Tübingen: Mohr/Siebeck 1972, 176 ff.

16 *Die Republik der Wirtschaft. Teil I: Von der Besatzungszeit bis zur Großen Koalition*, Tübingen: Mohr/Siebeck 1999, 5 ff.; cf., earlier K.W. Nörr, *Zwischen den Mühlsteinen. Eine Privatrechtsgeschichte der Weimarer Republik*, Tübingen: Mohr/Siebeck 1988.

17 As a paradigm example: Regulating Europe: Problems and Perspectives, *Jahrbuch zur Staats- und Verwaltungswissenschaft* 3 (1989), 159 ff. for which he developed the corresponding legitimising formula.

18 For an interim balance, see G. Majone, *Regulating Europe,* London: Routledge 1996. Since then, the conceptual edifice has been steadily perfected: cf., for example, G. Majone, Non-majoritarian Institutions and the Limits of Democratic Governance: A Political Transaction-Cost Approach, *Journal of Institutional and Theoretical Economics* 157 (2001), 57 ff.

19 For more details, see Ch. Joerges/G. Brüggemeier, Europäisierung des Vertrags- und Haftungsrechts (note 1 *supra*), Ch. Joerges, The Impact of European Integration on Private Law (note 1 *supra*).

2.3 Europe as a (Social) State and Legislator for Private Law?

"Hard Code Now!" This title sounded like a battle cry and was meant to. Ugo Mattei, who inscribed it on his banners,[20] is more conciliatory and circumspect in reality than the slogan he chose is. A European civil code ought to lay down binding provisions, but be content with a minimal programme and be process orientated. Only in this way could it fit the "social fabric of European capitalism". Would this, then, mean a code "with deep enough foundations and high enough vaulting" to include these social matters "in its conceptual edifice" to a sort of Otto von Gierke *redivivus*?[21] Otto von Gierke may be forgotten outside Germany; but his critique of the formalism of the German code would still seem to be alive and topical.[22]

Would the "social" aspects of private law be in a safe harbour in a European civil code? This is a question that does not concern private law alone, but is connected with the fate of the welfare state as a whole. We shall come back to this.[23] The difficulties that such a vision faces are however, so massive that there is no sense in putting them off. To anticipate the argument that we are developing: the normative quality of the constitutional "social private law" is dependent on the interplay of parliamentary legislation and the non-parliamentary production of law, on regulatory policy, special statutory law and codification, on expert communities and on the general public.[24] These circumstances are not present in the European context, and will not emerge in any near future. That this is the case follows simply from the "state of the (European) Union": this polity is not unitary, but plural[25] ("heterarchical", as some call it;[26] or "mixed", as others do[27]). In it, there are – relatively – autonomous political units, none of which are empowered with the *Kompetenz-Kompetenz* which would be needed for an authoritative resolution of jurisdictional conflicts. The result is a very specific disjunction of "society" and "state", of economic freedoms and political rights, market citizenship and political citizenship. Let us distance ourselves from the two approaches initially dealt with: Europe has never become a "market

---

20 U. Mattei, Hard Code Now!, *Global Jurist Frontiers*, Vol. 2: No. 1 (2002), Article 1.
21 O. v. Gierke, *Die soziale Aufgabe des Privatrechts*, Berlin 1889, 17.
22 Cf., Ch. Schmid, On the Legitimacy of a European Civil Code, *Maastricht Journal of Comparative Law* 8 (2001), 277 ff.
23 Sections 3.3 and 4 below.
24 Cf., Ch. Joerges, Formale Freiheitsethik, materiale Verantwortungsethik und Diskursethik im modernen Privatrecht, in: F.U. Pappi (ed.), *Wirtschaftsethik. Gesellschaftswissenschaftliche Perspektiven (Sonderheft der Christiana Albertina Universität)*, Kiel 1989, 127 ff.; The Science of Private Law and the Nation-State, in F. Snyder, *The Europeanisation of Law. The Legal Effects of European Integration*, Oxford/Portland: Hart 2000, 47 ff., 70 ff.); O. Gerstenberg, Public Intervention, Private Ordering and Social Pluralism, in Ch. Joerges/O. Gerstenberg (eds.), *Private governance, democratic constitutionalism and supranationalism*, Luxembourg: European Commission (Directorate-General Science, Research and Development; EUR 18340 EN), 1998, 205 ff.
25 As so well argued by N. Walker, The Idea of Constitutional Pluralism, *Modern Law Review* 65 (2002), 317 ff.
26 K.-H. Ladeur, The Theory of Autopoiesis. An Approach to a Better Understanding of Post-modern Law. From the Hierarchy of Norms to the Heterarchy of Changing Patterns of Legal Inter-relationships, EUI Working Paper Law 99/3.
27 G. Majone, Delegation of Regulatory Powers in a Mixed Polity, *European Law Journal* 8 (2002), 319 ff.

without a state" in which a supranational economic constitution can assign private law in its area; and it is even less the European social state described to the Nation States. Instead, it is a *tertium* which finds itself in a "constitutional moment" that will continue to last for some time yet.[28]

3 Three Sets of Examples

Verba docent, exempla trahunt. But it is by no means the case that the sets of examples from the case law of the ECJ discussed below could "confute" the paradigms sketched out in the first section, or represent some "higher law". This is because these paradigms merely refer to sets of ideas in which legal concepts and arguments can find a theoretical basis. To that extent, they compete with each other. But it is not to be expected, say, that one of them will totally dominate "practice", or that one tradition of thought will disappear without trace. Nevertheless, the analysis below pursues systematic and theoretical claims: they are intended to illustrate problems graphically with all three of the paradigms set forth in the previous section, thus preparing the transition to the view sketched out in the concluding section.

3.1 Centros and Überseering: Freedoms of Market Citizenship as Political Rights, and the Obsolescence of Traditional Private International Law

The ECJ's *Centros* judgment[29] is to be regarded as its most important,[30] or, at least, the most debated one since the legendary Cassis de Dijon decision of 1979.[31] Expectations of the subsequent *Überseering* judgment were correspondingly tense.[32] So much has been written that it would seem appropriate to start with the three theses that are to be established below: (1) This case law transforms economic freedoms into rights of political participation. (2) It strives towards a juridification of regula-

---

28 This scepticism does not, as P. Legrand's [European Legal Systems are not Converging, *International and Comparative Law Quarterly* 45 (1996), 52 ff.], result from presumed unbridgeable communication difficulties between common law and civil law. Nor is it meant, as, for instance, in H. Collins, European Private Law and the Cultural Identity of States, *European Review of Private Law* 3 (1995), 353 ff., as a rigid defence of the "cultural" ties of private law. Instead, it assumes "two kinds of social integration – cultural *and* political. The former denotes the kind of integration that is needed for individuals and groups that seek to find out who they are or would like to be..., the latter does not rest upon a particular set of values but on transcultural norms and universal principles", E.O. Eriksen and J.E. Fossum, The EU and Post-national Legitimacy, Oslo: Arena-Working Paper 26/2000, text accompanying notes 40 ff. It is in this sense that I understand M.W. Hesselink, *The New European Legal Culture*, Deventer: Kluwer 2001, 72 ff.
29 Case 212/97, judgement of 9 March 1999, [1999] *ECR* I-1459 – *Centros Ltd* v. *Ervervsog Selskabsstrylsen*.
30 A Celex search on 25 March 2002 indicated 112 commentaries. That figure was too modest, for it did not take into account, for instance, of H. Halbhuber's monograph *Limited Company statt GmbH? Europarechtlicher Rahmen und deutscher Widerstand – Ein Beitrag zur Auslegung von Art. 48 EG und zum Europäischen Gesellschaftsrecht*, Baden-Baden: Nomos 2001.
31 Case 120/78, [1979] *ECR* 649 – *Cassis de Dijon.*
32 Case 208/00 [2002] *ECR* I-99 19 – *Überseering BV* v. *Nordic Construction Company Baumanagement* GmbH (NCC).

tory competition. (3) It has the potential of "constitutionalising" the Europeanisation process through a law of justification that leaves orthodox supranationalism behind without seeking refuge in classical private international law.

3.1.1 Centros

The judgment in *Centros* concerns the core of the European legal *acquis*, namely the freedoms of market citizens which apply directly and ought therefore to take primacy over national law. Moreover, the decision counts as a prolongation and strengthening of a perception that has deeply penetrated the legal consciousness and awareness of economic law: it is held to serve the so-called negative integration, because the directly valid freedoms support review of the content of national law by the ECJ, exposing the law to regulatory competition. The justification would deserve a more detailed argument than space allows here.[33]

As so often occurs, the facts of this seminal case were trivial: a Danish married couple, Marianne and Tony Bryde, wished to import wine into Denmark but not pay the fee of the DK 200,000 (28,000 Euro) that Denmark requires for the registration of companies. The two then hit on the idea of "cocking a snoot" at their Danish Law.[34] They founded, and this was in May 1992, a private Limited company in England, the now legendary Centros Ltd., and set up a subsidiary in Copenhagen – for none of these steps did they require more than the minimum capital investment.

However, the Danish authorities refused registration; the Brydes went to court; after all the courts had been gone through, the Højesteret brought the question[35] of whether the refusal of registration was compatible with the guaranteed of freedom of establishment (Article 43 [ex 52] taken together with Articles 52 and 58 EC Treaty) before the ECJ in early June 1997. The ECJ's answer (given on 9 March 1999) read:

'It is contrary to Articles 52 and 58 of the Treaty for a Member State to refuse to register a branch of a company formed in accordance with the law of another Member State in which it has its registered office but in which it conducts no business where the branch is intended to enable the company in question to carry on its entire business in the state in which that branch is to be created, while avoiding the need to form a company there, thus evading application of the rules governing the formation of companies which, in that state, are more restrictive as regards the paying up of a minimum share capital'.[36]

---

33 The following owes much to Barbara Trefil (whose LL.M. Thesis on "Centros und die Niederlassungsfreiheit von Gesellschaften in Europa" Working Paper Law 2003, also at http://www.iue.it/PUB/law03-9.pdf.

34 Their conduct is interpreted with this degree of severity by Germany' *maître penseur* of private international law, G. Kegel in his editorial in *Europäisches Wirtschafts und Steuerrecht* Heft 9/1999 ["There is something rotten in the State of Denmark"].

35 Para. 13.

36 Sentence 1 of the tenor of the judgment ECJ [1999] I-1947.

3.1.2   Interpretation

The ECJ is seen by some[37] as cautiously continuing its earlier case law on freedom of establishment[38] or radicalising it in a questionable fashion.[39] The incorporation theory [*Gründungstheorie*] is seen as having won through against the *Sitztheorie* (company seat principle) with the help of the ECJ.[40] None of this is true, it is argued by others: in Denmark, the incorporation theory applied anyway, and recognition of the seat of the company principle through the Daily Mail decision[41] does not come into it: hence, it is business as usual for private international law (PIL).[42] Again, the ECJ is seen as opening the road to regulatory competition, so one would now have to expect Delaware effects in Europe.[43]

My first thesis[44] seeks to demarcate itself from the doctrinal dichotomy between European law and PIL, between thinking in terms of primacy and linkage and the associated policy dualism of "negative" and "positive" integration. The way the ECJ treated the conduct of the Bryde couple seems to me to make this sort of interpretation plausible. European law, says the criticism of the ECJ, has no business interfering with a purely internal Danish matter. The Brydes, who were pursuing no business interests in England, ought to have bowed to their home sovereign. But are the Brydes only Danes? Do they have the "right to the most favourable legal system",[45] just because they are not merely citizens of Denmark, but also citizens of the EU? This is the way that I, in fact, read the ECJ: there is nothing in itself abusive in a citizen of a Member State founding a company in accordance with another Members State's provisions which are more favourable for him. That is simply his right.[46]

Certainly, *Centros* concerned the incorporation of a company in England; the Brydes never intended to do business in England, but merely wished to start their ac-

---

37 Completeness can scarcely be achieved by portraying the range of opinions. Specifically on the response in Germany, see H. Halbhuber, National Doctrinal Structures and European Company Law, *Common Market Law Rev.* 38 (2001); a very comprehensive survey "from outside" on the overall development of company law is offered by J. Wouters, European Company Law: *Quo Vadis?*, *Common Market Law Rev.* 37 (2000), 257 ff.; more topically, B. Trefil (note 33).

38 Judgment of 10.07.1986, Case C-79/85, [1986] *ECR* 2375 – *Segers*.

39 An opinion to be found in E Steindorff, Centros und das Recht auf die günstigste Rechtsordnung, *Juristen Zeitung* 1999, 1140 ff.

40 Cf., for example, P. Behrens, Das Internationale Gesellschaftsrecht nach dem Centros-Urteil des EuGH, *Praxis des Internationalen Privat und Verfahrensrechts* 19 (1999), 323 ff.; this was the question the Federal High Court submitted to the EJC on 25.05.2000; cf., the *Überseering* decision, II.1.4 below.

41 Case C-81/87, judgment of 27.09.1988, [1988] *ECR* 5483 – *The Queen/Treasury and Commissioners of Inland Revenue, ex parte Daily Mail and General Trust PLC*.

42 Thus, for example, W. Ebke, Das Schicksal der Sitztheorie nach dem Centros-Urteil des EuGH, *Juristen Zeitung* 1999, 656 ff.; P. Kindler, Niederlassungsfreiheit für Scheinauslandsgesellschaften? Die Centros-Entscheidung des EuGH und das inernationale Privatrecht, *Neue Juristische Wochenschrift* 1999, 1993 ff.; W.-H. Roth, Case Note, *Common Market Law Rev.* 37 (2000), 147 ff.

43 It was especially paragraph 20 in Advocate General La Pergola's Opinion that inspired this sort of interpretation.

44 Above text before Section 3.1.

45 E. Steindorff, Centros und das Recht auf die günstigste Rechtsordnung, note 39 *supra*.

46 Para. 27; cf. para. 29.

tivities to Denmark. But can one call the freedom to exploit the provision of English law an abuse? No, the ECJ insists:

'[T]he fact that a national of a Member State who wishes to set up a company chooses to form it in the Member State whose rules of company law seem to him the least restrictive and to set up branches in other Member States cannot, in itself, constitute an abuse of the right of establishment. The right to form a company in accordance with the law of a Member State and to set up branches in other Member States is inherent in the exercise, in a single market, of the freedom of establishment guaranteed by the Treaty'.[47]

Is this "negative integration", interference with Denmark's constitutional autonomy, or new confirmation of the deregulatory effect of the freedoms?[48] Is the ECJ sending Europe's constitutional law off on the road to Delaware? Not really. For Denmark remains entitled to impose regulatory requirements on both its own – and on foreign – citizens, but has to adduce "compelling grounds of public interest". European law does not push Danish law aside, but places it under pressure of justification. It was this pressure that Denmark could not stand up to: it was completely unable to achieve the protection of creditors which, according to the Danish government's presentation, was the object of the Danish regulation – that was the ECJ's finding.[49] The ECJ acted as a constitutional court. It assumed the right to test Danish law according to whether it respects rights guaranteed at European level. However, the limits imposed on Denmark are limited. Denmark is entitled to protect its creditors and act against fraud – but in accordance with the provisos familiar to the readers of the case law on Article 28 [ex 30].[50] Denmark very soon, in May 2000, adopted a new regulation according to which companies wishing to do business in Denmark and having their main administrative centre there, must either deposit a caution amounting to DK 110,000 with the Danish bank authorities in the form of cash, government bonds or bank guarantees (which in the event of insolvency serve exclusively to meet tax demands), or else it must be clear that minimum assets of at least DK 125,000 are available.[51]

Merely putting new gloss on the old provisions? Danish commentators think so.[52] In its judgment of 3 February 2002, the Danish Supreme Court was silent on the issue of Centros' tax liability; it simply reprimanded that the forms had not been completed correctly.[53] What, then, is so "rotten" – in the State of Denmark – or elsewhere?[54]

---

47 Para. 35.

48 M. Baudisch discusses and contests this point in a very comprehensive study: From Status to Contract. A American Perspective on Recent Developments in European Company Law, Ms. New York (Columbia Law School) 2002.

49 Paras. 34-36.

50 Paras. 37-39; for a lucid analysis, cf., U. Forsthoff, Niederlassungsrecht für Gesellschaften nach dem Centros-Urteil des EuGH: Eine Bilanz., Europarecht 2000, 167 ff., 192 ff.

51 Cf., B. Trefil (note 33 supra), at 31 ff., with references to www.retsinfo.dk and a survey of the debate on the questionability in European law of the new regulations.

52 F. Hansen, From C 212 to L 212 – Centros Revisited, European Business Organisation Law Review 2 (2001), 141 ff., 156: "a flagrant violation of Article 43 EU".

53 Ugeskrift for Retsvæn 2002.1079H; Laurits Christensen (Copenhagen) and Hanne B. Jensen (Florence) kindly pointed me to the judgment.

54 G. Kegel, note 34 supra.

Denmark has to justify itself before its own citizens in the forum of the ECJ. It is entitled to pursue its regulatory interests, but it also has to show that the means it chooses serve the ends it pursues. What sort of law, then, are we dealing with here? Provisions that subject the case to the "geographically" best-suited jurisdiction? A legal innovation supported by comparative studies? Is what is at stake rather a European "conflict of laws" to the extent that it involves dealing with legal differences, a conflict of laws that seeks to reconcile Denmark's political autonomy with the granting of European citizenship rights to Danish citizens? In reshaping economic freedoms as rights to political participation, I see the constitutional core of the decision: private autonomy and political rights in democracies, so has Jürgen Habermas continually argued since *Between Facts and Norms*,[55] have to be conceived as having both an equivalent original dignity.[56] What does this mean in the European context? According to the *Centros* judgment, it means that a Danish citizen can bring his sovereign to court with the argument that the latter has no good reasons for denying him the use of the regulatory alternatives offered by another Member State. Adoption of Rudolf Wiethölter's term "law of just-ification" in order to conceptualise this type juridification of the Europeanisation process seems to me at least admissible.[57]

So much for the bright side of the *Centros* story. It is, however, not the only one. Neither the Danish legislator nor administrative practice, and not even the judiciary demonstrate themselves as deliberating actors ready, let alone eager, to learn from their European neighbours. It seems all the more important, then, that the ECJ can play its role convincingly. And this is one of the troubling impasses of the Europeanisation process: although the Court's statements convince normatively, it is questionable whether the Court will be able to cope factually with the supervision functions it has assigned to itself. I will have to come back to this question in all sets of the examples and in my conclusions.

3.1.3 The Consequences, and "Überseering"

What will the impact of *Centros* be on European company law? Will the courts of the Member States "implement" its deregulatory potential?[58] Will Europe's small firms flee to British law?[59] Will increasingly outlandish services be offered by limited com-

---

55 *Faktizität und Geltung*, Frankfurt a.M.: Suhrkamp 1992, 109 ff.; *Between Facts and Norms*, Cambridge, MA: MIT Press 1998, 82 ff., 133 ff.

56 Cf., his recent restatement in Constitutional Democracy: A Paradoxical Union of Contradictory Principles?, *Political Theory* 29, 766-781, as well as "So, why does Europe need a Constitution?", http://www.iue.it/RSC/EU/Reform02(uk).pdf.

57 S. Deakin, Regulatory Competition versus Harmonisation in European Company Law, *Cambridge Yearbook of European Law* 2 (1999), 231 ff. illustrates with the help of Centros his concept of "reflexive harmonisation" which risks, in my view, deducing normative conclusions from analytical concepts and factual observations. But, see M. Dougan, Vive La Différence? Exploring The Legal Framework For Reflexive Harmonisation Within The Single European Market, ms. Cambridge 2002; O. Gerstenberg, Expanding the Constitution Beyond the Court: The Case of Euro-constitutionalism, *European Law Journal* 8 (2002), 172 ff., 179 ff.

58 Cf., the case note by K. Nemeth, 37 *CMLRev.* (2000), 1277 ff.

59 This is discussed and disputed by M. Baudisch, From Status to Contract. An American Perspective on Recent Developments in European Company Law, ms. New York (Columbia Law School) 2002 (on file with the author).

panies incorporated in the UK?[60] Will the German model of company law that seeks to protect the public interest through mandatory organisational provisions and regulation be replaced by Anglo-Saxon corporate governance philosophies?

Can the ECJ be expected to have the answers to all these questions? To start with, it has had to face the legal "logic" of its views. In a reference for a preliminary ruling by the Federal High Court of 30 May 2002 (*Überseering*[61]), the ECJ was asked whether German law could prevent a Dutch plaintiff from suing for over 1,000,000 DM by, firstly, restricting in § 50 (1) of its *Zivilprozessordnung locus standi* to those legally competent [*rechtsfähig*] companies, and secondly, by prescribing that a company incorporated according to Dutch law could lose its legal capacity once it transferred its activities to Germany in a way which constitutes, according to German law, a transfer of its "seat" or legal headquarters [*Verwaltungssitz*].[62] In the conditions of an internal market, such legal principles seem downright incredible – if they were indeed as rigid or as stringent as the Federal High Court insinuates. As Advocate General Colomer noted, the German government had argued in the oral hearings that a company in the plaintiff's position could, in fact, continue to assert its rights under German law;[63] in addition, he also pointed out that, in German law, Überseering's passive *locus standi* continued to exist despite the new "seat" of the company.[64] But even if the ECJ had kept strictly to the preliminary question submitted to it, it would have been sufficient to rule that German law must not foreclose the Dutch company's rights to sue in Germany, and that German international civil procedural law, if prescribing such effects, was not discriminatory, but unreasonable. The arguments of the Advocate General are noteworthy in one further respect: the general reasons in favour of the "seat" theory (protection of creditors/protection of subsidiary companies/co-determination/avoidance of double taxation), which all have to be acknowledged as compelling reasons of general interest, simply are of no concern here.[65]

Advocate General Colomer's arguments and recommendations fit in with a Europeanisation practice that would respect the autonomy of Member States while nevertheless insisting on the compatibility of national policies with Community values.[66] By contrast, in its judgment of 5 November 2002, the ECJ used much stronger language. Its criticisms of German private international law and international procedural

---

60 Cf., D. Karollus-Bruner, Das steirische Bordell als Zweigniederlassung einer englischen "Private Limited Company", *ecolex* 2000, 725 ff.

61 BGH *Europäische Zeitschrift für Wirtschaftsrecht* 2000, 412; on which see the editorials by P. Behrens, *Europäische Zeitschrift für Wirtschaftsrecht* 2000, 385 und *Europäische Zeitschrift für Wirtschaftsrecht* 2002, 129.

62 Cf. para. 45 in Advocate General Colomer's opinion of 4.12.2001 in the Case C-208/00 – *Überseering*.

63 Para. 55; cf., more generally Bundesverfassungsgericht, decision of 2 September 2002 (1 BvR 1103/02), *Neue Juristische Wochenschrift* 48 (2002), 5333.

64 Para. 46.

65 Paras. 50 ff.

66 Cf., F.W. Scharpf, Autonomieschonend und gemeinschaftsverträglich. Zur Logik der europäischen Mehrebenenpolitik, in *idem, Optionen des Föderalismus in Deutschland und Europa*, Frankfurt a. M.: Campus, 131 ff.

law leave the possibilities addressed by Advocate General Colomer out of account, and sound correspondingly self confident, if not self-righteous: "A necessary precondition for the exercise of the freedom of establishment is the recognition of those companies by any Member State in which they wish to establish themselves."[67] German law ought not to disregard the point that the Dutch company never actually intended to transfer its seat.[68] Is one to understand the statement to the effect that, in the EU, it cannot be tolerated that each Member State determines "unilaterally", according to its *lex fori*, what legal significance it attaches to border-crossing actions, without taking into account the legal views of the Member States concerned and/or the interests of other Community citizens? This sort of civilising admonition is one thing. An unconditioned comprehensive conversion of German PIL to the incorporation theory would be another *problématique*.[69]

This issue arises once again in connection with the ECJ's discussion for the reasons adduced for the "seat" theory. To be sure, according to para. 92 of the judgment, it is "not inconceivable that overriding requirements relating to the general interest, such as the protection of the interests of creditors, minority shareholders, employees and even the taxation authorities, may, in certain circumstances and subject to certain conditions, justify restrictions on freedom of establishment". But the next paragraph goes on to say: "Such objectives cannot, however, justify denying the legal capacity and, consequently, the capacity to be a party to legal proceedings of a company properly incorporated in another Member State in which it has its registered office. Such a measure is tantamount to an outright negation of the freedom of establishment conferred on companies by Articles 43 EC and 48 EC." Did the ECJ wish to indicate that it seems no longer necessary to say anything about the rationale underlying the "seat" theory; that there is no longer any reason to take co-determination commitments seriously, because the regulation on the *societas europa* will come into force on the 8 October 2004,[70] and that, alongside, there is a Directive on Employee Participation?[71] An interpretation of the judgment which takes its practical outcome in the decision, and not its generalising doctrinal framework, as its rational would suit the Court's authority better.[72]

---

67 Case C-208/00, para. 59.
68 Case C-208/00, paras. 62, 63.
69 A *problématique* of huge dimensions at least in German perspectives; cf., for an overview D. Sadowski/J. Junkes/S. Lindenthal, The German Model of Corporate and Labour Governance, *Comparative Labour Law & Policy Journal* 22 (2000), 33 ff.
70 Council Regulation 2157/2001 of 8 October 2001.
71 Council Directive 2001/86 of 8 October 2001.
72 E. Schanze/A. Jüttner, Annerkennung und Kontrolle ausländischer Gesellschaften – Rechtslage und Perspektiven nach der Überseering-Entscheidung des EuGH, *Die Aktiengesellschaft* 2003, issue 1 Juristenzeitung, consider these concerns exaggerated and rather unhelpful for the development of a control theory moderated by European law ["*europarechtlich moderierte Kontrolltheorie*"] (cf. P. Ulmer, Schutzinstrumente gegen die Gefahren aus der Geschäftstätigkeit inländischer Zweigniederlassungen von Kapitalgesellschaften mit fiktivem Auslandsbesitz, *Juristen Zeitung*, 199, 662 ff.). The more one believes in the benefits of competition between regulatory systems or in the competence and capacity of a European judiciary, the more one would agree with their views. This is, to cite Theodor Fontane, a vast field, cf. Ch. Joerges, Interactive Adjudication in the Europeanisation Process? A Demanding Perspective and a Modest Example, *European Review of Private Law* 8 (2000), 1 ff. and below III.5.

3.2 De-Couplings and Rearrangements of Regulatory Law and General Private Law: Pronuptia and Courage

The second set of examples has to do with the tensions between private law and economic law, and between general and statutory private law. Such conflict constellations have been widely and intensively discussed, especially in Germany.[73] These tensions cannot be adequately understood as doctrinal problems which arise from imperfectly systematicised legal fields. They usually relate to regulatory functions of legal provisions, especially of economic law, which are in conflict with the background assumptions of "classical" private law.[74] Déjà-vu reactions are not, however, appropriate when one encounters such conflicts in the course of Europeanisation processes. It is a specific feature of the European multi-level system that, particularly in the course of the programme to "complete" the internal market being pursued in the mid eighties, practically the whole of economic law came under European direction. Consumer protection fits into this pattern. This explains why the European law community could ignore private law for so long.[75] Yet, the de-couplings of (European) regulatory law and statutory private law, on the one hand, from general (national) private law, on the other, were all to produce ever more disintegrative side-effect in national legal systems, the more resolutely the internal market policy was pursued.[76] And the question, therefore, inevitably also arose of the level at which, and the actors by whom, it is then to be dealt with – which also means what legitimation strategies come into consideration.

Let us again anticipate the findings of the analysis below in the form of theses. (1) Just as the "regulated" regulatory competition that the ECJ promotes in company law does not fit the guiding ideas of the *ordo*-liberal tradition, so the patterns for resolving conflicts between the European regulatory law and national private law do not fit the guiding ideas of functionalism and the models of a European "regulatory state". (2) Instead, we witness the emergence of a law of conflict of laws for "diagonal" conflict situations that makes European initiated regulatory policy – the law covered by EU competence – compatible with general private law – the sphere of competence of the Member States. Here, three answers are conceivable: a) European law and/or national law each insist on their own legitimacy (they reach for their *lex fori*); b) both pursue a strategy of conflict avoidance by each treating their own law restrictively; and c) they discover a principle or a rule that allows a conflict resolution which is compatible with the regulatory concerns of both legal layers.

The examples that demonstrate this pattern of conflict are legion. Let us here merely pick out two prominent cases involving tensions between European competi-

---

73 Cf., Ch. Joerges, The Science of Private Law and the Nation State, in Francis Snyder, *The Europeanisation of Law. The Legal Effects of European Integration*, Oxford/Portland: Hart 2000, 47 ff., 70 ff. But "Sonderprivatrecht" does by no means point to some German "Sonderweg"; here, it is sufficient to recall G. Calabresi's *The Common Law in the Age of Statutes*, Cambridge, MA/London 1982, 72 ff.

74 Cf., R. Wiethölter, Wirtschaftsrecht, in A. Görlitz (ed.), *Handlexikon zur Rechtswissenschaft*, München: Ehrenwirt 1972, 531 ff.

75 See Sections 2.1 and 2.2 above.

76 Cf., Ch. Joerges, Economic Law, the Nation-State and the Maastricht Treaty, in: R. Dehousse (ed.), *Europe after Maastricht: an Ever Closer Union?*, München: C.H. Beck 1994, 29 ff.

tion law and national private law. These examples will illustrate once again how limited the potential of the three paradigms set forth at the outset is to provide guidance in the justification of law in the Europeanisation process. European antitrust law has developed into an increasingly more complete system – so strong that, by now, the mere interest in getting it implemented has made the strengthening of the Member State level inevitable.[77]

The need to co-operate across the levels of governance in the EU has "always" existed in relation to the civil law implications of antitrust violations. To be sure, national legal systems, too, have to decide how far the objectives of antitrust law take primacy over private law. But in the EU context, the division of competences between the two levels of governance renders this issue more complex: to what extent can antitrust powers "intrude" on the realm of private law where that law remained national. Neither the principle of the supremacy of European law – a "vertical" conflict of law rule – nor PIL with its "horizontal" conflict rules are equipped to handle such constellations: what is involved here are "diagonal" conflicts.[78]

3.2.1 Dodging the Conflict: Pronuptia

Franchising has found legal form in Europe through the ECJ's *Pronuptia* decision, which declares the franchisees ties, which are regarded as essential to this business concept, to be outside the reach of Article 81 [ex 85], and franchising to be an innovative and, in general, pro-competitive business strategy.[79] The acceptability of franchising from the antitrust viewpoint has its price in civil law: imposing it effectively requires that the ties, which are legalised in antitrust terms, are not found unfair by law of contract.[80] These tensions between "competition justice" and "contractual justice" first emerged in car-dealing concessionaire contracts – they were reduced by including provisions to protect dealers in the relevant group exemptions.[81] In franchising law, this escape route was not sought. The resulting potential for conflict has, however, been kept latent. Yet the situation in itself is definitely potentially conflictual: the contract for marketing the Pronuptia collection that Ms. Irmgard Schillgalis had signed provided for territorial protection which can be taken as a precise precondition for the appropriateness of the ties that Ms. Schillgalis was being asked

---

77 Cf., The Commission's White Paper on modernisation of the rules implementing Articles 81 and 82 of the EC Treaty *(formerly Articles 85 and 86 of the EC Treaty)*, *OJ* C 132/1999; on its significance for integration policy, see R. Wesseling, *The Modernisation of EC Antitrust Law,* Oxford: Hart 2000, 168 ff., 174 ff.

78 Ch. Joerges in co-operation with A.Furrer/O.Gerstenberg, Challenges of European Integration to Private Law, *Collected Courses of the Academy of Law*, Den Haag-Boston-London: Kluwer, Vol. VII, Book 1, 281 ff., 311 ff.; Ch. Schmid, Diagonal Competence Conflicts between European Competition Law and National Regulation. A conflict of laws reconstruction of the dispute on book price-fixing, *European Review of Private Law* 8 (2000), 155 ff.

79 Cf., Case C-161/84, [1986], *ECR* 353 – *Pronuptia* and in the follow-up Group Exemption Regulation. 4087/88, *OJ* L 359/88, 46.

80 On the ECJ's case law, cf., Ch. Schmid, Die Instrumentalisierung des Privatrechts durch die Europäische Union, habilitationschrift submitted to the Law faculty of Munich, Germany in June 2004, Part 1, Section 1 C on file with authors.

81 Ch. Joerges, Relational Contracts Law in a Comparative Perspective: Tensions Between Contract and Antitrust Law Principles, *Wisconsin Law Review* 1985, 581 ff.

for; and the resale price maintenance throughout the system was also thoroughly in the interests of the franchisees. But even were one to regard the antitrust penalty of nullity of the contract as irrefutable, this in no way means that Ms. Schillgalis was not due at least compensation under enrichment law.[82]

This was the position that Pronuptia sought with extraordinary stubbornness to impose legally.[83] The Pronuptia suit, originally launched in Hamburg in December 1981, progressed through all the German courts, then to the ECJ and back again until, in 1994, the Oberlandesgericht Frankfurt allotted Pronuptia precisely the amount that the Hamburg district court had already tried to award it in 1981. "Justice delayed is justice denied"? "Postponed does not mean suspended"? Both questions can be answered in the affirmative. The German judicial system was not prepared to enrich Ms. Schillgalis unjustifiably in the name of an antitrust *effet utile*. However, from the viewpoint of EC antitrust law, nothing much can be objected to. The grip of antitrust law on Ms. Schillgalis' contract is not to be explained from the efforts to promote the sales of wedding dresses in the region outside Hamburg or even abroad. Nor is it intended seriously to disrupt the pricing polity of a franchise system. Instead, the point was to remove the uncertainties in antitrust law, which the development of a contractual arrangement that was thoroughly desirable in terms of competition policy could not properly cope with.[84] This objective was achieved by the decision. It did not concern a "true" conflict but only a false one.[85] The fact that it took so many years to get it straight is a high tribute levied by EU practice in the manufacture of law on its citizens.

3.2.2 Justi(ce)-fication in a Legal Vacuum: Courage

An agreement null and void under European competition law was also the point in the *Courage* case,[86] which, admittedly, was marked by a special feature that guaranteed it a place in EU legal history:[87] Bernhard Crehan, licencee of a Courage pub, not

---

82 § 817, 2 BGB does not run counter to this view as any *connaisseur* of that provision will confirm.

83 For a detailed history of the dispute, see W. Skaupy, Der Pronuptia-Prozess 1974-1995, *Betriebsberater* 1996, 1899 ff.

84 Cf., in detail, Ch. Joerges, Franchise-Verträge und Europäisches Wettbewerbsrecht: Eine Kritik der Pronuptia-Entscheidungen des EuGH und der Kommission, *Zeitschrift für das gesamte Handelsrecht und Wirtschaftsrecht* 151 (1987), 195 ff.; 223; Contract and Status in Franchising Law, in *idem* (ed.), *Franchising and the Law: Theoretical and Comparative Approaches in Europe and the United States*, Baden-Baden: Nomos 1991, 11 ff., 50 ff.

85 On the conceptual and conflicts of law theory still worth studying B. Currie, Notes on Methods and Objectives in the Conflict of Law, in *id.*, *Selected Essays on the Conflict of Laws*, Durham, N.C., 177–187 [cf., for a concise summary, his comment on Babcock v. Jackson, *Columbia Law Rev.* 63 (1963) 1233 ff., 1242 ff.]. For an instructive actualisation, cf., R. Wai, Transnational Liftoff and Juridical Touchdown: The Regulatory Function of Private International Law in a Era of Globalisation, *Colum J. Transnational Law* 2002, 209 ff., also H. Muir Watt, Choice of law in integrated and interconnected markets: a matter of political economy, this volume, ch. 10 (pp. 183ff.) each with further references.

86 Case 453/99, judgment of 20.09.2001 [2001] *ECR* I-6279 – *Courage v. Bernard Crehan.*

87 The case attracted much attention even in the run up to the ECJ decision; cf., for example, W. van Gerven, Substantive Remedies for the Private Enforcement of EC Antitrust Rules before National Courts, in C.-D. Ehlermann/I. Atanasiu (eds.), *European Competition Law Annual 2001: Effective*

only refused to pay £15,266 for beer supplied, but in a counter suit asked to be compensated for the drawbacks he had suffered because the "tied house" contract imposed a sole supplier obligation upon him for beer at prices considerably above those asked from free houses which were not tied to a sole brewery. The Court of Appeal (for England and Wales) that made the submission stated that, in English law, a party to an unlawful contract was not entitled to claim compensation for damages.[88] The legal position is, as it were, a mirror of the one in *Pronuptia*: There, EU antitrust law had to be enriched by law of contract; but here antitrust law had to equip itself with sanctions that were non-existent in English law. The judgment treats this as a matter of course: "As regards the possibility of seeking compensation for loss caused by a contract or by conduct liable to restrict or distort competition, it should be remembered from the outset that, in accordance with settled case-law, the national courts whose task it is to apply the provisions of Community law in areas within their jurisdiction must ensure that those rules take full effect and must protect the rights which they confer on individuals".[89] This statement is accompanied by an emphatic reference to the Community guarantees of subjective rights and the direct effect of the competition rules.[90] Yet the matter is not simply a sort of European octroi. The ECJ pays its respects to the procedural[91] and substantive[92] autonomy of national law. It takes account of the fact that the innovations that the European law requires differ from country to country, and tolerates legal divergences. It is manifestly concerned not to homogenise the legal systems, but to have each of the private law systems learn what they have to learn in order to lend European competition law its validity. And, as in *Centros*, it is individual rights that can be asserted by the citizens of the European Union in order to achieve a reshaping of their own law in each case.

3.3 The Logic of Market Integration and the Logic of Private Law Justification

It is always a delight to re-read: "Tucked away in the fairyland Duchy of Luxembourg and blessed, until recently, with benign neglect by the powers that be and the

---

Private Enforcement of EC Antitrust Law, Oxford/Portland: Hart 2002 and the references in A.P. Komninos, New Prospects for Private Enforcement of EC Competition Law: *Courage* v. *Crehan* and the Community Right to Damages, *CMLRev.* 39 (2002), 447 ff., 479 ff., 9 ff., to whose comprehensive assessment of the judgment we herein refer.

88 References on the English law can be found in A. Komninos (note 87), at 462.

89 Case C- 453/99 – *Courage*, para. 25.

90 Case C-453/99 – *Courage*, paras. 19, 20, 23.

91 "However, in the absence of Community rules governing the matter, it is for the domestic legal system of each Member State to designate the courts and tribunals which have jurisdiction and to lay down the detailed procedural rules governing actions for safeguarding the rights which individuals derive directly from Community law, provided that such rules are not less favourable than those governing similar domestic actions (principle of equivalence) and that they do not render practically impossible or excessively difficult the exercise of rights conferred by Community law (principle of effectiveness)", Case C-453/99 – *Courage*, para. 29.

92 "Similarly, provided that the principles of equivalence and effectiveness are respected ..., Community law does not preclude national law from denying a party who is found to bear significant responsibility for the distortion of competition the right to obtain damages from the other contracting party", C 453/99 – *Courage*, para. 31.

mass media, the Court of Justice of the European Communities has fashioned a constitutional framework for a federal-type Europe";[93] and even now that the ECJ has definitely become visible, respect has remained high: criticisms like those which national courts are accustomed to are exceptional phenomena. There are many reasons and explanations for this.[94] Assessments of the ECJ's performance usually refer to, and appreciate, its role as a promoter of the integration project. But this is not the only conceivable yardstick. The Court is exposed to very diverse expectations: its case law is not just to promote integration but also to guarantee the normative integrity of the integration process, to respond sensitively to political concerns. Can such a court at the same time operate as a court of ultimate review, earning the respect of the specialised courts of Member States? And with all that, can it alleviate the pangs of citizens seeking justice in courtrooms?

Specifically, consumer protection, which has been the pioneer and engine for the Europeanisation of private law, raises such questions. The two examples dealt with here concern two very prominent instances of European legislation, namely, the Clause Directive of 1993[95] and the Product Liability Directive of 1985.[96] Let us once again recall the outcome of the analysis: in the *Océano* decision[97] on the Directive on unfair terms in consumer contracts, the ECJ managed to implement the Directive's provision in national (Spanish) law by redefining the functions of courts in such a way that Spain's legal system could transform that intervention into an innovative reform. One can, in contrast, attribute to the decisions on the Product Liability Directive of 25 April 2002[98] the much more ambitious goal of taking on product liability law in the European system – an undertaking that, admittedly, would, in all likelihood, fail thoroughly.

3.3.1 Océano

Océano Grupo Editorial SA[99] was the first legal pronouncement, urgently awaited by the protagonists of European consumer policy, on the Directive about Unfair Terms in Consumer Contracts, adopted in 1993 after long preliminaries.[100]

---

93 E. Stein, Lawyers, Judges, and the Making of a Transnational Constitution, *American Journal of International Law* 75 (1981), 1 ff., 1.

94 Cf. only A.-M. Slaughter/A. Stone Sweet/J.H.H. Weiler 1998: *The European Court and National Courts – doctrine and jurisprudence: legal change in its social context*, Oxford/Portland: Hart, 1998; K.J. Alter, *Establishing the supremacy of European Law: the making of an international rule of law in Europe*, Oxford/New York: Oxford UP 2001.

95 Directive 93/13/ EEC of 5.04.1993 on unfair terms in consumer contracts *OJ* L 95/1993, 29.

96 Directive 85/374/EEC of 25.07.1985 on the approximation of the laws, regulations and administrative provisions of the Member States concerning liability for defective products, *OJ* L307/1988, 54; amended by Directive 1999/34/EC of the European Parliament and of the Council of 10.05.1999, *OJ* L 283/1999, 20

97 Cases C-240-244/98, Judgment of 27.06.2000, [2000] *ECR* I-4941– *Grupo Editorial SA* v. *Rocío Murciano Quintero et al.*

98 Case C-52/00 – *Commission* v. *France*; Case C-183/00 – *María Victoria González Sánchez* v. *Medicina Asturiana SA*; Case C-154/00 – *Commission* v. *Hellenic Republic*; see, also, Case C-203/99 – *Henning Veedfald* v. *Århus Amtskommune* – [2000] *ECR* I-3569.

99 Note 97.

100 M. Tenreiro/J. Karsten, Unfair Terms in Consumer Contracts: uncertainties, contradictions and nov-

The defendants to the underlying cases had entered into contracts for the purchase, by instalments, of an encyclopaedia for personal use. The instalment purchase contract was completed in 1995 but the instalments had not been paid. The purchaser filed suit in 1997 with the Juzgado de Primera Instancia No. 35 in Barcelona. This was in line with the conferral of jurisdiction on the courts in Barcelona in the contractual terms. The defendants, who came from all over Spain, did not turn up for the hearing scheduled in Barcelona.

Not a very tough story in itself, one might think. Yet the Juzgado saw itself barred from rejecting the suit. The "juicio di cogniciòn" is a summary procedure for legal cases with a small sum in dispute (between 80,000 and 8,000,000 Pesetas).[101] Admittedly, the Tribunal Supremo had repeatedly declared such venue clauses to be unfair. What was disputed, however, with whether the Juzgado was also entitled to make this finding when it had not been brought up in the proceedings by the defendants themselves. The question of whether it could pronounce nullity ex officio had been presented to the Juzgado by the Spanish Attorney General, and had received a negative answer.[102] Undaunted, it approached the ECJ with a preliminary ruling question as to whether Directive 93/13 required verification *ex officio*.

Before addressing that procedural issue one has, in the Advocate General's view,[103] to deal with the unfairness of the clause conferring jurisdiction to the Barcelona courts. This question was answered by the ECJ without further ado: the clause, not having been individually negotiated, was held to be unfair within the meaning of Article 3 of the Directive.[104] The importance of the fact that this clause was not contained in the indicative list in annex to the Directive was not explored by the ECJ. Similarly, the further question concerning the competence of the Spanish court submitted to the ECJ and discussed in great detail by the Advocate General,[105] caused no trouble: it would be contrary to the Directive's protective objectives if one were to require a consumer to appear before a court even though the venue clause requiring such appearance is unfair.[106] This holding may seem quite a modest step but is nonetheless a noteworthy reform: Spain is expected to adapt national procedural rules to consumer policy objectives agreed throughout Europe. Since Spain itself shared these objectives, it is at the same time merely a sort of self-correction, namely, the realisation of procedural requirements without which agreement to judicial review of general terms of business would not be credible.

---

elties of a directive, in H. Schulte-Nölke/R. Schulze (eds.), *Europäische Rechtsangleichung und nationale Privatrechte*, Baden-Baden: Nomos 1999, 223 ff.

101 Para. 16 in Advocate General Saggio's Opinion of 16.12.1999.

102 *Ibidem.*

103 *Ibidem* para. 20.

104 ECJ (note 99), paras. 21 ff.

105 *Ibidem* paras. 20-27.

106 ECJ, *ibidem*, paras. 25-29. – Spain had in 1995 (the time when the encyclopaedias were being sold) not complied with its obligation to implement the Directive. This, according to the ECJ (*ibidem*, para. 31), could, in the present case, be compensated by an interpretation of Spanish law "in accordance with the Directive"; cf. the interpretations by J. Stuyck in his annotation, *CMLRev.* 38 (2001),719 ff.

3.3.2 Product Liability

In its three judgments of 25 April 2002,[107] the ECJ seems to have enhanced the value of the, so far quite dormant, Directive 85/374/EEC[108] on product liability by asserting that this legislative act did not merely lay down minimum standards but instead aimed at "complete harmonisation". This came as a surprise: at the time, the very modest harmonisation effects had been minutely elaborated,[109] and the Directive was characterised as a product without much effect in terms of integration policy and rather defective in terms of liability law. There was, at any rate, broad agreement that the Directive did not affect the general law of tort, and specifically therefore also the general law of tort liability and its judicial extension in the Member States.[110]

This consensus has an objective basis. To be sure, product liability in tort law in the various countries overlaps with the Product Liability Directive. But the conceptual approach of, say, German law of tort on manufacturer liability and the conceptual design of the Product Liability Directive differ as significantly as do the procedures of national and European law. What is true of Germany is true equally of other jurisdictions, for instance, with regard to France and its *non cumul* principle. It is this very consensus which the ECJ now seems to wish to dismiss, that tends towards a position which was called the "fossilisation theory" [*Versteinerungstheorie*] at the time.[111] The decision on the Spanish law in particular[112] nourishes such fears.

The plaintiff had been infected by Hepatitis C virus in a clinic, because of a blood transfusion. She based her suit on Law No. 22/94 on civil liability for damage caused by defective products of 6 July 1994 that transposed the Directive, on the general liability provisions of Spanish civil law, and finally on the General Law No. 26 of 19 July 1984 for the Protection of Consumers and Users, which, in its turn, is based on a "objective liability regulation" according to which the suing party had only to prove its damage and a causal connection. She directed her action for compensation for damages against the owner of the medical establishment (Medicina Asturiana SA), not the manufacturer of the blood product (the Centro Comunitario de Transfusión del Principado de Asturias).

The submitting court found that the provisions of Law No. 22/94 that implemented Directive 85/374 were more restrictive than the older 1984 law. The *lex posterior* states that the older provisions "do not apply to apply to liability for damage caused by products defective within the meaning of the [new] law".[113] This perception brought it to the preliminary ruling question of whether Article 13 of the Product Lia-

---

107 Note 98 *supra*; [2002] *ECR* Case C-52/00, *ECR* [2002] I-3827 – Commission v. France; Case C-183/00, *ECR* [2002] I-3901 – Maria Victoria González Sánchez v. Medicina Asturiana SA; Case C-154/00, *ECR* [2002] I-3879 – Commission v. Greece.

108 Note 96 *supra*.

109 Cf., for example, H. Koch, Internationale Produkthaftung uznd Grenzen der Rechtsangleichung durch die EG-Richtlinie, *Zeitschrift für das gesamte Handels- und Wirtschaftsrecht* 152 (1988), 537 ff.

110 References in G. Brüggemeier, Produkthaftung und Produktsicherheit, *Zeitschrift für das gesamte Handels- und Wirtschaftsrecht* 152 (1988), 511 ff., 531 f.

111 G. Brüggemeier, *ibid.*, at 531.

112 Case C-183/00, judgment of 25.04.2002 – *María Victoria González Sánchez* v. *Medicina Asturiana SA*, [2002] *ECR* [2002] I-3901 – Maria Victoria González Sánchez v. Medicina Asturiana SA.

113 Case 183/00, para. 8.

bility Directive could "be interpreted as precluding the restriction or limitation, as a result of transposition of the Directive, of rights granted to consumers under the legislation of the Member State?"[114]

Oddly, there is no further mention in the sequel of the temporal conflict provision of the Spanish law just cited. Instead, the court employs the traditional principles on full harmonisation of the directives enacted under Article 100, old version, with its pre-emptive effects: Hence, "the margin of discretion available to the Member States in order to make provision for product liability is entirely determined by the Directive itself and must be inferred from its wording, purpose and structure".[115] And, accordingly, it is not some self-correction of Spanish law but the supremacy claim of Community law that is the basis for lowering the standard of protection in Spain. Is this then also to lead to the "fossilisation" of the general civil law which was forewarned in the early debate on the Product Liability Directive?[116] The ECJ does not, in fact, go that far:

> "The reference in Article 13 of the Directive to the rights which an injured person may rely on under the rules of the law of contractual or non-contractual liability must be interpreted as meaning that the system of rules put in place by the Directive, which in Article 4 enables the victim to seek compensation where he proves damage, the defect in the product and the causal link between that defect and the damage, does not preclude the application of other systems of contractual or non-contractual liability based on other grounds, such as fault or a warranty in respect of latent defects."[117]

Less dramatic questions are raised by the two parallel decisions. Both concerned the conformity with the Directive of transpositions going beyond its standards of protection: Greece had wanted to spare its citizens from the personal contribution of 500 Euro provided for in Article 9 I (b) of the Directive.[118] France additionally wanted to hold the distributor liable alongside with the manufacturer, and additionally to restrict the exemptions from liability foreseen in Article 7 of the Directive.[119]

These deviations would have been unproblematic had the Directive sought to lay down minimum standards of the European consumer protection. And indeed, had the Directive been adopted after the Single European Act and accordingly based on Article 100a (now 95), then the procedure pursuant to Sections 4 and 5 of that provision would have applied. But that was, after all, an old directive, the spiritual father of which had always stressed that it was aimed at the development of the internal market and only implicitly achieved consumer protection objectives.[120] Thus, Advocate Gen-

---

114 Case 83/00, para. 13. Article 13 states: "'This Directive shall not affect any rights which an injured person may have according to the rules of the law of contractual or non-contractual liability or a special liability system existing at the moment when this Directive is notified."
115 Cf., C-183/00, para. 25.
116 G. Brüggemeier, *supra* note 111.
117 Case183/00, para. 31.
118 Case 154/00, para. 6.
119 Case 52/00, para. 6 ff.
120 Cf., H.-C. Taschner, Die künftige Produzntenhaftung in Deutschland, *Neue Juristische Wochenschrift* 1986, 611 ff.; that it was also advisable to argue that way can be seen from B. Börner, Die Produkthaftung oder das vergessene Gemeinschaftsrecht, *Festschrift zum 70. Geburtstag von Hans Kutscher*, Baden-Baden: Nomos 1981, 43 ff.

eral Geelhoed – as also in Case C-183/00 – was able to bring the orthodox understanding of supremacy and pre-emption to bear.[121] The ECJ followed suit.[122] This is,
after all, not particularly tragic, since Article 13 of the Directive "does not preclude
the application of other systems of contractual or non-contractual liability based on
other grounds, such as fault or a warranty in respect of latent defects",[123] and because
Article 9 (1) (b) means only that those harmed "must bring an action under the ordinary law of contractual or non-contractual liability".[124] Should one expect the ECJ,
especially in view of the Spanish case,[125] to hold next that e.g. Germany's rules on
the manufacturers burden of proof are incompatible with the European directive?
Hardly so. Such a step would be damaging to product liability law – and to the ECJ's
authority.

3.4 Interim Comment

Exempla trahunt? The three groups of examples are intended to demonstrate the relevance and the limited interpretive power of the legitimation patterns submitted in
the first section. The three paradigms, we can summarise, have all left their traces but
none of them applied "in full" or exclusively. *Centros* and *Überseering* by no means
document willingness to expose law making in company law to mechanisms of regulatory competition. Neither *Pronuptia* nor *Courage* can be used to deduce primacy of
European competition policy over competing conceptions of contractual justice in
private law. And nowhere, and definitely not in the case law on consumer protection,
can one witness anything like the formation of a European (social) state. All three
paradigms are insufficiently complex analytically, and have defects in normative
terms. In the seemingly incomprehensible, jigsaw puzzle of viewpoints that come to
bear in the Europeanisation process, one can, however, certainly also find positive
messages. This, admittedly, presupposes the extension of the conceptual worlds hitherto employed.

4 Conclusions: Justice-Making Law for the Europeanisation of Private Law

Back to the beginning: when conceptualising the Europeanisation of private law, we
ought, said our initial thesis, to bear in mind the legitimation *problématique* that has,
at times explicitly, at times less visibly, been on the agenda of the integration project
from the outset, and which is now, since the success of the Human Rights Convention,[126] the Treaty of Nice,[127] the "post Nice process" and the "Convention pro-

---

121 Conclusions, Case C-154/00 para. 4; Cases C- 52/00 and C-183/00, paras. 27 ff.
122 Case C-154/00, para. 10; Case C-52/00, para. 14.
123 Case C-52/00 para. 22.
124 Case C-52/00 and Case C-154/00 both in para. 30.
125 Note 112 above.
126 *OJ* C-364/2000, 1.
127 *OJ* C-80/2001, 1.

cess"[128] being met with increasing academic and public attention. "Europe is not a state but it needs is a constitution" – this is not exactly a *communis opinio*, yet it is a formula that typifies the current discourse on European law.[129] "Europe already has a constitution that now needs to be developed further, but not necessarily in writing" – this is one of the more nuanced contrary positions.[130] Private lawyers are hard to hear in the current legal disputes over Europe's constitution. This indication of shortcomings is not without its ironies or its deeper significance: For, after all, it concerns a project which the founding fathers set going as a "economic community". To be sure, a key piece of the overflowing debates on the Europeanisation of private law is formed by the question of the advisability of a European Civil Code. As such, this is a constitutional question par excellence. It cannot be dismissed on the model of Paolo Cecchini's writings on the internal market,[131] i.e., via some estimate of the "costs of a non-code"; neither can we rely on the German experience of a pre-republican and pre-democratic history of private law unification. Unfortunately, the booming constitutional debate going on in public law offers limited help. Certainly, any internal market policy project, any directive, however technical and functionalist it may seem, regularly sparks off far-reaching controversies. But the constitutionalists, have lost the economy and society from their vision: their readiness to embrace a "constitution without a state" – a prospect which now hardly seems to offend anyone anymore – seems to promote a constitutionalism beyond and above conflicts over the economic and social conflict constellations, thereby strengthening the traditions of a non-political, economic or technocratic rationality that determine the integration process in the formative stage.

Such an abstract constitutionalism would call valuable achievements into question. The private and the public, the economic freedoms and political rights of citizens, can, in a democratic constitutional state, be understood as interdependent categories.[132] Private law has found its way into these contexts, finding its constitutional place in the interaction between legislation, case law, legal expertise and the political public.[133] The European constellation is different. But is it really of such a nature that economic freedoms must be understood as operating in a sphere which remains disconnected from political processes and beyond the reach of the political rights of European citizens? The answers to this question will depend on our understanding of the re-configuration of politics, economy and society that characterise the European Union, and on the functions of private law in this new environment.

This is a very abstract way to describe the theme of this section. In order some-

---

128 See http://european-conventiom.eu.int.

129 Quite symptomatically J. Habermas, "So, why does Europe need a Constitution?", note 56 *supra.*

130 J.H.H.Weiler, Prologue: Amsterdam and the Quest for Constitutional Democracy, in B. O'Keeffe/ P. Twomey (eds.), *Legal Issues of the Amsterdam Treaty*, Oxford/Portland: Hart 1999, 1 ff.; M. Poiares Maduro, Where to look for Legitimacy?, in E.O. Eriksen/J.E. Fossum/A. José Menéndez (eds.), *Constitution Making and Democratic Legitimacy*, Oslo: ARENA Report No 5/2002, 81 ff.

131 Cf., P. Cecchini/M. Catinat/A. Jacquemin, *The European challenge, 1992: the benefits of a single market*, Brookfield: Aldershot 1988.

132 References to Jürgen Habermas are insufficient as an explanation yet must suffice here; cf., the references in notes 4 and 56 *supra.*

133 Cf., the references in note 24 *supra.*

what to alleviate its abstractness, we shall anticipate the end result in two theses. The first is that we cannot conceive of the process of the Europeanisation of private law as the construction of a private law edifice with a unitary structure. Instead, we have to accept a multi-layer process in which very different sets of problems will have to be dealt with. The second is that the Europeanisation of private law has to base its legitimacy on the quality of the processes through which it comes about; we have to juridify these processes; we must, to rephrase the title of this essay, juridify the changes and innovations that the Europeanisation process brings about; we need a procedural law of Europeanisation.

Let me develop this argument in five steps:

(1)   the first refers to the analyses, widespread in political science, of the EU as a multi-level system; on these analyses, it bases the assertion that "orthodox" supranationalism and its hierarchical concepts of supremacy have to be replaces by a "deliberative" re-conceptualisation of supranationalism (Section 4.1).

(2)   A deliberative supranationalism promoting communication and co-operation – and dependent on them – must not rely on the "power of the better argument" alone. It needs a law with the potential to transform strategic interactions into argumentational interaction. The second step of the argument will go into this (Section 4.2).

(3)   The superiority of these categories to the paradigms presented in the introductory section will be defended in a retrospective look at the sets of examples discussed in the second section (Section 4.3).

(4)   Fourthly, we shall point to the emergence of genuinely transnational "governance arrangements", without, however, offering any comprehensive analysis (Section 4.4).

(5)   The vision of a (procedural) law of the Europeanisation process denotes a normative programme. Its defence does not imply the prediction that this vision will become reality (Section 4.5).

4.1   "Deliberative" Supranationalism

European integration research has kept on saying, for some years now, that the EU is to be understood as a "multi-level system of governance *sui generis*."[134] Jürgen Neyer, in particular, has enriched this debate in normative terms: if and because the powers of action and resources for action are located at various relatively autonomous levels in the EU, then coping with functionally interwoven problem situations will continually depend on communication between the actors competent in their various domains.[135] Such communication can be achieved in manifold ways. But Neyer is now seeking to make it plausible that, in the specific conditions of the EU,

---

134   For a summary, see M. Jachtenfuchs, The Governance Approach to European Integration, *Journal of Common Market Studies* 39 (2001), 245 ff., and F.W. Scharpf, Notes Toward a Theory of Multilevel Governing in Europe, *Scandinavian Political Studies* 24 (2001), 1 ff.

135   J. Neyer, Discourse and Order in the EU, A Deliberative Approach to Multi-Level Governance, *Journal of Common Market Studies* 41 (2003), 647 ff.

successful solutions to problems can be expected from the "deliberative" mode of communication based on universalisable motivations and tied down to rules and principles.[136] To be sure, the multi-level approach cannot be understood as revealing a "fact" to which legal constructions would have to orient themselves. This is especially true of Neyer's theoretical arguments. Nonetheless, the multi-level analysis does refer to problem situations that legal science confronts in similar fashion.[137] And the normative turn that Neyer gives to the multi-level approach does, at any rate, support the assumption that Europe need not sink into chaos if it relies on deliberative interaction instead of the formation of hierarchies.

4.1.1 Diagonal Conflicts

In delimiting and harmonising European and Member State powers, the parallels become particularly clear. Conflicts as to competencies are typified in the EU by the fact that the Member State defending its autonomy itself belongs to the Community against whose demands it is defending itself. Here, the principle of enumerated powers (Article 3-4; now 3-7), according to which the Community should act only in the areas specifically allotted to it, is quite often dysfunctional: activities oriented towards the solution of economic and social problems will often have to involve both Community and Member State powers. The resulting overlaps, in practice, compel the Community and Member States de facto to complex harmonisations of their activities: each can block the other, but neither can achieve solutions to the problems when acting alone.[138] "Diagonal" conflict constellations of this sort are an everyday experience in European law and European policy:[139] the Community holds powers that relate only to one segment of interdependent issues. The Member States hold partial powers that equally do not suffice to achieve a solution of problems autonomously.

---

136 Set out in the same sense and in more detail in his Habilitation Thesis on *Postnationale Politische Herrschaft*, Baden-Baden: Nomos 2004.

137 And has started to acknowledge this; cf., A. Furrer, *Zivilrecht im gemeinschaftlichen Kontext. Das Europäische Kollisionsrecht als Koordinierungsinstrument für die Einbindung des Zivilrechts in das europäische Wirtschaftsrecht*, Bern 2002, 56 ff., 155 ff., with references. Oddly (if not incomprehensibly) the comparative law tradition seems less impressed by all this than conflict of laws scholarship. At the same time, the conceptualisation of the EU as a multi-level system demonstrates with particular poignancy mutual influences between regulatory systems and the restructuring of international relations. Of course, generalising judgments on a discipline can always be falsified. The law will respond in some way real problems and legal science in turn will reflect on them, explicitly or more implicitly; cf. with further references H. Muir Watt, *ibidem*. (note 85); R. Michaels, Im Westen nichts Neues? 100 Jahre Pariser Kongress für Rechtsvergleichung – Gedanken anlässlich einer Jubiläumskonferenz in New Orleans, *Rabels Zeitschrift für ausländisches und internationales Privatrecht* 66 (2002), 97 ff.

138 The joint-decision trap: lessons from German federalism, *Public Administration* 66 (1988), 239 ff.; A. Benz, Politische Steuerung in lose gekoppelten Mehrebenensystemen, in R. Wehrle/U. Schimank (eds.), *Gesellschaftliche Komplexität und kollektive Handlungsfähigkeit*, Frankfurt a.M./New York: Campus 2000, 99 ff.

139 Cf., 3.2 and 3.3 above.

4.1.2 Deliberative Supranationalism I: European Law as Law of Conflict of Laws

It is a small step from this insight to an interpretation of legal provisions as precepts for a communication oriented, "deliberative" political style which can be more positively justified if set in its broader context. In the "post-national constellation" typified by economic interpenetration and interdependency, the extraterritorial effects of the decisions and omissions of democratic polities are unavoidable; but the burdens loaded unilaterally on to one's neighbour in each case cannot be justified by democratic processes internal to the state: "No taxation without representation" – this is a principle that imposes on the Member States of the EU the obligation to take account of the interests and concerns of non-nationals even within the national polity.[140]

But it is precisely this that is the normative core of these supranational rules and principles which legitimise European law, where it requires Member States to "apply" foreign law and to refrain from insisting on their *lex fori* and domestic interests.[141] This sort of restriction of a Member State's political autonomy is, however, limited. In particular, the case law on Article 30 (now 28) has repeatedly indicated[142] how the idiosyncrasies of individual states can be identified as such and reduced to a civilised level – "*autonomieschonend und gemeinschaftsverträglich*".[143]

The mediation between differences in regulatory policies and the diverse interests of the concerned jurisdictions that it achieves overcomes the one-sidedness of PIL-rules; it represents a truly European law of conflict of laws. It is "deliberative" if and because it does not content itself with appealing to the supremacy of European law; it is European because it seeks to identify principles and rules which make differing laws in the EU compatible; with this ambition it stands "above" national law because it indicates and declares binding a metanorm under which intra-European conflicts can be resolved.[144]

---

140 Cf., earlier Ch. Joerges, The Impact of European Integration (note 1), 390; and very similarly M. Maduro Poiares, Where To Look For Legitimacy?, note 130 *supra*.

141 Cf., the analyses by A. Furrer, *Zivilrecht im gemeinschaftsrechtlichen Kontext. Das Europäische Kollisionsrecht als Koordinierungsinstrument für die Einbindung des Zivilrechts in das europäische Wirtschaftsrecht*, Bern: Stämpfli 2002, 171 ff.; J. Fetsch, *Eingriffsnormen und EG-Vertrag*, Tübingen 2002, 126 ff., 139 ff. (on the conflict of laws principles, see 21 ff., 71 ff.); Ch. Schmid, Europäische Wirtschaftsverfassung und Privatrecht (note 74), ch. IV. – For a heuristic using American conflict of law methodologies for the structuring of European *Kollisionsrecht* cf., Ch. Joerges, "Deliberative Supranationalism" – Two Defences, *European Law Journal* 8 (2002), 133 ff., 135 ff. with references esp. to B. Currie, Notes on Methods and Objectives in the Conflict of Law, in *idem, Selected Essays on the Conflict of Laws*, Durham, NC: Duke UP, 177 ff. and B. Currie's particularly lucid summary of his position in his Comment on Babcock v. Jackson, *Columbia Law Rev.* 63 (1963) 1233 ff., 1242 ff.

142 See, for example, M. Maduro Poiares, *We the Court*, Oxford: Hart 1998, 150 ff.; J.H.H. Weiler, *The Constitution of Europe*, Cambridge: Cambridge UP 1999, 221 ff.

143 F.W. Scharpf, Autonomieschonend und gemeinschaftsverträglich, note 66 *supra*.

144 A law of conflict of laws which has a legally weak enforcement apparatus behind it is dependent on having it accepted as fragile: but this applies to all universal rules of conflict of laws, too.

4.2 Supranational Law

One of the analytical strengths of deliberative supranationalism is to conceive of the EU as a non-unitary polity in which Member States are not only "relatively" autonomous but also "relatively" different, in which cultural differences[145] can continue to exist.[146] This opens up realistic perspectives for the design of the European policy. It suggests "soft" forms of control that take account of the special features of national institutions and experience. At the same time, I believe, the compatibility with democracy of deliberative supranationalism is plain to see – indeed, it can be seen as a requirement for democracy, given that it seeks to enhance the influence of European citizens who are affected by decisions which they cannot influence.[147]

The legitimacy of a deliberative supranationalism which seeks to give voice to foreigners and seeks to promote deliberative political process in the EU is not really problematical. Instead, what is questionable is whether the EU's institutional circumstances and configurations of interests actually do favour such legitimated solutions to problems. The empirical dimension of this question must be left out of consideration here.[148] Though, we do wish to assert, at least, that important rules and principles of European law can be interpreted as institutionalisations of a deliberative style of politics, and thus that, in supranational European law, there is indeed a layer of law that does not merely favour deliberative interactions, but ties these interactions to substantive and enforceable rules.[149] This genuinely constitutional law includes the ban on discrimination in Article 12 [ex 6], the basic freedoms that have developed into civic rights, the European Human Rights Convention, and (probably in the foreseeable future) also the basic rights proclaimed in Nice. Also parts of it are the cooperation duties in Article 10 [ex 5], the ban on protectionism in Article 28 [ex 30]

---

145 See note 28.

146 This is how I read the plea for "constitutionalism pluralism" in N.Walker, The Idea of Constitutional Pluralism, *Modern Law Review* 65 (2002), 317 ff.

147 The critique by A. Peters, *Elemente einer Theorie der Verfassung Europas*, Berlin 2001, 660, of what she calls a "democracy of concern" ["*Betroffenheitsdemokratie*"] does not meet our argument, which aims to explain why a European law rule of mutual considerations would be democratic, rather than to derive participation rights from a diffuse "concern".

148 Cf., the references to the recent work of J. Neyer in notes 135 and 136 *supra*.

149 Deliberative Suprantionalism tends to undervalue perfectly legitimate validity claims of of suprantional law, argues Hans-W. Micklitz; cf., e.g., his Principles of Social Justice in European Private Law, *YEL* 19 (1999-2000), 167 ff. This objection is important, especially in the field of consumer protection. It seems to me, however, that our disagreement concerns the approaches to social protection in the EU, not the regulative idea of a „social" private law as such (cf., Ch. Joerges, Interactive Adjudication in the Europeanisation Process? A Demanding Perspective and a Modest Example, note 72 *supra*). – In his essay "Transnational Governance without a Public Law?" Ms. Heidelberg/Florenz 2002, Ch. Möllers [see, more recently, his Verfassunggebende Gewalt – Verfassung – Konstitutionalisierung, in A. von Bogdandy (ed.), *Europäisches Verfassungsrecht*, Heidelberg/New York: Springer (forthcoming), text accompanying notes 250 ff.] distinguishes between a "private law frameworks of public institutions" that understand the production of law or the generation of norms as the result of a spontaneous co-ordination processes) and a "public law framework" that conceives of the law as the outcome of authoritative legislative acts legitimated by majority decisions. Both forms could or should complement each other. The argument in the paper goes part of the way towards meeting this demand in that it insists on the indispensability of mandatory rules and principles governing interactions in the European polity.

and the mutual recognition obligation derived from this provision. All these legal positions are important not just because of their direct, both vertical and horizontal, effects, but also because they give guidance in the production of law, including legislative and executive law-making. They can be invoked in all modern and not-so-modern governance arrangements and constitute a protective shield against strategic patterns of argument.

4.3 Reinterpretations

Whether this conceptual framework is fruitful can be tested by using it to reinterpret the situation in the cases discussed in the second section, and contrasting it with the interpretations which keep to the traditional patterns of legitimation. In the requisite brevity:

Centros and *Überseering*[150] confirmed the fundamental importance of the freedoms in the TEU. At the same time, they show that this supranational or legal framework cannot be understood as rules capable of subsumption, or at any rate ought not to be understood that way: in the interpretation of the *Centros* judgment advocated above, the freedom of establishment is not merely an economic freedom, but also not an element of a European economic constitution – preordained for Member States and/or exposing their laws to processes of regulatory competition. Instead, it is more of a freedom that simultaneously acts as a political right, because it puts the citizens of a Member State in a position to place their sovereign under a compulsion to provide justification.[151] In this interpretation, what is involved is indeed a procedural law of justification, which sets first of all the courts and then the legislator (and then, if necessary, the courts again) in motion. Is this wishful thinking? To some degree; but one ought to bear in mind the implications of a more rigid interpretation which *Überseering* seems to suggest: if freedom of establishment were understood as a legal principle that could set aside the regulatory keystones of company law and historically and politically important concerns which the seat principle had defended,[152] then this "right" would not merely have disintegrative effects within some Member States but illegitimatise the Community and the integration project as a whole.

We have characterised the conflicts between European competition law and national private law in cases like *Pronuptia* and *Courage* as "diagonal" conflict constellations.[153] The "settlement" of this conflict occurred in the *Pronuptia* saga through sheer exhaustion. This is a mechanism which all legal systems use. But it is one which by no means does justice to the issues involved. What is at issue in cases like *Pronuptia* is whether European law incorporates elements of a law of franchisee protection as part of the European *ordre public* or tolerates such objectives where national contract law pursues them.[154] Again, we would then be witnessing a justification process emerging from the conflict between the two levels of governance in the EU; its legitimacy would rest either upon the insight that interests of franchisee

---

150 Section 3.1 above.
151 Section 3.1.2. above.
152 Section 3.1.3 above.
153 Section 3.2 above.
154 Ch. Joerges, Contract and Status in Franchising Law, note 84 above, 50 ff.

protection are not discredited by competition law, although such protection need not be uniformly shaped throughout all European jurisdictions. What was merely implicit in *Pronuptia* came openly to the fore in *Courage*: here the conflict of laws has led to the justi(ce)-fication of new private law that the Member States have to incorporates their "law of the land". In this case, the prescriptive claims of Community law are certainly more rigid, even though the incorporation it requires may take doctrinally different shapes.[155]

One can hardly interpret the competition law judgments as confirming the emergence of a European "regulatory state"; such an interpretation would be equally implausible with the consumer protection judgments (on the Directives on Unfair Terms in Consumer Contracts and on Product Liability.[156] In *Océano*, the ECJ encouraged semi-autonomous developments of national laws.[157] Its holdings on product liability – hopefully! –cannot, despite their strong language, change anything in the fact that Directive 85/374/EWG has only a complementary significance that cannot contribute much to the tasks of extending the law that continually arise in manufacturer liability in tort law. Whether these decisions will instigate new Community legislation in the field of product liability remains to be seen. Even if such activities are being initiated, the tensions between the "logic of market integration" and the "logic of a law of private law justi(ce)-fication" will not come to a rest. The European legal machinery is simply not equipped to cope with the many facets of this field in a comprehensive, let alone centralising, fashion.

4.4 Deliberative Supranationalism II: Constitutionalising "Transnational Governance Arrangements"

In many areas of regulatory policy, what is only rarely visible the realm of private law becomes plain: the building up of hybrid transnational governance arrangements, structured neither in purely private law terms not in purely public law terms, neither nationally nor European, neither purely governmental nor non-governmental,[158] in which societal and governmental actors adapt to a transnational reality which is no longer domesticisible nationally. What is so typical of regulatory policy also has to leave its traces in private law. Among the examples listed in Section 3, the one in franchising law is the clearest: this law is neither purely national nor purely European. Both the Commission, the ECJ and the Member State courts are involved in its making – not to mention the enterprise associations that work out the contractual arrangements to transport the various franchising concepts, which, at the same time, have to be kept compatible with European competition law and many kinds of national legal systems. Yet, the field is even broader. With increasing intensity, groups

---

155 Section 3.2.2 above.
156 Section 3.3 above.
157 Section 3.3.1 above.
158 On this term see Ph.C. Schmitter, What is there to legitimise in the European Union... and how might this be accomplished?", in Ch. Joerges/Y. Mény/J.H.H. Weiler (eds.) *Symposium: Mountain or Molehill? A Critical Appraisal of the Commission White Paper on Governance*, Jean Monnet Working Paper No. 6/01, 79 ff., 83 ff. (http://www.iue.it/RSC/Governance/; http://www.jeanmonnetprogram.org/papers/01/010601.html).

of academics and associations are having their say on the Europeanisation of private law, not merely "portraying, but also producing" law, and referring, for the legitimisation of their claims to involvement, not just to their scholarly reputation, but also intending their contributions to apply in legal practice and legal policy.[159] What can be observed in legislation has long been underway in the context of judicial law finding. Public jurisdiction can play only a very limited part in settling disputes in European contexts. All of this is more than, and different from, the type of conflict of laws just described, because these transnational governance arrangements do not just mediate between different given policies and law, but are to elaborate genuinely transnational responses to transnational problem constellations. This type of governance cannot be rejected as being outright illegal or illegitimate, not just because of their factual importance, but also because of their normative potential. The need to design a law that would "constitutionalise" such arrangements so that they deserve the recognition they claim is only gradually being realised – and all I wish to do here is to emphasise that we will have to face these challenges.[160]

4.5 Bottlenecks

All this "may be true in theory, but does not apply in practice", says Immanuel Kant famous General Maxim,[161] which may be appropriate here – even if one accepts all the benevolent reconstructions of the examples presented in the preceding sections. For everywhere, bottlenecks, weaknesses and omissions have also become visible: in such a complex organisation as the ECJ, there cannot be any unitary institutional self-perception. The interactions between the ECJ and the national courts are governed by formalist prescriptions and are vulnerable to strategic behaviour, be it of powerful private players, be it of governmental actors, be it of lower or higher courts: interactive adjudication does occur in the EU, although its quality is difficult to assess[162] and even more difficult to ensure.[163] And however careful courts may deliberate, they

---

159 For a comprehensive account, see K. Riedl, Europäisierung des Privatrechts: „Recht-Fertigung" wissenschaftlicher Vereinheitlichungsprojekte, Ph.D. Thesis, EUI-Florence 2003.

160 For the area of European risk regulation in the foodstuffs sector cf., Ch. Joerges, Zusammenfassung und Perspektiven: „Gutes Regieren" im Binnenmarkt, in Ch. Joerges/J. Falke (eds.), *Das Ausschußwesen der Europäischen Union. Praxis der Risikoregulierung im Binnenmarkt und ihre rechtliche Verfassung*, Baden-Baden: Nomos 2000, 349 ff., 363 ff..

161 I. Kant, Über den Gemeinspruch: Das mag in der Theorie richtig sein, taugt aber nicht für die Praxis (*Werkausgabe der Wissenschaftlichen Buchgesellschaft* Vol. 9, edited by W. Weischedel), Darmstadt 1971, 125 ff..

162 There are very many examples of a fortunate interaction in the European judiciary. And there are counter-examples and borderline cases: *Überseering* (see Section 3.1.3) and the recent judgments on the Product Liability Directive in den neuen Urteilen zur Produkthaftung (see Section 3.3.2) are certainly not particularly encouraging although they are not as disappointing as Case C-481/99, judgment of 13.12.2001 – *Georg und Helga Heininger v. Bayerische Hypotheken- und Vereinsbank* and the critique by G.-P. Calliess, The Limits of Eclecticism in Consumer Law: National Struggles and the Hope for a Coherent European Contract Law, *German Law Journal* 3/8, 1 August 2002, www.germanlawjournal.com). *Lasciate ogni speranza!?* Such a desperate outcry would be premature.

163 Ch. Joerges, "La langue de l'étranger" – Observations on the need to observe and understand discourses on foreign territories, Comments on Silvana Sciarra (ed.), *Labour Law in the Courts.*

are not in control of the processes of law production. They do much if they ensure the respect for Europe's legal commitments and help to identify and to defend procedural guarantees which promote deliberative interactions. Do all these practical troubles, then, ultimately militate in favour of the project of a European civil code? First of all, they are in favour of accepting the view that, in such a project, the very difficulties that arise are those that it is supposed to solve. The "classical" models of private law codification do not come into consideration for today's Europe. First, because Europe will not become some hierarchically structured polity, but will remain heterarchical and plural; there is no legislative actor with the vocation for universal legislation that would bring Europe under a unitary codified regime. Nor, however, is Europe some sort of cultural nation able to write down its code without having to wait for the formation of a state. The mixed position we find ourselves in – a "primary law" that is about to learn how to organise the interdependence of the freedoms of the "market citizens" with the aspirations of political citizenship in the European Union; and a heterarchical regulatory policy organised in networks; a patchwork of specific legislation tackling concrete problems which produces a host of disintegrative effects in national legal systems – this is the "state of the (European) Union". Is the quality of private law harmed thereby, and is the idea of equal originality [*Gleichurspüng-lichkeit*] of private autonomy and of political rights to be written off as theory? Will we be witnessing the generation of a "quilt", consisting of colourful yet disparate pieces, which have to be put together by people who are colour-blind?[164] This has by no means been established. The point is whether the development exceeds the learning capacities and productive imaginative power of those involved.

National Judges and the European Court of Justice, Oxford/Portland: Hart 2001, http://www.europeanbooks.org/index2.htm

164 Thus P. Schlechtriem, "Wandlungen des Schuldrechts in Europa" – wozu und wohin, *Zeitschrift für Europäisches Privatrecht* 10 (2002), 213 ff., 214.

CHAPTER 10

The Challenge of Market Integration for European Conflicts Theory[1]

Horatia Muir Watt*

1   The changing face of the conflict of laws

Today, Member States of the European Union are facing the fact that a quasi-federal or integrated political and economic structure bears necessarily on the way in which conflicts between the laws of component units are perceived and solved. To some extent at least, intra-European conflicts of laws are now seen to involve the allocation of regulatory authority within the Union, rather than the quest for the law most appropriate to the individual interests of the parties to a dispute. The private law paradigm dominant during the latter half of the twentieth century[2] appears to be giving way to a public law perspective, in which the conflict of laws enjoys, anew,[3] a "regulatory function".[4] Indeed, after shedding its "neutrality" in the 1970s by allowing in result-

---

* Professor at the University of Paris I (Panthéon-Sorbonne)
1   The theme developed in this paper is also the subject of a longer article published in the Columbia Journal of European Law 2003, entitled "Choice of law in integrated and connected markets". See also, for a further account "Les fondéments économique du droit international privé", Cours de l'Académic de Droit International de la Hague, 2004, forthcoming
2   The public/private divide has served an important purpose within the Continental European tradition in insulating private international law from political concerns. Traditionally, the applicable law is identified in the light of purely private interests; the choice remains indifferent to considerations of political economy. This is less true in the US, where the relationship between law and politics has been monitored by comity in the international arena, even serving as a rhetorical "bridge" in this context (see Joel R. Paul, "Comity in International Law", 1991 Harv Int'l L J 1), while federalism concerns have coloured the conflict of laws with political and public interest.
3   Both universalist theories at the turn of the century, then early twentieth century particularism, saw the function of the conflict of laws as residing in the allocation of legislative jurisdiction between sovereign states. The difference between the two doctrines was simply that the latter had definitively relinquished the universalist ideal, after the simultaneous discovery by Kahn and Bartin of conflicts of characterisation, thus severing the links between public and private international law. Allocation of sovereign authority, it was thought, could only be achieved by each individual state. Bartin, in particular, developed the idea that the local (French) system of private international law allocated legislative jurisdiction among the several states by acting functionally as a supranational legislator (see his *Principes de droit international privé selon la loi et la jurisprudence françaises*, 3 vol., Paris, 1930, 1932, 1935). The contradiction inherent in the very idea that any national system could define and share out legislative sovereignty among the several states soon gave way in the second half of the twentieth century to a redefinition of the function of the conflict of laws and the adoption of a purely private law perspective. The conflict of laws was then perceived merely to define the regime best suited to private interests in international situations (see the text below, n°4).
4   The term «regulatory function» appears in the title of an article by Robert Wai, "Transnational Liftoff and Juridical Touchdown: The Regulatory Function of Private International Law in a Era of Globalisation", 2002 Colum J. Transnat'l L 209.

selective considerations in private law,[5] private international law is now losing the "innocence" which served traditionally to keep it sheltered from the intrusion of state interests.[6] Interestingly if not unpredictability, the change is bringing the conflict of laws within Europe closer to its American counterpart, on which it had long looked askance for crossing the dividing line between choice of law and international, or interstate, politics.[7]

2   The presence of new quasi-federalist concerns within the European Union

Among the signs of the new quasi-federalist concerns present in European conflicts is the idea that certain traditional approaches, such as the use of nationality as a connecting factor, may be discriminatory,[8] thus mirroring current debate in the United State over the extent to which Currie's governmental interest analysis violates the principle of Equal Citizens by favouring personal connecting factors over territorialism.[9] Similarly, the debate which now focuses on the existence of "occult" conflict rules geared to the expansion of economic freedoms within the internal market expresses ideas about the proper balance of legislative authority among Member

---

5   The belief widely held in Europe that governments do not have a direct stake in outcomes in conflicts cases does not mean that legislators do not show concern for the implementation of substantive policies in private law. This gives rise to alternative choice of law rules, such as those designed to promote the interest of the child in the field of family relationships (par ex, articles 311-16 to 311-18 of the French civil code).

6   The phrase is coined by Herbert Kronke in his account of "Capital Markets and the Conflict of Laws", *Rec Cours Acad La Haye*, t286, 249-385, p.378.

7   A characteristic expression of the refusal to accept that state interests can be found in private law, can be found in Gerhard's Kegel's "The Crisis of the Conflict of Laws", *Rec Cours Acad. La Haye*, vol.112 (1964) p.91.

8   On the principle of non-discrimination in general, E. Brisbosia, E. Dardenne, P. Mgnette et A. Weyembergh (dir), *Union européenne et nationalités, Le principe de non-dsicitimnination et ses limites*, Bruylant, 1999; on the impact of the principle of non-discrimination on the use of nationality as a connecting factor, see M. Fallon "Les conflits de lois dans un espace européen intégré: l'expérience de la Communauté européenne", *Rec Cours Acad La Haye* vol 253 (1995) 9-281, n°62; M.P. Puljak, *Le droit international privé à l'épreuve du principe communautaire de non-discrimination en raison de la nationalité*, thèse Paris II, 2002, dir. Y. Lequette.

9   D. Laycock, "Equal Citizens of Equal and territorial States: The Constitutional Foundations of Choice of Law", 92 Colum. L. Rev. 249 (1992). It is doubtful, however, that use of a personal connecting factor in either context is discriminatory if it does not imply taking into account the content of the applicable law. Nationality or residence are not discriminatory per se in this context, if the applicable law is applied whatever its content. It would be discriminatory, on the other hand, to apply forum law to forum nationals or residents only when this law favours their case. This is the point on which Currie's governmental interest analysis becomes vulnerable to criticism. If, indeed, governmental interests are taken to signify that the forum state has a concern for favourable outcomes for forum residents, then there is indeed discrimination, as Lea Brilmayer has pointed out ("The Role of Sunbstantive and Choice of law Policies in the Formatiuon and Application of Choice of Law Rules" *Rec Cours Acad. La Haye*, vol. 252 (1995), p9). However, this may be distorting the real meaning of "interests" (H. Hill Kaye, "A Defence of Currie's Governmental Interest Analysis", *Rec Cours Acad. La Haye*, vol 215 (1989), p.9).

States – an issue which is subject to constitutional scrutiny in the United States. Indeed, it must not be forgotten that Currie's governmental interests theory was initially borrowed from constitutional case-law, according to which the application of the law of the forum in the absence of relevant state interests could violate the duty to provide Full Faith and Credit to the laws of Sister States.[10] Other analogies between the European and American approaches to the conflict of laws include the perceived need for a dual choice of law system, geared on the one hand to dealing with cross-border activities within the internal market, on the other to defining the scope of Community regulation vis-à-vis the law of third states.[11]

3. Change in perspective as the focus of this paper

All these shifts result in a significant change of perspective, which will be the focus of this paper. The idea is not to restate the many excellent studies[12] which already

---

10 See for example *Alaska Packers Assn v. Industrial Accident Comm'n of California*, Supreme Court of the United States, 1935, 294 US 532; then Allstate Insurance Co. v. Dick, Supreme Court of the United States, 1981, 449 US 302, requiring that there be "a significant contact or significant aggregation of contacts, creating state interests" for the application of forum law to be constitutional under Full Faith and Credit or the Due Process Clause of the Fourteenth Amendment.

11 At present, the state of Community law is particularly complex as decision –making in both these fields is multi-level. Not all the choice of law rules of the member States in fields which might affect the working of the internal market are harmonised as yet, and conflicts with third states are subject to community law only to the extent that it prohibits opting-out of harmonised protection. See on this last aspect, P. Lagarde, "Heurs et malheurs de la protection internationale du consommateur dans l'Union européenne », in *Le contrat au début du XXIème siècle, Etudes offertes à Jacques Ghestin*, 2000, p.511. A "close connection" with the territory of a Member State is usually required for consumer legislation to apply (see P. Lagarde, *op cit*). The reach of Community competition law is measured by a yardstick resembling the US "effects" test, which seems to have been adopted in fact if not explicitly by the Court of Luxembourg in the *Woodpulp* case (1988, case 89/85, 1988, ECR 5193). A similar cleavage between interstate and international conflicts –or rather, between conflicts subject to state or federal authority - has long existed in the United States, the former being to a certain degree constitutionalised (see FN 9 above), but not harmonised at a federal level. The latter, formulated at the federal level in terms of "prescriptive jurisdiction", are subject to the supposed constraints of public international law or comity: they involve defining the international reach of federal economic legislation, and, when a claim is not supported by the latter, leave no room for the enforcement of foreign public law.

12 The literature is so abundant that it is difficult to provide an exhaustive bibliography. See, in particular, J. Basedow, « Der kollisionrechtliche Gehalt der productfreiheiten im europaïschen Binnemarket: favor offerentis », RablesZ. 1995, p.1; M. Fallon, *op cit*; E. Jayme et Ch. Kohler, «L'interaction des règles de conflit contenues dans le droit dérivé de la Communauté européenne et des Conventions de Bruxelles et de Rome », Rev crit DIP 1995, p.1; H.U. Jessurun d'Oliveira, « The EU and a Metamorphosis of Private International law », in *Reform and Development of Private International Law, Essays in honour of Sir Peter North*, ed. James Fawcett, Oxford, p.111.P. Lagarde, « Heurs et malheurs... » cited above and book review, Rev crit DIP 1996, p.853; L. Idot, Le droit international privé communautaire: émergence et incidences », Petites affiches 12 déc. 2002, n°248, p.27; L. Radicati di Brozolo, «L'influence sur les conflits de lois des principes de droit communautaire de liberté de circulation », Rev crit DIP 1993.401; M. Wilderspin and X Lewis, « Les relations entre le droit communautaire et les règles de conflit de lois des Etats membres » Rev crit DIP 2002, p.1. Adde published after this paper was written, *Les conflits de lois et le système juridique communautaire*, dir. A. Fuchs, H. Muir Watt, E. Pataut, Dalloz, Thèmes et Commentaires, 2004.

monitor the impact of Community law on the conflict of laws – be such an impact "direct", in the form of secondary law pertaining to choice of law or jurisdiction, or "indirect" in the form of hidden principles or indeed the modified substance of public policy – but to consider the way in which the conflict of laws is gradually losing its private law trappings and becoming invested with public regulatory functions within the European Union. This evolution should provide food for thought for the drafters of a European Civil Code, who might pause to ask whether "private" international law still has its proper place in a codification of private law.[13] Of course, much of the "direct" contribution of Community law is part of the *acquis communautaire*, in particular, the various rules contained in consumer protection directives;[14] any new specifically European rules on the conflict of laws in the field of contract or products liability would require careful articulation with existing solutions.[15] But the issue arising here is a wider one. It is linked to the evolution affecting the uses of the conflict of laws, which is gradually moving beyond the type of concerns generally embodied in a private law code.

4   The global context: blurring the public/private law divide

The transformation of the conflict of laws is not limited to the intra-European context, which seems merely to accentuate changes already visible elsewhere. Globalisation is also bringing about a blurring of the public/private divide[16] in international litigation. A new generation of "collisions of economic regulation"[17] linked to unprecedented trans-national mobility of firms, goods, services and capital, challenges mainstream Continental European conceptions of choice of law as a tool geared to the resolution of purely private disputes.[18] Unchallenged throughout the major part of

---

13 The question might of course have been whether the conflict of laws is still needed within a European codification of private law, since the rationale of the European Civil Code lies in the need to eliminate conflicts as obstacles to the efficient functioning of the internal market. However, traditional conflicts of laws will remain, even in areas of harmonised law, as long as national measures of transposition are not identical, and are not interpreted identically. Moreover, the point made in this paper is that conflicts of laws within the internal market take on new forms and functions and remain as important, if not more important, than before.

14 See again, P. Lagarde, "Heurs et malheurs..", cited above.

15 Thus, the Groupe européen de droit international privé has proposed various amendments to articles 5- 7 of the Rome Convention in order to take account of new trends in intra-European conflicts (see Rev crit DIP2002.929 and 2001.774, obs. P. Lagarde).

16 Outside the Roman tradition, such a divide has of course been more easily dismantled. Among an abundant literature, see Duncan Kennedy, "The Stages of Decline of the Public/Private Distinction", 130 U Pa L Rev 1423 (1982); Mary Anne Glendon, "The Sources of Law in a Changing Legal order", 17 Creighton L Rev 663 (1983).

17 The expression was coined by Jurgen Basedow," Conflicts of economic regulation", 1994 Am J Comp L. 423; comp by the same author on this theme, "Souveraineté territoriale et globalisation des marchés: lde domaine d'application des lois contre les restrictions de concurrence", 264 *Rec Cours Acad La Haye* 9 (1997).

18 One reads with interest the following passage in Andreas D. Lowenfeld's work on "International Litigation and the Quest for Reasonableness", *Clarendon Press*, 1996, which provides excellent food for comparative thought on this point: "I do believe.. that Story was right to think of the conflict of laws as part of the law of nations, and that the term he introduced and that has gained currency in

the twentieth century,[19] the private interest paradigm can no longer explain the increasing interference of state policies in the field of transnational litigation. Of course, European legal theory has been more loath than American scholarship to embrace the idea that private law can also serve as a regulatory tool,[20] which explains the poor reception of governmental interests analysis this side of the Atlantic.[21] But, as it has been pointed out, fields such as antitrust, securities, banking law, export controls, products liability or environmental regulation, which can all affect private transactions, directly or indirectly, involve interests of an undeniably different order from those premised by traditional conflicts methodology,[22] introducing concerns previously identified as belonging to the field of public interests and as such beyond the pale of choice of law. In its strictest expression, the latter has been shielded from political concerns by the "public law taboo",[23] which led courts to decline to adjudicate other states' interests, at least when they give rise to the direct enforcement of foreign public rights.[24] The progressive emergence of an intermediate category of semi-public, internationally mandatory provisions, or "lois de police", has contributed somewhat to bridge the methodological gap; while remaining subject to specific unilateral methodology, foreign economic regulation has become amenable to application in domestic courts in private law litigation.[25] Beyond this concession, how-

---

Great Britain and throughout Europe is misunderstood by those who regard private international law as sharply distinct from public law or public international law. Thus my definition and approach are very different from those of Batiffol and Lagarde, who define private international law as the collection of rules applicable solely to private persons in their international relations" (p.3).

19 The idea that the conflict of laws is a "recipe" for achieving private law policies was expressed in Francescakis' seminal *Théorie du renvoi* in 1957 and characterises mainstream thinking to the present day (see, for example, in France, the Preface to *Grands arrêts de la jurisprudence de droit international privé*, by B. Ancel and Y Lequette, rejecting as corruptive the instrumentalisation of private international law by European Community law or human rights ideology). However, even prior to this clear challenge to sovereignty-based theories of multilateralism, of which the most characteristic is to be found in the work of Etienne Bartin (*Principes de droit international privé selon la loi et la jurisprudence françaises*, 3 vol., Paris, 1930, 1932, 1935), the conflict of laws was, paradoxically, considered to be limited to private relationships. This is clearly a legacy of von Savigny's Treatise of Roman Law (vol VIII).

20 That tort law for products liability, for instance, can be used to serves state interests (for instance, in protecting manufacturers or victims) is as banal in the US (see Hay, "Conflicts of Laws and State Competition in the Product Liability System", 80 Geo L R 617) as it is recent in the EU (see for example, Jane Stapleton, "Three Problems with The New Products Liability", Essays for Patrick Atiyah, Cane and Stapleton, Oxford, 1991, p.291). Newer still is the idea that the private law of contract can be used to regulate markets, through consumer protection, for example (see Hugh Collins, *Regulating Contracts*, OUP 1999).

21 See, again, Gerhard's Kegel's "The Crisis of the Conflict of Laws", *Rec Cours Acad. La Haye*, 1964, t.112, p.91.

22 Russell J. Weintraub, "The Extraterritorial Application of Antitrust and Securities Laws: An Inquiry into the Utility of a 'Choice-of-Law' Approach", 70 Tex L Rev 1799 (1992).

23 Philip J. McConnaughy, "Reviving the 'Public Law Taboo' in International Conflict of Laws" 35 Stan. J. Int'l L. 255; William S. Dodge, "Extraterritoraility and Conflict-of-Laws Theory: an Argument for Judicial Unilateralism", 39 Harv. Int'l J 101.

24 FA Mann, "The International Enforcement of ̈Public Rights", published in translation in 77 *Rev crit dr internat pr* 1 (1988).

25 The stimulus has been article 7§1 of the Rome Convention, which provides for the operation of foreign mandatory laws which override party choice of law. Similar provision is made in the Hague Agency Convention, 1978, art.16. But these texts concern claims initially framed in contract, so that

ever, the conflict of laws is traditionally presented as dealing exclusively with "private law relationships"; governments, it was thought, do not care directly about outcomes.[26] Such an assertion no longer holds true, however, as can be seen by the spectacular development of international judicial warfare[27] driven by state interests in ostensibly private litigation.[28] Despite recent attempts to define "new foundations" of the conflict of laws geared to the promotion of global welfare,[29] little can be done to stem the rise of unilateralism outside institutionalised cooperation.[30] The European Union provides such a context, however, and can thus be seen as an interesting testing ground for new solutions.[31] This is where the economics of federalism comes into the picture, suggesting new functions and scope for the conflict of laws.

5   The economics of federalism

Traditional "conflicts" rhetoric suggests that choice of law has a peace-keeping function between rival, mutually exclusive regulatory claims. The various theoretical models reinforce this impression: multilateralism carries a policy of alignment in order to produce decisional harmony out of chaos, whereas neo-statutist theories tend to pursue an agenda of political deference designed to induce reciprocity. Contemporary economic analysis, particularly the economics of federalism,[32] offers a reverse perspective, in which the idea that diversity is a source of disorder to be smoothed out wherever possible, is superseded by the conviction that competition between national legislators is basically salutary.[33] In a federal or vertically integrated structure, interjurisdictional competition appears as an alternative to centralized regulation. Far re-

---

the interference of foreign public law could arguably be considered as a case of incidental application (as both the United Kingdom and Germany argue, in opting out of article 7§1). On such incidental application of foreign public law, see H. Baade, "The Operation of Foreign Public law", 30 Tex Int'l L J 429 (1995).

26 Kegel, *op cit.*

27 See for example, J. Yoo, "Federal Courts as Weapons of Foreign Policy: the Case of the Helms-Burton Act", 1997 Hastings L. J. 747.

28 The notorious Laker litigation (see US Court of Appeals District of DC 1984, DC 577 F. Supp. 348; House of Lords 1985, AC 58) is ample evidence of the way in which courts perceive prescriptive jurisdiction to involve important state interests and engage if necessary in judicial warfare to protect it (here, through recourse to crossed anti-suit injunctions). But the doctrine of *forum non conveniens* can also serve to protect state policies, which explains increasing opposition to its use in cases where mass disasters are linked to the presence of forum multinationals in developing countries.

29 See Andrew Guzman's "Choice of Law: New Foundations", 90 Geo LJ 333 (2002).

30 As Guzman himself recognises (ibid).

31 Although sensitive areas such as competition law, securities regulation or products liability are now subject to a large extent to uniform or harmonised law at the European level, excluding or at least reducing interstate conflicts of laws in these fields, the conflict of laws is affected to some extent by the court of origin principle, which garants The working of the internal market. The question is therefore to what extent this change has influenced its scope and function.

32 See, for example, a classic among the abundant American literature relating this theme to the European Union, F.H. Easterbrook, "Federalism and European Business Law" (1994), 14 Internat Rev of Law and Economics 125.

33 While emphasising the importance of the conflict of laws, this perspective also reinstates comparative law as a source of informed choice.

moved from its traditional justifications, party choice in cross-border transactions is viewed through economic lenses as instrumental in stimulating such competition.

6   The conflict of laws as regulatory competition

The theme of regulatory competition, with the correlative question of the optimal level at which regulation should take place, has only recently begun to appear as a subject for debate in the European Union,[34] where it is more common to think of legal diversity as being at odds with the very idea of an internal market.[35] Borrowed from US scholarship,[36] it has generated new issues both as to the ways in which legislative authority should be allocated vertically within the European Union, emphasising the importance of subsidiarity,[37] and, paradoxically, as to the extent to which emulation between national legislators may be a factor of integration.[38] Desire for deregulation is linked to the perceived dangers of centralisation as giving rise to rent-seeking and problems of public choice, excessive bureaucratisation and an inability to respond to individual preferences.[39] Lowering the level at which regulation takes place in order to introduce more market pressure on legislators involves reintro-

---

34 See Wolfgang Kerber, "Interjurisdictional Competition within the European Union", in The Deregulation of Global Markets, Weimar Symposium 1998, Fordham International Law Journal 2000.217; A. Ogus, "Competition between national legal systems – a contribution of economic analysis to comparative law", 48 ICLQ 405 (1999); Jukka Snell, *Goods and Services in European Law, A Study of the relationships between the Freedoms*, Oxford, 2002, p. 35 et s. On the complex multilevel character of such competition, see Frey & Eichenberg on the concept of "FOCJ" (functional, overlapping, competing jurisdictions), in "FOCJ: Competitive Governments for Europe", 16 Int'l Rev L & Eco 315 (1996).

35 Indeed, until recently, a strong trend towards centralization of regulatory authority within the UE tended to make diversity suspect; integration seemed to imply harmonisation at highest level, and the attendant "death" of conflicts and comparative law (see, for the latter, Ch. von Bar, "From principles to Codification: Prospects for European Private Law", 8 Colum J Eur L 379 (2002); Symposium on Methodology and Epistemology of Comparative Law, Brussels, October 2002, to be published by Hart Publishing).

36 The volume of literature on this subject is impressive. See, in particular, the special issue of the Journal of International Economic Law (2000), devotes to "Regulatory competition in focus", with contributions by Daniel C. Esty, Richard L. Revesz, Damien Gerardin, Jonathan R. Macey, Alan O. Sykes, Joel P. Trachtman, concerning a wide range of different substantive fields. See too, Ulen, "Economic and Public Choice Forces in Federalism", 6 Geo Mason L Rev 921; and again, Frank H. Easterbrook, "Federalism and European Business Law", 14 Int'l Rev. L. & Econ. 125.

37 The links between subsidiarity and regulatory competition on various levels also give rise to an abundant literature. See, for example, R.Van den Bergh, "Subsidiarity as an Economic demarcation principle and the Emergence of European Private Law", 5 Maastricht Journal 129 (1998); George Bermann, "European Community law from a US Perspective", 4 Tul J Int'l & Comp L 5 (1995); Christian Kirchner, "The Principle of Subsidiarity in the Treaty on European Union: A Critique from the Perspective of Constitutional Economics", Tul J Int'l & Comp L 291 (1998), Breton, Cassone & Fraschini, "Decentralization and Subsidiarity: Toward a Theoretical Reconciliation", 19 U Pa J Int'l Econ L 21 (1998).

38 See Kerber and Van den Bergh, *op cit*, on competition as a learning process and its contribution to integration.

39 Kerber, p. 218.

ducing the conflict of laws in fields which might have been mapped out for unification. However, as a tool of political and economic integration, the conflict of laws has to fit into a sophisticated, multi-level scheme, which affects its traditional function in several ways. Firstly, by maintaining a field of free regulatory competition between national laws, it is instrumental in the vertical allocation of competences (1). Secondly, under the pressure of market integration, it serves simultaneously to promote fundamental market freedoms (2). Finally, extending its scope to the market for public goods, it must ensure that competition between national economic policies remains undistorted (3).

7 (1) Setting the vertical allocation of competences

As Stefan Grundmann has explained, the specific regulatory focus of European contract law[40] over the last decade has been the extension of party autonomy through the removal of obstacles to certain categories of cross-border transactions.[41] It rests upon a distinction between harmonised regulation at the European level, designed to cure market failures,[42] on the one hand, and national choice-facilitating rules[43] which remain amenable to the conflict of laws, and in particular to free party choice, on the other.[44] Regulation is thus "multi-level".[45] Party autonomy operates within a centralised regulatory framework designed to correct informational asymmetries by imposing minimum standards uniformly applicable throughout the Community, and to

---

40 We are not talking here about common substantive principles of private contract law, such as the Lando Commission's principles of European contract law, but "hard" Community law, in particularly the "acquis communautaire" in the filed of consumer protection, which regulates cross-border transactions within the internal market. On the very concept of European Contract law as being both wider (including areas such as competition law) and narrower (focussing on the correction of market failures) than what is generally perceived to constitue the private law of contract i national systems, see S. Grundmann, "The Structure of European Contract Law", 4 European Review of Private Law 505-528 (2001), at p. 515 et seq.

41 S. Grundmann, cited above. These are transactions which typically have a strong cross border dimension and take place in large numbers, such as sales, service contracts (insurance, investment banking, tourism...) commercial agency, contract questions in intellectual property etc. For a full analysis, see Grundmann, *Europaïsches Schuldvertragsrecht – das Europaïsches Recht der Unternehmensgeschefte (nebst Texten und Materialien zur Rechtsangleichung),* de Grutyer, Berlin, 1999.

42 The regulation of market failures is designed essentially to remedy informational asymmetries, through mandatory disclosure rules (on the priority given by the ECJ as from its Cassis de Dijon ruling in 1979, to mandatory disclosure over substantive protection, see Grundmann, p.513). Market failures are also addressed through Community rules against restriction of competition, caught by article 7 of the Rome Convention. State failure, as opposed to market breakdown, is addressed through subsidiarity.

43 These are essentially the rules of classical contract law pertaining to the formation and performance of the contract, and designed to help parties use their market freedom.

44 This distinction is fundamental to the 1980 Rome Convention on the law applicable to contractual obligations, which distinguishes the field of freedom of choice (article 3) from areas affected by internationally mandatory provisions (articles 5-7).

45 On multi-level regulation and its consequences for the conflicts of laws, see Ch. Joerges, "On the legitimacy of Europeanising Europe's private law: Considerations of a law of just-ification for the EU multi-level system", in *Global Jurist,* Berkeley Electronic Press, 2002.

eliminate restrictions on competition.[46] However, ensuring the full cross-border effect of party autonomy[47] also requires the removal of national regulatory barriers which interfere with the access to national markets. Regulation of market failure doubles up as a market integration issue.[48]

8 Over-regulation and multiple burdens

Community law therefore imposes a second, parallel, series of constraints on Member States, similar to those resulting within the United States from the dormant commerce clause,[49] according to which they must refrain from applying measures which will lead to over-regulation or multiple burdens restricting access to other European markets. Scrutiny under market freedoms may apply to any form of mandatory state regulation which is internationally enforceable under articles 5 to 7 of the Rome Convention, including national measures implementing Community directives (as for instance in the *Arblade* and *Mazzoleni* cases[50]), but does not apply to the choice-facilitating rules which fall within the scope of article 3 of the Rome Convention. As the *Alsthom Atlantique* case shows, national rules within this latter category are not subject to scrutiny under fundamental freedoms.[51] Thus, the conflict rule governing transactions on the internal market draws a double dividing line: it demarcates the scope of free choice, as opposed to internationally mandatory regulation, while simultaneously ensuring the vertical allocation of competence between Community law, designed to cure market failures (consumer protection, competition law), and regulation at the lower, Member State level, of the garden variety of contract law.[52] If the double line admittedly lacks clarity in some cases, it may be due to fluctuations in the case-law of the European Court of Justice as to the desirable extent of state com-

---

46 Protective legislation applicable to cross-border consumer contracts or international securities transactions, such as those adopted by European Community secondary legislation, are designed to eradicate informational asymmetries, which might otherwise lead to faulty choice – including choice of the applicable law. On the focus of Community law on disclosure rather than on substantive rules of consumer protection (mandated as far as national measures are concerned by the Court of Justice in *Cassis de Dijon* and as far as concerns the Community legislator by fundamental freedoms and proportionality), see Stefan Grundmann, "The Structure of European Contract Law", cited above. On similar developments in the field of securities regulation, see Niamh Moloney, *EC Securities Regulation*, Oxford EC Law Library, 2002.

47 Such is the primary function of internal market freedoms under the UE Treaty: see Grundmann, p.510.

48 On the fact that the integration issue sometimes eclipses substantive policies, in particular investor protection in the field of securities regulation, see Niamh Moloney, *op cit*.

49 On the requirements of the so-called "dormant" commerce clause, see

50 See for example, ECJ C-369/96 & 23rd November 1999, *Arblade*, C376/96 (concerning the 1986 commercial agency directive), ECJ C-376/96, 15th March 2001, *Mazzoleni* (extending the scrutiny to internationally mandatory rules of the forum-host state providing for minimum salary. The directive 96/71 of 16 December 1996 was not yet at issue here). The measures subject to scrutiny may include rules not traditionally seen as contract law, including rules of public law: see Grundmann, *op cit*, p.515.

51: ECJ *Alsthom Atlantique*, 24 Jan 1991, C-339/89.

52 See again, Grundmann, *op cit*, p. 515.

petition.[53] It is also true that the encounter between the economic dynamics of Community law and the more traditional private law concerns of the conflict of laws inevitably brings about shifts in traditional categories, which may also require time to settle.[54] Thus, pre-emptive law under market freedoms is not necessarily internationally mandatory within the traditional meaning of article 7 of the Rome Convention, whereas national public economic regulation may similarly be disqualified as such and, deprived of its mandatory character, subjected to party choice.[55]

9   (2) Ensuring the full extent of economic freedoms

Scrutiny of national law applicable to cross-border situations under market freedoms, in order to avoid reconstitution of regulatory barriers, has given rise to the well-known distribution of Member State regulatory authority under *Keck* and its progeny, in the form of mutual recognition. In the field of products, the home country may apply its regulation in relation to the product itself , whereas host country law prevails as far as selling arrangements are concerned.[56] As far as services are concerned, a similar division can be found, for example, in the field of financial services, where the host country may impose rules of conduct, while the service itself is shaped through prudential and supervisory requirements according to home country provisions.[57] Interestingly, such a design gives rise to the formulation of a new generation

---

53 See Jukka Snell, *op cit.* In implementing the economic freedoms, the Court of justice seems to hesitate between a model which fosters state competition, towards a more centralised model, in which EC scrutiny encroaches on cases in which there is no protectionist intent or effect, pre-empting choice of law and restricting party autonomy. Thus, the 1995 *Bosman* case implements a very expansive reading of the Treaty, based on the idea of market access, in which, practically, the very existence of a conflict of laws seems to generate EC competence. On the extent to which it may be necessary to distinguish the different freedoms: see Jukka Snell, *op cit.*

54 On these shifts, see Hans Ulrich Jessurun d'Oliveira, "The EU and a Metamorphosis of Private International Law", in *Reform and Development of Private International Law, Essays in Honour of Sir Peter North*, Oxford, 2002, p.111. See too Laurence Idot, *op cit*, p. 29, comparing the various civilian conflicts categories (personal status, property, contracts, torts) and their community law counterparts (goods, persons, services, capital).

55 Again, Grundmann, *op cit.* The allocation of regulatory competence between the home and host countries in the areas subject to scrutiny under the economic freedoms concerns points of both public and private law; a given determination of the applicable law may be pre-empted under the home country principle if it gives rise to a multiple burden for the importer, for example, whether or not it is technically a nationally imperative rule under article 7. Moreover, under the home country principle, according to which domestic consumers benefit from goods and services shaped by foreign regulation, national measures reinforcing the minimum requirements of directives loose their mandatory character, since those consumers will always be able to opt out of the scope of domestic regulation if they prefer a foreign offer. At the same time, regulatory competition among states may well extend to public goods.

56 See Jukka Snell, *op cit.*

57 An alternative approach is present in the 2002 Financial Distance Marketing Directive and in the 2000 e-Commerce Directive. The latter provides for the law of the Member State from which the Service is provided and allocates authority and jurisdiction to ensure compliance to the Member State of the suppliers' home. However, it does indicate that it does not provide rules of private international law. On this ambiguity, see Michael Wildespin & Xavier Lewis, "Les relations entre le droit communautaire et les règles de conflit de lois" Rev crit DIP 2002.1, p. 299; Corcoran & Hart, " The regulation of Cross-Border Financial Services in the EU Internal Market" 8 Colum J Eur L 221 at

of choice of law rules, which raise familiar issues of characterisation and definition of connecting factors.[58] Designed to prevent discrimination in the form of a double regulatory burden imposed on goods or services entering a foreign market, the new rules pre-empt divergent national conflicts solutions, and apply whatever the nature of the measures involved (public/private; mandatory/default).[59] Products and services may thus enter foreign markets freely, without being deprived of their original competitive advantage. At the same time, citizen preferences are maintained as host states are free to look for the most efficient marketing arrangements. Here again, the shifts in traditional categories become apparent: in exercising supervisory powers,[60] for instance in order to determine whether home country regulation has remained within the limits defined by *Keck*, host country authorities inevitably consider foreign public law.[61] The issue remains however as to whether a similar pattern should be extended so as to include rules relating to liability for products or services within the exclusive sphere of home country control. For instance, one may question whether the economic freedoms really require that products liability be subjected to the regulatory authority of the state of origin. The difficulties presently encountered in the elaboration of the "Rome 2" regulation on torts bear witness to strong differences of opinion on this point within the European Union.[62]

10 (c) Fostering undistorted competition for public goods[63]

Completion of the internal market and progress in technology have clearly brought about increased mobility of firms,[64] enhancing intra-European competition and im-

---

246; M. Fallon & J. Meesen , "Le commerce électronique, la directive 2000/31/CE et le droit international privé", Rev crit DIP 2002.465, at 484.

58 As in more traditional cases, these are not without difficulty, and require reflection upon the specific aims of division of regulatory competences (on the two possible readings of the Treaty on this point, the one, decentralised and anti-protectionist, the other a more intrusive "economic freedom" reading, see Jukka Snell, *op cit*). For instance, the 1995 *Alpine Investments* case (C-384/93, ECR I-1141) shows that the very notion of "selling arrangements" as distinct from product rules may be difficult; it has thus been proposed to sub-distinguish static and dynamic selling arrangements (see Jukka Snell, *op cit*, p. 94. For a different, interesting example of the formulation of a conflict of laws rule relating to takeovers, on cross-border bids, see Moloney, *op cit*, p.836.

59 See Jukka Snell, Stefan Grundmann, *op cit.*

60 The case-law concerning the extent of these supervisory powers shows that "eyes are on the prize" and the outcome is far from leaving states indifferent. See Jukka Snell, *op cit,*

61 On this point, see Jukka Snell, *op cit.*

62 See M. Wilderpsin and X. Lewis, *op cit*, arguing that the home country principle does not extend to private law rules of products liability. For the contrary view, see, for example, M. Wolf, "Privates Bankvertragsrecht im EG-Binnemarket", Zeitschrift fur Wirtschafts unbd Bankrecht, 1990.1941; J. Basedow, *op cit*. Other authors maintain that scrutiny under economic freedoms does not preclude the operation of the conflict of law rule; simply the applicable law will be subject to a control ex post, similar to the one required by the public policy exception (see for ex, H. D. Tebbens, "Les conflits de lois en matière de publicité déloyale à l'épreuve du droit communautaire", Rev crit DIP 1994.451). Since this paper was written, the proposal for a directive on services within the internal market (5.3.2004 exempts the non-contractual liabiling of service providers "in the case of an accident involving a person" from the country of origin principle.

63 For a complete account, see Kerber, *op cit.*

64 The ECJ's 1999 *Centros* case (case C-212/97, Rec 1999, I-1459, concl La Pergola) has to a certain extent remedied the problem of the high cost of mobility for firms within the European Union.

proving allocational efficiency.[65] In such a context, it becomes clear that the attractiveness of a given location, in terms of environmental concerns, quality of the workforce, infrastructures, etc, also depends on the economic policies of Member States.[66] The only way to limit such competition would be to centralise economic policy or raise barriers to mobility. Wolfgang Kerber has thus demonstrated very convincingly that the combined effect of deregulation and mobility leads to competition between Member States to attract businesses in the field of public goods.[67] Indeed, as he shows, an essential part of European integration seems to be that former monopolistic states are transformed into locations that must compete with others for goods and services.[68] This regulatory competition for public goods creates incentives to improve performance and ensures that governmental initiative really responds to citizens' preferences. An important difficulty arises, however, insofar as the "playing-field" made up of divergent economic policies is not level, and competition between Member States could thus be seen to be distorted;[69] clearly, rules of public law may create competitive advantages which are not subject to competition rules applicable to firms. However, the effects of an uneven playing field on competition can be corrected by allowing firms free choice of relevant provisions of public law.[70] At this point, it has been shown that the home-country rule, which at present ensures consumer choice of goods or services produced under foreign laws, is not necessarily optimal, as it cannot ensure undistorted regulatory competition unless it also allows for choice by producers.[71] The conflict of laws, expanding it scope beyond the traditional field of "private law", thereby has an important corrective or levelling function to play here, in order to ensure that state competition for public goods remains unrestricted. Thus, built into to a framework of mandatory requirements which ensure against market failure, the conflict of laws appears as an important deregulatory tool in the integrated market.[72]

---

65 Defined as efficient allocation of resources as factors of production move to their place of highest productivity.

66 Kerber, *op cit.*

67 Ibid.

68 Ibid.

69 The Treaty prohibits state aids, but this issue here is occult advantages which could not be eliminated without centralisation of Member States' economic policies.

70 Kerber, *op cit.*

71 As Wolfgang Kerber explains, *ibid*, p. 241, at present, the home country principle entails a distortion. States must allow consumer choice under the home country principle in cases of cross-border sales or providing of services. Thus, consumers always have a choice between different regulations, since foreign manufacturers may offer products under home country regulations. These regulations are aimed at consumer protection. They loose their mandatory character under the home country rule, precisely because consumers may choose, and become mere standards. However, domestic producers do not have similar choice of regulations, and remained governed by domestic rules. Mutual recognition thus entails the risk that national regulations for consumer protection actually subsidise national producers. This consequence could be avoided if producers could choose between different national regulations, for example, French firms could produce according to Italian standards without having to relocate to Italy.

72 The question is whether such an idea is sustainable outside context where centralised authority can correct market failures. Recent American scholarship has raised the issue of party choice in the field of economic law, such as in capital markets. The case has been put most strongly in the field of

11

In conclusion, the new functions which with the conflict of laws is invested within the internal market are linked in part to the appearance of complex patterns of regulation, which appear because the European Union is a multi-level system of governance.[73] Such a link suggests that story of change is only just beginning; conflicts of laws as we know them are bound to take on new forms, such as the "diagonal conflicts" between different levels of regulation described by Christian Joerges.[74] If traditional thinking in this field cannot of course be dismissed as obsolete, it is nevertheless already clear that as norm production begins to obey different structures,[75] new, more complex models will be required to cope with new constellations of conflicting laws. Christian Joerges' recent analysis of the *Centros* case[76] provides just such an example of the ways in which conflicts between national and Community law might be solved by less hierarchical, more deliberative solutions.[77] The same analysis demonstrates that conflicts may similarly be perceived as multi-dimensional; the *Centros* case is probably as much about political rights of the European citizen as about the exercise of economic freedoms within the Union.[78] This is a good example

---

securities, in favour of a system of "portable reciprocity" (Stephen J. Choi and Andrew T. Guzman, "Portable Recognition: Rethinking The International reach of Securities regulation", 71 S Cal L Rev 903, 1998) involving free choice of law by the issuer, thus delinking the applicable regulatory regime and the location at which the securities transactions take place. It is argued that because there is a considerable array of distinct preferences among investors and issuers alike, greater competition will lead to more efficient differentiation of regulatory regimes across the global market, each catering to different needs. The extent to which such competition is desirable remains controversial, however. Does regulatory competition really "empower investors" (Roberta Romano, « Empowering Investors: A Market Approach to Securities Regulation », 107 Yale LJ 2359, 1998) or does it generate harmful externalities with which the market itself cannot deal satisfactorily? Despite the seductiveness of the global competition thesis, the desirability of entrusting market failures to party choice is not entirely clear. The field of environmental protection offers clear empirical evidence that unbridled competition leads to sub-optimal regulation whenever there are important cross-border externalities, and similar demonstrations have been made in such areas as banking, antitrust or arbitration. At best, such evidence may indicate that it is unrealistic to generalize, and that the benefits to be gained from regulatory competition are field-specific.

73 Christian Joerges, *op cit.*

74 Christian Joerges has drawn attention to the new forms of "deliberative interaction" required in order to cope with the "functionally interwoven problem situations" that arise. The idea is that, since powers and resources for action are located a various autonomous levels within the Union, communication between actors each competent in their respective sphere is required in order to avoid paralysis of the system or chaos. "Deliberative supernationalism" is thus an alternative to the formation of hierarchies.

75 F. Ost & M. van de Kerchove, "De la pyramide au réseau? Vers un *nouveau* mode de production du droit ? », R.I.E.J. 2000, t44, p.1.

76 Case C-212/97, Rec 1999, I-1459, concl La Pergola.

77 *Op cit.*

78 In a section entitled "Freedom of market citizenship as political rights, and the obsolescence of traditional private international law"(II.I.2), Christian Joerges explains how, in the *Centros* case, Danish law is not pushed aside by European law, but placed under pressure of justification. The ECJ is acting here as a constitutional court. A Danish citizen can thus bring his sovereign to court with the argument that the latter has no good reasons to deny him the use of the regulatory alternatives offered by another member state. In order to conceptualise this type of justifiation of the

of the way in which present "flat thinking" about the law needs to be replaced by cognitive models capable of embracing complexity.[79] The implications of this idea reach far beyond the issue of conflict of laws. The question for the future may well then be not only whether conflicts can "fit" into a rational scheme of private law, but whether traditional tools – such as organised codes – can fit the new state of the law at all.

December 2002

Europeansiation process, Christain Joerges uses the term "Recht-Fertigungs-Recht" or "just-ification", suggested by Rudolf Wiethölter (essay, "Recht-Fertigungsen eines Gesellschafts-Rechts", Frankfurt a.M./Florence, 2002).

79 G. Samuel, English Private Law in the Context of the Codes, in *The Harmonization of European Private law,* Hart, 2000, ed. Van Hoeke & Ost, p.47. Using this idea in the field of Conflicts, see our contribution on "New Challenges in Public and Private International Legal Theory:Can Compara-tive Scholarship Help?", in Symposium on Methodology and Epistemology of Comparative Law, Brussels, October 2002, ed. M. Van Hoeke, to be published by Hart Publishing.

CHAPTER 11

The Constitutional Basis of a European Private Law

Vincenzo Zeno-Zencovich* & Noah Vardi**

1 Foreword

How will European private law emerge from the constitution-making process that has been taking place over the last years?

The answer is obviously of interest to private law scholars, but also to those who study the formation and evolution of legal systems, because of the circular interaction process between different aspects and levels of law.

If, from a historical point of view, we observe what has happened during the 20th Century in continental legal systems, we note the following elements:

a) The shift of the centre of gravity of private law from property towards contract and the use of contract as a dynamic and flexible element for the adaptation of the legal system to economic and social changes.
b) The growing process of "administrativisation" of private law in the sense that state intervention in the economy and in society has gradually bent private autonomy to its needs.
c) The constitutionalisation of several aspects of private law with the result that hierarchies of private juridical situations are modified and a new paramount source of law is created.

The first aspect is an *acquis* of modern private law; the second has been further strengthened by the sweeping community regulatory discipline which has covered extremely important areas such as competition, transport, energy, telecommunications, financial markets, transborder trade; the third must now be analysed in relation to the recent EU acts and their consequences, which seem to be confirmed by the draft of the European Constitution.[1]

---

*   Professor of comparative law – University of Roma Tre – Rome – Italy
** Research assistant in comparative law – University of Roma Tre – Rome – Italy
1   Considerations on the draft of the European Constitution refer to the draft Treaty establishing a Constitution for Europe, as adopted by consensus by the European Convention on 13 June and 10 July 2003 and submitted to the President of the European Council on 18 July 2003. These observations may very likely have to be reviewed against the light of the changes which shall be made to the final text to be approved.

2   A Catalogue of Fundamental (Private) Rights

The first issue to focus on concerns the question of which are the rights of a private nature that the December 2000 Nice Charter qualifies as "fundamental rights".[2]
This is a catalogue that from an objective point of view only partly coincides with the enumeration contained in the European Convention on Human Rights of 1950 and is the result both of the evolution of theory and practice of human rights in the past half-century[3] and of the review of the E.U. treaties, in particular the Treaty of Amsterdam.[4]

---

2   For a general treatment and a commentary on the Charter of Fundamental Rights of the European Union, out of an extremely vast bibliography on the Charter, see: R. Bifulco, M. Cartabia, A. Celotto, *L'Europa dei diritti. Commento alla Carta dei diritti fondamentali dell'Unione europea*, Bologna, 2001. See also F. Pocar "Commento alla Carta dei diritti fondamentali dell'Unione europea" in F. Pocar *Commentario breve ai Trattati della Comunità e dell'Unione europea*, Padova 2001; L. Ferrari Bravo, F.M. di Majo and A. Rizzo *Carta dei diritti fondamentali dell'Unione europea commentata con la giurisprudenza della Corte di giustizia CE e della Corte europea dei diritti dell'uomo e con i documenti rilevanti*, Milano 2001; G. Quinn and L. Flynn *The EU Charter on Fundamental Rights. Issues and Perspectives*, Oxford, 2001; G. F. Ferrari (editor) *I diritti fondamentali dopo la Carta di Nizza. Il Costituzionalismo dei diritti*, Milano 2001; A.W. Heringa and L. Verhey "The EU Charter: Text and Structure" in *Maastricht Journal of European and Comparative Law*, 2001;
3   On the protection of fundamental rights in Europe, with special reference to the European Convention on Human Rights, see: S. Bartole, B. Conforti and C. Raimondi *Commentario alla Convenzione europea per la tutela dei diritti dell'uomo e delle libertà fondamentali*, Padova 2001; R. Blackburn and J. Polakiewicz *Fundamental Rights in Europe. The ECHR and its Member States, 1950-2000*, Oxford, 2001. On the role of the European Court of Justice and of the European Court of Human Rights on this theme see: K. Lenaerts and E. de Smijter "The Charter and the Role of the European Courts" *Maastricht Journal of European and Comparative Law*, 2001; J.H.H. Weiler and N.J. Lockhart "Taking Rights Seriously. The European Court of Justice and its Fundamental Rights Jurisprudence" in *Common Market Law Review*, 1995. On the same theme with reference also to the Charter of Fundamental Rights, see: E. Pagano "Sui rapporti tra la Carta e i principi fondamentali elaborati dalla Corte di giustizia" in *Diritto pubblico comparato ed europeo*, 2001; R. Toniatti "La via giurisdizionale per la legittimazione dell'Unione europea" in *Diritto pubblico comparato ed europeo*, 2001. On the relation between the Charter of Fundamental Rights of the European Union and the ECHR see: P. Lemmens "The Relation Between the Charter of Fundamental Rights of the European Union and the European Convention on Human Rights – Substantive Aspects" in *Maastricht Journal of European and Comparative Law*, 2001; For a more general treatment of human rights in Europe see : P. Alston (ed.) *The EU and Human Rights*, Oxford, 1999; A. Tizzano "L'azione dell'Unione europea per la promozione e la protezione dei diritti umani" in *Il diritto dell'Unione europea*, 1999; F. Sudre *Droit international et européen des droits de l'homme*, Paris 1999; J.F. Renucci *Droit européen des droits de l'homme*, Paris 2001.
4   On the evolution and current state of fundamental rights in Europe after the Treaty of Amsterdam see: S. Negri "La tutela dei diritti fondamentali nell'ordinamento comunitario alla luce del Trattato di Amsterdam" in *Il diritto dell'Unione europea*, 1997; L. Azzena *L'integrazione attraverso i diritti ; dal cittadino italiano al cittadino europeo* Torino, 1998; A. Pizzorusso "Il rapporto del comitato Simitis" in *Diritto pubblico comparato ed europeo*, 1999; I. Pernice "Multilevel Constitutionalism and the Treaty of Amsterdam: European Constitution-Making Revisited?" in *Common Market Law Review*, 36, 1999; G. Tesauro "Eguaglianza e legalità nel diritto comunitario" in *Il Diritto dell'Unione europea*, 1999; M. C. Baruffi "Alla ricerca della tutela dei diritti fondamentali nel sistema comunitario" in *Diritti pubblico comparato ed europeo* 1999; P. Ridola "Diritti di libertà e mercato nella Costituzione europea" in *Quaderni costituzionali*, 2000; J.H.H. Weiler "Editorial: Does the European Union Truly Need a Charter of Rights?" in *European Law Journal*, 2000; K. Lenaerts "Respect for Fundamental Rights as a Constitutional Principle of the European Union" in *Columbia*

a) "Human dignity" (Article 1): the introductory article of the Charter is important, not so much for the principle it affirms, but rather for its function as an interpretative and creative key-note for the entire text of the Charter. It is an affirmation, that predictably (as the first commentators have already pointed out), is capable of being used in the same way as Articles 1 and 2 respectively of the German and Italian Constitutions have been.

b) The "right to integrity of the person" (Article 3): clearly the most significant impact will be on the delicate and controversial area of bioethics, which has, moreover, already been regulated by the 1997 Oviedo Convention. The properly private law aspects are, however, evident:

   i. the status of a person (with the prohibition of reproductive cloning);

   ii. the rights to one's own body (with the prohibition against making the human body a source of profit);

   iii. medical and health care contracts (for which "informed consent" becomes a constitutional pre-requisite);

   iv. tortious liability and damages for injury to the person (with the protection of both physical and psychological integrity);

c) Respect for private life (Article 7): this provision reproduces the analogous provision contained in the ECHR.

d) Respect for family life (Article 7): this again is a case of a pre-existing norm, but its extent should be considered with regard to the growing ferment of family law, especially between families based on marriage and other forms of union. The provision must be coordinated with Articles 9 and 33.

e) Protection of personal data (Article 8): the constitutionalisation of computer privacy – already part of the Spanish Constitution of 1978 – is further enriched by specifying the rights of the concerned subject and the role of consent.

f) Right to marry and right to found a family (Article 9): the Article must be read against the light of the analogous provision of the ECHR (Article 12), which, however, expressly indicates that "man and woman" are the subjects entitled to the right.

g) Freedom of expression and information (Article 11): the provision is interesting from a negative point of view, as the references to the protection of "other party's rights" or to "prevent the spreading of reserved information" which are contained in the analogous Article 10 of the ECHR have been suppressed. It is therefore predictable that there will be an impact on the extremely sensitive area concerning tortious liability of the media towards private persons, even though the principle contained in Article 52, 3rd paragraph, may lead back to the provisions of the ECHR.

h) Right to engage in work (Article 15): this Article must be read together with Articles 27 and 33. In the first place, one may ask if subordinated employment relations are part of the notion of private law. Without entering into the details of an over-subtle debate which has been carried out between many jurists, it must be

---

Journal of European Law, 2000; G. Telese "Dal Trattato di Amsterdam alla proclamazione dei diritti dell'Unione europea: recenti sviluppi nella codificazione dei diritti fondamentali in ambito comunitario" in Diritto pubblico comparato ed europeo 2001; A. Manzella, P. Melograni, E. Paciotti, S. Rodotà Riscrivere i diritti in Europa, Bologna, 2001.

observed that if a realistic approach is followed, it can be ascertained that in general, in the European landscape, employment law is structured as an autonomous branch of law in which the basic institutions of private law – especially contract – seem to have faded and are often unrecognisable.

On one hand it perhaps no longer appears necessary to proceed with a detailed analysis of the numerous articles previously mentioned. On the other hand, however one can understand to what degree the Charter on fundamental rights, by placing juridical situations (which previously were only contained in an implicit form in constitutional texts or were affirmed in texts of inferior standing, such as the European Social Charter or the Community Charter of Social Rights) in an eminent position, leads to a constitutionalisation of employment relations. This constitutionalisation process is evident when considering the draft of the European Constitution, where a specific Section on employment has been inserted in Part III.

i) Freedom to conduct a business (Article 16): the provision confines itself, in substance, to a reference to the *acquis communautaire*, and poses a question on the relation between the Charter and other Treaties of the Community, which will be examined further. While the effects on public governance of the economy are evident, the private law profile of major interest is represented by the pervasive influence of the principle of competition as both an incentive and a limit to the contractual activity of private business. It is clearly evident how contractual activity of an undertaking must take into consideration – in its concrete performance and effects – both consumer interests (with which the following Article 37 deals) and freedom of the market from restrictive agreements and abuse of dominant positions. The European law of contracts – should the principles currently affirmed by Articles 81 and 82 of the EC Treaty be constitutionalised – would be conceptually and practically influenced.

j) Right to property (Article 17): the heart of the liberal Constitutions of the 19th Century, moved to a decentralised position by the post-World War II Constitutions, excluded from the ECHR of 1950 and recovered only in Article 1 of the ECHR's first protocol, again finds recognition in the new text, which, however, confirms its nature as a "functional" right. Even though the new norm will have the importance that only application and interpretation will be able to give, certainly it will have to be considered in the formation of European private law and namely in the discussions on a project for a European civil code. Although the case law applying the 1st protocol of the ECHR may not be very far-reaching nor necessarily binding or even authoritative, from it emerge some important issues typical of private law, such as for example, the notion of "goods", the concept of "taking", and the determination of compensation. It could be worth considering how in the United States the Fifth Amendment and the principle of due process and the so-called "takings-clause" have been construed in a way to protect property, the latter being interpreted in extremely broad terms.

m) Equality between men and women (Article 23): the effects of the provision are clear in the domain of employment relations. Here, however the interest focuses on the effects in the area of family law and on some aspects which are still controversial, such as parental authority on minors, or the child's and wife's family name.

n) Children's rights (Article 24): the provision affirms one of the central principles of the international convention on the rights of the child of 1989, concerning the pre-eminent interest of the minor. Behind the rhetorical formulation, there will be implications in all proceedings in which there is a minor opposed to his parents, and in general, to adults. The effects therefore are not only on substantive law, but in perspective and to a considerable degree, on procedural law as well.

o) Consumer protection (Article 38): the brief provision constitutionalises the *acquis communautaire* in the field of consumer protection, with all the effects on the law of contracts and of tortious liability that have been widely studied.

p) Principle of proportionality (Article 52): it is interesting to observe that such a principle – cornerstone of all community activity – is now extended to the States and not only with reference to the traditional domain of public administration, but also to that of private law as well. The consequences, however, are quite different, as the principle is not used to moderate the intrusiveness of public power for the protection of its own interest, but, rather, in order to have one private situation prevail over another.

q) Abuse of rights (Article 54): the closing norm of the Charter elevates an idea, in this case the one of abuse of rights, to the rank of a fundamental principle; this has an historically justifiable precedent in the German Constitution. Here again the reach that the norm will have will be determined by its construction. However, by observing the extensive French case law, it can be understood that there are considerable implications in private law.

From this rapid overview one realises that the catalogue of "private law" fundamental rights is a rich one but covers only certain parts of civil law, especially those of persons and family, and far less so other areas. Is it a suitable structure for the building of a uniform European private law? The answer requires that the position of the Charter as a source of law be examined.

3 The European Charter in the European Constitutionalisation Process

Ever since its approval in Nice in December 2000 the Charter of Fundamental Rights of the European Union has found a prominent position among the community sources of law. Although its relation to the EU Treaty and to the EC Treaty is yet to be clarified, it is certainly not merely a programmatic declaration.[5] The idea is slowly gain-

---

5 On the effectiveness, the effects, and the future of the Charter of Fundamental Rights of the European Union, see: J. Dutheil de la Rochere "La Charte des droits fondamentaux de l'Union européenne: quelle valeur ajoutée, quel avenir?" in *Revue du Marché Comun et de l'Union européenne*, 2000; B. de Witte "The Legal Status of the Charter: Vital Question or Non-issue?" in *Maastricht Journal of European and Comparative Law*, 2001; A. Weber "Il futuro della Carta dei diritti fondamentali dell'Unione europea" in *Rivista italiana di diritto pubblico comunitario*, 2002; U. de Siervo "L'ambigua redazione della Carta dei diritti fondamentali nel processo di costituzionalizzazione dell'Unione europea" in *Diritto pubblico*, 2001; on the particular aspect of the effectiveness of the Charter in the external relations of European Union: J. Wouters "Editorial: The EU Charter of

ing ground – strengthened by several official documents – that the Charter is already binding on the EU institutions on the basis of the first paragraph of Article 51, and that it is one of the pillars for the construction of a future European constitution.[6] This now seems to be confirmed by the fact that the Charter has been incorporated in its totality in the draft of the European Constitution, forming Part II of the Constitution.

In the first place, one must remember the second paragraph of Article 52, which affirms that "Rights recognised by this Charter which are based on the Community Treaties or the Treaty on European Union shall be exercised under the conditions and within the limits defined by those Treaties".[7]

Fundamental Rights- some Reflections on its External Dimension" *Maastricht Journal of European and Comparative Law*, 2001; L.F. Besselink "The Member States, the National Constitutions and the Scope of the Charter" in *Maastricht Journal of European and Comparative Law*, 2001; on the personal scope of application of the Charter: D. Curtin and R. van Ooik "The Sting is Always in the Tail. The Personal Scope of Application of the EU Charter of Fundamental Rights" in *Maastricht Journal of European and Comparative Law*, 2001; E. Pache "Die Europäische Grundrechtscharta- ein Rückschritt für den Grundrechtsschutz in Europa?" in *Europarecht*, 2001; G. Sacerdoti "La Carta dei diritti fondamentali: dall'Europa degli Stati all'Europa dei cittadini" in *Diritto pubblico comparato ed europeo*, 2000; V. Atripaldi "La Carta dei diritti fondamentali: un processo verso una Carta d'identità europea" in *Diritto pubblico comparato ed europeo*, 2001; G.G. Floridia "«Nell'intenzion dell'artista, e agli occhi degli abitanti» (osservazioni sulla "Dichiarazione dei diritti" di Nizza)" in *Diritto pubblico comparato ed europeo*, 2001; A. Ruggeri "La 'forza' della Carta europea dei diritti" in *Diritto pubblico comparato ed europeo*, 2001;

6 On the debate concerning the existence and the need for a European Constitution, before the Charter of Fundamental Rights, see: D. Grimm "Does Europe Need a Constitution?" in *European Law Journal*, 1995 ; P. Häberle "Per una dottrina della Costituzione europea" in *Quaderni costituzionali*, 1999; J.C. Piris "Does the European Union Have a Constitution? Does it Need One?" in *European Law Review*, 1999; A. Barbera "Esiste una 'costituzione europea'?" in *Quaderni costituzionali*, 2000; A. Anzon "La Costituzione europea come problema" in *Rivista italiana di diritto pubblico comunitario*, 2000; *La Costituzione europea (Annuario A.I.C. 1999)*, Padova, 2000; J.H.H. Weiler *The Constitution of Europe*, Cambridge, 1999.
On the debate following the approval of the Charter of Nice, see, as part of the series "Verso la Costituzione europea" published by Il Mulino, 2001, the volumes edited by G. Bonacchi *Una Costituzione senza Stato*, Bologna 2001; U. de Siervo *La difficile Costituzione europea*, Bologna 2001; *Id. Costituzionalizzare l'Europa ieri ed oggi*, Bologna, 2001; S. Guerrieri, A. Manzella, and F. Sdogati *Dall'Europa dei Quindici alla Grande Europa. La Sfida istituzionale*, Bologna 2001; L. Torchia "Una Costituzione senza Stato" in *Diritto pubblico*, 2001; V.E. Parsi *Cittadinanza e identità costituzionale europea*, Bologna 2001; A.M. Petroni *Modelli giuridici ed economici per la Costituzione europea*, Bologna 2001; A. Quadro Curzio *Profili della Costituzione economica europea*, Bologna 2002; S. Gambino *Costituzione italiana e diritto comunitario*, Bologna 2001; U. de Siervo "I diritti fondamentali europei ed i diritti costituzionali italiani (a proposito della Carta dei diritti fondamentali)" in *Diritto pubblico comparato ed europeo*, 2001; A. Giovannelli "Dalla Carta dei diritti alla Costituzione europea" in *Diritto pubblico comparato ed europeo*, 2001; S. Mangiameli "La Carta dei diritti fondamentali dell'Unione Europea" in *Diritto pubblico comparato ed europeo*, 2001; T. Padoa Schioppa *Una Costituzione per l'Europa*, Bologna, 2001; A. Pizzorusso *Il patrimonio costituzionale europeo*, Bologna, 2002;

7 As in this context it is impossible to refer to the endless bibliography on the subject of European Union law, *ex multis*, may we refer to: G. Benacchio and V. Simoni *Repertorio di diritto comunitario civile e commerciale*, Padova 2001; P. Craig and G. de Burca *The Evolution of EU Law*, Oxford, 1999; on the constitutional aspects of the European Treaties see: K. Lenaerts and P. van Nuffel *Constitutional Law of the European Union*, London 1999; T. Tridimas *The General Principles of EC Law*, Oxford 2000; K.J. Alter *Establishing the Supremacy of European Law. The Making of an*

The norm apparently has a restrictive significance, however, in those cases where the community intervention is particularly deep, such as in the domains of competition and consumer protection for example, where the reference has an expansive reach.

It must be stressed however, that the current plurality of sources (namely EU Treaty, EC Treaty, and Charter of Fundamental Rights) gives rise to complications, especially on an interpretative level. This leads to the need for drawing up a single text containing, in addition to fundamental rights, the other provisions that are the central core of the Union, namely those on the institutions, their competences, and the common policies. In the draft of the European Constitution a single text has as a matter of fact been drafted. At first glance, however, it seems that the problem of coordinating the different existing norms has not quite been solved. On the contrary, it may be have been increased when one considers that Article 7 of the draft also recalls the ECHR, and affirms that the fundamental rights, as guaranteed by the ECHR, shall constitute general principles of the Union's law.

This may lead to confusion where the definitions of the principles do not fully correspond (especially as is the case between fundamental principles as drawn in the Charter and the previous statements in the ECHR). Closely related is the problem arising from the repetition of principles throughout the draft of the Constitution; it may not always be clear to determine what the hierarchy (if any) is between the norms which are taken from different sources throughout the draft.

This future European Constitution – the character and modality of approval of which are being discussed – should therefore absorb many principles from the EU and EC Treaty, putting certain problems and rules in a subordinate role. In this way, however, it is also possible that certain contents of the Charter may change, not so much as regards the contents as such, but rather for the simultaneous presence of other provisions of equal "constitutional" rank.

These remarks seem particularly valid for the traditional "four economic liberties" on which – also from a practical point of view – the development and success of the community policy of these last decades is based, and which are substantially ignored in the Charter, apart from a reference in Article 15, second paragraph, which is however limited only to physical persons. In the draft of the European Constitution, however, the four economic liberties stand in a symbolic position, as part of the opening articles concerning the Union's objectives.

From the point of view of the formation of European private law, the reference stands out if one considers that the Charter has a strong "social" character, which is not counterbalanced by equal importance that is given to economic initiative.

The result could be that private law becomes totally dominated by general interests, or in any case functionalised to them. The effects that must be considered are, as a matter of fact, not only the direct effects on regulation, but also the indirect ones determined by the fiscal policies which are necessary to ensure the high level of social rights contained in the Charter. If – as is normally the case – they will be fi-

---

International Rule of Law in Europe, Oxford 2001; P. Craig and C. Harlow *Lawmaking in the European Union*, The Hague 1998;

nanced by the higher taxation of economic activities, whatever contractual balance will be found by the contracting parties will be altered by tax pressure.

The consequences, from the point of view of competition between legal systems, can be easily imagined.

The European constitutional process, therefore, may have significant repercussions on the future of European private law and on the context in which it will have to operate.

4 Competences of the Union, Subsidiarity Principle and the European Civil Code

There is a final aspect that must be considered. In the last years one of the aspects – both theoretical and extremely practical – on which the debate has focused has been that concerning the competence of the EU institutions to proceed towards a unification/harmonisation of European private law.[8] Moreover, this not only as far as the le-

---

8   On European contract law and on the different projects for the codification of European private law see: O. Lando and H. Beale *Principles of European Contract Law,Parts I and II Combined and Revised*, The Hague-London-Boston, 2000; A.S. Hartkamp *Towards a European Civil Code*, The Hague, 1998; H. Kötz and A. Flessner *European Contract Law. Volume I. Formation, Validity and Content of Contracts; Contract and Third Parties* (trans. by P. Weir), Oxford, 1997; C. von Bar *The Common European Law of Torts. Vol.I: The Core Areas of Tort Law, its Approximation in Europe, and its Accomodation in the Legal System*, Oxford, 1998; *Id., The Common European Law of Torts. Vol.II: Damage and Damages, Liability for and without Personal Misconduct, Causality and Defences*, München-New York, 2000; M. van Hoecke and F. Ost *The Harmonisation of European Private Law*, Oxford-Portland-Oregon, 2000; F. Werro *L'Européisation du droit privé. Vers un code civil européen?*, Fribourg, 1998; *Id., New Perspectives on European Private Law*, Fribourg 1998; C. Jamin *L'harmonisation du droit des contrats en Europe*, Paris, 2001; S. Grundmann "The Structure of European Contract Law" in *European Review of Private Law*, 2001; Consiglio Nazionale Forense *La riforma dei codici in Europa e il progetto di codice civile europeo. Materiali dei seminari 2001.Raccolti da G. Alpa e E.N. Buccico*, Milano 2002;

As for the debate on the advisability of such a process see first of all the Communication: COMMUNICATION FROM THE COMMISSION TO THE COUNCIL AND THE EUROPEAN PARLIAMENT ON EUROPEAN CONTRACT LAW, in *COM/2001/0398 final, 11/07/2001*; and the answer of the COMMISSION ON EUROPEAN CONTRACT LAW and STUDY GROUP ON A EUROPEAN CIVIL CODE *Communication on European Contract Law: Joint Response of the Commission on European Contract Law and the Study Group on a European Civil Code*, Holte and Osnabrück, 19/12/2001; R. Sacco "Diversity and Uniformity in the Law" in *American Journal of Comparative Law*, 2001;

As for the methodology see: G. Gandolfi/ACCADEMIA DEI GIUSPRIVATISTI EUROPEI *Code Européen des contrats: avant-projet*, Milano 2001; M. Bussani and U. Mattei "The Common Core Approach to European Private Law" in *3 Columbia Journal of European Law 339*, 1998; O. Lando "The Common Core of European Private Law and the Principles of European Contract Law" in *21 Hastings International and Comparative Law Review 809*, 1998; *Idem* "Comparative Law and Law Making" in 75 *Tulane Law Review 1015*, 2001; U. Mattei "The Issue of European Civil Codification and Legal Scholarship: Biases, Strategies, and Developments" in *21 Hastings International and Comparative Law Review 883*, 1998; C. Kirchner "A 'European Civil Code': Potential, Conceptual, and Methodological Implications" in *31 U.C.Davis Law Review 671*, 1998; G. Alpa "European Community Resolutions and the Codification of 'Private Law'" in *European Review of Private Law*, 2000; J. Basedow "Codification of Private Law in the European Union: the Making of a Hybrid" in *European Review of Private Law*, 2001; C. von Bar "Le Groupe d'études sur un Code civil européen" in *Revue internationale de droit comparé*, 2001; A.Chamboredon and C.U. Schmid "Pour la création

gal instrument is concerned (directive/regulation) but especially regarding its compatibility with the subsidiarity principle that has so far guided community action.

These problems are even more relevant in the perspective of a European Constitution. Indeed, should the proposition – motivated by plausible arguments – be accepted, according to which the Union should only have the competences expressly enumerated, that these competences should be exercised subject to the principles of subsidiarity and proportionality, and that all the competences not assigned to the Union should remain with the Member States', (a proposition which seems to be confirmed by Article 3 and Article 9 of the draft of the European Constitution) it is easy to forecast that the path for a possible European civil code, or even only a European contract code, would be extremely difficult.

If indeed the actual Charter only considers a few aspects of private law; if the task of proceeding to the drafting of uniform texts will not be specifically assigned to the Union; if the Union's judicial structure will continue to remain frail, it is not easy to foresee what the outcome of the nonetheless extremely wide-ranging debates involving jurists from all over Europe, will be.

The solution might be – on an eminently political level – to include among the competences of the Union that of proceeding in the direction that many have invoked, but that many have also strongly criticised.

It would therefore be necessary to "constitutionalise" not only certain elements of European private law – which, as has been seen, are already present in the Charter – but also forms and procedures. This will of course animate the debate, especially regarding the relation between continental and the English legal systems.[9]

What has, so far, been said is quite understandable from the perspective of civil law systems which have always been characterised by – and worried by – the hierarchy of the sources of law and deductive logical processes.

Here the distance from the English common law – as opposed to the United States – can be felt, as it is not accustomed to using (or rather is uneasy at using) paramount principles and employing normative texts in a "creative" way.

There is also a further and substantial difference: while all the countries of continental Europe have written constitutions which are largely similar to one another, the United Kingdom has a completely different tradition based on constitutional practices and procedures.

These differences are not irrelevant from a practical point of view, when considering that for the complete adaptation of the English legal system to the European Convention on Human Rights of 1950 it has been necessary to wait almost half a century for the Human Rights Act of 1998.

From these brief remarks it is easy to understand that the idea of a European Con-

---

d'un 'Institut européen de droit' entre une unification législative ou non législative, l'emergence d'une science juridique transnationale en Europe" in *Revue internationale de droit comparé*, 2001; F. Sturm "Der Entwurf eines Europäischen Vertragsgestzbuchs" in *Juristen Zeitung*, 2001; K. P. Berger "The Principles of European Contract Law and the Concept of the 'Creeping Codification' of Law" in *European Review of Private Law*, 2001;

9   On European law from a perspective of the drawing closer of different juridical traditions, see, edited by B.S. Markesinis *The Clifford Chance Millenium Lectures. The Coming Together of the Common Law and the Civil Law*, Oxford-Portland-Oregon, 2000

stitution poses difficult questions of adaptation to the English context and raises doubts as to the effective impact that the subject described as "European private law" can have there.

Recognising the difficulties does not mean, however, that one should give up a perspective that seems increasingly to be imposed by the socio-economic unification. It is indeed possible to imagine different routes, which, starting from the core that will be determined by a European Constitution, will allow the drafting of texts on the basis of the *Restatements* model; or otherwise – but here too the political significance of the option is evident – an approach, not dissimilar from the one adopted for the single currency, that instead of aiming at a solution for the whole E.U., could propose ways of rendering uniform private law in civil law countries (which could be rapidly joined by most candidates to the Union), with the possibility for other Member States to adhere at a later stage.

CHAPTER 12

The Foreseeability Limitation on Liability in Contract

James Gordley*

1 Introduction

There is a rule in many legal systems that the a party who breaches a contract is only liable for damages that he could have foreseen at the time the contract was made. It was adopted in England in the famous case of *Hadley* v. *Baxendale*[1] whence it passed to the United States. It was adopted by the French Civil Code[2] whence it passed to the civil codes of Italy[3] and Spain.[4] It was included in early drafts of the German Civil Code but eliminated from the final draft.[5] It was rejected by the drafters of the new Dutch Civil Code.[6] Nevertheless, partly because of its ubiquity, and partly because of doubts about the German and Dutch solutions, this rule was accepted by the Convention on the International Sale of Goods,[7] the Unidroit Principles,[8] and the Lando Principles of European Law.[9] It seems destined to be part of a unified or harmonised European law if one should emerge.

I think this rule should be reexamined. There is much about it that should make us suspicious. I would like to examine the causes for suspicion and then suggest an alternative. In large part, the alternative is really a recognition that the rule has often played a valuable role, but not one that depends on whether harm is foreseeable. What should matter is whether the damages are disproportionate to the contract price.

2 Causes for Suspicion

2.1 The Rationale of the Foreseeability Rule

Traditionally, both civil and common lawyers have said that the rule rests on the claim that had the breaching party only known of the damages his breach might cause

---

* Shannon Cecil Turner Professor of Jurisprudence at the University of California, Berkeley.
1 [1854] 9 Exch. 341.
2 French Civil Code (*Code civil*) art. 1150.
3 Italian Civil Code (*Codice civile*) art. 1225.
4 Spanish Civil Code (*Codigo civil*) art. 1107.
5 See section 2.3, *infra*.
6 Harriet N. Schelhass, "Damages and Interest," in Daniel Busch, Ewoud H. Hondius, Hugo J. van Kooten, Harriet N. Schelhass & Wendy M. Schrama, eds., *The Principles of European Contract Law and Dutch Law A Commentary* (Nijmegen & Kluwer, 2002), 407-09.
7 art. 74.
8 art. 7.4.4.
9 art. 9.503.

he would not have contracted at all or would have contracted on different terms. As Roland, Starck and Boyer say, "le débiteur ne pas *vouloir* s'engager au-delà de ce qu'il a pu *prévoir*."[10] Alderson B. observed in his opinion in *Hadley* v. *Baxendale* that "had the special circumstances [leading to unforeseen injury] been known, the parties might have specially provided for the breach of contract by special terms, as to the damages in that case."[11]

That may be. But why assume that the breaching party is willing to be liable for the damages he does foresee unless he agrees to be? Yet, according to French and Italian authorities, foreseeability is all that is necessary.[12] In England and the United States it has occasionally been suggested that the breaching party must have implicitly assented to liability.[13] "On this view," Beatson notes, "the mere communication to a party of the existence of special circumstances is not enough: there must be something to show that the contract was made *on the terms* that the defendant was to be liable for the loss."[14] But this position is rejected by most English and American authorities including Beatson.

Sometimes, however, it is strange to think that a person is willing to be liable for harm simply because the possibility of it has been communicated to him or to his agent. In *Hadley* v. *Baxendale*, the plaintiff's mill was stopped because the mill shaft broke. The defendant was hired to transport it to be repaired. Suppose the plaintiff had explained exactly what had happened to the clerk who took his order. Are we to conclude the defendant wished to assume liability because its clerk did not object? Similarly, suppose that a farmer purchases lighting equipment for his tractor so that he can use it at night. Because the equipment arrives late, the farmer cannot plant and harvest his farm.[15] Or suppose a steamship company gives the agent of a telegraph company a message to be sent to its own agent in the Phillippines directing him to load extra cargo. Because it is not sent, and the steamship company loses the profit it could have made on the cargo.[16] These are the facts of two well known American cases. In each of them, the court refused to hold the defendant liable, noting, among other things, that the plaintiff might have communicated more information than he did. The farmer did not "bring home" to the seller the fact that he might be liable. The message was in cipher and, in any case, would not have conveyed to the agent the nature of plaintiff's business. But suppose each plaintiff had described the loss he might suffer. Does it follow that because the defendants were silent that they would

---

10 Roland, Starck and Boyer (1995), no. 444. Similarly, Terré, Simler & Lequette (1999), no. 538.

11 9 Exch. at 354-355.

12 Terré, Simler & Lequette (1999), nos. 538-539; Christofaro (1999) to art. 1225.

13 See section 2.2, *infra*.

14 Beatson (1998), p. 576.

15 Lamkins v. Internat'l Harvester Co, 182 S.W.2d 203 (Ark. 1944). This case was the model for Illustration 18 to § 351 of the Restatement (Second) of Contacts (1981). The Restatement agreed that the seller should not be liable and explained this result, not in terms of foreseeability, but by "the absence of an elaborate written contract and the extreme disproportion" between the "loss of profits" and "the price." See section 2.2, *infra*.

16 Kerr Steamship Co. v. Radio Corp. of America, 157 N.E. 140 (N.Y. 1927). In other cases, however, a telegraph company has been held liable on similar facts. E.g., *Fererro* v. *Western Union Tel. Co.*, 9 App. D.C. 455 (1896); *United States Tel. Co.* v. *Wenger*, 55 Pa. 262 (1867).

be willing to be liable for them? If not, why does the rule merely require that these losses be foreseeable?

This same objection can be made, not only to the traditional arguments for the requirement of foreseeability, but to the economic explanations of it that are currently popular in the United States. Supposedly the rule will lead to an "efficient" outcome. The "efficient" outcome is one which places risks or burdens on the party who can bear them the most cheaply.

Richard Posner, the founder of the law and economics movement, put the case of a photographer who hires a film studio to develop pictures of great value which he took in the Himalayas. If he is afraid the studio may ruin the pictures, he could take a number of precautions at relatively low cost. He could shoot more pictures on more rows of film and develop them at different times rather than in one batch. He will have no incentive to take them if he knows that the film studio must fully compensate him if they are ruined. The foreseeability rule "induces the party with knowledge of the risk either to either to take appropriate precautions himself, or, if he believes that the other party might be the more efficient preventer or spreader (insurer) of the loss, to reveal the risk to that party and pay him to assume it."[17] Posner described *Hadley* v. *Baxendale* as a case in which the miller was "imprudent" because he had not take the precaution of keeping an extra shaft on hand. "The court refused to imply a duty on the part of the carrier to guarantee the mill owners against the consequences of their own lack of prudence , though of course if the parties had stipulated for such a guarantee the court would have enforced it. The notice requirement of *Hadley* v. *Baxendale* is designed to assure that such an improbable guarantee really is intended."[18]

This argument, like the traditional one, assumes that the point of the foreseeability requirement is to allow the film studio or transporter to decide on what terms to contract. The photographer is supposed to inform the film studio of his potential loss only because the studio may be willing to assume liability for it in return for more pay. The miller is supposed to inform the carrier only because the court wants "assurance" that the carrier did not intend to be liable. But are the carrier or the studio to be liable merely because the have been informed, and the harm is therefore foreseeable, or on the supposition that, having been informed, they agreed, expressly or tacitly, to be liable? If they must expressly or tacitly agree, the rule is no longer one of liability for foreseeable harm. It is liability for harm for which one has agreed to be liable.

The same objection can be made to what is presently the most popular economic explanation of the rule. It was introduced by Ian Ayres and Robert Gertner. They describe the requirement of foreseeability as a "penalty default" "information forcing" rule. When the parties do not agree on a term expressly, a "penalty default" rule forces a term upon them which one of them does want to have in his contract. Normally, a court will try to read terms into a contract that the parties would have chosen for themselves. But it may have a reason to do otherwise. For example, it may believe that a party will be able to decide on such a term more accurately and at less cost than a court. To give him an incentive to do so, it may threaten that if he does not, it will

---

17 Posner (1998), p. 141.
18 *Evra Corp. v. Swiss Bank Corp.*, 673 F.2d 951, 957 (7th Cir. 1982).

read in a term he dislikes.[19] Or it may do so in order to force him to reveal information. The requirement that damages must be foreseeable to be recoverable will operate as a penalty default rule if it is inconsistent with the terms that fully informed parties would have chosen for themselves. If, in fact, the carrier were the most efficient bearer of the risk of loss, the parties would have wanted him to be liable. If the miller is told that the carrier will not be liable unless the miller informs him of the potential loss, the miller has an incentive, as the best informed party, to inform the carrier. The result will be efficient because, if the carrier is informed, he may be able to take some extra and economically reasonable precaution to prevent the loss.[20]

For Ayres and Gertner, the purpose the rule serves is simply to ensure that the carrier be informed of the loss so that he can take measures to avoid it. But suppose the miller is the party best able to take precautions or to bear the risk of loss. What is to prevent him from shifting the risk to the carrier by informing him? Ayes and Gertner are assuming, presumably, that if the carrier is informed, he will refuse to contract except for more remuneration than the miller would be willing to pay. Thus we are back to the assumption that the carrier will refuse unless he is willing to assume the risk.

2.2 Origins

One cause for suspicion, then, the is difficulty of finding a rationale for the foreseeability rule. Another is its origins. It grew out of a conjecture about a Roman rule that was not framed in terms of foreseeability but dealt with disproportionately high loss. It may have been adopted in England more out of a concern for disproportionate loss than out of a concern for foreseeability.

The Roman rule provided:

> 'In all cases which have a certain quantity or nature . . . damages are not to exceed twice the quantity; however, in other cases which appear to be uncertain judges are to require that the damages which was truly incurred be paid for.'[21]

There was much dispute in medieval and early modern Europe about what it meant to speak of "cases which have a certain quantity or nature" or "cases which appear to be uncertain." As Reinhard Zimmermann notes, "[g]enerations of lawyers have been mystified by the terms of this poorly drafted enactment."[22] Nevertheless, the rule did not mention foreseeability.

In the 16th century, however, the French jurist Du Moulin claimed: "the particular rationale of the limitation in the cases of what is certain is that most likely it was not foreseen or thought that greater damage would be suffered or that there was a risk beyond the principal object than the principal object itself."[23] As Zimmermann has noted, the 18th century jurist Pothier "generalised this idea and detached it from the

---

19 Ayres & Gertner (1989), pp. 96-97.
20 *Ibid.* p. 101.
21 C. 7.47.1.
22 Zimmermann (1990), p. 828.
23 Carolus Molinaeus, *Tractatus de eo quod interest* (1574), no. 60.

specific provisions" of the Roman text.[24] According to Pothier, "the person who owes a performance is only liable for the damages that one could have foreseen at the time of the contract that the party owed a performance would suffer."[25] The drafters of the French Civil Code took the rule from Pothier. They borrowed a great deal from him often *verbatim* and without much reflection. They had little time. Bonaparte had given them a short deadline, and, in fact, they produced their draft in four months.

We have, then, a rule that was once no more than a conjecture as to why one should not recover damages disproportionate to the contract price: the other party might not have foreseen them. That conjecture became the rule of the French Civil Code largely because it appealed to Pothier. But suppose the conjecture was wrong. Suppose what matters is not whether damages are foreseeable but whether they are disproportionate?

In deciding *Hadley* v. *Baxendale*, the court borrowed its rule from Pothier and the French Civil Code.[26] The circumstances make one wonder whether what really mattered was foreseeability. According to the head note of the case ""the plaintiff told the defendant that the mill was stopped." Is the headnote wrong, or was the court wrong to say that the loss was unforeseeable? Or did the court use Pothier's rule to reach a result that did not in fact turn on foreseeability?

It is interesting to watch the American *Restatement (Second) of Contracts* try to explain *Hadley* v. *Baxendale*. The *Restatement* accepts the rule that "(d)amages are not recoverable for loss that the party in breach did not have reason to foresee ... when the contract was made."[27] Nevertheless, it gives this illustration based on *Hadley*:

'A, a private trucker, contracts with B to deliver to B's factory a machine that has just been repaired and, without which B's factory, as A knows, cannot reopen. Delivery is delayed because A's truck breaks down. In an action by B against A for breach of contract the court may, after taking into consideration such factors as the absence of an elaborate written contract and the extreme disproportion between B's loss of profits during the delay and the price of the trucker's services, exclude recovery for loss of profits.'[28]

According to this explanation, the judge may deny recovery because the damages are disproportionate. Indeed, this illustration is offered, not as an illustration of the foreeseeability rule, but of an emendation of it in § 351(3) of the *Restatement*:

'A court may limit damages for foreseeable loss by excluding recovery for loss of profits, by allowing recovery only for loss incurred in reliance, or otherwise if it concludes that in the circumstances justice so requires in order to avoid disproportionate compensation.'

And so it turns out that in the minds of the American Restaters, *Hadley* itself must be explained, not by foreseeability, as the court said, but by the need o prevent recovery

---

24 Zimmermann (1990), p. 829.
25 Robert Pothier, *Traité des obligations* no. 160, in *Oeuvres de Pothier* 2 (Bugnet ed., 2d ed. Paris 1861) 497.
26 Zimmermann (1990), p. 830.
27 Restatement (Second) of Contracts § 351(1).
28 Restatement (Second) of Contracts § 351 Illustration 17. Similarly, see Illustration 18 described in note 15, *supra*.

of disproportionately high damages. Is it not possible that, whatever the judges who decided *Hadley* said, they the same concern in mind?

2.3 Application

One test of good legal rule is the way courts apply it. If they do so straightforwardly, it may be that they are satisfied that the rule produces the right results. If they strain to avoid applying the rule or they make exceptions, very likely, they are finding that some applications of the rule conflict with their sense of justice.

English courts, by and large, have followed the rule laid down in *Hadley* v. *Baxendale* without many qualms. There was a brief revolt. Not long after *Hadley*, an English court suggested that mere foreseeability might not be enough. In *British Columbia etc. Saw Mill Co. Ltd.* v. *Nettleship*,[29] plaintiff's saw mill could not be used because the defendant carrier failed to deliver a case containing parts. Bovill C.J. could have merely pointed out that the defendant was unaware that mill would not work without the parts contained in the case. He said, however, that the defendant was only liable for damages "to which he assented expressly or impliedly by entering the contract."[30] This suggestion was not taken up in later decisions. In 1949, in *Victoria Laundry (Windsor) Ltd.* v. *Newman Industries Ltd.*,[31] the rule was explained simply in terms foreseeability. As we will see later on, it was innocuous to do so in that case because the damages were probably not disproportionate. But in 1969, in *Koufos* v. *C. Czarinikow, Ltd. [the Heron II]*, the House of Lords allowed recovery for a loss suffered selling three thousand tons of sugar in Basrah when the vessel carrying it was delayed nine days and the price of sugar fell in the interval. Presumably, the result would be the same however great the drop in price might be, however volatile the market in question might be, however valuable, and therefore however vulnerable to price fluctuations, the cargo might be per pound or per cubic foot, whether or not the defendant charged simply by weight and bulk or included a premium to cover against price fluctuations. English judges pride themselves on their pragmatism. Yet American, French and German judges have been more willing to take pragmatic account of the importance of a disproportion in damages despite the rules they are supposedly applying.

In the United States, a suggestion like Bovill's was made by Oliver Wendell Holmes: the defendant is not liable unless one could infer that he tacitly agreed to be.[32] It has been accepted only in Arkansas.[33] Nevertheless, some American courts have been unwilling to award damages on the grounds that they are disproportionate even in cases in which they would seem to be foreseeable. In California, a franchisor was not allowed to recover damages for future royalties from a franchisee. To allow him to do so, the court said, would be unconscionable.[34] A federal court applying federal maritime law refused to allow recovery for loss caused by defects in a ship that

---

29 (1868) L.R. 3 C.P. 499.
30 (1868) L.R. 3 C.P. at 505.
31 (1949) 2 K.B. 528.
32 *Globe Refining Co.* v. *Landa Cotton Oil Co.*, 190 US 540, 543 (1903).
33 *Morrow* v. *First Nat'l Bank*, 550 S.W.2d 429 (Ark. 1977). *See* Farnsworth (1999), § 12.14.
34 *Postal Instant Press, Inc.* v. *Sealy*, 51 Cal. Rptr. 2d 365, 373 75 (Ct. App. 1996).

the defendant had certified to have no defects.[35] A federal court applying New York law denied recovery for injury to plaintiff's business caused by defendant's delivery of defective tires.[36] A Michigan court would not allow recovery for profits lost on a steam mill and "salt block" when the defendant failed to provide boilers on time.[37] An Illinois court would not hold the defendant, who failed to finish building a railroad, liable for the profits lost when the road could not be used.[38] An Alabama court did not allow recovery of lost profits from a defendant who failed to furnish a machine for drying bricks with as much capacity as promised.[39] Pennsylvania courts did not allow a miller to recover profits he lost when the defendant breached a contract to dress stones for his mill[40] or the owner of machinery to recover the profit he would have made had it been returned to him on time.[41] In all of these cases, the courts said that the reason for denying recovery was the disproportion. In all but three of them,[42] the court added that the defendant should not be liable unless he undertook to be liable for the damages which plaintiff sought. More cases could be cited.[43] Those mentioned, however, form a chain stretching back almost to *Hadley* v. *Baxendale*.

It is also worth noting the difficulties that judges have had reaching a sensible result and explaining why it is sensible in terms of foreseeability. Benjamin Cardozo, one of the most illustrious American judges, decided the case described earlier in which the defendant failed to send a telegram directing that cargo be loaded in the Phillippines.[44] He held that the telegraph company was not liable because the telegram was in cipher. It was not enough that "the length and cost of the telegram or the names of the parties would fairly suggest to a reasonable man that business of moment is the subject of the message."[45] There had to be [s]omething ... to give warning that the subject of the message is not merely business in general, but business of a known order." Cardozo did not explain why that must be. He did note that "the whole doctrine as to the need for notice [has] an air of unreality" since "neither the clerk who receives the message over the counter nor the operator who transmits it nor any other employee gives or is expected to give any thought to the sense of what he is receiving or transmitting." Nevertheless, "[t]he doctrine ... has prevailed for years so many that it is tantamount to a rule of property." Its advantage, he said was that companies have been relieved of liabilities that might otherwise be "crushing".[46] He did not explain why they are less crushing, or the companies less worthy of relief, if the clerk could have told from the message that it concerned business "of a known order."

In France, courts once held that the defendant must have been able to foresee the

---

35 *Sundance Cruises Corp.* v. *American Bureau of Shipping*, 7 F.3d 1077, 1084 (2d Cir. 1993).

36 *Armstrong Rubber Co.* v. *Griffith*, 43 F.2d 689, 691 (2d Cir. 1930).

37 *McEwen* v. *McKinnon*, 11 N.W. 828, 830 (Mich. 1882).

38 *Snell* v. *Cottingham*, 72 Ill. 161, 170 (1874).

39 *Moulthrop* v. *Hyett*, 17 So. 32, 33-34 (Ala. 1895) (adding that damages were remote and speculative).

40 *Fleming* v. *Beck*, 48 Pa. 309, 312 (1864).

41 *Armstrong & Latta* v. *City of Philadelphia*, 94 A. 455, 458 (Pa. 1915).

42 *Postal Instant Press*, *Armstrong*, and *Moulthrop*.

43 They are summarised in Gavin (1998), pp. 345-360.

44 Kerr Steamship Co. v. Radio Corp. of America, 157 N.E. 140 (N.Y. 1927).

45 157 N.E. at 141.

46 157 N.E. at 142.

cause of the harm but not its extent.[47] Even then, however, a passenger was denied recovery for loss of a suitcase that contained money.[48] Now courts say that there is no liability unless the amount of harm can be foreseen. A transporter is not liable for the contents if a racehorse dies[49] or the contents of a lost box are unusually valuable.[50] If the amount rather than the cause of harm must be foreseen, we have taken a step toward denying recovery when damages would be disproportionately large. The defendant is still supposed to be liable when damages are disprotionately large and yet foreseen. But sometimes, French courts have avoided that result. When a contractor's employee negligently set fire to plaintiff's chateau with a blow torch the *Cour de cassation* said it was unforeseeable that the owner would have to borrow money at interest to fix the damage or they he would lose rentals while it was being fixed.[51]

German law does not limit damages to those which were foreseeable. Preliminary drafts of the German Civil Code contained a version of the foreseeability rule:

> 'The liability for failure to perform of the person owing performance does not extend to compensation for harm the occurrence of which lay beyond the realm of probability given the awareness of the circumstances which that person had or should have had.'[52]

It was deleted because it was thought to be too restrictive.[53] In its place a second paragraph was added to what is now § 254. The first paragraph provides that damages may be reduced if the injured party was at fault. According to paragraph two, "This provision also applies if the fault of the injured party consisted of an omission to call to the attention of the party owing performance to the danger of an unusually serious injury of which that party neither knew nor should have known...." Foreseeability is supposed to matter, then, only if the plaintiff is at fault for failing to alert the defendant to a possibility of harm which he could not otherwise foresee. Even then, it is not supposed to matter unless the defendant could have prevented the harm had he been alerted.[54]

Nevertheless, sometimes this provision seems to be used in the same way that some American and French courts have used the foreseeability rule: to prevent recovery of disproportionately large damages. In one case,[55] the defendant was to translate a brochure concerning motor cycle parts into Dutch, French, English, Spanish and Italian. The defendant sought damages on the grounds that brochures it printed were unusable because the translation was faulty. The court said that the plaintiff was at fault for not calling the defendant's attention to the fact that it would print the bro-

47 Terré, Simler & Lequette (1999), no. 539.
48 Cour d'appel, Pau, 11 Aug. 1903, D.P. 1904.2.302
49 Cass. civ., 3 Aug. 1932, D.H. 1932.572.
50 Cass. civ., 7 July 1924, D.P. 1927.1.119.
51 Cass., 1 ch. civ., 11 May 1982, Gaz. Pal. 1982.2.612.
52 *Protokolle der Kommission für die zweite Lesung des Entwurfs des Bürgerlichen Gesetzbuchs* § 218, p. 292 (1897).
53 Antrag von Enneccerus in der XII. Kommission" no. 134 in H.H. Jakobs & W. Schubert, eds., *Die Beratung des Bürgerlichen Gesetzbuchs* (Berlin, 1978), pp. 117-118.
54 Grunsky (1994), § 254 no. 41.
55 Oberlandesgericht, Hamm, 28 Feb. 1989, N.J.W. 1989, 2006.

chures without having the translation checked. Was that really so unlikely? One suspects that the court's real concern was that: "the damage that threatened, and which occurred, was forty times as large as the fee for translation."

In another and well known case,[56] the plaintiff's agent gave his car keys to the night porter at the hotel where he was staying so that the car could be parked in a nearby garage, owned by a third party, and used by the hotel to provide parking for its customers. The agent left a collection of jewelry belonging to the plaintiff in the trunk. Although the agent found the trunk locked the next day, the jewelry had been stolen. The garage owner had given the porter a claim check meant to exclude liability but it was never handed to the agent. The plaintiff sued the hotel. The court remanded for a finding on whether the agent was at fault. According to the court, he might have been if he failed to tell the hotel about the jewelry. On the other hand, the hotel staff might have already known about it. The staff may also have been at fault for not telling him that the garage owner's exclusion of liability made it risky to leave the jewelry in the trunk. These grounds seem strange. If the trunk was found locked, very likely, the thief was someone with access to the agent's key. Telling the staff about the jewelry might have made the theft more likely. Moreover, it seems odd to think that the exclusion of liability made it significantly more likely that the garage or the hotel employed a thief. As before, the court may have been bothered by the disproportion between the value of the jewelry and the fee for parking the car. I have put variants of this case to German jurists and found them reluctant to decide for the plaintiff even on facts that would seem to exclude the agent's fault. Perhaps the judges of the *Bundesgerictshof* felt the same way.

These American, French and German cases may not be typical. It is hardly surprising that most of the time, American, French and German courts follow the rules supposedly in force in their legal systems. Nevertheless, they indicate that sometimes courts have balked at awarding disproportionate damages. That is a further reason to suspect that disproportion rather than foreseeability should matter.

3   An Alternative: Disproportionality Should Matter

Thus far we have seen that there is no good reason why foreseeability, in itself, should matter. We have also seen that the idea that it did matter was initially a conjecture by DuMoulin as to why disproportion mattered. His idea passed into the French Civil Code largely because it appealed to Pothier. Following Pothier and the Code, the foreseeability rule was accepted in English law *Hadley* v. *Baxendale*, a case that the American Restatement explains by disproportionality. Moreover, American, French and German cases sometimes seem to turn on disproportionality.

Du Moulin may have had it backwards. He thought disproportionality mattered because then losses are likely to be unforeseeable. Unforeseeability mattered because it indicates a lack of consent. Instead, we will argue, lack of foreseeability matters be-

---

56 Bundesgerichtshof, 29 January 1969, N.J.W 1969, 789. For an English translation by Tony Weir, see B.S. Markesinis, W. Lorenz & G. Dannemann, *The German Law of Obligations* vol. 1 (Clarendon Press 1997), p. 320-323.

cause it leads to disproportionality between the amount of the damages plaintiff claims and the price he was charged. Disproportionality matters because allowing these damages to be recovered is unfair.[57]

Elsewhere, I have discussed what it means for a contract to be unfair by drawing on Aristotle's concept of commutative justice.[58] In the Aristotelian tradition, commutative justice requires that in an exchange, the value of what each party gives should equal that of what he receives, thereby preserving each party's share of purchasing power. This idea – that the parties should exchange at a just price – has been misunderstood so often that we must be clear on what it did not mean to writers in this tradition. They did not mean that each party personally placed the same value on the goods he gave as on those he received. If they had, the parties would not exchange. As Aristotle said, the shoemaker does not exchange with the shoemaker but with the house builder.[59] Nor did they believe that the just price of goods was an intrinsic or stable property of them like their color. They identified the just price with the price on a competitive market[60] which, they knew, fluctuates from day to day and place to place in response to need, scarcity and cost.[61] Thus, although they believed that neither party became richer or poorer at the moment of the transaction, they knew that either might find himself richer or poorer the next day. The contract was fair in much the same way as a fair bet: the party who lost when prices rose could have won if they had risen.[62] Similarly, a term in a contract may impose a risk on one of the parties which, if it eventuates, will be make him poorer. Yet if he is compensated for bearing this risk, he is no poorer at the time of transaction, and the other party no richer, in the way that a person who bets at fair odds is at that moment no poorer or richer. An example is the seller's liability to the buyer if he unintentionally sold defective goods. Drawing on Aristotle's concept of commutative justice, Thomas Aquinas said he should be liable.[63] Otherwise, commutative justice is violated because the buyer paid the price of sound goods and received defective ones. A 16th century writer in the Aristotelian tradition, Luis de Molina, said that the seller might disclaim liability provided he reduces his price.[64] The buyer would then lose if the

---

57 Garvin (1998) and Kniffin (1988) also believe that disproportionality matters. According to Garvin it does because cognitive psychology shows that people are not as sensitive as they should be to the possibility of large losses. I do not see how, on the basis of this argument, one can tell which party should bear them. Kniffin believes, as I do, that imposing liability for a disproportionately large loss is unfair, although she does not explain unfairness in terms of commutative justice.

58 Gordley (2001), pp. 310-326.

59 Aristotle, *Nicomachean Ethics* V.v 1133ᵃ.

60 As noted by John Noonan, *The Scholastic Analysis of Usury* (Harvard Univ. Press,1957), 82-88; Raymond de Roover, "The Concept of the Just Price and Economic Policy," *Journal of Economic History* 18 (1958) 418.

61 Gordley (1991), pp. 94-102; Domenicus de Soto, *De iustitia et iure libri decem* (Andreas à Portonariis, 1553), lib. 6 q. 2 a. 3; Ludovicus Molina, *De iustitia et iure tractatus* (Sessas, 1614), vol. 2, disp. 348; All of these factors had been mentioned, albeit cryptically, by Thomas Aquinas, *In decem libros ethicorum expositio* (Angeli Pirotta, ed., Matriti, 1934), lib. 5, lec. 9; *Summa theologiae*, II-II, Q. 77 a. 3 ad 4. They were discussed by medieval commentators on Aristotle. Odd Langholm, *Price and Value in the Aristotelian Tradition* (Universitetsforlaget, 1979), 61-143.

62 Soto, lib. 6, q. 2, a. 3.

63 Aquinas, *Summa theologiae* II-II, Q. 77, a. 2.

64 Molina, vol. 2, disp. 353.

goods prove to be defective because the reduction in price would only reflect the probability of that event. But as of the moment of the transaction, the contract would be fair in the same way as a bet at fair odds. The price reduction would fairly reflect the risk that the buyer was assuming.[65]

I think we need something like this older idea of commutative justice to make sense of modern ideas about contractual unfairness. According to the Directive of the European Council on Unfair Terms in Consumer Contracts, "a contractual term that has not been individually negotiated shall be regarded as unfair if, contrary to the requirement of good faith, it causes a significant imbalance in the parties' rights and obligations...."[66] "Imbalance" here cannot mean that no risks may be placed on the consumer. What it must mean is that he is compensated for the risks placed on him so that, taking both the risks and the compensation into account, the contract is not imbalanced. To make sense of the Directive, then, we must say that a contract is not imbalanced when it is fair in the same way as a fair bet – each party is compensated for the risks that he bears – and an imbalanced contract is unfair. At that point, we are talking about commutative justice as it was understood in the Aristotelian tradition even if we do not use that expression.

We can now see why, if the damages for which a party may be liable are unforeseeable, a contract will be imbalanced in this sense and therefore unfair. Let us take, as an illustration, the English case of *Victoria Laundry (Windsor) Ltd.* v. *Newman Industries Ltd.*[67] Plaintiffs purchased a large boiler for £2,150 from defendants, who knew that the plaintiffs were launderers and dyers and that they wanted to put the boiler to use in their business in the shortest possible time. When the boiler was delivered late, the plaintiffs recovered for the loss of profits they would have made on their ordinary contracts but not on unusual and highly lucrative dyeing contracts they had entered into with the Ministry of Supply. The court said that the defendants could have foreseen the losses on their ordinary contracts but not those on the highly lucrative ones. Suppose the court was right. As a sensible businessman, knowing that he would be liable for plaintiff's losses on the ordinary contracts, the defendant would have charged a price for the boiler that reflected the risk of liability. Because he could not have foreseen the losses on the highly lucrative contracts with the Minister of Supply, he could not have adjusted the price to reflect plaintiff's potential losses on them. Since the risk of liability for these losses was not reflected in the price that the defendant charged, the contract would be imbalanced and therefore unfair if he were held liable for these losses. What matters, then, is that the losses on the unusually lucrative contracts were disproportionate to the contract price. They were disproportionate, not merely because they were high relative to the price, but that the price was not adjusted to charge for the risk of liability.

---

65 I am not reading modern concepts of probability into the minds of the earlier writers. The late scholastics of the 16th century described what we would call "expected value" in much the way we do, as gain or loss discounted by the probability that it will occur. *See* James Franklin, *The Science of Conjecture Evidence and Probability before Pascal* (Johns Hopkins Univ. Press, 2001), 286-88; James Gordley, "The Rule Against Recovery in Negligence for Pure Economic Loss: An Historical Accident," forthcoming in Vernon Palmer & Mauro Bussani, eds., *Recovery for Pure Economic Loss in European Tort Law* (Cambridge University Press).

66 93/31/EEC, 5 Apr. 1993, art. 3(1).

67 (1949) 2 K.B. 528.

This analysis treats the risk of breaching a contract and paying damages as a business risk. As in the case of other risks, a contract is imbalanced and unfair if the party who bears this risk is not compensated for doing so. We are supposing, then, that a party cannot simply eliminate the risk by deciding not to breach the contract. But that is surely true except in the case of a wilful breach. In the case of a negligent breach, he cannot altogether eliminate the chance that he or someone for whom he is responsible will act negligently. That is why people insure themselves against the consequences of their own negligence. If the contract creates what the French call an *obligation de résultat,* the breaching party will be liable for a non-negligent breach even in legal systems in which liability is said to be based on fault. If such risks are costs of doing business, like other risks, the defendant should not have to bear them without compensation. It is a different matter if the breach is committed with what the French call *dol.* If the defendant acted with *dol,* his breach was intentional and unjustified. He could eliminate the risk of this kind of breach by simply deciding to abide by his contract. There is no reason he should be charging extra in compensation for this risk, and if he did not, there is no more injustice in holding him liable than in holding him liable for deliberately destroying the plaintiff's property, even though the contract price did not compensate him for bearing the risk of doing so. French law, quite sensibly, recognises an exception to the foreseeability rule: the defendant is liable for unforeseeable damages caused by *dol.*[68] This exception was rejected by the Unidroit Principles but accepted by the Lando Commission.[69] If our approach is correct, the Commission made the better choice.[70]

In a case like *Victoria Laundry,* the defendant's inability to foresee the losses on the highly lucrative contracts mattered because, if the defendant could not foresee them, he could not charge an extra amount to compensate him for the risk he would be liable for them. It does not follow, however, that merely because the plaintiff had called a risk of loss to the defendant's attention, the defendant should be liable for it, and therefore should have charged extra. Normally, if the parties are sensible, and they both have their eyes open, they will place a risk on the party who can bear it most easily. Courts should do the same when the parties do not specify who is to bear a risk.[71] As Posner has observed, the party who can most easily bear a risk of loss is the one who can most easily prevent the loss or spread the risk of loss.[72] He can most easily spread the risk if he faces it over and over, and can, so to speak, self-insure against it by raising his price on each transaction in which the loss might occur. Suppose, if a manufacturer or seller breaches his contract, every customer will face a similar loss. The manufacturer or seller could normally bear that loss most easily. He can prevent it most easily and spread the risk by raising his prices for every customer. If the loss will be suffered by only one of his customers, however, while he may still be in the best position to prevent it, he is no longer in the best position to spread the risk that it will occur. If a customer calls this loss to his attention, he may, of course, agree to be liable for it in the event of breach and charge a suitably enhanced price.

---

68 French Civil Code (*Code civil*) art. 1150.
69 art. 9:503.
70 See Gordley (1998), pp. 198-208.
71 Gordley (2001), pp. 323-326
72 See section 2.1, *supra.*

Then, of course, he should be liable. But there is no reason why he should automatically be liable simply because the customer has told him about the loss. He may not be the best party to bear the risk. Moreover, if he did not raise his price, he was not compensated for bearing the risk. It would be unfair to hold him liable.

Moreover, even though normally the parties would want to place a risk on the party that can best prevent or spread it, they will not always want to do so. It depends on the costs of identifying the risk and adjusting the price to reflect it. These costs may be low enough to be outbalanced by the advantages of placing the risk on the right party. They are likely to be if the contract is an important one, or if, to perform, the manufacturer or builder or seller must already know a lot about the situation of a particular customer, or if many customers are facing the same loss and they are easy to identify. As Melvin Eisenberg has pointed out, however, one who is selling a large quantity of undifferentiated goods or services to many customers is unlikely to find it worth while to adjust his price because one of them may suffer a particularly severe loss if the contract is breached.[73] He is particularly unlikely to do so if the price he is charging is small. For that reason, it would be unreasonable to expect a carrier, a seller of lighting equipment, a telegraph company, or a parking garage to allow its clerks to adjust a price if they are informed that a mill is stopped, a farmer wishes to plow at night, or a steamship line needs to take on cargo in the Phillippines, or the trunk of a car contains jewelry.[74] Pricing such a risk would be difficult, and too costly for a high volume low price operation, even if the seller of the good or service could bear it most easily.

As a result, as Eisenberg observes,[75] if sellers were held liable for such risks, very likely, they would not customise their prices for high risk customers. They would raise the price for every customer to cover the losses they expect from a small number of contracts. That would also be unfair. Customers who will suffer a small loss if the contract is breached will have to pay an amount which reflects the risk that others will suffer a large one. If it is unfair for a seller to pay for such a loss when he has not been compensated for bearing it, then it is unfair for this loss to be shifted by raising prices for customers who run no risk of it.

4 The Harmonisation of European Law

One temptation that those interested in harmonising European law may face is to leave well enough alone. The Lando commission has already recognised the foreseeability rule as part of European law. Is it a step toward harmonising European law to criticise the rule? I think it is. We should recognise that the movement toward harmonisation has two methodologies. As Martijn Hesselink reports, it's "working method" is often based on a *presumptio similitudinis*. "[T]he Lando Commission has "concentrated on commonalities"; "the differences are not hidden altogether: they are spelled out in the comparative Notes" to the project.[76] Presumably, that is one reason the

---

73 Eisenberg (1992), pp. 592-593.
74 As noted by Garvin (1998), pp. 385-386.
75 Eisenberg (1992), pp. 592-593.
76 Hesselink & de Vries (2001), p. 30.

Commission adopted the foreseeability rule. It is so widespread. But as Hesselink also notes, "the emergence of the new discipline of European private law" has meant that "the object and methodology of European legal scholarship is changing rapidly from emphasis on formal deductive reasoning to a more substantive approach" of which "the functional approach to the law" is an example.[77] There are then, two methods, one based on ubiquity and the other on purpose. They can be made to work together. Often, one reason a rule is widespread is that it does serve a purpose. But because there are two methods, there is a danger of accepting ubiquitous rules as part of the "common core" of European law simply because they are ubiquitous, and taking a functional and substantive approach only when rules need to be harmonised because no one rule is widespread. That would lead to the wrong sort of harmonisation: everyone would do the same thing wrong. It would defeat harmonisation as Europeans have traditionally understood it. They have wanted the law to be a consistent expression of basic principles. National codifications have sought this kind of harmony as well as unity. One can hope that European law will achieve it and not merely uniformity.

BIBLIOGRAPHY: Ian Ayres & Robert Gertner, Filling Gaps in Incomplete Contracts: An Economic Theory of the Default Rule, *Yale Law Journal* vol. 99, pp. 87-130; J. Beaton, *Anson's Law of Contract* (27th ed., Oxford Univ. Press, 1998); Melvin Eisenberg, The Principle of *Hadley v. Baxendale, California Law Review* vol. 80 (1992), pp. 563-613; E. Allan Farnsworth, *Contracts* (3rd ed., Aspen, 1999); G. de Christofaro in Giorgio Cian & Alberto Trabucchi, *Commentario Breve al Codice civile* (4th ed., Cedam, 1999); Larry T. Garvin, Disproportionality and the Law of Consequential Damages: Default Theory and Cognitive Reality, *Ohio State Law Journal* vol. 59 (1998) pp. 339- 428; James Gordley, *The Philosophical Origins of Modern Contract Doctrine* (Clarendon Press, 1991); James Gordley, Responsibility in Crime, Tort and Contract for the Unforeseeable Consequences of an Intentional Wrong: A Once and Future Rule? in Peter Cane & Jane Stapleton, eds., *The Law of Obligations Essays in Celebration of John Fleming* (Clarendon Press, 1998), pp. 175-208; James Gordley, Contract Law in the Aristotelian Tradition, in Peter Benson, ed., *The Theory of Contract Law New Essays* (Cambridge Univ. Press, 2001), pp. 265-334; Wolfgang Grunsky, in Helmut Heinrichs, *Münchener Kommentar zum Bürgerlichen Gesetzbuch* (3d ed., C.H. Beck, 1994), vol. 2; M.W. Hesselink & G.J.P. de Vries, *Principles of European Contract Law* ([Deventer], 2001); M.N. Kniffin, "A Newly Discovered Unconscionability: Unconscionability of Remedy," *Notre Dame Law Review* vol. 63 (1988), pp. 247-76; Richard Posner, *Economic Analysis of Law* (5th ed., Aspen, 1998) Henri Roland, Boris Starck & Laurent Boyer, *Obligations 2 Contrat* (5th ed., Litec, 1995); François Terré, Philippe Simler & Yves Lequette, *Droit civil Les obligations* (7th ed., Dalloz, 1999); Reinhard Zimmermann, *The Law of Obligations Roman Foundations of the Civilian Tradition* (Juta, 1990).

---

77 *Ibid.* p. 9.

CHAPTER 13

E-Commerce

Christina Ramberg*

1 Introduction – E-commerce as a general topic or one to be regulated specifically

Modern means of communication, by email or websites are used increasingly, and the aim to remove legal obstacles to electronic commerce has been considered very important. In modern law-making, it is of course essential that electronic communication be permitted and facilitated.[1] Legislators throughout the world have been anxious to enable electronic communication and facilitate transactions by electronic means.[2]

Legislation concerning electronic commerce involves a number of problems. One particularly important factor is that the legislation should be media neutral or technology neutral.[3] This is to say, the legislator should not favour or discriminate between different means of such communication. It is essential that the legislator has an open mind and allows flexibility towards the development of new technical solutions. Experience shows that it has been very difficult for the legislator not to create new legislation that is closely linked to a particular technology. The Electronic Signature Directive is a prime example.[4] This Directive turns around a particular technique (1) for ensuring that electronic documents are not manipulated and (2) to trace who the sender of the document is. There are many available techniques to achieve these two goals, but the E-Signature Directive – despite its ambition to be media neutral – in practice only refers to one particular technology (PKI). This technology has not reached any significance in practice and the legislation thus becomes outdated and, instead of removing barriers to electronic communication, actually increases the barriers.

The information age is likely to contribute to fundamental changes in society and, as a consequence, lead to changes also in law. It is, however, vital that the legislation on e-commerce is made in close connection to the existing legal rules. It is possible to take any legal problem from the paper-world and ask how this problem could be solved in the electronic setting. The point of departure should not be how the legislation necessarily must be changed; rather the opposite approach is to be recommended, with a presumption that no changes are needed simply because the medium

---

* Professor of Commercial Law, University of Gothenburg, and member of the Coordinating Committee of SGECC.
1 I Walden, Regulating electronic commerce: Europe in the global E-conomy, (2001) E.L.Rev p. 541
2 See for instance one of the first policy papers, The White House, A Framework for Global Electronic Commerce, Jul.1, 1997 at http://www.iitf.nist.gov/eleccomm/eleccomm.htm;
3 M.B. Andersen, IT-retten, Copenhagen 2001, pp. 244 ff.; A Boss, The Uniform Electronic Transaction Act in a Global Environment, (2001) 37 Idaho Law Review 274-342.
4 1999/93/EC.

for communication is different.[5] With such an approach it becomes natural not to create special legislation applicable only to e-commerce transactions. It will in the future be difficult to distinguish electronic transactions from non-electronic transactions, and thus it is highly recommendable not to have separate legal regimes for them.

The existing legislation is often ambiguous. It is, for example, not altogether clear what the terms "writing" or "signature" mean. Do they include an electronic document or an email signature – or should the text be interpreted to only refer to paper with ink on it? Here we find two schools of thought. One argues that it is good and recommendable to interpret the texts according to the functional equivalent method. Thereby, special legislation will normally not be required which may hinder the development of new technology. The other school of thought argues that the world needs a higher degree of predictability. It is too uncertain how the legislation will be interpreted, and thus the legislator should provide extra guidance by specifically addressing the problem and to what extent the rule applies also to electronic documents. This school of thought argues that by making such technologically specific regulation e-commerce will be efficiently promoted. This is the well known conflict between generality and flexibility on the one hand and, on the other hand, exactness and predictability. The drawback with the second school of thought is that it is difficult to know how much predictability is necessary. Or in other words: how should the legislation address each and every particular form of technology.[6]

I should already at the outset explain that I am in favour of general rules that leave room for the reader of the text to interpret in a way that is in harmony with the rule's underlying purpose. As a consequence, I will be quite limited when it comes to suggestions for amendments in PECL. I will, however, frequently suggest that the PECL Comments address certain questions in order to explain how the text can be interpreted with respect to the technological solutions presently practiced.

This paper will analyse to what extent PECL and the ongoing work within the Study Group for a European Civil Code (SGECC) are suitable for e-commerce.

2   Method – Functional Equivalency

Harmonisation of law and research in e-commerce have much in common as regards methods. The work on the harmonisation of European law provides an excellent opportunity to analyse the apparently self-evident rules we have become accustomed to in national law. Analysing the problems from an electronic point of view provides a similar opportunity. The only way to reach consensus in work towards harmonisation is to go deep and under the present legal notions in order to find a common platform and then to dress this in modern language. In order to create understanding we must search for the often forgotten or implied policies behind a particular rule. This is of-

---

5   UNCITRAL Model Law on Electronic Commerce, Art 5.
6   A. Boss, The Internet and the Law, (1999) 23 Nova Law Review 585-624 at p. 608; P. Furberg, Lawmaking and IT: Reflections on the need for New Concepts and Categories of Thoughts, In Law and Information Technology. Swedish Views, SOU 2002:112 pp. 55-66; C. Ramberg, The E-Commerce Directive and formation of contract in a comparative perspective; T Smedinghoff, Online Law, Addison, Wesely, Developers Press 1999 pp. 4 ff.

ten surprisingly difficult. After the identification of the policies, it is quite easy to establish consensus about the best rule to adopt. Legislation on e-commerce requires that we use the same approach.

In e-commerce the functional equivalent method is described in the *UNCITRAL Model Law on Electronic Commerce* Art. 5: "Information shall not be denied legal effect, validity or enforceability solely on the grounds that it is in the form of a data message." This method asks from us lawyers that we do something quite extraordinary; to welcome any new technology with the presumption that it fits into the existing legal system.[7]

3 E-Commerce in a European Civil Code and How to Take into Account the Already Existing EU Directives

There exist today several Directives covering electronic commerce specifically (E-Signature Directive 99/93/EC, E-Commerce Directive 2000/31/ EC, Distance Selling Directive 97/7/EC, Financial Services Directive 2002/65/EC).These are all examples of hastily drafted Directives that unfortunately have been implemented quite differently in the different Member States. Some of them furthermore create severe problems, in particular the E-Signature Directive, in that it is not media neutral but specifically aimed at a particular technology (PKI digital signatures).

Despite these drawbacks, the Directives all have a common goal to enable electronic commerce and transactions to be made electronically. Naturally, a European Civil Code should adhere to this goal. A European Civil Code should also adhere to the goal of media neutrality. Furthermore a European Civil Code should be less fragmentary in nature and address the problems concerning e-commerce in a more coherent and structured way than has been possible in the present Directives.

The Directives related to e-commerce have all been differently implemented in the Members States. This is partly due to the fact that some of them are minimum Directives. It is also, however, due to the inconsistencies and difficulties in understanding the purpose of the Directives. A European Civil Code would enable us to have a common European legal structure for electronic transactions. Of course, it is particularly important that legislation on e-commerce is *exactly* the same in the whole Union. Since the electronic medium in itself does not recognise national borders, the rules on international private law become highly bureaucratic and foreign for the users of electronic mediums.

A European Civil Code should not only take into account the Directives related to e-commerce. It should also carefully try to harmonise its rules to the whole world's legislation on this topic. UNCITRAL had, in the beginning of the 1990's, an ambition to be the first to regulate a wholly new area of law and harmonise the rules before national legislators had had the time to create disparate regulations. UNCITRAL unfortunately and unavoidably came too late with its products (the Model Law on Elec-

---

7   A Boss, The Uniform Electronic Transaction Act in a Global Environment, (2001) 37 Idaho Law Review 275-342.

tronic Commerce and the Model Law on Electronic Signatures). It is, however, clear that the UNCITRAL work and the debates in the UNCITRAL negotiations have largely influenced many state's legislation on e-commerce. Prime examples are the US Uniform Electronic Transaction Act and the Canadian Uniform Electronic Commerce Act. Regrettably, the EU Directives have been less influenced by the UNCITRAL work.

Electronic communication and Internet transactions create problems for most areas of the law. Originally electronic communication was thought to be mainly a problem within the field of intellectual property law. Then we saw a lot of debate concerning criminal law (child pornography, for instance). We also remember the intense debate on the liability for Internet providers transmitting illegal information. These areas of law are outside the present work on a European Civil Code. I will in the following concentrate on some specific issues that are mainly dealt with in a general way in PECL and examine to what extent PECL encompass e-commerce satisfactorily and if changes or amendments are necessary. I will, whenever relevant, also note the problems that have so far arisen in the present work by the Study Group for a European Civil Code (SGECC). The main problems that will be dealt with are formal requirements, terminology and mistake in expression.

4 Formal Requirements

PECL are mainly free from formal requirements. PECL clearly adhere to the modern idea of a contract as something being able to emerge without formalistic features. This is a trend in modern contract law. It has taken many years (centuries) to slowly abolish the old Roman law concept of formal requirements.[8] One of the explanations for this slow development is of course that it is often wise for parties to make their contract in writing for evidentiary reasons. The writing helps to prove the *intention* to enter into a contract, the *content* of the contract and the *identities* of the parties to the contract.

Whenever discussing the legal effectiveness of electronic communication, it is extremely important to distinguish between validity and evidence. For some jurisdictions this distinction is fairly easy to make from a conceptual point of view. For other jurisdictions it is more difficult. I believe that the jurisdictions where there is no free admission of all types of evidence have more difficulties than others. We must acknowledge the close relationship between civil law and the law of evidence. No harmonisation is achieved if we all agree in the European Civil Code that contracts may be entered into without any formal requirements and at the same time have different rules in the national law of evidence as to what extent a contract's existence may be proved by electronic documents.

In the E-Commerce Directive (2000/31/EC) it is stipulated that the member states must allow contracts to be formed by electronic means. Art. 9 in the E-Commerce Directive, however, allows some exemptions to this rule. According to this exception

---

8 R. Zimmermann, The law of obligations: Roman foundations of the civilian tradition, pp. 68-95, 1996.

the member states may require that some types of contracts are committed to paper with ink and signed by old-fashion pen-technique. These exemptions are:

(a) contracts that create or transfer rights in real estate, except for rental rights;
(b) contracts requiring by law the involvement of courts, public authorities or professions exercising public authority;
(c) contracts of suretyship granted and on collateral securities furnished by persons acting for purposes outside their trade, business or profession;
(d) contracts governed by family law or by the law of succession.

Regrettably, most Member States have chosen to adopt the exemptions without making a thorough analysis as to *why* these contracts would benefit from not being able to be concluded electronically.

The E-Commerce Directive is problematic in two senses.

1. Some states have wrongfully thought that allowing contracts to be formed electronically requires that the parties use advanced electronic signatures according to the E-Signature Directive.
2. Some states take every opportunity to make use of the possibility to adopt an exemption whenever possible. The reason is probably that in this way they are not forced to put the relevant question: why should we not allow electronic contracting in relation to real estate transactions or in relation to personal security? But instead, the states adopting the exemptions can rely on tradition and without further concern prevent new technology. Another problem is that the allowed exemptions to a large degree include almost all possible transactions where there presently are form requirements of signature for concluding contracts.

5   Writing

In the traditional paper world the term 'writing' was uncomplicated and referred to documents written on paper by pencil, pen, etc. The problem is now whether electronic documents also constitute 'writing'. This problem has been examined in depth for the last ten years. The end result in most theoretical analyses as well as in legislative texts is that most electronic messages constitute 'writings' as long as they are understandable and can be saved. In other words, the prerequisite of 'writing' is fulfilled as long as the electronic message is able to fulfil the same functions as a paper message.

The EU Directives do not address the issue of "writing". PECL use the term "writing". In PECL, Art. 3:103 stipulates that notice may be given in writing or by any other appropriate means. According to Art. 3:104 a period of time set by a party in a written document for the addressee to reply or take other action begins to run from the date stated as the date of the document. Art 2:101 provides that a contract need not be concluded or evidenced in writing. Art 2:105 regulates merger clauses in written contracts and 2:106 written modification clauses. Art 2:207 refers to "letter or other writing" and its effect on late acceptances. Art. 2:210 concerns additional or different terms in a written confirmation after the conclusion of a contract. Art. 3:208 provides a rule on written confirmation about an agent's authority.

None of the provisions in PECL that refer to "writing" create any problems in relation to electronic documents. Notices provided by email are just as valid as those given in traditional letters, Art. 3:103. When an electronic document is dated (in an attachment at the top of the letter, or in an email at the heading of the email) the time period will start to run from that date, Art. 3:104. A contract can be concluded and evidenced by electronic messages, Art. 2:101. The provision in Art. 2:105 about merger clauses is applicable to electronic contracts where it is stipulated that the electronic contract embodies all the terms of the contract. With respect to written modification clauses, a modification is relevant also when it is made in an electronic message, Art. 2:106. A late acceptance in an electronic message may, similar to acceptances in traditional letters, form the basis for formation of a contract, Art. 2:207. Additions or different terms in an electronic confirmation may become part of the contract according to Art 2:210. And a third party may ask the principal in an electronic message whether the agent has *authority*, Art. 3:208.

PECL Art 1:301(6) stipulates that "'written' statements include communications made by telegram, telex, telefax and electronic mail and other means of communication capable of providing a readable record of the statement on both sides". This definition is very close to the definition in the UNCITRAL Model Law on Electronic Commerce Art. 6 ("accessible as to be usable for subsequent reference") and the US *UETA* Art. 2(13) ("retrievable in perceivable form"). All three in different words put emphasis on the fact that the document can be understood and saved. Maybe it is not recommendable to actually refer to the term "readable" since this normally would require that the content is understood with the use of somebody's eyes. I think it is better to phrase it as in the UNCITRAL Model Law on Electronic Commerce and UETA, where it is irrelevant which sense is used to understand the content, ears, fingers or eyes are all acceptable.[9] I see no reason why an electronic file that can only be heard, should also not fulfil a requirement of writing as long as it is possible to understand the content and to preserve it for others to hear at a later occasion.

There is one important factor that is not considered in PECL or the UNCITRAL Model Law on Electronic Commerce. This is the addressee's willingness to receive electronic messages of the relevant type and format. It is not difficult to imagine that the addressee simply does not regularly check his emails or that a certain email address is not in use or that the addressee is only able to read certain formats (certain types of electronic messages). If a notice is sent to an email address that is not in use, it would be unreasonable to hold the addressee to the legal consequences that would flow from a traditional letter being sent to his official mail address. Similarly, it would be unreasonable to have an additional term become part of the contract if the addition was sent in an electronic document format that the addressee was unable to open. This difficult and fundamental issue is dealt with in the US UETA Sec. 5 (b):

---

9   See www.uetaonline.com; and A. Boss, The Uniform Electronic Transaction Act in a Global Environment, 37 Idaho Law Review 275-342 (2001).

"This [Act] applies only to transactions between parties each of which has agreed to conduct transactions by electronic means. Whether the parties agree to conduct a transaction by electronic means is determined from the context and surrounding circumstances, including the parties' conduct."

This provision ensures that only addressees that are able and willing to communicate electronically will be exposed to the legal consequences of electronic messages. Furthermore, misspelled emails and emails to addresses that the addressee has not indicated that he uses, will not have legal consequences. Likewise, legal consequences will only flow from electronic messages sent to the addressee in a format that he has indicated that he is willing and able to perceive. The indication of willingness can be implicit, for instance by the addressee himself having communicated by email and there indicated a certain email address and used a certain format.[10]

As a conclusion with respect to writing, I strongly recommend that the definition of writing in PECL Art.1:301(6) be amended to expressly include a prerequisite of "the addressee's indication of willingness to receive messages of the relevant type and format". Furthermore, I suggest that the definition of "writing" in PECL Art. 1:301(6) be changed from "readable record" to "retainable in perceivable form". There is no need to be more specific in PECL. It is not advisable to include references in PECL to certain types of electronic documents that may or may not constitute "writing". It is better to focus on the main underlying reasons, which are that the content of a message can be perceived and retained.

6   Signature

PECL do not use the terms "signature" or "signs".[11] SGECC refers to signature in the draft chapter on personal security. It was considered essential to create a warning function in relation to a guarantee for another's debt when the guarantor is a private person providing the guarantee outside his profession. The formal requirement thus has a protective purpose. In the present draft (as of June 2002) the article stipulates:

(1)   The contract of guarantee must be in writing. At the end of the text, the guarantor itself must separately write out in letters [and by hand] the amount of his obligation and sign [the signature].
(2)   A security which does not comply with the preceding paragraph is void.

The SGECC's Coordinating Committee has vividly debated to what extent the contract of a guarantee should be able to be concluded electronically. It was agreed that a mere reference to "writing" and "signature" was ambiguous, since these terms actually do not say anything about "ink" and "paper". Some in the Coordinating Commit-

---

10 For a helpful list of examples of implicit indications of willingness to receive electronic messages, see www.uetaonline.com and the comments to Sec.5(b).
11 There is a mention of "signs" in Art. 2:104, but this is only as a reminder that a mere signature is not always sufficient to show that a term has been brought to the signer's attention.

tee thought that guarantees should be able to be made electronically, provided that the warning function also was preserved in the electronic environment. Others thought that the contract for a guarantee was of such nature that only old fashioned means of communication (ink on paper) should be allowed. This later opinion is reflected in the present draft. The present draft refers to "hand". The intention is to make clear that electronic communication is not allowed. I, however, claim that electronic signatures and electronic documents are also made by "hand" (in the case of a pen, the pen is held by the hand, and in the electronic cases, the hand touches a keyboard or screen). If the intention of the provision is to wholly exclude electronic guarantees, the text should explicitly state that a valid guarantee can only be made with a signature and a specified amount, both created by the use of pen and ink on paper.

Personally, I am of the firm opinion that the warning function can also be fulfilled in the electronic environment, by for instance requiring that the person writing his name with the help of a computer key board expressly also writes by himself "I hereby commit myself". Also the fact that a guarantor must with his own hand and the use of a computer keyboard fill in the box where the total maximum amount of the guarantee is specified, ought to fulfil a warning function similar to using a pen on paper filling in a box in a paper standard form. Against my firm opinion there stand opposing opinions of the same firmness.

This example is not only interesting from the point of view of electronic commerce. It also illustrates the working method in SGECC. Whenever the group is confronted with a question that cannot be agreed on by consensus, we take a vote in the Coordinating Committee and make a draft according to the majority. The Comments to the text clearly indicate the different available solutions and the arguments pro and contra. Such transparency will make it easier to make future changes in the text whenever modernisation is needed. If the final chapter for personal security makes it impossible to make electronic guarantees, I am personally confident that this provision will be changed rather soon.

Since PECL and SGECC are by and large informal and do not – apart from the case of personal guarantees – suggest any formal requirements with respect to signatures, the Directives on e-signatures and e-commerce become rather irrelevant. I would, however, like to stress that the E-Signature Directive does not stipulate that the only valid type of electronic signature is the one based on the PKI-technique. I would also like to point to the fact that the exceptions in the E-Commerce Directive Art. 9 are voluntary. The member states are allowed to make exceptions and require for such contracts to be formed with pen, ink and paper-signatures. The Directive, however, expressly discourages member states from making such exceptions, by requiring them to provide an explanation why it was considered necessary to do so (Art. 9). To this end, PECL as they presently stand are in harmony with these two Directives.

7   Terminology

Apart from formal requirements there are a couple of terms often used in contract law that cause some problems in the electronic context; these are "reach" and "dispatch".

7.1   Reach

When using traditional means of communication it is quite clear that a physical document should be delivered to a physical location where the addressee is physically located and has the opportunity of reading the message. The relevant moment in time is when the message reaches this physical location. In the electronic setting it is not self evident what location has the same practical characteristics as that physical location. Is it enough for the sender to dispatch the e-mail? Or does the e-mail have to pass through the sender's server out in the open network? What about closed networks? Is it required that the message enter the recipient's server? Or is it even necessary for the message to be located on the recipient's hard drive? And, if so, does it matter where this hard drive is located physically (at an airport, at the place of business, or at the addressee's home)?

Whenever the word 'reaches' is used in the PECL, the underlying purpose is to ensure that the addressee has an opportunity to read the message if he so chooses. It is not required that the recipient actually have read the message, but it is only required that the message has become accessible for reading (the distinction between 'reach the mind' and 'reach the desk' or 'reach the legal entity'). This leads to the effect that when a message has entered the recipient's sphere of control, it must be assumed to have reached the recipient.

Another reason for the PECL provision on "reach" is of evidentiary nature. It is possible (more or less easily, but at least conceptually) to prove when a message became accessible; it is very difficult to prove when someone actually addressed his mind to it.

An offer can be revoked if the revocation reaches the offeree before it has dispatched its acceptance, PECL Art. 2:202. In traditional means of communication this rule enables the offeror to withdraw his offer by a faster means of communication. He may, for instance, send an offer by ordinary mail ("snail mail") and then later withdraw it by sending a fax that reaches the offeree before the letter. The problem in relation to electronic means of communication is that there are rarely any practical means of faster communication than electronic messages sent by e-mail or communicated over websites or other EDI-arrangements. However, the question becomes of practical importance in situations where the offer is sent by traditional paper mail and the withdrawal is sent electronically.

Other provisions in PECL where the term "reach" poses similar problems are Art 1:303 about when a notice becomes effective; Art. 2:203 concerning the question of when a rejection leads to an offer lapsing; the Art. 2:205 stipulation that a contract is concluded when the acceptance reaches the offeror; Art. 2:206 about the point in time an offer becomes ineffective; Art. 2:207 concerning the effect of passiveness with respect to late acceptances; and 2:208 about the offeror's assent to modifications in an acceptance.

From a pragmatic point of view it is clear that the addressee of an electronic message may read it as soon as it is located on his server. He may have problems reaching his server, due to internal problems in the addressee's network system. This is normally within his 'sphere of influence'. This question has been dealt with in the UNCITRAL Model Law on Electronic Commerce Art. 15.[13] The crucial moment according to the Model Law is 'enters the designated information system'.

However frustrating it may be for the addressee that messages have arrived to his server but cannot be read by him due to internal problems, it is not appropriate to put the risk on the sender for the addressee's internal technical problems. The addressee must choose proper contractual partners (Internet providers), and design an appropriate internal technical environment to make sure that the internal communication functions satisfactorily. The sender of an electronic message ought not to have to assume this risk. It is quite similar to the situation in which a traditional letter reaches the postal box of an addressee, but the secretary picking up the mail loses it or distributes it to the wrong person in the office.

As explained above in relation to "writing", it is essential that the recipient of an electronic message has indicated his willingness to receive electronic messages of the relevant type and format. Only then should the recipient be burdened with the legal consequences of "reach".

As a conclusion, I suggest that the use of 'reach' in PECL be interpreted to correspond to the point in time when an electronic message has entered the addressee's server provided that the addressee has expressly or impliedly indicated that he is willing to receive electronic messages of the relevant type and format. I do not think that it is necessary to make an amendment in PECL by, for instance, including a definition of the term "reach" in Art 1:301. Instead the more precise meaning could be explained in the PECL Comments along the lines of UETA and the UNCITRAL Model Law on Electronic Commerce.

7.2 Dispatch

Quite similar to the term reach, is the term "dispatch". There are only three provisions in PECL using the term "dispatch": Arts. 1:303, 2:202 and 2:205. For these instances the relevant factor is not when the message enters the recipient's system, but when it leaves the sender's system.

---

13 Article 15. Time and place of dispatch and receipt of data messages
   (1) ...
   (2) Unless otherwise agreed between the originator and the addressee, the time of receipt of a data message is determined as follows:
   (a) if the addressee has designated an information system for the purpose of receiving data messages, receipt occurs:
   (i) at the time when the data message enters the designated information system; or
   (ii) if the data message is sent to an information system of the addressee that is not the designated information system, at the time when the data message is retrieved by the addressee;
   (b) if the addressee has not designated an information system, receipt occurs when the data message enters an information system of the addressee.
   (3) ...
   (4) ...
   (5) ...

Similar to what was explained in relation to 'reaches' and 'writing', it is necessary that the addressee has indicated his willingness to receive electronic notices of the relevant type and format. An electronic notice is not 'properly dispatched' according PECL Art. 1:303 if the addressee does not use electronic means of communication. Further, according to PECL Art. 2:202 an offeror may still revoke his offer when the offeree has dispatched an electronic acceptance if the offeror has not implicitly indicated that he is willing to receive such electronic acceptances.

My recommendation would be that no definition of 'dispatch' be included in PECL but that the exact point in time of "dispatch" is explained in the PECL Comments by using the definitions in UETA and the UNCITRAL Model Law on Electronic Commerce. Furthermore, the comments should refer to the prerequisite of "willingness to receive messages of the relevant type and format" as elaborated in UETA.

8 Mistake in Expression

One of the most problematic areas in connection with electronic commerce is that of mistake in expression. The good old principle that the mistaken party must bear the consequences of his mistake is now under pressure. The E-Commerce Directive, UETA and the UNCITRAL Model Law on Electronic Commerce address the problem of input errors. PECL, however, only refer the general principle.

Many users of electronic means of communication are aware of the speed with which Internet transactions are made. Many are also aware how easily something may go wrong. The 'send' button is clicked on too early, the 'Yes, I accept' box is clicked on by mistake and one kilogram of peppers is ordered instead of one piece of pepper. Worse things may happen. One of my students working in a bank office once ordered 10,000 Ericsson shares on the Stock Exchange (then worth approx. 200,000 euro) instead of ordering Ericsson shares to the value of 10,000 Swedish crowns (approximately 1,000 euro).

Two of the main features of electronic communication are speed and automation. Both these features increase the risks of making mistakes that cannot be easily corrected before they reach the addressee. Discussions in the legal literature and initiatives by legislative bodies indicate that electronic commerce might provide good reason for adjusting the present distribution of liability in connection with mistake and giving greater consideration to the mistaken party's need for protection.[14]

The problem of mistake has a long legal history. It has been difficult to strike the balance between, on the one hand, the interest of a mistaken party not to be bound by unintended expressions of promise and, on the other hand, the interest of a party relying on a promise to be able to act upon it. Contract law in most jurisdictions is based on the theory of intention and reliance. A contract is formed and the parties are bound by it because they *intended* to be bound and both *expressed* this intention. According to this theory a contract ought not to be formed when one of the parties in fact did not wish to be bound, but by mistake expressed such a wish, since there is a lack of mu-

---

14 See for references the following presentation.

tual consent. However, the party relying on the mistaken party's expression of intent could deserve protection, and in certain circumstances the mistaken party can be held responsible for his mistaken expression of intention. All jurisdictions strive towards finding a balance between the interest of the mistaken party only to be bound by his true intention, and the interest of the relying party to be able to rely on expressions of intention.[15]

Traditionally, the risk has been placed on the party making a mistake, the rationale being that such a rule creates an incentive to act carefully and prevents mistakes from being communicated. Another explanation for the rule is that the party to whom the mistake is communicated should be protected since it has no means of discovering the mistake. At the outset it may seem unfair to hold someone to a mistake. However, a party relying on the mistake incurs a loss and should be entitled to compensation. This is particularly the case when there was no mistake, but merely a change of mind. In practice, it is often hard to know whether a party who claims that it has made a mistake really did so or only changed its mind.[16] In this regard, there are two major problems. First, how can it be established that it was a mistake and not merely a change of mind? Second, the suitability of allocating the risk for mistake on the relying party depends on the type of contract and on how soon the mistake is discovered and brought to the other party's attention, i.e. to what extent the other party had reason and time to rely and act on the mistake.

For some types of contracts, it is in practice not critical if a party changes his mind and wishes to cancel a contract or withdraw an invitation or bid. The basic principle that promises are to be kept (*pacta sunt servanda*) is not crucial for all types of contracts, particularly not when notice of the mistake is provided at an early stage. In other words, when a party makes a mistake and soon afterwards informs the other party about it, the other party does not necessarily incur any losses; this is for example the case for the sale of consumer products such as cars, bikes and kitchen appliances. For such situations, it may seem unreasonably harsh to hold the promisor/consumer to his mistaken expression.

For other types of contracts it is absolutely vital that the parties be able to trust expressions of promises. This is the case, for example, in auctions and exchanges and for the sale of products exposed to rapid price variations, such as financial instruments and commodities. If there were an opportunity to escape from such contracts by referring to a mistake, parties would be tempted to do so when in reality they only made a bad bargain, i.e. the buyer could claim that he made a mistake when the prices fall after the purchase. If such contracts were not upheld, due to mistake, the party relying on the promise would incur losses; this is not a proper risk allocation since he was not at fault and had no means of protecting himself from the mistake made by the other party.[17]

A third type of contract is where an object that is not exposed to rapid price variations causes a party to bind himself to other contracts – with sub-contractors, or sup-

---

15 H. Zweigert and H. Kötz, An introduction to comparative law, 1998, 31.
16 E.A. Farnsworth, Changing your mind – the law of regretted decisions, 1988, *passim*.
17 C. Ramberg, Internet marketplaces – the law of auctions and exchanges online, Oxford University Press 2002, p. 125.

pliers – or in other ways involving taking passive actions, such as not committing himself to another contract due to the first contract making him 'fully booked'. Also for such transactions it is recommended that there be a restriction on the ability to escape from a contract because of a mistake.

Electronic communication can be conducted by persons typing messages on their computers in emailing or chat groups, or by an individual communicating with an automated system (such as for instance a website), or by two automated systems communicating (such as for instance in an EDI relationship). Individuals, as well as computer systems, can make mistakes. The individual may slip on the keyboard or with the mouse and click the box 'Yes' instead of the 'No'-box, or click on 'send' before the message is intended to be sent, or the figure '4' may be typed instead of '2', or an extra '0' may be typed inadvertently. Furthermore, computer systems may communicate mistakes due to being wrongly programmed or fed with inaccurate information.

In the 'good old days' – when we mainly communicated by paper messages – many mistakes could be corrected by informing the addressee about the mistake before he received the message containing the mistake, by for instance telephoning before the addressee read the message. The addressee was thus prevented from relying on the mistake. Such a means of correction is rarely available in the electronic environment since the addressee often receives the message with maximum speed and the addressee acts on it automatically and immediately. The trend towards imposing less liability on the party making mistakes in expression ('input errors') can be found in the E-Commerce Directive, Article 11(2) under which the 'service provider shall make available effective and accessible technical means allowing the person communicating with the service provider to identify and correct input errors prior to the placing of the order.' This protection can be contracted out of in business-to-business transactions, but is mandatory for consumers.

UETA goes even further in protecting the mistaken party. Section 10 on 'Effect of Change or Error' provides:

'If a change or error in an electronic record occurs in a transmission between parties to a transaction, the following rules apply:

(1))If the parties have agreed to use a security procedure to detect changes or errors and one party conformed to the procedure, but the other party has not, and the nonconforming party would have detected the change or error had that party also conformed, the conforming party may avoid the effect of the changed or erroneous electronic record.

(2) In an automated transaction involving an individual, the individual may avoid the effect of an electronic record that resulted from an error made by the individual in dealing with the electronic agent of another person if the electronic agent did not provide an opportunity for the prevention or correction of the error and, at the time the individual learns of the error, the individual:

(A) promptly notifies the other person of the error and that the individual did not intend to be bound by the electronic record received by the other person;

(B) takes reasonable steps, including steps that conform to the other person's reasonable instructions, to return to the other person or, if instructed by the other person, to destroy the consideration received, if any, as a result of the erroneous electronic record; and

(C) has not used or received any benefit or value from the consideration, if any, received from the other person.

(3) If neither paragraph (1) nor paragraph (2) applies, the change or error has the effect provided by other law, including the law of mistake, and the parties' contract, if any.

(4) Paragraphs (2) and (3) may not be varied by agreement.'

UETA indeed turns the traditional rule of mistake in expression upside down. It used to be that a mistaken party was bound by his mistake. Under UETA the burden is now shifted to the party relying on the mistake. The purpose is to create a strong incentive for website operators to introduce 'are-you-sure?' boxes in order to slow down the transaction and thereby reduce the risk of mistakes in Internet transactions. When such a security procedure is implemented on the website, the party making the mistake has to bear the risk. It is important to note that this provision is mandatory and parties may not deviate from UETA, Sect. 10 (not even in business-to-business transactions; also note the rule is not applicable to transactions subject to rapid price variations, UETA, Sec. 10, Comment 6).[18]

The UNCITRAL Model Law on Electronic Commerce also addresses the problem of mistake, in Article 13 dealing with the attribution of data messages.[19] This article is relevant to the problems discussed here but is difficult to interpret and understand. According to the Guide to Enactment, the intention of the article is not to interfere with the legal consequences determined by applicable rules of national law.[20] How-

---

18 See www.uetaonline.com and A. Boss, 'The Uniform Electronic Transaction Act in a Global Environment' (2001) 37 Idaho Law Review 68-70.

19 (1) A data message is that of the originator if it was sent by the originator itself.

(2) As between the originator and the addressee, a data message is deemed to be that of the originator if it was sent:

(a) by a person who had the authority to act on behalf of the originator in respect of that data messages; or

(b) by an information system programmed by, or on behalf of, the originator to operate automatically.

(3) As between the originator and the addressee, an addressee is entitled to regard the data message as being that of the originator, and to act on that assumption, if

(a) in order to ascertain whether the data message was that of the originator, the addressee properly applied a procedure previously agreed to by the originator for that purpose; or

(b) the data message as received by the addressee resulted from the actions of a person whose relationship with the originator or with any agent of the originator enabled that person to gain access to a method used by the originator to identify data messages as its own.

(4) Paragraph (3) does not apply:

(a) as of the time when the addressee has both received notice from the originator that the data message is not that of the originator, and had reasonable time to at accordingly: or

(b) in a case within paragraph (3)(b), at any time when the addressee knew or should have known, had it exercised reasonable care or used any agreed procedure that the data message was not that of the originator.

(5) Where a data message is that of the originator or is deemed to be that of the originator, or the addressee is entitled to act on that assumption, then as between the originator and the addressee, the addressee is entitled to regard the data message as received as being what the originator intended to send, and to act on that assumption. The addressee is not so entitled when it knew or should have known, had it exercised reasonable care or used any agreed procedure, that the transmission resulted in any error in the data message as received.

(6) The addressee is entitled to regard each data message received as a separate data message and to act on that assumption, except to the extent that it duplicates another data message and the addressee knew or should have known, had it exercised reasonable care or used any agreed procedure, that the data message was a duplicate. See www.uncitral.org.

20 Guide to Enactment, p. 48. See at www.uncitral.org.

ever at the same time paragraph (5) stipulates that the addressee is entitled to act on the assumption that the data message corresponds to 'what the originator intended to send'. As far as I understand, this is a rule on mistake 'interfering' with applicable rules of national law. Read together with paragraph (4), I come to the conclusion that the addressee may rely on an electronic message as long as he is acting in good faith and is unaware of any mistake. However, as soon as the addressee receives notice of the mistake, he is no longer entitled to rely and act on it. The effects of admitted action and reliance are not clear. It is uncertain whether an acceptance sent by the addressee during the period of time he is entitled to act on the assumption that the message (in this example, an offer) was correct results in a binding contract or only to compensation for damage.[21] Despite the problems in interpreting Article 13, it is worth noting that UNCITRAL addressed the problem of mistake in electronic communication as early as the beginning of the 1990s. Article 13 in the Model Law illustrates how difficult it may be to find a satisfactory solution to this problem.[22]

PECL are more traditional in their approach to mistakes and provide that the mistaken party bears the risk for mistakes in expression.[23] Those drafting PECL had probably not identified the new trend in regard to mistakes in the electronic setting. PECL leave only a limited opening for the risk to shift to the service provider (the website holder), by the reference to 'the mistake was caused by information given by the other party'. It could be argued that the inappropriate design of the website's interface caused the mistake. It would, however, have been preferable for PECL to have addressed this question more explicitly.

I do not suggest a special rule in PECL for e-commerce along the provision in UETA. Instead, I would favour a more general approach in PECL encompassing the underlying policies expressed in UETA. It is probably enough to add in the black letter text "the mistake was caused by the other party *or otherwise induced by him*". The reason that I do not suggest a special regime for e-commerce is that the rationale for not holding a person liable for input errors in e-commerce is equally valid irrespec-

---

21 A Boss, 'The Uniform Electronic Transaction Act in a Global Environment' (2001) 37 Idaho Law Review 49-50.

22 A newly initiated project in the UNCITRAL Working Group on Electronic Commerce deals with the question of mistake in automated transactions, Working paper 96, at www.uncitral.org.

23 Article 4:103: Mistake as to facts or law

(1) A party may avoid a contract for mistake of fact or law existing when the contract was concluded if:

(a) (i) the mistake was caused by information given by the other party; or

(ii) the other party knew or ought to have known of the mistake and it was contrary to good faith and fair dealing to leave the mistaken party in error; or

(iii) the other party made the same mistake, and

(b) the other party knew or ought to have known that the mistaken party,

had it known the truth, would not have entered the contract or would have done so only on fundamentally different terms.

(2) However a party may not avoid the contract if:

(a) in the circumstances its mistake was inexcusable, or

(b) the risk of the mistake was assumed, or in the circumstances should be borne, by it.

Article 4:104 (formerly Art 6.104): Inaccuracy in communication

An inaccuracy in the expression or transmission of a statement is to be treated as a mistake of the person who made or sent the statement and Art 4:103 applies.

tive of what medium that is being used. If the addressee of a mistake in expression has indirectly induced a mistake to occur, the mistaken party should not be held liable. In the PECL Comments the particular case of websites should be dealt with, explaining that a website could be deemed to have induced a mistake by having a procedure that is incomprehensible or ambiguous or lacks opportunity to correct input errors.

9   End Remark

I hope that this short paper has shown that it is not very complicated to regulate e-commerce in a media neutral way. For the SGECC e-commerce is mostly of interest since, due to its borderless nature, it clearly points to the need for harmonisation of substantive law. The traditional International Private Law rules are not suitable for solving borderless electronic transactions. So far, I have not seen any new International Private Law Rules that can solve the problems satisfactory. The only sustainable way forward is to harmonise law on an international scale. A European Civil Code is a good start. PECL and the ongoing work within SGECC illustrate that it is surprisingly easy to overcome the differences in national law and formulate common rules for Europe. If the rules were harmonised, electronic commerce would be greatly facilitated in Europe to the benefit of both business and consumers.

CHAPTER 14

A Diabolical Idea

Pierre Legrand*

> *For Casimir and Imogene,*
> *who do not believe in ghosts.*

> Why must all experience be systematised?
> – D.H. Lawrence[1]

> The thought world reduces itself to geometrical lines
> which appeal on account of their arrangement.
> A system like Kant's or Hegel's does not essentially
> differ from those games of patience through which
> women stave off the boredom of life with cards.
> – Anatole France[2]

> To find a form that accommodates the mess,
> that is the task of the artist now.
> – Samuel Beckett[3]

> [T]here is only one that would be one too
> many, which would be one and one only.
> – Werner Hamacher[4]

It is a famous English judge, Lord Mansfield, who once lamented that "the uncertainty of the law of evidence" was owing "to mistaken notes which have turned particular cases into general rules".[5] So is the irreducible epistemological *summa differentia* arising between the two main legal traditions represented within the Euro-

---

*   Professor of Law, Université Panthéon-Sorbonne. Anterior versions of this argument were published as "Against a European Civil Code", (1997) 60 Modern Law Review 44; "Sens et non-sens d'un code civil européen", Revue internationale de droit comparé, 1996, p. 779. I thank the editors of this volume for inviting me to restate my case. Needless to say, I am engaging in this exercise with my eyes wide open. But there are circumstances where it is more important to be the vanquished than the victor: better Prometheus than Zeus! This text appears in the version that was submitted for publication by the set deadline of December 2002.

1   "Etruscan Places", in *Mornings in Mexico and Etruscan Places*, ed. by Richard Aldington (London: Heinemann, 1956), pp. 114-15 [1927-28].

2   *Le jardin d'Epicure* (Paris: Calmann-Lévy, 1921), p. 56 ["*Le monde pensé se réduit à des lignes géométriques dont l'arrangement amuse. Un système comme celui de Kant ou de Hegel ne diffère pas essentiellement de ces* réussites *par lesquelles les femmes trompent, avec des cartes, l'ennui de vivre*"] (emphasis original).

3   Tom F. Driver, "Beckett by the Madeleine", Columbia University Forum, Vol. IV, No. 3, 1961, p. 23, col. 1.

4   "One 2 Many Multiculturalisms", in Hent deVries and Samuel Weber (eds), *Violence, Identity, and Self-Determination* (Stanford: Stanford University Press, 1997), p. 325.

5   *Crook* v. *Dowling*, (1782) 3 Doug. 75, p. 77; 99 E.R. 546, p. 546 (K.B.).

pean Community shown not to be the outcome of a purely stochastic process. On the contrary, *it has been wanted* in the sense that it is the result of resistances expressed by English lawyers who lived before us and who elected to withstand civilian influences on the common law in order better to affirm its Englishness, that is, its "connatural[ness] with the land".[6]

For the common law, the alternative narrative privileged by the civil law was always characterised by authoritative and general rules, formal and rigid structures, and the language of deduction. The civilian world-view was seen as being epistemologically dangerous on account of what was perceived to be its contemptible quest for absolutely certain knowledge.[7] Accordingly, the foundational discourse of the common law emphasised a rhetoric of antagonism so as resolutely to differentiate itself from "the parent civil law" – "the stronger and prior law" – thus claiming "its own identity through separation" and thereby forging its sense of self *"against"*.[8] "Put shortly: the Anglophone countries kept their distance from the relentless rationalisation of law on the continent which resulted from the alliance between Romanistic legal science and the absolute state".[9] Unsurprisingly, then, one finds in *Pollock and Maitland* "the prevalence of images of conflict in the descriptions of the relationship between the learned laws and the English Common Law".[10] Indeed, Peter Goodrich refers to the "construction of a negative national identity" against the Roman Church (not least in the wake of the Act of Supremacy of 1534) and against Roman and civil law.[11] This development finds its manifestation as early as Bracton who drew a clear demarcation between the English and the French observing that a murder victim was presumed to be French (*"Francigena"*) unless proven to be English through the process of "Englishry" (*"Englescheria"*).[12] The gradual institution of matters of fact as the basis for proper legal procedures and, through the protection given factual relations, the apprehension of anterior judicial decisions as mere recommendations or argumentative repertories progressively consolidated the common law's claim to distinction *as custom*.[13] Today, it remains the case that the common law is learned "not

---

6 Peter Goodrich, *Oedipus Lex: Psychoanalysis, History, Law* (Berkeley: University of California Press, 1995), p. 84. I reviewed this consequential book in [1996] Cambridge Law Journal 372.

7 E.g.: Peter Goodrich, "*Ars Bablativa*: Ramism, Rhetoric, and the Genealogy of English Jurisprudence", in Gregory Leyh (ed.), *Legal Hermeneutics* (Berkeley: University of California Press, 1992), pp. 43-82; *Id.*, "Poor Illiterate Reason: History, Nationalism and Common Law", (1992) 1 Social & Legal Studies 7.

8 Goodrich, *supra*, note 6, p. 160 [my emphasis].

9 Franz Wieacker, *A History of Private Law in Europe*, transl. by Tony Weir (Oxford: Oxford University Press, 1995), p. 393 [1952].

10 R.H. Helmholz, "The Learned Laws in 'Pollock and Maitland'", in John Hudson (ed.), *The History of English Law: Centenary Essays on "Pollock and Maitland"* (Oxford: Oxford University Press, 1996), p. 156. For Helmholz, Maitland was prepared to accept that "the Roman and Canon Laws stimulated the English lawyers to develop their own law", but took the view that this happened "as if from fear or revulsion against the *ius commune*": *id.*, p. 153.

11 *Supra*, note 6, p. 89.

12 *Bracton on the Laws and Customs of England*, transl. by Samuel E. Thorne, t. II (Cambridge, Mass.: Harvard University Press, 1968), pp. 379-382 [c. 1230].

13 For the importance of fact and procedure, see, e.g. Michael Lobban, *The Common Law and English Jurisprudence 1760-1850* (Oxford: Oxford University Press, 1991), pp. 61-79 and 257-289. For the customary character of the common law, see, e.g., J.G.A. Pocock, *The Ancient Constitution and the Feudal Law* (Cambridge: Cambridge University Press, 1957), pp. 30-55.

by study in the strict sense", but "by apprenticeship – hunting with experienced hunters [–] [... and ...] by participation in a kind of corporate retrospection".[14]

English law's sentiment of dissentience – its "protest in the name of lived time"[15] – also led common-law lawyers to *suppress* civilian influences on the common law, a disposition already apparent in Glanvill.[16] Nearly five centuries later, an anonymous tract – which the catalogues of the Bibliothèque Nationale de France, in Paris, and of the British Library, in London, both attribute to Coke – was boldly entitled *Argumentum Anti-Normannicum: or an Argument proving, from Ancient Histories and Records, that William, Duke of Normandy, Made no absolute Conquest of England by the Sword; in the sense of our Modern Writers.*[17] Bearing in mind Fernand Braudel's apophthegm that "a civilisation is characterised much more by what it disdains, by what it does not want, than by what it accepts",[18] I argue that the reiterated affirmation of difference from the civil-law tradition by the common law *regardless of historical evidence*, or the "Englishing of law",[19] constitutes in a significant way the foundation of the meaning that the common law ascribes to itself as common law: "England [...] can [not] appropriately be regarded as insular, if by that is meant an immunity to the influence of 'foreign' ideas. Yet [...] England [...] became insular in the particular sense in which its elite culture thematised the separateness, distinctiveness or 'peculiarity' of the English, as well as their unique destiny".[20] Johan Huizinga observed with characteristic perspicacity that any fantasy sustained by a culture is a valuable clue for coming to know that culture;[21] the energies directed toward imagination, projection, and a sense of idealised community also tell a story.[22] The contemporary challenge facing Europe is, therefore, to appreciate that English law not only is different, but that *it has wanted to be different* by taking the road not travelled. This willed particularism may or may not be a matter of regret. It is, however, a matter of historical record, which ought to command respect from those civilians

---

14 Walter J. Ong, *Orality and Literacy: The Technologizing of the Word* (London: Routledge, 1982), p. 9.

15 Charles Taylor, *Sources of the Self* (Cambridge, Mass.: Harvard University Press, 1989), p. 463.

16 *De Legibus et Consuetudinibus Regni Angliae*, ed. by George E. Woodbine (New Haven: Yale University Press, 1932), p. 184 [*c.* 1187], where the editor notes, for example, that Glanvill's prologue is often a silent imitation of the foreword to Justinian's Institutes and shows that the text borrows, without attribution, well-known passages from the Digest.

17 [Anonymous], *Argumentum Anti-Normannicum: or an Argument proving, from Ancient Histories and Records, that William, Duke of Normandy, Made no absolute Conquest of England by the Sword; in the sense of our Modern Writers* (London: John Darby, 1682).

18 Pierre Daix, *Braudel* (Paris: Flammarion, 1995), p. 279 [*"Une civilisation se caractérise beaucoup plus par ce qu'elle dédaigne, par ce dont elle ne veut pas, que par ce qu'elle accepte"*] (being the transcript of an interview with Jean-Claude Bringuier broadcast in August 1994).

19 Elizabeth L. Eisenstein, *The Printing Press as an Agent of Change* (Cambridge: Cambridge University Press, 1979), p. 360.

20 W.T. Murphy, "The Oldest Social Science? The Epistemic Properties of the Common Law Tradition", (1991) 54 Modern Law Review 182, p. 184

21 Johan Huizinga, *The Autumn of the Middle Ages*, transl. by Rodney J. Payton and Ulrich Mammitzsch (Chicago: University of Chicago Press, 1996), p. 62 [1919].

22 For a general reflection on the necessary and constitutive role of the unconscious in the delineation of political identity and destiny, see Jacqueline Rose, *States of Fantasy* (Oxford: Oxford University Press, 1996).

within the European Community agitating in favour of the *idée fixe* of civilianising (or, as they no doubt mean, "civilising") the common law.

Consider a proposal meeting with increasing favour in various political, professional, and academic circles: that of a European Civil Code.[23] Should the idea be supported? Not, it seems clear to me, if we accept that there are two main legal traditions within the European Community, that the notion of "legal tradition" includes, amongst other features, a discrete cognitive approach to law, and that the whole must accommodate the plurality of discourses within the parts. In other words, there exist both a civil-law and a common-law way of thinking about law, about what it is to have knowledge of law, and about the role of law in society. For example, as I have explained, the two main legal traditions differ in their understanding of rules.[24] Moreover, they foster incongruous views of the nature of rights, of legal reasoning, of the role of systematisation, of the significance of facts, and of the management of historical time.[25] An important feature of the civilian's contemporary epistemological construct is the civil code (although *not* a necessary one as Denmark, Finland, and Sweden continue to remind us). The code, as a purportedly self-contained and self-referential system, illustrates the deep-seated conviction held by civilian jurists that the lived experience ought no longer to be privileged (codes have "a Spartan quality that is unforgiving of spontaneity and insensitive to the foggy or the strange"),[26] that the lived experience can be reduced to propositional knowledge in the form of a panoptic and autarkic body of rules of law, and that it is useful to organise the lived ex-

---

23 E.g.: Resolution [of the European Parliament] on Action to Bring into Line the Private Law of the Member States, Off. J. E.C. 1989 C 158/400 (26 May 1989). Three more parliamentary resolutions have followed on 6 May 1994, 16 March 2000, and 15 November 2001. The idea of pan-national codification can be traced at least to [François] d'Olivier, *De la réforme des loix civiles*, t. I (Paris: Merigot, 1786), pp. 246-348. Olivier argued for a "Civil Code For All Peoples": *id.*, p. 273 ["*Code civil de tous les peuples*"].

24 "Alterity: About Rules, For Example", in Peter Birks and Arianna Pretto (eds), *Themes in Comparative Law: In Honour of Bernard Rudden* (Oxford: Oxford University Press, 2002), pp. 21-33.

25 "European Legal Systems Are Not Converging", (1996) 45 International and Comparative Law Quarterly 52, pp. 64-78. The occasional application of a civil-law rule to buttress common-law reasoning, as practised by late 19th-century English judges, for example, does nothing to blunt the epistemological distinction I address. E.g.: *Acton* v. *Blundell*, (1843) 12 M. & W. 324, p. 353; 152 E.R. 1223, p. 1234 (Exch., Tindal C.J.). See, e.g., Geoffrey Samuel, "Der Einfluß des Civil Law auf das englische Recht des 19. Jahrhunderts", in Reiner Schulze (ed.), *Französisches Zivilrecht in Europa während des 19. Jahrhunderts* (Berlin: Duncker & Humblot, 1994), pp. 287-313; Tony Weir, "Die Sprachen des europäischen Rechts", Zeitschrift für Europäisches Privatrecht 3 (1995), p. 373; Barry Nicholas, "Rules and Terms – Civil Law and Common Law", 48 Tulane Law Review 946 (1974), p. 947. *Cf.* R.H. Helmholz, "Continental Law and Common Law: Historical Strangers or Companions?", [1990] Duke Law Journal 1207, p. 1227: "[The borrowings] were normally the product of individual lawyers who made individual choices when the interests of their clients so required, and they also were the choices of judges looking for help in dealing with specific problems". This author adds: "Once planted in the common law, civil law doctrines quickly took on lives of their own": *id.*, pp. 1220-21. For a detailed examination of 19th-century English judicial practice, see Michele Graziadei, "Changing Images of the Law in XIXth Century English Legal Thought (The Continental Impulse)", in Mathias Reimann (ed.), *The Reception of Continental Ideas in the Common Law World 1820-1920* (Berlin: Duncker & Humblot, 1994), pp. 115-63.

26 Mark A. Schneider, *Culture and Enchantment* (Chicago: University of Chicago Press, 1993), p. 40.

perience (and the law) in this way.[27] "The need to codify finds its deepest roots in this love of order typical of the Cartesian spirit fond of perspectives, of plans, of logic, of the aesthetic beauty of the edifice even".[28] The common law, for its part, offers a challenge to the effort of structuring the world into a single determinate rationalisable order.

There is an array of reasons, largely historical and psychological, why a legal community is (or is not) attracted to a particular genre of cultural product. It is evident, however, that the specific cultural form that is retained – such as a civil code – has significant connections with the wider symbolic world within which a legal community operates. In this sense, matters of epistemology are not just questions of abstract reasoning; they also raise – perhaps primarily so – issues of social order. Whether as antecedent or effect, the absence of a civil code in England, for example, is not unrelated to sociological findings indicating that the English "feel definitely uncomfortable with systems of rigid rules", that there is even to be found in England "an emotional horror of formal rules", and that the English "pride themselves that many problems can be solved without formal rules".[29] And, whether as antecedent or effect, the presence of a civil code in Germany is not foreign to empirical studies showing that the Germans "have been programmed since their early childhood to feel comfortable in structured environments" and that they "look for a structure in their organisations, institutions, and relationships which makes events clearly interpretable and predictable" to the point where "even ineffective rules satisfy [the] people's emotional need for formal structure".[30] The French political geographer, André Siegfried, embraces in a succinct formula important aspects of the difference I wish to emphasise: "[The French] believe in written law, in Roman law, a law with sharp edges, based on suspicion, realism, pessimism, which contrasts with English law based on custom and trust".[31]

The depth of the fundamental differentiation between the civil-law and common-law *mentalités* is possibly best captured if we approach them as two *moralités*.[32] In this context, Michael Oakeshott's distinction between what he regards as "the two forms which [...] compose [...] the moral life of the Western world" is apposite.[33] The

---

27 *"Antiqui juris civilis fabulas"*, (1995) 45 University of Toronto Law Journal 311.

28 Louis Baudouin, "Originalité du droit du Québec", (1950) 10 Revue du Barreau 121, p. 123 [*"le besoin de codifier vient dans sa cause profonde de cet amour de l'ordre, propre à l'esprit cartésien amoureux des perspectives, des plans, de la logique, voire même de la beauté apparente de l'édifice"*].

29 Geert Hofstede, *Cultures and Organizations* (London: McGraw-Hill, 1991), pp. 145, 121, and 121, respectively.

30 *Id.*, pp. 121, 116, and 121, respectively.

31 "Introduction générale", in *Id.* (ed.), *Aspects de la société française* (Paris: L.G.D.J., 1954), p. 21 [*"Nous croyons au droit écrit, au droit romain, un droit aux arêtes dures, fondé sur la méfiance, le réalisme, le pessimisme, qui fait contraste avec le droit anglais fondé sur la coutume et sur la confiance"*]. The theme of "suspicion" is developed at length with specific reference to French political culture in Lucien Jaume, *L'individu effacé* (Paris: Fayard, 1997).

32 *Cf.* William Ewald, "Comparative Jurisprudence (I): What Was it Like to Try a Rat?", 143 University of Pennsylvania Law Review 1889 (1995), p. 1949: "The central task of comparative [legal studies], I think, is to interpret and make sense of the world's variety of [...] applied moral philosophies".

33 *Rationalism in Politics* (London: Methuen, 1962), p. 61.

one form of moral life is described by Hanna Fenichel Pitkin as "reflective, rational-istic, principled, and articulate".[34] Oakeshott outlines its workings thus: "the rule or the ideal is determined first and in the abstract [...]. This task of verbal expression [...] is not only to set out the desirable ends of conduct, but also to set them out clearly and unambiguously and to reveal their relations to one another. [...] For the right or the duty is always to observe a rule or realize an end, and not to behave in a certain concrete manner".[35] In its other form, argues Oakeshott, "the moral life is *a habit of affection and behaviour*; not a habit of reflective *thought*, but a habit of *affection* and *conduct*. [...] There is on the occasion, nothing more than the unreflective following of a tradition of conduct in which we have been brought up". How, then, is this par-ticular form of the moral life acquired? "No doubt [...] what is learnt (or some of it) can be formulated in rules [...]; but [we do not], in this kind of education, learn by learning rules [...]. What we learn here is what may be learned without the formula-tion of its rules". Oakeshott adds: "the sort of moral education by means of which habits of affection and behaviour may be acquired [...] gives the power to act appro-priately [...] but [...] does not give the ability to explain our actions in abstract terms"; moreover, "the habits of conduct which compose [a moral life in this form] are never recognized as a system". As Pitkin observes, the two *moralités* are constituted in dif-ferent ways. In the former case, it is "deductive" in the sense that the rules that struc-ture it are posited prior to the practices that apply it. Not so in the latter case where no rules pre-exist to the practice. What regularities arise emerge out of the practice itself and get their meaning from that practice.[36]

The civil-law and common-law traditions must, therefore, be seen as two discrete epistemological formations with the latter having elected, to borrow from Oakeshott once more, not to formulate itself as rules (although the possibility to do so was tech-nically open to it) and not to fashion itself as a system.[37] These two epistemologies are conditioned by, and constantly reinforce in their turn, deeply-embedded world-views within the societies in which they have developed to the point where there can be found, predictably, a pattern of congruence between a legal culture and a culture *tout court*.[38] A recent discussion of physical experimentation in France and England,

---

34 *Wittgenstein and Justice* (Berkeley: University of California Press, 1972), p. 52.

35 Oakeshott, *supra*, note 33, pp. 66-67. The quotations that follow in the body of the text are all from *id.*, pp. 61-64 [emphasis original].

36 Pitkin, *supra*, note 34, p. 52.

37 The fact that the two legal traditions have between them a certain number of describable relationships and that they can, *in this sense*, be seen as an inter-epistemological entity does not deprive them of their fundamental epistemological individuality. One such connection is underlined by Geoffrey Samuel who observes that whether in the civil-law or the common-law world law is about relations between individuals, on the one hand, and between individuals and things, on the other: *Epistemology and Method in Law* (Dartmouth: Ashgate, 2003), p. 15. Another parallel is mentioned by John Dewey who observes that both legal traditions operate by way of a logic relative to antecedents rather than to consequences: "Logical Method and Law", 10 Cornell Law Quarterly 17 (1924).

38 For an analysis of practices of rationality in France which is most relevant to an understanding of how the French think and think about law, see, e.g., Paul Rabinow, *French Modern: Norms and Forms of the Social Environment* (Cambridge, Mass.: MIT Press, 1989). For a comparison of the two major literary modes, the commentary and rhetoric, which correspond to the prevailing forms of doctrinal expression within the civil-law and common-law traditions, respectively, see generally Michel Charles, *L'arbre et la source* (Paris: Le Seuil, 1986).

showing that the credibility of experimental accounts has historically relied on different criteria in the two countries, affords a good example of the interdependencies that can be established between law and other fields of knowledge within a given culture.[39]

For the French, an experimental account produced in the 18th-century would be found convincing only if it had led its author to the formulation of a scientific law. The expectation within the interpretive community was that scientific measurements ought to reveal regularities sufficiently persistent to adopt the form of laws. The need to privilege this argumentative strategy regularly required physicists "to do violence to the narrative of measurements so that it would obey the discourse of the law".[40] In sum, for French physicists such as Coulomb, Laplace, or Lavoisier, "physical reality *can* and *must* be described in terms of simple, general, universal, and immutable laws".[41] The English, for their part, insisted that the persuasiveness of an experimental narrative must depend on the way in which it makes it possible for others to replicate the empirical demonstration on which it reports. Thus, an account would be regarded as credible only if it contained all the information, even in its finest detail, that would permit replication of the relevant experiment. Specifically, this concern for repetition led English physicists to use simple instruments since an instrument could not be considered as making proof if it could not be reproduced. Accordingly, when Cavendish felt constrained to resort to a complex instrument for his work on electricity, he promptly apologised. To summarise: "On the one hand, the oracles of natural law, eternal and universal, on the other the high priests of empirical *savoir faire*, able to generate everywhere and always the ritual of the production of the factual experiment, each time identical to itself".[42] Recall the way in which the French and English legal cultures continue to address the matter of factual data and replicate the differentiation between "guardians of the law and masters of the fact" just identified amongst physicists.[43] Indeed, the different approaches privileged by civilians and common-law lawyers concerning what it is to have knowledge of law have not been affected by increasing European legal integration at the level of rules and institutions. They still come to the interpretation of the law with an idiosyncratic "pre-understanding", Hans-Georg Gadamer's *"Vorverständnis"*.[44]

---

39 See Christian Licoppe, *La formation de la pratique scientifique: le discours de l'expérience en France et en Angleterre (1630-1820)* (Paris: La Découverte, 1996), pp. 299-304.

40 *Id.*, pp. 293-94 [*"faire violence au récit des mesures pour qu'il vienne se soumettre au discours de la loi"*].

41 *Id.*, p. 293 ["*une réalité physique pouvant et devant être décrite en termes de lois, simples, générales, universelles et immuables*"].

42 *Id.*, p. 304 [*"D'un côté les oracles de la loi naturelle, éternelle et universelle, de l'autre les grands-prêtres du savoir-faire empirique, capables de susciter partout et toujours le rituel de la production du fait d'expérience, chaque fois identique à lui-même"*].

43 *Id.*, p. 292 [*"Maîtres du faire et gardiens de la loi"*].

44 For Gadamer's theory of "pre-understanding", see his *Truth and Method*, 2d rev. ed. transl. by Joel Weinsheimer and Donald G. Marshall (London: Sheed & Ward, 1989), *passim* [1960] (hereinafter *Truth and Method*]. For the use of the German word, *"Vorverständnis"*, see his *Wahrheit und Methode*, 4th ed. (Tübingen: J.C.B. Mohr, 1975), *passim*. This notion is indebted to the Heideggerian idea of "fore-conception" (*"Vorgriff"*). See Martin Heidegger, *Being and Time*, transl. by John Macquarrie and Edward Robinson (Oxford: Blackwell, 1962), p. 191: "the interpretation has already

PIERRE LEGRAND

But, beyond reflecting the civilians' profound commitment to the aestheticisation of the legal and their predictable support for familiar legal forms, the proposal in favour of a European Civil Code is principally the product of two phenomena, both of which must be resisted.

First, this suggestion epitomises the advance of a European Community bureaucracy – consisting largely of uprooted civil servants and failed politicians often entertaining an ambivalent relationship with their national legal culture – which thrives on abstract generality, on false universals, and on illusory stability and predictability (Max Weber's *Beamtenstaats* rides again!). In this context, the European Civil Code becomes the agent of a dogma of (assumed) administrative efficiency for which particularisms undermine legal regulation.[45] It is meant to instrumentalise legal culture and to make culture subservient to the ethos of fiscal rectitude and commercial advantage. It is the support of a process of normalisation which is, effectively, a process of subjugation of the local that becomes stigmatised as deviant.[46] Writing with reference to the American *Restatements*, Lawrence M. Friedman observes how their authors "took fields of living law, scalded their flesh, drained off their blood, and reduced them to bones".[47] This approach to law-making is precisely that being advocated in the name of the "brusselisation" of law. As such, it propounds a distinctly impoverished view of law and of what it is to have legal knowledge.[48]

Second, the idea of a European Civil Code betrays fear, which manifests itself in at least two ways. There is the fear of what is unknown. For most civilians, the common-law tradition remains a curiosity – or, in the words of an Italian commentator, a "secret".[49] And civilians react to the unknown in the way that can be expected: they refuse to engage with it or to allow themselves to be questioned by it. The tendency is, therefore, to ignore the unknown or to minimise its impact. Cognitive psychology teaches that the search for similarities and differences relies on the recognition by the

---

decided for a definite way of conceiving [the entity we are interpreting], either with finality or with reservations; it is grounded in *something we grasp in advance* – in a *fore-conception*" [1927] (emphasis original). For an application of Gadamer's theory in a comparative context, see Charles Taylor, "Comparison, History, Truth", in *Philosophical Arguments* (Cambridge, Mass.: Harvard University Press, 1995), pp. 146-164. For a critical study of the notion of "pre-understanding" with specific reference to Gadamer, see Hans-Herbert Kögler, *The Power of Dialogue*, transl. by Paul Hendrickson (Cambridge, Mass.: MIT Press, 1996), *passim*.

45 *Cf.* Alexis de Tocqueville, "De la démocratie en Amérique", in *Oeuvres*, ed. by André Jardin, t. II (Paris: Gallimard, 1992), bk II, part IV, ch. 3, p. 814: "every central government worships uniformity; uniformity relieves it from inquiry into an infinity of details, which it would have to address if it made rules for men instead of indiscriminately subjecting all men to the same rule" ["*tout gouvernement central adore l'uniformité; l'uniformité lui évite l'examen d'une infinité de détails dont il devrait s'occuper, s'il fallait faire la règle pour les hommes, au lieu de faire passer indistinctement tous les hommes sous la même règle*"] (1840).

46 For a reflection on the link between bureaucracy and generalisation with specific reference to codification, see Pierre Bourdieu, *Raisons pratiques* (Paris: Le Seuil, 1994), p. 114.

47 *A History of American Law*, 2d ed. (New York: Simon & Schuster, 1985), p. 676.

48 A critic of my published work on European codification (*supra*, note *) is of the view that I am too kind toward Brussels bureaucrats: Vincenzo Zeno-Zencovich, "The 'Europeran Civil Code', European Legal Traditions and Neo-Positivism", (1998) 4 European Review of Private Law 349, pp. 351-352.

49 Vincenzo Arangio-Ruiz, *Istituzioni di diritto romano* (Naples: Jovene, 1980), p. 5 ["*un segreto*"] (being a reprint of the 14th ed.).

252

individual of a certain image of himself and on a measure of self-assertion. Thus, difference will be better accepted if it allows the enhancement of the individual in his own eyes and (seemingly) in the eyes of others. Hence, similarity by projection or projective identification, which consists in attributing to another features that we confer on ourselves, is the more current approach to cultural interaction.[50] The civilian, like any individual, is better able to accept the fact that the common-law lawyer belongs to his world than admit that he has something of the common-law lawyer in him. The result is a constant attempt by civilians to stress the imbrication of the civil law in the common-law world at different stages of the latter's history thereby attenuating the common law's claim to differentiation.[51] Truly, as Michel Serres acknowledges, "diversity fosters anxiety and unity reassures".[52] After all, "[t]he appearance of an alternative symbolic universe poses a threat because its very existence demonstrates empirically that one's own universe is less than inevitable".[53] But fear takes another form that is well-described in a French contribution to the *Harvard Law Review*, which appeared shortly after the First World War: "divergences in laws cause other divergences that generate unconsciously, bit by bit, these misunderstandings and conflicts among nations which end with blood and desolation".[54] The point of a

---

50 See Geneviève Vinsonneau, "Appartenances culturelles, inégalités sociales et procédés cognitifs en jeu dans les comparaisons inter-personnelles", Bulletin de Psychologie, 1994, t. XVIIII, No. 419, p. 422. For a philosophical reflection to the same effect, see Gadamer, *Truth and Method*, *supra*, note 44, p. 14: "To recognize one's own in the alien, to become at home in it, is the basic movement of spirit, whose being consists only in returning to itself from what is other".

51 E.g.: Reinhard Zimmermann, "Der europäische Charakter des englischen Rechts", Zeitschrift für Europäisches Privatrecht 1 (1993), p. 4. The strategy which consists in translating the common law into civilian terms and evaluating it by civilian standards can be spectacularly unpersuasive such as when it is posited that English scholarship about law is different from American scholarship (which it is, as Patrick Atiyah and Robert Summers have shown), that German scholarship about law is different from American scholarship (which it most certainly is), and that, *ergo*, English scholarship is *similar* to German scholarship. For these remarkable contentions, see Reinhard Zimmermann, "Savigny's Legacy: Legal History, Comparative Law, and the Emergence of a European Legal Science", (1996) 112 Law Quarterly Review 576, p. 584 [hereinafter: "Savigny's Legacy"]. For a discussion of scholarship about law in England and in the United States, see P.S. Atiyah and Robert S. Summers, *Form and Substance in Anglo-American Law* (Oxford: Oxford University Press, 1987), pp. 398-400.

52 *Eloge de la philosophie en langue française* (Paris: Fayard, 1995), p. 270 [*"Le multiple propage l'angoisse et l'unité rassure"*]. Cf. Edward Shils, *Tradition* (Chicago: University of Chicago Press, 1981), pp. 10-11, who remarks on "the metaphysical dread of being encumbered by something alien to oneself".

53 Peter L. Berger and Thomas Luckmann, *The Social Construction of Reality* (London: Penguin, 1966), p. 126.

54 Pierre Lepaulle, "The Function of Comparative Law", 35 Harvard Law Review 838 (1921-22), p. 857. For the making of a similar point after the Second World War, see Ernst Rabel, "Zum Geleit", Zeitschrift für ausländisches und internationales Privatrecht 15 (1949-50), p. 1: "After such fearful turmoil our age requires more than ever that the West consolidate its law-making powers. We must work with renewed courage toward the reconciliation of needless differences, the facilitation of international trade, and the improvement of private law systems" [*"Mehr denn jemals, nach einem noch schrecklicheren Wirrsal, braucht unsere Zeit die Zusammenfassung der rechtsbildenden Kräfte des Abendlands. Beherzter als früher muß an der Ausgleichung grundloser Gegensätze, an der Erleichterung des internationalen Rechtsverkehrs, an der Verbesserung der Privatrechtssysteme gearbeitet werden"*].

European Civil Code, then, becomes the taming of international tensions or, to put it more bluntly, the attenuation of the risk of war. The desire to assimilate the common-law tradition is thus linked, for civilians, to the fact that nationalist forms, which are associated with a territory, terrify.[55] Undeniably, the proposal advocating a European Civil Code is political in the sense that it purports to respond to perceived *political* imperatives.[56] Through the ages, there has been a thousand ways of eliminating "other" cultures. They all have had in common the desire to institute a unity, that is, a totalitarianism. Culture in the singular always represents *an act of power*.[57] Support for a European Civil Code, therefore, implies an attack on pluralism, a desire to suppress antinomy, an attempt at the diminution of specificity.[58] What is a European Civil Code if not a project seeking to produce a new separation between the legal-political function and the lifeworld and to reduce the diversity of legal discourses within Europe? How can the promotion of a formalistic and conceptualistic model, such as a pan-European civil code, not be understood as reflecting a decision to over-look the point of English exceptionalism, which is not to be found in unreflective na-tionalistic closure as much as in the specificity of a cultural tradition that has wanted to retain (and has wanted to convince itself that it was retaining) its pragmatic and individualistic character in defense against the slide into the strict legal and uni-versalising positivism characteristic of Continental civilian cultures?[59]

The power of a European Civil Code would lie not only in its ability to provide an officialised construction of reality, but also in its capacity to limit alternative visions of social life. The collection of legal norms within the new code would monopolise legal discourse in ways that would arbitrarily, but effectively, exclude alternative views of justice.[60] The common-law rationality would rapidly and decisively find it-self marginalised and common-law lawyers would soon be expected to transfer their fundamental epistemological loyalties to the civilian model – an intellectual forma-tion that remains ultimately inconsonant with their sense of justice.[61] The communion

---

55 Pierre Legendre, *Jouir du pouvoir: traité de la bureaucratie patriote* (Paris: Editions de Minuit, 1976), pp. 57 and 246.

56 For an argument focusing on the political character of national civil codes, see my "Strange Power of Words: Codification Situated", 9 Tulane European and Civil Law Forum 1 (1994).

57 Michel de Certeau, *La culture au pluriel* (Paris: Le Seuil, 1993), p. 213.

58 Indeed, Rodolfo Sacco underlines the incompatibility arising between the fact of legal particularism and the idea of codification: "Codificare: Modo superato di legiferare?", Rivista di diritto civile, 1983, p. 119.

59 See André-Jean Arnaud, *Pour une pensée juridique européenne* (Paris: Presses Universitaires de France, 1991), p. 152.

60 In this respect, the performative strength of a code would be far superior to that of any European directive or collection of directives. While a code readily conveys a sense of officialised coherence, solemn universality, and majestic permanence, for example, directives appear as discontinuous and contingent. For general observations on the "codification effect", see Pierre Bourdieu, "Habitus, code et codification", Actes de la recherche en sciences sociales, 1986, No. 64, pp. 41-43.

61 The sense, for the common-law lawyer, that a law grounded on texts inevitably operates a reduction-ism by substituting a legal treatment based on "habituality" or "ideality" (the text can not but capture what is regarded as the desirable solution either because it subsumes most situations as they arise or because it wishes to steer all situations in a certain direction) for a legal treatment based on "particu-larity" is already apparent in William Lambarde, *Archeion or, A Discourse upon the High Courts of Justice in England*, ed. by Charles H. McIlwain and Paul L. Ward (Cambridge, Mass.: Harvard

assumed to be epitomised by a European Civil Code would, in fact, represent, beyond the sum of words, the excommunication of the common-law way of understanding the world and the relegation to obsolescence of its particular insights.[62] Ironically, the officialised exclusion of the common-law rationality would be happening at a time when the interaction between civil-law and common-law cultures is possibly more sustained than at any other moment in European history.

Specifically, the idea of a European Civil Code can be criticised on at least six counts.

First, it is arrogant, for it suggests that the civilian re-presentation of the world is more worthy than its alternative and is, in short, so superior that it deserves to *supersede* its alternative.[63] The obvious objection arises: what recommends one discursivisation of reality over the other? It would be more heuristic to claim that the civil law and common law, as two competing forms of epistemological inquiry operating in part beneath consciousness, represent two modes of knowledge production potentially able to offer equally plausible accounts of the world in a context where it is not possible on the basis of reason to decide which of them can raise a more legitimate claim to validity. The civil-law and common-law traditions illustrate the conflict between systematic theory and historiography which, as Roberto Mangabeira Unger underlines, is really only a rendition of the larger opposition between universality and particularity in knowledge.[64] One can think of the civil-law and common-law traditions as two languages. Is it clear that understanding would be promoted if the variety of language present within the European Community was replaced by a commonality, say, through the adoption of German or French as a pan-European language?[65] *Is there not an element sacrificed to uniform thinking?* Is it not arguable that "a comprehensive polycentric culture consisting of many relatively independent member cultures which are in close contact with one another is in many respects superior to a homogeneous unified culture which is oriented only towards one center"?[66] Reality can not be apprehended in its quiddity which remains inscrutable; in fact, the etymology of the term informs us that reality is precisely that thing (*res*) which in the end *resists* understanding.[67] Reality, then, can only be constructed, not found. The meaning of any object or event is a function of the perspective or frame of reference in

---

University Press, 1957), p. 43: "For *written Lawes* must needs bee made in a generalitie, and be grounded upon that which happeneth for the most part, because no wisdome of man can fore-see every thing in particularitie, which Experience and Time doth beget" [1591] (emphasis original).

62   *Cf.* Iris Marion Young, *Justice and the Politics of Difference* (Princeton: Princeton University Press, 1990), p. 53: "Marginalization is perhaps the most dangerous form of oppression".

63   John Henry Merryman notes that many civilians are convinced that their legal tradition is "superior" to the common law. He adds that "[t]hat attitude itself has become part of the civil law tradition": *The Civil Law Tradition*, 2d ed. (Stanford: Stanford University Press, 1985), p. 3.

64   *Law in Modern Society* (New York: Free Press, 1976), pp. 21-22.

65   Joseph Vining, *The Authoritative and the Authoritarian* (Chicago: University of Chicago Press, 1986), p. 87.

66   Roland Posner, "Society, Civilization, Mentality: Prolegomena to a Language Policy for Europe", in Florian Coulmas (ed.), *A Language Policy for the European Community* (Berlin: Walter de Gruyter, 1991), pp. 124-125.

67   *Cf.* Bruno Latour and Steve Woolgar, *Laboratory Life: The Construction of Scientific Facts*, 2d ed. (Princeton: Princeton University Press, 1986), p. 260, note 17.

terms of which the object or event is *ascribed* meaning. Different languages, because they confront it in different ways, thus offer different accounts of reality. No language can pretend to exhaust reality; no language offers a standpoint from which reality would be wholly visible. Rather, each language represents a choice which conditions the answers to be given by reality. Although they all address reality, languages can never be reduced to a single description of it.

Imagine, for example, a spherical, bouncy object. An anglophone will call it "ball". A francophone will call it *"balle"*, *but only if it is small*. Otherwise, he will refer to it as a *"ballon"*. In other words, there is one spherical, bouncy object and two renditions of it through two languages ("ball" and *"balle"*). The descriptions vary to the extent that the word *"balle"* connotes the idea of smallness in the way the English "ball" does not. This illustration shows that the complexity of reality will not always be fully captured by a single language: the notion of size is not rendered by the English "ball". These narratives, then, are complementary more than they are adversarial in that their combination allows for a more insightful perspective on the reality they each attempt to re-present. Thus, the bilingual anglophone will better be able to explain what he sees – or will know more about the "ballness" of the ball – if he can say: "This is a ball, what the French would call a *balle*". Unsurprisingly, studies reveal that "bilinguals are more sensitive to semantic relations between words, are more advanced in understanding the arbitrary assignment of names to referents, are better able to treat sentence structure analytically, are better at restructuring a perceptual situation, have greater social sensitivity and greater ability to react more flexibly to cognitive feedback, are better at rule discovery tasks, and have more divergent thinking".[68] A rewarding analogy can be drawn between the bilingual and the bijuridical brain, which is similarly able to offer a more sophisticated interpretive grid than if steeped exclusively in one legal tradition. By complementing the findings of one partial perspective *qua* re-presentation of reality – say, the civil-law tradition – with the findings of another re-presentation of the world – for example, the common-law tradition – the European lawyer is in a position to create a global picture that is more comprehensive and, therefore, more insightful in terms of understanding reality. Specifically, it may help to appreciate the interaction between two individuals wishing to deal in widgets to be able to call not only on the idea of "meeting of the minds" (the orthodox view of what a contract is in the civil-law world), but also on that of "bargain, or exchange of promises" (the classical view of contract at common law). Difference, in other words, need not be perceived in antagonistic terms, as in the eyes of those who propose to suppress it through the adoption of a European Civil Code. It must be seen that difference need not be regarded as a malediction. While a dichotomy marks a "severance" and "isolates", difference is a "comparison" and "relates".[69] Because it is complementary, difference is salutary. In reminding lawyers that although there may be *one concept* of contract across Europe, there exist at least

---

68 François Grosjean, *Life with Two Languages: An Introduction to Bilingualism* (Cambridge, Mass.: Harvard University Press, 1982), p. 223. See generally Suzanne Romaine, *Bilingualism*, 2nd ed. (Oxford: Blackwell, 1995), pp. 107-118. *Cf.* John Edwards, *Multilingualism* (London: Routledge, 1994), pp. 66-71.

69 Clifford Geertz, *After the Fact* (Cambridge, Mass.: Harvard University Press, 1995), p. 28.

two conceptions of contract, difference fulfils a positive role. It contributes its own *vis affirmativa* allowing for a richer appreciation of reality.

Second, the proposal is misleading, for it suggests that, through a European Civil Code, Europe is returning to some golden age when it boasted a law common to its various constituent parts, the so-called *"jus commune"*. "There is no doubt, as Marie-France Renoux-Zagamé aptly underlines, that the history of the *jus commune* belongs in part to the history of representations, to the history of beliefs [...]. It is a matter of faith, to be studied as such".[70] Leaving to one side this mythological dimension, however, it remains that there *never* was a *jus* that was truly *commune*. "In terms of civil science [the] [c]ommon [l]aw was not only the *ius proprium* of England; it had in effect seceded from the *ius commune*".[71] As a result, "English lawyers were excluded from this lingua franca".[72] In the words of A.W.B. Simpson, "[u]niversity law, with th[e] exception [of equity], never had any profound influence upon the common law system".[73] In sum, "it is artificial to treat England as a true adherent of the *jus commune*".[74] The idea of a European Civil Code is, therefore, predicated on the *exclusion* of European legal history, which never featured a law common to all European states.[75] A European Civil Code partakes in an ahistoricist (or anti-historicist) re-in-

---

70 Marie-France Renoux-Zagamé, "La méthode du droit commun: réflexion sur la logique des droits non codifiés", Revue d'histoire des Facultés de droit et de la science juridique, 1990, p. 138 [*"Que l'histoire du droit commun relève pour partie de l'histoire des représentations, de l'histoire des croyances, cela ne fait pas de doute [...]. C'est* un phénomène de foi, *à étudier comme tel"*] (emphasis original). For the point about *jus commune* as spiritual fact, see also Paolo Grossi, *L'ordine giuridico medievale* (Rome: Laterza, 1995), pp. 227-229. *Cf.* John Henry Merryman and David S. Clark, *Comparative Law: Western European and Latin American Legal Systems – Cases and Materials* (Indianapolis: Bobbs-Merrill, 1978), pp. 104-105: "The idealization of [...] the *jus commune* is at the bottom of a special attitude which might be called 'the nostalgia of the civil lawyer.' It refers to a desire to reestablish a *jus commune* – a common law of mankind – in the West. [A] similar nostalgia is not a part of the culture of the common law".

71 Donald R. Kelley, *The Human Measure: Social Thought in the Western Legal Tradition* (Cambridge, Mass.: Harvard University Press, 1990), p. 182.

72 J.M. Kelly, *A Short History of Western Legal Theory* (Oxford: Oxford University Press, 1992), p. 180.

73 "The Survival of the Common Law System", in *Legal Theory and Legal History: Essays on the Common Law* (London: Hambledon Press, 1987), p. 394.

74 John Henry Merryman, "On the Convergence (and Divergence) of the Civil Law and the Common Law", in Mauro Cappelletti (ed.), *New Perspectives for a Common Law of Europe* (Leiden: Sijthoff, 1978), p. 198. See also J.W.F. Allison, *A Continental Distinction in the Common Law* (Oxford: Oxford University Press, 1996), p. 122; David Ibbetson and Andrew Lewis, "The Roman Law Tradition", in A.D.E. Lewis and D.J. Ibbetson (eds), *The Roman Law Tradition* (Cambridge: Cambridge University Press, 1994), p. 9; Donald R. Kelley, "Elizabethan Political Thought", in J.G.A. Pocock (ed.), *The Varieties of British Political Thought, 1500-1800* (Cambridge: Cambridge University Press, 1993), pp. 64-65: "There never was a serious threat of a 'reception' of Roman law [in England], and its political associations [with absolutism and popery] ensured that common lawyers would continue to resist its influence". *Cf.* Heinrich Brunner, "The Sources of English Law" in *Select Essays in Anglo-American Legal History*, t. II (Boston: Little, Brown, 1908), p. 42.

75 The argument claiming that there was once a common law of Europe is typically introduced without empirical foundations and appears reluctant to engage with what it apprehends as uncongenial or dissonant information. E.g.: Zimmermann, "Savigny's Legacy", *supra*, note 51, p. 600; Mireille Delmas-Marty, *Vers un droit commun de l'humanité* (Paris: Editions Textuel, 1996), p. 45. For a critical examination of undocumented argument in academic re-presentation, see generally Richard

vention of Europe, for what has long characterised Europe is precisely the cultural heteronomies within the whole.[76]

Third, to advance the idea of a European Civil Code is utopian, because it suggests that the legal cultures which purport to give normative strength to forms of behaviour developed in historically different contexts can be unified.[77] In fact, a European Civil Code would fail to effect the universal reach for which it stands, if only because the civil-law tradition, as it insists on its universality, is defining this universality in narrowly civilian terms – the common law being co-opted into participation in an experience from which it is specifically excluded, being asked to identify with a selfhood that defines itself in opposition to it, being required ultimately to identify against itself.[78] What good is a common text of reference when one legal tradition, the civil law, institutes the normal – the legislated text – as *its* referential source of law and the other, the common law, institutes the pathological – the case – as *its* prototypical source of law? What good is a common text of reference if it is internalised differently by the two legal traditions which it claims to unify – that is, if it is ascribed a different meaning because of the incompatible epistemologies at work?[79] And how could the internalisation process not differ when one legal tradition, the civil law, operates at the deductive or axiomatic stage, while the other, the common law, functions in the descriptive or inductive mode, which it regards as being most congruent with its sense of morality?[80] What point, then, a unitary text of reference in the absence of a unitary rationality and morality to underwrite and effectuate it? What good is a common rule when one legal tradition, the common law, has not even wished to acknowledge the notion of "rule"?[81] Addressing French civilians, Roger Perrot sounded an important warning: "We rather easily delude ourselves through the idea that men and institutions can be transformed by dint of cleverly examined juridical norms".[82]

F. Hamilton, *The Social Misconstruction of Reality* (New Haven: Yale University Press, 1996). A good illustration of the "confusion" surrounding the matter of *jus commune* appears from two articles by the same author published within a year or so of each other: Reinhard Zimmermann, "Civil Code and Civil Law: The 'Europeanization' of Private Law Within the European Community and the *Re-emergence of a European Legal Science*", 1 Columbia Journal of European Law 63 (1994-95); *Id.*, "Savigny's Legacy: Legal History, Comparative Law, and the *Emergence of a European Legal Science*", *supra*, note 51 [my emphasis].

76 E.g.: Jacques Derrida, *L'autre cap* (Paris: Editions de Minuit, 1991), *passim*.
77 Arnaud, *supra*, note 59, p. 298.
78 "Why can the common law not be civilian?", exclaims Reinhard Zimmermann: "*Statuta sunt stricte interpretanda?* Statutes and the Common Law: A Continental Perspective", [1997] Cambridge Law Journal 315. Needless to say, there is no attempt whatsoever by this author to articulate, clarify, or legitimise the common-law experience. Rather, the point of the article is to assert the superiority of the civil-law tradition with specific reference to the German model.
79 *Cf.* Volkmar Gessner, "Globalization and Legal Certainty", in *Id.* and Ali Cem Budak (eds), *Emerging Legal Certainty: Empirical Studies on the Globalization of Law* (Ashgate: Dartmouth, 1998), p. 436: "The implementation of international conventions is left to the judicial styles of courts and the claim consciousness of parties of different legal cultures in the world".
80 I borrow an argument applied to science in Robert Blanché, *L'épistémologie*, 3d ed. (Paris: Presses Universitaires de France, 1983), p. 65.
81 *Supra*, note 24.
82 Roger Perrot, "De l'empreinte juridique sur l'esprit de la société française", in Siegfried, *supra*, note 31, pp. 191-92 ["*nous nous berçons assez facilement de cette idée qu'on transforme les hommes et les institutions à coup de normes juridiques savamment étudiées*"]. According to Legendre, "the

In point of fact, unity can only arise from a commonality of experience, which assumes a commonality of meaning, which presupposes in turn a symbolic commonality. Meanwhile, "[a]t least until the one great, comprehensive, universal, political truth is revealed and accepted, every legal system is an expression of the culture that called it into being".[83] For example, external influences, rather than generate a kind of immanent rationalisation across legal cultures, lead to a local *métissage* which, because the elements in the mix are specific to a given historicity,[84] is itself idiosyncratic and, in the end, ethnocentric on account of an inevitable domestication process, itself a feature of every legal culture's inherent assimilative capacity.[85] Because a culture functions as an ongoing integrative process, what one encounters by way of an alternative experience is incorporated into an existing framework within which it is readily intelligibilised against the background of the whole, if at the cost of a measure of dissonance reduction. Indeed, the power of a culture inheres in its capacity to absorb data through a didactic of conflict resolution operating in its favour so that a new experience appears to conform to existing structures of thought and belief. This is why every culture continues to articulate *its* moral inquiry according to traditional standards of justification – a phenomenon which economists designate as "path dependence".[86] There is always at work, if you like, an active agent of articulation, and that agent lives locally.[87] (To those who do not like the idea of "culture", I ask: what is your competing model of social cohesion? Or do you not like the idea of "social cohesion" either?[88])

Fourth, the suggestion under consideration is retrograde in that it shows itself to be

---

French, more than any other people, believe in the transformative power of laws": Pierre Legendre, *Trésor historique de l'Etat en France* (Paris: Fayard, 1992), p. 63 [*"Les Français, plus qu'aucun autre peuple, croient à la puissance transformatrice des lois"*].

83 Paul D. Carrington, "Aftermath", in Peter Cane and Jane Stapleton (eds), *Essays for Patrick Atiyah* (Oxford: Oxford University Press, 1991), p. 114.

84 This observation suggests a more general remark: cultural diversity does not rest on cultural autonomy but rather on an original configuration of "interconnections": Ulf Hannerz, *Cultural Complexity* (New York: Columbia University Press, 1992), p. 266.

85 E.g.: F.S.C. Northrop, "The Comparative Philosophy of Comparative Law", 45 Cornell Law Quarterly 617 (1960), p. 657: "in introducing foreign legal and political norms into any society, those norms will become effective and take root only if they incorporate also a part at least of the norms and philosophy of the native society". See, e.g., my "What 'Legal Transplants'?", in David Nelken and Johannes Feest (eds), *Adapting Legal Cultures* (Oxford: Hart, 2001), pp. 55-70.

86 E.g.: Douglass C. North, *Institutions, Institutional Change and Economic Performance* (Cambridge: Cambridge University Press, 1990), pp. 92-100. See also Mark Granovetter, "Economic Action and Social Structure: The Problem of Embeddedness", 91 American Journal of Sociology 481 (1985). A good illustration of the point about cultural resistance is developed by Harald Halbhuber, "National Doctrinal Structures and European Company Law", (2001) 38 Common Market Law Review 1385.

87 E.g.: *L. v. DPP*, [2002] 3 W.L.R. 863 (Q.B.), p. 873: "The common law has traditionally adopted a practical and empirical approach to the questions that come to confront it, and granting the fullest possible weight to the Human Rights Act 1998 and to the Convention it enshrines, there is nothing in them that need compel judges to abandon that approach" (Poole J.). I am indebted to Geoffrey Samuel for this reference.

88 *Cf.* Jerome Barkow, *Darwin, Sex, and Status: Biological Approaches to Mind and Culture* (Toronto: University of Toronto Press, 1989), p. 142: "Culture is not a 'thing', not a concrete, tangible object. [...] To describe behaviour as 'cultural' tells us only that the action and its meaning are shared and not a matter of individual idiosyncrasy".

haunted by the ghosts of 19th-century scholarship's *Begriff*-stricken world. Because it privileges faith in a centralised political authority and in formalist truth, because it intimates that the whole of the law governing the daily lives of citizens can be reduced to a set of neatly-organised rules, a code is not a propitious endeavour for it runs against the more progressive view that law simply can not be captured by a set of rules, that "the law" and "the written rules" do not coexist, and that there is, indeed, much "law" to be found beyond the rules. By adhering to a "law-as-rules" representation of the legal world, a code becomes an epistemological barrier to an appreciation of the complexity of legal knowledge.[89] In other words, a code leads the jurist astray by implying that to have knowledge of law is to have knowledge of rules (and that to have knowledge of rules is to have knowledge of law!). Assuredly, it is not because there is the same *loi* or *Gesetz* (for example, a directive) that there is the same *droit* or *Recht*: *jus* is not reducible to *lex*. In its quest for rationality, foreseeability, certainty, coherence, and clarity, a civil code thus strikes a profoundly anti-humanist note. While the imperatives of certainty must evidently be borne in mind, the common-law experience illustrates that codes are not a prerequisite to their attainment. It is, in any event, simplistic to assume that codes beget certainty.[90] The making of a European Civil Code can only assume an operation performed "[u]nder the hypnotic spell of formal rationality", which gestures in the direction of scientificisation or technicisation and its reductive urge.[91]

A transnational construction like the European Community should rather be seen as offering the opportunity to *break* with the idea of a legal unity enforced in the name of abstract naturalism and to reach *beyond* a mode of apprehending social relations which has traditionally been linked to the state, such as a civil code.[92] Legal positivism and the closed system of codes, which the fetishism of rules commands, must be regarded as obsolete. Law has, after all, resolutely entered the era of complexity. Thus, legal monism (that is, the exclusive and unchallenged supremacy of written law) has given way to a multiplicity of legal sources, or to polyjurality. Likewise, political monism (that is, the unquestioned supremacy of the nation state) has yielded to the persuasion of supra-national and infra-national powers. Moreover, linear and deductive rationality have been replaced, for many, by a critical attitude to-

---

89 For a compelling argument establishing the epistemological inadequacy of the rule model, see Samuel, *supra*, note 37, *passim*. For the concept of "epistemological barrier", or *"obstacle épistémologique"*, see Gaston Bachelard, *La formation de l'esprit scientifique* (Paris: Vrin, 1989), *passim* [1938]. For an application to law, see generally Michel Miaille, *Une introduction critique au droit* (Paris: François Maspero, 1976), pp. 37-68.

90 For a demonstration of this assertion, see James Gordley, "European Codes and American Restatements: Some Difficulties", 81 Columbia Law Review 140 (1981); H.R. Hahlo, "Here Lies the Common Law: Rest in Peace", (1967) 30 Modern Law Review 241.

91 Lawrence M. Friedman and Gunther Teubner, "Legal Education and Legal Integration: European Hopes and American Experience", in Mauro Cappelletti, Monica Seccombe, and Joseph Weiler (eds), *Integration Through Law*, t. I: *Methods, Tools and Institutions*, bk 3: *Forces and Potential for a European Identity* (Berlin: Walter de Gruyter, 1986), p. 373.

92 Arnaud, *supra*, note 59, pp. 198-200 and 202. See also Bruno Oppetit, "Droit commun et droit européen", in *L'internationalisation du droit: mélanges en l'honneur de Yvon Loussouarn* (Paris: Dalloz, 1994), p. 314, who castigates European law for "expressing the most exacerbated legal positivism" [*"(l)e droit européen exprime le positivisme juridique le plus exacerbé"*].

ward thought processes. Finally, profectitious temporality (that is, the idea of time directed toward a future governed by reason and law) has made way for legal forms characterised by precariousness and provisionality.[93]

Fifth, the claims in favour of a European Civil Code are woefully under-theorised and reflect an ideological dogmatism devoid of almost any merit as scholarship. A few illustrations of this *"erudicion á vapor"* must suffice.[94] My first example draws on a paper by Ugo Mattei.[95] Referring in passing to his own work as "most distinguished",[96] this author argues that a European Civil Code means change, that change is inherently a good thing, that a European Civil Code, therefore, must be a good thing, and that any critique of that endeavour can accordingly be dismissed as... not a good thing, that is, in Mattei's words, as "conservative".[97] The extent of Mattei's simplism is well captured by the following sequence: "If we have conservative values, we regret change. [...] If we are progressive, [...] we acknowledge the change".[98] To suggest, as does Mattei, the so-called advocate of change driven by the regulatory and centralising impulse, that Europe's future requires taking a restricted view of the available forms of social ordering, privileging a formalist approach to law, remaining, in short, deeply mired in the kind of constricting positivistic outlook we are all only too familiar with, is extraordinary enough. To clamour for more conceptualism, more systemics, more discontinuity with the lifeworld, without discuss-

---

93 Michel van de Kerchove and François Ost, *Le système juridique entre ordre et désordre* (Paris: Presses Universitaires de France, 1988), p. 116.

94 The phrase is from Juan Bautista Alberdi, *El Proyecto de Código civil para la República Argentina* (Paris: Jouby & Roger, 1868), p. 5, where he refers to Anthoine de Saint-Joseph, *Concordance entre les codes civils étrangers et le Code Napoléon*, 2d ed. (Paris: Cotillon, 1856), 4 vol. – a two-thousand-page variation on the Leibnizian theme of the *theatrum legale* correlating by way of grid charts the legislative provisions of some sixty jurisdictions with those of the French civil code: "he has created instant erudition, mechanical erudition, so to speak, with which history is made almost as easily as music is played on a barrel-organ" ["*ha creado la erudicion á vapor, la erudicion mecánica por decirlo así, con que se hace historia casi con la facilidad con que se toca música en un órgano de Berberie*"]. For Leibniz's comparative ambitions, see Gottfried Wilhelm Leibniz, *Nova methodus discendae docendaeque jurisprudentiae* (Glashütten im Taunus, Germany: Detlev Auvermann, 1974), no. 29, p. 54 [1748]. There are always those who are more impressionable. Indeed, one author praised Saint-Joseph's work for having established "the perfect concordance which exists between the various modern legislations" ["*la parfaite concordance qui existe entre les différentes législations modernes*"] thus showing "how easy it would be to draft a single code for Europe" ["*combien il serait facile (...) de faire un seul code pour l'Europe*"]: Ernest Moulin, *Unité de législation civile en Europe* (Paris: Dentu, 1865), p. vi. This author was apparently unaware of the existence of the common-law tradition and had certainly not read Tocqueville who, visiting England in 1833 and 1835, concluded that it was "unique amongst all modern nations" ["*singularis(é)e (...) au milieu de toutes les nations modernes*"], remarked on the "peculiarities" of its laws, of its spirit, and of its history" ["*les particularités de ses lois, de son esprit et de son histoire*"], and concurred with Montesquieu who had written of England that it "hardly resemble[d] the rest of Europe" ["*(un pays qui) ne ressemble guère au reste de l'Europe*"]: Alexis de Tocqueville, *L'ancien régime et la Révolution* (Paris: Gallimard, 1967), p. 160 [1856].

95 Ugo Mattei and Anna di Robilant, "The Art and Science of Critical Scholarship: Post-Modernism and International Style in the Legal Architecture of Europe", (2002) 10 European Review of Private Law 29.

96 *Id.*, p. 49.

97 *Id.*, p. 29.

98 *Id.*, pp. 44-45.

ing how codification can ever transcend the reification that inevitably follows from the urge toward systematisation and the aspiration to deductive certainty (not to mention the accompanying phenomenon of fixation on the fact and on the letter of the code that comes with the adoption of any theological system) is perhaps taking us somewhere into false consciousness. Does the adoption of a unique model not militate *against* change in the way the presence of competitive models does not? Is it not the case, for example, that the adoption of a unique institutional model of the coherentist type inevitably tends to favour a substantial measure of inertia in the face of social change if only because of the difficulty of generating a consensus around any amendment to the model? Is it not the case, especially in a *dirigiste* context, that the coercive power of homogeneity must see the need to keep contest alive and protect difference by affirmatively encouraging oppositional discourse?[99] There is more. What of Paul B. Stephan's point to the effect that "[n]o matter what the task of technocratic reformers, we must expect interest groups to have the capacity either to thwart rules that they find threatening or to capture the process for their own purposes"? What of Stephan's further point that "[i]nternational unification instruments display a strong tendency either to compromise legal certainty or to advance the agendas of interest groups" such that "[i]n either case they offer no obvious gains as compared to rules produced through the national legislative process"?[100] Where does this leave the European Civil Code? Is it so clear that pan-European codification can express "the 'new'", that it can stand for "progress"?[101] Is there not something to be said, for example, for the fact that diversity in private-law allocations of business risks across European laws reflects diversity in business expectations across national borders, which in turn translates an "embeddedness" of economic transactions within local culture such that the challenge for any pan-European framework is precisely to account for the dissonance of cultural practices of (business) law?[102]

For my second illustration, I borrow from Mathias Reimann who argues that the law of Europe must be that of the civil-law tradition. The author, having observed that "*Europeans* [he means, of course, "civilians"!] tend to submit more willingly to state regulation and to establish legal norms that are relatively general and strict", and having noted that "*[i]n Western Europe* [he means, of course, "on the Continent"!!] [...] the drive to understand the basic concepts is alive and well", concludes that "if Europeans are to pursue the goal of a uniform private law", it remains that "continental jurists must preserve their own civilian tradition".[103] One is left to ponder whether

---

99 For a general argument along these lines, see Jane Mansbridge, "Using Power/Fighting Power: The Polity", in Seyla Benhabib (ed.), *Democracy and Difference* (Princeton: Princeton University Press, 1996), pp. 46-66.

100 "The Futility of Unification and Harmonization in International Commercial Law", 39 Virginia Journal of International Law 743 (1999), p. 788.

101 Mattei and di Robilant, *supra*, note 95, p. 58.

102 For a persuasive argument to the effect that formalism is an unsatisfactory regulatory tool for business transactions, see Hugh Collins, "Formalism and Efficiency: Designing European Commercial Contract Law", (2000) 8 European Review of Private Law 211. To his credit, even a staunch advocate of European codification like Claude Witz shows concern for the demands of localism: "Plaidoyer pour un code européen des obligations", D.2000.Chr.79, p. 82.

103 "American Private Law and European Legal Unification – Can the United States Be a Model?",

Reimann is aware of the presence of the common-law tradition within the European Community and, if he is, what role he ascribes to it.[104]

In my third example, the author is clearly aware of the presence of the common-law tradition in Europe and, in fact, seeks to demonstrate an appreciation for English law with a view to showing his readership what English law is really like (in other words, how English law is really like the civil law).[105] Regrettably (and somewhat pathetically), the author approaches the common-law tradition in general, and English law in particular, uncluttered by any first-hand knowledge whatsoever. As a result, the reader is treated to a slipshod concoction of genuinely extraordinary claims. Thus, in the first two paragraphs of the relevant part of the text, that is, over a mere twenty-six lines and seven footnotes, the author manages to refer to the Royal Courts "invent[ing] the rule of precedent" in order "to impose the common law"; to observe that "contemporary legal evolution in England [...] is characterised by a development of State law and seems to be similar to what may be called a kind of 'codification' of private law"; to note that "[p]rivate law is understood as the law regulating relations between individuals (which is the core of the law in common law countries")"; to inform us that "criminal law [...] [is] already codified by Statute"; to remark that "[t]he legislator can nowadays modify a precedent"; and to underline that "the judge cannot normally disobey a statutory legislation [sic]".[106] There is more along the same lines in the next paragraph and there is worse on the pages that follow. What can one usefully say beyond making the elementary point that the author projects his familiar terms and categories in an attempt to ascribe meaning to a foreign legal experience which he does not, and can not, understand simply by making cursory reference to a hodge-podge of introductory texts (including the well-known student primer by "William Glanvill"!)?[107] Even leaving to one side the author's historical misreadings and simplifications concerning precedential authority, the language of "rule", "State", and "private law", on the one hand (there is also a reference to "the system of common law"),[108] and the images of a "core law" and of a judge "disobeying" the statute, on

---

(1996) 3 Maastricht Journal of European and Comparative Law 217, pp. 229, 231, 234, and 234, respectively [my emphasis].

104 Reimann is far from being alone in seemingly "forgetting" about the common law in Europe. Consider, say, Peter Häberle, *Europäische Rechtskultur* (Baden-Baden: Nomos, 1994). On p. 12, this author identifies four constitutive elements of what he terms a "European Legal Culture": 1. *"Die Geschichtlichkeit"*, or the historical dimension; 2. *"Die Wissenschaftlichkeit-juristische Dogmatik"*, or "dogmatic", that is, doctrinal or didactic legal science (note that the three relevant pages include nine footnotes referring to twenty-two texts, all of them in German); 3. *"Die Unabhängigkeit der Rechtsprechung"*, or the independence of the judiciary; 4. *"Die weltanschaulich-konfessionelle Neutralität des Staates- Religionsfreiheit"*, or the ideological neutrality of states on the matter of confessionality and freedom of religion. Now, there is no "legal science" in England and there is an established Church. How, then, to account for the author's criteria?

105 Anthony Chamboredon, "The Debate on a European Civil Code: For an 'Open Texture'", in Mark Van Hoecke and François Ost (eds), *The Harmonisation of European Private Law* (Oxford: Hart, 2000), pp. 63-99.

106 *Id.*, p. 71.

107 *Ibid.* The theoretical argument about the impossibility of "co-presence" in communication is helpfully summarised in Patricia J. Huntington, *Ecstatic Subjects, Utopia, and Recognition* (Albany: SUNY Press, 1998), p. 299.

108 *Supra*, note 105, p. 70, note 34.

the other – not to mention the striking capitalisation of "Statute" –, reveal cognitive flaws that are nothing short of staggering in a chapter purporting to expatiate with intellectual authority on the matter of legal integration within the European Community. Where does this *"charabia"* leave one? Should one really have to reply to an argument to the effect that recent English statutes have anything in common with codes (apart from also consisting of words, perhaps)? Should one really have to reply to a claim that proves so ignorant of United States or Canadian law as to argue that the non-existent category of "private law" is more significant in New York or in Toronto than, say, constitutional or administrative law? Should one really have to address the point about judicial disobedience and "statutory legislation" (whatever this may mean for the author) and the further statement about statute "nowadays" being able to modify precedent (what was it like *before?*). The very fact that this text was allowed to appear in print, unedited, is extremely revealing and reminds us that civilians actually think they know about the common law and actually feel competent to write about it (in English, if you please) and actually feel able to pronounce on its similarity *vis-à-vis* the civil-law tradition, thereby disclosing a comprehensive attitude *preceding* the facts which are supposed to call it forth. Indeed, why could one not learn about the common law in the very same way one does about the distinction between the *"action paulienne"* and the *"action oblique"*, that is, by reading a few introductory texts squarely focused on the "black-letter" description of the law? Law is a science, is it not? *Le droit est une science, n'est-ce pas? Das Recht ist eine Wissenschaft, nicht wahr?* Yet, the kind of sloppy and jejune "argument" I address can boast at least two virtues. It provides my doctoral students with an example of what comparison-at-law must emphatically *not* be like (although I already had many such illustrations in stock for them). It also points to the outer limits of Donald Davidson's interpretive principle of charity.[109]

My fourth illustration refers to the Joint Response of the Commission on European Contract Law and the Study Group on a European Civil Code to the European Commission's Communication on European Contract Law.[110] It is difficult to imagine that the European Commission would take seriously a report which explains that the Commission on European Contract Law and the Study Group on a European Civil Code "are bringing to light in particular the existence of common European legal norms" while simultaneously asserting that "[e]xamples of [...] dislocations in the effective functioning of the internal market are so numerous that it is hardly possible [...] to provide more than an appropriate selection" and proceeding to devote nearly sixty printed pages to an enumeration of "differences between the contract laws of the Member States" – a presentation which, according to the report itself, "show[s] significant diversity on many fundamental points".[111] The intellectual credibility of this document is not helped by its acknowledgement that the research teams "have not undertaken any empirical studies to assess the magnitude of any of [the] costs"

---

109 *Inquiries into Truth and Interpretation* (Oxford: Oxford University Press, 1984), p. 197.
110 Christian von Bar and Ole Lando, "Communication on European Contract Law: Joint Response of the Commission on European Contract Law and the Study Group on a European Civil Code", (2002) 10 European Review of Private Law 183.
111 *Id.*, pp. 188, 195, 194, and 198, respectively.

repeatedly claimed to be attributable to legal diversity.[112] It is hardly reassuring to be told by the research teams that "[they] consider it to be a safe assumption, supported by anecdotal evidence, that significant cost factors are involved and that these costs factors are operative in practically all sectors of the market economy".[113] Along the same superficial lines, this report informs us that it "do[es] not distinguish between cross-border matters and matters which are purely domestic within one jurisdiction".[114] Apparently, "[t]here is a multitude of reasons for preferring that approach in the creation of binding European private law",[115] although not a single such reason is offered in support of the claim. The report also regrets that "legal terms and their particular nuances vary from jurisdiction to jurisdiction" ("[w]hy should each European legal system have to cope with different concepts of damage?" – why indeed?) and pleads for the creation of a "shared private law vocabulary", while (safely) eschewing the matter of the language in which this vocabulary ought to be formulated (as well as the question of local accents – which, presumably, must also be made to disappear in short order so as better to contain transaction costs!).[116] Most importantly, perhaps, the report advances the view that a common law of Europe can be "impartial", "dispassionate", and "neutral" – a set of assumptions disclosing an unhealthy mixture of credulity and complacency (which I work hard to dispel in my *first-year* students).[117] As for the statement that "[u]ltimately law is only that which is binding and only a binding text will have profound practical impact", it can only leave the reader dumbfounded.[118] One would have thought that even hardened positivists would have acknowledged the profound impact that the various *Restatements* have had on United States law although not in the least binding, especially so in a context where these positivists themselves argue that "all progress in overcoming the outlined problems [arising from legal diversity in Europe] depends on the creation of a restatement of law".[119] Less surprising, however, is the summary disqualification of the common-law tradition on account of its "weaknesses".[120] Since no exemplification has been deemed necessary, I can only suppose that these "weaknesses" are self-evident, that they exist beyond any need to be stated or restated.

Sixth, the idea of a European Civil Code contravenes the letter and – rather more importantly – the ethos of European Community law. The fundamental points underlying the Treaty of Rome are that there should be an opening of economic borders within the European Community; that the Member States should recognise each other's law; and that "market citizens" should have the opportunity to select the legal regulation that best suits them. This structure, therefore, assumes difference across the legal "systems" of the various Member States. Moreover, the Treaty of Rome itself accepts the presence of differences across legal "systems" within Member States,

---

112 *Id.*, p. 198.
113 *Id.*, pp. 198-199.
114 *Id.*, p. 235.
115 *Ibid.*
116 *Id.*, pp. 211 and 230, respectively.
117 *Id.*, pp. 222, 222, and 228, respectively.
118 *Id.*, p. 232.
119 *Id.*, p. 231.
120 *Id.*, p. 234.

for the Treaty's concern with the harmonisation of laws expressed in Article 94 (formerly 100) acknowledges either that these differences are insurmountable or that they ought not to be fully transcended. (In this respect, the doctrine of "direct effect" developed by the European Court of Justice arguably suffers from a legitimacy problem.) Indeed, "harmonisation" does not connote the idea of a "common meeting point" and certainly means neither "uniformity" nor "equivalence". It does not, therefore, require any "convergence" of national laws in order to materialise. The preamble of the 1992 Treaty of European Union and Article 7 of the protocol on subsidiarity and proportionality appended to the 1998 Treaty of Amsterdam both recognise the inevitability or value of legal pluralism as do, in effect, all European directives by conceding a national margin of appreciation to the Member States.[121] Besides, the European Court of Justice, which is entrusted with the interpretation of the Treaty of Rome (as subsequently amended), has no adjudicative power to eliminate differences across the laws of the various Member States not even as regards those Member States' readings of European Community law itself. According to Article 234 (formerly 177) of the Treaty, its role is strictly consultative. Once the European Court of Justice has pronounced on what it regards as the correct interpretation of European Community law, it falls to the national courts, embedded as they are in diverse legal cultures, to apply the law, including European Community law. Again, the structure of this interpretive framework shows how differences across legal "systems" are not meant to be erased. (The European Court of Justice's proactive stance in favour of the assimilation of laws across Member States, therefore, also raises a serious issue of legitimacy.)

***

The European Community represents a particular articulation of universality which is almost entirely market-oriented and economistic, emphasising trade and investment and the economies of production and distribution. In this spirit, the prevailing concern is for the systematic unification of all that is perceived to be calculable and controllable. A symptom of this ethically deficient globalism, or uncreditable cosmopolitanism, is the proposal in favour of a European Civil Code.[122] The paradox, however, is that such universalisation depends on the promotion of a perspective of

---

121 In fact, the piecemeal, at times spasmodic, character of European Community interventions regularly causes the disintegration of "systemic" interdependencies within the various Member States both within law and between law and other discourses. Given that the nature or extent of these discontinuities depends upon the particular discursive configuration governing locally, every Community measure generates new, if unintended, differences *across* the discursive configurations (including law) prevailing in the various Member States. The production of "difference" across Member States is, therefore, inherent to European law-making. See Gunther Teubner, "Legal Irritants: Good Faith in British Law or How Unifying Law Ends Up in New Divergences", (1998) 61 Modern Law Review 11.

122 Another example, taking us beyond Europe, concerns the Unidroit *Principles of International Commercial Contracts*: "The objective of the Unidroit Principles is to establish a balanced set of rules designed for use throughout the world irrespective of the legal traditions and the economic and political conditions of the countries in which they are to be applied": Governing Council of Unidroit, 'Introduction', in Unidroit, *Principles of International Commercial Contracts* (Rome: International Institute for the Unification of Private Law, 1994), p. viii. Meanwhile, of course, the United States and Canadian experiences, amongst others, continue to demonstrate that the success of a common market does not depend on the fashioning of a common commercial law.

the whole which is totally oblivious of the historical fact that legal traditions reveal moral preferences which are culturally embedded and which, on that account, are incompatible and incommensurable, that is, *incommiscible*.[123] In other words, the European Community's agenda in favour of uniformisation rests on the effective denial of sites of contestation within itself. The common-law experience, although it belongs to the universality that is sought, is not allowed to shape the universalisation process; it is, thus, simultaneously empowered and disempowered.[124] In suggesting the adoption of a European Civil Code, civilians foster a modality of experience which is uniquely theirs, for "[c]odification is anathema to the common law mind".[125] In the process, they impugn the common-law tradition and its rationality, an epistemological configuration which demonstrates that there is no historical or practical necessity for a legal culture to operate by way of general rules or under the sway of highly-conceptualised systems and which shows that it is perfectly possible, for example, to "conceive an injury was done one when an impartial spectator would be of opinion he was injured".[126] Why, then, should the common law be made to think of law as a science? Why should common-law lawyers have to learn to think like civilians when both legal traditions are inherently valid and legitimate? But even more is at stake. To expect common-law lawyers to show allegiance to the civilian model while the culture they inhabit continues to propound its moral inquiry according to established standards of justification – "based not on ideas and principles but on tradition, experience, and reasonableness of conduct"[127] – is, in effect, to invite common-law lawyers to surrender cultural authority and to accept unprecedented marginalisation *within their own culture*. And to what extent is it even *possible* for a common-law lawyer to undergo an apostasy? At this juncture, a civilian may test his own capacity for thinking otherwise: if he were entrusted with the codification of the common law, would it ever occur to him to proceed *alphabetically*? Why not? After all, as Bernard Rudden wryly observes, "the alphabet is virtually the only instrument of intellectual order of which the common law makes use"...[128]

---

123 For an apposite illustration of the brand of "incommensurability" I address in the text, see Alasdair MacIntyre, *Whose Justice? Which Rationality?* (Notre Dame, Indiana: University of Notre Dame Press, 1988), p. 380: "The translator from language-in-use A to language-in-use B of [...] a scheme [of naming] will have to explain the scheme of naming in A to those whose language is B in terms of the beliefs of the members of this latter community. The scheme of naming in A, that is, will have to be explained in terms of its differences from naming in B, but so to explain will be to exhibit A's scheme of naming as lacking in justification, as in some ways defective. To understand the translation-plus-explanation into B will entail for those whose language is B rejecting the beliefs so explained". See also Charles Taylor, "Rationality", in Martin Hollis and Steven Lukes (eds), *Rationality and Relativism* (Oxford: Blackwell, 1982), p. 98.

124 See Judith Butler, "Universality in Culture", in Joshua Cohen (ed.), *For Love of Country* (Boston: Beacon Press, 1996), p. 50.

125 Martin Loughlin, *Public Law and Political Theory* (Oxford: Oxford University Press, 1992), p. 47. Even statutes, despite their proliferation, still arouse the diffidence of common-law lawyers. E.g.: Jack Beatson, "The Role of Statute in the Development of Common Law Doctrine", (2001) 117 Law Quarterly Review 247.

126 Adam Smith, *Lectures on Jurisprudence*, ed. by R.L. Meek, D.D. Raphael, and P.G. Stein (Oxford: Oxford University Press, 1978), p. 17 [1762-63].

127 Wieacker, *supra*, note 9, p. 394.

128 Bernard Rudden, "Torticles", 6/7 Tulane Civil Law Forum 105 (1991-92), p. 110. See also Alan

The specificity of Europe lies not in the abolition of difference, but in the deft management of it,[129] in the acceptance of a co-existence of non-harmonised rationalities on its territory, and in the steady practice of a politics of inclusion ensuring an equal presence for the two main legal traditions represented in its midst. If only on ethical grounds, difference must be understood, and the temptation to reduce it resisted.[130] Indeed, Europe's distinctive circumstances throughout its history have repeatedly involved the recognition of insurmountable alterities arising from within.[131] In the words of Jacques Derrida, "the *duty* to answer the call of European memory dictates respect for difference, the idiomatic, the minority, the singular and commands to tolerate and respect everything that does not place itself under the authority of reason".[132] Indeed, this author insists on the fact that "this responsibility toward memory is a responsibility toward the concept of responsibility itself which regulates the justice and the justness of our behaviour, of our theoretical, practical, ethico-political decisions".[133] The aim must now be, therefore, not only to re-activate the aptitude to value difference in Europe, which is disappearing as fast as the move toward a European Civil Code is gaining strength, but moreover to nurture the willingness of civilians to open themselves to a different way of thinking about the law.[134] Of course, a legal tradition can be criticised. But it should first be understood on the epistemological basis of what it takes to be true or correct – which requires that it be taken *seriously* with the benefit of a realisation by the jurist from another tradition of the existence of his own cognitive and affective biases and against a relativisation of his own ontological premises.

If they are not to be placed under a damaging and self-imposed handicap while engaging with a pluricentric world consisting in part of the common-law tradition, civil-

---

Watson, *Legal Transplants*, 2d ed. (Athens, Georgia: University of Georgia Press, 1993), p. 70. E.g.: *The Book of the General Lawes and Libertyes Concerning the Inhabitants of the Massachusets*, ed. by Thomas G. Barnes (San Marino, California: The Huntington Library, 1975) [being a reprint of the 1648 ed.], which ranges from "Abilitie", "Actions", "Age", and "Ana-Baptists" to "Wolves", "Wood", "Workmen", and "Wrecks of the Sea". *Halsbury's*, the leading English legal abridgement, also operates alphabetically.

129 I apply Clifford Geertz, *Local Knowledge* ([New York]: Basic Books, 1983), pp. 215-216.

130 Jean Pouillon, "L'oeuvre de Claude Lévi-Strauss", *Les Temps Modernes*, 1956, No. 126, p. 152.

131 Certeau, *supra*, note 57, p. 202.

132 Derrida, *supra*, note 76, pp. 75-77 [*"le devoir de répondre à l'appel de la mémoire européenne (...) dicte de respecter la différence, l'idiome, la minorité, la singularité (... et) commande de tolérer et de respecter tout ce qui ne se place pas sous l'autorité de la raison"*] (emphasis original).

133 *Id.*, *Force de loi* (Paris: Galilée, 1994), p. 45 [*"Cette responsabilité devant la mémoire est une responsabilité devant le concept même de responsabilité qui règle la justice et la justesse de nos comportements, de nos décisions théoriques, pratiques, éthico-politiques"*].

134 Much sensitisation remains to be done as is shown by a civilian openly rejoicing that the use by the British courts of "a typically common law phenomenon" such as "contempt of court" should have been repudiated "[i]n the European Court of Human Rights, a college of judges mostly of a continental-type professional mould" and that law-making within the European Community, "largely the work of civil law trained jurists", should "becom[e] directly part of British law". What effectively amounts to the countermanding of one experience of legal ordering by another is termed "convergence" and saluted without more ado as "an obvious and natural phenomenon": Alessandro Pizzorusso, "The Law-Making Process as a Juridical and Political Activity", in *Id.*, (ed.), *Law in the Making* (Berlin: Springer-Verlag, 1988), p. 42. The reference to the European Court of Human Rights decision is to the *Sunday Times* case: *Times Newspapers Ltd* v. *United Kingdom*, European Court of Human Rights, 1979, Series A, No. 30 [judgement of 26 April 1979].

ians must show themselves to be receptive to the otherness of the common-law mind, notably (but certainly not exclusively) because it helps them to define *themselves* by directing attention to what they are *not* and, therefore, by illustrating that they are *not* everything there is to be.[135] Civilians must regard the common-law tradition as presenting an alternative *for* them (in the sense of a contrapuntal cognitive and experiential possibility that is defensible and potentially enriching) as opposed to an alternative *to* them (in the sense of an inchoate and impertinent apprehension of the legal that must be regretted and obliterated).

The civil-law world must recognise in the common-law tradition the existence of a different, equally legitimate approach to the assuagement of the human need for order rather than see in it nothing more than a peripheral – and, therefore, expendable – phenomenon. Civilians must attempt to penetrate the web of meaning of the common-law tradition and of the European societies it has served through its past and present historical conditions, that is, to learn to empathise with, or even admire, the common-law world as "an anthropological reality of extraordinary complexity".[136] Specifically, European civilians who, to borrow from George Steiner, live with the common law "in the brittle familiarity of mere acquaintance",[137] could reflect with profit on the profound merits of a legal tradition which does not necessarily expect its expositors to be acting, in the words of Pierre Legendre,[138] as mere "children of the text" and which can, therefore, accommodate a critique that "understands and analyzes the law not simply for professional ends but also as a specific genre of human relationship and as an activity or form of life".[139] But perhaps in seeking to assimilate the common-law tradition, civilians are actually succumbing to the repressed desire to liberate themselves from the tutelage of Justinian whose Digest – not to mention his ban against commentaries on it – continues to confine academics throughout the civil-law world to the drone of the *repetitor?*

The reflection which these interrogations invites is, of course, vastly more complicated than designing a "cognitive intoxicant" such as a European Civil Code with a view to smothering the common-law world within a largely immutable and unified system of concepts and categories through the institution of a homogeneous legal culture.[140] Fidelity to the historical situation itself demands that the civil-law and common-law discourses, each with its own internal grammar, be apprehended as reflecting different world-views and be acknowledged as entitled to pursue their respective realisation. The central question remains: how can they each be accommodated *on their own terms* so that one is not found to be doing violence, even insidiously, to the other? Clearly, syntheses can also be forged from the distances and differences between the constituent points, and not only by the old method of

---

135 See Homi K. Bhabha, *The Location of Culture* (London: Routledge, 1994), p. 52

136 Ugo Mattei, *Common Law: il diritto anglo-americano* (Turin: UTET, 1992), p. 3 [*"una realtà antropologica di straordinaria complessità"*].

137 George Steiner, "Cake", in *The Deeps of the Sea and Other Fiction* (London: Faber & Faber, 1996), p. 202 [1964].

138 Pierre Legendre, *Les enfants du texte* (Paris: Fayard, 1992).

139 Goodrich, *supra*, note 6, p. 8. For excellent illustrations of the kind of inquiry I have in mind, see Murphy, *supra*, note 20; David Sugarman, *In the Spirit of Weber: Law, Modernity, and "The Peculiarities of the English"* (Madison, Wisconsin: Institute for Legal Studies, University of Wisconsin-Madison Law School, 1985).

140 The expression is Schneider's: *supra*, note 26, p. 40.

centralised regulation. In the name of respect for culture and for *mentalité* – in the name of respect for the *life of the law* itself – Europe as it seeks to define a new legal order must identify referents that are beyond the two main legal *mentalités* and that are also of them. It must privilege a politics of imagination and sensitivity which might well take the form, for example, of a centrifugal construct, a decentralisation that would be better attuned to the thick texture of relationships, events, and places – rather than a centripetal legal integration based on the formulation of authoritative rules divorced from their socio-historical rationales and the practical context within which they operate.[141]

If I may be permitted some etymological word-play, let me suggest that the way forward for European legal integration does not lie with *Ordnung*, but rather with *Ortung*. As *"Ord-"* suggests *"Reihe"* and *"Rang"*, *"Ort-"* connotes *"Spitze"*, that is, by extension, *"Gegend"* and *"Platz"*. What is needed is, indeed, a focus on the law as it is situated, as it is located. What is wanted is an accentuation of the *"Ort-"* of the law, a re-assertion of the *genius loci*. A strategy of European legal integration for today is one that will feature Keats's "negative capability", a "quality" he regarded as "form[ing] a Man of Achievement" and which is present "when man is capable of being in uncertainties, Mysteries, doubts".[142]

The French philosopher, Jean-François Lyotard, has written that our times – which he refers to as the "postmodern" era (not a period that enjoys the virtue of easy definability) – reveal an incredulity toward meta-narratives.[143] Such scepticism, it is to be fervently hoped, will find itself reinforced in the face of the extravagant irresponsibility that would be involved in the adoption of a European Civil Code which represents, at least etymologically, a *diabolical* idea.[144] As Michael Green recalls, "[a] civilization [...] attempts to melt down different peoples, ethnic groups, and cultures who do not share the same fundamental beliefs, values, and attitudes into a common framework of beliefs and values"; "[i]t attempts to break down intrinsic and organic systems of meaning and replace them with those of the dominant culture".[145] But simple formulas will not solve complex situations. That different meanings and practices should flow from a unitary text, for example, ought not to surprise, because globalisation of the world can not change the reality of varied historical traditions. This is why the feasibility of European legal integration rapidly becomes as problematical as the idea of integration of European societies itself. The integration of a group of legal cultures does not appear any more realistic than would the integration of the different world-views privileged by a wide range of societies. *How, indeed, can indigenous ways of thinking that have contributed crucial ingredients of person-*

---

141 E.g.: Stephen Toulmin, *Cosmopolis* (Chicago: University of Chicago Press, 1990), p. 206.

142 [John Keats], *The Letters of John Keats*, ed. by Hyder Edward Rollins, t. I (Cambridge, Mass.: Harvard University Press, 1958), p. 193 [being a letter to his brothers, George and Tom Keats, dated 21 or 27 December 1817].

143 *La condition postmoderne* (Paris: Editions de Minuit, 1979), pp. 7-8. A stimulating introduction to postmodernism is offered by Charles Jencks, *What is Post-Modernism?*, 4th ed. (London: Academy Editions, 1996).

144 A "symbol" is a sign that unites. I call a "diabol" a sign that divides, for instance, a European Civil Code fostering the estrangement of the common law from a European Community in thrall to the civil-law ethos.

145 Michael K. Green, "Codes of Civilization and Codes of Culture", in Roberta Kevelson (ed.), *Codes and Customs* (New York: Peter Lang, 1994), pp. 112 and 113, respectively.

hood, that have supplied a sense of self-esteem and identity, that have defined success within a community be unified? In the face of a globalisation that operates in a deracinating world of contracts, transaction costs, and externalities, it falls to identity politics to fulfil a humanising role and to admonish posited law to recognise its own limits in acknowledgement of the fact that allegiance to a legal tradition is a defensible way of organising one's place in the moral universe.

"Cultural Pluralism or Brave New Monotony?", asks Paul Feyerabend.[146] For the self-respecting comparatist, envisaging as he must law as culture, cherishing as he must the value of difference as *principium comparationis*, and advocating as he must a morality of alterity by reading legal traditions *against* one another and by rejecting the strategy of compulsive reduction of otherness to sameness, the reply should be easy. In the face of incommensurability across legal traditions, the *understanding of diversity* must be seen as the only way to attenuate the heterogeneity of meaning that acts as an impediment to communication and to foster the respect due the variety of lived experiences that sustain (inter)subjective world-views and practices across European interpretive communities. The civil-law and common-law discourses, each with its own internal grammar, *must* be apprehended as reflecting different world-views. The question is: how can each of them be accommodated on their own terms so that one is not found to be doing violence to the other, that is, to be *terrorising* the other?[147] Charles Taylor offers useful guidance: "the adequate language in which we can understand another society is not our language of understanding, or theirs, but rather what one could call a language of perspicuous contrast".[148]

To stress difference as a value, to militate in favour of the recognition, respect, and implementation of difference in all its complex ramifications, is not to subvert the Enlightenment commitments to human emancipation and liberty and is not *a fortiori* to insist upon a return to a pre-Enlightenment cast of mind which denied parity for all before the law and favoured exclusion based on status. Nor is it to promote indifferentist relativism or to stand against Europeanisation or to display pessimism. My argument lies elsewhere. Given that the diversity of legal traditions and the diversity of forms of life in the law they embody remain the expression of the human capacity for choice and self-creation, I seek affirmatively to encourage oppositional discourse in the face of a totalitarian rationality which, while claiming to pursue the ideal of impartiality by reducing differences in the lifeworld to calculative and instrumental unity, effectively privileges a situated standpoint – that favouring regulation and juridification – which it allows to project as universal.[149] I contend that this exercise

---

146 Paul Feyerabend, *Farewell to Reason* (London: Verso, 1987), p. 273. For an insightful reflection on this theme, see Hugh Collins, "European Private Law and the Cultural Identity of States", (1995) 3 European Review of Private Law 353.

147 *Cf.* Lyotard, *supra*, note 143, p. 103: "Terror means the efficiency derived from the elimination or the threat of elimination of a partner out of the game of language we were playing with him. He will be silent or will assent not because he has been disproved, but because he has been threatened not to be allowed to play" [*"On entend par terreur l'efficience tirée de l'élimination d'un partenaire hors du jeu de langage auquel on jouait avec lui. Il se taira ou donnera son assentiment non parce qu'il est réfuté, mais menacé d'être privé de jouer"*].

148 Charles Taylor, *Philosophy and the Human Sciences: Philosophical Papers 2* (Cambridge: Cambridge University Press, 1985), p. 125.

149 *Cf.* Seyla Benhabib, *Situating the Self* (Cambridge: Polity Press, 1992), pp. 152-153: "Universalistic

must be apprehended for the fiction that it is and that one must accept, therefore, that a universalisation can only prove persuasive if it will work *through* difference rather than against it by acknowledging as equally meaningful each legal tradition's characteristic discursive formation. Only in deferring to the non-identical can the claim to *justice* be redeemed.

Today's comparatists in law faculties throughout Europe are expected to subscribe to a script of underlying European unity and ultimate European transcendence where particularism is assumed to be epiphenomenal and fated to play but a peripheral role in the future of human affairs. It is easy to sympathise with the desire for a more orderly, circumscribed world. The obsession to find and impose order possibly answers a most basic human drive (in fact, the common law is an order too – as is the alphabet). But it is quite another thing to underwrite the search for a monistic unifying pattern not unlike the Platonic or Hegelian belief in a final rational harmony, that is, to endorse reason acting as the corrosive solvent of custom and allegiance. And this is why the programmatic engagement that I advocate must aim for a relentless disruption of the immoderate confidence in regulatory formalisation somnolently reiterated by those who seek to rob the law of its historical integrity. Should I repeat that in the face of the purported elimination of differentiated sites of deliberation with a view to facilitating the *imperium* of assimilationist efficiency, my conviction in the enabling virtuosity of participatory pluralism is anything but naive, for I appreciate that one of the integrationists' animating desires as they pursue their irredeemably suburban enterprises is specifically to avoid gaining contextual knowledge and thick understanding. Indeed, such cognitive deficit is constitutive of "doing law" for these individuals, which means that remedying one's ignorance by addressing the complex questions that have been avoided heretofore can hardly be a genuine option as this would entail that one is no longer "doing law": "to be really good at 'doing law', one has to have serious blind spots and a stunningly selective sense of curiosity".[150] As I have suggested elsewhere, civilians may well prove, ultimately, to be uneducable.[151]

---

moral theories in the Western tradition from Hobbes to Rawls are substitutionalist, in the sense that the universalism they defend is defined surreptitiously by identifying the experiences of a specific group of subjects as the paradigmatic case of the human as such".

150 Pierre Schlag, *The Enchantment of Reason* (Durham, N.C.: Duke University Press, 1998), p. 140. For a textbook example of the avoidance strategy which Schlag stigmatises, see von Bar and Lando, *supra*, note 110. But see, for example, Teubner, *supra*, note 121; Nicholas Kasirer, "*Lex*-icographie *mercatoria*", 47 American Journal of Comparative Law 653 (1999); *Id.*, "The Common Core of European Private Law in Boxes and Bundles", (2002) 10 European Review of Private Law 417; Yves Lequette, "Quelques remarques à propos du projet de code civil européen de M. von Bar", D.2002.Chr.2202.

151 "Are Civilians Educable?", (1998) 18 Legal Studies 216. In the years since this article was written, which I have spent living and teaching in two civil-law jurisdictions, it has become increasingly clear to me that one must dispense with any expression of doubt. For a recent observation to the same effect, see Barbara Herrnstein Smith, *Belief and Resistance* (Cambridge, Mass.: Harvard University Press, 1997), p. 119: "For those who conduct their intellectual lives primarily or exclusively through transcendental rationalism, that set of densely interconnected, mutually reinforcing ideas (claims, concepts, definitions, and so forth) operates as a virtually unbreachable cognitive and rhetorical system, or, one might say, as a continuously self-spinning, self-repairing, self-enclosing web. [...] Everything in the system fits together tightly and securely. Whatever does not fit *into* the system is identified by the system as irrelevant or unauthentic. [...] The rigorous, unremitting work of Reason creates a tight, taut web, intertextual and interconceptual" [emphasis original].

CHAPTER 15

The "Social" Side of Contract Law and the New Principle of Regard and Fairness

Brigitta Lurger*

1   Status Quo of European and National Contract Law

1.1   The EC-Directives

Since the second half of the 1980s, the EC has adopted a number of directives which protect the interests of consumers in a contractual setting. The first was, in 1985, the Doorstep Selling Directive.[1] It was followed by the Consumer Credit Directive in 1987,[2] the Unfair Contract Terms Directive in 1993,[3] the Timesharing Directive in 1994,[4] the Distance Selling Directive in 1997,[5] the Injunctions Directive in 1998,[6] and the Consumer Guarantees Directive in 1999.[7] The final step so far was the adoption of the Distance Selling Directive for Financial Services in 2002.[8] Besides these eight directives, further directives have to be taken into account which also realise consumer protection, but which not only protect consumers but also businesses as customers. Among those are: the Advertising Directives,[9] the Product Liability Directive,[10] the Insurance Directives,[11] the Package Travel Directive,[12] the Credit

---

*   Dr. Brigitta Lurger, Univ.-Prof. Mag., LL.M. (Harvard), Universität Graz
1   Directive 85/577/EEC of 20 December 1985 to protect the consumer in respect of contracts negotiated away from business premises, *OJ* 1985 L 372, p. 31.
2   Directive 87/102/EEC of 22 December 1986 for the approximation of the laws, regulations and administrative provisions of the Member States concerning consumer credit, *OJ* 1987 L 61, p. 14.
3   Directive 93/13/EEC of 5 April 1993 on unfair terms in consumer contracts, *OJ* 1993 L 95, p. 29.
4   Directive 94/47/EC of 26 October 1994 on the protection of purchasers in respect of certain aspects of contracts relating to the purchase of the right to use immovable properties on a timeshare basis, *OJ* 1994 L 280, p. 83.
5   Directive 97/7/EC of 20 May 1997 on the protection of consumers in respect of distance contracts, *OJ* 1997 L 144, p. 19.
6   Directive 98/27/EC of 19 May 1998 on injunctions for the protection of consumers' interests, *OJ* 1998 L 166, p. 51.
7   Directive 1999/44/EC of 25 May 1999 on certain aspects of the sale of consumer goods and associated guarantees, *OJ* 1999 L 171, p. 12.
8   Directive 2002/65/EC of 23 September 2002 concerning the distance marketing of consumer financial services and amending Directives 97/7/EC and 98/27/EC, *OJ* 2002 L 271, p. 16.
9   Directive 84/450/EEC of 10 September 1984 relating to the approximation of the laws, regulations and administrative provisions of the Member States concerning misleading advertising, *OJ* 1984 L 250, p. 17; Directive 97/55/EC of 6 October 1997 amending Directive 84/450/EEC concerning misleading advertising so as to include comparative advertising, *OJ* 1997 L 290, p. 18.
10 Directive 85/374/EEC of 25 July 1985 on the approximation of the laws, regulations and administrative provisions of the Member States concerning liability for defective products, *OJ* 1985 L 210, p. 29, amended by Directive 99/34/EC of 10 May 1999, *OJ* 1999 L 141, p. 20.
11 Directive 92/49/EEC of 18 June 1992 on the coordination of the laws, regulations and administrative provisions of the Member States relating to direct insurance other than life assurance and amending

Transfer Directive[13] and the E-Commerce Directive.[14] A few Directives include protective provisions only in favour of entrepreneurial parties: the Commercial Agents Directive[15] and the Late Payment Directive.[16]

Almost all of the mentioned directives were based on the Internal Market competence of Art. 95 EC-Treaty, respectively on old Art. 100a and – before its insertion into the Treaty – on old Art. 100 EC-Treaty. Considering that all but one[17] of the consumer protection directives are so-called "minimum directives" permitting the Member States to keep or introduce stronger protective measures in favour of the consumer or other customer, their positive impact on the functioning of the Internal Market and their capacity to improve, simplify and promote cross-border trade and competition on the European market can be questioned. Their main aim is more the improvement of the protection of the consumer or weaker party in the Member States and not so much the improvement of the functioning of the Internal Market. Recent decisions of the European Court of Justice (ECJ) concerning the use of Art. 95 EC-Treaty as a basis of competence for Community measures[18] raise serious doubts as to the legality of the use of this competence norm for consumer protection directives.[19]

The point to be made here is that a remarkably large part of the customer protection introduced into contract law by the directives mentioned is not meant to protect or to protect *only* consumers, but operates in favour of businesses as contract parties. The protection of the directives reaches from the commercial agent to the insurance client, the capital investor and bank customer, to the businessman booking a package travel arrangement, the e-commerce customer and the creditor in general. The most common reason for the introduction of protective measures in favour of business clients is the lack of specialised knowledge in the respective branch of business on the side of the customer who is confronted with a contract party who is an expert in the field. Sometimes also the market power or the superior negotiating power of the other party stand behind a protective provision.

Directives 73/239/EEC and 88/357/EEC, *OJ* 1992 L 228, p. 1 (third non-life insurance Directive); Directive 92/96/EEC of 10 November 1992 on the coordination of the laws, regulations and administrative provisions of the Member States relating to direct life assurance and amending Directives 79/267/EEC and 90/619/EEC, *OJ* 1992 L 360, p. 1 (third life assurance Directive); since 19 December 2002 Directive 2002/83/EC of 5 November 2002, *OJ* 2002 L 345, p. 1, is in force and replaces Directive 92/96/EEC.

12 Directive 90/314/EEC of 13 June 1990 on package travel, package holidays and package tours, *OJ* 1990 L 158, p. 59.

13 Directive 97/5/EC of 27 January 1997 on cross-border credit transfers, *OJ* 1997 L 43, p. 25.

14 Directive 2000/31/EC of 8 June 2000 on certain legal aspects of information society services, in particular electronic commerce, in the Internal Market, *OJ* 2000 L 178, p. 1.

15 Directive 86/653/EEC of 18 December 1986 on the co-ordination of the laws of the Member States relating to self-employed commercial agents, *OJ* 1986 L 382, p. 17.

16 Directive 2000/35/EC of 29 June 2000 on combating late payment in commercial transactions, *OJ* 2000 L 200, p. 35.

17 Distance Selling Directive for Financial Services 2002.

18 ECJ 5 October 2000 (Tobacco Advertising Directive) Case C-376/98 (Germany/Parliament and Council), *ECR* 2000, I-8419.

19 W-H Roth, Europäischer Verbraucherschutz und BGB, *Juristenzeitung* 2001, p. 477; Lurger, *Grundfragen der Vereinheitlichung des Vertragsrechts in der Europäischen Union*, Wien 2002, pp. 81 *et seq.*

This expansion of protection of parties in European contract law – and also in national contract law – which reaches far beyond the protection of consumers, has led *Grundmann* to reconsider the term of "consumer protection" altogether: He suggested to rename the whole field of consumer or customer protection and call it simply "market law" or "exterior business law" ("Marktrecht", "Unternehmensaußenrecht").[20] He considers this market or exterior business law, which deals with the contractual relations of businesses with other market actors – consumers or others, to be part of general civil law. *Franz Bydlinski* argues on the same lines when he denies the notion of the consumer and the idea of consumer protection the ability to produce the necessary interior and exterior systematic for the formation of a special sub-discipline of private law.[21] The same result is reached by a recent study by *Krejci*.[22]

The key question for a future European Civil Code or European Contract Code is, therefore, not only if and how to include consumer protection law into its basic concepts and principles, but if and how to include the whole field of *customer* protection into its contract law rules. What is the role of protective provisions in contract law in general? Are they a mere exception or the rule? How can their scope be defined? Should and how can their fragmented and selective character that is caused by the directives be transformed into more general concepts in order to fit into a codification of contract law? Where are the limits for a protective approach to contractual relations?

1.2 National Contract Law

A majority among the EU Member States possess a codified contract law which is often part of a general codification of civil law.[23] In many cases this codification dates back to times when consumer protection was not an issue. In some countries, the first individual measures of consumer protection were adopted as early as around the end of the 19th century.[24] Most of the national consumer protection legislation, however, which, over time developed into a more comprehensive protection system, was not adopted earlier than in the 70s and 80s of the former century. The most common approach to consumer protection legislation was and still is not to integrate these new measures into the general codification of contract law, but to place them in sepa-

---

20 Grundmann, Verbraucherrecht, Unternehmensrecht, Privatrecht – warum sind sich UN-Kaufrecht und EU-Kaufrechts-Richtlinie so ähnlich?, *Archiv für die civilistische Praxis* 202 (2002), pp. 40 (43, 56 *et seq.*); Grundmann, Europäisches Handelsrecht – vom Handelsrecht des laissez faire im Kodex des 19. Jahrhunderts zum Handelsrecht der sozialen Verantwortung, *Zeitschrift für das gesamte Handelsrecht und Wirtschaftsrecht* 163 (1999), pp. 635 (668 *et seq.*); Grundmann, The Structure of European Contract Law, *European Review of Private Law* 2001, pp. 505 (515 *et seq.*); as "Unternehmensaußenrecht" (exterior business law) in Grundmann, *Europäisches Schuldvertragsrecht*, Berlin / New York 1999, part 1, notes 14 *et seq.*

21 F. Bydlinski, *System und Prinzipien des Privatrechts*, Wien 1996, pp. 718 *et seq.*

22 Krejci, Ist das Verbraucherrecht ein Rechtsgebiet?, in: Eccher/Nemeth/Tangl (Ed.), *Verbraucherschutz in Europa, Festgabe für Heinrich Mayrhofer*, Wien 2002, pp. 120 *et seq.*

23 Like in France, Belgium, Italy, Spain, Portugal, Greece, Netherlands, Austria, Germany.

24 An example is Austria: Schuhmacher, *Verbraucher und Recht in historischer Sicht*, Wien 1981, pp. 55 *et seq.*; Kalss/Lurger, *Rücktrittsrechte*, Wien 2001, pp. 35 *et seq.* with further references.

rate statutes. These specialised statutes most often deal with only one contract type or with a specific situation in which protection is needed (e.g. consumer credits, credit sale, doorstep selling, general contract terms). From the 70s until now, the number of single protection statutes grew constantly and, in the last two decades, came under the strong influence of the EC directives. As in EC legislation, the scope of protective measures was expanded to many groups of customers who are not consumers, but businesses.

Soon, the vast number of separate regulations made the field obscure and they were justifiably criticised for their confused, unsystematic and sometimes even contradictory character.[25] Some countries, such as Austria,[26] Spain,[27] France[28] and Greece,[29] introduced "Consumer Protection Acts" in which they tried to collect more or less all protection measures in favour of consumers. These consumer protection acts are not systematic codifications of consumer contract law, but rather compilations of protective provisions which by their character often remain fragmentary and incoherent. Nor do they include protective measures in favour of business customers. The consumer acts approach of these countries and the specialised statutes approach of many others have in common that the notion of consumer is not mentioned or dealt with in any place in the Civil Code. The fields of protective contract law in favour of consumers and customers and of the (much older) „general" or „ordinary" contract law are kept as two separate bodies of law. Nevertheless, the „ordinary" contract law applies as a general basis also to consumer and other separately regulated contracts and supplements the fragmentary character of the specialised protective statutes.

Most recently, some Member States adopted a new approach to consumer protection, namely the inclusion of protective provisions in their civil codes: Forerunners were the Dutch. The parts on obligations and property law of the Nieuwe Burgerlijk Wetboek (NBW) entered into force in 1992 and cover commercial as well as consumer contract law.[30] Consumer protection rules are not collected in a separate chapter of the Code, but are to be found in many different places among the „ordinary" rules: as e.g. in the provisions concerning general contract terms (Arts. 6:236 ff NBW), the sales contract (Arts. 7:5 f, 7:11, 7:13, 7:18, 7:21, 7:24 f, 7:28, 7:35 NBW), the personal guarantee (Arts. 7:857 ff NBW), package travel arrangements (Arts. 6:500 ff NBW), product liability (Arts. 6:185 ff NBW) and misleading advertising (Arts. 6:194 ff NBW).

In 2000, the Germans introduced the notions of „consumer" and „entrepreneur" to their Civil Code (§§ 13, 14 BGB) before they integrated, in 2002, as part of a comprehensive modernisation of their law of obligations,[31] the whole set of EC consumer

---

25 Lurger, *Vertragliche Solidarität*, Baden- Baden 1998, pp. 58 *et seq.*; Kalss/Lurger, *Rücktrittsrechte*, Wien 2001, pp. 12 *et seq.*; Bourgoignie, Propositions pour une loi générale sur la protection des consommateurs en Belgique, *Revue européenne de droit de la consommation* 1997, pp. 97 *et seq.*

26 Konsumentenschutz-Gesetz 1979, BGBl 1979/140 as amended by BGBl I 2002/111.

27 Ley General para la defensa de los consumidores y usuarios, BOE Nr 176/1984.

28 Code de consommation, L. No 93-949 du 26 juillet 1993, D. No 97-298 du 27 mars 1997.

29 Statute No 2251/94, Etk No 191/16 November1994.

30 Hondius, in: Heusel (Ed.), *Neues europäisches Vertragsrecht und Verbraucherschutz*, Trier 1999, p. 19.

31 „Schuldrechtsmodernisierungs-Gesetz", 26 November 2001, BGBl I, p. 3138, in force as of 1 January 2002.

protection directives into their code:[32] In the German BGB you now find the rules on unfair clauses in pre-formulated and general contract terms (§§ 305-310), on doorstep selling, distance selling and e-commerce contracts (§§ 312-312f BGB, Art 339 ff EGBGB), on the rights of withdrawal (§§ 355-359), timesharing contracts (§§ 481-487), consumer credits (§§ 491-507), warranties in general (amended under the influence of the directive) and consumer warranties in sales contracts (§§ 433-445, 474-479, 633-651) and on package travel contracts (§§ 651a-651m). The method of this massive integration of consumer protection rules into the civil code rather resembles that of a compilation, not that of a real codification or systematisation. This can be easily explained by the short time of preparation and encountered justified criticism by the literature.[33]

In Italy, the Unfair Contract Terms Directive and the Consumer Guarantees Directive were implemented by insertion of new provisions in the Codice Civile (Arts. 1469 *bis* – 1469 *sexies*; 1519 *bis* – 1519 *nonies*[34]), which mainly replicate the text of the Directives and do not strive for coherence with the general contract law of the code. Insurance contracts are regulated by the Code, whereas other rules of consumer and customer protection can be found in separate statutes.[35] The Swiss Codification („Obligationenrecht" – OR) contains a few separate sections dealing with consumer protection issues (such as doorstep selling and credit sales in Arts. 40a-40f, 226a-227h OR). All other consumer protection legislation is located in separate statutes. The Austrian Civil Code does not mention consumers at all, all provisions pertaining to consumers are collected in a Consumer Protection Act. But the implementation of the Consumer Guarantees Directive recently led to a reform of the general rules on warranties and guarantees in the Civil Code (§§ 922-933b ABGB) with special provisions for consumers having been inserted in the Consumer Protection Act.[36] The Scandinavian Member States, Denmark, Sweden, and Finland, have strong and early national traditions of consumer protection. Apart from that, the unified Contract Act of those countries contains in its § 36 a wide general clause enabling the judge to annul or modify unfair contracts in favour of one of the parties. The narrower general clause of § 33 allows for the annulment of contracts concluded under such circumstances which make the reliance on the contract appear a violation of good faith. Due to these general clauses and other provisions of the Contract Act, the idea of party

---

32 Schulze/Schulte-Nölke, Schuldrechtsreform und Gemeinschaftsrecht, in: Schulze/Schulte-Nölke (Ed.), *Die Schuldrechtsreform vor dem Hintergrund des Gemeinschaftsrechts*, Tübingen 2001, pp. 1 (17 *et seq.*); Dörner, Integration des Verbraucherrechts in das BGB, in: Schulze/Schulte-Nölke (Ed.), *Die Schuldrechtsreform vor dem Hintergrund des Gemeinschaftsrechts*, Tübingen 2001, p. 177 (179 ff.).

33 W-H Roth, Europäischer Verbraucherschutz und BGB, *Juristenzeitung* 2001, p. 475 (489); Micklitz, Vertragsschlußmodalitäten, in: Micklitz/Pfeiffer/Tonner/Willingmann (Ed.), *Schuldrechtsreform und Verbraucherschutz*, Baden-Baden 2001, pp. 191 (194, 240 *et seq.*).

34 D.Lv. 2.2.2002, n. 24 implementing the Consumer Guarantees Directive 1999/44/EG.

35 As for example: D.P. R 24.3.1988, n. 224 (product liability); L. 10.4.1991, n. 126 (consumer information); D.Lv. 15.1.1992, n. 50 (door-to-door selling); D.Lv. 25.1.1992, n. 73 and D.Lv. 17.3.1995, n. 115 (product safety); usury statutes (L. 7.3.1996, n. 108, D.P. R. 29.1.1997, n. 51, D.P. R. 11.7.1997, n. 315, L. 23.2.1999, n. 44); D.Lv. 15.3.1995, n. 111 und D. 23.7.1999, n. 349 (package tours); L. 30.7.1998, n. 281 (collective legal protection, injunctions); D.Lv. 9.11.1998, n. 427 (timesharing); D.Lv. 1999, n. 181 (distance selling contracts).

36 BGBl I 2001/48 (Gewährleistungsrechtsänderungs-Gesetz); in force as of 1 January 2002.

protection (which is not restricted to consumers) appears to be also solidly rooted in general contract law.[37] The dividing line, therefore, between general contract law and special protection statutes for consumers appears to be less marked in the Scandinavian countries than in other Member States.

In most Member States a strong tension between the older general rules of contract law, centering on the traditional principle of freedom of contract, and the huge number of specialised protective legislation in favour of consumers and other customers, which severely limits private autonomy, can be observed. About 95 per cent of all contracts are concluded between businesses or between businesses and consumers.[38] In some countries, the general contract law rules of the respective Civil Codes apply, without any qualifications and limitations by special legislation, only to contracts between two consumers, i.e. to about 5 per cent of all contracts, because special rules for commercial contracts are to be found in the Commercial Codes („Handelsgesetzbuch", „Code de commerce", „Código de Commercio"), and special rules for consumer contracts in the various consumer protection statutes. In all countries, specialised legislation in favour of consumers and other customers contributes a great deal to the massive decrease in importance of the contract law of the Civil Codes.[39] Many countries also deplore the unsystematic and fragmentary nature of EC legislation which is at odds with the principles and aims of their national general contract law.[40] The EC directives show "disintegrative" effects on the exterior and interior system of national private law.[41] The rules of the directives and the national rules of

---

37 § 36 Contract Act serves as a basis for Wilhelmsson's theory of "social force majeure": Wilhelmsson, "Social Force Majeure" – A New Concept in Nordic Consumer Law, *Journal of Consumer Policy* 13 (1990), pp. 1 *et seq.*; Wilhelmsson, Need-Rationality in Private Law?, *Scandinavian Studies in Law* 33 (1989), pp. 227 *et seq.*

38 Grundmann, Verbraucherrecht, Unternehmensrecht, Privatrecht – warum sind sich UN-Kaufrecht und EU-Kaufrechts-Richtlinie so ähnlich?, *Archiv für die civilistische Praxis* 202 (2002), p. 40 (68).

39 Roth, Transposing "Pointillist" EC Guidelines into Systematic National Codes – Problems and Consequences, *European Review of Private Law* 6 (2002), p. 761 (774); Basedow, *Die Reform des deutschen Kaufrechts*, Köln 1988, p. 87; Irti, *L'età della decodificazione*, Mailand 1980, p. 36.; Remy, La recodification civile, Droits, *Revue française de théorie, de philosophie et de culture juridiques* 26 (1998), pp. 4, 10 *et seq.*; Pizzio, La protection des consommateurs par le droit commun des obligations, *Revue trimestrielle de droit commercial et de droit économique* (1998), pp. 56 *et seq.*; Collard-Dutilleul/Delbecque, Contrats civils et commerciaux, *Précis Dalloz*, vol. 3., Paris 1996, note 5; Terré/Simler/Lequette, Droit civil – les obligations, *Précis Dalloz*, vol. 7, Paris 1999, note 9 (pp. 11 *et seq.*); Cornu, L'évolution des contrats en France, *Revue internationale de droit comparé* 1979, see the special issue of Journées de la Société de législation comparée, pp. 447 *et seq.*; Wilhelmsson, Consumer Protection and the Rules and Principles of General Contract Law, in: Wilhelmsson, *Twelve Essays on Consumer Law and Policy*, Helsinki 1996, pp. 129 *et seq.*; Behr, Das BGB im Jahr 2096, in: Schlosser (Ed.), *Bürgerliches Gesetzbuch*, Heidelberg 1896-1996 (1997), pp. 205 *et seq.*; Joerges, *Verbraucherschutz als Rechtsproblem*, Heidelberg 1981, pp. 57, 126 *et seq.*; Joerges, Der Schutz des Verbrauchers und die Einheit des Zivilrechts, *AG* 1983, pp. 66 *et seq.*

40 Roth, Transposing "Pointillist" EC Guidelines into Systematic National Codes – Problems and Consequences, *European Review of Private Law* 6 (2002), pp. 761 (767 *et seq.*).

41 Joerges, Desintegrative Folgen legislativer Harmonisierung: ein komplexes Problem und ein unscheinbares Exempel, in: Schulte-Nölke/Schulze (Ed.), *Europäische Rechtsangleichung und nationale Privatrechte*, Baden-Baden 1999, pp. 205 *et seq.*; Christoph Schmid, Desintegration und Neuordnungsperspektiven im europäischen Privatrecht, in: *Jahrbuch Junger Zivilrechtswissenschaftler*, Stuttgart 1999 (2000), pp. 33 (34 *et seq.*); The difference between outer and inner system of private law goes back to Heck, *Begriffsbildung und Interessenjurisprudenz*, Tübingen 1932, pp. 139 *et seq.*;

contract law are – in contrast to national special statutes and the rules of the codification – not assigned to each other in an exterior system.[42] Additionally, EC rules are not in harmony with internal principles and values of national contract law. This results in internal contradictions and the pressure to adjust national rules to the intruding "alien element", a "legal irritant" as the phenomenon was called by *Gunther Teubner*.[43]

1.3 Main Categories of Protection Instruments

There definitely is a need for further systematisation of the often incoherent or even contradictory field of consumer and customer protection on the national as well as on the EC level. The recently published Action Plan of the EC Commission "A More Coherent European Contract Law"[44] emphasises this necessity and proposes further measures to achieve this goal. The Commission indicates that time has come for a serious systematisation and consolidation of contract law directives rather than for a further expansion of the protective regime to additional situations or contracts. One first contribution to this effort can be made by dividing the protection instruments used in the directives – and also in autonomous national law – into five main categories: duties to inform, rights of withdrawal, mandatory interventions in the contractual stipulations (like control of unfair terms or mandatory contents of the contract), formal requirements, and provisions concerning the burden of proof. The order of the first three instruments reflects the intensity by which they limit the private autonomy of the parties:

The provision regarding the duty to inform is the „softest" of all instruments, because it least interferes with the freedom of contract of the parties. Information obligations improve the quality of the contractual decision of a responsible customer. After the receipt of the information, they leave the customer to the general rules of contract law, especially to the principle of *"pacta sunt servanda"*. Some neo-liberal authors as well as some exponents of economic analysis of law recommend limiting the protection of weaker parties, as much as possible, to improving the quality of their information. Information obligations occupy an important position even in relatively progressive consumer protection systems, like the Austrian, German or Scandinavian, which in addition rely heavily on more intrusive protective measures.

However, according to the prevailing view in Europe, the duty to inform is not sufficient to effectively protect weaker parties in some situations. The directives as well as autonomous national provisions therefore introduced a number of rights of withdrawal in favour of consumers and customers. They serve different goals: they allow for the undoing of a subjectively wrong contract decision made by a consumer or cus-

---

further: Larenz/Canaris, *Methodenlehre der Rechtswissenschaft*, vol. 3 (1995), pp. 263; Canaris, *Systemdenken und Systembegriff in der Jurisprudenz*, vol. 2, Berlin 1983, pp. 19, 40 *et seq.*; F. Bydlinski, *System und Prinzipien des Privatrechts*, Wien 1996, pp. 9, 31 *et seq.*

42 Christoph Schmid, Desintegration und Neuordnungsperspektiven im europäischen Privatrecht, in: *Jahrbuch Junger Zivilrechtswissenschaftler*, Stuttgart 1999 (2000), p. 33 (37).

43 Teubner, Legal Irritants: Good Faith in British Law or How Unifying Law Ends up in New Divergencies, *Modern Law Review* 61 (1998), pp. 11 *et seq.*

44 12 February 2003, COM(2003) 68 final.

tomer in a situation of surprise or over-haste, or when there was a lack of information or a lack of understanding of the weight and the long-term character of a contractual commitment. In some jurisdictions, the exercise of a right of withdrawal is also possible in cases of mistakes about future events, when the entrepreneur unilaterally modified the content of the contract, or as some sort of notice of termination in long-term contracts. Rights of withdrawal generally supplement and perfect the provision of information and the protection of the freedom of decision of the customer; they sometimes go further and sanction unfavourable and burdensome contracts with their termination.[45] If rights of withdrawal are employed by the legislator in a restrained and functional manner, the intensity of their interference with the freedom of contract lies between that of information duties and mandatory interventions in the contractual stipulations. If they are granted too generously they allow for opportunistic and unfair behaviour by the customer.

The problems with the duties to inform and rights of withdrawal lie in their great number, their almost unlimited diversity and in their fragmentary character. The great number of duties to inform often leads to high costs for the ascertainment of the legal situation, to legal uncertainty and also to their ineffectiveness, because a customer who has been showered with information, does not actually know much more afterwards. The different regulation of the details of these protection instruments as well as their provision in the one and not in another similar situation often lack reasonable justification.

The interventions in the contractual stipulations by mandatory legal provisions consist of (a) fixation of parts of the rights and duties of the parties by the law, which cannot be modified by party agreements less favourable to the customer, and of (b) the control of the (pre-formulated and other) terms of the agreement by general clauses or a list of unfair terms exemplifying the general clause. Both types of provisions constitute relatively sharp limitations of freedom of contract.

Formal requirements are often employed to make one of the first three instruments more effective. They, for instance, increase the value of information the entrepreneur has to provide to the customer.[46] Or they go beyond this merely supplementary function and serve an independent goal, as the protection of the customer from haste, the non-deliberate entry into a one-sided and burdensome commitment (such as a personal guarantee) or the protection of both parties from problems of proof. Meanwhile, the great number and diverse shaping of formal requirements is only a little less worrying than that of the duty to inform and rights of withdrawal: They also create legal uncertainty and contain unjustified differentiations. The shifting of the burden of proof to the entrepreneur is a somewhat rarely used instrument. It aims to favour the enforcement of rights by consumers and other weaker parties.

Rights of withdrawal and interventions in the contractual content strongly undermine the principle of *"pacta sunt servanda"*. Due to the unclear and confusing legal situation, businesses often do not know whether a contract concluded with a customer will „hold" or not.

---

45 Kalss/Lurger, Zu einer Systematik der Rücktrittsrechte insbesondere im Verbraucherrecht, *Juristische Blätter* 1998, 89-97 (part 1), 153-174 (part 2), pp. 219-233 (part 3); Kalss/Lurger, *Rücktrittsrechte,* Wien 2001, pp. 39 *et seq.*

46 Mankowski, Formvorschriften und Europäisches Privatrecht, in: Schulte-Nölke/Schulze (Ed.), *Europäisches Vertragsrecht im Gemeinschaftsrecht,* Trier 2002, p. 181 (201).

2 The New Principle of Contract Law and What to Call It

2.1 The Characteristics of the New Principle

The legal status quo of "protective contract law" as outlined above raises difficult questions not only on the level of coherence and clarity of the individual provisions and on the level of the implementation of directive provisions in the respective national systems, but also on the level of principles. The two areas of traditional general contract law and of the younger customer protection law have been kept separate in most legal systems, including EC law, because they are not based on the same set of values and principles: In traditional contract law freedom of contract is considered the dominant principle, whereas customer protection statutes focus on the partial restriction of this freedom in order to realise their protective goals. Recent developments of integration of consumer protection rules in the codifications of contract law in the Member States (see section 1.2. above) express the justified conviction of those states that, at the present stage, a reintegration and systematisation of the whole of contract law must take place in order to avoid much of the problems described above.[47] At the very beginning of this process, on the European as well as on the national level, lies the task of reconstruction of the set of basic values of contract law, or, in other words, the clarification of the relationship between the principle of freedom of contract and protection of the parties.[48]

Both the huge practical importance of those parts of contract law that serve the protection of the interests of weaker parties and also their being anchored in the constitutional systems of many Member States and the EU, lead me to the conclusion that "party protection" or "protection of contractual fairness" can be nothing less than a principle of contract law, to be situated on the very same level as the principle of freedom of contract and without any signs of subordination to the latter.[49] The enormous practical importance of protection of the parties in contract law is evidenced not only by the broad field of customer protection as described so far, but also by other fields, such as labour law and the protection of tenants. The catalogues of fun-

---

47 Möllers, European Directives on Civil Law – The German Approach: Towards a Re-codification and New Foundation of Civil Law Principles, *European Review of Private Law* 6 (2002), p. 777 (785); Lurger, Integration des Verbraucherrechts in das ABGB?, in: Fischer-Czermak/Schauer (Ed.), *ABGB – auf dem Weg in das 3. Jahrtausend, Reformbedarf und Reform,* Wien 2003 (forthcoming).

48 Lurger, Prinzipien eines europäischen Vertragsrechts: liberal, marktfunktion, solidarisch oder ...?, *Electronic Journal of Comparative Law* (March 1998) vol 2.1, http://law.kub.nl/ejcl/art21-1.html; Lurger, *Grundfragen der Vereinheitlichung des Vertragsrechts in der Europäischen Union,* Wien 2002, pp. 393 *et seq.*

49 Lurger, *Grundfragen der Vereinheitlichung des Vertragsrechts in der Europäischen Union,* Wien (2002), pp. 241 *et seq.,* 376 *et seq.;* Lurger, *Vertragliche Solidarität,* Baden- Baden 1998, pp. 132 *et seq.;* Lurger , Prinzipien eines europäischen Vertragsrechts: liberal, marktfunktional, solidarisch oder ...?, *EJCL* 1998, http://law.kub.nl/ejcl, pp. 7 *et seq.;* Lurger, Grundfragen der Vereinheitlichung des Vertragsrechts in der Europäischen Union, in: Martiny/Witzleb (Ed.), *Auf dem Wege zu einem Europäischen Zivilgesetzbuch,* Berlin/ Heidelberg 1999, p. 141 (155 *et seq.*); Hesselink, *Principles of European Contract Law,* Deventer 2001, pp. 49, 53 *et seq.;* Hesselink, The Horizontal Effect of ‚Social Rights' in European Contract Law, Paper presented at the conference „Diritti fondamentali e formazione del diritto privato europeo" at the Università Roma III, on 18 June 2002.

damental rights of many Member States include rights which correspond not only to the principle of contractual freedom, but also to the principle of party protection: as e.g. general guarantees of social solidarity,[50] consumers' and workers' rights,[51] the protection of human dignity, the general right to protection of personality ("Persön-lichkeitsrecht") or the right to equality.[52] These fundamental rights often not only bind the legislator, but also exercise indirect horizontal effects through the general clauses of contract law (good faith, good morals etc, see below). And they serve as guidelines for the interpretation of existing, and the development of new, contract law rules. According to Art. 6 EU Treaty, the Community respects the common constitutional traditions of the Member States and the European Convention on Human Rights. Express social rights can be found in the European Charter of 18 October 1961[53] and in the Community Charter of Fundamental Social Rights of Workers of 1989,[54] to which the Community and the EU feel attached (Art. 136 EC Treaty, Sect. 4 Preamble of EU Treaty). On 7 December 2000, the European Parliament, the Council and the Commission with the approval of the European Council proclaimed the "Charter of Fundamental Rights of the European Union" as formulated by the European Convention. This comprehensive Charter, which does not yet have formally binding force, will henceforth – voluntarily – be taken into account by the EU institutions and is intended to become part of a future EU Constitution.[55] Chapters I to III of the EU Charter contain classical freedom rights. The general "right of liberty and security" of Art. 6 also covers the protection of freedom of contract, probably also in the wider sense of protection of the "material" contractual freedom of weaker parties. Chapter IV on solidarity and social rights does not formulate a similar general right (as Art. 6). It contains a number of fundamental rights of workers and rights of access to several public social, health and education services. In its Art. 38 the Charter confirms the principle of consumer protection.

This new principle of contract law developed as the reverse side of a formally understood freedom of contract, which latter – in its most extreme form – was shaped by the economic liberalism of the 19th and early 20th centuries. The protection principle aims to compensate the limited or completely missing substantive freedom of decision of a weaker contract party; sometimes it even succeeds in the restoration of this freedom of decision. When the market mechanism or other factors do not motivate one party to treat the other party fairly and considerately, this fairness and regard

---

50 E.g.: Art. 2 of the Italian Constitution; Arts. 20, 28 of the German Grundgesetz.
51 E.g.: Arts. 40-51 of the Spanish Constitution; Arts. 19-23 of the Dutch Grondwet; Preamble of the French Constitution of 27 October 1946.
52 Lurger, *Grundfragen der Vereinheitlichung des Vertragsrechts in der Europäichen Union*, Wien 2002, pp. 241 *et seq.*; Hesselink, *Principles of European Contract Law*, Deventer 2001, pp. 49, 53 *et seq.*; Hesselink, The Horizontal Effect of 'Social Rights' in European Contract Law, Paper presented at the conference „Diritti fondamentali e formazione del diritto privato europeo" at the Università Roma III, on 18 June 2002.
53 529 UNTS Nr 89; ETS Nr 35; for further references see: Samuel, *Fundamental Social Rights*, Strasbourg 2002; Prouvez, The European Social Charter, an Instrument for the Protection of Human Rights in the 21st Century?, *International Commission of Justice Review* 1997, pp. 30 *et seq.*
54 ABl Nr C 120/51 *et seq.* = EuGRZ 1989, pp. 205 *et seq.*
55 Philippi, *Die Charta der Grundrechte der Europäischen Union*, Baden-Baden 2002, p. 16 with further references.

must be imperatively prescribed by the law. Thereby, the freedom of contract of one party is limited for the benefit of the other party. The two principles of contractual freedom and party protection and fairness are in *partial conflict* with each other: Mandatory protective provisions, in particular the duty to inform, can succeed in restoring the full substantive freedom of contract of the weaker party and thereby render any further intervention into the contractual stipulations unnecessary. Additionally, the exercise of regard and fairness can also be in the interest of and thus intended by the entrepreneur, who wants to win new and keep old customers. If this is not the case (no restoration of contractual freedom, no self-interest of the business to comply with standards of fairness) mandatory protective provisions must intervene directly in order to compensate the weaker party's restricted freedom at the expense of the freedom of the entrepreneur. Only in this latter situation does a direct conflict between the two principles arise.

The idea of a more or less one-sided protection of the interests of one of the parties can also be found in various parts of the traditional contract law codes:[56] examples are the general principles of good faith, "good morals" and unconscionability ("Treu und Glauben",[57] "bonne foi",[58] "buona fede",[59] "regole della correttezza",[60] "redelijkheid en billijkheid",[61] "gute Sitten",[62] "bonnes moeurs"[63] "buon costume",[64] "goede zeden",[65] §§ 33, 36 of the Nordic Contract Law[66] etc), in the *"laesio enormis"* provision (§§ 934, 935 Austrian ABGB), the change of circumstances provisions, the notice of termination in long-term contracts and the breach of contract rules.[67] The principle is not restricted to mandatory legal provisions. Dispositive law is not a set of neutral fall-back rules, but secures the material balance, the regard and fairness in contractual relations. It has guiding and justice functions.[68] In the area of control of

---

56 For the German BGB see: Dörner, Integration des Verbraucherrechts in das BGB, in: Schulze/ Schulte-Nölke (Ed.), *Die Schuldrechtsreform vor dem Hintergrund des Gemeinschaftsrechts*, Tübingen 2001, p. 177 (178) with further references; for the Austrian ABGB: Lurger, *Vertragliche Solidarität*, Baden- Baden 1998, p. 85, 133 *et seq.*; Lurger, *Grundfragen der Vereinheitlichung des Vertragsrechts in der Europäischen Union*, Wien 2002, pp. 353 *et seq.*

57 § 242 German BGB; § 241 BGB establishes the general duty of the parties to show regard ("Rücksicht") for the rights, legal "goods" ("Rechtsgüter") and interests of the other party.

58 Art. 1134 French Code Civil.

59 Arts. 1337, 1366, 1375 Italian Codice Civile.

60 Art. 1175 Italian Codice Civile.

61 Book 6 Art. 248 Dutch NBW.

62 § 138 German BGB, § 879 Austrian ABGB.

63 Art. 1133 French Code Civil.

64 Arts. 1343, 1418 Italian Codice Civile.

65 Book 3 Art 40 Dutch NBW.

66 See section 1.2 above.

67 Lurger, Grundfragen der Vereinheitlichung des Vertragsrechts in der Europäischen Union, in: Martiny/Witzleb (Ed.), *Auf dem Wege zu einem europäischen Zivilgesetzbuch*, Berlin/Heidelberg 1999, p. 141 (155 ff.); Lurger, *Grundfragen der Vereinheitlichung des Vertragsrechts in der Europäischen Union*, Wien 2002, pp. 353 *et seq.*

68 „Leit-, Ordnungs- und Gerechtigkeitsfunktionen": Kramer, Funktion, rechtliche Problematik und Zukunftsperspektiven der Innominatverträge, in: Kramer, *Zur Theorie und Politik des Privat- und Wirtschaftsrechts,* Wien 1997, pp. 147 (162 *et seq.*); Raiser, *Das Recht der Allgemeinen Geschäftsbedingungen* Hamburg 1935, Neudruck 1961, pp. 293 *et seq.*; Ennecerus/Nipperdey, *Allgemeiner Teil*

unfair clauses in general or pre-formulated contract terms, the dispositive contract law develops – at least according to the Austrian and German doctrines – indirectly mandatory effects:[69] Hereby, the greater the difference in power between the parties, the less the stronger party may depart from the dispositive model.[70]

2.2 The New Principle as Part of a Larger Spectrum of Innovations in Contract Law

The new principle of party protection is one key element of a larger spectrum of innovations in contract law that developed over the last decades:

(1)   The EC fundamental freedoms led to a process of rationalisation, functionalisation and policy orientation in contract law.[71] What counts with respect to the fundamental freedoms are not traditions of regulation and formal or abstract concepts, but the functional orientation of the norms with respect to the Internal Market. Thereby, a perspective is introduced to national contract law that was non-existent before. This process reinforces the general materialisation of contract law triggered by the protection idea. Protective provisions also lead to a decline of the abstract nature of contract law and the notion of contract by taking into account various special circumstances of the contract and the qualities of the parties.

(2)   Another characteristic of modern contract law is the care for the material balance of the contract during the time of contract conclusion and during performance.

(3)   The binding force of the contract is often unilaterally relaxed in favour of a weaker party.

(4)   Transparency and information occupy a central role in contract law.

(5)   Third parties are integrated in the distribution of contractual responsibility (e.g. responsibility of the seller for the producer's advertising, three or multi party contracts[72]). These latter developments relativise the central idea of traditional

---

des Bürgerlichen Rechts I/2, vol. 15, Tübingen 1959/1960, pp. 1011 ff.; Lurger, *Vertragliche Solidarität*, Baden- Baden (1998), pp. 85, 116.

69   Kramer, Die „Krise" des liberalen Vertragsdenkens, in: Kramer, *Zur Theorie und Politik des Privat- und Wirtschaftsrechts*, Wien 1997, pp. 69 (113 *et seq.*); P Bydlinski, Beschränkung und Ausschluss der Gewährleistung, *Juristische Blätter* 1993, pp. 560 *et seq.*; Basedow, Über Privatrechtsvereinheitlichung und Marktintegration, in: Immenga/Möschl/Reuter (Ed.), *FS für Mestmäcker*, Baden-Baden 1996, p. 355.

70   Kramer, (Die „Krise" des liberalen Vertragsdenkens, in: Kramer, *Zur Theorie und Politik des Privat- und Wirtschaftsrechts*, Wien 1997, p. 69 (114)) calls this phenomenon "relative Geltungsintensität" (relative intensity of applicability).

71   Lurger, Konflikte um Macht und Wissen als Grundelemente von Vertragstheorie und Verfassungswirkungen, in: *Jahrbuch Junger Zivilrechtswissenschaftler*, Stuttgart 1995 (1996), p. 17 (36); Hesselink, *The New European Legal Culture*, Deventer 2001, pp. 73 *et seq.*; Joerges, Die Europäisierung des Privatrechts als Rationalisierungsprozess und als Streit der Disziplinen, *Zeitschrift für europäisches Privatrecht* 1995, p. 181; Christoph Schmid, Desintegration und Neuordnungsperspektiven im europäischen Privatrecht, in: *Jahrbuch Junger Zivilrechtswissenschaftler*, Stuttgart 1999 (2000), p. 35.

72   Three or more party contracts, as e.g. several banking transactions, credit sales agreements, are

contract doctrine, the principle of *pacta sunt servanda*. They give rise to a flexible contract law which intensifies the competition between the different enterprises, and has been, for that reason, called "competitive" contract law.[73] Furthermore, the traditionally very sharply drawn line between the moment of contract conclusion and the stage of contract performance gets blurred.

(6)   The legal interests protected by contract law are expanded to cover all financial interests and the substantive freedom of decision of the weaker party.[74] This elevation of the substantive freedom of decision of the weaker party to an officially protected value of contract law was recently laid down expressly in the new § 241 (2) of the German BGB in the form of an obligation of the other party to show regard for this freedom.

2.3   What Should it be Called?

The new principle of "party protection" is closely linked to notions such as fairness, regard, good faith, material balance of the agreement, and co-operation between the parties. It amounts to a general obligation of one party not to act exclusively in her/his self-interest, but to have regard for the needs and interests of the other party. This obligation shows traces of "altruism"[75] and "solidarity",[76] but is not a fully fledged form of these. Both terms are expressions of rather extreme forms of unselfishness. The term "solidarity" is closely associated with certain phenomena in ethics, sociology and public law. If applied to contract law, the term "solidarity" could mislead the reader to expect that such kind of contract law would deal with transfers of assets from richer to poorer parties, with sacrifices of groups of society made in support of other groups, or it could evoke the false impression that "contractual solidarity" is the same as a communitarian view of private law.[77] The traditional term of "solidarity"

---

extremely important in practice, but are (almost) ignored by the traditional civil codes. There is a definite necessity for legislative action.

73   Micklitz, Der Vertragsbegriff in den Übereinkommen von Brüssel und Rom, in: Schulte-Nölke/Schulze (Ed.), *Europäisches Vertragsrecht im Gemeinschaftsrecht*, Trier 2002, pp. 39 (41 *et seq.*); Micklitz, Ein einheitliches Kaufrecht für Verbraucher in der EG?, *Europäische Zeitschrift für Wirtschaftsrecht* 1997, p. 236; Micklitz, Die Fernabsatzrichtlinie 97/7/EG, *Zeitschrift für Europäisches Privatrecht* 1999, pp. (875) 885; Kalss/Lurger, *Rücktrittsrechte*, Wien 2001, p. 130.

74   Kalss/Lurger, *Rücktrittsrechte*, Wien 2001, p. 129.

75   "Altruism" is a term used by CLS: see Dalton, *An Essay in the Deconstruction of Contract Doctrine*, Yale Law Journal 94 (1985), pp. 997 (999 *et seq.*, 1032, 1065 ff., 1094 *et seq.*); Kennedy Duncan, *Form and Substance in Private Law Adjudication*, Harvard Law Review 89 (1976), pp. 1685 (1712 *et seq.*, 1733); Kennedy Duncan, *The Political Stakes in "Merely Technical" Issues of Contract Law*, European Review of Private Law 5 (2001), pp. 7 (13 *et seq.*); Singer, *The Player and the Cards: Nihilism and Legal Theory*, Yale Law Journal 94 (1984), pp. 1 (30, 46 ff.); Gordon, *New Developments in Legal Theory*, in: Kairys (Ed.), The Politics of Law, New York 1982, p. 281 (288); Feinman, *The Significance of Contract Theory*, Cincinnati Law Review 58 (1990), p. 1283 (1311); Kelman, A Guide to Critical Legal Studies, Cambridge 1987, pp. 54 *et seq.*

76   Lurger, *Vertragliche Solidarität*, Baden-Baden 1998, pp. 132 ff.; Lurger, *Grundfragen der Vereinheitlichung des Vertragsrechts in der Europäischen Union*, Wien 2002, pp. 373 *et seq.*; Hesselink, *Principles of European Contract Law*, Deventer 2001, pp. 49, 53 *et seq.*

77   Walzer, The Communitarian Critique of Liberalism, *Political Theory 1*, Cambridge 1990, p. 6; Benhabib, Autonomy, Modernity, and Community: Communitarianism and Critical Social Theory in Dialogue, in: Honneth/McCarthy (Ed.), *Zwischenbetrachtungen im Prozeß der Aufklärung. Jürgen*

has already so many established meanings and connotations that do not really or not completely coincide with the role and functioning of customer protection in contract law. It is therefore not advisable to use this old pre-defined term for a rather recently established principle of contract law.[78]

A terminological alternative can be found in the works of *Wilhelmsson* who uses the term "social contract law".[79] Here again it must be stated that, even though the author describes exactly what I here called customer protection and protection of the weaker party, the term "social" is commonly understood in a sense which is not convergent with our contract law principle. Customer protection is not a measure of social policy in the traditional sense: It does not only concentrate on the protection of the really poor and needy. The low social position of a party can play a certain role, but is not the central justification for protective measures in contract law, whereas traditional social policy measures see neediness as the main basis for transfer payments or similar distributive measures. Additionally, the whole of contract law is not "social", it is still also individualistic and allows for the operation of the principal of private autonomy.[80]

I suggested, therefore, to call the new contract principle "principle of regard and

---

Habermas zum 60.Geburtstag Frankfurt/M 1989, p. 385; Zahlmann (Ed.), *Kommunitarismus in Diskussion*, Berlin 1992; Honneth (Ed.), *Kummunitarismus*, vol. 2, Frankfurt am Main 1994; Gutmann, "Keeping 'em down on the farm after they've seen Paree": Aporien des kommunitaristischen Rechtsbegriffs, *Archiv für Rechts- und Sozialphilosophie* 83 (1997), p. 38 with further references; von Kube, The Legitimacy of the Communitarian Critique – or: Can a Liberal Theory of Social Justice Accomodate the Public Trust Doctrine?, *Archiv für Rechts- und Sozialphilosophie* 83 (1997), p. 68 with further references.

78 Lurger, *Grundfragen der Vereinheitlichung des Vertragsrechts in der Europäischen Union*, Wien 2002, pp. 373 *et seq.*

79 Wilhelmsson, *Social Contract Law and European Integration*, Aldershot 1995; Wilhelmsson, Questions for a Critical Contract Law – and a Contradictory Answer: Contract as Social Cooperation, in: Wilhelmsson (Ed.), *Perspectives of Critical Contract Law*, Aldershot 1993, pp. 9 *et seq.*; Wilhelmsson, Control of Unfair Contract Terms and Social Values: *EC and Nordic Approaches, Journal of Consumer Policy* 16 (1993), pp. 435 *et seq.*; Wilhelmsson, "Social Force Majeure" – A New Concept in Nordic Consumer Law, *Journal of Consumer Policy* 13 (1990), pp. 1 *et seq.*; Wilhelmsson, Need-rationality in Private Law?, *Scandinavian Studies in Law* 33, Dartmouth 1989, pp. 223 *et seq.*; Wilhelmsson, The Philosophy of Welfarism and its Emergence in the Modern Scandinavian Contract Law, in: Brownsword/Howells/Willhelmsson (Ed.), *Welfarism in Contract Law*, Aldershot 1994, pp. 63 *et seq.*; Wilhelmsson, Consumer Images in East and West, in: Micklitz (Ed.), *Rechtseinheit oder Rechtsvielfalt in Europa? Rolle und Funktion des Verbraucherrechts in der EG und den MOE-staaten*, Baden-Baden 1996, pp. 53 *et seq.*; Wilhelmsson, Consumer Protection and the Rules and Principles of General Contract Law, *Journal of Behavioral and Social Sciences* 38 (1992), pp. 150 *et seq.* = Wilhelmsson, *Twelve Essays on Consumer Law and Policy*, Helsinki 1996, pp. 120 *et seq.*; Wilhelmsson, Consumer Law and Social Justice, in: Ramsay (Ed.), *Rethinking Consumer Law in the Global Economy* (1997) = Wilhelmsson, *Twelve Essays on Consumer Law and Policy*, Helsinki 1996, pp. 191 *et seq.*; Wilhelmsson, Contribution to a Green Sales Law, in: Wilhelmsson, *Twelve Essays on Consumer Law and Policy*, Helsinki 1996, pp. 267 *et seq.*; Wilhelmsson, Critical Studies in Private Law: *A Treatise on Need-rational Principles in Modern Law*, Dordrecht 1992; Lurger, *Grundfragen der Vereinheitlichung des Vertragsrechts in der Europäischen Union*, Wien 2002, pp. 427 *et seq.*

80 Lurger, *Grundfragen der Vereinheitlichung des Vertragsrechts in der Europäischen Union*, Wien 2002, p. 376.

fairness" ("Rücksichtnahme und Fairness").[81] The most proper translation of the German word „Rücksichtnahme" would be „consideration", a term which cannot be used because of its traditional legal meaning of „counter-performance" (doctrine of consideration of common law systems). The terms "regard and fairness" avoid unwanted associations with broad general solidarity or social policy and name two key elements of the new obligations of the parties. The parties are not meant to fully co-operate in the contract, to completely give up their own interests (altruism), or to behave in accordance with solidarity or social ideas in the traditional sense. What is expected of them is to behave fairly (in good faith) and to take into consideration the interests of the other side.

3   How Does the Principle of Regard and Fairness Operate?

3.1   The Limitation of the Two Main Principles as the Key Question for a Future Contract Code

The description and naming of the new principle that is – at least partially – the counter-principle to the principle of freedom of contract does not solve one central question: how far should we go in protecting "weaker" parties and in demanding regard and fairness of the other side? When is the pursuit and promotion of a party's own interests still legitimate, and when is it to be considered unfair and inconsiderate? The answer to this question is of great import not only for the proper functioning of our markets, which are to a great extent driven by individualistic choices of free market actors, but also for the shaping of large areas of social life: What conditions can customers expect in their professional or every day consumer markets? From which dangers are they protected and from which not? Which of their interests and choices will be supported by the law?[82]

The question of where to set the limits to contractual freedom, on the one hand, and to the obligations of regard and fairness, on the other, is not a rare or exceptional question, but rather a very frequent question occuring almost everywhere in the discipline. A few examples:

(1)   How far does the duty to inform the customer go? Does the entrepreneur have to take into account the visibly extreme lack of knowledge and experience of a customer, e.g. by telling her/him that the product is actually not the one she/he needs or is not the cheapest on the market? To gather information often requires talent and financial resources. Would it, therefore, not be economically more efficient and also fair to be able to profit from one's own information by not disclosing it to the other party?

(2)   How far can rights of withdrawal go, how far can their time limits be ex-

---

81 Lurger, *Grundfragen der Vereinheitlichung des Vertragsrechts in der Europäischen Union*, Wien 2002, pp. 376 *et seq.*

82 Collins, *The Law of Contract*, vol. 3, London 1997, pp. 9, 22, 101 *et seq.*; Collins, Social Market and the Law of Contract, *Archiv für Rechts- und Sozialphilosophie-supplement* 49 (1992), pp. 85 *et seq.*

tended?[83] In which situations can rights of withdrawal and the implied limitations of the other party's freedom be justified by the protection of the customer's material freedom of decision or other interests?

(3)   When may contract law intervene in the contents of the contractual stipulations of the parties considering that the customer is already protected by many duties to inform and by a right of withdrawal? Which parties still have to be protected against their own contractual choices in such a situation? Is the image of a dependent, ignorant, not self-responsible, hasty consumer justified or does the rather harsh restriction of contractual freedom hamper the proper functioning of the market? Do interventions in the contents of the agreement really (only) protect the material freedom of choice of the customer or can they legitimately also serve other goals, such as the protection of the financial interests of the customer or the realisation of distributive justice?

(4)   Who should bear the risk for a lack of information or for a mistake of one party? Which are the interests really protected by the rules of mistake? This leads back to the question of how much information an entrepreneur can be required to give, but also to the question of how far the law can go in securing a materially balanced exchange or distributive justice.

(5)   If a party, due to a change of circumstances, is unable to perform or loses any interest in the contract should she/he bear loss or damages or should she/he be helped by the other party? If a weaker party is completely unable to pay back her/his loan because of an unexpected deterioration of her/his social and financial situation, should the loss be partially shifted to the creditor? *Wilhelmsson* and *Reifner* answer this latter question in the affirmative (*social force majeure*).[84]

(6)   What is a breach of contract and what is not (dispositive law)? If, e.g., the buyer cannot resell the products because they do not comply with safety or health standards on her/his market should she/he be able to hold the seller liable? How far should the remedies for breach of contract go and how strongly should they take into account the interests of the breaching party? Should opportunistic behaviour (e.g. "efficient breach") of one of the parties be allowed, or mildly or severely sanctioned?

The search for an appropriate limitation of the two principles of freedom of contract and regard and fairness is, on the one hand, of great significance for the reform and future development of the national contract law systems of the Member States. As described above (ch. 1.2.), in many countries the separate development of a special con-

---

83 EuGH 13.12.2001, Case C-481/99 (Heininger/Bayerische Hypo- und Vereinsbank AG), *ECR* 2001 I-9945.

84 Wilhelmsson, "Social Force Majeure" – A New Concept in Nordic Consumer Law, *Journal of Consumer Policy* 13 (1990), pp. 1 *et seq.*; Wilhelmsson, Need-Rationality in Private Law?, *Scandinavian Studies in Law* 33 (1989), pp. 227 *et seq.*; Wilhelmsson, Control of Unfair Contract Terms and Social Values: EC and Nordic Approaches, *Journal of Consumer Policy* 16 (1993), pp. 435 *et seq.*; Krüger, *Norsk kontraktsrett*, Bergen 1989, pp. 402 *et seq.*; Reifner, *Alternatives Wirtschaftsrecht am Beispiel der Verbraucherverschuldung. Realitätsverleugnung oder soziale Auslegung im Zivilrecht*, Darmstadt 1979, pp. 321 *et seq.*

tract law protecting customers is considered unsatisfactory and new ways to improve the coherence and transparency of contract law are proposed and realised. The integration of protective contract law into the general (codified) contract law cannot be successful as a mere transcription or compilation of existing rules, but must start with an exploration of the underlying principles. It is only on this basis that the reform or re-codification can work its way up to more detailed questions in shaping the diverse rules.

The same applies to the project of developing a (uniform, harmonised or "soft") European contract law. If there is no agreement among the Member States, as so far seems to be the case, on how far the principle of regard and fairness should be extended and where to set its limits, the attempt to formulate detailed rules of contract law appears to be an unprincipled, non-transparent and arbitrary approach, being unable to encompass the real social and economic issues of a modern contract law system and, thus, being also unable to develop real persuasive force. The major part of existing European contract law is protective in its character. It can, therefore, be fairly said that the question of how to connect and integrate its driving principles to the general rules of contract law is one of the key issues for the development of a more comprehensive European contract law.

3.2 Personal and Situational Elements in the Protection System

The integration of protective contract law in a more coherent set of general contract law rules can be facilitated by a distinction of personal and situational elements. Protective provisions most often contain a combination of these two types of elements:[85] (a) The *person oriented element* relates to the personal qualities of the parties which cause a situation of imbalance materialising in a one-sided lack of information, lack of abilities or experience. But a situation of imbalance caused by personal qualities is by itself not a sufficient basis for the provision of party protection. (b) Every protective measure has to be justified by a *situation oriented element* in addition: the protection aims to avert certain dangers which materialise at the stage of contract conclusion or at the stage of performance of the contract.

The relationship between the two elements should be seen as a flexible interdependent system. The personal element can be very weak or inexistent, if the situation-related danger is very strong, or if a certain situation brings one party in the position of inferiority or dependence on the regard and fairness of the other party or if it reveals a formerly concealed state of imbalance. Examples are: the control of pre-formulated or general contract terms in contracts between businesses, the protection of the creditor in cases of delay in payment, change of circumstances, and the Austrian *laesio enormis*. The stronger the personal inferiority of a party is the more intensive the protection also has to be in situations which constitute only medium or small dangers.

The personal quality represented by the *notion of "consumer"* is a relatively reliable indicator for the existence of personal inferiority. It is rather easy to handle and creates legal security. Therefore, it would be wrong to eliminate the notion of "con-

---

85 Lurger, *Vertragliche Solidarität*, Baden-Baden 1998, pp. 77 *et seq.*

sumer" from the legal system altogether, e.g. in favour of a more comprehensive notion of "customer". It is true that in exceptional cases single consumers, who are e.g. themselves experienced in the relevant branch of business, comparatively more highly educated than the other party or lawyers, are not in need of special or stronger protection than business parties. But to establish a rule that singles out these cases and exempts them from the protective regime for consumers[86] would most probably be a violation of all EC consumer directives, which do not provide such an exception.

Another question points in the opposite direction: should, and in which types of cases should, consumer protection measures be extended to small or all businesses whose knowledge and experience in the respective branch is similarly inferior to that of the other contracting party as is that of consumers? Two types of solutions can be considered: (a) One could try to define certain "personal requirements" for these businesses (e.g. very small businesses, businesses not acting in their proper trade) under which they qualify for the complete application of the consumer protection regime. (b) Or one could solve the problem on a more situation or contract type oriented basis: the starting point being that consumer protection generally does not apply to businesses. But certain protective measures, which may be very similar to those provided for consumers or comparatively more moderate, apply when a situation proves to be dangerous also for business customers. This latter approach is the one adopted by EC legislation so far. The EC directives consider protective measures in favour of business parties to be primarily necessary when the type of contract concluded typically implies a strong imbalance of knowledge and experience or a certain situation of dependence of the parties. This may be e.g. the case in insurance contracts, commercial agency contracts, delayed payments, or transfers of funds by banks. Among the Member States, only a minority (France, Greece) follow the first approach, whereas a majority follows the second, mostly contract type based, approach. The second approach has the advantage of avoiding the considerable difficulty of drawing a line between businesses that qualify for consumer protection and those that do not.

The preferable second approach as traced out by the EC so far is fragmentary. The question has therefore to be posed which types of contracts or other circumstances generally create "dangerous" situations for business customers in which protection should be provided. With respect to contract types, one could say by way of generalisation that the contracts involved are normally rather complex and complicated; they involve a long-term commitment or considerable investment of the customer and imply a high degree of specialisation on the side of the supplier of the services or goods. Non-contract type based protection often focuses on situations of dependence (of various character) which are likely to be abused by the other party.

In the area of protection of business customers, it has to be equally considered that some customers may not be in the typical need of protection assumed by the protective provisions, due to certain personal characteristics: this may e.g. be the case when

---

86 Franz Bydlinski, *System und Prinzipien des Privatrechts*, Wien 1996, pp. 733 *et seq.*; Koziol, Sonderprivatrecht für Konsumentenkredite?, *Archiv für die civilistische Praxis 188* (1988), pp. 201; Chazal, Le consommateur existe-t-il?, *Recueil Dalloz, Chronique*, Paris 1997, p. 266; Lurger, *Vertragliche Solidarität*, Baden-Baden 1998, p. 81.

the customer is a large group of companies disposing of a high degree of expertise among its staff. In such cases the respective customers should be excluded from the protective provisions. The EC insurance directives are a good illustration of that approach.

Based on these general deliberations, more detailed proposals for a systematisation and integration of protective contract law can be developed:[87] as e.g. the formulation of a general duty to inform followed by a more detailed list of simplified and systematised special information duties, a unification and modernisation of the system of sanctions for the violation of information duties (damages, mistake, right of withdrawal), the simplification and systematisation of the diverse rights of withdrawal,[88] provisions for the control of unfair contract terms and for breach of contract which integrate the special protection afforded to consumers, the regulation of modern types of contract in the civil codes. These further proposals cannot be dealt with here and are explained in more detail in the abovementioned footnotes.

4 Conclusion

The national contract law of the Member States generally consists of two rather separate parts of contract law: the "general" or "ordinary" contract law (most often part of their civil codes) and the contract law of special statutes which is protective in its character. EC contract law can be mainly found in this second area. In the last decades, the EC directives have heavily influenced the development of the special statutes of the Member States. The area of protective contract law, in EC as well as in national law, cannot be reduced to the field of consumer protection, but also includes the protection of business customers in various situations. The protection of consumers and other customers is based on the same ideas, has the same characteristics and instruments. The field of protective contract law has become so large that its application is by no means an exception, but rather the rule on the market. 95 per cent of all contracts concluded are contracts between businesses and consumers or between businesses and businesses.

The separation of the two areas of contract law creates numerous problems on the national as well as on the European level. The best way out of this crisis can be seen in a systematisation and integration of protective contract law in the "general" contract law rules. This systematisation and integration should not only be at the heart of national reforms of contract law, but are also the only way towards a European Contract Code.

Systematisation and integration must start on the level of principles and not with a mere comparison of national or EC rules. Customer protection is an expression of the general "principle of regard and fairness" which is in partial conflict with the other great principle of contract law: the principle of freedom on contract. Both principles

---

87 Lurger, Integration des Verbraucherrechts in das ABGB?, in: Fischer-Czermak/Schauer (Ed.), *ABGB – auf dem Weg in das 3. Jahrtausend, Reformbedarf und Reform*, Wien 2003, chapter E (forthcoming); Lurger, *Vertragliche Solidaritat*, Baden-Baden 1998, pp. 61 *et seq.*

88 Kalss/Lurger, *Rücktrittsrechte*, Wien 2001, pp. 67 *et seq.*

are rooted in the catalogues of fundamental rights of most member states and the EU. The key question is how to limit these principles in cases of conflict: When is the pursuit and promotion of a party's own interests still legitimate and how much regard for the interests of the other party can be demanded? The answers given to that question have a great impact on the functioning of markets and the shaping of our society in general. The limits of the principle of regard and fairness can be better ascertained by a distinction between the personal and the situational elements of protective provisions. These two elements operate in a flexible system and link the protective instrument to the danger to be averted by it.

The efforts made so far to prepare a European contract law (Lando-Principles, Study Group on a European Civil Code etc) have neglected the area of protective contract law, its underlying principle of regard and fairness and the problem of its systematisation and integration in the "general" contract law rules. Thus, a discussion on the political, economic and social implications of contract law was almost completely avoided. There seems to be no common consensus among the Member States about the key question of limitation of the two contract law principles. As long as a discussion about these fundamental questions is not initiated on a European level and does not lead to the development of a common basis, proposals for uniform contract law rules will lack contact with the underlying values and political issues of contract law. They will leave the impression that they are incoherent and arbitrary and will have little chance to convince the relevant political actors in the EU and the Member States of their quality and desirability. Nothing can be safely built on a basis that does not yet exist or must at least be considered shaky.

BIBLIOGRAPHY: Basedow, *Die Reform des deutschen Kaufrechts*, Köln 1988; Basedow, Über Privatrechtsvereinheitlichung und Marktintegration, in: Immenga/Möschl/Reuter (Ed.), *FS für Mestmäcker*, Baden-Baden 1996, pp. 347 *et seq.*; Behr, Das BGB im Jahr 2096, in: Schlosser (Ed.), *Bürgerliches Gesetzbuch*, Heidelberg 1896-1996 (1997), pp. 203 *et seq.*; Benhabib, Autonomy, Modernity, and Community: Communitarianism and Critical Social Theory in Dialogue, in: Honneth/McCarthy (Ed.), *Zwischenbetrachtungen im Prozeß der Aufklärung. Jürgen Habermas zum 60.Geburtstag* Frankfurt/M 1989, pp. 385 *et seq.*; Bourgoignie, Propositions pour une loi générale sur la protection des consommateurs en Belgique, *Revue européenne de droit de la consommation* 1997, pp. 97 *et seq.*; Bydlinski Franz, *System und Prinzipien des Privatrechts,* Wien 1996; Bydlinski, Beschränkung und Ausschluss der Gewährleistung, *Juristische Blätter* 1993, pp. 560 *et seq.*; Bydlinski, *System und Prinzipien des Privatrechts*, Wien 1996; Canaris, *Systemdenken und Systembegriff in der Jurisprudenz*, vol. 2, Berlin 1983; Chazal, Le consommateur existe-t-il?, *Recueil Dalloz, Chronique*, Paris 1997; pp. 260 *et seq.*; Collard-Dutilleul/Delbecque, Contrats civils et commerciaux, *Précis Dalloz*, vol. 3., Paris 1996; Collins, Social Market and the Law of Contract, *Archiv für Rechts- und Sozialphilosophie-supplement* 49 (1992), pp. 85 *et seq.*; Collins, The Law of Contract, vol. 3, London 1997; Cornu, L'évolution des contrats en France, *Revue internationale de droit comparé* 1979, special issue of Journées de la Société de législation comparée, pp. 447 *et seq.*; Dalton, *An Essay in the Deconstruction of Contract Doctrine*, Yale Law Journal 94 (1985), pp. 997 *et seq.*; Dörner, Integration des Verbraucherrechts in das BGB, in: Schulze/Schulte-Nölke (Ed.), *Die Schuldrechtsreform vor dem Hintergrund des Gemeinschaftsrechts*, Tübingen 2001, pp. 177 (179 f); Dörner, Integration des Verbraucherrechts in das BGB, in: Schulze/Schulte-Nölke (Ed.), *Die Schuldrechtsreform vor dem Hintergrund des Gemeinschaftsrechts*, Tübingen 2001; Duncan, *Form and Substance in Private Law Adjudication*, Harvard Law Review 89 (1976), pp. 1685 *et seq.*; Duncan, *The Political Stakes in "Merely Technical" Issues of Contract Law*, European Review of Private Law 5 (2001), pp. 7 *et seq.*; Ennecerus/ Nipperdey, *Allgemeiner Teil des Bürgerlichen Rechts* I/2, vol. 15, Tübingen 1959/1960; Feinman, *The Significance of Contract Theory*, Cincinnati Law Review 58 (1990), pp. 1283 *et seq.*; Gordon, *New Developments in Legal Theory*, in: Kairys (Ed.), The Politics of Law, New York 1982, pp. 281 *et seq.*; Grundmann, Europäisches Handelsrecht – vom Handelsrecht des laissez faire im Kodex des 19. Jahrhunderts zum Handelsrecht der sozialen Verantwortung, *Zeitschrift für das gesamte Handelsrecht und Wirtschaftsrecht* 163 (1999), pp. 635 *et seq.*; Grundmann, The Structure of European Contract Law, *European Review of Public Law* 2001, pp. 505 *et seq.*; Grundmann, *Europäisches Schuldvertragsrecht*, Berlin /New York 1999; Grundmann, Verbraucherrecht, Unternehmensrecht, Privatrecht – warum sind sich UN-Kaufrecht und EU-Kaufrechts-Richtlinie so ähnlich?, *Archiv für die civilistische Praxis* 202 (2002), pp. 40 *et seq.*; Gutmann, "Keeping 'em down on the farm after they've seen Paree": Aporien des kommunitaristischen Rechtsbegriffs, *Archiv für Rechts- und Sozialphilosophie* 83 (1997), pp. 37 *et seq.*; Heck, *Begriffsbildung und Interessenjurisprudenz*, Tübingen 1932; Hesselink, *Principles of European Contract Law*, Deventer 2001; Hesselink, The Horizontal Effect of ‚Social Rights' in European Contract Law, Paper presented at the conference „Diritti fondamentali e formazione del diritto privato europeo" at the Università Roma III, on 18 June 2002; Hesselink, *The New Europe European Legal Culture*, Deventer 2001; Hondius, in: Heusel (Ed.), *Neues europäisches Vertragsrecht und Verbraucherschutz*, Trier 1999; Honneth (Ed.), *Kummunitarismus*, vol. 2, Frankfurt am Main 1994; Irti, *L'età della decodificazione*, Milano 1980; Joerges, Der Schutz des Verbrauchers und die Einheit des Zivilrechts, *AG* 1983, pp. 57 *et seq.*; Joerges, Desintegrative Folgen legislativer Harmonisierung: ein komplexes Problem und ein unscheinbares Exempel, in: Schulte-Nölke/Schulze (Ed.), *Europäische Rechtsangleichung und nationale Privatrechte*, Baden-Baden 1999, pp. 205 *et seq.*; Joerges, Die Europäisierung des Privatrechts als Rationalisierungsprozess und als Streit der Disziplinen, *Zeitschrift für europäisches Privatrecht* 1995, pp. 181 *et seq.*; Joerges, *Verbraucherschutz als Rechtsproblem*, Heidelberg 1981; Kalss/Lurger, *Rücktrittsrechte*, Wien 2001; Kalss/Lurger, Zu einer Systematik der Rücktrittsrechte insbesondere im Verbraucherrecht, *Juristische Blätter* 1998, 89-97 (part 1), ppp. 89 *et seq.* (part 3), pp. 219 *et seq.*; Kelman, A Guide to Critical Legal Studies, Cambridge 1987; Koziol, Sonderprivatrecht für Konsumentenkredite?, *AcP* 188 (1988), pp. 183 *et seq.*; Kramer, Die „Krise" des liberalen Vertragsdenkens, in: Kramer, *Zur Theorie und Politik des Privat- und Wirtschaftsrechts*, Wien 1997; pp. 69 *et seq.*; Kramer, Funktion, rechtliche Problematik und Zukunftsperspektiven der Innominatverträge, in: Kramer, *Zur Theorie und Politik des Privat- und Wirtschaftsrechts,* Wien 1997; Krejci, Ist das Verbraucherrecht ein Rechtsgebiet?, in: Eccher/Nemeth/Tangl (Ed.), *Verbraucherschutz in Europa, Festgabe für Heinrich Mayrhofer*, Wien 2002, pp. 120 *et seq.*; Krüger, *Norsk kontraktsrett*, Bergen 1989; Kube von, The Legitimacy of the Communitarian Critique – or: Can a Liberal Theory of Social Justice Accomodate the Public Trust Doctrine?, *Archiv für Rechts- und Sozialphilosophie* 83 (1997), pp. 67 *et seq.*; Larenz/Canaris, *Methodenlehre der Rechtswissenschaft*, vol. 3 (1995); Lurger, Prinzipien eines europäischen Vertragsrechts: liberal, marktfunktional, solidarisch oder ...?, *EJCL* 1998, http://law.kub.nl/ ejcl, pp. 7 *et seq.*; Lurger, *Grundfragen der Vereinheitlichung des Vertragsrechts in der Europäischen Union*, Wien 2002; Lurger, Grundfragen der Vereinheitlichung des Vertragsrechts in der Europäischen Union, in: Martiny/Witzleb (Ed.), *Auf dem Wege zu einem Europäischen Zivilgesetzbuch*, Berlin/ Heidelberg 1999, pp. 141 (155 *et seq.*); Lurger, Integration des Verbraucherrechts in das ABGB?, in: Fischer-Czermak/Schauer (Ed.), *ABGB – auf dem Weg in das 3. Jahrtausend, Reformbedarf und Reform*, Wien 2003 (forthcoming); Lurger, Konflikte um Macht und Wissen als Grundelemente von Vertragstheorie und Verfassungswirkungen, in: *Jahrbuch Junger Zivilrechtswissenschaftler*, Stuttgart 1995 (1996), pp. 17 *et seq.*; Lurger, Prinzipien eines europäischen Vertragsrechts: liberal, marktfunktion, solidarisch oder ...?, *Electronic Journal of Comparative Law* (March 1998) vol 2.1, http://law.kub.nl/ejcl/art21-

1.html; Lurger, *Vertragliche Solidarität* , Baden-Baden 1998; Mankowski, Formvorschriften und Europäisches Privatrecht, in: Schulte-Nölke/Schulze (Ed.), *Europäisches Vertragsrecht im Gemeinschaftsrecht*, Trier 2002, pp. 181 *et seq.*; Micklitz, Der Vertragsbegriff in den Übereinkommen von Brüssel und Rom, in: Schulte-Nölke/Schulze (Ed.), *Europäisches Vertragsrecht im Gemeinschaftsrecht*, Trier 2002, pp. 39 *et seq.*; Micklitz, Die Fernabsatzrichtlinie 97/7/EG, *Zeitschrift für Europäisches Privatrecht* 1999, pp. 875 *et seq.*; Micklitz, Ein einheitliches Kaufrecht für Verbraucher in der EG?, *Europäische Zeitschrift für Wirtschaftsrecht* 1997, pp. 229 *et seq.*; Micklitz, Vertragsschlußmodalitäten, in: Micklitz/Pfeiffer/Tonner/Willlingmann (Ed.), *Schuldrechtsreform und Verbraucherschutz*, Baden-Baden 2001, ppp. 191 *et seq.*; Möllers, European Directives on Civil Law – The German Approach: Towards a Recodification and New Foundation of Civil Law Principles, *European Review of Private Law* 6 (2002), pp. 777 *et seq.*; Philippi, *Die Charta der Grundrechte der Europäischen Union*, Baden-Baden 2002; Pizzio, La protection des consommateurs par le droit commun des obligations, *Revue trimestrielle de droit commercial et de droit économique* (1998), pp. 56 *et seq.*; Prouvez, The European Social Charter, an Instrument for the Protection of Human Rights in the 21st Century?, *International Commission of Justice Review* 1997, pp. 30 *et seq.*; Raiser, *Das Recht der Allgemeinen Geschäftsbedingungen* Hamburg 1935, Neudruck 1961; Reifner, *Alternatives Wirtschaftsrecht am Beispiel der Verbraucherverschuldung. Realitätsverleugnung oder soziale Auslegung im Zivilrecht*, Darmstadt 1979; Remy, La recodification civile, Droits, *Revue française de théorie, de philosophie et de culture juridiques* 26 (1998), pp. 3 *et seq.*; Roth W-H, Europäischer Verbraucherschutz und BGB, *Juristenzeitung* 2001, pp. 477 *et seq.*; Roth, Transposing "Pointillist" EC Guidelines into Systematic National Codes – Problems and Consequences, *European Review of Private Law* 6 (2002), pp. 761 *et seq.*; Samuel, *Fundamental Social Rights*, Strasbourg 2002; Schmid Christoph, Desintegration und Neuordnungsperspektiven im europäischen Privatrecht, in: *Jahrbuch Junger Zivilrechtswissenschaftler*, Stuttgart 1999 (2000), pp. 33 *et seq.*); Schuhmacher, *Verbraucher und Recht in historischer Sicht*, Wien 1981; Schulze/Schulte-Nölke, Schuldrechtsreform und Gemeinschaftsrecht, in: Schulze/Schulte-Nölke (Ed.), *Die Schuldrechtsreform vor dem Hintergrund des Gemeinschaftsrechts*, Tübingen 2001, pp. 1 *et seq.*; Singer, *The Player and the Cards: Nihilism and Legal Theory*, Yale Law Journal 94 (1984), ppp. 1 *et seq.*; Terré/Simler/Lequette, Droit civil – les obligations, *Précis Dalloz*, vol. 7, Paris 1999; Teubner, Legal Irritants: Good Faith in British Law or How Unifying Law Ends up in New Divergencies, *Modern Law Review* 61 (1998), pp. 11 *et seq.*; Walzer, The Communitarian Critique of Liberalism, *Political Theory 1*, Cambridge 1990, pp. 6 *et seq.*; Wilhelmsson, "Social Force Majeure" – A New Concept in Nordic Consumer Law, *Journal of Consumer Policy* 13 (1990), pp. 1 *et seq.*; Wilhelmsson, Consumer Images in East and West, in: Micklitz (Ed.), *Rechtseinheit oder Rechtsvielfalt in Europa? Rolle und Funktion des Verbraucherrechts in der EG und den MOE-staaten*, Baden-Baden 1996, pp. 53 *et seq.*; Wilhelmsson, Consumer Law and Social Justice, in: Ramsay (Ed.), *Rethinking Consumer Law in the Global Economy* (1997), pp. 191 *et seq.*; Wilhelmsson, Consumer Protection and the Rules and Principles of General Contract Law, in: Wilhelmsson, *Twelve Essays on Consumer Law and Policy*, Helsinki 1996, pp. 129 *et seq.*; Wilhelmsson, Consumer Protection and the Rules and Principles of General Contract Law, *Journal of Behavioral and Social Sciences* 38 (1992), pp. 150 *et seq.*; Wilhelmsson, Control of Unfair Contract Terms and Social Values: EC and Nordic Approaches, *Journal of Consumer Policy* 16 (1993), pp. 435 *et seq.*; Wilhelmsson, Critical Studies in Private Law: *A Treatise on Need-rational Principles in Modern Law*, Dordrecht 1992; Wilhelmsson, Need-Rationality in Private Law?, *Scandinavian Studies in Law* 33 (1989), pp. 223 *et seq.*; Wilhelmsson, Questions for a Critical Contract Law – and a Contradictory Answer: Contract as Social Cooperation, in: Wilhelmsson (Ed.), *Perspectives of Critical Contract Law*, Aldershot 1993, pp. 9 *et seq.*; Wilhelmsson, *Social Contract Law and European Integration*, Aldershot 1995; Wilhelmsson, The Philosophy of

Welfarism and its Emergence in the Modern Scandinavian Contract Law, in: Brownsword/ Howells/Willhelmsson (Ed.), *Welfarism in Contract Law*, Aldershot 1994, pp. 63 *et seq.*; Wilhelmsson, *Twelve Essays on Consumer Law and Policy*, Helsinki 1996; Wilhelmsson, Contribution to a Green Sales Law, in: Wilhelmsson, *Twelve Essays on Consumer Law and Policy*, Helsinki 1996, pp. 267 *et seq.*; Zahlmann (Ed.), *Kommunitarismus in Diskussion*, Berlin 1992.

CHAPTER 16

Basics First Please! A Critique of Some Recent Priorities shown by the Commission's *Action Plan*

Ugo Mattei*

Being asked to contribute to the new edition of *Towards a European Civil Code,* a well deserved "classic" in the field of European Private Law, is at the same time an honour and an important occasion for me. It gives the opportunity to convey a message to everybody concerned with the field. The opportunity must not be missed, because with the polarisation of scholarship, the multiplicity of venues of publication, and the many sub-fields that divide up private law, one can never assume that ideas are known and circulate. I will therefore seize the opportunity by offering a short laundry list of priorities around which I have articulated my work in the field in the last few years.[1]

This is a moment where many things are happening in the domain of European private law, and the landscape around us is rapidly changing. In this paper I will therefore present some of these changes in order to provide some context to a story, that of the European Civil Codification process, that started unfolding only from 1989, the year of the first recommendation of the European Parliament, and that is therefore less than fifteen years old. I apologise to the reader for two aspects of this piece. First, a certain preaching vein, that is occasioned by the fact of being myself an old boy in this young field. Second, a tone that is occasionally deviant from the usual style of legal scholarship and sounds more like exposure than objective observation. I find myself in a somewhat more militant phase of my career and I therefore try to put myself in the shoes of the losers of every social game that I observe. Exposure is my recipe for not being captured by the dominant discourse and rhetoric.

The European Commission seems to have changed its attitude dramatically in the last decade. From an initial stage of plain disinterest, with only the Parliament involved in the attempt to introduce some official input in the field (1989, 1994), the Commission is now experiencing a moment of extensive activism. A green paper, spelling out some options produced in 2001, was followed by an official call for inputs by the scholarly community. The issue on the table was if "contracts" would be a sufficient field for efforts of harmonisation, or whether neighbouring fields, such as property or torts, were also in need of being tackled. The imposing scholarly apparatus organised around the "Study group on the European Civil Code" started to work on the issue (with an agreed six months time-frame) but before its results were due, the Commission decided that contracts were enough. An *Action Plan* was produced in February 2003.

---

* Alfred & Hanna Fromm Distinguished Professor of International and Comparative Law, University of California, Hastings. Professore Ordinario di Diritto Civile, Università di Torino.
1   I have collected this work in the book Ugo Mattei, *The European Codification Process. Cut & Paste*, Kluwer, 2003. Part of this article reproduces the concluding chapter of the book.

A new notion, that of "Common Frame of Reference" was created. The scholarly community is now debating the term.[2] Is it a disguised term for "Common Civil Code"? Is it a disguised term for "Common Core"? After the scholarly creativity, inspired by the Americanisation process, brought to the table of the European debate a variety of "soft notions" such as "Restatement", "Model Codes", "Default Codes", "Competition between Legal Orders" etc., the Commission is now adding a new wave of neologisms.

The Action Plan is a disappointing document indeed. One suspects that the Commission has intervened in the field not so much to help its development, but on the contrary to limit and channel the debate, in order to avoid real reform happening, after the early more critical voices defending the status quo (the Savignys and the postmoderns) have lost momentum in the Academic debate. Antonio Gambaro, in his inaugural lecture as a member of the Accademia Nazionale dei Lincei in Rome, points to the shortcoming of the codification technique that the Commission seems to suggest. A European code with no ambition of fundamental reform will only add another rule in the already complex scenario of European private law. There is nothing dramatic or new in this (think about the Vienna Convention). This is however very contradictory to the proclaimed goal of reducing transaction costs.

The issue that a number of commentators, concerned with legitimacy and pluralism, were pointing at, that of inclusion of *subordinate* European legal cultures, has been plainly ignored.[3] Reactions to the Commission's proposals are from the usual people in the usual countries. I respectfully submit, as a top priority, a *proactive* effort to reach such cultures, especially after new members have joined, to include legal cultures that are completely at the margins of academic networks. The Commission *must not* rely on spontaneous networking. It has to take the initiative to produce the tools for creating communication between the hegemonic and the subordinate European cultures. Proactive steps must be taken in order to put all European legal cultures on a basis of substantial equality in the production of European private law. At least an official catalogue of Academic legal institutions through Europe *should be produced now*.

Why is the commission ignoring the scholarly input, even if it ostensibly requires it? Why this obsession with contract law only, without even an effort to understand what scholars have been pointing out for years, that this notion is itself entirely variable across systems and that therefore it is senseless to skip broader issues?

There are different explanations. Legal hegemony of the English language, coupled with the imperialism of Economics in social sciences, is conspiring to produce the development of an all-inclusive non-technical notion of contract as a fundamental legal framework for a free market. Contract is successfully competing with institutional ideas of corporation and with public law ideas of hierarchy, in the governance of markets.[4] Outsourcing, downsizing, and privatisation, all put an economic

---

2   In May 2003 for example, an international seminar on this issue was hosted by the University of Catania Law School under the auspices of the Jean Monnet program.

3   See M. Bussani, in Grundmann Stuyck, (eds.), An Academic Green Paper on European Contract law (2002). See also U. Mattei, hard Code Now! In Global Jurist Frontiers 2002, <www.bepress.com>.

4   See the "nexus of contracts theory" as developed by Easterbrook & Fishel, The Economic Structure of Corporate Law (1991).

notion of "contract" at the centre of the scene. Contracts are the tool through which the surrender of the political process to market forces is maintaining a façade of legality.

Like all bureaucratic institutions, DG 24 – the branch of the Commission that is now involved in the civil code process –, also struggles for survival and possibly expansion. The political wind has changed, and its past contribution to the protection of consumers, has been challenged as paternalistic and formalistic by the political forces that control – together with the global financial institutions setting the rules of the game[5] – the political process at Brussels.

The scholarly community of lawyers concerned with consumer's protection has been depicted as a clique of radicals paving with intellectual hurdles the pathway to a full unfolding of the free market harmony. DG 24 needs to distance itself from that perception in order to survive. The attitude that promotes contract as the only institutional structure deserving attention, and that of ill-disguised preference towards *soft* non- binding solutions, can all be explained by a political move towards market neutrality and its neo-conservative implications.[6]

The context of the Action Plan is also characterised by major trends in legal scholarship. In just a few years, remarkable developments have happened even in the sociological and anthropological aspects of legal scholarship.

The early part of the decade has been characterised by a strong pattern of resistance of local legal values imbedded in positivism. At the Hague conference convened by the Dutch Ministry of Justice, in 1997, for example, every invited speaker proposed his national code or legal model as the pattern for everybody.[7] This early attitude was supported by a variety of nostalgic scholarly attitudes that resisted, on different grounds, the idea of a Common Civil Code. In the last few years, the wind has changed. A new generation of "European private law scholars", who are neither the most distinguished local private lawyers, nor the traditional group of private comparative law specialists, has seised the field.[8] This generation expresses itself mostly in English and is largely Americanised in its style. Many of the soft attitudes expressed by the Green book and by the Action Plan are the product of the impressive impact of policy arguments (mostly efficiency) that this new generation has imported from the US. At the Leuven conference that organised the Academic feedback to the Commission's call, the new attitude was apparent.[9] Positivism is now mostly gone in the predominant discourse, but together with it, the sense that the market should be governed by the law and not the other way around has also gone. The baby seems to be lost with the bathwater!

This attitude is at work in much of the present day production of European private

---

5   See for a critical discussion of the reactive philosophy behind globalisation U. Mattei, *A Theory of Imperial Law. A Study on U.S. Hegemony and the Latin Resistance*, in 10 Indiana J. Global Legal Studies (2002) and Global Jurist Frontiers 2003.

6   The little attention given to the development of a European judicial process capable of effective enforcement of rights and the parallel attention towards ADR responds to the same political logic. See L. Nader, *The Life of the Law* (2002).

7   See the papers published in European Review of Private Law in 1998.

8   See the reconstruction by M. Hesselink, *The New European Legal Culture* (2002).

9   See the papers collected in Grundmann & Stuyck, *op cit.*

law. A sort of carefree attitude motivated by pragmatism and desire to visibly appears, as protagonists of the ongoing debate (itself the product of the ongoing process of privatisation of Academic research) are producing a wave of proposals in a large variety of domains that follow the following efficient strategy: a) comparing only a few solutions (mostly from hegemonic countries) and promoting the outcomes of the comparison to "common core" status. b) looking at the US as an example of creativity, adaptability and "everything goes" attitude to policy proposals (the so called marketplace of legal ideas!).

There are dangerous cryptic political implications of this shift from Parochialism to Americanisation. One must not be nostalgic about the former, but should be careful about the latter too. In particular, it is crucial to have a sense of the reality of American law in order to avoid importing at face value its description from the protagonists of the American debate. There is a need of first hand knowledge of US law that requires the use of sophisticated comparative tools. Just as for any other legal system, American law is not necessarily what American legal scholars tell us it is. In particular, American law is not as *soft* as it appears if one only looks at the details of the enforcing mechanisms. Nor is American law necessarily as technical and neutral as it might appear, if only one understands the political powers that capture its production as strongly as everywhere else. American legal scholars, as happens to all the élites within hegemonic contexts, are proud of their system. Most of their work reflects this pride. The picture that emerges is therefore very much distorted for the purposes of transplants. European legal scholarship must carefully check what it is buying and promoting.

The Americanised European legal discourse, moreover, has lost contact with the everyday working of practicing lawyers through Europe. Positivism is still the dominant European practical attitude towards the law, and in many countries (most of the subordinate ones) it permeates the academic discourse as well.

For the scholarly community the recommendation is always the same. Attempt to understand before offering your conclusions. This is true for the purposes of finding the common core as well as for American inspired creative policy suggestions, such as many coming from my fellow European law and Economics scholars. If the selection of priorities is the province of the political process, the understanding of the basic issues is the province and responsibility of legal scholarship.

I believe that a first recognition of such basic issues is the most important task that the scholarly community can do in this early phase of the process.

Europe is experiencing, in the post-cold war years a contradictory process, if looked upon from a global perspective. On the one hand, it is now the institutional structure of a market of almost half billion people, with a larger GDP than the US, experiencing a continuous process of integration from the legal and economic perspective. On the other hand, divisions and rivalry between the most important Member States, the lack of efficient and legitimate institutions of policymaking, a persistent and unbearable democratic deficit, are responsible for political Europe increasingly becoming a province of a US led Empire.

In this scenario, it is hard to believe that the process of Civil Codification can be perceived as a top priority, when such fundamental issues such as common defence, a common foreign policy, a common immigration policy, comparable standards in education and social protection, are neither solved not even discussed openly. Nevertheless, the observation that there are more important questions to tackle at the present moment should not discourage action in the domain of private law.

To begin with, private law is one of the fundamental domains in which the problems of externalities arise. It is the very basic legal structure of the market, so that issues of environmental harm and labour standards (just to talk about two of the most socially loaded areas of the law) find in the private law regime the proper venue of discussion.

A civil code that does not approach, in its fundamental philosophy, the political choices that are mandated today by such important areas of externality production, simply fails in its role to provide a proper legal regime for a sustainable market.

A civil code is an important aspect of the cultural identity of a community. Europe is in desperate need of such an identity building exercise, from the perspective of anybody who is interested in providing a viable alternative to the present, very exploitive, pattern of capitalist development. Once again, the development of a civil code – a thorough de facto economic constitution – offers a chance to discuss the choices that are in front of us, refusing to be captured by the present rhetoric of unavoidability. Dismantling the social institutions of capitalism in favour of the return to a laissez faire philosophy, as has consistently happened since the end of the Cold War, is not a necessity. It is only reactionary politics.

It is true that many of the issues that are to be faced during a complicated process such as codification are of a somewhat "technical"[10] nature, so that public awareness of their political implications can only be limited. Nevertheless, it is extraordinarily important for at least the scholarly and legal community at large to be aware of the fundamental political implications of the different options. This is particularly crucial these days when a large variety of discourses and rhetorical devices are a-critically imported from the United States either as trendy cultural movements, or as self-serving solutions imposed or marketed by the all mighty transnational economic actors, together with their faithful servants – the mega-law firms.

A variety of different "professional projects", make the "invisible hand" of legal and economic integration work against the common interest favouring, on the contrary, a variety of "rent-seeking" attitudes. Many of the present day discussions about the civil code are hiding behind the rhetoric of merely technical stakes, a variety of such professional projects. Critical scholarship must expose and relentlessly challenge this hidden attitude.

Historical experience shows that in order to produce a Civil Code there is not only the need for a strong legal community, capable of understanding the technical aspects of the enterprise. There is the need of a political will, capable of injecting into the Code a degree of political legitimacy, an internal political philosophy, and a recognisable political function in the landscape of the sources of law. We find such visible political inspiration and symbolism in all the great codifications, from the French, to the German, to the Italian, to the Mexican, to the DDR of 1975, just to offer the most visible examples. Most importantly, a Codification, with its inevitable aspect of innovation, break with the past, and revolt against a previous order, inherently reflects a desire for progress, to move away from a status quo that is perceived as non-desir-

---

10 See, however, D. Kennedy, *The Political Stakes in "Merely Technical" issues of Contract Law*, 10 Eur. Rev. Priv. Law, 7 (2002)

able, technically and politically.[11] In 1804 France was trying to move beyond the class privileges of the ancién regime. In 1900 Germany was attempting a new start as a mighty unitary empire, away from political divisions and warfare. In 1942 Italy was reacting against the bourgeois and liberal legal order. A similar social revolt, though grounded in a socialist rather than in a fascist philosophy, characterised 1950s Mexico. The DDR produced, in 1975 an advanced and innovative Civil Code, in an attempt to overcome bourgeois formalism, professionalism and faked economic equality. That code certainly shows the existence of a ripe and respectable academic legal culture, and sounds like an indictment of the hasty intellectual purge carried on after reunification.

While there are examples of relatively a-political codes, such as perhaps the post-cold war Dutch one, or the Uniform Commercial Code in the United States, history shows that there is a need for political inspiration for a Code that claims a strong personality, and that important political stakes might be present even in self-portrayed technical enterprises. There is little doubt that within Karl Llewellyn's UCC the balance of power between State and national regulators of the rising business superpowers was al least in part at stake. Such a need of political inspiration, to be sure, does not mean that there is a need or a desire of an autocratic political rule, such as that in place in most of the previous examples discussed. A political platform capable of inspiring a "not merely technical" codifying exercise can be brought about from the historical moment that a given community is living, from the tensions and the stakes of such moment, as reflected by constitution-making exercises that might, and indeed do, appear wearing new clothes in the present post-modern condition. In particular, political inspiration can be brought about in comparison with other experiences, from a desire of identity of the European community in the post cold war international order.

It would seem natural to seek such a guideline in a Constitution. Unfortunately, the European constitutional process carried on by the Convention and its presidium is nothing more that the product of a political oligarchy, lacking democratic legitimacy and promoting the executive power to constitutional status. It misuses the label "Constitution" for something that is little more than the charter of an "Old Boys" club, seeking, in a mythological European past legitimisation for the privileges of the present ruling élite. Unfortunately, colonialism, racism and authoritarianism show that the European past is less than commendable and the present attitude towards anybody born outside the walls of fortress Europe make the future too dark to be inspirational for someone seeking values for a "real" Constitution.

Despite these serious problems of political legitimacy, the European charter of rights offers a first important political mandate for a codification enterprise that might be sufficient for the purpose of a private law codification governing the common market. The social nature of European capitalism, despite the rejection of some of the most classic ideas, such as the social function of property rights, is re-asserted in the charter and is claimed as a strong aspect of European identity.[12] Both the politi-

---

11 On the issue of the Code's break with the past, the best pages are still due to R.B. Schlesinger *et al.* Comparative Law, ed. (1998).
12 European social capitalism is well described by M. Albert, *Capitalisme contre capitalisme*, (1980).

cal aspiration and the previous path that the Code would break with, are therefore a given. The community of legal scholars should interpret, apply and put in practice such political aspirations in the next years of the European codification process. I believe that sensitivity towards the path and a clear perception of the challenges for the future are the fundamental intellectual tools for carrying on such enterprise. There is in the Charter, and there should be in the Code, a wish to break with internal divisions, but also – more important in private law – a wish to break with two decades of quite a-critical assumption that long term social capitalism "the European way" (as opposed to short term global "financial capitalism") was too expensive to afford. There is also, to be sure, a political mandate to re-assert primacy of rights enforced by an effective institutional system, over a model of development based on more exploitation, and cryptic continuation of our shameful colonial past.

The European civil code has many lessons to learn from the past in order to accomplish such challenges for the future. To begin with, it is imperative to overcome the great abyss between the common law and the civil law traditions in order to profitably learn from both experiences. The code should reflect contributions from all the legal traditions of Europe, and I would suggest, also from those non European traditions that a ripe community of legal scholars well grounded in comparative law, might be able to understand as useful for our task.

European legal scholarship (or science as once was said) should learn to think more freely, should break the still present cages of formalism, should challenge the established taxonomies and all the artificial boundaries such as those between private law and public law or between substantive and procedural law. The task in front of us is to produce a code capable of becoming the milestone of 21st century social and political regulation of market forces. We are in need of a regulation of market transactions capable of making them serve the interest of everybody and not only of strong economic actors nor, I would add, of Europeans only. Sustainable development worldwide requires such an effort to be started before it is too late.[13]

Many things that traditional formalist (particularly civilian) cages of learning have precluded from consideration in the process of preparation of a code, should be approached and thoroughly explored for possible introduction in the would-be document. Remedies, access to justice, environmental law, protection of diffused interests, fundamental antitrust regulations and many other connected fields should all be thoroughly explored. I have provided no guidance in these fields in my scholarship because of limited forces. I would nevertheless continue to insist on the need for tackling *now* a serious discussion on the way in which a European machinery of justice should look like in order to offer an appropriate public domain venue for the vindication of individual and social rights.

There are many basic questions to be explored. Issues that are located at the semantic level of the codification process. There is no question that the problem of multi-lingualism does introduce new and unexplored challenges. Nevertheless, once again, challenges can be met.[14] The need is to produce a piece of work that is not

---

13 See S. Rodotá, Un Codice per l'Europa? Diritti nazionali, diritto europeo, diritto globale, in Codier, Una Riflessione di Fine millennio (P. Cannellini e B. Sordi eds.) 2002, 541

14 See A. GAMBARO <<Ivra et deges>> nel processo di edificazione di von diritto privato evropeo, Evropa e Dintto Puvato, 1398, 993.

based on tacit knowledge and tacit assumptions such as those shared by the users of a local language. Once again, options might have to be more thoroughly spelled out, and in the process of doing so, through breaking out as much as possible from monolingual cages, new lessons might be learned.

The European codification process is an exercise of learning by doing. It is however an exercise that needs to be done within a conscious political plan to accomplish the result. Private enterprises can not damage, unless they attempt to gain a legitimacy that they do not have. The codification process should start, I believe, with an official and responsible act of appointment of a multinational committee, well funded and supported, which should explore the best venue to gain legitimacy and to thoroughly involve the many stakeholders in the issue. The appointment should be a joint act of the Commission, the Parliament, and the Council. As always happened in the history of law, scholars are ready to be used.

Part 2 – Substantive Law

A – Family Law and Law of Succession

CHAPTER 17

Is Unification of Family Law Feasible or even Desirable?

Dieter Martiny*

1 Introduction

1.1 The Concept of a 'European Family Law'

Family law as such is still not a matter of general concern in the development of European civil law. It is often only discussed in the context of European human rights,[1] fundamental rights in the EU[2] or private international law.[3] However, compared to the past,[4] one has become more and more aware of the problems originating from the diversity of family law in Europe and the methods to improve the current situation. Nevertheless, the scepticism towards unnecessary attempts at legislative unification and the creation of a state of sameness still overshadows the issue. Does a unification mean, as Hein Kötz once phrased the question, that in the future, marriages of Sicilians, Danes, and Irish will be contracted or dissolved according to the same rules?[5] One's initial response is likely to be 'no'. Admittedly, European citizens enjoy different rights and have different obligations in their respective countries. Consequently, they may qualify as married in one country, but are deemed single in another; they are allowed to adopt or have a child recognised as legitimate here, but not there. This reality, however, albeit the manifestation of a rich cultural diversity, has its drawbacks and is increasingly felt as an obstacle to the free movement of persons.[6] Recognising this, an increasing number of resolutions of the European Parliament have been concerned with questions of family law.[7] The Parliament, however, has provided unsystematic guidance as to how these issues are to be tackled. It has, more or

---

* Professor Civil Law, Private International Law and Comparative Law at Europa Universität Viadrina, Frankfurt, Germany.

1 Cf. Hohnerlein (2000), pp. 252 ff.; McGlynn (2000), pp. 223 ff.,

2 Cf. McGlynn (2001), pp. 582 ff.

3 See Boele-Woelki (2002-I), pp. 17 ff.; Kohler (2002), pp. 709 ff.; Dethloff (2003), pp. 37 ff.; Jänterä-Jareborg (2003), pp. 194 ff.

4 See Hondius (1995), pp. 173 ff.; Martiny (1995), pp. 419 ff.

5 Kötz (1993), pp. 95.

6 Cf. Boele-Woelki (2002-II), pp. 179 ff.

7 See the Resolution on a European Charter of Rights of the Child of 8 July 1992, *OJ* 1992, C 241/67, the Resolution on the Abduction of Children of 9 March 1993, *OJ* 1993 C 115/33, the Resolution on Women and Parental Co-responsibility of 29 October 1993, *OJ* 1993, C 315/652, the Resolution on Abduction of Children of Bi-national Marriages of 1996, *OJ* 1996, C 261/157, the Resolution on measures to protect minors in the European Union of 12 December 1996, *OJ* 1996, C 20/170 and the Resolution on the Protection of Families and Children of 28 Jan. 1999, *OJ* 1999, C 128/79. Cf. also Resolution on the Contribution of Civil Society in Finding Missing or Sexually Exploited Children, *OJ* 2001, C 283/1; McGlynn (2000), pp. 223 ff.

less, recommended 'searching for possibilities to harmonise family law at the European level';[8] it has also instigated the 'drafting of national and international provisions';[9] demanded the creation of a 'coordinated mechanism among our European countries in the area of family law';[10] and, in the same breath, has pledged its commitment for the ratification of existing treaties.[11] Given this uncertainty, it is hardly surprising that little consensus has developed until now as to the proper course of action. Some legal scholars have issued a call for a 'European Family Law'[12] or, at least, a partial unification.[13] Others banish such ideas to the realm of utopia[14] and believe that merely an accommodation is possible.[15] However, the process of 'Europeanisation of family law' is now being discussed on a broader basis.

1.2. Unification and Approximation of Family Law

The idea of a unification of family law is in principle nothing new.[16] In the light of the European Convention for the Protection of Human Rights and Fundamental Freedoms (ECHR) some commentators have found an implicit recognition of the contours of a 'European Family Law'.[17] Few developments in creating additional substantive law, however, have occurred. Accordingly, European family law was in the past often only understood as the principles of this convention and other international instruments, and not as substantive law as such.[18]

When one ponders more closely the possibility of a unification of family law, a variety of questions arise. Which uniform rules already exist? If and with respect to which subject matters is there a need for unification? What barriers would need to be overcome? Which institutions possess the corresponding competencies? Within what framework could a unification or even an approximation occur? Any attempt to try to provide answers to these questions must consider the diversity of approaches to family law, which implicitly raises still another subset of issues of a general nature, such as the differences between common law and civil law countries. These issues will only be discussed in this paper to the extent they touch on the peculiarities of family law. This is also not the place to analyse what in particular belongs to the field of family law (in contrast to family policy); nor will individual domestic solutions be examined. Before discussing a potential unification of family law, it may be worthwhile to first consider the alternatives to such an ambitious undertaking.

---

8 Resolution of 29 October 1993 (*supra* n. 7) no. 3.
9 *Ibid* no. 5.
10 Resolution of 28 Jan. 1999 (*supra* n. 7) no. 24.
11 Resolution of 1996 (*supra* n. 7) no. 28.
12 See Pintens (1993), pp. 209 ff.; Basedow (1994), pp. 197 ff.; Pintens (1999), pp. 238 ff.; Boele-Woelki (2002-II), pp. 171 ff.; Kuchinke (2002), pp. 589 ff.; Martiny (2002), pp.191 ff.
13 Remien (1991), pp. 33 ff.
14 See Sosson (1992), p. 34 (regarding parent and child law). For a related, sceptical view see also Meulders (1991), p. 26. Contra Verschraegen (1994), pp. 23 ff.
15 See in particular Rieg (1990), p. 475. – Cf. also MeuldersKlein (2003), pp. 105 ff.
16 See Neuhaus (1963), pp. 427 ff.; Müller-Freienfels (1968-69) 175 ff.; reprinted in: (1978) 79 ff.
17 Compare Jayme (1979), p. 2425; Jayme (1981), pp. 222 ff.
18 See Hamilton & Standley (1995), pp. 548 ff.

1.3. The Alternative of Rules Governing Conflicts of Law

A decision foregoing a unification of family law in an otherwise unified European economic and social sphere would inevitably entail deciding issues of family status and maintenance obligations under the private international law and civil process rules of the respective domestic jurisdictions. In this respect, a unification of the rules governing conflicts of laws must be considered. This alternative, thriving on the variances in substantive legal rules, involves only a relatively limited incision into any one domestic legal system and mitigates the differences among legal systems. It avoids, at a minimum, the possibility that issues regarding personal status – such as the recognition of marriages or paternity as well as marital property relationships – could be subject to divergent rules governing conflicts of laws. A solution can be most easily attained through an acceptance of general international rules regarding international civil procedure. There remain, in any event, the difficulties of the domestic forum in understanding and correctly applying unfamiliar foreign rules and principles. It is therefore often argued that private international law solutions will prove increasingly inadequate.[19]

The *Hague Conference on Private International Law* has exerted the greatest influence on the development of a 'European International Family Law' through the standardisation of the rules of conflicts of laws pursuant to multilateral treaties.[20] For our purposes, reference need be made to the Hague Conventions on the Protection of Minors,[21] on Maintenance Obligations,[22] on the Civil Aspects of International Child Abduction,[23] on Inter-Country Adoption,[24] on the Protection of Children[25] and the Convention on the International Protection of Adults.[26] Although membership in the Hague Conference extends outside the European continent, the participation of its

---

19 Cf. Boele-Woelki (1997), pp. 1 ff.; Dethloff (2003), pp. 37 ff.

20 See Dyer (1992), pp. 95 ff.; Lipstein (1993), pp. 586 ff.

21 Hague Convention Concerning the Powers of Authorities and the Law Applicable in Respect of the Protection of Minors of 5 October 1961, United Nations Treaty Series (*U.N.T.S.*) 658 (1969) 144, BGBl. II (1971), 219.

22 Hague Convention on the Law Applicable to Maintenance Obligations of 2 October 1973, *AJCL* 21 (1973), p. 596; Hague Convention on the Recognition and Enforcement of Decisions Relating to Maintenance Obligations of 2 October 1973, *U.N.T.S.* 209 (1973) 1021, reprinted in: *AJCL* 21 (1973), p. 156.

23 Hague Convention on the Civil Aspects of International Child Abduction of 25 October 1980, *U.N.T.S.* 1343 (1983) 89, BGBl. II (1990), 207.

24 Hague Convention on Protection of Children and Co-Operation in Respect of Intercountry Adoption of 29 May 1993 I, BGBl. II (2001) 1034. Austria, Belgium, Cyprus, Czech Republic, Denmark, Estonia, Finland, France, Germany, Ireland, Italy, Latvia, Lithuania, Luxembourg, Monaco, Netherlands, Poland, Portugal, Slovakia, Slovenia, Spain, Sweden and the United Kingdom are signatories to this convention.

25 Convention on Jurisdiction, Applicable Law, Recognition, Enforcement and Co-operation in respect of Parental Responsibility and Measures for the Protection of Children of 19 October 1996 *Rev.crit. dr.i.p.* (1996), p. 813. Austria, Belgium, Cyprus, the Czech Republic, Denmark, Estonia, Finland, France, Germany, Greece, Ireland, Italy, Latvia, Lithuania, Luxemburg, Monaco, the Netherlands, Poland, Portugal, Slovakia, Slovenia, Spain, Sweden and the United Kingdom are signatories to this convention.

26 Convention on the International Protection of Adults of 13 January 2000. France, Germany, and the United Kingdom, Netherlands and the United Kingdom are signatories to this convention.

states in drafting, and their ready willingness to adopt, these conventions has given them an esteemed place in the work of the conference.

On the *European Union level* today there is an increased unification of the rules governing conflicts of laws in family matters. The creation of a European international family law is the result of a closer co-operation and of approximation within the European 'area of Freedom, Security and Justice'. It is evidenced by the Council Regulation on jurisdiction and the recognition and enforcement of judgments in matrimonial matters and in matters of parental responsibility ('Brussels II').[27] Maintenance obligations are covered by the Council Regulation on jurisdiction and the recognition and enforcement of judgments in civil and commercial matters ('Brussels I').[28] The new competencies under Article 61 lit. c and 65 EC Treaty are also the basis for projects in the development of uniform conflicts rules and procedural rules in the fields of matrimonial property law and the consequences of the dissolution of non-married couples.[29]

In the past treaties such as the Convention concerning the Enforcement of Maintenance Obligations[30] were designed merely to remedy deficiencies in areas which have not, or have only partially, been addressed by the Hague Conventions. Since EU Regulations deal at least in some respects (e.g., child abduction) with the same subjects as the Hague Conventions today there is a more or less open conflict with the Hague Conference. It has not been easy to co-ordinate the European Regulations with existing conventions of the Member States since difficult questions of competence have arisen. In any case, an expanded activity of the European Union in the field of private international law will probably only lead to a unification of the rules of conflicts of laws in a relatively small number of subject areas – certainly no substitute for a basic unification of domestic substantive law among its members. The harmonisation of European private international law can therefore only be considered as an intermediate step along the path to more integration.[31]

Another problem is raised by the ambitiousness of some of the European proposals and their intention to overcome the existing limits of international civil procedure. Especially recognition of foreign decisions shall be granted without the traditional control mechanism of exequatur proceedings.[32] There are warnings, however, that mere recognition, by ignoring the existing differences between the legal systems, will

---

27 Council Regulation (EC) No. 1347/2000 of 29 May 2000 on jurisdiction and the recognition and enforcement of judgments in matrimonial matters and in matters of parental responsibility for children of both spouses, *OJ* 2000, L 160/19. Entry into force 1 March 2001.

28 Cf. Council Regulation (EC) No. 44/2001on jurisdiction and the recognition and enforcement of judgments in civil and commercial matters of 22 December 2000 (entry into force 1 March 2002), *OJ* 2001, L 12/1.

29 Programme of measures for implementation of the principle of mutual recognition of decisions in civil and commercial matters, *OJ* 2001, C 12/1. – Cf. Kohler (2002), pp. 709 ff.; Boele-Woelki (2002-II), pp. 173 ff.; Jänterä-Jareborg (2003), pp. 194 ff.; Tenreiro/Ekström (2003), pp. 183 ff.

30 Convention on the Simplification of Procedures for the Enforcement of Maintenance Payments of 6 November 1990, Trb. (1991), no. 58; cf. Brückner (1994), pp. 179 ff.

31 Cf. Boele-Woelki (2002-II), pp. 173 ff.

32 For family litigation (e.g. on maintenance claims and visiting rights), see Presidency Conclusions – Tampere European Council 15/16 October 1999 under no. 34 and Programme of measures (*supra* n. 29).

lead to new tensions and contradictions.[33] Given the fact that there is a strong tendency for simplification and recognition, however, at least in the long run there will be growing pressure for a unification or at least an approximation also on the level of substantive law.

2 Existing Uniform Rules

A unification of family law would be totally, or at least partially, superfluous if sufficient uniform international laws already existed. Such is not however the case. Much attention has been devoted to the United Nations Convention on the Rights of the Child of November 20, 1989.[34] This comprehensive multilateral treaty not only facilitates the human rights protection of the child, but also contains, in its 54 articles, a number of substantive family law provisions.[35] The guiding principle of the convention is that the 'best interests of the child' shall be the primary consideration in all actions concerning children.[36] This treaty, to be sure, advances specific values such as non-discrimination, as well as common parental responsibility, thereby influencing the development of uniform substantive law. Domestic family law as such remains, nonetheless, largely untouched.

Another important document is the ECHR,[37] which all Community Member States have ratified and which has come to enjoy the 'status of a constitution of basic rights for Europe'.[38] Its Article 8 demands respect for private and family life. Article 12 protects the right to marry. Article 14 prohibits discrimination against children born out of wedlock. The convention's impact with respect to the unification of laws is primarily twofold: Firstly, and most importantly, the specific domestic practices of individual national legal orders are called into question. Secondly, and partially in light of the foregoing, the provision for the collective enforcement of a number of human rights and fundamental freedoms facilitates the development of a common European consciousness and promotes a basic understanding regarding rights to be respected in family law legislation.[39]

The European Court of Human Rights, terming the ECHR a 'living instrument', has made it possible for the Court, in applying the treaty, to consider subsequent social developments, to conform provisions to changed perceptions of what is just, and to develop the meaning of the particular guarantees. The Court has found, for example, that there is a positive obligation inherent in an effective 'respect for family life' arising from the convention. In the *Marckx* case, where the Court held that Bel-

---

33 Kohler (2002), pp. 709 ff.

34 Int. Leg. Mat. 28 (1989), 1448; BGBl. II (1992), 121.

35 Cf. Art. 2 (prohibition on discrimination), Art. 3 (guarantee of protection and social assistance), Art. 7 (recording in register), Art. 8 (protection from interference in family relations), Art. 12 (significance of the child's wishes).

36 Art. 3(3). Cf. McGoldrick (1991), pp. 135 ff.; Longobardo (1991), pp. 370 ff.; Rubellin-Devichi (1994).

37 European Convention for the Protection of Human Rights and Fundamental Freedoms of 4 November 1950, ETS No. 5; BGBl. II (1952), 685, 953.

38 Götz (1994), p. 269.

39 Cf. Jayme (1981), p. 223 ; McGlynn (2003), pp. 228 ff.

gium had an affirmative duty to provide a system of inheritance rules which safe-guard the illegitimate child's integration into the family, the British member of the Court, Sir Fitzmaurice, pleaded in a dissenting opinion to treat Article 8 of the convention merely as a defensive right and not to read a 'whole code of family law' into the article.[40] Fortunately the case law of the Court has developed in a manner that fails to heed his warning, and today the ECHR constrains countries in their legislation governing parent and child relations. However, within the parameters set down by the Court, there is still plenty of room for a variety of individual domestic statutory solutions.[41]

In the past, the ECHR has had a meaningful practical significance for countries that have no well-established national bill of rights in family matters. This applies particularly to the Netherlands[42] and, to a certain extent, to the former discussion in the United Kingdom, where the ECHR has only recently been incorporated into domestic law.[43] In Austria, on the other hand, the ECHR has been accorded constitutional status.[44] In short, the real achievement of the European Convention on Human Rights resides primarily in its provision of a constitutionally guaranteed catalogue of fundamental values coupled with the operational machinery for their enforcement. The convention's rules have been particularly influential in strengthening and facilitating developments in matters of according equal status to illegitimate children as well as of joint custody and the position of non-married fathers. In spite of these developments towards a European constitutional family law, a number of discrepancies remain in the substantive domestic law of the contracting states. It must also be borne in mind that constitutional principles serving as non-discrimination *rules in family matters* are an important starting-point but that they alone cannot result in differentiated solutions in family law.

3 The European Union

The European Union has at its disposal a refined apparatus for the harmonisation of laws. These instruments serve, however, primarily economic aims. The harmonisation of family law is not mentioned in the Treaty Establishing the European Community (EC Treaty). Even so, family issues are linked to other policies of the Community and at least indirectly impacted. A relationship can already be found at the fundamental rights level. The Union is obliged to respect fundamental rights as guaranteed by the ECHR, and as they result from the constitutional traditions common to the Member States.[45] These rights, including the protection of the family, now

---

40 See the dissenting opinion of Sir Fitzmaurice in the case of *Marckx* v. *Belgium, Eur. Ct. H.R.* (ser. A) 31 (1979), 1 (45), reprinted in: *Eur.GrundRZ* (1979), p. 454 (463); *NJW* (1979), p. 2449; cf. also Remien (1991), p. 22.

41 Cf. Meulders (1991), pp. 26-27.

42 See Smits & Vlaardingerbroek (1995), pp. 119 ff.; Remien (1994), pp. 333 ff. (containing further references).

43 Human Rights Act 1998 (c. 42). – Cf. also Warbrick (1994), pp. 34 ff.; Thorpe (1994) 509 ff.; Fahrenhorst (1994) 8 ff.

44 For further references see Berger (1985), pp. 142 ff.; Fahrenhorst (1994), p. 11.

45 Art. 6 (2) (ex-art. F (2)) Treaty of European Union.

constitute a part of Community law. Today, there are also provisions in the Charter of Fundamental Rights of the EU that deal with the family, e.g. Article 7 (respect for private and family life), Article 9 (right to marry and right to found a family), Article 24 (rights of the child) and Article 33 (protection of the family). [46] In short, although the European Union presently does not have its own body of unified substantive family law, it does possess an established constitutional family law. [47]

The primary objectives assigned by the EC Treaty to the Community are the creation of an economic and monetary union, but the Community is also given the task of promoting a high level of social protection, raising standards of living and the quality of life, and increasing solidarity among the Member States – all of which touch on the situation of families. The Union, in any event, only possesses the authority to harmonise domestic laws 'to the extent necessary for the function of the common market',[48] by which the power to issue Regulations touching primarily on the economic sphere is meant.[49] No mention is made of a harmonisation of substantive civil law as such, and certainly not of family law.[50] One cannot maintain that personal status or the marital property relationship between spouses directly impacts the 'functioning of the common market' and, therefore, that a harmonisation is necessary. The only provisions in the Treaty which at present could conceivably form the basis for a further unification of family law are those regarding co-operation in judicial and legal matters (Art. 61 lit. c, 65 EC Treaty).[51]

The European Parliament has requested the drafting of a European Civil Code, which would cover areas 'relevant' to the Community's activities, such as the law of obligations.[52] Family law is not mentioned in the Parliament's resolutions on a codification of civil law; nor is it expressly excluded. This silence speaks, nevertheless, against including family law in the project. A call for the unification of family law merely on the grounds that the subject is generally included in continental European civil law codifications is not a serious argument. For the time being at least, the European Parliament is likely to continue to limit its activities with respect to family law to compiling and ratifying declarations on fundamental rights and specific family problems. It should not be underestimated that the European Parliament has also become increasingly interested in issues with transborder aspects, e.g. in respect to custody and contact and supports at least a partial codification of European international

---

46 Charter of Fundamental Rights of the European Union of 7 Dec. 2000, *OJ* 2000, C 364/1. Cf. Herzog (2001), pp. 7 ff.; McGlynn (2001), pp. 582 ff.
47 For a more detailed discussion see Verschraegen (1994), pp. 43 ff. As to the former situation see O'Higgins (1990), pp. 1645 ff.
48 See the description of the general activities of the European Union in Article 3 par. 1 (h) of the EC Treaty as well as the provisions of Articles 94 and 95 (ex-art. 100 and 100a) regarding the approximation of laws.
49 Cf. Götz (1994), pp. 266 ff.
50 Pintens (2003-II), p. 22. – For an argument as to why the Community has neither the need nor the competence to regulate family law matters see Verschraegen (1994), pp. 26, 29. Article 149 and 150 (ex-art. 126 and 127) of the EC Treaty mention youth but only in the context of financial measures.
51 As to Art. 29 ff. (ex-art. K.1 ff.) Treaty on European Union see Beaumont (1995), pp. 268 ff.
52 See the Resolution of 26 May 1989, *OJ* 1989, C 158/400, reprinted in: *RabelsZ* 56 (1992), p. 320; *ZEPR* (1993), p. 613.

family law. However, at present even the advocates of a harmonisation of European family law do not propose the drafting of a binding uniform law.[53]

Even though there is no clear dividing line in Community law between conflicts of laws and substantive norms, the former omission of international family law from the Community's activities was subject to criticism. It is increasingly recognised that uniform rules in the Member States are necessary for the resolution of problems of international jurisdiction, the recognition of foreign judgments, conflicts of laws in marriage, parental custody and adoption matters.[54] Today the European Union has a competence for Regulations in the field of private international law. For the sensible field of family matters there is still a restriction as to the degree of unanimity in the adoption of new Regulations. But despite this restriction the field of family law is now expressly mentioned.[55]

Merely because the European Union does not have the express competence for family law questions does not mean that national legislatures are unrestrained in how they proceed with such matters. The Union has not been granted the responsibility for the transliteration of foreign names[56] or for domestic civil process law.[57] In a number of cases involving these matters, the European Court of Justice has, nonetheless, held that certain national laws in discriminating against foreign nationals violate the non-discrimination clause, the freedom of establishment, as well as the freedom to provide services. It is not is not the legal subject matter itself which is the controlling factor in the determination of whether a situation is within or outside the jurisdiction of the Community but whether Community freedoms set forth in the EC Treaty are impacted.[58] The willingness of the Court of Justice to strike down national legislation on this basis is, however, generally limited to those situations where principles such as the ban on discrimination in Article 12 (ex-art. 6) of the Treaty and the aforementioned freedoms are affected. Domestic family laws which discriminate on grounds of nationality[59] or make arbitrary distinctions between domestic and foreign activities could be set aside on this basis.

---

53 Cf. Boele-Woelki (2002-II), p. 179; Martiny (2002), p. 199.
54 Pirrung (1993-I), p. 130.
55 See Art. 67 par. 5 EC Treaty in the version of the Treaty of Nice of 26 Feb. 2001, *OJ* 2001, C 80/ 1.
56 Case 168/91, Christos Kostantinidis, *ECR* 1993-I (30 March 1993) 1191 (in reliance upon Article 52 of the EC Treaty), reprinted in: *IPRax.* (1994), 113 (with a comment by Böhmer (80)); *ERPL* 3 (1995), 483 (with comments by Gaurier (483), Schockweiler (496), and Loiseau (504)); *ZEPR* (1995), 89 (with a comment by Pintens regarding the use of a name for trade purposes and the applicability of Article 3 of the CIEC Convention Concerning the Recording of Family and Given Names in Civil Registers of 13 September 1973 (*U.N.T.S.* 1081 (1978) 274, *BGBl.* II (1976), 1473); see also Streinz (1993), pp. 243 ff.
57 See Case 20/92, Hubbard v. Hamburger, *ECR* 1993-I (1 July 1993) 3777; reprinted in: *IPRax.* (1994), p. 203 (with a comment by Kaum (180) on the compatibility of former section 110 of the German Code of Civil Procedure (cautio iudicatum solvi) with Articles 12, 49 and 50 (ex-art. 6, 59, and 60) of the EC Treaty); Case C-398/92, Mund & Fester v. Hatrex Internationaal Transport, *ECR* 1994-I (1994) 467, reprinted in *IPRax.* (1994), p. 439 (with comment by Geiger on the compatibility of former section 917(II) of the German Code of Civil Procedure (civil arrest) with Articles 12 and 293 (ex-art. 6 and 220) of the EC Treaty and the Brussels Convention.
58 See Case 186/79, Cowan v. Trésor public, *ECR* (2 February 1989) 220, reprinted in: *EuR* 24 (1989), p. 356; *NJW* (1989), p. 2183 (concerning victim compensation); Basedow (1994), pp. 197 ff.
59 *Ibid.*

The lack of any specific competence for the family matters has not meant that these issues have not been considered from time to time by the Union.[60] Both the European Parliament[61] and various committees at the Commission have devoted their time and resources to dealing with family issues in the context of the establishment of a European common market.[62] Community law in matters of immigration, employment, and social security have serious implications for the rights of family members.[63] Definitions of 'spouse' and 'dependent' are, by way of illustration, contained in the Regulations regarding the freedom of movement and freedom of establishment.[64]

The Community, besides being constrained by the lack of an express grant of responsibility for family matters, is further limited by the principle of subsidiarity to taking action only when it can do so better than the Member States acting individually (Article 5 EC Treaty). Such measures are also subject to the principle of proportionality, which means that even when the Community is authorised to intervene, it must do so in the least intrusive manner possible. Community action regarding family law matters is, thus, most conceivable for those inter-country topics that cannot be adequately resolved through the application of national rules of conflicts of laws and substantive law. In any event, a unification of substantive law itself is probably unnecessary as long as adequate solutions are afforded by rules of conflicts of laws.[65]

4 Other European Institutions

The *Council of Europe*, whose influence extends beyond the borders of the European Union, has played an important role in the alignment of European family law. This organisation has drafted a series of treaties dealing with both rules of conflicts of laws and substantive law matters.[66] With respect to the latter, the Convention on the

---

60 See for the Presidency Conclusions of the Laeken European Council of 2001 Pintens (2003-II), pp. 26 ff.; cf. also Resolution on Family Policy in the European Community of 9 June 1983, *OJ* 1983, C 184/116. Cf. also Kohler (1992), p. 227; Conclusions of the Council and of the Ministers Responsible for Family Affairs Meeting Within the Council of 29 Sept. 1989, *OJ* 1989, C 277/2.

61 See Resolution on Single Parent Families of 8 July 1986, *OJ* 1986, C 227/31; Resolution on the Problems of Children in the European Community of 13 December 1991, *OJ* 1992, C 13/534.

62 Cf. the reply issued by the Commission in connection with the roundtable on international adoptions, *OJ* 1994, C 251/37; *OJ* 1994, C 352/45 (regarding the European Observatory on National Family Policies). Cf. also McGlynn (2000), pp. 229 ff.

63 See O'Higgins (1990), pp. 1643 ff.; Castillo (1990), pp. 361 ff.; McGlynn (2003), pp. 219 ff.

64 See Art. 10(a) of Regulation 1612/68 of the Council adopted on 15 Oct.1968, *OJ* 1968, L 257/2 (regarding the freedom of movement for workers within the Community); cf. Kohler (1992), pp. 227 ff.; Verschraegen (1994), pp. 26 ff.; Jessurun d'Oliveira (2000), pp. 527 ff. The European Court of Justice has not found any general social development that would justify stretching the reach of the term 'spouse' to cover a cohabitee. Case 59/85, The Netherlands v. Reed, *ECR* (17 April 1986) 1283 (1300-01). See also Proposal for a European Parliament and Council Directive on the right of Union citizens and their family members to move and reside freely within the territory of the Member States, *OJ* 2001, C 270 E.

65 For a view critical of a unification of family law in light of the principal of subsidiarity see Verschraegen (1994), pp. 25 ff.

66 For further information see Harremoes (1992), pp. 9-15; Schrama (1998), pp. 54 ff.; Requena (2000),

Adoption of Children of 1967,[67] the Convention on the Legal Status of Children Born out of Wedlock of 1975,[68] the Convention on the Exercise of Children's Rights of 1996[69] and the Convention on Contact Concerning Children of 2002[70] are worth mentioning. The Council has also been active through its making recommendations on particular issues submitted to it.[71] The Council is, nevertheless, limited in that the multilateral conventions proposed and adopted by it bind only those states which have chosen to ratify them. The norms of the conventions, in effect, rarely have automatic direct effect at the national level in the way that Community enactments do. The Council is basically limited to formulating general policy principles. Even if the Council's entire record does not appear particularly extraordinary, it remains the only European body that, in addition to its usual responsibilities, has attempted to tackle questions relating to the unification of family law in any significant manner.

The *Commission Internationale de l'Etat Civil* (CIEC) endeavours to address not only problems of the law of civil status, but has also taken on issues of marriage law, paternity, and the right to bear a name. This body, whose membership is comprised of sixteen European countries,[72] has drafted treaties of both substantive as well as of a purely conflicts of laws' nature; it has also delivered a series of recommendations on these subjects.[73] On the whole, however, the work of the CIEC has been confined to a relatively limited field and has been geared to serving the needs of the practice.[74] A general codification of family law is not to be expected from this organisation.

---

pp. 53 ff.; Pintens (2003-II), pp. 16 ff.; cf. also Furgler (1977), pp. 913 ff.; Rieg (1990), pp. 480 ff.; Kropholler (1975), pp. 68 ff.

67 Convention on the Adoption of Children of 24 April 1967, *U.N.T.S.* 634, 255, European Treaty Series No. 58; BGBl. II (1980), 1093. Signatories include Austria, Czech Republic, Denmark, Germany, Greece, Ireland, Italy, Latvia, Liechtenstein, Malta, Norway, Poland, Portugal, Romania, Sweden, Switzerland and the United Kingdom.

68 European Convention on the Legal Status of Children Born out of Wedlock of 15 October 1975, Rev.dr.unif. 1975 I 278, European Treaty Series No. 85. This convention has been ratified by Austria, Cyprus, Czech Republic, Denmark, Greece, Ireland, Liechtenstein, Lithuania, Luxembourg, Norway, Poland, Portugal, Romania, Sweden, Switzerland, United Kingdom.

69 European Convention on the Exercise of Children's Rights of 25 January 1996, European Treaty Series No. 160, cf. Baer & Marx (1997), pp. 1185 ff. This convention has been ratified by the Czech Republic, Germany, Greece, Latvia, Poland, Slovenia and Turkey.

70 European Convention on Contact Concerning Children of 15 May 2003, European Treaty Series No. 192. Cf. Requena (2000), pp. 61 ff.

71 Cf. Resolutions and recommendations adopted by the Committee of Ministers and Recommendations adopted by the Parliamentary Assembly under www.coe.int. – Cf. Kropholler (1975) 72.

72 These countries include the member states of the European Union (Austria, Belgium, Germany, France, Greece, Hungary, Italy, Luxembourg, the Netherlands, Poland, Portugal, Spain, United Kingdom), Member Candidates as Hungary and Poland as well as Croatia, Switzerland and Turkey. Cf. Protocol of 25 September 1950 concerning the CIEC and the supplementary protocol of 25 Sept. 1952, *U.N.T.S.* 932, 21; BGBl. II (1974), 915; cf. also Simitis (1969), pp. 30 ff.

73 For a list of these recommendations see Bischoff (1992), pp. 90 ff.; von Bar (1987) no. 66; Kropholler (1975), p. 77.

74 As to the proposal to establish a European birth, marriage and death register cf. Teschner (2002), pp. 289 ff.

5 Academic Research

In respect to family law there has always been an intensive comparison of law. A possible harmonisation of family law matters is mainly discussed within in the framework of the Council of Europe (cf. *supra* 4). However, since 2001 the Commission on European Family Law (CEFL), which is composed of experts in the field of family and comparative law from most of the European Union Member States and other European countries, tries to further the harmonisation of family law.[75] The Commission endeavours to survey the current state of comparative research and looks for a common core of European family law. A main goal of the search is the creation of a set of Principles of European Family Law that are thought to be most suitable for the harmonisation of family law within Europe.

6 Basic Issues in a Unification of Family Law

6.1 Increasing Convergence

In contrast to other legal subject areas, such as the law of carriage and the law on securities, which by their very nature are global and thereby render a substantive unification within reach, family law is a more intrinsically local matter.[76] A variety of factors facilitate the impression of domestic sources being unique and incompatible with a unification, including national customs, the incorporation of different views into laws, religious and emotional bonds, as well as lack of foreign ties.[77] Upon closer examination, these factors may be overemphasised. Comparative law has certainly called into question claims about the uniqueness of one's own legal system.[78] The transcontinental reception of individual concepts from the roman and canon law, as well as the common law, demonstrates that even in the area of family law, foreign legal ideas are capable of transference and furthers the process of unification.[79] 'Cultural constraints' are varyingly strong in different fields of family law.[80] In short, clinging onto one's own national legal traditions might have no other source than an innate mistrust of the imposition of foreign rules onto one's own native legal order.[81]

It is true that in some respects the family law of the new Central and Eastern European Union Member States still reflects the origin of a socialist background. However, in many respects as to the non-discrimination of sexes or children born out of wedlock there are no conflicts with modern trends. In some fields, especially in marriage law and matrimonial property law there are reforms underway which bring

---

75 Boele-Woelki (2002-II), pp. 178 ff.; Pintens (2003-I), pp. 504 ff. See http://www2.law.uu.nl/priv/cefl/
76 Philipps (1965), pp. 137 ff., 158 ff.
77 Cf. Ferid (1962), p. 205; Taupitz (1993), p. 11.
78 Cf. Müller-Freienfels (1968-69), pp. 181 ff. = (1978), pp. 86 ff.; Grossen (1991), pp. 96 ff.; Simitis (1994), pp. 420 ff. Cf. also Bradley (1999) 127 ff.
79 For a more detailed discussion see Luther (1981), pp. 254 ff.; Antokolskaia/De Hondt/Steenhoff (1999); Martiny (2002), pp. 191 ff.
80 Boele-Woelki (2002-II), pp. 176 ff.; Schwenzer (2003), pp. 143 ff.
81 Zitelmann (1888), p. 202 (concerning marital property and testate law).

more flexibility. An existing basis of common values has already been mentioned. Developments in European countries, as well as in other industrial and post-industrial societies, confirm shared trends in the changing nature of the family: the tendency towards smaller families, the increase in the number of single-parent households, the significant percentage of children born out of wedlock, and the increasing acceptance of unmarried cohabitation.[82] This convergence of living and familial relationships has meant that legislators the world over have been confronted with similar problems. Today there are also signs of a more international orientated milieu of lawyers, e.g. there are specialised lawyers within the national Central Authorities and 'liaison magistrates' dealing with international child abduction cases.

It is true that there is a close connection between family law and the field of national family, labour market and social policy. It therefore seems to be unrealistic to develop legal solutions not adapted to the societal background where these concepts should play a role.[83] On the other hand, not every legal question is so related to a unique background which prevents harmonisation. Furthermore, the different societal background is also subjected to change and tendencies of convergence. Flexibility and reasonable restrictions in uniform rules can avoid an unrealistic level of details in the rules.

Merely because one does not advocate a unification of family law at a supranational level does not necessary mean that one is against an accommodation of national legal norms to these changed circumstances.[84] Allowing this process of adjustment to societal change to occur in a manner commensurate with a country's own national development facilitates a substantive convergence and the preservation of a distinctive legal consciousness, while avoiding the imposition a prescribed legal order and disregard of the national context. Since these individual accommodation processes proceed in an uncoordinated fashion, no standardisation in legal form, let alone in detail, can be assured – not to mention that the reform debates in the individual countries need not proceed simultaneously, nor need they necessarily reach the same result. What is occurring can best be described as an 'unintended parallelism' in view of comparable social conditions.[85]

Despite any major convergence that may be occurring today, the perseverance of purely national solutions remains immense. A need for unification exists, above all, in those areas where existing national rules fail to adequately address the challenges facing the Common Market with respect to families.[86] This is particularly the case for newer transborder problems that do not lend themselves to an adequate resolution through resort to a single national legal order.

6.2 Relationship to a European Codification of Civil Law

Family law does not comprise a legal system by itself. In a number of European countries, this topic has been arranged primarily within the framework of a compre-

---

82 Kuisten (1996), pp. 115 ff.; Schwenzer (2003), pp. 143 ff. – Cf. the citations in Dopffel & Martiny (1994), pp. 575 ff.
83 Cf. Bradley (1999), pp. 127 ff.; McGlynn (2000), pp. 235 ff.; Bradley (2003), pp. 65 ff.
84 Cf. Neuhaus (1970), p. 256; Luther (1981), pp. 265 ff.
85 Will (1991), pp. 84 ff.
86 Cf. Taupitz (1993), p. 537; Neuhaus (1970), pp. 255 ff.

hensive codification of civil law. This is the situation in Austria, Belgium, France, Greece, Germany, Italy, Luxembourg, the Netherlands, Portugal, and Spain. A different approach has been taken in the northern countries of Denmark, Finland, and Sweden, where separate statutory enactments have been promulgated to deal with specific aspects of family law,[87] as well as in Great Britain and Ireland. In the former Socialist countries there is generally a separate Family Code. Only when an initial decision has been made to go ahead with a general European codification of civil law, will the consequences for family law become apparent.

A further decision will then have to be made regarding the extent and depth of any unification of family law. It is conceivable that family law could form a subordinate part of a universal codification. On the other hand, in view of the difficulty posed by the subject matter, one could forego a broad codification and undertake, from the beginning, only a limited unification; for example, with respect to particular aspects of the law of marriage. The rejection of a universal codification – thereby restricting any standardisation to specific, perhaps less controversial issues – would make the task easier. A piecemeal codification of this nature could, at any rate, give rise to co-ordination difficulties. This could also happen to the proposal of an introduction of a European family law as an additional optional regime.[88]

6.3 Relation to Other Fields of Law

Many rules of family law are exceptions to general principles of the law of obligations and personal and real property, or they have a tight connection to particular rules of procedural, administrative, and social security law. Family law no longer serves its former, purely civil law functions; it is today increasingly bound up, in a variety of ways, with other branches of law.[89] This is particularly true with respect to the intervention rights of authorities as well as the provision of social benefits. Family law is also intensively intermingled with procedural law, another area that has still not been unified. In view of these barriers of a legal-technical nature, decisions will have to be made as to whether a unification of family law in the European Union is meaningful without a unification of these other legal subject matters.

7 Family Law Subject Matters

7.1 Family Law and the Law Concerning Persons

The legal developments and reforms of the last decades have made a unification of family law easier to achieve.[90] Not only have the former political blocs disappeared,[91] but the major moral debates among the Member States in regulation of fam-

---

87 See Agell (2001), pp. 313 ff.
88 Cf. de Groot (2001), pp. 626 ff.
89 Cf. Bradley (1999), pp. 127 ff.; McGlynn (2000), pp. 235 ff.; Bradley (2003), pp. 65 ff.
90 Cf. Pintens (1995), pp. 542 ff.
91 The former controversy regarding a unification, including one with the former socialist states, is discussed in Rieg (1990), pp. 495 ff.

ily law matters have quietened down.[92] Apart from a few obstinate running fights, controversies no longer centre around the justifications for sexual equality, the necessity of according equal status to out-of-wedlock children,[93] or the permissibility of divorce. The points of contention today are more concerned with the implementation and consequences of these principles. Since a basic agreement regarding general principles does not preclude differing individual statutory solutions, the tasks involved in achieving a unification have not become easier: The basic issues having been resolved, the focus has shifted to a number of subsidiary complications and the deficits of past reform legislation. Current issues that have yet to be settled include the consequences of divorce, successive family relationships,[94] the formation of new families, single-parent families, and an increasing variety of living and family arrangements. Demographic changes also make inevitable a reform of the rules regarding the custodianship for the elderly.[95] There is, in sum, no shortage of issues that could form the basis of a discussion on unification. The following overview of some of the more significant areas of family law will show that each has been impacted to a different degree by unification tendencies.

7.2   Matrimonial Law

7.2.1   Formation of Marriage

A unification of matrimonial law was considered by the Council of Europe early on, but without anything being done.[96] Recent reforms in the law of marriage include the removal of impediments to marriage and other formalities.[97] The disparities between obligatory civil ceremonies (as practised in Germany) and the permissibility of religious ceremonies (as allowed in most European countries) have become less important.[98] The attention devoted to this topic in political and legal spheres has correspondingly decreased.

7.2.2   Marital Property Law

While English and Irish law, in allowing general contract and property laws to govern – with of course the possibility for equitable distributions – do not contain special regimes for matrimonial property, all other Member States in the European Union have enacted their own specific statutory marital property regimes. The net result is a con-

---

92 The same may also be said for the debates within Germany itself. See Simitis (1994), pp. 442 ff.
93 Cf. Resolution on Discrimination between Single Mothers and Married Women as regards Filiation in Certain Member States of 11 February 1983, *OJ* 1983, C 68/120.
94 See Sosson (1993), pp. 395 ff.
95 See on the Council of Europe's Recommendation on Principles Concerning the Legal Protection of Incapable Adults of 1999, Requena (2000), pp. 59 ff. – Cf. also Rood-de Boer (1989), pp. 207 ff.; Schulte (1989), pp. 591 ff.
96 See Neuhaus (1970), pp. 253 ff.; Neuhaus (1979), pp. 3 ff.
97 Cf. Müller-Freienfels (1968-69), pp. 197 ff. = (1978), pp. 102 ff.; Neuhaus (1970), pp. 259 ff.; Rieg (1990), p. 487; Coester (1988), pp. 122 ff.
98 As to the different forms for the contraction of marriages recognised under Italian law see Luther (1994), pp. 7 ff.

fusing plethora of property systems.[99] If a spouse participates significantly in transborder transactions in a unified economic region, divergent rules regarding spousal administration of marital property and liability for debts could constitute an impediment to commercial transactions within the Common Market.[100] As a result, marital property law is often mentioned as a possible subject for a unification.[101] However, due to the extreme complexity of this field, no concrete plans are in the making for the realisation of such a project. Furthermore, there is still a lack of sufficient experience in the European internal market as to the necessity for a co-ordination of the systems of marital property law. These systems represent primarily community of after-acquired property and, to a lesser extent, separate property regimes (as practised in England).[102] A unification could, at a minimum, prescribe a series of basic types of property regimes. Each European legislator could declare one of these types to be the national marital legal property regime. Spouses would then be entitled to elect treatment under one of the other regimes and make alternative contractual arrangements.[103] Another possibility would be the development of a 'European' system of matrimonial property that would be recognised in all Member States as a supplement to their respective domestic regimes.[104]

7.2.3 Divorce

With the exception of Malta, divorce is possible today everywhere in Europe. Significant divergences, especially as once existed in Ireland, Italy and Spain, have disappeared,[105] and a certain consensus concerning divorce has developed in the Community.[106] With respect to the grounds for divorce, the doctrine of irretrievable breakdown has become widely accepted. A party's desire not to continue with a marriage is honoured; and after a period of living apart, the marriage is presumed to have broken down.[107] Also widespread is a system that allows different divorce grounds with the provision for various types of divorces, as practised in Austria, Belgium, and France.[108] French law, as an illustration, recognises, in addition to divorce by mutual consent, divorce on the basis of breakdown of the community as well as fault-based

---

99 See Verbeke/Cretney/Grauers/Malaurie/Ofner/Savolainen/Skorini-Paparrigopoulou/van der Burght (1995), pp. 445 ff.; Agell (1998), pp. 7 ff.

100 For a discussion of the debate in Germany at the time of the adoption of the Civil Code between supporters of a unified property law regime and those advocating a regional system see Motive zu dem Entwurfe eines Bürgerlichen Gesetzbuches IV (1896) 133 ff.

101 Cf. Zajtay (1955), pp. 162 ff.; Remien (1991), p. 33.

102 A common tendency is in the participation of spouses in earnings on property. Müller-Freienfels (1968-69) 199 ff. = (1978), pp. 105 ff.; Henrich (2002), pp. 1521 ff.

103 Henrich (2002), pp. 1521 ff.

104 See Consortium Asser – UCL No. 2.1 ff. – Cf. for 'international marriages' Agell (1995), pp. 63 ff.; Agell (1996), pp. 313 ff.; Agell (1998), pp. 1 ff.

105 Luther (1981) 258-59; Müller-Freienfels (1968-69), pp. 201 ff. = (1978), pp. 107 ff.

106 See the Country Reports concerning the CEFL Questionnaire on 'Grounds for Divorce and Maintenance Between Former Spouses', http://www2.law.uu.nl/priv/cefl. Cf. Pintens (2003-I), pp. 334 ff.; Martiny (2003), pp. 529 ff.

107 See Meulders-Klein (1989), pp. 7-58; Grossen & von Overbeck (1988), cf. also Jayme (1981), p. 223; Luther (1981), p. 259.

108 See Meulders-Klein (1989), pp. 12 ff.; Schwenzer (1987), pp. 42 ff.

divorce.[109] Among these countries, however, there remains only a limited consensus in their legal orders. Neither this nor the fact that other countries (such as England and Germany) have only a single category of divorce grounds should be a formidable barrier to a unification. There remains, however, the difficulty that also in respect to the consequences of divorce there exist various solutions.

Divorce by mutual consent was once deemed suspect because of the concern that the continuation of the marriage would then be left at the parties' disposal. Today the consensus prevails that estranged spouses should be given the opportunity to work out between themselves the arrangement for their divorce, usually subject to some form of judicial approval.[110]

One of the main consequences of divorce involves child custody determinations. In this respect, Germany was not the only country that needed to do away with the rule that custody was to be awarded to only one parent. After reforms here and in other countries, joint custody is increasingly recognised.[111] Many countries, the Netherlands for example,[112] have asserted the 'protection of family life' demanded by Article 8 of the ECHR in enacting reforms.[113]

7.2.4   Non-Marital Cohabitation

Aside from a recommendation of the Council of Europe concerning agreements for non-marital cohabitation,[114] little in the way of a co-ordination has been achieved in this area, which has meanwhile become a preferred topic of comparative legal study.[115] Substantively the issue is to what extent rules that have been drawn up to govern marriages shall be applied to unmarried couples living together. A few countries, Sweden for example, provide for their equal application in most significant respects.[116] Others, such as Germany, have avoided placing unmarried cohabitation on the same footing as marriage, or at least have avoided enacting statutory rules dealing with the matter. It is conceivable that a more unified view of the law could eventually develop here.[117] In the meantime, no consensus regarding the type and the scope of an equalisation should be expected.

7.2.5   Registered Partnerships

In the controversial matter of registered partnership laws for homosexual couples, legislation could be passed in many European countries within a relatively short pe-

---

109 Cf. Arts. 229 ff. Civil Code. For reform proposals see Boulanger (2002), pp. 590 ff.
110 For more details see Verschraegen (1991), pp. 588 ff.; Dethloff (1994). – Cf. also Luther (1981), pp. 259 ff.
111 Cf. Art. 287 of the French *Code civil*, § 1671 German Civil Code; see also Meulders (1991) 18 ff.; Dopffel & Martiny (1994), pp. 583 ff.
112 See Hoge Raad [Supreme Court] 4 May 1984, *NJ* 1985 no. 510 p. 1650; see also Breemhaar (1987), pp. 69 ff.; Remien (1994), pp. 338 ff.
113 Cf. Fahrenhorst (1988), pp. 238 ff.; Brötel (1991), pp. 185 ff.; Rieg (1990), p. 493.
114 Recommendation regarding the validity of such contracts, R (88)3; cf. also Harremoes (1992), p. 14.
115 See only Müller-Freienfels (1987), pp. 259 ff.; Rubellin-Devichi (1989); Rubellin-Devichi (1990).
116 Cf. Håkansson (1989), pp. 9 ff.; Bradley (1990), pp. 154 ff.
117 See Luther (1981) 265.

riod. One explanation for this development is that the elimination of discrimination on the grounds of sexual orientation now laid down in Article 13 EC Treaty was persuasive.[118] Nevertheless, there are at least two basic models used. One is the partnership laws of the Nordic countries that basically apply the same legal rules to homosexual couples as for traditional marriage and has found followers also in countries like Germany. On the other hand there is the French 'pacte civil de solidarité' (pacs) which has limited effects and is also open to heterosexual couples.[119] The Dutch position recognising also full civil marriage for same-sex partners is unique at least for the moment.

7.3   Parent and Child

7.3.1   Consequences of Divorce for Children

It is obvious that with the growing number of divorces the consequences of divorce and separation for children become more and more important. Thus, they are no longer only a subject of national family law. Within the European Council, the European Union and the Hague Conference there is an increasing awareness of the growing transborder dimensions of questions of custody, access and contact, child abduction and maintenance enforcement (cf. 1.3). The complicated interplay of rules of different origin shows that in the long run a harmonisation of substantive law and procedural rules would also be desirable.

7.3.2   Out-of-Wedlock Children

The equalisation of the rights of out-of-wedlock children has been a matter of great concern.[120] In this respect, reference should be made not only to the United Nations Convention on the Rights of the Child and the Council of Europe Convention on the Legal Status of Children Born Out of Wedlock,[121] but also to the *Marckx* judgment of the European Court of Human Rights.[122] At the time of the decision, Belgian law provided that out-of-wedlock children were to be regarded as their mother's own if the

---

118   See Resolution of the European Parliament of 8 February 1994, *OJ* 1994, C 61/40-43. – But see also the restrictive judgments in case C-249/96, Grant v. South-East-Trains, *ECR*, 1998-I (17 Feb. 1998), 621 (no obligation of railway company to grant the same travel concessions to homosexual partners as to heterosexual partners of staff members); case C-122/99 P, D. and the Kingdom of Sweden v. Council of the European Union, *ECR* 2001-I (31 May 2001) (no household allowance provided for in the Staff Regulations of the Officials of the EC for Swedish partner of the same sex). Cf. Jakob (2002), pp. 505 ff.; Pirrung (2002), pp. 605 ff.

119   Cf. Verschraegen (1994); Basedow/Hopt/Kötz/Dopffel (2000); Boele-Woelki/Fuchs (2003); Pintens (2003-II), pp. 12 ff.

120   See Pintens (1993) 205 ff. The Resolution on the Problems of the Children in the European Community suggests that the law of parentage should be co-ordinated at the European level, *OJ* 1992, C 13/534 (no. 26).

121   The Convention of 15 October 1975 (*supra* n. 68), provides that maternity is to be merely by fact of birth (Art. 2); paternity is to be determined on the basis of either recognition or through judicial decree (Art. 3). In addition, the convention provides that illegitimate children are not to be discriminated against in child support and testate matters (Arts. 6, 9).

122   *Marckx v. Belgium* (*supra* n. 40); see also Jayme (1979), pp. 2425 ff.; Pintens (1993), pp. 205 ff.; Sturm (1982), pp. 1150 ff.

mother formally recognised her maternity. Even after recognition illegitimate children were not regarded as a part of their parents' family and so their rights as regards inheritance and gifts *inter vivos* were significantly less than those of legitimate children and other family members. The Court held that these restrictions failed to secure protection of the right to family life, as required by Article 8 of the ECHR. This article, it was held, protects the illegitimate as well as the legitimate family. The Court also found a violation of the non-discrimination provision of Article 14 because of the unjustified discrimination between legitimate and illegitimate children. Eight years were to pass, however, before Belgium finally amended its laws on illegitimacy to conform with the Court's decision.[123] The decision also motivated other countries to bring their legislation into line with the ECHR.[124] Although French and Italian law still have not adopted the rule *mater semper certa est*, the position of illegitimate children in these countries has improved.[125] After the reform of 3 Dec. 2001, French law now also guarantees the same succession rights to children of adulterous unions that are given to children born in wedlock and thus follows a judgment of the ECHR.[126]

Another shared legal development involves the rules for the establishment of paternity. An automatic presumption of paternity in situations where the child could have been conceived during a marriage is widely accepted. The application of this presumption, however, has been restricted in certain circumstances,[127] while the right to contest paternity has been expanded. The latter are both subject to an actual determination of paternity.

Today many jurisdictions provide the possibility for a grant of parental custody to the fathers of out-of-wedlock children.[128] The limits of this parental responsibility and contact with the child are still a matter to be solved by the ECHR.[129]

7.3.3 Adoption

The law of adoption has been recently characterised by a movement towards easing adoption procedures.[130] A certain amount of uniformity already exists, for example,

---

123 See Pintens (1994), pp. 2 ff. (containing further references). For the particulars of the delayed legislative incorporation of the Marckx decision see *Vermeire* v. *Belgium*, 214-C Eur. Ct. H.R. (ser. A) (1991) 74, reprinted in: *EuGRZ* (1992) 12; see also Polakiewicz (1992) 149-90.

124 Cf. Meulders-Klein (1996), pp. 487 ff.; Rieg (1990), pp. 484 ff.

125 Cf. arts. 323, 334-38 of the French *Code civil*. For a summary of the reform of January 8, 1993, see Ferrand (1994), pp. 43 ff.; C. Steindorff (1993), pp. 319 ff.

126 Case 34406/97, *Mazurek* v. *France*, Eur.Ct.H.R., Reports of Judgements and Decisions 2000-II p. 1, reprinted in *Droit de la famille* (2000), p. 20 Annotation Lamy, *FamRZ* (2000), p. 1077 Annotation Vanwinkelen.

127 See *Rasmussen* v. *Denmark*, Eur. Ct. H.R. (ser. A) 87 (1984) 1 (14 *et seq.*); cf. Meulders-Klein (1990), pp. 138 ff.; Pintens (1993), pp. 207 ff.

128 See Coester (1993), pp. 542 ff.; Meulders (1991), pp. 21 ff.; Schwenzer (1987) 253 ff.; cf. also Jayme (1981), p. 225; Brötel (1991), pp. 278 ff.; Henrich (1994), pp.190 ff.

129 Cf. Case 25735/94, *Elsholz* v. *Germany*, Eur.Ct.H.R., Reports of Judgements and Decisions 2000-VIII p. 345, reprinted FamRZ (2001), p. 341 Annotation Vanwinkelen; Case 31871/96, *Sommerfeld* v. *Germany*, Eur.Ct.H.R. (2001), reprinted FamRZ (2002), p. 381 Annotation Rixe. – Cf. Hohnerlein (2000), p. 259.

130 Cf. Rieg (1985), pp. 511 ff.

among the signatories to the European Adoption Convention of 1967.[131] This treaty permits only 'full adoptions', a provision aimed at ensuring complete acceptance in the adoptive family through the severance of ties to the biological parents. Several European countries, clinging to their civil law traditions, also allow simple adoptions.

This brief overview of family law issues demonstrates that an appreciable convergence with respect to certain principles has occurred and that some uniformity among European countries has already been achieved. Actual unification of individual family law norms is, nevertheless, still the exception rather than the rule. The situation in Europe, as in the past, is the existence of different substantive rules. Even in those instances where some uniformity exists among these rules, their particulars diverge.

8. Means of Achieving a Unification

8.1. Treaties

In principle, lawmaking within the community is not limited to regulations, directives and decisions; originally Member States could also conclude agreements among themselves regarding matters connected with the Treaty.[132] Until recently the unification of international family law within the European Union has been achieved exclusively through the implementation of treaties. In former years the European Parliament has, for example, requested a separate treaty dealing with international child abduction, which would supplement and be more effective than the Hague Convention of 1980 and the Luxembourg Convention of 1980.[133] However, before the number of treaties is further increased, it may also be worthwhile to consider whether the possibility of ratifying and effectively implementing existing treaties has been exhausted.[134] For example, the Convention on the Recovery of Maintenance, which has meanwhile entered into force, has been criticised as having been an unnecessary duplication of already existing multilateral treaties.[135] In addition, today there is a competence of the European Union which restricts the competence of the Member States.

While unification of substantive family law through the use of a treaty is theoretically conceivable, the tediousness of drafting and agreeing upon provisions for such a treaty, coupled with its limited chances for ratification and the purely framework character which any rules are likely to take, suggests that a meaningful and effective unification of family law is not to be achieved by this means.

8.2 Regulations

Regulations now play a major role in European international civil procedure. Especially in the field of international family law procedure, several instruments are in

---

131 See *supra* n. 67.
132 Cf. Art. 293 (ex-art. 220) EC Treaty.
133 See numbers 27 and 28 of the Resolution of 9 March 1993 (*supra* n. 7) (supporting an expanded role for international mediation in family matters).
134 Cf. Castillo (1990), p. 365.
135 See Sumampouw (1992), pp. 315 ff.

force and there are new initiatives for community legislation (cf. 1.3).[136] E.g., the Council and Commission initiated a preliminary study on the possibility of drawing up a legal instrument on the law applicable to divorce (April 2004) and intend to draw up a preliminary study on jurisdiction and the law applicable to matrimonial property and successions (April 2004).

8.3 Directives

Although binding directives have been the most effective instrument for creating a common European civil law, they have until now played no role with respect to family law matters as a result of the Union's lack of competence. Were a unification to be limited to the promulgation of guiding principles, directives would be a potential tool for achieving this goal.

8.4 Framework Rules and Model Laws

No international organisation has yet to put together a model family law. While model laws lack binding force under international law, they may be adopted into domestic law by individual legislatures. In the European context it is not clear what organisation, if any, would take on the risk of such a project. In the United States, where each of the individual state legislatures possesses the competence for family law matters, a series of model laws have been drafted.[137] Some of these uniform laws, which are often very detailed, focus on interstate matters, such as the enforcement of maintenance obligations[138] or the jurisdiction for custody procedure.[139] Others attempt a comprehensive unification of the law with respect to an entire subject area.[140] The latter, at any rate, are seldom adopted by the individual states, with the result that the degree of unification varies throughout the nation. Even though these efforts have not resulted in any comprehensive unification on a countrywide basis, they have contributed a significant sense of comprehension and transparency to the process of legal reform and its implementation.

8.5. Restatements and Principles

The variety of domestic laws in Europe makes it imperative that a general overview of existing laws be put together. In the United States, this has been achieved in many

---

136 See Council Regulation concerning jurisdiction and the recognition and enforcement of judgments in matrimonial matters and in matters of parental responsibility repealing Regulation (EC) No.1347/2000 of 27 November 2003, *OJ* 2003, L338/1. For more detailed information see Kohler (2002), pp. 709 ff.

137 Such uniform acts are approved by the National Conference of Commissioners on Uniform State Law. Cf. Müller-Freienfels (1968-69), pp. 184, 192 = (1978), pp. 89, 97.

138 All 50 states and the District of Columbia have adopted the Uniform Interstate Family Support Act of 1996; U.L.A. 9 (Part I) (1988 & Supp.) 229. – Cf. also new version of 2001.

139 The Uniform Child Custody Jurisdiction Act 1968 has been adopted in all 50 states and the District of Columbia. See U.L.A. 9 (Part I) (1988 & Supp.) 113-114. – See also new Jurisdiction and Enforcement Act of 1997

140 See, e.g., the Uniform Parentage Act 1973, U.L.A. 9B (1988) 287 (adopted by eighteen states). – Cf. new version of 2002.

areas with the aid of 'Restatements of the Law', authored by the American Law Institute. A restatement lays out what the law in a general area is, how it is changing, and what direction the reviewers think this change should take. Although restatements have been used primarily for subject matters outside of family law, 'Principles of the Law of Family Dissolution' have been developed.[141] At the European level efforts are being made for compilation of a restatement covering the law of obligations. There would be, it seems, no reason for rejecting a further restatement on family law. A stock-taking of this nature could serve not only to describe and accompany, but also to influence, the process of change within European legal systems. At the same time, one would need to bear in mind that the wealth of laws which would need to surveyed, coupled with rapidly changing legislative reforms, could doom this undertaking, from the outset, to failure.

Another alternative is the establishment of non-binding principles for selected fields of family law.[142] European principles generally contain a set of rules with a commentary. Insofar as they are based on a compilation of the existing national solutions they are, to a certain extent, interchangeable with Restatements. The establishment of such principles, which is preferred by the Commission on European Family Law, is faced not only with the necessity of selecting an appropriate field of law,[143] with the difficulties of gathering information on national laws but also with a plethora of additional methodological questions. The aim is to find as far as possible a practicable 'common core' of European solutions. The principles, however, cannot fix only the status quo. In the case of divergent solutions it is also unavoidable to make a decision what is to be regarded as the 'better law' in the future.[144] Work in the field of divorce law has started in 2002.[145] Future subjects could be parental responsibility and non-marital cohabitation.

9   Conclusion

The awareness of an emerging 'European family law' has risen in the last years. However, this field of law is still comprised of fragmentary legal principles of disparate nature and variant origin. While several of them attempt to prescribe detailed substantive law provisions, others merely convey a basic decision taken by the promulgating institution. Some instruments and procedures are simply geared towards an accommodation of national legal systems; very few strive towards any sort of actual unification of these systems. National developments are, at the same time, proceeding in a manner that merely attempts to accommodate, in a piecemeal fashion, changing societal practices and foreign legal developments.

The European Union, as discussed, has now a competence in the field of international family but has still not been authorised to undertake a unification of substan-

---

141 American Law Institute, ed., Principles of the Law of Family Dissolution – Analysis and Recommendations (2002). – Cf. also Krause (1992), p. 223; Maxwell (2003), pp. 249 ff.
142 Cf. Boele-Woelki (2002-II), pp. 179 ff.; Pintens (2003-I), pp. 329 ff.
143 See Antokolskaia (2002), pp. 4 ff.
144 For more details see Antokolskaia (2003), pp. 159 ff.
145 Cf. Boele-Woelki (2002-I) pp. 17 ff.; Boele-Woelki/Braat/Sumner I, II (2003).

tive family law. In any event, one should not overlook the progress that has been made in overcoming transnational issues in Europe. A certain degree of unification has already been achieved within the Union especially on the law of international civil procedure. Several Regulations are already in force. With the aim of facilitating the free movement of persons and the free circulation of judgments, a broader unification of international family law is currently in preparation. To this extent there will also be indirect pressure in the direction of a harmonisation of domestic family law. The work of the Hague Conference has also been significant in the area of rules of conflicts of laws. Another important player has been the Council of Europe, which has promoted mainly the unification of substantive law through a series of treaties and recommendations. These have, unfortunately, only been of isolated significance.

In spite of an intensifying debate on a 'Europeanisation of family law' and an increasing number of calls for a 'European solution', a comprehensive concept is still not in sight and not to be expected in the near future. For the time being, all indicators point to a retention of the present division of responsibilities in family law, leaving intact the current practice of diversified, and sometimes overlapping, activities carried out by an assortment of national, supranational and international bodies and commissions. The chances of success for a broader unification seem to be best with respect to those common, clearly delineated issues that require a joint effort for their successful resolution. In the meantime, the development of European family law will continue to take place through a process of reciprocal influence and interaction among the Member States, with the result that much of the present diversity of solutions in the individual legal orders will continue into the future.

BIBLIOGRAPHY: Agell, Towards Uniforming Spouses' Property Rights, Especially in International Marriages?, in: Council of Europe, ed., Proceedings of the 3rd European Conference on Family Law (Strasbourg 1995), pp. 63-80 = Matrimoni trasfrontalieri e regimi patrimoniali: Verso un diritto uniforme?, *Rivista di diritto civile* 42 (1996), pp. 313-334; Agell, The division of property upon divorce from a European perspective, in: *Liber Amicorum Meulders-Klein* (Brussels 1998), pp. 1-20; Agell, Is there one system of family law in the Nordic countries?, *European Journal of Law Reform* 3 (2001), pp. 313-330; Antokolskaia, Would the harmonisation of family law in Europe enlarge the gap between the law in the books and the law in action?, *Die Praxis des Familienrechts* (2002), pp. 261-292; Antokolskaia, The „better law" approach and the harmonisation of family law, in: Boele-Woelki, ed., *Perspectives for the Unification and Harmonisation of Family Law in Europe* (Antwerpen et al. 2003), pp. 159-182; Antokolskaia/De Hondt/Steenhoff, Een zoektocht naar Europees familierecht, *Report for the Dutch Association of Comparative Law* (Deventer 1999); von Bar, *Internationales Privatrecht* I (Munich 1987); Basedow, Konstantinidis v. Bangemann oder die Familie im Europäischen Gemeinschaftsrecht, *ZEPR* (1994), pp. 197-199; Basedow/Hopt/Kötz/Dopffel, eds., *Die Rechtsstellung gleichgeschlechtlicher Lebensgemeinschaften* (2000); Beaumont, Brussels Convention II – A New Private International Law Instrument in Family Matters for the European Union or the European Community?, *Eur. L. Rev.* (1995), pp. 268-288; Berger, Auswirkungen der Europäischen Menschenrechtskonvention auf das österreichische Zivilrecht, *JBl.* (1985), pp. 142-155; Bischoff, La Commission Internationale de l'Etat Civil (C.I.E.C.), in: Ganghofer, ed., *Le droit de la famille en Europe – Son évolution depuis l'antiquité jusqu'à nos jours* (Strasbourg 1992), pp. 85-93; Boele-Woelki, De weg naar een Europees familierecht, *Tijdschrift voor familie- en jeugdrecht* (1997), pp. 2-9; Boele-Woelki, The Road Towards a European Family Law, *1.1 Electronic Journal of Comparative Law* (1997);

Boele-Woelki, Divorce in Europe: Unification of Private International Law and Harmonisation of Substantive Law, *Liber Amicorum I. S. Joppe* (Deventer 2002), pp. 17-29 (referred to as Boele-Woelki (2002-I)); Boele-Woelki, Comparative Research-Based Drafting of Principles of European Family Law, in: Faure/Smits/Schneider, eds., *Towards a European Ius Commune in Legal Education and Research* (Antwerpen/Groningen 2002), pp. 171-189 (referred to as Boele-Woelki (2002-II)); Boele-Woelki/Fuchs, *Legal Recognition of Same-Sex Couples in Europe* (Antwerpen 2003); Boele-Woelki/Braat/Sumner, *European Family Law in Action* I, II (Antwerpen 2003); Boucaud, La protection de l'enfant en Europe, *Annuaire européen* 38 (1990), pp. 21-38; Boulanger, Au sujet de la réforme française du divorce – La notion de rupture dans les droits européens et la survie des éléments subjectifs, *Dalloz Doctrine* (2002), pp. 590-592; Bradley, Radical Principles and the Legal Institution of Marriage – Domestic Relations Law and Social Democracy in Sweden, *Int. J. L. Fam.* 4 (1990), pp. 154-185; Bradley, Convergence in Family Law: Mirrors, Transplants and Political Economy, *Maastricht Journal of European and Comparative Law* 6 (1999), pp. 127-150 = *Oxford University Comparative Law Forum* (2001) 2; Bradley, A family law for Europe? Sovereignty, political, economy and legitimation, in: Boele-Woelki, ed., *Perspectives for the Unification and Harmonisation of Family Law in Europe* (Antwerpen et al. 2003), pp. 65-104; Breemhaar, Das Sorgerecht für minderjährige Kinder nach niederländischem Recht, *Das Standesamt* (1987), pp. 69-70; Brötel, *Der Anspruch auf Achtung des Familienlebens* (Baden-Baden 1991); Brückner, *Unterhaltsregreß im internationalen Privat- und Verfahrensrecht* (Tübingen 1994); Castillo, La protection des enfants dans la Communauté européenne, *Revue du Marché Commun* (1990), pp. 361-365; Coester, Probleme des Eheschließungsrechts in rechtsvergleichender Sicht, *Das Standesamt* (1988), pp. 122-129; Coester, Entwicklungslinien im europäischen Nichtehelichenrecht, *ZEPR* (1993), pp. 536-553; Consortium Asser – UCL (ed.), '*Etude sur les régimes matrimoniaux des couples mariés et sur le patrimoine des couples non mariés dans le droit international privé et le droit interne des Etats membres de l'Union Européenne – Analyse comparative des rapports nationaux et propositions d'harmonisation*' (Offre no. JAI/A3/2001/03), Den Haag/Louvain-La Neuve (2003). Dethloff, *Die einverständliche Scheidung* (1994); Dethloff, Arguments for the unification and harmonisation of family law in Europe, in: Boele-Woelki, ed., *Perspectives for the Unification and Harmonisation of Family Law in Europe* (Antwerpen et al. 2003), pp. 37-64; Dopffel & Martiny, Rechtsvergleichung – Kindschaftsrecht im Wandel, in: Dopffel, ed., *Kindschaftsrecht im Wandel – Zwölf Länderberichte mit einer vergleichenden Summe* (Tübingen 1994), pp. 575-661; Dyer, L'évolution du droit international privé de la famille en Europe au cours du "premier siècle" de la Conférence de La Haye de droit international privé: les avatars des Conventions de La Haye, in: Ganghofer, ed., *Le droit de la famille en Europe – Son évolution depuis l'antiquité jusqu'à nos jours* (Strasbourg 1992), pp. 95-103; Fahrenhorst, Sorge- und Umgangsrecht nach der Ehescheidung und die Europäische Konvention zum Schutze der Menschenrechte und Grundfreiheiten, *FamRZ* (1988), pp. 238-242; Fahrenhorst, *Familienrecht und Europäische Menschenrechtskonvention* (Paderborn 1994); Fallon, Droit familial et droit des Communautés Européennes, *Revue trimestrielle de droit familial* (1998), pp. 361-400; Ferid, Methoden, Möglichkeiten und Grenzen der Privatrechtsvereinheitlichung, *ZRVgl.* 3 (1962), pp. 193-213; Ferrand, Die Entwicklung des französischen Kindschaftsrechts, in: Schwab & Henrich, eds., *Entwicklungen des europäischen Kindschaftsrechts* (1994), pp. 41-57; Furgler, L'évolution actuelle et les perspectives d'harmonisation du droit de la famille au sein de l'Europe, *Diritto di Famiglia e della Persone* 6 (1977), pp. 913-938; Götz, Auf dem Weg zur Rechtseinheit in Europa?, *JZ* (1994), pp. 265-269; de Groot, Op weg naar een Europees personen- en familierecht?, *Ars Aequi* 44 (1995), pp. 29-33; de Groot, Auf dem Wege zu einem europäischen (internationalen) Familienrecht, *ZEPR* (2001), pp. 618-627; Grossen, The Contribution of Comparative (or Foreign Law) Studies to Family Law Reform, in: *Droit sans frontières – Es-*

says in Honour of I. Neville Brown (Birmingham 1991), pp. 95-101; Grossen & von Overbeck, eds., *Révision du droit du divorce. Expériences étrangères récentes* (Zurich 1988); Hamilton & Standley, European family law, in: Hamilton/Standley/Hodson, ed., *Family Law in Europe* (London *et al.* 1995), pp. 548-597; Harremoes, Le Conseil d'Europe et le droit de la famille, in: Ganghofer, ed., *Le droit de la famille en Europe – Son évolution depuis l'antiquité jusqu'à nos jours* (Strasbourg 1992), pp. 9-15; Henrich, Entwicklungslinien des deutschen Kindschaftsrechts im europäischen Kontext, in: Schwab & Henrich, eds., *Entwicklungen des europäischen Kindschaftsrechts*, (1994), pp. 185-199; Henrich, Zur Zukunft des Güterrechts in Europa, *FamRZ* (2002), pp. 1521-1526; Herzog, Europäischer Grundrechtsschutz für Ehe und Familie, *Jahrbuch Bitburger Gespräche* (2001), pp. 7-14; Hohnerlein, Konturen eines einheitlichen Europäischen Familien- und Kindschaftsrechts, *The European Legal Forum* (2000/2001), pp. 252-260; Hondius, Naar een Europees personen- en familierecht, in: *Drie Treden – Over politiek, beleid en recht* (Zwolle 1995), pp. 173-180; Håkansson, Die rechtliche Behandlung der nichtehelichen Lebensgemeinschaften in Schweden, in: Blaurock, ed., *Entwicklungen im Recht der Recht der Familie und der außerehelichen Lebensgemeinschaften*, (1989), pp. 9-20; Jakob, Die eingetragene Lebenspartnerschaft im Europarecht, *FamRZ* (2002), pp. 507-508; Jänterä-Jareborg, Unification of international family law in Europe – a critical perspective, in: Boele-Woelki, ed., *Perspectives for the Unification and Harmonisation of Family Law in Europe* (Antwerpen *et al.* 2003), pp. 194-216; Jayme, Europäische Menschenrechtskonvention und deutsches Nichtehelichenrecht, *NJW* (1979), pp. 2425-2429; Jayme, Die Entwicklung des europäischen Familienrechts, *FamRZ* (1981), pp. 221-226; Jessurun d'Oliveira, Freedom of Movement of Spouses and Registered Partners in the European Union, in: Basedow *et al.*, ed., *Private Law in the International Arena* (The Hague 2000), pp. 527-543; Killerby, The Council of Europe's Contribution to Family Law (Past, Present and Future), in: Lowe/Douglas, eds., *Family Across Frontiers* (The Hague 1996), pp. 13-25; Killerby, Family law in Europe. Standards set by the Member States of the Council of Europe, in: Liber Amicorum *Meulders-Klein*, (Brussels 1998), pp. 351-378; Kohler, L'article 220 du traité CEE et les conflits de juridictions en matière de relations familiales: premières réflections, *Riv.dir.int.priv.proc.* 28 (1992), pp. 221-240; Kohler, Auf dem Weg zu einem europäischen Justizraum für das Familien- und Erbrecht, *FamRZ* (2002), pp. 709-713; Kötz, Rechtsvergleichung und gemeineuropäisches Privatrecht, in: Müller-Graff, ed., *Gemeinsames Privatrecht in der Europäischen Gemeinschaft* (1993), pp. 95-108; Krause, Family Law, in: Clark/Ansay (eds.), *Introduction to the Law of the United States*, (Deventer, Boston 1992), pp. 219-261; Kropholler, *Internationales Einheitsrecht* (Tübingen 1975); Kuchinke, Über die Notwendigkeit, ein gemeineuropäisches Familien- und Erbrecht zu schaffen, *Europas Universale rechtsordnungspolitische Aufgabe im Recht des dritten Jahrtausends, Festschrift für Alfred Söllner zum 70. Geburtstag* (München 2000), pp. 589-612; Kuisten, Changing Family Patterns in Europe – A Case of Divergence?, *European Journal of Population* 12(1996), pp. 115-143; Lipstein, One Hundred Years of Hague Conferences on Private International Law, *ICLQ* 42 (1993), pp. 553-653; Longobardo, La convenzione internazionale sui diritti del fanciullo, *Diritto di Famiglia e della Persone* 20 (1991), pp. 370-427; Luther, Einheitsrecht durch Evolution im Eherecht und im Recht der eheähnlichen Gemeinschaft, *RabelsZ* 45 (1981), pp. 253-267; Luther, Italienisches Familienrecht, *Jahrbuch für Italienisches Recht* 7 (1994), pp. 3-45; Martiny, Europäisches Familienrecht – Utopie oder Notwendigkeit?, *RabelsZ* 59 (1995), pp. 419-453; Martiny, Die Möglichkeit der Vereinheitlichung des Familienrechts innerhalb der Europäischen Union, in: Martiny/Witzleb, eds., *Auf dem Wege zu einem Europäischen Zivilgesetzbuch*, (Berlin, 1999) pp. 177-189; Martiny, The Harmonisation of Family Law in the European Community. Pro and Contra, in: Faure/Smits/Schneider, eds., *Towards a European Ius Commune in Legal Education and Research* (Antwerpen/Groningen 2002), pp. 191-201; Martiny, Divorce and maintenance between former spouses – initial results of the Commission on European Family Law, in: Boele-Woelki, ed., *Perspectives for the Unification and Harmonisation of Family Law in Europe* (Antwerpen *et al.* 2003), pp. 529-550; Maxwell, Unification and harmonisation of Family Law principles: the United States experience, in: Boele-Woelki, ed., *Perspectives for the Unification and Harmonisation of Family Law in Europe* (Antwerpen *et al.* 2003), pp. 249-267; McGlynn, A Family Law for the European Union, in: Shaw, ed., *Social Law and Policy in an Evolving European Union* (Oxford 2000), pp. 223-241; McGlynn, Families and the European European Union charter of Fundamental Rights: Progressive change of entrenching the status quo?, *Eur. L. Rev.* 26 (2001), pp. 582-598; McGlynn, Challenging the european harmonisation of family law: perspectives of „the family", in: Boele-Woelki, ed., *Perspectives for the Unification and Harmonisation of Family Law in Europe* (Antwerpen *et al.* 2003), pp. 219-238; McGoldrick, The United Nations Convention on the Rights of the Child, *Int. J. L. Fam.* 5 (1991), pp. 132-169; Meulders, Vers la co-responsabilité parentale dans la famille européenne, *Revue trimestrielle de droit familial* (1991), pp. 5-28; Meulders-Klein, La problématique du divorce dans les législations d'Europe occidentale, *Rev. int.dr.comp.* 41 (1989), pp. 7-58; Meulders-Klein, The Position of the Father in European Legislation, *Int. J. L. Fam.* 4 (1990) pp. 138-153; Meulders-Klein, The Status of the Father in European Legislation, *AJCL* 44 (1996), pp. 487-520; Meulders-Klein, Towards a European Civil Code on Family Law? Ends and means, in: Boele-Woelki, ed., *Perspectives for the Unification and Harmonisation of Family Law in Europe* (Antwerpen *et al.* 2003), pp. 105-117 ; Müller-Freienfels, The Unification of Family Law, *AJCL* 16 (1968-69), pp. 175-218; Müller-Freienfels, *Familienrecht im In- und Ausland – Aufsätze* I (Frankfurt am Main 1978), pp. 79-124; Müller-Freienfels, Cohabitation and Marriage Law – A Comparative Study, *Int. J. L. Fam.* 1 (1987), pp. 259-294; Neuhaus, Europäisches Familienrecht? Gedanken zur Rechtsvergleichung und Rechtsvereinheitlichung, in: *Festschrift Dölle* II (1963), pp. 419-435; Neuhaus, Europäische Vereinheitlichung des Eherechts, *RabelsZ* 34 (1970), pp. 253 -263; Neuhaus, *Ehe und Kindschaft in rechtsvergleichender Sicht* (1979); O'Higgins, The Family and European Law, *New Law Journal* (1990), pp. 1643-1646; Philipps, *Erscheinungsformen und Methoden der Privatrechts-Vereinheitlichung* (Frankfurt am Main 1965); Pintens, Entwicklungen im europäischen Abstammungsrecht, *Das Standesamt* (1993), pp. 205-210; Pintens, Die Entwicklung des belgischen Kindschaftsrechts, in: Schwab & Henrich, eds., *Entwicklungen des europäischen Kindschaftsrechts*, (1994), pp. 1-31; Pintens, Droit des successions, des donations et des testaments en Europe – de la diversité à l'unité?, in: Fédération royale des notaires de Belgique, ed., *Les relations contractuelles internationales – Le rôle du notaire* (Antwerpen 1995), pp. 532-; Pintens, Rechtsvereinheitlichung und Rechtsangleichung im Familienrecht. Eine Rolle für die Europäische Union?, *ZEPR* (1998), pp. 670-676; Pintens, Von Konstantinidis bis Grant. Europa und das Familienrecht, *ZEPR* (1998), pp. 843-848; Pintens, Over de Europeanisatie van het familierecht, *Tijdschrift voor familie- en jeugdrecht* (1999), pp. 238-243; Pintens, Grundgedanken und Perspektiven einer Europäisierung des Familien- und Erbrechts, *FamRZ* (2003), pp. 329-336, 417-425, 499-505 (referred to as Pintens (2003-I)); Pintens, Europeanisation of family law, in: Boele-Woelki, ed., *Perspectives for the Unification and Harmonisation of Family Law in Europe* (Antwerpen *et al.* 2003), pp. 3-33 (referred to as Pintens (2003-II)); Pintens/du Mongh, Family and Succession Law in the European Union, in: Blanpain/Pintens, eds., *International Encyclopaedia of Laws. Family and Succession Law* (The Hague, 1997); Pirrung, Sorgerechts- und Adoptionsübereinkommen der Haager Konferenz und des Europarats, *RabelsZ* 57 (1993), pp. 124-154 (referred to as Pirrung (1993-I)); Pirrung, Internationales Privat- und Verfahrensrecht der Scheidung in den Europäischen Gemeinschaften – eine Skizze zum Erfordernis einer neuen internationalen Rechtsgrundlage, in: *Grensoverschrijdend privaatrecht – Opstellen aangeboden aan Mr. van Rijn van Alkemade* (Deventer 1993), pp. 189-204 (referred to as Pirrung (1993-II)); Pirrung, Registrierte Partnerschaften vor den Europäischen Gerichten, *Estudos em homenagem à de Magalhães Collaço* I

(Coimbra 2002), pp. 605-621; Polakiewicz, Die innerstaatliche Durchsetzung der Urteile des Europäischen Gerichtshofs für Menschenrechte, *Zeitschrift für ausländisches öffentliches Recht und Völkerrecht* 52 (1992), pp. 149-190; Remien, Möglichkeiten und Grenzen eines europäischen Privatrechts, *Jahrbuch Junger Zivilrechtswissenschaftler* (1991), pp. 11-421; Remien, Niederlande – Die Wirkungen des Vater-Mutter-Kind-Verhältnisses im niederländischen Privatrecht, in: Dopffel, ed., *Kindschaftsrecht im Wandel – Zwölf Länderberichte mit einer vergleichenden Summe* (Tübingen 1994), pp. 333-385; Requena, Activities of the Council of Europe in the Field of Family Law, *Cal. W. Int. L. J.* 31 (2000), pp. 53-65; Rieg, L'adoption dans les principales législations européennes – Introduction comparative, *Rev.int. dr.comp.* 37 (1985), pp. 511-524; Rieg, L'harmonisation européenne du droit de la famille: mythe ou réalité?, in: *Conflits et harmonisation – Mélanges en l'honneur d'Alfred E. von Overbeck* (Fribourg (Switzerland) 1990), pp. 473-499; Rood-de Boer, Veroudering in Europa en de implicaties voor de rechtspraktijk, in: Franken *et al.*, eds., *Themis en Europa – Een opening van nieuwe grenzen?*, (Zwolle 1989), pp. 207-220; Rubellin-Devichi, ed., *Les concubinages en Europe – Aspects socio-juridiques* (Paris 1989); Rubellin-Devichi, ed., *Des concubinages dans le monde* (Paris 1990); Rubellin-Devichi, Le principe de l'intérêt de l'enfant dans la loi et la jurisprudence françaises, *JCP* (1994) I no. 3739; Schrama, De Raad van Europa en het familierecht, *Tijdschrift voor familie – en jeugdrecht* (1998), pp. 54-59; Schulte, Reform of Guardianship Laws in Europe – A Comparative and Interdisciplinary Approach, in: Eekelaar & Pearl (eds.), *An Aging World – Dilemmas and Challenges for Law and Social Policy* (Oxford 1989), pp. 591-608; Schwenzer, *Vom Status zur Realbeziehung* (Baden-Baden 1987); Simitis, Die Internationale Kommission für Zivilstandswesen (C.I.E.C.), *RabelsZ* 33 (1969), pp. 30-72; Simitis, Familienrecht, in: Simon, ed., *Rechtswissenschaft in der Bonner Republik – Studien zur Wissenschaftsgeschichte der Jurisprudenz* (Frankfurt am Main 1994), pp. 390-448; Smits & Vlaardingerbroek, The Influence of Human Rights on Dutch Family and Child Law, *Journal Social Welfare Fam.L.* 17 (1995), pp. 119-126; Sosson, La filiation dans les pays membres de la Communauté européenne, *Revue trimestrielle de droit familial* (1992), pp. 5-34; Sosson, The Legal Status of Step Families in Continental European Countries, in: Eekelaar & Sarcevic (eds.), *Parenthood in Modern Society – Legal and Social Issues for the Twenty-first Century* (Dordrecht *et al.* 1993), pp. 395-405; Schwenzer, Methodological aspects of harmonisation of family law, in: Boele-Woelki, ed., *Perspectives for the Unification and Harmonisation of Family Law in Europe* (Antwerpen *et al.* 2003), pp. 143-158; C. Steindorff, Familienrechtsreform in Frankreich – Das Gesetz vom 8. Januar 1993, *FuR* (1993), pp. 319-25; Streinz, Gemeinschaftsrecht und deutsches Personenstandsrecht, *Das Standesamt* (1993), pp. 243-249; Sturm, Das Straßburger Marckx-Urteil zum Recht des nichtehelichen Kindes und seine Folgen, *FamRZ* (1982), pp. 1150-1159; Sumampouw, The EC Convention on the Recovery of Maintenance: Necessity or Excess?, in: *Essays on National and International Procedural Law – Essays in Honour of Voskuil* (Dordrecht *et al.* 1992), pp. 315-336; Taupitz, *Europäische Privatrechtsvereinheitlichung heute und morgen* (Tübingen 1993); Tenreiro/Ekström, *Unification of private international law in family law matters within the European Union*, in: Boele-Woelki, ed., *Perspectives for the Unification and Harmonisation of Family Law in Europe* (Antwerpen *et al.* 2003), pp. 183-193; Teschner, Zur Harmonisierung des Personenstandswesens in der Europäischen Union und der Vision eines „Europaregisters", *Das Standesamt* (2002), pp. 289-292; Thorpe, The Influence of Strasbourg on Family Law, *Fam. L.* (1994), pp. 509-512; Verbeke, Perspectives for an International Marital Contract, *Maastricht Journal of European and Comparative Law* (2001), pp. 189-200; Verbeke/Cretney/Grauers/Malaurie/Ofner/Savolainen/Skorini-Paparrigopoulou/van der Burght, European Marital Property Law Survey 1988-1994, *ERPL* 3 (1995), pp. 445-482; Verschraegen, *Die einverständliche Scheidung in rechtsvergleichender Sicht* (Berlin 1991); Verschraegen, *Gleichgeschlechtliche "Ehen"* (Wien 1994); Warbrick, Rights, the European

Convention on Human Rights and English Law, *Eur. L. Rev.* (1994), pp. 34-47; Will, Autonome Rechtsangleichung in Europa, in: Schwind, ed., *Österreichs Weg in die EG, Beiträge zur europäischen Rechtsentwicklung* (Wien 1991), pp. 84-109; Zajtay, Rechtsvergleichung im ehelichen Güterrecht, *Annales Universitatis Saraviensis* 4 (1955), pp. 154-167; Zitelmann, Die Möglichkeit eines Weltrechts, *Allgemeine Österreichische Gerichts-Zeitung* 1888, 193 -195, 201-203, 209-212.

CHAPTER 18

Harmonisation of the Law of Succession in Europe

Alain Verbeke* & Yves-Henri Leleu**

1 Comparative Law, *Ius Commune* and Harmonisation

With the concept of harmonisation, we refer to a wide variety of methods and techniques which attempt to realise, to a variable degree, an approximation of differing national legislations in a certain area of law.[1]

First of all, there is the influence of the existing apparatus of international courts or supranational authorities that may realise or improve the convergence between national legislations through judgments, decisions or resolutions. Secondly, there is the increasing tendency of national legislations to grow more or less spontaneously towards each other based on comparative analysis. Finally, a uniform act, regarding conflict of laws or effectively unifying material law, elaborated in an international treaty will lead to unification, which is the most extreme form of harmonisation, making one unified set of rules in lieu of the differing legislations. Application of these methods of harmonisation to the area of the law of succession will be discussed in the third section of this contribution.

To find an answer to the question whether or not the harmonisation of a certain field of law is feasible, one must start from comparative legal research, pursued according to the functional-typological methodology.[2]

Such a functional approach examines the function of a legal rule or institution in society and inquires whether this rule properly fulfils this function. Unlike the dogmatic method, this research is problem-oriented, not norm-oriented. With the typological method, one tries to find 'typical solutions'. These types are independent from one particular legal system. One chooses a type-determining criterion in order to tran-

---

* *Professeur Ordinaire* at the Catholic University of Leuven and Full Professor of Private and Comparative Law at the University of Tilburg; co-director of Research Alliance Contracts & Property (with Prof. B. Tilleman); Director of the Institute for Contract Law and co-director of the Center for Construction Law; attorney-at-law at the Bar of Brussels.

** Professor of Private Law at the University of Liège (Ulg).

1 On these methods, see David, The methods of unification, *AJCL* 1968-69, p. 13; Glenn, Unification of Law, Harmonisation of Law and Private International Law, in: *Liber memorialis François Laurent* (Brussels, Story-scientia 1989), p. 783; Goode, Reflections on the harmonisation of commercial law, *ULR* 1991, p. 57; Kötz, Alternativen zur legislatorischen Rechtsverheinheitlichung, *RabelsZ* 1992, p. 215; Zweigert, Grundsatzfragen der europäischen Rechtsangleichung, ihrer Schöpfung and Sicherung, in: *Vom deutschen zum europäischen Recht, Festschrift für Hans Dölle*, II, (Mohr, Siebeck 1963), pp. 410 ff.

2 Canaris, Comparative Law, unification and scholarly creation of a new jus commune, *N.I.L.Q.* 1981, 283; Drobnig, Methodenfragen der Rechtsvergleichung im Lichte der 'International Encyclopaedia of Comparative Law', in: *Ius privatum gentium. Festschrift für Max Rheinstein* (Tübingen, Mohr 1969), p. 221. See for a different approach of harmonisation, from the perspective of human rights: Van Grunderbeeck. *Beginselen van personen- en familierecht. Een mensenrechtelijke benadering*, Antwerp. Oxford, Intersentia 2003. p. 625 ff., n° 829 ff.

scend the differences between legal systems and to bring these systems together under a common denominator: the type.

The number of typical solutions will vary according to the legal systems involved and according to the nature of the analysed problem.

In a context of more or less socially, economically, politically and culturally comparable societies, such as the modern Western capitalist world, it is likely that the social problems to be regulated and solved by legal rules are similar. If, then, the analysed problem is one of a morally neutral nature, it is very likely that the solutions found for that problem will be very similar too. This has been called a *praesumptio similitudinis*, a presumption of similarity of legal solutions for social problems in the Western world.[3] Thus, for such social problems in the Western world, one would find only few 'typical solutions', since there are not hundreds of different legal anwers to the same social problem.

This may sound somewhat misleading, since, of course, any legal solution for any social problem is determined and influenced by moral, social, economic, cultural, historical and political values.[4] A legal rule can never be the legal rule, as if it were the only possible solution, but will always be just one legal rule, one possible solution from several others. Why this solution has been chosen in a particular legal system, and not another one, is precisely the consequence of the social context and all kinds of values and interests involved. Any legal rule is merely a choice, it is a political choice; in the best case, it is a fair compromise balancing all the interests involved.

However, some social problems are more influenced by particular moral and traditional values than others. In such a case, the similarity between legal solutions becomes less likely. Problems existing in the context of family relationships tend to be of the latter nature.

The typical solutions discovered by comparative legal research may reveal some general common principles of law, common to several legislations. These general principles have been denominated as comparative law notions,[5] general superior concepts,[6] *rein Rechtsvergleichenden Kategorien*,[7] forming a modern version of *ius commune*.[8]

---

3   Zweigert & Kötz, *Introduction to Comparative Law*, I, *The Framework* (Oxford, Clarendon Press 1987), p. 36.

4   Watson, *Legal Transplants. An Approach to Comparative Law* (Edinburgh, Scottish Academic Press 1974), pp. 4-5.

5   Rozmaryn, Communication at the conference of the international association of legal science on the legality rule, *Rev.int.dr.comp.* 1958, p. 70.

6   Von Caemmerer/Zweigert, Evolution et état actuel de la méthode du droit comparé en Allemagne, in: *Le livre du centenaire de la société de législation comparée*, II, *Evolution internationale et problèmes actuels du droit comparée* (Paris, L.G.D.J. 1971), pp. 290-291.

7   Drobnig, *RabelsZ* 1969, p. 380.

8   Koopmans, Towards a New 'Ius Commune', in: De Witte/Fonder (eds.), *Le droit commun de l'Europe et l'avenir de l'enseignement juridique* (Deventer, Kluwer 1992), p. 43; Oppetit, Droit commun et droit européen, in: *L'internationalisation du droit, Mélanges Y. Loussouarn* (Paris, Dalloz 1995), p. 311; Schulze, Allgemeine rechtsgrundsätze and europäisches Privatrecht, *ZEPR* 1993, p. 442; Van den Bergh, Ius Commune, a History with a Future?, in: De Witte/Fonder (eds.), *Le droit commun de l'Europe et l'avenir de l'enseignement juridique* (Deventer, Kluwer 1992), p. 593; Zimmerman, Das römisch-kanonische ius commune als Grundlage europaischer Rechtseinheit, *JZ* 1992, p. 8. Cornu, Un code civil n'est pas un instrument communautaire, *Dalloz* 2002, 351; Compare with Legrand, Sens et non-sens d'un code civil européen, *Rev.int.dr.comp.* 1996, p. 806. See also

The more these general transnational principles are found, the more the feasibility of a unified legal rule for a particular problem becomes likely. The more such unification seems feasible, the more it is desired.[9] Therefore, in contract law, where such a *ius commune* is present to a certain extent, the efforts for unification have been intense.[10] Also the European Parliament encourages unified codification as regards private law, especially contract law.[11]

The social problem to be solved by the law of succession is the issue of transferring, how and to whom, property after death. Even considering all of Europe as part of the modern Western capitalist world, the social problem involved is of a morally and culturally more delicate nature than contract law. Perhaps even more than family law, the law of succession is a field reserved to local rules and customs, a field in which the desire or need for unification seems to be, at best, moderate.[12]

Since the legal rules for these social problems are, to a larger degree than other problems, determined and dictated by moral and cultural values, there seem to be few general principles, not to speak of a *ius commune*. Therefore, both the feasibility of a unified family and/or succession law as well as its desirability are very often questioned.[13] Because of its deep roots in the fundamental social and cultural values of a society, it is argued that family and succession law should remain national (or regional in a federal system) legal matters.

However, this traditional view should be reconsidered. Family law as a whole is opening up more and more, looking over the boundaries and integrating new and modern ideas and concepts.

Since the seventies, especially in the field of family law, under the strong influence of the European Treaty on Human Rights and the Council of Europe, there has been an undeniable evolution towards common general principles, such as equality of spouses, economical and financial marital solidarity, equality of all children irrespective of the means of descent (see section 3.1.3). These principles offer a (limited) basic *ius commune*,[14] affecting not only family law or marital property law, but also, although to a lesser extent, the law of succession.

Brauneder, *Europäisches Privatrecht: historische Wirklichkeit oder zeitbedingter Wunsch an die Geschichte?* (Rome 1997), Saggi, Conferenze e Seminari, No. 23.

9 Although some authors object to unification or harmonisation if there is no practical need for such venture. See Kahn-Freund, Common Law and Civil Law. Imaginary and Real Obstacles to Assimilation, in: *New perspectives for a Common Law of Europe*, Capelletti (ed.) (London, European University Institute 1978), p. 141.

10 Lando, Principles of European Contract Law. A first step towards a European Civil Code?, *Revue de droit des afaires internationales/International Business Law Journal* 1997, pp. 189 ff.; Lando/Beale (eds.), *The Principles of Contract Law*. 1, (The Hague, Martinus Nijhoff 1995); Lando, Principles of European Contract Law, *Rabels, Z* 1992, pp. 261 ff.; Schulze, Le droit prive commun européen, *Rev. int. dr.comp.* 1995, pp. 8 ff.

11 Cauffman, De Principles of European Contract Law, *Tijdschrift voor privaatrecht* 2001, 1231; Hondius, Beginselen van Europees privaatrecht, *Tijdschrift voor Privaatrecht* 1994, pp. 1455 ff.; Storme, Beginselen van Europees overeenkomstenrecht, *Tijdschrift voor privaatrecht*, 2001, 1311. Compare Cauffman, *De eenzijdige belofte in het Europees Privaatrecht* (Ph.D. thesis Leuven 2004; to be published Antwerp/Oxford, Intersentia).

12 Remien, Illusion and Realitat eines europäischen Privatrechts, *JZ* 1992, pp. 277 ff. Compare Puelinckx-Coene, *La protection de la famille dans le domaine des successions*, general report on the 6th Conference on family law, Strassbourg, Council of Europe, 2002, No. 52 ff.

13 Luther, Einheitsrecht durch Evolution im Eherecht, *Rabels, Z* 1981, pp. 253 ff., p. 258.

14 Ost, La jurisprudence de la cour européenne des droits de l'homme: amorce d'un nouveau 'ius

Numerous reforms of national legislation regarding divorce and abortion have narrowed the gap between local legal systems. Also (although exceptionally) some judgments of the European Court of Justice are of importance to the areas of family law and succession law (see section 3.1.2). In some federal countries, such as Germany and Switzerland, family and succession law are federal matters. In those federations where it is not, as in the United States, there are several attempts to bridge the disparity of local state law through uniform acts.[15]

Specifically in the field of succession law, already more than 30 years ago, on 29 December 1972, the Benelux countries agreed on a regulation regarding simultaneous death (commorientes). Somewhat later, with the Treaty of Washington of 26 October 1973, a uniform act regarding the form of an international will was presented (see sections. 2.3.1 and 3.2). Recently, it has been rightly argued that the issue of transfer of assets of the deceased should not be treated as a matter of the continuation of the person of the deceased nor as an issue of family solidarity, but that it should be approached as a problem of settlement and liquidation of an estate, bringing this matter within the ambit of economic and bankruptcy law.[16]

In the following section, the typical solutions for some important questions and problems of succession law will be analysed. This should provide us with the information needed to answer the question of whether we can go any further on the unification path as far as the law of succession is concerned.

This question will be explored in the final section. Here we will look at several options for harmonisation and unification of national laws. We will conclude with a concrete suggestion as to the method that might be considered for harmonising of the law of succession.

2   Typical Solutions in Succession Law

2.1   Transfer of the Estate

A preliminary problem to be solved in succession matters is the question of how the estate of the deceased is transferred to his heirs. This problem has been comparatively examined.[17] A distinction should be made between the transfer of assets of the succession and the liability for the debts of the deceased and his estate.[18]

---

commune'?, in: De Witte/Fonder (eds.), *Le droit commun de l;'Europe et l'Pavenir de l'enseignement juridique* (Deventer, Kluwer 1992), p. 683; Van Grunderbeeck (2003), pp. 3 ff.

15 Family law: see Uniform Marriage and Divorce Act, Uniform Marital Property Act, Uniform Premarital Agreement Act (Clark, *Domestic Relations*, (St. Paul, West, 1988), second edition; Verbeke, *Goederenverdeling bij echtscheiding* (Antwerp, Kluwer 1994, second edition); Verbeke, Perspectives for an International Marital Contract, *Maastricht Journal of European and Comparative Law* 2001, 189-200; Succession law: Uniform Probate Code (see section 3.2).

16 Leleu, *La transmission de la succession en droit comparé* (Antwerp/Brussels, Maklu/Bruylant 1996), No. 154, p. 491, No. 864, p. 500, No. 979, p. 565; Watté, La faillite internationale: quelques observations sur l'application du Traite néerlando-belge du 28 mars 1925 et l'interprétation de la 'lex concursus' étrangère, Revue Critique de Jurisprudence Belge 1993, p. 457, No. 6; Didier, La problématique de la faillite internationale, *Revue de droit des affaires internationales* 1989, p. 20.

17 Leleu (1996); Leleu, La transmission de la succession en droit comparé, *Revue du Notariat Belge* 1996, pp. 46 ff.

18 Leleu, Nécessité et moyens d'une harmonisation des règles de transmission successorale en Europe, *EPRL* 1998.

Regarding the transfer of assets, two criteria are used to distinguish between three typical solutions. The first criterion concerns the directness of transferring the estate, i.e. directly to the heirs (without an intermediate person) or indirectly, passing the estate through an intermediary. A second aspect is the immediateness of the heir's ownership, immediately upon the death of the decuius or deferred to a moment somewhat later. Thus, the three typical solutions are: 1. the French type of direct and immediate transfer; 2. the Austrian type of direct but deferred transfer; 3. the English type of indirect and deferred transfer.

As to liability for the debts of the deceased, the criterion relates to the extent of such liability, in particular whether it is limited to the hereditary goods (intra vires) or whether it might transcend (ultra) this boundary (vires) and involve the personal property of the heir. Again three typical solutions may be distinguished: 1. the French type tending towards unlimited liability; 2. the German type tending towards limited liability; 3. the English type of strictly limited liability.

2.1.1 Direct and Immediate Transfer by Virtue of Law (French Type)

This first type is the one where the estate is transferred directly and immediately, by virtue of law or *ipso iure*, to each one of the heirs. This is the French type, also known in countries like Belgium, the Netherlands, Greece, Germany and Switzerland. No initiative is required from the heirs or legatees. They are 'seized' by the deceased: 'Le mort saisit le vif, son hoir le plus proche habile a lui succeder'.

Acceptance of the succession is not required to become the owner of an inheritance. Acceptance is mere confirmation of the ownership acquired by virtue of law. However, accepting or not accepting the succession is very relevant to liability for the debts of the succession. Acceptance implies liability. In this respect, the French type tends towards unlimited liability (*ultra vires*), i.e. liability of the heir with his personal property. Therefore, it may be important to renounce the succession (or to accept under the privilege of inventory limiting the liability *intra vires*). To the contrary, in Germany, a somewhat unique solution tending towards limited liability (*intra vires*) is in force, protecting the personal estate of the heirs.

Typical for the French type is also the dissociation between ownership and possession of hereditary goods. The mechanism of the saisine vests in some of the heirs or legatees the right of possession of the succession, while other heirs or legatees, also owners of the succession, do not have this right and must request delivery of their share. This saisine may also be found in the Belgian system,[19] but is unknown to the German, Swiss and Greek succession laws, where each heir or legatee by virtue of law also receives the right of possession, although the effect thereof is limited through the theory of Erbschein, requiring each heir to prove his quality as an heir. New legislation in France (december 3rd, 2001) regulates the *acte de notoriété*, being notarial confirmation of the quality as an heir, besides the *attestation d'hérédité*, the latter being functionally similar to the *Erbschein*.

---

19 See e.g. Verbeke/van Zantbeek, Belgium, in: Hayton (ed.) *European Succession Laws* (Bristol, Jordans 2002, second revised and expanded edition), No. 3.12-3.14.

2.1.2   Direct but Deferred Transfer (Austrian Type)

In this type, the ownership of the estate is transferred directly to the heirs and legatees, not passing through an intermediate person, but this transfer does not occur immediately upon death, but only at a later moment, after an initiative has been taken by the heir, this initiative being his acceptance of the succession (aditio hereditatis). In Italy and Spain, this acceptance may be silent. In Austria, however, an additional formality is required, being a court decision, the Einantwortung, explicitly transferring the succession to the heirs.

A disadvantage of such a system is the vacuum that arises between death and the acceptance of the succession. During that period, there is a hereditas jacens to be administered by a curator or one of the heirs. In Italy, acceptance operates retroactively to the moment of death, while in Austria, the court decision transfers the estate from that moment. An advantage of the Austrian judicial intervention is that the transfer of the succession occurs in a controlled and orderly manner. There is no need for a saisine, as in the first type.

Regarding liability for the debts of the deceased, the countries of this second type follow the French type tending towards unlimited liability.

2.1.3   Indirect and Deferred Transfer (English Type)

Finally, in the third type, the estate passes through the hands of an intermediate person, the personal representative. Heirs and legatees have to await the settlement and payment of the hereditary debts before having the net result of the succession transferred to them.

The first transfer of the succession, to the personal representative, occurs through a probate procedure where the court awards a grant appointing the personal representative. This may be the executor appointed in the will of the deceased, or in the absence of such designation, an administrator, being a family member appointed by the court. The executor or the administrator administers and settles the succession as a trustee, paying off the debts.

Heirs and legatees are only creditors of the net result of the succession. They have a claim upon the administrator to pay out their share of this net result. This is the second transfer of the succession, now to the heirs and legatees, obtaining by assent the ownership of their share in the succession.

It is quite clear that this type of transfer of assets does imply a strictly limited liability for the debts of the deceased. The heirs will never be liable with their personal assets, since they only receive their share in the net result of the succession, after the settlement of the estate and payment of the debts involved.

2.2   Intestate Rights. Position of the Surviving Spouse

In the absence of a will, the intestate succession will be transferred to the heirs, designated according to the legal principles on the devolution of a succession.

Basically, these principles are founded on consanguinity with preference to descendance, excluding more distant relatives.[20]

---

20 Spellenberg *et al.* Recent Developments in Succession Law, in *Law in Motion* (Antwerp, Kluwer 1997). A.II and IV.2.

One of the common principles that have been growing during the last decades in family law is the tendency towards equality of illegitimate with legitimate children. Therefore, equal inheritance rights for children born out of wedlock are generally admitted.[21]

Another generally accepted rule is the need to protect the surviving spouse. Although not a blood-related person, the spouse is recognised to have a legitimate claim towards the succession of his or her partner. In considering the position of the surviving spouse, one should also take into account what the surviving spouse receives through the liquidation of the marital property system.

The inheritance rights of the surviving spouse vary and may be quite modest in some countries.[22] First, there are countries where the spouse is limited to rights of usufruct (enjoyment and benefit) of the fruits and revenues of the succession. If there are descendants, in Belgium the spouse receives usufruct of the entire estate, while in France since the new Act of 3 December 2001 the surviving spouse can choose between such usufruct over the entire estate or a share in full ownership of one quarter of the succession.[23] In several countries, e.g. in Germany, Austria, Denmark, Sweden, Italy, Portugal, Greece, the surviving spouse invariably receives a share of the succession in full ownership. The size of this share varies according to the number of other heirs. In England, the surviving spouse receives the personal chattels and an amount of money, smaller or larger according to the number of other heirs. In the US Uniform Probate Code the entire succession is awarded to the surviving spouse if there are common descendants or other blood relatives than parents.

An interesting intestate system (called the *wettelijke verdeling*) has been introduced in the Netherlands by the recent Acts of 3 June 1999 and 18 April 2002, coming into force as of 1 January 2003. All assets and debts are awarded by virtue of law to the surviving spouse, leaving the children with a claim towards that spouse, to be paid in principle upon death of that spouse.[24]

2.3 Wills and Forced Heirship

Anyone who has legal capacity can make a will, thereby instructing precisely how and to whom his estate should be transferred. There are two major problems to be solved.

1. What are the formal requirements in order to make a valid will?
2. Are there any material limitations as to the content of the will, or in other words,

---

21 Spellenberg *et al.* (1997), B.I.

22 See Hayton (ed.), *European Succession Laws* (Bristol, Jordans 2002, second revised and expanded edition); Verbeke, *De legitieme ontbloot of dood? Leve de echtgenoot!*, Ars Notariatus CXIII (Deventer, Kluwer 2002), pp. 4-14 (see also first edition in *Tijdschrift voor Privaatrecht* 2000, 1111-1236 with summary in English).

23 In Luxembourg, the same choice exists, but the spouse can take a larger share in full ownership, depending on the number of children (one half if there is one child and one third if two children and one quarter if more than two children). In Spain (not taking into account regional legislation) the surviving spouse only receives usufruct over one third of the succession if there are descendants.

24 Besides the abundant literature and comments in Dutch, see Nuytinck, *A short introduction to the new Dutch succession law* (Deventer, Kluwer 2002).

is there a reserved part of forced heirship awarded by law to a certain category of heirs?

2.3.1 Formal Requirements

Four types of will may be distinguished: the holographic will, the witnessed will, the closed and international will and the public or notarial will.[25]

The holographic will must be written and signed personally by the testator. This type of will exists in most European countries, although the formal requirements are not as strictly applied in all of them. It does not exist in the Netherlands and Portugal, where the intervention of a notary is always required. Such a will is also unknown in Common Law jurisdictions, e.g. England and Ireland.

Typical for these Common Law jurisdictions is the witnessed will. It may be written personally, but also typed or even written by a third person. Even the signature does not have to be personal since a facsimile suffices. Essential here is the simultaneous presence of witnesses at the moment of signing the will, their confirmation of this signature and their signing of the will. A similar type of will is known in Austria and Denmark.

The closed will, written or typed by the testator or a third party and signed by the testator, must be put in a closed envelope and presented to a notary and several witnesses. Such a will is known in the Netherlands,[26] France, Denmark, Italy, Spain, Portugal, Greece. Some of these countries also recognise the international will created by the Treaty of Washington of 26 October 1973 (see sections 1 and 3.2). Other countries, like Belgium, have replaced the closed will with this international will.

Finally there is the public will, in most countries drafted by a notary but signed personally by the testator. In Austria, a public will can also be made by a judge. Under Belgian and French law, the will must be dictated by the testator to the notary. In other countries, like Germany and Austria, delivery of a document confirmed by the testator to be his will, is sufficient. Generally, the presence of witnesses is required.[27]

2.3.2 Material Limitations. Forced Heirship[28]

One should distinguish between the Anglo-American legal systems where the freedom of will has traditionally been unlimited, and to a large extent still is. As opposed to that, the civil law countries defend the notion of forced heirship, thereby stating

---

25 Pintens, Erfrecht, schenkingen en testamenten in Europa. Van verscheidenheid naar eenheid?, in: *Les relations contractuelles internationales. Le rôle du notaire*, (Antwerp, Maklu 1995), pp. 521-524; Verbeke/van Zantbeek, Belgium, in: Hayton (ed), *European Succession Laws* (Bristol, Jordans 2002, second revised and expanded edition), No. 3.101-3.115.

26 The new Dutch Inheritance Act does not require the presence of witnesses, not for a *closed* nor for a *public will*.

27 However not in the Netherlands.

28 See: *Examen critique de la réserve successorale*. I. *Droit comparé* II *Droit belge*; III *Propositions* (Brussels, Bruylant 1997 and 2000); Verbeke, *De legitieme ontbloot of dood? Leve de echtgenoot!*, Ars Notariatus CXIII (Deventer, Kluwer 2002) (see also first edition in *Tijdschrift voor Privaatrecht* 2000, 1111-1236 with summary in English).

that the estate does not exclusively belong to the deceased but at least partially also to his family that may not be deprived of the entire estate.[29]

Thus, in the Anglo-American jurisdictions, freedom of will is not restricted, but those persons whom the deceased was bound legally or morally to support during his lifetime may claim a right of maintenance from the estate. The courts are given a discretionary power to award a so-called family provision.[30]

Despite the common feature of forced heirship in civil law countries, there remains also in this matter a wide variety of national legislations. However, an evolution towards some common principles seems to be gaining ground.

There is a tendency towards reducing class of heirs entitled to a forced heirship. Descendants are invariably recognised as being entitled to a forced heirship. Often also the surviving spouse is protected through a reserved right. Forced heirship rights for ascendants have been limited[31] or abandoned. Reserved rights for brothers and sisters are very rare and seem to have been increasingly excluded.

Also the principle of a property entitlement upon hereditary assets has been abandoned in several countries. Thus, the German Pflichtteil represents only a claim in money for the protected heir. He has no property rights upon the assets of the succession. Quite analogously, under the new Dutch legislation, in force since 2003, the protected heir is reduced to a creditor of the succession. In France the entitlement of a protected heir to the assets of the succession is limited to the relationship towards third parties. In the internal relationship between heirs, the forced heirship right has been reduced since 1971 to a right in value.

Belgian law still applies rather completely (with few exceptions) the traditional Napoleonic forced heirship property right upon the assets of the succession. The Belgian experience proves that this is an outdated principle, entailing several practical problems and very often leading towards inequitable results for several of the heirs in question.[32]

3 Harmonisation of the Law of Succession

3.1 Convergence

3.1.1 Application of European Community Law

The first issue under consideration is whether European Community Law, based on the Treaty of Rome, might offer a solid foundation for the harmonisation of succession law.[33] This may sound somewhat strange since the basic mission of the Euro-

---

29 Spellenberg *et al.* (1997), B.III.
30 For England: Inheritance (Family Provisions) Act 1938 and 1975.
31 In the German legal family only the parents are protected. In Belgium, ascendants have no reserved claim in relation to the surviving spouse. While the new French legislation has increased the intestate position of the surviving spouse (see above), it has not restricted the reserved claim of ascendants.
32 See *Examen critique de la réserve successorale*, II and III, *Propositions* (Brussels, Bruylant 1997 and 2000).
33 Compare Pintens/Du Mongh, *Family and Succession Law* in the European Union, in: *International*

pean Community/Union is situated in the economic area. However, Article 235 of the Treaty is broad and vague enough to enlarge the competence of the Community. In the Treaty of Maastricht (Art. 3, h) the Community has been given the competence to realise the approximation of national legislations as far as this may be needed for the functioning of the common market and with respect for the subsidiarity principle.

(a) In two resolutions, the European Parliament has supported the idea of the approximation of national private law by developing a European Code of private law.[34] In the first place, unification of the law of obligations and contracts is stimulated, since this may clearly affect and improve the functioning of the common market. However, the Parliament is of the opinion, interpreting the Treaty and the free movement of persons rather extensively, that also unification in the area of family law is desirable,[35] in order to obtain a better guarantee of the freedoms and liberties inscribed in the Treaty.[36] Regarding the law of succession, there has only been minor consideration thereof in the Resolution of 14 December 1994. According to the European Parliament, such unification should be realised by multilateral treaty, based on Article 220 of the Treaty of Rome (see section 3.2).[37]

(b) As opposed to the Parliament, the European Commission is far less enthusiastic as regards the desirability of unification of European family and succession law.[38] The attitude of the European Commission is rather negative since it considers this field to be 'emotionally charged'.[39] Nevertheless, the Commission seems to have some concern about the diversity of national succession laws. Thus, in a recommendation of 7 December 1994, the Commission requested the Member States of the European Community to facilitate the transmission of small and medium companies in order to avoid their liquidation and growing unemployment. This would not only require measures in the areas of company and tax law, but also in the field of family property law, in particular concerning restrictions on transfers between spouses, the prohibition on contracting as regards a succession which has not yet occurred and the forced heirship property rights upon hereditary assets rather than rights in value or money's worth.[40]

Encyclopedia of Laws. Family and Succession Law (The Hague/London/Boston, Kluwer Law International 1997); Pintens, Rechtsvereinheitlichung und Rechtsangleichung im Familienrecht. Eine Rolle für die Europäische Union?, ZEuP 1998, 670.

34 Resolution of 6 May 1994, OJ 1994, C 205/518; Resolution of 26 May 1989, OJ 1989, C 158/400.
35 E.g. parental authority. See Resolution of 29 October 1993, OJ 1993, C 315/652; Resolution of 14 December 1994, OJ 1994, C 18/96.
36 Resolution of 14 December 1994; Resolution of 29 October 1993; Resolution of 9 March 1993, OJ 1993, C 115/33; Resolution of 8 July 1992, OJ 1992, C 241/67.
37 Resolution of 9 March 1993, nos. 27-28.
38 See, however, one initiative: Sosson, Les Politiques familiales des Etats membres de la Communauté européenne. Modèles familiaux et droit civil: la fillation et ses effets (Brussels, C.O.F.A.C.E. 1990); Sosson, La filiation dans les pays membres de la Communauté européenne. Etude de droit interne comparé, Revue Trimestrielle de Droit Familial 1992, p. 5.
39 Question, No. 861/92, 14 April 1992, OJ 1993, C 40/17. Compare with Question of Kostopoulos, No. E-3630/93, OJ 1994, C 251/37, regarding the Greek Law on adoption; Bangemann, ZEPR 1993, p. 383; Basedow, Konstantinidis v. Bangemann oder die Familie im europäischen Gemeinschaftsrechts, ZEPR 1994, pp. 197 ff.
40 OJ 1994, C 400; OJ 1994, C 400/6. See: Leleu, Les pactes successoraux en droit comparé, in: Les relations contractuelles internationales. Le rôle du notaire, (Antwerp, Maklu 1995), p. 545; Leleu, La réduction et le rapport en valeur. Reflexions critiques en vue d'une r6forme legislative, in: Examen critique de la reserve successorale, II, Droit belge (Brussels, Bruylant 1997), p. 213.

In addition, the Commission has repeatedly suggested that the Community should adhere to the European Convention on Human Rights.[41] In the recent Treaty of Amsterdam, some rules regarding human rights have been included.[42]

(c) Based on Article 189 of the Treaty of Rome, the European Council of Ministers can issue a regulation, a directive or a decision. Through directives, the company law of the Member States has been harmonised.[43] Rules have profoundly modified national competition law and social legislation. In the area of family law, harmonisation of national legislation could be based on the objective of effective integration of the European employee in the foreign Member State of his residence. However, such basis seems to be very weak since some link with the economic objectives of the Community is required. Although the Court of Justice in Luxembourg has recognised, based on a wide interpretation, the Community's competence in certain areas of family law and even in succession law (see section 3.1.2), it remains doubtful that the Treaty offers an acceptable basis for the harmonisation of national legislation in the field of succession. Additionally, the principle of subsidiarity (Art. 3B of the Treaty of Rome) might prevent such initiative by the Community,[44] since the Member States themselves possess the necessary instruments to realise the objective of the unification of private law.

3.1.2 Influence of International Courts

(a) As has been pointed out already, the European Court of Justice has considered itself competent to decide matters of family law, if these rules affect a right guaranteed under the Treaty. This has been done in two cases, one relating to the law of names (Konstantinidis)[45] and the other concerning the administration of an international succession (Hubbard).[46] In both cases, the plaintiff challenged national legislation that imposed restrictions on him because of his nationality, thus restricting his freedom of establishment as an employee (Art. 52 of the Treaty) or his freedom of provision of services (Art. 59 of the Treaty).

---

41 Communication of the Commission of 19 November 1990, *Bull. E.C.*, 10-1990, No. 1.3.218 and I 11990, No. 1.3.203; Memorandum of the Commission of 4 April 1979, *Bull. E.C.*, suppl. 2/79.

42 Regarding the draft of the Amsterdam Treaty, see Dehousse, La conference intergouvernementale apres la reunion de Rome, *JT* 1997, p. 266, column 1.

43 See Drobnig, *Private Law in the European Union*, Forum Internationale, No. 22, (Kluwer, Deventer 1996), p. 4; Oppetit, Droit commun et droit europ6en, in *L'internationalisation du droit. Mélanges Y. Loussouarn* (Paris, Dalloz 1995), p. 316.

44 In this sense: Collins, European Private Law and the Cultural Identity of States, *ERPL* 1995, p. 355; Martiny, Europaïsches Familienrecht – Utopie oder Notwendigkeit?, *RabelsZ* 1995, p. 436. Gaudissart, La subsidiarité: facteur de (dés)intégration européenne?, *JT* 1993, p. 173; Lenaerts/Van Ypersele, Le principe de subsidiarité et son contexte: Etude de l'article 3B du traité CE, *Cahiers de Droit Européen* 1992, p. 3.

45 ECJ 30 March 1993 (Konstantinidis), *ZEPR* 1995, p. 90, annotation Pintens, *ECR* 1993-1, p. 1191, *ERPL* 1995, p. 483, annotation Gaurier/Schockweiler/Loiseau. See Aps, Bescherming van het recht op naam in bet Europees recht, *Burgerzaken & recht* 1995-96, p. 85; Pintens, Der Fall Konstantinidis. Das Namensrecht als Beispiel für die Auswirkung des Europaïschen Gemeinschaftsrecht auf das Privatrecht, *ZEPR*, 1995, p. 91.

46 ECJ 1 July 1993 (Hubbard/Hamburger), *ECR* 1993, I, p. 3777, *Rev. Crit. dr. int. pr.* 1994, p. 663, annotation Droz, *JT* 1994, p. 36, annotation Ekelmans, *Tijdschrift voor Notarissen* 1994, p. 187, annotation Bouckaert.

In the Hubbard case, an English solicitor operating as an administrator of a succession in Great Britain, was forced to pay a judicial deposit to cover the costs of proceedings in Germany which were instituted in pursuit of hereditary assets. The Court decided that Articles 59 and 60 guaranteeing freedom of provision of services, oppose a national rule that requires a judicial deposit from a professional, if solely based on the fact that this professional is a citizen of another Member State.[47] Furthermore, the Court stated that the fact that the litigation concerned a matter of succession law is not a bar to the Court's competence based on the freedom of the provision of services.

Even before these two cases, the Court of Justice had already established that the power of the Community may transcend the strictly economical framework of Articles 2 and 3 of the Treaty of Rome in order to further the integration of a foreign employee in the social life of his country of residence.[48] Thus, it seems to be the opinion of the Court that if a right guaranteed under the Treaty can be claimed, all discrimination based on nationality is forbidden, even if such discrimination results from a rule in an area of law which does not form part of the objectives of the Treaty.[49]

Nevertheless, harmonisation through the European Court of Justice's case law will remain very modest. For succession law, the connection with the economic objectives and liberties of the Treaty is simply too weak.[50] Moreover, since the Court can only intervene in concrete litigation, its influence and impact will always be coincidental without any reference to a concrete project or model of harmonisation or unification.[51]

(b) Another important court is the European Court of Human Rights, which has stimulated the convergence of the national legislation of the Member States of the Council of Europe in a number of private law areas.[52] In the field of family law, this Court has forced several Member States to reform their legislation to a considerable extent.[53] Its greater influence on family law, as opposed to the European Court of

---

47 For a criticism, see Leleu (1998), No. 60.

48 See ECJ 11 July 1985 (Mutsch), *ECR* 19854, p. 2691; *ECJ* 12 February 1989 (Cowan), *ECR* 1989-I, p. 221.

49 *ECJ* 21 March 1972 (Sail), *ECR* 1972, (p. 119), p. 136, No. 5.

50 See Kohler, L'article 220 du Traité CEE et les conflits de juridictions en matière de relations familiales: premieres réflexions, *Riv. dr. int. priv. proc.* 1992, pp. 232-233, note 28.

51 In this sense: Weatherhill, Prospects for the Development of European Private Law. Through 'Europeanisation' in the European Court – the case of the Directive on Unfair Terms in Consumer Contracts, *ERPL* 1995, p. 308. See also: Martiny, Europaïsches Familienrecht – Utopie oder Notwendigkeit?, *RabelsZ* 1995, p. 434; Schwartz, Perspektiven der Angleichung des Privatrechts in der Europäischen Gemeinschaft, *ZEPR* 1994, p. 576.

52 In this sense: Jayme, Die Entwicklung des europäischen Familienrechts, *FamRZ* 1981, p. 223.; Van Grunderbeeck (2003).

53 Concerning Belgian law and the consequences of the Marckx case: Leleu, Erfrechtelijke discriminatie van buitenhuwelijkse kinderen: Quousque tandem, Gallia, abutere patientia nostra?, *Tijdschrift voor privaatrecht* 2001, 1353; see Rigaux, La loi condamnée, *JT* 1979, p. 513; Senaeve, Van Marckx tot Vermeire. 12,5 jaar rechtspraak van her Straatsburgse Hof, *Tijdschrift voor familie- en jeugdrecht* 1991, p. 195, p. 244; Senaeve, Het personen- en familierecht, de Grondwet en bet E.V.R.M., in: *Gezin en recht in een postmoderne samenleving,* (Ghent, Mys & Breesch 1994), p. 331. In the Netherlands, this evolution has been anticipated (Act of 27 October 1982). In France, after being condemned by the European Court of Human Rights to abolish all discriminations in the field of

Justice, results from the fundamental rights and liberties guaranteed by the Treaty. Fundamental human rights are substantially affected by family and penal law.

Technically, the Strasbourg Court's influence is realised by the direct applicability of the Treaty in the Member States, the binding force of its judgments towards a Member State involved in litigation (Art. 53),[54] the interpretative authority of such judgments in other Member States[55] and especially by the method of evolutive interpretation of the Treaty; this is a form of judicial activism enabling the Court to apply the Treaty to new situations and thus to create new law. In the area of succession law, certain devolution rules might infringe on the respect for the family life (Art. 8)[56] and some rules on the distribution of a succession might violate the respect for the property rights of the heir (Art. 1 of the First Protocol).[57]

However, the Court leaves a large margin of appreciation to the Member States to bring their legislation into line with the Treaty.[58] There remains a broad freedom of choice for the Member State as to the means to be used.[59] Therefore, this Court cannot effectively realise the unification of national law. It merely imposes some kind of convergence of national legislations, forcing them to look in the same direction.

3.1.3 Spontaneous Convergence

Such convergence of different national legislations not only occurs as a result of the influence of supranational jurisdictions and authorities or the application of supranational law. Comparative law learns that in comparable societies the solutions to problems are limited (see section 1). A more extensive use of the comparative legal method upon the reform of national legislation has increased the impact of foreign law and even led to the reception of foreign solutions and institutions. Thus, national rules are growing spontaneously towards each other.[60]

---

succession against children born out of wedlock (Eur. Ct. H. R., 1 February 2000 (Mazurek) *Dalloz*, 2000, 332, note Thierry, *Revue trimestrielle de droit familial*, 2000, 390, note Leleu), the French legislature now treats all forms of filiation equally (new Inheritance Act of 3 December 2001).

54 See Leuprecht, The Execution of Judgements and Decisions, in: *The European System for the Protection of Human Rights*, Mc Donald/Matscher/Petzold (eds.) (Dordrecht, Martinus Nijhoff 1993), p. 793.

55 For further details, see: Cohen-Jonathan, Quelques considerations sur l'autorite des arress de la Cour europeenne des Droits de l'Homme, in: *Liber Amicorum Marc-André Eissen* (Brussels, Bruylant 1995), pp. 53 ff.; Goedertier, Het interpretatief gezag van het arrest Marckx, annotation on the judgment of the Cour de cassation of 7 April 1995, in: *Mensenrechten. Jaarboek van het Interuniversitair centrum Mensenrechten* (Antwerp, Maklu, 1997), p. 407.

56 Eur. Ct. H.R., 13 June 1979 (Marckx), A, No. 31, § 52, 59; Eur. Ct. H.R., 29 November 1991 (Vermeire), A, No. 214-C, § 25.

57 Eur. Ct. H.R., 28 October 1987 (Inze v. Austria), A, No. 126, § 38, 45; Eur. Ct. H. R., 1 February 2000 (Mazurek), see footnote 53. For further analysis, see Leleu (1998), No. 64; Leleu (2001), 1357 ff.

58 See Ganshof van der Meersch, Le caractère 'autonome' des termes et la 'marge d'appréciation' des gouvernements dans l'interprétation de la Convention européenne des Droits de l'Homme, in: Mélanges en l'honneur de G.J. Wiarda (Köln, Heymanns 1988), p. 201; Kastanas, Unité et diversité: notions autonomes et marge d'appréciation dans la jurisprudence de la Cour européenne des Droits de l'Homme (Brussels, Bruylant 1996).

59 See Callewaert, Article 53, in *La Convention européenne des Droits de l'Homme*, Pettiti/Decaux/Imbert (eds.) (Paris, Economica 1995), p. 850.

60 See Van Grunderbeeck (2003), p. 4.

Spontaneous convergence also exists in the field of succession law. In the second section we pointed to the evolution towards common principles such as the protection of the position of the surviving spouse, the equality of children born in and out of wedlock, the reduction in the class of heirs entitled to a forced heirship and the evolution towards abolition of the principle of distribution of the hereditary goods.[61] No such tendancy of convergence, however, can be discerned regarding the issue of transfer of the succession.[62]

3.2 Unification

Article 220 of the Treaty of Rome, allowing Member States to enter into international conventions related to the objectives of the Community could offer a solid basis for the unification of the law of contracts. The European Parliament has invoked Article 220 as a basis for a convention regarding guardianship and abduction of children.[63]

In our opinion, the law of succession is not sufficiently linked to the economic objectives of the Treaty of Rome in order to base a convention regarding succession law thereon. However, this article does not prevent or forbid Member States from entering into international conventions related to succession law. It is quite clear, however, that the need for uniform acts in the field of family and succession law is much less pressing than it is in other areas of private law related to business and economy.[64]

It has been argued that the unification of laws should not be realised by the unification of substanitve law but rather by the unification of the principles of private international law.[65] The law to be applied to a transnational conflict is designated according to the national rules on conflict of laws (private international law) of the country of the judge or authority deciding the case.

However, also on the level of conflict of law rules, unification of conflict rules regarding family and succession law is not so simple, given the wide variety of conflict rules in that field. Therefore, in the Treaty of Brussels of 27 September 1968, family

---

61 In the same sense M. Puelinckx-Coene (2002), No. 53-55
62 See the analysis of Leleu (1998), No. 69.
63 Resolution of 29 October 1993, B; Resolution of 9 March 1993, No. 28. See Martiny, Europäisches Familienrecht – Utopie oder Notwendigkeit? *RabelsZ* 1995, p. 442; Meulders, vers la co-responsabilité parentale dans la famille européenne, *Revue Trimestrielle de Droit Familial* 1991, p. 26.
64 See Goode, Reflections on the harmonisation of commercial law, *ULR*, 1991, p. 54. Examples are: Uniform Act on the Formation of Contracts for the International Sale of Goods, The Hague, 1 July 1964; Uniform Act on the International Sale of Goods, The Hague, 1 July 1964. In some countries, these treaties have been revoked upon the adoption of the United Nations Convention for the International Sale of Goods (Vienna, 11 April 1980; although this convention does not contain any uniform act). For the text of these treaties, see Watté/Erauw, Les sources du droit international privé belge et communautaire (Antwerp/Brussels, Maklu/Bruylant 1996), nos. 186-188, pp. 161-196. For further details: Van der Velden, Her Weense koopverdrag 1980 en zijn rechtsmiddelen (Deventer, Kluwer 1988).
65 Catala, La communauté induite aux acquêts, *Les petites afiches* 1992, No. 58, p. 84, No. 11; Glenn, Harmonisation of law, foreign law and private international law, *ERPL* 1993, p. 47; Jayme/Kohler, Europäisches Kollisionsrecht 1994. Quellenpluralismus und offene Kontraste, *IPRax* 1994, p. 405; Kohler, Zum Kollisionsrecht internationale Organisationen: Familierechtliche vortragen im europäischen Beamtenrecht, *IPRax* 1994, p. 416. See also: Jessurun d'Oliveira, Towards a European Private International Law? in: De Witte/Forder (eds.), *Le droit commun de l'Europe et l'avenir de l'enseignement juridique* (Deventer, Kluwer 1992), p. 265.

matters, except for alimony, are omitted from the field of application. Also the Treaty of The Hague of 2 October 1973 on the administration of successions has a very limited objective and success.[66] The Treaty of The Hague of 1 August 1989 regarding the law applicable to successions is an attempt to unify the conflict rules. The Treaty has only been ratified by the Netherlands, and it made a reservation regarding the rules of transfer of the estate.[67]

The technique of a multilateral treaty proposing a uniform act does not directly affect national legislation. The states which sign and ratify it should integrate it in their national legislation. To achieve effective unity, the Member States of the treaty should abolish their national legislation and replace it by the uniform act. They should not make any reservation. In order to preserve unity, there should be a supranational authority or court to determine the interpretation of the treaty.[68] The existence of an official publication, enabling Member States to exchange information, might also facilitate the application of a uniform act.[69]

The 1973 Treaty of Washington regarding international wills is a very valuable attempt to unify one aspect in the area of succession law.[70] However, the unification is not as effective as it could be, since several Member States have simply added this form of will to the existing wills which remain in force (see section 2.3.1). Also the rules for interpreting the uniform act are not identical in all Member States.[71]

A greater and more successful and effective unification has been realised by the American Uniform Probate Code unifying the rules of transfer of succession (see also section 1).[72] This should set an example for Europe, without forgetting, however, that the conditions in Europe are not as favourable as in the United States, where unification takes place within one federation.[73] Being part of such a federation may explain

---

66 Ganshof, La convention de la Haye du 2 octobre 1973 sur l'administration internationale des successions, *Revue du Notariat Belge* 1975, p. 490; Watté, *Les successions internationales. Conflits de lois. Conflits de juridictions*, in *Répertoire Notarial*, t. XV, l. 14/3 (Brussels, Larcier 1992), No. 227, pp. 181-183; Lalive, L'administration des successions internationales, *Annales suisses de droit international* XXVIII, p. 66.

67 This Treaty forms part of Dutch private international law: Art. 1 of the Wet Conflictenrecht Erfrecht (see Stille, Het nieuwe Nederlandse internationale erfrecht, *Tijdschrift voor familie- en jeugdrecht* 1996, p. 216).

68 E.g. the Office central du chemin de fer deals with problems of interpretation of the international convention concerning transportation of passengers and luggage by railway (Bern, 25 February 1961).

69 UNIDROIT publishes the Uniform Law Review. In the United States, similar publications attempt to improve the application of uniform acts (e.g. *Uniform Commercial Code Journal*).

70 For Belgium, see the Act of 2 February 1983 (Vander Elst, Le testament international, *JT* 1984, p. 257). For France, see the Act of 1 December 1994 (Byk, La forme internationale du testament, *JCP*, Edition notariale 1994, doctr., p. 331).

71 Compare with Art. 15 of the uniform act. See Watté, *Les successions internationales. Conflits de lois. Conflits de juridictions*, in *Répertoire Notarial*, t. XV, l. 14/3 (Brussels, Larcier 1992), No. 51, p. 85.

72 Wellman, The Uniform Probate Code. A Possible Answer to Probate Avoidance, *Indiana Law Journal* 1969, pp. 191 ff.; see also Reimann, Amerikanisches Privatrecht and europäisches Rechtseinheit. KSnnen die USA als Vorbild dienen?, in: Zimmermann (ed.), *Amerikanische Rechtskultur and europäisches Privatrecht* (Tübingen, Mohr 1995), pp. 132 ff.; Clark/Lusky/Murphy, *Gratuitous transfers. Wills, intestate succession, trusts, gifts, future intrests and estate and gift taxation* (St. Paul, West 1985), p. 624.

73 See Reimann, Amerikanisches Privatrecht and europäisches Rechtseinheit. Können die USA als

why the differences between the state legislations are less far-reaching than in Europe; why efforts aimed at the approximation of laws seem to be more evident and desirable; why there is a tradition of organisations and institutions charged with the unification of law.[74] Furthermore, the common language, legal tradition and education are factors which facilitate unification to a very considerable extent.[75]

4 Conclusion

True unification of differing national legislations, in our view, can only be realised by the adoption of a uniform act, elaborated in an international treaty that is signed and ratified by several countries, committing themselves to integrating that uniform act in their internal legislation. This method seems to offer an acceptable compromise between the autonomy of the Member State and the need for precision in order to obtain an effective unification of the law.

The emergence of some common principles in the field of succession law (see sections 1 and 2) shows that there might be a solid basis for the unification of some parts of the law of succession. Following the example of the uniform act regarding international wills, certain aspects of the law of succession could be subjected to the long procedure aiming at an international treaty promulgating a uniform act.

We believe in the feasibility of such a uniform act for those aspects where some kind of similar orientation is growing (see section 3.1.3). It might even be possible to elaborate such a uniform act regarding issues where no convergence nor common principles seem to appear, such as the transfer of the succession. A proposal in this regard has even been made already.[76]

Vorbild dienen?, in: Zimmermann (ed.), *Amerikanische Rechtskultur and europäisches Privatrecht* (Tübingen, Mohr 1995), p. 147. More optimistically: Weigand, The Reception of American Law in Europe, *AJCL* 1991, p. 229.

74 The National Conference of Commissioners on Uniform State laws was founded in 1892. With the American Bar, it has achieved several successes: the Uniform Commercial Code (see Malcolm, The Uniform Commercial Code in the United States, *ICZQ* 1963, p. 226); in family law, the Uniform Marriage and Divorce Act and the Uniform Marital Property Act (see Verbeke, *Goederenverdeling bij echtscheiding*, second edition, (Antwerp, Maklu 1994), No. 28, p. 38); Verbeke, Die Guteraufteilung nach Billigkeit aus Anlaß den Ehescheidung. Judicial application of statutory factors for an equitable distribution of marital property upon dissolution of the marriage on divorce in New York. An Illustration, ZVgl. 1989, pp. 170-214. The American Law Institute is responsible for the research and preparation of uniform acts and is charged with the publication of the Restatements of Laws which synthezise, codify and unify the Common Law rules regarding the law of contract, tort, property, trust and conflict of laws. For each unified area of law, there is a law journal publishing all the necessary information in order to obtain a more or less uniform application (see also *supra*).

75 Concerning the influence of legal education on the unification of law: De Witte/Fonder (eds.), *Le droit commun de l'Europe et l'avenir de l'enseignement juridique* (Deventer, Kluwer 1992); Oppetit, Droit commun et droit européen, in: *L'internationalisation du droit. Mélanges Y. Loussouam* (Paris, Dalloz 1995), p. 318; Sacco, Droit commun de l'Europe et composantes du droit, in *Nouvelles perspectives d'un droit commun de l'Europe*, Capelletti (ed.) (Brussels, Bruylant/Sijthoff 1978), p. 107; Van Gerven, Casebooks for the common law of europe. Presentation of the project, *ERPL* 1996, p. 67.

76 See Leleu (1998).

B – Contract Law – General Issues

CHAPTER 19

Formation of Contracts

Rodolfo Sacco*

1 Introduction: What Do We Mean by a Contract?

The purpose of the following pages is to explain how the rules on formation of contracts could be drawn up. First of all, we shall try to clarify what we mean by a contract and what would be the scope of rules concerning contract. In doing so, we have to deal with two problems:

a) does the contract include gratuitous agreements such as gifts, loans for use, gratuitous deposits? In England, a gift is not considered a contract, whereas in France a *donation* is a contract. Moreover, how can we label an agreement for the transfer of property to a fiduciary person? Is it a *contrat?* If not, why not? A common law lawyer will certainly shudder at the idea of a 'contract of trust', settled between a settlor and a trustee! Nevertheless, I do not know which definition of 'contract' is the most suitable to omit the trust; neither do I know which logical arguments would justify such a definition;

b) will the rules under discussion be applied only to agreements which can be considered as a source of obligations? Or will the agreement be sufficient to create securities *(hypothèques,* mortgages, *gages,* pledges), or to transfer movable property or property in land? Or, at least, will the agreement be sufficient to create or to transfer property?

In assessing these issues, the Vienna Sales Convention is of no assistance. In fact, it does not deal with gratuitous or fiduciary agreements. Moreover, as everyone is aware, it does not even mention whether a contract of sale conveys property (in specific goods) or not. Not even the Unidroit Principles are of much help in this respect, because they only cover commercial contracts. They do not consider gratuitous agreements and they do not deal with transfer of property. Furthermore, even though they deal with 'commercial contracts', they do not elaborate on the scope of this concept.

However, a European Civil Code would have to explain to the reader, at least in broad terms, what it means when it refers to a contract. Being a real Code, it would override and repeal every national Code, and one could not rely on the national law of the parties, nor on that of different states. We can only suppose that the concept of 'contract', with all its own qualifications, is bound to appear in the Code as a necessary but incomplete requirement for the transfer of property, in conformity with the opinion of Prof. Drobnig (at least in the field of movables) in the first edition of To-

---

* Professor of Law at the University of Torino

wards a European Civil Code.[1] A contract in these terms sounds very much like one or more promises.

We can furthermore consider that any well-grounded (reliable) promise creates a liability which remains the same when the promise is followed by a counter-promise (as in a contract of sale), when it is isolated without being gratuitous (e.g. a promise of a reward depending on a performance) and when the promise is entirely gratuitous. A contract defined in such a manner is much more restrictive than the Franco-Italian *contrat/contratto*, as it does not include those agreements reached for the purpose of transferring or producing a *droit réel* (for this reason it could not include the Anglo-American sale of goods, nor the German *Übergabe* or *Auflassung*). On the other hand, it is much more comprehensive than the Anglo-American contract, as it includes forms of bailment and gratuitous promises and it operates in the constitution of a trust. It corresponds to the Austrian and Swiss *Vertrag*, to the German *obligatorischer Vertrag* and to the Russian *dogovor*.

2 Offer and Acceptance: In General

How is a contract concluded? Schlesinger produced two extremely useful volumes on the subject.[2] They demonstrate how several problems remain unsolved. It is clear, first of all, that a contract of gate, a lease, and a partnership agreement are considered to have been concluded only when the offer is followed by an acceptance. In order that both the seller and the purchaser are under a specific obligation, the former must in fact promise and the latter must counter-promise.

A problem, well-explained in the work of Schlesinger, exists for those contracts in which only one of the two parties is under an obligation. What is the rule for such contracts? How do we deal with a contract of suretyship, in which the sponsor receives nothing in exchange for the promise? How do we deal with an offer to reward the promisee, whether he performs his services or not? In these circumstances only one party is under an obligation, as only one has promised to do something. In short, how, in the above-mentioned situations, is the contract concluded? Is it necessary that the party who is not under an obligation communicates his acceptance?

2.1 Solutions in the Various Legal Systems

The more important historical codifications require the *promisor* to declare his assent. Article 1108 of the *Code Napoléon* stated:

> 'Quatre conditions sont essentielles pour la validité d'une convention: le consentement de la partie qui s'oblige; ...' ('Four requirements are necessary for the validity of an agreement; the assent of the party who promises; ...').[3]

The German *Bürgerliches Gesetzbuch* also favours such a solution. Hence, its § 516

---

1 Chapter 20, p. 360.
2 Schlesinger (1968), *passim.*
3 The 1882 Italian Commercial Code (Art. 36) and the 1942 Italian Civil Code (Art. 1333) are openly in favour of the assent of the party who promises as a sufficient element.

(1) defines the *Schenkung* (donation, meant as a liberal promise), and the second sentence adds: 'If the attribution *–Zuwendung* – comes without the other party's assent, the author of the act of attribution has the right to fix a suitable deadline for the acceptance. On the expiry date the donation is considered to have been accepted, provided the other party has not refused'. The authority of the Principles of European Contract Law is now supporting the classical Codes' definitions.[4]

It is obvious that this is the natural solution. The promisee, who does not agree to an obligation, is better protected by a rule that makes the promise effective even if not accepted, provided he is allowed to refuse. The promisor, in turn, is better protected by a rule that strengthens his will every time the addressee does not disagrees with this.

Court decisions assist the literal tenor of the classical codes. This can be seen with regard to the 'unilateral contract' of the common law. In England, a promise on condition of performance on the part of the promisee, without a counter-promise, is considered an offer calling for an act, opposite to the offer calling for an acceptance. A performance on the part of the offeree is qualified as an acceptance, even when it is performed within the only domain of the offeree, and even when the fulfilment of the condition is unintentional.[5] One cannot ignore the fact that in this case the qualification of an unintentional action as an acceptance is artificial. The performance of the promisee is silent and it may represent several things. Perhaps the promisee performed the action because he had a personal interest or desire in doing so. Perhaps he wanted to carry out a favour for the promisor. However, a study as to his intention is not necessary, nor relevant. The performance concludes the contract and the assent of the promisee is not necessary. A contract is therefore reduced to a promise, under a condition of performance by the offeree and followed by the fulfilment of the condition.

When a promise is gratuitous, common law is not inclined to acknowledge its effectiveness, as it lacks consideration (unless the promise is solemn). However, with regard to gratuitous suretyships, for the last few decades the creditor has been protected by a solution founded on reliance. Paragraph 90 of the American Restatement explains this clearly.[6] Subsequent cases support the rule.[7] Donation is further discussed in section 3. We can already take note that in England a deed, a liberal act (valid – lacking consideration – thanks to its solemn form), operates without the necessity of acceptance, and this reminds us of the German *Schenkung*. Even in France the non-liberal promise, not depending on the counter-promise, operates without the necessity of acceptance. The most remarkable test case on the matter is provided by Req. 29, March 1938.[8]

---

4   Art. 2.107.

5   *Carlill* v. *Carbolic Smoke Bali Co.* [1893] 1 Q.B. 256. The offeror put a pharmaceutical product on sale, promising anyone who caught influenza in spite of using the product a sum of money. The offeree used the product and he nevertheless caught influenza.

6   'A promise which the promisor should reasonably expect to induce action or forbearance on the part of the promisee or a third person and which does induce such action or forbearance is binding if injustice can be avoided only by enforcement of the promise.'

7   *Trenholm* v. *Klopper*, 129 N.W. 436 (1911); *Bishop* v. *Easton*, 37 NE 665 (1984).

8   In D. 1939, D.P., I, 5. The landlord offered the tenant a reduction in rent for the future; the tenant did not provide an answer.

In Germany, a proposal which is not bound to be followed by a counter-promise is considered effective, even if not accepted. The commentators refer to § 151 BGB: 'The contract is concluded through the acceptance of the offer, and the acceptance does not have to be declared to the proposer if such a declaration is not to be expected according to the normal usage'. The German courts assume that when a promise does not depend on a counter-promise, no declaration of acceptance is expected.[9]

Some recent legislative texts refer to definitions of contract that seem to require the acceptance of a proposal in any case. The new Dutch Civil Code states in Article 6:217(1) that 'a contract is formed by an offer and its acceptance.' In order to assess what an acceptance is, we can read Article 3:33 (' A juridical act requires an intention (...) manifested (...) by a declaration') and to know what a declaration is (*verklaring*, in Dutch) one should read Article 3:37(1); the declaration 'may be inferred from conduct'. One should take Article 6:5(2) and Article 6:253(4) into account to understand the meaning of this rule, such as a promise to perform a natural obligation and a promise to a third party beneficiary. The assent of the party who promises is unquestionably enough, unless the performance is refused by the party who would benefit.

The Unidroit Principles admit that a contract may be concluded either by the acceptance of an offer or by the conduct of the parties whenever it is sufficient (Art. 2:2.1). The rule as to what is sufficient to show agreement is to be found in Article 2:2.6, according to which 'a statement made by other conduct of the offeree indicating assent to an offer is an acceptance. Silence or inactivity does not in itself amount to acceptance.'

2.2 Which Solution Should Be Preferred?

The logical and ideal definition of the *Code Napoléon* has therefore not persuaded the recent legislators, who have preferred other solutions. They seem to be fascinated by the notion that a contract implies two requirements: offer and *acceptance*, and since acceptance (in their words) has no specific meaning, they probably explain that it may be a declaration, a conduct or an act. Needless to say, they are not able to explain which conduct amounts to acceptance. Therefore, the legislator remains silent and leaves it to whoever has to interpret the legislation to develop a legal doctrine as regards the conduct. With regard to this, France and Germany have already established the following rule: the fact that a proposal is made exclusively in the party's interest is sufficient to conclude that the silence of that party amounts to assent. This explanation has prevailed in the above-mentioned important decisions.

The French and German view leads to a correct but artificial result. The party's silence does not and cannot mean anything more than this. Respecting this logic, one would not be inclined to say: 'in the given circumstances, silence means the will to accept.' One would rather say: 'in the given circumstances, the declaration of acceptance is not necessary.' This incorrect language, which so many have silently accepted, praises the 'implied declaration', which is absurd from a logical point of

---

9   Three decisions of the German Supreme Court provide a good example, RG 19 April 1907, K. VII, 348/06; RG 10 November 1910, K. IV, 652/09, JW 1911, n. 2, p. 87; RG 12 December 1924, Seuff. A. 79, n. 89; in addition to BAG 3 August 1961, DB 1961, p. 1262.

view. To raise the issue effectively we must ask ourselves the following: when every or any form of acceptance is absent and when there is no form of denial of the proposal, shall the court hold that the contract exists or not? Since the answer is the former, it is not logically correct to state that the formation of a contract implies acceptance.

The curious might wonder why the simple and logical solution of Article 1108 of the *Code Napoléon* has not been unquestionably accepted. The answer highlights two points.

a) In the lawyer's ideology every person is the ruler of his juridical sphere. Therefore, nothing can enter or leave his sphere without his declared consent. It follows that the offeree cannot become a creditor if he has not declared his acceptance. This ideology rests on a perfectly acceptable premiss. Anyway, it is not impossible to silence the ideological lawyer and force him to agree with Article 1108 of the *Code Napoléon*. The independence of the citizen certainly and unquestionably requires a tool which he can use to safeguard his liberty; but the right means by which to safeguard him from other people's promises is the power of refusal. Article 1108 of the *Code Napoléon* certainly does not imply that *le consentement de la partie qui s'oblige* (the assent of the party who promises) also works when the promisee refuses the promise!

b) Several commentators all over Europe[10] find it convenient to define a contract as a bilateral formation of a legal act. Nevertheless, their seemingly convenient definition somewhat confines them. Having to face the problem of a contract consisting of just one promise and followed by nothing, they are forced to state that the declarations are in any case two-fold. Since this is false, they inform us that they define a declaration as 'something void', that is, the offeree's silence.

Why then do commentators adhere to this definition? They search through their collection of ideas (so deep-rooted they seem to be innate!), and they discover that the contract is an agreement. An agreement implies two intentions. Such arguments, of Byzantine and certainly not Roman origin, have muddled, in France as well, the reading of Article 1108 of the *Code Napoléon*.

Yet, the conceptual genotype of 'agreement' is not the only conceptual genotype to be used as regards the contract! In addition, there is the equation 'contract equal to exchange' (which appears in the promise on condition). Apart from the agreement and the exchange there is also the equation 'contract equal to promise able to produce a reliance' (which appears in a not for value suretyship). Academics have written books and formed their opinions while referring to the agreement genotype, or have combined the two genotypes based on agreement and exchange. Some legislators have followed these definitions.

The case-law of all the mentioned countries has instead followed the genotype of the promise that has produced a reliance thereon. Unconsciously, they practically translate those rules that have been well stated by the most important legislators. Unfortunately, however, the decisions of the courts are couched in conventional text-

---

10 See the survey in R. Sacco and G. De Nova (2003), I, pp. 243 ss. Other voices are not missing.

book language. This, in turn, leads to the notion of the agreement being highlighted and subjects this notion to an adjustment making use of the instrument of tacit declaration.

2.3 Contents of the Future European Civil Code

What should the European Code state on the matter? The future Code will have to use those solutions adopted by the courts of all or nearly all the European countries, and which take their inspiration from very noble conceptual genotypes. It will have to formulate these solutions in a correct manner. Therefore, it will have to start from a rule and a statement, both of them similar to the *Code Napoléon*.[11] It might express itself in the following words: 'an agreement enables the parties to contract obligations, according to the promises they have made. If one party places obligations up himself, the promise binds him, unless the promisee rejects it'.

3   Offer and Acceptance: The Gratuitous Nature Thereof

The above suggested explanation of the conclusion of a contract in general may also be applied to donation. The laws of all the mentioned countries suggest that a donation needs to be in a solemn form. Yet, once the form is respected, the donor's declaration should be sufficient to bind him, § 516 BGB is evidence of this. The rules pertaining to English and American deeds also provide evidence for this.

A possible exception could come from the French rules on donation. In France a donation is void if not 'explicitly accepted' (Art. 932 and Art. 938 of the *Code Napoléon)*. However, such a necessity is probably due to the fact that the French donation immediately transfers property to the donee. Property differs from a credit since it carries all sorts of obligations with it. It is perfectly understandable that the French legislator protects the donee – the recipient of a transfer – declaring the agreement is not complete before the moment of acceptance. However, in the proposed European Civil Code it will not be necessary to wait for an acceptance in order to state that the donation has been completed, if the contract has effect only between the parties.

4   Acceptance, Transfer and Receiving

The European Code will have to state the moment at which the acceptance becomes effective. The French legislator has never decided in general whether the offeree's declaration becomes effective from the moment it is sent or from the moment the offeror receives the acceptance. The German legal system has set down the receiving rule in its legislation (§ 130 BGB). Under English law, generally speaking, an accep-

---

11   A slightly different version is found in the Italian Civil Code, Art. 1333 (Contract binding on the offeror only): An offer for the purpose of forming a contract that creates obligations only for the offeror is irrevocable(...).The offeree can reject the offer (...). In the absence of such rejection the contract is concluded'.

tance is effective from the moment it is known to the offeror;[12] furthermore, acceptance sent by post is also effective, since the postal service is considered to be an 'agent' of the addressee.[13]

Which solution may be the best, if we are to draw up standard rules? If pure 'will' was once considered to be the main element of the contract, nowadays reliance, together with receiving the promise, is considered to be the only evidence of the contract's existence. The Vienna Sales Convention (Art. 18.2) and the Unidroit Principles (Art. 2:2.6 (2)) provide evidence for this. Article 3:35 of the Dutch Civil Code agrees. The solution will therefore be the one based on receipt. However, the moment the acceptance is sent might be very important in considering whether or not the proposal is irrevocable (see section 5); and the place at which the acceptance is sent might be the place where the contract is considered concluded and left to the competence of the court having jurisdiction over that particular place.

5 Revocation of the Proposal

The European Civil Code will have to state if and until when a proposal remains revocable. Two centuries ago, revocability of the proposal was undisputed. Irrevocability was considered to be an obligation and an obligation can only result from a contract. Even if the proposer undertook not to revoke, an obligation could not result, because the promise not to revoke was not supported by any consideration (the common law system), and because of a lack of acceptance (the continental approach).

The continental system was the first to realise that a proposal could include an implied promise not to revoke, that such a promise could create reliance upon it and that, therefore, it must produce an obligation, independent of the acceptance. Towards the end of the 19th century this solution had already been accepted both in France and in Germany. The Germans codified this approach in their *Bürgerliches Gesetzbuch* (§ 145).

Succeeding events have not reinforced the notion of irrevocability of the proposal. In Germany, citizens avoid the statutory rule of § 145 by means of the non-committal (*freibleibend*) warning. In France, the general rule of irrevocability has been replaced by the notion that the proposer is under an obligation for a short period of time only. Meanwhile, the English legal system seems to be willing to re-examine its position.[14]

The Vienna Sales Convention (Art. 15) and the Unidroit Principles (Art. 2.4) have chosen – with no opposition from the German delegates, nor from the Anglo-American representatives – a solution that states the rule of revocability in general terms, but does not admit revocation once excluded, either explicitly or by fixing a deadline for acceptance and even when it is reasonable for the offeree to rely on the offer as being irrevocable and the offeree has acted in reliance thereon. The solution chosen by the uniform law bas been welcomed. Article 6:220 of the Dutch Civil Code is based on it. The solution of the Vienna Sales Convention could also be accepted in

---

12 *Entores Ltd.* v. *Miles Far East Corporation* [1955], 2 All. ER 493, [1955], 2, QB, 327.
13 *Household Fire and Carriage Accident Insurance Co.* v. *Grant* [1879],4 Ex. D. 210.
14 In 1973, the suggestion of a revision came from the Law Revision Committee. The Law Commission became involved in 1975: Twelfth Ann. Report (1977), § 16.

the European Civil Code. The revocation should be effective if it 'reache[d] the offeree before he has dispatched an acceptance' (Vienna Sales Convention, Art. 16; Unidroit Principles Art. 2:2.4).

6   Battle of Forms

The European Code will have to regulate the conflict between standard contract terms referred to in the offer and in the acceptance (the so-called battle of forms). Should the standard terms of the two parties not coincide (and normally they do not), one might imagine that whereas the acceptance does not correspond to the proposal, no contract bas been concluded. However, such a conclusion seems to be too strict. In exchanging their declarations the parties believe that they have reached an agreement. Moreover, if one of the parties commences performance and the other party does not oppose it, it becomes a factual contractual relationship, which somehow has to be governed.

Generally speaking, the following solution seems to be rather successful: a reply to an offer, which contains additional or different terms which do not materially alter the terms of the offer, is an acceptance, unless the offeror objects to the discrepancy; and the terms of the contract will be the terms of the offer with the modifications contained in the acceptance (Vienna Sales Convention, Art. 19(2); Art. 6:225 (2) of the Dutch Civil Code). If we apply this rule to the battle of forms, we have to consider the acceptor's standard terms to be effective.

Nevertheless, the subject of the battle of forms deserves its own solution. Article 19(2) of the Vienna Sales Convention applies in the situation where the acceptor draws the proposer's attention to the discrepancy between the offer and the acceptance. The provision does not apply when the acceptance simply refers to the acceptor's standard contract terms.

With regard to the battle of forms the following solution then seems proper: should the standard contract terms of the two parties not agree, neither of the terms will be applied. This is, essentially, the solution proposed by the Unidroit Principles (Art. 2.22).

7   Formation of Contracts and Good Faith

A European Civil Code must beware of faint and general expressions such a 'good faith', 'good custom', and so on. Such formulations, however, would be useful to the national courts to recycle the national rules, apparently defunct. However, where the preparation and conclusion of contracts is concerned, some rules on the principle of good faith should be embodied in the Civil Code, in order to avoid leaving unsolved the many questions that could arise. Let us consider, for example, the following situations:

a) a person enters into negotiation without the intention of concluding an agreement;
b) a person unfairly abandons negotiation;

c) a person pronounces declarations (of contractual revocation, for instance) so that the counterpart cannot prove what has happened;

d) a person revokes a proposal, or withdraws acceptance, or turns down a proposal, or omits a refusal or an acceptance, because he is threatened or deceived and the counterpart wishes to take unfair advantage of this situation;

e) a person takes unfair advantage of a mistake or misinformation, a lack of reflection or fear on the part of the counterpart, or makes a mistake, even beyond the typical farms of threat, fraud, mistake.

Embodying rules on the principle of good faith could go some way in finding a solution to the above problems.

BIBLIOGRAPHY: P.S. Atiyah, *An Introduction to the Law of Contract*, 1981; C.W. Canaris, Schweigen im Rechtsverkehr als Verpflichtungsgrund, in: *Festschrift Wilburg*, 1975, pp. 77-78; H. Coing, *EuropäischesPrivatrecht*, 2 volumes, 1985 and 1989, 1, Rap. 19, e 11, Kap. 22; Corbin, *On Contracts*, 1950-1962; J. Ghestin, *Les obligations. Les contrat: formation*, 2nd ed., 1988; E.A. Kramer, Schweigen als Annahme eines Antrags, *Jura* 1984, p. 235; R. Sacco and G. De Nova,. *Il contratto*, 2 vol., 3rd ed., 2003; R.B. Schlesinger, *Formation of Contract*, 2 vol. (1968); W.B. Sirnpson, *A History of the common Law of Contracts*, 1975.

CHAPTER 20

The Pre-Contractual Stage

J.H.M. van Erp*

1 Introduction

When discussing the common core of European private law,[1] the law of contract is one of the most clear examples of the possible existence of such more or less "common" law. These, as Lipstein would prefer to call them, common aspects of European law[2] are no doubt based upon a shared legal heritage. However, a critical remark should be made at the outset. The feeling that when one looks at the principles and rules of contract law and finds it surprisingly easy to recognise familiar principles and rules in a foreign legal system might very well prove to be a, what Schlesinger in his famous work on Formation of Contracts has called 'booby-trap'.[3] As will be seen later, it has now – in the light of all the research done in this field by, among others, the United Nations Commission on International Trade Law (Uncitral), the International Institute for the Unification of Private Law (Unidroit) and the Commission on European Contract Law[4] – become relatively less of an effort to describe in a formal

---

* LLM (Tilburg, 1977), DrSc (Tilburg, 1990). Professor of civil law and of European private law, Maastricht University; Deputy Justice in the Court of Appeals 's-Hertogenbosch, the Netherlands. Research and writing for this chapter was done in part during a stay as a vacation visitor of Wolfson College, University of Cambridge (UK), as a visiting scholar at the University of California, School of Law (Boalt Hall), Berkeley (USA) and during a stay as a visiting professor at Cornell University Law School, Ithaca, New York in the autumn of 1995. This is the revised version of Chapter 8, The Formation of Contracts, in the first edition of this book. The chapter was updated and revised for the third edition.

1 Cf. for the Netherlands as one of the "older" publications on a developing European private law: Van Erp, Europees privaatrecht in ontwikkeling?, in: Franken, Gilhuis, Peters (eds.), Themis en Europa, een opening van nieuwe grenzen? (Zwolle, 1989), pp. 61 ff. In the second edition of this book I only made a reference to Drobnig, Private law in the European Union, Forum Internationale, No. 22 (September 1996), (The Hague, 1996) as one of the most recent publications about status, ambit and perspective of a common European private law. Since then, the amount of literature on this new legal area has become overwhelming and it is still growing.

2 Lipstein, European legal education in the future: teaching the "common law of Europe", in: De Witte/Forder (eds.), The common law of Europe and the future of legal education/Le droit commun de l'Europe et l'avenir de l'enseignement juridique (Deventer, 1992), pp. 255 ff.

3 Schlesinger, Formation of contracts, A study of the common core of legal systems, Conducted under the auspices of the General Principles of Law Project of the Cornell Law School, Vol. I, p. 56 (Dobbs Ferry, N.Y., 1968).

4 Cf. the (United Nations) Vienna Sales Convention and its history, documented by Honnold, Documentary history of the Uniform Law for International Sales, The studies, deliberations and decisions that led to the 1980 United Nations Convention with introduction and explanation (Deventer, 1989); Unidroit (International Institute for the Unification of Private Law), Principles of International Commercial Contracts (Rome, 1994); O. Lando and H. Beale (eds.), Principles of European Contract Law, Parts I and II, Combined and Revised, Prepared by the Commission on European Contract Law, (The Hague, London, Boston, 2000).

way the common rules regarding contract formation. Essentially, it might be argued, contract law can even be subsumed under one formal (backbone) rule: a contract comes into existence after the sequence of offer and corresponding acceptance. But formal rules do not give a complete picture of legal reality. Their application differs from one legal system to another. To give one striking example: the English common law does not recognise any duty to negotiate in good faith, as was only some years ago decided in a unanimous, single speech, decision by the House of Lords.[5] This is a clearly different approach (perhaps it would be better to say: different attitude) than can be found in continental legal systems.

In the following pages it is the process leading to the conclusion of a contract that will be analysed. This is the so-called "pre-contractual stage", from which various legal consequences might ensue. Very often this pre-contractual stage is characterised by negotiations, which can be very brief or extremely lengthy. The way a legal system looks at this process influences how that legal system perceives its rules on offer and acceptance. Are they seen as formal rules from which deviation is hardly possible or as a mere model (example) of how a contractual relationship may come into existence?[6] A legal system might also consider the whole contractual relationship as an ongoing process. In that view performance of a contract will not always mean that the contractual relationship has come to its end. It might very well be that the former contractual partners somehow still owe one another certain duties. That might be called the "post-contractual stage", the – at least in some respects – mirror image of the pre-contractual stage.[7]

The structure of this chapter will be as follows. First some introductory remarks about the more formal side of contract formation will be made.[8] This will be followed by an analysis of formation as a process. It will be seen that where, e.g., Dutch, French and German law follow a more substantive approach, English law tends to be more formal. At the end of this chapter it will be attempted to find a middle course between the civil law and (English) common law approach.

2 The Freedoms which Find their Expression in a Market Economy

All the Member States of the European Union share the economic view that a market economy will, at the end, result in the most efficient and fair distribution of labour, goods, services and capital. The type of market economy, however, might differ from

---

5   *Walford* v. *Miles* [1992] 2 W.L.R. 174; cf. Van Erp, Good faith: A concept "unworkable in practice"?, 1 Tilburg Foreign Law Review 215 (1992), with erratum in 1 Tilburg Foreign Law Review 406 (1992).

6   See in this respect R. Savatier, La théorie des obligations en droit privé économique (Paris, 1979), pp. 145 ff., where he not only writes about the "schéma classique de l'offre et de l'acceptation", but also about the "complexité corrigeant le schéma classique de négociation".

7   Cf. for German law, the so-called "culpa post contractum finitum"; see D. Medicus, Bürgerliches Recht (Cologne, Berlin, Bonn, Munich, 1996), p. 24.

8   See for a more elaborate discussion of the rules on offer and acceptance the chapter in this book on the formation of contracts by Sacco.

one country to another: some Member States favour state interference in certain areas of economic life, where others would oppose it fiercely. Consequently, privatisation and deregulation have gone further in some countries than in others. Still, the basic private law freedoms related to a market economy are shared by all and are the basis of the economic integration within the European Union. Müller-Graff calls these freedoms "compatible institutions of private law" and mentions "freedom of contract, the freedom of competition, the freedom of association and the guarantee of property rights as well as the existence of equivalent basic ideas in legal reasoning concerning conflicts in private relations such as the principle 'pacta sunt servanda', liability in torts or protection of property".[9] They are used as an already existing common legal basis for economic integration within the EC.

Given that, when describing formation of contracts, the starting-point is the freedom to enter (or not to enter) into a contract as well as the freedom to decide about its content, the question arises when this freedom is being surrendered and consequently a binding relationship comes into existence. Since the end of the 19th century it can fairly be stated that all legal systems in Western Europe demand a rather formal procedure for this surrender of freedom. There has to be a sequence of an offer followed by a corresponding acceptance of this offer and only through this formal sequence a contractual relationship can arise. Of course there are divergencies in the further elaboration of, e.g., what constitutes an offer, when an offer (or, as the case may be, an acceptance) can be withdrawn, under what circumstances an offer will be irrevocable, but basically the mechanism is clear.[10] The whole purpose of this mechanism is to ensure certainty. It should be clear exactly when a contract comes into existence, so that the line between freedom and being bound to someone else is unambiguous. This means that, in principle, pre-contractual dealings do not result in any binding legal relationship and that – generally speaking – between negotiating parties no general duty of disclosure as to essential information exists. It also means that, once being bound, the law will enforce the contract even under unforeseen circumstances. However, this rigidity in its extreme form no longer exists, although some legal systems are still more rigid in this respect than others. It is being realised more and more that a contract is an ongoing relationship, with, e.g., a duty to co-operate,[11] which develops itself in time.[12]

---

9   Müller-Graff, Common private law in the European Community, in: De Witte/Forder (eds.), The common law of Europe and the future of legal education/Le droit commun de l'Europe et l'avenir de l'enseignement juridique (Deventer, 1992), pp. 239-240.

10   A good example of this mechanism can be found in the new Dutch Civil Code. Cf. for the English and French translation of the relevant provisions of the code (articles 3:32 ff. on juridical acts, 6:217 ff. on the formation of contracts and 6:232 on general conditions), Haanappel/Mackaay, Nieuw Nederlands Burgerlijk Wetboek, Het vermogensrecht/New Netherlands Civil Code, Patrimonial law/ Nouveau Code Civil Néerlandais, Le droit patrimonial (Deventer/Boston, 1990). A brief discussion of the new Dutch Civil Code, especially in the area of contract law, can be found in Whincup, the new Dutch Civil Code, 142 New Law Journal 1208 (1992).

11   Cf. Bateson, The duty to co-operate, The Journal of Business Law 1960, p. 187, Honnold, Uniform law for international sales under the 1980 United Nations Convention, pp. 407-408 and pp. 430-431 and Legrand, Information in formation of contracts: a civilian perspective, in: Essays in honour of Jacob S. Ziegel, 19 Canadian Business Law Journal/Revue Canadienne du Droit de Commerce 318 (1991), p. 331.

12   Cf. Van Erp, Contract als rechtsbetrekking, Een rechtsvergelijkende studie/Contract as a form of legal

In civil law systems the softening of the mechanism of offer and acceptance as the exclusive test for the formation of a contract took place by the development of the (more special) duty to perform and enforce a contract in good faith towards an overall duty to act in good faith once a legally relevant relationship came into existence. This meant that also negotiating parties could be bound by this duty.[13] As a consequence of this overall duty to act in good faith a duty of disclosure can arise – at least in certain specific situations – to provide the other party with highly relevant information, thus securing the conclusion of a contract by informed consent. The requirement of *informed* consent can be seen as the modern expression of the freedom of contract. Surrender of freedom has to be free itself and it can only be so if one knows what is given up and which legal ties are being established. Again: some legal systems demand in this respect more than others, as will be briefly discussed hereafter.

3 Formation of Contracts: A More General Comparative Perspective

The idea behind a European Civil Code or –what I would prefer –a European private law Restatement[14] should be to state basic principles or standards applicable in general to any type of contract, be it inter (Member) State or strictly domestic.[15] This necessarily means that these principles must be fairly abstract and general, in order to encompass as much as feasible the different legal traditions in Europe (common law, civil law, the law of the Nordic countries, the mixed legal system of Scotland, the laws of the new Member States and the laws of future Member States). However, I am very much afraid that it will prove to be extremely difficult to avoid stating principles which are so general that they might lose any meaning in legal reality. A technique which could avoid this hazard is to counterbalance the openness of the standard

---

relationship, A comparative study (doctoral thesis; Zwolle, 1990) where some of the developments which will be described later in this chapter are also discussed with further references, to which can be added Bridge, Does Anglo-Canadian contract law need a doctrine of good faith?, 9 Canadian Business Law Journal/Revue Canadienne du Droit de Commerce 385 (1984), p. 417 ("To the extent that contract transcends its written expression, agreement can no longer be regarded as an event: it must be seen as a process.").

13 There is some circularity in reasoning to be detected here. The very moment that the step is taken that contracting parties, by the fact of their contract negotiations, enter into a legally relevant relationship, good faith is their basic norm of behaviour. See Hoge Raad (Netherlands Supreme Court) 15 November 1957, Nederlandse Jurisprudentie 1958, 67 (*Baris* v. *Riezenkamp*). On the other hand, their relationship can be said to be legally relevant, because good faith governs their pre-contractual dealings. See Hoge Raad 18 June 1982, Nederlandse Jurisprudentie 1983, 723 (*Plas* v. *Valburg*). Cf. for German law, Loges, Die Begründung neuer Erklärungspflichten und der Gedanke des Vertrauensschutzes (Schriften zum Bürgerlichen Recht, Band 136; doctoral thesis; Berlin, 1990), pp. 80 ff.

14 Cf. Remien, Illusion und Realität eines europäischen Privatrechts, 47 Juristen Zeitung 277 ff. (1992).

15 In this way an attempt might be made to avoid the intricacies of private international law, although I have doubts as to whether this attempt can ever be successful. Even if European private law would apply in the general way as is here advocated, its standards will be of such a general nature that the national laws of the Member States by sheer necessity will have a forceful supplementary role to play. Thus revitalising the old conflict of laws questions.

by formulating guiding (policy-weighing) factors. This is a technique which is at present widely used in case law all over the European Union.[16]

How could these standards, with regard to the formation of contracts, look like? As mentioned above, the Vienna Sales Convention, the Unidroit Principles for International Commercial Contracts and the Principles of European Contract Law can be taken as a solid base to build upon. But not, unfortunately, without further rethinking. The rules about formation of contracts as, e.g., laid down in the Vienna Sales Convention are – obviously – meant for international commercial contracts, not for purely domestic contracts and not for consumer contracts.[17] In addition these are rules for contracts of sales of goods, not for other types of contract and not even for sales of immovables.[18] Moreover and perhaps even more important than what just has been mentioned, it should be pointed out that formation of a contract can take place without offer and acceptance. After lengthy and complex negotiations it is sometimes nearly impossible to trace the final offer and/or the final corresponding acceptance. Then there are situations where contracts come into existence by the only fact that people behave as if there was a contract: the, what in German law is called, "faktische Vertragsverhältnisse" (*de facto* contractual relations).[19] And, finally, the "neat divisions of offer, acceptance and invitation to treat"[20] are not really well applicable in case of a multipartite agreement or to explain efficiently the possible binding nature of a contract in relation to third parties. Of course it can be argued, and to a certain extent rightly so, that the basic model of offer and acceptance will apply in most of the above mentioned types of situation. Still, it could make a difference whether these provisions would be applied, let us say, in a strictly commercial setting or in a consumer context. For that reason when formulating European private law one should take the internationally accepted model of offer and acceptance not as a legal tenet, but as a starting-point for further elaboration of principles depending upon the different types of situations just specified. The abstract standard of offer and acceptance could thus be exemplified according to the type of contract, e.g. – as was mentioned

---

16 Cf. Remien *ibid.*, p. 281. From an English perspective even the acceptance of a European restatement clearly would mean a considerable step towards their European counterparts. Traditionally English lawyers are not in favour of abstract principles. Besides *Walford* v. *Miles*, already referred to, this can be seen in *Murphy* v. *Brentwood District Council* [1990] 3 W.L.R. 414, a case in the area of the tort of negligence. For an American view see Llewellyn, The case law system in America (Gewirtz, ed., translated from the German by Ansaldi; Chicago/London, 1989), pp. 84 ff., discussing certainty and clarity in American law (§ 60) and legal compendiums and legal certainty (§ 61).

17 As to the distinction between civil law and commercial law it can very well be argued that it no longer proves to be as strict as it originally was. Cf. for a comparative analysis Kozolchyk, The commercialisation of civil law and the civilisation of commercial law, 40 Louisiana Law Review 3 (1979).

18 This remark does not apply to the Unidroit proposals, as these contain general principles for international commercial contracts.

19 Examples are boarding a bus, or parking one's car in a parking garage. Cf. Larenz and Wolf, Allgemeiner Teil des bürgerlichen Rechts (Munich, 1997), pp. 597 ff., Brox, Allgemeiner Teil des BGB (Cologne, Berlin, Bonn, Munich, 1999), pp. 99 ff. and, for English law, Atiyah, The rise and fall of freedom of contract (Oxford, 1979, reprint 1985), pp. 693 ff., esp. 734 ff.

20 Bridge, Does Anglo-Canadian contract law need a doctrine of good faith?, 9 Canadian Business Law Journal/Revue Canadienne du Droit de Commerce 385 (1984), p. 418.

earlier – by formulating different applicable guiding factors.[21] American experience precedes us, as was pointed out by Lücke.[22]

'(...) the United States legal system has some special characteristics which make it necessary for lawyers to embrace broad principles and policies, deeper reasons, abstract approaches and ethical terminology. The United States Bill of Rights is itself expressed in such terms. Moreover, it is probably only by attention to broad principles that some degree of unity can be achieved for the United States legal system with its huge and relentless flow of reported cases and its many separate systems of common law. Also, a homogenous society will find it easier to leave basic assumptions unspoken than does a multicultural one like that of the United States. The comparative method has proved useful in meeting that undoubted need, as have other factors such as the strong influence of the "national" law schools and the associated flow of high quality academic writing.'

If these remarks by Lücke are true for the United States, where the law in the respective states (except Louisiana) is primarily based on the common law as the shared legal tradition, even more should they be true for Europe where a prevailing legal tradition does not exist. What Lücke writes here is also a clear caveat. We should not let ourselves be deceived by the prima facie similarities in formal rules on offer and acceptance. Divergence in legal tradition, related to a divergence in legal atmosphere or, in other words, a different social, economic and political climate does influence ideas as to the role of, in our case, the law on formation of contracts.[23] The result of this divergence are deep-seated conflicting modes of thought in the several European traditions and these will not change the very moment a European restatement will be published.[24]

To illustrate this I will give two examples, which will be discussed in the next paragraph: the legal consequences of negotiating in contradiction with the requirements of good faith and, closely related to this problem area, the acceptance of a general duty of disclosure during contract formation. It seems for the present that in particular on the one hand English law and on the other hand Dutch, French and German law take an approach to these questions which can almost be qualified as antagonistic. Therefore and because it seems to me quite an impossible task to discuss in

---

21 Different guiding factors might also be formulated for the different legal systems as such, as socio-economic circumstances might differ from one Member State to another.

22 Good faith and contractual performance, in: Finn (ed.) Essays on contract (Sydney, 1987), pp. 155 ff, p. 156.

23 Cf. the discussion between Bridge and Tancelin about the introduction of good faith in Anglo-Canadian contract law, 9 Canadian Business Law Journal/Revue Canadienne du Droit de Commerce 385 ff. and 430 ff. and cf. Lord Goff of Chievely, Opening address (second annual Journal of Contract Law conference in London in September 1991), 5 Journal of Contract Law 1992, 1. See also the book review by Hooley of O'Connor's book Good faith in English law (Dartmouth, 1990), 49 The Cambridge Law Journal 515, referring to the already mentioned article by Bridge.

24 On the other hand, it might very well be that after the introduction of a European Civil Code or Private Law Restatement the differences in legal attitude gradually change. This phenomenon was noted by Frier, Interpreting codes, 89 Michigan Law Review 2201 (1991), as one of the long term consequences of the introduction of the UCC in the United States. Cf. in this respect for a view on developments in English legal practice Bingham, L.J., "There is a world elsewhere": the changing perspectives of English law, 41 International and Comparative Law Quarterly 513 (1992).

only a few pages all of the national legal systems in Europe a comparison will be made between these four European Member States to illustrate my earlier remarks.[25]

4 Pre-Contractual Dealings: The (Non-)Existence of a Duty to Negotiate in Good Faith and a General Duty of Disclosure

4.1 The Duty to Negotiate in Good Faith[26]

Traditionally, one of the basic distinctions between continental legal systems and the English legal system has been the absence in English law of both academically and judicially developed general concepts, like good faith. It was argued that, because English law had known a constant case by case evolution rooted in judicial practice, which had only at a fairly late stage been rationalised by academic legal scholars, common law meant practical law to solve practical problems, not speculative law to solve theoretical problems. The latter was to be found on the continent, where academic legal writing, strongly influenced by moral concepts based on canon law and general precepts based on roman law, had shaped legal practice, which had to suffer a further practical setback when even more theoretical codes were introduced. As has clearly been shown by others, this picture of the differences between English law and other legal systems is, remarkably enough, rather theoretical and incorrect. English law is far more influenced by Roman law than is sometimes admitted,[27] continental legal systems are far more practice oriented than might seem[28] and English law did develop general concepts in equity. Let us elaborate the last mentioned point somewhat further, in order to clarify what is meant. A reference might be made here to the discussion of the so-called "maxims of equity" in the first (1868) and the 28th edition (1982) of Snell's Principles of Equity. In the first edition Snell mentions 11 such

---

25 Although in the legal areas on which this chapter will focus among others the law of the United States would also offer a most rewarding object of comparative study, this legal system cannot be further discussed for the reasons mentioned in the text.

26 A clearly written overview of the various approaches in Europe can be found in Kötz, Europäisches Vertragsrecht I (Tübingen, 1996), pp. 10 ff. (about various theories to explain the binding nature of a contract as well as liability in case of "*culpa in contrahendo*") and pp. 50 ff. (a more general comparative discussion of liability for broken down negotiations). See also the chapter in this book on good faith written by Hesselink; Zimmermann and Whittaker, Good faith in European contract law (Cambridge, 2000), especially their introductory chapter 'Good faith in European contract law: surveying the legal landscape' (pp. 8 ff.); Gordley, The enforceability of promises in European contract law (Cambridge, 2001), which can be seen as a companion volume to the earlier mentioned book on Good faith in European contract law. For a recent comparison between English and French law see Giliker, Pre-contractual liability in English and French law (The Hague, London, New York, 2002).

27 See Gorla and Moccia, A 'revisiting' of the comparison between 'continental law' and 'English law' (16th-19th century), 2 The Journal of Legal History 143 (1981), Moccia, English law attitudes to the 'civil law', *ibid.*, pp. 157 ff. and Gordley, The philosophical origins of modern contract doctrine (Oxford, 1991).

28 Cf. Frier, Interpreting codes, 89 Michigan Law Review 2201 (1991). He points out (p. 2213/4), as was said earlier, that a code (like the continental codes or the American Uniform Commercial Code) results in what he calls an "expanded interpretive community": the judiciary, the bar and (academic) legal authors.

maxims, arguing[29] that the "ingenuous student will find no difficulty in tracing almost every maxim or head of equity to that great maxim, the keystone of the whole arch, – 'Equity suffers no wrong without a remedy'". In the 28th edition Baker and Langan mention 12 maxims ('equity acts in personam' is added) and defend[30] that "it would not be difficult to reduce them all under the first and the last, 'Equity will not suffer a wrong to be without a remedy', and 'Equity acts on the person'".[31] It is also quite revealing to read what Jessel M.R. said in Re Hallet's Estate,[32] acknowledging that equity was invented by judges.[33] In his own words: "(...) it must not be forgotten that the rules of the Courts of Equity are not, like the rules of the Common Law, supposed to have been established from time immemorial. It is perfectly well known that they have been established from time to time – altered, improved, and refined from time to time. In many cases we know the names of the Chancellors who invented them. No doubt they were invented for the purpose of securing the better administration of justice, but still they were invented." Of course I do realise that equity developed into a system of rules, laid down in precedents, with its own specific character next to the common law. The point I am trying to make, nevertheless, is that English law is able to transform general norms[34] in workable rules, not unlike continental judges transform good faith in workable "sub-regulations", as, e.g., described by Alpa.[35] The fact that a code system uses (even must use) open ended principles and standards does not necessarily mean that it is unable to produce practical solutions or that the judges who have to apply these principles and standards are hampered in their creativity. For that reason I cannot but disagree with Bridge[36] when he argues: "General principles, such as good faith, can serve the purposes of innovation and creativity in a civil law system that are carried forward by a more creative judiciary in the common law tradition." My first reaction – as an academic, but also as a Deputy Justice – to this statement would be to say that judicial creativity can be limited as much by the binding nature of precedents as by the binding nature of a statute, as a code essentially is.[37] But foremost I would reply that I strongly believe that a discus-

---

29 Snell, The principles of Equity, Intended for the use of students and the profession, (London, 1868), p. 12.
30 Baker and Langan, Snell's Principles of Equity (London, 1982), p. 28.
31 See for a brief historical practice note on the maxim 'he who comes into equity must come with clean hands' Starke, 63 The Australian Law Journal 854 (1989).
32 (1880) 13 Ch. D. 696, 710.
33 Cf. also Gardner, An introduction to the law of trusts (Oxford, 1990), p. 34 (note 34).
34 Snell (first edition, 1868, p. 12), even describes a maxim of equity as an "active and comprehensive aphorism".
35 Italian report about pre-contractual liability, in: Hondius (ed.), Precontractual liability, Reports to the XIIIth congress international academy of comparative law (Montreal, Canada, 18-24 August 1990)(Deventer/Boston, 1991), pp. 195 ff., p. 200.
36 Bridge, Does Anglo-Canadian contract law need a doctrine of good faith?, 9 Canadian Business Law Journal/Revue Canadienne du Droit de Commerce 385 (1984), p. 414.
37 I refer to a feeling expressed by Lord Goff of Chievely, already mentioned, that in English law the introduction of a good faith principle in contract law is beyond the powers of the English judiciary. Cf. Lord Goff of Chieveley, Opening address, ibid., p. 4. Reflecting upon this submission I cannot help but feeling intrigued by the fact that in Germany (and later in the Netherlands) the most influential force in developing good faith as a general norm applying to the whole of the contractual process was – remarkably enough for a code system – not the legislature, but on the contrary the judiciary.

sion about whose judges are more creative is an unnecessarily negative as well as an unproductive approach which tends to move analysis away from a more fundamental discussion of good faith in a comparative context.[38]

Why this, perhaps at first sight somewhat provocative, introduction to the subject which we are discussing in this paragraph? Although it only until recently seemed likely that the above mentioned traditional distinction between English law and continental legal systems was gradually disappearing, this proved to be a deceptive impression in regard to the role of good faith in contract law. An illustration of this at first converging, then diverging development in the area of good faith is being offered by a case about the incorporation of a general condition in a contract, *Interfoto Picture Library Ltd.* v. *Stiletto Visual Programmes Ltd.*[39] In that case Bingham L.J. said that "English law has, characteristically, committed itself to no such overriding principle (i.e. that in making and carrying out contracts parties should act in good faith, J.v.E.) but has developed piecemeal solutions in response to demonstrated problems of unfairness." But he added:[40] "The tendency of the English authorities has, I think, been to look at the nature of the transaction in question and the character of the parties to it; to consider what notice the party alleged to be bound was given of the particular condition said to bind him; and to resolve whether in all the circumstances it is fair to hold him bound by the condition in question. This may yield a result not very different from the civil law principle of good faith, at any rate so far as the formation of the contract is concerned." Developments like this case led a legal writer like O'Connor in a book published in 1990 to defend the thesis that English law had come very close to introducing a general good faith concept.[41] Before O'Connor also Lücke[42] had defended the introduction of good faith in the common law. But there also were other voices. Lücke wrote partly as a reaction to an, already mentioned, article written by Bridge, 'Does Anglo-Canadian contract law need a doctrine of good faith?'.[43] The answer which Bridge gave to this question was distinctively negative: introduction of good faith as a general norm of behaviour in contract law would disrupt the "complex amalgamation of doctrine, case law and legislation, which is beyond the realistic range of instant human achievement." He did see a role for good faith "in articulating contract theory and in defining the goals that our con-

---

38 A discussion about whose language is better equipped for comparative law analysis runs the same risks. Cf. for an attempt to avoid this unproductive type of discussion about legal languages Remien, Rechtseinheit ohne Einheitsgesetze? – Zum Symposium "Alternativen zur legislatorischen Rechtsvereinheitlichung", 56 Rabels Zeitschrift 300 (1992), p. 307.

39 [1989] 1 Q.B. 433 (1987), 439.

40 *Ibid.*, p. 445.

41 O'Connor, Good faith in English law (Dartmouth, 1990), critically reviewed by Hooley, 49 The Cambridge Law Journal 515 (1990).

42 Good faith and contractual performance, in: Finn (ed.), Essays on contract (Sydney, 1987), pp. 155 ff. See for the role of good faith in Australian contract law, which seems to be more receptive to this concept than English and Anglo-Canadian law, Carter/Harland, Contract law in Australia (Chatswood, 2002), pp. 88-89, p. 521, pp. 649 ff. and pp. 673-674; cf. also Starke, Current topics, The current activities of Unidroit, 64 The Australian Law Journal 685 (1990), 686. Starke mentions that Unidroit will incorporate good faith in its principles for international commercial contracts and that Australian contract law is no longer hostile to this idea.

43 9 Canadian Business Law Journal/Revue Canadienne du Droit de Commerce 385 (1984).

tract law is harnassed to serve". However, legislative adoption along the lines of United States law or continental codes would be "an abuse of the comparative legal method", it would fail "to address the role and function of good faith in differently constituted societies",[44] which would result in the introduction of a "highly selective legal transplant without regard to the whole of a country's legal tradition".[45] Another English author, Cartwright, writing in 1991 also disagreed with O'Connor and basically agreed with Bridge: "There is no general rule in English law that a party has to bargain in good faith, or to comply with a principle of fair and open dealing."[46] He went, however, on saying: "(...) even if English law does not enforce a rule of fair dealing , it does take account of *un*fair dealing."

Less than two years after the publication of O'Connor's book and one year after the publication of Cartwrights book, it appears that the latter was right after all, at least as far as the non-recognition of good faith is concerned. The House of Lords made unequivocally clear that introduction of good faith in English contract law would and, even stronger, could not happen. The case, already mentioned earlier, in which this was decided is *Walford* v. *Miles*.[47] The case is about the legal consequences, if any, of a contract to negotiate and the final breakdown of negotiations. In a single speech by Lord Ackner, the following was said about the possible acceptance in English law of a duty to negotiate in good faith: "A duty to negotiate in good faith is as unworkable in practice as it is inherently inconsistent with the position of a negotiating party."[48] *Walford* v. *Miles* did make it possible to conclude a so-called "lock

---

44 Bridge, *ibid.*, p. 426. Cf. the comments to this paper by Farnsworth and Tancelin, *ibid.*, pp. 426 ff. and pp. 430 ff. See also Hassan, The principle of good faith in the formation of contracts, 5 Suffolk Transnational Law Journal 1 (1980)

45 Bridge, *loc. cit.*, p. 414. See further Klapisch, Der Einfluß der deutschen und österreichischen Emigranten auf contracts of adhesion und bargaining in good faith im US-amerikanischen Recht, Zugleich eine Darstellung der vorvertraglichen Haftung in den USA (Arbeiten zur Rechtsvergleichung, Schriftenreihe der Gesellschaft für Rechtsvergleichung, Band 152) (Baden-Baden, 1991), esp. pp. 157 ff. Here the author discusses the reasons why American law did not develop a doctrine of culpa in contrahendo as it is known in German law. Cf. also Zimmermann, "Common law" und "civil law", Amerika und Europa – Zu diesem Band, in: Zimmermann, Amerikanische Rechtskultur und europäisches Privatrecht (Tübingen, 1995) pp. 1 ff.

46 Cartwright, Unequal bargaining, A study of vitiating factors in the formation of contracts (Oxford, 1991), pp. 224-225, referring in a footnote to the already mentioned case of *Interfoto* v. *Stiletto Visual Programmes*.

47 [1979] 2 W.L.R. 174. Looking at English history, bearing in mind that English law is being seen as an uninterrupted continuing flow of cases, one cannot but be surprised by this categorical denial of good faith as a general concept in contract law. Good faith, still more utmost good faith, has always been accepted as a fundamental norm of behaviour in insurance law. The historical landmark case is *Carter* v. *Boehm* (1766) 3 Burr. 1905. Here Lord Mansfield even remarked: "The governing principle (i.e. that a concealment will avoid a policy, J.v.E.) is applicable to all contracts and dealings. Good faith forbids either party by concealing what he privately knows, to draw another into a bargain, from his ignorance of that fact, and his believing the contrary. But either party may be innocently silent, as to grounds open to both, to exercise their judgment upon." See also Cohen, Precontractual duties: two freedoms and the contract to negotiate, in: Beatson/Friedmann (eds.) Good faith and fault in contract law (Oxford, 1995), pp. 25 ff.

48 The words that good faith is a concept "unworkable in practice" might refer to a remark by the Canadian author Waddams, Pre-contractual duties of disclosure, in Cane/Stapleton (eds.), Essays for Patrick Atiyah (Oxford, 1991), pp. 237 ff., p. 254: "It is true that the law, in its general objectives, represents a community sense of morality, but actual legal rules must also be fair and *workable in*

out agreement". This is a contract by which one party promises the other party not to negotiate (further) with third parties. It does not, however, give the other party a positive right to continuation of the negotiations. As a lock out agreement is a contract it is only valid if supported by valuable consideration.

Walford v. *Miles* was followed by the Court of Appeal in *Pitt* v. P.H.*H. Asset Management Ltd.*[49] In the latter case a lock out agreement between a vendor and a prospective purchaser of a cottage was held to be concluded and legally binding. The consideration found to be valuable[50] for the vendor was that he was freed from the "nuisance value" of a threat by the purchaser to ask for an injunction to continue the negotiations only with the latter and to be freed from the "nuisance value" that the prospective purchaser might withdraw from the negotiations, at the same time informing a third party that it no longer had any competitors (allowing that party to lower its offer). It was further seen as valuable consideration that the purchaser promised to exchange documents within two weeks after the vendor had sent a draft contract of sale to him. It is clear from *Pitt* v. *P.H.H. Asset Management* that English law only accepts liability from broken down negotiations in cases where existing lines of case law would allow this: e.g. by accepting a validly concluded lock out agreement. A general doctrine of good faith negotiations is not accepted.

In sharp contrast with English law is Dutch law,[51] following the direction as indicated by French, Italian[52] and more in particular by German law.[53] The Dutch Supreme Court (Hoge Raad) decided in 1957[54] that the pre-contractual stage was a legal relationship governed by good faith. Then in 1982[55] it was decided that the negotiating process could be divided in three stages: an initial stage, where determining negotiations would not lead to any claim for damages, an intermediate stage where

---

practice with a reasonable degree of regularity, and reasonably inexpensive to apply. Justice is the general objective of the law, but the search for justice is not advanced by the adoption of rules that are so expensive to apply that they put its attainment out of practical reach." (Italics mine, J.v.E.) Adding (*ibid.*): "What is needed is a set of rules sufficiently in conformity with the community sense of morality not to produce results perceived as outrageous, while at the same time preserving sufficient content to be workable and reasonably inexpensive of regular application, and maintaining a fair degree of security of property transfers."

49 [1994] 1 W.L.R. 327.

50 Under English law a binding contract only comes into existence if there is "do ut des": an exchange of performances or promises to perform. This is what is meant when it is said that a contract has to be supported by "consideration".

51 Cf. Van Dunné, Dutch report in: Hondius (ed.) Precontractual liability, Reports to the XIIIth congress international academy of comparative law (Montreal, Canada, 18-24 August 1990), pp. 223 ff. and the general report by Hondius, *ibid.*, pp. 1 ff., p. 23. See also Hartkamp and Tillema, Contract law in the Netherlands (The Hague/London/Boston, 1995), pp. 71-72.

52 See art. 1337 Italian C.C.: "Le parti, nello svolgimento delle trattative e nelle formazione del contratto, devono comportarsi secondo buona fede."

53 Cf. for French law Ghestin,Traité de droit civil, Les obligations, Le contrat; formation (Paris, 1988), pp. 249 ff. and for German law Esser/Schmidt, Schuldrecht, Band I, Allgemeiner Teil (Heidelberg, 1984), pp. 435 ff., Larenz, Lehrbuch des Schuldrechts, Erster Band, Allgemeiner Teil (Munich, 1987), pp. 106 ff. and Loges, *loc. cit.*, pp. 39 ff. For Israeli law see Rabello, La théorie de la "culpa in contrahendo" et la loi israélienne sur les contrats 1973, Revue internationale de droit comparé 1997, 37 ff.

54 Hoge Raad 15 november 1957, Nederlandse Jurisprudentie 1958, 67 (*Baris* v. *Riezenkamp*).

55 Hoge Raad 18 June 1982, Nederlandse Jurisprudentie 1983, 723 (*Plas* v. *Valburg*).

negotiations might be determined under the condition that the other party's reliance expenses were paid and an ultimate stage where it was no longer in accordance with good faith when the negotiations would be ended and the other party's expectation damages had to be paid in case no contract ensued after all. This third stage, almost – so it seems – of a quasi-contractual nature, has not only attracted quite some attention in the Netherlands, but also abroad.[56] A first remark which should be made in regard to this stage is that courts will be very cautious when they have to decide whether in a particular case such a stage was apparently reached.[57] A second remark concerns the test to decide if this ultimate stage is reached. In 1982 it was formulated as follows: "if the parties, from both sides, could trust that some contract would, in any case, ensue from the negotiations". This test has in following cases been rephrased.[58] Relevant now is only the reliance by the party who is being confronted with a party who determines the negotiations. As a consequence of this reformulation of the reliance test it is no longer necessary that both parties relied on a positive outcome of their pre-contractual dealings: multilateral reliance has been replaced by unilateral reliance as a precondition for liability. Unilateral reliance by itself is, however, not sufficient. It should also be considered to what degree and in which manner the party who ended the negotiations caused the other party's reliance. And further it should be considered if there were any justified interests on the side of the first mentioned party justifying the break down of the discussions, also in the light of possible unforeseen circumstances which arose while the parties were negotiating.[59]

This approach to pre-contractual liability comes very close to older and present German (case-)law. The leading German decision in this area is the so-called "Linoleum case".[60] This was a case about a customer and her child who were injured by rolls of linoleum which fell on top of them after a salesman had moved those in order to show them the roll of linoleum the customer wanted to see. The German Supreme Court ruled that the injury occurred at a moment that the parties were preparing a

---

56 Farnsworth, Precontractual liability and preliminary agreements: fair dealing and failed negotiations, 87 Columbia Law Review 217 (1987), p. 221.

57 See Hoge Raad 14 June 1996, Nederlandse Jurisprudentie 1997, 481 (*De Ruiterij* v. *MBO*).

58 See, e.g, the *De Ruiterij* v. *MBO case.*

59 It is interesting to note that this change in emphasis from the reliance of both parties to the reliance of the party who has to face that someone else breaks down the negotiations in fact means a change in emphasis from an examination of the parties' mind to a questioning of one party's behaviour. A comparable trend away from the state of mind of the victim of an error or fraud to an examination of the other party's behaviour can also be seen in French law. Cf. Legrand, Pre-contractual disclosure and information: English and French law compared, 6 Oxford Journal of Legal Studies 322 (1986), p. 337 and Legrand, Information in formation of contracts, Essays in honour of Jacob S. Ziegel, 19 Canadian Business Law Journal 318/Revue Canadienne du Droit de Commerce (1991), pp. 332-333. For German law see the decision by the Bundesgerichtshof (German Supreme Court) 10 July 1970, Neue Juristische Wochenschrift (NJW) 1970, pp. 1840-1841. The German Supreme Court ruled that the behaviour of both parties has to be judged in the light of what good faith requires. If one party declares that he is willing to conclude a contract and by doing so causes his counter-party to rely on the final conclusion of the contract, the counter-party has to make clear within a reasonable time if he is also willing to conclude the contract. Reliance, though justified it may be for some time, cannot last forever.

60 Reichsgericht (German Supreme Court) 7 December 1911, amtliche Sammlung der Reichsgerichtsrechtsprechung (RGZ) 78, 239.

sales contract. The relationship between the parties was therefore not merely coincidental, but was quasi-contractual. The salesman was therefore obliged to take care of the health and property of the customer. This is an application of the "culpa in contrahendo" doctrine: parties engaged in contract negotiations are bound by a duty of care not to injure the other party or cause damage to the other party's property. The range of culpa in contrahendo in German law has been extended to a very large degree.[61] To give but one example: under the doctrine of culpa in contrahendo also a third party, who does not take part in the negotiations, can claim damages in case of injury. This was decided by the German Supreme Court in the "saladleaf case".[62] A child accompanied her mother while the latter was buying groceries. The child fell over a saladleaf and got injured. Although only the mother was – strictly speaking – in a pre-contractual relationship with the supermarket, the child was protected by the same duty of care which the supermarket owed its customers.[63] In comparison with Dutch law, the money compensation which can be awarded is somewhat more limited. Generally speaking only losses ("negatives Interesse") can be claimed, although in some cases it seems that a claim for lost profits could also be awarded.[64]

4.2 The Duty to Disclose Essential Information

Reflecting upon the non-acceptance of a general duty to negotiate in good faith and the reasons given by the House of Lords as well as several common law authors, the question arises what causes this more or less sudden reversal of convergence to divergence between common and civil law. Does the present trend perhaps indicate – it is for the time being only tentatively suggested – that, at least in regard to contract law, there is a certain desire to preserve an historically evolved feeling of self-identity as a case law system? Before answering this question it is useful to look at another example of the present trend in English contract law to move away from other legal systems: the refusal to accept a general duty of disclosure in the pre-contractual stage. The present position of English law is quite clear, as was affirmed in *Banque Keyser Ullmann S.A.* v. *Skandia (U.K.) Insurance Co. Ltd.* and *Bank of Nova Scotia* v. *Hellenic Mutual War Risks Association (Bermuda) Ltd.*[65] Basically, with an exception

---

61 Even to such a degree that D. Medicus, Grundwissen zum Bürgerlichen Recht, (Cologne, 1995), p. 128 qualifies culpa in contrahendo as a type of "Mehrzweckinstrument mit gefährlich weitem Anwendungsbereich" (muti-purpose instrument with a dangerously wide field of application).

62 Bundesgerichtshof (German Supreme Court) 28 January 1976, Entscheidungen in Zivilsachen (BGHZ) 66, 51. See for cases applying the *culpa in contrahendo* doctrine also: Bundesgerichtshof 12 July 1977, NJW 1977, 2259; Bundesgerichtshof 23 October 1985, NJW 1986, 586. Cf. D. Medicus, Grundwissen zum Bürgerlichen Recht, *loc. cit.*, pp. 127 ff.; D. Medicus, Bürgerliches Recht (Cologne, 1996), pp. 139 ff.; Palandt-Heinrichs, Bürgerliches Gesetzbuch (Munich, 2002), Comments under § 276; Palandt-Heinrichs, Gesetz zur Modernisierung des Schuldrechts (Munich, 2002), Comments under § 311; Haas, Medicus, Rolland, Schäfer, Das neue Schuldrecht (Munich, 2002), pp. 116 ff; R. Schulze, Bürgerliches Gesetzbuch, Handkommentar (Baden-Baden, 2003). Comment under § 311.

63 Culpa in contrahendo is here extended by applying the doctrine of contracts with protective effect towards third parties. Cf. Medicus, Bürgerliches Recht, *loc. cit.*, pp. 623 ff.

64 Cf. Palandt-Heinrichs, *loc. cit.*, § 276; Medicus, Grundwissen, *loc. cit.*, p. 130.

65 [1991] 2 A.C. 249, [1990] 3 W.L.R. 364, H.L. (E.) and [1991] 2 W.L.R. 1279, H.L. (E.), both concerning a duty to inform in the case of an insurance contract.

for, e.g., insurance contracts, the principle as laid down in *Smith* v. *Hughes*[66] still applies.[67] In the words of Cockburn C.J.:[68] "I take the true rule to be, that where a specific article is offered for sale, without express warranty, or without circumstances from which the law will imply a warranty – as where, for instance, an article is ordered for a specific purpose – and the buyer has full opportunity of inspecting and forming his judgment, if he chooses to act on that judgment, the rule caveat emptor applies." Or, as Blackburn J. put it in even stronger words:[69] "(...), whatever may be the case in a court of morals, there is no legal obligation on the vendor to inform the purchaser that he is under a mistake, not induced by the act of the vendor."

Very much the same as we saw while looking at the non-acceptance in English law of a general contractual standard of good faith, we can see here that English and Anglo-Canadian authors are supportive of the approach taken by the House of Lords. Nicholas, although realising the gap between English law and French law, certainly seems to be sustaining the English piecemeal acceptance of a duty of disclosure.[70] Also Waddams[71] favours the incremental approach, based on the further development of existing situations in which a duty to disclose has been accepted, which approach "has more to recommend it than the revolutionary."

Looking at French and German law, one cannot but conclude that in those legal systems an unmistakably different attitude is to be found.[72] It is argued by authors like Ghestin and Legrand[73] that a general duty of disclosure of essential information

---

66 (1871) LR 6 QB 597.

67 See also Cartwright, Unequal bargaining, A study of vitiating factors in the formation of contracts pp. 90 ff.
    Two decisions underlining the approach taken by the House of Lords are *Barclays Bank Plc.* v. *Khaira* [1992] 1 W.L.R. 623 (Chancery Division; the Court of Appeal struck out a notice of appeal) and *Barclays Bank Plc.* v. *O'Brien* [1992] 3 W.L.R. 593, C.A. In the last mentioned case Purchas L.J. on the one hand refused to categorise the existing case law in this area, but on the other hand did rephrase the authorities by putting forward what he called "propositions" (*ibid.*, pp. 635-636).

68 *Smith* v. *Hughes, ibid.*, p. 603.

69 *Smith* v. *Hughes, ibid.*, pp. 606-607.

70 Nicholas, The pre-contractual obligation to disclose information, 2: English report, in: Harris/Tallon, Contract law today, Anglo-French comparisons (Oxford, 1989), pp. 166 ff.; cf. also Fabre-Magnan, Duties of disclosure and French contract law: Contribution to an economic analysis, in: Beatson/ Friedmann (eds.) Good faith and fault in contract law (Oxford, 1995), pp. 99 ff.

71 Waddams, *loc. cit.*, p. 256. See also Waddams, Precontractual duties of disclosure, 19 Canadian Business Law Journal 349 (1991) (a summary of his contribution to the Essays in honour of Patrick Atiyah) and the comments on Waddams' article by Farnsworth, 19 Canadian Business Law Journal/ Revue Canadienne du Droit de Commerce 351 (1991). Also, as was the case with the introduction of a general concept of good faith, it seems that Australian contract law is more receptive towards a general duty of disclosure than its English and Anglo-Canadian counterparts. Cf. Finn, Good faith and nondisclosure, in: Finn (ed.), Essays on torts (Sydney, 1989), pp. 150 ff.

72 See for Swiss law: Wahrenberger, Vorvertragliche Aufklärungspflichten im Schuldrecht (unter besonderer Berücksichtigung des Kaufrechts), zugleich ein Beitrag zur Lehre von der culpa in contrahendo (Dissertation, Zürich, 1992), pp. 57-58.

73 Ghestin, Traité de droit civil, Les obligations, Le contrat; formation, pp. 502 ff., Ghestin, The pre-contractual obligation to disclose information, 1: French report, in: Harris/Tallon (eds.), Contract law today, Anglo-French comparisons (Oxford, 1989), pp. 151 ff., p. 166; Legrand, Pre-contractual disclosure and information: English and French law compared, 6 Oxford Journal of Legal Studies 322 (1986), p. 337 and also Information in formation of contracts, Essays in honour of Jacob S. Ziegel, 19 Canadian Business Law Journal/Revue Canadienne du Droit de Commerce 318 (1991), pp. 332-

necessary for an informed consent to contract does exist in French law. Ghestin summarises French law in the following way:[74] "To sum up, a party who was or (having regard especially to any professional qualification) ought to have been aware of a fact which he knew to be of determining importance for the other contracting party is bound to inform the latter of that fact, provided that he was unable to discover it for himself or that, because of the nature of the contract, the character of the parties, or the incorrectness of the information provided by the other party, he could justifiably rely on that other to provide the information." A conclusion which, no doubt, could also have been formulated for German law[75] or Dutch law.

How this gap between English law and other legal systems might be bridged, in spite of the seemingly antagonistic approach, will be suggested in the next paragraph.

5   Final Remarks: How to Bridge the Gap Between English Law and the Other European Legal Systems?[76]

In regard to the role of good faith and pre-contractual duties to inform English law and continental legal systems seem, as was remarked earlier, no longer to converge but to diverge. Nicholas[77] has put forward that the basic distinction between English and French law is that English law departs from an economic viewpoint and French law from a moral viewpoint, at the same time referring to the difference in conceptual structures between the two legal systems. Adding to this analysis reference can be made to what Finn has said[78] about the common law as inclined to cherish virtues like individual responsibility and self-reliance and to what was remarked by Farnsworth[79] namely that the common law traditionally favoured the goals of finality, certainty and practicality by generally not requiring disclosure. Legrand, in contrast, has characterised French law, comparing it with English law, as positive (it accepts an obligation of information), altruistic (acceptance of a duty to share certain information between partners) and concrete (it is not as much the nature of a contract which is decisive if a duty of disclosure will be accepted, but the character of the parties: 'professionel' vs. 'profane').[80] He considers this approach as the legal reaction to a since the 1950's changed society in which the liberal classical economic model of (enlightened) laissez-faire was replaced by the welfare model of the mixed

---

333. See also for a comparison of French-Canadian with American law Legrand, De l'obligation précontractuelle de renseignement: aspects d'une réflexion métajuridique (et paraciviliste), 21 Ottawa Law Review/Revue de droit d'Ottawa 585 (1989, partly discussing the opposite of a duty of disclosure: the right to remain silent about certain secrets).

74 Ghestin, The pre-contractual obligation to disclose information, p. 166.

75 Cf. Larenz, Lehrbuch des Schuldrechts, *loc. cit.*, pp. 110 ff. and the (critical) study by Loges, passim.

76 Or, so might be asked, 'how to tunnel the channel?', to refer to a successful, albeit costly, attempt to bring England and the continent closer together.

77 Nicholas, *loc. cit.*, p. 184; cf. also the conclusions, *ibid.*, pp. 187 ff.

78 Finn, *loc. cit.*, p. 159.

79 Comments on professor Waddams' "Precontractual duties of disclosure", Essays in honour of Jacob S. Ziegel, 19 Canadian Business Law Journal/Revue Canadienne du droit de Commerce 351 (1991), p. 352.

80 Pre-contractual disclosure, *loc. cit.*, p. 349; Information in formation, *loc. cit.*, p. 346.

economy, where the community and the individual share responsibilities, creating a what Legrand calls "esprit de solidarité". Another aspect of this changed society is that it has become highly technological, thus causing a division, already suggested, between "experts" (those who possess knowledge and are able to use it) and "profanes", i.e. their counterparts, those who do not possess knowledge and even if they would, do not know how to use it to its maximum. Also, finally, this changed society is more concerned about consuming than about the improvement of producing.[81]

Considering all this, slowly the impression starts to build up that somehow there might be more to the differences in development of English law compared to other legal systems than meets the eye. Perhaps it is too straightforward simply to presume that the background of conceptual diversity at least partly can be explained by a desire to preserve a feeling of self-identity. It could very well be that Bridge is right after all when he characterises (common law) Canada – and probably England – as "differently constituted societies" in comparison to French law Canada, the (mostly common law, but partly French law) United States, (common law) Australia and countries with a (French, German or Swiss type) code system, arguing that this is the cause of conceptual diversity. A diversity that would make it "an abuse of the comparative legal method" to introduce a general concept of good faith in England and (common law) Canada. To me it is not altogether clear what Bridge exactly means by societies which are "differently constituted", but my submission is that the social-economic phenomena, as tentatively described by Legrand, indeed might be close to the heart of the problem. Perhaps England and common law Canada did develop their own particular legal system because of the type of society which existed at the time. In England, certainly, the feudal system did influence legal concepts to a large degree. But are England and common law Canada – both modern, democratic societies with a free market economy, like all the other countries in Europe as well as the United States[82] and Australia – really so different from other societies even at the present day? If the answer is yes (but the answer would require a study of far more length and depth than is here possible), this would mean that legal harmonisation within Europe desperately needs the development and implementation of a common social, economic and technological policy, in order to establish the common extra-legal basis for a European private law.[83]

This does not mean that for the time being harmonisation as to the requirement of good faith in contract negotiation and formation, as well as to a general duty of (pre-contractual) disclosure would be impossible. It only means that it can absolutely not be done in the form of a code.[84] This would prove to be too compelling for in particu-

---

81 Pre-contractual disclosure, *loc. cit.*, p. 330, Information in formation, *loc. cit.*, p. 331.

82 See for a recent overview of the developments in American law: Hillman, The richness of contract law, An analysis and critique of contemporary theories of contract law (Dordrecht/Boston/London, 1997), pp. 143 ff.

83 It could very well be argued that the European Union already is moving in that direction after the Treaties of Maastricht, Amsterdam and Nice.

84 See in this respect P. Legrand, Against a European Civil Code, Modern Law Review 1997, pp. 44 ff. This is different, of course, within a particular national legal system, if pre-contractual liability has already been accepted in case law. Reference can be made to German law, where § 311 of the Civil Code after the reform of the law of obligations now incorporates pre-contractual liability.

lar England and Ireland. Principles, on the other hand, might work well, because they leave more interpretive freedom than rules. They would allow both English and other judges to opt either for an implementation by incremental development (using the principles as background notions) or for an acceptance as such (in the way as now happens in, e.g., Dutch, German and French law).[85] Therefore, I would support the principles regarding pre-contractual dealings proposed by Unidroit and the "Lando Commission".[86] On the one hand, these principles demand good faith behaviour in general, whereas, on the other hand, bad faith (i.e. explicitly not acting in good faith) behaviour in negotiations is specifically excluded.[87] In regard to commercial transac-

---

85 By taking this approach, also differences of opinion within a particular legal system in regard to whether good faith is an explicit or implicit (underlying) principle could perhaps be overcome. Cf. for such a discussion in Scots law the various contributions in Forte, Good faith in contract and property law (Oxford/Portland, Oregon, 1999). See, e.g., MacQueen, Good faith in the Scots law of contract: An undisclosed principle?, *op cit.*, pp. 5 ff.; Thomson, Good faith in contracting: A sceptical view, *op cit.*, pp. 63 ff.

86 Unidroit Principles of International Commercial Contracts, Articles 1.7 and 2.15 read as follows: "(Article 1.7, Good faith and fair dealing)
(1) Each party must act in accordance with good faith and fair dealing in international trade.
(2) The parties may not exclude or limit this duty."
"(Article 2.15, Negotiations in bad faith)
(1) A party is free to negotiate and is not liable for failure to reach an agreement.
(2) However, a party who negotiates or breaks off negotiations in bad faith is liable for the losses caused to the other party.
(3) It is bad faith, in particular, for a party to enter into or continue negotiations intending not to reach an agreement with the other party."
Principles of European Contract Law, Article 2:301, which reads:
"(Article 2:301: Negotiations contrary to good faith)
(1) A party is free to negotiate and is not liable for failure to reach an agreement.
(2) However, a party which has negotiated or broken off negotiations contrary to good faith and fair dealing is liable for the losses caused to the other party.
(3) It is contrary to good faith and fair dealing, in particular, for a party to enter into or continue negotiations with no real intention of reaching an agreement with the other party."

87 Unidroit (International Institute for the Unification of Private Law), Principles of international commercial contracts (Rome, 1994). For a further explanation of these principles see Bonell, An international restatement of contract law, The Unidroit principles of international commercial contracts (New York, 1994), pp. 79 ff. (observance of good faith and fair dealing in international trade) and pp. 91 ff. (policing the bargaining behaviour). For a brief comment on the Principles of European Contract Law from a Dutch perspective see: Mak, Article 2:301, in: Busch, Hondius, Van Kooten, Schelhaas and Schrama (eds.), The Principles of European Contract Law and Dutch law. A commentary (Nijmegen/The Hague, London, New York, 2002), pp. 129 ff. Cf. about good faith in international commercial sales law also Honnold, Documentary history of the Uniform Law for International Sales, The studies, deliberations and decisions that led to the 1980 United Nations Convention, with introduction and explanation (Deventer, 1989), pp. 369-370; the same author, Uniform law for international sales under the 1980 United Nations Convention (Deventer/Boston, 1991), pp. 146 ff. and Ercüment Erdem, La livraison de marchandises selon la Convention de Vienne, Convention des Nations Unies sur les contrats de vente internationale de marchandises du 11 avril 1980 (Travaux de la faculté de droit de l'Université de Fribourg, Suisse, no. 101; Fribourg, 1990), pp. 51 ff. An interesting development in the area of consumer protection which should be mentioned here is the EC Council Directive on Unfair terms in consumer contracts, dated 5 April 1993, *OJ* L 95/29. In this directive consumers are given protection against so-called "unfair contract clauses". These are clauses which have not been individually negotiated and which, against the requirements of good faith, create a significant divergence between the rights and duties for the parties to the contract.

tions (dealings between professional parties) I would like to add, however, that I agree with Giliker that courts should take into consideration commercial practices and appreciate realistically "the parties own perception of their risk".[88]

Let us hope that the harmonisation effort in the area of European private law proves to be far less of a burden than it sometimes looks like. For this hope to come true it is however a conditio sine qua non that comparative research does not end where it unveils conceptual divergency, but that it also attempts to overcome otherwise seemingly insuperable obstacles to harmonisation by including in its analysis a thorough study of social, economic and political factors relevant to the functioning of a legal system.

---

88 Giliker, *loc. cit.*, p. 180.

CHAPTER 21

Agency

Michael Joachim Bonell*

1   Introduction

The law of agency, emphatically described as "a subject of never-ending fascina-tion"[1] if not even "a legal miracle",[2] broadly speaking deals with the situation where a party enters into legal relationships with another party by acting not personally but through an intermediary. As such it represents an essential supplement to general contract law and may be seen as the legal response to the division of work indispens-able in modern societies.

Yet despite the fact that the practical needs it is meant to meet are basically the same everywhere, the law of agency differs, at least at first sight, significantly among the various jurisdictions, leading to considerable linguistic difficulties and conceptual confusion.[3]

Notions such as "agency", "*Stellvertretung*", "*représentation*", "*rappresentanza*", "*vertegenwoordiging*" or the like, only apparently express the same concept, while in fact they have quite different meanings within the respective legal systems.

Thus, the common law notion of "agency" has a very broad meaning, covering all cases where a person, the principal, consents that another person, the agent, acts on its behalf so as to affect its relations with a third party, irrespective of whether or not the agent reveals to the third party the identity or even the very existence of the prin-cipal.[4]

---

*   Professor of Law, University of Rome I "La Sapienza"; Chairman of the UNIDROIT Working Group for the Preparation of Principles of International Commercial Contracts. The views expressed in this article are those of the author and do not necessarily reflect the opinions of the other members of the Working Group.

1   R. Goode, Commercial Law, 2nd ed. (1995), p. 166.

2   E. Rabel, Die Stellvertretung in den hellenistischen Rechten und in Rom, in Gesammelte Aufsätze IV (edited by W. Wolff) (1971), pp. 491 *et seq.* (p. 492).

3   W. Müller-Freienfels, Zum heutigen Stand des Stellvertretungsrechts und den Reformvorhaben, in W. Müller-Freienfels, Stellvertretungsregelungen in Einheit und Vielheit (1982), pp. 1 *et seq.* (p. 59i) speaks of a "babylonische Sprachverwirrung".
     Even such an authoritative text as the Principles of European Contract Law (cf. *infra*) could not avoid a somewhat confusing terminology: in a chapter entitled "authority of *agents*" they never use the term *agency* and speak instead of *representation*, further distinguishing between *direct* and *indirect* rep-resentation depending on whether an *agent* acts *in the name of a principal* or an *intermediary* acts *on instructions and on behalf of but not in the name of* a principal, or the third party neither knows nor has reason to know that the *intermediary* acts as an *agent* (emphasis added).

4   Cf. Bowstead and Reynolds on Agency, 17th ed. (2001), p. 2: "The word 'agency', to a common lawyer, refers in general to a branch of law under which one person, the agent, may directly affect the legal relations of another person, the principal, as regards yet other persons, called third parties, by acts which the agent is said to have the principal's authority to perform on his behalf and which when done are in some respect treated as the principal's acts").

By contrast, civil law systems traditionally distinguish between "direct" and "indirect" agency – *rectius*: *Stellvertretung, représentation, rappresentanza* or *vertegenwoordiging* – depending on whether the agent, when dealing with the third party, acts in the name of the principal or in its own name, and only in the first case provide that the agent's acts directly bind the principal, while in the second case it is the agent who becomes party to the contract with the third party even if the third party knows that it is dealing with an agent.[5]

Doubts may arise as to whether such conceptual contrasts are really justified or whether the time has not come to try to find a common ground between the common law and civil law approaches to the law of agency. [6]

Efforts to achieve international unification in this field have so far produced rather limited results. Two international conventions dealing with agency have been adopted but both have met with little success in practice. The 1978 Hague Convention on the Law Applicable to Agency (hereinafter the "Hague Convention"), laying down uniform conflict of laws rules with respect to agency relationships in general, has entered into force but only in a very small number of States.[7] On its part, the 1983 Geneva Convention on Agency in the International Sale of Goods (hereinafter the "Geneva Convention"), based on a draft prepared by UNIDROIT and containing uniform substantive law rules on agency in the context of the conclusion of international sales contracts, has not even entered into force, lacking the required number of ratifications.[8]

However, recently some fresh and promising attempts to develop internationally acceptable rules in the field of agency have been made. Both the Principles of European Contract Law (hereinafter the "European Principles") and the UNIDROIT Principles of International Commercial Contracts (hereinafter the "UNIDROIT Principles"), aiming at laying down rules of general contract law within the European Union and at a universal level, respectively, contain a specific chapter on "Authority of Agents". Actually, only the chapter of the European Principles has been pub-

---

5   For the distinction e.g. between "*direkter oder unmittelbarer Stellvertretung*" and "*indirekter oder mittelbarer Stellvertretung*" in German law, see K. Larenz/M. Wolf, Allgemeiner Teil des Bürgerlichen Rechts, 8th ed. (1997), p. 864; between "*représentation parfaite*" and "*représentation imparfaite*" in French law, see Ph. Malaurie – L. Aynes, Cours de droit civil, t. VI, Les obligations, 10th ed. (1999), pp. 392 *et seq.*; between "*rappresentanza diretta*" and "*rappresentanza indiretta*" in Italian law, see M.C. Bianca, Diritto civile, III, Il contratto, 2nd ed. (2000), pp. 93-95 and 120-123; between "*directe vertegenwoordiging*" and "*middellijke vertegenwoordiging*" in Dutch law, see Asser – van der Grinten, Vertegenwoordiging en rechtspersoon, 7th ed. (1990), Nos. 1-17, 102.

6   In this sense expressly W. Müller-Freienfels, Zum heutigen Stand, *cit.*, p. 21: "In der Gegenwart wachsen [...] die Zweifel, ob die scharfe Konfrontation beider Rechte noch länger begründet ist und nicht vielmehr eine Hauptaufgabe unserer Zeit darin liegt, einen wirklichen Kompromiss zwischen den common law- und den civil law – Systemen hier zustandezubringen".

7   Namely, Argentina, France, Portugal and The Netherlands (for the entry into force of the Convention three ratifications were sufficient).

8   The Convention has been ratified by five States (France, Italy, Mexico, South Africa and The Netherlands) but requires ten ratifications for entry into force. – For a first commentary on the Geneva Convention, including references to its preparatory work, see M. J. Bonell, The 1983 Geneva Convention on Agency in the International Sale of Goods, in 32 The American Journal of Comparative Law (1984), pp. 717 *et seq.*

lished,[9] while the corresponding chapter of the UNIDROIT Principles is contained in the new enlarged edition of the UNIDROIT Principles expected to be published by June 2004.[10]

In the following, the two sets of rules will be critically analysed in order to see to what extent they follow solutions traditionally adopted at domestic level or take an innovative approach, laying the path for a new, internationally acceptable law of agency. In this context, special attention will also be paid to the Geneva Convention, which despite its failure to enter into force remains an important point of reference for any uniform law project in this field, and to the Draft Restatement Third of Agency (hereinafter the "Draft Restatement Third"), presently under preparation under the auspices of the American Law Institute[12] and aiming at "re-stating" the current law of agency in the United States.[13]

2 Authority of Agent Distinct from Underlying Contract

Both the European Principles and the UNIDROIT Principles, rather than providing a comprehensive set of rules on agency, focus on the authority of an agent to bind its principal in relation to a contract with a third party. In other words, they are concerned only with the external relations between the principal or the agent on the one hand and the third party on the other,[14] and not with the internal relations between the principal and the agent which continue to be governed by the otherwise applicable law.[15]

---

9   Cf. O. Lando – H. Beale (eds.), Principles of European Contract Law, Parts I and II (2000), Chapter 3.
10 Cf. UNIDROIT 2003, Study L – Doc. 91.
11 The new edition of the UNIDROIT PRINCIPLES, containing 5 new chapters (Authority of agents; Set-off; Assignment of rights, transfer of obligations and assignment of contracts; Third party rights; Limitation periods, respectively) together with additional provisions on inconsistent behaviour and release by agreement, will be submitted to the Governing Council of UNIDROIT at its next session in April 2004 for final approval.
    The chapter on the authority of agents will become Section 2 of Chapter 2 of the UNIDROIT PRINCIPLES. Hereinafter the individual articles of the chapter will be quoted in their final numbering
12 Reporter for the Draft Restatement Third is Professor Deborah DeMott. Specific references hereinafter to the Draft Restatement Third are to Tentative Draft No. 2 (March 14, 2001), except for those in notes n. 48 and n. 52, which are to Tentative Draft No.4 (March 17, 2003) and in note n. 96 which is to Tentative Draft No. 3 (March 18, 2002). Note that so far not all the envisaged chapters of the Draft Restatement Third have been prepared. With respect to issues addressed hereinafter which have not yet been dealt with in the Draft Restatement Third, reference is made to Restatement Second of Agency (1957).
13 This all the more so since, as pointed out in the Reporter's Notes to the Introduction (cf. Draft Restatement Third, p. 13), "[u]nlike the Restatement Second of Agency, this Restatement also makes explicit references to foreign law for purposes of comparison".
14 Cf. Article 3:101(1) and (3) of the European Principles, and Article 2.2.1(1) and (2) of the UNIDROIT Principles.
15 Cf. Comment 1 to Article 2.2.1 of the UNIDROIT Principles, pointing out that "[t]he rights and duties as between the principal and the agent are governed by their agreement and the applicable law which, with respect to specific types of agency relationships [...] may provide mandatory rules for the protection of the agent." The same Comment specifically refers to the so-called commercial agents which within the European Union are protected by a number of mandatory provisions imposed by EC directive 86/653.

This approach, which is the same as that taken by the Geneva Convention[16] but not by the Draft Restatement Third,[17] is based on the so-called principle of separation ("*Trennungsprinzip*"), i.e. the distinction between the unilateral act of the principal's granting the authority to an agent to affect its relations with a third party, and the underlying contract that may or may not exist between the agent and the principal.

This principle, while adopted in most, though not all, civil law systems,[18] is as such unknown in common law systems.[19] However, as pointed out,[20] the contrast between the two systems lies "rather in the nature and extent of the conclusions drawn from the initial reasoning than in the reasoning itself". Indeed, also at common law the authority of an agent stems not from any contract between principal and agent (for indeed there need not to be one) but from the unilateral grant of authority.[21]

Where civil law and common law systems really diverge is with respect to the so-called abstract nature of the authority ("*Abstraktion der Vollmacht*"), i.e. the impossibility of the principal to invoke against third parties the limitations of the agent's authority as established in the internal relationship. It should, however, be noted that this principle, which is the most important corollary of the *Trennungsprinzip*, is fully recognised as such only in some civil law systems and even then only with respect to the holder of a statutory commercial authority.[22] At any rate it is not accepted by either the European Principles or the UNIDROIT Principles.[23]

Both the European Principles and the UNIDROIT Principles expressly state that they do not deal with cases where the agent's authority is conferred by law or arises from judicial authorisation.[24] A consequence of this approach, which corresponds to the Geneva Convention and the Draft Restatement Third,[25] is that also the authority of the directors of a corporation – to the extent that it is governed by special statutory provisions of the *lex societatis*,[26] – is outside their scope.[27]

---

16 Cf. Article 1(1) and (3) of the Geneva Convention.

17 Cf. Draft Restatement Third, § 1.01 ("Agency Defined") and Comment c to § 1.01 stressing that "[a]gency [...] entails inward-looking consequences, operative as between the agent and the principal, as well as outward-looking consequences, operative as among the agent, the principal, and third parties with whom the agent interacts". Consequently also the Draft Restatement Third, like the Restatement Second of Agency (1957) (cf. chapter 14 and chapters 1-13, respectively), will cover both the "inward-looking" and the "outward-looking" consequences of agency.

18 See, also for further references, M.J. Bonell, The 1983 Geneva Convention, *cit.*, pp. 718-720.

19 Cf. Bowstead and Reynolds on Agency, *cit.*, pp. 13 *et seq.*

20 Bowstead and Reynolds on Agency, *cit.*, p. 16.

21 Bowstead and Reynolds on Agency, *cit.*, p. 15; similarly Draft Restatement Third, Comment b to § 3.01 ("Actual authority may exist although there is no contract between a principal and agent; a relationship of agency does not require that the principal or the agent receive consideration from the other").

22 See for further references M.J. Bonell, The 1983 Geneva Convention, *cit.*, p. 719.

23 See Articles 3:204 (1), 3:205 and 3:209 of the European Principles and Articles 2.2.5 (1), 2.2.7 and 2.2.10 of the UNIDROIT Principles, on the agent acting without authority, on conflicts of interest and termination of authority, respectively.

24 See Articles 1:101(2) of the European Principles and Art. 2.2.1(3) of the UNIDROIT Principles

25 Cf. Articles 3 and 4 of the Geneva Convention; Draft Restatement Third, Comment f2 to § 1.01.

26 Cf., e.g., Section 35 A of the English Companies Act 1985, Article 98 of the French *Code des Sociétés* (as amended in 1969), § 82 of the German *AktG* (as amended in 1968) or Article 2384 of the Italian Civil Code (as amended in 1969), all implementing Article 9 of the EEC Directive 68/151 of 9 March 1968. – For some references on U.S. law see Draft Restatement Third, Reporter's Notes on Introduction, pp. 15-16.

27 Thus, for instance, if under statutory law a corporation is prevented from invoking against third

This does not mean, however, that in practice there might not still be cases where the two instruments apply even if the principal is a corporation. This is true first of all whenever the competent organ of a corporation confers authority on an *ad hoc* basis on one of its members or employees to act on behalf of the corporation.[28] Moreover and more importantly, as long as there is no conflict between the special statutory provisions on the directors' authority and the rules contained in the two instruments, there is nothing to prevent the latter from being applied instead of the former.[29]

3   Actual and Apparent Authority

The granting of the agent's authority by the principal is not subject to any particular requirements of form and may be either express or implied.[30]

An implied authority exists whenever the principal's intention to confer the authority on an agent can be inferred from the terms of the express authority or the principal's conduct (e.g. the conferment on the agent of a particular task) or other circumstances of the case (e.g. a particular course of dealing between the two parties or a general trade usage). The broader the mandate conferred on the agent, the wider the scope of its authority.[31]

A particular case of implied authority, for which express provision is made in both the European Principles and the UNIDROIT Principles, is the agent's right to appoint subagents, with the only limitation that the agent may not entrust its subagents with tasks which the agent is reasonably expected to perform itself.[32]

Actual authority, be it express or implied, is at least theoretically to be distinguished from so-called apparent authority.[33] This latter concept refers to a situation

---

parties any limitation to the authority of its directors (as is the case according to the statutory provisions cited *supra* in note n. 23), that corporation would not be permitted to rely on Article 3:204(1) of the European Principles or Article 2.2.5(1) of the UNIDROIT Principles to claim that it is not bound by an act of its directors which falls outside the scope of their authority.

28   Cf. Comment B to Article 3:101 of the European Principles.

29   Cf. Comment 5 to Article 2.2.1 of the UNIDROIT Principles, which by way of example refers to the case where a party dealing with a foreign corporation, unaware of the special statutory provisions governing the authority of that corporation's directors, in order to establish that the corporation is bound by the contract, invokes the rule on apparent authority of agents as contained in Article 2.2.5 (2), provided that the requirements therein laid down are met.

30   Cf. Article 3:201(1) of the European Principles and Article 2.2.2 (1) of the UNIDROIT Principles. Similarly, Article 9 of the Geneva Convention and § 3.01 of the Draft Restatement Third.

31   Accordingly, both instruments expressly provide that the agent's authority extends to all acts necessary in the circumstances to achieve the purposes for which the authority was granted: see Article 3:201(2) of the European Principles and Article 2.2.2 (2) of the UNIDROIT Principles.

32   Article 3:206 of the European Principles and Article 2.2.8 of the UNIDROIT Principles.

33   On the difficulty in drawing in practice a clear border line between cases of implied authority and cases of apparent authority see M.J. Bonell, The 1983 Geneva Convention, *cit.*, p. 740; H. Kötz, European Contract Law, I, (translated from German by T. Weir), 1997, p. 235, rightly pointing out that "it is really a question of juristic taste whether or not one treats it as a pure fiction to say that particular conduct on the part of the principal falls within an implied grant of authority: the critical question in all cases is how a proper third party would reasonable interpret the situation presented to him".

where the principal has no intention to authorise the agent to act on its behalf with a third party, but nevertheless by its statements or conduct *vis-à-vis* the third party causes the third party reasonably to believe that such intention actually existed.[34]

As stated in the Comments to the UNIDROIT Principles,[35] as well as in the Comments to the Draft Restatement Third,[36] the apparent authority is especially important where the principal is not an individual but an organisation. In dealing with a corporation, partnership or other business association a third party may find it difficult to determine whether the persons acting for the organisation have actual authority to do so and may therefore prefer, whenever possible, to rely on their apparent authority. For this purpose the third party only has to demonstrate it was reasonable for it to believe that the person purporting to represent the organisation was authorised to do so, and this belief was caused by the conduct of those actually authorised to represent the organisation (board of directors; executive officers; partners; etc.). Whether or not the third party's belief was reasonable will depend on the circumstances of the case (position occupied by the apparent agent in the organisation's hierarchy; type of transaction involved; acquiescence of the organisation's representatives in the past; etc.).

There is a difference in the way the European Principles and the UNIDROIT Principles approach apparent authority.

The European Principles put apparent authority, at least with respect to its effects, on the same footing as actual authority.[37] While this approach is similar to, though not identical with, that of the Draft Restatement Third,[38] the UNIDROIT Principles, like the Geneva Convention,[39] express the concept of apparent authority in terms of estoppel by conduct or prohibition of *venire contra factum proprium*.[40] To be sure,

---

34 For further references on what is known as *Rechtsscheinvollmacht* in German law, as *mandat apparent* in French law or as *procura apparente* in Italian law see M.J. Bonell, The 1983 Geneva Convention, *cit.*, pp. 739-740; H. Kötz, European Contract Law, *cit.*, pp. 234-237.

35 Comment 2 to Article 2.2.5 of the UNIDROIT Principles.

36 Draft Restatement Third, Comment c and e to § 3.03.

37 Cf. Article 3:201(3) of the European Principles: "A person is to be treated as having granted authority to an apparent agent if the person's statements or conduct induce the third party reasonably and in good faith to believe that the apparent agent has been granted authority for the act performed by it." See also Comment D, according to which "[a]n agent who has apparent authority will have power to bind the principal as much as if the agent had express authority[...]".

38 Actually the Draft Restatement Third distinguishes between "apparent authority" (cf. § 2.03: "Apparent authority is the power held by an agent or other actor to affect a principal's legal relations with third parties when a third party reasonably believes the actor has authority to act on behalf of the principal and that belief is traceable to the principal's manifestations") and "estoppel to deny existence of agency relationship" (cf. § 2.05: "A person who has not made a manifestation that an actor has authority as an agent and who is not otherwise liable as a party to a transaction purportedly done by the actor on that person's account is liable to a third party who justifiably is induced to make a detrimental change in position because the transaction is believed to be on the person's account, if (1) the person intentionally or carelessly caused such belief, or (2) having notice of such belief and that it might induce others to change their position, the person did not notify them of the facts"). – For the somewhat similar distinction between *Anscheinsvollmacht* und *Duldungsvollmacht* in German law, see K. Larenz/M. Wolf, Allgemeiner Teil des Bürgerlichen Rechts, *cit.*, pp. 920-929.

39 Cf. Article 14(2) of the Geneva Convention.

40 Cf. Article 2.2.5(2) of the UNIDROIT Principles: "[...] [W]here the principal causes the third party reasonably and in good faith to believe that the agent has authority to act on behalf of the principal

this does not affect the position of the third party since under both approaches the principal may not invoke against the third party the agent's lack of actual authority. Yet the situation is different as far as the principal is concerned: while under the European Principles the principal may sue the third party on the contract concluded by the apparent agent, under the UNIDROIT Principles it would not be entitled to do so.

On closer examination however the difference is a more theoretical than practical one. Indeed, even under the UNIDROIT Principles any action by the principal against the third party could be considered an implied ratification of the contract concluded by the apparent agent and as such be admitted.

4 Effects of Agent's Acts

More substantial are the differences between the European Principles and the UNIDROIT Principles with respect to the effects of the acts of the agent.

The European Principles distinguish between "direct representation" and "indirect representation" depending on whether the agent acts "in the name of a principal" or merely "on instructions and on behalf of, but not in the name of a principal",[41] and only in the first case provide that the agent's acts bind the principal and the third party directly to each other,[42] while in the second case as a rule it is the agent – *rectius*: "intermediary" – who is bound to the third party and vice versa.[43]

By contrast, under the UNIDROIT Principles it is irrelevant whether or not the agent acts in the name of the principal.[44] For the establishment of a direct relationship between principal and third party it is sufficient that the agency is disclosed, i.e. the third party knows or ought to know that the agent is acting on behalf of a principal whether identified or not.[45] Only where the agency is undisclosed, i.e. the third party neither knows nor ought to know that the agent is acting as an agent, the agent's acts affect merely the relations between the agent and the third party. [46]

---

and that the agent is acting within the scope of that authority, the principal may not invoke against the third party the lack of authority of the agent." – See also Comment 2, stating that "[a]pparent authority [...] is an application of the general principle of good faith (see Article 1.7) and of the prohibition of inconsistent behaviour (see Article 1.8 [...]". – For a similar approach at domestic level see e.g. Article 3:61 (2) of the Dutch Civil Code; Bowstead and Reynolds on Agency, cit., pp. 308 *et seq.* (but see at p. 317: "There can be no doubt that the prevailing approach in England has been in terms of representation and estoppel [...], but its theoretical underpinnings are shaky, even if the need for such reasoning is undoubted, and in the long run reconsideration may be needed").

41 Cf. Article 3:102 of the European Principles. – "Direct representation" is dealt with in Articles 3:201 to 3:209, "indirect representation" in Articles. 3:301 to 3:304 of the European Principles.

42 Article 3:202 of the European Principles. – Note that according to Article 3:203 the same rule applies where an agent enters into a contract "in the name of a principal whose identity is to be revealed later", provided that the principal's identity is revealed "within a reasonable time after a request by the third party".

43 Article 3:301(1)(a) of the European Principles.– Note that according to Article 3:301(1)(b) the same rule applies where "the intermediary acts [...] on instructions from a principal but the third party does not know and has no reason to know this [...]".

44 In this sense expressly Article 2.2.1(1), last sentence, of the UNIDROIT Principles.

45 Article 2.2.3 (1) of the UNIDROIT Principles.

46 Article 2.2.4 (1) of the UNIDROIT Principles. – Note that that according to Article 2.2.3(2) of the

As one can see, the European Principles seem to take the traditional civil law approach, whereas the UNIDROIT Principles, following the Geneva Convention,[47] in this respect come close to the common law approach, as reflected also in the Draft Restatement Third.[48]

Yet there are significant departures from the respective models.

Thus, the European Principles, in conformity with similar rules to be found in some, but by far not all, civil law systems,[49] even in cases of indirect representation grant the principal and the third party the right of direct action against each other whenever the intermediary becomes insolvent or commits a fundamental non-performance towards one or the other.[50] On the other hand, contrary to both the Geneva Convention[51] and the Draft Restatement Third,[52] under the UNIDROIT Principles in cases of undisclosed agency the principal's right of direct action against the third party is excluded altogether,[53] while the third party only exceptionally may sue the principal, namely when in contracting with the agent it was led to believe that it was dealing with the owner of a business but later discovers that it had in fact been dealing with the owner's agent. More precisely, "where [...] an agent, when contracting with the third party on behalf of a business, represents itself to be the owner of that business, the third party, upon discovery of the real owner of the business, may exercise also against the latter the rights it has against the agent".[54]

UNIDROIT Principles the same rule applies where the agent, with the consent of the principal, undertakes to become the party to the contract. In practice this will be the case where the principal wants to remain anonymous and decides to act through a so-called commission agent, or where the third party insists that the agent "confirms" the contract concluded on behalf of a principal with whom the third party does not want to deal directly.

47 Cf. Articles 12 and 13 (1) of the Geneva Convention, which correspond almost literally to Articles 2.2.3 and 2.2.4 (1) of the UNIDROIT Principles.

48 Cf. §§ 6.01 and 6.02 of the Draft Restatement Third, dealing with the cases where an agent acts on behalf of a "disclosed" or of an "unidentified" principal, respectively, and providing that in both cases parties to the contract are the principal and the third party. – According to § 1.04 (2) of the Draft Restatement Third, "a principal is disclosed if, when an agent and a third party interact, the third party has notice that the agent is acting for a principal and has notice of the principal's identity", and "a principal is unidentified if, when an agent and a third party interact, the third party has notice that the agent is acting for a principal but does not have notice of the principal's identity".

49 For further references see M.J. Bonell, The 1983 Geneva Convention, cit., pp. 734-737.

50 Cf. Articles 3:302 and 3:303 of the European Principles. – The two articles also provide that, if the conditions for such a direct action are fulfilled, the intermediary must disclose to its principal or to the third party the name and address of the third party or of the principal, respectively, and that the third party may raise against the principal the same defences it has against the intermediary, and the principal may raise against the third party the same defences the intermediary has against the third party or the principal has against the intermediary.

51 Cf. Article 13 (1) (a) in conjunction with Article 13 (2) of the Geneva Convention.

52 Cf. § 6.03 of the Draft Restatement Third, according to which, even where the agent acts on behalf of an "undisclosed" principal, parties to the contract are not only the agent and the third party but also the principal, unless otherwise agreed between the agent and the third party. – According to § 1.04 (2) of the Draft Restatement Third, "a principal is undisclosed if, when an agent and a third party interact, the third party has no notice that the agent is acting for a principal".

53 Cf. Article 2.2.4 (1) of the UNIDROIT Principles.

54 Cf. Article 2.2.4(2) of the UNIDROIT Principles. – For a similar rule at domestic level see e.g. with respect to German law, K. Schmidt, Handelsrecht, 3rd ed. (1987), pp. 112 et seq. ("unternehmensbezogene Geschäfte"); with respect to Italian law, Article 2208, second sentence, Civil Code

The insistence of the European Principles on the formal requirement of a *contemplatio domini* for the agent's act directly to bind the principal may come as somewhat of a surprise. This not only because its rejection was considered one of the most important achievements of the Geneva Convention,[55] but also in view of the fact that even within the civil law systems its importance in practice, at least with respect to commercial transactions, is rather doubtful.[56] It is true that by granting, in case of default by the intermediary, the principal and the third party a direct right of action even where the intermediary acted in its own name, the distinction between direct and indirect representation loses much of its original significance.[57] The question however remains: why then make such a distinction at all?[58]

The approach taken in this respect by the UNIDROIT Principles may appear simpler and more linear. In disposing of the dichotomy of direct/indirect representation and providing that, as a rule, in all cases of disclosed agency the agent's acts directly bind the principal and the third party to each other, they take into account that in practice the distinction between the agent acting (expressly or impliedly) in the name of the principal or (expressly or impliedly) in its own name but still on behalf of a principal, is often rather artificial and at any rate difficult to prove. What really matters from an economic point of view is whether the third party knows or ought to know that the person with whom it is contracting has the authority to act, and actually acts, not in its own interest but in that of another person.[59] Moreover, in this way the UNIDROIT

("*atti [...] pertinenti all'impresa*"). The leading case in U.S. law is Grinder v. Bryans Road Bldg. & Supply Co., 432 A.2d 453 (Md. App. 1981).

55 See M. Evans, Explanatory Report to the Convention on Agency in the International Sale of Goods, in: Uniform Law Review, 1984, II, p. 119, where the relevant provisions of the Convention are referred to as "the most original part of the instrument".

56 For further references see M.J. Bonell, The 1983 Geneva Convention, *cit.*, pp. 736-737; more recently, H. Kötz, European Contract Law, *cit.* (who may however go too far when stating at p. 239 that "[a]lthough continental systems treat agency as disclosed only if the agent acts 'in the name of' the principal, this does not mean that the precise name of the particular principal has to be stated when the deal is closed. It is sufficient if the third party was made aware by all the circumstances that rights and liabilities were to attach to a principal and not to the agent").

57 This may explain why even an attentive writer like A. Hartkamp, Indirect Representation According to the Principles of European Contract Law, the UNIDROIT Agency Convention and the Dutch Civil Code, in Festschrift für Ulrich Drobnig zum siebzigsten Geburtstag (1998), pp. 45 *et seq.* (pp. 46-47), seems to pay little if any importance to the different approach taken in this respect by the Geneva Convention on the on hand and the European Principles on the other.

58 It will be interesting to see how the dichotomy of direct/indirect representation, as adopted in the European Principles, will be received in the English and Irish legal milieux: for a first positive appraisal, though not by a common lawyer but by a Dutch lawyer, see D. Busch, Indirect Representation in the Lando Principles, in Electronic Journal of Comparative Law http://www.ejcl.org/. Rather sceptically, Bowstead and Reynolds on Agency, *cit.*, p. 10, who after recalling the different approach taken in this respect by the European Principles on the one hand and the UNIDROIT Principles (and the Geneva Convention) on the other, points out in that "[the] dichotomy between direct and indirect representation is unlikely to be attractive to common law systems which tend to reach the result of direct representation with more facility than the civil law."

59 Cf. F. Pollock, Principles of Contract Law (1876), p. 429 ("[...] the true leading distinction is whether the agent is known to be an agent or not, rather than whether the principal is named or not." More recently, and from a comparative perspective, H. Kötz, European Contract Law, *cit.*, pp. 219-220 ("Yet can it be right to draw [...] a such sharp distinction between acting in one's own name and acting in the name of someone else? In both cases the agent is acting in the interest of his principal, on his behalf, and pursuant to his instructions [...] the economic aim is the same in the two cases").

Principles avoid the rather involute approach of the European Principles which, after stating the rule that in case of indirect representation there is no direct relationship between the principal and the third party, introduce precisely such a direct relationship by way of exception in practically all relevant cases.

Yet despite these conceptual differences, the only issue with respect to which the UNIDROIT Principles differ in substance from the European Principles is the case of so-called undisclosed agency, i.e. where the third party neither knows nor ought to know that the agent is acting as an agent.

Indeed, while the European Principles, in case of default of the agent/intermediary, grant also the undisclosed principal a right of direct action against the third party, the UNIDROIT Principles even in such cases stick to the general rule according to which if the third party neither knows nor ought to know that the agent is acting as an agent, the contract binds only the agent and the third party. The latter solution has been justified on the ground that in international commerce it would often contravene a party's reasonable expectations if, after entering into a contract with a person it believed to be the principal, it was subsequently confronted with another person claiming to be the principal but whose existence had until then been completely unknown to it.[60] Moreover, it was argued, the only case where the third party has a compelling interest in suing the undisclosed principal, i.e. when it discovers that the person with whom it was contracting was not the owner of the enterprise but only the owner's agent, is taken care of also by the UNIDROIT Principles.[61]

Only practice will show whether these arguments are valid or not.

5   False agent

The acts of an agent acting without authority or exceeding its authority do not affect the legal relations between the principal and the third party. Both the European Principles and the UNIDROIT Principles lay down this obvious rule[62] which may be found also in the Geneva Convention.[63]

With respect to the consequences such acts will have for the false agent itself, it is a generally recognised principle that, failing a subsequent ratification by the principal, the false agent is liable for damages to the third party who without fault believed

---

60 Cf. UNIDROIT 1999, Study – Misc. 21, paras. 266-274; UNIDROIT 2000, Study – Misc. 22, paras. 866-883.

It is worth noting that not even the common lawyers of the Working Group insisted on the retention of the doctrine of undisclosed principal which, though known in their legal systems, they conceded might be inappropriate in the context of international contracting. Similar views were also expressed by the two external experts consulted on this issue: cf. UNIDROIT 1999, Study L – Doc. 63/Add.1, containing the comments of Professor D. De Mott ("I do not think that deleting this aspect of the doctrine represents a major loss...") and of Professor F. Reynolds ("[I]f the common law doctrine of the undisclosed principal were abandoned, nothing very dramatic would be lost. Like the doctrine of consideration, it tends to be taken much more seriously by civil law comparative lawyers than by common lawyers [...]").

61 Cf. Article 2.2.4 (2) of the UNIDROIT Principles. – For the discussion leading to the adoption of this provision, cf. UNIDROIT 2001, Study – Misc. 23, paras. 13-25.

62 See Article 3:204(1) of the European Principles and Article 2.2.5(1) of the UNIDROIT Principles.

63 Article 14(1) of the Geneva Convention.

that the false agent had actual authority. Differences however exist as to the exact nature of such liability and the measure of damages to be paid. On the one hand there are legal systems in which the liability of the false agent is viewed as a consequence of the non-performance on its part of the obligation to warrant, *vis-à-vis* the third party, the existence of authority. Consequently the third party is entitled to require performance of the contract by the false agent itself or payment of damages for the latter's failure to perform.[64] On the other hand, there are legal systems which consider the liability of a false agent rather as a sort of pre-contractual liability ("*culpa in contrahendo*") on account of the agent's failure to reveal to the third party its lack of authority. Consequently these systems limit the damages to so-called negative or reliance interest, i.e. the loss suffered by the third party due to its reliance without fault on the validity of the contract.[65]

By stating that, provided the third party did not know nor ought to have known that the agent had no authority or was exceeding its authority, the false agent is liable for damages that will put the third party in the same position as if the agent had acted with authority, both the European Principles[66] and the UNIDROIT Principles [67] clearly opt for the first of the two above-mentioned approaches.

This solution, which is in full accordance with the Geneva Convention,[68] seems better to reflect the actual needs of trade practice. Indeed, especially in cases where the contracts involved are of a highly speculative nature or refer to goods or services of considerable value and importance for the parties, third parties who are unaware that they are contracting with a false agent would not be adequately protected if they could seek from the latter only reimbursement of the expenses incurred during the negotiations or damages for lost opportunities in concluding the same type of transaction under the same or more advantageous conditions. These losses would be, after all, difficult to prove.

6   Conflict of Interest

It is inherent in any agency relationship that the agent, in fulfilling its mandate, is under a fiduciary duty to act in the interest of the principal to the exclusion of its own interest or that of anyone else if they conflict with one another.

Contrary to the Geneva Convention which is silent on this matter, both the European Principles and the UNIDROIT Principles deal with the case where the agent, when concluding the contract, acts in a situation of conflict of interests with the principal.

---

64 This is the solution adopted by English law (cf. Bowstead and Reynolds on Agency, *cit.*, p. 505); in the same sense see also Article 3:70 of the Dutch Civil Code. The situation is less clear with respect to U.S. law (cf. §§ 329 and 330 of Restatement Second of Agency).

65 In this sense see Article 1398 of the Italian Civil Code; yet the same solution also prevails among other civil law systems where the agent was not aware of its lack of authority: for further references see H. Kötz, European Contract Law, *cit.* pp. 237-238.

66 Article 3:204(2) of the European Principles.

67 Article 6 of the UNIDROIT Principles.

68 Article 16 of the Geneva Convention.

However, in conformity with their focus on the external relationship between the principal or the agent on the one hand and the third party on the other, the two instruments address only the impact the agent's involvement in a conflict of interests may have on such external relationship, leaving issues such as the agent's duty of full disclosure *vis-à-vis* the principal and the principal's right to damages from the agent to the provisions to be found in other of their chapters or to the law governing the internal relationship between principal and agent.[69]

Both the European Principles and the UNIDROIT Principles lay down the general rule according to which "[i]f a contract concluded by an agent involves the agent in a conflict of interests of which the third party knew or could not have been unaware, the principal may avoid the contract [...]".[70] While the European Principles indicate two situations in which a conflict of interests between the agent and the principal is presumed, i.e. where the agent also acts as agent for the third party, or where the contract is with itself in its personal capacity,[71] the UNIDROIT Principles do not make mention of such presumptions.[72] The two instruments do however concur in excluding the principal's right to avoid the contract whenever the principal has consented to or could not have been unaware of the agent's involvement in the conflict of interests, or the agent has disclosed to the principal the conflict of interests and the latter had not objected within a reasonable time.[73]

The solution adopted by the European Principles and the UNIDROIT Principles represents a sound compromise between the two extreme positions to be found on the matter at domestic level. Indeed, on the one hand they reject the rather rigid solution provided by e.g. German and Dutch law according to which, albeit only in specific conflict of interests situations, the agent's acts do not bind the principal at all,[74] thereby taking into account that in practice there are many situations of possible conflict of interests but that in all cases the third party may have a legitimate interest in upholding the contract. On the other hand, by providing that under certain conditions the principal is entitled to set aside the contract,[75] they avoid the excessive flexibility of the common law systems under which the remedies available, if any, depend on the circumstances of the case.[76]

---

69 See Comment 5 to Article 2.2.7 of the UNIDROIT Principles referring among others to the general provision on good faith (Article 1.7) and the chapter on damages (Articles 7.4.1 *et seq.*) as contained in the UNIDROIT Principles.

70 Article 3:205(1) of the European Principles and Article 2.2.7(1) of the UNIDROIT Principles.

71 Article 3:205(2) of the European Principles.

72 Yet see Comment 1 to Article 2.2.7 of the UNIDROIT Principles stating that "[t]he most frequent cases of potential conflict of interests are those where the agent acts for two principals and those where the agent concludes the contract with itself or with a firm in which it has an interest [...]".

73 Article 3:205(3) of the European Principles and Article 2.2.7(2) of the UNIDROIT Principles.

74 See § 181 of the German Civil Code and Article 3:68 of the Dutch Civil Code (both specifically referring to the case where the agent concludes the contract with itself ("*Insichgeschäft*")). – As to other cases of abuse of the agent's authority ("*Missbrauch der Vertretungsmacht*") in German law, see K. Larenz/M. Wolf, Allgemeiner Teil des Bürgerlichen Rechts, pp. 894-897.

75 For an antecedent of this rule in domestic law, see Article 1394 of the Italian Civil Code.

76 See, also for references to other common law jurisdictions, Bowstead and Reynolds on Agency, *cit.*, p. 194; similarly § 399 *et seq.* of the Restatement Second of Agency.

7 Ratification

It is a generally accepted principle that acts by an agent acting without authority or exceeding its authority may be authorised by the principal at a later stage.

Contrary to the Geneva Convention and the Draft Restatement Third which contain rather lengthy provisions on ratification,[77] both the European Principles and the UNIDROIT Principles are much more concise on the subject.[78]

To begin with, while the Geneva Convention expressly states that ratification is not subject to any requirement as to form,[79] neither the European Principles nor the UNIDROIT Principles contain a similar provision. Yet this does not mean that they adopt a different solution: in fact both instruments contain a general provision according to which not only contracts but also unilateral statements or any other acts are not subject to formal requirements.[80]

Ratification may be either express or implied from the principal's words or conduct,[81] and though normally communicated to the agent, to the third party, or to both, it is not necessary to do so provided that it is manifested in some way and can therefore be ascertained by probative material.[82]

All four instruments provide that on ratification the false agent's act produces the same effects as if it had initially been carried out with authority.[83]

The fact that ratification produces the same effects as authorisation, i.e. to bind the principal and the third party directly to each other as from the moment the agent had acted, has two important consequences. First, once ratification has come to the attention of the third party the principal may no longer revoke it[84] since revocation would amount to a unilateral withdrawal from a binding contract; secondly, the third party may refuse partial ratification[85] since it would amount to a proposal by the principal to modify the terms of the contract as originally agreed.

Yet are there time limits within which the principal must ratify, and may the third party refuse ratification before it occurs? The answers to these questions differ considerably in the four instruments.

The Geneva Convention provides the most elaborate solution, distinguishing between the case where the third party, when contracting with a false agent, was aware of the lack of authority or was not. If unaware, the third party not only may at any

---

77 Cf. Article 15 of the Geneva Convention and §§ 4.01–4.07 of the Draft Restatement Third.

78 Cf. Article 3:207 of the European Principles and Article 2.2.9 of the UNIDROIT Principles.

79 Article 15 (8) of the Geneva Convention.

80 So expressly Article 1.2 of the UNIDROIT Principles; similarly Article 2:101 (2) in conjunction with Art. 1:107 of the European Principles.

81 Cf. Comment 1 to Art. 2.2.9 of the UNIDROIT Principles; Comment A to Art. 3:207 of the European Principles; Art. 15 (5), first sentence, of the Geneva Convention

82 So expressly Comment 1 to Art. 9 of the UNIDROIT Principles; similarly Comment A to Art. 3:207 of the European Principles; Comment d to § 4.01 of the Draft Restatement Third.

83 Cf. Article 3:207 (2) of the European Principles; Article 2.2.9 (1), second sentence, of the UNIDROIT Principles; Article 15 (1), second sentence, of the Geneva Convention; § 4.02 (1) of the Draft Restatement Third.

84 So expressly Article 15 (5), second sentence, of the Geneva Convention and Comment b to § 4.02 of Draft Restatement Third, and Comment 3 to Article 2.2.9 of the UNIDROIT Principles.

85 So expressly Article 15 (4) of the Geneva Convention and § 4.07 of the Draft Restatement Third, but in the same sense see Comment 2 to Article 2.2.5 of the UNIDROIT Principles.

time before ratification inform the principal that it would not accept ratification, but may also refuse a ratification that has not been made within a reasonable time.[86] If it was aware, the third party may object to ratification by the principal only after the expiration of the time period agreed upon for ratification or, failing such an agreement, after a reasonable period of time unilaterally specified by it.[87]

The Draft Restatement Third provides that the third party may in any case withdraw from the transaction made with the false agent,[88] and that ratification, in order to effective, must in any event occur before a material change in circumstances that would make it inequitable to bind the third party.[89]

The European Principles do not address at all the question of a time limit for ratification in general, and only exceptionally, i.e. where the principal by its conduct gave the third party reason to believe that the agent's act was authorised, the third party is granted the right to request confirmation of the agent's authority with the effect that, if the principal does not reply without delay, the agent's act is treated as having been authorised.[90]

Finally, the UNIDROIT Principles in all cases grant the third party the right to set a reasonable time limit within which the principal must ratify if it intends to do so.[91] Moreover, if at the time of the agent's act the third party neither knew nor ought to have known of the lack of authority, it may at any time before ratification indicate to the principal its refusal to become bound by a ratification.[92]

The solution adopted by the UNIDROIT Principles seems preferable to the surprisingly agnostic position taken in this respect by the European Principles. The rule according to which the third party, irrespective of whether or not it knew that it was dealing with a false agent, may set as reasonable time limit for ratification is intended to balance the principal's interest in ratifying at any time and the third party's interest in not being kept in limbo indefinitely.[93] Moreover, it is only fair to grant a third party, who was unaware that it was dealing with a false agent, also the right to withdraw from the contract prior to ratification: any other solution would unduly favour the principal who would be the only person to be able to speculate on the market developments between the time of the conclusion of the contract by the false agent and its decision to ratify or not to ratify the transaction.[94]

Finally, while both the European Principles and the UNIDROIT Principles state that they are concerned only with the effects of ratification on the three parties directly

---

86 Article 15, para. 2 of the Geneva Convention.

87 Article 15, para. 3 of the Geneva Convention.

88 Cf. § 4.05 of the Draft Restatement Third.

89 Ibidem.

90 Cf. Article 3:208 of the European Principles .

91 Article 2.2.9 (2) of the UNIDROIT Principles.

92 Cf. Article 2.2.9 (3) of the UNIDROIT Principles: "Where, at the time of the agent's act, the third party neither knew nor ought to have known of the lack of authority, it may, at any time before ratification, by notice to the principal indicate its refusal to become bound by a ratification."

93 Comment 3 to Article 2.2.9 of the UNIDROIT Principles.

94 This is also the solution prevailing among civil law systems: see, for further references H. KÖTZ, European Contract Law, cit., p.234. Yet see in the same sense also § 4.05 of the Draft Restatement Third, while even with respect to English law, traditionally opposed to the idea of the third party being entitled to withdraw from the contract, doubts as to the appropriateness of such a solution have recently be expressed: see Bowstead and Reynolds on Agency, cit. p. 77.

involved in the agency relationship, i.e. the principal, the agent and the third party and do not affect the rights of other third persons,[95] neither of the two instruments address the question, expressly dealt with by the Geneva Convention and the Draft Restatement Third, of the effectiveness of the ratification of an act which at the time of ratification can no longer be carried out, nor the somewhat related question of the ratification of acts carried out on behalf of a corporation or other legal person before its creation.[96] However, under both the European Principles and in the UNIDROIT Principles basically the same results will be achieved in applying provisions of a more general character to be found in the two instruments.[97]

8   Termination of Authority

Also with respect to termination of the agent's authority, the approach taken by the European Principles and the UNIDROIT Principles is not entirely the same.

To be sure, the two instruments agree on the basic principle according to which termination is not effective in relation to the third party unless the third party knew or ought to have known of them.[98] In other words, whatever the grounds for the termination of the agent's authority, the agent's acts continue to affect the legal relationship between the principal and the third party as long as the third party is unaware nor ought to know that the agent no longer has authority.[99]

Obviously, no problem arises where the principal or the agent give notice to the third party of the termination. In the absence of such notice it will depend on the circumstances of the case whether the third party ought to have known of the termination.[100] Only the European Principles provide that the third party must be deemed to have knowledge of termination when it was made public or communicated in the same manner as the granting of authority itself.[101]

---

95 Cf. Article 3:207 (2) of the European Principles and Comment 4 to Article 2.2.9 of the UNIDROIT Principles.

96 Article 15 (6) of the Geneva Convention provides that "[r]atification is effective notwithstanding that the act itself could not have been effectively carried out at the time of ratification", while Article 15 (7) of the Geneva Convention provides that "[w]here the act has been carried out on behalf of a corporation or other legal person before its creation, ratification is effective only if allowed by the law of the State governing its creation". "By contrast, according to § 4.04 of the Draft Restatement Third "[a] person may ratify an act if (a) the person existed at the time of the act, and (b) the person had capacity [...] at the time of ratifying it."

97 See in particular Article 4:101 of the European Principles and Article 3.3. of the UNIDROIT Principles, stating the general principle that the mere fact that at the time of the conclusion of a contract the performance of the obligation assumed was impossible or a party was not entitled to dispose of the assets to which the contract relates does not affect the validity of the contract, and Article 1:103 of the European Principles and Article 1.4 of the UNIDROIT Principles, both acknowledging the predominance of mandatory rules of national, international or supranational origin (e.g. the applicable company law rules concerning pre-incorporation contracts).

98 See Article 19 of the Geneva Convention, Article 3:209, opening sentence, of the European Principles and Article 2.2.10(1) of the UNIDROIT Principles, respectively.

99 So expressly Comment 2 to Article 2.2.10 of the Unidroit Principles. – For basically the same principle at domestic law see, e.g., Article 1396 of the Italian Civil Code; Article 3:76 of the Dutch Civil Code; Bowstead and Reynolds on Agency, *cit.* pp. 570 *et seq.*; § 3.11(2) of the Draft Restatement Third.

100 So expressly Comment 2 to Article 2.2.10 of the UNIDROIT Principles.

101 Article 3:209 (2) of the European Principles. – Note that according to this provision such presump-

The two instruments also concur in providing that, notwithstanding the termination of its authority, an agent remains authorised to perform the acts that are necessary to prevent harm to the principal's interests.[102]

By contrast, differences exist with respect to the actual grounds for termination or, more precisely, as to whether to deal with them at all or to refer in this respect to the otherwise applicable law.

While the Geneva Convention specifically enumerates three rather self-explanatory grounds for termination[103] and for any other possible cases refers to the otherwise applicable law,[104] the European Principles provide an exhaustive list of grounds for extinction of the agent's authority.[105] On their part, the UNIDROIT Principles do not indicate at all what the grounds for termination are, leaving them to be determined entirely by the applicable law.[106]

The self-restraint shown by the UNIDROIT Principles seems justified in view of the fact that, as pointed out in the comments,[107] domestic laws vary considerably as to what exactly constitutes a ground for termination of the agent's authority. On the contrary, the more ambitious approach taken by the European Principles may be criticised for admitting circumstances as grounds for termination which are not recognised as such at domestic level and, more importantly, for excluding others which in fact do operate at domestic level.[108]

---

tion should apply only where the agent's authority has been "brought to an end" by the principal, the agent or both, but one fails to see the reason why the same rule should not apply also to other grounds of termination, such as the expiry of the period of time for which the authority was granted or the insolvency of the principal or the agent, etc.

102 Cf. Article 20 of the Geneva Convention, Article 3:209 (3) of the European Principles and Article 2.2.10 (2) of the UNIDROIT Principles.

103 Cf. Art. 17 of the Geneva Convention which provides that the authority is terminated (a) when this follows from any agreement between the principal and the agent, (b) on completion of the transaction or transactions for which the authority was created, and (c) on revocation by the principal or renunciation by the agent, whether or not this is consistent with the terms of their agreement.

104 Cf. Article 18 of the Geneva Convention.

105 Cf. Article 3:209 (1) of the European Principles: "An agent's authority continues until the third party knows or ought to know that: (a) the agent's authority has been brought to an end by the principal, the agent, or both; or (b) the acts for which the authority has been granted have been completed, or the time for which it had been granted has expired; or (c) the agent has become insolvent or, where a natural person, has died or become incapacitated; or (d) the principal has become insolvent."

106 Cf. Comment 1 to Article 2.2.10 of the UNIDROIT Principles: "There are several grounds on which the agent's authority may be terminated: revocation by the principal, renunciation by the agent, completion of the act(s) for which authority had been granted, loss of capacity, bankruptcy, death or cessation of existence of the principal or the agent, etc. What exactly constitutes a ground for termination [...] is to be determined in accordance with the applicable laws (e.g. the law governing the internal relations between principal and agent; the law governing their legal status or personality; the law governing bankruptcy, etc.).

107 Comment 1 to Article 2.2.10 of the UNIDROIT Principles, *cit.*

108 The most striking example of a ground for termination of the agent's authority admitted by the European Principles but by far not generally recognised as such, at least without further qualifications, at domestic level, is "insolvency" of either the principal or the agent: thus, e.g., under English law the agent's insolvency terminates the agent's authority only "in some situations" (cf. Bowstead and Reynolds on Agency, *cit.* pp. 552, 566-567). As to the exclusion by the European Principles of grounds for termination which on the contrary are generally admitted at domestic level, suffice it to mention the death or supervening mental incapacity of the principal (see for further references H.

9 Conclusions

Two decades after the adoption of the Geneva Convention the prospects of bringing about greater uniformity in the law governing agency relationships of an international character, are greater than ever.

Though prepared by different groups of experts, and with diverse legal backgrounds and objectives in mind,[109] the European Principles and the UNIDROIT Principles present many points of convergence.

On a number of issues, such as the granting of the agent's authority by the principal, the liability of the false agent, and conflict of interests, the European Principles and the UNIDROIT Principles lay down provisions which correspond even literally.

With respect to other questions, such as apparent authority, ratification and termination, the differences between the two instruments are more of form than of substance.

The sole significant point of divergence is the European Principles' distinction between direct and indirect representation as opposed to the UNIDROIT Principles' distinction between disclosed and undisclosed agency. Yet again, from an operational point of view, the only case where the two instruments lead to substantially different solutions concerns the undisclosed principal.

It is true that, given the non-binding nature of both the European Principles and the UNIDROIT Principles, also their rules on authority of agents will in practice be applied only by virtue of their persuasive value. Nevertheless, the importance of the two sets of rules from both a theoretical and a practical point of view is manifest. Suffice it to mention that the European Principles may in the near future become part of a European Civil Code,[110] while the UNIDROIT Principles are already being recognised in international arbitration practice as a particularly authoritative source of "general principles of international commercial contracts" or the *lex mercatoria*.[111]

Kötz, European Contract Law, *cit.*, p. 231) or the dissolution of both the principal and the agent if they are a body corporate (see e.g. Bowstead and Reynolds on Agency, *cit.*, pp. 552 and 565).

109 The European Principles are intended to be applied as "general rules of contract law in the European Union" (cf. Article 1:101(1)), while the UNIDROIT Principles are intended to "set forth general rules for international commercial contracts" (cf. Preamble, para. 1).

110 Cf. O. Lando, Principles of European Contract Law and UNIDROIT Principles: Similarities, Differences and Perspectives, Centro di Studi e di Ricerche di Diritto Comparato e Straniero: Saggi, Conferenze e Seminari, 49, (2002), pp.10 *et seq.*

111 See for further references, M.J. Bonell The UNIDROIT Principles in Practice (2002), pp. 31-33. – For an update of international case law relating to the UNIDROIT Principles see <http://www.unilex.info>.

CHAPTER 22

Defects of Consent in Contract Law

Muriel Fabre-Magnan* & Ruth Sefton-Green**

The mere fact that an offer has been accepted does not suffice to establish that a valid contract has been concluded; in addition many legal systems require that the contract is not vitiated by defects of consent. Some legal systems place consent itself at the heart of the contract: consent must be free and enlightened.[1] Some legal systems focus on the invalidity of legal acts.[2] Other systems, which put the emphasis on the contract and not on the parties' consent, talk of the contract being free from vitiating factors.[3] Defects of consent prevent the conditions of validity of a contract from being satisfied and thus run the risk of upsetting the security of transactions.[4]

This chapter will examine three defects of consent, mistake, fraud and duress, in the main legal traditions of Europe. Although these concepts can be grouped together under the heading of defects of consent, they are in fact rather different. First, it should be noted that some legal systems have a unitary notion of defects of consent,[5] whereas others do not.[6] Secondly, some defects may be more controversial than others in the sense that fraud for instance is less likely to raise divergent views than say mistake. Thirdly, each defect may not necessarily have the same end-goal: protection, punishment or deterrence may be at stake.

Despite a number of differences, mistake, fraud or duress are all grounds for avoiding the contract. In the light of increasing discussion about the possibility of a European Civil Code, it is necessary to examine two hypotheses in order to make sure that we are going in the right direction.

First, even if these three categories do not cover exactly the same situations everywhere, the same circumstances seem to allow a party to set aside the contract by invoking one or another of these defects. If in fact, each legal system adopts the same practical solutions, even if the ways and means of arriving at the solution are differ-

* Professor at the University of Nantes. Field of Specialisation: Law of Obligations, Jurisprudence. Correspondance Address: Maison des Sciences de l'Homme Ange Guépin – 21, Bld Gaston Doumergue – B.P. 76235 – 44262 Nantes Cedex 2 (France) – Email: <muriel.fabre-magnan@wanadoo.fr>.

** Senior Lecturer at the University Paris I (Pantheon-Sorbonne). Field of Specialisation: Comparative Law of Obligations. Correspondance Address: UMR de droit comparé de Paris – 9, rue Mahler, 75004 Paris (France) – Email: <Ruth.Sefton-Green@univ-paris1.fr>.

1 This is the case of French and German law. The corollary is denoted by the theory of *vices du consentement* and *Willensmangel* respectively.

2 This is the case of Nordic laws (see Chapter 3 of the Nordic Contract Acts 1915-1939).

3 This is true of English law.

4 J. Cartwright, *Defects of Consent and Security of Contract: French and English Law Compared*, in *Themes in Comparative Law. In Honour of Bernard Rudden* (ed. P. Birks and A. Pretto) OUP 2002, pp. 153-164.

5 E.g. French, German and Italian law.

6 This is generally accepted to be the case in English law; for the contrary view, see note 12, *infra*.

ent, due to different traditions, may it not be contended that no harm would arise if such legal concepts were harmonised? However a closer look at the similarities reveals underlying differences, which may force us to re-evaluate the effects of harmonisation.

Secondly, differences in defects of consent are obvious from the outset. It may be that the differences are really as striking as they first appear and lead sometimes, if not always, to quite divergent results. It may be too easy to rely on a broad similarity of solutions since the means used are important and characterise each national legal system. Once again, this may lead to a reassessment of the need for and the way to harmonise, or even unify, national legal systems by using a European Civil Code.

In an attempt to examine the differences and assess their relative significance, the place and importance of defects of consent in the law of contract must be examined. Next the underlying policy and end-goals of defect of consent will be investigated. These two enquiries should enable us to proceed to a critical assessment: is it going to be possible to harmonise or unify defects of consent in a European Civil Code?

1   The Place and Importance of Defects of Consent in the Law of Contract

Defects of consent concern the formation of contracts. In all European legal systems, several types of defect in consent are distinguished. To refer only to some of the main systems, it appears that the following defects of consent exist: in English law: *mistake*, *misrepresentation*, *duress* and *undue influence*; in French law: *erreur* (mistake), *dol* (fraud) and *violence* (threat); in German law: *irrtum* (mistake), *arglistige taüschung* (fraud) and *widerrechtliche drohung* (illegitimate threat); in Dutch law: *dwaling* (mistake), *bedreiging* (threat), *bedrog* (fraud) and *misbruik van omstandigheden* (abuse of circumstances); in Italian law: *errore* (mistake), *dolo* (fraud) and *violenza* (threat). In order to situate defects of consent in the law of contract, mistake, fraud and duress will be briefly identified. These three categories need refining in the light of developments in positive law.

1.1   Mistake

In English law the circumstances in which a contract is void for mistake are restrictive. Two categories of mistake are distinguished at common law. The existence of a separate doctrine of equitable mistake has recently been denied.[7]

In the first type of mistake, both parties made the same mistake so that they actually agreed on the same thing but their agreement cannot have its normal effect: their mistake is often said to nullify consent. As the parties made the same mistake, it is often said that there is mutual[8] or common mistake. The mistakes which can thus nul-

---

7   *Great Peace Shipping Ltd v. Tsavliris Salvage (International) Ltd* (2002) 4 All ER 689, CA.
8   A few authors reserve this term for mutual misunderstanding, i.e. when both parties made a mistake but not the same one.

lify consent are very limited:[9] There must be a fundamental shared mistake of fact, mainly as to the existence of the subject-matter.

In the second type, the mistake prevented the parties from reaching an agreement so that this mistake is often said to negative agreement. Mistake negatives consent when the parties never had the same thing in mind. Either one party only has made a mistake, for instance as to identity of the other (there is a unilateral mistake), or both have made mistakes but different ones, for instance one party intended to deal with one thing and the other with a different one (in other words, there was a misunderstanding). Misrepresentation is another means of identifying mistake in English law. However, mistakes caused by misrepresentation are mostly treated as misrepresentations, not as mistakes.[10] The conceptual classification may lead to exaggerating differences or overlooking similarities. It is submitted that negligent and innocent misrepresentation may be better understood as belonging to mistake. An operative misrepresentation consists in a representation of existing or past fact, made by one party to the other which induces the latter to enter into the contract. In addition, the representation must be unambiguous and material and the misrepresentee must have relied on it.[11]

French law frequently uses mistake as a ground for relief. *Erreur* is a false assessment of reality made by a contracting party. Some mistakes are so important that there has never been any agreement: they are usually called *erreur-obstacle* (they are an obstacle to the formation of contract) even though judges never use this vocabulary. Such mistakes may concern the very nature or identity of the subject-matter of the contract.

Amongst mistakes vitiating consent, article 1110 of the French Civil Code identifies two main types of mistake: those relating to the subject matter of the contract (*erreur sur la substance*) and those relating to the other party (*erreur sur la personne*). *Erreur sur la substance* was initially limited to mistakes about the material out of which the subject-matter of the contract was made. Its scope has been widely extended to include mistakes as to the essential qualities (*qualités substantielles*) of the contract's subject-matter which caused its conclusion. This kind of mistake is often a ground for annulling a contract. On the contrary, an *erreur sur la personne* only constitutes a defect of consent where the person with whom the contract was concluded is essential (contracts concluded *intuitu personae*, i.e. in consideration of the person). Despite this restrictive approach, this type of mistake has been extensively interpreted.[12]

Other types of mistake, such as to value or to motive will not suffice to annul the

---

9 See *Bell* v. *Lever Brothers Ltd.* [1932] A.C. 161. For a more recent case, see *Associated Japanese Bank International Ltd* v. *Crédit du Nord SA* [1989] 1 W.L.R. 255, 266-267, 268, where it was said that the former case decided that a mistake might render a contract void provided it rendered the subject-matter essentially and radically different from what the parties believed to exist: *Chitty on Contracts*, 5-017.

10 Except R. Goff and G. Jones, *The Law of Restitution* (1998), Ch. 9 and J. Cartwright, *Misrepresentation* (2002), 1.02.

11 *Chitty on Contracts*, 6-004 ff.

12 The courts have accepted both mistakes as to the identity of the person and also as to the essential attributes of the person (qualifications, background, solvency, etc.).

contract, unless it can be established that the latter was part of the conditions for concluding the contract. An operative mistake may not be recognised by the courts if it is considered that the mistaken party's behaviour is inexcusable.[13]

The German concept of "mistake" means an "incorrect understanding of the reality of the situation".[14] In German law, different types of mistakes are mentioned by §119 and §120 BGB. These provisions are rather unclear and have given rise to different opinions. § 119 BGB is divided into two definitions: the first clause covers the so-called "mistake in declaration or expression" as to meaning or to content (the party does not say, write or act as he intended), the second "mistake as to subject matter" or *error in substantiali qualitate* (here the complaining party has said what he wanted to say but he was wrong to say what he said).[15] The latter kind of mistake is judged by an objective criterion, that is a quality or characteristic generally considered fundamental.

A slightly different version of mistake is given by, for example, article 1428 of the Italian Civil Code, which states that a contracting party whose consent was given by mistake can ask for the contract to be annulled when the mistake is fundamental (*essenziale*) and recognisable (*riconoscibile*) by the other contracting party. The Code enumerates the different kinds of fundamental mistakes; moreover, the requirement that the mistake is recognisable is assessed according to whether the parties exercised reasonable and proper care at the time the contract was made (article 1431). The Italian Supreme Court tends either to exclude the presence of a mistake or consider the mistake not essential when it is inexcusable (*inescusabile*).[16]

An actionable mistake allows the mistaken party to annul the contract under all the legal systems considered. In addition, under German law, the mistaken party's right to annul is qualified by the payment of negative interest (*vertrauensinteresse*) to compensate the non-mistaken party's reliance on the contract, (§ 122 I) if the non-mistaken party did not know or could not have known of the mistaken party's mistake (§ 122 II).

It should be clear that each legal system has a somewhat different view of mistake: French law allows unilateral and uninduced mistakes, subject to the bar of the mistaken party's inexcusable behaviour. It does not take into account how the mistake was caused. The emphasis continues to lie on intention and the will theory of contract whereas German law includes a different element: that of the parties' reliance on the contract. English law only allows unilateral mistake if it is caused by innocent or negligent misrepresentation. Otherwise the criterion that the mistake must be shared to be operative means that mistake is rarely admitted. Italian law introduces yet another criterion, which is perhaps comparable to the question of how the mistake was caused. It is necessary to consider whether the non-mistaken party knew about the

---

13 J. Ghestin, *La formation du contrat* (1993), No. 523.

14 § 119 para. 1 BGB. Larenz and Wolf (1997), p. 664.

15 Of course, these two subsections represent the tension between the theory of declaration (*Erklärungstheorie*) and the will theory (*Willenstheorie*) respectively. The same tension is found in Austrian law in § 871 ABGB.

16 Cass. 16.5.1960, n.1177, *GI*, I, 1, 112 noted by G. Amorth.

mistake. Article 4: 103 of the Principles of European Contract Law[17] ("PECL") attempts to synthesise and combine all the identifiable elements of mistake.[18]

1.2 Fraud

In English law, fraud is not treated as a general defect of consent since it is subsumed as an instance of misrepresentation. A person may complain if he was induced to conclude a contract by a fraudulent misleading statement[19] i.e. when the misrepresentor did not honestly believe in the truth of what he stated.[20] The usual remedy for misrepresentation is the rescission of the contract but damages may also be granted in the case of fraudulent misrepresentation.[21]

Under French law, article 1116 of the Civil Code sets out the conditions of *dol* (fraud). It is usually acknowledged that for *dol* to vitiate consent, the fraud must have induced a mistake in the other party's mind. However, an important difference between fraud and mistake is that, while mistake must concern the essential qualities of the subject-matter, fraud may be invoked even when the resulting mistake would not have given the right to annul the contract if it had been spontaneously made (e.g. mistake as to value or as to motives). Thus, strictly speaking, fraud is not in itself a defect of consent but the cause of such a defect.

Several requirements are necessary for the contract to be annulled. First, it must be proved that without fraud, the aggrieved party would not have entered into the contract. Secondly, the deceiving party's intention to deceive must be established. Finally, fraud must have been committed by a party to the contract, a third party's fraud can only be invoked if he was an accomplice of a contracting party.

Dol can result from acts (*manœuvres*), lies (*mensonges*) or from fraudulent non-disclosure of material facts (*réticence dolosive*). Lies must be made on purpose to induce the other party to contract. They must also be sufficiently important: as under English law, mere 'puffs' (*dolus bonus*) do not give right to relief. The most complex type of fraud is *réticence dolosive* (fraudulent non-disclosure), which is a failure to inform. It is no longer disputed that under French law *dol* may result from remaining silent and failing to dispel a known misunderstanding of the other party.[22]

---

17 *The Principles of European Contract Law, Part I and II, Combined and Revised*, Prepared by the Commission of European Contract Law, edited by O. Lando and H. Beale, Kluwer Law International, 2000.

18 Article 4: 103 of the PECL sets out three alternative conditions for mistake to be operative: – the way in which the mistake was caused; or whether the non-mistaken party knew of the mistake; or whether both parties made the same mistake. One of these conditions is further cumulated with the knowledge by the non-mistaken party of the significance of the mistake. A mistake will not be operative if the mistaken party's behaviour is inexcusable or the risk of the mistake was assumed or should have been assumed

19 See J. Cartwright, *Misrepresentation*, Ch. 4.

20 See *Derry* v. *Peek*. (1889) 14 App.Cas. 337, 374. According to Lord Herschell, 'fraud is proved when it is shown that a false representation has been made knowingly, or without belief in its truth, or recklessly, careless whether it be true or false'.

21 *Archer v. Brown* (1985) QB 401.

22 As the *Cour de cassation* [Supreme Court] has regularly held since a case dated 1st April, 1954 (Bull. civ., V, No. 223, p. 171): '*dol* may consist of the silence of one party concealing from the other a fact which, if it had been known by him, would have prevented him from entering into the contract;

German law is very similar to French law and §123 BGB provides that anyone who has been induced to make a declaration of will by fraudulent deceit (*arglistige Täuschung*) may have this declaration annulled. As under French law, fraud must result in a mistake of the other party but this mistake does not have to be fundamental and may be for instance a mere mistake about the value. Fraud by a third party may lead to annulling the contract if the other contracting party knew about the fraud or should have known about it (§123 II BGB); this is similar to French law except that the requirement is less strict in German law since mere knowledge by the third party suffices.

Three conditions must be satisfied for relief to be granted. There must have been a deceit (*täuschung*), which may be due to acts or even non-disclosure. The deceit must be fraudulent (*arglistig*) i.e. made for the purpose of inducing the other party to enter into the contract or at least knowing that it would have this effect and it must have actually induced the other party to contract. Moreover, if a mistake has been caused by the fraudulent deceit, the mistaken party is relieved from paying the negative interest to the non-mistaken party, whose reliance is no longer deemed worthy of protection.

It is submitted that fraud is the least controversial of the defects of consent considered. More precisely, the legal systems diverge less in their attitude towards fraud and agree that fraudulent behaviour is reprehensible and must be treated severely. However, there is of course some divergence about what actually characterises fraud, not in terms of the intention to deceive but in terms of what kinds of behaviour, acts, omissions, including silence, can be considered fraudulent. This issue must be combined with that of the duty to disclose: it is no doubt for this reason that article 4:107 of the PECL refers to fraudulent misrepresentation, or fraudulent non-disclosure of information.[23]

1.3 Duress

In English law duress and undue influence may be presented together under this category. In both cases, the consent of a party to a contract has been obtained by some form of pressure which the law regards as illegitimate or improper.

Duress is a common law defect of consent. It was first limited to actual or threatened physical violence to the person of the contracting party, subsequently threats made to the victim's property were also included. More recently, a principle of economic duress has become recognised by case law and this is the most significant form of duress. Economic duress often arises in cases of contractual modification and is sometimes used when the condition of consideration has not been satisfied.[24] All threats can be considered as a duress provided that they are illegitimate and that they actually left the coerced party with no other reasonable alternative than to conclude the contract.

---

but such silence must relate to a circumstance or a fact which the other party could reasonably be expected not to know'.

23 The text specifies that such misrepresentation can be by words or conduct; fraudulent non-disclosure is assessed by the fact that it should have been disclosed in accordance with good faith and fair dealing.

24 *Chitty on Contracts*, 7-014.

Equity has added a remedy in cases of *undue influence*, which is also a form of illegitimate pressure. This undue influence, contrary to duress, implies no violence: it concerns cases 'where influence is acquired and abused, where confidence is reposed and betrayed'[25] (for instance when a husband persuades his wife to guarantee his business).[26] The onus of proving undue influence generally lies on the aggrieved party except when there may be a rebuttable presumption in cases where a special relationship (for instance of a fiduciary nature) exists between the parties. Equitable relief against duress *sensu lato* includes unconscionable bargains when one party has taken advantage of a particular weakness of the other.[27] The weakness or inequality is sometimes measured in terms of power derived from information.

In French law *violence* prevents consent from being given freely (article 1112 of the Civil Code). The victim knows perfectly well that he is making a bad bargain but he has no other reasonable option for he has been threatened with something worse. *Violence* i.e. the harm feared may be physical, moral (like a threat of defamation) or pecuniary (fear of economic loss). Threats may be aimed at the person who is to sign the contract or to persons close to him.

Fear must be actual and serious enough to induce the victim to enter into the contract. There is a contradiction in the Civil Code as to whether the test must be objective or subjective: article 1112 mentions both that the fear must have influenced a reasonable person and also that the age, sex and condition of the victim must be taken into account. Judges have chosen mainly to apply a subjective test.

The constraint must be illegitimate and, for instance, reverential fear of parents does not suffice to establish a defect of consent. There are also complex rules about the legitimacy of the threat to exercise a right, particularly a threat to sue, which is considered to be legitimate, so long that there is no abuse (for instance to try to obtain much more than what is due).

Lastly, the origin of the pressure may be diverse. It may come from the contracting party or from a third party. There is some debate as to whether the constraint may also arise from external circumstances in which the plaintiff finds himself. A typical example of necessity (*état de nécessité*) is where the captain of an endangered vessel has to accept unreasonable terms for her to be rescued. There are very few cases. More recently, there has been an evolution towards admitting economic duress (*violence économique*), when one of the parties is economically dependant on the other.[28] For this defect of consent to give a right to relief, it must be established that one party has actually taken advantage of the other by extorting unconscionable terms.[29]

---

25 *Chitty on Contracts.* See in particular *Allcard* v. *Skinner* (1887) 36 Ch.D. 145, 171.

26 For the leading cases on surety cases are *Barclays Bank plc* v. *O'Brien* (1994) 1 AC 180, HL ; *Royal Bank of Scotland* v. *Etridge* (No 2) (2001) 3 WLR, HL.

27 G. H. Treitel, pp. 382-85.

28 See Civ. 1ère, 30 May 2000, Bull. civ., I, No. 169: under French law a "settlement cannot be annulled for *lésion* ; the first judges had refused to annul a settlement for *contrainte économique* ; the Cour de cassation censured this decision: " *en se déterminant ainsi, alors que la transaction peut être attaquée dans tous les cas où il y a violence, et que la contrainte économique se rattache à la violence et non à la lésion, la cour d'appel a violé les textes susvisés* ".

29 See Civ. 1ère, 3rd April 2002, Bull. civ., I, No. 108: " *seule l'exploitation abusive d'une situation de dépendance économique, faite pour tirer profit de la crainte d'un mal menaçant directement les intérêts légitimes de la personne, peut vicier de violence son consentement* ".

German law admits the concept of illegitimate threat (*widerrechtliche Drohung*). §123 BGB states that anyone whose declaration of will has been illegitimately induced by means of threat can have this declaration annulled. Rules are once again very similar to those under French law. Several requirements are usually necessary for the victim to be granted relief: there must be a threat which is often described as the 'perspective of a harm whose realisation depends on the will of the author of the threat';[30] the threat must be made to induce the victim's declaration of will illegitimately (even though the author of the threat may think he is acting lawfully); it must also have actually compelled the victim to make this declaration of will (a subjective test is applied); it may emanate from a third party. However the *Bundesgerichtshof* [Federal Court of Justice] judged that mere use of a state of constraint of fact (*Ausnutzung einer tatsächlichen Zwangslage*) is not enough to be considered as a threat.[31] Sometimes German law uses §138, paragraph 2 BGB to refer to the exploitation (*wucher*) of a person's difficulty.[32]

It has been suggested that one difference between the legal systems considered is whether or not defects of consent are treated as part of a unitary theory. The significance of this difference needs to be examined further. One approach would be to examine the other conditions of validity of contract to see how defects of consent fit in as a whole in each legal system's view of contract. In French law for example, the *vices du consentement* are combined with the concepts of *cause* and *objet*. In English law, the concept of consideration has a part to play in establishing the conditions of existence of a contract. In German law, there is not one concept that corresponds to the French *cause*. The general clauses of the BGB relating to immorality and illegality are often invoked to nullify legal acts of all kinds where French law relies on the *cause*.[33] When considering the PECL it becomes clear that a third (not to say fourth) requirement (after offer and acceptance) has been omitted. This may have the effect of highlighting the defects of consent by increasing their role. Conversely, it may be unrealistic to expect defects of consent to fill the conceptual gap. Moreover, it may be that the presence of a unitary theory about defects of consent reveals something about a legal system's tradition or approach to the contract itself. For example, it is arguable that French law's unified vision of *vices du consentement* stems from the will theory being at the heart of the contract, at least traditionally, which would explain why consent (and the subjective intention of the parties) is highlighted. German law emphasises reliance as being a constituent part of the contract. This is illustrated by the use of negative or reliance interest. English law plausibly gives priority to party autonomy but an objective approach to contract is adopted.[34] Moreover, English law has not developed its theory of contract in the same way, notably because of systematic and historical considerations, i.e. the way in which the common law emerged by a gradual process. It is implausible that a common law system should arrive at a

---

30 D. Medicus (1992), Rdn. 814.
31 BGH 7th June 1988, NJW 1988.2599, 2601.
32 K. Zweigert and H. Kötz, *An Introduction to Comparative Law* (1998), p. 428.
33 §§134, 138 BGB are used in these circumstances. See H. Kötz and A. Flessner, *European Contract Law*, vol 1 (1997), pp. 154ff.; Zweigert and Kötz, *An Introduction to Comparative Law* (1998), p. 381.
34 *Chitty on Contracts*, 2-001.

unified version of defects of consent when their very existence and recognition is dependent on the hazards of case law. If a more coherent version of defects of consent were to be adopted, this may create inconsistencies elsewhere in the law or disturb a present internal equilibrium.

Defects of consent need also to be put into perspective in view of new developments of the law. Recognition is being increasingly given, at least in a number of legal systems, to duties to inform or duties of disclosure which form part of a larger new field of precontractual liability.[35] Not only must a place be found for defects of consent in relation to other conditions of validity of contract but also in relation to other questions about their function and purpose. Lastly, in France, defects of consent have been elaborated within a general theory about the formation of contracts. In Germany, defects of consent are not just limited to the formation of contracts but apply to all legal acts, of which the theory of *Willenserklärung* (declarations of will) forms a necessary ingredient. In Dutch law, for example, these two different conceptual viewpoints are merged since mistake (*dwaling*) belongs to a section about the formation of contracts whereas the other defects of consent apply to legal acts in general. One question which should be addressed is what place is left to defects of consent in view of the specialisation of contracts, a modern phenomenon to be found in all European legal systems, partly as a result of European secondary legislation. Certain consumer contracts provide for cancellation rights,[36] for example, does this mean that remedies for defects of consent will be invoked less often? Are remedies for defects of consent cumulable with the remedies provided for by the Directive on consumer sales and associated guarantees?[37] To answer this question an enquiry into whether remedies for defects of consent are both sufficient and efficient must be made.

A comparative overview of defects of consent highlights the inadequacy of legal categories since selecting three main defects has shown the categorisation to be deficient: is it satisfactory and uncontroversial to include misrepresentation with mistake? The PECL clearly adopts this position.[38] A close look at Dutch law is revealing in this respect since relief is mainly given for a mistake perceived as a consequence of a misrepresentation or failure to disclose information.[39] Do English, French and German laws of mistake fit the same pattern? A closer look shows that French law admits mistake much more often than English law, even if misrepresentation is included in the calculation. Fraud is from this point of view somewhat easier in the sense that it coincides with a moral issue, thus leaving less room for national legal systems to diverge. No one would disagree that the intention to deceive should be reprimanded. Duress is also less controversial than mistake since if illegitimate pressure has been exercised on one party by the other few would deny that relief should

---

35   This may derive from a principle of good faith, see R. Zimmermann and S. Whittaker, *Good Faith in European Contract Law*, CUP, 2000, or from an independent duty to disclose, see R. Sefton-Green, *Mistake and Duties to inform in European Contract Law*, CUP, forthcoming.

36   See for example, the European Directive on distance selling, 97/7/EC

37   Directive 1999/44/EC.

38   Note that article 4:104 treats inaccuracy in communication as a form of mistake. Article 4:106 states that if incorrect information has caused a loss but not a fundamental mistake, damages are recoverable, unless the giver of the information had reason to believe that the information was correct.

39   Article 6:228 BW. In addition, Dutch law has a version of shared mistake in article 6:228 c.

be granted. Differences of opinion may lie as to what kinds of pressure may be considered illegitimate, whether economic pressure is included, how far and in what circumstances the constrained party should be protected, etc. These are questions of policy and underlying values. The PECL use three criteria: threats (article 4:108), excessive benefit and unfair advantage (article 4: 109).

Finally, it is submitted that even if a legal system contains a unitary view of defects of consent, this does not prevent each defect from being viewed differently within each legal system. *A fortiori*, in a system that does not contain a unified theory of defects of consent, this must be even truer. In French law for example, *erreur* and *dol* both induce a mistake whereas *violence* does not since the victim of violence is aware that he is concluding a disadvantageous contract but he has no other choice. In another respect, it has been submitted that *dol* is different from the others in that the law takes into account the defendant's conduct: it looks at how the *dol* caused the mistake (it may be classified as "defendant-sided" relief), whereas, in contrast, *erreur* and *violence* would illustrate a "claimant-sided" ground of relief as they focus on the vitiation of the claimant's consent.[40] In fact, *dol* could also be put on the same side as *violence*, as opposed to *erreur*, as the former two are not exactly defects of consent but the cause of such defects (mistake for *dol* and constraint for *violence*) . In English law, only defects that have been caused by the other contracting party (shared mistake apart), misrepresentation of whatever kind, duress, and undue influence will suffice to annul the contract (defendant-sided relief).[41] Despite appearances to the contrary, it is arguable that English law does take a consistent view of defects of consent in the sense that procedural unfairness is a key factor and justifies annulment.[42] In German law, the claimant/defendant-sided relief distinction is blurred since the protection of each party is weighed against each another. Moreover, even where claimant-sided relief is emphasised, this is counterbalanced by a recognition of the claimant's own behaviour (assessed in terms of the assumption of risks or the duty to pay negative interest). This analysis diminishes the significance of a unitary theory of defects of consent and highlights the critical issue of the underlying values in each legal system.

2 The Underlying Policy and End-Goals of Defects of Consent

All European legal systems acknowledge that consent may be defective. They even seem to be very similar in this respect as the same defects appear almost everywhere: mistake, fraud or duress for instance are grounds for avoiding the contract all over Europe. Even if these main categories do not cover exactly the same situations everywhere, the same circumstances seem to allow a party to set aside the contract by invoking one or the other of these defects. This provides the perfect illustration for the

---

40 This distinction and language come from P. Birks and N. Y. Chin, *On the Nature of Undue Influence*, in J. Beatson and D. Friedmann (eds), *Good Faith and Fault in Contract Law*, OUP (1995), pp. 57 ff., at p. 58 and is used again by J. Cartwright, *supra* note 4.

41 *Idem.*

42 See for example, J. Cartwright, *Unfair Bargaining*, Clarendon, 1991.

increasingly popular idea according to which all systems of law, particularly all European systems of law, adopt the same solutions in practice, even if the ways and means are different, due to different traditions.

But on looking closer, this harmony is only superficial. Even if defects of consent are widely accepted as a ground for annulling a contract, legal traditions vary considerably as to the degree of protection to be afforded to the parties. Thus, the circumstances in which a contract is in fact set aside differ greatly in the different countries and the difference is not merely one of degree.

The end-goals of defects of consent need to be examined more closely. It has already been suggested that the purpose of these defects may include protecting the victim, punishing the party whose conduct the law finds reprehensible (fraudulent and negligent behaviour, using illegitimate pressure, etc.) or even deterring a contracting party from acting in a morally and legally blameworthy way. It is often considered that remedies for defects of consent are drastic and require a *post hoc* intervention, in some ways too late since annulling the contract has the effect of upsetting the transaction.

As far as mistake is concerned, some legal systems, such as English law, clearly give priority to legal security over and above individual party intention. Another way of expressing this idea is to say that there has to be a good reason to undo the contract at the expense of one party.[43] German law takes this view to some extent, or at least balances up the protection offered to the mistaken and non-mistaken party by the existence and requirement of paying negative interest. Both English and German law may pay attention to the assumption of risks by the parties which influence whether or not annulment will be granted. French law seems to disregard legal security or at least give priority to the protection of the mistaken party. French law does not pay attention to the cost for a non-mistaken party of losing the contract; it only examines the cost to a mistaken party to have to go on with a disadvantageous contract. This can be explained by the value given to individual will and free consent: there can be no contract without a proper consent.

So far as fraud is concerned, protection is reinforced by punishing the other party, in the form of damages, which are cumulated with a claim for annulment.[44] English, French and German law coincide in protecting the victim from the other party's misbehaviour and the latter is treated severely as a consequence. When dealing with fraud, the law takes into account the way in which the parties behave, their standards of behaviour and the presence (or not) of procedural fairness. This last criterion is also clearly present in some forms of duress.

So far as duress is concerned it has already been pointed out that the value protected is sometimes the victim's consent (French law of duress, the overborne-will theory of duress once recognised by English law). However, in some legal systems the emphasis is once again on procedural fairness or its absence, in the way in which

---

43 See J. Cartwright, *Defects of Consent and Security of Contract: French and English Law Compared, in Themes in Comparative Law. In Honour of Bernard Rudden* (ed. P. Birks and A. Pretto) OUP 2002, p. 159, who points out that the issue in English law is " why should the non-mistaken party lose the contract ? ".

44 This is true of all legal systems. Moreover, in German law, fraud disbars the fraudulent party from being compensated for his negative interest, see *supra*.

the contract has been obtained. This is clearly the case if the illegitimate nature of the pressure is highlighted (German law, English economic duress) or the way in which a weaker party has been exploited (English undue influence). This means that more generally the law protects the victim in certain situations when a contractual imbalance is present. It is plausible that this idea is subsumed in the PECL by the general principles of good faith and fair dealing. It must be recognised however, that such principles are open-ended and subject to a variety of interpretations.

Furthermore, it may be necessary to consider if attitudes towards the aggrieved party are not becoming more entrenched in the sense that the status and the capacity of the parties are taken into account to justify annulment. If for the most part the idea of the parties equal footing is set aside, protection may be founded rather on the nature and status of the parties: whether they are professionals or consumers. Likewise the law may enquire whether they are in situations giving rise to rebuttable presumptions of exploitation which has the effect of reversing the burden of proof incumbent on the aggrieved party. Another element the law uses is the knowledge by one party of the other's weakness (whether informational or of bargaining power). As a corollary, a mistaken party who is in a strong position may find that his mistake is considered inexcusable. If defects of consent are evolving in this direction, it may be possible to suggest that proper consent is required only for certain categories of persons. This would indicate that a system of two-tier protection exists: one where parties are not on equal footing; the other where they are. The presumption that the parties are on equal terms (a postulate of 19th century freedom of contract) no longer subsists; on the contrary it has been reversed. This is important when examining the content of the PECL as a potential instrument for harmonisation since they were designed principally to meet the needs of the international business community, who are for the most part on equal footing.[45] They contain no special provisions as to consumer contracts. This might mean that the existing protection offered by defects of consent would be reduced, were such principles to be adopted. To summarise, these differences of outlook and underlying values (to whom should protection be given and in what circumstances) prevail over an enquiry into black letter rules. These differences are an amalgamation of philosophical political, social, historical and cultural considerations[46] that are a constituent of each legal system which may not be easily reducible or digestible in one text.

3 The Codification of Defects of Consent

Because mutual consent is the very essence of the formation of contract, the elaboration of rules to determine whether consent has been properly given or not has long been the central preoccupation of academics and judges alike. The result is a complex set of rules, often providing for arcane exceptions and subtle distinctions.

Therefore, unification cannot be achieved simply, and as a preliminary step, a

---

45 O. Lando and H. Beale, *op cit.*, note 18, Introduction, pp. xxv.
46 For a discussion the impact of culture on the law, see P. Legrand, *Fragments on Law-as-culture*, W.E.J. Tjeenk Willink, 1999.

methodology must be developed. Obviously, no easy solution exists and arbitrary choices will sometimes have to be made.

A preliminary and essential question is that of the language to be used: a European Civil Code should not be drafted in only one language, but in enough languages to represent the main legal traditions: three would probably suffice. There can be no serious (nor proper) harmonisation without taking into account the diversity of our cultures and thus of our languages. If the aim is to enable national legal systems to adopt the European Civil Code these historical and cultural diversities must be taken into account and not erased.

Many methods of harmonisation, which have too often been used for unification in the European Union must be firmly rejected. For instance, attempting to retain only common rules which can be found in the European legal systems would result in the adoption of the least developed system, thus affording minimum protection and leaving aside all improvements which may have developed over decades or even centuries in other countries. On the contrary, a cumulative approach which would try to integrate all European rules would result in an inefficient system of tremendous complexity. In the light of European directives laying down minimum protection requirements, it may be useful to bear in mind the danger that harmonising legal rules and values may lead to lowering the common denominator rather than raising the standards expected of contracting parties.[47] In this respect the implementation of the Directive 1999/44 must be mentioned in conjunction with defects of consent since reinforcing a consumer buyer's remedies in relation to conformity of the goods may have an impact on the need felt to invoke remedies for defects of consent. In other words, consumers may turn to the protection offered by the Directive rather than relying on defects of consent.

Contrary to what is usually suggested, it is not possible to achieve a European Civil Code, particularly on the question of defects, by looking for a mythical hard core of law which would "naturally" be common to all European countries since, as already seen, the underlying values of the different countries are in reality very different.

The adoption of unique rules[48] for all European countries is in reality a political choice. This should be borne in mind so that this choice is made clearly and not left to depend either on the dominant nationality or language in harmonisation commissions, or on the culture of the person who is in charge of drafting a given article. We all have long-rooted traditions and deep-seated prejudices: it is neither satisfactory nor possible to avoid them completely but it is better to be aware of their actual influence.

A balance should be found between protection and certainty. Some principles present no difficulty as they can be found in all systems and there is certainly no reason to rule them out, but on many issues, a political choice will be necessary to decide how far to protect parties to a contract, i.e. which circumstances justify relief for defects of consent.

---

47 See for example, the ECJ's decision of 25 April 2002, *Commission of the European Communities* v. *French Republic*, case C-52/00.

48 For a very enlightening distinction between unification, uniformisation and harmonisation, see A. Jeammaud, *"Unification, uniformisation, harmonisation?"* in *Vers un code européen de la consommation, Bruylant,* Bruxelles, 1998, p. 35.

Another general remark must be made about the use of standards, a method which is often applied for unification. It is important to stress that the use of standards, in order to achieve unification, should remain limited since judges will tend to apply them according to their own traditions. In other words, it is certainly not enough to achieve unification to agree on basic standards: what is to be unified is not only the concepts mentioned in European Codes but also the reality which they cover. More generally, making a European Code does not suffice to achieve unification. To agree on unified standards or even on unified principles is certainly not a sufficient guarantee that these standards and principles will be uniformly applied by national judges. The only way of really and practically achieving unification between the European systems of law would be to rely on a European Supreme Court to indicate how to apply these principles in specific cases. The function of such a Court would be to unify the law but to do so its decisions would have to bind national courts. This would perhaps lead us further than we really want.

Achieving unification in satisfactory conditions is not easy. Some codifications have been the consequence of an internal and bloody revolution, although of course codification can be achieved more peaceably as the recent example of the Netherlands shows. The importance of a Civil Code should not be underestimated as it is linked to our civilisation.[49] What makes the process far more difficult in the context of a European Civil Code however is that unification cannot result from simply deciding which system of law should prevail. Once again, there are not only technical choices to be made between the European systems of law but also political ones: in many instances, it will be necessary to decide which solution shall prevail.

It has already been suggested that a code will not suffice to achieve unification, but can unification be achieved without a code? The coexistence of different legal rules and values is not necessarily an impediment to the proper functioning of a legal order; indeed it is arguable that it can even contribute to its success.[50] If unification cannot be achieved, then harmonisation may be a preferable option. Does harmonisation require the existence of a code? If the 19th century reforms of the judiciary in England and Wales are used as an illustration (the "fusion" of Common Law and Equity[51]), the answer is again negative. Moreover, will a European Civil code be acceptable to all European legal systems? The utility and the progress resulting from legislative law reform must be balanced against more evolutionary progress, leaving the law to adapt over time. As Lord Goff has suggested "statutory law reform is likely to lead to ossification of the law, precluding gradualist development which is capable of ironing out those wrinkles with which old age disfigures law, like all liv-

---

49 It has been shown that, historically, civilisation is the empire of civil law: Cf. A. Supiot, *Critique du droit du travail*, PUF, Les voies du droit (1994), p. 68, who quotes P. Legendre, *L'Empire de la vérité*, Paris, Fayard (1983), p. 171.

50 Perhaps a Darwinian survival of the fittest theory may be applied to the continuity of legal species. Overtime, certain rules may be weeded out because they are uncompetitive or inefficient or simply because they no longer represent legal, cultural and political values.

51 For the view that this fusion is a fallacy, see R. P. Meagher, W.M.C. Gummow et J.R.F. Lehane, *Equity, Doctrines and Remedies*, Butterworths, 3rd edn .(1992), para 221. Even a recent attempt to go beyond the fallacy controversy shows that the fusion has not yet achieved unity: see A. Burrows, *We do this at Common law but that in Equity*, *OJ LS* 2002, p.1.

ing creatures".[52] Although this is specially true of the Common Law tradition even in Civil Law traditions, as Portalis acknowledged in his famous preliminary discourse, "les codes des peuples se font avec le temps; mais, à proprement parler, on ne les fait pas".

BIBLIOGRAPHY: *English law*: J. Beatson, *Anson's Law of Contract*, OUP, 28th edn (2002); H.G. Beale, W. D. Bishop and M. P. Furmston, *Contract, Cases and Materials*, Butterworths, 4th edn (2001); J. Cartwright, *Misrepresentation*, Sweet and Maxwell (2002); *Chitty on Contracts*, vol. I, *General principles*, Sweet and Maxwell, Chitty 29th edn (2004) (edited by H. Beale et al.); R. Goff and G. Jones, *The Law of Restitution*, Sweet and Maxwell, 6th edn (2002); G.H. Treitel, *The Law of Contract*, London, Sweet and Maxwell, 11th edn (2003).
French law: J. Carbonnier, *Droit civil, Les obligations*, Thémis, PUF, 22nd edn (2000); J. Flour et J.-L. Aubert, *Droit civil, Les obligations, 1. L'acte juridique*, Armand Colin, 10th edn (2002), with Eric Savaux; J. Ghestin, *Traité de droit civil, Le contrat: formation*, LGDJ, 3rd edn (1993); Ph. Malaurie, L. Aynès and Ph. Stoffel-Munck, *Droit civil, Les obligations*, Defrenois, 2003; F. Terré, Ph. Simler and Y. Lequette, *Droit civil, Les obligations*, Précis Dalloz, 8th edn (2002).
German law: H. Brox, *Allgemeiner Teil des Bürgerlichen Gesetzbuchs*, Carl Heymann Verlag, 24th edn (2000); W. Flume, *Allgemeiner Teil des Bürgerlichen Rechts*, t. 2: *das Rechtsgeschäft*, Springer, 4th edn (1992); K. Larenz, *Allgemeiner Teil des Bürgerlichen Rechts*, Beck, Larenz/Wolf 8th edn (1997); D. Medicus, *Allgemeiner Teil des Bürgerlichen Rechts*, Müller Juristischer Verlag, 7th edn (1997); M. Pédamon, *Le contrat en droit allemand*, LGDJ (1993); Cl. Witz, *Droit privé allemand, 1. Actes juridiques, droits subjectifs*, Litec (1992).
Italian law: P. Gallo, *I vizi del consenso*, in *I Contratti in generale*, a cura di E. Garbielli – *Trattato dei contratti*, diretto da P. Rescigno, Torino (1999); U. Mattei, Consenso viziato, lesione e abuso della controparte, *Rivista di Diritto Civile*, 1988, II, 653; V. Pietrobon, *Errore, volontà e affidamento nel negozio giuridico*, Padova (1990); R. Sacco, *Trattato di Diritto Civile, Le Fonti delle Obbligazioni, Il contratto*, 2 tomi, with G. De Nova, Torino, Utet (1993).
Comparative Law: H. Kötz and A. Flessner, *European Contract Law, vol 1: Formation, Validity and Content of Contracts; Contract and third Parties*, translated by T. Weir; Clarendon Press, Oxford (1997); O. Lando and H. Beale (eds), *Principles of European Contract Law*, Part I and II, Dordrecht, Kluwer Law International(2000); R. Zimmermann, *The Law of Obligations, Roman Foundations of the Civilian Tradition*, OUP (1996); K. Zweigert and H. Kötz, *An Introduction to Comparative Law*, 3rd edn, translated by T. Weir, OUP (1998).

---

52 Child & Co Lecture, May 1986, p. 12.

CHAPTER 23

Illegality and Immorality in Contracts: Towards European Principles

Hector L. MacQueen*

1 Introduction

In 1996 I was asked to prepare a position paper for the Third Commission on European Contract Law on the question of whether the *Principles of European Contract Law* (PECL) should deal with the topic of illegal and immoral contracts. Article 4:101 of PECL (published later, in 1999[1]), the first article in the chapter on Validity, already stated that 'This chapter does not deal with invalidity arising from illegality, immorality or lack of capacity', obviously leaving open the question of whether or not the Principles would at some future date contain provisions on these subjects. The article thus contrasted with the more absolute statement in the Unidroit *Principles of International Commercial Contracts* (1994) that 'These Principles do not deal with invalidity arising from ... (c) immorality or illegality'.[2] Similarly the Vienna Convention on the International Sale of Goods (CISG) contains no provision on illegality and immorality. The reason for what seemed then to be an exclusionary approach to the topic of illegality and immorality in the major instruments on international contract law appeared to be a perception that, while most or all western legal systems have relevant rules broadly to the effect that illegality and immorality are grounds upon which a contract may be invalidated, the specific treatment of these topics varies from country to country, each having its own statutory and other provisions on when and which contracts are illegal and its own conception of what is immoral.[3] Further, the content of that specific treatment varies over time, as legislation and moral concepts change.

It was the submission of my paper to the Third Commission that nonetheless PECL should deal with the topic of illegality and immorality. While PECL is an attempt to create an independent legal order, the system cannot be divorced from the reality of national and, in the case of the European Union within which the Principles are predominantly intended to apply, Community law regulation. Thus PECL already recognises the possibility of illegality and immorality in Article 1:103, which allows effect to be given to certain mandatory rules of any country with which a contract

---

* Professor of Private Law, University of Edinburgh; Member, Commission for European Contract Law 1995-2001.
1 O. Lando and H. Beale (eds.), *Principles of European Contract Law Parts I and II* (1999).
2 It is also understood that the forthcoming additions to the Unidroit Principles do not include any provisions on illegality or immorality.
3 See e.g. K. Zweigert and H. Kötz, *Introduction to Comparative Law* (3rd revised edn., trans T. Weir, 1998), pp. 380-382.

otherwise governed by the Principles has a close connection, taking as its main example the case of a contract illegal in the country of its performance.

Article 1:103 distinguishes between two types of mandatory rules: (1) those national mandatory rules which may be rendered *inapplicable* by the parties' choice of the Principles to govern their contract, where this is allowed by the law which would otherwise be applicable; (2) those rules which *are* applicable regardless of the law governing the contract according to the relevant rules of international private law. This distinction follows Article 7 of the Rome Convention on the Law Applicable to Contractual Obligations 1980, which provides that when applying the law of one country under the Convention, effect *may* be given to the mandatory rules of another country with which the situation has a close connection if and in so far as under the law of the latter country these rules *must* be applied whatever the law applicable to the contract. In considering whether to give effect to such mandatory rules, regard is to be had to their nature and purpose and to the consequences of their application or non-application. But nothing in the Convention restricts the application of the rules of the law of the forum in a situation where they are mandatory irrespective of the law otherwise applicable to the contract. Note should also be made of Article 16 of the Convention, which states that the application of a rule of law of a country specified by the Convention may be refused only if such application is manifestly incompatible with the public policy (*'ordre public'*) of the forum. There thus emerges overall a distinction between those rules which are mandatory but may nevertheless be set aside, and those which are super-mandatory and cannot be set aside.

Further, as Zweigert and Kötz remark, 'every legal system must reserve the right to declare a contract void if it is legally or morally offensive',[4] and every system which I investigated in preparing my paper did in fact do so. Zimmermann had noted of the Continental systems that 'the codes invariably tackle this problem by way of general clauses, which (also invariably) use the key concepts of illegality and immorality'.[5] While English Common Law had no equivalent to general clauses, the standard texts on contract all included chapter headings such as 'Illegality', or 'Statutory Invalidity', under which were embraced further concepts such as 'immorality' and 'public policy'.[6] The same was true for Scottish and Irish texts.[7] So, if PECL was to form a truly comprehensive system of contract law and a basis for a future European civil code, texts on illegality and immorality had to be included.

Another potential benefit of articulating some principles about the invalidity of illegal and immoral contracts, I suggested, would be the encouragement of national and European Union legislators formulating regulations for market transactions to take into account whether or not the sanctions enforcing such regulations should or

---

4 *Ibid.*, 380.
5 'The Civil Law in European codes', in D.L. Carey Miller and R. Zimmermann (eds.), *The Civilian Tradition and Scots Law* (Berlin 1997), 267.
6 See e.g. G.H. Treitel, *The Law of Contract* (11th edn., 2003), chs. 11 and 12; E. McKendrick, *Contract Law* (4th edn., 2000), ch. 15.
7 For Scotland see W.W. McBryde, *The Law of Contract in Scotland* (2nd edn., 2001), ch. 19; *The Laws of Scotland: Stair Memorial Encyclopaedia*, vol. 15 (1996), paras 763 ff. For Ireland see R. Clark, *Contract Law in Ireland* (4th edn., 1998), Part 5 (Public Policy), chs 14 (Illegal Contracts) and 15 (Void Contracts).

should not include the invalidity of relevant contracts, a common problem revealed by comparative study being the silence of regulatory legislation on this particular matter. PECL would thus serve its purpose as a background framework against which specific legislation could be made more conceptually consistent.

My proposal was accepted by the Commission, although not without debate; and that debate continued throughout the five years of work which followed. Indeed, at the final meeting of the Third Commission at Copenhagen in February 2001, a vote had to be taken on a motion that, such were the difficulties attendant upon this subject, there should be no provisions on illegality in PECL. Fortunately for me, this motion was defeated by a large majority; but the debate showed the complexity of the issues involved. In essence, they were about the extent to which contracts might be invalidated on grounds of illegality and immorality in a 'soft law' instrument such as PECL, and to which an unofficial body might presume to go beyond and perhaps around positive legal provisions in national and international systems of law.

The result which is printed in the appendix to this article is thus to some extent a compromise between, first, those members of the Commission who saw our work as laying the basis for a future European civil code, i.e. as prospectively hard law; second, those who saw our system as primarily effective in cross-border transactions and as therefore essentially confined to solving specific problems arising in that context; and, finally, those who thought that we were going beyond our capacity as an unofficial group by presuming to over-ride existing national and international rules. The chapter contains five articles. The first (Article 15:101) begins, not with illegality or contrariety to positive law as such, but rather with what would be called in some systems immorality, in others public policy or *ordre public*; here it is described as 'fundamental principles of law'. Guidance as to these fundamental principles may be obtained from such European documents as the EC Treaty, the European Convention on Human Rights, and the European Union Charter on Fundamental Rights. However, by avoiding any attempt to list those contracts to be regarded as contrary to fundamental principles of law, the public policy underpinning principles recognised as fundamental may change over time, in accordance with the prevailing norms of society as they develop. The second Article (15:102) is concerned with the case where in some way a contract infringes a rule of positive law, and declares what the effects of such infringement may be. This reflects a view that fundamentally this whole area of law is primarily concerned with the public good, with contrariety to positive law being a specific area of this requiring particular treatment as a result of certain characteristics. The third Article (15:103) recognises the possibility of severability in illegal contracts, i.e. that if a contract is tainted only in part the remainder of the contract continues to be valid and enforceable unless this would be unreasonable in all the circumstances. The fourth Article (15:104) provides for restitution in appropriate cases of performances rendered under the ineffective contract. Finally, the fifth Article (15:105) recognises a further possibility when the invalidity takes effect, namely that one of the parties may be unfairly out of pocket as a result of entry into the ineffective contract, and accordingly provides for a right to damages to cover this kind of case.

2 Contrariety to Fundamental Principles

The first Article of Chapter 15 of PECL begins, not with illegality or contrariety to positive law as such, but rather with what would be called in some systems immorality, in others public policy or *ordre public*. This reflects a view that fundamentally this whole area of law is primarily concerned with the public good or, as I put it in a Scottish fashion in my original position paper, the 'common weal', with contrariety to positive law being a specific area of this requiring particular treatment as a result of certain characteristics. But the debate within the Commission had great difficulty with this concept. One reason is that the relative concepts operating within the various national systems are not at all the same: immorality, public policy and *ordre public* capture distinct ideas and associations, at least partly reflecting different national and social traditions. Another issue was how the Commission might be able to express European – as distinct from national or local – ideas of morality, public policy and *ordre public* which would command general assent. On the other hand, it was clear that to confine the Principles strictly to issues of legality or conformity with specific rules of law would probably be too narrow; certainly so if PECL was to form the basis of a future European civil code on contract.

The end result of the debate is Article 15:101. This formulation is intended to avoid the varying national concepts of immorality, illegality at common law, public policy, *ordre public* and *bonos mores*, by invoking a necessarily broad idea of fundamental principles of law found across the European Union, including European Community law. Guidance as to these fundamental principles may be obtained from such documents as the EC Treaty (e.g. in favour of free movement of goods, services and persons, protection of market competition), the European Convention on Human Rights (e.g. prohibition of slavery and forced labour (art 3), and rights to liberty (art 5), respect for private and family life (art 8), freedom of thought (art 9), freedom of expression (art 10), freedom of association (art 11), right to marry (art 12) and peaceful enjoyment of possessions (First Protocol, art 1)) and the European Union Charter on Fundamental Rights (which includes many of the rights already mentioned and adds such matters as respect for personal data (art 8), freedom to choose an occupation and right to engage in work (art 15), freedom to conduct a business (art 16), right to property (art 17), equality between men and women (art 23), children's rights (art 24), rights of collective bargaining and action (art 28), protection in the event of unjustified dismissal (art 30), and a high level of consumer protection (art 38)).

Merely national concepts as such have no effect upon contracts governed by the Principles and may not be invoked directly, although comparative study can give further help in the identification and elucidation of principles recognised as fundamental in the laws of the Member States. Thus Article 15:101 extends to contracts placing undue restraints upon individual liberty (for example, being constraints of excessive duration or covenants not to compete), upon the right to work, or upon being otherwise in restraint of trade, contracts which are in conflict with the generally accepted norms of family life and sexual morality, and contracts which interfere with the due administration of justice (e.g. champertous agreements in England, *pacta de quota litis* elsewhere). All of these grounds of invalidity can be found across the European legal systems,[8] and it seems right to see them as reflecting general European norms.

It is necessary to recognise the limits of public policy in order to prevent it becoming a means of giving effect to a purely intuitive sense of 'justice between man and man',[9] as opposed to a sufficiently clearly defined and reasonably certain legal concept. However, by avoiding any attempt to list those contracts to be regarded as contrary to fundamental principles of law, the public policy underpinning principles recognised as fundamental may change over time, in accordance with the prevailing norms of society as they develop and become apparent through other legal texts. Also, because PECL already contains rules about contracts conferring excessive benefit or unfair advantage (Article 4:109) and unfair contract terms not individually negotiated (Article 4:110), these situations fall outside the scope of Article 15:101.[10]

Regulation under the concept of fundamental principles of law should, it is suggested, be distinguished from good faith as a control device in contract law, although the precise dividing line may require further clarification. A possible starting point for analysis may lie in the idea that the former is about social and moral standards quite apart from the relationship of the contracting parties, whereas good faith, although also concerned with objective community standards (and itself thus perhaps a manifestation of public policy), applies them much more directly to the specifics of the relationship between the parties.[11] So good faith looks to matters such as duties of disclosure, the interpretation of and filling of gaps in contracts, standards of performance, the prevention of unfair surprise, and the abuse of contractual powers; whereas the public policy concept of fundamental principles of law deals with more abstract questions such as the prevention of crime and other wrongs, the protection of marriage and family life, the right to work, and the proper administration of justice and other public services.

PECL avoids the national concepts of nullity (absolute or relative), voidness, voidability and unenforceability, and uses instead a concept of 'ineffectiveness'. Ineffectiveness extends to non-enforcement of the contract where enforcement (as distinct from the contract itself) would be contrary to principles regarded as fundamental in the laws of the Member States of the European Union. It is important to note that the ineffectiveness applies to the contract only in so far as it or its enforcement would be contrary to fundamental principles: thus, for example, a contract in restraint of trade could still be effective so long as the restraint involved was not an undue constriction of the covenantor's liberty or of competition. But once the contract is found to be contrary to the fundamental principles, the judge or arbitrator is given no discretion to determine the effects upon the contract: such a contract is to be given no effect at all. The intentions and knowledge of the parties are irrelevant.

---

8   See further H. Kötz and A. Flessner, *European Contract Law*, vol. 1 (1997), pp. 155-161.
9   The famous phrase of Stratford C.J. in the South African case of *Jajbhay* v. *Cassim* 1939 AD 537 at 544; see it used also by Smalberger J.A. in *Sasfin (Pty) Ltd* v. *Beukes* 1989 (1) SA 1 (AD) at 9G.
10 Cf e.g. the position in South African law, where the lack of legislative regulation of unfair contracts has led to the use of the common law concept of public policy to give the courts some control in this area. See in particular *Sasfin (Pty) Ltd* v. *Beukes* 1989 (1) SA 1 (AD).
11 See Alfred Cockrell, 'Second-guessing the exercise of contractual power on rationality grounds', (1997) *Acta Juridica* 26 at 42-43.

3 Contrariety to Mandatory Rules of Law

Article 15:102 is concerned with the case where in some way a contract infringes a rule of positive law which is mandatory under international private law rules and Article 1:103 of PECL (already referred to in my introductory remarks).

The first point to note is the relation with Article 15:101. Many contracts are illegal, in the sense that they contravene an applicable statute, without necessarily being contrary to any fundamental principle. Article 15:102 deals with such contracts. It is implicit in the structure of Articles 15:101 and 15:102 that, if the infringement of a statute also involves a violation of a fundamental principle within the meaning of Article 15:101, it is that Article which applies. In practice, therefore, Article 15:102 deals with less important violations of the law than Article 15:101. Indeed, given the extent of statutory regulation in modern States, some infringements covered by Article 15:102 may be of a merely technical nature. This means that a more flexible approach can be taken to the effects of an infringement; this is what Article 15:102 is about. It does not say *when* a contract is illegal (that is a matter for the otherwise applicable law); it deals with the *effects* of the illegality once that illegality has been identified.

In determining the effects of an illegality upon a contract, regard is to be had first to what the mandatory rule in question lays down upon the matter. This provision arises from the need to respect the provisions of the applicable law, whether PECL is seen as essentially a soft law system available for use in cross-border transactions, or as a basis for a future European civil code. If the mandatory rule provides expressly for the effect of an infringement, then that effect follows. If, for example, the relevant rule expressly states that infringement invalidates a contract, or if it provides that contracts are not to be invalidated by any infringement, then these consequences follow. Thus, for example, Article 81 of the EC Treaty prohibits agreements between undertakings which have as their object or effect the prevention, restriction or distortion of competition within the common market and declares such prohibited agreements to be 'automatically void'. Conversely, the legislation may provide that the criminal offence which may be committed in the course of forming or performing a contract does not of itself make the contract void or unenforceable or prevent any cause of action arising in respect of any loss.[12]

But the rule in question may not provide expressly for the effects upon a contract of an infringement of the rule. It is therefore necessary for the Article to deal with this second situation. It does so by addressing itself to the person (judge or arbitrator) with power to determine matters arising under the contract. If the matter is never referred to a judge or arbitrator it would seem (on the assumption that the matter is not within Article 15:101) that the contract is not affected by the infringement. The general policy has to be that contracts are valid unless otherwise provided, and in this situation there is no Article or mandatory rule of law which provides for invalidity.

Where Article 15:102(2) is brought into operation, the judge or arbitrator is given a discretion to declare the contract of full effect, or of some effect, or of no effect, or

---

12 See e.g. UK Package Travel, Package Holidays and Package Tours Regulations 1992 reg 27, implementing Council Directive 90/314/EEC on package travel, package holidays and package tours.

to be subject to modification. In reaching a decision on these matters, the judge or arbitrator is to have regard to all the relevant circumstances and, in particular, to those spelled out in Article 15:102(3), under which an appropriate and proportional response to the infringement may be spelled out.

Article 15:102(2) gives the judge or arbitrator a choice from a range of possible effects, including that of leaving the contract wholly unaffected and fully enforceable. Equally, the contract may be given some but not complete effectiveness: for example, it may be enforceable by one of the parties only, or only in part, or only at a particular time. It may be that some remedies, such as specific performance, are not available, while others, such as damages for non-performance, are. It may be decided that the contract is of no effect at all (the phraseology is intended to cover both nullity and unenforceability), or that its enforceability is subject to modification by the judge or arbitrator.

This approach was controversial in the Commission because it seemed to arrogate to PECL a power to depart from, or over-ride, the applicable positive law in the sense that that law might *impliedly* state what its effects upon infringing contracts were to be. There were also serious doubts about doing this by way of a discretion vested in the judge or arbitrator deciding the particular case. So it was particularly useful that in the period during our deliberations there should be published by the Law Commission of England and Wales its Consultation Paper No. 154, *Illegal Transactions: The Effect of Illegality on Contracts and Trusts* (1998).[13] The Commission's provisional proposals were also to the effect that courts should have a discretion to decide whether or not illegality should act as a defence to a claim for contractual enforcement. But the discretion should be structured by requiring the court to take account of specific factors:

(1)   the seriousness of the illegality involved;
(2)   the knowledge and intention of the party seeking enforcement;
(3)   whether denying relief will act as a deterrent;
(4)   whether denial of relief will further the purpose of the rule rendering the contract illegal; and
(5)   whether denying relief is proportionate to the illegality involved.

All of these were factors that should probably be taken into account in determining what the implied effect of a legislative prohibition upon a contract should be, and the idea of a discretion structured in this way thus entered the thinking towards European principles. The influence of the English proposals is apparent in Article 15:102, although we have not slavishly copied them and have highlighted in particular the purpose of the rule which the contract infringes (see (a)-(c) in Art 15:102(3)). Also, the judge or arbitrator is enjoined to take into account all the relevant circumstances in determining the effect of the infringement of the law upon the contract. Thus the list of factors is not exclusive, while the factors mentioned may well overlap in application.

---

13 See further *The Illegality Defence in Tort* (Law Com CP No. 160, 2001); a report giving the Law
    Commission's conclusions on the whole topic is anticipated in due course.

Let us take the factors briefly in turn, bearing in mind that they apply in considering the effect of illegality upon, not only the contract itself, but also the remedies of restitution and damages (see further below):

3.1 Purpose of the Rule

Where the rule in question contains no express provision about the effects of the illegality, the legislative intent will have to be determined in accordance with the usual rules on the interpretation of the law. A purposive approach is to be adopted. The intention of the Principles is that consideration should always be given to whether, in the absence of an express statement on the point, enabling the rule to take full effect requires the contract to be set aside, or restitution or damages denied.

3.2 For Whose Protection Does the Rule Exist?

This factor is closely related to the issue of the purpose of the rule. If, for example, the rule in question merely prohibits one party from entering or making contracts of the kind in question, it does not follow that the other party may plead the illegality to prevent the contract taking effect. Take, for example, a consumer protection statute which prohibits the negotiation or conclusion of loan agreements away from business premises. The aim of the statute is to protect consumers from 'cold selling' by home-visiting or telephoning salesmen of credit acting on behalf of consumer credit companies. While such companies are unable to enforce agreements entered in such circumstances, the consumer for whose protection the prohibition exists may do so. Likewise the consumer should be able to get restitution and/or damages.

3.3 Existence of Other Sanctions

If the rule in question provides for a criminal or administrative sanction against the wrongdoer, the imposition of that sanction may be enough to deter the conduct in question without adding the ineffectiveness of the contract or denying restitution or damages. The goal of deterrence is usually better achieved through such sanctions than by way of private law. Often such sanctions will take into account the degree of blameworthiness of the party concerned, and this may be a more appropriate response to the conduct than rendering the contract wholly or partially ineffective or denying other remedies.

3.4 Seriousness of the Infringement

If the infringement is minor or very slight, that may point to the contract being given effect. Thus, when a shipowning company is in breach of statutory regulations as to the maximum load to be carried by ships but only by a very small amount, it should not be disabled on this ground alone from recovery of freight for the voyage. If on the other hand the infringement had major or serious consequences, that might suggest that there should be some effect upon the contract.

3.5 Was the Infringement Intentional?

Subject to the other factors in the case, in particular the purpose of the law in issue, there is a stronger case for the illegality rendering the contract ineffective if it was known to or intended by the parties than if both were unaware of the problem. More complex is the situation where one party knows of the infringement and the other does not, where much may depend upon which of them is trying to enforce the contract. The most difficult situation is the contract for an illegal purpose. If it is lawful for A to sell a weapon or explosive material to B, and these materials may be lawfully used (for example, in self-defence or in construction work), the fact that B intends to use the goods illegally ought not to affect the validity of the contract of supply. If however at the time of contracting A is aware of or shares B's illicit purpose (e.g. supplies Semtex to a person whom A knows to be an active member of a terrorist organisation), then there may be some deterrence from entering the contract (on credit terms at least) if A cannot compel B to pay for material supplied; but it may be appropriate to allow A to seek restitution.

3.6 Relationship Between Infringement and Contract

This factor requires examination of whether or not the contract expressly or impliedly stipulates for an illegal performance by one or both of the parties. Thus a contract of carriage which can only be performed by overloading the ship or lorry may be more readily seen as consequentially ineffective (although possibly the case might be addressed by an appropriate modification of the contract).

4 Severability

Article 15:103 restates a principle found in most European systems' rules on illegality and immorality, the principle of severability. Consistently with the general intention of minimising the impact of illegality and immorality upon transactions, the Article here provides the possibility that if a contract is tainted only in part the remainder of the contract continues to be valid and enforceable unless this would be unreasonable in all the circumstances. This is also consistent with the approach to avoidance in Article 4:116. Circumstances that might be taken into account include whether or not the contract has any independent life without the invalidated part; whether the parties would have agreed to a contract consisting only of the remaining parts of the contract; and the effect of partial invalidity upon the balance of the respective obligations of the parties as performance and counter-performance.

5 Restitution

Much more of a radical departure from the conventional response to illegality and immorality is Article 15:104. If the prohibitions and rules of other legal orders commonly fail to state the effect upon contracts that infringe their requirements, it is even more common for them to fail to state what are the remedial consequences of a finding of invalidity for the contract where one or both parties have commenced performance of the obligations under it. In general, for reasons ranging from deterrence, punishment or protection of the dignity of the courts to a notion that parties to an illegal or immoral transaction have placed themselves outside the legal order, the national systems of Europe have commenced their analysis of this problem from the traditional basis of Roman law, which denied restitution and left the parties in whatever position had been achieved at the time the invalidity was recognised (*ex turpi causa melior est conditio possidentis*). But restitution, or unwinding the performances rendered under the illegal contract, often appears to be a more appropriate response to the invalidity. Denial of restitution can leave the effects of the illegality standing, quite contrary to the policy underlying the prohibition in question.[14] Suppose that a statute declares that any contract using an abolished system of weights and measures is to be void, and A sells goods to B in a contract using the abolished system of weights and measures to determine the quantity of goods to be delivered and the price, whereupon B, having taken delivery and consumed the goods, refuses to pay. If A has no action for the contract price, denial of restitution would allow B to have the benefit of an illegal transaction without paying for it.[15]

Article 15:104 therefore provides for restitution in appropriate cases of performances rendered under the ineffective contract. The paragraph is based upon the general provisions contained in Article 4:115 (Validity) rather than the more specific provisions of Articles 9:307 to 9:309 (Non-performance). Nevertheless the rule or principle rendering the contract ineffective is to be examined to see whether or not it requires denial of restitution. The same considerations as those used under Article 15:102 to judge whether or not a contract should be invalidated (where the applicable mandatory rule does not expressly regulate that question) are to be applied to the question of whether there should be restitution. Article 15:104(4) further enables the judge or arbitrator to refuse restitution to a party who knew or ought to have known of the illegality in question.

Detailed application of restitutionary principles – for example, whether defences such as change of position are available – is left to the applicable law of unjustified enrichment. Similarly, the Articles contain no provisions about the transfer of property and ownership under illegal transactions. If however a European civil code is to develop, both of these aspects of the unwinding of illegal transactions will require much further work.[16]

---

14 See, for valuable recent discussions of the issue, H.J. van Kooten, 'Illegality and restitution as a matter of policy considerations', [2001] 9 *Restitution Law Review* 67-75; and the contributions of W.J. Swadling and G. Dannemann on the subject in D. Johnston and R. Zimmermann (eds.), *Unjustified Enrichment: Key Issues in Comparative Perspective* (2002), pp. 289-324.

15 The example comes from the Scottish case of *Cuthbertson* v. *Lowes* (1870) 8 M 1073.

16 The Unjustified Enrichment chapter being produced by the Osnabruck team in the Study Group towards a European Civil Code will contain provisions on illegality. See further the Group's website, http://www.sgecc.net.

6 Damages

Restitution will not be necessary in every case, since benefits will not necessarily have been transferred between the parties when the invalidity takes effect; yet one of the parties may be unfairly out of pocket as a result of entry into the ineffective contract. For example, suppose that legislation requires the suppliers of certain chemicals to hold licences indicating compliance with safety and environmental standards. Contracts made by suppliers holding no licence are declared to be null. A Ltd, which has recently been deprived of its licence by government action, nevertheless enters a contract for the supply of the chemicals to B Ltd, which is unaware of A Ltd's fall from grace and buys from it because its price is lower than that of the only other licensed supplier, C Ltd. B intends to use the chemicals for industrial purposes leading on to profitable contracts of its own, and spends money preparing its premises to handle the material safely. A's illegal conduct is discovered and the contract with B is declared null before either delivery or payment have taken place. B is unable to make the intended further contracts.

Article 15:105 accordingly provides for a right to damages to cover this kind of case, another innovation of this scheme. The remedy parallels that given for invalidity under Chapter 4 of PECL. It would be inappropriate for the damages to extend to the positive or expectation interest of the party, since putting the party in the position as if the contract had been performed (PECL Article 9:502) would be to enforce the illegal or immoral contract. The aim of the damages should therefore be like that of restitution, to put the party as far as possible in the position as if the contract had not been made, that is, to protect the negative or reliance interest. Thus in the illustration above, while B cannot recover the expectation loss of profit on these further contracts, it may recover its incidental reliance expenditure on preparing its premises and any other costs associated with having contracted with A. These might include a figure for the loss of the opportunity to contract with C (as distinct from the extra cost of contracting with C or the profits which would have been earned had B concluded the contract with C rather than A).

A party who knows or ought to have known of the illegality of the contract cannot, however, recover damages. But there seems no reason in principle why a party should not cumulate a restitutionary with a damages claim. If in the above example B had in addition made payment in advance to A, it should be entitled to recover that sum as well as its incidental expenditure.

7 The *Code Européen* des Contrats

PECL is not the only set of unofficial contract principles available for consideration in the development of a European civil code. Account must also be taken of the work of a group headed by Professor Giuseppe Gandolfi of Pavia, which was published as *Code Européen des Contrats* in 2001,[17] and is based upon the Italian Civil Code and the Code of Contract Law drafted in the late 1960s by Harvey McGregor QC for the

---

17 G. Gandolfi (ed), *Code Européen des Contrats: Livre Premiere* (Pavia, 2001).

English and Scottish Law Commissions.[18] This too contains provisions on illegality and immorality (Articles 140, 143, 144 and 160), and these contrast, at least presentationally and probably also substantively, with the PECL model, being more obviously in line with traditional approaches to the subject, in particular those found in Continental Europe.

Thus, under Article 140, unless the law states otherwise, a contract is void (that is, wholly without contractual effect *ab initio*[19]) if (a) it is contrary to public policy or morals or a mandatory rule adopted for the protection of the general interest or for situations of primary importance for society, or (b) it is contrary to any other applicable mandatory rule. A penal prohibition which affects the contract as such – for example, a prohibition on the conclusion of a contract without prior authorisation by a public body – also avoids the contract; but where performance of a contract forms part of an illegal activity, a party not involved in that activity may, by way of the remedies for non-performance, seek the performance due to him under the contract. Void contracts can generally be validated under Article 143 if the parties remove the cause of nullity and agree to perform, but not if the ground of voidness is that under (a) above. Article 144 provides for a regime of severability, enabling a clause to be void without necessarily similarly affecting the remainder of the contract if that remainder can have an autonomous existence and the parties' purpose can be reasonably realised. Again, however, this does not apply to contracts which are void under Article 140(1)(a). Article 160 provides for a general right of mutual restitution of performances rendered under a void contract, but in paragraph 9 states that 'parties who have performed contractual duties which constitute offences liable to prosecution or which are against morality or public policy – but not against economic public policy – and the party who has made performance for a purpose which even only as to himself presents those characteristics, have no right to any restitution under this Article'. It is not clear how far this is to be squared with the absolute voidness of contracts infringing Article 140(1)(a). Finally, there seems to be no provision for a right of damages in cases of illegal or immoral contracts, except under Article 161 for third parties who in good faith have relied on the appearance of a contract (essentially a tortious or delictual liability rather than one between the apparently contracting parties).

In general, the Gandolfi approach is more absolute and less discretionary than the PECL one. Gandolfi gives much greater impact to illegality and immorality than PECL, which is designed to minimise their effect on contracts to what is clearly required by legal policy in the matter. Where PECL confines absolute ineffectiveness to the case of contrariety to fundamental principles and otherwise follows either the express provisions of the infringed statute or a structured discretion which can go so far as to make the contract effective, voidness is the general sanction of the Gandolfi code unless the law says otherwise. The voidness may be tempered in favour of an innocent party in cases of illegal performance, while there can be validation where the cause of the voidness is removed and a void clause may be severed to leave the remainder of a contract enforceable; but even these possibilities are excluded where

---

18 H. McGregor, *Contract Code drawn up on behalf of the English Law Commission* (Milan, 1993).
19 See Art. 141(1).

the contract is contrary to public policy or morals or a mandatory rule adopted for the protection of the general interest or for situations of primary importance for society. Especially with the last of these, there is still room for debate, uncertainty and, ultimately, the exercise of discretion; but the overall emphasis on nullity is very apparent. This is much narrower than PECL, which may allow enforcement despite illegality and has a general principle of severability. The Gandolfi emphasis on nullity also leads conceptually to the remedy of restitution provided for in Article 160, but again the remedy is absolutely denied in certain cases of illeagality and immorality, while PECL in contrast ties its availability to what the policy factors in the particular case may require.

8   Conclusion

The contrasting approaches of PECL and the Gandolfi code take us back to the debate with which this contribution began, and which it is clear will have to be undergone again if and when the time for a European Civil Code finally comes. Experience across Europe suggests that illegality and immorality are areas in which satisfactory general rules are difficult to formulate in any detail, and even harder to apply. It is perhaps worthy of note that in at least some of the world's mixed legal systems there has been a recent trend towards a more discretionary and flexible approach to the subject, based upon a recognition of the primacy of public policy concerns in all respects.[20] As far as possible, a proper balance between the requirements of certainty of approach, sensitivity to change, and flexibility of outcome has to be achieved in Europe. The 'structured discretion' approach seems to me to have important advantages over absolutely fixed rules, applying as it does not only to the effect of the illegality upon the contract, but also to the remedies which may be necessary to achieve equity between the parties so long as they too are not also contrary to the underlying policy of the legal instrument or fundamental principle in question. Whether however this will be acceptable to those raised in the Continental traditions remains to be seen.

---

20 See H.L. MacQueen and A. Cockrell, 'Illegal contracts', in R. Zimmermann, D. Visser, and K. Reid (eds.), *Mixed Legal Systems in Comparative Perspective: Property and Obligations in Scotland and South Africa*, forthcoming.

APPENDIX

Principles of European Contract Law
Part III
Chapter 15

Illegality

Article 15:101: Contracts Contrary to Fundamental Principles

A contract is of no effect to the extent that it is contrary to principles recognised as fundamental in the laws of the Member States of the European Union.

Article 15:102: Contracts Infringing Mandatory Rules

(1)　Where a contract infringes a mandatory rule of law applicable under Article 1:103 of these Principles, the effects of that infringement upon the contract are the effects, if any, expressly prescribed by that mandatory rule.

(2)　Where the mandatory rule does not expressly prescribe the effects of an infringement upon a contract, the contract may be declared to have full effect, to have some effect, to have no effect, or to be subject to modification.

(3)　A decision reached under paragraph (2) must be an appropriate and proportional response to the infringement, having regard to all relevant circumstances, including:

    (a)　the purpose of the rule which has been infringed;

    (b)　the category of persons for whose protection the rule exists;

    (c)　any sanction that may be imposed under the rule infringed;

    (d)　the seriousness of the infringement;

    (e)　whether the infringement was intentional; and

    (f)　the closeness of the relationship between the infringement and the contract.

Article 15:103: Partial Ineffectiveness

(1) If only part of a contract is rendered ineffective under Articles 15:101 or 15:102, the remaining part continues in effect unless, giving due consideration to all the circumstances of the case, it is unreasonable to uphold it.

(2) Articles 15:104 and 15:105 apply, with appropriate adaptations, to a case of partial ineffectiveness.

Article 15:104: Restitution

(1)　When a contract is rendered ineffective under Articles 15:101 or 15:102, either party may claim restitution of whatever that party has supplied under the contract, provided that, where appropriate, concurrent restitution is made of whatever has been received.

(2)　When considering whether to grant restitution under paragraph (1), and what concurrent restitution, if any, would be appropriate, regard must be had to the factors referred to in Article 15:102(3).

(3)　An award of restitution may be refused to a party who knew or ought to have known of the reason for the ineffectiveness.

(4) If restitution cannot be made in kind for any reason, a reasonable sum must be paid for what has been received.

Article 15:105: Damages

(1)   A party to a contract which is rendered ineffective under Articles 15:101 or 15:102 may recover from the other party damages putting the first party as nearly as possible into the same position as if the contract had not been concluded, provided that the other party knew or ought to have known of the reason for the ineffectiveness.

(2)   When considering whether to award damages under paragraph (1), regard must be had to the factors referred to in Article 15:102(3).

(3)   An award of damages may be refused where the first party knew or ought to have known of the reason for the ineffectiveness.

CHAPTER 24

Standard Form Conditions

Thomas Wilhelmsson*

1   Introduction

Traditional contract thinking is built on the ideal of individual contracting. Each part of the contract is thought of as expressly agreed upon by the parties. As is well known, however, probably a rather small percentage of all contracts is actually made in this way. Modern mass transactions require standardised conditions.

The content of the concept 'standard form conditions' can be defined in various ways. In those countries having special rules on standard form conditions, a legal definition of such conditions is required. Comments on some of these definitions will be presented later. Here, in the introduction, it suffices to list some stipulative criteria in order to indicate the scope of the following discussion. For this purpose standard form conditions can be described as contract terms which are intended for use in several future contractual relationships. The conditions are designed to be used in relation to any of several different contract parties, of which at least one has not participated in the drafting of the terms.

Before the widespread use of computers, the technical term 'pre-printed conditions' was sometimes used, in a sloppy use of language, more or less as a synonym for standard form conditions. It should, however, be stressed that it is seldom relevant in this context what typographical method of presentation is used. Standard form conditions may be pre-printed as specific documents, they may be used in connection with other documents or on packages, or they may just be pre-formulated and stored in the memory of a computer.

Some practical problems related to the use of standard form conditions may follow already from their poor adaptation to the concrete situation and the needs of the parties involved. The most prominent problem, and the one which has given rise to recurrent discussions on standard form contracting, is, however, the potential one-sidedness of the conditions. The business using standard form conditions may use them as a means to impose conditions which are unfavourable to or even unfair on the other party.

Various kinds of rules and principles have been developed in order to cope with the specific problems connected with standard form contracting. From a traditional contract law perspective, the basic question is, obviously, how a set of rules developed by one party to the contract, or by an organisation completely outside the contractual relationship, can become a part of an individual contract (the incorporation problem). In business-to-business relationships this problem sometimes occurs in a more special form, when both parties rely on their own standard form conditions (the battle-of-the-forms problem). Furthermore, the interpretation of standard form condi-

---

*   Professor of Civil and Commercial Law, University of Helsinki

tions cannot be as closely tied to the intention of the parties as the interpretation of individual contract terms (the interpretation problem). These problems obviously need to be addressed in any analysis of the law concerning standard form conditions. However, as the main problem in this context is the often unbalanced nature of the conditions, it is natural also to deal with the question of how to bring about the use of more balanced conditions (the fairness problem), although this problem is not necessarily limited to the sphere of standard form contracting alone.

Various methods are used to achieve fairness in contracting. In this chapter only the use of a general clause giving the courts the right to adjust unfair contract terms will be discussed. Mandatory legislation outlawing certain specific terms will not be analysed, as such legislation often relates to specific contract types, and such an analysis would become too detailed in this context. In addition, the discussion of the fairness principle in this chapter is limited to cover only the use of the principle as a typical private law remedy. In other words, the very important question of the enforcement of the principle through other means than adjustment by a court in an individual case will not be touched upon here. Although the distinction private law/public law is largely outmoded and one could well defend the inclusion of various kinds of collective enforcement mechanisms in a private law context, there does not seem to be much point in discussing a harmonisation of such different methods as the German organisational action (*Verbandsklage*), the French *Commission des clauses abusives* and the possibilities to outlaw unfair terms by decree,[1] the British Director General of Fair Trading[2] and the Nordic Consumer Ombudsmen. Even the EC Unfair Contract Terms Directive has refrained from any attempt to harmonise this field and simply requires the Member States to ensure that 'adequate and effective means exist to prevent the continued use of unfair terms'.[3]

2   Procedural or Substantive Solutions?

The solutions of the problems related to the use of standard form conditions are not only practical, but have a theoretical/ideological aspect as well. The various rules are closely connected with variations in basic contract ideology (in the contract paradigm). Any regulation of standard form conditions has to be positioned in relation to the parameters of this paradigm.

The use of standard form conditions poses obvious problems for traditional contract thinking, which emphasises autonomy and the will or consent of the parties as basic legitimating factors behind the binding force of contracts. How can one, with such a starting point, accept that a party who might even not have read the conditions and knows nothing about their content can be bound by them? In fact the need for regulation of the incorporation, battle-of-the-forms, interpretation and fairness prob-

---

1   *Loi sur la protection et l'information des consommateurs de produits et de services* of 10 January 1978 (Nos. 78-23). This method has, however, hardly been used in practice; see e.g. Zweigert & Kötz (1998), p. 339.
2   For a good overview of the achievements, see e.g. Bright (2000).
3   Council Directive 93/13/EEC of 5 April 1993 on unfair terms in consumer contracts, *OJ* 1993, L95/29, Art. 7.

lems is to a large degree a consequence of this anomaly between contract ideology and contract practice.

The search for solutions to the problems may, however, proceed on two lines. On the one hand one might attempt to develop the rules within the traditional paradigm. One would then use various methods, such as the obligation to provide information, in an effort to guarantee a more genuine consent to the conditions than that contained in a mere reference to them. When deciding whether and to what extent standard form conditions bind the other party, the focus of the decision would in this case be on the events at the time when the contract was made. If the party referring to the conditions follows the rules of the game at this stage the conditions become binding irrespective of their content. Because of their neutrality as to the content of the conditions, these kinds of solutions may be termed formal or procedural solutions.

The other way of reacting to the problems is to transcend the traditional procedural contract paradigm and to analyse the question of the binding force of the conditions with direct reference to the content of the conditions. Then the (un)fairness, (un)balanced character, (un)suitability, etc. of a term in the conditions, or of the conditions as a whole, would be relevant when deciding whether the term or the conditions are considered binding. Such a content-oriented solution can be termed a substantive solution.

Most national as well as international solutions contain both procedural and substantive elements. Obviously, up-to-date legislation on standard form contracting would need both kinds of elements. The emphasis may, however, differ. The following presentation of the concrete rules attempts to show various reflections of this dichotomy in the legal systems.

The relation between the procedural and the substantive approaches is a leading theme of the analysis.[4] A discussion concerning possible future rules on standard form contracting cannot take place on practical terms alone, without any connections to the deep-structure of contract thinking. It is important to discuss explicitly the proper balance between the procedural and substantive elements in the rules.

3   Special Provisions on Standard Form Conditions?

Before proceeding to analyse the solutions to the specific problems connected with the use of standard form conditions, a general policy issue should be mentioned which at least to some extent is connected with the balancing of procedural and substantive elements. This is the issue whether, and to what extent, one should have special rules on standard form contracting that differ from those that apply to individual contracts.

As a specific problem, the phenomenon of standard form conditions provoked discussion as early as at the beginning of the 20th century.[5] Legal doctrine has since

---

4   As should be clear from the above, the dichotomy procedural/substantive used here refers to the distinction between rules and arguments related to the making of the contract on the one hand and rules and arguments related to the content of the contract on the other. Of course both kinds of rules are substantive if this term is used as it is in the traditional dichotomy between procedural law and substantive law.

5   The French lawyer Raymond Saleilles (1901) proposed that the phenomenon that he called *contrat d'adhesion* should be distinguished from contract law proper.

then tried to come to terms with this phenomenon in various ways.[6] To some extent this promoted the development of certain specific nuances in contract law when applied to standard form conditions.

Later some countries developed specific legislation on standard form conditions, of which the German Act on General Conditions from 1976 was probably the most important.[7] This Act, which dealt with both the incorporation and interpretation problems, as well as with the fairness problem, only applied to standard form conditions (general contract conditions). Later, in the German *Schuldrechtsreform*, these provisions were included in the *BGB* in a specific chapter on general contract conditions.[8] These are defined as contract conditions which are pre-formulated for a multitude of contracts and which one party sets for the other when the contract is concluded (§ 305). Provisions on general conditions (*algemene voorwaarden*) have been included in a specific part of the new Dutch civil code as well.[9]

The German Act has had a strong influence on the content of the EC Unfair Contract Terms Directive. The preparation of the Directive started from the assumption that all consumer contracts, both standard form contracts and individually negotiated contracts, should be covered.[10] However, this was criticised, especially in German doctrine: the fairness control of individually negotiated contracts was said to be in conflict with private autonomy and the functioning of the market economy.[11] This criticism lead to the result that the scope of application of the adopted Directive was restricted to contracts which have 'not been individually negotiated' (Art. 3). In other words, the Directive is focused on standard form conditions and excludes individual terms from its scope. However, the definition of the scope of the Directive is not limited solely to standard form conditions. It covers also such individual terms set forth by the seller or supplier concerning which there has been no negotiation. The scope of the Directive therefore is relatively broad, covering all cases where the consumer did not have a real possibility of influencing the content of the disputed term.[12] Even 'pre-formulated' oral agreements seem to be covered.[13]

The central provision of the Unfair Contracts Terms Directive has been adopted more or less intact in the Principles of European Contract Law. The fairness rule in the Principles is applicable to all terms which have not been negotiated individually (Art. 4:110). In other words, the Commission on European Contract Law sticks to the exclusion of individually negotiated terms from the scope of the principle of fairness,

---

6   In German legal doctrine Raiser (1935) soon became a leading monograph. Among the numerous works written on the subject, Kessler (1943), Hondius (1978), Rakoff (1983) and Bernitz (1993) are some of the best known. See also for more references, e.g., Zweigert & Kötz (1998), pp. 333 ff.

7   *Gesetz zur Regelung des Rechts der Allgemeinen Geschäftsbedingungen*, BGBl 76 I 3317.

8   *Gesetz zur Modernisierung des Schuldrechts*, BGB Arts. 305-310.

9   See the Dutch Civil Code, Arts. 6:231-247.

10 See the 1990 proposal: *OJ* 1990, C 243/3.

11 Brandner & Ulmer (1991), pp. 652 ff.

12 The Commission has in fact claimed that 'the rather broad definition of non-negotiated terms in the common position will make it possible to cover the majority of cases which raise problems for consumers', Communication from the Commission to the European Parliament, Re: Common position of the Council on the proposal for a Directive on unfair terms in consumer contracts.

13 According to the preamble of the Directive 'the consumer must receive equal protection under contracts concluded by word of mouth and written contracts'.

but extends its application to other contracts than consumer contracts. The same limitation of scope appears also in the rules on the incorporation problem (Art. 2:104) and the interpretation problem (Arts. 5:103 and 5:104).[14] In the Principles the exact meaning of the term 'individually negotiated' is not defined,[15] and it should therefore probably be understood in the same way as this term in the Directive.

Finally, the UNIDROIT Principles contain a relatively extensive regulation of the incorporation problem (Art. 2.19-2.22) as well as an interpretation rule (Art. 4.6). The rules on incorporation apply to 'standard terms', which are defined as 'provisions which are prepared in advance for general and repeated use by one party and which are actually used without negotiation with the other party' (Art. 2.19(2)). The coverage of this is not as extensive as that in the Principles of European Contract Law, as it is more clearly restricted to standard form contracting proper.

As this presentation already shows, the need for some specific provisions on standard form conditions (or on terms which have not been individually negotiated) seems to be largely recognised. There is an obvious practical need for at least some rules on the incorporation problem and the connected battle-of-the-forms problem. However, when discussing the fairness problem, and to some extent also the interpretation problem, one may question to what extent one should restrict the scope of the rules only to standard form conditions. In general, such limitations emphasise the procedural approach: the question of how the contract was made – individually negotiated or not – becomes a key issue. The criticism of the earlier drafts of the Unfair Contract Terms Directive shows very clearly how the restriction of its scope to cover only contract terms which have not been individually negotiated reflects a strong commitment to the procedural contract paradigm. As long as the terms of the contract have actually been negotiated, the law is not interested in the substantive outcome of the contract. A more substantive approach, on the other hand, would focus more directly on the fair content of the contract, and would therefore not limit the scope of the fairness provision only to contracts that have not been individually negotiated. The relationship between procedural and substantive elements is discussed further below in the analysis of the solutions to the fairness problem.

In those cases where there is a need for specific provisions on standard form contracting, e.g. concerning the incorporation problem, the wording of the provision on scope used in the Unfair Contract Terms Directive and in the Principles of European Contract Law is preferable to a pure focus on 'standard form conditions' or 'standard terms'. A wording which refers to terms which have 'not been individually negotiated' is more flexible and more clearly reflects the nature of the problem. From the point of view of the party that cannot influence the content of the terms, it is relatively irrelevant whether the terms were pre-formulated for repeated use or drafted for the present contract only. In fact, with today's use of computerised documents, this party may not even be able to know which terms were standardised in this sense.

---

14 In addition, the term 'individually negotiated' is also used in Art. 2:105 on merger clauses. See also Art. 2:209 on conflicting general conditions, where the reference to the lack of individual negotiation is made part of a definition of general conditions.

15 It is also not discussed in the comments; see Lando & Beale (2000), p. 266. The comment on Art. 5:103 mentions briefly that the provision 'may also apply to a contract of adhesion which has been drawn up for the particular occasion but which is non-negotiable', Lando & Beale (2000), p. 294.

In addition, a flexible definition of the scope of the incorporation rule is more in line with a flexible fairness rule, as the extent of actual negotiations certainly is one factor to be taken into account even within a more substantive paradigm.

Finally, it should be expressly mentioned that the Unfair Contract Terms Directive as a consumer protection measure only covers consumer contracts. However, as both the Principles of European Contract Law and the UNIDROIT Principles, as well as German law, show, it is not necessary to restrict the scope of the rules on standard form conditions to consumer contracts only.[16] The type of relation may of course be taken into account in the details of the rules and in their application.

4　The Incorporation Problem

In practice, there are many ways for a party to attempt to incorporate standard form conditions into an individual contract, ranging from having the conditions printed in the contract document to only short – or in some cases even implied – references to the conditions in the contract. This is not the place to discuss the specific legal niceties of the techniques of incorporation found in various jurisdictions. Instead, we can take a closer look at some more or less common general solutions which are designed to create some consistency between the recognition of standard form conditions and the ideals behind the procedural contract paradigm.

Seen from this perspective, the problem is how to construct some form of consent of one party to the conditions imposed by the other. From a practical point of view it seems impossible to require genuine consent in all cases, in the sense that a party should have read the conditions, understood them and accepted them, as in many situations parties do not bother even to read the conditions. On the other hand it would not be acceptable to give force to more or less 'secret' norms that are totally beyond the reach of the party. Consequently, the usual compromise solution is to construct a kind of potential consent. It is seen as a minimum requirement for the conditions to become binding on a party that this party has had at least an opportunity to acquaint itself with the conditions when the contract was made.

In fact such a rule is applied in many countries. German law expressly requires that a party shall have the opportunity in a reasonable way to become acquainted with the conditions in order to be bound by them.[17] A similar rule can be found in the Dutch Civil Code.[18] The doctrine and practice in the Nordic countries have developed on the same lines.[19] Even secondary EC law recognises, at least indirectly, the need to have access to the standard form conditions. In the Annex to the Unfair Contract

---

16　Neither does it seem necessary to adopt an express limitation of the scope of certain provisions in relation to rather precisely defined medium-sized and big businesses (Dutch Civil Code Art.6:235), as such 'on/off' rules produce unnecessary disparities in the system. These factors can be taken into account in a more flexible manner in the application of provisions with a general scope.

17　After the *Schuldrechtsreform* this provision is in *BGB* § 305(2): '*die Möglichkeit...in zumutbarer Weise...von ihrem Inhalt Kenntnis zu nehmen*'.

18　Art. 6:233(b). The Dutch Civil Code also contains provisions defining reasonable opportunity (Art. 6:234(1)) that seem very detailed and technical.

19　See e.g. Bernitz (1993), p. 32 and Wilhelmsson (1995-II), p. 67.

Terms Directive, which contains an 'indicative' list of terms that may be regarded as unfair, example (i) states that a term which has the object or effect of 'irrevocably binding the consumer to terms with which he had no real opportunity of becoming acquainted before the conclusion of the contract' is unfair.[20] The Electronic Commerce Directive, again, even requires that the conditions 'must be made available in a way that allows him [the recipient] to store and reproduce them'.[21] Against this background it is not surprising that the Principles of European Contract Law require that the party invoking standard form conditions has taken 'reasonable steps to bring them to the other party's attention before or when the contract was concluded' and state that a mere reference is not sufficient in this respect (Art. 2:104). If the other party does not have knowledge of the terms, they 'must be included in the document or other steps taken to inform the party of them.'[22] Although there are jurisdictions where this requirement has not been adopted,[23] it seems justified as a minimum rule if one wishes to respect, at least as a fiction, the ideas behind the traditional procedural contract paradigm.

However, one may well go further within the procedural paradigm. A so-called 'red hand rule', which is designed to prevent a party using onerous terms to sneak them into the contract without the knowledge of the other party, is in force in a number of countries. According to German law surprising terms – terms which the other party should not expect – are not binding.[24] Such terms become effective only if the party who wishes to rely on them specifically informs the other party before the conclusion of the contract. Similar rules are to be found in other countries as well.[25] The UNIDROIT Principles seem to go even a short step further (Art.2.20): terms which the other party could not reasonably have expected must be expressly accepted by that party in order to become effective – merely waving the 'red hand' is not sufficient.

Rules like these are certainly necessary in a legal regulation on standard form conditions nowadays. They represent a step in the direction of including substantive elements – is the term onerous/uncommon? – in the framework of a procedural paradigm. It is therefore rather disappointing that, for example, the Principles of European Contract Law lack an explicit 'red hand rule'. However, the general requirement of the Principles, mentioned above, that the party invoking terms which have

---

20 This has been said to imply that even such standard forms that are signed by the consumers may be regarded as unenforceable if the contract form was presented to the consumer at such a late point in the contracting process that he had no opportunity to become acquainted with its content; see Padfield (1995), p. 178.

21 Directive 2000/31/EC of the European Parliament and of the Council of 8 June 2000 on certain legal aspects of information society services, in particular electronic commerce, in the Internal Market (Directive on electronic commerce), *OJ 2000*, L 178/1, Art. 10(3).

22 Lando & Beale (2000), p. 150.

23 As in common law; see e.g. Adams (1994), p. 243; *Thompson* v. *LMS* [1930] 1 KB 41 is illustrative.

24 *BGB* § 305c(1).

25 See for Austria *ABGB* § 864a; for England e.g. *Interfoto Picture Library* v. *Stiletto Visual Programmes* [1988] 1 All ER 348 and *AEG (UK)* v. *Logic Resource* [1996] C.L.C. 265; and for the Nordic countries Bernitz (1993), pp. 36 ff., and Wilhelmsson (1995-II), pp. 87 ff. The provision on unreasonably onerous terms in the Dutch Civil Code Art. 6:233(a) seems to be related both to the rule described here and to the fairness rule analysed below.

not been individually negotiated should have taken 'reasonable steps' to bring them to the other party's attention (Art.2:104) might be interpreted as implying such a rule.[26]

The acceptance of a 'red hand rule' should not, however, be seen as a radical departure from a traditional procedural contract paradigm, but rather as an attempt to take such a paradigm seriously. The basic problem of a procedural paradigm, that is the fact that even informed consent, when given by a party in an inferior bargaining position, may not ensure that the contract is fair, is not solved by the 'red hand rule'. It therefore represents only a partial solution to the problems under consideration and does not eliminate the need for a substantive fairness provision.

5   The Battle-of-the-Forms Problem

In connection with the incorporation problem one should also mention the specific problem of conflicting general conditions. Which conditions should apply when, in the process of concluding the contract, both parties have referred to their own standard conditions but no explicit choice has been made at that stage?

This 'battle-of-the-forms' problem is not uncommon in commercial relations. It is therefore surprising that the solutions in Europe are very different and often relatively unsettled.[27] In some countries, such as the Netherlands, the 'first shot' rule is preferred: if offer and acceptance contain references to different conditions, the second reference usually has no effect.[28] In others, like England, the 'last shot' rule most often prevails.[29] The Nordic countries again may be mentioned as examples of partially unsettled and partially very individualising approaches, where ultimately assessments *in casu* will be decisive.[30]

The first shot rule and the last shot rule are both extremely procedural solutions. The timing of the reference to the conditions in the contracting procedure becomes a very crucial factor. A more substantive approach, which takes the content of the conditions of both parties into account, seems more practical and in line with what today's contract paradigm needs.

It is therefore certainly to be welcomed that traditional solutions that focus only on the procedure in which the conditions were introduced in the contracting process have been replaced in the UNIDROIT Principles by a substantive method which compares the content of the conditions. As a main rule here the contract is considered to have been concluded on the basis of those standard terms 'which are common in substance' (Art. 2.22). This 'knock out' rule, focusing on what is 'common in sub-

---

26 The examples in the Comments do not, however, give any support for this; see Lando & Beale (2000), pp. 149 ff.
27 A good comparative analysis is made by Göranson (1988).
28 Dutch Civil Code Art. 6:225(3).
29 See *B.R.S.* v. *Arthur Crutchley* [1967] 2 All E.R. 285, as well as *Butler Machine Tool Co.* v. *Ex-Cell-O Corporation (England) Ltd.* [1979] 1 All E.R. 965.
30 See e.g. Göranson (1988), pp. 134 ff., 170 ff. Lando & Beale (2000), p. 185 contains an illustrative summary of many of the various positions taken in Nordic law.

stance', has also been adopted in the Principles of European Contract Law (Art. 2:209). The reference to substance in these rules is intended to make clear that differences in wording are not relevant as long as the substance is (more or less) the same.[31]

Of course the common substance rule solves only a part of the problem, as in many cases the disagreement between the parties is related precisely to the fact that the substance of their conditions is different.[32] In such cases the 'knock out rule' leads to a gap in the contract which should be filled with non-mandatory law.[33] In this respect also, substantive deliberations concerning the content of the contract, not the procedure when the contract was made, should be decisive.

6 The Interpretation Problem

Traditionally courts have often tried to relieve the problems connected with the use of standard form conditions with the help of specific approaches to the interpretation of such conditions.

The rule on interpretation of standard form conditions *in dubio contra stipulatorem* or *contra proferentem* is very widely accepted in European jurisdictions.[34] It has also, applied to consumer relations, been introduced in EC law through the Unfair Contract Terms Directive (Art. 5). Both the Principles of European Contract Law (Art. 5:103) and the UNIDROIT Principles (Art. 4.6) mention it. It clearly belongs to the common European legal heritage.

In this context, however, one may ask whether it is a good idea to restrict the scope of this rule only to standard form conditions (or terms not individually negotiated). In contrast to the other above-mentioned examples the UNIDROIT Principles do not contain such a limitation, but offers a more general rule on interpretation according to which contract terms 'supplied by one party' should be preferentially interpreted against that party. Such a rule puts in more general terms the party that was responsible for the unclearness at an interpretative disadvantage.[35] In contrast to a rule restricted only to standard form conditions, it does not convey the impression that problems of balance due to one-sided drafting do not exist within individually negotiated contracts.

When speaking of legislation, one may even question whether the rule is important enough – especially after the introduction of a substantive fairness principle – and not too self-evident to be expressly enacted.[36] As the Unfair Contract Terms Directive

---

31 Lando & Beale (2000), p. 183, where also an example concerning the difficulties in deciding what is 'common in substance' is given.

32 This is underlined by Hellner (1993), p. 51.

33 E.g. by the Principles of European Contract Law; see Lando & Beale (2000), p. 183.

34 See e.g., as examples on legislation, the German *BGB* § 305c(2), the Austrian *ABGB* § 915 and the Italian *CC* Art. 1370.

35 See e.g. the extensive analysis by Huser (1983), pp. 553 ff. For a general legislative formulation, see e.g. Austrian law, *ABGB* § 915 and Spanish law, *CC* Art. 1288.

36 However, on the controversies in implementing this rule from the Unfair Contract Terms Directive, see Hondius (1997), p. 124.

has resolved this matter for EC law, at least with regard to consumer contracts where an express enactment can be defended with reference to informational needs,[37] it need not be further discussed in this context.

A brief reference to the rule that individually negotiated terms take preference over standardised ones, which seems to be an equally generally accepted rule of interpretation,[38] is also sufficient in this context. This rather self-evident rule can hardly be disputed; one may, however, doubt the need for express enactment. Of course, in consumer relationships and similar contexts it might, from an informational point of view, be useful to emphasise expressly, for example, that oral agreements can supersede standard form conditions.

7   The Fairness Problem

These remedies to the problems connected with the use of standard form conditions, which are basically procedural, can only solve some of the problems of unfairness in contracting. As P.S. Atiyah has noted, 'it is no longer possible to accept without serious qualification the idea that the law is today solely concerned with the bargaining process and not with the result.'[39]

In many countries more or less vaguely worded general clauses allow the courts to intervene against unfair contract terms. In Germany, terms in standard forms are not to be given effect if contrary to good faith, they place the other party at an unreasonable disadvantage.[40] The famous provision in the Nordic Contracts Acts[41] § 36 uses the concept of unfairness: contract terms which are unfair or whose application leads to unfairness shall not be applied. However, there are also countries which traditionally have not given such a power to the courts – or where the courts have not taken it – except within very strict limits. The obvious example is English law. In spite of its name, the Unfair Contract Terms Act 1977 does not contain any general recognition of the fairness principle, but is applicable only to exclusion clauses.[42]

However, today the Unfair Contract Terms Directive has established a contractual fairness principle for the whole European Union, at least in the field of consumer law. In this area English law has also been forced to recognise the principle of fairness.[43]

---

37 This argument is used by Hondius (1987), pp. 232 ff.
38 See e.g. *BGB* § 305b, the Principles of European Contract Law Art. 5:104 and the UNIDROIT Principles Art. 2.21.
39 Atiyah (1986), p. 346.
40 *BGB* § 307.
41 In Sweden *Lag om avtal och andra rättshandlingar på förmögenhetsrättens område* (1915:218), in Finland *Laki varallisuusoikeudellisista oikeustoimista* (228/1929).
42 The attempt of Lord Denning to create a doctrine of inequality of bargaining power in *Lloyds Bank v. Bundy* [1975] QB 326 was rejected by the higher courts; see e.g. *National Westminster Bank v. Morgan* [1985] AC 686.
43 See e.g. on English law Department of Trade and Industry, Implementation of the EC Directive on unfair terms in consumer contracts (93/13/EEC), A Consultation Document (1993), Introduction: 'The main effect of the Directive will be to introduce for the first time a general concept of fairness into the UK law of contract'.

The formula used in the Directive resembles the German one to some extent: a term 'shall be regarded as unfair if, contrary to the requirement of good faith, it causes a significant imbalance in the parties' rights and obligations arising under the contract' (Art. 3). This formula is later reproduced in the Principles of European Contract Law (Art. 4:110)[44] and here enlarged to cover not only consumer contracts but commercial contracts as well (as long as the terms have not been individually negotiated). Through the Directive and the Principles the substantive paradigm for controlling unfair terms is recognised as a part of the European legal culture.

However, there are good grounds to question the procedural limitation of the scope of the fairness principle to cover only contracts that have not been individually negotiated.[45] The fairness provisions in the Nordic Contracts Acts give the courts the power to adjust both standardised and purely individual contract terms and this power has been used in practice, both in consumer and business relations. Even negotiated terms may, due to imbalances in bargaining power, be so unfair that they should not be upheld as such. A substantive contract paradigm accepts the possibility that a court may intervene in such cases as well. A general fairness rule is also more practical in the sense that difficult problems of interpreting and applying the limitations can be avoided. In this context a strict legal definition of 'standard form conditions' or 'individual negotiation' is unnecessary, as the concrete facts in connection with the making of the contract can be taken into account as arguments in the assessment of fairness.

In fact the Principles of European Contract Law can be said to be more traditionally procedural than the Unfair Contract Terms Directive in this respect. The Directive is only a minimum Directive, and one of the main reasons for the limitation of its scope to terms which have not been individually negotiated was the difficulty in reaching unanimity with respect to the fairness control of individually negotiated contracts.[46] However, what is only a minimum in the Directive is made the rule in the Principles! Therefore one may claim that the Principles at this point represent a relatively traditional, procedurally geared approach to contract law.

Another feature of the Directive and its reflection in the Principles is liable to the same criticism for its emphasis on traditional procedural thinking instead of on a straightforward substantive approach to the unfairness of contracts. The Directive (Art. 4(2)) and the Principles (Art. 4:110(2)) exclude so-called core provisions of the contract from their sphere of application. The fairness test is not concerned with the definition of the main subject matter of the contract and the adequacy of the price. This reflects the procedural idea that the parties at least to some extent negotiate or are aware of those parts of the contract whose content should be determined by the market.[47] These assumptions, however, are not so obviously based on reality that they

---

44 The Principles, however, refer to 'the requirements of good faith and fair dealing'.
45 See also Zweigert & Kötz (1998), p. 345.
46 The Preamble to the Directive notes that it was necessary to restrict the Directive to contractual terms that have not been individually negotiated because national laws only allowed partial harmonisation. In its Communication to the Parliament the Commission regretted this limitation in the Directive; see COM(92) 66 final.
47 See e.g. Brandner & Ulmer (1991), p. 656.

would convince a person who thinks the courts should not enforce substantively unfair bargains.[48] Here, again, the Principles are more conservative than the Directive, as they make a rule out of a minimum requirement.

In addition, some other aspects of the Directive, such as the focusing of the fairness test on 'the circumstances attending the conclusion of the contract' (Art. 4(1))[49] and certain procedural interpretations of the good faith requirement,[50] reveal attempts to cling as tightly as possible to the procedural paradigm even within the substantive fairness provision.[51]

In a way, the fairness provision presents in a nutshell a fundamental conflict of approaches to contract law in Europe. On the one hand a substantive fairness provision is required if the law is to properly reflect the partially welfarist values of late 20th century contract law. On the other hand, the models which are given by the Unfair Contract Terms Directive and the Principles of European Contract Law still emphasise the procedural elements so strongly that some, for example in the Nordic countries, may look at them rather as steps backwards in the development of contract law.

8 Conclusion

On many basic points, the rules on standard form conditions in the various European countries seem relatively similar, especially after the adoption of the Unfair Contract Terms Directive. There are, however, without question, important differences between, for example, the English legal climate, which favours private autonomy, and the Nordic countries' more ready acceptance of substantive fairness control of contract terms (with Germany probably somewhere in between). Some of these differences may contribute to useful learning processes in European law, as the Unfair Contract Terms Directive shows. These learning processes do not, however, necessarily lead to the adoption of identical rules. Although it would be advantageous from the point of view of businesses dealing in the internal market to have similar ground rules concerning the use of standard form conditions throughout the market, the goal can hardly be a 'free movement of standard forms' as such. One certainly has to place some requirements on language of the conditions, at least in consumer relations.[52]

---

48 E.g. in the fairness-friendly Nordic countries the scope of the general clauses in the Contracts Acts § 36 is not limited in such a way.

49 See more closely e.g. Wilhelmsson (1995-I), pp. 148 ff.

50 See the preamble to the Directive: 'whereas, in making an assessment of good faith, particular regard shall be had to the strength of the bargaining positions of the parties, whether the consumer had an inducement to agree to the term...' A strongly procedural interpretation of the good faith requirement is recently given by the House of Lords; *The Director General of Fair Trading v. First National Bank plc* [2001] UKHL 52.

51 However, in the first decision of the ECJ, *Océano Grupo Editorial SA* v. *Rocio Murciano Quintero*, and other cases, Joined Cases C-240/98 to C-244/98, the reasoning of the court was rather substantive (in the sense of this chapter, that is, it was oriented towards the content of the term; the decision concerned an issue connected with procedural law, the fairness of a jurisdiction clause).

52 See e.g. Howells & Wilhelmsson (1997), pp. 109 ff.

Looking at the various solutions, one may wish to press for a clearer emphasis on substantive elements than is the case in many jurisdictions today. Above all, there are good grounds to question whether the fairness provision should be confined to standard form contracting alone. Rather one should look at the fairness provision as a substantive (content-oriented) ground rule in any modern contract paradigm, within which one may take into account also procedural elements, such as whether the contract was standardised or individually negotiated by the parties.[53] A fairness provision which is not limited to certain types of terms or to certain parts of the contract would be the cornerstone of such an approach.

One might even take a step further in the substantive direction by taking seriously the question why one should accept as a starting point that businesses and/or their organisations should have the right to create a legal order for themselves in which they are in a better position than they would be according to non-mandatory law.[54] This does not mean that the use of standard form conditions as such should be abandoned. On the contrary, rational contracting in a society of mass distribution, production and consumption certainly requires the use of standardised conditions. One can, however, question the use of standardised terms which have the sole or primary purpose of improving the legal position of the party using the terms in relation to the other party. This would imply a change in the burden of proof (or rather the burden of reasoning) relating to the (un)fairness of the conditions. Instead of taking the binding force of the conditions as a starting point and requiring the other party to show that they are unfair if it does not want to be bound by them, one could put the burden on the party who uses the conditions. The point of departure for such a substantive paradigm would be the principle that terms which put the other party in a less favourable position than it would be under non-mandatory law should be considered binding only if the party using them can justify their use. Such justifiable grounds could relate for example to the legitimate need to make precise and well-suited rules for a particular type of contractual relation.

BIBLIOGRAPHY: J.N. Adams, Unconscionability and the Standard Form Contract, in R. Brownsword, G. Howells & T. Wilhelmsson (eds.), *Welfarism in Contract Law* (1994), pp. 230-247; P.S. Atiyah, *Essays on Contract* (1986); U. Bernitz, *Standardavtalsrätt* (6th ed., 1993); H.E. Brandner & P. Ulmer, The Community directive on unfair terms in consumer contracts: some critical remarks on the proposal submitted by the EC Commission, 28 *CMLR* (1991), pp. 647-662; S. Bright, Winning the battle against unfair contract terms, 20 *Legal Studies* (2000), pp. 331-352; H. Collins, Good Faith in European Contract Law, 14 *Oxford Journal of Legal Studies* (1994), pp. 229-254; U. Göranson, *Kolliderande standardavtal* (1988); J. Hellner, *Kommersiell avtalsrätt* (4th ed., 1993); E. Hondius, *Standaardvoorwaarden* (1978); E. Hondius, *Unfair Terms in Consumer Contracts* (1987); E. Hondius, Unfair contract terms: towards a European Law. Introduction, 5 *European Review of Private Law* (1997), pp. 121-134; G. Howells & T. Wilhelmsson, *EC Consumer Law* (1997); K. Huser, *Avtaletolking* (1983); F. Kessler, Contracts of Adhesion – Some Thoughts About Freedom of Contract, 43

---

53 In addition to the private law rules, an efficient regulation of standard form contracting would require various rules addressing such questions as authority control, collective action, etc. As mentioned in the introduction to this chapter this very important aspect will not be analysed here.

54 The theme of Kessler (1943).

Colum.L.Rev. (1943), pp. 629; O. Lando & H. Beale (eds.), *Principles of European Contract Law, Parts I and II* (2000); A. Padfield, The Impact on English Contract Law of the EC Directive on Unfair Terms in Consumer Contracts, 5 *Journal of International Banking Law* (1995), pp. 175-182; L. Raiser, *Das Recht der allgemeinen Geschäftsbedingungen* (1935); T.D. Rakoff, Contracts of Adhesion: An Essay in Reconstruction, 96 *Harvard Law Review* (1983), pp. 1173-1284; R. Saleilles, *De la déclaration de volonté* (1901); T. Wilhelmsson, *Social Contract Law and European Integration* (1995-I); T. Wilhelmsson, *Standardavtal* (2nd ed., 1995-II); K. Zweigert & H. Kötz, *An Introduction to Comparative Law* (3rd ed., 1998).

CHAPTER 25

Interpretation of Contracts

Claus-Wilhelm Canaris* & Hans Christoph Grigoleit**

1 Theoretical Background

1.1 Interpretation as Part of General Hermeneutics and its Characteristics

The issue of interpretation arises when there is an ambiguity in the content of a contract. This is an omnipresent phenomenon of contract law: Even a thoroughly drafted and apparently precise contract may, under close scrutiny, prove to be in need of interpretation. Virtually every understanding of a contract includes – albeit often unsaid – an interpretation. In fact, the mere statement that a contract does not require or allow interpretation constitutes in itself an act of interpretation and the result of such an interpretation. From a philosophical point of view, therefore, the topic of interpretation of contracts forms a part of hermeneutics, i.e. the general theory of understanding human expressions. Indeed, there are some hermeneutic insights which also guide the interpretation of contracts. The founding principle of hermeneutics, for instance, that the interpretation of a word may be influenced by its context, applies to a contract just the same as to a piece of literature. The idea that a text can be "more intelligent than its author" and, accordingly, often has a meaning which the author was totally unaware of sometimes proves as useful for contracts as for other sorts of texts.

More important, however, than such connections with the general theory of hermeneutics are the peculiarities of the interpretation of contracts. For the recipient of a love letter, for example, it only matters whether its author *really* meant his or her words, even if this understanding has found no outward expression but has remained purely inward. As opposed to this, a contract could obviously not fulfil its legal and economic function if the purely internal understanding of the author were decisive in every case. A similar statement can be made about the ambiguity of words. For example, a poet may use ambiguities on purpose as a stylistic device so that the interpreter has to highlight them, whereas the parties of a contract, and therefore also its interpreter, should avoid ambiguities as far as possible. Finally, the autonomous significance of interpreting contracts as compared to other fields of hermeneutics becomes obvious if one looks at the phenomenon of "gaps". While a gap in a contract may potentially be filled by "constructive" interpretation (cf. 3.3.2), a scholar of literature would thoroughly misunderstand his job if he supplemented a drama by a scene which the author himself failed to write or whose text was lost. The interpretation of contracts is therefore primarily determined by *legal* requirements and value judgements. Consequently, the *legal* principles on which contractual interpretation is based have to be considered first.

---

* Professor of Civil, Trade, Labour Law and Law Philosophy at the University of Regensburg.
** Professor of Civil, Trade and Company Law, European Private Law, University of Regensburg.

1.2 Self-Determination and Freedom of Contract as Starting Point

The interpretation of contracts must comply with their function which is primarily to enable the parties to govern their legal relations by themselves. Nowadays, the principle of freedom of contract applies as a general rule, in all European legal systems.[1] This is aptly expressed in Art. 1:102 (1) PECL: "Parties are free to enter into a contract and to determine its contents, subject to the requirements of good faith and fair dealing, and the mandatory rules...". Similarly, Art. 2.1. CEC states: "Les parties peuvent librement déterminer le contenu du contrat, dans les limites imposées par les règles impératives, les bonnes mœurs et l'ordre public...". While the Treaty of the European Communities does not explicitly guarantee the principle of freedom of contract, it is generally accepted as a fundamental underlying idea[2] because the exercise of the expressly stated Community freedoms is only conceivable on the basis of freely negotiated contracts.

1.2.1 The Justification of Freedom of Contract

The principle of freedom of contract has several roots. From an ethical point of view, it is based upon the idea that the state must respect the autonomy of the individual. This assumption can be derived from the dignity of man and his right of "free development of his personality", of "pursuit of happiness" or similar concepts. These rights are violated if the state does not generally leave it to the individuals to regulate their relations themselves, but rather prescribes every detail; because by doing so the state turns into a guardian of the individuals, and this is irreconcilable with their dignity – a notion that has won nearly complete recognition in Europe since the age of enlightenment. Thus, freedom of contract is an expression of the legal self-determination of the human being and a sub-category of the autonomy of the individual.

In addition, the principle of freedom of contract has a foundation in political theory. It corresponds both to the ideas of democracy and of separation of powers. *Democracy* and freedom of contract are based upon the same basic values: on legal liberty and on the equality of the citizens. *Hans Kelsen* justly called the contract a "markedly democratic method of creating rights and duties" because the "subjects that are to be bound participate in the creation of the binding rule".[3] The link to the idea of democracy also becomes quite obvious if one considers the classic wording of Art. 1134 CC: "Les conventions légalement formées tiennent lieu de loi (!) à ceux qui les ont faites". The principle of *separation of powers* is strengthened considerably by a free contractual exchange[4] – in particular if the principle of competition is obeyed as well. This is because freedom of contract counterbalances the concentration of power in the government by shifting, within its area of operation, the competence to take legal decisions from the government to the citizen.

---

1 Cf. the overview in PECL, 2000, pp. 99 *et seq.*
2 Cf. ECJ Judgment of 05/10/1999 (*Spain/Commission*), C- 240/97, ECR 1999 p. I-6571, 6634 (No. 99); *Grundmann* JZ, 1996, 274, 278; 591.
3 Cf. *Kelsen*, Reine Rechtslehre, 2nd ed. 1960, p. 285.
4 See *Bydlinski*, Privatrecht und umfassende Gewaltenteilung, 2. Festschrift für Wilburg, 1975, 53, 67.

Finally, modern welfare economics accentuate and describe more precisely the *social* function of free contracting. According to the *Pareto*-criterion, the *voluntary* exchange by contract is the paradigm of economic efficiency. The individual exchange and its efficiency correspond on the collective level with the institution of the market: The mechanism of the market brings the independent transactions to perfection and, when operating ideally, creates optimal *Pareto*-efficiency. Thus, contract and market guarantee an efficient distribution of resources and a maximisation of social wealth, while, of course, not exhaustively solving the problem of just distribution.[5] Accordingly, the primary postulate of the *Coase* theorem to the legal system is that it should allow the voluntary exchange of goods and make it as easy as possible by lowering the cost of transactions.[6]

1.2.2 The Aim of Interpretation: Ascertaining the Intention of the Parties

If the right of self-determination is taken seriously it necessarily includes the freedom to pursue and to agree to something unreasonable – just as the vote in a democratic decision is not subject to any control of reasonableness. Not reason but the intentions of the parties, therefore, form the basis of the contract according to the maxim: "Stat pro ratione voluntas".[7] This implies that the legal system only has to make sure that the decision of the parties is as free as possible not only in its legal but also in practical circumstances.

This assumption is in accordance with the fact that the economic goal of efficiency is to achieve at the greatest possible compliance with the individual preferences. Thus, the assessment of personal utility is left to the sole discretion of the individual. It is no contradiction that this utility is also measured by its monetary value, because money, in economic theory, merely has an instrumental character in relation to the individual evaluation of the utility. The individual determines the monetary value of his utility in the context of the transaction. However, this again does not preclude discussion on the issue of just distribution.

Accordingly, it is not legitimate to impose "reasonable" solutions upon the parties by means of interpretation. Rather, the goal of interpretation is to determine the intention of the parties – primarily the actual, alternatively the hypothetical intention. Only if this fails, may one resort to the "reasonable" intention; because it has then to be assumed that the parties are rational actors and thus intended something reasonable in case of doubt. The prevalence of the actual over the reasonable intention is generally acknowledged in all European legal systems[8] and also forms the basis of the rule of Art. 5:101 (1) – (3) PECL and of the similarly phrased rule of Art. 8 CISG (for more detail see 2.1. and 2.2.). Under Italian law, to give another example, it is widely held that the rule of Art 1366 CC "il contratto deve essere interpretato secondo buona fede" is subordinate to Art 1362 CC "Nell'interpretare il contratto si deve indagare

---

5   Concerning the relation of freedom of contract and market to just distribution see detailed *Canaris*, Die Bedeutung der iustitia distributiva im deutschen Vertragsrecht, 1997, pp. 63 *et seq.*

6   Cf. In more detail e.g. *Posner*, Economic Analysis of Law, 5th ed., 1998, § 1.2. = pp. 12 *et seq.*; *Eidenmüller*, Effizienz als Rechtsprinzip, 2. Aufl:, 1998, pp. 41 *et seq.*

7   Cf. *Flume*, § 1, 5.

8   See the overview given in PECL, 2000, pp. 290 *et seq.*; *Kötz*, p. 166.

quale sia stata la commune intenzione delle parti...".[9] By contrast, it is questionable that Art. 39.4. CEC rules: "En tout état de cause, l'interprétation du contrat ne doit aboutir à un résultat qui soit contraire à la bonne foi ou au bon sens". If the parties intended such a result in an agreement it is not the task of interpretation to correct it; rather this may happen, if at all, according to the rules of law concerning the nullity of contracts.

1.3 Legal Certainty, Protection of Reliance and Individual Responsibility as Correlatives of Self-Determination

1.3.1 The Problem of a Diverging Understanding by the Parties

There are (at least) two parties involved in a contract. Therefore the intention of only one party cannot form by itself the authoritative criterion for the interpretation of the contract because it constitutes a purely psychological internal state and, as such, is generally not discernible by the other party. Thus, one cannot simply resort to the internal intention of the declaring party if the addressee understood the declaration differently. Conversely, the understanding of the addressee cannot be authoritative if it differs from that of the declaring party. Both assumptions directly result from the principle of freedom of contract and from the idea of self-determination. If contract terms which one of the parties neither intended nor could discern were regarded as authoritative, then his freedom of contract would be disregarded and his self-determination would virtually be turned into heteronomy.

On the other hand it would go too far to consider a contract invalid whenever the parties understood its terms differently. This would largely deprive the contract of its suitability as an instrument for effectively regulating the relations between the parties. It is therefore a compelling imperative of legal certainty to hold a party to a contract under certain circumstances, even if he was mistaken about its terms. Closely related is the notion that a party has to be protected in his reliance on the effectiveness and the terms of the contract if he understood it "correctly". It is generally fair and reasonable to hold the erring party to the "correct" terms because of, and insofar as he is responsible for, his "incorrect" understanding. Like every freedom, the freedom of contract and, accordingly, contractual self-determination correspond with responsibility, which restricts self-determination as far as it is necessary to protect individual reliance and the functioning of the markets.

1.3.2 The Balancing Approach

What is the measure to determine the "correct" understanding of the contract if both parties have a different perception of it? One could take the perspective of a non-involved third party, but this would be in conflict with the fact that the declarations are generally – i.e. apart from special situations such as the declarations in commercial papers or in a corporate contract (see below 2.4.1) – not made to be received and un-

---

9 Cf. *Cian/Trabucchi*, Art. 1366, sub II. Some authors, however, attribute priority to the *interpretazione secondo buona fede*; see e.g. *Bianca*, p. 420 and 424.

derstood by an "outsider" but by the addressee. Therefore, it is consequent to take the addressee's perspective as the relevant point of view, because the contract is an act of communication with this party only and it concerns only his or her interests. To define this perspective more precisely, one has to assume that the addressee seeks to understand the meaning of the declaration in a reasonable way and in good faith. On the one hand, it is not expecting too much of the declaring party under the postulate of individual responsibility to be bound by a reasonable and fair understanding and on the other hand, only reliance in such an understanding deserves protection by the law.

Therefore, this view has two sides. The declaring party *as well as* the addressee is held to an understanding which the latter party was able to have and ought to have had when a reasonable standard of good faith is applied. The test works *equally* for and against *both* parties: As little as the declaring party can allege his or her understanding when it is not reasonable or against good faith, he is not to be held to an unreasonable or unfaithful understanding the addressee might have had and vice versa. In this manner, the conflict described under 1.3.1 is resolved in a fair balance. Thereby, it is useful, but not necessary, to emphasise the notion of good faith besides the criterion of reasonability. The latter concerns more the aspect of rationality whereas the former has a connection to the principle of fairness. This is to say that a self-centred understanding of the contract may still seem reasonable from the perspective of one of the parties, but it is not an understanding in good faith and therefore the legal order cannot take it as a standard for the interpretation of a contract.

Art. 5:101 (3) PECL, which is modelled after Art. 8 (2) CISG, similarly refers to the perspectives of the parties by stating that "the contract is to be interpreted according to the meaning that reasonable persons of the same kind as the parties would give to it in the same circumstances". This view is generally shared in all European legal systems.[10] Under Portuguese law, for instance, the rule of Art. 236 CC almost literally corresponds to Art. 5:101 (3) PECL. Obviously, the main problem for interpretation is to find out what a reasonable and fair understanding of a contract is. To give an answer to this question all circumstances of the individual case may be relevant (see in more detail below sub 2.1).

A different matter is whether a party may avoid the contract by reasons of mistake if he or she has misunderstood the content of the contract. Some legal systems, such as the German, the Swiss and de facto the Italian as well, have special rules for such a mistake ("Inhaltsirrtum"), whereas most legal systems and Arts. 4:103 PECL, 151 CEC treat such a mistake like other mistakes.[11] This issue belongs to the doctrine of mistake which is the subject of another chapter of this book.[12] It should be emphasised in this context, however, that the rules of interpretation are to be applied with priority, i.e. a remedy on the grounds of mistake may only be taken into consideration if the contract cannot be interpreted in accordance with the assumptions of the mistaken party.[13]

---

10 See the overview in PECL, 2000, p. 291 and the citations in note 19.

11 See *Kramer*, Der Irrtum beim Vertragsschluß – eine weltweit rechtsvergleichende Bestandsaufnahme, 1998, pp. 87 *et seq.*

12 See chapter 22 by *Muriel Fabre-Magnan*.

13 See e.g. *PECL*, pp. 230 *et seq.*

1.3.3 "Subjective" and "Objective" Interpretation: The Will Theory and the Theory of Declaration

A theory of interpretation which is based on the actual intention of the parties is often called "subjective", whereas a theory which emphasises the external signs of the communicative act, such as the literal meaning of declaration in particular, is characterised as "objective". This antagonism pervades the entire history of interpretation, while the prevalence of one position over the other sometimes changed.[14] It is characteristic that Roman Law knew two different maxims of interpretation as the proposition of *Papinian* "In conventionibus contrahentium voluntatem potius quam verba spectari placuit"[15] and the word of *Paulus* "Cum in verbis nulla ambiguitas est, non debet admitti voluntatis quaestio".[16]

Historically, the objective approach with its focus on the literal meaning of the words has been the starting point. This is related to the fact that in legal systems whose development has not yet reached an advanced level there is obviously a strong leaning to formalism and therefore an overemphasis of the role of the literal meaning of contract terms. In the course of legal and judicial development, however, the modes of interpretation have become more refined and more flexible. Correspondingly, the idea of freedom of contract – which is the underlying principle of "subjective" interpretation – had to gain acceptance bit by bit against the original notion that only certain types of contracts are admissible.

Systematically, there are different issues underlying the conflict between "subjective" and "objective" interpretation. The first problem is the formalism caused by overemphasising the literal meaning of the contract. The result of such formalism can be that the parties are bound to the terms of the contract even if they have mistakenly phrased them or made them cover a situation which neither of the parties could have reasonably meant. Modern laws in principle reject such formalism. The French Code Civil, for instance, rules in Art. 1156: "On doit dans les conventions rechercher qu'elle a été la commune intention des parties contractantes, plutôt que de s'arrêter au sens littéral des termes". This formula is matched by the Italian rule of Art. 1362 CC almost literally and, likewise, the German BGB demands in § 133 BGB, "nicht an dem buchstäblichen Sinne des Ausdrucks zu haften".[17] Nevertheless the historical approach of formalism still has a certain influence today, albeit in modified forms (see 2.4.1 below).

The term "objective" interpretation fulfils a different function when it is used to describe the perspective of a reasonable party as the basis of interpretation. This perception is not about overemphasising the literal meaning of a declaration, but about its divergence from the intention of the declaring party. In this respect the "objective" approach takes into account that the declaring party has not appropriately expressed his intention and therefore the addressee cannot reasonably consider the actual intention as relevant for the interpretation of the contract. In modern contract law, this as-

---

14 A comprehensive historical analysis is provided by *Zimmermann*, pp. 621 *et seq.*
15 Pap. D. 50, 16, 219.
16 Paul. D. 32, 25, 1.
17 With the same wording under Austrian law § 914 ABGB.

pect of "objective" interpretation has prevailed for good reason, as we just have described above under 1.3.2. Yet, this "objective" approach does not proceed "formalistically" in the sense of being strictly bound to the literal meaning, but it allows an unlimited variety of other criteria to be considered in addition and besides the meaning of the words (see in more detail under 2.1).

With respect to this function of "objective" interpretation, one can draw a certain parallel to the dispute between the will theory and the theory of declaration, which played a major role in the 19th century legal discourse especially in Germany. This dispute has, however, no practical consequences for the theory of interpretation. This is to say that even the advocates of a strict will theory cannot argue that the intention of the declaring party determines the terms of the contract even if it could not have been recognised by the addressee. Doing so would mean to disregard the intention of the latter and would therefore be contradictory to its own premise. Even on the basis of a strict will theory, therefore, differences between the intention of a party and the "objective" meaning of his declaration can only have a practical impact on the question whether the contract is invalid or subject to rescission, which is answered to the affirmative under German law by § 119 Abs. 1 BGB ("Inhaltsirrtum"). The dispute between the will theory and the theory of declaration therefore becomes only relevant for the doctrine of unilateral mistake and does not prejudice the issue of interpretation.[18]

1.4   The Object of Interpretation

Interpretation is not only about the content of an agreement, but also about the logically prior question whether or not a contract has been formed at all. In some cases it may be doubtful whether a declaration is to be understood as an offer or just as an invitation to the other party to make an offer of his own (*invitatio ad offerendum*), in other cases it may be questionable whether a declaration is an offer to enter into a contract or just a declaratory message to confirm that an alleged contract has been formed before etc. To answer such questions, the same rules and criteria apply as to questions about the content of a contract.

The same applies if the parties did not express themselves in words, but merely through a certain conduct. It is common currency in contract law that a conclusive form of conduct – for example a certain motion of the head or raising a hand in a public auction – may be sufficient to imply a binding contract. This is, for example, expressly emphasised in Art. 2:102 PECL and in § 863 (1) of the Austrian ABGB. There may often be doubts about whether the conduct shown is in fact conclusive. This, too, is a problem of interpretation and therefore one has to ask how the other party reasonably had to understand the conduct in question.

2   The Rules of Interpretation

The rules of interpretation in the different European legal systems largely overlap, as all national approaches are based on the described principles and their implications.

---

18   To the same effect *Kötz*, p. 171 with note 22; *Ghestin*, no 386.

2.1 General Principle: The Intention as Seen from the Perspective of the Addressee

Corresponding to the principles discussed above (see 1.3.), most European legal systems and the PECL attempt to strike a balance between subjective and objective considerations.[19] The fundamental point for determining the content of a contract is the actual intention of parties (Arts. 2:101 (1) (a), 5:101 (1), (2) PECL). The goal of interpretation, therefore, is to establish what the intention of each party was at the time of contracting. As far as their intentions correspond, they form the content of the contract. The objective aspect of interpretation concerns the perspective that is adopted in order to determine the intention of each party. In this context, the content of each declaration has to be determined separately and the perspective of the addressee has to be adopted (cf. above 1.3.2). It is crucial how the addressee could reasonably understand the declaration in view of the individual circumstances of the case (Arts. 2:102, 5:101 (3), 6:101 (1) PECL).

In ascertaining the perspective of a reasonable addressee, it is generally irrelevant whether the declarant knew or could have known that perspective. The declarant is protected sufficiently by the rule that his reasonable perspective is relevant for the interpretation of the corresponding declaration of the other party. If the two declarations do not correspond, the parties do not consent and no valid contract is formed.[20]

When establishing the meaning of a contract, the judge must consider all circumstances which allow one to draw conclusions with regard to the intentions of the parties at the time of contracting. Special consideration has to be given to the circumstances of the negotiations. In certain cases, circumstances which occurred before the state of negotiations – e.g. particular practices which the parties have established between themselves – or after conclusion of the contract – e.g. the specific handling of a certain aspect of performance mutually agreed upon – may also be taken into account.[21] It should, however, be emphasised that, from a theoretical perspective, those circumstances, regardless of when they occurred, are only circumstantial evidence as to the *parties' intentions at the time of contracting*.

The content of a declaration is to be determined objectively only to the extent that the addressee can reasonably rely on the "normal" use of language, "the regular" meaning of a certain conduct etc. It is therefore not justifiable to use an "absolutely objective" standard, i.e. a standard which is entirely independent from the individual situation and purely based on the declaration itself or its wording. Moreover, it is almost impossible to obtain such an "absolutely objective" perspective. In evaluating an act of communication, it is generally unavoidable to respond to the individual circumstances of the case, e.g. the branch of trade involved, the objectives of the parties etc. Otherwise, there is little chance to identify the meaning of words and of other means of expression used. This is in keeping with the general rules of hermeneutics

---

19 See e.g. *Beatson*, p. 31; *Treitel*, pp. 8-9; *Ghestin*, No. 390; *Ghestin et al.*, 2001, nos. 9 *et seq.*, *Mazeaud, H. et al.* No. 123; *Cian/Trabucchi*, Art. 1362, sub X. Moreover Art. 4.1, 4.2 Unidroit Principles.

20 Such a dissent, however, is rare, because usually the reasonableness test defines identical perspectives for either party; for examples see below sub 3.1.

21 This is substantially laid down under Spanish law in Art. 1282 CC.

under which an act of communication is to be understood only with reference to its context. These aspects are neglected or at least unduly simplified when the subjective approach to interpretation is, as it is commonly done, contrasted with the objective approach. At a closer look, it is the subjective perspective of the addressee that matters and this perspective is objectified only to a certain extent, i.e. by the standard of reasonable understanding.

The wording, however, is necessarily the starting point of interpretation. It is of particular importance because it is the manifestation of the party's intention. In balancing against other criteria, the language used is normally to be given a rather significant weight. The wording may not impetuously be disregarded by arguing the reasonableness of a solution which is far from or even not at all in accordance with the text. This point may be demonstrated by using an example drawn from the Comments to Art. 5:101 (3) PECL, given there as an illustration of the objective method:[22]

A clause in an insurance contract provides that the policy covers the theft of jewellery only if there has been "clandestine entry" into the place where the jewellery was. An individual, A, pretends to be a telephone repairman and presents himself at Madame B's home to repair her telephone. A distracts B with some pretext and takes the opportunity to steal her jewels. The insurance company refuses to pay up, on the basis that there has been no "clandestine entry". *On a reasonable interpretation entry gained by fraud is a form of "clandestine entry".*

This example shows the risk of not taking the wording of the contract seriously, while the interpreter realises his own evaluation of a reasonable term. By its literal meaning, the term "clandestine entry" hardly encompasses "entry gained by fraud". One would use the term "clandestine" if the victim did not notice the entry of the thief, but not if she voluntarily admitted him into her home not realising his identity and intentions. "Entry gained by fraud" may surely not be considered to be within the core meaning of the expression "clandestine entry", but at its periphery at most. Therefore, the parties' interests and the purpose of the contract clause must be analyzed thoroughly. In this respect, significant differences between the two situations become evident. If B did not suspect that an unknown person had entered her home, she had no reason to take special care to protect her jewels from theft. On the other hand, if she deliberately admits a telephone repairman into her home, the need to lock the jewels away or keep an eye on them is apparent. The crucial factor in interpreting the ratio of the expression is the aspect of control: It is immaterial whether the thief really is a telephone repairman or just pretends to be, whereas it is decisive that B, despite being aware of an unknown person's presence, left the jewels unguarded and let herself be distracted by some pretext. This could have happened with a real telephone repairman as well. With respect to the purpose of the insurance, B's need and worthiness of protection against theft by a pretender is almost as low as against theft by a real telephone repairman and not nearly as high as against theft by unknown intruders. Thus, the case is much closer to a situation which is definitely not covered by the insurance than to one which falls into the core meaning of the clause. That is why with respect to the purpose of the insurance contract and the clause in question, its

---

22 Cf. PECL, 2000, p. 289.

wording is to be construed narrowly. Theft after "entry gained by fraud" is therefore not covered by the insurance. This example shows how the criteria of reasonableness may be applied in a rational and methodical manner: The usual meaning of the words and the purpose of the clause to be interpreted must be combined with the double comparison of the situation in question with those definitely within and those definitely without the scope of the clause. Moreover, in the example, B cannot successfully invoke the *contra proferentem* rule (cf. below 2.4.2). Although the contract was phrased by the insurer, there are no remaining doubts which justify the application of the *contra proferentem* rule after careful analysis of its wording and purpose and taking into account the parties' interests.

2.2 The Prevalence of the Recognised Intention over the Objective Meaning

If the parties' intentions correspond, but deviate from the regular understanding of their declarations, then neither party reasonably relies on the objective meaning of the contract. In such a situation, therefore, the corresponding intentions of the parties have priority over the "regular" or "correct" meaning of the declaration (*falsa demonstratio non nocet*). This priority is based on the above assumption that there is no "absolutely objective" perspective underlying the interpretation. What matters is the individual perspective of the addressee. This perspective is not purely shaped by the "bare" declarations, but also by all the circumstances which allow conclusions concerning the actual intention of the other party.

The priority of the corresponding intentions is largely agreed upon in all European legal systems.[23] One formula, which is often used (e.g. in Art. 5:101 (1) PECL and in Art. 39 II CEC), states that the corresponding intentions of the parties have priority over the literal meaning of the words.[24] If, for instance, the object of a sale is denominated as "Haakjöringsköd" and both parties take it for granted that this refers to *whalemeat*, even though "Haakjöringsköd" – according to the general use of language – means *sharksmeat*, then the contractual agreement is about whalemeat.[25] This also applies if the parties knowingly use the term sharksmeat in the wrong sense in the written contract (e.g. if they fear that trading openly with whalemeat might damage their reputation). In such situations, the priority of the corresponding intentions is in line with the generally recognised rule of simulation (Art. 6:103 PECL):[26] The true intentions of the parties prevail even if they have stipulated otherwise in an apparent contract.

The same applies if one of the parties realises or if it is obvious to him that there are certain intentions underlying the other party's declaration that contradict the normal understanding (Art. 5: 101 (2) PECL).[27] Here, the interpretation deviating from

---

23 For an overview see PECL, 2000, p. 290. For limitations see below 2.4.1. Under English law, the principle of *falsa demonstratio non nocet* is implemented with respect to written contracts by the equitable relief of rectification; see *Beatson*, pp. 339 *et seq.*

24 Cf. e.g. under French law Art. 1156 CC. Under Swiss law Art. 18 (1) OR.

25 Cf. RG 8.6. 1920, RGZ 99, 147.

26 For an overview see PECL, 2000, p. 307.

27 BGH 26.10.1984 BGH NJW 1984, 721. Under English law, again, the rules on rectification concerning unilateral mistakes lead to similar results; see Beatson, pp. 340 *et seq.* For an overview see PECL, 2000, p. 291.

the normal understanding does not correspond to the *common* intention. Yet, the addressee's reliance on the regular use of language is not worthy of protection. Rather, the addressee can reasonably be expected to reveal the discrepancy if he prefers not to be bound to the intention of the other party. In a modified version of the example given above, this means that the seller owes whalemeat if the buyer knows that the seller mistakenly uses the term "Haakjöringsköd" for whalemeat, notwithstanding that the buyer intends to enter into a contract about sharksmeat (which might be the case because sharksmeat is more valuable).

2.3   General Remarks Concerning the Definition of Further Rules

Before we turn to the discussion of further rules of interpretation, some general characteristics of the law of interpretation have to be considered.

2.3.1   The Problem of Defining Precise Rules of Interpretation

Although the principles discussed under 2.1 and 2.2 appear to be widely accepted and quite well founded, it is difficult to phrase them in more concrete terms and to complement them by further rules. The reason for this difficulty lies in the nature of communication and its fundamental dependence upon the circumstances of the individual case.[28] It is possible to establish general rules, for instance by establishing pragmatic guidelines based on the experience of normal communication. However, the number of potential rules is practically unlimited. Moreover, any rule is prone to mistakes due to peculiarities of the case and must allow for a wide range of exceptions.

It is therefore not surprising that, even in continental systems, interpretation is largely governed by general principles and judge-made law.[29] The most recent codification, the Dutch Burgerlijk Wetboek, deals very briefly with the topic of interpretation.[30] The draftsmen of the German Civil Code (BGB) deliberately abstained from stating detailed rules of interpretation since they wanted to avoid instructing the judiciary in "practical logic".[31] Nevertheless, detailed rules can be found in Arts. 1156 *et seq.* of the French CC, in Arts. 1362 *et seq.* of the Italian CC and in Arts. 1281 *et seq.* of the Spanish CC. The PECL also provide rules related to interpretation in Arts. 2:102, 5:101-107 and so does the CEC in Arts. 39-41. It is noteworthy that only limited binding force is attributed to the French rules of interpretation.[32] The Cour de Cassation holds that a judgment does not have to be reversed purely on the ground that rules of interpretation have not been observed.[33] The rules in the PECL are – in parts – consciously drafted in a way that courts may abstain from applying them in exceptional cases.[34]

---

28 Cf. *Zimmermann*, pp. 638 *et seq.*
29 For an overview PECL, 2000, p. 290 sub 1.
30 Art. 3:35 BW refers to the perspective of a reasonable addressee.
31 Cf. Motive I, p. 155.
32 Cf. *Ghestin et al.*, No. 35 *et seq.*
33 See Cass. civ., 19.12.1995, Bull. civ., I, No. 466, p. 324.
34 Cf. PECL, 2000, p. 294.

A clear line has to be drawn between "real" rules and the mere enumeration of aspects that ought to be taken into consideration in the process of interpretation. In Art. 5:102 PECL, some factors are named that must be taken into account when interpreting a contract.[35] This kind of list is supposed to outline circumstances that are of particular importance in determining the perspective of the reasonable addressee. Yet, such a list will always be exemplary and very general, as demonstrated by Art. 5:102 PECL. The perspective of the addressee is characterised by an indefinite number of individual factors. Moreover, the choice of possible factors will always be the self-explanatory expression of common sense. Thus, there is little use in enumerating the factors relevant to interpretation: where such an enumeration is specific, it will always be incomplete; where it is general, it will only state the obvious.

The difficulty in setting up a precise scheme of rules also affects the question whether interpretation is a matter of fact or a matter of law. This distinction is relevant especially with regard to the scope of review of the trial court's decision on appeal. Interpretation is always based on facts, namely, the subjective intentions of the parties and other individual circumstances of the case. The core question of interpretation, whether a binding contract has been formed on the established facts and what its content is, necessarily requires an additional legal judgment.[36] This follows directly from the assumption that the perspective of the reasonable addressee determines the outcome of interpretation. Because of the numerous and particular circumstances that potentially need to be taken into consideration, it is difficult, however, to clearly distinguish fact-finding from the application of law. As a consequence, findings of trial courts concerning interpretation should be reviewed with restraint, in a similar way as with findings of fact. In order to secure the priority of the trial judge's verdict, some legal systems deal with interpretation as a matter of fact, but nevertheless allow some limited review on appeal.[37] It is more accurate and therefore preferable to regard interpretation as a matter of law while limiting reversion of the trial court's findings to cases in which the result of interpretation is *evidently* inconsistent with a legal rule.[38]

2.3.2 Interpretation as a Balancing Approach

Admittedly, there is no strict concept of priority between the different aspects which play a role in the process of interpretation such as the meaning of the words, the purpose, the context or the origins of a contractual clause. These aspects are more or less loosely combined with one another. At one time a certain aspect prevails and another time a different aspect. Often the aspects are weighed by their persuasiveness. So there may be cases where a "weak" argument drawn from the meaning of the words of the agreement has to step back behind a "strong" argument derived from the purpose of the clause or the contractual context, but in other cases a narrow understanding of the words may prevail, because the purpose of the clause does not speak

---

35 Similarly with regard to the question whether or not a statement constitutes a contract see Art. 6:101 (1) PECL. See also Art. 4.3 Unidroit Principles.
36 Similarly *Bianca*, p. 413.
37 E.g. under French law; cf. *Ghestin et al.*, 2001, nos. 14 *et seq.*
38 Cf. *Larenz/Wolf*, § 28 No. 132. For an overview see PECL, 2000, p. 290 sub 1.

clearly enough for the opposite or is even vague or indistinct. Hence, interpretation is a process of balancing.

Inevitably, a balancing approach bears considerable uncertainties. But this does not mean that interpretation of contracts evades rational inspection or is even an irrational and purely decisionistic procedure. Rather, balancing works as does reasoning in general: one gathers as many arguments as are worth considering, weighs them by their persuasiveness and strikes a balance between them if they are in conflict. Yet, the uncertainties of the balancing approach explain why it is so difficult to develop abstract and clear rules for interpretation. They also explain why it is preferable to leave some discretion to the trial judge in the process of interpretation and to limit the scope of judicial review on appeal.

Even though there is no strict priority between the different aspects of interpretation, some of them carry special weight from an abstract point of view without regard to the particulars of a case. First of all, this applies to the meaning of the words of the agreement. The words used are usually the manifestation of parties' intention as well as the object of their reliance (see 2.1 above). In addition, the meaning of the wording marks the border line with "constructive" interpretation, which may only be passed under certain conditions (see below 3.3.2). Thus, to overcome the hurdle of the literal meaning, very strong arguments are needed. The situation is similar with respect to arguments which are drawn from the purpose of a contractual clause or the purpose of the entire contract, since the parties use the contract as a means to pursue their specific goals. Moreover, the focus on the purpose of legal arrangements generally prevails in modern jurisprudence. In many cases, however, the purpose remains unclear or can only be determined on the basis of other aspects such as the literal meaning of the words, the context or the origin.

Even though some of the criteria, such as the meaning of the words or the purpose, have important weight, they nevertheless remain elements within the process of balancing. Therefore, they may have to step back behind other arguments if those turn out to be stronger in the particular case. This would be different in the case of a clear rule. If, for example, a rule stated that one has to consider only the aspects expressed in a written document and that one may only refer to external aspects if they are known to everyone – as it is stated with respect to the interpretation of negotiable instruments (see below 2.4.1 ad finem) –, it would clearly follow, that external circumstances in the process of formation of the contract would not be allowed to be taken into account. In this case, interpretation is not guided by a "more or less" as in a balancing process when reasons have to be weighed against each other, but by a "yes or no".

2.4 Some Rules of Interpretation

2.4.1 Limits of Interpretation: Clauses Claires et Précises; Parol Evidence Rule; Merger Clauses; Formal Requirements

The Roman Law principle *cum in verbis nulla ambiguitas est, non debet admitti voluntatis quaestio*[39] is still effective especially in the French doctrine of *clauses*

---

39 Paul. Dig. 32, 25, 1.

claires et précises. As far as a contractual clause *in a written contract* is phrased unambiguously, the Cour de Cassation holds that there is no interpretation to be carried out and only the objective meaning is relevant. Thus, there is an *irrebuttable* presumption that the unambiguous clause is the correct and complete expression of the parties' intentions.[40]

Prima facie, the French doctrine appears to be an exception to the rule that the corresponding intentions of the parties have priority over the objective meaning of the declarations. This would be irreconcilable with the principles governing interpretation: If one party can prove that both parties had corresponding intentions which deviate from the unambiguous meaning of the written declarations, none of the parties has reasonably relied on the objective meaning. However, this objection does not prove strong if one takes a closer look at the doctrine of *clauses claires et précises*, since it is held permissible under this rule to consider external circumstances to determine whether or not the term in question is ambiguous.[41] This is unavoidable also from a practical point of view, as there is no purely objective standard which allows a determination of the plain meaning of the words used. This leads to the second objection: The doctrine of *clauses claires et précises* is inconsistent because it presupposes a "regular" interpretation for determining the plain meaning or, respectively, an ambiguity, while claiming that interpretation is not allowed.[42] This contradiction becomes apparent in a case where the Cour de Cassation decided on a shipment of sugar damaged on transport. There was a precise term in the contract providing for an allocation of transport risks. Contrary to the wording of the contract, however, the buyer was willing to accept delivery and to pay in full despite the damage the shipment had suffered, because the price of sugar had risen and therefore acceptance of the damaged shipment was preferable to rescission of the contract. The court ruled that, on the one hand, the clause concerning transport damages was *clear*, but, on the other hand, that the clause, being inconsistent with the apparent intentions of the parties in the situation given, was subject to interpretation.[43]

The obvious question is why the doctrine of *clauses claires et précises* has nevertheless not yet been abandoned. An important aspect might be that interpretation under French law is a matter of fact and thus there is, as a general rule, no review on appeal.[44] The conclusion that a declaration is unambiguous in a certain sense is a means to reverse the decision of the trial court on appeal. Thereby, interpretation becomes – not openly but practically – subject to a review of evident mistakes on appeal as has been argued above.

Related, but not identical to the doctrine of *clauses claires et précises* is the parol evidence rule which has played an important role particularly in the English legal tradition. Under this concept, extrinsic (parol) evidence is, as a general rule, not admissible to add to, vary, subtract from or contradict the terms of a written document.[45]

---

40 Cf. in detail *Ghestin et al.*, nos. 25 and 28. With regard to a similar practice under Italian law see *Bianca*, p. 420; *Cian/Trabucchi*, Art. 1362 sub X 1.See also Art. 39 (1) CEC.
41 Cf. *Ghestin et al.*, No. 27; *Mazeaud, H. et al.*, No. 345.
42 Cf. with more details *Ghestin et al.*, No. 25.
43 Cf. Req., 15.4. 1926, S. 1926, I, pp. 151 *et seq.*
44 Cf. *Ghestin et al.*, No. 15.
45 E.g. *Jacobs* v. *Batavia and General Plantations Trust* [1924] 1 Ch. 287, 295. Under French law a

Here, the objection mentioned above is equally valid, i.e. none of the parties reasonably relied on the objective meaning in case they had corresponding intentions that were "wrong", or if they agreed on further terms of contract not embodied in the written document. Again, it has to be added that an interpretation which claims to leave aside circumstances that are not embodied in the written document is practically impossible. Accordingly, the rigid ban on external circumstances also had to be loosened under English law by way of recognising many exceptions. In 1986, the Law Commission even started doubting whether the parol evidence rule has any actual binding effect at all.[46] It has to be admitted, however, that usually the parties consider the written document the complete and final expression of their legal relationship. Yet, this assumption can be appropriately accounted for by regarding it a rebuttable presumption:[47] Whoever claims circumstances not embodied in the written document to be valid bears the burden of proof for this claim.

This legal situation generally remains unchanged if the parties agree on a written form clause or a merger clause. Such a clause only implies a higher probability that the parties intend to restrict the content of their agreement to what is stated in the written document, thereby cancelling or excluding other (deviating) agreements. Such an intention, however, is subject to modifications: There is always the possibility that the parties – contrary to the clause – intend to leave certain other agreements intact or to provide new terms on certain issues after conclusion of the contract. The written form clause and the merger clause can be justified – like any other term of contract – on the basis of mutual consent and, therefore, they can be altered by mutual consent at any time.

It follows that a written form clause and the merger clause only strengthen the presumption of the written agreement being complete. This is in line with tendencies in most European legal systems[48] and with Art. 2:106 PECL concerning clauses that aim to exclude other amendments to the contract than written ones. Not fully convincing, however, is the regulation of Art. 2:105 (1) PECL which attributes *unconditional* validity to individually stipulated merger clauses. This rule – along with its legislative ratio – demonstrates, again, that a rigid rule intending to limit interpretation to the written document is inadequate. The first indication for this can be found in Art. 2:105 (3) PECL, stating that declarations made at an earlier stage can be used for the interpretation of the contract. Furthermore, the merger clause is set aside according to Art. 2:105 (4) PECL if otherwise reasonable reliance of one party would be infringed. Finally, there is a reference in the comments on the PECL that a merger clause is also ineffective with respect to stipulations made separately from the contract.[49] Again, these restrictions qualify the merger clause as giving rise to a rebuttable presumption, but do so in an unnecessarily complicated manner.

---

similar rule is stated in Art. 1341 CC. This provision, however, does not apply if there is an ambiguity in the contract; cf. Req., 31.3. 1886, S. 1886, I, p. 260; *Ghestin et al.*, No. 28.

46 Cf. *Beatson*, pp. 132-134, 160-163; *Treitel*, pp. 176-183.

47 This is substantially realised under Spanish law in Art. 1281 CC, stating the prevalence of the "intención evidente de los contratantes" over the literal meaning; cf. *Paz-Ares Rodriguez et al.*, Art. 1282, sub II. To the same effect *Beatson*, p. 132.

48 Cf. PECL, 2000, pp. 153 *et seq.*

49 Cf. PECL p. 152.

There is an additional problem if written form is required by law with regard to the contract to be interpreted. In this case, the question is what kind of relationship exists between interpretation and the legal requirement of form. In order to answer this question, two sub-questions need to be distinguished (which is often neglected): First, the content of the contract must be determined. Second, it has to be established whether the contract is valid with *that* specific content. With regard to the first sub-question, the content of the contract is to be determined on the basis of the general rules on interpretation of written documents. At this level, the requirement of form does not pose any restriction on interpretation. The starting point is therefore the presumption of the written document being correct and complete. This presumption is rebutted if one of the parties proves by way of external evidence that the actual intentions of the parties deviate from, or go beyond, the objective content of the written document. At the level of interpretation, there is no need to disregard extrinsic evidence due to the form requirement,[50] as form requirements are generally not aimed at binding the parties to something that contradicts their corresponding intentions. Having established the content of the contract, one may turn to the second sub-question, i.e. whether the contract, with the terms given, is valid or invalid due to a breach of the form requirement. Generally, there can be no breach of the form requirement only on the ground that circumstances not embodied in the written document are relevant in order to determine the content of the contract, for it is practically impossible to phrase a written clause that is not in any need of interpretation on the basis of external circumstances. Thus, the requirement of form must, at least, be limited to ensuring that the actual intention is somehow indicated in the written document.[51] Yet, even if there is no such indication in the document with regard to a certain point, the contract is not necessarily invalid. Rather, the validity of the contract should be determined depending upon the specific form requirement and its objective.[52] This objective may frequently but not always render the contract invalid. For example, under German law the contract of sale of real estate remains valid even though the actual piece of land has been designated wrongly in the written document, if it can be established what piece of land the parties actually wanted to refer to.[53] This is because the requirement of form governing real estate sales aims to alert the parties to the general risks of such contracts and makes them seek legal advice by a notary public, and this ratio is fulfilled even if the technical designation of the piece of land is wrong.

Finally, particular caution is necessary with regard to cases where third parties who did not originally participate in the conclusion of the contract rely on its content and where the transaction is specifically designated to evoke such reliance. This is especially relevant with respect to negotiable instruments and corporate contracts. With regard to negotiable instruments, for instance, the general rule is that extrinsic circumstances can only be considered in the process of interpretation if they are known to anyone.[54] A similar rule applies to corporate contracts if legitimate interests

---

50 Cf. e.g. *Cian/Trabucchi*, Art. 1362 CC, sub IX 5.
51 See BGH 9.4.1981, BGHZ 80, 242, 245.
52 Cf. in detail *Lüderitz*, pp. 192 *et seq.*; *Larenz/Wolf*, § 28 nos. 82 *et seq.* = pp. 355 *et seq.*
53 Cf. BGH 25.3.1983 BGHZ 87, 150, 152 *et seq.*
54 Cf. e.g. BGH 30.11.1993, BGHZ 124, 263; OGH 1.12.1977, OGH SZ 50/157 (1977); *Baumbach/Hefermehl*, Wechselgesetz und Scheckgesetz, 22. Aufl. 2000, Introd. No. 56; *G.H.Roth*, Grundriß des österreichischen, Wertpapierrechts, 2. Aufl., 1999, p. 27.

of third parties, for example future shareholders or creditors, require such a restriction.[55] In these cases, the third party might be solely depending on the content of the written agreement alone as the basis for his dispositions. Generally, the third party has no access to the individual circumstances accompanying the conclusion of the contract and, therefore, his perspective differs from the point of view of the original parties to the contract. The original parties do not deserve the regular protection by law if (and because) they exchanged offer and acceptance with the initial concern that third parties might rely on their declarations. In these cases, it is justified to generally have regard only to the written content of the contract and to circumstances obvious to anybody while other external circumstances are to be disregarded.

2.4.2 Interpretation Contra Proferentem

It is widely accepted that an ambiguous clause is to be construed against the party on whose initiative it was inserted into the contract. This rule has its foundation in the Roman law principle "Cum quaeritur in stipulatione, quid acti sit, ambiguitas contra stipulatorem est".[56] The *contra proferentem* rule is laid down in Art. 5:103 PECL and in Art. 40 (3) CEC. Moreover, this rule is an integral part of the already existing Community law in Art. 5 of the Directive 93/13 on Unfair Terms in Consumer Contracts. In the European jurisdictions, the *contra proferentem* rule is to be found not only in regulations that implement Directive 93/13, but also in other contexts.[57]

The *contra proferentem* rule is mainly based upon the concept of deterrence. The party who introduces a clause into the contract can and should ensure its transparency and, respectively, avoid the uncertainty associated with ambiguous terms. This uncertainty is detrimental, since the other party is not sufficiently aware of the scope of his rights and duties when concluding the contract. Also, it is more difficult for the other party to evaluate the outcome of a dispute. The *contra proferentem* rule, moreover, preserves the legal status quo which would exist without the clause in question. If one party introduces a clause, it usually worsens the other party's existing legal position by establishing duties or limiting rights. The *contra proferentem* rule aims to achieve that the other party's 'well-earned' legal position is only restricted to an extent that is made perfectly clear in the contract. This idea is sometimes also expressed by demanding that clauses which limit essential duties or rights of one party have to be interpreted narrowly.[58] Accordingly, disclaimer clauses are often construed very restrictively.[59] Of course, this always bears the risk that the restrictive interpretation de facto serves to implement a legal prohibition.

---

55 Cf. e.g. OGH 25.11. 1997 AG 1998, 199; *J. Farrar/B. Hannigan* Company Law, 4th ed. 1998, p. 117; *G. Resta*, Gli atti costitutivi e gli statuti, in G.Alpa/G.Fonsi/G.Resta, L'interpretazione del contratto, 2nd ed., Milan, 2001, p. 450. In detail see *K. Schmidt* Gesellschaftsrecht, 4. Aufl., 2002, § 5 I 4 = pp. 87 *et seq.*

56 Cels. D. 34, 5, 26. With regard hereto *Zimmermann*, pp. 639 *et seq.*

57 Cf. under English law *Tan Wing Chuen* v. *Bank of Credit and Commerce Hong Kong Ltd.* [1996] 2 B.C.L.C. 69. Under French law Art. L. 133-2 C. consom.; with more details *Ghestin et al.*, 2001, No. 40. Under Italian law see Art. 1370 CC. Under Spanish law Art. 1288 CC. Under Austrian law § 915 ABGB. Furthermore Art. 4.6 Unidroit Principles.

58 Cf. *Palandt-Heinrichs*, BGB, 2002, § 133, No. 23.

59 See *Hollier v. Rambler Motors* (A.M.C.) Ltd. [1972] 2 Q.B. 71; *Beatson*, 2002, pp. 170-174; *Treitel*, p. 202.

The *contra proferentem* rule only applies to terms which were not individually negotiated (Art. 5:103 PECL; Art. 39 III CEC). If a term was negotiated between the parties there is no unilateral responsibility for an unclear formulation. Individual negotiation of a term also reduces the need for protecting the affected legal position.

Some rules connect the interpretation against one of the parties with the role this party plays in a specific contract. For example, there are rules in French Law which, in case of doubt, provide for an interpretation against the creditor (Art. 1162 CC) or against the seller (Art. 1602 CC). The idea of the *contra proferentem* rule might provide a certain justification for these rules which originate in Roman Law. In many cases, however, the contract is negotiated in detail or the debtor or the buyer is responsible for the drafting of the contract. If this is the case there is – possibly with the exception of promises without recompense[60] – no plausible reason to put the creditor or the seller at a disadvantage. In a liberal contract system, interpretation cannot depend on social aspects, namely on the relative economic strength of the parties, not to mention that creditor and seller are not necessarily economically more powerful than debtor and buyer. Consequently, the rule on uncertainty contained in Arts. 1162, 1602 (2) CC can, if at all, only be justified as an inaccurate version of the *contra proferentem* rule.[61]

2.4.3 Further Rules of Interpretation

Numerous other rules of interpretation are practised beyond those already discussed. For instance, the proposition that an individual agreement takes preference over terms which were not subject to individual negotiations (Art. 5:104 PECL) is important and widely recognised.[62] This idea is based on the legitimate reason that the individual negotiation of the parties allows a more precise conclusion with regard to the intention of *both* parties than an abstract reference. According to another, equally convincing rule, an interpretation which avoids rendering the agreement void or meaningless is generally to be preferred (Art. 5:106 PECL; Art. 40 II CEC).[63] This is based on the generally justified assumption that the parties want to achieve the goals of the contract by reasonable and legal means.[64]

Apart from this, it should be emphasised again that one cannot expect rules of interpretation to give precise guidelines in making decisions. Therefore, one should be cautious when formulating them in binding form. For example, the rule in Art. 5:107 PECL and Art. 4.7 Unidroit Principles that, as far as contracts in various languages are concerned, the original version generally is authoritative, is unconvincing. The underlying assumption that the original version reflects the intention of the parties most clearly is speculative. In particular, this rule fails to consider that the parties

---

60 There are provisions specifically demanding an interpretation in favour of such promisor e.g. in Art. 41 s. 1 CEC, under Italian law (Art. 1371 CC), under Portuguese law (Art. 237 CC) and under Austrian law (§ 915 ABGB).

61 See with the same result *Kötz*, pp. 174 *et seq.*

62 For an overview over the jurisdictions see PECL, 2000, p. 295.

63 To the same effect under English law *Lord Napier and Ettrick* v. *R.F. Kershaw Ltd.* [1999] 1 W.L.R. 756, 763. Under French law Art. 1157 CC. Under Spanish law Art. 1284 CC.

64 Cf. e.g. *Ghestin et al.*, No. 33.

have usually drafted the contract in different languages *in order to have a better understanding*. As another example, the norm of Art. 5:105 PECL,[65] stating that the interpretation has to show consideration for the contract as a whole, appears to be superfluous since it is not a genuine rule but only one obvious aspect which has to be taken into consideration for interpretation (see 2.3.1). Aspects like these, which are only potentially relevant to interpretation, can be compiled into catalogues such as Art. 5:102 PECL. From the point of view put forward here, however, it is preferable to abstain from this kind of regulation for reason of the self-evidence and almost unlimited number of such potentially relevant criteria.

3 Dealing with Gaps in the Contract

It is not always possible to solve the problems of interpretation by reverting to the wording of the contract or to the clear and concurring intention of the parties. In practice, contracts often contain gaps.

3.1 Lack of Agreement Despite Interpretation

A gap in the contract may arise in case the parties' intentions diverge and this divergence cannot be resolved by means of interpretation. In such a case, there is no agreement with respect to one element of the contract. As a general consequence, the contract is void.[66]

Such a dissent occurs extremely rarely. Normally, a dissent is ruled out either because the parties notice their disagreement or because the rules of interpretation demand that both declarations be understood in the same sense. In general, the corresponding interpretation of both declarations is ensured by the rule that each declaration has to be interpreted from the perspective of a reasonable recipient. In most cases, it follows that the same circumstances of the case are decisive for both parties. That means that the perspectives of the reasonable recipient and, accordingly, the meanings of the declarations are the same for both parties.

Under German law, for instance, a dissent has been found in a case where both parties wanted to conclude a contract for the sale of tartaric acid by telegram. Both parties wanted to sell but due to the shortened language they failed to notice the equal intention of the other party.[67] This case rather underlines, however, how seldom such a dissent occurs: Before the telegraphic declarations were exchanged one party had sent a price list to the other. Thus, one of the parties had made it clear that he wanted to sell and not to buy. Taking this into account, it would have been more appropriate to treat both declarations as congruent with the other party as buyer on the basis of the perspective of an objective recipient.[68] By comparison, the English case *Raffles v. Wichelhaus* seems to be a more justifiable example for a dissent. Here the parties en-

---

65 Similarly in French law Art. 1161 CC and in Spanish law Art. 1285 CC.
66 Under English Law see *Cundy* v. *Lindsay* (1878) 3 App Cas 459; *Beatson*, pp. 321-323. Under French law *Ghestin*, No. 495. Under Spanish law Art. 1284 CC.
67 Cf. RG 5. 4. 1922, RGZ 104, 265.
68 Cf. *Medicus*, Rn. 438.

tered into a contract on the sale of a cargo of cotton 'to arrive ex Peerless from Bombay'. Unknown to both parties, there were two ships called 'Peerless' which arrived at the agreed port of Liverpool at different times. If both parties really had different ships in mind and if there were no indications which allowed an unequivocal determination of the ship the contract was void.[69] Finally, in France, a dissent occurred in a case where the parties' intentions did not correspond with respect to the currency in which the price was to be paid. Due to a currency reform, the agreement could have referred either to old or to new Francs.[70]

3.2 The Applicability of Suppletive Law in Case of a Gap

The case of differing declarations has to be strictly distinguished from the situation that the parties have not made any provisions at all with respect to certain questions. This may be the case either because they did not consider the question at all or because they deliberately abstained from dealing with it. As long as this gap does not affect fundamental elements of the contract such as, in particular, the parties, the subject matter of the contract, and the price, the contract is enforceable (cf. Art. 2:103 PECL). In that case, the questions for which no provisions were made have to be solved under the rules provided by law.[71]

All European legal systems contain supplemental rules to complete contractual arrangements. In France, e.g., they are called règles supplétives, in England terms implied in law,[72] and in Germany dispositives Gesetzesrecht. The necessity of these rules becomes obvious if one takes into account that the parties can never provide for all eventualities. Thus, the existence of suppletive law prevents contractual incompleteness (or voidness respectively) and thereby reduces the cost of negotiations and drafting. Suppletive law can, however, only achieve its goals if it responds to the typical interests which can be attributed to the parties of the particular type of contract. Therefore its content has to reflect the kind of arrangement which reasonable parties would have made if they had thought of the issue in question. Moreover, suppletive law serves to guarantee the fairness of contracts. While the *parties* generally do not have to justify the content of their contracts in terms of substantive justice in a legal system governed by freedom of contract, the opposite obviously applies to the *legislator* (respectively to objective law). If one specifies the applicable form of justice, contract law is primarily to be governed by the rules of *commutative* justice, whereas the appeal to principles of *distributive* justice is restricted to rare exceptions.[73]

In continental Europe, suppletive law is to be found mainly in the codifications of private and commercial law. It is not possible, however, to achieve a comprehensive codification because the parties can construct the contract freely according to their own interests. Moreover, even a detailed elaboration of all known types of contracts

---

69 Cf. 2 H & C. 906, 159 Eng.Rep 375 (1864).
70 Cf. Cass. com., 14 janvier 1969, Bull. civ. IV, No. 13, p. 13.
71 In order to justify the rules of suppletive law, it is inaccurate and not necessary to refer to the actual intentions of the parties; for a more detailed discussion see *Ghestin et al.*, No. 42.
72 Cf. *Treitel*, pp. 188-194.
73 Cf. *Canaris*, Die Bedeutung der iustitia distributiva im deutschen Vertragsrecht, 1997, pp. 45 *et seq.*, 75 *et seq.*, 125 *et seq.*

would go far beyond the scope of a concise codification. Therefore, the body of suppletive law in a code will necessarily be subject to further concretisation by judicial case law which will grow in importance with increasing age of the codification. English Law shows that the supplementation of contractual gaps on the basis of objective law is possible and necessary even in the case where the pertinent rules are not codified at all.[74]

3.3 Ascertaining the Non-Explicit Content of a Contract

The rules of suppletive law do not always offer legal results that meet the particular requirements of the case at hand. Therefore, courts often attempt to derive particular solutions from the actual contract itself, i.e. from the common intention of the parties, even if the parties did not express their ideas explicitly.

3.3.1 Completion of the Contract on the Basis of Implied Intent

As stated above (cf. 1.4), the content of a contract can be derived not only from the explicit declarations but also from the conduct of the parties. This kind of implied intention does not necessarily have to concern the conclusion of the contract as a whole. Rather, it is possible to derive implied provisions from the agreement which – in addition to its express terms – have to be acknowledged as a binding element of the contract because they reflect the *actual intention* of the parties (cf. Art. 6:102 (a) PECL). In particular, this is the case when a certain term is a necessary precondition for the meaningful performance of the explicit agreement. This kind of connection justifies the assumption that the parties actually intended the provision in question. The more obviously the explicit agreement depends on a term not explicitly agreed upon, the more likely the conclusion is justified that, according to the actual intention of the parties, the condition is an unexpressed element of the contract as well.[75] An obvious example is the case of a car rental contract, which obliges the lessor to hand over the ignition key to the lessee even in absence of an explicit term to do so. This kind of recourse to implied elements of a contract is an essential tool of contractual interpretation. If it were not possible to consider these supplements, the parties would be forced into using an excessive amount of wording which would make the drafting process unnecessarily complicated and expensive.

Another important source of determining non-explicit intentions are the usual customs of a particular field of commerce. Provided that a solution to a specific question is established by custom, it is generally justified to assume that the parties were implicitly referring to the customary solution (Art. 1:105 (2) PECL; Art. 32 (1) lit. c CEC).[76]

---

74 In more detail on suppletive law see *Kötz*, pp. 176 *et seq.*

75 Cf. Art. 32 (1) lit.d CEC. Furthermore, see the definition of the term implied in fact in *Shirlaw* v. *Southern Foundries* (1926) Ltd. [1939] K.B. 206, 227: "Prima facie that which in any contract is left to be implied and need not be expressed is something so obvious that it goes without saying; so that, if while the parties were making their bargain, an officious bystander were to suggest some express provision for it in the agreement, they would testily suppress him with a common 'Oh, of course!'."

76 Cf. under English law ("term implied by custom") *Treitel*, pp. 194-195. Under Spanish law see Art.

3.3.2 Reference to the Hypothetical Intention by Constructive Interpretation

Yet, often the connection between the express terms of the contract and a certain problem is not compelling enough to justify a solution on the basis of the parties' actual intention. Some jurisdictions, however, nevertheless provide for contractual complementation by way of interpretation in such cases.[77] For instance, when filling gaps by constructive interpretation, the German BGH reverts to the rule which the parties themselves would have agreed upon with regard to the contract and the maxims of good faith and common usage.[78] On this basis, the Court ruled , for example, that two doctors who had swapped their practices were barred from opening a new practice in the immediate vicinity of the old one for a period of two to three years.[79] The French Cour de Cassation allows for considerable freedom in the interpretation of contracts as well. For instance, in a case where a radio station had contracted with an author to compose a radio play and had accepted the play without objections and paid for it, the court used the idea of contractual interpretation to find that the radio station actually had to broadcast the play even though there was no explicit agreement on that issue.[80]

In such cases, the only basis of interpretation can be the parties' *hypothetical* intention. However, in many cases, the distinction between the (implied) actual and the hypothetical intention of the parties is merely a gradual one. Therefore, a clear line cannot always be drawn.[81] It is a characteristic feature of constructive interpretation that the supplementary rule cannot be deduced exclusively from the contractual provisions. Instead, it requires an additional normative judgment with respect to the content of the agreement which goes beyond the reasonable recipient's perspective. For example, the German BGH reverts to the principle of good faith and common usage in this context. Moreover, Art. 6:102 PECL points in the same direction stating that implied terms of a contract cannot only arise from the intention of the parties but also from good faith and fair dealing.[82]

It is, however, not only difficult to distinguish constructive interpretation from the case of implied intent, but also from the provisions of suppletive law. The reason is the additional normative assessment which is necessary in both cases. In some cases, it can even be doubtful whether a distinction is fruitful at all or whether the method of constructive interpretation in fact uses the contract and its interpretation to covertly formulate rules of objective law. This objection is not to be taken lightly. The reference to the parties' intention conceals that constructive interpretation profoundly

---

1287 CC. To the same effect under French law Art.1160 CC; Art. 1159 CC additionally refers specifically to the custom "...dans le pays où le contrat est passé".

77 See for an overview PECL, 2000, p. 305.
78 Cf. BGH 18.12.1954, BGHZ 16, 71, 76.
79 Cf. BGH 18.12.1954, BGHZ 16, 71, 76.
80 Vgl. Cass. civ., 1ʳᵉ, 2 April 1974, Bull. civ., I, No. 109.
81 Critically in general on the distinction, *Bianca*, pp. 412 *et seq.*
82 In Art. 6:102 PECL (b) "the nature and purpose of the contract" is stated as an independent consideration. This is unnecessarily complicated. Either the implied term results self-evidently from "the nature and purpose of the contract"; then it follows from the actual intention of the parties (see (a)). If this is not the case, the implied term needs an additional normative justification, which means that it has to be justified by objective principles such as good faith and fair dealing.

interferes with the contract in two ways: on the one hand, the omission of a contractual term is, generally speaking, just as meaningful as a positive agreement. Thus, the court has to disregard this *negative exclusiveness*[83] of the agreement if it implies constructive clauses into the contract. On the other hand, even if one generally acknowledges the need for a complementing clause, there is always a certain discretion with respect to the particular legal result. Here again, constructive interpretation takes the solution of the pertinent issue away from the parties' autonomy and negotiation.[84] It follows that constructive interpretation is only permissible under restrictive conditions. It is, in particular, not possible to justify it by *normative considerations alone*. Rather, the parties' particular declarations have to indicate clearly and specifically that the constructive interpretation would have complied with the hypothetical intention of both parties at the time the contract was concluded.[85]

The distinction between constructive interpretation and suppletive law becomes particularly important in legal systems where mechanisms for the adjustment of contracts in the case of unforeseen circumstances exist in suppletive law, i.e. apart from interpretation. Those mechanisms of adjustment, such as the German rules of the 'foundation of the transaction' ('Wegfall der Geschäftsgrundlage'; cf. § 313 BGB), are justly governed by strict requirements, which should not be circumvented by constructive interpretation. If, however, a specific mechanism for the adjustment of contracts to exceptional circumstances is missing, as, for instance, still appears to be the case in France, constructive interpretation can function as a "safety valve" with respect to an overly strict reading of the principle of pacta sunt servanda. By contrast, the open acknowledgement of a legal rule for contractual adjustment is preferable because, in many cases, the recourse to the parties' intention is merely fictitious.

3.3.3 Collateral Contractual Duties

All European legal systems acknowledge that the contract is not only the source of principal, but also of collateral duties which need not be described explicitly. These duties are simply founded on the parties' intentions if, in case they are not observed, performance cannot be perfected properly. The obvious example is again the duty to hand over the keys in a car rental. These duties, however, have to be distinguished from duties which cannot be derived directly from the principal duty and which aim at a more general protection of the other party's rights and legally protected interests while performing the contract. An example would be the duty of a painter not to damage the principal's furniture by drops of paint.

---

83 The aspect of negative exclusiveness is laid down in Art. 1283 of the Spanish CC.

84 Recently, it has been suggested to solve the problem of judicial interference by establishing certain duties of the parties to adapt or amend the contract by negotiation. Cf. e.g. Art. 157 CEC; in detail *Nelle*, Neuverhandlungspflichten, 1994. Generally, solutions by negotiation are always desirable. However, there is no evidence that it is possible to establish legal duties which, on the one hand, are judicially workable and, on the other hand, can efficiently facilitate the process of working towards a voluntary agreement. Moreover, one has to keep in mind, that duties to negotiate can never guarantee the successful conclusion of a voluntary compromise and, thus, will never fully replace judicial interference.

85 More detailed on the necessary limitations to constructive interpretation see Palandt-*Heinrichs*, BGB, 61. edition, 2002, § 157 Nos. 8-10.

This second group of collateral duties is also acknowledged in all European legal systems. With respect to the issue of interpretation, the most important question is whether it is possible to imply from the parties' intentions a general contractual duty to take reasonable care. This would correspond to the French doctrine that derives a general obligation de sécurité from the contract.[86] Moreover, a famous English example for the contractual construction of such a duty is the *Moorcock* case. In this case, the defendant was contractually obliged to unload the plaintiff's ship at his jetty. When the tide went out the ship stranded and was damaged. The court established liability of the defendant on the ground of breach of his implied duty to take reasonable care.[87]

Yet there are two important arguments against a general duty of care *based on the contractual agreement*. First, there is generally no sufficiently clear indication to this end in the parties' declarations, in other words: establishing such a duty based on contract is fictitious. In terms of the parties' intentions, there is a clear difference between a general duty of reasonable care and other collateral duties directly aimed at achieving the contractually defined goal of performance. Accordingly, it is sufficient to have the parties bound to the contractual goal of performance in order to establish duties adhering directly to the principal duty, whereas establishing a general duty of reasonable care requires balancing the parties' conflicting interests.[88] Second, it is objectionable to make the duty of care depend on whether or not a contract was concluded. For example, there would be no relevant reason to deny liability if the ship had been damaged at a time when the negotiating parties had not concluded a contract yet. Even if the contract was invalid, e.g. if the parties without noticing had actually reached no agreement on the price, the question of liability should not be dealt with differently.

The reason for the frequent assumption of a general contractual duty of reasonable care is that liability in contract can usually be established more easily than liability in tort. Liability in tort is restricted, as compared to contractual liability, in some European legal systems with respect to the principal's responsibility for his agent, the compensation of pure economic losses and/or the burden of proof.[89] On the basis of the reasons given above, however, the question whether the collateral duties are contractual in their origin does not address the right issue. Rather, one should ask whether the rules of contractual liability – if they in fact provide a more "liberal" framework – apply even though the duties in question are not contractual in their origin, but imputed by law. This position has gained more and more support in recent times and was statutorily recognised under German law on the occasion of the reform of contract law in 2001 (see §§ 241 II, 311 II, III BGB). The reason for this legally imputed liability under the rules of contract law is that the parties necessarily grant each other an opportunity of interfering with the legal goods and interests of the other

---

86 Cf. *Ghestin*, 2001, No. 48.
87 Cf. (1889) 14 PD 64.
88 Cf. the criticism on the Moorcock decision by *Treitel*, p. 193. Under French law, there is a dispute on the contractual character of l'obligation de sécurité as well; see *Ghestin*, 2001, No. 48 and footnote 310.
89 See for a comparative analysis *v. Bar*, Gemeineuropäisches Deliktsrecht, vol. I, 1996, pp. 405 *et seq*, 459 *et seq*. With regard to the aspect of interpretation *Kötz*, 1996, pp. 184 *et seq*.

that goes beyond the actual contractual performance and cannot reasonably be provided for in advance. The duty of reasonable care is correlated with this opportunity. It protects the parties' reliance on the beneficial effects of mutual cooperation and helps creating such reliance. The recognition of a duty of reasonable care and the resulting liability under the rules of contract law thus support and facilitate the conclusion of contracts. This concept allows one to establish a duty of care even in cases where no contract has been concluded yet or where the contract is invalid. It suffices that the parties – while negotiating or performing a contract – grant each other the opportunity to interfere with the legally protected interests of the other. The details of this issue, however, are beyond the scope of our topic in this article.[90]

BIBLIOGRAPHY: *Académie des Privatistes Européens* (Coordinateur: *G. Gandolfi*) Code Européen des Contrats, 2001 (quoted: CEC); *J. Beatson* Anson's Law of Contract, 28th edition, 2002; *C.M. Bianca*, Diritto Civile, III, Il Contratto, 2nd ed. 2000; *G. Cian; A. Trabucchi* Commentario breve al codice civile, 5th ed. 2001; *J. Ghestin* Traité de droit civil, La formation du contrat, 3rd edition, 1993; *J. Ghestin et al.* Traité de droit civil, Les effets du contrat, 3rd edition, 2001; *W. Flume* Allgemeiner Teil des Bürgerlichen Rechts, II, 4th ed. 1992; *H. Kötz* Europäisches Vertragsrecht vol. I, 1996; *O. Lando; H. Beale* (eds.) Principles of European Contract Law, I and II, 2000 (quoted: PECL); *K. Larenz; M. Wolf* Allgemeiner Teil des Bürgerlichen Rechts, 8th edition, 1997; *A. Lüderitz* Auslegung von Rechtsgeschäften, 1966; *H. Mazeaud et al.* Leçons de droit civil, Tome II, 1st vol., Obligations. Théorie générale, 9th edition, 1998; *D. Medicus* Allgemeiner Teil des BGB, 8th ed., 2002; *Paz-Ares Rodriguez et al.* Comentario del Codigo Civil, 2nd ed., 1993; *G.H. Treitel* The Law of Contract, 10th edition, 1999; *R. Zimmermann* The Law of Obligations, Roman Foundations of the Civilian Tradition, 1990.

---

90 With regard to the position asserted here see *Canaris*, JZ 1965, pp. 475 *et seq.*; *Canaris*, 2nd Festschrift für Larenz, 1983, pp. 27, 85 *et seq.* For a recent and detailed analysis see e.g. *Krebs*, Sonderverbindung und außerdeliktische Schutzpflichten, 2000.

CHAPTER 26

The Concept of Good Faith*

Martijn W. Hesselink**

1 Introduction

Most European civil codes contain a general good faith provision.[1] In addition, some codes contain specific rules in which reference is also made to the concept of good faith. Moreover, many specific rules in the codes are said to be special applications of good faith.

Most systems make a distinction between subjective good faith and objective good faith. Subjective good faith is usually defined as a subjective state of mind: not knowing nor having to know of a certain fact or event. It is of relevance particularly in property law (*bona fide* acquisition). Objective good faith, the concept that the general good faith clauses refer to, is usually regarded as a norm for the conduct of contracting parties: 'acting in accordance with or contrary to good faith'. Some systems have even emphasised this distinction by introducing separate terminology for objective good faith (*Treu und Glauben, correttezza, redelijkheid en billijkheid*). In France, however, such a distinction is not usually made.[2] The English common law traditionally does not recognise a concept of objective good faith. However, the concept has recently been introduced into English law by statute.[3]

In this paper I will discuss whether a European Civil Code or a Code of Contracts, if it were to be enacted,[4] should contain a provision on objective good faith. Therefore I will examine first how the concept of objective good faith is understood in the

---

* This is a revised and updated version of my contibution to the second edition of this book ('Good Faith', in: Hartkamp et al. (eds.), *Towards a European Civil Code*, 2nd. ed., Nijmegen and The Hague, London, Boston 1998, pp. 285-310). The present version was pre-published, as Chapter 7, in my *The New European Private Law, Essays on the Future of Private Law in Europe* (Kluwer Law International, The Hague, London, Boston 2002), pp. 193-223.

** Amsterdam Institute for Private Law (*AIP*), *Universiteit van Amsterdam*, the Netherlands.

1   See Art. 1134, Section 3 French Civil Code; § 242 German Civil Code; Art. 2 Swiss Civil Code arts. 1175 and 1375 Italian Civil Code; Art. 288 Greek Civil Code; Art. 762, Section 2, Portuguese Civil Code; arts. 6:2 and 6:248 Dutch Civil Code. See also Art. 1.7 UP and Art. 1.201 PECL.

2   The same holds true for observations which many English lawyers make on the concept of good faith. They often speak of 'acting in bad faith' when referring to the conduct of contracting parties where most continental European lawyers would speak of 'acting contrary to good faith'.

3   Unfair Terms in Consumer Contracts Regulations 1994, *SI* 1994/3159 which implemented EC Council Directive 93/13/EEC. See Gunther Teubner, 'Legal Irritants: Good Faith in British Law or How Unifying Law Ends Up in New Divergences', *MLR* 1998, pp. 11 ff.

4   On the desirability of a European Civil Code or a European Code of Contracts see my *The New European Private Law*, Chapter 5 (based on 'The Politics Of European Contract Law: Who Has An Interest In What Kind Of Contract Law For Europe?', in Stefan Grundmann & Jules Stuyck (eds), *An Academic Green Paper on European Law* (The Hague, London, New York 2002), 181-191, and Chapter 8 (based on 'The Structure Of The New European Private Law' in: Ewoud Hondius and Carla Joustra (eds.), *Netherlands Reports to the Sixteenth International Congress of Comparative Law*, Antwerp, Oxford, New York, 2002, pp. 7-23).

various countries (II). Then I will give a brief account of how good faith is applied by the courts (III). Finally, I will raise the question whether the traditional view of good faith constitutes an adequate representation of the way in which good faith actually operates (IV). The answer to that question will determine my final conclusions (V).

2 Good Faith in Theory

2.1 Introduction

Objective good faith is usually regarded as a normative concept (2.2). However, a general good faith clause is not an ordinary rule like most others in the code. It contains an open norm (2.3), it is said, the content of which must be established through concretisation (2.4) into functions and groups of typical cases (2.5).

2.2 Normative Concept

In all systems objective good faith is usually regarded as a normative concept. Indeed good faith is often seen as the highest norm of contract law, or of the law of obligations or even of all private law. For that reason many provisions in the code which make no explicit reference to good faith are nevertheless said to be based on it.

Good faith is often said to be in some way connected with moral standards. On the one hand, it is said to be a moral standard itself, a legal-ethical principle;[5] good faith means honesty, candour, loyalty et cetera. It is often said that the standard of good faith basically means that a party should take the interest of the other party into account.[6] On the other hand, good faith is said to be the gateway through which moral values enter the law.[7]

Reference is thereby sometimes made to the Aristotelian concept of equity.[8] Actually, some systems do not distinguish between equity and good faith; they regard them as the same objective standard.[9] It is then said that abstract rules may lead to an

---

5   See e.g. Joachim Gernhuber & Barbara Grunewald, *Bürgerliches Recht; Ein systematisches Repertorium*, 4th ed., München 1998, p. 106 (*grundlegendes rechtsethisches Prinzip*); Giorgio Cian & Alberto Trabucchi, *Commentario breve al codice civile*, 5th ed., Padova, 1997, Art. 1175, I, 1 (*principio etico-giuridico*).

6   See e.g. Arndt Teichmann, in: *Soergel Bürgerliches Gesetzbuch mit Einführungsgesetz und Nebengesetzen,* Vol. 2 *Schuldrecht I (§§ 241-610)*, 12 th ed., Stuttgart, Berlin and Köln 1990, § 242, No. 4; C. Massimo Bianca, *Diritto Civile*, III, *Il contratto*, Milano 1987 (reprinted in 1992), No. 224; A.S. Hartkamp, *Verbintenissenrecht* (in: *Asser* series), Vol. II, *Algemene leer der overeenkomsten*, 11th ed., Deventer 2001, No. 300; Michael P. Stathopoulos, *Contract law in Hellas*, The Hague, London and Boston, Athens 1995, No. 51.

7   See e.g. Helmut Heinrichs, in: *Palandt Bürgerliches Gesetzbuch*, 61st ed., München 2002, § 242, No. 3; François Terré & Philippe Simler & Yves Lequette, *Droit civil, Les obligations*, 6th ed, Paris 1996, No. 414; Art. 1.106 PECL, Comment, A.

8   Aristotle, *Nicomachean Ethics*, V, x.

9   In France, accessory duties like the duty to inform or the duty of care, are founded by the courts on Art. 1134, Section 3 (*bonne foi*) and Art. 1135 (*équité*) alternatively, and sometimes on both. In the Netherlands the new Civil Code merged the concepts of *goede trouw* (Art. 1374, Section 3 old BW)

unjust result in a specific case, and that good faith may provide the basis for an exception on the facts of that particular case. For that reason it is sometimes argued (as it was for early Equity in England)[10] that a decision based on good faith cannot serve as a precedent, as it is only meant to prevent injustice in a particular case, and that therefore no effort should be made to determine the content of the good faith norm in more general terms. However, this view is not generally accepted and the next Section will show that it does not correspond with the way in which good faith operates in practice.

Finally, in some systems good faith is regarded – and actually used by the courts – as a means through which the values of the Constitution enter into private law.[11]

2.3   Open Norm

At first sight, the theoretical status of good faith may seem quite unclear to an outsider since the terminology used by legal authors is far from unitary. Good faith is said to be a norm,[12] a (very important)[13] principle,[14] a rule,[15] a maxim,[16] a duty,[17] a rule or standard for conduct,[18] a source of unwritten law,[19] a general clause.[20] To an

---

and *billijkheid* (Art. 1375 old BW) into the new concept of *redelijkheid en billijkheid* (objective good faith) (arts. 6:2; 6:248 BW).

10 See J.H. Baker, *An Introduction to English Legal History*, London 1979 (reprinted in 1988), p. 89; S.F.C. Milsom, *Historical Foundations of the Common Law*, 2nd ed., London 1981, p. 90.

11 For Germany see e.g. Herbert Roth, in: *Münchener Kommentar zum Bürgerlichen Gesetzbuch*, 4th ed., München 2001, § 242, Nos. 52 ff.; for Italy see e.g. M. Cantillo, *Le Obbligazioni*, in: *Giurisprudenza sistematica di diritto civile e commerciale* (founded by Walter Bigiavi), Vol. I, Torino 1992, p. 207. See further my *The New European Private Law*, Chapter 6 (published as 'The Horizontal Effect Of Social Rights In European Contract Law', in Martijn W. Hesselink, Edgar du Perron, Arthur Salomons (eds.), *Privaatrecht tussen autonomie en solidariteit*, pp. 119-131, and in *Europe e diritto privato* 2003, pp. 1-18.

12 See e.g. Karl Larenz, *Lehrbuch des Schuldrechts*, Vol. I *Allgemeiner Teil*, 14th ed., München 1987, p. 129 (*Norm*); Jacques Herbots, *Contract Law in Belgium*, Deventer, Boston and Bruxelles 1995, No. 109 ('norm').

13 See e.g. Art. 1.106 PECL, Comment, A ('a basic principle running throughout the Principles'); Dieter Medicus, *Schuldrecht I; Allgemeiner Teil*, 12th ed., München 2000, No. 125 ('ein den einzelten Rechtsvorschriften übergeordnetes Prinzip'); C. Massimo Bianca, *Il contratto*, No. 223 ('un principio di ordine pubblico che supera anche la legge').

14 See e.g. A.S. Hartkamp, *Verbintenissenrecht II* (in: *Asser* series), Nos. 300, 301, 304 (*beginsel*); Michael P. Stathopoulos, *Contract law in Hellas*, No. 50 (*principle*).

15 See e.g. A. Menezes-Cordeiro, 'Rapport portugais', *Travaux de l'association Henri Capitant, Tome XLIII, année 1992. Journées louisianaises de Baton-Rouge et La Nouvelle Orléans, 'La bonne foi'*, Paris 1994, p. 338 (*règle*); Art. 1.106 PECL, Comment, A (*rule*).

16 See Jean Carbonnier, *Droit Civil*, Vol. IV *Les Obligations*, 22nd ed., Paris 2000, No. 113: *maxime*.

17 See e.g. Philippe Malaurie & Laurent Aynès, *Cours de droit civil*, part IV, *Les obligations*, 10th, Paris 1999, No. 622 (*devoir*); C. Massimo Bianca, *Il contratto*, No. 223 (*obbligo giuridico*).

18 See e.g. C. Massimo Bianca, *Il contratto*, No. 223 (*precetto di condotta*); A. Menezes-Cordeiro, 'Rapport portugais', p. 337 (*règle de conduite*); Michael P. Stathopoulos, *Contract law in Hellas*, No. 52 ('criterion of conduct').

19 See e.g A.S. Hartkamp, *Verbintenissenrecht II* (in: *Asser* series), No. 305.

20 See e.g. Konrad Zweigert & Hein Kötz, *Einführung in die Rechtsvergleichung*, 3rd ed., Tübingen 1996, p. 149 (*Generalklausel*); Massimo Bianca, *Il contratto*, No. 223 (*clausola generale*); Michael P. Stathopoulos, *Contract law in Hellas*, No. 50 ('general clause').

English lawyer – often accused by his continental European colleagues of making inconsistent use of terminology – this may seem rather confusing.

However, on closer inspection, the picture is less confused than it seems. It is generally agreed that a general good faith clause does not contain a rule, at least not one like most other rules in the code. It is not, like other rules, susceptive to subsumption since neither the facts to which it applies nor the legal effect that it stipulates can be established *a priori*. Good faith is therefore usually said to be an open norm, a norm the content of which cannot be established in an abstract way but which depends on the circumstances of the case in which it must be applied, and which must be established through concretisation.[21] Most lawyers from a system where good faith plays an important role, will therefore agree that these differences in theoretical conception do not matter very much. Indeed, many authors are themselves not very consistent in their indication of the status of good faith. What really matters is the way in which good faith is applied by the courts: the character of good faith is best shown by the way in which it operates.

2.4   Concretisation

As said, the abstract standard of good faith must be concretised in order to be able to be applied. The court determines what good faith requires in the circumstances of the specific case (*Einzelfallgerechtigkeit*).[22] However, the judge is not allowed to simply decide the way which seems most equitable to himself. He has to determine the requirements of good faith in such an objective way as possible.[23] In the Netherlands the code therefore provides in a specific provision what should be taken into account in determining what good faith requires in a particular case.[24] In addition to that, in most systems, particularly in Germany, scholars both in private law and in jurisprudence have developed methods for rationalising and objectivating the decisions of the court. The purpose of these *Methodenlehren* is to render the application of the law in general, and of general clauses like good faith in particular, as rational and objective (and thereby predictable) as possible, instead of leaving it to the subjective judgment of the individual judge. The generally agreed method for rationalising is that of distinguishing functions and developing groups of cases in which good faith has previously been applied (*Fallgruppen*). In doing so legal doctrine has developed an 'inner system' of good faith,[25] which is regarded as the content of that norm.

In Germany this operation has already been accomplished to a large extent. Com-

---

21   See e.g. Helmut Heinrichs, in: *Palandt Bürgerliches Gesetzbuch*, § 242, Nos. 3 and 13, and Giorgio Cian & Alberto Trabucchi, *Commentario breve al codice civile*, Art. 1175, II, 1.

22   See e.g Arndt Teichmann, in: *Soergel Bürgerliches Gesetzbuch*, § 242, No. 6.

23   See e.g. Karl Larenz, *Lehrbuch des Schuldrechts I*, pp. 126 ff.

24   Art. 3:12 BW: 'In determining what reasonableness and equity require, reference must be made to generally accepted principles of law, to current juridical views in the Netherlands, and to the particular societal and private interests involved'. (Translation P.P.C. Haanappel & E. Mackaay, *New Netherlands Civil Code Patrimonial Law*, Deventer and Boston 1990).

25   The term inner system (*Binnensystem*) is taken from Jürgen Schmidt, in: *J. von Staudingers Kommentar zum Bürgerlichen Gesetzbuch mit Einführungsgesetz und Nebengesetzen; Zweites Buch Recht der Schuldverhältnisse; Einleitung zu §§ 241 ff.; §§ 241-243*, Berlin 1995, § 242, No. 87.

pare Palandt/Heinrichs:[26] 'In einer jetzt fast 100jähriger Rechtsentwicklung ist der Inhalt des § 242 durch Herausarbeitung von Funktionskreisen und durch Bildung von Fallgruppen präzisiert und im wesentlichen abschließend konkretisiert worden.' The effort of concretisation has made the content of the good faith norm quite comprehensible. The result is a system of sometimes quite specific duties, prohibitions, (sub)rules and doctrines which are all part of the content of good faith. It is said to have made decisions on the basis of § 242 BGB agreeably predictable (legal certainty) and rational.[27]

It is often emphasised, however, that concretisation will not and indeed should not lead to the fossilisation of good faith. First of all, it would be an illusion to think that concretisation will ever lead to a limited set of clearly distinguishable rules.[28] But, it is said, more importantly good faith should remain an open norm in order to be able to continue to play its important role of making the law flexible. The inner system of good faith should not become a strait-jacket.[29]

It should be added that the process of concretisation has not been totally identical in all countries. Whereas in Germany and in the Netherlands legal doctrine rather reacts to court decisions and tries to regroup them, and thus they build up a system (a rather more inductive approach), French and Italian legal doctrine seem to follow the more deductive approach of asking themselves what, in theory, the content of the duty of good faith, or the good faith standard could be, and thus they build up a system of sub-duties et cetera, in which the legal decisions are given their place at a later stage, the Italian authors thereby relying heavily on the achievements of German courts and legal doctrine.

2.5 Functions and Fallgruppen

Most systems distinguish between several functions of good faith. Here again French law takes a somewhat different position since there the approach seems to be rather one of distilling sub-duties from the general duty of good faith.[30] But, as said, in most other systems legal doctrine has distinguished several functions of good faith. It is interesting to see that the number of functions attributed is usually three.

In Germany a distinction made by Siebert has been *grundlegend*. He distinguished three functions of § 242 BGB:[31] 1) supplementation of duties; 2) limitation of rights;

---

26 Helmut Heinrichs, in: *Palandt Bürgerliches Gesetzbuch*, § 242, No. 2.

27 See Arndt Teichmann, in: *Soergel Bürgerliches Gesetzbuch,* § 242, No. 7.

28 See J. Gernhuber, *Bürgerliches Recht; Ein systematisches Repertorium für Fortgeschrittene*, 3rd ed., München 1991, p. 167: 'Die Vorstellung einer totalen Vertypung ist eine reine Utopie'.

29 See Herbert Roth, in: *Münchener Kommentar*, § 242, No. 32.

30 The subduties most often mentioned are the duty of loyalty (*obligation de loyauté*) and the duty to cooperate (*obligation de coopération*). See e.g. Y. Picod, *Le devoir de loyauté dans l'exécution du contat*, Paris 1989, *passim*; François Terré & Philippe Simler & Yves Lequette, *Les obligations*, nos. 415-416; A. Rieg, 'Articles 1134 et 1135' in: *Jurisclasseur, Contrats et obligations* (1989), nos. 86-104; B. Starck & H. Roland & L. Boyer, *Droit civil, Les obligations, 2. Le Contrat*, 3rd ed., Paris, 1989, nos. 1140-1146. The (important!) duty to inform (*obligation de renseignement*) is usually regarded as a subduty of the duty to cooperate. See e.g. François Terré & Philippe Simler & Yves Lequette, *Les obligations*, No. 430). See on these duties, *infra*, III, A, 4.

31 See W. Knopp & W. Siebert, in: *Soergel Bürgerliches Gesetzbuch*, 10th ed., Stuttgart, Berlin, Köln and Mainz 1967, § 242, Nos. 34 ff.

3) *Wegfall der Geschäftsgrundlage*. In addition to these three functions there is good faith interpretation which is based on § 157 BGB. This distinction has essentially been followed by most scholars.[32] Some authors have defined one or more of the functions differently, while others have split the first function into two functions, thus arriving at a quadripartition.

In Italy scholars distinguish between a supplementing function (*funzione integrativa*) and an evaluating function (*funzione valutativa*) of good faith. However, not both are recognised by all scholars. As a matter of fact, a fierce debate has taken place between scholars who regarded a *funzione valutativa* as the exclusive role of good faith,[33] and those who wished that a *funzione integrativa* be recognised.[34] However, today both functions seem to have been recognised by the courts.[35] In addition the code provides for good faith interpretation (Art. 1366).

In the Netherlands good faith has a supplementing function (or effect, as it is usually called: *aanvullende werking*)[36] and a limiting function (*beperkende werking*).[37] In addition, good faith plays a role in interpretation.[38] Before the adoption of the 1992 Civil Code the limiting effect was the object of a lively debate amongst legal scholars, somewhat similar to the debate in Italy. Some authors favoured a broad concept of good faith interpretation and held the *beperkende werking* to be superfluous;[39] others upheld the necessity of a separate limiting or correcting function.[40] The *Hoge Raad* took the latter view, just like the legislator who explicitly recognised the *beperkende werking* in the new code.[41]

Also in Belgium good faith is usually said to have three functions:[42] an interpreta-

---

32 See explicitly F. Wieacker, '*Zur Rechtstheoretischen Präzisierung des § 242*, in: *Recht und Staat in Geschichte und Gegenwart; Eine Sammlung von Vorträgen und Schriften aus dem Gebiet der gesamten Staatswissenschaft*, 193/194, Tübingen 1956, p. 22; Joachim Gernhuber & Barbara Grunewald, *Bürgerliches Recht*, Nos. 4 ff; Dieter Medicus, *Schuldrecht I*, No. 132.

33 See in particular U. Natoli, *L'attuazione del rapporto obbligatorio*, in: *Trattato di diritto civile e commerciale diretto dai professori Antonio Cicu e Francesco Messineo*, vol. XVI, t. 1, Milano 1974, pp. 14 ff. See also e.g. L. Bigliazzi Geri, 'Buona fede nel diritto civile', pp. 171-172; U. Breccia, *Le obbligazioni*; in: *Trattato di diritto Privato a cura di Giovanni Iudica e Paolo Zatti*, Milano 1992, p. 3.

34 See in particular Stefano Rodotà, *Le fonti di integrazione del contratto*, Milano 1969, *passim*, especially chapter 2 (pp. 111 ff.). See also, e.g. A. Di Majo, *Delle Obligazioni in Generale, arts. 1173-1176*, in: *Commentario del codice civile Scialoja-Branca*, Bologna/Roma 1988, p. 322; C. Massimo Bianca, *Il contratto*, p. 223.

35 See e.g. Cass., 18 July 1989, n. 3362, Foro it., 1989, I, 2750, notes Di Majo and Mariconda. See e.g. Giorgio Cian & Alberto Trabucchi, *Commentario breve al codice civile*, I, 2; M. Cantillo, *Le Obbligazioni*, p. 210.

36 See A.S. Hartkamp, *Verbintenissenrecht II* (in: *Asser* series), Nos. 307 ff.

37 See A.S. Hartkamp, *Verbintenissenrecht II* (in: *Asser* series), Nos. 312 ff.

38 See A.S. Hartkamp, *Verbintenissenrecht II* (in: *Asser* series), Nos. 280 ff.

39 J.M. Van Dunné, *Normatieve uitleg van rechtshandelingen; Een onderzoek naar de grondslagen van het geldende verbintenissenrecht*, Deventer 1971, *passim*; H.C.F. Schoordijk, *Het algemeen gedeelte van het verbintenissenrecht naar het Nieuw Burgerlijk Wetboek*, Deventer 1979, pp. 21 ff.

40 See in particular P. Abas, *Beperkende werking van de goede trouw*, Deventer 1972, *passim*.

41 See Art. 6:2, Section 2, and Art. 6:248, Section 2 BW. See *Parl. Gesch. Boek 6*, pp. 43 ff.

42 See e.g. Jacques Herbots, *Contract Law in Belgium*, No. 272; Jacques Périlleux, 'Rapport belge', in: *Travaux de l'association Henri Capitant, Tome XLIII, année 1992. Journées louisianaises de Baton-Rouge et La Nouvelle Orléans, "La bonne foi"*, Paris 1994, p. 250.

tive function (*fonction interprétative*), a supplementing function (*fonction complétive*) and a restricting or limiting or mitigating function (*fonction restrictive, limitative, modératrice*). Sometimes a fourth function is distinguished that would allow the courts in certain circumstances to change the content of the contract, but this function, just as the *imprévision* theory, has not been accepted by the majority of authors and the courts.[43]

In a famous lecture published in 1956 Wieacker made an effort to specify the theoretical status of § 242 BGB.[44] That lecture is usually regarded as the theoretical foundation for Siebert's trichtonomy. What Wieacker did was to assimilate the functions of good faith to those which Papinian had attributed to the praetorian law.[45] In a well-known passage Papinian had said:[46] 'Ius praetorium est, quod praetores introduxerunt adiuvandi vel supplendi vel corrigendi iuris civilis gratia propter utilitatem publicam (...)'. Wieacker stated: 'Auch § 242 BGB wirkt *iuris civilis iuvandi, supplendi* oder *corrigendi gratia.*' Similar to the *ius praetorium*, Wieacker said, good faith has three functions: 1) 'die sinngemäße Verwirklichung des gesetzgeberischen Wertungsplanes durch den Richter' (*officium iudicis*); 2) 'alle Maximen richterlicher Anforderung an das persönliche rechtsethische Verhalten einer Prozeßpartei' ((*praeter legem*); 3) 'rechtsethische Durchbrüche durch das Gesetzesrecht' (*contra legem*). That trichtonomy looks very similar to the distinctions made in Italy, the Netherlands, and Belgium: interpretation, supplementation, correction. In Greece and in Portugal good faith does have an interpretative, a supplementing and a correcting role, although legal authors do not seem to think so explicitly in terms of three functions of good faith. Therefore, ignoring the subtleties, one could regard this trichtonomy as the European common core.[47]

It should be remarked, however, that the way in which Wieacker elaborates the assimilation of the functions of good faith to the three functions distinguished by Papinian as he continues his lecture is somewhat surprising. He regards the supplementation of duties as *iuvare*, whereas under Roman law and under contemporary law in Italy, the Netherlands, Greece, and Belgium this is regarded as *supplere*. Accordingly, he regards the *exceptio doli* (abuse of right) as *supplere*, whereas under Roman law and under contemporary law in Italy, the Netherlands and Belgium this is seen as *corrigere*. Several explanations may be given for this choice, which is followed by most German scholars: one being that the *exceptio doli* actually supplements a norm ('you must not abuse your right'), another that a distinction should be made between abuse of right and correction, because in the latter case (e.g. unforeseen circumstances) no reproach is made to the conduct of the party who requests performance. However, the most likely reason seems to lie in the fact that Wieacker

---

43 See Jacques Périlleux, 'Rapport belge', p. 248.
44 F. Wieacker, '*Zur Rechtstheoretischen Präzisierung des § 242*, especially p. 20 ff.
45 Followed explicitly by Dieter Medicus, *Schuldrecht I*, No. 132. See, previously, *RG*, 26 May 1914, *RGZ* 85, 108.
46 D. 1, 1, 7.
47 P. Schlechtriem, *Good Faith in German Law and in International Uniform Law*, in: Centro di studi e ricerche di diritto comparato e straniero (diretto da M.J. Bonell), *Saggi, conferenze e seminari*, 24, Roma 1997, p. 8, has suggested Wieacker's distincion of functions as a tentative understanding of how good faith might work under the UNIDROIT Principles or CISG.

was determining the functions of § 242 BGB, and not those of good faith. Therefore he did not regard concretisation (interpretation), which is not based on § 242 but on § 157 BGB, as the first function (*iuvare*), thus making the others move down one place, and creating space for (and actually adding) another (fourth) function.[48]

In most systems good faith is said to have three functions. Between the systems, and within each system, there is some difference of opinion about the exact definition of each of the functions. But it seems fair to say that in Europe usually three functions of good faith are distinguished, each of which correspond to one of the functions Papinian attributed to the *ius honorarium* with respect to the *ius civile*: 1) concretisation/interpretation (*adiuvare*); 2) supplementation (*supplere*) (mainly of duties, e.g. duties to be loyal, to protect, to co-operate, to inform); 3) correction/limitation (*corrigere*) (prohibition of abuse of right; *Fallgruppen* include: *venire contra factum proprium non valet*,[49] *dolo agit qui petit quod statim redditurus est, tu quoque*, prohibition of excessive disproportion). In addition, sometimes (in Germany and by some Belgian authors) a fourth function is added[50] in order to distinguish between the correction/limitation of a right for one's own (present or past) improper behaviour (*exceptio doli generalis* (*praesentis*) and *exceptio doli specialis* (*praeteriti*) respectively) and the correction/limitation of the right of an 'innocent' party (mainly when there is a change of circumstances or other *Unzumutbarkeit*).

3 Good Faith in Practice

Good faith has had great success in many European legal systems during the 20th century. In most countries the number of cases where the good faith clause has been applied has grown explosively over the last few decades. Also the field of application has been growing considerably in many systems. In the various systems good faith has been applied in virtually all fields of contract law (A), and sometimes even far outside it (B). In the following a few examples will be given of the way in which

---

48 Siebert actually regarded *Wegfall der Geschäftsgrundlage* merely as a sub-group of the cases on abuse of right (W. Knopp & W. Siebert, in: *Soergel Bürgerliches Gesetzbuch*, No. 40).

49 This *Fallgruppe* has been accepted in many jurisdictions. For Germany see e.g. Herbert Roth, in: *Münchener Kommentar*, § 242, Nos. 322 ff.; for the Netherlands ('*rechtsverwerking*') see e.g. A.S. Hartkamp, *Verbintenissenrecht II* (in: *Asser* series), Nos. 320 ff.; for Italy see e.g. A. Di Majo, *Delle Obligazioni in Generale*, arts. *1173-1176*, p. 341; for Spain ('*prohibición de ir contra los actos propios*') see e.g. L. Díez-Picazo & A. Gullón, *Sistema de Derecho Civil*, Vol. II, Madrid 1998, pp. 433 and 438 ff; for Portugal see e.g. A. Menezes-Cordeiro, 'Rapport portugais', p. 341; for Switzerland see e.g. Theo Mayer-Maly, in: Heinrich Honsell, Nedim Peter Vogt and Thomas Geiser (eds.), *Kommentar zum Schweizerischen Zivilgesetzbuch I*), Basel and Frankfurt am Main 1996, art. 2, Nos. 48 ff. Compare for Greece Michael P. Stathopoulos, *Contract law in Hellas*, No. 50. In France the principle has been recently discovered. See Martine Behar-Touchais (ed.), *L'interdiction de se contredire au détriment d'autrui*, Paris 2001.

50 See the four functions distinguished by Helmut Heinrichs, in: *Palandt Bürgerliches Gesetzbuch*, § 242, No. 13 (who, however, in addition to these functions of § 242 *BGB*, distinguishes a separate role for § 157 *BGB*, regarding § 157 *BGB* as a provision dealing with *Wollen* and § 242 *BGB* as dealing with *Sollen* (see No. 18)): 1) *Konkretisierungsfunktion*; 2) *Ergänzungsfunktion*; 3) *Schrankenfunktion*; 4) *Korrekturfunktion*.

good faith has been applied. It is clear that this account will be nowhere near exhaustive.[51]

3.1   Contract Law

3.1. 1 Formation

Many systems recognise a general duty of precontractual good faith.[52] Some codes contain a specific provision on precontractual good faith,[53] in other systems the duty of precontractual good faith has been established by the courts.[54] On the basis of this general duty they usually recognise a precontractual duty to inform.[55] Moreover, they hold that a party may be liable if it breaks off negotiations in a manner contrary to precontractual good faith.[56] In some systems it is held to be contrary to good faith under certain circumstances to invoke the non receipt of the acceptance of an offer (*exceptio doli specialis (praeteriti)*).[57]

3.2.2 Validity

A violation of the duty of good faith may lead to invalidity. For example, in many systems, before the introduction of statutory rules, standard terms could be held void on the basis of the general good faith clause,[58] and today in these statutes the test for

---

51 The same is true for references. See for more details M.W. Hesselink, *De redelijkheid en billijkheid in het Europese privaatrecht*, Deventer 1999, pp. 65-397 with references to many cases from various European jurisdictions.

52 See M.W. Hesselink, 'Precontractual Good Faith', in: Hugh Beale *et al.* (eds.) *Cases, Materials and Text on Contract Law*, Oxford and Portland, Oregon 2002, Chapter 2, Section 2 (pp. 237-293).

53 See Art. 1337 Italian Civil Code; Art. 197 Greek Civil Code; Art. 227 Portuguese Civil Code; Art. 2.15 UP; Art. 2:301 PECL. The German doctrine of *culpa in contrahendo*, which was frequently said to be based on good faith, has now been codified in § 311 (2) (*new*) BGB.

54 See for France, e.g. Com., 20 March 1972, *Bull. civ.* IV, No. 93; *J.C.P.* 1973, 17534, note Schmidt; *R.T.D. civ.* 1972, p. 722, observation Durry; for the Netherlands, e.g. HR, 15 November 1957, *NJ* 1958, 67, note Rutten; for Spain L. Díez-Picazo & A. Gullón, *Sistema de Derecho Civil*, Vol. II, p. 68.

55 For France, e.g., Cass. com., 8 november 1983, *Bull. civ.* IV, No. 298, p. 260; for the Netherlands e.g. HR, 30 November 1973, *NJ* 1974, 97, note GJS (under the new code good faith is no longer necessary as a basis; see now Art. 6:228(1)(b)); for Italy Rodolfo Sacco & G. De Nova, *Il contratto*, Vol. I, pp. 434 ff.; for Greece Michael P. Stathopoulos, *Contract law in Hellas*, No. 86; for Portugal J. De Matos Antunes Varela, *Das Obrigações em geral*, Vol. I, 9th ed., Coimbra 1996, No. 67.

56 See for France, e.g., Civ. I, 12 April 1976, *Bull. Civ.*, I, No. 122, *Def.*, 1976, a. 31434, No.5, p. 389, note Aubert; for Italy, e.g., Cass., 17 June, 1974, 1781, *Foro padano* 1975, I, 80, note Prandi, Temi, 175, 408, note Fajella; for the Netherlands, e.g., HR 18 June 1982, *NJ* 1983, No. 723, note Brunner; *AA* 32 (1983), 758, note Van Schilfgaarde; for Spain L. Díez-Picazo & A. Gullón, *Sistema de Derecho Civil*, Vol. II, p. 69; for Greece, Michael P. Stathopoulos, *Contract law in Hellas*, No. 86; for Portugal J. De Matos Antunes Varela, *Das Obrigações em geral*, Vol. I, No. 67.

57 See for Germany, *RG*, 13 July 1904, *RGZ* 58, 406; for the UP, Art. 1.7, Illustration 1.

58 See for Germany e.g *BGH*, 29 October 1956, *BGHZ* 22, 90 = *NJW* 1957, 17; for the Netherlands e.g *HR*, 20 February 1976, *NJ* 1976, 486, note G.J. Scholten, *AA* 1976, p. 476, note Van der Grinten; for Greece, Michael P. Stathopoulos, *Contract law in Hellas*, No. 34.

the unfairness of a term often lies in good faith.[59] Further, a violation of a pre-contractual duty to inform, based on good faith, may lead to invalidity for mistake or fraud (see above).[60] On the other hand, good faith may limit invalidity. The right to offer an adaptation in order to avoid invalidity is often based on good faith.[61] In the Netherlands under the old code conversion was based on the general good faith clause.[62]

3.2.3 Interpretation

In most systems good faith plays a role in interpretation. Many systems contain a statutory provision on good faith interpretation;[63] in other systems the role of good faith in interpretation has been established by the courts.[64] Particularly the objective method of interpretation is often based on good faith. In addition to 'objective' interpretation in some systems there is a concept of supplementing interpretation (*ergänzende Vertragsauslegung*), also based on good faith.[65] It amounts to what could be called 'gap filling'. If a contract does not contain any specific provision for a question that arises, the gap in the contract is filled by way of supplementing interpretation. Some authors have suggested a doctrine of good faith interpretation that is even broader, operating not only in case of gaps.[66]

3.1.4 Content

English textbooks on contract law usually contain a chapter entitled 'Content' that deals with the express and implied terms of the contract.[67] The UP have followed this example.[68] Legal systems in the French tradition speak of the effects of the contract.[69] Both for common law and civil law a distinction can be made between au-

---

59 See in Germany Art. 9 *AGBG*; in Portugal arts. 16 and 17 statute 1985 (see A. Menezes-Cordeiro, 'Rapport portugais', p. 349). For consumer contracts see also EC Council Directive 93/13/EEC, Art. 3, Section 1, which has been implemented in all EU jurisdictions.

60 In Greece, the test for mistake is (partially) based on good faith (Art. 142 CC; Michael P. Stathopoulos, *Contract law in Hellas*, Nos. 114 ff.).

61 Art. 144 Greek Civil Code explicitly says so (see Michael P. Stathopoulos, *Contract law in Hellas*, No. 121). See on Art. 1432 Italian Civil Code e.g Guido Alpa & M. Bessone, *I contratti in generale; Effetti, Invalidità e risoluzione del contratto*, Vol. II, Torino 1992, No. 36; on art. 6:230 Dutch Civil Code e.g. J.B.M. Vranken, 'Nietige overeenkomsten binden tot wat de goede trouw meebrengt', *NJB* 1990, p. 489.

62 See e.g. *HR*, 8 July 1987, *NJ* 1981, 284. Art. 3:42 of the new code is said to be based on good faith. See *Parl. Gesch. Boek 3*, p. 199 (M.v.A. II).

63 See § 157 German Civil Code; Art. 1366 Italian Civil Code; Art. 200 Greek Civil Code.

64 See for the Netherlands e.g. *HR*, 20 May 1994, *NJ* 1995, 691, note Brunner.

65 For Germany see e.g. *BGH*, 25 June 1980, *BGHZ* 277, 301; for Greece, see Michael P. Stathopoulos, *Contract law in Hellas*, No. 154; for the UNIDROIT Principles see Art. 4.8 UP. The PECL do not contain a similar provision.

66 See in the Netherlands J.M. Van Dunné, *Verbintenissenrecht I*, pp. 137 ff.

67 See e.g. G.H. Treitel, *The Law of Contract*, 10th ed., London 1999, Chapter 6; M.P. Furmston, *Cheshire, Fifoot and Furmston's Law of Contract*, 14th ed., London, Edinburgh and Dublin 2001, Chapter 6; Ewan McKendrick, *Contract Law*, 4th ed., London 2000, Part II.

68 Chapter 5 is called 'Content'.

69 The PECL have not made a choice: see Chapter 6 which is entitled 'Content and Effects'.

tonomous and heteronomous terms or effects of the contract. In Italian textbooks the determination of the heteronomous effects is usually called *integrazione* (supplementation or completion),[70] the term *interpretazione* being reserved for the determination of the autonomous effects.

In many systems good faith is regarded as one of the most important sources of heteronomous effects, or implied obligations as the Principles call them. The good faith duties most often incurred in the various legal systems are a duty of loyalty,[71] a duty of care,[72] a duty to co-operate[73] and a duty to inform.[74] The duty of loyalty protects the expectation interest. It obliges a party to secure performance or, more broadly, to ensure that the other party will have the use of the contract that he could reasonably expect from it. The contractual duty of care protects the negative interest. It obliges a party to take care that the person and the property of the other party do not suffer any damage during the performance. The adoption of a contractual duty of care is usually determined by the wish of the courts to provide victims (particularly when they are injured) with the protection tort liability (e.g. limited vicarious liability) or ordinary contractual liability (limited to impossible or late performance) does not provide or which is inaccessible (*non cumul*). In Germany there are even some who favour the adoption of a third track of liability (*dritte Spur*), which lies between contractual liability and tort liability, for a violation of a *Schutzpflicht* which arises whenever there is a special relationship (*Sonderverbindung*) between two ore more persons.[75] The duty to co-operate was first proposed by Demogue, in a famous for-

---

70 See C. Massimo Bianca, *Il contratto*, Chapter 8; Rodolfo Sacco & G. De Nova, *Il contratto*, Vol. I, Part 5, II.

71 See for Germany e.g. *BGH*, 28 April 1982, *NJW* 83, 998 (*Leistungstreuepflicht*); for France e.g. *Cass. soc.*, 30 April 1987, *Bull. civ.* V, No. 237, p. 152; *R.T.D. Civ.* 1988, 531, obs. Mestre (*devoir de loyauté*); for Italy e.g. *Cass.*, 18 July 1989, n. 3362, *Foro it.*, 1989, I, 2750, notes Di Majo and Mariconda (*obbligo di salvaguardia*); for Portugal A. Menezes-Cordeiro, 'Rapport portugais', p. 344; for Greece Michael P. Stathopoulos, *Contract law in Hellas*, No. 155; for Denmark Ole Lando, 'Each contracting party must act in accordance with good faith and fair dealing', in: *Festskrift till Jan Ramberg*, Stockholm 1996, p. 351.

72 See for Germany e.g. *BGH*, 10 March 1983, *NJW* 83, 2813 = *MDR* 1982, 1000 = *LM* BGB § 242 (Be), No. 47 (*Schutzpflicht*) and since January, 2002, § 241(2) BGB (*new*) (*Pflichten aus dem Schuldverhältnis*): 'Das Schuldverhältnis kann nach seinem Inhalt jeden Teil zur Rücksicht auf die Rechte, Rechtsgüter und Interessen des anderen Teils verpflichten.' See for France e.g. *Civ. I*, 17 January 1995, *D.* 1995, 350, note Jourdain; *D.* 1996, *Somm.* 15, obs. Paisant; *R.T.D. civ.* 1995, 631, obs. Jourdain (*obligation de sécurité*). See for Greece Michael P. Stathopoulos, *Contract law in Hellas*, No. 155; for Portugal, A. Menezes-Cordeiro, 'Rapport portugais', p. 344. In Italy the *obbligo di protezione* only plays a very limited role; see for an example where such a duty is said to have been adopted *Cass.*, 11 May 1973, n. 1269, *Giust. civ.*, 1973, I, 1306.

73 See for Germany e.g. *BGH*, 25 June 1976, *BGHZ* 67, 35; for France e.g. Paris, 26 June 1985, *R.T.D. civ.* 1986, 100, n. 2, obs. J. Mestre; for Italy *Cass.*, 9 March 1991, n. 2503, *Foro it.*, 1991, I, 2077, note Bellantuono.

74 See for France e.g. *Cass. I*, 18 December 1985, *Bull. civ.* I, No. 357; for Germany e.g. *BGH*, 7 December 1989, *LM* BGB § 242 (Be), No. 71 = *NJW* 1990, 1906 = *MDR* 1990, 690; for Italy e.g. *Cass.*, 8 August 1985, n. 4394, *Giur. it.* 1987, I, 1, 1136, note Romano; for Portugal see A. Menezes-Cordeiro, 'Rapport portugais', p. 344.

75 Claus-Wilhelm Canaris, 'Ansprüche wegen "positiver Vertragsverletzung" und "Schutzwirkung für Dritte" bei nichtigen Verträgen, Zugleich ein Beitrag zur Vereinheitlichung der Regeln über die Schutzpflichtverletzungen', *JZ* 1965, pp. 475-482, p. 479, proposed a theory of an *einheitliches gesetzliches Schutzverhältnis*, based on good faith: 'Alle Schutzpflichten finden ihre Grundlage in

mula:[76] 'Les contractants forment une sorte de microcosme; c'est une petite société où chacun doit travailler pour un but commun qui est la somme des buts individuels poursuivis par chacun, absolument comme dans la société civile ou commerciale', and it was first 'codified' by the Principles.[77] It follows from the nature of this duty that it is more important in relational, long-term contracts, in particular long-term commercial contracts,[78] than in simple exchange contracts. Finally, the duty to inform does not only operate during the pre-contractual stage, but also during performance.[79]

3.1.5   Privity

In Germany the doctrine of *Vertrag mit Schutzwirkung zugunsten Dritten*, which was adopted on the basis of good faith,[80] considerably relaxed the privity of contract by broadening the possibility of a third party to profit from a contract between two other parties.[81] Under this doctrine certain third parties are included in the protection which a party to a contract has to provide for his partner and which makes full vicarious liability possible (*Schutzpflicht*; see above).[82] In the Netherlands, under certain conditions a party may invoke a limitation clause against a third party.[83]

---

einem einheitlichen Schutzverhältnis, das mit der Aufnahme des geschäftlichen Kontaktes beginnt und sich über mehrere Stufen – Beginn der Vertragsverhandlungen, Vertragsschluß, Eintritt in das Erfüllungsstadium – verdichtet; es entsteht unabhängig vom Willen der Parteien, ist also "gesetzlicher" Natur, und findet seine Rechtfertigung im Vertrauensgedanken und seine positiv-rechtliche Grundlage in § 242 BGB'.

76 R. Demogue, *Traité des obligations en général, II Effets des obligations*, Part VI, Paris, 1931, No. 3 (p. 9). Compare however, the reaction by Jean Carbonnier, *Droit Civil*, Vol. IV *Les Obligations*, 22nd ed., Paris 2000, No. 114 (p. 227): 'L'outrance peut perdre une idée juste. On s'étonnera qu'à une époque où le mariage s'était peut-être trop transformé en contrat, d'aucuns aient rêvé de transformer tout contrat en mariage.'

77 Arts. 5.3 UP and 1:202 PECL.

78 See Nagla Nassar, *Sanctity of Contract Revisited: A Study in the Theory and Practice of Long-Term International Commercial Transactions*, Dordrecht, Boston and London 1995, pp. 156 ff. See, generally, Ian Macneil, 'Contract Adjustment of long-term economic relations under classical, neoclassical and relational contract law', (1978) 72 *Northwestern University LR*, p. 854.

79 More precisely: in addition to a duty to give the other party information that may determine his consent, there may also be a duty to inform the other party in order to assure that a party obtains what he could expect from the performance. See M. Fabre-Magnan, *De l'obligation d' information dans les contrats; Essai d'une théorie*, Paris 1992, 281.

80 The courts have based it on § 157 *BGB* (*ergänzende Vertragsauslegung*), but the majority of legal doctrine, maintaining that there cannot be said to be a gap in the contract, regards § 242 *BGB* as the real foundation (see e.g. Karl Larenz, *Lehrbuch des Schuldrechts I*, p. 227).

81 See, for Portugal, A. Menezes-Cordeiro, 'Rapport portugais', p. 337.

82 A well-known example is the vegetable leaf case (*BGH*, 28 January 1976, *BGHZ* 66, 51), where the doctrines of *culpa in contrahendo* and *Vertrag mit Schutzwirkung für Dritte* were combined in order to find laibility against a supermarket, where the child of a (potential) customer was injured because it had slipped on a vegetable leaf that an employee of the supermarket had dropped.

83 See e.g. *HR*, 12 January 1979, *NJ* 1979, 36, note Bloembergen; *AA* 1979, p. 556. Exceptions to the privity principle like this one are said to be based on good faith (see A.S. Hartkamp, *Verbintenissenrecht II* (in: *Asser* series), No. 386).

3.1.6   Performance

In most systems if the parties have not made adequate provisions regarding the time and place of performance et cetera, and if the code does not provide for any specific regulations either, such rules are usually based on good faith or equity. However, one may ask whether a separate heading 'performance' is necessary in addition to 'content'. The (rules on) rights and duties which the code adds to what the parties have agreed upon may be spelled out under the heading 'content'.

In the UP the second section of the chapter on performance deals with hardship. However, since the effect of hardship may not only be that a party is no longer under a duty to perform a still existing obligation, but also that the obligations are changed or even the contract terminated, it seems more appropriate to distinguish hardship as a separate doctrine.

3.1.7   Hardship

During the course of the 20th century a doctrine of hardship was adopted in most European systems. Often it was based on good faith, either because the courts based their doctrine on the general good faith clause[84] or because a specific code provision referred to the concept of good faith[85] and is regarded as a *lex specialis* of the general good faith clause.[86] Indeed, the problem of unforeseen circumstances is often cited as the paradigm example of the operation of the concept of good faith and of the need for such a concept.

3.1.8   Remedies for Non-Performance

On the one hand, in many systems some of the remedies for non-performance are based on good faith. The right to withhold performance forms the most significant example. Most systems recognise an *exceptio non adimpleti contractus*. In some systems this remedy (which is actually a defence) is or was based on good faith.[87] In ad-

---

84 See for German law, e.g. *BGH*, 8 February 1984, *NJW* 1984, 1746 = *MDR* 1985, 47 = *LM* BGB § 242 (Bb), No. 108. See now § 313 *BGB* (*new*) (Störung der Geschäftsgrundlage): '(1) Haben sich Umstände, die zur Grundlage des Vertrags geworden sind, nach Vertragsschluss schwerwiegend verändert und hätten die Parteien den Vertrag nicht oder mit anderem Inhalt geschlossen, wenn sie diese Veränderung vorausgesehen hätten, so kann Anpassung des Vertrags verlangt werden, soweit einem Teil unter Berücksichtigung aller Umstände des Einzelfalls, insbesondere der vertraglichen oder gesetzlichen Risikoverteilung, das Festhalten am unveränderten Vertrag nicht zugemutet werden kann. (2) Einer Veränderung der Umstände steht es gleich, wenn wesentliche Vorstellungen, die zur Grundlage des Vertrags geworden sind, sich als falsch herausstellen. (3) Ist eine Anpassung des Vertrags nicht möglich oder einem Teil nicht zumutbar, so kann der benachteiligte Teil vom Vertrag zurücktreten. An die Stelle des Rücktrittsrechts tritt für Dauerschuldverhältnisse das Recht zur Kündigung.'

85 See Art. 388 Greek Civil Code; Art. 437 Portuguese Civil Code; Art. 6:258 Dutch Civil Code.

86 See for the Netherlands *Parl. Gesch. Boek 6*, p. 974 (M.v.A. II); for Greece Michael P. Stathopoulos, *Contract law in Hellas*, No. 60, No. 292.

87 For both German and Dutch law the reason for this lies in the fact that the relevant provisions (§ 320 *BGB* and Art. 6:262 *BW* respectively) are seen as *leges speciales* of the general right to withhold (§ 273 *BGB* and Art. 6:52 *BW* respectively), which in turn is regarded as a *lex specialis* of the general

dition, Germany and the Netherlands recognise a more general right to withhold performance which is said to be a *lex specialis* of the general good faith clause.[88] Further, the German doctrine of *positive Vertragsverletzung* is often said to be (ultimately) based on good faith.[89]

On the other hand, the exercise of a remedy may be limited by good faith. In many systems a party is not allowed to terminate the contract or withhold its own performance for a merely minor non-performance. In some systems this is conceived as an exception to the general right to terminate or to withhold, based on good faith.[90] Moreover, the right to request specific performance may be limited by good faith.[91] Furthermore, in France the invocation of a *clause résolutoire* is limited by good faith.[92] Finally, in some systems the right (and its modalities) to end a contract which was concluded for an indeterminate period – not a remedy for *non-performance*, of course – is based on good faith.[93]

3.2 Outside Contract Law

It is often thought, particularly by common law lawyers, that good faith typically operates in contract law. Good faith is often seen, partly due to its collocation in codes of the French legal family, as a counterbalance to the rigour of the *pacta sunt servanda* rule. Although this may be an important role, in most systems the field of application of good faith is far from limited to contract law. First, many codes already themselves indicate that the obligor and obligee to *any* obligation have to meet the standard of good faith in their conduct.[94] This means that a person who is liable in tort towards another person (e.g. because he has injured him or damaged his property) or who has been unjustifiedly enriched at the expense of another person has to

---

good faith clause (see *infra*). Under the old code the Dutch *Hoge Raad* based the *e.n.a.c.* on the general good faith clause (see *HR*, 30 June 1978, *NJ* 1978, 693, note G.J. Scholten). Also in France the *e.n.a.c.* is sometimes based on good faith (see Philippe Malaurie & Laurent Aynes, *Les obligations*, No. 722).

88 For Art. 273 German Civil Code, see Helmut Heinrichs, in: *Palandt Bürgerliches Gesetzbuch*, § 273, No. 1; for Art. 6:52 Dutch Civil Code, see *Parl. Gesch. Boek 6*, p. 205 (T.M.).

89 See e.g. *BGH*, 13 November 1953, *BGHZ* 11, 80 = *NJW* 1954, 229; Claus-Wilhelm Canaris, 'Ansprüche wegen 'positiver Vertragsverletzung' und 'Schutzwirkung für Dritte' bei nichtigen Verträgen', pp. 475-482, p. 479; E. Kramer, in: *Münchener Kommentar*, 'Einleitung Band 2', No. 73. See now § 280 (*new*) *BGB*. See for Portugal A. Menezes-Cordeiro, 'Rapport portugais', p. 340.

90 See for the Netherlands e.g. *HR*, 10 August 1992, *NJ* 1992, 715; A.S. Hartkamp, *Verbintenissenrecht II* (in: *Asser* series), No. 516. See for Germany e.g. Herbert Roth, in: *Münchener Kommentar*, § 242, Nos. 438 ff. See explicitly § 320 *BGB* (*e.n.a.c.*).

91 See for the Netherlands *HR*, 5 January 2001, *NJ* 2001, 79 (Multi Vastgoed/Nethou); A.S. Hartkamp, *Verbintenissenrecht I* (in: *Asser* series), no 639.

92 See, e.g., *Cass. Civ. III*, 15 December 1976, *Bull. Civ. III*, No. 465, *R.T.D. Civ.* 1977, 340, obs. Cornu.

93 For Germany see e.g. *BGH*, 15 June 1951, *LM*, § 242 (Bc) BGB, No. 1; for the Netherlands see e.g. *HR*, 21 April 1995, *NJ* 1995, 437.

94 See § 242 German Civil Code, in the Section on the content of obligations in general; Art. 1175 Italian Civil Code, in the title on obligations in general; Art. 288 Greek Civil Code, in the Section on the law of obligations in general; Art. 762, Section 2, Portuguese Civil Code, in the Section on performance of obligations in general; Art. 6:2 Dutch Civil Code, in the title on obligations in general.

act in accordance with good faith. However, in addition to that, in some systems the field of application is even broader.[95] In the Netherlands good faith has been applied in, for example,[96] the law of succession, company law, bankruptcy law, property law and private international law. Hartkamp concludes that good faith must be held to be applicable in the whole of patrimonial law.[97] German law goes even further. There good faith operates not only in the whole of private law (e.g. family law, labour law, commercial law, copyright law),[98] but even outside it, in administrative law, tax law, procedural law (not only civil procedure) et cetera.[99] In other words: it is applicable in all fields of the law, except maybe in penal law.[100]

In Germany an effort has been made to limit the field of application of good faith in a rational way. The solution was found in the *Sonderverbindung* (special relationship). It was said that only in the case of a 'special connection' between two or more persons, which is defined as a relationship of mutual trust similar to a contractual relationship, does their conduct have to meet the standard of good faith.[101] That standard being higher than the one generally prevailing in society (i.e. between 'strangers'), the *gute Sitten* (*boni mores*), the violation of which leads to tort liability. The *Sonderverbindung* concept was adopted by the courts. However, in their wish to apply the good faith standard (and all the duties, doctrines, and rules that come with it!) in many situations, they have broadened the concept considerably. As a result now not only neighbours, but also, e.g. plaintiff and defendant, competitors in a market, and a citizen and the State are said to have a special relationship.[102] It is therefore held that the concept of the *Sonderverbindung* has failed to limit the field of applica-

---

95   See Martijn W. Hesselink, *De redelijkheid en billijkheid in het Europese privaatrecht*, p. 382 ff, where I give examples from various European jurisdictions of applications of good faith in property law, family law, company law, procedural law, public law, international law.

96   See, for more examples, A.S. Hartkamp, *Verbintenissenrecht II* (in: *Asser* series), No. 304.

97   A.S. Hartkamp, *Verbintenissenrecht II* (in: *Asser* series), No. 304.

98   See already *Reichsgericht*, 26 May 1914, *RGZ* 85, 108 (117): 'Das System des Bürgerlichen Gesetzbuchs wird durchdrungen von dem Grundsatze von Treu und Glauben mit Rücksicht auf die Verkehrssitte und von dem Grundsatze der Zurückweisung jeder Arglist im weitesten Sinne. Die §§ 157, 226, 242, 826 erscheinen nur als besondere Ausprägungen eines allgemeinen Prinzips. (...) das allgemeine Prinzip beherrscht alle Einzelbestimmungen und muß gerade in ihnen lebendige Wirkung üben, zur Klärung, Erweiterung, Ergänzung oder Beschränkung des vereinzelten Wortlauts'. Compare the Swiss Civil Code which has put the general good faith clause right at the beginning (Art. 2).

99   See for examples, e.g. Arndt Teichmann, in: *Soergel Bürgerliches Gesetzbuch*, § 242, nos. 65-106; Herbert Roth, in: *Münchener Kommentar*, § 242, Nos. 57 ff. Compare the *Travaux de l'association Henri Capitant, Tome XLIII, année 1992. Journées louisianaises de Baton-Rouge et La Nouvelle Orléans, 'La bonne foi'*, Paris 1994, that discuss good faith in contract law, penal law, fiscal law, administrative law, and international law, in several systems.

100 See e.g. Helmut Heinrichs, in: *Palandt Bürgerliches Gesetzbuch*, § 242, No. 1 ('eine das gesamte Rechtsleben beherrschenden Grundsatz'). It is often said that only (substantive) penal law seems to be excluded from the application of good faith, as a result of the *nulla poena sine lege* principle. See e.g. Jürgen Schmidt, in: *J. von Staudingers Kommentar*, § 242, No. 237, and Y. Loussouarn, 'Rapport de synthèse', in: *Travaux de l'association Henri Capitant, Tome XLIII, année 1992. Journées louisianaises de Baton-Rouge et La Nouvelle Orléans, 'La bonne foi'*, Paris 1994, p. 18.

101 See e.g. Helmut Heinrichs, in: *Palandt Bürgerliches Gesetzbuch*, § 242, No. 6; Karl Larenz, *Lehrbuch des Schuldrechts I*, p. 128.

102 See for other examples e.g. Jürgen Schmidt, in: *J. von Staudingers Kommentar*, § 242, Nos. 159 ff.

tion of good faith and that its field of application must therefore be regarded as being unlimited.[103]

4   An Alternative View

4.1   Introduction

Section 3 shows that in all systems the courts have developed many – often very important – new rules and doctrines on the basis of the general good faith clause, in contract law and far outside it. These rules at first sight do not seem to have very much in common. In particular there seems to be nothing else that distinguishes them from other rules than the fact that the courts, when adopting them, have mentioned a general good faith clause as their basis. However, in the traditional view, as shown in Section 2, all these rules are regarded as concretisations of good faith, as the content of the open good faith norm. Here I will argue that good faith as it has developed cannot be regarded as a norm and that it does not make sense to regard rules like those mentioned in Section 3 as the content of an open good faith norm. What are usually called the three functions of good faith are in reality the normal tasks of the judge. There is no inner coherence between so-called good faith rules and doctrines. Instead of trying to develop an inner system of good faith that is supposed to concretise the open norm, legal doctrine should try to give the rules and doctrines that the courts have developed while invoking good faith their proper place in the system of the code.

4.2   The Judge and the Code

Immediately after the enactment of the codes in Europe it was thought that the only thing the courts had to do was to apply the law, which they could find in the codes. This led to the traditional civil law view that the courts do not create the law, they merely apply it. Today, however, it is broadly accepted that this traditional view may be in conformity with the ideals of Enlightenment (separation of powers), but not with reality: also in civil law systems the courts do not only apply the law, they also create it.

As a matter of fact, in civil law as in common law systems, applying the law necessarily implies creating it. This follows from the simple fact that a court has to make a decision in every case that comes before it. In continental European legal systems the courts have to resolve cases by applying the rules from the code. This means that they have to apply abstract rules to concrete cases. A rule may be conceived as an abstract formula that links certain legal consequences to certain facts: if facts a, b and c occur the legal effect will be x (e.g.: 'a person who promises to do something but then breaks his promise must repair the damage'). In applying a rule to a certain fac-

---

103 See e.g. Jürgen Schmidt, in: *J. von Staudingers Kommentar*, § 242, No. 163; Dieter Medicus, *Schuldrecht I*, No. 130. In *BGH*, 22 October 1987, *BGHZ*, 102, 95 (102), the *BGH* explicitly left open the question whether a *Sonderverbindung* is required for the application of § 242 *BGB*.

tual situation the judge may have to face three major problems. First, it may occur that he has some doubts as to whether the facts presented before him correspond to the facts as defined in the rule (e.g.: does silence constitute a promise?), or whether the remedy which the plaintiff requests corresponds to the legal effect as defined in the rule (e.g.: is lost profit part of the damage that must be repaired?). Secondly, it may be that not all the facts mentioned in the rule have occurred, but some others have, which he regards as equivalent, so that he finds it suitable that the same legal effect should follow in this case (or he regards the remedy requested as equivalent to the remedy mentioned in the rule). Thirdly, it may occur that all the facts mentioned in the rule have indeed occurred, but also some other facts which, in the eyes of the judge, mean that the legal effect indicated in the rule should not follow. Thus the court may find it necessary to interpret (concretise), to supplement and to correct the abstract rule in order to reach an acceptable result. This necessarily follows from the fact that it has to apply a system of abstract rules to a concrete case.

If a judge decides in a certain case to concretise, supplement or correct the law in a certain way, would he be doing justice if he refused to do so in a following similar case? The answer is no, in most systems it is thought that justice requires like cases to be treated alike.[104] Therefore a court in civil law countries is bound by *stare decisis* just as much as a common law court. But if a court should decide in the same way as it decided in a precedent similar case, this means nothing less than that the court with its earlier decision has established a new rule, a rule which is a concretisation, a supplementation or a correction of an existing rule.[105] Thus the concretisation, supplementation, and correction of the law has become part of the law. Therefore the conclusion must be that the application of the law necessarily implies the creation of law.[106]

The same wish to treat like cases alike and different cases differently in accordance with the differences, also means that the law – be it common law or civil law – has to be a system:[107] rules are related to each other, according to the similarities and

---

104 In most systems the right to equal treatment is even constitutionally protected. See e.g. in the Netherlands art. 1 *GW*. For the EU see Chapter III (Equality) (arts. 20-26) Charter of Fundamental Rights of the European Union (Nice, 2000), especially art. 20 (Equality before the Law): 'everyone is equal before the law'. See also art. 14 ECHR.

105 The rule is new in the sense that its existence was not known before. Unless one believes in natural law there seems to be no reason to take the view that the judge discovers a pre-existing concretisation, supplementation, or a correction to or of the rule. In that latter (rather fictitious) view all three problems could be regarded as questions of interpretation. For a debate on this issue (and on other related issues) see M.J. Borgers & I. Giesen & C.E.C. Jansen & F.G.H. Kristen & F.W.J. Meijer & T.H.D. Struycken & F.M.J. Verstijlen & J.B.M. Vranken, 'Vragen aan Hesselink over zijn alternatieve visie op de functies van de redelijkheid en billijkheid en de taak van de rechter', *NJB* 2000, pp. 2029-2031 and M.W. Hesselink, '"Wat is recht etc.?"; Antwoorden op vragen van Tilburgers over rechtsregels, rechtspraak en rechtsvorming', *NJB* 2000, pp. 2032-2040.

106 For this reason it is important that the judge indicates the facts that were decisive in persuading him to adopt a certain interpretation, supplementation, or correction of the law. Legal certainty depends on the extent to which the judge makes it explicit which facts are decisive (i.e. which facts constitute elements of the new (sub-)rule) (and on consistency of course: *stare decisis*). A summary justification of a legal decision fits in with the idea that the courts merely apply the law, but is no longer justified when it is recognised that the courts create the law when applying it.

107 This is not a factual but a normative statement, based on the (fundamental) idea of equality.

differences of the cases to which they apply.[108] The difference between civil law and common law is that most civil law systems have (temporarily) fixed their system of rules in a code in which the system is made more explicit; in most codes, particularly the German BGB and the new Dutch BW, as a result of a higher degree of abstraction. The creation of new rules (concretisations, supplementations, and corrections of existing rules) leads to new ramifications of the system. What has been said with regard to rules applies accordingly to the system. Clearly, the need to treat like cases alike may mean that as a result of the concretisation, supplementation, and correction of a rule other rules, located in other places within the system, are also adapted accordingly. Moreover, just like rules, the system as such (which is, as said, nothing more than the formalisation of the wish to treat like cases alike) may be concretised, supplemented and corrected. Again, this is equally true for civil law as it is for common law. The fact that in civil law systems the legislator at a certain point in time has fixed the system does not mean that it will remain unchanged and closed. Just as the legislator cannot make rules that will remain unchanged in their application neither can it make a system that does not change when it is applied.

From the time when it was discovered that the courts (occasionally, it was thought) do create rules, civil lawyers have been trying, on the one hand, to determine why and when a judge is allowed to create law, and, on the other, to find a way by which to render the court's judgment as rational and as objective as possible, by developing – sometimes descriptive, but usually prescriptive – analyses of the decision-making by the judge. However, both these efforts presuppose that judge-made law is an anomaly. But, as we have just seen, that presumption is incorrect. Therefore there is no need for a justification that goes any further than the (constitutional) attribution to the judge of the power to resolve disputes on the basis of the law in the code. Also, there is no need to develop a prescriptive method for guaranteeing the objectivity and rationality of the court's judgment. We should merely recognise that we have confidence in the subjective judgment of our judges – in particular those in our Supreme Courts – with regard to the interpretation, supplementation and correction of the law, and in the way our judicial system is organised (e.g. the selection and training, the career system, the plurity of judges, the duty to provide the grounds for the decision in question, and the appeal system).[109]

---

108 In the same sense David Howarth, 'The General Conditions of Unlawfulness', in: A.S. Hartkamp *et al.* (eds.) *Towards a European Civil Code*, 2nd ed., Nijmegen and The Hague, London, Boston 1998, pp. 397 ff. See also J.H. Baker, *An Introduction to English Legal History*, p. 89, who says that in England the law has been regarded as a system since Tudor times.

109 This latter point has been the subject of criticism. See especially M.J. Borgers & I. Giesen & C.E.C. Jansen & F.G.H. Kristen & F.W.J. Meijer & T.H.D. Struycken & F.M.J. Verstijlen & J.B.M. Vranken, 'Vragen aan Hesselink over zijn alternatieve visie op de functies van de redelijkheid en billijkheid en de taak van de rechter' (see also Oliver Remien, *ZeuP* 2001, p. 420). In reply to those critics I have further developed this point in my article '"Wat is recht etc.?"; Antwoorden op vragen van Tilburgers over rechtsregels, rechtspraak en rechtsvorming'. I will not pursue this point any further here since the questions of how a judge must operate when he creates new rules and whether in doing so he has discretion, are not specific to judge-made law 'on the basis of good faith' (they arise in all cases where judges make new rules), and since my main claims regarding the nature of good faith, which I will make in the remainder of this Section IV and in the Conclusions (V), do not depend on this point. One may very well accept these claims without accepting that courts, when

4.3   Functions of Good Faith or Tasks of the Court?

It is interesting to see that these three activities with regard to the law – concretising (or interpreting), supplementing, and correcting – which follow from the normal task of the judge (i.e. to apply the law), correspond to the three tasks that Papinian attributed to the *praetor* with regard to the written law in Rome. The *praetor* (and other magistrates) had to help (concretise), supplement and correct the *ius civile*, and the results of these three operations were regarded as new law which was called *ius honorarium*.

As I said before, Wieacker transplanted the Papinian trichtonomy into modern German law. However, he did not do so in order to indicate the tasks of the judge with regard to the law in the code, or to show the relationship between German judge-made law and the law in the code, but rather in order to indicate the functions of modern good faith. Good faith, Wieacker said, concretises, supplements and corrects the law. And, as shown above, this view has not only been followed by most German legal scholars, it is also the common view in most European legal systems, albeit that there the contract (and not the law) is often regarded as the object of interpretation, supplementation and correction by good faith.[110]

However, if the functions of good faith are the same as the tasks of the judge, i.e. interpreting, supplementing or correcting the law, does it then still make sense to regard good faith as a specific norm?

4.4   Good Faith is not a Norm

Good faith is usually said to be an open rule or open norm (see above, Section 2).[111] From the use of the term 'open norm' one could conclude that there must be a category of open norms which can be distinguished from other norms which are not open. However, such a conclusion would not be correct: all norms are more ore less open. Every norm could be placed on a scale which ranges from totally open to totally closed: a norm is more open when fewer situations are excluded from its applicability. The closer a rule gets to one of both extremes, the less it makes sense to speak of a rule: a totally closed rule (all cases but one are excluded) is an order, a totally open rule (no case excluded) is equivalent to the (potential) law. Although all norms are more or less open there are some norms which are usually explicitly called 'open', like *gute Sitten* in Germany, the *zorgvuldigheidsnorm* in the Netherlands, 'a reasonable time' in the Unidroit Principles, 'unfair term' in the European Directive. Often the legislator has deliberately formulated them in an open manner, usually because it was not yet able to determine which cases should be covered by the rule. The content of more open (or abstract) rules becomes clearer by their concretisation.[112]

---

creating new rules, have discretion and/or do actually decide according to their own subjective views.

110 I will come back on this later.

111 A norm is only part of a rule, the other part being the effect of non-compliance with the norm. The term 'general clause' reflects openness on both sides.

112 This is true for any rule (since all rules are more or less open) and accounts for the fact that after a certain period of time during which is apllied a code becomes unworkable: the system of the

Through application, sub-rules are developed which are interconnected. Thus a sub-system of the rule is developed. Therefore, as a result of its application, every rule will become the top of a subsystem.[113] Thus through a process of concretisation it becomes more and more clear what the content of the norm is.

However, the particularity of the general good faith clause as it has developed in many European legal systems is that – unlike other 'general clauses' – it does not contain (or no longer contains) a rule, because it is completely open: with regard to the premises (the norm) as well as with regard to the effects it is totally open.[114] Section 3 has given an impression of the variety of norms and legal effects that have been based on good faith by the courts. Statements, which are sometimes uttered to the effect that a general good faith clause makes the whole of contract law superfluous, or that the concept of equity could replace the whole law, are correct to the extent that in its field of application (see *infra*) good faith may be applied in *any* factual situation to establish *any* legal effect. In other words: any rule could be based on it. There is no difference between saying 'good faith requires' and 'justice requires' or 'the law requires'.[115]

The cause of good faith having become a completely open norm, and therefore having ceased to be a norm at all, probably lies in the fact that the content of good faith is said to consist of three functions which in reality are the tasks of the judge with regard to the law. Had the courts given real content to the good faith norm (e.g. leaving it a norm for the way in which an obligor has to perform), instead of calling the three main tasks of the judge its content, it would have been a real (open) norm. However, the assimilation of the functions of good faith with the tasks of the judge has resulted in good faith becoming a completely open norm. In every system where the content of good faith is said to consist of these three functions good faith is a completely open norm, i.e. no norm at all.[116]

Therefore, it seems, because of the way in which good faith has developed in most

---

code has developed huge subsystems with ramifications that often reach a degree of abstraction that is so low that they nearly touch the ground of the facts. Hence the call for recodification.

113 See as an illustration the commentaries on the various Civil Codes: the text of each article effectively serves as a heading for a very detailed account of a particular branch of the law, each of which may discuss hundreds of cases and cover dozens of pages of fine print.

114 The fact that good faith is not a norm may explain why its formulation or its place in the code of the general good faith clause does not seem to have been of any importance for its 'application' in most systems.

115 If, for example in a case of application of good faith in its corrective function, Parliament had allowed the same exception in the code, that would have been the result of a debate among MPs, who had all expressed their opinion about what would be most just, and then voted, whereas, if the need for this exception is 'discovered' by a judge in a concrete case lying before him, the judge has to state that the objective standard of good faith requires the exception instead of frankly admitting that in his view justice so requires.

116 The content of no other norm has been said to consist of functions which in reality are the tasks of the judge. This may explain why no other norm has become a totally open norm. Very broad concepts like *boni mores* and *zorgvuldigheidsnorm* are not completely open: not only is the norm not completely open, also their effect (in terms of remedies) is limited. As a result, the inner systems of provisions like § 826 BGB and art. 6:162 *BW* do not 'compete' (see *infra*, Section F) with the system of the code. See further my *De redelijkheid en billijkheid in het Europese privaatrecht* pp. 423f.

European legal systems (see above), it can no longer be regarded as a norm. In reality, good faith is not a norm but a mouthpiece (a *porte parole*) for new rules (see for a few examples Section 3).[117] However, if the general good faith clause is not a rule, it does not make sense to say that a decision is based on it. In reality such a decision is based on the new rule. Therefore the court should mention the new rule, and formulate it as explicitly as possible.

4.5 Field of Application Unlimited

It is clear that good faith, as is the case with the judge, should fulfil these three tasks with regard to the whole of private law, not only with regard to contract law. The assimilation of the functions of good faith with the normal tasks of the judge therefore explains why it has proved to be impossible in most countries to limit the field of application of good faith. The idea that the field of application of good faith should be limited follows from the conception of good faith as a standard for conduct which is higher than the one prevailing between strangers, and which should therefore be limited to contractual and similar situations. If, however, concretisation, supplementation, and correction of the law are regarded as the functions of good faith, there is no reason why good faith should only operate in a limited field of the law. Any rule is subject to interpretation, supplementation, correction, or, to put it in terms of rights and obligations: rights and obligations are never abstract, but always subject to concretisation, supplementation and limitation. To give an example, it is clear that not only a contractual right but any right should not be abused (i.e. any abstract right has certain limits).[118]

---

117 In the same sense Jürgen Schmidt, in: *J. von Staudingers Kommentar*, § 242, Nos. 176 ff.; Christian E.C. Jansen, 'Good Faith in Construction Law: the Inaugural King's College Construction Law Lecture' (1999) 15 *Const. L.J.*, pp. 347 ff, on p. 358; H.J. de Kluiver, 'Goede trouw en rechtspersonenrecht', in: *A-T-D; Opstellen aangeboden aan Prof.mr. van Schilfgaarde*, Deventer 2000, pp. 225 ff.; W. Snijders, *WPNR* 6376 (1999), pp. 792 ff, see on p. 793, who agrees in principle, but regards the present version as being too radical; Duncan Kennedy, 'The Political Stakes in "Merely Technical" Issues of Contract Law', 10 *ERPL* (2002), pp. 7-28, on p. 19 ('the phrase good faith has no content at all'); Simon Whittaker & Reinhard Zimmermann, 'Good faith in European contract law: surveying the legal landscape', in: Reinhard Zimmermann & Simon Whittaker (eds.), *Good Faith in European Contract Law*, Cambridge 2000, pp. 7-62, p. 32: 'All in all, therefore, § 242 BGB is often needed merely for a transitory phase until a new rule is sufficiently well established to be able to stand on its own legs: so that "figuratively speaking, the statutory foundation of § 242 could be withdrawn without any risk of having the judge-made edifice collapse" [reference to Hein Kötz]. All in all, therefore, § 242 BGB is neither 'queen of rules' nor 'baneful plague' but an invitation, or reminder, for courts to do what they do anyway and have always done [reference to the present essay]: to specify, supplement and modify the law, i.e. to develop it in accordance with the perceived needs of their time.' See also H. Merz, *Berner Kommentar, Einleitungsband*, Bern 1966, Art. 2 ZGB, No. 42 (*Durchgangsfunktion*). Critical are P. van Schilfgaarde, 'Deel 4 van Hesselink', *WPNR* 6377 (1999), pp. 811 ff; J.H. Dalhuisen, *RM Themis* 1999, pp. 332 ff, Oliver Remien, *ZeuP* 2001, pp. 418ff; M.J. van Laarhoven & W.M. Nieskens-Isphording, *NTBR* 2001.

118 In some systems the prohibition of the abuse of a right is seen as one of the rules contained in good faith. In some others it is seen as a separate doctrine. It is clear, however, that it is simply equivalent to the third task of the judge: in certain circumstances he has to make an exception to the right. Of course, the question in which circumstances a right should be limited ('the test for abuse') depends entirely on the right involved. Usually, a property right is thought to be more sovereign than

4.6 Rejection of an Inner System of Good Faith

Section 3 has shown that the courts have developed many new rules and doctrines on the basis of good faith, which for an outsider at first sight do not seem to have much in common. Section 2 has shown that all these rules are usually regarded as sub-rules of good faith, as part of the content of the good faith norm. However, if, as maintained here, good faith is not a norm, and if the functions of good faith in reality are the normal tasks of the judge, it does not make any sense to regard these new rules as the content of the good faith norm.

This also means that it does not make much sense to develop a sub-system of good faith either.[119] As said, the content of more open rules becomes clearer by their concretisation into a subsystem of rules et cetera.[120] However, the sub-system of a completely open rule inevitably turns out to be a parallel system of the law, which covers the whole field of law in which it applies, but in an alternative manner.[121] The result of the concretisation of good faith would be just another system of law, parallel to the system of the code, but not self-sufficient.[122]

'Good faith rules' have nothing more in common that distinguishes them from other rules than that the courts, when adopting them, have mentioned the general good faith clause as their legal basis. In particular, good faith rules are not fairer or more equitable or more moral than other rules.[123] Therefore, the sum of good faith rules and doctrines has no inner coherence. It is frequently assumed that good faith rules are necessarily or normally altruistic rules which impose solidarity and counterbalance party autonomy.[124] However, this is not necessarily the case. Indeed, it is more a question of which is the rule and which is the exception.[125] Most civil codes, especially those which were enacted in the 19th century, were almost exclusively

---

a contractual right. But the mechanism is the same: an abstract right does not exist in certain concrete circumstances. It is sometimes said that an existing right may not be invoked in certain circumstances. That terminology, however, reflects the idea of a higher norm ('you should not abuse your right') setting aside the lower norm ('you have a right'). This difference in terminology reflects the debates in Germany (*Innentheorie/Außentheorie*) and in France (Planiol/Josserand). In Germany one approach won the debate, in France it was the other.

119 For this reason the rules in Section 3 were not presented in the shape of a tentative three functions plus *Fallgruppen* subsystem of European good faith but according to the structure of a possible European contract law. This approach is not correct, of course, in the sense that these rules must be seen in their own system.

120 Jürgen Schmidt, in: *J. von Staudingers Kommentar*, § 242, nos. 192 ff, uses the term 'inner system' (*Binnensystem*).

121 See Jürgen Schmidt, in: *J. von Staudingers Kommentar*, § 242, nos. 194.

122 Compare for equity F.W. Maitland, *Equity; also The Forms of Action at Common Law; Two Courses of Lectures*, Cambridge 1920, pp. 18-19, and for *ius honorarium*, M. Kaser, 'Ius honorarium' und 'ius civile', *SZRA* 101 (1984), pp. 1-114, p. 4.

123 See Jürgen Schmidt, in: *J. von Staudingers Kommentar*, § 242, No. 195.

124 See especially Duncan Kennedy, 'Form and Substance in Private Law Adjudication', and more recently, Marietta Auer, 'Good Faith: A Semiotic Approach', 10 *ERPL* (2002), pp. 279-301.

125 Simon Whittaker & Reinhard Zimmermann, 'Coming to terms with good faith', in: Reinhard Zimmermann & Simon Whittaker (eds.), *Good Faith in European Contract Law*, Cambridge 2000, p. 699.

based on the idea of party autonomy. As a result, most concretisations, supplementations and corrections were inspired by concerns of solidarity. However, to the extent that contemporary private law is increasingly based on solidarity courts may well decide to concretise, supplement and correct those rules, on the basis of good faith, in a more autonomy-oriented way.[126]

Good faith shows the perceived weak spots of a legal system which the courts felt they had to repair by supplementation and correction on the basis of good faith.[127] In this respect 'the content of good faith' is very similar to equity in old English law and *ius honorarium* in Roman law.[128] And it is striking to see how much of what has been said on equity and on the *ius honorarium* is equally true for good faith in many civil law systems today. See, for example, Maitland on equity:[129] 'we ought to think of equity as supplementary law, a sort of appendix added on to our code, or a sort of gloss written round our code. (…) Equity without common law would have been a castle in the air, an impossibility. For this reason I do not think that any one has expounded equity as a single consistent system, an articulate body of law. It is a collection of appendixes between which there is no very close connection. (…) To have acknowledged the existence of equity as a system distinct from law would in my opinion have been a belated, a reactionary measure. (…) I think, for example, that you ought to learn the many equitable modifications of the law of contract, not as part of equity, but as part, and a very important part, of our modern English law of contract', and Kaser on *ius honorarium*:[130] 'Das *ius honorarium* ist stofflich kein geschlossenes Ganzes, kein System. (…) Während man dem *ius civile* zwar das Merkmal einer gewissen Kohärenz, wenn auch, wie der notwendig gewordene Hinzutritt des *ius honorarium* beweist, nicht das der Vollständigkeit zuerkennen darf, bleibt das *ius honorarium* eine bloße Summe von miteinander nicht, jedenfalls zumeist nicht notwendig, zusammenhängenden Einzelerscheinungen.' The 'content' of present-day good faith could be regarded as a new *ius honorarium* or as civil law's equity.[131] As

---

126 See, as a recent Dutch example, *HR*, 1 October 1999, *NJ* 2000, 207 (Geurtzen/ Kampstaal) where the concept of good faith was used to limit the effect of a (protective) statutory rule, thus reinforcing party autonomy. See further my *The New European Private Law*, Chapter 3 (previously published as 'The Principles of European Contract Law: Some Choices Made by the Lando Commission', in: Martijn W. Hesselink, Gerard de Vries, *Principles of European Contract Law*, Deventer 2001, pp. 5-95, and in *Global Jurist Frontiers*: Vol. 1: No. 1, Article 4), Section VI, B, 3.

127 Compare Simon Whittaker & Reinhard Zimmermann, 'Coming to terms with good faith', p. 677 (with a focus on contract law, the subject of their study): 'a legal system which is generally at ease with its own legal rules for the creation and regulation of contracts will have much less of a need to have a recourse to a general legal principle such as good faith; if the legal rules are seen as generally good (however this is conceived), there will be no need to correct or to supplement them.'

128 In the same sense with regard to equity now also Simon Whittaker & Reinhard Zimmermann, 'Coming to terms with good faith', p. 675.

129 F.W. Maitland, *Equity*, pp. 18-21.

130 M. Kaser, '"Ius honorarium' und "ius civile"', pp. 4, 72.

131 Of course, it is hardly surprising that the *ius honorarium* should be comparable to the good faith rules, since 'the functions of good faith' are parallel to those of the *ius honorarium* (see *supra*, Section C). However, there are differences as well. The most important one seems to be that the *ius honorarium* in principle contained all the law created by the magistrates, whearas today the courts do not base all their new rules on good faith (see *infra*, Section G).

said, it shows the perceived weak spots of a legal system which the courts felt had to be repaired by supplementation and correction on the basis of good faith.

Legal doctrine, instead of bringing the new rules developed on the basis of good faith in connection with each other, and becoming involved in discussions on whether a decision may be based on good faith and, if yes, on which good faith article or on which function etc., should relate them to the rules or doctrines that are concretised, supplemented or corrected by them.[132] In Germany, the present commentator to § 242 *BGB* in the prestigious Staudinger commentary has come to the same conclusion.[133] The 11th edition (1961) of that commentary, by Weber, counted 1553 pages. J. Schmidt, the present commentator, rightly says that ideally the commentary to § 242 *BGB* should be limited to a few phrases explaining that good faith is not a norm, and should then refer, for a discussion of rules which the courts have adopted mentioning § 242 *BGB*, to the commentary to the rules that were changed by them.[134]

In addition to these theoretical objections, in many countries there will soon be a practical need for abolishing the inner system of good faith. As a result of the enormous number of cases 'based on good faith' it will no longer be manageable. However, this number will inevitably continue to rise in all systems where the tasks of the judge with regard to the law are regarded as the functions of good faith. More and more lawyers will question the sense of a distinction between the rules of the code and the rules that are said to be the content of the good faith norm.[135] Therefore it seems likely (and indeed desirable) that the same will happen to good faith as happened to equity and *ius honorarium*: when the distinction is no longer held to be justified and in addition will prove to be impractical, it will be abolished.[136] German law may already have reached that point.

However, the rejection of an inner system of good faith does not mean that the efforts made by legal doctrine over the last century have been useless. First of all, it has been of great importance that scholars have formulated the rules or even doctrines which were adopted in cases where the general good faith clause was 'applied'. Secondly, many parts of the inner system of good faith may be directly transferred into the system of the code, particularly to its general provisions (e.g. the *Fallgruppe* of *venire contra factum proprium*),[137] and, for contract law, into the chapter on content (e.g. the obligations to be loyal, to protect, to co-operate, to inform). That is not only true for rules, but also for entire doctrines. This is shown where countries have adopted a new code: many doctrines that were adopted on the basis of good faith under the old code have been given their proper place in the new code, e.g. *culpa in*

---

132 On this approach see Simon Whittaker & Reinhard Zimmermann, 'Good faith in European contract law: surveying the legal landscape', p. 32: 'Whilst a radical adoption of this approach would probably go too far, and might also be impractical, the development is heading, in some respects, in this direction.'

133 Jürgen Schmidt, in: *J. von Staudingers Kommentar*, § 242, No. 236.

134 No. 241.

135 Compare once again, on equity, F.W. Maitland, *Equity*, p. 20.

136 It should be submitted, however, that in this respect good faith is closer to the *ius honorarium* than to equity, since the practical need for the abolition of the distiction is less urgent because good faith rules are not, like equity was untill the Judicature Acts of 1873 and 1875, administered by a separate jurisdiction.

137 Compare Dieter Medicus, *Schuldrecht I*, No. 135.

contrahendo,[138] *e.n.a.c*,[139] hardship,[140] *Schutzpflicht*,[141] the duty to co-operate,[142] *Vertrag mit Schutzwirkung für Dritte*.[143] Incidentally, if good faith really were a norm it would have been much more logical for these legal systems to have placed all the good faith sub-rules in one section under a heading like 'Good faith concretisations'.

4.7 Good Faith is a Cover

Good faith is not the highest norm of contract law or even of private law, but no norm at all, and is merely the mouthpiece through which new rules speak, or the cradle where new rules are born. What the judge really does when he applies good faith is to create new rules. These new rules are concretisations, supplementations and corrections to the rules and system of the code. One may ask why the courts mention the good faith clause when they develop these new rules and doctrines. Why did the courts say – and are still saying – that they apply good faith instead of openly saying that they are interpreting, supplementing and correcting the law? Several reasons can be given. They all show that good faith has not only been a mouthpiece but also a cover.[144] Judges in continental European systems have felt uncomfortable with their role as creators of law. First, there is the traditional civil law view with regard to the role of the judge: the judge's task is to apply the law (*trias politica*). Therefore, the courts may have felt uncomfortable in creating law instead of merely applying it, and they were encouraged to feel this way by legal doctrine.[145] Secondly, civil law judges may have felt somewhat at fault when they changed or created new rules because the law created by them was not democratically legitimised. Therefore, it was much easier for them, instead of openly declaring that they changed the law, to state that they merely applied it, invoking the general good faith clause in the code which had been adopted by the democratically elected legislator, and attributing to it the functions of concretising, supplementing and correcting the law. A third reason why the judge felt uncomfortable, and probably the most significant one, lies in the sanctity of contract. In many of the cases where the courts have 'applied' good faith (particularly those in the first period) they have more or less radically interfered with the binding force of what parties had freely agreed to (the most typical example: unforeseen circumstances).[146] They therefore preferred to say that the highest norm of contract law required that in the given case the contractual right could not be exercised rather than

---

138 See § 311 (2) (*new*) *BGB*.

139 See Art. 6:262 Dutch Civil Code.

140 See Art. 6:258 Dutch Civil Code, § 313 (*new*) *BGB*, Art. 6:111 PECL, Art. 6.2.1 UP.

141 See § 241(2) (*new*) *BGB*.

142 See Art. 5.3 UP and Art. 1.202 PECL.

143 See § 311 (3) (*new*) *BGB*.

144 See Herbert Roth, in: *Münchener Kommentar*, § 242, No. 26: 'Deckmantel richterlicher Rechtsfortbildung'. In the same sense Brigitta Lurger, *Grundfragen der Vereinheitlichung des Vetragsrechts in der EuropäischenUnion*, Wien, New York, 2002, p. 383: 'Deckmantel für einen immensen Bestand an richterlicher heteronomer Rechtsetzung'.

145 The same ideals of the Enlightenment also explain why the *Methodenlehre* has been developed. It was clearly aimed at rendering the judgment as objective as posssible, as close as possible to the mere application of the law. See e.g. the efforts made by Karl Larenz, *Lehrbuch des Schuldrechts I*, pp. 126 ff.

146 In all systems the emancipation of good faith occurred together with the decline of party autonomy.

to bluntly state that in their view it would be just to accept an exception to the abstract rule *pacta sunt servanda*. Then there is the argument of convenience. It is much easier for a judge to just mention the general good faith clause as the rule he applies than to formulate the new rule (*Die Flucht in die Generalklauseln*).[147] Finally, it should not be forgotten that many judges actually believed that good faith is a truly existing supreme norm, a belief that fitted perfectly in a European tradition of Aristotelian and Christian belief in natural law.

On the other hand, the question arises why the courts did not invoke the general good faith clause in all the cases where they interpreted, supplemented and corrected the law. Firstly, the courts only invoked good faith when they thought that the new rule could not realistically be based on another provision in the code.[148] That is why good faith interpretation of the law is fairly rare. The courts usually only invoke good faith when they want to supplement or correct it. Secondly, if one looks at the (often explosive) expansion of the field of application and the number of applications of the general good faith clause over the last few decades it seems that the courts themselves have been asking the same question: why not also use good faith as a foundation for change in fields of law other than contracts?

The discussion as to whether good faith has a supplementing and correcting function has served as a facade for the question whether the judge may supplement and correct the law (first: the contract). In other words, the emancipation of the judge has taken place under the cover of the emancipation of good faith and equity. The judge as a creator of new rules which supplement or correct the law has entered the scene behind the mask of good faith. Today all European code systems have accepted a supplementative and a corrective function of good faith;[149] the pretensions of the Enlightenment have been overcome. It seems that in this post-modern age the time has come to recognise that what the judge is doing is nothing to be ashamed of and that he can remove his good faith mask.

Rightly, in some systems it has been pointed out that if there had been no general good faith clause the courts would have adopted the same new rules.[150] Indeed, most of these new rules have been adopted in other systems without the use of the doctrine of good faith.[151] On the other hand, still other systems with a general good faith

---

147 J.W. Hedemann, *Die Flucht in die Generalklauseln; Eine Gefahr für Recht und Staat*, Tübingen 1933, pp. 60, 66.

148 See Herbert Roth, in: *Münchener Kommentar*, § 242, No. 20; Jan Smits, *Het vertrouwensbeginsel en de contractuele gebondenheid*, Arnhem 1995, p. 101.

149 Including France. See e.g. the cases on *clauses résolutoires* mentioned *supra* which date from the 1970s. Since then the increase in the application of art. 1134 (3) *Cc*, which had been dormant for almost two centuries, has been explosive. See Christophe Jamin, 'Une brève histoire politique des interprétations de l'art. 1134 du CC', *D.* 2002, pp. 901-907, and M.W. Hesselink, 'De opmars van de goede trouw in het Franse contractenrecht', *WPNR.* 6154 (1994), pp. 694-698. In addition French law recognises the concept of *abus de droit*.

150 Michael P. Stathopoulos, *Contract law in Hellas*, No. 50; Jürgen Schmidt, in: *J. von Staudingers Kommentar*, § 242, No. 181.

151 To give only a few examples among the 'good faith applications' discussed *supra*, in Section III: in some systems including present Dutch law the precontractual duty to inform is based directly on the mistake provision; in several countries including Germany liability for breaking off negotiations is based on a specific doctrine (*culpa in contrahendo*) or on tort; in many systems objective interpretation is not based on good faith; English law has developed the doctrine of implied terms without

clause did not adopt the same rule.[152] This shows that the real question is whether the new rule should be adopted. In resolving this question the general good faith clause is of no assistance.[153]

5 Conclusion

The main conclusion must be that if the role of the judge as a creator of rules is fully recognised, there is no need for a general good faith clause in a code or restatement of European private law.[154] It may even do harm because it gives the courts an excuse for not formulating the rule which they apply. If, however, there is still some doubt as to the power of the courts, a good faith clause could be useful in order to assure that the judge may create new rules. This may be of particular importance for a new code for Europe where the European Court of Justice and the other courts may need extensive powers right from the beginning. It would then be logical not to put the article in the chapter on contract law, but right at the beginning as one of the first preliminary provisions of the code, just like in Switzerland. The wording would not matter much; experience shows that any phrase containing the words 'good faith' will suffice. However, if good faith were to have only such an *Ermächtigungsfunktion*,[155] it could

---

the concept of good faith; in some countries statutory provisions on unfair terms were adopted without making any reference to good faith; in most systems the relaxations of privity are not based on good faith; in various countries including Italy a rule on hardship was adopted by the legislator or the courts without basing it on good faith; in several countries including England the availability of remedies (for English law particularly: specific performance) may be limited but on a different basis than good faith (for English law: the discretionary character of an equitable remedy).

152 These observations, which as said are based on comparative research (see my *De redelijkheid en billijkheid in het Europese privaatrecht, passim*), have now also been confirmed by the results of the Trento project. See especially Simon Whittaker & Reinhard Zimmermann, 'Coming to terms with good faith', especially pp. 653 ff.

153 Neither is a provision like Art. 3:12 *BW*: 'In determining what reasonableness and equity require, reference must be made to generally accepted principles of law, to current juridical views in the Netherlands, and to the particular societal and private interests involved'. (Translation P.P.C. Haanappel & E. Mackaay, *New Netherlands Civil Code Patrimonial Law*; 'reasonableness and equity' is the term which the new code uses for 'objective good faith'). Quite apart from whether these factors are specific for law making 'on the basis of good faith'(should they not always play a role when courts create new rules?), these factors can hardly be said to provide any guidance. 'Principles of law' (e.g. in the sense in which Ronald Dworkin understands them) either do not exist or cannot be known or are usually in conflict with each other (e.g. the principles of autonomy and solidarity). 'Current juridical views in the Netherlands' are manifold: we have quite a broad spectrum of political parties and we live in a strongly individualised and multicultural society. And 'private interests involved' (i.e. especially the interest of the parties) are usually diametrically opposed (that is why they have gone to court in the first place). And even if all these factors could be determined and weighed objectively, does a judge really have enough time to study the programmes of the political parties, hold opinion polls, visit various communities et cetera?

154 However, it may be worthwhile to anchor a general principle of solidarity in the most general part of the code next to the principle of autonomy. In the same sense see Brigitta Lurger, *Grundfragen der Vereinheitlichung des Vertragsrechts in der EuropäischenUnion*, p. 385. Such a principle, although admittedly quite broad and open, would nevertheless retain some distinct normative coherence especially if conceived in opposition to party autonomy. See further my *The New European Private Law*, Chapter 3, Section VI, B, 2.

155 The term is taken from H. Merz, *Berner Kommentar, Einleitungsband*, Art. 2 ZGB, No. 22.

be argued that it would be more straightforward instead of using good faith terminology to provide expressly that the courts may interpret, supplement and correct the code where necessary. It may be argued that for the sake of tradition the term 'good faith' should be used. However, since this term may lead to hostile reactions from common law lawyers (however unjustified) 'equity' may be an acceptable compromise, since it is part of both the civil law and the common law traditions. It is submitted, however, that this term has the disadvantage of having a strong natural law connotation.

Secondly, this paper shows that the concept of good faith in itself should not keep common law and civil law lawyers divided. On the one hand, common law lawyers should not fear the concept of good faith. The adoption of a general good faith clause in itself does not say anything about which rules will speak through its mouth.[156] Good faith does not differ much from what the English lawyers have experienced with equity. The real question is whether the rules adopted by the courts mentioning good faith should be included in a European code or restatement. It does not make any more sense for a common law lawyer to fight the concept of good faith than it would have been to fight the whole of equity. Rather, good faith serves as a guarantee against the rigidity that the English fear from a code. On the other hand, civil law lawyers should not insist too much on including a good faith provision in a code or restatement of European private law. If they fully recognise what the courts do when they 'apply' good faith they should acknowledge that it should not be necessary that a court mentions the words 'good faith' when it creates a new rule which supplements or corrects the law.[157] Common law lawyers do not believe that the law should be exclusively made by the legislator, nor do they consider it necessary that all the law should be democratically legitimated. This may largely explain why English law has not needed the concept of good faith.

Finally, it has become clear that it is not possible to say anything on the 'content' of European good faith without knowing the system that it will be operating in.[158] Ideally it should be empty. All the rules mentioned in Section III, for example, if accepted, could (and indeed should) be given their proper place in a code or restatement of European private law.[159]

---

156 In the same sense now Whittaker & Reinhard Zimmermann, 'Coming to terms with good faith'., p. 687 : 'the recognition of a principle of good faith does not require a particular result in the circumstances, it merely allows the possibility of a particular result, leaving the court to decide whether or not it should be brought about. From this perspective, it could indeed be argued there would be no *substantive* legal change were English or Scots law to accept a general principle of contractual good faith (…).'

157 The same is true for a (separate) doctrine of abuse of right: if the courts are only prepared to limit a right if they can say that the right is set aside by a higher norm (the prohibition of abuse), such a doctrine should be maintained. If, however, a court is prepared to say that the right given in abstract terms by the code is limited in certain situations, then such a doctrine is not necessary.

158 On the question whether the 'content' of good faith necessarily consists of altruistic rules which impose solidarity and counterbalance party autonomy see my *The New European Private Law*, Chapter 3, Section VI, B, 3.

159 In the same sense see Brigitta Lurger, *Grundfragen der Vereinheitlichung des Vetragsrechts in der EuropäischenUnion*, p. 384.

CHAPTER 27

Hardship

Denis Tallon*

1 Introduction

Hardship is a controversial notion – and has been for more than one century. 'The basic French case on *imprévision*, the 'Canal de Craponne' case, dates back to 1876[1] and the well-known German case-law to the twenties. And it has engendered a huge amount of literature; it is still a major subject of discussion of the law of contract, a subject which shall have to be tackled by the drafters of a European Civil Code. Various reasons explain why the question is so important nowadays. First, there is an increase in long term contracts, which are more sensitive to unforeseen events. Some events affect a great number of contracts: the closing of the Suez canal, the oil crisis, the Gulf war, the implosion of the communist countries of Europe, to mention a few.[2] These events have stressed the disadvantages of conflicting legal systems. Secondly, despite the huge quantity of energy spent on the subject, the theory – or theories – of hardship remains hazy and unsettled. It is difficult to opt for one policy or another. The Unidroit Principles of International Contract and the Principles of European Contract Law (PECL)[3] have given a similar answer to the problem, but after long discussions and many hesitations. The moment has come to try and dissipate some misunderstandings. First of all, it is necessary to propose a definition of what is meant by hardship (2). This having been done, there remains to determine the place it must occupy in a modern theory of contract (3).

2 What is Hardship?

The very first thing to be done is to agree on what is meant by hardship or *imprévision* – I shall use the two terms indifferently. The general idea is that the performance of a contract has become 'harder' because of the occurrence of supervening events which could not have been foreseen at the time of the contract. The difference

* Professor emeritus, University Panthéon-Assas (Paris II), Former Director of the *Institut de Droit Comparé de Paris*.
1 Civ. 6 March 1876, D.P. 1876.1.93; S.1876.1.161.
2 See specially J. Bel and I. de Lamberterie, in: *Contract Law Today*, D. Harris & D. Tallon, ed., chap. 4: The Effect of Change of Circumstances in Long Term Contracts, Oxford 1989, pp. 195-241 (pp. 217-267 of the French version: *Le contrat aujourd'hui. Une comparaison franco-anglaise*, Paris 1987).
3 Arts. 6.2.1 to 6.2.3, Unidroit Principles of International Commercial Contracts (Rome, 1994); Art. 6.110 PECL (former article 2.117), The first part, *Performance, Non-performance and Remedies*, have been published in 1995 (O. Lando, H. Beale, ed., Martinus Nijhoff publishers). See the texte of Art. 6.110 in the annex. There is a slight difference between Art. 2.117 and Art. 6.110, which is explained, under 3.2.

to force majeure is that performance is still possible though much more onerous. There is first a question of terminology (2.1). Then the notion itself has to be clarified (2.2).

2.1 Terminology

Whereas *force majeure* is now considered as an adequate way to designate the complete impossibility situation (even in the English language: see Article 7.1.7. Unidroit Principles), there is no generally admitted term in the various European legal systems for the hardship situation. This leads to much confusion. In the leading system in this matter, German Law, hardship is referred to as the *Wegfall des Geschäftsgrundlage,* that is to say the disappearance of the basis of the contract. It is the justification of the rule which is used to describe it. In French law, the normal term is *imprévision* or, to expand the formula, *révision pour imprévision:* it is the unforeseen character of the event which is stressed. The Italian code speaks of excessive onerosity, that is the effect on the performing party. For PECL, it is change of circumstances. Unidroit Principles use hardship, both in the English and the French versions (as it also uses *force majeure* in both). Yet the word hardship has no legal meaning in England. The term is mostly used for hardship clauses.[4] It only suggests that performance is 'harder'. No such word appears in Treitel's Contract and in Beale, Bishop and Furmston's Case Book, the expression 'relief in the case of hardship' appears in the chapter Discharge by Frustration.[5] But what is the difference between hardship and frustration (or frustration of the purpose, of the venture ....)? And to make things worse, the Americans use the term impracticability.[6] There is a paradox here: the English language, which appears to be the new *lingua franca* for Contract law, has no appropriate word, perhaps because it does not really know the notion.

2.2 A Unique Notion?

Through the centuries, *force majeure* has acquired a coherent aspect, both as to its conditions of existence (with more or less rigour) and its effect: it is *tout ou rien.* Either the obligor is liberated or he has to perform as promised. As Lando wrote, 'there is a need for a more lenient tule',[7] when performance is still possible. But there is no general consensus on what this rule should be. A comparative survey shows a variety of solutions.[8] First, the more radical: the contract must be performed, however onerous the performance may be, unless there is *force majeure.* This is the French solution for private (as opposed to administrative) contracts.[9] This strict application of *the force obligatoire du contrat* is of course an incentive for the parties to introduce adequate clauses in their contract: indexation clauses, hardship clauses, or even just a

---

4   See the International Chamber of Commerce brochure: Force majeure and Hardship, ICC Publication No. 421, 1985.
5   H.G. Beale, W.D. Bishop, M.V. Furmston, *Contract – Cases & Materials,* Chapter 16: Discharge by Frustration, pp. 459-499, 4th ed. 2001.
6   Restatement Second, Contracts, §§ 261 ff.
7   *Towards a European Civil Code,* Nijmegen 1994, pp. 210 ff.
8   See for instance the ICC brochure referred to in note 4.
9   A. de Laubadère et Y. Gaudemet, *Traité de Droit administratif,* T.I., 16th ed. 2001, Nos 1408-1493.

duty to renegociate the contract. This duty may be considered as imposed by the general obligation of good faith, which is to be found in many systems or even the rarer duty to collaborate, as defined by Article 1. 201 PECL. But if negotiation fails, the contract stands. As we shall see, renegociation is a useful preliminary step to a more radical solution. By itself, it is insufficient, even if the party who refuses to negotiate or breaks the negotiation abusively may be liable in damages. Then we have the stranger system – to the foreign observer – of frustration. Frustration, according to Lord Radcliffe 'occurs when the circumstances in which performance is called for would render it a thing radically different from that which was undertaken by the contract'.[10] This is not so different from the *Wegfall des Geschäftsgrundlage,* but the result is not at all the same, for it always leads to the discharge of the contract. It is understandable that the Anglo-American doctrine has some trouble in reconciling the doctrine of frustration or impracticability with that of impossibility *or force majeure.* Both lead to the disappearance of the contract.[11] The more radical solution is that of German Law; lt has been elaborated by the *Reichgericht* during the monetary crisis of the twenties.[12] In case of hardship, the court may either terminate the contract or readjust it in order to allocate the unforeseen burden equitably between the parties. This solution has been adopted by many codes (Art. 388, Greek Civil Code, Art. 107 Algerian Civil Code and now by § 313 of the reformed BGB) or by case law (Switzerland, Austria). The ltalian Civil Code (Art. 1467), in case of excessive onerosity, says that the judge may terminate the contract but the other party may offer an equitable indemnity in order to save the contract.

We see that apart from the duty to negotiate which may be combined with both, there are three issues: the contract stands, the contract disappears, the contract may be modified. These two last solutions are radically different. The first is a kind of enlarged *force majeure,* with the same result. In the second, the risk is shared between the parties. lt gives the court *a pouvoir modérateur* in equity. So that the same word, hardship, covers two very different notions, corresponding to two different conceptions of contract and two different conceptions of the function of the judge. In my view, one should only speak of hardship when revision is possible. Same thing with imprévision. But it remains to be seen if such an institution is desirable and ought to be introduced in a European Civil Code.

---

10 In Davis Contractors Ltd v. Farenham UDC (1956) 2 All ER 145, HL.; on the English doctrine of Frustration, Mc Kendrick, ed., *Frustration and Force Majeure – Their Relationship and a Comparative Assessment,* 1991. lt has been suggested that the courts also have the power to adapt the contract (Zweigert & Kötz (1996), p. 550), but no example bas been given and some judges – such as Lord Radcliff – have given, obiter, an opposite opinion.

11 Aluminium Co of America v. Essex Group, 499 F Supp 53 (1980, US Dist. Ct, WD Pa 1980). E.A. Farnsworth, Contracts, 2nd ed., 1990, pp. 506, 527 and note 48; Restatement 2nd Contracts. §§ 261 ff.

12 K. Larenz, *Lehrbuch des Schuldrechts, I,* Allgemeiner Teil, 14th ed., 1997, pp. 320 ff. The German case law on this point has been integrated in the BGB by the recent reform of the Law of Obligations, in the new § 313, with the title: "Störung der Gesschäftsgrundlage". The new Civil Code of the Russian Federation has adopted hardship along the same lines: art. 451.

3   The Best Choice?

A comparative survey should be made (3.1), in order to appreciate the choice made in PECL and by Unidroit and explain why it is thought to be the best (3.2).

3.1   Comparative Survey

Is there a tendency to recognise hardship – in the full meaning of the term? The argument was put forward by those who wanted the French courts to overrule the Canal de Craponne precedent.[13] And René David showed in 1974[14] that the French position was more and more isolated. This should be qualified. For R. David qualifies under the heading of *imprévision* both the German solution and the English frustration, which is not really hardship or *imprévision*. And in recent times, the tendency is not so marked. Of course, the Dutch Civil Code has abandoned the French tradition on this point and adopted the German one;[15] but the new Civil Code of Quebec has deliberately rejected hardship.[16] In the European Union, the balance is in favour of hardship[17] and the new members reinforce the pro-hardship camp as the three of them accept revision for hardship.[18] But there is still France, Belgium and Luxembourg on the other side, and on the same side, though separate, Great Britain and Ireland. So that there is a need for harmonisation.

If we now turn to international instruments, we find the same contrast. As we shall see in more detail further on, both the Unidroit Principles and PECL have adopted revision, but the Vienna Convention on International Sale of Goods has not. Article 79 CISG is rather unclear but it is widely interpreted as excluding hardship.[19] The problem is to determine if this is a deliberate rejection, or a lacuna. If it is a lacuna, there being no disposition in the Convention, the relevant municipal law must be applied. And good faith could not be used as a support for revision, as it is not recognised as a general principle of CISG. Thus, we can say that there is no

---

13 My article in the Mélanges Alain Sayag is an attempt in this direction.
14 René David, L'imprévision dans les droits européens, in: *Mélanges en l'honneur d'A. Jauffret,* Paris, 1974, pp. 211-219.
15 Art. 6.258 s.1: 'Upon the demand of one of the parties, the judge may modify the effects of a contract, or he may set it aside in whole or in part on the basis of unforeseen circumstances which are of such a nature that the cocontracting party, according to criteria of reasonableness and equity, may not expect that the contract be maintained in an unmodified form. The modification or the setting aside of the contract may be given retroactive force'. Translation of Haanappel & Mackaay, Nieuw Nederlandsch Burgerlijk Wetboek, Centre canadien de droit comparé, Deventer-Boston, 1990; A.S. Hartkamp & M.-M. Tillema, *Contract Law in the Netherlands,* 1995, No. 51 and Nos. 170-173.
16 J.-L. Baudoin, *Les Obligations,* 4th ed., 1993, Nos. 424 ff.
17 The notes under Art. 6.110 (ex 2.117) give a short survey of the situation in the (then) twelve members of the EU.
18 Case-law in Austria; statute law (the model contract law of Nordic countries) for Finland and Sweden (as well as Denmark).
19 J. Honold, Uniform Law for International Sales under the 1980 UN Convention, 2nd ed., 1994, 572; B. Audit, La Vente internationale de marchandises .... Paris, 1990, Nos. 182 ff.; C. Witz, Les premières applications jurisprudentielles du droit uniforme de la vente internationale, Paris 1995, No. 87. R. David, in his article, p. 224 and pp. 228-229, considers that Art. 74 of ULIS is very similar to Art. 79 CISG, allows imprévision, but with the meaning he gives to this notion.

una.nimity on the subject even if there is a strong trend towards recognition of revision. And 1 think it is the best choice, as we shall see by a short review of Article 6.111 PECL.

3.2   The Rule in PECL and in Unidroit Principles

Article 6.110 PECL (ex-article 2.117 in the first version of the first part of PECL) is placed in the chapter 'Contents and Effects' of the contract. It has been a difficult text to draft and the final version is the result of many modifications.[20] Unidroit articles are very similar, which is not surprising: the two working parties have worked in close cooperation and often with the same people. There is a difference in form: Unidroit Principles have divided the matter in three articles, and a small differenee in substance: Unidroit Article 6.2.2 assimilaties the events which have occurred before the conclusion of the contract but which have become known after to events which have occurred after (as did ex-article 2.117 PECL) whereas Article 6.110 reserves hardship for posterior events, the prior ones being dealt with under the ruie on mistake.[21]

Article 6.110 gives a short definition for hardship. It adopts the l'excessive onerosity' formula of Italian Law, thus leaving a large power of appreciation to the courts. lt was considered impossible to be more precise owing to the great variety of circumstances. Further directions would have been regarded as vague.

The procedure is in two stages. The first is the attempt to find a negotiated solution, with its own remedy in case of failure, the second one is the judicial procedure. The court has the same wide power as under German law. The only difference is that PECL have not formulated a preference for revision, as the German Courts do,[22] it being felt that it was illusory to try to bind the judge by such a wish. The important thing is that the judge must try to 'distribute in a just and equitable manner the losses and gains resulting from the change of circumstances'. This is indeed the core of the institution. Hardship is a remedy in equity (in the general sense of the word). And it is equity which will guide the judge in choosing termination (and he has a further choice as to date and conditions) or adaptation, according to the circumstances.

How can this power be justified? I do not want to reopen the old debate but comparative law may bring some further arguments in favour of the PECL conception of hardship. First of all, good faith plays and increasing role in the law of contract.

Hardship is a typical daughter of good faith. The performing party who pays with devalued money is not acting in good faith as any other debtor who is liberated through an unforeseen 'windfall' at the creditor's expense. Hardship is also in conformity with the trend to give the judge a *pouvoir modérateur* every time excesses are to be feared (for instance, in France and Germany in case of excessive penalty clauses). And where revision has been widely admitted, the dangers imagined by some have not been noticed. For instance, the floodgate argument (a great increase in litigation)

---

20 Such as the last minute change in Art. 6.110 as to the date of the event.

21 Change of circumstances and mistake are of course closely related. H. Kötz, *Europäisches Vertragsrecht, I, p.* 228, J.C.B. Mohr, 1996.

22 This preference has been constantly repeated by the Supreme Court; it is now to be found in § 313 BGB.

or a growing insecurity of transactions. Of course there are safeguards. The principle of sanctity is affirmed and hardship is always presented as an exception, to be restricted to extreme cases of 'excessive onerosity'. This is due to the prudence of the judges, always afraid of being taxed with arbitrariness. This prudence is to be found in the German case-law and in the *jurisprudence* of the French administrative courts: cases are few. Things are generally settled by agreement. The mere fact that the judge may intervene drives the parties to come to an agreement. It is a general observation that whenever the law gives the judge large powers, he uses them with moderation: see the abuse of rights in France, the conservative use made by the Swiss judge of Article 1-2 of the Civil Code, etc.

The real danger lies elsewhere. It is to be feared that such a text as article 6.110 will be used very differently by the judge or arbitrator according to his national legal background either in appreciating what is excessive onerosity or in choosing readjustment of the contract rather than termination. But this is inevitable; it is to be hoped that progressively there will emerge a common European legal culture. Hardship is a good example of a difficult exercise in unification of the law. Little by little the notion gets clearer. And it shows how instructive is the comparative approach.

BIBLIOGRAPHY: Bibliography of literature in French in: J. Ghestin, *Traité de droit civil, Les effets du contrat,* par J. Ghestin, with the collaboration of M. Billiau and C. Jamin, 2nd ed., 1995, No. 263, notes 1 and 2; comparative bibliography in Zweigert & *Kötz, Einführung in die Rechtsvergleichung,* 3rd ed., 1996, § 37, p. 516, and the developments pp. 516-537. Adde: Ph. Stoffel-Munck, *Regards sur la théorie de l'imprévision,* Aix-Marseille, 1994; J.M. Perillo, *Hardship and its Impact on Contractual Obligations: A Comparative Analysis,* Centro di Studi e Ricerche di Diritto Comparato e Straniero, Saggi, Conferenze e Seminari, No. 20, Rome, 1996; D. Tallon, La révision du contrat pour imprésivion au regard des enseignements récents du droit comparé, *Droit et vie des affaires, Etudes à la mémoire d'Alain Sayaq, Paris, 1997, pp. 403-417.*

CHAPTER 28

Non-Performance (Breach) of Contracts

Ole Lando*

1 The Subject Matter

The terms which parties to a contract agree upon will generally govern their relationship. Some contracts contain many and elaborate terms, some do not. A contract for the construction of an off-shore oil rig will generally contain hundreds, if not thousands of pages of contract terms. A contract whereby a buyer merely faxes the seller: "Send me 1000 bales of cotton", which the seller then does, contains few terms. In the first contract almost everything is settled. The contract terms describe in great detail the quality of the performance and the terms of payment. They stipulate how to solve unforeseen contingencies, such as unexpected sea-bed or stream conditions, and technical improvements, which may call for changes in the planned performance. There are also terms on breach (non-performance) by one party and its consequences. In the second case, the sale of cotton, the contract only provides the quantity and type of the commodity. The law or usages will tell the parties how much cotton there must be in a bale, and which qualities the cotton must have. Law rules or usages will provide the terms and place of delivery, and the terms of payment.

The rules of law will also prescribe the conditions and the consequences of non-performance. We are dealing with these rules here. Most of them are non-mandatory. The parties may derogate from them, and this is often done in the written contract. In many countries, however, the courts show a tendency to construe the written contract terms in the light of the rules of law. A party who wishes to free himself from any of the consequences which the law will attach to his non-performance must be specific. In case of doubt the law rules will apply. And some rules are mandatory in the sense that the customer cannot waive certain rights or remedies which the rules confer upon him

In the Principles of European Contract Law (PECL) the Commission on European Contract Law (CECL) has set up a structure and terms for a future European Code in relation to the "breach of contract"[1] In doing this the CECL has been guided by two main considerations. The first is to have a structure which is compatible with that of the CISG. The second is to use one which in principle may apply to all kinds of contracts and not only to the sale of goods.

---

* Professor emeritus at the Copenhagen Business School; President of the Commission on European Contract Law.

1 See Lando & Beale (eds.), *Principles of European Contract Law*, Part 1 & 2, The Hague 2000 and on these Principles , Hartkamp, *Principles of Contract Law*, *supra* chapter 7.

2   The System and Terminology Proposed

2.1   The Obligations of the Parties

If the contract has not set a time for the parties' performance the law will do it. Furthermore, it is expressed or implied that the performance, whether it be about services, goods, industrial property rights etc., must have a certain quality and quantity. The buyer will have to receive them when tendered and to pay for them. Many contracts contain other obligations, such as a duty for one party to provide the other party with documents relating to his performance and to give him the necessary information. The party receiving the information may have a duty not to disclose it to others. A seller of goods, services and intangibles may have a duty to obtain an export license, a buyer to get an import license. A buyer may have to open a credit in favour of the seller. If the person who is to perform – the debtor – has to deliver tangible or intangible goods, these goods must be free from any rights and claims of a third party.

2.2   The Failure to Perform and the Non-Performance

If the contract is not performed in accordance with these express or implied terms, the failure to perform may be due to the debtor's fault; or it may have causes for which he cannot be blamed, but for which he nevertheless must bear the risk. The failure to effect due performance may also have been caused by the person who is to receive performance – the creditor- either by his fault or by other causes for which he bears the risk.

The legal systems will allocate detrimental consequences to the defaulting party if that party is in fault or carries the risk. The failure to perform may give the other party – the aggrieved party – certain rights against the defaulting party. The aggrieved party may have a right to damages for the loss he suffers from the other party's failure to effect due performance. If he accepts a tender of performance not conforming to the contract he may reduce his own performance. Furthermore, he may withhold his performance until the other party makes a due performance. Under certain conditions he may terminate the contract, i.e. choose not to perform his own obligations and not to claim performance by the other party,[2] see on termination the following Chapter by Hugh Beale. The aggrieved party may finally have a right to specific performance, that is to claim that the contract be performed as agreed. All these rights are here called remedies.

The law gives these remedies to the creditor when for reasons for which the debtor carries the risk the latter fails to effect due performance. If, for instance, the seller of scrap iron does not deliver it, the buyer may terminate the contract, buy the iron from another source and claim damages from the seller for the loss he has suffered. The same remedies may also be accorded to the seller when the buyer fails to receive performance. If a buyer of scrap iron refuses or is unable to receive it, the seller may

---

2   Sometimes termination has the consequence that each party must return what he has received from the other party, see e.g. CISG Art. 81 (2).

terminate the contract, sell the iron to another purchaser and claim damages from the buyer for the loss he has suffered.

The situations where there is a failure to effect due performance which gives the aggrieved party one or more remedies we call situations of non-performance.[3]

In the case of the scrap iron we face a problem of terms. The seller who has a duty to deliver the iron also has a right to get rid of it. The buyer who has a right to get the iron also has a duty to remove it or receive it. Both parties are therefore "debtors" and "creditors" in relation to the same performance, and there is non-performance if they fail to perform their duties.

There are cases where the debtor's failure to perform gives the party who is to receive performance no rights or remedies. Thus where identified goods are to be delivered, and due to a contingency for which the seller is not liable, they perish before delivery but after the risk has passed, the buyer who has to pay the price has no remedies. The performance has failed, but there is no non-performance since there is no remedy. Sometimes a party's failure to receive performance or to contribute in other ways to the debtor's performance (*mora creditoris*), will not give the debtor any remedy. The effect of the failure is that the creditor does not get the performance he has contracted for, but the debtor, who is prevented from effecting due performance, cannot force his performance upon the creditor; nor can he terminate the contract or claim damages. If he gets his counter-performance as stipulated in the contract he has no remedy. Thus, if a pianist who has been engaged to come and play in the bride's home at a wedding party, is dismissed, because the couple has decided not to marry, the pianist who gets his fee, cannot force the couple to listen to his performance, nor can he – under normal circumstances – claim damages because he was denied the opportunity to perform. The refusal of the bride to admit him to play in her home causes a failure in his performance, but since it does not give him any remedies caused by that failure we will not call it a non-performance, neither on his part nor on the part of the couple.

2.3 Duty to Achieve a Specific Result and Duty of Best Efforts (Obligations de Résultat and Obligations de Moyens)

The debtor's duty varies depending upon the nature of the obligation incurred. Sometimes the debtor must bring about a specific result, and he carries the risk that it is achieved. If he fails there is a case of non- performance. In many legal systems the seller's duty to deliver conforming goods at the right time is a duty to achieve a specific result, and if he fails he is strictly liable.[4]

In other cases a party is bound only by a duty of best efforts. He must then make the efforts that a normal person would reasonably be expected to exert in similar circumstances. If he is a professional he will have to live up to the standards of the profession or trade, but he will not have to bring about a specific result. If he has made

---

3   This is the terms used in PECL and the Unidroit Principles of International Commercial Contracts (hereinafter Unidroit Principles), published in 2004 by UNIDROIT in Rome. CISG uses "breach of contract".

4   In case of force majeure the contract disappears, which will exonerate the debtor; see on French law 3.5 below.

his best efforts he has performed his duty and the creditor must bear the risk for the non-achievement of the desired result. A doctor's attempt to cure his patient is to be made with his best efforts. and if he has done so there is due performance even if the patient is not cured.[5]

This distinction between what the French call an *obligation de résultat* and an *obligation de moyens* shows typical degrees of duties in contract. In some contracts part of a party's obligation is one of *résultat* and part of it one of *moyens*. A party, who has undertaken to deliver a computer with a programme which is aimed at performing certain functions, is strictly liable for the defects in the hardware but, unless he has warranted that the software can perform the desired functions, he is only obliged to make his best efforts to achieve that result.

In some laws there are further distinctions to be made. There are situations where the creditor can terminate a contract or claim a reduction of the price if the result is not achieved, but where the debtor is liable in damages only for fault.[6]

2.4 The Excused Non-Performance

Even the debtor who must achieve a specific result is not always liable in damages for non-performance. He is generally not liable for non-performance of any of his obligations if he proves that the failure to perform was due to an impediment beyond his control and that he could not have taken the impediment into account at the time of the conclusion of the contract, or have avoided or overcome it or its consequences, see CISG 79.[7] For instance, the seller is not liable in damages if, after the conclusion of the contract, an unforeseen embargo is placed on scrap iron which prevents the seller from delivering it to the buyer's country.

Where the aggrieved party cannot claim damages for non-performance of an obligation, he also cannot as a rule claim specific performance of the same obligation . The non-performance is excused. However, the aggrieved party may still withhold his own performance, in this case his payment of the purchase price. In case of a temporary impediment, which excuses the debtor, the creditor's right to specific performance is not lost, but only postponed. When the impediment disappears the creditor may claim performance and if he does not get it, damages for delay. If, however, the impediment lasts so long that the non-performance becomes substantial, as for example if the embargo persists, the aggrieved party may terminate the contract. He may then refuse to receive the iron even if, once the embargo is repealed, the defaulting party wishes to deliver it. In this respect the defaulting party carries the risk for the non-performance.

---

5 Terré, Simler, Lequette *Droit civil, Les obligations*, (hereinafter Terré) 6.ed 1996 no 6.

6 See German BGB § 276. This is probably also the general rule in Nordic law; see Gomard, *Obligationsret* Vol. 2 1995 141 ff., Ramberg & Herre, *Köplagen* 1995 105 ff.

7 CISG Art. 79 has retained the right to claim performance in cases of the excused non-performance. This is criticised by Tallon in Bianca & Bonell, *Commentary on the International Sales Law*, Milan 1987, 588 and Huber in von Caemmerer/ Schlechtriem, *Kommentar zum Einheitlichen UN-Kaufrecht*, 2d ed. München 1995 Art 28 Rn 26 ff., hereinafter Schlechtriem/Huber, but see Stoll *idem*. Art. 79 Rn. 55 ff. and Schlechtriem, *Commentary on the UN Convention on the International Sale of Goods (CISG)* Oxford 1998 (hereinafter *Schlechtriem Commentary*) Art 79 notes 55-57.

Thus non-performance of an *obligation de résultat* may be divided into two categories: the excused and the non-excused. In the former case the aggrieved party may neither claim damages nor specific performance but he may have the other remedies; in the latter cases he may have all the remedies

2.5 The Proposed Structure

There are now the following categories

	Failure to perform	
Non-performance		"Remedy-less" failures
Non excused	Excused	
REMEDIES:	REMEDIES	
Specific Performance		
Damages		
Withhold Performance	Withhold Performance	
Termination	Termination	
Reduction	Reduction	

It is to be noted that the creditor's failure to receive performance may be a non-performance on his part. The failure to receive performance may, however, also be "remedy-less". The division between the non-performance and the other cases of a failure to perform lies between the failures which give the aggrieved party a remedy and the "remedy-less" failures.

As far as the *obligations de moyens* is concerned, the debtor's failure to achieve the desired result does not give the creditor any remedies if the debtor has exerted his best efforts. In that case there is due performance. If the result has not been achieved because the debtor did not exert his best efforts there is a non-performance and the creditor may claim damages and exercise other remedies.

The Commission on European Contract Law (CECL) discussed whether to provide rules on specific performance of a non-monetary obligation. In the common law countries specific performance is a remedy which is left to the discretion of the court that will only grant it when damages are inadequate to satisfy the creditor's needs. In the civil law countries it is considered to be the obvious remedy. However, the members agreed that in all the Member States the enforcement mechanisms are heavy handed, and therefore seldom required and seldom awarded. It was nevertheless agreed that it should be a right which was to be tied to rules and not to be left to the discretion of the court. PECL therefore provides for specific performance both of a monetary and a non-monetary obligation see Arts. 9; 101 and 9:102

Under PECL Art 9:102 (l) the aggrieved party is entitled to specific performance of an obligation other than one to pay money, including the remedying of a defective performance.

Para 2 provides that specific performance cannot be obtained where;

(a) performance would be unlawful or impossible; or
(b) performance would cause the debtor unreasonable effort or expense; or
(c) performance consists in the provision of services or work of a personal character or depends upon a personal relationship; or

(d)   the aggrieved party may reasonably obtain performance from another source.[8]

In the Comments it is said that the exception under (c) is explained by the consideration that an order to perform personal services or work would be a severe interference with a party's personal freedom. Further, such performance rendered under coercion would often be unsatisfactory, and finally it would be difficult for a court to control the proper enforcement of the order.

2.5 Mixed Situations

There are situations where a failure to perform is partly due to *mora creditoris*, partly to causes for which the debtor carries the risk, and there are cases of non-performance which are partly excused and partly not-excused.

Thus, a construction of a house may be delayed beyond the time set for its completion, partly because the owner failed to provide in time the necessary instructions to the builder (*mora creditoris*), partly because the builder was unable to do the work within the time schedule agreed upon. When administering the remedies available for the owner, one will have to assess the relative importance of the *mora creditoris* of the creditor and the non-performance caused by the debtor.

There are also cases where force majeure is only one of the factors which have delayed performance and caused a loss for the aggrieved party. For instance, the seller of the scrap iron has been prevented from delivering it by an embargo of short duration. During that period the buyer cannot claim delivery of the iron and he cannot claim damages for the loss he sustains during that period. Once the embargo has been repealed the buyer may claim that the seller effects performance[9] and, if the seller does not perform, he will be liable in damages for the further loss the buyer now suffers. Such mixed situations do not disturb the structure.

3   The Structure of CISG and Some Legal Systems

The structure and the terms described above are those used in PECL and in the Unidroit Principles of International Commercial Contracts.[10] In national systems the terms and the structures for non-performance differ considerably.[11] When preparing the first drafts of the "Uniform Law for the International Sale of Movable Goods" Ernest Rabel[12] and his fellow draftsmen established a system which was modelled upon the Common Law and the law of the Scandinavian Countries, notably their Sale

---

8   PECL I & II 394 ff.
9   This may be one of the reasons why some authors find it sensible that Art 79(5) on *force majeure* does not exclude the claim for specific performance, .see Schlechtriem, Commentary art 79, note 55. In my view this is not a valid explanation; during the embargo the buyer can neither claim performance nor damages.
10   Principles of International Commercial Contracts published 2004 by Unidroit.
11   See Zweigert & Kötz, *Einführung in die Rechtsvergleichung*, 3 ed. Tübingen 1996 § 36.
12   See Rabel, *Das Recht des Warenkaufs*, I-II (Tübingen 1957 and 1958), Vol I, 118 ff., 329 ff, 380 ff., Vol II 368 ff., and *Schlechtriem/ Huber* (*op cit.* note 7) Art. 45 Anm. 1-13.

of Goods Act from 1905-07. This system has roughly been followed in later drafts, in the Uniform Law of the International Sale of Goods from 1964 (ULIS) and in the CISG.

3.1 CISG

In CISG the terms "remedy" ("*moyens*")[13] and "right" ("*droit*") are used for what is here called a remedy. Most of the remedies are described in CISG Arts. 45 ff and 61 ff, which mention specific performance, termination, in CISG called avoidance, re-duction of the aggrieved party's own performance, and damages. The party's right to withhold his own performance until the other party performs his obligation is pro-vided for in Art. 58, which is located in Section II of Chapter III, and which, unlike the system of PECL, is not reckoned among the "remedies for breach of contract".

Art. 80 provides that a party cannot rely on the failure of the other party to perform to the extent that such failure was caused by the first party's act or omission. There-fore, when CISG Art. 45 provides the remedies which the buyer may exercise "if the seller fails to perform any of his obligations under the contract or this Convention", it is understood that these remedies are not available for the buyer if the seller's failure to perform was due to contingencies for which the buyer carries the risk. Thus the remedies do not operate if a buyer who has bought goods on FOB conditions does not provide the ship on which the goods are to be carried. In this case the seller has no obligation to deliver the goods on board a ship.

In CISG "breach" (non-performance) is not tied to the remedy of damages. Even in case of an excused non-performance, where the aggrieved party cannot claim dam-ages, he may terminate the contract. The fact that CISG only exempts a defaulting party from liability in case of force majeure (Art. 79 (1) means that the seller's and the buyer's obligations are treated as "obligations de résultat".

In spite of the many points of resemblance in results of the civil and the common law, as far as the remedy of specific performance is concerned the delegates that in 1980 made CISC could not agree on common rules.. Art 46 gave the buyer an un-qualified right to require performance, but Art 28 provided that if in accordance with the provisions of the Convention one party is entitled to require performance of any obligation by the other party, a court is not bound to enter a judgment for specific performance unless the court would do so under its own law in respect of similar con-tracts of sale not governed by the Convention. Thus Art 28 preserved the common law courts' discretion.

This partition was unnecessary. The civil law countries could have admitted that specific performance should be restricted to the situations for which this remedy is needed in practice and have admitted the exceptions provided in PECL art 9:102 (2). The common law countries could have conceded that in the other situations specific performance should be a right which the court would have to grant the aggrieved party.[14]

---

13 *Remedy*: e.g. Titles of Sections III of Part II, Chapters II and III, Articles 45 (2) and (3), 47 (2) and (3) and 70. *Right*: e.g. Articles 45 (1) (a) and 61 (1) (a).

14 See Lando in Bianca-Bonell (eds.) *Commentary on the International Sales Law*, Milan 1987 237.

3.2

The System under the New *Dutch Civil* Code (BW) which came into force in 1992 is similar to that of PECL. The "neutral" term for all situations of failure to perform is called "*niet-nakoming*". The failure which gives the aggrieved party a remedy (non-performance) is called "*tekortkoming in de nakoming,* see Art. 6:74, 6:265 and 6; 262ff...

Failure to perform (*niet-nakoming*) which is caused by the creditor excludes him from the right to terminate, see Art. 6:266, and the debtor from being in "default", see Art. 6:61. This means that a failure to perform caused by the creditor will prevent him from exercising any remedy

The aggrieved party may terminate the contract, reduce or withhold his performance even in cases where the defaulting party is not liable in damages. In the BW the rules on liability for damages are provided in Arts. 6:74 ff. Art. 6:74 provides that the aggrieved party cannot claim damages if the non-performance cannot be attributed (*toegerekend*) to him. Art. 6:75 provides that a non-performance cannot be attributed to the debtor if it does not result from his fault, and if he cannot be held liable for it by the rules of law or by legal act, or prevailing opinion in society or in the particular trade.[15] The debtor is always excused in case of force majeure. *Force majeure* will also in practice prevent the creditor from claiming specific performance. The typical example of liability following from a legal act is the assumption of liability by a contract clause. The term "prevailing opinion" refers to legal rules laid down by the courts before book 6 of the new BW came into force. It covers a variety of situations arising in the various specific contracts, some of which have received general application. Thus the courts have applied the French distinction between the "*obligations de résultat*" and "*the obligations de moyens*". When performing an "*obligation de moyens*" the debtor is liable for the fault of his servants and employees and others whom he had entrusted performance, see art. 6:76, and generally for the tools he has used in performance, see Art. 6:77.

3.3

The terms and structure of the *Nordic* laws are close to that of PECL. The main rule regarding liability for damages still seems to be that the non-performance must be imputed to the debtor but there are many cases where the liability is strict, as in CISG. The distinction between "*obligations de résultat*" and "*obligations de moyens*" – though noted by a well known Swedish author[16] – has not been adopted in practice, but the rules provide similar results.

3.4

Before 2002 the provisions on non-performance of the *German* Civil Code (BGB) §§ 275-292 only addressed impossibility which relieved the debtor of the duty to per-

---

15 „*in het verkeer geldende opvatting*"
16 Rohde, *Lärobok i Obligationsrätt,* 4 ed. 1975 27 ff.

form, and delay in performance.[17] The Code did not provide an inclusive term for non-performance which could, among other things, have included a defective performance. In general the creditor did not have any remedy against a debtor who could show that the impossibility or the delay could not be imputed to him.

A reform of the rules on obligations of the BGB came into force on Jan.1 2002. The amended Code follows in several respects the system and the rules of CISG and PECL. It introduces the concept of *Pflichtverletzung*. *Pflicht* means duty and *Verletzung* violation. This has been done although *Pflichtverletzung* appears to imply fault, and that was not intended.[18] since there is *Pflichtverletzung* even if the non-performance cannot be imputed to the debtor. *Pflichtverletzung* is now the inclusive term for non-performance which among other things includes a defective performance.

BGB § 275 provides that performance cannot be obtained in so far as it is impossible for the debtor or for everybody. Furthermore, the debtor may refuse to perform, if performance will cause the debtor an effort which, contrary to the requirement of good faith and fair dealing, is disproportionate to the interest of the creditor in getting the performance. When assessing the effort to be required of the debtor it is to be considered whether the impediment may be imputed to the debtor. Finally, the debtor may refuse a performance of a personal character if it cannot reasonably be claimed when balancing the impediment facing the debtor against the interest of the creditor in getting the performance. As stated, the debtor may be liable in damages even if performance cannot be required.

The fault rule is retained as far as damages are concerned. Under § 276 of the new BGB the debtor is in general only liable in damages for his intentional or negligent behaviour. The fault rule, however, only applies to the remedies of damages. Fault is no longer required when due to a non-performance the aggrieved party terminates the contract, claims a price reduction in case of defects, or withholds his performance. The fault rule does not apply when a less strict, or a stricter, liability has been agreed upon or is to be inferred, especially if the debtor has assumed a guarantee or the risk for procuring the performance; see § 276. A seller of generic goods will in general have assumed such a procurement risk, and is strictly liable for delay and defects.. Also here, the debtor is excused if the non-performance is due to an unforeseeable and insurmountable impediment beyond his control. A seller of a specific object is in general not strictly liable for non-performance which cannot be imputed to him but also he is subject to the rules on vicarious liability in § 278. A fault-rule similar to the one in BGB § 276, is also applied in Nordic law; see section 3.3 above.

Also in German law there are contractual duties, which are only obligations de moyens. The debtor has to make his best efforts, but his duty goes no further.

3.5

In *France* the term *"inexécution"* covers both a non-performance and a "remedyless" failure to perform.

---

17 On the system of the old BGB, see Schmidt-Räntsch, *Das neue Schuldrecht, Anwendung und Auswirkungen in der Praxis*, 2002 (hereinafter Schmidt-Räntsch), p. 3 no. 11.
18 See on this criticism *Schmidt-Räntsch* pp. 107 ff., nos.303 ff.

The party who has to provide an *obligation de moyens* performs his contract if he exerts his best efforts. If he does not, the creditor has all the remedies available under French law and so has a party whose contracting partner fails to perform an obligation de résultat, irrespective of whether the latter is in fault or not. However, as happens in some other legal systems, force majeure destroys the foundation of the contract. The effect of force majeure is that the contract is extinguished and that none of the parties need to make a declaration to that effect. The failure it causes is therefore not treated as an *"inexécution"*.[19]

In case of the debtor's non-performance the creditor may claim specific performance,[20] and remedy is facilitated by the liberal use of judicial penalties (*astreinte*).[21] Therefore it is probably used more frequently in France than in many other countries.

Unless the parties have agreed otherwise a contract must be terminated for breach by a court. A court will only do so as a last resort and may in stead award damages to the aggrieved party.

3.6

In the *Common Law* some authors use the term remedy to describe the various types of relief which an aggrieved party can obtain in case of a breach of contract. Such relief may be the very performance he contracted for or something in substitution of the promised performance, i.e. damages and restitution.[22] Other authors use the term remedy for other rights of an aggrieved party as well, for instance the right of an aggrieved party to withhold his own performance and to terminate the contract.[23] They all agree, however, that breach implies that the debtor is liable in damages. There is no breach unless the aggrieved party would be entitled to claim damages.

Frustration, which destroys the foundation of the contract,[24] will free the debtor. It is therefore not a breach of contract. Apart from this, it is the prevailing view in the Common law that contract liability is strict liability.[25] There are, of course, contracts under which the duty is not to achieve a specific result but to use one's best efforts – such as employment and services contracts. These contracts do not seem to have been treated very differently from the way they have been in France and the other countries.

Specific performance is a discretionary remedy. It is generally granted in cases of the purchase of land but in other cases only where damages are an inadequate remedy because of the difficulty of quantifying the damages or where the debtor may not be "good for the money".[26]

---

19 Terré, no. 558.
20 Terré, nos. 1009 ff.
21 Idem no. 1025.
22 *Farnsworth on Contracts*, Boston 199o Vol. III, 152.
23 Beale, *Remedies for Breach of Contract*, London 1980, 152.
24 Treitel, p. 847.
25 *Restatement of the Law, Second, Contracts*, 1981 Vol. II 309.
26 See Chitty on Contracts 28 ed. 1999 28.oo1 ff.

3.7 *Force majeure* and hardship

As mentioned above, in France, England and other legal systems force majeure and frustration destroy the foundation of the contract. CISG, and the laws of the Nordic countries, take a different attitude. If a party is exonerated under Article 79 (1) or (2) this will affect the other party's right to claim damages only. The aggrieved party may still "exercise any right other than damages", see Art. 79 (5). This means that CISG, although it does not expressly say so, treats "force majeure" as a "breach", i.e. a non-performance, and that the aggrieved party who wishes to terminate the contract must give notice to the other party. The attitude of PECL is very similar. As a rule a notice of termination is required. However, Art 9.303 (4) provides that if a party is excused due to an impediment which is total and permanent, the contract is terminated automatically and without notice at the time the impediment arises

Some *force majeure* situations may affect only part of the performance and some, such as strikes and embargoes, may be temporary. It may be uncertain whether an impediment is total or partial, definitive or temporary. The rules in CISG on notice of termination for breach are well fitted for such situations. As long as the goods are not delivered the buyer will not loose his right to terminate, see Art 49 (2). When it becomes apparent that the delay is, or will be, a fundamental one, the aggrieved party may give notice of termination, and if the defaulting party asks him whether he wishes to uphold the contract, he will have to inform the latter if he wishes to terminate, see Art. 26.

Hardship is treated by *Denis Tallon* in the preceding Chapter. In addition to rules on *force major* covering impossibility and quasi-impossibility some legal systems have relieved the debtor when performance, though not impossible, has become excessively onerous, (Italy: *essesivamente onorosa*[27]) or so different that the economic basis on which the contract was made has lapsed, (Germany, *Störung der Geschäftsgrundlage*).[28] A hardship rule is found in Dutch law[29] and a similar rule on imprévision in French administrative law.[30] Relief in case of hardship is also provided in PECL Art 6:111 and in the UNIDROIT Principles Arts 6.2.1-6.2.3. CISG has no separate provision on hardship. It has been argued that Art 79 dealing with "exemption" stands somewhere between the very tough French rule on force majeure governing civil contracts and the more lenient German rule on *Störung der Geschäftsgrundlage*.

---

27 Italian Civil Code Art 1467.
28 See new BGB § 313 and Schmidt- Räntsch 201.
29 Civil Code of 1992 Art 6:250.
30 See Nicolas, *The French Law of Contract* 2nd ed. 1992 208.

CHAPTER 29

Limitation Periods

Michael Joachim Bonell*

1 Introduction

The topic of limitation of actions, statute of limitations, prescription or, simply, limitation periods – the terminology varies among the different jurisdictions and is an issue in itself[1] – has long been neglected in the international unification process. Not only has no attempt been made to lay down uniform rules dealing with the subject in a general and comprehensive manner, but even in the context of harmonising the law of specific types of contracts the question as to when the rights or claims arising from such contracts may become time-barred has normally not been addressed at all[2] or only partly regulated, e.g. by fixing the length of the limitation periods and their starting dates, while leaving all the other issues to the otherwise applicable domestic law.[3]

The only exception in this respect is the 1974 United Nations Convention on the Limitation Period in the International Sale of Goods (as amended by the 1980 Protocol) (hereinafter the "UN Limitation Convention"), which is complementary to the 1980 United Nations Convention on Contracts for the International Sale of Goods (CISG) and provides a comprehensive set of rules on the limitation periods with respect to international sales contracts. Yet, notwithstanding its undoubted intrinsic merits, the UN Limitation Convention has in practice met with rather limited success: so far no more than one third of the Contracting States of CISG have adopted it, among which only a few of the major trading nations,[4] and – more importantly – it has in practice been rarely, if at all, applied by courts or arbitral tribunals.[5]

---

* Professor of Law, University of Rome I "La Sapienza"; Chairman of the Working Group for the preparation of UNIDROIT Principles of International Commercial Contracts. The views expressed in this paper are those of the author and do not necessarily reflect the opinions of the other members of the Working Group.

1 See *infra* § 2.
2 See, e.g., the 1964 Uniform Laws on the International Sale of Goods (ULIS) and on the Formation of Contracts for the International Sale of Goods (ULFC); more recently, the 1988 Ottawa Conventions on International Financial Leasing and on International Factoring.
3 See e.g. Article 3 (6) of the 1924 Convention for the Unification of Certain Rules Relating to Bills of Lading ("Hague Rules"); Article 29 of the 1929 Warsaw Convention for the Unification of Certain Rules Relating to International Carriage by Air; Article 32 of the 1956 Convention on the Contract for the International Carriage of Goods by Road (CMR); Article 20 of the 1978 UN Convention on the International Carriage of Goods by Sea ("Hamburg Rules").
4 As of 16 June 2003 the total number of ratifications of the (amended version of the) UN Limitation Convention was 24 (comprising 11 Eastern European States, 5 Central and South American States, 6 African States plus the United States of America and Norway).
5 Suffice it to mention that CLOUT, the UNCITRAL collection of case law on UNCITRAL texts, does not report any decision on the UN Limitation Convention as compared to the more than 200 decisions referring to CISG contained therein.

The reasons why limitation regimes continue to be the realm of domestic laws, with very few, if any, successful attempts to bring about uniformity at international level, are manifold.

One reason may be that in some legal systems the limitation rules are considered to be a matter of procedural law, and that even where they are part of the substantive law they are generally of a strictly mandatory character.[6]

Yet the most serious obstacle to any unification or harmonisation of the various national limitation regimes has hitherto proven to be their very content. Suffice it to mention that just within the area of contract law alone, domestic laws traditionally provide different limitation periods not only with respect to the various types of contract,[7] but also to claims relating to one and the same type of contract.[8] Moreover the variety of the respective time limits is such that, at least nowadays, it does not seem to correspond to any rationale[9] but rather reflects more or less arbitrary choices made by legislatures over the centuries.[10]

Recently, however, there have been developments which indicate that there might be room for a new and more uniform approach to the subject, at least in the field of contract law.

To begin with, a number of countries have adopted or are about to adopt a more simplified and rational limitation regime.[11] This is the case, in particular of the relevant sections of the new Civil Codes of Quebec, the Netherlands and the Russian Federation, of the 1998 Belgian Law on *verjaring* and – most recently – of the

---

6   For further references see R. Zimmermann, Comparative Foundations of a European Law of Set-Off and Prescription (2002), p. 163 Fns. 219-220.

7   See e.g. the Italian Civil Code which sets a general limitation period of 10 years (Art. 2946) but at the same time provides some 30 exceptions (ranging from 1 to 5 years) mainly for different types of service contracts. The same was the case for the German BGB (until the recent reform) which in addition to a general limitation period of 30 years (§ 195) provided for a shorter 2 year period for some 17 types of contracts, mainly service contracts (§ 196). – For an exhaustive comparative overview in Europe see A. Danco, Die Perspektiven der Anspruchsverjährung in Europa (2001), pp. 115-148.

8   This is the case, for instance, of sales contracts where many legal systems provide different limitation periods which sometimes range between six month and thirty years, depending on whether the claim relates to a case of invalidity of the contract, non-conformity of the goods or any other breach: see the comparative overview in H. Müller-Chen, in P. Schlechtriem, Kommentar zum Einheitlichen UN-Kaufrecht, 3rd ed. (2000), p. 888 Fn.1.
   With reference to claims for non-conformity the situation is further complicated by the coexistence in many legal systems of real limitation periods, within which the claims must be exercised, and other – normally much shorter – time limits, within which the buyer must give notice to the seller of the defects of the goods on pain of the loss of the claims altogether: see, for a comprehensive comparative analysis A. Danco, *op cit.*, pp. 202 *et seq.*

9   Indeed, think of the Italian Civil Code which e.g. distinguishes between the remuneration of teachers for lessons given monthly, daily or hourly" and "remuneration of teachers for lessons given for more than a month" providing a limitation period of 1 year in the first case (Art. 2955 n. 1) and of 3 years in the second (Art. 2956 n. 4), or provides a limitation period of 1 year for "rights arising from a transport contract with no further qualifications" (Art. 2951 (1)) and of 18 months for the same rights "if the transport begins or ends outside Europe" (Art. 2951 (2)).

10 As R. Zimmermann puts it, "[…] the relevant provisions still reflect the somewhat haphazard history of the subject" (cf. Comparative Foundations, *cit.* p. 66).

11 More precise references in R. Zimmermann, Comparative Foundations, *cit.*, pp. 66 *et seq.*

amendments introduced into the German BGB in the context of the General Reform of the Law of Obligations which entered into force in 2002. As to law reform projects, mention may be made of the proposals submitted by the Ontario Law Reform Commission, the New Zealand Law Reform Commission and, most recently, by the English Law Commission.[12]

Obviously the various domestic laws are not all the same. Yet, apart from differences of detail, they do have common features which, as will be seen below, are also present in the most recent uniform law instruments in this area. These "international trends" may be summarised as follows:[13] uniform limitation periods for all kinds of claims, at least in the area of contract law;[14] a rather short (3 or 4 years at most) "general" limitation period, starting at the time the obligee knows or ought to have known of its claim;[15] a "maximum" or cut-off limitation period (normally 10 years), starting at the time the claim accrues and after which the claim is at any rate time-barred;[16] and lastly, extensive freedom of the parties to modify by agreement the limitation regime.[17]

At international level there are principally two initiatives worth mentioning. Both the UNIDROIT Principles of International Commercial Contracts (hereinafter "the UNIDROIT Principles") and the Principles of European Contract Law (hereinafter "the European Principles"), aiming at laying down rules of general contract law at universal level or within the European Union, respectively, contain a chapter dealing with the effect of the lapse of time on rights or claims.[18] Actually, only the chapter of the European Principles has been published,[19] while the corresponding chapter of the UNIDROIT Principles[20] is contained in the new enlarged edition of the UNIDROIT Principles expected to be published by June 2004.[21] Like the other chapters of the respective instruments, also these two sets of rules are of a non-binding nature. Nevertheless they deserve the greatest attention, if only because they represent the first attempt at international level to provide a comprehensive limitation regime covering, in the UNIDROIT Principles, all rights or claims arising from international com-

---

12 For a critical analysis of this project which was published in 1998, see N. Andrews, Reform of Limitation of Actions: The Quest for Sound Policy, in 57 Cambridge Law Journal (1998), pp. 589 *et seq.*

13 Cf. R. Zimmermann , Comparative Foundations, *cit.*, p. 85; for similar remarks see also E. H. Hondius, General Report, in E. H. Hondius (ed.), Extinctive Prescription, *cit.* pp. 1 *et seq.* (p. 20 *et seq.*) ; A. Danco, *op cit.*, pp. 200-201. Critically, at least with respect to some of these trends, N. Andrews, Reform of Limitation of Actions, *cit.*, pp. 596 *et seq.*

14 Further references in R. Zimmermann, Comparative Foundations, *cit.*, pp. 89 *et seq.*

15 Further references in R. Zimmermann, Comparative Foundations, *cit.*, pp. 86-89; 92-95.

16 Further references in R. Zimmermann, Comparative Foundations, *cit.*, pp. 99 *et seq.*

17 Further references in R. Zimmermann, Comparative Foundations, *cit.*, pp. 163 *et seq.*

18 The Reporters on the two chapters were P. Schlechtriem and R. Zimmermann , respectively.

19 Cf. O. Lando – E. Clive – A. Prüm – R. Zimmermann (eds.), Principles of European Contract Law, Part III (2003), Chapter 14.

20 Cf. UNIDROIT 2003, Study L – Doc. 91.

21 The 2004 edition of the UNIDROIT Principles, containing 5 new chapters (Authority of agents; Set-off; Assignment of rights, transfer of obligations and assignment of contracts; Third party rights; Limitation periods, respectively) together with additional provisions on inconsistent behaviour and release by agreement, can be ordered at www.unidroit.rome@unidroit.org.

mercial contracts,[22] or even, as in the European Principles, any right to performance of an obligation be it of contractual or extra-contractual origin.[23]

Hereunder the two sets of rules will be examined in more detail in order to indicate their (few) differences and (many) similarities. Whenever appropriate, regard will also be had to the UN Limitation Convention which, though restricted to international sales contracts, represents the most ambitious attempt to unify the law of limitation of actions or prescription at legislative level. Moreover, some concluding remarks will be devoted to the scope of application of the three instruments and to the question how to avoid in practice possible conflicts or undue interference among them.

2   The Terminology Issue

With respect to the effects of the lapse of time on rights or claims common lawyers speak of "limitation of actions" or "statute of limitations", while civilian lawyers, following the Roman term *"prescriptio longi temporis"*, use the terms *"prescription (extinctive ou libératoire)"* (French), *"prescrizione"* (Italian), *"Verjährung"* (German), *"bevrijdende verjaring"* (Dutch), and the like.[24] Yet does this mean that also in English the term "prescription" (with or without the addition of adjectives such as "extinctive", "negative" or "liberative") can be used as a synonym,[25] or at least the functional equivalent,[26] of the terms "limitation of actions" or "statute of limitations"?

Doubts may arise for at least two reasons. First because, while in the common law systems the consequences of the obligee's inactivity over a certain period of time are of a procedural nature, in the civil law systems the lapse of time affects the obligee's substantive right.[27] Secondly, and more importantly, because for common lawyers the term "prescription" has an entirely different meaning from the above mentioned corresponding terms used on the continent: in fact it denotes the process whereby limited rights of use over another's land may be acquired,[28] rather resembling therefore, though not entirely coinciding with, the civil law terms of *"prescription acquisitive"* or *"usucapion"* (French), *"usucapione"* (Italian), *"Ersitzung"* (German), *"verkrijgende verjaring"* (Dutch).[29]

As will be illustrated in more detail below,[30] all three international instruments

---

22 Cf. Art. 10.1 of the UNIDROIT Principles ("[...] rights governed by these Principles [...]").
23 Cf. Art. 14:101 of the European Principles ("[a] right to performance of an obligation ('claim') [...]") and Comment D ("This Chapter applies not only to contractual claims but also to other rights to performance [...]").
24 For further references see R. Zimmermann, Comparative Foundations, *cit.*, pp. 69-71 Fns. 41 and 45.
25 Cf. E. H. Hondius (ed.), Extinctive Prescription. On the Limitation of Actions (1995).
26 So R. Zimmermann , Comparative Foundations, *cit.*, p. 70.
27 See *infra* § 7.
28 See A. McGee, England, in E. H. Hondius (ed.), Extinctive Prescription, *cit.*, pp. 133 *et seq.* (p. 135): "[...][F]or a Common Lawyer the term 'extinctive prescription' has an odd ring. 'Prescription' is a term usually used in the common law to denote the process by which limited rights of use over another's land (such as easements) may be acquired."
29 For further references see R. Zimmermann, Comparative Foundations, *cit.*, pp. 69-71 Fn. 41 and 45.
30 See *infra* § 7.

here under consideration reject the purely procedural approach and consequently deliberately avoid the use of the traditional English terms of art "limitation of actions" or "statute of limitations". Yet while both the UN Limitation Convention and the UNIDROIT Principles for the reasons indicated above also refrain from using in their English version the term "prescription",[31] and instead adopt the neutral term "limitation period(s)",[32] the European Principles surprisingly enough use the term "prescription".[33] It remains to be seen how this rather peculiar terminology will be received in practice.[34]

3   Limitation Periods as Distinct from Other Time Limits

Both the UNIDROIT Principles and the European Principles provide in a number of cases that a party entitled to exercise a right must do so within a certain time limit, on pain of loss of the right itself.

Under the UNIDROIT Principles, for instance, notice of avoidance for defects of consent and gross disparity must be given "within a reasonable time, having regard to the circumstances, after the avoiding party knew or could not have been unaware of the relevant facts or became capable of acting freely",[35] the request for renegotiation of the contract in case of hardship "shall be made without undue delay",[36] notice of the intention to cure must be given by the non-performing party "without undue delay",[37] the request of performance of a non-monetary obligation must be made "within a reasonable time after [the party entitled to performance] has, or ought to have, become aware of the non-performance",[38] and notice of termination for breach of contract must be given "within a reasonable time after [the aggrieved party] has or ought to have become aware of [...] the non-conforming performance".[39] Similar provisions, which in some cases even literally correspond, may be found also in the European Principles.[40]

---

31 Actually, the non-use in the UNIDROIT Principles of the term "prescription" is also due to the fact that in particular Islamic laws are traditionally very strict in excluding that rights could be lost by the mere passage of time, so that the adoption of a neutral term for the chapter was considered to be essential in order to be acceptable in those legal systems: cf. UNIDROIT 1999, Study L – Misc. 21, para. 293.

32 Cf. the full title of the UN Limitation Convention ("Convention on the Limitation Period in the International Sale of Goods") and the title of Chapter 10 of the UNIDROIT Principles ("Limitation Periods").

33 Cf. the title of Charter 14 of the European Principles ("Prescription"), but the terms "prescription" and "period of prescription" are also used throughout the chapter.

34 The Comments, after stating that possible alternative options could have been the terms "extinctive prescription", "negative prescription", "liberative prescription" and "limitation of claims", merely state that "[f]or the sake of simplicity and since these Principles do not deal with acquisitive prescription the term 'prescription' is generally used without any further qualifying adjective" (cf. Comment A to Art. 14:101 of the European Principles).

35 Cf. Art. 3.15(1) of the UNIDROIT Principles.

36 Cf. Art. 6.2.3(1) of the UNIDROIT Principles.

37 Cf. Art. 7.1.4(1)(a) of the UNIDROIT Principles.

38 Cf. Art. 7.2.2 of the UNIDROIT Principles.

39 Cf. Art. 7.3.2(2) of the UNIDROIT Principles.

40 Cf. Arts. 4:113; 9:102 (3); 9: 303 (2) of the European Principles.

These time limits – which at domestic level are known as forfeiture, *délais prefixes* (French), *Ausschlußfrist* (German), *decadenza* (Italian), *verval* (Dutch), etc. – should not be confused with the limitation periods. Not only are they in general much shorter than the latter but, being designed to meet different policy needs, are not subject to the rules e.g. on suspension or on modifications by parties' agreement, provided for limitation periods.

Accordingly the UNIDROIT Principles expressly state that "[Chapter 10] does not govern the time within which one party is required under these Principles, as a condition for the acquisition or exercise of its right, to give notice to the other party or perform any act other than the institution of legal proceedings."[41] A similar provision is to be found in the UN Limitation Convention,[42] while the European Principles address the issue only in the Comments, though basically in the same way.[43]

4 Duration and Commencement of the Limitation Periods

It is generally accepted that the principal components of any limitation regime are the length of the limitation periods, when they begin to run, whether and under which circumstances they may be suspended or begin to run afresh, and whether they may be shortened or extended by parties' agreement. It is likewise undisputed that these components are closely interrelated, so that they cannot be considered in isolation but have to be assessed in relation one to the other.[44]

This is true above all of the length and the commencement of the limitation periods. Indeed, at least from the point of view of the obligee, a limitation period of say 3 or 4 years may be considered rather short or even too short, if calculated from the date on which the obligee's right or claim accrues, while the same period would appear in a different light if the starting date was that on which the obligee discovers or should have discovered its right or claim. Conversely, for the obligor even a short period of 3 or 4 years but starting to run on the obligee's discovery of its right or claim may prove to be too long, unless there is a further cut-off or "maximum" period of say 10 years after which the rights or claims are in any case time-barred.

All three international instruments basically adopt a so-called two-tier system, i.e. provide for a rather short "general" limitation period combined with a "maximum" cut-off period.

---

41 Cf. Art. 10. 1(2) of the UNIDROIT Principles.

42 Cf. Art. 1 (2) of the UN Limitation Convention: "This Convention does not affect a particular time-limit within which one party is required, as a condition for the acquisition or exercise of his claim, to give notice to the other party or perform any act other than the institution of legal proceedings".

43 See Comment D to Article 14:101 of the European Principles ("The Principles contain a number of time limits (see Article 2:206 on the time limit for acceptance; Article 4:113 on the time limit for notice of avoidance; Article 9:303(2) on the time limit for notice of termination and Article 9:102(3) on the time limit for the right to seek specific performance). These time limits do not constitute prescription periods [...]").

44 Cf. R. Zimmermann , Comparative Foundations, *cit.*, p. 76; similarly E. H. Hondius (ed.), Extinctive Prescription, *cit.*, p. 8 (citing the English Report): "The whole of the [...] law of limitation of actions may be encapsulated in the answers to five questions: When does time start to run? Can the running of time be suspended? How long is the limitation period? What happens when time expires? Can the limitation period be overriden"?

The general limitation period, under both the UNIDROIT Principles and the European Principles, is 3 years,[45] while under the UN Limitation Convention it is 4 years.[46] This difference may be regretted, but can be explained by the fact that 3 years have only recently become absolutely prevalent at domestic level, whereas, even at the time when the UN Limitation Convention was adopted, 4 years represented in the context of sales contracts basically a compromise solution between the industrialised countries of the North, advocating a (much) shorter period, and the less developed countries of the South, in favour of a (much) longer period.[47]

Yet there is another quite significant difference between the UN Limitation Convention on the one hand, and the UNIDROIT Principles and the European Principles on the other. While under the former the general limitation period begins to run when the claim accrues, i.e. with respect to claims for breach of contract on the date on which the breach occurs, and with respect to claims for non-conformity of the goods on the date of delivery,[48] the latter basically make the commencement of the general limitation period dependent on the obligee's actual or constructive knowledge of its claim.[49]

There are again both historical and substantive reasons for this difference. Indeed the so-called accrual test not only prevailed in the past, but may still be accepted with respect to sales contracts where the non-conformity of the goods can normally be established rather easily upon delivery or shortly thereafter. By contrast, the so-called discoverability test, which recently has become more common, seems definitely more appropriate at least with respect to works and service contracts – the main target of both the UNIDROIT Principles and the European Principles – where defects may come to light years after performance.

To be sure, the discoverability test does not operate in exactly the same manner under the UNIDROIT Principles and the European Principles. Whereas the former openly state that the general limitation period begins "on the day after the day the obligee knows or ought to know the facts as a result of which the obligee's right can be exercised",[50] the latter provide that the general period of prescription begins to run "from the time when the debtor has to effect performance or, in the case of a right to damages, from the time of the act which gives rise to the claim",[51] but at the same time specify that "[t]he running of the period of prescription is suspended as long as the creditor does not know of, and could not reasonably know of: (a) the identify of the debtor; or (b) the facts giving rise to the claim [...]".[52] The approach taken by the UNIDROIT Principles may be preferred as being more linear; what ultimately matters is, however, the practical result which is the same under both instruments.

---

45 Cf. Art. 10. 2(1) of the UNIDROIT Principles; Art. 14:201 of the European Principles.

46 Cf. Art. 8 of the UN Limitation Convention.

47 R. Loewe, Internationales Kaufrecht (1989), p. 199. – Interestingly enough, while on that occasion also the United Kingdom called for a 6 year period, the English Law Commission is now proposing at domestic level the adoption of a general limitation period of 3 years.

48 Cf. Arts. 9 (1) and 10 (1) (2) of the UN Limitation Convention.

49 Cf. Art. 10. 2 (1) of the UNIDROIT Principles and the combination of Arts. 14:203 and 14:301 of the European Principles.

50 Cf. Art. 10. 2 (1) of the UNIDROIT Principles.

51 Cf. Art. 14:203 of the European Principles

52 Cf. Art. 14:301 of the European Principles

The "maximum" limitation period (or, in the words of the UN Limitation Convention, the "general limit of the limitation period") is, under all three international instruments, 10 years.[53] Yet, as will be illustrated more in detail below,[54] there are significant differences among them as far as the operation of such maximum period is concerned.

5 Party Autonomy

As mentioned above, limitation rules have traditionally been considered mandatory in nature, while only recently has there been a growing tendency at domestic level to grant parties considerable freedom to shorten or extend the length of limitation periods.

The change in attitude towards the role of party autonomy in this field is evident also at international level.

While the UN Limitation Convention basically excludes the possibility of any modification of the limitation periods by the parties,[55] both the UNIDROIT Principles and the European Principles permit the parties ample freedom to alter them. Thus under the UNIDROIT Principles the parties may shorten or extend both the general and the maximum limitation period, the only limits being that the former cannot go below one year and the latter below 4 years or beyond 15 years.[56] The solution adopted by the European Principles is very similar, the sole difference being that the limitation period may be extended up to 30 years on account, evidently, of the fact that the European Principles also cover claims of non-contractual origin.[57]

On closer examination however even under the UN Limitation Convention the parties are ultimately free to adopt the limitation regime of their choice. According to Article 3 (2) the parties may by an express agreement exclude the application of the Convention in its entirety: if they do so, it is up to the relevant rules of private international law to determine the otherwise applicable domestic law and those rules normally grant the parties the right to make their own choice.[58]

---

53 Cf. Art. 10. 2 (2) of the UNIDROIT Principles; Art. 14:307 of the European Principles; Art. 23 of the UN Limitation Convention.

54 See *infra* § 6.

55 Cf. Art. 22 (1) of the UN Limitation Convention. However even under this Convention "[t]he debtor may at any time during the running of the limitation period extend the period by a declaration in writing to the creditor" (Art. 22(2) and the parties may in an arbitration agreement stipulate that "[...]arbitral proceedings shall be commenced within a shorter period of limitation than that prescribed by this Convention, provided that such clause is valid under the law applicable to the contract of sale" (Art. 22 (3).

56 Cf. Art. 10. 3 of the UNIDROIT Principles.

57 Cf. Art. 14:601 (1) (2) of the European Principles.

58 Cf. Arts. 3 (1) and 10 (1) lit. (d) of the 1980 Rome Convention on the Law Applicable to Contractual Obligations, stating, respectively, "[t]he contract shall be governed by the law chosen by the parties [...]" and "[t]he law applicable to the contract [...] shall govern in particular [...] prescription and limitation of actions". For similar provisions see Arts. 7 and 14 lit. (d) of the 1994 Inter-American Convention on the Law Applicable to International Contracts.

6 Suspension and Renewal of the Limitation Periods

It is generally recognised that the course of the limitation periods may be affected by certain acts of either the obligor or the obligee or by external circumstances. More precisely, in some cases the running of the limitation periods is suspended for the duration of the event that caused suspension, while in others the limitation periods starts to run afresh as a result of the occurrence of the event.

With respect to possible causes of suspension there is a wide convergence among the three international instruments.

They all concur that the commencement of judicial or arbitral proceedings by the obligee to assert its right against the obligor causes the suspension of the limitation period for the duration of the proceedings.[59]

The UN Limitation Convention expressly provides that the suspension effect is conditional upon the proceedings ending with a decision binding on the merits of the claim.[60] The same solution seems to have been adopted by the European Principles,[61] while the UNIDROIT Principles in this respect take a more flexible approach: by stating that "[s]uspension lasts until the proceedings have been terminated by a final decision of the court or otherwise",[62] they admit the suspension of the limitation period not only where the judicial or arbitral proceedings end with a decision on the merits but also in all other cases which according to the applicable rules of procedure terminate the proceedings, including the withdrawal of the claim, settlement, a stay of proceedings, etc.[63]

The three instruments also agree that the limitation period is furthermore suspended whenever the obligee is prevented from pursuing its right by an external impediment, such as force majeure, death or incapacity.[64]

The UNIDROIT Principles and the European Principles admit yet another cause for suspension. More precisely, under the UNIDROIT Principles the limitation period is also suspended when the parties agree to engage in alternative dispute resolution, i.e. in "[...] proceedings whereby the parties request a third person to assist them in their attempt to reach an amicable settlement of their dispute",[65] while the European Prin-

---

59 Cf. Arts. 10. 5 and 10. 6 of the UNIDROIT Principles; Art. 14:302 of the European Principles; Arts. 13 -18 of the UN Limitation Convention.

60 See Art. 17 of the UN Limitation Convention ("Where a claim has been asserted in legal proceedings within the limitation period [...] but such legal proceedings have ended without a decision binding on the merits of the claim, the limitation period shall be deemed to have continued to run").

61 See Art. 14:302 (2) of the European Principles ("Suspension lasts until a decision has been made which has the effect of res iudicata, or until the case has been otherwise disposed of") in conjunction with Comment A (3) "[...] Where the proceedings end without a decision on the merits of the claim (because the action is procedurally defective or because it has subsequently been withdrawn) the creditor merely has what remains of the old period of prescription to bring a new action".

62 So expressly Art. 10. 5 (2) of the UNIDROIT Principles (but see for a similar provision with respect to arbitration proceedings Art. 10. 6 (2) of the UNIDROIT Principles).

63 Cf. Comments to Arts. 10. 5 and 10. 6 of the UNIDROIT Principles

64 Cf. Art. 10. 8 of the UNIDROIT Principles; Arts. 14:303, 14:305 and 14:306 of the European Principles; Art. 21 of the UN Limitation Convention

65 Art. 10. 7 of the UNIDROIT Principles. – The definition of alternative dispute resolution proceedings is taken almost literally from Art. 1 (3) of the 2002 UNCITRAL Model Law on International Commercial Conciliation. Note that the same Model Law contains an Article X ("Suspension of limitation period"), the content of which basically corresponds to Art. 10. 7 of the UNIDROIT Principles.

ciples go even further in providing that in order for there to be suspension it is suffi-cient that "[...] the parties negotiate about the claim, or about circumstances from which a claim might arise [...]".[66]

To be sure, to admit mere negotiations between the parties as a cause for suspen-sion of the limitation period had originally been proposed also for the UNIDROIT Prin-ciples but was ultimately rejected for basically two reasons: first, on the ground of the difficulty of defining the very concept of negotiations and of exactly determining the time when they begin and when they end;[67] secondly, because it was felt that it should be left to the parties, whenever they enter into more or less formal negotia-tions with a view to settling their dispute, to agree in each given case whether or not the limitation period be suspended, and if so, for how long.[68]

Finally, under all three instruments acknowledgement by the obligor of the obligee's right or claim causes the renewal of the limitation period with the conse-quence that the time which has elapsed before the acknowledgement is no longer taken into account and a new limitation period begins to run.[69] The acknowl-edgement, which may be either express or implied, e.g. by partial performance or payment of interest,[70] must of course take place before the expiration of the limitation period:[71] as pointed out in the Comments to Article 10.4 of the UNIDROIT Principles, if the parties want to undo or refute the effects of a completed limitation period they have to create a new obligation, e.g. by a novation or recreation of the time-barred right.[72]

On the contrary, where the three instruments present considerable differences is the extent to which the various grounds for suspension or renewal may affect not only the general limitation period of 3 or 4 years, but also the maximum period of 10 years.

The most rigorous approach is definitely that taken by the UN Limitation Conven-tion, according to which the 10 year time limit is absolute in the sense that it applies even where the Convention itself provides for the suspension or renewal of the gen-eral limitation period.[73]

---

66 Art. 14:304 of the European Principles ("If the parties negotiate about the claim, or about circum-stances from which a claim might arise, the period of prescription does not expire before one year has passed since the last communication made in the negotiations").

67 Significantly enough in this respect also the European Principles merely state that "[t]he term 'ne-gotiations' has to be interpreted widely. It covers any exchange of opinion which may reasonably lead the claimant to believe that the claim has not been finally rejected by the other party. Conciliation proceedings [...] should also be taken as covered by the term negotiations" (cf. Comment to Art. 14:304).

68 Cf. UNIDROIT 1999, Study L, Misc. 21, para. 334; UNIDROIT 2002, Study L, Misc. 24, paras. 107 – 118.

69 Cf. Art. 20(1) of the UN Limitation Convention; Art. 10. 4 UNIDROIT Principles; Art. 14:401(1) European Principles.

70 So explicitly Art. 14:401(1) European Principles, yet the same is true not only of the UNIDROIT Principles but also of the UN Limitation Convention which, though requiring as a rule the written form (Art. 20 (1), admits that the obligor's intention to acknowledge may be inferred also from such other acts (Art. 20 (2)).

71 So explicitly Art. 20 (1) of the UN Limitation Convention and Art. 10. 4 of the UNIDROIT Principles.

72 Cf. Comment 3 to Art. 10. 4 of the UNIDROIT Principles.

73 Cf. Art. 23 of the UN Limitation Convention.

By contrast, both the UNIDROIT Principles and the European Principles take a more flexible approach and admit an exception to the operation of the maximum limitation period in the case of judicial or arbitral proceedings commenced by the obligee against the obligor and of acknowledgement of the obligee's right or claim by the obligor. More precisely, in the case of judicial proceedings the maximum limitation period may be extended virtually indefinitely depending on the length of the proceedings,[74] while in the case of acknowledgement the limitation period will be exceeded by the beginning of a new general limitation period of three years.[75]

7 Effects of Expiration of Limitation Periods

The effects of the lapse of time on rights or claims are differently conceived in the various legal systems. While in the common law systems the consequences of the obligee's inactivity over a certain period of time are of a procedural nature, i.e. the obligee is prevented from pursuing its right in court, in the civil law systems the lapse of time affects the substantive right, either by extinguishing it altogether (so-called strong effect) or by granting the obligor the right to refuse performance (so-called weak effect).[76]

However, as rightly pointed out,[77] on closer examination the differences between the various approaches are of a more theoretical than practical nature. Indeed, within the civil law systems it is the weak substantive approach which is more and more prevailing, and the acceptance that the effect of the lapse of time is a defence considerably attenuates the differences between the procedural and the substantive approaches.

All three international instruments here under consideration reject the purely procedural approach and, faced with the alternative between a "strong" and a "weak" substantive approach, adopt the second solution, i.e. reject the idea that the obligee's right or claim is extinguished and instead consider the expiration of the limitation periods as a defence which the obligor may invoke against the obligee. This is expressly stated in the UNIDROIT Principles, according to which "[t]he expiration of the limitation period does not extinguish the right"[78] and "[f]or the expiration of the limitation period to have effect, the obligor must assert it as a defence".[79] But substantially the

---

74 Cf. Arts. 10. 5 and 10. 6 of the UNIDROIT Principles; Art. 14:307 of the European Principles. – This is also the reason why, contrary to the UN Limitation Convention which provides that if, at the time the legal proceedings ended, the limitation period has expired or has less than one year to run, the obligee is entitled to an additional one year period from the date the proceedings ended (cf. Art. 17 (2)), neither the UNIDROIT Principles nor the European Principles contain a similar rule.

75 Cf. Art. 10. 4 of the UNIDROIT Principles; 14:401(2) of the European Principles.

76 Cf. R. Zimmermann, Comparative Foundations, cit., p, 69 et seq.

77 Cf. R. Zimmermann, Comparative Foundations, cit., pp. 73-75.

78 Cf. Art. 10. 9 (1) of the UNIDROIT Principles; see also Art. 10. 1 (1) of the UNIDROIT Principles stating that "[t]he exercise of rights governed by these Principles is barred by expiration of a period of time, referred to as 'limitation period' [...]".

79 Cf. Art. 10. 9 (2) of the UNIDROIT Principles; see also Comment 2 to Article 10. 9, explaining that "[t]he effects of an expiration of a limitation period do not occur automatically, but only if the obligor raises the expiration as a defense. This can be done in any proceeding and also outside of a proceed-

same provisions can be found also in the European Principles[80] and in the UN Limitation Convention.[81]

There are at least two important consequences which follow from this basic decision.

First, precisely because the expiration of the limitation periods does not extinguish the obligee's right or claim but only bars its enforcement if the obligor invokes it as a defence, the obligee may, even after the expiration of the time limits, generally rely on its right or claim as a defence, for instance, as a ground for retention of a performance owed by it to the obligor.[82]

Yet may the obligee even set off its time-barred right or claim against a right or claim asserted by the obligor? All three instruments do expressly address the issue, but while the UN Limitation Convention ultimately refers for the answer to the applicable domestic law,[83] both the UNIDROIT Principles and the European Principles, relying on their respective rules on set-off,[84] positively state that "[t]he obligee may exercise the right of set off until the obligor has asserted the expiration of the limitation period".[85]

Secondly, since the effects of the expiration of the limitation periods do not operate *ipso iure*, the obligor which performs its obligation may not subsequently change its mind and reclaim its performance on the ground that the obligee's right was already time-barred.[86]

8 Scope of Application

With respect to the scope of application of the three instruments, a first question which arises concerns the relationship between the UN Limitation Convention, on the one hand, and the chapter on limitation periods in the UNIDROIT Principles and the European Principles, on the other.

The situation is clear whenever the formal requirements for the application of the

---

ing, as by refusing a request of the obligee to perform. The existence of the defense can also be the subject of a declaratory judgement."

80 Cf. 14: 501 (1) of the European Principles ("After expiry of the period of prescription the debtor is entitled to refuse performance").

81 Cf. Art. 25(1) of the UN Limitation Convention ("[...] [N]o claim shall be recognized or enforced in any legal proceedings commenced after the expiration of the limitation period") in combination with Art. 24 ("Expiration of the limitation period shall be taken into consideration in any legal proceedings only if invoked by a party to such proceedings").

82 Cf. Art. 9 (3) of the UNIDROIT Principles ("A right may still be relied on as a defence even though the expiration of the limitation period for that right has been asserted") and Comment 3 to Art. 9; Art. 25(2) of the UN Limitation Convention.

83 Cf. Art. 25 (2), lit. (a) and (b) of the UN Limitation Convention.

84 Cf. Art. 8. 5 of the UNIDROIT Principles; Art. 13:106 of the European Principles.

85 So expressly Article 10. 10 of the UNIDROIT Principles, but see similarly Article 14:503 of the European Principles according to which "[a] claim in relation to which the period of prescription has expired may nonetheless be set off, unless the debtor has invoked prescription previously or does so within two month of notification of set-off".

86 Cf. Art. 10. 11 of the UNIDROIT Principles; Art. 14:501 of the European Principles; Art. 26 of the UN Limitation Convention.

UN Limitation Convention are met, i.e. the contract is an international sales contract entered into between two parties whose places of business are in two different Contracting States or the rules of private international law make the law of a Contracting State applicable to the contract.[87] In this case the Convention will prevail, and in view of its mandatory nature this will occur even if the parties, either because they are unaware of its existence or because they do not know that their contract falls within its scope of application, refer to the UNIDROIT Principles or the European Principles, including the respective chapters on limitation periods or prescription, as the applicable law.[88]

In all other cases, i.e. with respect to international sales contracts not governed by the UN Limitation Convention or to all other kinds of contracts, it ultimately depends on whether a domestic court or an arbitral tribunal is seized of the case.

Domestic courts traditionally tend to consider the parties' reference to either the UNIDROIT Principles or the European Principles as a mere agreement to incorporate them into the contract and to determine the law governing the contract on the basis of their own conflict-of-laws rules. As a result, they will also apply the respective chapters on limitation periods or prescription only to the extent that the rules contained therein do not affect the provisions of the proper law from which the parties may not derogate.[89]

By contrast, arbitral tribunals, which are not necessarily bound to base their decision on a particular domestic law, may well apply the UNIDROIT Principles or the European Principles, including the chapters on limitation periods or prescription, as "rules of law" governing the contract irrespective of whether or not they are consistent with the particular domestic law otherwise applicable. The only mandatory rules the arbitral tribunals may take into account, also in view of their task of rendering to the largest possible extent a decision capable of enforcement, are those which claim to be applicable irrespective of the law otherwise governing the contract ("*loi d'application nécessaire*"). Yet none of the national limitation rules should fall under this notion.[90]

To be sure, international arbitrators may – and actually increasingly do – go even

---

87 Cf. Arts. 2 and 3 of the U.N. Limitation Convention (but see also the restrictions of Arts. 4, 5 and 6).

88 As already noted, according to Article 3 (2) of the UN Limitation Convention, if the parties wish to exclude the Convention in its entirety, they must do so "expressly".

89 This at least is still the prevailing view under the 1980 Rome Convention on the Law Applicable to Contractual Obligations: see most recently, also for further references, F. De Ly, Choice of law clauses, Unidroit Principles of international commercial contracts and Article 3 of the Rome convention, in Etudes offertes à Barthélemy Mercadal (2002), pp. 133 *et seq.*

The situation may soon change if, following the inquiry currently being conducted by the EC Commission, there is sufficient support for the proposal to amend Art. 3 (1) of the Rome Convention so as to expressly permit the parties to choose as the applicable law not only the law of a particular country, but also principles and rules of supranational or a-national character, such as international conventions not yet in force, general principles of law or the UNIDROIT Principles: see *Green Paper by the Commission of the EC on the Rome Convention of 1980 on the law applicable to contractual obligations into a Community instrument and its modernisation* of 14 January 2003 (COM (2002) 654 final), Question 7, pp. 21-22.

90 Cf. also for further references, M.J. Bonell, An International Restatement of Contract Law, 2nd ed. (1997), pp. 192 *et seq.*

further and apply the UNIDROIT Principles and – though to a much lesser extent – the European Principles even in the absence of an express choice to this effect by the parties, either because the contract is governed by "general principles of law", "*lex mercatoria*" or the like, or because, in the absence of any choice of law clause in the contract, they consider these two instruments to be "the most appropriate rules of law" to be applied.[91]

What still remains to be seen is the relationship between the UNIDROIT Principles and the European Principles in all cases in which the UN Limitation Convention does not apply.

Obviously, no problem arises as long as the parties themselves express their preference for one or the other set of rules, e.g. by referring to the UNIDROIT Principles or to the European Principles, including the respective chapters on limitation periods or prescription, as the law governing their contract. Yet even in the absence of such a choice by the parties the fear that the co-existence of the two sets of rules might cause uncertainty or even conflicts in practice is largely unfounded. Like most of the other chapters of the UNIDROIT Principles and the European Principles, also those on limitation periods or prescription do not present substantial differences, and even if they differed with respect to a specific issue one might opt for one or the other solution depending on whether the dispute involves parties at least one of which is non-European, or is a purely intra-European one. As a matter of fact, while the European Principles are formally limited to the member States of the European Union,[92] not only do the UNIDROIT Principles claim to lay down rules for international commercial contracts, but they are already being recognised in arbitration practice as a particularly authoritative source of "general principles of international commercial contracts" or the *lex mercatoria*.[93]

9 Conclusions

Despite its practical importance the topic of limitation periods – rightly defined as "the gateway to justice"[94] – has long been neglected in the international unification process.

Only recently there have been developments which indicate that there might be room for a new and more uniform approach to the subject, at least in the field of contract law.

Apart from the UN Limitation Convention, which is limited to sales contracts, there are principally two initiatives worth mentioning. Both the UNIDROIT Principles and the European Principles, dealing with contracts in general, contain a chapter on limitation periods.

The two set of rules, which present only few differences and many convergences, reflect the most recent and advanced international trends in the field. This is true with

---

91 Cf. M. J. Bonell, The UNIDROIT Principles in Practice (2002), pp. 31-33.
92 Cf. O.Lando-H.Beale (eds.), Principles of European Contract Law, Parts I and II (2000), Introduction.
93 For an update of international case law relating to the UNIDROIT Principles see <http://www.unilex.info>.
94 N. Andrews, Reform of Limitation of Actions, *cit.*, p. 590.

respect to all the principal components of any modern limitation regime, i.e. the duration and commencement of the limitation periods, the extent to which parties may modify them, the causes for the suspension and renewal of the limitation periods and the effect of their expiration.

Admittedly both the UNIDROIT Principles and the European Principles have no binding force and are applied only by virtue of their persuasive value. Yet the practical experience shows that the arbitral tribunals increasingly base their decisions on the UNIDROIT Principles and – though to a much lesser extent – the European Principles, and this not only if expressly chosen by the parties as the law governing the contract, but also because they consider these instruments as the "most appropriate rules of law" to be applied in a truly international or transnational context. The inclusion in the UNIDROIT Principles and in the European Principles of an additional chapter on limitation periods cannot but increase the attractiveness of the two instruments and contribute to greater uniformity of the limitation rules with respect to international commercial contracts.

C – Contract Law – Specific Contracts

CHAPTER 30

Towards Principles of European Sales Law

Viola Heutger & Christoph Jeloschek*

1 Introduction

A working team within the framework of the Study Group on a European Civil Code has embarked on the task of creating Principles of European Sales Law. But one may be inclined to argue that most of the work has already been done, as the impact of international instruments of sales law on this research project cannot be overlooked. If one purports to search for common rules and principles in sales law one cannot avoid dealing with the standards that have been set in Europe so far. What comes to mind first is the Consumer Sales Directive (hereinafter referred to as 'the Sales Directive' or 'the CSD'), which the European Parliament and the Council of the European Union have enacted on 25 May 1999.[1] Even though this Directive only aims at harmonising *consumer* sales law it cannot be denied that, by doing so, a large domain of the law of sales as such has been covered. In addition to that, the United Nations Convention on the international sale of goods (hereinafter referred to as 'the CISG') has been ratified by most of the Member States of the European Union, thus unifying *international commercial* sales.[2] And in the third place, there are also general principles of contract law, such as the Principles of European Contract Law, which, albeit not drafted for sales law as such, can provide a basis for common European rules.

But do these instruments indeed amount to the establishment of a *European* Sales Law? At first sight, the answer is in the negative, as there is no such thing as a comprehensive system of rules covering the contract of sale in Europe. Nonetheless, there are important fragments on the European level, such as the Sales Directive and other Directives touching upon sales transactions.[3] These Directives have one thing in common, as they aim at the protection of consumers.

Upon leaving behind the mere European plane, the case for a common sales law looks stronger, though. The CISG constitutes a truly universal body of sales law. Not only has it been ratified by 62 countries, but it also been applied frequently in the

---

*   The authors are researchers at the Molengraaff Institute for Private Law, University of Utrecht/The Netherlands. They take part in the working team on sales law within the framework of the Study Group on a European Civil Code (see below at 3.).

1   Directive 1999/44/EC on certain aspects of the sale of consumer goods and associated guarantees (*OJ* L 171, 7.7.1999, p. 12).

2   Ireland, Portugal, and the UK being the exceptions.

3   For instance the Directives on unfair contract terms, contracts negotiated away from business, distance selling, late payments, and e-commerce. For further references and an overview of the important community acquis in the area of private law, see the Communication from the Commission to the Council and the European Parliament on European Contract Law, COM (2001) 398 final, Annex I.

more than two decades since its enactment.[4] This success and level of harmonisation notwithstanding, the CISG cannot be considered a constituting part of a European sales law. On the one hand, it has been drafted for the world community at large, thus applying to a spectrum of diverse economies, ranging from the developing world to the most industrialised nations.[5] On the other hand, the CISG remains restricted to the international cross-border trade, i.e. sales transactions concluded between commercial parties on the international plane.

Where does this leave us with the introductory question? It seems as if neither European law nor international sales law can be deemed amounting to a comprehensive European sales law. This view is, however, rather simplistic, for it has already been pointed out that there are bits and pieces that could eventually result in such a body of sales law. This contribution will attempt to refine this picture by investigating the fragments already in existence, the ultimate aim being twofold.

One the one hand, we will establish whether there is indeed a need for a truly European sales law (2). To this end, we will first discuss policy considerations on a European level, such as the existence of a common currency and the amount of cross-border consumer shopping. Then we will analyse briefly the two instruments of sales law mentioned above, the Sales Directive and the CISG, by comparing them in order to point out some of the differences, lacunae, and problems in their application. The results from this analysis are then applied as a yardstick for the discussion of an attempt at creating a set of European Principles of Sales Law (3). In our concluding remarks, we would like to show whether, and to what extent, this research project has managed to overcome the problems raised in this contribution (4).

2   Is There a Need for It?

2.1   A Common Currency: A Boast for European Sales Law

Before delving into the more legal arguments as regards the shortcomings of the Sales Directive and the CISG, it is worthy – and necessary if law is to serve the social and economic needs of society – to reflect upon some economic factors that are often put forward in pursuit of a greater unification of the laws in Europe.

One of the most important, and for the European peoples certainly most evident, recent developments in Europe has been the ascent of a common currency. As a result, it is a reality since 2002 that most sales transactions within the eleven countries of the European Monetary Union are settled in €. Not only does the common currency therefore bear witness of the ever-deepening market harmonisation, but it will also stimulate further the internal market.[6]

---

4   The ever-growing databases dedicated to the application of the CISG bear witness of this development, see www.unilex.info and www.cisg.law.pace.edu.

5   As it has been pointed out above, three out of the 15 Member States have not ratified the CISG. Out of the 10 candidate countries, which are about to join the EU in 2004, all but two, Cyprus and Malta, have ratified the CISG.

6   See Consumer Policy Strategy 2002-2006 at p. 8: 'Cross-border opportunities should, therefore, become more evident for consumers'.

In sum, the Euro has definitely facilitated comparison of prices and thus, torn down an important obstacle to cross-border shopping. To some, it now seems only logical to continue by harmonising other equally important aspects of sales transactions, such as the legal framework within they are embedded. In other words, Europe has a common currency, but no common rules for sales transaction; disparities in sales law are thus seen as another hurdle to cross-border trade that needs to be dismantled.

2.2 The Cross-Border Debate: The Tale of the Active Consumer

Yet, a note of caution seems to be in place. Phrased as a critical question: is it actually true that a European body of sales law will result in a sudden surge in consumer cross-border transactions? From the Community's point of view, the answer is certainly in the affirmative. Consumers are said to be 'keen to benefit from the large market by purchasing goods in Member States *other than their State of residence*'.[7] This is but one statement in a long line of similar euphemistic odes to the so-called active consumer.

> 'The active consumer, who seeks to make use of the advantages of the large European market by obtaining products and services abroad, therefore plays a fundamental part in the construction of Europe by preventing the artificial reconstruction of new borders and the commercial partitioning of markets. [...] Therefore his acts must be supported and facilitated by removing existing barriers as far as possible, i.e. the linguistic, cultural, psychological and legal barriers which prevent consumers from profiting from the advantages of the large market, and by giving it added vitality, by obtaining products and services beyond national borders.'[8]

These words seem convincing, even more so as they have been written by the administrator in charge of the early harmonisation efforts of what has now become the Sales Directive. But on the other hand, they smack of wishful thinking and are arguably a bit far-fetched, to say the least. In fact, above statement already contains references to a host of factors that are capable of impeding cross-border transactions. In the present context, one question is essential: do *legal rules* inhibit cross border shopping?[9] In answer to this question, it cannot be overlooked that the real barriers to consumers buying abroad are practical, rather than legal in nature.

First of all, *geographical accessibility* is a key-factor to be taken into account. Consumers do not regularly engage in long, drawn-out 'hunting-and-gathering' campaigns to purchase goods. The large bulk of consumers shopping abroad, with the exception of those who live in border regions, are tourists or businessmen on business trips.

---

7   Recital 4 of the CSD.

8   M. Tenreiro, Guarantees and after-sales service: brief analysis of the Green Paper presented by the Commission, Consumer Law Journal 1995, p. 81.

9   This question, and some arguments, have been taken from R. Bradgate, Harmonisation of legal guarantees: a common law perspective, Consumer Law Journal 1995, pp. 95-97. Cf. R. Cranston, The Green Paper on guarantees, Consumer Law Journal 1995, p. 110, who also mentions a possible exception, the sale of cars that is.

Second, *language* plays an in important role in consumer transactions. The consumer wants to both understand and make him understood. He will therefore be inclined to conduct the necessary conversation in his native tongue, which facilitates building up of trust.

Third, there is the issue of *logistics*. After having overcome all the previous hurdles, how can the consumer get the goods back home? If they are small there is no problem in doing that yourself. But when it comes to big house-hold appliances, the picture looks different. Sellers will most likely be neither willing nor in a position to ship them to the consumer's place of residence in another country. In any event, asking for repair or maintenance service will prove quite difficult once the consumer is back at home.

And last, there are *legal obstacles*. It is argued that consumers have no confidence when buying abroad.[10] But is this also due to the consumer's fear of alien law being applied to his sales transaction? To start with, does the consumer actually know his own law at all?[11] Without engaging on a debate about this fundamental issue, it can be argued that the uncertainty of foreign law, i.e. the fact that these rules may be different and not known, is definitely not the first thing that comes to mind when consumers shop abroad. A little case should illustrate this point.

A, an eminent scholar from country X, walks down the famous *Via Condotti* in Rom with his wife. Suddenly, she becomes aware of a beautiful robe that is remarkable not only for its uniqueness, but also given the price. They enter the shop, and his wife, to her great joy, finds out that the robe suits her well. How likely is it that considerations of a legal nature will play a dominant role in A's mind when he considers buying the robe for his wife, never mind the fact that he is a scholar after all? [12]

In concluding this discussion, the active consumer has so far not been able to live up to his name. The scope for cross-border shopping remains rather limited, not at least because the consumer is a 'creature of habit', who likes to shop close to home in a language he understands. It seems as even the Commission has admitted to this point by now:

---

10 The Directive on unfair contract terms being a perfect example: according to recital 5, 'generally speaking, consumers do not know the rules of law which, in Member States other than their own, govern contracts for the sale of goods or services; whereas this lack of awareness may deter them from direct transactions for the purchase of goods and services in another Member State'. Cf. Consumer Policy for 2002-2006, p. 9 with reference to a GALLUP survey in January 2002.

11 It was argued that consumers often do not know the difference between the legal guarantee and the commercial guarantee (Green Paper 1993 at p. 13). But even if consumers actually do not know their own law, they might still *believe* that it is better than the law of other Member States (this point has been made by T. Wilhelmsson in his contribution to a conference held in Utrecht on February 21, 2003 (with reference to the study in Eurobarometer 117, 2002).

12 This example has been given by Roy Goode in his Inaugural Lecture in Utrecht on February 11, 2003 (published in the *Ius Commune* Lectures on European Private Law 8: Roy Goode, Contract and Commercial Law: the Logic and Limits of Harmonisation, June 2003). See also G. Howells, Editorial: Consumer Guarantees, Consumer Law Journal 1995, p. 78: 'the eventual directive can hopefully concentrate on the needs of all European consumers whether they purchase at home or are among the few active consumers who travel the union in search of bargains'.

'Cross-border shopping will not replace routine shopping, except for those who live very near borders. But even just making cross-border shopping a realistic possibility can itself have a major knock-on impact on competition in local markets. Even if a small percentage of consumers shop abroad, it will have an effect on the prices in each Member State's overall market.'[13]

It is to be hoped, as suggested by the Commission, that the advent of new communication technologies will improve this situation, and eventually make the tale of the active consumers come true.[14] But even here, a caveat is in place. The undoubted IT-revolution does not necessarily mean that consumers flock to shopping online, as there are, once again, also other difficulties involved. To name just one, a sale is often combined with a credit agreement to enable the buyer to finance the purchase of the goods. In this case, a cross border transaction becomes more complex due to different national rules of contractual liability and retention of title clauses.

2.3 Two Instruments of Unified Sales Law – A Brief Overview

2.3.1 The Consumer Sales Directive[15]

Article 1 paragraph 1 CSD lays down the purpose of the Sales Directive as

the approximation of the laws, regulations and administrative provisions of the Member States [...] *in order to ensure a uniform minimum level of consumer protection* in the context of the internal market.[16]

---

13 Consumer Policy for 2002-2006, p. 9. Cf. press-release 'Unlocking the potential of cross-border shopping in the EU' (IP/02/1683): 'Cross-border shopping still appears to be stuck at a stubbornly low level' [quote Commissioner David Bryne].

14 Recital 4 of the CSD. Besides, the fear is voiced that, in the absence of harmonised rules, 'the development of the sale of goods through the medium of new distance communication technologies risks being impeded'. Cf. Consumer Policy for 2002-2006, p. 8 with reference to actual figures: Internet use and its household penetration rates are on increasing and have reached 38% by the end of 2001.

15 For the discussion about the initial proposal in the Green Book, see Journal of Consumer Policy 1995, nos. 3 and 4; As regards the final phase of the legislative process, i.e. the implementation, see European Review of Private Law (ERPL) 2001, nos. 3 and 4. And finally, the most comprehensive discussion of this subject-matter to date in S. Grundmann/C.M. Bianca (Hrsg.), EU-Kaufrechts-Richtlinie Kommentar, Verlag Dr. Otto Schmidt, Köln, 2002 (this commentary is actually published in four languages: see Hart and Intersentia for the English edition; Bruylant and L.J.D.G. for the French edition; and Giuffrè for the Italian edition).

16 *Emphasis* added. It becomes clear from the title itself that only consumers are dealt with. The motivation for this is laid down in the recitals of the Directive. First of all, it is based on Article 95 ECT aiming at an achievement of a high level of consumer protection. Then after having stressed the ubiquitous 'magical' formula of the internal market (recital 2), and after having pointed out the potential distortion of competition due to the differences in the law of consumer sales (recital 3), the importance of the consumer in the completion of the internal market is underlined (recital 4). Besides, recital 5 speaks of 'the creation of a common set of minimum rules of consumer law [...] that will strengthen consumer confidence [...]'.

This ambitious endeavour – i.e. establishing, at least parts of, a uniform consumer sales law – has actually come a long way, as a quick look at the legislative history of the Sales Directive reveals. It all started with a survey made in 1993, trying to find out why consumers in the European Union were reluctant to purchase in another Member State.[17] It did not come as a big surprise that most of the interviewed persons mentioned possible difficulties in exercising their rights and the uncertainty of possible lawsuits. The European Commission did not negate this call for action and put forward a proposal for a Directive in 1996.[18] It instigated a heated debate that eventually resulted in a common position of the European Council in 1998.[19] Finally, after having consulted the Conciliation Committee, the European Parliament and the Council reached an agreement in March 1999, which was subsequently enacted as Directive 1999/44.

The Member States were rather late in implementing the Sales Directive: only three countries – Austria, Finland, and Germany – managed to abide by the deadline of January 1, 2002. A year later, eight Member States have still not complied with their obligations to transpose this piece of European legislation.[20] On the one hand, one could argue that this is just 'business as usual', since Member States are notoriously late, and sloppy one might add, in transposing EU Directives.[21] Less sarcastically, one could, on the other hand, argue that this is a clear sign that the process of European harmonisation as such has reached its limits: while Member States grapple with the transposition of one instrument into the peculiarities of their national laws, another 'threat' to the unity thereof is already at their door-step.[22]

2.3.2 The UN Convention on the International Sale of Goods

The CISG has been drafted at an international conference in Vienna in 1980, and entered into force on January 1, 1988. As already mentioned above, the CISG constitutes a truly universal body of sales law, as it has been ratified by a large number of countries worldwide. In fact, the efforts to harmonise the international law of sales

---

17 In fact, the efforts to tackle the area of consumer goods guarantees and after-sales services that eventually resulted in the Green Paper bearing the same name, COM (93) 509 final, go even further back in time, see M. Tenreiro, Guarantees and after-sales service: brief analysis of the Green Paper presented by the Commission, Consumer Law Journal 1995, p. 79.

18 Proposal for a European Parliament and Council Directive on the sale of consumer goods and associated guarantees, *OJ* No C 307, 16.10.1996, p. 8. After the Opinion of the Economic and Social Committee, *OJ* No C 66, 3.3.97, p. 5, and the Amendments by the European Parliament, *OJ* C 104, 6.4.1998, p. 30, the Commission published an Amended Proposal, *OJ* C 148, 14.5.1998, p. 12.

19 Common Position adopted by the Council on 24 September 1998, *OJ* C 333, 30.10.1998, p. 46; cf. Decision by the European Parliament on the Common Position, *OJ* C 98, 9.4.1999, p. 226.

20 Which thus promoted the Commission to start infringement proceedings against Belgium, France, Ireland, Luxembourg, the Netherlands, Portugal, Spain, and the UK (see press-release IP/03/3 6 January 2003).

21 It took the French legislator, for instance, an impressive 10 years to implement the Directive on product liability, see Commission *v* France, C-52/00, 25 April 2002.

22 For a practical example of the different modes of implementing Directives, and the often far-reaching consequences thereof, see E. Hondius/C. Jeloschek, Towards a European Sales Law – Legal Challenges posed by the Directive on the Sale of Consumer Goods and Associated Guarantees, ERPL 2001, pp. 157-161.

date back to the last century, leading from the early comparative studies carried out by *Ernst Rabel* to the Hague sales law, the ULIS, and eventually arriving at the CISG.[23]

Without foreclosing an analysis of the scope of application (see 2.4.1 below), it should be noted that the CISG is essentially an instrument of international commercial sales law. This character has to be taken into account when applying the CISG, as is expressly provided for in Articles 7 and 9 CISG (international character and trade usages, respectively).

The CISG consists of four parts, which in turn are divided into chapters and sections.[24] In contrast to the Sales Directive, some issues of general contract law are also dealt with, such as the formation of sales contracts.

2.4   Limits of Existing Unified Sales Law

2.4.1   Scope

It follows from the name of the Sales Directive that two main subject matters are tackled, certain aspects of the sale of consumer goods and associated guarantees.[25] When looking at the first thrust of the Sales Directive, i.e. the sale of consumer goods, the question that comes to mind is which aspects of sales law it covers. The ambit of the Sales Directive can be characterised by several elements as it regulates sales of consumer goods concluded between consumers and professional sellers.

Article 1 paragraph 4 extends the *scope of sales* to contracts for the supply of goods to be manufactured or produced.[26]

Consumer goods are any tangible movables with four exceptions in Article 1 paragraph 2 sub (b): goods sold by way of execution or otherwise by authority of law; water and gas, unless they are sold in a limited volume or set quantity; electricity; and finally – as an option for the Member States (Article 1 paragraph 3) – second-hand goods sold at public auction with consumers having the opportunity of attending in person.

---

23 For a detailed account of the history of the harmonisation of international sales law, see for instance the introduction in p. Schlechtriem (ed.), Kommentar zum Einheitlichen UN-Kaufrecht, 3rd edition, Verlag C.H. Beck, München, 2000.

24 Part I: sphere of application and general provisions, Part II: formation of the contract, Part III: sale of goods, Part IV: final provisions.

25 The Sales Directive addresses commercial guarantees in Article 6 by basically setting out transparency requirements in paragraphs 2 to 4. The 'main' clause in paragraph 1 boils down to stating the obvious: 'a guarantee shall be legally binding […]'; one can assume that most, if not all, Member States already acknowledge such a legal consequence. However, the Sales Directive might force the national legislators to codify rules on commercial guarantees, which are actually known but hardly ever regulated as such.

26 It remains controversial whether the Sales Directive does not even cover regular contracts for work. The administrator in charge of the Sales Directive points to the drafting of the Directive along the lines of the CISG (D. Staudenmayer, NJW 1999, p. 2394). Therefore Art. 1 (4) CSD should not go beyond the ambit of its 'sibling' in Art. 3 CISG, which applies only to *Werklieferungsverträge* in the meaning of German law. However, it cannot be overlooked that the Sales Directive applies also to *certain* contracts for work, since installation falls also under the ambit of conformity, and thus, under the Sales Directive's rules on buyer's rights in the case of non-conformity.

Let alone this restriction to certain goods, one has to keep in mind that the Sales Directive purports to regulate only *certain aspects* of consumer sales. Basically, it establishes the principle of conformity with the contract and a minimum socket of rights in the case of non-conformity.[27] The seller's right of redress is also dealt with, but it arguably lacks teeth.[28]

The *consumer* is defined by means of an objective and subject element as 'any natural person who, in the contracts covered by this Directive, is acting for purposes which are not related to his trade, business or profession', Article 1 paragraph 2 sub (a). His counterpart, the *seller*, is 'any natural or legal person who, under a contract, sells consumer goods in the course of his trade, business or profession', Article 1 paragraph 2 sub (c).

The CISG defines its sphere of application in Article 1 CISG as follows:

(1) This Convention applies to contracts of sale of goods between parties whose places of business are in different States:
(a) when the States are Contracting States; or
(b) when the rules of private international law lead to the application of the law of a Contracting State.
(2) – (3) [...]

This definition is qualified further by Articles 2 to 6 CISG: Article 2 excludes certain types of sale from the ambit, such as sale by auction, sale on execution, sale of certain financial instruments, sale of ships, vessels, hovercraft or aircraft, and sale of electricity in sub (b) to (f). Article 3 includes contracts for the supply of goods to be manufactured or produced, the *Werklieferungsverträge*, subject to certain conditions. Article 4 clarifies that the '[...] Convention governs only the formation of the contract of sale and the rights and obligations [...] arising from such a contract [...]'; sub a and b expressly exclude matters of validity and property. Article 5 excludes liability for death and personal injury.

Consumer transactions do not, in principle, fall under its ambit. This is made clear by Article 2 sub (a), which excludes 'goods bought for personal, family or household use', *unless* the seller 'neither knew nor ought to have known that the goods were bought for any such use'.

---

27 The Sales Directive identifies non-conformity of the goods with the contract as the main source of dispute (recital 6).

28 Article 4 merely states that the national laws shall provide for a right of redress on the part of the final seller *vis-à-vis* the previous seller(s). There is, however, no indication as to how that shall be achieved. Recital 9 *in fine* makes sure that the freedom of contract within the marketing chain shall not be infringed. Accordingly, it is up to the respective national legislator to regulate this matter. This provision has been fiercely criticised arguing that the now stricter regime of the buyer's right in conjunction with the existing rules on redress might result in shifting the economic burden of non-conformity to the final seller instead of the manufacturer.

2.4.2 Lacunae and Further Problems of a Substantive Nature

It therefore follows that both instruments are rather restricted in their application. But let alone such considerations of scope, there are plenty of lacunae and other problems relating to the substance of the rules. Due to contraints of space, we can but hint at a few of these issues without purporting to sketch a complete picture. Furthermore, we will confine the brief discussion to the shortcomings of the Sales Directive, as it is the most recent, and arguably most modern instrument of sales law, which has also been inspired by the CISG.

When looking at the Sales Directive, one cannot but remark two things. On the one hand, a lot of proposals have been dropped in the course of the legislative history, such as the manufacturer's liability, after-sales services, and network liability.[29] These rules have been considered too radical, at least for the time being. It is interesting to note, however, that they have not been filed in the dustbin of history, as the Sales Directive itself contains reminders of the great ideas to come.[30]

On the other hand, it seems as if even the water-down comprise of the Sales Directive still managed to stir a lot of trouble.[31] To mention but a few: the seller's right to redress enshrined in Article 4 has turned out to be controversial, as some Member States have seen it necessary to implement it, whereas others have dismissed it completely.[32] Besides, the Sales Directive has introduced some black letter rules on guarantees, which had previously been somewhat 'under-regulated' on the national level.

In addition to these shortcomings, the Sales Directive contains some important gaps, as certain important issues are not addressed at all. To name but a few of these lacunae: risk is not covered (see recital 14 CSD); the right to damages is not addressed in Article 3 CSD; and as in the CISG, issues of property are not addressed at all.

2.4.3 Mandatory Nature

Pursuant to Article 8 paragraph 2 CSD, 'Member States may adopt or maintain in force more stringent provisions [...] to ensure a higher level of consumer protection'. At first sight, this so-called minimum protection clause seems to make sense, as the Sales Directive aims only at creating a certain minimum level of consumer protection in sales law across Europe. Not only does this leave the Member States with greater freedom, but clauses of this nature have become a common feature of European consumer legislation.

---

29 All these topics featured in the Green Paper 1993, see pp. 86-88, 97, and 100, respectively.

30 Article 12 CSD states that the Commission will prepare a report on the Directive by mid-2006, which 'shall examine, *inter alia*, the case for introducing the producer's direct liability [...]' (cf. recital 23). What is more, many commentators have deplored that the more ambitious ideas have not been implemented. See for instance R.Bradgate/C. Twigg-Flesner, Expanding the Boundaries of Liability for Quality Defects, Journal of Consumer Policy 2002, pp. 345-377.

31 Cf. E. Hondius/C. Jeloschek, Towards a European Sales Law – Legal Challenges posed by the Directive on the Sale of Consumer Goods and Associated Guarantees, ERPL 2001, pp. 157-161.

32 For example. Germany and Austria have included specific provisions in their sales law (§ 478 BGB and § 933b ABGB). The Netherlands have even tightened their old rule on redress further (Art. 7:25 BW); whereas no such rule can be found in English law after the implementation of the Sales Directive.

The devil, however, lies in the detail. It is not always clear what amounts to 'more stringent provisions'. In fact, one often cannot but wonder 'whether the trains of thought depart from the same platform'.[33] What is more, such divergent views may eventually result in diverging implementations of the same legal text, thus running counter to the intended harmonisation in a given field of law.

In contrast to the mandatory nature of the Sales Directive, the CISG has a different starting point, which reflects its commercial character. Pursuant to Article 6 CISG, parties can either 'exclude the application of this Convention or [...] derogate from or vary the effect of any of its provisions'.[34]

2.4.4 Evaluation of Findings

In sum, there are now two separate bodies of sales law in existence in today's Europe: the CISG deals with international commercial sales, whereas the Sales Directive targets consumer sales within the European internal market. These two instruments are clearly situated on opposite poles of a spectrum that ranges from purely private transactions on a national level to commercial transactions transcending the borders. It therefore seems as if these two instruments could not possibly clash with each other.[35]

But despite the difference in nature, that is the emphasis on consumers v. commercial transactions, both legal instruments are quite alike. That does not come as much of a surprise, bearing in mind that the CISG has served as a model for the drafting of the Sales Directive on a European level. But since this contribution is to explore the need for, and a possible basis of, a comprise European regime of sales law, it is necessary to briefly discuss the arguably different starting points of both instruments. In other words, is either of them fit to meet the challenges of the European markets in the 21st century?[36] In our point of view, there are some precautions to be taken.

First of all, the CISG may not reflect today's values and considerations anymore. Not only has it been in force for 20 years, but the drafting process started way back in the last century.[37] In addition to that long time span, a compromise had to be reached on a worldwide basis. In other words, a balance had to be struck between rich and poor states, between different politic systems, economic models, social systems, and legal concepts.[38] One could now argue that the Sales Directive has re-ignited the dis-

---

33 E. Hondius/C. Jeloschek, Towards a European Sales Law – Legal Challenges posed by the Directive on the Sale of Consumer Goods and Associated Guarantees, ERPL 2001, p. 159 with the example of the hierarchy of remedies established by the Sales Directive.

34 Thus, the CISG is a so-called opt-out instrument.

35 But see A. Janssen, Kollision des einheitlichen UN-Kaufrechts mit dem Verbraucherschutzrecht am Beispiel der Richtlinie über den Verbrauchsgüterkauf und -garantien, VuR 1999, pp. 324-327.

36 Such challenges include the opening of the EU to the East, and the strategic goal for the EU for this decade 'to become the most competitive and dynamic knowledge-based economy in the world capable of sustainable economic growth with more and better jobs and greater social cohesion' (as expressed at the special European Council held in Lisbon March 23-24, 2000).

37 Cf. 2.3.2 above.

38 Some provisions bear witness to these differences, such as Art. 44 CISG. For a detailed analysis, see J.C. Reitz, A History Of Cutoff Rules as a Form of *Caveat Emptor*: Part I – The 1980 U.N. Convention on the International Sale of Goods, The American Journal of Comparative Law (1988), pp. 437-472.

cussion, eventually adopting new rules in an ever-changing time, tailored to the European needs. But as it has already been mentioned, the CISG was one of the main sources of inspiration, a development that can be witnessed in different national legal systems as well.[39] Thus, it remains doubtful whether the Sales Directive indeed reflects the true spirit of consumer protection.[40]

Secondly, both instruments are geared at a rather special context. The Sales Directive regulates sales of consumer goods concluded between consumers and professional sellers; whereas the CISG, in contrast, applies to the international sale of goods, which excludes consumer transactions.[41] This difference is also reflected in the mandatory nature of the provisions in either instrument. In addition, the Sales Directive and the CISG are rather restricted as regards the object of sale, as they deal exclusively with the sale of goods, which in turn are restricted again by excluding certain types of goods.[42]

Thirdly, the Sales Directive regulates only certain issues right from the outset, thus leaving some essential problems unresolved. On the contrary to that, the CISG can be seen as a rather independent body of sales law.[43] However, let alone its restricted scope of application discussed above, it has to be kept in mind that the provisions of this Convention have to be read in the light of the commercial cross-border character, in particular taking into account the needs and ends of commercial sales. Bearing in mind these caveats, it seems as if the CISG as it stands does not render itself fit for being the sole pillar of a European sales law.

3 An Example of European Sales Law: The Proposal by the SGECC

3.1 The Study Group on a European Civil Code (SGECC)

What has just been discussed is not a mere phantasm of a few committed comparative lawyers. In fact, several groups have embarked upon the task of putting flesh on the

---

39 Cf. the New Dutch Civil Code of 1992 (*Nieuwe Burgerlijk Wetboek*) or Nordic Sales law.

40 P.S. Atiyah/S.N. Adams/H. McQueen, The Sale of Goods, 10th edition, Pearson Educational Limited, Essex, 2001: 'Perversely, given that it is a consumer protection measure, both the warranty content and the remedial scheme are derived from the [CISG], which was drafted to deal with sales between business'. Nonetheless, it should not be forgotten that the Sales Directive has also introduced some revolutionary elements geared at protecting the consumer, such as a regime on commercial guarantees (Art. 6 CSD), liability for public statements (Art. 2 (2) d CSD), a reversal of burden of proof for the first six months after delivery (Art. 5 (3) CSD), the installation clause (Art. 2 (5) CSD).

41 In particular, the Sales Directive does *not* cover sales contracts between professionals, sales between consumers, and sales where the seller is not acting as a professional. The CISG does *not* cover national sales transactions, international sales between consumers, and international consumer sales.

42 The CISG limits the scope of application to typical goods of trans-national trade, which are not subject to registration duties or other procedures. This certainly does not reflect the European need of a modern, comprehensive regulation, since the trade in ships, vessels, space objects, electricity, all of which are excluded from the scope of application of the CISG, are also important in the internal market.

43 The CISG covers a wide range of issues, including a separate chapter on formation. However, certain issues are still left to national sales law, such as issues of passing of property or rules on evidence.

bones of the mere academic theories of harmonisation of European Private Law.[44] In this final part of our contributions, we would like to focus on the work of one group in particular, the so-called Study Group on a European Civil Code (hereinafter: 'the SGECC').[45]

Their efforts to present practical examples of how to harmonise different fields of the law have already crystallised in quite advanced drafts.[46] Since the sales draft constitutes only a part of the work carried out by the SGECC, we will first address the entire project as such. The aim of the SGECC is to produce a codified set of *Principles of European Patrimonial Law* complete with commentary and comparative annotations.[47] For the time being, the outcome of the research is presented in English, and will later also be translated into other languages. Within this framework, a working team on sales law started carrying out comparative research on sales contracts in 1999.[48]

3.2 A Brief Introduction to the Research Project on Sales Law

After having analysed the national reports drafted following several questionnaires, the working team presented a position paper on Principles of European Sales Law to the Co-ordinating Committee of the SGECC.

In order to deal with the different aspects of sales contracts, the relevant topics were divided into small sub-chapters of the final set of rules. At the first stage, the

---

44 The so-called *Gandolfi* Group, also known as the *Accademia dei Giusprivatisti Europei*, published their results in 2001 (Code européen des contrats/Avant-projet, Livre premier, Giuffrè, Milano). The *Acquis Group* is working on a pure research level, see www.jura.uni-freiburg.de/newsletter/NEPL. *Walter van Gerven* contributed to the teaching of European private law by means of several case books (*Ius Commune* Case Books of the University of Maastricht and Leuven, Editor Walter van Gerven; for further information see Pierre Larouche, Ius Commune casebooks for the common law of Europe, in EUI Working Papers, Law No. 99/7, p. 87 ff.). The aim of *SECOLA* is to serve as a platform for discussion, see www.secola.org. The so-called *Common Core* Project is even active outside the European Union, striving to work out the common core of different fields of European private law. This group convenes every July in Trento/Italy for their annual conference, see www.jus.unitn.it/dsg/common-core/.

45 The SGECC, chaired by Prof. Christian von Bar/Osnabrück, is a European-wide network of academics conducting comparative law research in private law of the various legal jurisdictions of the Member States, candidate countries, European Law and international instruments, such as the United Nations Convention on Contracts for the International Sale of Goods.

46 Preliminary results are available on the SGECC's website www.sgecc.net. By the end of 2003, the outcome of two working groups will be published in two volumes, one dealing with personal securities and another dealing with unjustified enrichment.

47 The American Restatements have inspired the way of presenting the research results. However, the work carried out by the Study Group can be seen as more than just a *re*-statement of European patrimonial law, as it does not only compile existing legal solutions, but also comes up with novel approaches. The research undertaken by the Study Group takes into account national contract laws including case law, academic writing, legislation, established contractual practice, existing EC acquis, and relevant international instruments.

48 For a description of the working team and their work, see Viola Heutger, Konturen des Kaufrechtskonzeptes der Study Group on a European Civil Code: Ein Werkstattbericht, ERPL, 2003, pp. 155-173. In fact, the question of the need for a European Sales Law was already raised years before: see for instance Hans W. Micklitz, Ein einheitliches Kaufrecht für Verbraucher in der EG?, Europäische Zeitschrift für Wirtschaftsrecht 1997, pp. 229-237.

working team elaborated these sub-chapters, such as general provisions, conformity, remedies, obligations of the buyer and the seller, etc.

By the end of 2000, the working team was able to present the first indicative black letter rules on sales law, which were based both on their comparative research and on the support and expertise by their advisors. This preparatory initiative has been re-fined throughout the last years; as a matter of fact, the core topics characterising a sales contract are at the final stage of drafting.[49] The ultimate outcome will have to pass the so-called Drafting Committee, which ensures consistency with other drafts prepared by the SGECC.

In addition to the national reports, the CISG served as the starting point for the drafting process because of its wide acceptance and its influence on various national sales laws and on the Sales Directive itself. However, deviations from the CISG have been considered necessary insofar as a given rule posed problems in the non-commercial or European context. Besides, the working team has deemed the Sales Directive a minimum standard of consumer protection. In other words, the choices made in the Sales Directive were accepted as compelling for consumer sales law at least.

The sales draft is designed to operate within the framework of general contract law as promulgated by the Principles of European Contract Law (hereinafter: 'the PECL').[50] Thus, certain subject matters of general, i.e. non sales-specific interest, such as validity or formation, are regulated in the PECL and will not be repeated in the sales draft.

3.3 The Aim of the Working Group on Sales Contracts

The principles of European sales law are to serve different purposes. On the one hand, they will be an academic answer to the ongoing process relating to the EU-wide harmonisation of contract law. On the other hand, they could also be a model law for further comparative activities within European contract law. The research undertaken will have to show which rules are better designed to meet the needs of international and national commerce alike. In sum, the sales draft attempts to create a truly uni-form sales law, bridging the differentiation into different settings, different parties to the contract, and different object of sales. To that end, a balance is struck between the two poles of the sales spectrum, the commercially orientated CISG and the consumer orientated Sales Directive. It follows from these considerations that the principles of sales law – despite from heavily drawing on the CISG and its ever-growing case law

---

49 The website of the SGECC provides information about the ongoing process, see http://www.sgecc.net. It should be noted that the current draft does not tackle all aspects of sales law, since some accessory issues still have to be worked out. Therefore connected problems, such as financing the purchase or the possibility of introducing a direct liability of manufacturers, require further research to be carried out in the years to come.

50 In fact, the SGECC can be considered a continuation of the work of the so-called *Lando Commission*, which embarked upon drafting common European rules on contract law. The PECL consist of three parts; Part 1 was published in 1995, combined Parts I and II in 1999, and finally Part III in 2003. As already mentioned, the SGECC bases its work on the PECL as a common, general chapter for the outcome of the research undertaken.

– did not copy the CISG slavishly. Instead, deviations are introduced where deemed necessary.

3.4 Some Flashlights on the Draft

To start with, it is remarkable that neither CISG nor the Sales Directive offers a definition of sale. The draft, however, starts with such a definition whereby an attempt is made to summarise the essence of sale: the seller undertakes to transfer property and the buyer undertakes to pay the price. It is imporpant to note that, other than in the CISG and the Sales Directive, issues of property are therefore addressed (albeit fleshed out in a separate chapter on property). Further obligations of the parties are set out in greater detail in separate sections. Rules on barter are to fall under the ambit of the sales draft.[51]

The sales draft covers all sales transactions irrespective of the status of the parties involved: commercial contracts; consumer contracts; and private contracts, i.e. transactions between private parties. Consumer sales are addressed by specific rules, which either deviate from, or complement the general rules. One important consequence of the consumer protection regime is that the parties may not derogate from the rules to the detriment of the consumer.[52] In contrast, commercial sales are not regulated as a category in their own right. The idea behind this uniform approach is to counteract the increasing fragmentation into several specialised branches of sales law.

Along the lines of both the CISG and the Sales Directive, the sales draft focuses on goods. It should be noted, however, that these rules on the sale of goods in the strict sense have been extended considerably. On the one hand, certain objects have been included in the definition of goods, such ships, aircraft and space objects, animals, liquids and gases. This explicit enumeration makes sure that these objects are well within the scope of goods, defined as 'corporeal movables', while this may remain doubtful under certain national and international sales laws. On the other hand, the sales draft also applies *with appropriate modifications* to contracts of sale involving objects that are explicitly excluded from the CISG and the Sales Directive (such as shares, electricity, information, to name but a few). By and large, this wider approach has been adopted in order to reflect the economic realities of the Internal Market; what is more, the sales rules may also be extended to further types of sales later on.

Conformity of the goods is addressed in a separate section, which amongst others lays down the principle of, and the relevant time for, conformity of the goods. Cases of partial delivery and partial non-conformity are also deemed non-conformity. Fur-

---

51 It will be decided later whether contracts such as leasing and hire purchase should also be included. This decision will depend on the progress of the SGECC as a whole, in particular on the participation of further working teams.

52 Time and again, it has been argued that harmonised rules on European Private Law should take the form of 'soft law' along the lines of the American Restatements. Consumer protection, however, calls for specific rules of a binding nature to safeguard consumers' rights. In comparison, the PECL contain only few absolutely mandatory provisions, e.g. the fairness test for standard terms in Article 4:110 PECL, and the rule on exclusion or restriction of remedies in Article 8:109 PECL.

thermore, the section on conformity contains a regime on examination and notification of the lack of conformity, including an absolute time limit of two years running from delivery. This regime is novel in that it contains a separate set of rules for consumer sales, which attempts to accommodate the solutions offered by the Sales Directive and the CISG. As a result, a consumer never loses his rights to damages and price reduction upon failure to notify non-conformity.

The remedial regime is split into two parts, remedies for non-conformity and remedies for any other non-performance on the part of the seller, notably late delivery. As a general principle, specific performance by means of repair or replacement prevails over the other remedies, i.e. termination of the contract, price reduction and damages. In consumer sales, the buyer may choose between repair and replacement, while this choice is otherwise up to the seller. Since commercial sales have not been regulated as a separate category, it was seen necessary to limit the liability of non-professional sellers in damages.

The section on guarantees goes a step further than the Sales Directive. A guarantee as defined by the sales draft is a voluntary instrument used by any person in the commercial chain of distribution. The draft provides for default rules in the case when the guarantor does not specify the content of the product guarantee. Thus, the draft has remedied one of the main shortcomings of the Sales Directive, i.e. the default content of the commercial guarantee.

The section on the seller's remedies, following the CISG, provides for a seller's right to make specifications if the buyer failed to do so.

As a general rule the risk of loss or damages to the goods passes when control over the goods is handed over to the buyer. Loss of or damage to the goods after the risk has passed to the buyer does not discharge the buyer from the obligation to pay the price, unless the loss or damage is due to an act or omission of the seller. Passing of risk is therefore not dependent on the obligation to pay the price. Risk passes even before the payment of the price and also when the buyer is not excused in not taking delivery. Accordingly, the buyer may not postpone the passing of risk by not accepting due delivery of the goods. Since transparent regulations on the passing of risk are very important in in the field of transportation law, the section on passing of risk provides special rules for carriage of goods and sales in transit.

Finally, the last section deals with preservation of the goods, which denotes a refined version of the CISG and the approach by the PECL. If a party is unwillingly left in possession of goods, it is not allowed to expose them to loss, damage or theft. Besides, it must take reasonable steps for their preservation, e.g. by taking them back into its own custody.

After having sketched the rough structure of the proposal, it may prove helpful to discuss briefly the application of a future European sales law. Basically, two options are possible. First, the Principles of European Sales law may serve as an *optional* instrument in cross-border transactions, allowing the parties to simply refer to this instrument as the applicable law. Thus, the parties have the free choice to use these principles, which do not supersede national sales laws as such. Doing so should be more advantageous than resorting to the CISG, for the draft, as exemplified above, offers a more comprehensive regulation. Besides, also consumers should have the free choice, since the rules have been aligned carefully with European standards of consumer protection. The second option is far-reaching in that a EU-wide sales law would govern all sales transactions, domestic and trans-national ones alike. Such a European Sales Law would be a real European codification without any local restriction within the internal market. In addition, it would take the place of both the CISG and the Sales Directive.

In essence, the choice is ultimately a political one, which has to be made by legislators and not by academics. Still, we would like to express our preference for the first option, the adaptation of a "soft law" instrument. This optional instrument would have the advantage of becoming a forerunner or test case for a more far-reaching regulation. Not only would it show whether businesses are interested in a set of common rules, but it would also denote a more democratic way of arriving at harmonisation in Europe.

4 Conclusions

At the beginning of this contribution, we have asked whether the existing instruments of unified sales law, the Sales Directive and the CISG, amount to the establishment of a European Sales Law. In our opinion, the answer is in the negative, since neither the CISG nor the Sales Directive seems to be fit to meet the challenges of the European markets in the 21st century. This holds true for mainly three reasons. First, the Sales Directive does not amount to a comprehensive regulation of European sales law, leaving unanswered many an important issue, such as risk and damages. Second, it is also limited to a specific scenario, i.e. the sale of consumer goods. Not only are private and commercial transactions left out of consideration, but certain goods are also exempted, notably energy. And last, the CISG, although being more comprehensive a regulation than the Sales Directive, has been drafted for the international commercial context, thus excluding non-commercial, notably consumer transactions.

We would like to argue that there is a need for a truly European sales law, the main reason being the ever-growing fragmentation of sales law. In effect, the increasing specialisation of rules over the last decades could result in no less than four different bodies of sales law characterised by the following relationships: (1) private party – private party; (2) consumer – business (consumer sales); (3) business – business (national commercial sales); (4) business – business (*international* commercial sales). Since the Sales Directive and the CISG already cover situations 2 and 4, there seems to be little room left for national rules to apply. Basically, the non-harmonised parts of sales law concerns situations 1 and 3, and the goods that do not fall within the scope of the CISG or the Sales Directive.

Against that rather chaotic, and increasingly confusing background of diverse set of rules it makes sense that new developments in the law tend to harmonise the different fields again. And what better opportunity is there than using Principles of European Sales Law as a vehicle of unification or disentanglement?

The main question is how this could be achieved. Here, it is time to turn back to the impact of the international instruments. Since both the CISG and the Sales Directive regulate very important parts of sales law, it seems to make sense to take them as a model rather than creating new rules from scratch.[53] By doing so, one can kill two birds with one stone. On the one hand, such a procedure can benefit from the experiences and results of those instruments. One can keep the rules that have proven workable and effective, and focus on the controversial issues instead. On the other hand, the new rules will not have to compete against the old ones, which will result in a quick and successful reception thereof.

Against that background, a future European Civil Code – or less enthusiastic: a harmonised set of rules – therefore cannot afford to ignore the international instruments already in existence. Bearing this caveat in mind, the SGECC has attempted to come up with a set of Principles of European Sales Law, which combines the Sales Directive and the CISG. At the end of the day, these endeavours are still an academic exercise, albeit with a view to creating a set of unified rules in European Private Law that is *prêt-a-porter*.

However, critics have often voiced their concern about the legitimacy of private individuals, and scholars in particular, to act as legislators. Let alone the fact that the ECC project does not claim to be the lawmaker, it is important to note that its role has gained considerable weight when taking into account recent developments on the Community level.

In February 2003, the Commission launched the so-called 'Action Plan on a more coherent European contract law', which is yet another important step towards harmonisation of European Private Law.[54] In fact, the research undertaken by the Working Team on sales law is closely interconnected to the objectives set out in this Action Plan. Accordingly, one of the main issues is to improve the quality of the EC *acquis communitaire* in the area of contract law. In doing so, a 'common frame of reference' should help to establish European concepts, principles, definitions and terminology.[55] This compilation may later even lead to an optional instrument on the European level.[56]

Not only has the SGECC already elaborated such an optional instrument, but the work undertaken also provides for such a 'common frame of reference' for European Sales Law, as it contains references to national legal systems and jurisdictions in addition to the actual black letter rules. As a result, the Principles of European Sales Law will fall nothing short off a common European sales law, which is based on a very detailed analysis of the European *acquis communautaire*, various European legal

---

53 The Sales Directive has to be considered an important landmark in the landscape of European Private Law. Not only has the European legislator tackled somey very important issues, but for the first time he also regulated a larger and coherent field of law. One could even argue that the Sales Directive falls nothing short of a uniform sales law for consumer goods, its minimum character and certain shortcomings notwithstanding. Seen from this point of view, the Sales Directive proves to be a remarkable climax of the making of a European Private Law, adding to the pieces of legislation already in existence.

54 http://europa.eu.int/comm/consumers/policy/developments/contract_law/. This Action Plan was the result of a process of consultation and discussion about the way in which problems resulting from divergences between national contract laws in the EU should be dealt with at the European level. This initiative dates back to July 2001 when the commission launched its Communication on European Contract law.

55 Action Plan, Nos. 59 to 68.

56 Action Plan, No. 96.

systems, general principles like those drafted by the Commission on European Private Law (PECL) and UNIDROIT, as well as international instruments such as the United Nations Convention on the international sale of goods (CISG). Last, but not least, the Principles of European Sales Law have defined common concepts and terminology in the course of the research, which may offer a perfect point of departure for any future instrument. It is to be hoped that they meet the expectations of the Commission and thus, can contribute to the ongoing process of developing further the *acquis communitaire*, and ultimately, an optional instrument. Ideally, such a set of rules should constitute a comprise between the diverging interests of consumers and commercial parties, which could modernise European sales law by bringing it into line with the economic challenges of the 21st century.

C – Contract Law – Specific Contracts

CHAPTER 31

The Case for a European Insurance Contract Code[*]

Jürgen Basedow[**]

The internal market, which the European Community was supposed to establish by the end of 1992, is defined by the implementation of some basic freedoms. Under Article 14 para. 2 (ex 7 a) of the EC Treaty[1] "the internal market shall comprise an area without internal frontiers in which the free movement of goods, persons, services and capital is ensured in accordance with the provisions of this Treaty." This target clearly includes insurance markets, and the Community made great efforts to achieve that goal. This it finally did after the adoption and transformation of numerous directives by the mid-nineties. I shall describe that process in more detail in the first part of this paper (1). From an economic perspective the existence of a Single Market is perhaps less clearly indicated by the guarantee of some basic freedoms such as the freedom of establishment or the freedom to provide services, but rather by the effective existence of transnational business. In the second part of my paper I will therefore explore the internal insurance market from this point of view. I will try to explain the finding, i.e. a deficit of market integration, by the subsisting differences between national insurance contract laws within the European Community. These differences are even increasing as more and more Member States enact new legislation on insurance contract law[2] (2). This observation raises concern and directs our inquiry to the goals and perspectives of European policy in this field (3). My resulting plea for renewed harmonisation efforts may appear untimely since former attempts in that direction have proven unsuccessful. A further part of this paper will therefore indicate reasons for my proposition that the prospects for an approximation of insurance contract law in the European Union are much brighter today than they were 20

---

[*] This paper was first published in the Journal of Business Law 2001, 569.
[**] Director of the Max-Planck Institute for foreign private and private international law, Hamburg, and Professor of Law, University of Hamburg.
[1] Treaty Establishing the European Economic Community, Done at Rome on March 25 1957, 298 U.N.T.S. 11, lastly amended by the Treaty of Amsterdam of October 2, 1997, *OJ* EC 1997 C 340/ 1. The present Art. 14 was inserted by the Single European Act of February 17 and 28, 1986, *OJ* EC 1987 L 169/1.
[2] Within the European Economic Area comprehensive acts were recently adopted, *inter alia* in Member States such as Belgium (Loi sur le contract d'assurance terrestre of 25.6.1992, Moniteur belge of 20.8.1992), Finland (Lag om försäkringsavtal Nr. 543 of 28.6.1994, Finlands Författningssamling 1994, 1450), Greece (Law no. 2496 of 16.5.1997; an English translation prepared by *Manessiotou/ Murray* from the law firm of *Rokas & Partners* is on file with the author), Luxembourg (Loi du 27.7.1997 sur le contrat d'assurance, Memorial 1997 A No. 65) and Norway (Lov om forsikrings-savtaler Nr. 69 of 16.6.1989, Norsk Lovtidend 1989 I, 494). Further drafts are under preparation in various countries, see e.g. the German draft Act reforming the insurance contract law, BT-Druck-sache 13/8163 of 2.7.1997; *Reimer Schmidt*, Gedanken zur Arbeit an einem neuen Versiche-rungsvertragsgesetz, ZVersWiss 1998, 55. For a collection and translation of the European Laws see Basedow, below note 13, vol. III (2003).

years ago (4). An outline of a European Insurance Contract Act (5) will be followed by a final discussion of the pros and cons of the codification project with particular reference to a common law perspective (6).

1 The Single Insurance Market – A Survey

The way towards an internal market for the insurance industry has been marked by three generations of Community directives. First, in the seventies, we witnessed the implementation of the freedom of establishment which became effective when the restrictions on the creation of agencies and branches were abolished.[3]

However, all efforts made to put into effect the freedom to provide services, i.e. the provision of insurance cover by insurers established in one Member State for clients domiciled in others, were doomed to failure. This was due to the strong and common interests of all participants: insurance companies feared the competition of foreign competitors; under the country-of-origin rule which is inherent in the Community freedoms these foreign competitors might have been able to offer their services at much lower rates. Customers worried about the transparency of the market and feared that the domestic standard of protection would decline if foreign companies were allowed to enter the market without any form of control performed by an insurance authority of the host state. Last but not least, the governments of the Member States wanted to preserve the national insurance industries as prime borrowers who had always been reliable partners when new state loans were issued but who might be less willing to lend their support once under attack from foreign competition. It was not before 1986 that the European Court of Justice, in a courageous decision, declared the direct applicability of the freedom to provide services in the field of insurance.[4] Finally, the coalition advocating the preservation of the status quo was weakened. Starting with the second generation of directives in 1988/1990, the conditions for the exercise of the freedom to provide services were created.[5]

The third generation of directives went further, by promoting the harmonisation of certain areas of market control regulation, to the effect that today the country-of-ori-

---

3   First Council Directive of 24 July 1973 on the coordination of laws, regulations and administrative provisions relating to the taking-up and pursuit of business of direct insurance other than life assurance (73/239/EEC), Official Journal of the European Communities (*OJ* EC) 1973. L 228/3; First Council Directive of 5 March 1979 on the coordination of laws, regulations and administrative provisions relating to the taking-up and pursuit of the business of direct life assurance (79/267/EEC), *OJ* EC 1979 L 63/1; see below, note 6.

4   European Court of Justice (*ECJ*), 205/84 (*Commission* v. *Federal Republic of Germany*), ECR 1986, 3755, considerations 25, 52.

5   Second Council Directive of 22 June 1988 on the coordination of laws, regulations and administrative provisions relating to direct insurance other than life assurance and laying down provisions to facilitate the effective exercise of freedom to provide services and amending Directive 73/239/EEC (88/357/EEC), *OJ* EC 1988 L 172/1; Second Council Directive of 8 November 1990 on the coordination of laws, regulations and administrative provisions relating to direct life assurance, laying down provisions to facilitate the effective exercise of freedom to provide services and amending Directive 79/267/EEC (90/619/EEC), *OJ* EC 1990 L 330/50; see below, note 6.

gin principle is implemented. This means that the state of origin of an insurance company will exclusively be responsible for its admission, supervision and control. By tying the Member States to a common European standard of market supervision, acceptance by the host Member States is ensured.[6]

What was the role of insurance contract law in this development? The Commission's formula was twofold. For insurance involving transportation and large risks, the Commission focused on a conflict of laws solution dispensing with the harmonisation of substantive law. In its 1979 draft directive, the Commission suggested to guarantee the freedom of choice of law, in the first place, and to apply the law of the company's state of origin where no choice was agreed to by the parties.[7] As to other risks, especially in relation to consumer insurance, a different solution was advocated. According to the Commission, choice of law was excluded here, and the applicable law was the law of the company's state of origin. At the same time, the harmonisation of insurance contract law would guarantee the protection of basic rights of the insured once he agreed upon a policy governed by a foreign law.[8] After a long debate, the Commission eventually concluded, however, that for reasons of consumer protection, the future conflict of laws rule could not refer to the law of the company's state of origin. The applicable contract law should rather be the law of the state in which the risk is situated[9] which in most cases is the law of the consumer's habitual residence. However, the harmonisation of the substantive law of insurance contracts was still considered needed to encourage acceptance of a gradual extension of the free choice of law which the Commission continued to regard as a necessary prerequisite for the effective exercise of the freedom to provide services.[10]

This proposition too has come under attack.[11] According to the critics, the freedom of choice of law in the field of consumer insurance is not a prerequisite, but rather an obstacle to the effective implementation of the freedom to provide services since consumers would not buy policies subject to foreign law by a choice of law clause. 'The target of allowing the free choice of the applicable law could, therefore, hardly be regarded as a sufficient justification for the harmonisation of the substantive law of insurance contracts.[12] The failure of the substantive harmonisation approach had other reasons as well. It turned out to be extremely difficult due to its entanglement with

---

6   Council Directive (92/49/EEC) of 18 June 1992 on the coordination of laws, regulations and administrative provisions relating to direct insurance other than life assurance and amending Directive 73/239/EEC (88/357/EEC), *OJ* EC 1992 L 228/1 (third directive on non-life insurance); Council Directive (92/96/EEC) of 10 November on the coordination of laws, regulations and administrative provisions relating to direct life assurance and amending Directive 79/267/EEC (90/619/EEC), *OJ* EC 1992 L 360/1 (third directive on life assurance). The three directives on live assurance mentioned in notes 3 and 5 and in this note have been consolidated in Directive 2002/83/EC of 5 November 2002 *OJ* EC 2002 L 345/1.

7   Cf. Proposal for a council directive on the coordination of laws, regulations and administrative provisions relating to insurance contracts (*OJ* EC 1979 C 190/2, consideration 2); the same point of view in: "Errichtung des Gemeinsamen Marktes für Schadensversicherungen" (so called *Schwartz* document), ZVersWiss 1972, 101, 109 *et seq.* and 111 *et seq.*

8   Cf. *Schwartz* document (note 7) ZVersWiss 1972, 112.

9   Cf. Proposal 1979 (note 7) consideration 3.

10   Cf. Proposal 1979 (note 7) consideration 4.

11   Cf. *Steindorff,* Rechtsangleichung in der EG und Versicherungsvertrag, ZHR 114 (1980) 447-483.

12   *Steindorff* (note 11) ZHR 144 (1980) 455.

the general law of obligations. These difficulties were particularly emphasised by those who lobbied for a continuous policy of protection of national markets; since the Commission was not sufficiently prepared by comparative research it could not give a serious reply to these arguments.[13] Moreover, the harmonisation of insurance contract law lost importance in the course of time, in particular after the ruling of the European Court of Justice in 1986[14] which exerted considerable pressure to implement the single insurance market within a few years before the end of 1992. Other areas of harmonisation, such as the admission and supervision of companies, the control of solvability, investment policy, and technical reserves acquired primary importance in this period of time constraints.

Eventually, a solution was adopted which is entirely based on the conflict of laws. That conflicts regime is limited to risks located in the European Economic Area while risks in other countries are subject to the general rules of private international law as laid down in the Rome Convention of 1980.[15] Moreover, the regime of the directives only deals with intra-community relations but has been extended, by some Member States, to insurance contracts concluded with insurance companies outside the European Union. While it allows for a choice of the applicable law with regard to transportation and large risks, all other risks, and in particular those in the field of consumer insurance, are governed by the law of the policyholder; the choice of another law will usually be without effect.[16] This solution can hardly be characterised as a harmonisation of private international law. This is because the Court of Justice had permitted the Member States in 1986, for reasons pertaining to the public good, to avoid the country-of-origin rule which is inherent in the free movement of services, and to provide for the application, to the insurance contract, of the law of the host state.[17] The latter conflicts rule was clearly meant, by the Court of Justice, to be an exception to the country-of-origin principle and to permit a kind of national reservation commanded by the public interest of the host state. The second generation of insurance directives has, however, turned this exception into the general rule, purporting that it would serve the implementation of the free movement of services. It should however be clear that this has nothing in common with the initial concept of the Commission since the target of an approximation of the substantive law of insurance contracts was no longer pursued. The Commission withdrew the draft directive relating to this matter in 1993.[18]

---

13 The study by *Berr*, Le contrat d'assurance dans la C.E.E. (1974) did not cover the required parts of the topic and was very soon outdated, cf. now Basedow/Fock, Europäisches Versicherungsvertragsrecht, vols. I-III (2002-2003).

14 Cf. note 4.

15 Rome Convention (of the EC Member States) of 19 June 1980 on the law applicable to contractual obligations, *OJ* EC 1980 L 266/1.

16 Cf. Art. 7 of the directive (88/357/EEC) and Art. 32 of the directive (2002/83/EC) (note 6); see also the articles in *Reichert-Facilides/Jessurun d'Oliveira* (ed.), International Insurance Contract Law in the EC. Proceedings of a comparative conference held at the European University Institute, Florence, May 23 to 24, 1991 (1993) as well as *Reichert-Facilides* (ed.), Aspekte des internationalen Versicherungsvertragsrechts im Europäischen Wirtschaftsraum (1994); cf. *Basedow/Drasch*, Das neue Internationale Versicherungsvertragsrecht: NJW 1991, 785 ff.

17 *ECJ* (note 4) para. 40 *et seq.*

18 Cf. *OJ* EC 1993 C 228/4, 14.

2 The Single Insurance Market – An Appreciation

Whoever tries to assess the practical importance of the European Insurance Market at a distance of some years from its establishment will be disillusioned. According to EUROSTAT, the European Union's agency responsible for statistics, most of the European insurance companies prefer to organise their activities in other Member States by means of subsidiaries or branches, instead of directly acquiring transborder business from their headquarters. Such cross-border transactions contribute only 0.13 per cent of the total turnover of German non-life insurance companies. It is only for smaller Member States, such as Luxembourg, Belgium and Ireland, that the percentage of such transactions plays an important role.[19]

The statistical data confirm the assessment of the internal market for insurance made by the European Commission and by the Economic and Social Committee of the European Union. At the end of 1997 the Commission issued a draft communication which addressed the doubts relating to the interpretation of some basic concepts such as the free movement of services and the public interest. These doubts are said to be liable for barring insurance companies from making effective use of the basic freedoms granted by the treaty although the third generation of insurance directives purported to foster the use of such freedoms.[20] In a carefully prepared opinion of early 1998, the Economic and Social Committee revealed a series of obstacles and problems which hamper the realisation of the internal market in this area.[21] The opinion points out that all attempts have failed which were meant to guarantee the consumers the right of equal access to insurance coverage in every Member State outside their countries of domicile or origin.[22] In practice, this means that many consumers who addressed foreign insurance companies asking for coverage met with a refusal.

This assessment can by no means be regarded as surprising. With regard to cross-border contracts, an insurer usually has to face two categories of special risks. First, the overall damages in a given sector may differ from domestic experience due to particular economic, social, and cultural conditions of the foreign environment. To obtain information on these differences requires time and depends on the volume of business contracted abroad. Second, the insurer has to deal with the foreign contract law of the policyholder's country which is applicable under the relevant conflict of laws rules and which determines the interpretation and the effects of the policy. In the case of insurance which rightfully has been characterised as a "legal product",[23] the contract and the law by which it is governed are more than the legal framework of a transaction, more than the mere "selling arrangements" as described by the European Court of Justice in the *Keck* decision.[24] Under the test advocated in that case the con-

---

19 Cf. "Grenzüberschreitendes Versicherungsgeschäft noch bescheiden" FAZ Nr. 187 of 14.8.1998, S. 26.

20 Draft Commission Interpretative Communication: Freedom to provide services and the general good in the insurance sector, *OJ* EC 1997 C 365/7.

21 Opinion of the Economic and Social Committee on "Consumers in the insurance market", *OJ* EC 1998 C 95/72, 77 sub 2.1.9.

22 Note 20, p. 73 sub 1.7.

23 Cf. *Dreher,* Die Versicherung als Rechtsprodukt (1991).

24 *ECJ* 24.11.1993, C-267/91 and 268/91 (*Keck* and *Mithouard*), E.C.R. 1993 I, 6097, 6131, considerations 15 and 16.

tract law is more related to the product itself since it defines the extent of coverage which is the product offered by the insurer. Having to cope with 15 different insurance contract laws within the European Union might be as important for an insurance company as the accommodation of 15 different national foodstuff Acts for a producer of chocolate bars, tinned chicken soup or fruit yoghurt.

The producer of foodstuff must either adjust his products to the changing requirements of the different foreign markets and their respective legal frameworks or must dispense with export of his products to these countries. In the same way, insurance companies operating from their home bases must either invest in the costly adaptation of their policies to the foreign insurance contract laws, or must abandon the idea of expanding their activities to the foreign markets if they are unwilling to incur such costs. It appears that the costs of adaptation would not be much higher if the insurance company decides to set up a branch or subsidiary in the foreign market, i.e. if it makes use of its freedom of establishment. On the other hand the profit to be expected from a permanent establishment in the foreign market would be higher than the profit which can be made from a limited number of cross-border transactions. For practical and commercial reasons the insurance companies will therefore either continue their activities in national confinement, or they will establish a branch or subsidiary in a foreign market which conducts business within that state on an equally national basis. Due to the applicability of different national insurance contract laws, it would appear highly unlikely that an insurer would assemble policies from different countries into one pool of risks subject to a uniform coverage. The creation of such multi-state risk pools would, however, be the true advantage offered by cross-border underwriting activities, i.e. by an effective exercise of the freedom to provide insurance services. Such multi-state risk pools could be commercially feasible although the insurer secures only very little business from each Member State. But under the present conditions no insurance company will be willing to pay for costly legal advice on the insurance contract laws of 14 foreign member states in order to obtain a few new customers from each of them. At present, the insurance companies therefore have only the choice between continuing purely national business activities and the establishment of a branch or subsidiary abroad. Although cross-border transactions are particularly favoured by the intangible character of financial services they therefore remain exceptional in that field.

After all, the internal market for consumer insurance exists on paper only since the conflict of laws approach taken by the second generation of directives has failed.[25] While this is also true for the insurance of smaller commercial risks, the implementation of the free choice of law in the field of high volume and transportation risks allows the insurance companies to assemble those multi-state risk pools governed by a single law, usually that of the insurer, which are therefore subject to a uniform coverage.

---

25 *Reichert-Facilides,* Europäisches Versicherungsvertragsrecht, in: Festschrift für Drobnig (1998) pp. 119, 131.

3   Goals and Perspectives

In the light of the preceding analysis, it is difficult to understand why the European Commission takes the view that the conflict of laws solution adopted by the second generation of directives is an efficient approach. Efficiency according to this assessment apparently is not measured by reference to the target of the Single Market. In this respect it should be clear that the mandate of Art. 14 (ex 7a) of the EC Treaty to accomplish an internal market is still unfulfilled in the area of small commercial insurance and consumer insurance, and therefore should still be on the agenda of the Union. Future action should focus on the following targets. First, insurance companies must have an effective opportunity to form risk pools consisting of participants from different Member States. The pooling of a great number of risks which is the basis of all insurance activities must not be hampered by national borders. The policies of an all European, multi-state risk pool must essentially be determined by the same product related rules, i.e. the same contract law.

Second, the consumer should have the opportunity to choose between competing offers from different Member States which should be comparable one to the other. In order to allow for the comparison an outlay of costs for information and consultation may be necessary which should not be disproportionate to the significance of the policies. Thus, the consultation of an experienced insurance agent could be justified in the case of an industrial fire insurance while it might be regarded as an unreasonable expenditure if it is required to make private liability or household equipment policies comparable.

Third, the special interest in promoting continuity for all the parties involved has to be taken into account, in particular if a "euromobile" policyholder has his domicile in different Member States throughout his life and intends to renew or supplement his policy with the same insurance company. Whereas the present legal situation requires a change of the applicable law for every contract made after a cross-border change of domicile, the interest of both parties to maintain contractual continuity within the European internal market should be safeguarded.[26]

What options are open to European legal policy to achieve these goals? A first approach would follow the example given by the conflict of laws rules relating to transportation and large risks which are based on the principle of free choice of law. Under this model, insurance companies would very likely insert choice of law clauses into their policies declaring their own national law applicable. Therefore, transnational risk pools would in fact be governed by one single law of contract, i.e. the law of the insurer. Although this approach would help to attain the first goal, the second target, i.e. the consumer's choice between several comparable offers would not be achieved. For the consumer would not be in a position to compare the private liability insurance policy offered by a German company and governed by German law, and a competing offer made by a British company under the laws of England. Such a comparison would probably surpass even the talents of an expert in the field of com-

---

26 Cf. *Basedow*, Das österreichische Bundesgesetz über internationales Versicherungsvertragsrecht – Eine rechtspolitische Würdigung, in: *Reichert-Facilides* (ed.), Aspekte des internationalen Versicherungsvertragsrechts im Europäischen Wirtschaftsraum (1994) pp. 89, 91 *et seq.*, 99 *et seq.*

parative law. Establishing comparability would require an unreasonable expenditure in terms of time and money. While the risk of ignorance of the applicable law is allocated to the insurance company under the present conflict of laws rules, this approach would shift that risk to the policyholder. Therefore the second target can hardly be said to be furthered. As knowledge of this fact would spread, consumers would rather refrain from buying policies from foreign insurance companies, and we could not expect an increase in the number of cross-border transactions.

Moreover, that transfer of risk to the consumer would be in contradiction to the goal of a high level of consumer protection mandated by Art. 95 (ex 100a) of the Treaty. Quite to the contrary, the level of consumer protection would be reduced, particularly because litigation arising from the insurance contract would cause a split of jurisdiction and applicable law. While the courts in the country of the insured have a concurrent jurisdiction (Art. 8) or even the exclusive international jurisdiction (Art. 11) under the Brussels or Lugano Conventions,[27] they would probably have to apply foreign law, i.e. the law of the insurer stipulated in the policy in most cases. The lawyers of the forum state would undoubtedly lack the specific knowledge required for giving advice on the applicable law. Moreover the costs of applying foreign law would be unjustifiably high for the court system, too.[28] The free choice of law therefore cannot be regarded as an appropriate solution for insurance contracts concerning smaller business risks and consumer risks.

A second option would be the harmonisation of the substantive law of insurance contracts. The Economic and Social Committee has declared its preference for this solution. According to its opinion, the deficits of the Single Market are due to the lack of Community provisions on contracts of insurance, in particular a minimum of harmonisation of the substantive law.[29] In fact, the harmonisation of essential points of insurance contract law would help to make consumers trust in the comparability of policies offered by insurance companies in different Member States. Whether they actually compare the details is of secondary importance, for there is reason to believe that the trust in the comparability of policies will enable consumers to focus on essential issues such as the definition of risk and the premium, and to make their choice on this basis. On the other side of the market, the harmonisation of the substantive law of insurance contracts will reduce the risk which insurance companies face under the present conflict of laws rules when they assemble risks from various Member States into all-European risk pools. Take the extreme case of a complete harmonisation or even unification by an EC regulation – the practical result would be the same as if the free choice of law were accepted, i.e. the application of one single contract law to all policies which are part of the all-European risk pool.

But even if this target is out of reach it can be said that every single step in this direction could help to reduce the uncertainties and distortions which currently exist

---

27 Cf. the Lugano Convention of September 16, 1988 on Jurisdiction and the Enforcement of Judgments in Civil and Commercial Matters, Bundesgesetzblatt 1994 II, 2660; see now Arts. 9 and 12 of Regulation (EC) No. 44/2001 of the Council of 22 December 2000 on jurisdiction and the recognition and enforcement of judgments in civil and commercial matters, *OJ* EC 2001 L 12/1 which has replaced the Brussels Convention on March 1st, 2002.

28 Cf. *Steindorff* (note 11) ZHR 144 (1980) 450 *et seq.*

29 Opinion (note 20) *OJ* EC 1998 C 95/72, 77 sub 2.1.9.

due to divergent interpretations and effects given to the same insurance policy in different Member States. Finally, a harmonisation would support the continuity interests of the above mentioned "euromobile" policyholders. It is true that the harmonisation of substantive law would not change the conflict of laws rules. There would therefore still be a change in the applicable law with regard to renewed or supplementary policies when such persons move from one Member State to the other. Such changes would be more easily acceptable, however, if the policyholder could be confident that the essential substantive rights and obligations arising from the contract would continue under the new law.

It would appear after all that the second approach, i.e. a renewed attempt at the harmonisation of the law of insurance contracts, is to be preferred. Neither considerations of subsidiarity nor those of proportionality (Arts. 5 paras 2 and 3, ex 3b EC Treaty) can be accepted as valid objections to this proposal. With regard to subsidiarity it should be recalled that the mandate to establish an internal market has yet to be fulfilled in the insurance sector and that the Member States are not able to create that internal market by themselves. Moreover, experience from other areas of uniform law tells us that we should not rely on intergovernmental cooperation and in particular not on the instrument of an international convention in a Community of 15 or even more Member States if we really want to achieve harmonisation. Bearing all this in mind it is difficult to maintain that the principle of subsidiarity could bar harmonisation measures adopted by the Community.[30]

The principle of proportionality requires a more careful review of the situation. As pointed out above, the internal market is already established in the fields of large risks and transportation risks where the free choice of law is admitted by the conflict of laws rules of the second generation of directives. Harmonisation measures cannot therefore be regarded in these areas as "necessary" within the meaning of Art 5 para. 3 (ex 3b) of the EC Treaty. For reasons of proportionality the Community would therefore have to focus on insurance contracts covering consumer risks and small commercial risks. The perspective outlined here is not very attractive. Next to the existing national insurance contract laws which would continue to apply to transport and large risks, the Community would introduce its own legislation on the insurance of small commercial risks and consumer risks. The Member States are of course not precluded from extending, at the national level, the Community legislation to the area of large risks and transport insurance. But it might equally be worthwhile to consider the possibility of a common understanding of the proportionality principle which would allow the Community to enact comprehensive legislation not limited to certain types of risk.

---

30 Cf. the disillusioning report about the harmonisation process promoted by means of agreements within the Council of Europe: *Taschner*, Richtlinie oder Internationale Übereinkommen? Rechtsinstrumente zur Erreichung der Ziele der Europäischen Union. Rheinische Friedrich-Wilhelms-Universität. Zentrum für Europäisches Wirtschaftsrecht. Vorträge und Berichte No. 66 (1996).

4   Outlook on Political Implementation

After the failure of former harmonisation efforts in the eighties, the proposition made in this paper will certainly raise the question as to whether and why the chances of success of a renewed attempt at harmonisation are better today. If we compare the present situation with that of 1980 we can in fact discover some differences in the political and economic environment which allow for some optimism.

In the first place it should be recalled that the establishment of the Single Market has to be viewed, not as an accomplished fact, but rather as a process which is still under way. In the course of this process political interest focused, at a first stage, on the greatest and most conspicuous obstacles for the realisation of the basic freedoms. These are national market regulations of a public law character such as the former German statute requiring foreign insurance companies to maintain a separate domestic establishment for doing business in Germany. As such regulations are being abolished, the market actors, both insurers and policyholders, are becoming more sensitive to other national regulations which equally impede the access to foreign markets, although perhaps in a less intense and less visible way. In the eighties the differences in contract law may not really have mattered as compared with differences relating to the regulation of premiums, investment policy or technical reserves. But after the harmonisation in those areas they are seen as quite an important barrier to the implementation of the single insurance market today.

A second change concerns the attitude of the insurance industry towards the single insurance market. At the end of the 1980s the official positions taken by the industry associations were characterised by the fear of foreign competition and a strong reluctance towards the implementation of the freedom to provide services and the deregulation necessary for this purpose. This defensive attitude has given way in the last few years to the rising conviction that deregulation and European integration offer new business opportunities to domestic companies in foreign markets. As this more offensive approach gains support, the industry is loosing interest in the maintenance of legal differences between Member States which were formerly welcomed as tools of protectionism. Quite to the contrary, the industry itself will lobby for the harmonisation of the legal framework.

The introduction of the EURO is a third change of fundamental importance that will probably accelerate the process of harmonisation.[31] The indication of insurance amounts and premiums in national currency gives clear evidence of the separation of national markets which exist even for intangible goods such as insurance. Many consumers feel a psychological barrier, which is often underestimated, to insure their risks with a foreign insurance company. Once this barrier is eliminated by the introduction of the European currency the direct comparison between domestic and foreign policies will suggest itself to a lot of people. Their demand for comparable policies will increase and can be satisfied by a harmonisation of the substantive contract law.

Another recent development which may have a fundamental impact on financial

---

31   Cf. in a general perspective *Duisenberg*, The Euro as a Catalyst for Legal Convergence in Europe: International Business Lawyer 2000, 483, 486 *et seq.*

services in general and insurance in particular is the internet. While insurers have made use of the new instrument only with great caution until now, its potential appears to be tremendous and perhaps unlimited in all sectors of standardised insurance such as private liability insurance, motorvehicle insurance, household insurance etc. The effect of the more frequent use of the internet for the making of insurance contracts will be similar to that of the EURO: transborder comparison of similar products offered by insurance companies established in different Member States will become a matter of course for consumers. It will be less and less acceptable for them that insurance coverage which is so readily available via the internet, which can easily be compared in terms of a premium expressed in the same currency and which looks so similar on the monitor, still is so different by virtue of different national laws.

A fifth change has come about in the general environment relating to the law of contracts. It cannot be denied that the interaction between the law of insurance contracts and the general law of obligations renders harmonisation of the former a particularly difficult task. On the other hand there are some signs which announce a forthcoming europeanisation of the general law of obligations, in particular the adoption of the principles of European contract law by the so-called Lando Commission[32] and of the Principles of International Commercial Contracts by the Institute for the Unification of Private Law (UNIDROIT) in Rome.[33] These developments were entirely unexpected in 1980 when the first speculations on a common private law for Europe had not even been published.[34] Today, the national civil codes and common law no longer seem to be as untouchable as they were at that time.[35] It would therefore appear doubtful whether these traditional fortresses of legal nationalism can still be used against the europeanisation of the law of insurance contracts. When doubts arise in the application of Community measures on the law of insurance contracts the proper approach today would no longer appear to assess the meaning of the Community acts in the light of a national system of contract law; instead, the interpretation should be guided by the principles of European contract law of the Lando Commission.[36]

As compared with the early eighties, things have finally changed in so far as the Community has already taken some initial steps towards a European law of insurance contracts. This relates, in the first place, to some specific rules of contract law contained in several insurance directives. They address issues such as the required minimum information and the right of cancellation in life insurance, minimum coverage

---

32 See below, note 46; on this topic cf. *Zimmermann*, Konturen eines europäischen Vertragsrechts, JZ 1995, 477 *et seq.*

33 UNIDROIT Principles of International Commercial Contracts (1994); German translation of these provisions in ZEuP 1997, 890; cf. *Bonell*, An International Restatement of Contract Law (2nd ed. 1997).

34 *Kötz*, Gemeineuropäisches Zivilrecht, in: Festschrift für Zweigert (1981), pp. 481 *et seq.*

35 Cf. several articles in *Hartkamp et al.* (ed.) Towards a European Civil Code (2nd ed. 1998); *Drobnig*, Private Law in the European Union (Forum Internationale No. 22, 1996); *Basedow*, Codification of Private Law in the European Union: The Making of a Hybrid: European Review of Private Law 9 (2001) 35 *et seq.*

36 Cf. *Basedow* The Renaissance of Uniform Law: European Contract Law and Its Components: Legal Studies 18 (1998) 121, 133 ff., 139 *et seq.*

and the scope of liability in the compulsory liability insurance of car owners as well as some aspects of the insurance of litigation expenses.[37] In the second place the directive on unfair terms in consumer contracts of 1993[38] will apply to insurance contracts as a matter of principle, as can be concluded from preliminary consideration no. 19.[39] In its opinion the Economic and Social Committee recently referred to the abundant case law of national courts in the area of unfair terms in general conditions of insurance.[40] It is safe to assume that the European Court of Justice will sooner or later have to interpret the directive in its application to standard terms of insurance, and there is no need to explain the obvious interaction between the review of standard insurance terms and the law of insurance contracts. In the third place, guidance for a future European law on insurance contracts is given by the block exemption regulation for the insurance industry of 1992.[41] Art. 5 et seq. of this regulation specify the conditions which model insurance terms must fulfil in order to be exempted from the prohibition of cartels and concerted practices in Art. 81 (ex 85) of the Treaty. Since the contract terms set forth in the lists of the regulation are mainly inspired by considerations of competition it is not possible to draw final conclusions on the contractual fairness of such terms. It can however be stated that the massive use of blacklisted terms runs counter to a competitive orientation of the European insurance market. There are authors who in fact take the view that the black list of Art. 7 of the Regulation equally serves the protection of individual rights of the insured.[42]

This short outline of changes which have occurred in the political, economic, and legal environment leads to the conclusion that the renewed efforts for a harmonisation of the substantive law of insurance contracts may be more successful than previous attempts. Since the Community is still under an obligation to establish the internal market in the insurance sector, such efforts should be made.

5 Outline of an European Insurance Contract Act

The first step towards a future harmonisation is the reflection on some preliminary questions of methodology. The answers to these questions mainly depend upon the legal basis for harmonisation in the framework of the European Community. Previous

---

37 Cf. *Reichert-Facilides* (note 25) p. 128 and note 56.
38 Council Directive (93/13/EEC) of 5 April 1993 on unfair terms in consumer contracts, *OJ* EC 1993 L 95/29.
39 Cf. *Brandner*, Auswirkungen der EU-Richtlinie über mißbräuchliche Vertragsklauseln auf Versicherungsverträge, in *Basedow/Schwark/Schwintowski* (ed.), Versicherungswissenschaftliche Studien 2 (1995) p. 67; *Kieninger*, Die Kontrolle von leistungsbeschreibenden Versicherungsbedingungen nach der AGB-Richtlinie – Fortschritt oder Rückschritt? ZEuP 1994, 277. It should however be borne in mind that the English version of Directive 93/13 differs from the German version as far as preliminary consideration no. 19 is concerned.
40 Opinion (note 20) *OJ* EC 1998 C 95/72, 83 *et seq.* sub 3.7.3.2. and 3.7.3.3.
41 Commission Regulation No. 3932/92 of 21 December 1992 on the application of Art. 85 (3) of the Treaty to certain categories of agreements, decisions and concerted practices in the insurance sector, *OJ* EC 1992 L 398/7.
42 *Windhagen*, Die Versicherungswirtschaft im europäischen Kartellrecht (1996) 169 *et seq.*; *Veelken* in Immenga/Mestmäcker (ed.), EG-Wettbewerbsrecht I (1997) p. 664 para. 44.

legislation of the Community was essentially based upon what is now Art.47 (ex 57) and 55 (ex 66) EC.[43] These provisions empower the Community to enact legislation which aims at the implementation of the freedom of establishment and the freedom to provide services which is not covered by Art. 95 (ex 100 a) EC, see section 2 of that provision. Arts. 47 (2) and 55 EC would appear to provide the appropriate basis for a future harmonisation of insurance contract law as well, as that legislation would mainly purport to foster an effective use of the aforementioned basic freedoms of both policyholders and insurance companies. In the framework of Title IV on the free movement of persons, the Treaty of Amsterdam[44] has introduced Art. 65 EC which deals with judicial co-operation in civil matters and might equally serve as a basis for future legislation relating to private law. Art. 65 EG is however primarily concerned, not with harmonisation or unification, but with the compatibility of national legal systems which remain distinct from each other. As the requirement of "cross-border implications" and the exemplary list contained in Art. 65 indicate, this provision focuses upon the conflict of laws and not on a comprehensive harmonisation or unification of substantive rules.[45]

The only form of legislation that is available under Art. 47 (2) EC is the directive; as opposed to Arts. 65 and 95 EC, the adoption of regulations is excluded. It is difficult to conceive any piece of comprehensive legislation in the form of a directive. The directive is the appropriate form for Community acts which deal with isolated issues such as the right of a consumer to withdraw from a contract made at his doorstep. It makes sense that such fragmentary rules must and can be implemented by the Member States in the way they chose in accordance with their national legal systems. But this is different if the Community decides to create a comprehensive framework for insurance contracts in order to increase the confidence of consumers that they benefit from a more or less identical protection throughout the Community. For that purpose a text of immediate application is needed which is invested with the same authority in all Community languages. Since regulations cannot be issued on the basis of Art. 47 (2) EC and the second-best solution of a directive does not appear very attractive, an amendment of Art. 47 allowing for the adoption of regulations would appear desirable. Alternatively one might think of a pragmatic solution to be adopted in the absence of an appropriate legislative basis: a draft directive of the Community could be taken as a blue print for an international treaty of the Member States, and the Community would then, by virtue of a directive adopted under Art. 47 (2) EC, put the Member States under an obligation to ratify that treaty. The resulting mix of legislative forms would certainly blur the borderline between Community action and intergovernmental co-operation, but it would have the advantage of combining the

---

43 See the Directives cited above in fns. 3, 5 and 6.

44 Treaty amending the Treaty on European Union and the Treaty Establishing the European Community. Done at Amsterdam on 2 October 1997, *OJ* EC 1997 C 340/1.

45 See *Basedow*, The Communitarisation of the Conflict of Laws Under the Treaty of Amsterdam: Common Market Law Review 37 (2000) 687-708, 699 s.; the Action Plan of the Council and the Commission on how best to implement the provisions of the Treaty of Amsterdam on an area of freedom, security and justice, *OJ* EC 1999 C 19/1 in this respect leaves some doubts as to the intentions of the Community institutions, cf. *Betlem/Hondius*, Europees Privaatrecht na Amsterdam: Nederlands Juristenblad 1999, 1137, 1144.

immediate applicability of an international convention with the enforceability of Community acts. Outside the field of harmonization of national laws one could finally think of an optional insurance act adopted as a Community regulation based upon Art. 308 EC; it would add to the existing national regimes and could be chosen by the parties as an alternative to the applicable national law.[45a]

The preparation of a draft European Insurance Contract Act is essentially independent from its eventual implementation. Irrespective of the subsequent role of the Community institutions such preparation should be initiated by a committee of neutral experts from different Member Countries. A very successful example for that work has been provided by the Commission of European Contract Law chaired by Professor Ole Lando from Copenhagen. That Commission has recently published the third part of its "Principles of European Contract Law" which deal with various aspects of general contract law such as the formation of contracts, the authority of agents, validity and interpretation, performance and remedies for non-performance.[46] The method of that group is similar to that applied by the American Law Institute in the preparation of the various restatements of the law.[47] The group aims at the drafting of statute-like rules which may be regarded as a restatement of the law in Europe, and which is supported by comments and comparative notes. A similar working group called the "Project Group *Restatement of European Insurance Contract Law*" was established in 1999 in Innsbruck, Austria. Its first chairman was the late Professor Fritz Reichert-Facilides of that University, and it is currently composed of academics from twelve different European countries.[48] It aims at working out common principles of European insurance contract law, relying on comparative studies of the national laws of the EC Member States, some Member States of the European Economic Area and Switzerland. These rules are compiled in a so-called Restatement. The project forms part of a more comprehensive endeavour which is ambitiously called the Study Group on a European Civil Code by some of its members. The real scope of that study group is limited, however, to the law of contracts, non-contractual obligations, and securities, both personal and in mobile equipment.[49] Since major parts of traditional civil codes such as real property, family law and succession are not covered, a denomination of the project as a Restatement of European Commercial Law would perhaps be more appropriate.

Being integrated in this more comprehensive project the Restatement of European Insurance Contract Law does not purport to provide an all-embracing regulation of the insurance contract from the preliminary negotiations until its termination. Instead, the project group has decided to abstain from the drafting of rules for specific issues wherever the Principles of European Contract Law[50] contain general rules which also provide for viable and satisfactory solutions with regard to insurance contracts.

45a Cf. *Basedow*, Insurance contract law as part of an optional European Contract Act: LMCLQ 2003, 498-507.

46 *Lando/Beale* (eds.), Principles of European Contract Law Parts I & II (2000); Lando/Clive/Prüm/Zimmermann (eds.), Principles of European Contract Law Part III (2003).

47 For a closer analysis of the ALI see *Schwartz/Scott*, The Political Economy of Private Legislation: U.Pa.L.Rev. 143 (1995) 595-652.

48 On that group, see http://www.uibk.ac.at/c/c3/c305/restatement/portal.html.

49 Cf. *von Bar*, Die Study Group on a European Civil Code, in: Festschrift für Henrich (2000) 1-11.

50 See above note 46.

Moreover the Restatement of European Insurance Contract Law will only contain provisions which are either absolutely mandatory or which provide for a minimum protection of the policyholder. This limitation is due to the fact that a major part of national provisions on insurance contract law are mandatory and thereby provide a serious obstacle to trans-border insurance business. The need for harmonisation is particularly urgent in this respect while differences between dispositive rules may be overcome by a careful drafting of the policies. Given the almost unlimited freedom of contract in English insurance law, the mandatory character of the restatement will probably raise concern in England. But a closer look will reveal that the rules approved by the project group are much more in line with the reality of English law than might appear at first sight. This is due to the fact that the Restatement will be limited to consumer insurance including small business insurance along the demarcation line drawn by EC directives.[51] As a consequence of its limited scope the restatement is much more easily compatible with the practice of consumer insurance in the United Kingdom as reflected by the Statement of General Insurance Practice of 1986 of the Association of British Insurers.[52] It should also be borne in mind that the European Community, when implementing its policies and activities, is under an obligation to take into account requirements of consumer protection and to ensure a high level of consumer protection in this context, see Art. 153 (1) and (2) EC.

Contrary to some proposals[53] the Restatement is not limited to transborder insurance contracts. Those proposals were inspired by the traditional view of uniform law as a substitute for the conflict of laws. In the European Community, however, the unification or harmonisation of law aims primarily at the implementation of the basic freedoms and at the removal of all kinds of distortions of competition as pointed out by the preliminary considerations of various directives.[54] It follows that for the purposes of harmonisation, the Community must not distinguish transnational and purely internal fact situations.[55] With regard to insurance it can be stated more specifically that the creation of all-European riskpools which would be an objective of Community action in this field calls for a harmonisation of the legal framework for all intra-community insurance contracts, whether internal or international.

6 A European Insurance Contract Act and the Common Law

Would the European Insurance Contract Act outlined above be regarded as a code? Would it therefore trigger similar discussions as those that have made England refrain from codification in the past?[56] At first sight the answer would be clearly in the nega-

---

51 See Art. 5 d) of Directive 73/239/EEC, as amended, above note 3.

52 Reproduced in *Hodgin*, Insurance Law (1998) 241 *et seq.*

53 *Reichert-Facilides* (note 25) 119, 133; generally *Drobnig*, Private Law in the European Union (Forum Internationale No. 22, 1996) 21.

54 See consideration no. 6 of Directive 88/357/EEC (above note 5); consideration no. 30 of Directive 92/49/EC (above note 6); consideration no. 16 of Directive 90/619/EEC (above note 5); consideration no. 27 of Directive 92/96/EC (above note 6).

55 In the same sense *Schwartz*, 30 Jahre EG-Rechtsangleichung, in: Festschrift für von der Groeben (1987) 333, 363 s.

56 See e. g. *Hahlo*, Here lies the Common Law: Rest in Peace: Mod. L. Rev. 30 (1967) 241-259 with

tive. The European Insurance Contract Act would of course cover a broader area than any one of the previous directives adopted with regard to contract law. But its method would be the same: it would fix minimum standards with regard to specific issues of insurance contract law, and it would in particular not purport to provide solutions for all questions that may arise in connection to such contracts. Therefore, the act as such would not compel Member States to deviate from the traditional way they transform EC directives. Britain could continue her practice and implement such a directive by means of subordinate legislation.[57] Nor would such a directive appear to pose new problems relating to the structure and interpretation of the law.

A closer look, however, reveals some additional problems. As pointed out before, the European Insurance Contracts Act should rather be adopted in the form of a directly applicable instrument, possibly a regulation if an amendment to the treaty so permits. It should moreover form part of a more comprehensive set of Principles of European Contract Law, and the whole project would come close to the idea of a European Commercial Code. Therefore, the proposal for a European Insurance Contract Act will encounter the same objections that are raised against the general project. Although this paper is not the appropriate place for discussing these objections in depth, the debate should not go unnoticed. The criticism is essentially threefold. First, some argue that the myth of the common law being based upon a long tradition of social experience cannot be reconciled with the claim to prospective certainty and completeness which is said to be inherent in the logical structure of the codes.[58] Second, the systematic structures of the common law are said to be too different from those of civil law codes in order to accommodate a common European scheme. In particular, the basic concepts of the civil law such as tort or property or the demarcation of private law and public law are said to be meaningless to the common law.[59] Third, it appears doubtful to some authors whether the harmonisation or unification of texts really brings about a convergence of the law in action. The differences existing in legal methodology, procedural enforcement, in the social, economic and political environment are said to provide for future divergences to the effect that a future European code of obligations will have "dans quelques décennies un sens français, un sens allemand, un sens écossais etc."[60]

In response to this criticism some short remarks must suffice here. If the common law cherishes, as it does, practical experience instead of logical deductions, it would follow that the feasibility and prospective effects of harmonisation should be predicted from previous experience and not from logic. In particular we should expect

---

a comment by *Gower*, pp. 259-262; *Kerr*, Law Reform in Changing Times: L. Q. Rev. 96 (1980) 515-533.

57 See sect. 2 (2) of the European Communities Act 1972; cf. *Hartley*, The Foundations of European Community Law (4th ed. 1998) 252 s.

58 This criticism has repeatedly been expressed and varied by *Legrand*, see e.g. Against a European Civil Code: Mod. L. Rev. 60 (1997) 44; *id.*, European Legal Systems are not Converging: Int. Comp. L. Q. 45 (1996) 52.

59 *Samuel*, English Private Law in the Context of the Codes, in van Hoecke/Ost (eds.), The Harmonisation of European Private Law (2000) 47-61.

60 *Malaurie*, Droit romain des obligations. Droit français contemporain des contrats et l'Europe d'aujourd'hui: La semaine juridique – édition générale 2000 I 246, p. 1415, 1420; *Teubner*, Legal Irritants: Good Faith in British Law or How Unifying Law Ends up in New Divergences: Mod. L. Rev. 61 (1998) 11.

the critics to look at 100 years of application of uniform law conventions. Unfortunately, however, the opponents appear to have one thing in common: they apparently have very little practical experience with the interpretation of those conventions which prevail in important areas of commercial law such as shipping, aviation, road transport, intellectual property and, more recently, also in the sale of goods. A careful analysis of court practice gives evidence of a wide-spread effort to take into account foreign precedent and thereby promote uniformity of application.[61] While it is obviously more difficult to achieve that uniformity or harmony in an international context than at the national level, solutions such as the reference procedure of the European Court of Justice or international arbitration can cope with that problem and will have to be developed further. As to the structural differences between civil law and common law they certainly present a serious problem and obstacle to the harmonisation in some parts of private law. But this problem does not concern the law of contract and therefore cannot impede a progressive harmonisation in this field. After all, it appears that some defenders of the status quo are primarily seized by nostalgic apprehensions expressed for example by Pierre Legrand in the following statement: "En Europe, la tradition de common law, dans ce qu'elle a de magique et de mystérieux, est en train de s'éteindre comme une lampe a l'huile au petit matin."[62] But this is not true. The style of adjudication will remain unaltered after the adoption of a European Code of obligations. As demonstrated by the Sale of Goods Act English courts will continue to find the law in their way as continental courts will continue to apply their methods. But it is essential that they take notice of each other.

---

61 See *Basedow*, Depositivierungstendenzen in der Rechtsprechung zum Internationalen Einheitsrecht, in: Canaris et al. (eds.), 50 Jahre Bundesgerichtshof – Festgabe aus der Wissenschaft vol. II (2000) 777-798.
62 *Legrand*, La leçon d'Appollinaire, in: *id.*, Fragments on Law-as-Culture (1999) 117, 129.

CHAPTER 32

Service Contracts

Marco B.M. Loos*

1 Introduction

In the academic world the development of European principles has been placed high on the agenda for some years now. Many different groups of researchers have researched the question whether a (more) uniform European private law is feasible and to be desired. The main stream of publications indicates that such uniformity is both needed and feasible, even though there will be big problems on the road ahead.

A further step was made at a one-day conference in The Hague, organised by the Dutch presidency of the European Union.[1] On the initiative of Prof. Dr. Chr. von Bar (University of Osnabrück, Germany), the *Study Group on a European Civil Code* was formed, aiming at the development of a Restatement of European principles with commentary, which could then form the basis of such a code, if there was the political will for this. It was recognised that in a modern European Code – if such were ever to be enacted – a regulation of service contracts would be needed since these form an important element of national and transborder trade, but at this point they lack coherent regulation. This leads to difficulty both on a national and on a European level. For this purpose, the Tilburg Working Team on Services was established,[2] working in close co-operation with the Working Team in Amsterdam (Long Term Commercial Contracts, in particular Commercial Agency, Franchising and Distribu-

---

* Marco Loos is a senior researcher at the Amsterdam Institute for Private Law, University of Amsterdam, and one of the team managers of the Tilburg Working Team on Services of the Study Group on a European Civil Code, led by prof. Christian von Bar of Osnabrück University. This contribution was submitted on 1 March 2003.

1 The opening speech by the Dutch Minister of Justice is published on the website of the Dutch Ministry of Justice, see http://www.minjust.nl:8080/C_ACTUAL/SPEECHES/SP0006.htm.
2 The Working Team on Services is led by Prof. Maurits Barendrecht (team leader, in particular responsible for Construction) and further consists of Marco Loos (team manager, national reporter for the Netherlands and responsible for the drafts on Storage and Processing), Chris Jansen (team manager and responsible for the drafts of the General Chapter and in part on Design), Andrea Pinna (national reporter for France and responsible for the draft on Information and Advice), Rui Cascaõ (national reporter for Portugal, responsible for the draft on Treatment) and Roland Lohnert (national reporter for Germany, in part responsible for the draft on Design). The Working Team is greatly helped by the national reports prepared by Georgios Arnokouros (Utrecht/Greece), Odavia Bueno Diaz (Amsterdam/Spain), John Dickie (Utrecht/England and Wales), Christoph Jeloschek (Utrecht/Austria), Manola Scotton (Amsterdam/Italy), Hanna Sivesand (Utrecht/Sweden), and Aneta Wiewiorowska (Utrecht/Poland). Further contributions were made during the joint meetings of the Working Teams, consisting of the members mentioned before, and of prof. Martijn Hesselink (Amsterdam), Viola Heutger (Utrecht), prof. Ewoud Hondius (Utrecht), Jacobien Rutgers (Amsterdam) and Muriel Veldman (Amsterdam).

tion) and the Working Team in Utrecht (Sales Contracts).[3] This being said, it becomes clear that the development of Principles in the field of service contracts will not be easy, for these rules will have to be build almost from scratch. In this paper I will set out how the Working Team on Services has tried (and is still trying) to deal with this and other problems. I will do so by first describing the existing situation at a national (2) and a European level (3). Under 4 and 5, I will explain our method of research and how we decided whether a topic should be regulated. Finally, under 6, I will indicate the contents of the General Chapter on Services.

2   Lack of Coherent Regulation at the National Level

Many of the existing codifications contain some provisions that might form the basis of a general system of services (e.g. § 675 of the German *Bürgerliches Gesetzbuch*, Article 1779 of the French *Code civil* and Articles 7:400 ff. of the Dutch *Burgerlijk Wetboek*). These provisions, however, are of a rudimentary nature and often only apply insofar as the contract has not been regulated elsewhere in the Code. The lack of a common framework at a national level can partly be explained by the fact that services were of less fundamental importance in the days when the great national codifications (above all the French *Code civil* and the German *Bürgerliches Gesetzbuch*) were created. At that time it was felt there was no need for regulation in this area. The types of contract that occurred in those days can be characterised by the fact that nearly all of them concerned contracts of an incidental nature, whose performance could be completed in a relatively short period after entering into the contract.[4] Long term contracts, which form an important subcategory among service contracts,[5] only began to emerge in the course of the 20th century, and in particular since the end of World War II. The great national codifications therefore contain hardly any provisions regarding such contracts. Consequently, each time a new service contract was developed, lawyers – who often operated only in that specific area of law – had to invent applicable rules on an *ad hoc* basis.[6] In doing so, they generally ignored – or perhaps: were ignorant of – solutions that had been found for other services. Regulations for specific services, developed by courts and occasionally by legislators, have

---

3   All three Working Teams thus consist of a team leader, one or two team managers and several national reporters coming from (Candidate-) Member States of the European Union. The three Working Teams have exchanged reporters in order to benefit as much as possible from the presence of researchers from a large number of European jurisdictions. The Working Teams are sponsored by the *Nederlandse Organisatie voor Wetenschappelijk Onderzoek*, the *Centraal Onderzoeksfonds* of the University of Amsterdam and the Onassis Foundation.

4   E.g. a sales contract.

5   E.g. financial services and insurance law. In this paper, I will not touch any further upon the relation between services and long term contracts.

6   By 'lawyer', I mean a professional provider of legal services, by 'attorney', the lawyer who represents his client as his authorised agent in and out of court, and by 'notary', the lawyer who (often in the performance of a public office) drafts legal documents for his clients and who advises them, but who does not normally act as his client's agent. Cf W.B. Fisch, 'Professional services,' in W. Lorenz (ed), *International Encyclopedia of Comparative Law*, Vol. VIII, Specific contracts, Chapter 9; Mohr Siebeck/Martinus Nijhoff, Tübingen/Dordrecht/Boston/Lancaster; 1999, no 2, p. 4.

developed more or less autonomously ever since. The current specific regulations for medical services, construction law and insurance law do not, therefore, have a common background.

This in itself need not have been problematic if academics had, from the start on, tried to fill the gap by trying to build a bridge between the services, comparing solutions found in one area to solutions in other areas and by implementing similar solutions for similar problems. Most academics, however, also specialise in a particular field of services and are therefore inclined to deal with only those contracts or types of contracts that have been regulated by legislators or have been developed by courts. Generalists, operating at the more abstract level of the Law of Obligations, sometimes refer to service contracts, but usually only to illustrate the general Law of Obligations.[7] Academic works linking specific services to the abstract level of the Law of Obligations are rare. A coherent, overarching system of service contracts has therefore not been developed.

3   Deepening the Problem: Transborder Contracts

At the national level, there is no uniformity in the Law of Services. The drawbacks that this causes deepen when the relationship has an international dimension.[8] Unless the parties have determined differently, the law applicable to the service contract will most likely be that of the country where the provider of the service has its seat.[9] The lack of system in the substantive law, however, makes it difficult for the client to properly estimate the content of the foreign rule. A cautious client may consider that by entering into a contract with a foreign provider of the service, he is bound to encounter greater uncertainties than he would have when contracting with a provider from his own country.

Admittedly, there are other, more practical explanations why the number of transborder service contracts is at present rather limited. One such explanation is undoubtedly that it is often impractical for a client to seek a counterpart abroad: a private person, living in Bavaria, is not likely to hire a Greek attorney to handle his divorce or to contact a Danish paperhanger. But even when both the client and the provider of the service are large commercial companies and the service required is not one that

---

7   To give an example, taken from Principles of European Contract Law: if a non-performance 'substantially deprives' the creditor of what he was entitled to expect under the contract and the debtor could or should have foreseen that result, the non-performance is considered to be fundamental (Art. 8:103 *lit* b PECL), which authorises the creditor to terminate the contract under Art. 9:301 PECL. In order to explain when a non-performance *substantially deprives* the creditor of his legitimate expectations, Comment C to Art. 8:103 PECL illustrates that notion by using 4 cases of non-performance in service contracts.

8   The fact that in case of a legal dispute between a client and the provider of a service, (at least) one of the parties will have to appear in front of a court in another country is inevitable in an international setting and will therefore not be discussed below. One needs, however, to put this in perspective: it is probably easier for a citizen of Trier to have to travel to a court in Luxembourg than to a court in Berlin.

9   Cf. Art 4, paragraph 1 and 2, of the Rome Treaty on the Law applicable to contractual obligations, 19 June 1980, *OJ* EC 1980, L 266/1.

has to be performed in the presence of the client, transborder service contracts seem to be rare. It is plausible that this is partially due to the lack of a set of rules that is common to all Member States and the uncertainty this causes for (at least one of) the parties. To substantiate this, one may point to the developments within the field of the provision of financial services. In this area of law, some standardisation has taken place due to the 'adoption' of Anglo-Saxon model contracts. Nowadays, transborder provision of financial services is common practice. This might imply that a certain frequency of transborder contracts is necessary before a general call for regulation or harmonisation arises. After the development of such regulation, the number of transborder contracts could rise considerably. Empirical research would have to show whether this is correct. However, it appears that the existence of a sufficiently clear legal framework is necessary for international service relations to flourish.

A sectoral approach to services prevails not only at the national, but also at the European level.[10] A general harmonisation was considered,[11] but encountered so much resistance[12] that the Commission was forced to withdraw the proposal. In doing so, the Commission indicated it was contemplating the possibility of draft directives on specific types of services, such as construction law and medical law.[13] Although nearly every harmonising activity in the Law of Services would mean an improvement to the present situation, there are important drawbacks to such a development. Sectoral regulation has the disadvantage that a generic approach will not be forthcoming for a long time, and consequently that the existing lack of coherence and system in the Law of Services will continue. As has been the case so far, applicable rules for newly emerging types of services would have to be established on an *ad hoc* basis and the different areas within the Law of Services would continue to develop autonomously.[14]

4   Searching for European Rules on Service Contracts

With that in mind, while preparing the start of our research in order to draft common Principles on Service Contracts, we thought it wiser to choose a more general approach. The question then arose as to *how* to approach services on a European level. Should one focus the search for 'the better rule' by aiming at the specific contracts presently dealt with in the existing codifications? This seemed to be tempting since these codifications usually deal with the same contracts. Yet, as a starting-point for

---

10 Cf. the impressive overview by P.-Chr. Müller-Graff in Chapter 5 of this book. Exceptions are, among others, the directive on distance selling (Directive 97/7/EC of 20 May 1997, *OJ* 1997, L 144/ 19) and the e-commerce directive (Directive 2000/31/EC of 8 June 2000, *OJ* 2000, L 178/1), which more or less apply to all types of services concluded in a certain way.

11 Proposal for a Council Directive in liability for services, *OJ* 1991, C 12/8.

12 Cf. the critics mentioned by E.H. Hondius in the General Introduction to this book.

13 COM (94) 260.

14 G. Betlem and E. Hondius, 'European Private Law after the Amsterdam Treaty,' *European Review of Private Law* 2001, pp. 3 ff., argue that there already is a lot of European legislation in the field of private law, but the technical quality of that legislation is meagre and the different regulations are often inconsistent with each other.

comparative research, we thought it to be unwise. Legal institutions such as the Dutch *opdracht* and the German *Auftrag* may be homophonous, but fulfil different functions in the respective legal systems,[15] whereas huge linguistic differences exist between the German *Auftrag* and the French *mandat*, but these legal institutions do fulfil similar functions.[16] The tasks performed by the providers of services may lead to further obscurity. For instance, an English *solicitor* may be compared to a continental attorney, but also performs tasks that in other Member States of the European Union are performed by a notary,[17] whereas it is not the solicitor but the barrister who appears in an English court.[18] Furthermore, nowadays a company often provides a number of services within the framework of one contract, some of which were originally provided by others, sometimes combined into new, integrated contract types: 'design and build'-contracts in construction law, legal advice by accountants, storage, distribution and value-added logistics by forwarding agents,[19] etc. A traditional approach to the services will often lead to problems of qualification of the contract. These observations suggested that in *developing* a Law of Services, one had better look at the activities that are carried out and to compare from a functional point of view the rules that govern these activities. On the basis thereof, common rules may be developed. Of course, this need not say anything about the final outcome of the research, since one could try to generalise, in the end, the rules developed on the basis of this functional approach. If that were possible, the traditional problem of qualification would also become less important: if the same rules apply anyway, the need for qualification would to a large extent fade.

On the basis of these assumptions, we decided to direct our attention to what we considered to be the functional basic obligations of which the existing service contracts are composed. Preliminary research[20] showed that most services could essentially be brought back to ten basic types, which for the time being we described as follows:

a. Advice: the presentation of information in such a manner that the client – whether or not on the basis of a reasoned recommendation – is capable of deciding upon the course of action to follow;
b. Agency: acting for the account of the other party in order to legally bind the other party directly or indirectly;[21]

---

15 Cf. M.B.M. Loos, 'Dienstverlening: de overeenkomst van opdracht,' in E.H. Hondius, G.J. Rijken (eds.), *Consumentenrecht*, Kluwer, Deventer, 1996, no 7.3, p. 133.

16 Cf. M. Fontaine, Codifying 'Modern' Contracts, in the second edition of this book, p. 373.

17 Cf. J.M. Barendrecht and E.J.A.M. van den Akker, *Informatieplichten van dienstverleners*, Tjeenk Willink, Deventer, 1999, no 18.

18 Cf. W.B. Fisch, 'Professional services,' in W. Lorenz (ed), *International Encyclopedia of Comparative Law*, Vol. VIII, Specific contracts, Chapter 9; Mohr Siebeck/Martinus Nijhoff, Tübingen/Dordrecht/Boston/Lancaster; 1999, no 24, pp. 13-14.

19 Cf. E.J.M. van Beukering-Rosmuller, 'Logistieke dienstverlening,' *Tijdschrift Vervoer en Recht* 1998, pp. 91-96.

20 See M.B.M. Loos, Towards a European Law of Service Contracts, *European Review of Private Law* 2001, vol. 4, pp. 565-574.

21 Clearly, we here meant the *internal* relation between the agent and the principal, not the external relation with a third party.

c. Construction: the process of combining parts to form a larger structure;

d. Design: the service of creating something that is intended as a guide for making something else;

e. Information: the collection, analysis and providing of information to another person;

f. Intermediation: bringing two or more parties into contact with each other and enabling them to establish a certain connection;

g. Processing: the treatment of an existing good in order to effect or prevent some change in that good, thus adding value to the good concerned or maintaining it;

h. Storage: placing and leaving goods in the hands of somebody else for preservation, later use or disposal;

i. Transportation: carriage of persons, goods or information from one place to another by means of a transportation vehicle or telecommunication medium;

j. Treatment: all the processes that are applied to a person or animal in order to change the physical or mental health of that person or animal.

The functional approach we intended to use implied that we would then, per basic type, put and – try to – answer a number of questions, such as the following. On the basis of which norms should the quality of the service provided be measured? To what extent do duties to inform or warn exist? In what way should conflicts of interest be dealt with? How can a service relation be adjusted to changes in the circumstances?

Of course, we realised that several objections to this analysis could be made. First of all, there are services that probably cannot be brought into one or more of these basic types. Examples that we thought of at the time were the contract by which a party takes upon itself the obligation to 'educate' somebody else. In a way, educating somebody is providing information, but it is more than that, nor is it advice. Other examples are the 'entertainment contract' a performer of arts concludes with a theatre, and the contract a person visiting that performance concludes with that same theatre. Surely, this is not intermediation, even though one could argue that it would meet the description given above.

Secondly, we realised that one of the types that we did identify, could in reality be considered to only form a subcategory of another type. An obvious candidate for such a conclusion would be the distinction between *advice* and *information*, since advice necessarily has to be preceded by the collection, analysis and provision of information by the party providing the advice. In that respect, advice may be seen as information plus something else (as, in a way, education is or can be). Our research in the end confirmed that idea, which means that advice and information will ultimately be dealt with in one single chapter, in which some provisions only apply for advice and most provisions to both advice and information. We also had envisaged that perhaps no legally relevant difference would be found between *construction* and *processing* and/or *construction* and *design*. However, ultimately we concluded that these types ought to be treated separately.

Thirdly, we considered the possibility that we had failed to recognise a type that actually should be distinguished from the types enumerated. We would have to facilitate our research in such a manner that we would be able to deal with such a conclusion and, if need be, to adjust our work. During our research, we indeed found there to be such a type, namely supervision of the performance of a service by yet another party.

Still, applying a functional approach to services, dealing with the questions mentioned above at the level of the activity performed, proved to have an important advantage: one does not focus so much on the legal qualification of a specific service nor on the profession of the provider of that service, but primarily on what *actually* happens. Moreover, as indicated above, the approach made it possible to conduct a comparative study: whether a last will and testament is drafted by a common law *solicitor* or by a civil law *notary* is not all that relevant in a functional approach of the service. In other words, the functional approach enabled us to overcome national classifications and characterisations.

The approach, however, also had important disadvantages, some of which were already pointed out to us even before we started our research. The most serious disadvantage proved to be that it was very hard to collect the necessary information. Especially for advice and information, we found that many national legal systems often did not deal with these activities explicitly, let alone in a more or less systematic way. This was, of course, to be expected, given the lack of a coherent legal framework in the Member States, as indicated above under 2. Moreover, it turned out that sometimes we expected materials to be available, but we simply could not get access to it. For the latter problem, Sweden provides a good example. Because most construction cases are dealt with by arbitration tribunals and their rulings are not open to the public, the reporter could not present much more information than indicating what the current state of legislation was and how that ought to have worked out in practice, based on the rare cases that did go to civil courts.

Another, also rather serious, problem is the fact that this type of research is very time-consuming. We have had the privilege of having been able to work with talented young researchers from several jurisdictions, but they have had to work on their Ph.D.-dissertations and on reports on sales and long-term contracts as well.[22] Moreover, from some jurisdictions we were not able to engage researchers, which implies that these jurisdictions have not been studied as thoroughly as we had hoped for.

5   Developing Rules for European Rules on Service Contracts

In an area with so much fragmentation, and given the problems indicated above, it will be hard to cover every possible problem that could arise in any service contract. Because of these problems, which became apparent rather soon, we decided that we could not deal with all of the types identified above. We therefore decided not to deal specifically with agency (in the meaning set out above), intermediation, supervision, and not to deal with transport at all. Moreover, we decided not to touch upon financial services, with the exception of obligations to advise and inform resulting from

---

22   It is fair to say that in fact the time available for their work on their theses was rather restricted, especially in the first years of their appointment. Moreover, the amount of work to be done in the field of services meant that the Services Working Team trespassed on much of the researchers' time in these years.

such contracts. Some limitation would further follow from the possibility to fall back on the already existing Principles of European Contract Law (PECL), which the Study Group on a European Civil Code takes as the starting point of its work. The PECL will therefore serve as a general framework for all specific contracts, including service contracts. Even so, this still left a large number of aspects that could be covered, with, in theory, an enormous number of rules to establish. Covering *all* aspects would simply exceed our – and our researchers' – powers.

A way out could be to try to generalise rules developed for specific types of services to a more abstract level. This would, on the one hand, make both the rule and the composition of the services chapters more complex and less understandable, but on the other hand would decrease the chances of inconsistencies or unintended differences. Generalisation would therefore ultimately diminish qualification problems. Yet, in generalising rules, information and guidance for the parties when drafting their contracts will get lost. Furthermore, in the case of over-generalisation, subtleties needed for specific services may also be lost, requiring either derogations in the specific chapters for these individual types of services, or forcing the parties to continue to draft their own contracts in order to derogate from inadequate rules. It appeared there was no way we could win... Yet, the only way forward seemed to be to try to strike a balance between generalisation on a general level, specification if needed on the specific level of individual services, and absence of regulation if no real need for rules could be established.

This meant that choices would have to be made. We thought about criteria for these choices for quite some time. The following seemed relevant to us:

First, there are '*instrumental*' criteria, which refer to the usefulness of rules for service contracts:

1. The amount of service activities the rules cover. This criterion points to rules that cover many kinds of services and services that are commonly provided.
2. The rate at which parties address the subject of a rule themselves in their contracts. This criterion, however, points in two different directions: on the one hand, the development of default rules is less pressing when most parties deal with the problem themselves in their contracts. On the other hand, the more parties regulate the problem in a similar manner, the more it seems prudent – from an efficiency point of view – to draft the common answer to that problem as a default rule, so that the parties don't need to invest time and money to come up with such a rule for their contract.
3. Facilitation of future developments of the law. In some instances it will not be feasible to find a general solution for the problem at hand. It might then still be worthwhile to deal with the problem, because the development of the law will be stimulated if the problem has a name and a place in the Principles.
4. Stimulation of the parties to behave in a certain manner. Service contracts are characterised by the fact that parties have to co-operate to achieve a common goal. Rules that can stimulate the parties to such co-operation may be considered worthwhile, even when they do not have a direct remedial effect. This criterion is closely connected with the following one.
5. Usefulness of the rule for the application of other rules in the part of the Principles dealing with services. Some rules may help one of the parties in proving

a breach of contract by the other party. The breach of a duty to inform, for instance, is hard to prove, but that proof is easier if the party under that duty is obliged to keep record of its actions and to provide those records when so asked by its counterpart.

Other criteria deal with the *connection to other parts* of the envisaged code on which the whole Study Group is working:

6. Is the subject matter of the rule already sufficiently dealt with by the PECL or by other parts of the Principles? If, for instance, the rules on *negotiorum gestio*[23] provide adequate answers for certain gratuitous services, contract law may step back, whereas a more restricted scope of *negotiorum gestio* will lead to a stronger need for rules in contract law.
7. Do the PECL or the other parts of the Principles refer to or presuppose rules in the law of services?

Still other criteria deal with the *political and social acceptability* of the Principles, which of course is of great importance if the Principles are ever to be a basis for the development of a European Civil Code:

8. Protection of weaker parties against stronger parties abusing their dominant market power. Of course, existing consumer law must be included throughout the Principles, but structural imbalance of power and dependency of a party on the service provided by the other party is not restricted to consumer law: small and medium-sized enterprises (SME's) are often in the same or a similar position as consumers. That could be cause for mandatory rules protecting such a party. In this respect, it is typical that one of the leading cases on the role of fundamental rights in contract law pertains to the position of a commercial agent.[24]
9. A problem may be considered 'essential' from the point of view of the law of certain Member States. For instance, in some countries the question whether the price is sufficiently determined or determinable from the contract has been the subject of fierce litigation. That could be a reason to include specific rules dealing with such a situation.
10. The opposite may also be relevant: it could be essential, from the perspective of a Member State, *not* to deal with a problem. This criterion refers to national sensitivities as to, for instance, the role of contract law versus tort or property

---

23 I.e. benevolent intervention in another's affairs, *gestion d'affairs, Geschäftsführung ohne Auftrag, zaakwaarneming, gerencia, gerenza.*

24 Cf. BVerfG 7 February 1990, BVerfGE 81, 242 (Handelsvertreter). In this case, the German Constitutional Court considered that if one of the contracting parties has such a dominant position that it can unilaterally determine the content of contractual agreements, then the other party is forced to agree to something it does not want. In such a case, the law of contract cannot lead to a just settlement of the interests of both parties. If, because of that, fundamental rights are endangered, mandatory law must intervene in order to protect those fundamental rights.

law, but also to the role that fundamental rights and constitutional law play in contract law.[25]

Finally, as mentioned above, criteria as to the *comprehensibility* of the Principles may play a role, especially regarding the level of abstraction:

11. Comprehensibility and complexity of the rule. Generalisation of rules will lead to a higher level of abstraction. Such a rule may therefore be less understandable for the user of the Principles.
12. On the other hand, the chance of inconsistencies or unintended differences may diminish by generalisation, thus leading to less qualification problems.

As indicated, these criteria may point in different directions and their individual weight – which may differ from one topic to another – cannot be easily determined. We have more or less had to feel our way through the mists. In doing so, we decided that it was necessary to develop on the one hand a General Chapter on Services and on the other hand specific chapters for some specific services. In order to do so, however, we have had to partly change our approach. While still focusing on types of services, we decided that within each type we would focus our attention on typical providers of such services. This meant that for construction, we focused on the construction of immovable property by building contractors; for design, we primarily considered the services of architects; in the case of processing, we looked especially at repair, maintenance and similar services; for storage we focused on commercial storage; for treatment on the treatment provided by doctors. Finally, for information and advice, we focused on the services of lawyers, notaries, and, again, those of doctors.

On the basis of this, we drafted rules that in any case can and will cover the services of the 'typical provider' of such a type of services. With that, a core scope of application of a Specific Chapter is given. For other providers of similar services, these rules are to be applied with appropriate modifications, in a manner not different from what would be considered analogous application in other instances. Moreover, and more importantly, where – on the basis of the rules developed for these typical providers – a common denominator could be established, more general rules were drafted for the General Chapter on Services. These rules could then also be applied to those services for which we did not draft specific rules.

At this point in time[25] in the last stage of the research, we are returning to the level of the specific chapters and are now checking to see how the rules that are drafted for the General Chapters work out for the specific services, that is both for the services from which the general rule was deduced and the services for which such a rule was not developed. Remaining differences between the specific chapters are being identified and reconsidered. On the basis thereof, we now have to decide whether a specific provision on a topic is needed in one or more of the specific chapters, either in addition to the rule in the General Chapter or in derogation thereof. Moreover, current

---

25 Reference may be made to the Handelsvertreter case, mentioned in the previous footnote, and to the Bürgschaft decision of the same court, cf. BVerfG 19 October 1993, BVerfGE 89, 214 (Bürgschaft).
26 March 2003.

drafts of these specific chapters are aligned with the newly drafted provisions in the General Chapter, so as not to contain different concepts where no different meaning is intended. This work is still so much in progress that it is not yet possible to give an indication as to the content of the specific chapters. For the General Chapter, this is much more clear.

6 Lifting a Corner of the Veil: a Sketch of the Content of the General Chapter on Services

What, then, will be regulated in the General Chapter? In a first article, the definition of services and the scope of this General Chapter will be indicated. The article will indicate that it applies in particular to such contracts where a service will be performed in exchange for remuneration; the Chapter will be applied with appropriate modifications to gratuitous services. A matter of debate is still how the Chapter is to be applied if a service is to be rendered in the course of the execution of another contract, e.g. the installation of computer hardware or kitchen appliances purchased on the basis of a sales contract. At present, it is envisaged that the Chapters on Service Contracts, with appropriate modifications, apply to the parts of the contract that involve services (e.g. the installation), whereas the rules on sales contracts govern the actual purchase of the computer or kitchen appliances.

A second article will be dedicated to the determination of the price. Moreover, we have tried to draft provisions that regulate when the service provider is merely under an obligation of means (obligation of best efforts) and when he is under an obligation to achieve a certain result, and what the consequences are of applicability of the one or the other provision.

Other articles pay attention to the fact that services contracts may be long term contracts (think of contracts whereby a party provides administration services to a client) or are performed over a longer period of time (think of doctors providing treatment, and construction companies building a house or railway line): does the client have the right to give directions or instructions as to the way the service is to be performed once the contract has been concluded, and is the service provider obliged to follow such directions or instructions? Can parties end their contractual co-operation unilaterally and if so, what are the consequences for the price that is due? Is it possible to force a change of the contract upon the other party even if there is not (yet) a case of hardship? It should be noted that Article 6:111 PECL provides a basis for changes of the contract in case of change of circumstances, but does so only in exceptional cases. In case of long term contracts in which parties need to closely co-operate, a more flexible adjustment of contractual terms may be needed. If such a provision is missing, contracting parties will be enticed to simply end the contract.

These and other articles also relate to the fact that in the case of services, parties often need to work together to achieve the goal for which the client has had the service carried out. Some provisions are drafted to stimulate the steady flow of communication between the parties and to stimulate the necessary co-operation, including both precontractual and contractual obligations to warn and investigate in order for the service to be performed properly, provisions as to what co-operation may be expected of the other party and obligations to warn against, for instance, bad instructions from the client.

Finally, we have drafted provisions introducing obligations to investigate the conditions under which the contract is to be performed (e.g., in the case of the construction of a house, is the soil solid enough for the construction of that house or is piling necessary) and to make use of materials of sufficient quality and of personnel that is qualified to carry out the service. These obligations as such do not have a direct remedial effect – breaching these obligations normally does not lead to a separate claim – but primarily stimulate a proper execution of the contract. That does not mean that a breach of such obligations does not have consequences. Firstly, such a breach could, and often will, lead to a breach of the standard of care or to the absence of the envisaged result; liability will then follow from that. Moreover, if from the non-performance of such a secondary obligation it is clear that there will be a fundamental non-performance, Article 9:304 PECL (Anticipatory Non-Performance) allows the client to terminate the contract already at that time.

However, and more importantly, such provisions may also serve to *prevent* a breach of the standard of care or to prevent that the result is not achieved: if, for instance, the client (or an architect supervising the work on the client's behalf) becomes aware that the bricks used in the construction of a house are of such quality that the walls that are erected with theses bricks will not be strong enough to support the roof of the building, the client may demand specific performance of the obligation to use materials that are adequate and functional for the proper performance of the contract. As such, specific performance of such an obligation is closely related to the doctrine of anticipatory breach. It should be noted, however, that there has been considerable opposition to such provisions to be included in the Principles.

7   Conclusion

Regulation of services contracts is – certainly when compared with sales law – still a relatively new area of contract law. At present, a common and coherent framework exists neither at the national nor at the European level, and the Law of Services is rapidly developing in different directions. One could doubt, therefore, whether it is at all feasible to create a uniform regulation of service contracts, without relapsing into a haphazard construction of legal provisions. The approach we have taken to overcome that problem may to some people look like science fiction. Yet, at the time it seemed to us to be the only approach that could actually lead to uniform rules covering the multitude of services, without these rules being normatively empty. Whether we succeeded in developing such rules, is for others to decide.

D – Restitution

CHAPTER 33

Towards a European Civil Code (Third Edition) Unjustified Enrichment

Eric Clive*

1 Introduction

1.1 Update

In the second edition of this book I put forward some ideas for a possible treatment of the law of unjustified enrichment in a new European civil code.[1] At that time this was but a dream. Now the dream has become, if not reality, at least work in progress. The Study Group on a European Civil Code, under Professor Christian von Bar, has done a great deal of work on the subject of unjustified enrichment and parts of a possible text have been considered at three meetings of the Co-ordinating Committee.[2] In this new edition I try, with Professor von Bar's permission, to take account of the work done within the Study Group. It must be emphasised, however, that this is work in progress, that much remains to be done[3] and that decisions and choices of approach made in the earlier stages may possibly be changed later in the light of work on the later stages. It must also be emphasised that, unless otherwise stated, any views expressed in this chapter are my own and not those of the Study Group or any part of it.

1.2 Terminology

The term "unjustified enrichment" is preferable to "unjust enrichment." The latter suggests that some sort of vague moral criterion is being employed. Although it is un-doubtedly true that there is a moral underpinning to the law on unjustified enrich-ment, it is not the case that the actual rules apply a moral criterion directly. This part

---

* Visiting Professor in the School of Law at the University of Edinburgh. Formerly a full-time member of the Scottish Law Commission. Member of the Advisory Council on Unjustified Enrichment and *Negotiorum Gestio*, and of the Co-ordinating Committee and Drafting Committee, for the Study Group on a European Civil Code. Field of Specialisation: Private Law.
1 For an excellent critical discussion, see Schäfer (2001) at pp. 714-719; 736-737.
2 At Oxford in December 2001, Oporto in December 2002 and Leuven in December 2003. The pre-paratory work was done, and preliminary drafts prepared, by Professor Stephen Swann and Professor Christian v. Bar of Osnabrück University with the Working Team on Extra-Contractual Obligations. The drafts were discussed by the Advisory Council on the Law of Unjustified Enrichment and *Negotiorum Gestio* at several meetings.
3 So far the only provisions that can be said to have been agreed by the Co-ordinating Committee are those on the basic rule, on enrichment and disadvantage and on attribution of enrichment to disad-vantage. The meaning of "unjustified" has been discussed and a provisional approach agreed but texts have to be revised.

of the law is concerned with enrichments of one person at the expense of another which are regarded as legally unjustified and hence reversible. There are many enrichments which could be said to be unjust but which are not regarded, and could not reasonably be regarded, as unjustified for the purposes of the rules on reversible enrichments. For example, enrichments of one person at the expense of another due to harsh laws on taxation, bankruptcy or prescription might sometimes be regarded as unjust but will certainly not be unjustified.

The term "unjustified enrichment" is also preferable to "restitution"[4] which, if used in its ordinary sense of giving something back, describes only one method of reversing an unjustified enrichment – a method, moreover, which is not applicable in all cases of unjustified enrichment. In that respect, "restitution" is too narrow. It is also too wide, because the technique of restitution, or giving back something, may apply in contexts other than unjustified enrichment.[5]

1.3 Possibility of a European Approach

Building on Roman law texts, the work of the natural lawyers and later writers, and the demands of justice in actual cases, jurists throughout Europe have recognised that it is advantageous to have a general obligation to redress unjustified enrichment or at least to have a general principle to underpin specific rules.[6] Although specific rules and approaches vary, as is only to be expected, the results reached are generally similar.[7]

More important even than this long shared tradition is the functional utility, indeed necessity, of rules on this subject. Without such rules there would be cases where assets or value would end up in the wrong hands without any possibility of a legal remedy. People would be left with a sense of grave injustice and in certain cases would be tempted to resort to extra-legal methods in order to redress the situation.

From the point of view of the form of the law and the state of European academic discourse there is also much to be said for a new basic framework, preferably of a simple and robust nature. The present state of the law in some European countries favours "the creation of sophisticated theoretical empires which are beginning to spin out of control".[8]

1.4 Location in Code

Provisions on unjustified enrichment are part of the law on obligations and would appear in the part of the code dealing with that subject – probably after obligations

---

4   E.g. in English law. See Goff and Jones (2002). But see now Birks (2003) esp. at pp. 4, 16, 238-242.
5   See for French law, Malaurie (1991). There may well, for example, be a contractual obligation of restitution.
6   See Gallo (1992); Zimmermann (1995); Zweigert and Kötz (1998) pp. 538-565; and Schlechtriem, Coen and Hornung (2001). At one time English law could be described as an exception – an almost unique case – (as by von Caemmerer (1966) at p. 574), but things have changed. See Goff and Jones (2002) Chap. 1.
7   See Schlechtriem, Coen and Hornung (2001).
8   Schlechtriem, Coen and Hornung (2001), p. 377 fn. 2.

based on contract and obligations arising out of harm caused to another but before obligations arising out of benevolent intervention in another's affairs.[9] They could appropriately be given a Book of their own.[10] Once such provisions were in place, some rules in the Principles of European Contract Law would cease to be necessary[11] and some others might require modification.[12]

1.5 Various Approaches Possible

It is not necessary to work for long on the topic of unjustified enrichment before realising that, although there is likely to be broad agreement as to the results to be reached in real life, there are many different ways of organising the rules necessary to achieve these results. For example, essential restrictions can be built into the definition of enrichment or left until later and built into the rules on when an enrichment is unjustified or on defences or on how an enrichment is to be reversed. The choice between the different approaches is likely to be based on considerations such as ease of understanding and ease of use. Other things being equal, an approach which leads the reader gently into the subject, leaving complex qualifications and refinements until later, is likely to be preferable to an approach which puts people off by launching straight into the most technical and difficult aspects of the subject. Also, an approach which begins with a broad general rule, and introduces necessary qualifications later, is likely to be preferable to an approach which begins with a list of special rules or remedies for particular cases.

2 Primary Division of Subject Matter

2.1 Repetition: Unjustified Enrichment

In some European laws a distinction is drawn between repetition of the undue and the redress of unjustified enrichment (or enrichment without cause) in a narrower sense.[13] The reasons for this are partly historical: repetition of the undue comes

---

9 *Negotiorum gestio.*

10 In the second edition I suggested that the rules on unjustified enrichment might appear along with those on benevolent intervention in another's affairs in a Book called something like "Other Sources of Obligation". That remains an option, of course, but now seems less attractive, partly because it is convenient for a project on a draft European civil code to be able to publish separate Books on discrete topics as the work progresses.

11 Those providing for restitution in the case of invalid or ineffective contracts.

12 The rules providing for restitution after contracts terminated for fundamental non-performance might, for example, remain as contract law rules but might provide for the application by analogy of the rules on unjustified enrichment.

13 The French Civil Code dealt only with repetition of the undue (arts. 1376-1381) but case law, beginning with the famous *affaire Boudier* (Req. 15 June 1892, D.P. 92, 1, 596), recognised a general remedy for enrichment without cause. The Italian Civil Code deals separately with payment of what is not due (arts. 2033-2040) and enrichment without cause (arts. 2041 and 2042). The Netherlands CC also deals separately with undue payment (arts. 6.4.2.1-6.4.2.9) and unjustified enrichment (art. 6.4.3.1). All of these codes deal also with *negotiorum gestio*. In the uncodified Scottish law a

straight from the *condictio indebiti* of the Roman law whereas recognition of a general obligation to redress unjustified enrichment came later. Historical accident would not justify the retention of this distinction in a new European civil code if there is no functional reason for it. Two functional reasons may be suggested for retaining the distinction, but neither seems sufficient.

First, it may be argued that the measure of recovery has to be different in the two cases. In the case of repetition of the undue, what was received must be returned and there is no question of limiting the obligation to the value which remains in the hands of the recipient at some later point. In the case of unjustified enrichment in the narrower sense, it may be said, the focus of attention has to be on the enrichment remaining in the hands of the enriched party at a certain time. However, this argument assumes a particular answer (and not necessarily the best answer) to some quite difficult questions about the measure of recovery. Moreover, it elevates a technical matter – the ascertainment of enrichment in different types of case – to a fundamental point of principle.

Secondly, it may be argued that there is a reason of convenience for dealing separately with repetition of the undue and the redress of unjustified enrichment. Repetition of the undue covers many cases which arise in practice, including the common case of mistaken payments. It is convenient to deal with these cases separately. There is no point in complicating the rules for such simple cases by submerging them in more general rules which have to cater for unusual cases. This argument is unattractive in the context of a new code. It is normally better to begin at a general level and proceed to particular cases which may require special treatment. Moreover, it may be unduly optimistic in assuming that all cases involving repetition of the undue will be simple cases.

There is no compelling functional reason for dealing separately with repetition of the undue and other cases of unjustified enrichment. The retention of what is not due is just one way in which a person may be enriched at the expense of another without legal justification. To draw a distinction between this case and others at the primary level of the subject matter just perpetuates an awkwardness in the law and leads to drafting difficulties.[14] There are important elements in the law on unjustified enrichment, such as the concepts of enrichment and disadvantage (or detriment) and justification and certain defences, which apply to all types and it therefore seems expedient to have one category for the treatment of these general elements.

2.2 Performance: Other Cases

A similar distinction which might be considered for use in a European civil code is the distinction between enrichment by receipt of another's performance and enrich-

---

somewhat similar distinction is drawn between restitution or repetition on the one hand and recompense for unjustified enrichment on the other. Stewart (1992), p. 25.

14 What, for example, is to be covered by repetition of the undue? The Netherlands CC covers transfer of property, payment of money and the performance of any other prestation without legal ground (art. 6.4.2.1) but the rules for "other prestations" cannot be exactly the same as for transfers or payments and there is therefore a need to resort to the application of some rules "*mutatis mutandis*" and the addition of a special rule (art. 6.4.3.8).

ment by other means, in particular by interfering with another's patrimonial rights. This type of distinction is used in German law.[15] However, if enrichment by receipt of another's performance, without legal justification, is just one type of unjustified enrichment, and if there are elements common to all types of unjustified enrichment, then it seems unnecessary and undesirable to use this distinction as the basis of a primary division of the subject matter for legislative purposes, however useful it may be for explanatory purposes or for certain subsidiary rules.

2.3 Other Divisions

Other primary divisions are possible. For example, one could divide the subject into (1) cases based on conscious transfer (2) cases based on failed bilateral contracts (3) cases based on the recovery of gifts (4) cases based on improvements to another's property and (5) cases based on enrichment by wrongs.[16] Divisions of this type are helpful for explaining existing laws and may be useful at a secondary level in a new code but do not seem to be necessary or desirable at the primary level.

2.4 Conclusion

It is suggested that the most logical and expedient solution is to have no primary division but to begin the code provisions with a general obligation to reverse unjustified enrichment. This unitary approach to the subject is the one adopted so far by the Study Group on a European Civil Code.

3 The General Principle

The general principle might be to the effect that a person who has been enriched at the expense of another person is bound, if the enrichment is unjustified, to redress the enrichment. This principle could, with some justification, be regarded as part of the common European legal heritage.

There are various possible ways of expressing the general principle. The formula currently under consideration by the Study Group on a European Civil Code does not talk of an unjustified enrichment "at the expense of" another. Instead it talks of an unjustified enrichment which is "attributable to another's disadvantage".

The advantage of using "attributable to another's disadvantage" rather than "at the expense of" is that it separates out more clearly two quite different elements. The element of "disadvantage" or detriment is concerned with a practical state of affairs – the mirror image of enrichment. The element of "attributability" is concerned with abstract notions of causation or connection. Keeping these two elements separate has certain drafting advantages over the more compact "at the expense of" formula.[17]

---

15 It is used in the BGB art. 812 although no significance there attaches to the distinction. It has subsequently been used as the basis of the influential Wilburg/von Caemmerer typology. For surveys in English, see Zimmermann (1985); Dickson, (1987); and Zimmermann and du Plessis (1994).

16 See Schlechtriem, Coen and Hornung (2001).

17 If "at the expense of" is used it is necessary to provide or explain that certain enrichments which

One common situation which is covered more clearly under the approach adopted by the Study Group than under an "at the expense of" approach is enrichment by lawful competition. A new business moves into an area where there is an existing business and does well. It takes customers from the existing business. In a popular sense it could be said that the new business is enriched at the expense of the old. This impression has to be negated in the text, or at least in the comments. However, no one would even be tempted to say that the enrichment of the new business was attributable to the disadvantage or detriment suffered by the old. It is attributable to its own qualities and competitive advantages.

The general principle mentioned above, however drafted on points of detail, may appear at first sight to be an alarmingly broad one. It must be remembered, however, that it is limited, not only by the requirements built into it (enrichment on the one side; disadvantage on the other; a sufficient connection between the two; lack of justification) but also by the subsequent provisions in the Book on unjustified enrichment.[18] It must also be remembered that, in accordance with the normal principle, it would be for the claimant to establish the ingredients of the claim.

4 Enrichment

A fundamental choice has to be made between an "economic" or "net worth" approach to the concept of enrichment and a more "itemised" or "discrete" approach. On the "economic" approach a person would not be enriched unless there was some increase in the net value of that person's patrimony. The receipt of some valueless or burdensome property would not be an enrichment. The receipt of an unwanted service would not be an enrichment. The receipt of a wanted service which had the effect of saving expenditure on an equivalent service would be an enrichment. On the more "itemised" or "discrete" approach the receipt of any property which increased the recipient's assets, even if it was economically valueless or burdensome, would count as an enrichment, as would the receipt of any service, even one which was unwanted and which did not involve any saving of expenditure.

I am on record as preferring an economic approach.[19] The topic was thoroughly discussed within the Advisory Council on Unjustified Enrichment and *Negotiorum Gestio* of the Study Group on a European Civil Code. There was support for both views. In the end the itemised approach was preferred. That decision was subsequently approved by the Co-ordinating Committee. This way of proceeding has certain advantages. It leads to a simpler definition of enrichment and a more straightforward solution to the problem of corporeal property which ends up in the wrong hands.[20] It also leads to a more obvious solution to the problem of enrichment

---

might be thought to be at the expense of another in ordinary language are not so regarded for the purposes of this branch of the law.

18 This is made clear in the draft rules under consideration by the Study Group.

19 See the second edition of this book at p 386.

20 A person who has, in error, transferred property which has no value or which is actually burdensome to the recipient can still require its return. It might, after all, be of some value or use to the transferor even if not to the transferee.

coupled with a countervailing disadvantage. It is easier to see on this approach that there can be enrichment on both sides in such situations.[21] It does mean that the problem of unwanted services has to be dealt with at a later stage. That is not necessarily a bad thing. Such situations are unusual and there is something to be said for leaving them until the end rather than complicating the initial provisions by trying to deal with them at the beginning.

So there are reasons for the itemised approach adopted by the Study Group. At the same time it has to be said that this approach immediately distances the law from ordinary thinking, which is not a good thing in a new code. People who have paid a fair price for a product or service do not normally think of themselves as enriched by the receipt of what they have paid for. People who have unwanted graffiti painted on their walls do not normally think of themselves as enriched by the accretion of paint or the receipt of an artistic service. However, the decision having been made, the important thing now is to make the itemised approach work. That places a considerable burden on the provisions on justification considered below. It has to be made very clear that the millions of "enrichments" obtained daily in Europe under fair contracts are legally justified and do not even begin to give rise to problems of unjustified enrichment.

The definition of enrichment currently under consideration by the Study Group on a European Civil Code is as follows:

(1)   A person is enriched by:
    (a)   an increase in assets or a decrease in liabilities;
    (b)   receiving a service or having work done;
    (c)   making use of another's assets; or
    (d)   being spared a decrease in assets or an increase in liabilities.
(2)   In determining whether and to what extent a person obtains an enrichment, no regard is to be had to any disadvantage which that person sustains in exchange or subsequently.

It will be noted that, consistently with the general approach adopted, the first paragraph does not regard a mere increase in the value of a person's property as an enrichment in itself. It is thought, however, that in all, or practically all, cases where the increase in value is attributable to another person's disadvantage there would be an actual increase in assets or a receipt of services. For example, if X's property has increased in value because Y has, in error, built something on it, X would in fact have received property, in the form of building materials, and services in the form of building work.

The second paragraph makes it clear that, for example, a person can be treated as being enriched under a void transaction even if consideration was given, and that accordingly in such circumstances each party to the transaction may be regarded as being enriched.

---

21   One classic case is where something has passed from each party to the other under a void contract. Of course, even on the "economic" approach, this problem can be solved by a specific provision.

5   Disadvantage

The concept of disadvantage or detriment is the converse of the concept of enrichment. Already, therefore, the bits begin to fall into place. Once it has been decided that enrichment is to be defined as set out above it becomes relatively easy to conclude, as is currently the case in the Study Group's draft, that:

(1)   A person is disadvantaged by:
    (a)   a decrease in assets or an increase in liabilities;
    (b)   rendering a service or doing work;
    (c)   another's making use of that person's assets; or
    (d)   foregoing an increase in assets or a decrease in liabilities.
(2)   In determining whether and to what extent a person sustains a disadvantage, no regard is to be had to any enrichment which that person obtains in exchange or subsequently.

6   Attributability

When is the enrichment of one person attributable to the disadvantage or detriment of another?

Cases involving only two parties are normally straightforward. There is no real problem in the case of enrichments by the receipt of property or money which is transferred to the enriched person by another because in such cases the enrichment of the transferee is clearly attributable to the disadvantage of the transferor. Nor is there any problem in the case of the receipt of services. It is obvious that the enrichment of the recipient is attributable to the disadvantage of the person providing or paying for the services. Similarly, in the case of an enrichment by having one's debt paid by another it is clear that the enrichment of the debtor is attributable to the disadvantage of the person who pays. In all of these cases there is an obvious loss on one side which corresponds to, and is causally linked to, the enrichment on the other.

The position is slightly less obvious in the case of enrichments by making use of another person's assets. In such cases there may be no equivalent loss on the other side. The classic cases are the unauthorised use of another's property for free storage or accommodation, or the unauthorised use of another's vehicle or transport system for free transport.[22] The property may have been lying empty. There may have been spare capacity on the vehicle or transport system. There may be no actual loss to the person of whom advantage has been taken. If, however, "enrichment" is defined as including making use of another's assets and "disadvantage" is defined as including having one's assets used by another person[23] there can be no doubt that the enrichment of the user is attributable to the disadvantage of the person whose assets are used. Again, the disadvantage on one side corresponds to, and is causally linked to, the enrichment on the other. Nor is this simply a matter of applying abstract defini-

---

22   See e.g. (Germany) RGZ 97, 310 (use of railway track); (France) Req. 11 Dec. 1928, DH 1929, 18 (use of water pipes); (England) *Phillips* v. *Homfray*, (1883) 24 Ch.D. 439 (use of underground roads and passages).
23   See above.

tions. In a real economic sense the person whose assets are used without payment can be regarded as being deprived of the payments which would normally have been received from legitimate users. It seems reasonable that the unauthorised user should be under an obligation to redress the unjustified enrichment arising from the unauthorised use.

Another situation which is neatly solved by having separate rules on enrichment, disadvantage and attribution, but slightly less easily solved if an "at the expense of" formula is adopted[24] is where one person uses another's assets in such a way as to destroy them or dispose of them to a third party who acquires a good title to them. It is clear that in such cases the enrichment of the person using the assets is attributable to the disadvantage of the person who loses them.[25]

Cases of intercepted benefit are also neatly solved by the above technique. If X intercepts a payment which should be made to Y, and does so in such a way that X's assets are increased and Y has to forego an increase in assets,[26] it is clear that the enrichment of X is attributable to the disadvantage of Y.

The provision on attribution currently under consideration by the Study Group on a European Civil Code distinguishes between the relatively simple cases involving only two parties and the more complicated cases involving three or more parties. It is as follows.

Section 2: Attribution of Enrichment to Disadvantage

Art. 2: 201: Particular Instances of Attribution Involving Only Two Persons

An enrichment is attributable to another's disadvantage in particular where:
(a)   an asset of that other is transferred to the enriched person by that other;
(b)   a service is rendered to, or work is done for, the enriched person by that other;
(c)   the enriched person makes use of that other's asset;
(d)   an asset of the enriched person is improved by that other; or
(e)   a liability of the enriched person is discharged by that other.

Art. 2: 202: Particular Instances of Attribution Involving More than Two Persons

An enrichment is also attributable to another's disadvantage in particular where:
(a)   the enrichment is obtained from a third person and as a consequence the disadvantaged person loses a right against the third person to the enrichment; or
(b)   a third person makes use of another's asset so as to divest that disadvantaged person of their asset and vest the same or a like asset in the enriched person.

---

24 See the second edition of this book at pp. 387-388.
25 It might be argued that a person who breaches a contract interferes with the patrimonial rights of the other party. However, the rules on the measure of redress (see below) ought to prevent the law on unjustified enrichment from being used to subvert the rules on damages for breach of contract.
26 This will turn on whether Y still has rights against the person (Z) who is bound to pay. If Y still has these rights then Y suffers no disadvantage. The enrichment of X will then be attributable to the disadvantage of Z, not Y.

Art. 2: 203: Irrelevance of Difference in Nature or Value

An enrichment may be attributable to another's disadvantage even though the enrichment and disadvantage are not of the same nature and value.

The words "in particular" in Article 2:201 will be noted. They leave room for the development of the law by the recognition of other cases where one person's enrichment should, on policy grounds, be regarded as attributable to another person's disadvantage. But they also leave some potentially important questions unresolved.

One troublesome category of case is where the use of Y's asset by X results in X being spared a great loss. Suppose, for example, that X, during a storm, makes unauthorised use of a length of rope belonging to Y in order to secure X's yacht and save it from certain destruction. There is a disadvantage to Y – having the rope used by X. There might be said to be two advantages or enrichments to X. First, X has the use of the rope. This is an enrichment in itself. Secondly, X has been spared a decrease in assets. This is also an enrichment. There is no doubt that X's enrichment in the form of the actual use of Y's asset is attributable to Y's disadvantage in having the asset used. However, for there to be the necessary attributability it is not necessary that the enrichment and the disadvantage should be the mirror image of each other. They need not be of the same type or have the same value.[27] So it is possible to argue that X's enrichment in being spared the loss of the yacht is also attributable to Y's disadvantage in having the rope used. It would also, however, be possible to argue that the chain of causation between Y having his rope used and the saving of the yacht is broken by X's actions and that only X's enrichment in the form of using the rope is attributable to Y's disadvantage. Any further enrichment of X is attributable to what X does with the rope, not to the mere fact that he has the use of it. It is not clear from the Article which of these views is to be preferred. It may not matter much if the measure of redress is regulated in an appropriate way.[28] What seems clear is that by one means or another it has to be made clear that X is not bound to pay Y the value of the yacht.

Another possible criticism which might be made of the provisions on attributability is that they do not deal in a clear and satisfactory way with the case where one person has benefited as a result of a contract made between two other persons. A typical case is where the tenant of a property contracts with a builder to do work on the property. The tenant becomes insolvent and the builder attempts to recover from the owner on the ground that the owner has been enriched by having assets increased or services provided. In general there are good reasons for not imposing an obligation to redress the indirect enrichment which arises in this type of case. To allow the builder to recover from the owner might subvert the rules on the distribution of assets in insolvency (if the tenant had a good claim against the owner) or deny the owner defences which might have been available against the tenant (if the tenant had no good claim against the owner). There is also a danger of double liability or double recovery and a danger of widening the scope of unjustified enrichment in an unpredictable way. It might therefore be suggested that it could be useful to have a short

---

27 See draft Article 2:203.
28 See below.

provision in the code to make it clear that in this type of situation the enrichment of the owner is not regarded as attributable to the disadvantage of the builder.[29] However, here as elsewhere, the necessary restriction can be introduced in different ways and at different points. It would be possible to say that the enrichment of the owner is attributable to the disadvantage of the builder but that the enrichment is legally justified. This is the approach currently favoured by the Study Group.

6 Absence of Justification

6.1 The Importance of "Unjustified"

The term "unjustified" is of crucial importance in the law on unjustified enrichment. There is an obligation to redress or reverse an enrichment attributable to the disadvantage of another only if the enrichment is unjustified. There is no such obligation if the enrichment is justified.

There are two basic approaches to this question.

6.2 An "Unjustified If", or "List of Grounds", Approach

One approach is to have a list of grounds which make a relevant enrichment unjustified.[30] The list might, for example, cover (a) transfers[31] made in error or as a result of force or fear[32] (b) transfers made without legal capacity to make them[33] (c) transfers made on the basis of a contract or obligation or gratuitous disposition which is void or retrospectively avoided (d) transfers made under an express or implied reservation of a right of recovery[34] (e) taking or using property without consent[35] and (f) transfers made for a purpose which is not realised or does not materialise.[36] There are various ways of organising such a list, some more attractive than others. For example, categories (a) to (d) could be grouped together under some such heading as "Defective transfers" to give three main types of case – (1) defective transfer cases (2) taking and using cases and (3) failure of purpose cases.

---

29 There is a difference between national legal systems on this point. Zweigert and Kötz (1998), pp. 563-564; Whitty (1994).
30 A "relevant enrichment" is an enrichment of one person which is attributable to the disadvantage of another.
31 The word "transfers" is here used in a wide sense to include, for example, performance of a service.
32 The error might be of fact or law. Typical cases would be payments by mistake to the wrong person and payments made twice by mistake.
33 It is assumed for the purposes of categories (a) and (b) that there is no underlying contract or obligation which is void or retrospectively avoided.
34 E.g. X receives a demand for payment of a large sum. X knows or believes that the payment is undue but it would have grossly inconvenient consequences (e.g. loss of reputation, loss of a good credit rating, cessation of supplies) not to pay immediately. So X pays under protest and under the express or implied reservation of a right of recovery.
35 E.g. using another person's property without their consent.
36 E.g. paying for a counter-performance, or reasonably expected benefit or purpose, which does not materialise. One classic example is a transfer in anticipation of a marriage which does not occur.

The list could be a closed one, in the interests of certainty, but that could be risky as it is difficult to foresee every possible case. A closed list would also prevent non-legislative development of the law. An open list – ending with a category of suitably defined "other cases" – would be better in this respect but the final category would be difficult to frame and would run the risk of subverting any restrictions built into the preceding grounds or, indeed, subverting the whole approach.

A "list of grounds" approach cannot be used on its own because an enrichment caused by one of the listed factors might still be justified. For example, a payment made as a result of a mistaken assumption that it is due under a contract might turn out to be actually due by virtue of a statute or under the terms of another contract. Such a payment ought not to be recoverable. Similarly, a use of another's property without that person's consent may nonetheless be justified under a law allowing, say, suppliers of gas or electricity to take certain measures required for safety reasons.

6.3 An "Unjustified Unless" or "Absence of Basis" Approach

Another approach might be to take as a starting point the proposition that an enrichment of one person at the expense of another is unjustified unless there is a good legal cause or basis for it. There would be a legal cause for the enrichment if the enriched person was entitled to it by virtue of a contract or obligation; or by virtue of a gift, testamentary disposition or other gratuitous act; or by virtue of an enactment, court decision or rule of law.[37] Of course, none of these bases would provide justification if it turned out to be void from the beginning or was avoided retrospectively. Qualifications and refinements to this basic rule would be provided.[38] For example, it might have to be made clear that the mere transfer or acquisition of property in certain specified ways (depending on the relevant rules on property) is not in itself legal cause.[39]

The idea of legal cause is not, however, enough in itself.[40] It does not deal with opportunistic claims by those who conferred an enrichment incidentally or knowingly, without any contract or purpose of donation, in acceptance of the risk of non-payment.[41] For example, a flat-dweller who incidentally provides warmth to the flat above should not be allowed to claim from the proprietor of that flat a sum representing the saving on the latter's heating bills. Similarly, a person who paints a neighbour's house, unasked, while the neighbour is on holiday should not (in the absence of any claim based on the doctrine of benevolent intervention in another's affairs)[42]

---

37 For example, the laws on prescription or bankruptcy will often provide justification for an enrichment of one person at the expense of another. The laws on succession may do the same.

38 Note that under the Principles of European Contract Law there would be legal cause for a payment under a prescribed obligation. This is because prescription does not extinguish the obligation but merely entitles the debtor to refuse performance. See Article 14:501.

39 One of the main functions of the law on unjustified enrichment is to reverse the effects of valid transfers of property which are unjustified. Another function is to redress the sometimes inequitable results of doctrines such as *confusio*, *commixtio*, or *specificatio*.

40 See von Caemmerer, (1966) pp. 576-577.

41 See Mazeaud (1969) para. 701 and the Scottish case of *Edinburgh and District Tramways Co Ltd* v. *Courtenay* 1909 SC 99.

42 *Negotiorum gestio.*

be able to force the neighbour to pay for unwanted work.[43] Enrichments of this type are justified, not by a legal cause, but by something else. That "something else" could be expressed in various ways[44] one way being by reference to the consent of the disadvantaged person to the sustaining of the disadvantage.

One version of this "unjustified unless" approach was suggested in the second edition of this Book. Another version was presented to the Co-ordinating Committee at its Oporto meeting. The essence of this version was that an enrichment of X attributable to the disadvantage of Y would be regarded as unjustified unless (a) Y had consented to it or it had taken place with Y's actual or deemed authority or (b) X had a right to obtain it from Y or was legally entitled to it.[45] This was supplemented by detailed provisions covering those cases where the consent or apparent consent of Y fell to be disregarded.

6.4 The Present Position of the Study Group

The "unjustified unless" approach presented to the Oporto meeting failed to win acceptance. The Committee considered that the rules were too compact and therefore difficult for a reader to understand without a prior knowledge of laws on unjustified enrichment. It was suggested that the text should be "unpacked" and should set out clearly the circumstances in which an enrichment would be unjustified, in terms which were more specific and more accessible to the non-expert. There was also some concern that the draft rules did not make clear their relationship with the rules in the Principles of European Contract Law, especially the rules on invalid and illegal contracts. Finally, some members considered that in a free society people ought not to be required to justify enrichments: respect for the status quo required that the reversal of an enrichment should be required only if there was a specific ground for reversal, and not merely if there was an absence of justification for the enrichment.

The approach which found favour with the Co-ordinating Committee at its meeting in Leuven in December 2003 is to have a list of the grounds on which an enrichment will be considered unjustified. The list would be combined with a provision that an enrichment is not unjustified, even if one of those grounds exists, if the enriched person obtains it as a result of another's performance of a contract or obligation, or as a result of a gratuitous disposition or as a result of another's benevolent intervention in the enriched person's affairs[46] or if the enriched person is entitled to retain it under an enactment or rule of law,[47] without liability to account for it or pay compensation.[48] A

---

43 See Gallo (1992), p. 455.
44 See e.g. Clive (1996) pp. 50-57, Birks (2003) pp. 140-141.
45 This is a rather gross over-simplification of what was suggested, designed simply to give the main idea. Paragraph (b) is, of course, very like the idea of legal cause. Para (a) makes it easy to deal with opportunistic claims by those who have incidentally enriched others while doing something primarily for their own benefit. Such persons have consented to the disadvantage.
46 In such a case the rules on benevolent intervention would apply.
47 Perhaps there should also be a reference here to court decrees, which may sometimes have the effect of vesting assets directly in a party rather than just creating an obligation to transfer.
48 The last words may need to be reconsidered. If a power supply company has a statutory right to lay a pipe across another's land on payment of compensation at an amount fixed by statute it ought not to be liable to pay more under the law on unjustified enrichment. Its enrichment ought to be regarded

contract, obligation or gratuitous disposition[49] would not justify an enrichment if it was void or avoided with retrospective effect.[50]

It has not yet been decided whether the list of grounds is to be open or closed. A draft of a residual "other cases" provision is to be presented to the next meeting. This is rather an important question because if the "other cases" category is too wide – if, for example, it covered "any other case where the enrichment is without a legal basis and the disadvantaged person did not consent to the disadvantage" – then there would be little point in the list of specific grounds and one might as well abandon it in the text, revert to an "unjustified unless" approach and include the list as illustrative material in the comments. There was discussion of the contents and arrangement of a draft list but it is probably too early to say what form it will eventually take. There will have to be some reflection and reformulation in the light of the discussion at the meeting.

It is ironic that the Study Group should favour a "list of grounds" approach just as English law, for long the bastion of this approach, is being congratulated by one of its leading commentators for having abandoned it in favour of an "absence of basis" approach.[51]

7 Redress Due

7.1 General

There is also room for a range of different solutions when it comes to the redress due.

It is tempting at first sight to concentrate on the enrichment and ignore the fact that the enrichment is reversible only to the extent that it is attributable to the disadvantage. In some cases, concentrating on the enrichment alone and ignoring the disadvantage will produce the right results. Where there is a transfer of assets from the one party to the other the return of the property (with any fruits) would be the appropriate way of reversing the enrichment. It is only necessary to look at the enrichment and to provide for its return. However, in cases involving the use of another's assets or the provision of services the matter is more complicated.

The difficulty can be illustrated by the following example. X, a caravan owner, seizes a fire extinguisher from a neighbouring caravan belonging to Y and uses it to put out a fire in his own caravan. It seems clear that X ought not to be obliged to pay

---

as justified by the statute. There may also have to be refinements to cover certain cases where an enrichment to which a person is entitled (e.g. under the rules on acquisition of property by specification or accession) should nonetheless be reversible. This depends on what is eventually provided in the Book on property.

49 It should be considered whether the same rule should not apply to an enactment (e.g. subordinate legislation which may be *ultra vires*) or court decree.

50 However, a contract which was terminated for fundamental non-performance could still justify an enrichment. The rules on restitution after such termination would be for contract law to determine although, of course, the contract law could always incorporate some or all of the unjustified enrichment rules by reference. There would seem to be little sense in having two regimes of unjustified enrichment – a sophisticated one for avoided contracts and a primitive one for terminated contracts.

51 See Birks (2003).

Y the value of what X has been saved (the loss of the caravan) but only a reasonable sum for the unauthorised use of Y's asset (the fire extinguisher). This result can be achieved by saying that it is only X's enrichment in the form of the use of the fire extinguisher which is attributable to Y's disadvantage in having the extinguisher used.[52] However, the appropriate result could be achieved more directly and unsubtly by providing that the amount of the redress is the lesser of the enrichment and the disadvantage.[53]

The notion of attributability does not solve all problems. Consider the following example. X is enriched by being spared the burning down of his house. The enrichment was due to the actions of Y, who has agreed to buy the house and who discovered the fire while looking over the property prior to taking entry. Y smothered the initial flames with his coat. Y lost the coat and also provided a fire-fighting service. He acted in error, thinking (wrongly) that the property and risk had already passed to him. So it was not a case of benevolent intervention in another's affairs and, for the purposes of unjustified enrichment, his consent falls to be disregarded. There was a fire-fighters' strike at the time and it is admitted that, if Y had not put out the flames, there would have been no way of preventing the total destruction of the house. It seems clear that X should not have to pay Y the value of the house but only the value of the coat and a reasonable remuneration for the service provided. How can this be achieved? One way is to say, as suggested in the previous example, that in general the redress due is the lesser of the enrichment and the disadvantage. Whatever approach is adopted it is clear that some way must be found of dealing with the type of case where the enrichment on the one hand is out of all proportion to the disadvantage on the other.

On principle, the redress ought to be quantified at the time when the obligation arises, which would be when the conditions for it are fulfilled and not when a claim is made or an action commenced.[54] However, principle has to be qualified by considerations of equity. There are situations where it would be unfair to require full redress, particularly where the enriched person has been in good faith throughout and has either changed position in reliance on the enrichment or has suffered a diminution in the enrichment without compensating advantage. Some provision for such cases will be necessary.

7.2 Specific Cases

In the case of payment of money the enrichment on one side corresponds to the loss on the other and the appropriate redress is the repayment of the amount paid with interest.

In the case of a transfer of property to the enriched person the appropriate redress is the return of the property in substantially the same condition, where that is possible

---

52 See the discussion of attributability, above.

53 This was the approach recommended in the previous edition of this book.

54 There may never be an action. Some existing laws use a value-surviving test as the starting point. See Zimmermann and du Plessis (1994) pp. 38-42; Malaurie (1991) pp. 50-51. But this can be criticised. See Visser (1992) p. 187; Clive (1996) pp. 95-96.

without expenditure on it. The enriched person should also be bound to account for any benefit derived from the property.

The case of enrichment by the receipt of unwanted services ought normally to be covered by the rules on justification. I ought not to be regarded as obtaining an unjustified enrichment merely because someone has knowingly thrust an unwanted service on me, taking the risk of not being paid for it.[55] However, in cases where there is an error and a service intended for one person is received by another it may be necessary to deal with the problem in the provisions on the amount of the redress due. On principle, if the receipt of the service resulted in a saving of expenditure by the recipient then the redress due ought to be the amount of that saving or the amount of the disadvantage to the service provider whichever is the lesser. If it did not result in any saving then it is submitted that nothing ought to be due by the recipient unless the recipient was in bad faith in allowing the service to continue when it could have been prevented or stopped. The person making the error rather than the recipient in good faith of an unwanted and (to that person) valueless service ought to bear the loss.

Other cases can give rise to considerable difficulty and perhaps the best solution is to fall back on the general principle that the redress due is the amount of the enrichment to the extent that it is attributable to the disadvantage to the claimant and does not exceed the amount of that disadvantage, both the enrichment and the disadvantage being quantified at the time when the obligation to redress the unjustified enrichment arises rather than at the time of any claim or proceedings. Where appropriate, the amount of the disadvantage will have to be taken to be the amount which the claimant could reasonably have expected to be paid for any services or materials provided or for any permission to use assets.

7.3 Modification of Normal Rules

There are at least three cases where some modification of the normal rules on redress is required. Others may be suggested – or it may be considered by some that a more general modification is required – but there are obvious dangers in introducing too much flexibility.

The first case is where the enrichment was the result of an invalid juridical act and the purpose of the invalidating rule would be frustrated if full redress were required. For example, a contract by a minor may be invalid. To require the minor to make full redress would frustrate the policy of protecting minors from their own inexperience. Other examples can be found in the area of illegal or immoral contracts.

The second case is where the enriched person has, in good faith,[56] actively changed position in reliance on the enrichment, or has passively suffered a diminution in the enrichment due to circumstances beyond his or her control. For example, a person who has received an erroneous credit to a bank account and who has not noticed the error may have incurred certain extra and irrecoverable expenditures in rea-

---

55 This is covered by draft Article 3: 103(2).

56 A person who receives funds, knowing they are not due, and passes them on to someone else would not be in good faith and could not rely on this rule. The same result would be reached as in the Dutch case of *Sociale Verzekeringsbank* v *Stichting St. Jansgeleen*, HR 31 March 1978, NJ 1978,363.

sonable reliance on the enrichment, or a person who has received an erroneous transfer of property may have suffered uninsured damage to the property.

The third case is where the conduct of the claimant has been such that it would be unreasonable or inequitable to require full redress. For example, the claimant may have lured the enriched person into an enrichment situation for the claimant's own advantage or may have wrongfully forced the enriched person into an enrichment situation.[57]

8   Other Matters

8.1   Third Party Enriched or Disadvantaged as a Result of Void Contract

Suppose that a painter does work on a property under a contract with the tenant. Can the painter, instead of claiming payment from the tenant under the contract, choose to claim payment from the owner of the property on the basis of unjustified enrichment? It is clear that this is not possible if the contract is valid. Even if the owner can be regarded as enriched, the rule providing that an enrichment is not unjustified if it results from the performance of a valid contract would prevent the painter from recovering. What happens, however, if the contract turns out to be void or is avoided with retrospective effect? Could the painter then claim from the landlord? The principle accepted by the Study Group is that the nullity of the contract should make no difference. The disadvantaged party's claim should still be against the other party to the apparent contract and not against the third party. It is proposed to have a special rule to enable this result to be achieved. Similar problems can arise the other way round when a third party is disadvantaged as a result of a void contract between two other parties. For example, something done under a void contract between two parties, one of whom is acting as agent for an undisclosed principal, may cause a disadvantage to the principal. The special rule will cover that situation too. The claim for reversal of the enrichment will be the agent's,[58] just as any claim for counter-performance under the contract would have been, and the principal will have a claim against the agent. It is for consideration whether rights under the law on unjustified enrichment should be exercisable by or against the third party in any case where equivalent contractual rights would have been so exercisable had the contract been valid.[59]

8.2   Transferred Enrichment

Although there are good reasons for not having a general obligation to redress indirect enrichments – such as enrichments arising from the performance of a contract between two other people – there is one situation in which an obligation based on indirect enrichment might be regarded as appropriate. That is where the first enriched

---

57 See Mazeaud (1969), para. 700.
58 And the disadvantage would have to be deemed to be suffered by the agent.
59 As may happen under e.g. PECL Art. 3:302 or 3:303.

person has transferred the benefit of the enrichment to another person who takes gratuitously or in bad faith.

8.3 Remedies and Procedure

Remedies and procedures should presumably be left, in general, to other laws. Some specific matters might, however, be dealt with in the rules on unjustified enrichment. It might be useful, for example, to allow a direct action by a true creditor against a usurping creditor who had wrongly received payments from many debtors of the true creditor. This would be more efficient than reversing the many individual payments made in error. It might also be useful to make it clear one way or the other whether claims for unjustified enrichment are to be regarded as subsidiary to other claims.[60]

9   Conclusion

There are many different ways in which provisions on unjustified enrichment could be drafted. A good start has been made on one possible way by the Study Group on a European Civil Code. Personally, I would have preferred an "economic" or "net worth" approach to the question of enrichment and an "unjustified unless" or "absence of legal basis" approach to the question of absence of justification, but there are advantages and disadvantages in all approaches and the decisions of the Study Group are defensible and understandable. The challenge now is to ensure that these decisions, and the decisions still to be made on such questions as redress and defences, are translated into a text which achieves good results without being too complicated and impenetrable.

BIBLIOGRAPHY: J. Beatson, *The Use and Abuse of Unjust Enrichment* (1991); P. Birks, *An Introduction to the Law of Restitution* (rev'd edn., 1989) *Unjust Enrichment* (2003); E. von Caemmerer, Problèmes Fondamentaux de l'Enrichissement sans Cause, 18 Revue Internationale de Droit Comparé (1966), pp. 573-592; E.M. Clive, *Draft Rules on Unjustified Enrichment and Commentary* (published by the Scottish Law Commission as an Appendix to its Discussion Paper No. 99 on Judicial Abolition of the Error of Law Rule and its Aftermath, 1996); B. Dickson, The Law of Restitution in the Federal Republic of Germany: a Comparison with English Law, 36 International and Comparative Law Quarterly (1987), 751-787; P. Gallo, Unjust Enrichment: A Comparative Analysis, 40 American Journal of Comparative Law (1992), 431-465; Goff (Lord) and G. Jones, *The Law of Restitution*, (6th edn. 2002); F. Goré, *L'Enrichissement aux Dépens d' Autrui*, (1949); M. Malaurie, *Les Restitutions en Droit Civil*, (1991); H. L. and J. Mazeaud, *Leçons de Droit Civil* (4th edn 1969) Tome 2(1) (*Obligations*); S. Meier and R. Zimmermann, Judicial Development of the Law, *error iuris* and the Law of Unjustified Enrichment, 115 Law Quarterly Review 556; F.L. Schäfer, *Das Bereicherungsrecht in Europa* (2001): P. Schlechtriem, *Restitution und Bereicherungsrecht in Europa* (Vol. I, 2000; vol. II, 2001). P. Schlechtriem, C. Coen and R. Hornung, Restitution and Unjust En-

---

60   National laws differ greatly on this point. Many take the view that a remedy based on unjustified enrichment is not available if another legal remedy is available, but this can be criticised. See Schrage (1994), pp. 219-221.

richment in Europe, 9 European Review of Private Law (2001) 377-415; E. Schrage, Restitution in the new Dutch Civil Code, 2 Restitution Law Review (1994), pp. 208-221; W. J. Stewart, *Restitution* (1992); D. Visser, Responsibility to Return Lost Enrichment, 1992 *Acta Juridica*, 175-187; N. R. Whitty, Indirect Enrichment in Scots Law, 1994 Juridical Review, pp. 200-229, 239-282; R. Zimmermann, A road through the enrichment-forest? Experiences with a general enrichment action, 18 Comparative and International Law Journal of Southern Africa (1985), pp. 1-20; Unjustified Enrichment: the Modern Civilian Approach, 15 Oxford Journal of Legal Studies (1995), pp. 403-429; R. Zimmermann and J. du Plessis, Basic Features of the German Law of Unjustified Enrichment, 2 Restitution Law Review (1994), pp. 14-43; K. Zweigert and H. Kötz, Introduction to Comparative Law (3rd rev'd edn., translated by T. Weir, 1998), Vol. II.

E – Tort

CHAPTER 34

The General Conditions of Unlawfulness

David Howarth*

1   Introduction

Several European legal systems believe that it is a necessary condition of extra-contractual civil liability that the defendant's act was 'unlawful'. The most prominent example is the German *Bürgerliches Gesetzbuch*, with its requirement that the defendant's act be *widerrechtlich* (§823 I) or, if intentional and not otherwise prohibited, *gegen die guten Sitten* (§826). In England the position is similar, at least according to the conventional view that defendants must be found to have been subject to a 'duty of care', that is, they can only be liable if they are subject to a legal duty to be careful which they have breached. In such systems, the question of lawfulness is often connected with the question of the kinds of interest the law protects against interference, but it is also connected with the questions of liability for omissions, immunities from suit and the liability of public authorities.[1]

But not all European legal systems believe that it is necessary to have a separate requirement of unlawfulness. The best example is the French Civil Code, whose general clauses on delictual liability rely exclusively on the concepts of fault, control, causation and damage.[2] The French system has to deal with the same problems as the others, for example the recoverability of pure economic loss and compensation for psychiatric harm, but manages to do so without straying beyond its own vocabulary. It can deal with issues of protected interests, for example, by using its category of 'damage' and the omissions issue under the heading of 'causation'.

But there is also an important difference between English law and German law, at least as English law has developed over the last 25 years. In German law the main method for limiting liability is that conduct is not said to be unlawful unless it violates one of a set of specified protected interests listed in the code. In English law the courts have a developed a much broader method of saying that there should be no duty of care unless it is 'just, fair and reasonable' that there should be such a duty. The German method leads to pressure to extend liability by widening the meaning of the listed interests or by adding examples to the final clause that recognises 'other interests'. The English method, in contrast, has allowed the courts to develop an ex-

---

*   Lecturer, Department of Land Economy; Fellow, Clare College, Cambridge.

1   Portuguese, Greek and, by interpretation, Italian law have similar structures to English and German law. See see C. von Bar, (1998) pp. 27-37. Dutch law also requires an 'unlawful act' for liability in tort (art. 6:162 BW), but defines such an act as 'the violation of a right or an act or omission violating a statutory duty or an unwritten rule of law pertaining to proper social conduct' (except where justified) (art. 6:162 II BW), a definition so wide that it seems to provide for little control.

2   Some Scandinavian systems also seem to have quite general liability, e.g. the Finnish SKL chap. 2, § 1, s. 1 and the Swedish SKL chap. 2, § 1 (the Danish code, however, mentions 'unlawfulness'). Von Bar, however, sees parallels with the German conceptual scheme in the elaboration of these provisions (C. von Bar (1998) p. 270), although the parallel seems somewhat tenuous.

traordinary creative negativity, for it means that there is no logical end to the reasons – economic, constitutional or pragmatic – that can be given for denying liability.

The purpose of this chapter is primarily to discuss whether it is necessary for a modern European system of civil responsibility to use a separate concept of unlawfulness. It proposes what amounts to a compromise between the English and French approaches, but it is conscious of the many pitfalls of codification, and warns against an over-ambitious view of what codification can achieve. It looks first at three causes for scepticism about the project of European codification, and on the basis of that discussion, turns to the main question, namely to establish what is the best approach to the unlawfulness issue.[3]

2 Codification, Harmonisation and Diversity

Questions have been raised about the legal basis of the harmonisation of European private law, especially in the light of the *Tobacco Advertising* case.[4] These doubts are not resolved in any obvious way by the draft of the proposed European Constitution.[5] Indeed, the new Constitution makes it clear that even where harmonisation is permissible, it is subject to the principles of subsidiarity and proportionality.[6] Therefore, even if a legal power conferred on the EU can be found for a harmonising measure such as a European Civil Code, the question arises whether the harmonisation of tort law would conform to the principle of subsidiarity[7] and the principle of proportionality.[8]

There are, admittedly, strong arguments for the harmonisation of contract law, especially commercial contracts. Harmonisation of contract law might arguably enhance trade within the EU because it would eliminate the need for traders to discover the consequences of particular sorts of deal in different parts of the Union. It would also eliminate negotiation and disputes about which national law is to govern the contract.[9]

---

3   Another preliminary point that might be taken up at this stage is whether there ought to be any tort liability at all – see Atiyah (1997). For the author's (negative) view of Atiyah's radical proposal to abolish tort law actions for personal injury, see D. Howarth, 'Towards a Guilt-Free Society', *Times Literary Supplement* 5 June 1998, pp. 11-12 and 'Three Forms of Responsibility: On the Relationship Between Tort Law and the Welfare State' [2001] *Cambridge Law Journal* 553-580.

4   Case C-376/98, *Germany* v. *Parliament and Council*, 2000 E.C.R. I-8419. See S. Weatherill (2001).

5   Draft Treaty for establishing a Constitution for Europe (18 July 2003), arts III-64 and III-65 seem to be fundamentally the same as ex-articles 94 and 95.

6   Draft Treaty for establishing a Constitution for Europe art. 1-9(iii)

7   Subsidiarity will mean 'the Union shall act only if and insofar as the objectives of the intended action cannot be sufficiently achieved by the Member States, either at central level or at regional and local level, but can rather, by reason of the scale or effects of the proposed action, be better achieved at Union level' (art 1-9(iii)).

8   Proportionality will mean that 'the scope and form of Union action shall not exceed what is necessary to achieve the objectives of the Constitution' (art 1-9(iii)).

9   For a summary of the arguments, see European Commission, *A More Coherent European Contract Law: An Action Plan* (2003/C 63/01), summarising responses to its green paper *Communication From The Commission To The Council And The European Parliament On European Contract Law* (COM(2001) 398).

But there is a question mark over whether there are equivalent arguments about tort liability, especially if one is attempting to make a case for the harmonisation of the whole of tort law, rather than just of some sub-categories of liability. One can plausibly argue that harmonisation of products liability enhances intra-EU trade by reducing the uncertainties of trading in other European jurisdictions. One can even argue that if road traffic accident law were to be harmonised, it would reduce uncertainty for the road haulage industry – although such an argument does not seem to justify harmonisation beyond accidents in which one party is a commercial operator.[10] There is perhaps also an argument for harmonisation of professional liability for certain sorts of internationally tradable service, such as accountancy, especially if there is harmonisation in other aspects of the regulation of those particular professions. But it is difficult to see what the benefit would be in bringing together the law on, for example, the liability of householders for accidents that occur on their property. It seems unlikely that cross-border purchases of property would be much affected by such a harmonisation. Similarly, there seems little benefit in harmonising liability for professions whose services are little traded across different jurisdictions, health services for example, especially where the structure of state support for the provision of those services is different – direct state provision of services as against insurance-based provision, for example. And the liability of the public authorities themselves seems so enmeshed in different approaches to public law, and even constitutional law, that harmonisation of this single question in isolation would likely produce widely different practical results in different jurisdictions

One argument in favour of harmonisation is that liability rules can seriously affect the viability of investment projects, and so harmonisation would enhance the free movement of capital. Liability rules about environmental damage, for example, might greatly affect the rate of return on investments in certain industries. Indeed arguments of this sort have already been used to justify an EU-wide approach to environmental liability.

Another argument is that all harmonisation of liability rules helps to create a single market in insurance, since insurance companies would not need specialised knowledge of the legal systems of different countries and would find it less risky to offer liability insurance across borders.

There is also an argument from the free movement of persons and the free establishment of enterprises. Common liability regimes could play a role in encouraging the free movement of professionals by reducing one source of uncertainty about the costs of practice in another country. It would also play a role in encouraging the free movement of lawyers. The less the difference in law between jurisdictions, the lower the barriers to entry for lawyers from those jurisdictions.

Another argument is that there is a legal technical reason for harmonisation, namely that the line between contractual and extra-contractual liability is not easy to draw. Certain rules, for example those about the effects of contracts on third parties and those about giving misinformation in the course of contractual negotiations, can be classified either way. If contract law is harmonised, a number of standard issues

---

10 Moreover, whether, on environmental grounds, the road haulage industry is one which policy-makers would want to help is an important separate question.

which in some systems count as extra-contractual may end up as harmonised anyway. For example, because of the way the National Health Service works, and because English law allows third parties to sue in contract only in very limited circumstances,[11] medical accident cases in England count as extra-contractual, as cases in tort. But if a harmonisation of contract law were to include the issue of the rights of third parties and to take a more expansive view of the issue than English law does at present, the result might be that some medical cases in England would thenceforth count as contractual and therefore would have been harmonised. Would it make sense in those circumstances for other medical cases not to be the subject of harmonised law? More generally, service providers are often potentially liable both in contract and in tort, on the basis of a negligence rule. Systems of law usually strive to keep the concept of negligence applicable in contract the same as that applicable in tort, so that as little as possible should turn on the legal technicalities of classification. If contract harmonisation were to include a particular way of thinking about negligence, anomalies would occur if the concept of negligence applied by the non-harmonised national tort law were different.[12]

Finally, there are political arguments in favour of a Code, arguments which draw their strength from support for the process of European unification. First, it might be claimed that a harmonised and complete civil code is a necessary condition of the formation of a European citizenship. The argument would be that, on the analogy of the French code, citizenship requires that citizens have the same rights and responsibilities, and that any variation in these rights and responsibilities undermines the essential unity of the state on which equal citizenship has to be based. Secondly, there is the argument that a European Code would divert the attention of European lawyers, and perhaps other Europeans, away from the legal systems of other parts of the world, and in particular of the United States of America, and onto Europe itself. The Code is a way of driving European lawyers together and driving them away from the United States.

But the validity of these arguments is not universally accepted. On the investment argument, for example, evidence is lacking that doctrinal differences in tort law cause very much difference in investment levels themselves, especially given the possibility of much bigger differences of approach to the enforcement of rights.[13]

As for the legal technical argument, the question for policy makers in each case is whether the degree of anomaly which results from cases crossing the contract-tort divide is sufficient to justify what otherwise would be a violation of the principle of subsidiarity. For many policy-makers, the cure would seem worse than the disease, or, more technically, it would violate the principle of proportionality. In addition, be-

---

11 Contracts (Rights of Third Parties) Act 1999.
12 Cf. O. Lando and C. von Bar *Communication on European Contract Law: Joint Response of the Commission on European Contract Law and the Study Group on a European Civil Code* (2002) para 38 (http: //europa.eu.int/comm/consumers/cons_int/safe_shop/fair_bus_pract/cont_law/comments/5.23.pdf)
13 The difference in litigation rates across different European countries has often been noted. See e.g. E. Blankenburg in D. Nelken (1997), S. Deakin, C. Lane, and F. Wilkinson, Contract Law, Trust Relations, and Incentives for Co-operation: A Comparative Study, in S. Deakin and J. Michie, *Contracts, Co-operation, and Competition: Studies in Economics, Management, and Law* (1998; Oxford University Press, Oxford).

hind the doctrinal difference between tort and contract there lies a practical, economic difference, that what matters is not whether the rule itself counts as contractual or extra-contractual but whether it is easy for the parties to contract around it. The higher the transactions costs of agreeing a rule different from the one used by the court, the more likely it is that the court's rule will be the rule that governs the parties' behaviour. 'Tort' situations are often ones in which such transactions costs are high (road accidents are the clearest example), so that a mistake in tort law is likely to have a much greater and more lasting effect than a mistake in contract law. Harmonised tort law has greater risks than harmonised contract law.

More generally, uniformity itself has great costs. It stifles innovation and prevents adaptation to local conditions. The US Supreme Court speaks often of the individual states as being 'laboratories' for testing different rules and interpretations of rules.[14] Europe is learning, as the enshrinement of subsidiarity in the draft Constitution illustrates, that uniformity is often the enemy of truth and that it can only be justified if its benefits are overwhelming and it is the only way to achieve an important end. These conditions do not seem obviously to be present in the case of extra-contractual civil liability.

A single market in professional services and insurance, though desirable, is not in itself sufficient reason to destroy diversity of opinion on some of the most difficult questions legal systems have to face. And it is not necessary in any case to have complete uniformity for barriers to entry to be lowered or to create pan-European markets in those services. It is sufficient that the differences are understandable and limited. Insurance, for example, even within one country, already has to cope with the uncertainty created by the possibility that the law might change over time. And the example of the United States, where tort law, and much else in the law, varies from state to state, shows that it is not necessary to have complete uniformity before lawyers find it practicable to take jobs in new jurisdictions. The question is merely one of degree – what does it cost, including how long does it take, for a lawyer to be trained sufficiently to understand the different system? In the US it typically takes only months for a lawyer to qualify for practice in a new state.

The USA also provides a counter-example to those who say that a common private law code is essential to build a common European citizenship. Private law varies from state to state in the USA and yet there is no doubt that Americans feel a sense of common citizenship. American citizenship is built on common participation in the political system, on the institutions that arise out of public law and on the practices – election campaigns, for example – which have grown up around them. Private law has played little part in American citizenship. Even the Supreme Court of the United States, in many ways a key institution in Americans' sense of themselves, has very little private law business. The individual states are sovereign in the substance of private law and subject to federal control only if the exercise of that sovereignty

---

14 *New State Ice Co.* v. *Liebmann* (1932) 285 US 262, 311. See also *Cruzan v. Director, Missouri Dept. of Health* (1990) 497 US 261, 292 (O'Connor J. concurring). See also G. Schwartz, Considering the Federal Role in American Tort Law (1996) 38 *Arizona Law Review* p. 917 (arguing for state-to-state variation in most tort law, but for uniformity in products liability) and H. Perlman, Products Liability Reform in Congress: An Issue of Federalism (1987) 48 *Ohio State Law Journal* p. 503 (arguing for state-to-state variation even in products liability).

breaches the federal constitution.[15] In addition, the draft European constitution makes it clear that European citizenship is supplementary to national citizenships, not a replacement of them.[16] Europe is not taking the route of the French republican tradition, a tradition that demands uniformity as the price of citizenship.

The argument from attention, however, that the Code is a way of driving European lawyers together and to thinking more about one another than they think about the rest of the world, is a plausible argument for those who accept the premise that European integration is itself a desirable political end. One can expect, however, those who oppose European integration to oppose the Code for precisely the same reason.

3   Codification and Judicial Reason

English lawyers are notoriously suspicious of codification and that suspicion increases when the codification proposed concerns concepts, such as unlawfulness, at a high level of abstraction.[17] Many of these suspicions are in no way affected by assurances, which may or may not be true and which this chapter takes up below, that there is a large degree of agreement among European legal systems about what the results of particular cases should be. The suspicions spring from a conception of the view of the relationship between the courts and the rest of the state. These are concerns about the dynamics of law, not about comparative statics.

The most obvious criticism English lawyers make against codification is that it stifles the law and makes more difficult the task of reacting to new circumstances and new cases. In practice, of course, codification presents no more or less difficulty in adapting the law to new circumstances than do the English rules of precedent. But one might sympathise with the English attitude if codification were to be combined with rigid rules of precedent. English lawyers would indeed be heavily constrained and their imaginative powers stretched to breaking point if they had to deal not only with an authoritative text but also with a strict doctrine of *stare decisis* about what that text meant.

Part of the problem has been the strength of the literalist tradition of statutory interpretation in England. If the words of a statute are 'in themselves precise and unambiguous', judges have claimed that there is no need for 'interpretation' beyond the 'natural and ordinary meaning' of the words.[18] Many, and perhaps all, legal systems use the 'ordinary meaning' method to some degree,[19] but it is a question of balance. Until recently, the English approach tended to treat the purpose of the statute as a secondary consideration, to be resorted to only where there was ambiguity. There are

---

15 Or, technically, if it breaches a (constitutionally valid) federal statute where a federal statute has ousted state law. The federal courts also obtain some private law business through the 'diversity' route, but they have no power to oblige the state courts to accept their view of state law. Their job is merely to predict what the highest state court would say about the case. For a non-technical summary, see D. Sloviter, A Federal Judge Views Diversity Jurisdiction through the Lens of Federalism, (1992) 78 *Virginia Law Review* p. 1671.

16 Draft Treaty establishing a Constitution for Europe art. I-8.

17 See e.g. B. Markesinis' chapter in the first edition of this book.

18 Tindal C.J. in the *Sussex Peerage Case* (1884) 11 Cl. & Fin. 85 at 143

19 See generally MacCormick and Summers (1991)

signs, however, that the literalist, non-purposive tradition is dying, a process which contact with other European legal cultures has at least accelerated.[20] Purposive interpretation of statutes, as well as using all information currently available at the time of the application of the statute, regardless of what was available at the time the statute was passed, are now established principles of English statutory interpretation.[21]

The problem of binding precedent, however, deserves further attention. English lawyers have a strong interest in retaining their rules of precedent. It is what they are trained in and what they understand. The ability to understand precedents, to make them dance to the tune of one's client's interest or to justify the decision one has decided to reach, is highly prized. Even the more mundane skill of predicting what a dull judge will do with a dull case is often a matter of reading the case law in its most obvious and least subtle sense. English lawyers do not want to give up one of their most precious assets. Even if codification combined with the rules of precedent did not make the law intolerably inflexible, the rules of precedent themselves are psychologically and economically important for English lawyers and codification is thus perceived as a threat.[22]

There may not be a way around the problem of the economic interest of common lawyers in their way of thought. But there is a way reducing the apparent distance between their way of thinking and other ways of thinking about law. One must understand why precedent is important. Pierre Legrand goes wrong in his characterisation of the common law as free decision, and of common law decisions as lacking *toute dimension canonique*.[23] This is a myth originating in the work of the American Legal Realists, and especially in a superficial reading of the work of Karl Llewellyn.[24] It is true that the reasons for the decisions of the common law courts are binding only 'on their own facts', that is, only in cases where the facts are the same. It is also true that a judge who really wanted to could always re-cast the facts of the case at hand so that they appear different from the facts of the case cited to the court as a binding precedent. But the doctrine of precedent goes deeper than mere verbal manipulations. The point of the doctrine is that there is a fundamental principle of justice that like cases should be treated alike. The question whether the case at hand is a 'like case' is therefore a serious one, requiring mature reflection, not just a verbal game to played according to the whim of the judge. It is undoubtedly possible for a judge to distinguish a case on a trivial and irrelevant point – the parties' physical appearance, for example, or the time of year of the hearing – but the judge would be wrong to do so, would be reversed on appeal and would be unlikely to be promoted. Legrand is right

---

20 *R (on the application of Quintavalle) v. Secretary of State for Health* [2003] UKHL 13 especially per Lord Steyn at para. 21.

21 *R (on the application of Quintavalle) v. Secretary of State for Health* [2003] UKHL 13.

22 Cf the response of the Law Society of England and Wales, as reported in *A More Coherent European Contract Law: An Action Plan* (2003/C 63/01, to the concept of a European Civil Code – "In particular, English legal practitioners fear that the global significance of English common law would suffer. To them it would be disproportionate, in the very least, to impose a mandatory European contract law on Member States. One contributor claims that a mandatory scheme would risk undermining the existing 'export' of English common law, which provides contracting parties worldwide with greater legal certainty than do legal systems in the civil law tradition."

23 Legrand (1996) at p. 786

24 E.g. *The Common Law Tradition* (1960; Little, Brown, Boston).

that English judges are fond of 'common sense' and dislike 'strict logic', but they can also find themselves deciding a case 'with regret' when there is no honest way of avoiding the conclusion that, if like cases are to be treated alike, the judge must find for the party the judge personally thinks ought to lose.[25]

But even in English law, the principle of treating like cases alike is only one principle of justice among many. It can be overridden if the reasons for changing a rule are overwhelming. The House of Lords has since 1966 accepted that it is not bound by its own previous decisions. It may depart from them if new information has come to light, including information about the effects of the previous decision, or new arguments have been developed not taken into account by the court deciding the original case.[26] Below the level of the House of Lords, the doctrine is more relaxed than often appreciated. Only the Court of Appeal technically binds itself. One High Court judge does not bind another High Court judge. Treating like cases alike is an important conception of justice in the common law but it is not the only one and it is certainly not constitutive of the common law.

The question is whether other European legal systems see the principle of treating like cases alike in a way so very different from English law. Formally, there might be some distance between systems. French law notoriously denies judges the power to make law,[27] although leading judges have called for the abrogation of the rule against regulatory decisions, for the sake of reducing the case load of the highest courts and increasing the clarity of the case law.[28] It also refuses to allow failure to follow previous judicial decisions to count as a ground for appeal.[29] But the practical position is very different. In the higher courts the judges are not given to great changes and give weight to the general tendency of the cases.[30] Judges in lower courts who decide cases contrary to the tendency of the higher courts know that in all probability they are wasting both their time and the time of the parties.[31] Past cases are often cited, including their specific facts, by counsel in argument both orally and in writing.[32]

---

25 A classic example is the judgment of Diplock L.J. in *Pook* v. *Owen* [1968] 1 All E.R. 261, [1968] 2 W.L.R. 691, disagreeing with the free decision approach of Lord Denning M.R. Sometimes all the judges in a case express their 'regret' about the decision they come to – see e.g. *R.* v. *Royal Borough of Kensington and Chelsea ex parte Casey* (Court of Appeal 4 October 1994), in which the words of Leggatt L.J. are particularly telling for those who confuse the common law judge with the khadi: 'No-one reading these papers can fail to feel compassion for Miss Casey's predicament but, within the constraints to which the Borough is subject, there is, in my judgment, no prospect that they failed to fulfil their duty ... Accordingly, though with regret, I would dismiss the application'. See also the speech of Lord Lloyd of Berwick in the titanic case *Westdeutsche Landesbank Girozentrale* v. *Islington London Borough Council* [1996] A.C. 417.

26 For a perhaps extreme example of overruling, see *R* v. *Howe* [1987] AC 417. For a more traditional view, a refusal to overrule even when the majority of the court thought the previous decision to be wrong, see the somewhat confusing *R.* v. *Kansal (no. 2)* [2001] UKHL 62.

27 Code civil art. 5.

28 J. Bel, Le Bicentaire de la Révolution: retour aux sources pour la Cour de Cassation D. 1989 Chron. 105.

29 E.g. most recently, *Le Collinet* v. *Compagnie d'assurances Rhin et Moselle* (2000) D. 2000, 593.

30 Cf. P. Matter (procureur general) addressing the Chambres reunites in the celebrated *Jand'heur* case (Cass. Ch. Réunies 12 Feb 1930, D.1930.I.57).

31 See F. Terré, (2003) p. 283.

32 See E. Steiner (2002) p. 82.

Formally, *la jurisprudence* is not a source of law, but it is *une autorité priviligiée*.[33] The reality, according to some writers is that *'la jurisprudence est une source du droit, mais il ne faut pas le dire'*.[34] In 1979 Tunc said that the decisions of the highest French courts did not have the precedential value of equivalent English decisions, but they did have at the precedential value of American decisions.[35] And 1975 was before the occurrence of all but one of the cases in which the House of Lords has invoked its 1966 power to overrule itself.

Any European Code or European Restatement which included explicitly a general clause that the principles to be followed in interpreting and applying its substantive rules include that like cases should be treated alike and that rules should be interpreted in the light of their purposes and using all current information would do little violence to practice either side of the Channel. English lawyers would still have their case law, but by making the basis of precedent more explicit, linking it to a specific purpose alongside other purposes, there would be less danger of excessive rigidity.

But one can see the question of the role of case law as merely a special case of the second and more important English argument against codification that flows from differing conceptions of legal dynamics. This is the argument that codification leads to a reduction in the degree to which courts discuss the law openly, and thus to a reduction in its rationality.[36] Whatever French courts do with case law, they do not discuss it at the length indulged in by their English counterparts.

English lawyers coming across French and Italian decisions immediately remark on the sparseness of their reasoning. The facts are presented baldly and without comment on their reliability. The Code is cited and quoted without discussion of previous interpretations of the relevant articles. A single apparently unchallengeable interpretation of the Code is made (or sometimes merely implied) and the result announced. Even the more expository style of the German courts has little of the appearance of a debate between opposing points of view, an impression confirmed by the lack of dissenting judgments at least outside the Constitutional Court. If one questions the lack of debate and the lack of any admission of uncertainty in the judgments of these courts, even when the courts are radically changing their view of the question at hand, the usual reply is that the job of the courts is to interpret the will of the legislator, as expressed in the Code, not to debate the merits of different approaches. The English lawyer finds this incomprehensible. It is inherent in the common law view of the legal world that the law is a matter of dispute, and that the court's job is to decide which of the parties has the better view, arguing if possible from previous decisions, but if not, from what would be the best rule. As far as the common law is concerned, there is no relevant 'legislator', since the whole point of the common law is that, although it can be affected by statutes, it is not enacted. There is no legislator's will to find, and the process of deciding what the law is cannot simply be an exercise in political obedience.

The response of the non-common lawyer to the mystery of unenacted law is either that it must be a version of 'custom' (which it is not) or that there must be something

---

33 J. Carbonnier, *Droit Civil* vol 1 (1988; PUF Paris) § 144.
34 P. Jestaz, La Jurisprudence, ombre portée du contentieux, D. 1989 Chron 149.
35 La méthode du droit civil: analyse des conceptions françaises, Rev. int. dr. comp. 1975 p. 817.
36 Cf. Rudden (1974).

profoundly undemocratic in the common law tradition. If courts are not applying the law as decided by a democratic legislature, what is the source of their authority? In the conventional non-common law view, pace Gény, courts are interpreters, not legislators.[37] In contrast, common lawyers tend to think of their non-enacted techniques and methods of interpretation as bulwarks of freedom against the incursions of a capricious state.[38] The common lawyer, in turn, suspects that there is something dishonest about the judgments of courts in codified countries. Legal interpretation necessarily involves making choices, but, except for courts applying codes derived from the Swiss code[39] with its explicit authorisation of judges to act as legislators if necessary, the form of these courts' judgments gives the impression that no conscious choice is taking place.[40] The problem is only made more acute when the common lawyer learns that oral and written argument in these systems is far more relaxed and expansive than the judgments themselves. There appears to be an uneasy gap between argument and decision.

The laconic nature of court judgments in the French and other codified civil law jurisdictions is often explained by the prohibition contained in many codes against the practice of refusing to decide a case on the ground that the code does not cover the case – in other words the doctrine of comprehensiveness of the Code.[41] But by itself such an explanation is incomplete. One might accept that the Code has no gaps but also allow explicit judicial debate about what it means in novel or difficult cases. Why is such debate excluded? One distinct possibility is that the real driver is the doctrine of collegiality, the prohibition on explicit dissent, for it is often the case that judges will agree on the result of a case more readily than they can agree on the reasons for the result, so that the only way to produce a judgment on which they can all agree is to keep it as short as possible. But that in turn raises the question of what the doctrine of collegiality is meant to achieve? The point, it seems, is to maintain the impression that there is no alternative to the decision the court makes, an impression that is demonstrably false.

Another distinct possibility is that when judges explain themselves in an expansive way, they will end up making general rules, contrary to the prohibition in the Code against regulatory decisions. But when one delves deeper, it seems that the reason civil lawyers give for the rule against regulatory decisions is that such decisions might be seen to be contravening the principle of the separation of powers.[42] The trouble with that explanation is that it presupposes a specific and not altogether obviously correct conception of the doctrine of the separation of powers, the conception that the branches of government should be functionally separate and pure, largely for reasons connected with the democratic mandate of the legislative branch. Another,

---

37 Rudden, *ibid.*, Terré (2000) para. 472.
38 See Allan (1992) pp. 40-43 (Allan's view is that common law reasoning provides a form of constitutional protection, rather as one would expect from a theory of autopoiesis).
39 Art 1.2 ("A défaut d'une disposition légale applicable, le juge prononce selon le droit coutumier et, à défaut d'une coutume, selon les règles qu'il établirait s'il avait à faire acte de législateur.").
40 Rudden (1974) p. 1010 at p. 1027. See also A. Touffait and A. Tunc, Pour une motivation plus explicite des décisions de justice, notamment celles de la Cour de Cassation, (1974) *Rev. trim. dr. civ.* p. 487.
41 See art. 4 Code Civil. See e.g. Rudden (1974).
42 See E. Steiner (2002).

more pragmatic version of the separation of powers is that it is a way of checking and balancing state power.[43] The point is for the branches of government to control one another, so that power is not concentrated. On that conception, as long as the legislature can change the law as laid down by the courts, the principle is fulfilled even if the courts make law. There is no necessary link, however, between this pragmatic conception of the separation of powers and any particular distribution of those powers. In the British constitutional system, the legislature always has the last word – in the end policy trumps principle – whereas in most constitutional systems the last word lies with the procedure for the amendment of the constitution itself. But in both distributions of power, some dialogue occurs between branches of government. The main question is whether the dialogue is seen as a positive process to be developed or, as seems to be implied by the pure functionalist view of the separation of powers, as something to be denied and discouraged.

There is a connection between the more pragmatic view of the separation of powers and the common law's view of the authority of law. The authority of the common law is itself dialogic. What matters ultimately is not the formal origins of the law but the strength of its arguments from principle. There can be no substantive authority in precedent for a decision about a novel case. The strength of such a decision depends on the strength of the reasons the court gives, reasons which are subsequently tested in further cases.

What common lawyers are objecting to in codification is therefore not codification itself but a non-dialogic view of law, both in the form of court judgments and in underlying constitutional doctrines. What they fear is that codification implies a reduction of dialogue because of the doctrine of comprehensiveness and the pure functionalist view of the separation of powers. But that is not the end of the debate. The question is whether it is possible to construct a version of a code which allows for greater dialogic rationality.

At this point some might object that we have bumped up against a fundamental difference between common law and civil law. The common law takes rationality to mean ratiocination. A rational decision, on this view, is one which has been actively thought about and made on the basis of plausible reasons. Civil lawyers, it is claimed, take rationality to mean systemisation. More plausibly, as Max Weber pointed out more than 80 years ago, the heart of the difference between common law and civil law is the difference between calculability and systemisation.[44] According to Weber, the needs of business and everyday life for law to be calculable, to be capable of sufficient clarity and predictability to help people work out how to act, are best met by a 'formal, empirical case law'. Systemisation, Weber claimed, meets the needs of legal theorists in universities for the purely intellectual satisfactions of coherence and might in practice work against the interests of calculability. Systematic logic can move law away from life, case law moves it back.

But, as the Swiss Code shows, it is technically possible for a code to concede that it is not comprehensive[45] and for case law to be given an explicit role in the develop-

---

43 See A. Hamilton, J. Madison and J. Jay, *The Federalist* (1788) Numbers 47-51 (2003; Cambridge University Press, Cambridge) pp. 234-255.
44 Weber (1978) p. 855.
45 Swiss Civil Code Art 1.2 – see above n. 39.

ment of the law.[46] Such a move also implies a more dialogic view of the separation of powers. Whether such a development is desirable is a question of constitutional law and politics, perhaps beyond the expertise of private lawyers, but it is certainly a view which has inherent attractions.[47]

In addition, it is not impossible for people with different views to learn from one another. The desire to systematise reflects an attachment to the value of consistency, which is itself a virtue to which the common law aspires. Requiring consistency is another way of saying that like cases should be treated alike. Indeed, common law judges are no less susceptible than judges or academics in other systems to the fault of going too far in the search for consistency and of making sense out of nonsense.[48] More importantly, the existence of writers such as Birks[49] on the one hand and Capitant[50] on the other show that learning, and thus change, are possible. The real difference between the systems comes down to one point: that if consistency can only be achieved by suppressing debate, by abstracting to a level where meaninglessness sets in, common lawyers on the whole prefer an honest exposition of the law's incoherence, with perhaps an appeal for the legislature to step in to reform the law, to an attempt to give the mere appearance of system.

One suspects that Weber identified another possible motive of some of those opposed to moves towards European legal integration: 'Wherever the two types of administration of justice and of legal training have had the opportunity to compete with one another, as for instance in Canada, the Common Law way has come out on top and has overcome the Continental alternative rather quickly'.[51] Although Pierre Legrand has been concerned to preserve the special characteristics of the common law from an alleged continental conspiracy to sweep it away,[52] perhaps the real problem will turn out to be protectionism in favour of the civil law. Law is one of the few professions, and one of the few university disciplines, that is partially exempt from global competition. Is it really English lawyers, with their trained instinct for the needs of business, who will lose from European integration?

4   Convergence, Euro-Scepticism and the Code

The other preliminary objection to European codification concerns comparative statics rather than dynamics. Codification is, inevitably, modification.[53] If a new code proposes too much modification for the legal system of any particular state, it will

---

46 Swiss Civil Code Art 1.3 ("[L'application de la loi] s'inspire des solutions consacrées par la doctrine et la jurisprudence").

47 Cf J. Habermas, *Between Facts and Norms* (1996; Polity Press, Cambridge) ch. 3.

48 See D. Howarth, Making Sense out of Nonsense, in H. Gross and R. Harrison, *Jurisprudence: Cambridge Essays* (1992; Oxford University Press, Oxford).

49 See Birks (1985) p. 2.

50 See the introduction to the first edition of *Les grands arrêts de la jurisprudence civile* (reproduced in the 10th edition (F. Terré and Y. Lequette eds.) 1994; Dalloz, Paris).

51 Weber (1978) p. 892.

52 Legrand (1996) pp. 803-804.

53 Terré (2003) p. 338.

probably be politically unacceptable. The question therefore arises, how much change can lawyers from particular systems be expected to be tolerate.

4.1 Convergence

One answer to such concerns is the so-called convergence thesis, that European legal systems are coming together in the answers they give to concrete cases, though not, perhaps, in the way they arrive at those answers. If the convergence thesis is correct, it should be possible to construct a text that at least captures that convergence and that minimises the gap between from the previous position in each Member State and the position of the text.

There are some obvious examples of convergence in civil responsibility.[54] For example, most European legal systems have adopted objective fault rules and several are working towards the American 'Learned Hand' formula for judging fault.[55] Most systems have adopted proportionate rules for contributory negligence. But there are also obvious areas of divergence. One area, discussed in detail elsewhere in this volume, is traffic accidents. Most jurisdictions have some form of strict liability for traffic accidents, but the texts vary widely, especially on the recoverability of non-economic loss. There is also disagreement about whether contributory negligence should apply.[56] In England, in even greater contrast, fault is still required, the courts having declined an opportunity in the 1950s to move to a stricter liability regime using the trespass torts.[57]

In the particular area of law on which this chapter focuses, the requirement of unlawfulness, the evidence of convergence is equivocal. At the most abstract level, there is the still the obvious difference between the Anglo-German approach and the French approach. The German and English systems have moved somewhat closer together over the last 50 years, especially with the adoption in German law of the 'duty of care' concept.[58] But French law remains adamantly opposed to what it sees as arbi-

---

54 See generally, B. Markesinis (ed.), *The Gradual Convergence* (1994; Oxford University Press, Oxford).

55 The 'Learned Hand' test for fault is that conduct should be judged to have been unreasonable if its expected benefits for all concerned were less than its expected costs for all concerned, understanding that 'costs' means the harm the conduct could cause discounted by the likelihood that it would occur. See *Conway* v. *O'Brien* (1940) 111 F.2d 611 and *US* v. *Carroll Towing* (1947) 159 F.2d 169 (though the version in the latter case is too formulaic for many tastes).

56 One should note in passing that systems such as French law which, when they apply strict liability to the defendant, largely exclude contributory negligence by the victim, are subject to criticism from an economic point of view. Strict liability, although it has some advantages, tends to reduce the incentive for owners of property to take care of it, since they know that if their property is damaged, someone else will be liable to pay for its repair or replacement. Contributory negligence doctrines can help to restore appropriate incentives to care for one's own property. If a system of strict liability for property damage lacks a contributory negligence rule, one can expect unreasonable behaviour by some property owners. See S. Shavell, *Economic Analysis of Accident Law* (1987; Harvard University Press, Cambridge, Mass.) pp. 12-13, 36-40.

57 *NCB* v. *Evans* [1951] 2 KB 861. Learner drivers are held to a near to strict standard, however – *Nettleship* v. *Weston* [1971] 2 QB 691.

58 K. Lipstein, Protected interests in the Law of Torts [1963] *Cambridge Law Journal* 85.

trary exclusions from liability, preferring to limit liability solely by using concepts such as damage, fault and causation.

As for the detailed law, a very complex picture emerges. There is some evidence of convergence on the recoverability of some forms of harm. For example, presumably because of the transnational nature of psychiatry and its underlying sciences, there is a growing consensus on the recoverability of psychiatric harm, although English and, probably, German law still maintain some restrictions on liability for psychiatric harm caused by ricochet,[59] and French law still goes much further than English or German law in compensating psychic pain which does not amount to psychiatric illness at all.[60] There is also a growing consensus in favour of the protection of dignitary rights, especially rights of privacy, and, although few countries go as far as the German courts in protecting such interests, the English courts, inspired in part by the incorporation of the European Convention on Human Rights into domestic law, have recently come around to the view that some privacy interests need to be protected in their own right.[61]

Nevertheless, there are areas in which there is little or no convergence. Take the effect of the violation of a criminal or administrative statute on civil responsibility. Superficially, there are resemblances between the various systems. For example, German, French and English law all seem to use the notion that statutes should only give rise to liability for the type of loss the statute intended to prevent and only if the statute meant to protect the claimant.[62] But not only have such theories come in for heavy criticism in at least two of those jurisdictions,[63] the similarity they appear to produce pales into insignificance when compared with the differences in the various systems' underlying theory about the relationship between criminal infractions and fault-based civil liability. In French law, if the defendant injures the plaintiff in the course of committing a crime, the plaintiff has a right to compensation regardless of how the case would have been resolved in the absence of the law establishing the crime.[64] In Germany, the claimant has to show fault as well as breach of the criminal law, so that strict liability crimes cannot create strict liability torts.[65] In England, in contrast, the courts have developed a mania for denying that statutes, especially those which create obligations on the state but also those which create crimes, have any effect whatsoever on the private law rights of the plaintiff.[66] Similar reluctance in the

---

59 See C. von Bar (2000) pp. 66 ff.
60 See e.g. G. Viney and P. Jourdain (1998) pp. 25 ff., 58 ff., 132 ff. See F. Terré, P. Simler and Y. Lequette (1999) p. 643 for a case of a person who successfully sues for the suffering caused by the loss of an animal. See C. von Bar (2000). 389 for a similar Italian case.
61 See especially *Campbell* v. *MGN Ltd* [2002] EWCACiv 1373, [2003] QB 633.
62 See B. Markesinis and H. Unberath (2002) pp. 885 ff. and R. Youngs, *Sourcebook on German Law* (1994; Cavendish, London) p. 362 for German law; Viney (1995) p. 174 for French law.
63 Viney (1995) p. 175, Howarth (1995) pp. 334-338.
64 Either as a *partie civile* who had been directly and personally injured as a result of the crime, or, in the civil courts, as a result of the principle that the penal jurisdiction has primacy over the civil. Terré, Simler and Lequette (1999), pp. 773-776. There are, of course, subtleties when one looks at the detail. Viney (1995), pp. 111-274.
65 BGB § 823 II.
66 See D. Howarth and J. O'Sullivan (2000) ch 12. For another example, see *Cullen* v. *Chief Constable of the Royal Ulster Constabulary (Northern Ireland)* [2003] UKHL 39.

field of public authority liability can sometimes be observed,[67] but the great reluctance of the English courts to allow private rights of action on the basis of statutory
rules is exceptional.[68]

Another area of divergence is liability for omissions. In English law, liability for
'nonfeasance' as opposed to 'misfeasance' is problematic. For the most part there is
no difficulty in English law with omissions that can be reconstrued as acting badly.
For example, a car driver who omits to brake can be said to have 'driven badly', and
thus to have commited a careless act. But problems arise in cases of failures to warn
about dangers and failures to rescue, including failures by governmental bodies. The
traditional doctrine is that there is no liability for failure to warn or to rescue unless
there was a pre-existing special relationship between the parties. As Lord Keith once
said, in the absence of such a relationship, such as that between family members,
there is no liability in negligence 'on the part of one who sees another about to walk
over a cliff ... and forbears to shout a warning'.[69] It is controversial whether such a
relationship can arise solely out of the defendant's occupation or social role, although
some judges are willing to set as a test whether it would be reasonable for the victim
to rely on the defendant to look after the victim's safety.[70] The underlying justification for this doctrine is largely libertarian, that the state has no business criticising
citizens for their bad characters, only for their harmful actions. But the rule has been
extended to benefit even the public rescue services, so that, remarkably, in England
the fire brigade is not liable if injury results when it fails for no good reason to attend
a fire.[71] Similarly, local authorities are not liable if they carelessly fail to exercise
their statutory powers to improve road safety,[72] although the rule does not apply
where the authority created the danger itself,[73] or, more generally, where the authority provides a service in a careless way.[74] The position is different in German and
French law.[75] In German law, although formally there is no duty to warn or to rescue,
the theory of the *Verkehrssicherungspflichten* has reached the point where one can
say that a duty to act arises not only where there was an undertaking to protect the
victim or a prior special relationship which implies such an undertaking, but also
where the defendant, no matter how innocently, had created or allowed to continue
the conditions from which the risk of harm arose. The English case *Stovin* stands in
stark contrast with a venerable German case[76] in which a local authority was held li-

---

67 See e.g. E. Deutsch, Compensation for Pure Economic Loss in German Law, in Banakas (1996) chs.
    3 and 4, pp. 66 and 82 and, for Italian law, *Curti* v. *Ciampi* Trib, Milano 6 Apr. 1982.
68 For an outline of the law across Europe on these subjects, see C. von Bar (1998) pp. 39-50.
69 *Yuen Kun Yeu* v. *AG(HK)* [1988] AC 175.
70 *Barrett* v. *Ministry of Defence* [1995] 3 All ER 87, 95.
71 *Capital and Counties plc* v. *Hampshire County Council* [1997] 2 All ER 865, [1997] 3 WLR 331.
    The fire brigade is, however, liable if it acts positively to make the situation worse. For somewhat
    unconvincing reasons, the same rule does not apply to ambulances, or, indeed, to national health
    service hospitals – *Kent* v. *Griffiths* [2000] 2 WLR 1158 [2000] 2 All ER 474.
72 *Stovin* v. *Wise* [1996] AC 923.
73 *Kane* v. *New Forest DC* [2001] 3 All ER 914.
74 E.g. *Barrett* v. *Enfield London Borough Council* [1999] 3 All ER 193 and *Phelps* v. *Hillingdon LBC*
    [2000] 4 All ER 504. For further discussion, including discussion of the point that *Stovin* is not really
    distinguishable from these cases, see D. Howarth and J. O'Sullivan (2000) pp. 114-118.
75 See J. Kortmann (2001).
76 *RG* 23 February 1903, *RGZ* 54, 53.

able to a citizen who slipped on an icy footway because of the authority's 'power of disposition' over the footway. But German law does not go as far as French law. French law, like German law, but not English law, has a criminal law statute which makes it a crime wilfully to fail to render or to obtain assistance to an endangered person when such was possible without danger to himself or others.[77] In French law, unlike German law, following the principle of the primacy of penal law, violation of this statute gives rise to civil liability.[78] More generally, although French commentators draw a distinction between *abstention dans l'action* and *abstention pure et simple*, roughly the same as the English distinction between omissions and pure omissions, the courts merely apply the test of fault without an intermediate concept of 'duty of care' or '*Verkehrssicherungspflichten*'.[79] Although many of the cases can be analysed as concerning the creation of dangers or *abstention dans l'action*,[80] and the courts are sometimes careful to use other concepts to refuse liability,[81] the widely accepted position is that liability for *abstention pure et simple* should be a matter solely of the application of the fault standard.[82]

There is also some divergence on the place of intentionality in civil liability. Some systems, notably the French, make very little use in civil responsibility of the distinction between intentional and careless fault.[83] In contrast, English and German law make much of the distinction. In both systems, intentional fault counts as fault for the purpose of ordinary civil responsibility, (§ 823 BGB in Germany and the tort of negligence in England, despite its name), but where there is intentional fault, some of the restrictions on the recoverability of various types of harm are dropped. In addition, concepts of remoteness, that is the normative aspect of causation, may be relaxed.[84] The German system, however, also includes the elusive element that the defendant's act had to be *contra bonos mores*. The overall effect is that where there is intentionality, the results achieved by the various systems are closer than where there is no intentionality, since intentionality removes restrictions on liability in some systems that do not exist in the first place in other systems.

One must also consider the complex question of pure economic loss.[85] Superfi-

---

77 Nouveau Code Pénal arts. 223-5 ff. (originally Code pénal art. 63 al. 2.).

78 Terré, Simler and Lequette (1999) p. 648, and J. Kortmann (2001).

79 Viney and Jourdain (1998) pp. 333-341. Cf. Terré, Simler and Lequette (1999) pp. 648-649.

80 E.g. Civ. 2, 6 Oct. 1960, D.60.721 in which it is said, 'En dehors de toute obligation légale ou réglementaire, l'abstention d'une mesure de prudence engage la responsabilité de son auteur lorsque le fait omis a eu pour effet de porter atteinte à la sécurité d'autrui' but which might be interpreted as a case involving the creation of a danger.

81 See Civ. 2nd, 17 Feb 1982, cited in Viney and Jourdain (1998) at p. 339, and, more generally, J. Kortmann, (2001).

82 Viney and Jourdain (1998) at pp. 338-341; H. Mazeaud, L. Mazeaud and A. Tunc, *Traité Théorique et Pratique de la Responsabilité Civile* (6th edn 1965), No. 544.

83 Viney and Jourdain (1998) pp. 545-95. Intentionality might be relevant in French law in deciding issues of what English law would call 'remoteness' – causation in the sense of responsibility – but not issues of fault. See P. Malaurie and L. Aynès (1999-2000) p. 46. Foreign writers sometimes say that the French doctrine of *abus des droits* depends on intentionality, but this is not necessarily so. See Terré, Simler and Lequette (1998) p. 663.

84 For English law see Howarth (1997). For German law see Markesinis and Unberath (2002) pp. 985-986.

85 See E. Banakas (1996), M. Bussani, V. Palmer and F. Parisi (2003).

cially, there is a serious divergence. The common law and German law start with the presumption that pure economic loss should not be recovered, whereas the French, Italian and Dutch codes apparently offer unlimited recovery. In reality, however, there is more agreement than there appears to be.[86] Both English and German law allow the recovery of 'impure' economic loss, that is economic losses such as the lost future earnings of victims of personal injury where the economic loss can be interpreted as measuring the value of an injury to an interest that the law protects. German law also compensates harm to 'an established and operating business', as does English law though often in the guise of the protection of intellectual property, confidentiality and reputation. English and German law also give much broader protection against pure economic loss when the interference was intentional. Furthermore, German law protects against pure economic loss by characteristic extensions of the law of contract to situations which would not count as contractual in other systems, for example in its *culpa in contrahendo* and third party beneficiary doctrines, achieving, for example, wide protection against the effects of negligent advice. The concept of *Liquidation des Drittschadens* also helps third parties by treating interests in contract in some circumstances as interests in property. English law has taken a number of steps in the same direction. The rule against the recoverability of pure economic loss is subject to a broad exception that such losses are recoverable where the defendant can be said to have 'assumed responsibility' for the loss.[87] The concept of 'assumption of responsibility' is still developing, but we know that it is an 'objective' concept, in the sense that the absence of a conscious taking of responsibility is not fatal. It seems that the concept is related to the idea of 'objective' consensus in contract, under which what matters is not so much what the parties thought but rather how the situation would have looked to a reasonable person in the position of the other party.[88] It replaces the 19th century position, that there is a fundamental difference between the risks taken by property owners and the risks taken by those with merely contractual rights, with distributions of risk founded on social expectations. Since the rise of the assumption of responsibility concept, cases which have frequently been taken as fixed points of the English approach, for example *Spartan Steel* v *Martin* on the 'broken cable' problem, can no longer be taken to be canonical.[89]

At the same time, the apparently generous rules of French and Italian law are often not as generous as they look.[90] In both countries, liability is restricted by requirements that the damage must be certain and directly caused by the defendant's fault.

---

86 For English and German law compared on this topic, see Markesinis and Unberath (2002) pp. 203-356.

87 *Henderson* v. *Merrett* [1995] 2 A.C. 145, [1994] 3 All E.R. 506, *White* v. *Jones* [1995] 2 A.C. 207, *Williams* v. *Natural Life Health Foods Ltd* [1998] 1 W.L.R. 830, [1998] 2 All E.R. 577.

88 D. Howarth and J. O'Sullivan (2000) pp. 225-226, and D. Howarth (2001) pp. 568-569.

89 See for doubts about the validity of *Spartan Steel*, D. Howarth and J. O'Sullivan (2000) p. 188 and D. Howarth (2001) pp. 564-565. *Spartan Steel* has not been mentioned by the House of Lords since the development of the 'assumption of responsibility' approach to pure economic loss in *Henderson*. It is now perhaps best seen as a 'loss of use' case, subject to a possible assumption of responsibility by the claimant contained in the contract for the supply of electricity.

90 See Christian Lapoyade Deschamps, La réparation du préjudice économique pur en droit français, and P.-G. Monateri, Economic Loss in Italy, in Banakas, (1996).

French cases thus produce results that would not be unfamiliar to English lawyers brought up on the 19th century orthodoxy of *Cattle* v *Stockton*,[91] which held that there was no liability for negligently causing the plaintiff's contract with a third party to become more onerous. Thus, for example, the French state unemployment insurance fund was found to have no direct case against those who cause personal injury to people who lose their jobs as a result.[92] A creditor has no claim against a defendant who kills his debtor.[93] No action lies, at least for a *partie civile* suing on the basis of a criminal statute, for loss of financial support against a defendant who injures (but does not kill) a relative of the plaintiff.[94] One should also take into account the restrictive effect of the rules of no option and *non-cumul*, under which, subject to a few exceptions, no delictual action can arise if the dispute is covered by a contract between the parties.[95] Even in Italy, the results of the cases do not reflect the liberality of the official doctrine. In the famous *Meroni* case, for example, in which the theoretical possibility was admitted that a creditor could win compensation from a defendant who wrongfully injured his debtor (in that case, a footballer employed by the plaintiff), the plaintiff in the event lost the case because of the lack of clear causation.

The overall position on convergence on the duty of care question is, therefore, that there is a similarity, perhaps even a growing similarity, between the results achieved by different European legal systems, but that large areas of dissimilarity of result still exist. The unknown, but crucial, factor is the degree to which the dissimilarities express differences of value and approach so important that they would represent insuperable barriers to further convergence. If the doctrines concerned are controversial or unpopular, there will be less objection to jettisoning them.

Let us look at the three examples where English law seems to diverge from French law: the civil consequences of the breach of criminal statutes, pure omissions and the place of intentionality. In the first example, there appears to be little problem. The English attitude to the civil consequences of breaches of criminal law is frequently criticised and its loss would be far from universally regretted.[96] The position on pure omissions is slightly different. Although the application of the idea to the organs of the state might be seen as illegitimate, the English position is deeply rooted in con-

---

91 (1875) L.R. 10 Q.B. 453.

92 Viney and Jourdain (1998) p. 138 (citing 2 Civ. 28 [avril] 1982). See now loi 5 juillet 1985 (Viney and Jourdain (1998) p. 139, G. Viney and P. Jourdain (2002) pp. 285-322. The new law, however, does not affect the position reached in the case itself – see Viney and Jourdain (2002) p. 303. English law in this situation, since a statute of 1989, is that the state is entitled to recoup out of the damages paid to the plaintiff any social security payments made to the plaintiff as a result of the accident. Effectively, the defendant subsidises the state.

93 Viney and Jourdain (1998) p. 135 (though n.b. the exception in favour of workers thrown into unemployment by the death of their employer, *ibid.* at p. 136).

94 1 Civ. 5 Mar. 1963.

95 See Terré, Simler and Lequette (1999) pp. 771-773, Malaurie and Aynès (1999-2000), pp. 519-521. Oddly, English law has abandoned its equivalent of non-cumul – *Henderson* v. *Merrett* [1995] 2 AC 145.

96 G. Williams, The Effect of Penal Legislation in the Law of Tort (1960) 23 *Modern Law Review* 233; The Law Commission, Report no. 21: *The Interpretation of Statutes* (1969; H.M.S.O., London); K. Stanton, *Breach of Statutory Duty in Tort* (1986; Sweet and Maxwell, London); R. Buckley, Liability in Tort for Breach of Statutory Duty (1984) 100 *Law Quarterly Review* 240.

ceptions of the proper scope of legal compulsion. On the other hand, recent British governments have been committed to forms of 'communitarianism' which see state guidance of the formation of character as legitimate.[97] It may be that a move to the French position on duties to rescue and warn would result in little difficulty at the political level. The place of intentionality is more complex. Some writers insist that intention to harm is an independent wrong-making factor in any conduct, a factor separate from negligence.[98] Others say that it would be possible for English law to move away from its insistence on the existence of separate 'intentional' theories of liability, as long as some adjustments were made to the state of the law on remoteness (normative causation), punitive damages and the liability of state officials.[99]

In any case, one suspects that the plausibility of finding a consensus on the basis of convergence is greater than a straightforward comparative analysis of the law might suggest. Some Member States might welcome the opportunity to rid their law of rules or results that diverge from those in the rest of Europe. The United Kingdom government's hostile reaction to the prospect of the harmonisation of private law seems largely a reflection of generalised Euro-scepticism and a preference for market solutions than a detailed evaluation of individual rules.[100] Lawyers must ask themselves whether politicians will think, when they have the text of a restatement or a code before them, that the differences between the systems are as significant as lawyers believe them to be.

4.2 Legal Culture

There is, however, another answer to the question of modification which aims at a higher level of analysis. This answer maintains that even if the rules themselves are converging, the underlying legal cultures remain very different.[101] In the absence of convergence among cultures, any similarity in the rules is likely to be accidental and short-lived.[102]

The problem with this line of argument is that although it takes genuine historical differences, it exaggerates their present-day and future effects. Although widely accepted, many of the alleged fundamental differences between European legal cultures, especially between common law and civil law traditions, are misconceived. It is not true, for example, that the common law is obsessed with the facts of particular

---

97 See J. Arthur and R. Bailey, *Schools and Community: The Communitarian Agenda in Education*, (2001; Falmer Press, London) at pp. 20-26, 47-57. See also Citizenship and Character Education in British Education Policy, http://www.ittcitized.info/Commarticles/James_Arthur.pdf

98 See e.g. J. Finnis, Intention in tort law, in D. Owen (ed.) *The Philosophical Foundations of Tort Law* (1997; Oxford University Press, Oxford).

99 See Howarth (1997).

100 See European Commission, *A More Coherent European Contract Law: An Action Plan* (2003/C 63/ 01) pp. 26, 28 and 31.

101 The term 'legal culture' is, of course, a highly contested one. See e.g. the exchange between R. Cotterrell and L. Friedman in D. Nelken (1997). Here I am referring to the characteristic styles of working of a legal profession and a judiciary, including their characteristic mental resources, rather than the attitudes of the public at large to the legal system or to any specific rules or results.

102 See Legrand (1996) and also Legrand, European Legal Systems Are Not Converging [1996] *ICLQ* p. 52

cases whereas civil law ignores facts and is only interested in abstract rules.[103] Some writers in England are dedicated to academic systemisation and elaboration and are very distrustful of using case after case as the basis for debate. When Peter Birks says that 'a mass of cases makes for unintelligible law'[104] and that 'the movement from simple to complex is more easily understood and controlled than are attempts to reason with materials whose basic structures have never been exposed or even looked for' he is not urging English lawyers to stick close to the facts of cases. On the other side of the Channel, by way of complement, there are writers who have for years been producing collections of decisions of the French courts, so that students can become familiar with legal decision-making as it applies in hard cases.[105] Admittedly, English judges tend to produce more elaborate statements of the facts than French or Italian judges, just as they produce more elaborate legal analyses. But the reasons for that elaboration are related to the tradition of open rational debate rather than to an obsession with fine distinctions of precedents. Above all, it is important to compare like with like. To compare, as Legrand does, English judges with French academic writers is not valid. French judges are not great systemisers either – for one thing the Code tells them not to be.[106] In any case, judges everywhere are wary of over-generalisation, because they know that they do not know what kind of case the future will bring.

It is also erroneous to believe, with Legrand, that whereas civil lawyers deal in subjective rights, the common law does not understand rights but only remedies and 'causes of action'. Not only do common lawyers deal everyday with rights created by statutes, for example the right not to be unfairly dismissed, many common law countries, now since 1998 including England itself, deal with the concept of human rights on a day-to-day basis. And it is also not true that when common lawyers speak of 'rights' they have in mind some inferior or popular meaning of the word, as opposed to the civil lawyer's supposedly elevated notion of the 'subjective right' as a form of state sovereignty delegated to the individual. Rather, common lawyers are often conscious that the word 'right' has a number of sharply different meanings and are prop-

---

103 Legrand says that no-one in France is taught, or is interested in the facts of cases like *Jand'heur*. But who in England is taught or knows the exact facts of much re-interpreted cases such as *Rylands* v. *Fletcher* (1866) L.R. 1 Ex. 265, (1868) L.R. 3 HL 330? Also, how many English students could say, without a moment's hesitation, which of the parties in *Donoghue* v. *Stevenson* [1932] A.C. 562 was Donoghue and which Stevenson? In England, many cases are known only for the abstract rules they establish. Legrand also says that the French case reference system, which uses the name of the court and the date rather than the parties' names, illustrates a deep cultural difference between the systems, but he himself uses the name of a party to refer to a case (*Jand'heur*) even when writing in French in a French journal!

104 Birks (1985) p. 2.

105 Capitant says the introduction to the first edition of *Les grands arrêts de la juridprudence civile* (Terré and Lequette (eds) (1994; Dalloz, Paris)): 'Mais ce n'est pas seulement en tant que source alimentaire du Droit que le juriste doit étudier la jurisprudence. Son examen présente pour lui un second et précieux avantage. Il lui permet en effet de saisir sur le vif la formulation et l'évolution des rapports juridiques. Il y voit en action la lutte des intérêts, la complexité des relations humaines, les mobiles qui déterminent les conclusions de ces rapports, les conflits qu'ils suscitent. Dans un procès, l'examen des faits qui ont provoqué le différend est aussi profitable que l'étude de la solution adoptée par les juges.'

106 Code Civil art. 5.

erly aware of the errors that can creep into legal reasoning about rights when it is unaware of these equivocations in meaning.[107] If common lawyers are less susceptible to these errors because of their more discursive style of argument, that is not a fundamental difference in culture but an opportunity for others to learn. Moreover, even if some civil lawyers think that the exposition of subjective rights is their only task, it is difficult to see how that approach fits with the reality of their codes. The French Civil Code, for example, contains rights, duties, powers, immunities and instructions to judges. The central article on delictual liability, art. 1382, is expressed in terms of a duty, as is art. 1377, the central article on restitution. And, incidentally, both articles are similar in form to that of a 'cause of action'.

There are also attempts to ground fundamental differences in legal culture in the impossibility of fully understanding another legal culture from the inside and to say that there is no convergence because of such differences. Such attempts are self-defeating. If it is impossible to understand a foreign legal culture, it must also be impossible to say whether it is so very different from one's own. More generally, it makes no sense to claim that comparison is impossible simply because one has concluded that a foreign system is foreign. To do so means that one has already done a comparison.[108]

Of course, foreign legal cultures are difficult to understand. So is one's own legal culture, which was once for all of us very strange. People cross cultural barriers and learn new cultures all the time. It is not just that people migrate from one place to another. The internal barriers of culture, across different classes for example, can be very strong. But language and personal history are no barrier to absorbing new cultures even in the law. The 'English' judges Legrand wants so much to be stuck in English political and cultural history contain a large number of foreigners, including, in recent years, Germans, Scots and Afrikaans-speaking South Africans, all of whom have both learned a new culture and have contributed to it.

Admittedly learning a new culture can be slow and painful, and it is often the case that when learning a new culture one feels less comfortable with rejecting part of it and shaping changes in it than one does with a culture in which one has been established longer. Cultures seem less controversial and more like unchanging objects of study to those who are new to them. It is also the case that one carries around much baggage from the cultures one has already acquired, so that although one might already have acquired some useful tools of analysis and understanding, existing patterns of thought can sometimes slow down the understanding of new patterns of thought. But it cannot be correct to say that only those participants in a culture who have never been tainted by another culture have a true understanding of that culture. Indeed, the opposite seems closer to the truth, that those who have nothing with which to compare their culture lack an essential element in understanding what they are doing, because they lack any notion of what else they might do.

What lies behind these somewhat exaggerated claims of the impossibility of comparison and of an apparently purist communalism, is, however, a genuine, though un-

---

107 See W.N. Hohfeld, Fundamental Legal Conceptions as Applied in Judicial Reasoning (1913) 23 *Yale Law Journal* p. 16 and (1917) 26 Yale Law Journal p. 710 (reprinted as *Fundamental Legal Conceptions* (1964; Yale University Press, New Haven).

108 Cf H.P. Glenn, Are Legal Traditions Incommensurable? (2001) 49 *Am. J. of Comp. L* 133.

doubtedly political, concern about diversity. Although legal cultures, like all cultures, constantly change, and although people constantly adapt to change, the existence of multiple centres of legal authority can be seen as a possible source of continuing diversity of legal culture. It is, of course, no guarantee of diversity, for few would claim that the legal culture of the United States is as diverse as its number of jurisdictions. The structure of US legal education and the existence of the federal legal system have a harmonising effect. But there is a fear that the imposition of common legal texts will reduce diversity in legal culture. Indeed, since those who favour a common legal text often envisage that the text will be translated into action in the same way wherever the text is authoritative, it might plausibly be claimed that harmonisation of legal culture is part of their aim.

But we should doubt whether these fears are justified. The link between common legal texts and common legal cultures is far from automatic.[109] European Union law has been the supreme law of EU Member States for decades, and yet those who wish to see the preservation of separate national legal cultures still see enough difference between those cultures to be able still to call for the preservation of those differences. The destruction of national legal cultures requires more than the creation of codes: it requires a common system of legal education, a common system of training of the judiciary and the development of common norms of judicial style. The threat, therefore, of a common text to the diversity of legal cultures is, it seems, merely this: that it provides a basis for future attempts to establish such common education and training programmes.[110]

One possibility for counteracting the potential for a common text to provide foundations for a uniform legal culture is to make it clear from the outset that, at least with regard to extra-contractual liability, there will be no unified appellate structure, so that the ultimate authority for the meaning of the text in each jurisdiction will be the highest court of that jurisdiction and not, for example, the European Court of Justice. Such a text would provide a common starting point and would facilitate the use of decisions from other jurisdictions as persuasive authority, so increasing the chances of courts making similar interpretations, but it would not bludgeon good ideas out of existence and would not require any change in local judicial styles. Uniformity could only be achieved by persuasion, and would be rare, but also impressive, when it happened. The situation would be similar to that in the United States, especially with regard to the various Restatements and even the Uniform Commercial Code, that the law differs from state to state but, because of the use of common starting points and vocabulary, the variations are largely comprehensible for those from other jurisdictions. Indeed, if European legal cultures really are as diverse as those who wish to preserve them say they are, one would expect a wide variety of interpretations simply because the common text, as a form of legal transplant, would be oper-

---

109 This, I take it, is the main conclusion arising out of the debate about legal transplants. See e.g. D. Nelken and J. Feest, *Adapting Legal Cultures*, (2001; Hart, Oxford), especially D. Nelken, Towards a Sociology of Legal Adaptation.

110 Cf. O. Lando and C. von Bar, *Communication on European Contract Law: Joint Response of the Commission on European Contract Law and the Study Group on a European Civil Code* (2002) para. 80 (http://europa.eu.int/comm/consumers/cons_int/safe_shop/fair_bus_pract/cont_law/comments/5.23.pdf) (proposing a European Legal Academy and Institute).

ating in different contexts, just as the same species of plant grows differently in different soils and climates.[111] One would also certainly expect different levels of litigation and enforcement.[112]

This position might disappoint those who seek a uniform code interpreted in a uniform way and producing uniform results, but uniformity is not a virtue in itself, especially if it stifles innovation and adaptation to different conditions. In any case, one might doubt whether any existing legal systems produce the same practical effects throughout their jurisdictions – is English contract law applied by the courts in Cambridge in the same way as it is applied in Oxford? Does Italian contract law produce the same commercial behaviour in rural Sicily and urban Turin? Dogmatic hopes are not the same as real behaviour.

Also, a common text without any attempt to impose harmonised interpretation or a common legal culture would respond proportionately to the problem of assisting the provision of legal services across boundaries and the movement of lawyers from one Member State to another. It would help foreign lawyers to identify points of difference, so reducing the time needed for re-training, but without undermining all the benefits of diversity.

4.3 Social Attitudes to the State

There is, however, a level of analysis beyond the level of legal culture on which critics such as Legrand have concentrated. More important than differences in mentality between lawyers are social attitudes in the population at large towards the relationship between society and the state, or between everyday life and the law. The problem can be illustrated by a social psychological study conducted during the 1960s which tried to find out what young people in different countries thought the function of the law was by asking them what they thought their society would be like if there was no law.[113] The study found that views differed dramatically from country to country. In particular, British young people thought that the function of law was to control people's innate selfishness, whereas German young people thought it was to give people a structure for their lives. The difference between British and German young people is stark and fundamental. On one side is the view that law's function, and by extension the function of the state, is to impress on citizens the importance of other citizens' interests. This means that the law should provide solutions to particular disputes which would be more fair and just than would ensue from the unencumbered interplay of power and wealth. It also means that the law should use solutions that take into account the interests of those who are not parties to the dispute itself. On the other side is the view that the function of the law and the state is to structure

---

111 Cf. G. Teubner, Legal Irritants: Good Faith in British Law Or How Unifying Law Ends Up in New Divergencies, (1998) 61 *Modern Law Review* 11; B. Markesinis, Why a code is not the best way to advance the cause of European legal unity, (1998) 5 *European Review of Private Law* 519; C. Harlow, Voices of Difference in a Plural Community (2002) 50 *Am. J. Comp. L.* 339 at p. 347 ff., (reinterpreting Legrand's impossibility thesis and drawing on Teubner and Markesinis).

112 See above n. 13.

113 J. Adelson and L. Beall, Adolescent Perspectives on Law and Government (1970) 4 *Law and Society Review* p. 495, at pp. 500-504.

relationships between citizens and to give them meaning. If there was no law, according to the young people who took this view, people would not know what to do or what to think. The former view sees the law as intervening in a pre-existing social life in order to counteract in-built tendencies to asociality and injustice. The latter sees law as creating social relationships, as constituting society rather than just regulating it.[114]

These two views of law reproduce themselves in two intellectual traditions in sociological jurisprudence. According to theorists from Durkheim to Niklas Luhmann, the central problem in modern societies is how to cope with increasing complexity and contingency. This view sees law as the central solution to the problem. Thus Luhmann:

> 'Law is essential as structure, because people cannot orientate themselves towards others or expect their expectations without the congruent generalisation of behavioural expectations. This structure has to be institutionalised at the level of society itself because it is only here that we can build beyond pre-conditions and create those establishments which domesticate the environment for other social systems. It therefore changes with the evolution of societal complexity.'[115]

The other view is that of scepticism about the necessity for law. It is best illustrated by the work of Stewart Macauley and his followers.[116] They are interested in the extent to which the law impinges on day-to-day activity, especially in business, They find that law is far less important in the maintenance of social relationships, including economic relationships, than the effects of reputation and the desire to deal again with the same people. The threat of losing one's reputation for fair dealing and co-operativeness is worse than the threat of having to pay compensation. Law operates only in the background, and only exceptionally. Life goes on without it. The most im-

---

114 The two views mentioned in the text are not the only possible views of law and the state. Adelson and Beall also report the views of American adolescents, who seem to hold a third, mixed, view. Like German adolescents, they made no strong distinction between the 'law' (or the state) and the 'community', although they took a more democratic view of the relationship between the two. On the other hand, more like English youths, the Americans conceived of the law as a restraint on individualism, but they took a more optimistic view of individualism than the English. In sum, these Americans were optimistic libertarians, believing that human society is naturally benign and democratic and that only minimal intervention is necessary to achieve perfect happiness. Another possible view, which one might posit on the basis of the work of, for example, Heyderbrand and Deakin, Lane and Wilkinson (see above n. 13) is that the law is an alien intervention into ordinary social life, (defined, for example, in terms of family and friends) and is therefore often conceived of as a purely coercive presence designed to operate in the interest of a ruling clique. Note that all four views correspond to a view of what the 'rule of law' (or a *Rechtstaat*) means. The first view (that of the German adolescents) implies a state constituted by law, with no power or even existence, outside the law. The second ('English') view implies that the rule of law requires that state power can be mobilised by individuals on their own behalf only by legal means, rather than by bribery, extortion or nepotism. In the third ('American') view, it means the restraint of the 'state' by the long-term consensus views of the 'community'. Under the fourth view, the rule of law is seen as a sham, as domination in disguise.

115 Luhmann (1985) p. 105.

116 See e.g. S. Macauley, Non-contractual relations in business, (1963) 28 *American Sociological Rev.* p. 55, Beale and Dugdale, Contracts between businessmen, (1975) 2 *Brit. J. Law & Society* p. 45.

portant finding of this line of research, which fits, incidentally with the findings of transactions costs economics,[117] is that that people in business do not plan every last detail of their deals, because to do so would be too costly and too aggressive. Contrary to the Durkheim-Luhmann view, some ambiguity and uncertainty is good for establishing and maintaining social relationships, and constitutes a rational response to complexity.[118]

These two views of the relationship between law and society feed into views of codification. The 'English' view implies, first, that the job of the code is provide solutions to the problems that often present themselves in court, and, secondly, that complexity should be met not with an attempt to solve every problem in advance, but with a system of decision that trusts someone to decide future cases fairly. Consistency is an element of fairness but not identical with it. All this points to an open-ended non-comprehensive view of the law. The 'German' view, in contrast, implies a comprehensive code, because otherwise people will be wandering lost, confused and unguided. In the absence of detailed law, it is feared that society will be anomic.

It is, of course, a mistake to treat these models as more than ideal-types. It is not the case that all English people accept the 'English' view of the relationship between law and society or that all German people accept the 'German' view. As with all such differences, views can change dramatically over time. As Luhmann pointed out,[119] the intimate connection between law and social structure is to some extent put at risk by the realisation that the law is a matter of political choice, that it is 'positive' – an experience the attempt to design a code itself brings to the fore. Describing a difference as 'cultural' does not make it impervious to intentional or unintentional change.

Nevertheless, these differences in attitudes fit with, and complement, other cultural traits. For example, the anthropologist Edward Hall developed a scale to describe how much communication goes on within different societies at a tacit, taken-for-granted level.[120] Hall calls 'high-context' societies in which people prefer implicit means of communication to explicit means of communication. Those in which people prefer everything to be spelled out he calls 'low context'. Very high context societies include China and Japan. The Mediterranean countries are high context, with England a middle-ranking society. The USA is relatively low-context. Germany, however, is the lowest context country of all, where there is a very strong preference for the spelling out of details – an attitude which reinforces, and perhaps is reinforced by, expectations about what the law will contain and what the role of the courts will be.

The dilemma faced by European codification is this: the 'English' solution offers

---

117 See Williamson (1985).

118 Note that both views can be found in the work of Max Weber: see Weber (1978) p. 336, where Weber says: 'Form the purely theoretical point of view, legal guarant[ee] by the state is not indispensable to any basic economic phenomenon. The protection of property, for example, can be provided by the mutual aid system of kinship groups', but he goes to say that a modern market economy requires a calculable legal system because of the decline of other forms of association. Luhmann takes the latter statement as axiomatic. Macauley's approach treats both statements as empirical.

119 Luhmann (1985) p. 160.

120 *Beyond Culture* (1976; Doubleday, New York); *Understanding Cultural Differences* (1990; Intercultural Press, Yarmouth, Maine).

by far the better answer to the problem of complexity, but Europe as a whole is probably a 'low-context' place in which spelling out solutions seems required.

It is unrealistic to imagine that answers to every legal problem can be found in advance, especially when technological and social changes are constantly producing new, previously unheard of problems. On the other hand, the fact that new problems cannot fully be anticipated should not make us retreat into silence or into making the law up as we go along. There are well-known principles for dealing with such circumstances. As Herbert Simon[121] and Oliver Williamson say,[122] people are rational but only boundedly so. As Williamson recommends, instead of attempting to answer all questions in advance, we should set up 'governance' structures, that is procedures for decision-making in which we repose our trust. We can give these structures some basic principles to take into account, and require them to subject decisions on new topics to full, rational and open discussion, but in the end the most important aspect of the structure is the procedure for deciding. This implies an 'English' solution – a code which deals with known problems but allows judges to develop new solutions to new problems.

But the cross-border nature of a European code, laying down rules across linguistic and other cultural boundaries, means that it has to deal with an underlying society which has not very much in common and which will therefore require a high level of explicitness if it is to communicate successfully.[123] This implies a 'German' solution, designing a code that has sufficient detail that it could constitute social life, not just regulate it.

The dilemma seems to be that an open-textured code capable of dealing with the complexity of pan-European everyday life will not be widely understood, but a comprehensive code capable of dealing with a low-context pan-European society will fail to cope with social change and cultural difference. But perhaps there is not such a misfit here as first appears. The problems posed by the first solution are not as difficult to deal with as the problems posed by the second. With the first solution, one sets up conditions under which it becomes important to strive to communicate better, a problem to which one can envisage solutions (cross-boundary discussions either of an institutional or informal kind, for example). The second solution provides no such automatic self-correction apart from constant, and destabilising, legislation. But the first solution also reinforces the suggestion that there should a long period in which any Code should only be in the form of a Restatement or a Uniform Law, and, because it is important that any decision-making structure should retain high levels of confi-

---

121 *Administrative Behavior* (3rd ed.) (1976; Macmillan, New York) at xxvii; *Models of Bounded Rationality* (2 vols) (1982; MIT Press, Cambridge, Mass.) and *Models of Man* (1957; Garland, New York).

122 Williamson (1985).

123 One should add, however, that there are indications that Europeans are becoming more alike in terms of some important political values, and to have less and less in common with, for example, citizens of the United States. Compare the map produced in R. Inglehart and W. Baker, Modernisation, Cultural Change, and the Persistence Of Traditional Values (2000) 65 *American Sociological Review*, p. 19 at p. 29 with the apparently later map in *The Economist* 4 Jan. 2003 ('Special Report: Living with a superpower – American values'). The researchers themselves insist on the existence of an 'English-speaking' group, but it is difficult to see the justification of such a cluster in the data, which persistently place Britain much closer to Austria and Italy than to the USA.

dence, that, at least for those states which want to, there should be no appeal on interpretation above the national courts. Admittedly, the first solution will be difficult to
adapt to for societies used to higher levels of explicitness in their rules, but, where no
supranational appeal structure exists, it should be possible to allow states to supplement any Restatement or Code with extra rules, spelling out their own domestic solutions.

One might object that an open-textured code backed by no supranational appellate
structure is not a Code at all. But the point of such a Code is not to impose uniformity, which can be seen as harmful in any case, but to provide a common starting
point out of which common understanding might arise – and if common understanding does not arise, at least there might be a clarification of differences. The aim of the
Code would be to neutralise the surface questions of what verbal formulae should be
used and to help us pay more attention to the more important questions of what the
best solutions are to the disputes at hand, and, ultimately, to the underlying questions
of what sort of society we want to live in. No-one would claim that we are in a position to come to common conclusions on those more important questions, but if we are
to make progress some common starting point is necessary, and a common starting
point needs some content, not just a procedure. Furthermore, if the Code is to succeed
in attracting attention and in provoking debate, it needs to make changes in the existing legal position in all Member States – a Code which can be treated as making no
difference will provoke no discussion at all.

Perhaps the process of making a Restatement or a Code is more important than the
text itself. The crucial point is that cultural differences cannot even start to be sur-
mounted unless the cultures concerned become capable of reflecting on themselves,
of seeing themselves as others see them.[124] The kind of communication between lawyers that a fully-fledged Code requires, with its shared assumptions both about the
nature of law and the relationship between law and society, is impossible as long as
those attempting to communicate do not realise that there are differences between
them. But as soon as they realise what the differences are, communication, and negotiation, become possible. The key is to make sure that the prior period of coming to a
cultural understanding, the period of talking about the difficulties of making a Code
rather than doing anything concrete, lasts long enough to give the idea of cultural
compromise a chance. We are still in that period.

5   A Separate Unlawfulness Requirement?

Assuming that any draft European Civil Code or Restatement should, therefore, aim
to allow dialogue to flourish, so that it should aim neither to decide all cases in advance nor to leave so much open that it will be if no help in defining a common starting point, we can now return to the strategic question posed at the beginning of this
chapter. Should such a code adopt the German approach, which is close to the conventional view of the English approach and to the Italian approach, and require that

---

124 See G. Delanty, Habermas and Occidental Rationalism: The Politics of Identity, Social Learning and
     the Cultural Limits of Moral Universalism, (1997) 15 *Sociological Theory* p. 30 at p. 47.

the defendant's behaviour be 'unlawful' or 'unjustified'? Should it go further along the same route and require that the defendant's behaviour interfered with one or more of a specific list of protected interests of the claimant? Or should it adopt the elegant French formulation, forget about unlawfulness and limit itself to fault, causation and damage?[125] In the light of the conclusions of the previous section, any answers offered her can only be starting points for discussion. But their can be no discussion without starting points.

Let us begin with the idea of building from a list of protected interests. The advantage of doing so, an advantage which applies to all unlawfulness clauses, is that it gives the legislature some control over the extent of liability. It allows the legislature to exclude forms of loss which, according to the dominant political thinking at the time, should not be recoverable. The difficulty with this approach is that it leads to the Code going out of date very quickly, and, as German law has experienced, great pressure for 'creative' readings of the Code that undermine the original but outdated intentions of the legislature. For example, conduct which at one era seems like the encouragement of admirable stoicism might seem at another era like unfeeling heartlessness. In the 19th century, much of what we now see as mental illness was seen as weakness of character. In the First World War, soldiers suffering from what we now call post-traumatic stress disorder were condemned as cowards. Should the law fix one generation's moral psychology in concrete? Similarly, to protect physical interests but not non-physical interests may have made sense once, but in an age when wealth and power lie in such things as computer programs, which are not easily classified as physical or non-physical, such distinctions become useless and an obstruction to justice.

Moreover, many arguments about whether a duty should be recognised, although correct in themselves, are not robust enough to justify a general rule about the whole protectable interest. Arguments about economic incentives, for example, rarely, if ever, work for whole categories of loss, or even against whole categories of defendant. If allowing the recovery of pure economic loss against accountants acting as auditors in take-over cases wastes more resources than it saves (which it may or may not), it does not follow automatically that the law should allow no recovery against accountants in all cases. Economic arguments are often very sensitive to the facts, and as such are difficult to turn into convincing general rules about protectable interests.

One recent attempt, for example,[126] claims that we should have a rule that pure

---

125 Note that the following discussion assumes that fault-based liability will remain the norm. It continues to be the case that, throughout Europe, fault-based liability is the 'default option' for civil liability, the regime which applies in the absence of specific provision for a stricter regime (as often happens for e.g. traffic accidents, environmental harms and products). There is some tendency for the scope of strict liability to expand (e.g. the Dutch Civil Code seems to have adopted the American rule, derived from an English case, *Rylands* v. *Fletcher*, which is interpreted differently in England, that there should be strict liability for those who have control over dangerous substances – see J. Spier, How to keep liability within reasonable limits: A brief outline of Dutch Law, in J. Spier (ed) *The Limits of Liability: Keeping the Floodgates Shut* (1996; Kluwer, The Hague and London)). But fault still reigns supreme as the general rule. Furthermore, despite the fashion to decry fault-based liability, it retains, especially in its 'objective' or 'reasonable behaviour' form, not only an inherent moral appeal but also, in many types of case, inherent economic advantages over strict liability.

126 M. Bussani, V. Palmer and F. Parisi (2003).

economic loss should be recoverable wherever it is more than purely 'private' loss. This rule builds on the idea that in many situations of pure economic loss there are other people in the society who gain, so that those who cause pure economic loss are not necessarily causing losses for the society as a whole. For example, where a ship destroys a bridge which connects the mainland to an island on which the plaintiff is running a restaurant, so that the plaintiff loses customers, many writers say that recovery should be denied because there are other restaurateurs who will gain from the plaintiff's loss. There is no social loss, only 'private' loss.[127] But the difficulty with this rule is not only that it is often very difficult to say that no social loss has occurred (what about, for example, the social losses flowing from a general reduction in faith in market transactions), it is also that it fails to take into account the fact that even where there is social loss, the cost of transferring that loss from plaintiffs to defendants might be so great that it wipes out any benefit gained from imposing liability. Whether the transfer of a particular loss through liability is worthwhile looking at total costs and benefits cannot be decided merely by looking at whether the loss was 'social' or 'private'.

Another objection to the use of the idea of protected interests is that it does not capture the full range of arguments in favour of excluding the possibility of liability. The English courts use a very wide range of arguments to deny liability even when the defendant has been at fault. The formal rule is that it has to be 'just, fair and reasonable' to treat the defendant as having been subject to a duty of care, but, in reality, the courts have used a very wide range of arguments to deny liability, including economic arguments, constitutional arguments and arguments from the overall coherence of the law. Not counting arguments that are really arguments about the moral consequences of the existence of other important causes of the harm to the plaintiff ('remoteness' arguments), and also not counting arguments that have lost their contemporary relevance, such as the argument that it would be against Biblical teaching to allow a wife to sue her husband, English courts have used all of the following to deny the liability of a faulty defendant, in addition to arguments that particular kinds of interest should not be recognised or not fully recognised: that liability would encourage too much litigation and a cultural change towards American levels of litigiousness; that liability should not expand too quickly; that liability in the circumstances at hand would offend popular sensibilities (in particular, the sensibilities of travellers on the London Underground); that pure omissions should not attract liability; that liability would not produce better behaviour by defendants and would therefore waste resources (the 'defensiveness' arguments); that liability would obstruct the defendant's exercise of its public functions; that liability would put the courts in the position of making policy decisions which are constitutionally the province of other institutions; that liability would undermine the position established between the parties by some other branch of the law (e.g. contract law, nuisance law, procedural law); and that the defendant, for example a judge or a witness, should be immune from suit.[128] Regardless of whether they are convincing, these arguments can only be

---

127 Strictly, this is not so – there is a social loss because the diners are obliged to eat at restaurants which are not their first choice.

128 For all these and more, see D. Howarth (2001) at pp. 527-587.

converted into arguments about protected interests in convoluted and artificial ways.

Turning to 'unlawfulness' similar considerations apply. If 'unlawful' means 'in violation of protected interests', it falls because of the same arguments that applied to the protected interest theory. If it means 'not justified by some other rule of law that allows the conduct no matter how faulty', one must ask which rules of law should count as justifying faulty conduct. If the answer is any rule which the court decides can justify the result, the word 'unlawful' is empty of meaning. If it means, on the other hand, a rule specifically laid down elsewhere in the Code, the Code would then suffer from a type of inflexibility in the opposite direction to that produced by the protected interest theory, that it would be impossible without legislation to bring forward new reasons for denying liability in the light of new facts or the wide adoption of new values.

The Code must, admittedly, have some room for widely recognised defences, such as the contributory fault of the plaintiff, explicit prior consent of the plaintiff to the defendant's faulty conduct and the fact that the parties were engaged in a joint criminal enterprise.[129] This might be thought to lead to the Italian solution that the defendant's fault has to be 'unjustified', but the difficulty with that approach is precisely what happened in Italy, namely that it was taken to mean the same as the protected interest approach.

Why not, therefore, simply adopt the French approach? Why not say nothing about 'unlawfulness' and rely on loose expressions such as fault, causation and damage to allow the courts to come up with the reasons they need to deny liability? The English position on pure omissions, for example, or the inefficacy of certain incentives can be covered by fault. Types of loss that ought to be excluded can be dealt with under damage or causation. It is noticeable that in the recent *Perruche* dispute, about whether disabled children could sue doctors whose negligence robbed the children's parents of the chance to abort them, the entire debate was carried on in the French courts in terms of damage and causation.[130] The equivalent cases in England are decided as matters of public policy controlling the duty of care, on the question of whether the law should endorse the position that a person's life is worthless.[131] Indeed, in recent related cases, the courts have taken to using what they call the 'distributive justice' argument, the argument that popular opinion would strongly disapprove of allowing plaintiffs of the sort appearing in the case to gain compensation when others facing similar burdens in life but who cannot find someone to blame, get nothing.[132]

---

129 Other defences which are sometimes used, such as necessity, are not required since they can be incorporated into the Court's view of whether there was fault.

130 See Ass. plén., 17 novembre 2000; Ass. plén., arrêt No. 478 du 13 juillet 2001; Ass. plén., arrêt No. 479 du 13 juillet 2001; Ass. plén., arrêt No. 480 du 13 juillet 2001; Ass. plén., arrêt No. 485 du 28 novembre 2001; Ass. plén., arrêt No. 486 du 28 novembre 2001. See now Loi No. 2002-303 du 4 mars 2002.

131 *Mckay* v. *Essex Area Health Authority* [1982] 1 QB 1166 (e.g. Ackner L.J.: 'I cannot accept that the common law duty of care to a person can involve, without specific legislation to achieve this end, the legal obligation to that person, whether or not *in utero*, to terminate his existence. Such a proposition runs wholly contrary to the concept of the sanctity of human life').

132 *McFarlane* v. *Tayside Health Board* [2000] 2 A.C. 59. See also, however, *Parkinson* v. *St James and Seacroft University Hospital NHS Trust* [2001] EWCA Civ 530, [2002] QB 266 and *Rees* v. *Darlington Memorial Hospital NHS Trust* [2002] EWCA Civ 88, [2003] QB 20.

But there are serious objections to the French approach. There are important concerns about transparency and candour, for it is clear from the arguments presented to the courts, for example in the *Perruche* cases, that much more than fault, causation and damage is really being taken into account.[133] In addition, an argument that says that there should be no liability even if the defendant acted unreasonably is a completely different type of argument from one which says that the defendant acted reasonably in the first place. The former is more general than the latter. It considers the consequences of liability for other people whose lives could be affected by the adoption of the rule proposed in the case, not just the effects of the defendant's decision to act or not to act. To conflate the two requires one to believe that the defendant should have contemplated not just the effects of his actions on the plaintiff and people similarly situated but also the effect of legal liability for his kind of action on society as a whole. The defendant's decision to act is different from the court's decision whether or not to impose liability.

It is true that the French approach can act as protection against certain types of injustice which the English duty of care approach can perpetrate. For example, where a public authority negligently harms a large number of citizens, English courts have been tempted by the argument that there should be no liability because the sums involved would be so large that they would affect political decisions about the level of taxation and the distribution of public spending. The objection to liability seems to be that the sums involved are too large – an objection it is very difficult to frame in terms of fault, causation and damage. The French approach, although it lacks candour in itself, is perhaps better suited to forcing the legislature to act candidly. For example if the legislature thinks that the size of damage awards against public authorities means that the courts are impinging on political decisions, it is open to the legislature to impose a cap on damages against public authorities. But this advantage is outweighed by the disadvantages of failing to distinguish between the particular and the general, most importantly that it makes the law incomprehensible. It is an approach which can only survive by giving as few reasons as possible, which is itself an argument against it.

How can a Code escape this dilemma: either use a concept such as unlawfulness and risk meaninglessness or inflexibility, or refuse to use such a concept and risk incoherence or deception?

One possibility is to adopt the simple French definition of when there should be liability but then to construct a list of the arguments the legislature finds convincing against liability even when the defendant's conduct was unreasonable, combined with an instruction to the court to apply the arguments in appropriate cases. The idea is to reverse the pattern of the German code and the English duty of care theory. Instead of there being a presumption against liability for fault with certain defined exceptions, there would be a presumption in favour of liability for fault but with explicit examples of when there should be no liability. The examples of no liability should, however, be as close as possible to the form of arguments that can be made, rather than attempting to settle cases in detail in advance. The court could be invited to take

---

133 The arguments of the *avocat général, Mr. Sainte-Rose,* in the *Perruche* cases are particularly wide-ranging. They take in, for example, considerations of moral philosophy and the politics of eugenics.

into account the stated principles or points when deciding whether the general clause should apply or not. For example, an example of no liability could be where liability would upset the expectations that the parties had reasonably formed on the basis of their previous dealings with each other. Such a principle would provide a form of consent defence and would deal with that part of the pure economic loss problem which in England is dealt with under the rubric of 'no assumption of responsibility' and in France by the use of the rule of *non-cumul*. Another example of no liability might be where to impose liability would demonstrably and significantly affect the economic welfare of the community at large – which would deal with the central problem of pure economic loss. Another could be where the imposition of liability would demonstrably and significantly lower overall standards of public service to an extent not justified by any improvement in public safety which the imposition of liability might reasonably be expected to secure – which would deal with 'defensiveness' arguments. One could even attempt to sum up the protected interest or type of harm approach and the 'distributive justice' argument by saying that there should be no liability for harms which, according to prevailing standards, are too trivial or inconsequential to merit the intervention of the law.

One might also draft an exception for pure omissions – that is failures to warn or rescue – either with the English 'special relationship' rider or the German rule that the exception does not apply where the defendant created the risk, or both. On the other hand, given the ultimately political nature of the doctrine, it might be wiser expressly to leave the question open for future development in national courts and legislatures.

Of course, careful consideration needs to be given to all the proposed examples of non-liability. Some of the arguments used in the English courts to deny liability notoriously make little sense when examined closely, especially the famous 'floodgates' arguments.[134] To argue that a defendant should not be liable because it created too much risk, or caused too much damage to too many people, is perverse. To argue that rights depend on the capacity of the courts to process claims is even worse. The real concern that underlies the floodgates argument is, however, one which it is difficult to draft into a Code. It is that an ever-expanding law of civil responsibility both reflects and encourages a change in social values which some people take to be harmful, namely the tendency to blame others for our misfortunes and to refuse to take responsibility for the vicissitudes of our own lives. The problem with this argument is that it produces an unjustified presumption in favour of the present pattern of liability. It tells the court 'no more liability' without asking whether existing liabilities are more or less justified than the proposed new form and whether it would be inconsistent to carry on with an existing form of liability and yet to deny a similar new one. There are better ways of dealing with the problem, for example the proposed example of non-liability where the harm is too trivial by prevailing standards to justify the intervention of the law or the proposed example that liability would be economically harmful to the community as a whole.

Indeed all the proposed examples of non-liability require detailed political debate. There are decisions to be made about the extent to which wider economic arguments

---

134 See D. Howarth (2001) at pp. 527-529.

should be allowed to override the principle of fault. Legislators might consider that small losses in economic efficiency are worthwhile if they come from upholding the principle that wrongdoers should bear the costs of their actions. European law already recognises, for example, the principle of 'the polluter should pay',[135] which is a principle of political justice rather than a strictly economic principle.

A separate question is whether to include a general exception along the lines of the English rule that there should only be a duty of care where it is 'just, fair and reasonable' for one to exist. A general exception would allow the courts to develop new arguments which have not yet occurred to lawyers for refusing liability. As long as claimants are allowed to put all of their arguments to the court, there is no inherent human rights objection to such an approach.[136] One might object that such a rule would result, as it has in England, in much uncertainty about the scope of the law, especially in novel cases. But the law is inherently uncertain in novel cases. In any case the situation would be different from the formal position in England because under the proposed rule there would be a presumption in favour of liability for fault, not against. This means that, other things being equal, potential defendants should expect that they will be liable for the harmful consequences of their unreasonable conduct and that the only way to guarantee escaping liability would be to act reasonably. In addition, uncertainty would be reduced by adopting as a principle of interpretation of the Code that like cases should be treated alike. On the other hand, a general exception would have the disadvantage of allowing in arguments of dubious merit, such as the floodgates argument. It might be possible, however, at some risk, admittedly, of over-burdening the text, for arguments identified as unacceptable to be included in the Code itself or, if a Restatement was being constructed, in authoritative comments to the text.

6 Causation and Remoteness

Special care needs to be taken in respect of causation. Most European legal systems distinguish between two sorts of causation: factual causation (or 'equivalence' causation) and normative causation ('remoteness', 'adequate cause', 'legal cause' or 'proximate cause'). The first kind of causation, although it is notoriously difficult to formulate precisely and is the topic of endless debate in its own right, poses no immediate problem for the unlawfulness question. Its function is to eliminate from consideration cases in which, even if the defendant had reached the standard of conduct required by the law, the plaintiff would still have suffered to the same extent. The second sort of causation, however, does pose problems. It concerns responsibility more than causation. It asks whether the defendant should still be found to be legally responsible for the harm in the light of the other factual causes of the harm.

Some legal systems, notably the English and the German, have developed an elaborate jurisprudence around questions of normative causation. There are interesting parallels between the two. Both, for example, have a tendency to link together

---

135 Draft Treaty establishing a Constitution for Europe art III-129(2).
136 *Z* v. *UK* [2001] FLR 612 (E.C.H.R.).

questions of normative cause and duty of care, and to say in cases in which the normative cause issue results in the defendant escaping liability altogether that the defendant had no duty because the harm was beyond the scope of the duty.[137] Also, in both countries there is a school of thought that believes that all questions of normative cause can be decided by asking whether the harm was, in a more or less sophisticated way, foreseeable.[138]

A European Code should make explicit the distinction between the two sorts of causation, since the courts would probably make the distinction for them anyway. But it is not easy to decide how to formulate the normative causation issue. The problem is that there are fundamental and persuasive objections even to the concepts the English and German systems have in common. To say that cases in which the presence of other causes completely exonerates the defendant should count as cases in which there is no duty of care or in which there is no unlawfulness is open to the powerful criticism that it obscures the nature of the argument against liability. It is again a question of the general and the particular. Unlike other duty of care cases, there is no question of an immunity for a *type* of defendant or a refusal to recognise a *type* of harm or a general assessment of the effects of a *type* of liability on society as a whole. Normative causation cases are very sensitive to the facts of the case. The question is whether to exonerate the defendant not because of the nature of what the defendant did, but because of the coincidence of what others did.

As for foreseeability, if the experience of the English courts in tort law over the past 35 years has shown one thing it is that foreseeability alone cannot solve the problems of normative causation.[139] The best example is that of third party interventions. The plaintiff is placed in danger by the fault of the defendant, but the damage is inflicted by the additional fault, often the deliberate fault, of a third party. Is the defendant liable for the harm? If one applies just a foreseeability test the results strike many judges as unjust. Thus, where a bus company carelessly left an empty bus unattended with its ignition keys in place and its doors unlocked, so that thieves stole the bus and killed someone as they drove it wildly around, the English courts decided that the bus company could not be held responsible for the death.[140] But is it really true, as some judges suggested, that the results of the actions of the thieves were 'unforeseeble'? Similarly, when a landlord failed to secure empty property, so that wrongdoers broke in and used it as a base to rob the landlords' neighbours, the court decided that the landlord was not responsible. The court struggled, however, to explain why the harm was 'unforeseeable'.[141] Where young criminals escaped from a correctional facility because of the carelessness of the guards, the House of Lords found in favour of plaintiffs whose property the criminals damaged in the course of

---

137 See D. Howarth (2001) at pp. 508-509 and 520-524. Markesinis and Unberath (2002) 108-109, pp. 113.

138 Howarth (1995) pp. 114, Markesinis and Unberath (2002) at p. 113, U. Magnus (2000) at p. 65. German law has, however, long recognised the normative nature of these questions (see U. Magnus (2000) at 65f, Zweigert and Kötz (1987) at p. 642). English law is still struggling. See *Jolley* v. *London Borough of Sutton* [2000] 3 All ER 409.

139 Many German lawyers come to the same conclusion. See Magnus (2000) at p. 65-67.

140 *Topp* v. *London Country Bus* [1993] 3 All E.R. 448. The same result is obtained in French law – see Terré, Simler and Lequette (1999) pp. 693 and 756 (lack of *direct* causation).

141 *P. Perl* v. *Camden L.B.C.* [1984] Q.B. 342.

their escape. The court added, however, that there would have been no equivalent claim for the victims of the young criminals' subsequent crimes, even though nothing could be more foreseeable than the recidivism of young offenders.[142]

Attempts to qualify 'foreseeability' by terms such as 'reasonable' have only added to the confusion, as have attempts to quantify it by requiring that the intervention should be 'highly likely' or 'obvious'. Older cases, and some more recent ones, use the word 'direct', as did the highest French courts in the *Perruche* litigation.[143] Those who drafted the BGB rejected notions of directness in causation as vague and unscientific, but the whole question of this type of causation is normative and hence not scientific in the first place. If a third party deliberately intervenes in the situation to harm the plaintiff, the issue is whether it is just to hold the admittedly careless defendant wholly responsible for the harm. To say that the defendant did not 'directly' cause the harm, or that the third party's act 'broke the chain of causation' are ways of saying 'no' to that question.

At this point a European Code faces a three-way strategic choice. One way forward is to accept that foreseeability cannot by itself solve the problem of normative causation and to launch into the very difficult and intricate task of capturing more precisely the conditions under which damage should be declared to be 'indirect'. Another way forward is simply to include the word 'direct' and leave it to the courts to work out what it means. A third way forward, adopted briefly by the French courts, is to apply the idea of proportionality to such cases, in the same way as it applies in many jurisdictions to contributory negligence. Instead of declaring the defendant to have been responsible or not responsible for the harm, the court would declare a percentage figure to represent the defendant's share in responsibility for the harm. The proportionality approach might even apply to interventions by natural events. If the third approach is adopted, the further question would arise about the guidance to be given to the courts in making apportionments.

An additional and important complication is that the issue interacts with the issue of joint and several liability as opposed to proportionate several liability. Under joint and several liability, if more than one person is responsible for the harm, every defendant is potentially liable for the whole loss. The plaintiff may choose to proceed against only one of the defendants for the whole loss or against more than one for a part of the loss. Plaintiffs thus have discretion in how to assemble their compensation (though, of course, they may not collect more than 100% of the loss). The idea is that if the plaintiff finds that one or more of the defendants are insolvent or have fled the jurisdiction or are otherwise not worth pursuing, the plaintiff can proceed against the other defendants for the whole loss. The risk of some defendants turning out to be not worth suing falls on the other defendants, who are, after all, wrongdoers, not on the innocent plaintiff. There is a potential injustice in joint and several liability that a minor wrongdoer can end up bearing the whole loss, but this injustice can be alleviated by introducing contribution among defendants.

In proportionate several liability, in contrast, the risk of defendants who are not worth suing shifts to the plaintiff. Each defendant is responsible only for his own

---

142 *Home Office* v. *Dorset Yacht* [1970] A.C. 1004.
143 See above n. 130.

court-determined share of the loss. The plaintiff proceeds against each defendant separately, so that if a defendant has disappeared, the plaintiff is the loser, not the other defendants.

Proportional several liability fits more simply with a proportionate remoteness rule than with a non-proportional rule. But it is possible to combine either joint and several liability or proportional several liability with non-proportional remoteness. The effect would be to exclude completely from liability those defendants who can take advantage of the normative causation rules, but to deal with those defendants left in after the application of those rules in either a proportional way or a joint and several way.

At this stage it is more important to pose the questions than to draft the Code. The choices are significant in financial terms. Insurance companies might see more advantages in the harmonisation of these rules than in the harmonisation of the liability rules themselves. The consequences of adopting any particular combination, however, are not entirely clear. It is possible, for example, that the adoption of proportional several liability will reduce incentives to behave carefully in the first place, although economic theory would predict that under a fault rule, any level of damages greater than the costs of the required further precautions would be enough to induce reasonable behaviour, since, under a fault rule, defendants can avoid all the costs borne by victims as long as they act reasonably. On the other hand, it has been argued that a non-proportional, joint and several liability regime, because it is so harsh to minor defendants, does tend to push the courts into holding such minor defendants not to be liable at all.[144]

One possibility would be to try to discover the best approach by inserting a fixed number of options in the Code from which Member States could choose. We could then learn from the results. The codification of much of the rest of the law would help by holding some other factors constant. Undoubtedly some interests would prefer immediate harmonisation, but a period of experiment would be better than a leap in the dark.

7   Conclusion

This chapter has considered the question of whether, and if so, how, a projected European Civil Code, or indeed a European Restatement, should deal with the most general aspects of extra-contractual civil liability. It has argued that the reasons in favour of harmonising extra-contractual civil liability are not as strong as those in favour of harmonising contractual liability, but that some degree of approximation might have economic advantages in terms of the free movement of legal services and lawyers and political advantages in drawing the attention of lawyers towards the European Union. It has argued, however, for a high degree of discretion to be left at the level of the Member State, to maximise the space for diversity and experimentation. In particular, it has argued that any code should be open-textured, contain options and not be subject to a compulsory supranational appellate jurisdiction. Instead the Code should aim

---

144 Howarth (1994).

at increasing cross-boundary understanding and encourage cross-boundary borrowing of ideas by providing a common starting point for analysis. Furthermore, the Code should encourage debate by refusing to purport to solve all problems in advance and by acknowledging openly the role of the courts in developing the law. It should also state openly that the courts should endeavour to treat like cases alike unless there are strong reasons for departing from previous decisions.

On the question of what the Code should say about extra-contractual civil liability, this chapter has argued that, like the French Code, there should be a presumption in favour of liability for damage caused by fault, but it has also argued that, unlike the French Code, there should be explicit provision for exceptions from the general principle. It has proposed possible examples of such exceptions, drawing principally from English law, but it has also warned against the adoption of all the arguments against liability used by the English courts. It has, however, pointed out that the German protected interest approach cannot cope with the full range of points that can be raised against the application of the general principle and recommends drafting the Code in terms of arguments rather than interests. It leans towards adopting a general 'just, fair and reasonable' clause to allow the courts to develop new reasons to deny liability. It warns of the interaction between the general rule and causation, recommending the formal separation of factual and normative concepts of causation. It offers options for dealing with normative causation within the Code, but warns against simplistic applications of the concept of foreseeability. It also calls attention to a related problem, the question of joint and several liability as opposed to proportionate several liability.

Such proposals cannot expect immediate and unanimous consent. Indeed, since, unlike other proposals, they do not adopt either the form or the substance of any existing European legal system, one can expect them to be rejected on all sides. All one can reasonably hope is that they advance the debate and that the debate itself helps to reduce the misunderstandings that we Europeans have of one another's legal systems. The project will only succeed if we give the debate sufficient time to clear up such misunderstandings and to allow us to arrive at the point at which we can reflect on our own systems in the light of others. One fears that, even with the advance of understanding in other areas of private law, especially in contract, we are still very far from that point. It would indeed be a serious mistake to treat extra-contractual liability as if it was simply a minor adjunct of contractual liability whose problems posed no additional technical and political difficulties. These proposals are put forward only as a step towards that understanding. The destination is still a long way off.

BIBLIOGRAPHY: T. Allan, Law, *Liberty and Justice*, (1992; Oxford University Press, Oxford); Patrick Atiyah, *The Damages Lottery* (1997, Hart, Oxford); E. Banakas, *Civil Liability for Pure Economic Loss* (1996; Kluwer, London); C. von Bar, *The Common European Law of Torts volume 1* (1998; Clarendon Press, Oxford); C. von Bar, *The Common European Law of Torts volume 2* (2000; Clarendon Press, Oxford); P. Birks, *Introduction to the Law of Restitution* (1985; Oxford University Press, Oxford); M. Bussani, V. Palmer and F. Parisi, Liability for Pure Financial Loss in Europe: An Economic Restatement, (2003) *51 American Journal of Comparative Law* p. 113; D. Howarth, My Brother's Keeper: Liability for the Acts of Third Parties, (1994) 14 *Legal Studies* p. 88; D. Howarth, *Textbook on Tort* (1995; Butterworths, London); D. Howarth, Is there a future for the intentional torts? in P. Birks (ed.), *The Classification of Obligations* (1997; Oxford University Press, Oxford); D. Howarth, The Duty of Care in A. Grubb *et al*, *The Law of Tort* (2001; Butterworths, London) D. Howarth and J.

O'Sullivan, *Hepple, Howarth and Matthews' Tort: Cases and Materials* 5th edition (2000; Butterworths, London); J. Kortmann, Liability for Nonfeasance; a comparative study (2001) *Oxford U Comparative L Forum 1* at ouclf.iuscomp.org; P. Legrand, Sens et Non-sens d'un Code Européen (1996) 4 *Rev. int. dr. comp.* p. 779; N. Luhmann, *A Sociological Theory of Law* (King and Albrow trans., 1985; RKP, London); N. MacCormick and R. Summers, *Interpreting Statutes: A Comparative Survey* (1991; Dartmouth, Aldershot); U. Magnus, Germany, in J. Spier (ed.) *Unification of Tort Law: Causation* (2000; Kluwer, The Hague); P. Malaurie and L. Aynès, *Droit Civil: Les Obligations* (1999-2000 ed.; Cujas, Paris); B. Markesinis and H. Unberath, *The German Law of Tort* (4th ed., 2002; Oxford University Press, Oxford); D. Nelken, *Comparing Legal Cultures* (1997; Dartmouth, Hampshire); B. Rudden, Courts and Codes in England, France and Soviet Russia, (1974) 48 *Tulane Law Review*, p. 1010; E. Steiner, *French Legal Method* (2002; Oxford University Press, Oxford); F. Terré, P. Simler and Y. Lequette, *Droit Civil; Les Obligations* (7th ed. 1999; Dalloz, Paris); F. Terré, *Introduction générale au droit* (6th ed. 2003; Dalloz, Paris); G. Viney, *Traité de droit civil: Introduction à la responsabilité* (2nd ed. 1995; L.G.D.J., Paris); G. Viney and P. Jourdain, *Traité de droit civil: Les Conditions de la Responsabilité* (2nd ed. 1998; L.G.D.J., Paris); G. Viney and P. Jourdain, *Traité de droit civil: Les effets de la responsabilité* (2002; L.G.D.J., Paris) S. Weatherill, The European Commission's Green Paper on European Contract Law, (2001) 24 *J. Consumer Policy* p. 339; M. Weber, *Economy and Society* (Roth and Wittich trans., 1978; UCLA Press, Berkeley); O. Williamson, *The Economic Institutions of Capitalism* (1985; Free Press, New York); K. Zweigert and H. Kötz (trans. T. Weir), *An Introduction to Comparative Law* (2nd ed. 1987; Oxford University Press, Oxford).

CHAPTER 35

Product Liability – A History of Harmonisation

Geraint Howells*

1   Introduction

Throughout the three editions of this book this chapter has been somewhat different from many of the others. Rather than discussing whether harmonisation of product liability is desirable or practical or debating how best it can be achieved, it has instead dealt with a topic (product liability) which has in fact, since 1985, been the subject of a harmonising directive. Rather than rehearse old debates, this short paper seeks to focus on three issues. First, what has the product liability experience taught us about the need for harmonisation and particularly about the degree of harmonisation required for internal market reasons? Second, how has the Community monitored its legislation and determined whether it needs to be amended? Finally, we will use the central concepts of defect and development risks to consider whether the courts (both national and European) have been able to develop a harmonised approach to interpretation and what can be done to enhance a common development of European principles.

2   How Much Harmonisation is Necessary?

The Product Liability Directive was introduced as an internal market measure under art. 100 of the Treaty. The drafter of the Directive Prof. Taschner has on many occasions subsequently spoken of his firm belief that the measure is an internal market and not a consumer protection measure. Thus the first recital to the directive states that 'the existing divergences may distort competition', although it does go on to note that this may entail a differing degree of consumer protection.

One unfortunate side-effect of this has been that product liability has not been within the sweep of directives for which the consumer protection Directorate General (DG-SANCO) is responsible. This is regrettable given that it has clear overlaps with other directives under the umbrella of DG-SANCO – most obviously it complements the General Product Safety Directive[1] and in the private law field sits along side directives on sale of goods[2] and unfair term.[3] This split of competences might have important consequences for any future development of European private law. At the

---

* LLB, Barrister, Professor of Law, University of Sheffield and barrister, Gough Square Chamber, London.
1 Directive 2001/95: *OJ* 2002 L11/4 amending Directive 92/59.
2 Directive 1999/44: *OJ* 1999 L 171/12.
3 Directive 1993/13: *OJ* 1993 L95/29.

very least the Commission needs to improve the way it co-ordinates work between the different directorates.

Germany v. *European Parliament and Council*[4] confirmed that the internal market Treaty provision could only be invoked where either this was necessary to eliminate barriers (or potential barriers) to trade or to prevent distortions in competition. Product liability does not directly impose barriers to trade as it makes no specific requirement of products other than they are not defective. Thus the justification must rest upon the distortion of competition ground. Such distortions must be 'appreciable'.[5] One might be sceptical about the necessity (as opposed to the desirability) for product liability harmonisation given that the US manages to work with a single market containing differing product liability regimes. Indeed certain product liability rules were already common throughout Europe. For instance, most systems had a regime of contractual liability for defects and a tort regime based around fault liability. Possibly instances like the development of a de facto strict liability regime in countries like France and the reversal of the burden of proof in Germany provided sufficient excuse for harmonisation.

The US experience should, however, teach us that the single market does not require complete uniformity of product liability law; indeed it needs to be appreciated that the impact of product liability goes beyond substantive rules and depends on issues such as damages, procedural rules and access to justice. We shall see that the Directive was nevertheless intended to be a maximal harmonisation directive not allowing states to increase protection other than in areas where this was provided for expressly by the Directive. It will be argued that this is unjustified. All that the internal market requires is that the rules in the Member States be within a sufficiently narrow band so that they do not create appreciable distortions in competition. Given this, it does indeed seem bizarre that the directive did not find it necessary to harmonise whether pain and suffering damages could be recovered, but thought it essential that that consumers could not use the Directive to recover the first 500 Euros of property damage in any state!

The lack of discretion of Member States to increase protection has been confirmed in three recent decisions of the European Court of Justice. In *Commission* v. *France*,[6] the French implementing law was condemned for allowing recovery of the first 500 Euro; for making suppliers liable on the same basis as producers; and, for imposing the extra condition that the producer must prove that he took appropriate steps to avert the consequences of a defective product in order to invoke the compliance with mandatory requirements and the development risks defence. Similarly Greece was condemned for not introducing the 500 Euro threshold.[7] In *González Sanchez* v

---

4 C-376/98, [2000] *ECR* I-8419, [2000] All ER (EC) 769. For a fuller discussion of this decision by the present author see 'Federalism in USA and EC – The Scope for Harmonised Legislative Activity Compared' (2002) 6 *European Review of Private Law* 601. At the same time the Court decided the case of *R* v. *Secretary of State for Health, ex parte Imperial Tobacco and others* , C-74/99, [2000] *ECR* I-8599 in which the English High Court had referred the question of the same directive's validity.

5 Judgment at para. 168.

6 Case C-52/00, [2002] *ECR* I-3827.

7 *Commission* v. *Greece*, C-154/00 [2002] *ECR* I-3879.

Medicina Asturiana SA[8] a victim of infected blood was not allowed to continue to rely on an earlier Spanish law which had been repealed when the Directive was implemented.

The discussion in the above cases centred on an interpretation of art. 13, which provides:

> 'This Directive shall not affect any rights which an injured person may have according to the rules of the law of contractual or non-contractual liability or a special liability system existing at the moment when this Directive is notified.'

The Court in *Commission* v. *France* states that art. 13 does not allow Member States to maintain a general system of product liability different from that provided for in the Directive. It goes on to state that contractual and non-contractual liability can, however, exist on grounds such as fault or a warranty for latent defects. It also states that the special liability scheme exception is limited to specific schemes limited to a given sector of production. Given that France extended liability in an act implementing the Directive, the Court's decision could be easily justified on the basis that the law increases the protection beyond the permitted maximum levels by rules introduced after the notification of the Directive. It is more problematic, however, to justify the Court's other statement that art. 13 does not give Member States the possibility of maintaining a general system of product liability different from that provided for in the Directive. It is well known that the French system of contractual and tortious liability had developed to an extent where its protection probably surpassed that of the Directive. Some French commentators now interpret this decision as meaning that the existing liability system must be reinterpreted so as not to exceed the protection of the directive.[9] This would be remarkable. The French system might be labelled by jurists as a special liability system, but it is really only the accumulation of a set of contractual and non-contractual rules, whose continued validity had seemingly been expressly preserved by art. 13. Art. 13 might, admittedly, put a break on the future interpretation of those rules by the courts, but surely should not affect existing jurisprudence. Indeed, it might even be argued that it would be going too far to limit the national courts interpretation of laws which only incidentally provide liability for defective products. For example, should the development of warranty law be impeded because it happens to have knock-on effects in product liability which exceed the protection offered by the Directive? In the United Kingdom, for instance, one might argue that for parties to a contract a claim in satisfactory quality is an easier route than establishing a defect under the Consumer Protection Act 1987. Does the European Court seriously intend that English sales of goods law needs to be reformed or its development modified because of its product liability consequences? What the Court seems to have failed to appreciate is that product liability is not a simple topic that can be boxed off and delimited within the scope of a directive; rather product liability claims can typically be based on a wide range of contractual and tortious claims.

---

8   Case C-183/00, [2002] *ECR* I-3901.
9   See Note C. Larroument, Dalloz 2002 no.31 pp. 2464 at 2465.

Similarly the result in *Sanchez* can be justified, but the reasoning might be questioned. Sanchez was in effect complaining that Spain had implemented the Directive by repealing the more protective rules in its 1984 law. It seems perfectly permissible to argue that whilst art. 13 permits Member States to maintain existing systems of liability in place it does not require them to do so. They would clearly seem to be free to decide that existing laws should be repealed in favour of the Directive's standard. However, the Court seems to have gone further and indicated that the Spanish Government would not have been able to maintain its 1984 rules in place if it had wanted to do so. It states that the special liability system is limited to specific sectors and continues:

'.... system of producer liability founded on the same basis as that put in place by the Directive and not limited to a given sector of production does not come within any of the systems of liability referred to in Article 13 of the Directive. That provision cannot therefore be relied on in such a case in order to justify the maintenance in force of national provisions affording greater protection than those of the Directive.'[10]

Whilst the special liability system was clearly intended to cover cases like the pharmaceutical regime, it is baffling how the existing Spanish system could fail to be anything other than a species of non-contractual liability whose continued existence was specifically provided for by art. 13. It would be an elementary mistake to only define as non-contractual liability, liability based on civil codes or the common law. Thus whilst the decision can be justified as defending the right of Spain to choose not to maintain its existing laws, it should have held that Spain would have had the right to have done so if it had so desired.

From an internal market perspective there would seem to be no reason why product liability has to be absolutely uniform, so long as the range of liability is sufficiently narrow so as not to distort competition. Insisting on complete uniformity might even be viewed as a disproportionate response. The only crucial issue of substantive law, which might appreciably affect competition is the development risks defence and this is specifically addressed in the Directive. Other important issues such as the heads of damages available, particularly non-material damage, have been the subject of consultation recently and their approximation could be valuably reviewed.

One of the foci of a recent study carried out by the Commission[11] was the relationship between the strict liability regimes and contractual and non-contractual claims. It would be surprising if the issue of whether the Directive should be the sole source of redress in product liability cases should not be on the Commission's agenda, especially given the tone of the recent European Court judgments and the general move towards total harmonisation directives in order to promote the internal market. However, in product liability such a move is both unnecessary and would generate much complexity. Total or maximal harmonisation is only really necessary where rules affect the form of the goods or services so that modification or adaptation to design,

---

10 Judgment para. 33.
11 The scope of the study was envisaged in COM (2000) 893 at 29-31. This study was carried out by the law firm Lovells and the present author acted as a consultant: see report at http://europa-eu-int/comm/internal-market/en/goods/liability/report-2001-en.pdf.

labelling or packaging may be required to permit market access. Otherwise rough equivalence of laws will usually suffice. The idea that traders should be able to trade into any Member State without having to have knowledge of national laws on the basis that they can assume them to be the same across Europe is unrealistic. It is illusory in theory and unrealistic in practice.

Indeed boxing off product liability laws and trying to create a uniform European regime is impracticable. The contours of product liability overlap with other areas to such an extent that saying an issue falls within product liability and not other areas like service or environmentally liability will be problematic and equally it will be hard to prevent areas like sale of goods law and negligence from having an impact.

3 Modernisation

The fact that Europe was able to enact a directive on product liability at all was indeed a major achievement, given the fear of a US style liability crisis in the minds of many governments and industries. The fact that its content was ambiguous was understandable given that it was responding to a thalidomide problem and yet had to include a development risks defence option to ensure there was sufficient support for the directive's adoption. This was also to be expected given its inspiration had in part at least come from the US. The US had settled on strict product liability in the Second Restatement of Torts in 1964. However, the jurisprudence from the US was confused; unsurprisingly given the variety of state and federal courts which addressed the issue. In particular there was no agreement on the respective roles of consumer expectations and risk:utilty in judging product defects. More fundamentally from a historical perspective it is clear that the drafters of the Second Restatement had been seeking a rather modest reform, limited to tidying up the existing sales law and overcoming the evidential problems consumers faced with regard to proving how product defects arise.[12] Subsequently the US addressed this issue in the Restatement of Torts (Third) (Product Liability) and somewhat contentiously sought to bring order to its product liability system by distinguishing between types of defects – manufacturing, design and failure to warn – and in effect restricting strict liability to manufacturing defects. There has been and continues to be much debate as to whether this is the correct restatement of the court's jurisprudence and whether it will be accepted by the courts. Even if the drafters of the Second Restatement had not foreseen their reform would lead to challenges to product designs and warnings with the attendant broader social impact, this was certainly how the new rules were utilised by many courts. It would seem hard to turn the clock back and view strict liability as having only a marginal impact.

For our purposes it suffices to note, that the EC Product Liability Directive was therefore introduced at a time when product liability jurisprudence was in an embryonic state and at least with some reliance on US theories, which the US itself has revisited and revised. The Directive also had more than the usual scars from the

---

12 G. Priest, 'Strict Products Liability: The Original Intent' (1989) 10 (order nr. 230).

political compromises that 'distinguish' EC legislation. There were overt options on the development risks defence, the exclusion of primary agricultural produce and game and a ceiling on personal injury damages. Other important matters left to national law included the practically important topic of recovery of non-material damages. The Directive also included some significant restrictions, such as the ten year long-stop on liability and some other minor irritable aspects such as the exclusion of the first 500 Euro of property damage. The central concept of defect was itself subject to the accusation of opaqueness for in defining defectiveness in terms of when a product does not provide the safety which a person is entitled to expect' it could easily be accused of being circuitous by including in the definition the very question the definition should be providing the answer to. Moreover, the development risks defence, introduced against the Commission's better judgment, threatened to undermine the strict liability regime which underpinned the reforms. Fortunately, the Directive had made plenty of provision for its review. The Directive was to be reviewed every five years[13] and the options on the development risk and cap on personal injury after 10 years.[14]

The sole reform to-date has been the removal of the exclusion of primary agricultural produce and game.[15] This was intended to respond to the "mad cow" BSE crisis, although how any victim of CJD could be expected to invoke the Directive is baffling. They would have to identifying which beef, consumed many years before, was infected and responsible for the disease. It smacks more of knee-jerk political reaction than any serious attempt to reform product liability law. The Commission's first report on the directive had been a very scant document[16] relying on an impact study[17] to suggest that given the limited experience to-date it was not appropriate to propose reforms. The European Parliament had called for a substantial revision of the Directive when debating the limited reform for primary agricultural produce and game. Although the Commission did not share this view it promised to open up discussion in the form of a Green Paper.[18] This Green Paper canvassed an amazing array of possible reforms, from the modest to the potentially dramatic, but its very breadth seemed to indicate a lack of focus and drive to bring about reforms. This seems to support the view that the Commission wanted to air the issues, but had no urgent desire to see reform. The European Parliament's Committee on Legal Affairs and the Internal Market nevertheless still seems keen on reform.[19] The Commission subsequently issued a Report outlining the responses to the Green Paper and setting out some future steps.[20] One of these was to commission a study on the workings of the directive and future reforms will no doubt have to await the response to that study. Another study on the economic impact of the development risks defence was undertaken.

---

13 Art. 21.
14 Art. 15(3) and 16(2).
15 Directive 99/34 *OJ* 1999 L 141/20.
16 COM (1995) 617.
17 Available at www.europa.eu.int/comm/internal_market/en/goods/liability/index.htm
18 COM (1999) 396.
19 See its report on the Green Paper of 1 March 2000, A5-0061/2000.
20 COM(2000) 893.

The author was a consultant to the latest Commission study, which should be public by the time this article is published.[21] Without going into the details of that report, it can be noted from general observations that there is no great clamour for major reform. The guiding spirit behind the original directive (Prof. Taschner) is no longer at the Commission and although active in academic circles seems fairly pleased with the law he introduced. As we have seen the Commission were dragged into a more extensive review of the law. Industry has not experienced any major disasters. Injured parties tend on the whole to fail on causation issues rather than because there is no potential ground for liability. There have been no major scandals, where an aspect of the directive, like the ten year limitation period, for instance, has caused obvious injustice.

The courts have, of course, faced problems with some product claims. The most tricky product related claims to-date have concerned blood products, where the risk has resulted from public health scares infecting the blood and blood products with diseases such as Hepatitis C, AIDS and new variant CJD. As the problem is a by-product of a public health problem, the blood industry has been fortunate to escape widespread calls for reform to the law to make it liable. This is in stark contrast to the way the pharmaceutical industry was treated in the wake of the thalidomide children, where the industry was seen as the cause of the problem. Of course this does not mean that the blood industry should not be responsible for those infected by its products. Indeed this has happened in a significant English case.[22] Simply the blood issue has been seen as a specific social problem not requiring general reform of the law of product liability.

Some important reform issues are on the agenda. France[23] and Denmark[24] in particular seem concerned that the strict liability regime should be capable of being extended to all suppliers. Another major issue is the repeal of the development risks defence, which the Commission is undertaking a specific study into. The ten year limitation period could also be seen as a potential source of injustice. It would also be useful to ensure non-material damages were recoverable in all countries; although there is a trend in this direction anyway given the reforms to civil liability in Germany.[25]

There could also be a number of minor reforms that would clarify the law. Most obvious is the exclusion of the first 500Euro from a property damage claim. There is even confusion as to whether this is in fact a threshold, which when breached allows recovery in full (as applies in the United Kingdom) or whether it should be a deduction like an insurance excess as it is treated in the other states. The simplest solution would be to abolish it, especially given that the rationale for the exclusion as a way to

---

21 See http://europa-eu-int/comm/internal-market/en/goods/liability/report-2001-en.pdf.

22 A v. *National Blood Authority*, [2001] 3 All ER 289.

23 Following the recent ECJ court case.

24 During their Presidency of the Council they proposed an amendment making it clear that Member States could impose liability on intermediaries to Council: see www.health.fgov.be/WHI3/krant/krantarch2002/kranttekstoct2/021023m05eu.htm.

25 The Zweites Schadenersatz-ÄnderungsGesetz would amend s. 8 of the Product Liability Law so as to allow compensation for non-material damage under the conditions set out in the new s. 253(2) of the Civil Code.

reduce claims for small amounts is not very convincing. One can see minor clarifications like this taking place. One would be sceptical about more fundamental reforms to the legislation given the lack of enthusiasm from the Commission combined with a lack of clamour for reform from any interest groups. Although it must be said that the lack of voice from the consumer side may be explained by the fact that the consumer groups that lobbied for the earlier reforms have now moved on to newer sexier topics and have not been involved in the application of the law which has been carried out by private practitioners. This leaves the question of whether the courts can by themselves bring order to his area of law. This will be tested by their approach to the central jurisprudential topics of defect and development risks.

4   Defect and Development Risk

The concept of defect and the development risks defence can be criticised for vagueness, but their very imprecision could provide the opportunity for the Courts to develop a meaningful approach. The European Court of Justice in particular could be an important source of guidance for the development of product liability law given its ability to bind the Member States' courts to the view of liability it espouses.

The Court has not been called upon to consider the concept of defectiveness directly. In addition to the cases on maximal on minimum harmonisation discussed above, it has decided that a hospital could be liable when a fluid caused a kidney destined for a transplant to become unusable.[26] Its most relevant decision for our purposes was, *Commission* v. *United Kingdom*,[27] when it was called upon to determine whether the English version of the development risks defence, in s. 4(1)(e), Consumer Protection Act 1987 was too generous to the producers (by judging defendants in the light of producers of similar products and by introducing the notion of expectancy of discoverability rather than a test of mere discoverability). The Court found that the Commission had not made out its case. One of its reasons for so holding perhaps indicates that the Court is not entirely au fait with the nature of personal injury litigation, at least in the United Kingdom. The Court considered it significant that there had not been a pattern of cases establishing that the English courts would interpret the provision at variance with the Directive. However, product liability cases are not so numerous that they trouble the courts on a regular basis and product liability cases raising the development risks defence are even rarer. Most product liability cases are settled by negotiation and the possibility that the defence will be generously construed will affect those negotiations and thus should have been sufficient justification for the Commission to bring infringement actions.

Nevertheless, the judgment could be approved if it provides sufficient guidance on the scope of the defence to ensure that United Kingdom courts will indeed interpret the defence in line with the strict liability rationale which underpins the Directive and to which the development risks defence was intended to be a strict exception, with

---

26 *Henning Veedfald* v. *Århus Amtskommune*, C-203/99, [2001] *ECR* I-3569 note G, Howells (2002) 6 *European Review of Private Law* 847.

27 C-300/95, [1997] *ECR* I-2649.

the burden of proving the defence placed on the defendant. Here we have an irony, for whilst we shall see that the European Court was not particularly demanding on when the defence could be invoked, this judgment was picked up by Mr Justice Burton and used as a reason for giving the defence a limited scope in *A* v. *National Blood Authority*.[28]

Some of the language of Advocate-General Tesauro in particular seemed to smack of negligence. For instance, he talked about the producer having to bear all *foreseeable* risks.[29] Whilst some aspects of the decision confirm the narrow scope of the defence – such as identifying the standard expected with the most advanced state of knowledge[30] – the court also introduced the concept that for knowledge to defeat the use of the defence it must be accessible.[31] Whilst such an interpretation may be necessary if one desires to prevent the defence being defeated even where a producer is blameless, it nevertheless gives a broad interpretation to the defence. The defect had to have been discovered and not merely have been discoverable. Indeed such knowledge must have been accessible to the defendant. Advocate-General Tesauro would have, for example, excluded findings in a Manchurian scientific journal.[32] In the English *National Blood* case Mr Justice Burton suggested that this might be a bad example in a case involving a product for which Manchuria was famous, but equally unpublished documents or research retained within the laboratory or research department of a particular company might be regarded as 'Manchurian'.[33] One might not like it, but the case law does seem to have settled on a clear interpretation of the development risks defence to the extent that it excludes inaccessible information; even if some uncertainty still surrounds what is meant by inaccessible.

One difficulty is whether the development risks defence can apply to manufacturing defects or, as Mr Justice Burton preferred to refer to them, non-standard products.[34] The German Supreme Court decided that there was no need to refer to Luxembourg the question of whether the defence applied to manufacturing defects, namely the undiscoverable crack in a mineral bottle. The failure to refer a matter which was far from obvious is regrettable.[35] Burton agreed with the German court's conclusion that the defence should not apply on the basis that the risk was a known one. However, in such cases he would have allowed the defence potentially to apply on one occasion before the defect became known. If the issue had been referred, the European Court might have provided guidance and prevented the need for the point to be litigated across Europe with national courts all potentially producing their own slightly distinctive interpretations.

In his own case Burton J was faced with the argument that the defence should ap-

---

28 [2001] 3 All ER 289.
29 Opinion at para. 22.
30 Judgment para. 26.
31 Judgment, para. 29.
32 Opinion para. 23
33 Para. 49.
34 Para. 36.
35 J. Stapleton describes the decision as extraordinary for merely asserting the defence did not apply: 'Restatement (Third) of Torts: Product Liability, An Anglo-Australian Perspective' (2000) 39 *Washburn LJ* 363 at 383.

ply as it was impossible to detect the defect in the particular product given the lack of a test for the Hepatitis C virus. He held that the defence did not apply once the risk was known, even if there was no ability to detect it in individual products. This was a potentially viable defence, because the defence talked about the state of scientific and technical knowledge being such as 'to enable the existence of the defect to be discovered'; so it could be argued that it was not enough for the risk to be known, it must also have been possible to detect actual defects. Burton J noted that the Amsterdam County Court[36] had allowed such a defence in a case of HIV infected blood but he rejected the court's reasoning. He also distinguished an Australian case where the undiscoverability of Hepatitis A in individual oysters[37] allowed a similar defence to apply on the basis that the defence was differently worded in the Australian law. Instead the English judge relied on the opinion of Advocate-General Tesauro in *Commission* v. *United Kingdom*. Earlier we criticised him for talking in terms of foreseeable risks because this smacked of negligence, but in one respect it works to the claimants advantage for once risks are foreseeable it is clear that the defendant had the choice of stepping up experimentation or insuring. Burton found the development risks defence inapplicable to foreseeable risks.[38]

The reader will have noticed frequent references to the decision of Mr Justice Burton. This is not only an important decision on the particular issue of liability in England and Wales for infected blood, but is also significant because of the way the judge approached the case. For instance, he by-passed the English implementing statute and went straight to the directive. Questionable as this may be, it shows he was open to the influence of European law. Equally, he referred to many academic writings, which is unusual for British judges and is obviously to be applauded. Moreover he also relied on continental and US scholarly writing and as we have seen was well informed and willing to learn from continental case law. Again this is a very healthy approach which should be emulated by all national judges faced with complex and ambiguous laws with an EC origin that have yet to be authoritatively determined by the European Court of Justice.

Indeed on the issue of defectiveness he adopted the approach of a German writer and treated the judge as the 'appointed representative of the public at large'.[39] What the public were entitled to expect could be more or less that what they actually did expect.[40] Avoidability was not a relevant circumstance in assessing defectiveness.[41] Standard products were differentiated from non-standard products.[42] On the facts the blood containing Hepatitis C was treated as non-standard and defective because it was not sufficient that the medical profession knew of the risk. The public would not expect blood to be infected and would have expected to be informed of the risk and this had not been done. The impact any warnings, through the media or at the time of supply, might have had is not spelt out by the judge. It is certainly arguable that the

---

36 *Scholten* v. *The Foundation Sanquin of Blood Supply*, 3 Feb. 1999.
37 *Graham Barclay Oysters Pty* v. *Ryan*, 102 FCR 307.
38 Para. 74.
39 H. Bartl, *Produkthaftung nach neuem EG-Recht*, (1989).
40 Para. 31 (vii).
41 Para. 63.
42 Para. 80.

case might not be so favourable to future claimants where warnings are supplied.[43]

Without going into detail in assessing the judgment one can at least see that this judgment should be widely read across Europe. One might also think the judgment throws up issues that only the European Court can settle for the whole of Europe. Thus we need to consider (i) the relationship between national case law and European case law, and, (ii) also the use of comparative jurisprudence. The former is a constitutional issue, which raises broader questions about access to the European Courts. The latter can perhaps be addressed by the development of a data base on European product liability law drawing on the experience of the CLAB data base in unfair terms. The Commission in the Green Paper had proposed the establishment of an expert group, but a database would in any event seem a more useful and openly available tool. Such a database has now been established by the British Institute for International and Comparative Law.[44]

There is also some evidence of different practices emerging about how courts determine the issue of defectiveness. The question is whether the fact a product when used as intended causes unexpected harm should be seen without more ado as evidence of a defect? In the United Kingdom this is certainly not the case. For instance, in a case involving a condom that broke it was not enough that the condom ripped as people should know they are not 100% safe.[45] That may be a fair decision on its facts. Less easy to accept is a decision that a breast implant that leaks cannot be held to be defective until the claimant shows what caused the defect.[46] That risks taking us back to the dark days of negligence and the evidential difficulties that strict liability was intended to address. It is to be hoped that such a result would not be reached after the *National Blood* case as the public would not expect breast implants to leak unless they were defective. By contrast the French courts seem to take a different approach. For instance, the Court of Appeal in Toulouse presumed that tyres that exploded were defective[47] and equally the Tribunal de grande instance in Aix-en-Provence found liability when a glass window in a fireplace exploded without having to determine the exact cause.[48] Similarly the Green Paper cites a Belgium case in which the defect was inferred from the abnormal behaviour of an aerated beverage bottle that exploded.[49] Of course these can be viewed as simply instance as one or other of the courts getting things wrong, but they do perhaps suggest a different approach between jurisdictions. The issue of burden of proof is an issue the Commission has mentioned in the Green Paper and Follow up report.[50] However, there is much more work that needs to be done in unpicking the relationship between burden of proof in establishing defectiveness and the related issue of proving a causal relationship between defects and damage.

---

43 See, G. Howells and M. Mildred, "Infected Blood: Defect and Discoverability: A First Exposition of the EC Product Liability Directive" (2002) 65 *Modern Law Review* 95-105.
44 See http://www.biicl.org/index./asp?contentid=411.
45 *Richardson* v. *LRC Products Ltd., unreported decision of Mr Justice Kennedy 2 Feb. 2002.*
46 *Foster* v. *Biosil*, 59 BMLR 178.
47 7 November 2000.
48 2 October 2001.
49 *Op cit.* at p. 21.
50 *Op cit.* at 21-22 and 13-16 respectively.

5 Conclusions

The Product Liability Directive has undoubtedly been a good thing from the consumer perspective.[51] Without the Directive it is unlikely that all Member States would have introduced strict liability and certainly it would not have arrived in so coherent a form. Yet doubts still remain about the degree to which product liability needs to be harmonised. Does the internal market demand uniformity, equivalence or merely that laws are harmonised to within broad bands of compatibility? The law looks silly at present by demanding that the first 500 Euro of property damage should not be recovered in any state, whilst leaving recovery of non-material damage to national law. This question of the extent of harmonisation is one which needs to be addressed in relation to all forms of internal market law. Within the private law field, the indirect impact private law rules have on traders might suggest a fairly relaxed regime as regards harmonisation might be justified.

However, the tendency seems towards increased harmonisation and within the field of product liability increased competence of the European legislator at the expense of the national legislator. That places greater emphasis on the need to ensure the European laws are of a good quality and that efficient mechanisms exist for modernising them. Modernisation of EC product liability law to-date has been restricted to the inclusion of primary agricultural products and game. The reasons for the lack of reform may indeed lie in the acceptance by all parties that the system is working well and not causing major problems. It may also be partly a result of the long lead time for such actions (although this becomes less significant as the directive ages; the lack of litigation in the field may indeed mean that not enough experience has been gained to support calls for major reforms. One difficulty is that consumer groups in particular may simply not have had the time to devote to assessing the impact of the Directive. Indeed whilst it is easy to spot victims whose claims fail, the more difficult task may be to detect where people are failing to bring their claims to court. The problem may simply be that consumer groups have diverted their attention to other more immediately pressing topics. Although the Commission has investigated the area thoroughly, after the promptings of the European Parliament, one cannot help but feel that rather than rely on the initiative coming from the Commission alone there should still be room for national initiatives.[52]

Finally we have noted that some of the core terms – defect and development risks – remain ambiguous. Guidance in the form of further legislative initiative or case law of the European Court of Justice might be welcomed, but cannot be guaranteed. It is likely that national case law will remain sporadic and so national courts may well be eager to engage in cross-border dialogues if there are easy means of doing so available. In order to assist this process the Commission should set up the necessary communication structures, such as the development of case law databases. Indeed out of such necessity might actually come some of the most constructive practical moves towards the integration of European private law.

---

51 However, it is also said to lack practical impact. M. Reimann, "Product Liability in a Global Context: The Hollow Victory of the European Model" (2003) 11 *European Review of Private Law* 128.

52 See, T. Wilhelmsson, "Private Law in the EU: Harmonised or Fragmented Europeanisation?" (2002) 10 *European Review of Private Law* 77.

CHAPTER 36

Economic Analysis of Tort Law and the European Civil Code

Michael Faure*

1 Introduction: The Contribution of Law and Economics of Tort Law to the Harmonisation Debate

In this paper I address the potential contribution of the economic analysis of law to the debate concerning the need for the harmonisation of tort law in Europe. The focus of this paper will indeed mainly be on this harmonisation issue. It is important to stress this since the economic analysis of law could be useful to a study of European integration at various levels.

1.1 A Search for Principles

A first important advantage of the economic analysis of tort law is that it enables a debate concerning the economic functions of tort law. The economist will not immediately analyse all the legal refinements of the tort law system, which has the advantage of focusing on goals and functions of tort law at a more general, abstract level.

Economic analysis of tort law has for instance stressed that the goal of tort law should be the prevention of accidents. This focus on the reduction of accident costs has the advantage that law and economics will focus on the main principles that underlie the tort law system. Thus economic analysis could, for instance, explain why many European tort systems have chosen a strict liability regime for hazardous activities and have kept a negligence/fault regime for non-hazardous activities. Economic analysis of tort law builds on the well known theories of Calabresi,[1] Landes/Posner[2] and Shavell[3] who argue that a strict liability rule will especially be useful in case of hazardous activities. Strict liability is considered by economists as the tool to provide incentives to injurers to adopt an optimal activity level.

By focusing on these relatively straightforward ideas, economic analysis of law can make clear what economic background underlies (usually implicitly) specific rules of tort law. It is precisely in this way that I believe economic analysis of tort law can contribute to European integration and hence to a possible European Civil Code. Indeed, if it would be possible to identify the economic reasons for a specific liability regime (to which, I argue, economics can offer a useful tool) the comparative

---

* Maastricht University.
1 Calabresi, G., *The costs of accidents, a legal and economic analysis*, New Haven, Yale University Press, 1970.
2 Landes, W. and Posner, R., "The positive economic theory of tort law", *Tort and Law Review*, 1981, 851-924.
3 Shavell, S., *Economic Analysis of Accident Law*, Cambridge, Harvard University Press, 1987.

lawyer could verify whether differences between the tort rules in various legal systems are in fact merely optical differences (whereby only the use of legal technique differs) or whether these differences are the result of varying values and preferences. Differences concerning the legal technique used are often related to various legal traditions and are hence the result of, to put it simply, dogmatic and doctrinal traditions within a specific legal system. On the other hand these dogmatic and doctrinal differences should not be underestimated. Some will argue that these differences in legal culture are so important that they are even unbridgeable.[4] Here I see a useful task for economic analysis of law. Law and economics can show that, although there are important differences between the legal systems as far as the specific legal technique is concerned, the underlying (economic) balance of interest and preference can often be similar. By, thus focusing on the functions and goals of liability law in the various legal systems, law and economics may, by merely scrutinising the legal techniques which are used to achieve a specific result, show that differences between some legal systems are not as huge as one may at first sight believe.

The negative aspect of this benefit of the economic analysis of tort law is that economics will indeed simplify the working of tort law by not addressing the details of the legal technique. There is the unavoidable disadvantage of the economic analysis which focuses on functions and goals and hence usually not on legal detail. Undoubtedly this focus on principles of tort law and on the instrumental goals tort law (more specifically the prevention of accidents) will lead some lawyers to argue that economics hereby simplifies the more nuanced and refined legal reality of tort law. Partially that is undoubtedly the case. One could equally argue, however, that the simplification may, more specifically from an integration perspective, have the major advantage of focusing precisely on the underlying similarities in a tort law system. Behind the surface of various legal techniques similar principles, goals and preferences can hide. By focusing on these underlying principles instead of on the peculiarities of the legal technique used, I believe the economic analysis of tort law can contribute to a "bridging of the unbridgeable".[5]

Within the scope of this contribution I will not focus on the basic economic analysis of tort law. This analysis is now widely accepted within the European academic world. Many traditional tort lawyers now also make use of economic arguments.[6] It seems, however, more interesting to stress the possible contribution of the economic analysis of tort law to the European integration process and more particularly to the European Civil Code.

1.2 Critical Analysis of the European Tort Law

A second benefit of the economic analysis of tort law for European integration concerns the simple fact that economic methodology can be used to take a critical look at

---

4 This – debated – point of view has repeatedly been defended by Legrand; see (among others) Legrand, P., "The impossibility of legal transplants", *Maastricht Journal of European and Comparative Law*, 1997, 111.

5 See Van Gerven, W., "Bridging the unbridgeble. Community and national tort laws after Francovich and Brasserie", *International Comparative Law Quarterly*, 1996, 507-544.

6 See e.g. as far as Germany is concerned Kötz, H. and Wagner, H., *Deliktsrecht*, 9th edition, Neuwied, Luchterhand Verlag, 2001, 17-20.

existing European legislation and thus to provide a critical perspective for judging European legislation.

1.2.1 Example: Product Liability

Economic analysis could for instance be used to verify whether the European Directive on Product Liability was actually necessary to realise a market integration, as it claims. From an economic point of view it can easily be argued that it is relatively doubtful whether the European Directive can reach the goal of harmonisation. The lowering of administrative costs which could be reached as a result of harmonisation can never be achieved through the European Product Liability Directive. Everyone (also tort lawyers) agree that there are so many uncertainties and references to national law within the directive that it can never reach the goal of harmonisation of marketing conditions.[7] The harmonisation of marketing conditions, which was mentioned many times in the considerations preceding the directive, was probably only the formal goal in order to give the European authorities competence in this area. Since, however, this directive could never reach a harmonisation of marketing conditions, its most important goal was probably the desire of the European bureaucracy to show that they were able to produce a legislative document in an important area of private law, namely product liability. The recent green paper and the following report of the Commission to the Council concerning product liability have, however, made it clear that, with the exception of Austria, the national legislation implementing the directive is hardly used. The product liability directive therefore does not serve any practical goals.[8] This is just one example to show that economics can provide an interesting input for judging the efficiency of European legislation. Law and economics scholars have also examined other European legislation in the area of private law, such as the European initiatives in the area of the liability for the suppliers of services.[9] Law and economics can obviously fulfil this critical role not only for already existing European legislation, but also for new legislation to come, such as the contents of a European Civil Code.

2 Positive Versus Normative Analyses

The way law and economics will provide this critical analysis is by using the efficiency criterion. On the basis of the efficiency criterion it will be established whether a certain legal regime will promote social welfare or not. Many lawyers argue that, though this may be an interesting criterion, it is not decisive, since the goal of law is

---

7 See for a more detailed analysis Faure, M., "Product liability and product safety in Europe: harmonisation or differentiation?", *Kyklos*, vol. 53, 2000, 467-508.

8 For more details see Faure, M., "Product liability and product safety in a federal system: economic reflections on the proper role of Europe", in Marciano, A. and Josselin, J.M. (eds.), *The economics of harmonising European Law*, Cheltenham, Edward Elgar, 2002, 131-177.

9 See Curran, C.H., "The burden of proof and the liability rule for suppliers of services in the EEC", *The Geneva Papers on Risk and Insurance*, 1994, 85-98.

certainly not just to promote efficiency. However, in this respect it is important to make a difference between the positive economic analysis of law on the one hand and normative economic analysis on the other hand. In a positive economic analysis economics is used to analyse the economic effects of the law as it is, without necessarily indicating that efficiency is a value by which legal rules can be judged. Such a positive economic analysis can be highly useful since it often includes effectiveness tests. Thus economic analysis allows us, as an example, to test whether the goals set by the (European) legislator can actually be reached with the instruments used. This information is obviously useful for any assessment of a legal framework. In a normative economic analysis, efficiency is used as a criterion to judge legal rules. Many lawyers may have more difficulties with that. But even if one accepts that the law serves purposes other than efficiency, economic analysis can still provide useful information, for example, on the costs and benefits of a specific legal regime.

2.1 Division of Labour Within Federal Systems

A third and important contribution of the economic analysis of law to the European integration process is that economics has focused a lot of attention on the division of competences within federal systems. This is a topic which, in a European legal perspective, is obviously relevant to the subsidiarity principle. From an economic perspective the question which is addressed in the economics of federalism is what the optimal level would be for specific types of regulation.

This literature, which deals with the optimal division of competences within federal systems, seems also quite relevant for the harmonisation debate concerning tort law. Law and economics scholars have indeed paid quite a bit of attention to the possible goals, functions and economic effects of a harmonisation of tort rules.[10]

The economic criteria which are advanced in the literature in favour of harmonisation can indeed also be applied to the various areas of tort law, such as environmental liability, product liability or medical malpractice. In all of these cases it is possible to indicate, with the use of economic instruments, what the possible benefits of harmonisation may be. It is understandable that so far the harmonisation debate has more specifically concentrated on domains such as environmental liability and product liability. Those are two areas were we can typically expect "transboundary torts", meaning that the argument in favour of harmonisation may be stronger precisely in those areas. Moreover, product liability has so far been one of the only areas of tort law where the European Commission has successfully enacted legislation leading to a (partial) harmonisation. With respect to environmental liability the European Commission is also undertaking initiatives in the direction of a (more modest) harmonisation. See in this respect the well-known White Paper on Environmental Li-

---

10 See for instance as far as environmental law is concerned Faure, M., "Harmonisation of environmental law and market integration: harmonising for the wrong reasons?", *European Environmental Law Review*, 1998, 169-175; Faure, M. and De Smedt, K., "Should Europe harmonise environmental liability legislation?", *Environmental Liability*, 2001, 217-237 and see for the area of medical malpractice Faure, M., "Kompensationsmodelle für Heilwesenschäden in Europa mit Ausblick auf die EG-Rechtsharmonisierung", *Zeitschrift für Europäisches Privatrecht*, 2000, 575-600.

ability issued by the European Commission on 9 February 2000.[11] Meanwhile this White Paper has resulted in a real draft directive on the prevention and restoration of significant environmental damage.[12]

It is, however, not only interesting to apply the economic criteria for centralisation on typical transboundary torts, such as environmental liability and product liability. Economics can equally be used to answer the question whether Europe should strive for a more general harmonisation of (parts of) general tort law. This is of course not an academic question at all, given the initiatives towards a European Civil Code.

The economics of federalism seems to be a particularly appropriate way of looking at harmonisation efforts in Europe because the European Commission has been using economic arguments to justify its harmonisation efforts for some time. More specifically the argument has long been advanced that harmonisation of law, including private law, is necessary in order to harmonise the conditions of competition within Europe. One aspect of this paper is devoted to an analysis of whether this "economic" argument for the harmonisation of the conditions of competition is indeed a valid economic justification for harmonisation. Moreover, applying the economics of federalism to the harmonisation of tort law within Europe also has the advantage that a balanced view can be presented of the need to harmonise tort law. Indeed, economic analysis does not come up with black or white statements in favour of or against harmonisation, but allows balanced criteria to be advanced on the basis of which those areas and topics which may be good candidates for harmonisation are indicated.

Of course the reader should be aware that applying the economics of federalism to the harmonisation issue means that I will only provide "one view of the cathedral".[13] As was mentioned above, I do not deal with the basic economic analysis of tort law. Moreover, the harmonisation issue is addressed only from an economic angle in this paper. Although I have argued above that I think that economics can provide an interesting contribution to the harmonisation debate, I want to repeat that I realise that this really is just one view of the cathedral. One may indeed well argue that there may be other, non-economic, arguments for a harmonised liability system, such as the belief that this will lead to a higher degree of victim protection than Member States could achieve when using national liability law. But even if non-economic arguments are advanced to justify European harmonisation, it seems important that in future European documents these reasons are clearly explained within the scope of the subsidiarity principle.

---

11 White Paper on Environmental Liability, COM (2000) 66 final, Brussels, 9 February 2000. For comments, see Rice, P., "From Lugano to Brussels via Arhus: Environmental Liability White Paper published", *Environmental Liability*, 2000, 39-45; Rehbinder, E., "Towards a community environmental liability regime: the Commission's White Paper on Environmental Liability", *Environmental Liability*, 2000, 85-96 and Faure, M., "The White Paper on Environmental Liability: efficiency and insurability analysis", *Environmental Liability*, 2001, 188-201.

12 See on that proposal Bergkamp, L., "The Proposed Environmental Liability Directive", *Environmental Liability Law Review,* 2002, 294-314 and 327-341.

13 Paraphrasing the words of Calabresi and Melamed (Calabresi, G. and Melamed, D., "Property rules, liability rules and inalienability: one view of the cathedral", *Harvard Law Review*, 1972, vol. 85, 1089-1128).

3 Some Lessons from the Economic Debate

European private law and the trend towards harmonisation have a lot of support in Europe today. For many traditional lawyers differences between the legal systems are undesirable and they plead in favour of a harmonisation, also in the field of tort law.[14]

Symptomatic in that respect is of course the project for the European Civil Code. Within this contribution I will not deal with the complicated question through what kind of legal techniques such a harmonisation of tort law in Europe could be realised; I will also not deal with the issue on which domains of tort law the differences between the Member States would be the greatest today. However, I would like to address the question, using economic analysis, of whether a harmonisation of tort law is indeed desirable and if so for which domains. One can indeed not escape the impression that today for many lawyers, especially those enthusiastic for a European Civil Code, this question seems implicitly to be answered in the positive. I believe, however that the economic perspective, more particularly the economic theory of federalism can provide an important contribution to the harmonisation debate. Economics can, more specifically, indicate which areas of tort law might be good candidates for harmonisation and which not.

What are the most important results of this economic literature?[15]

3.1 Starting Point: Respect Various Preferences

The starting point for the economist addressing the question of centralisation seems to be totally different than that of many policymakers (or certainly politicians) at the European level. The starting point for the economist is that differences are as such not bad, on the condition that these differences in legal systems also reflect varying preferences of citizens.[16]

The starting point for a law and economics scholar is therefore that differences between legal systems should in principle be respected. Furthermore, economists would even argue that these differences can increase the quality of the legal system since legal systems will compete to offer their citizens the highest quality of legal rules.[17]

---

14 See for instance Janssen, M., "Auf dem Weg zu einem Europäischen Haftungsrecht", *Zeitschrift für Europäisches Privatrecht*, 2001, 30-65; Koziol, H., "Das Niederländische BW und der Schweizer Entwurf als Vorbilder für ein künftiges Europäisches Schadenersatzrecht", *Zeitschrift für Europäisches Privatrecht*, 1996, 587-599; Magnus, U., "European perspectives of tort liability", *European Review of Private Law*, 1995, 427-444 and see also Nieuwenhuis, J.H., "Wat is een onrechtmatige daad? Europese perspectieven", *RMThemis*, 1998, 242-248.

15 Obviously it is not possible within the scope of this paper to deal with the very rich economic literature concerning harmonisation. Therefore within this contribution I will merely present the most important results of the economics of federalism. Those interested in the details are referred to the literature in footnotes.

16 This idea is, by the way, also to be found in the work of many lawyers. See in this respect for instance the interesting inauguration address of Smits, J., *The good Samaritan in European private law*, Deventer, Kluwer, 2002, 43, who argues in favour of a "praise of diversity".

17 See in that respect Ogus, A., "Competition between national legal systems. A contribution of economic analysis to comparative law", *The International and Comparative Law Quarterly*, 1999, 405-418; Ogus, A., "The contribution of economic analysis of law to legal transplants", in Smits, J. (ed.),

Some will of course react to this idea by saying that it is doubtful whether the fact that, for instance, in Portugal lower amounts for non-pecuniary losses would be awarded than say in Germany, really reflects the preferences of the Portuguese citizens. This would then mean that national legislation would not sufficiently reflect the preferences of its own citizens. This is, however, a very dangerous reasoning, at least if this were to be used as a reason for harmonisation. Indeed, if it is considered that the national (in my example Portuguese) legislator or judge is not be sufficiently capable of establishing the amount of non-pecuniary losses in accordance with the preferences of the citizens of his own country, the whole democratic nature of the decision making process in the particular state, in the example Portugal, is actually put in doubt. Moreover, even if one were to agree with these critics of the preference argument that national legislators and judges are not capable of producing legislation which really reflects the preference of the citizens, there is still no reason to assume that the European legislator would do better in that respect. Why should we assume that European bureaucrats in Brussels would be more able to find out what the preferences are of the Portuguese than Portuguese legislators and judges could? Here one can notice that the supporters of harmonisation are in fact of the opinion that they would know better than national legislators or judges what is good for the European citizens. Such a harmonisation argument seems, however, dangerous and paternalistic since it disrespects national preferences.

From an economic perspective the starting point should therefore remain a decentralisation. Starting from Tiebout's model,[18] there is reason to believe in what Van den Bergh calls a "bottom up federalisation", assuming that in principle the local level is optimal, since the local level has the best information on local problems and on the preferences of citizens. Decision making should be moved to a higher level only when there is a good reason.[19] Economic theory has indeed suggested that there may be a variety of reasons why the local level is not best suited to take decisions and that there are occasions when central decision making can lead to more efficient results.

I will now apply these criteria for centralisation and relate them to the harmonisation of tort law in Europe.

3.2 Transboundary Externalities or Race for the Bottom? Centralisation!

Law and economics certainly does not provide a one-sided argument against harmonisation. Economics argues that in many cases this idea of a competition between na-

---

The contribution of mixed legal systems to European law. Antwerp, Intersentia, 2001, 27-37 and Van den Bergh, R., "Subsidiarity as an economic demarcation principle and the emergence of European private law", *Maastricht Journal of European and Comparative Law,* 1998, 134.

18 The model of C. Tiebout (A pure theory of local expenditures, *Journal of Political Economy,* 1956, 416) has been used by many scholars, such as Van den Bergh, as the basis for their economic theory of harmonisation.

19 A major American supporter of this "presumption in favour of decentralisation" is Revesz. See, e.g., Revesz, R., "Environmental Regulation in Federal Systems", in Somsen, H. (ed.), *Yearbook of European Environmental Law,* 2000, 1-35 and Revesz, R., "Federalism and Environmental Regulation: An Overview", in Revesz, R., Sands, Ph. and Stewart, R. (eds.), *Environmental Law: The Economy and Sustainable Development,* 2000, 37-79.

tional legislators will not produce optimal results. Economic theory has, for instance, indicated that this will be the case if there are transboundary externalities.[20] The mere existence, however, of transboundary externality does not as such justify a total harmonisation of tort law. It merely provides an argument for the regulation of transboundary accidents at the central level.[21]

A second argument in favour of harmonisation lies in the fact that without centralisation a ruinous competition between legal systems could take place whereby states would compete with each other to attract industry with inefficient standards. This risk of a destructive competition is also indicated in the literature as "race for the bottom".[22] The basic idea is that local governments would compete with lenient legislation to attract industry. The result would be an overall reduction of the quality of legislation below efficiency level.[23]

It is, however, very unlikely that within the European context such a race for the bottom would emerge with tort law. This argument indeed supposes that states compete with each other to attract industry with inefficient tort rules. First, there is no empirical evidence whatsoever that Member States would willingly enact inefficient legislation in the area of tort law in order to attract industry. Second, empirical studies have indicated that the location decision of firms is based on a large number of criteria, such as the tax climate, transport, infrastructure and labour. These are obviously much more important in the location decision of firms than legislation in the field of private law.[24] Third, it is much more likely that states would engage in a so-called "race for the top", specifically in the area of tort law. Indeed, the primary interest of states is probably to issue legislation protecting the own citizens (who have to support politicians by re-electing them). It is indeed the own citizens of a Member State who can become victims of accidents and can therefore have a primary interest in a victim-friendly tort law.[25]

3.3 Harmonisation of Marketing Conditions? No!

An important advantage of the economic analysis of federalism is that the literature has paid a lot of attention to the traditional European argument that a harmonisation of all kinds of rules would be necessary because differences between rules would create an unequal marketing condition. The argument goes that if legislation is different, the costs for industry would differ as well, and the conditions of competition within

---

20 See Faure, M., "Towards a harmonised tort law in Europe? An economic perspective", *Maastricht Journal of European and Comparative Law*, 2001, 334.

21 See for this "transboundary only" argument Van den Bergh, R., *supra* note 17, 144-145.

22 See – among others – Rose-Ackerman, S., *Rethinking the progressive agenda, the reform of the American regulatory state*, Macmillan Inc./Simon & Schuster, 1992, 166-170.

23 For a detailed discussion of this argument see Esty, D. and Geradin, D., "Environmental protection and international competitiveness. A conceptual framework", *Journal of World Trade*, 1998, vol. 32/3, 16-19.

24 Compare Jaffe, A., Peterson, S., Portney, P. and Stavins, R., "Environmental regulation and the competitiveness of US manufacturing: what does the evidence tell us?", *Journal of Economic Literature*, 1995, vol. 33, 132-163.

25 See on this argument for the race for the top Vogel, D., *Trading-up. Consumer and Environmental Regulation in a Global Economy*, Cambridge, Harvard University Press, 1995.

the common market would not be equal. Levelling the playing field for European industry was therefore the central message for a long time. This argument of harmonisation of marketing conditions can be found in many European directives as the justification for action at European level.[26]

This argument has been thoroughly examined by economists and has been rejected as a wrong justification for harmonisation.[27] Nevertheless this argument for the harmonisation of conditions of competition has been used for a long time in Europe to justify European harmonisation in many areas. To some extent this can be understood on grounds of European legal reasoning. Indeed, it was for a long time necessary to give Europe competence to intervene in specific areas. The disadvantage of this argument is of course that the argument is so general and unbalanced that it has no distinctive power whatsoever. The argument could in fact justify much (largely unnecessary) harmonisation of all kinds of legal rules, since one could of course always argue that a legal rule has some influence on the conditions under which products or services are marketed. However, empirically the argument is not very convincing either. The legal literature agrees that if one takes, for instance, the European Directive on Product Liability (which was again based on the harmonisation of conditions of competition argument) it is relatively clear that this goal can never be achieved by this directive.[28]

The argument of the harmonisation of conditions of competition also wrongly supposes that an integrated market could only exist if the marketing conditions would be totally equal for all players. That should of course not necessarily be the case. There is, in addition, a strong counter-argument, in that there are many examples showing that economic market integration is possible (without the distortions predicted by the race-for-the-bottom argument) with non-standardised legal orders. Public choice scholars have often advanced the Swiss federal model as an example where economic market integration goes hand in hand with differentiated legal systems.[29] It is apparently possible to create a common market without the total harmonisation of all legal rules and standards. That is not to say that there may not be other arguments in favour of the harmonisation of tort law in Switzerland. Notably, the reduction-of-transaction-costs argument – to be discussed below – may well constitute a powerful reason to prefer one Federal Swiss tort law instead of 26 different cantonal systems. There-

---

26 It is for instance to be found literally in the considerations preceding the European Directive on Product Liability.

27 In particular Revesz has examined the weakness of this "harmonisation of conditions of competition" argument and has also indicated that European scholarship has tried to rephrase this argument in "race for the bottom" terms (see Revesz, R., "Federalism and regulation: some generalisations", in Esty, D. and Geradin, D. (eds.), *Regulatory competition and economic integration, comparative perspectives*, Oxford, Oxford University Press, 2001, 3-29.

28 Almost all authors agree on that point. See Duintjer Tebbens, H., "De Europese Richtlijn Produktaansprakelijkheid", *Nederlands Juristenblad*, 1986, 373-374; Storm, P., "Een gebrekkig produkt", *Maandblad voor Ondernemingsrecht*, 1985, 245; Van Wassenaer van Catwijck, A.J.O., "Produktaansprakelijkheid", in *Serie Praktijkhandleidingen*, Zwolle, 1986, 81 and Martin Casals, M. and Solé Feliu, J., "Responsabilidad por productas en España y (des)armonizacion Europea", *Revista de responsabilidad civil y seguros*, 2001, vol. 4, 1-17.

29 Frey, B., "Direct Democracy: Politico-Economic Lessons from Switzerland", *American Economic Review*, 1994, 338-342.

fore, clear steps towards harmonisation of tort law can be seen in Switzerland as well.[30] Note, however, that this is not because harmonisation would be necessary to make market integration possible.

Further, even if one were to take the (political) "common market" goal as a starting point and tort law were to be harmonised on that ground, this would still not create a level playing field since differences in, for example, energy sources, access to raw materials and atmospheric conditions will still lead to marketing conditions that favour trade.[31]

3.4   Reduction of Administrative Costs? If Possible: Yes!

3.4.1   Bottom Up Instead of Top Down

From an economic perspective, probably the most important argument for a harmonisation of tort law (for issues that are not transboundary) is that such a harmonisation could lead to a reduction of administrative costs.[32] One could indeed easily argue that in Europe today many liability rules exist which do in fact reflect similar values and preferences, but are technically different as a result of the differences in underlying doctrines and the legal techniques used. If it were possible to uniform liability rules which do indeed reflect similar values and preferences at relatively low costs this should indeed be considered as an important advantage. This is of course the leading thought behind many initiatives which have been developed by many academic tort lawyers in Europe and who examine whether it is possible to proceed to a harmonisation of tort law.[33]

Many of these harmonisation projects are undertaken by academic lawyers who examine the existing differences between tort rules in the legal systems and try to find the largest common denominator. Such an approach, looking for a common denominator on the basis of comparative legal studies and of case law[34] seems far more

---

30 See Wininger, B., "L'architecture de l'Avant-projet de loi sur la responsabilité civile", *Revue de Droit Suisse*, 2001, 299-326; and see Koziol, H., *supra* note 14, 592-593.

31 So Van den Bergh, R., "Economics in a Legal Strait-Jacket: The Difficult Reception of Economic Analysis in European Law", paper presented at the workshop Empirical Research and Legal Realism: Setting the Agenda, Haifa, 6-9 June 1999, 10.

32 A somewhat related argument deals with economies and diseconomies of scale in administration. See in that respect Rose-Ackerman, S., *supra* note 22, 165-166.

33 Within the scope of this contribution it is obviously not possible to mention all the projects that aim to achieve a harmonisation in the area of private law. As far as tort law is concerned an overview of the various initiatives is provided by Janssen, M., *supra* note 14, 31-65. A European group on tort law, coordinated by Prof. Helmut Koziol (of Vienna) develops European principles of tort law. See Spier, J. and Haazen, O., "The European group on tort law ('Tilburg group') and European principles of tort law", *Zeitschrift für Europäisches Privatrecht*, 1999, 469-493. Another initiative is the major project concerning the European Civil Code supervised by Prof. Christian von Bar (from Osnabrück). See for their view on the issue of harmonisation of tort law Von Bar, Ch., "Konturen des Deliktrechtskonzept der Study Group on a European Civil Code", *Zeitschrift für Europäisches Privatrecht*, 2000, 515-532.

34 For comparisons of tort rules on the basis of case law see Van Gerven, W., Lever, J., Larouche, P., von Bar, Ch. and Viney, G., *Cases, materials and texts on national, supranational and international*

promising than the approach followed by the European Commission so far. The "top down" approach of the European Commission forcing Member States to implement European legislation as laid down in directives has not proven to be very successful, especially in the area of private law. The approach chosen by the various academic study groups seems much more aimed at the search for a ius commune in tort law. Hence, their search for the common roots of the tort law systems in Europe can be considered as a "bottom up" approach. If these academic study groups were to succeed in proving that many differences between the legal systems are merely of a technical nature and can therefore be considered as often pointless incompatibilities not related to differences in values or preferences, such a harmonisation attempt, namely looking for the largest common denominator in tort law, seems far more promising than the approach followed so far by the European Commission.

3.4.2 Input of Economic Analysis

The advantage of the work of the study groups is that most of this work is also based on a specific conceptual idea of tort law. On that basis the different groups formulate proposals for the various areas of tort law as a more or less coherent framework. A major disadvantage of the European approach today is that one has the impression that the Commission at one moment presents a European Product Liability Directive, then thinks it might be a good idea to work on the liability for services and the next morning considers a directive on consumer sales. If one sees the approaches followed in these different European initiatives it becomes clear that they are so different that a fundamental vision on the function and goals of tort law is totally lacking.[35] An approach aimed at a lowering of administrative costs whereby a largest common denominator would be sought, respecting differences between national values and preferences, would also have the advantage that an almost traditional hostility against the europeanisation of tort law could be more easily overcome. Indeed, it is clear that the resistance to harmonisation will be much stronger when national legal systems have to give up national rules which are strongly rooted in national values or tradition. This may be totally different if the national rules are replaced by another rule which is formulated, in a technically different way but still reflects the same values and preferences. If one therefore accepts that the opportunities for harmonisation (from the perspective of lowering administrative costs) should especially be seen where preferences do not differ, but only legal techniques are different, the economic approach to tort law can be very helpful to achieve this goal. Indeed, as has been explained above, the economic analysis of tort law has the advantage of focussing on functions and goals of tort law and hence, enables the study of tort law at a higher

---

tort law. Scope of protection, Oxford, Hart Publishing, 1998 and Van Gerven, W., Lever, J. and Larouche, P., Cases, materials and texts on national, supranational and international tort law, Oxford, Hart Publishing, 2000.

35 That was an important point of criticism of the current European tort law as developed by the European Commission. See Koziol, H., "Ein Europäisches Schadenersatzrecht – Wirklichkeit oder Traum", JBl, 2001, 32-33 and Widmer, P., "Die Vereinheitlichung des Europäischen Schadenersatzrechts aus der Sicht eines Kontinental Europäers", Revue Héllenique de Droit International, vol. 52, 1999, 99.

level of abstraction. Thus this higher level of abstraction, essential for the economic analysis of tort law, may well enable the focus on the common roots between the various legal systems. Hence, the economic approach to tort law can provide an important contribution to the search for a ius commune of tort rules in Europe.

3.4.3 Examine the Costs of Harmonisation!

Whether the harmonisation attempts will be successful in the long run is hard to predict today. Some scholars are very pessimistic and stress the differences between the legal systems (and legal cultures) in Europe to argue that these will inhibit a harmonisation of private law.[36] From an economic perspective one can easily argue that many legal rules often serve the same goal and could therefore be harmonised, certainly if only the legal techniques used differ and not the underlying values and preferences. However, in some cases these differences can be rooted so deeply in the legal cultures and traditions that the costs of harmonisation could be extremely high, maybe even prohibitive. In addition, the administrative costs of harmonisation need to be taken into account. From an economic perspective it can be held that the argument of harmonisation based on the potential reduction of administrative costs (through a simplification by uniform legal rules) is of course valid only when the marginal costs of this harmonisation are indeed lower than the marginal benefits of such a unification.[37]

4   Possibilities and Limits of Harmonisation: A Few Tips

Within the scope of this book it seems interesting to point out a few suggestions following from economic analysis for the work on a European Civil Code.

4.1   Focus on Areas where Preferences do not Differ

First, it seems important primarily to focus on those areas of tort law where preferences apparently do not differ. One could think of the choice between a strict liability regime on the one hand and negligence/fault on the other hand. If it could be established that the legal systems largely agree on the area where a strict liability regime should be applied, then one could argue that the differences in form are merely technical and do not reflect varying preferences, so that this area would be a good candidate for harmonisation.[38]

---

36 See Legrand, P., *supra* note 4, 111.

37 See in this respect also Van den Bergh, R., *supra* note 17, 146-148.

38 I certainly do not want to argue that there are no differences between the Member States as far as the cases are concerned to which a strict liability rule applies. Some might argue that the differences, say, between France and the United Kingdom in that respect are huge (for an overview, see Koch, B. and Koziol, H. (ed.), *Unification of Tort Law, Strict Liability*, The Hague, Kluwer Law International, 2002 and see Van Gerven, W., Lever, J. and Larouche, P., *supra* note 34, 467-687 and see Von Bar, Ch., *The Common European Law of Torts, II*, Oxford, Clarendon, 2000, 333-432.). The point is only made that if there were – factual – agreement, say, on the strict liability of the guardian of a dangerous installation, this would mean that preferences on that point do not appear to differ.

The same could be argued, for example, concerning the weighing of interests the judge has to undertake in a negligence case when he has to establish a standard of care for a particular behaviour and when the wrongfulness of the behaviour of the defendant has to be established. If the research groups find out that, although the wordings and principles are dramatically different, the underlying methodology is similar, harmonisation might be possible.[39] However, the way in which a judge in a particular legal system will interpret this duty of care may again be strongly linked to differing preferences. Thus it would be possible, to be specific, to indicate that whatever methods judges use to establish negligence in a particular case, it may still be possible that, say, in a medical malpractice case the appropriate care required from a physician in Portugal may well be totally different from the care required from a physician in Germany.[40] This shows that it may be possible to call for centralisation, but that this centralisation should not necessarily be equated with harmonisation.[41] The previous example shows that it would, for example, be possible to centralise the way judges deal with the negligence standard, but this could be combined with a differentiated application of the duty of care in specific cases.[42] Thus one could use a *flexible system*[43] with a harmonisation of some general notions at the European level, but on the other hand retain a sufficient degree of flexibility to account for diverging preferences between Member States.

The major advantage of such a system would of course be that only the method in which the judge examines e.g. whether there is negligence is harmonised (which may already lead to a reduction of administrative costs because optical differences between the legal rules are removed), but at the same time differences in preferences are respected. A disadvantage is of course that differing outcomes will remain; however, if these differing outcomes correspond to differing preferences this should be considered more as an advantage than as a disadvantage. I do realise, however, that many "true believers" in harmonisation will not be very happy with this proposal. It means indeed that national judges, taking into account the preferences of national citizens can still give a different interpretation of the unified norm. Koziol for in-

---

39 See on that point generally, Koziol, H. (ed.), *Unification of Tort Law: Wrongfulness*, The Hague, Kluwer Law International, 1998 and for a comparison of the wrongfulness concept in Austria and Germany, Koziol, H., *supra* note 35, 2001, 29-38 and Lewisch, P., "A comparison of the Negligence Concept of the German BGB and the Austrian ABGB in an Economic Perspective", paper presented at the Annual conference of the European Association of Law and Economics in Vienna, September 2001, as well as Van Dam, C.C., *Aansprakelijkheidsrecht. Een grensoverschrijdend handboek*, Den Haag, Boom Juridische Uitgevers, 2000, 143-150.

40 Comparative research has indicated that this is indeed the case. See Faure, M. and Koziol, H. (eds.), *Cases on Medical Malpractice in a Comparative Perspective*, Vienna/New York, Springer, 2001.

41 This was correctly argued in the context of environmental liability by Arcuri, A., "Controlling environmental risk in Europe: the complementary role of an EC environmental liability regime", *TMA*, 2001, 37-45.

42 See, however, Koziol, H., *supra* note 35, 33, who argues that a harmonisation effort could not suffice with mere vague notions whereby the normative choices in specific cases would be left to the national legislators or judges. Spier, J. and Haazen, O.A., *supra* note 33, 484 also see this problem where they argue "the use of standards as a smoke-screen for deep disagreement creates a false consensus".

43 This idea of a flexible system in tort law comes from the Austrian scholar Wilburg, W., *Die Elemente des Schadenersatzrechts*, 1941 and *Entwicklung eines beweglichen Systems im bürgerlichen Recht*, 1950. See also Koziol, H., "Rechtswidrigkeit, bewegliches System und Rechtsausgleichung", *JBl*, 1988, 619.

stance holds that for him a harmonisation has not been successful when only vague notions are harmonised and when the normative choices in a specific case are still left to the national judges or legislators.[44] Also Spier and Haazen realised this problem where they argue "the use of standards as a smoke-screen for deep disagreement creates a false consensus".[45]

I do, however, believe that such a flexible system with a harmonisation of general notions at the European level creates important advantages. On the one hand it can enable a reduction of administrative costs by removing optical differences created by various legal dogmas, but at the same time a sufficient amount of flexibility is still retained, taking into account the various preferences of the citizens in the Member States.

4.2   Where Preferences Differ: Don't Touch!

There are, moreover, probably areas in tort law where the differing preferences are much stronger than the reduction of transaction cost benefits. Take the example of the amounts awarded for non-pecuniary losses. Many have argued that there are still considerable differences between the Member States in that respect. However, it is relatively difficult to argue that these differences themselves lead to huge economic problems. Again, one could argue that these differences reflect differing national preferences and therefore there seems to be no point in favour of harmonisation in this area. In this case the differences are probably not just differences in legal technique and can therefore not be reduced to pointless incompatibilities. It is therefore difficult to see any transaction cost benefit from harmonisation there, whereas the disadvantages (in terms of not respecting national preferences) under harmonisation would be huge. From an economic perspective there would thus not be an argument to harmonise, say, the specific amounts awarded in the various cases of non-pecuniary losses.

In the framework of a comparison of amounts awarded for non-pecuniary losses in Europe it could indeed be established that serious differences still exist, both with respect to the question whether some victims (and their relatives) are entitled to compensation for non-pecuniary losses, but also as far as the amounts awarded are concerned.[46] Some have therefore argued that it is unacceptable that within Europe a victim who, for example, suffers the loss of an arm would receive less in, say, Portugal than in, say, Germany. They implicitly argue that there is no reason to treat those victims differently and that the call for harmonisation of the amounts awarded for non-pecuniary losses is justified.[47]

---

44 See Koziol, H., *supra* note 35, 33.

45 See Spier, J. and Haazen, O.A., *supra* note 33, 484.

46 For an overview of the current differences between the Member States as far as the amounts awarded for pain and suffering are concerned see Rogers, H.W.V. (eds.), *Damages for Non-Pecuniary Loss in a Comparative Perspective*, Vienna, Springer, 2001.

47 This argument is made by Magnus, U. and Fedtke, J., "German Report on non-pecuniary loss", in Rogers, H.W.V. (ed.), *Damages for non-pecuniary loss in a Comparative Perspective*, 2001, 109-128, and in Magnus, U., "Towards European Civil Liability", in Faure, M., Schneider, H. and Smits, J. (eds.), *Towards a European Ius Commune in legal education and research*, Antwerpen, Intersentia, 2002, 205-224; also compare Magnus, U., *supra* note 14, 427-444.

What can, again, be said about this argument from an economic perspective? *First* of all one should remember that the differences in amounts awarded for non-pecuniary losses are certainly not pointless, but may reflect differing preferences of the citizens in the various states. In this respect one should, *second*, also remember that Coase taught that every increase in protection can always be passed on via the price mechanism.[48] In other words if, for example, in the area of product liability, one would argue that the Portuguese should pay higher amounts for non-pecuniary losses for victims of product accidents, this would lead to an increase in prices. Indeed, the manufacturer will add the additional damage costs to the price of the products. The effect therefore is that consumers pay a higher price for the protection awarded. It may well be that consumers in Portugal are not willing to pay this higher price. A European intervention forcing all Europeans to come up to, say, the German level, would therefore amount to paternalism.

Third, there may well be specific reasons why certain countries have relatively low amounts of non-pecuniary losses and others have higher. To some extent this may be related to the level of social security. It is difficult to judge, but looking at the difference between the US system and the European system, some claim that the high amounts for non-pecuniary losses in the US constitute to some extent compensation for the fact that there is no general basic social security system in the US. Nevertheless, no one would claim that the European level of non-pecuniary losses should come up to the American level.

Some argue that given the higher amount of travel in Europe today (tourism), it cannot be understood why, say, a German professor would receive less for his pain and suffering if he were to have an accident in Portugal rather than in Germany.[49] That fact is, again, hardly an argument in favour of harmonisation. Indeed, the fact that the Portuguese would choose a lower level of damage awards for pain and suffering than the Germans reflects differing preferences. There is no reason why the Portuguese would – paternalistically – have to come up to the German level, just to please the German tourist. The latter can, moreover, being aware that they will not enjoy the same level of protection abroad as in Germany, seek additional protection – if they so desire – in the form of a voluntary first party insurance. Such insurance for tourists is widely available on the market. The mere fact of tourism can therefore hardly be considered as an argument in favour of harmonisation.

In sum, contrary to what is sometimes assumed, there may be very clear reasons why some countries have lower or higher levels of compensation for non-pecuniary losses than others. If this corresponds to differing preferences, one can, at least from an economic perspective, see no need for a general harmonisation merely based on the reason that the existence of such differences is "unjust".[50] The example, again, shows that harmonisation cannot be addressed in black and white statements. Some issues may be harmonised at relatively low cost, whereas others (which are closely related to preferences) can be differentiated. In the area of compensation for non pe-

---

48 Coase, R., "The problem of social cost", *Journal of Law and Economics*, 1960, 1-44.
49 See – again – Magnus, U. and Fedtke, J., *supra* note 47, 109-128.
50 For a similar analysis, see Hartlief, T., "Comments on Magnus, U., 'Towards European Civil Liability'", in Faure, M., Schneider, H. and Smits, J. (eds.), *Towards a European Ius Commune in legal education and research*, Antwerpen, Intersentia, 2002, 225-230.

cuniary losses harmonisation[51] could lead to a paternalistic measure and to disrespect for the preferences of citizens. Even a call for the need to provide the same minimum protection to all accident victims within Europe can hardly justify such a paternalistic measure. However, with this statement and the reference to the need for providing a basic level of victim protection we have left the area of economics. Indeed, the reader should recall once more that in this paper I have only provided "one view of the cathedral".

It is indeed still thinkable that other, non-economic arguments would be advanced to argue that a harmonisation of e.g. pain and suffering would still be necessary in Europe, for instance to guarantee the minimum level of protection to all European victims. Those who would advance this argument should, however, realise that Europe today does not provide such a minimum protection to accident victims either. Social security is indeed to an important extent not yet harmonised. Also the compensation after industrial accidents or occupational diseases can still be very different between the Member States. If one would therefore argue that a minimum level of protection of accident victims is necessary it seems more indicated to focus on those areas first instead of pleading for a harmonisation of compensation for non-pecuniary losses.

4.3 No Harmonisation of Conditions of Competition

In this chapter I have merely addressed the question of whether a harmonisation of tort law is needed from an economic perspective. This is not totally useless, since the European Commission itself has long advanced an economic reason (harmonisation of marketing conditions) to justify European action. That reason is, as I have tried to show in this chapter, particularly weak.

The conclusion at the normative level, however, should not necessarily be that there is no need for any European action at all with respect to tort law.[52] My main problem is that the Commission still seems to be stuck in the old jargon of the "harmonisation of conditions of competition", whereas that seems to be a weak reason for harmonisation. There may be other, non-economic, reasons to justify harmonisation. But then these goals and expectations should be spelled out more specifically. Even those who dream of a European tort law as a political ideal (and who should realise that this may violate the preferences of citizens) can still benefit from economic analysis. Economics can help to show whether the methods of harmonisation chosen in a particular case can lead to the goals advertised. Moreover, those who blindly follow an unbalanced harmonisation dream should also be aware of the fact that in some cases they may (probably unknowingly) be instruments in the hands

---

51 See also Hartlief, T., *supra* note 50 and Hartlief, T., "Op weg naar een Europees aansprakelijkheidsrecht?", *TPR*, 2002, 945-953.

52 Compare Spier, J. and Haazen, O.A., *supra* note 33, 477: "Nor is convergence or unification of private law ever strictly speaking necessary... If we favour convergence of European private law, we deem it simply *desirable*, perhaps highly desirable, but nothing more". This desirability of the harmonisation of private law in Europe is, however, highly criticised – inter alia – by Smits, J.M., "Waarom harmonisering van het contractenrecht (via beginselen) onwenselijk is", *Contracteren*, 2001, 73-74.

of powerful lobby groups who can benefit from harmonisation. In this respect the important lesson from the public choice school, that whenever inefficient regulatory measures are enacted there is usually a special interest group that benefits from this action, should not be forgotten.[53]

4.4 Take the Subsidiarity Principles Seriously!

Finally there remains one important lesson from economics, being that the subsidiarity principle which is often heard, but not practised in Brussels should be taken seriously within the European harmonisation debate. Many talk about subsidiarity, but when it comes to providing serious arguments why a certain issue should be better regulated at the European level than at the level of the Member States, a serious answer is usually lacking. In addition it is important that serious attention is also given to the correct legal basis for harmonisation attempts with respect to tort law. If these issues are taken seriously the conclusion will probably be that a general harmonisation of tort law is problematic (and as I have argued, not necessary) and that a more nuanced approach of a limited harmonisation of certain general notions seems more promising. Such a balanced approach seems moreover to offer the necessary flexibility, which will allow the differing preferences of citizens in the Member States to be respected. One of the goals of this contribution was to show that within the shaping of such a nuanced approach (which could take the form of general tort rules in a European Civil Code) it is possible to harmonise to a certain extent and at the same time keep the necessary flexibility. Law and economics may prove to be a very helpful instrument in this exercise.

BIBLIOGRAPHY: Arcuri, A., "Controlling environmental risk in Europe: the complementary role of an EC environmental liability regime, *TMA*, 2001, 37-45; Bergkamp, L., "The Proposed Environmental Liability Directive", *European Environmental Law Review*, 2002, 294-341; Calabresi, G., *The costs of accidents, a legal and economic analysis*, New Haven, Yale University Press, 1970; Calabresi, G. and Melamed, D., "Property rules, liability rules and inalienability: one view of the cathedral", *Harvard Law Review*, 1972, vol. 85, 1089-1128; Coase, R., "The problem of social cost", *Journal of Law and Economics*, 1960, 1-44; Curran, C.H., "The burden of proof and the liability rule for suppliers of services in the EEC", *The Geneva Papers on Risk and Insurance*, 1994, 85-98; Duintjer Tebbens, H., "De Europese Richtlijn Produktaansprakelijkheid", *Nederlands Juristenblad*, 1986, 373-374; Esty, D. and Geradin, D., "Environmental protection and international competitiveness. A conceptual framework", *Journal of World Trade*, 1998, vol. 32/3, 16-19; Faure, M., "Harmonisation of environmental law and market integration: harmonising for the wrong reasons?", *European Environmental Law Review*, 1998, 169-175; Faure, M., "Product liability and product safety in Europe: harmonisation or differentiation?", *Kyklos*, vol. 53, 2000, 467-508; Faure, M., "Kompensationsmodelle für Heilwesenschäden in Europa mit Ausblick auf die EG-Rechtsharmonisierung", *Zeitschrift für Europäisches Privatrecht*, 2000, 575-600; Faure, M., "The White Paper on Environmental Liability: efficiency and insurability analysis", *Environmental Liability*, 2001, 188-201; Faure, M., "Towards a harmonised tort law in Europe? An economic perspective", *Maastricht Journal of European and Comparative Law*, 2001, 339-350; Faure, M. and De Smedt, K., "Should

---

53 See for a discussion of harmonisation attempts from a public choice perspective Van den Bergh, R., *supra* note 17, 148-151.

Europe harmonise environmental liability legislation?", *Environmental Liability*, 2001, 217-237; Faure, M. and Koziol, H. (eds.), *Cases on Medical Malpractice in a Comparative Perspective*, Vienna/New York, Springer, 2001; Faure, M., "Product liability and product safety in a federal system: economic reflections on the proper role of Europe", in Marciano, A. and Josselin, J.M. (eds.), *The economics of harmonising European Law*, Cheltenham, Edward Elgar, 2002, 131-177; Frey, B., "Direct Democracy: Politico-Economic Lessons from Switzerland", *American Economic Review*, 1994, 338-342; Hartlief, T., "Comments on Magnus, U., 'Towards European Civil Liability'", in Faure, M., Schneider, H. and Smits, J. (eds.), *Towards a European Ius Commune in legal education and research*, 2002, 225-230; Hartlief, T., "Op weg naar een Europees aansprakelijkheidsrecht?", *TPR*, 2002, 945-953; Jaffe, A., Peterson, S., Portney, P. and Stavins, R., "Environmental regulation and the competitiveness of US manufacturing: what does the evidence tell us?", *Journal of Economic Literature*, 1995, vol. 33, 132-163; Janssen, M., "Auf dem Weg zu einem Europäischen Haftungsrecht", *Zeitschrift für Europäisches Privatrecht*, 2001, 30-65; Koch, B. and Koziol, H. (ed.), *Unification of Tort Law, Strict Liability*, The Hague, Kluwer Law International, 2002; Kötz, H. and Wagner, H., *Deliktsrecht*, 9th edition, Neuwied, Luchterhand Verlag, 2001; Koziol, H., "Rechtswidrigkeit, bewegliches System und Rechtsausgleichung", *JBl*, 1988, 619; Koziol, H., "Das Niederländische BW und der Schweizer Entwurf als Vorbilder für ein künftiges Europäisches Schadenersatzrecht", *Zeitschrift für Europäisches Privatrecht*, 1996, 587-599; Koziol, H. (ed.), *Unification of Tort Law: Wrongfulness*, The Hague, Kluwer Law International, 1998; Koziol, H., "Ein Europäisches Schadenersatzrecht – Wirklichkeit oder Traum", *JBl*, 2001, 32-33; Landes, W. and Posner, R., "The positive economic theory of tort law", *Tort and Law Review*, 1981, 851-924; Legrand, P., "The impossibility of legal transplants", *Maastricht Journal of European and Comparative Law*, 1997, 111; Lewisch, P., "A comparison of the Negligence Concept of the German BGB and the Austrian ABGB in an Economic Perspective", paper presented at the Annual conference of the European Association of Law and Economics in Vienna, September 2001; Magnus, U., "European perspectives of tort liability", *European Review of Private Law*, 1995, 427-444; Magnus, U. and Fedtke, J., "German Report on non-pecuniary loss", in Rogers, H.W.V. (ed.), *Damages for non-pecuniary loss in a Comparative Perspective*, 2001, 109-128; Magnus, U., "Towards European Civil Liability", in Faure, M., Schneider, H. and Smits, J. (eds.), *Towards a European Ius Commune in legal education and research*, Antwerpen, Intersentia, 2002, 205-224; Martin Casals, M. and Solé Feliu, J., "Responsabilidad por productas en España y (des)armonizacion Europea", *Revista de responsabilidad civil y seguros*, 2001, vol. 4, 1-17 ; Nieuwenhuis, J.H., "Wat is een onrechtmatige daad? Europese perspectieven", *RMThemis*, 1998, 242-248; Ogus, A., "Competition between national legal systems. A contribution of economic analysis to comparative law", *The International and Comparative Law Quarterly*, 1999, 405-418; Ogus, A., "The contribution of economic analysis of law to legal transplants", in Smits, J. (ed.), *The contribution of mixed legal systems to European law*. Antwerp, Intersentia, 2001, 27-37; Rehbinder, E., "Towards a community environmental liability regime: the Commission's White Paper on Environmental Liability", *Environmental Liability*, 2000, 85-96; Revesz, R., "Environmental Regulation in Federal Systems", in Somsen, H. (ed.), *Yearbook of European Environmental Law*, 2000, 1-35; Revesz, R., "Federalism and Environmental Regulation: An Overview", in Revesz, R., Sands, Ph. and Stewart, R. (eds.), *Environmental Law: The Economy and Sustainable Development*, 2000, 37-79; Revesz, R., "Federalism and regulation: some generalisations", in Esty, D. and Geradin, D. (eds.), *Regulatory competition and economic integration, comparative perspectives*, Oxford, Oxford University Press, 2001, 3-29; Rice, P., "From Lugano to Brussels via Arhus: Environmental Liability White Paper published", *Environmental Liability*, 2000, 39-45; Rogers, H.W.V. (ed.), *Damages for Non-Pecuniary Loss in a Comparative Perspective*, Vienna, Springer, 2001; Rose-Ackerman, S., Rethinking the progressive agenda, the reform of the American regulatory state, Macmillan Inc./Simon &

Schuster, 1992; Shavell, S., *Economic Analysis of Accident Law*, Cambridge, Harvard University Press, 1987; Smits, J.M., "Waarom harmonisering van het contractenrecht (via beginselen) onwenselijk is", *Contracteren,* 2001, 73-74; Smits, J., The good Samaritan in European private Law, Deventer, Kluwer, 2002; Spier, J. and Haazen, O., "The European group on tort law ('Tilburg group') and European principles of tort law", *Zeitschrift für Europäisches Privatrecht,* 1999, 469-493; Storm, P., "Een gebrekkig produkt", *Maandblad voor Ondernemingsrecht,* 1985, 245; Tiebout, C., "A pure theory of local expenditures", *Journal of Political Economy,* vol. 64, 1956, 416-424; Van Dam, C.C., Aansprakelijkheidsrecht. Een grensoverschrijdend handboek, Den Haag, Boom Jurische Uitgevers, 2000; Van den Bergh, R., "Subsidiarity as an economic demarcation principle and the emergence of European private law", *Maastricht Journal of European and Comparative Law,* 1998, 129-152; Van den Bergh, R., "Economics in a Legal Strait-Jacket: The Difficult Reception of Economic Analysis in European Law", paper presented at the workshop Empirical Research and Legal Realism: Setting the Agenda, Haifa, 6-9 June 1999; Van Gerven, W., "Bridging the unbridgeble. Community and national tort laws after Francovich and Brasserie", *International Comparative Law Quarterly,* 1996, 507-544; Van Gerven, W., Lever, J., Larouche, P., von Bar, Ch. and Viney, G., *Cases, materials and texts on national, supranational and international tort law. Scope of protection,* Oxford, Hart Publishing, 1998; Van Gerven, W., Lever, J. and Larouche, P., Cases, materials and texts on national, supranational and international tort law, Oxford, Hart Publishing, 2000; Van Wassenaer van Catwijck, A.J.O., "Produktaansprakelijkheid", in *Serie Praktijkhandleidingen,* Zwolle, 1986, 81; Vogel, D., Trading-up. Consumer and Environmental Regulation in a Global Economy, Cambridge, Harvard University Press, 1995; Von Bar, Ch., "Konturen des Deliktrechtskonzept der Study Group on a European Civil Code", *Zeitschrift für Europäisches Privatrecht,* 2000, 515-532; Von Bar, Ch., *The Common European Law of Torts, II,* Oxford, Clarendon, 2000; Widmer, P., "Die Vereinheitlichung des Europäischen Schadenersatzrechts aus der Sicht eines Kontinental Europäers", *Revue Héllenique de Droit International,* vol. 52, 1999, 99; Wilburg, W., Die Elemente des Schadenersatzrechts, 1941; Wilburg, W., Entwicklung eines beweglichen Systems im bürgerlichen Recht, 1950; Wininger, B., "L'architecture de l'Avant-projet de loi sur la responsabilité civile", *Revue de Droit Suisse,* 2001, 299-326.

CHAPTER 37

Environmental Liability and the Private Enforcement of Community Law

Gerrit Betlem*

1 Introduction

This Chapter examines legal developments at EC level relevant to possible environmental liability provisions in a possible future European Civil Code. It updates the second edition of *Towards a European Civil Code* in that both legislative and judicial contributions during the period 2000-2003 are covered. First, a chronological account of events is provided. Then there is a discussion of the June 2003 Council Common Position. As will be seen, the Common Position is, from a private law perspective, perhaps most noteworthy for what it does not contain, i.e. tort as an enforcement tool for public law standards. Accordingly, the remainder of this Chapter will focus not on legislative but on judicial developments in the Europeanisation of (environmental) liability law within the framework of empirical research into the deterrent effect of liability and an international Convention requiring effective access to justice to combat violations of environmental law by both private bodies and public authorities (the Aarhus Convention). That being said, the draft Environmental Liability Directive will nonetheless have an impact on private law in at least two respects: its applicability will have to be coordinated with product liability regimes and it may give rise to claims before civil courts with a view to recognition and enforcement abroad (below § 2).

1.1 Chronology

A short reminder of the recent history of environmental liability law at Community level may be useful. As noted in *Towards II*, legislative progress has been very slow. Indeed, many commentators were not sure whether a proposal for a Directive would ever be adopted. The political climate in the first year of the 2000s, however, differed from that in the 1990s in that there was a growing public concern over e.g. the environmental consequences of the various pollution incidents that have occurred over the years and the possible effects of releases of genetically modified organisms (GMOs) on public health and the environment. The increase in public awareness of environmental matters provides an incentive for regulators to establish rules on environmental liability.

The first time that harmonisation of environmental liability law was mentioned in

* Reader, European Private Law, University of Exeter. Field of Specialisation: European private (international) law. Correspondence Address: University of Exeter, School of Law, Amory bld., Rennes Drive, Exeter EX4 4RJ, UK, e-mail: G.Betlem@exeter.ac.uk

an EC legislative instrument was in 1984 in Article 11(3) of Directive 84/631,[1] pursuant to which the Council was under a duty to regulate the liability for damage caused by waste. Although this obligation has applied since 6 December 1984, legislative progress has so far only resulted in an Amended Proposal for a Council Directive on civil liability for damage caused by waste.[2] In any event, this duty to legislate is no longer in force as Directive 84/631 has been replaced by Council Regulation 259/93 on the supervision and control of shipments of waste within, into and out of the European Community.[3] The Regulation does not, however, contain any reference to a regime for the liability of producers of waste. Liability is thus governed by the legal systems of the Member States. The Commission is proposing a complete overhaul of the Regulation in light of obligations under international law (the Basel Convention regime). But even here no harmonisation of the liability rules is being considered. The 2003 Proposal for a Waste Shipments Regulation is explicitly without prejudice to national or Community law on liability. Nonetheless, it presumes that adequate liability rules are in place as it does require operators to furnish evidence of insurance against liability for damage to third parties.[4]

In 1994 the European Parliament called for legislation in this area and adopted a resolution calling on the Commission to submit a proposal for a directive on civil liability for environmental damage.[5] It took until 9 February 2000 for the Commission to publish the final version of the White Paper on Environmental Liability.[6] The White Paper was an important step in preparing legislation. As will be seen, the Commission opted for a so-called horizontal regime, covering damage to the environment resulting from harmful activities generally, instead of deciding for sector-specific liability rules such as those for liability for damage caused by GMOs or waste. The document sets out the structure of a possible future EC environmental liability regime. It contains the core elements and principles of a horizontal environmental liability directive. The regime as proposed is set up as a framework regime with minimal requirements and standards and is to be completed over time and on the basis of experience with its initial application. The regime outlined in the White Paper has a closed character and is linked to relevant EC environmental legislation. It covers two areas: damage caused by activities that bear an inherent risk of causing damage to the environment and that are subject to EC law, and damage to natural resources but only insofar as these are protected by Community law. A strict liability applies for damage caused by inherently dangerous activities and a fault-based liability for damage to (what is called) biodiversity caused by an activity not listed as dangerous. The regime will not be applied retroactively. Environmental damage that was caused in the past is considered to be a matter that should be dealt with by the Member States.

---

1 Council Directive 84/631 on the supervision and control within the European Community of the transfrontier shipment of hazardous waste, *OJ* 1984 L 326/31.
2 *OJ* 1991 C 192/6; see for an extensive commentary V. Wilmowsky & Roller (1992).
3 *OJ* 1993 L 30/1 (as amended); in force since 1 May 1994.
4 Proposal for a Regulation of the European Parliament and of the Council on Shipments of Waste, COM(2003) 379 of 30/06/03, Arts. 25(3), 26(8) and Annex II, No. 16.
5 EP Resolution on preventing and remedying environmental damage, *OJ* 1994 C 128/165. See also Opinion of the Economic and Social Committee on the Green Paper, *OJ* 1994 C 133/8, para. 2.2.1.
6 COM(2000) 66, http://europa.eu.int/comm/environment/liability/.

In January 2002, the European Commission adopted a Proposal for a Directive on Environmental Liability.[7] The draft Directive marks the first formal step in the legislative process after the Commission issued its White Paper (as mentioned). The White Paper outlined some of the key elements of an effective and practicable EU-wide environmental liability regime, including damage to persons, goods and soil pollution, and also damage to nature. What is interesting (or perhaps regrettable), however, is that the civil liability regime of the White Paper is not reflected in the 2002 Proposal. The current proposal underlines that "this Directive shall not give private parties a right of compensation" relating to (threatened) environmental damage at all; although it leaves intact any rights of recourse or contribution by operators against other polluters in situations of multiple party causation (Arts. 3(8) and 11(3)). It is confined to actions by public authorities against operators (which generally means proceedings under a public law regime, though this varies from jurisdiction to jurisdiction).[8] What is thus clearly excluded is any role whatsoever for civil liability as a tool of private enforcement by private actors against polluters and as a mechanism to overcome barriers to access to justice. As will be seen below, this is incompatible with the Aarhus Convention, to which the EC is a signatory.

This is particularly strange, for a number of reasons. First, the draft Directive was produced while the EC had already signed the Aarhus Convention and which, it is suggested, does require a private action to be available to non-public bodies to ensure compliance with environmental law by other non-public bodies (to be further discussed below § 3).

Secondly, the complete exclusion of civil claims by private parties negates a commitment made by the Commission to the European Parliament that a general liability regime would cover damage caused by GMOs; the EP therefore agreed not to press for liability provisions in the revised GMO Directive.[9] Although the European Parliament is considering numerous amendments to the Proposal, which, if agreed, may include civil actions by private claimants against polluters, it remains to be seen what will come of them.[10]

To be sure, one of the reasons for this shift from private to public law is the fact that tort law nowadays operates in a regulatory context.[11] Crudely summarised, the

---

7 COM(2002)17, Brussels, 23 January 2002, *OJ* 2002 C 151 E/132.

8 See also Lee (2003).

9 Betlem & Brans (2002). Directive 2001/18/EC of the European Parliament and of the Council of 12 March 2001 on the deliberate release into the environment of genetically modified organisms and repealing Council Directive 90/220/EEC, *OJ* 2001 L 106/1, recital 16, of the preamble which reads: "The provisions of this Directive should be without prejudice to national legislation in the field of environmental liability, while Community legislation in this field needs to be complemented by rules covering liability for different types of environmental damage in all areas of the European Union. To this end the Commission has undertaken to bring forward a legislative proposal on environmental liability before the end of 2001, which will also cover damage from GMOs."

10 See in particular the Draft Opinion of 16/10/02 of the Committee on the Environment, Public Health and Consumer Policy for the Committee on Legal Affairs and the Internal Market by Mihail Papayannakis, available at www.europarl.eu.int. The EP, in second reading under Article 251 EC Treaty, will consider the Proposal further following the political agreement of a Common Position by the Council at its 2517th session on 13 June 2003 in Luxembourg, see Minutes 10273/03 (Press 165).

11 See generally Cane (2002-2).

historical development of environmental protection law is that it started with private law alone. In the common law world with the torts of nuisance and trespass, in civilian jurisdictions with the general provisions of the law of delict,[12] coupled with the doctrine of abuse of rights and maxims such as *sic utere tuo ut alienum non laedas*. But the emphasis shifted substantially from private to public law enforcement from the 1960s onwards,[13] mainly because tort law was not regarded adequate for environmental protection purposes. Some authors currently advocate a return to an all-or-nothing situation in the sense of only regulation and no tort law at all.[14] Others prefer a complementary role for tort alongside, and in conjunction with, public law regulatory regimes.[15] It is nevertheless true that environmental law is, and is likely to remain, clearly dominated by regulatory command and control regimes with tort or delict as at most the junior partner.

That does not mean, however, that there is no longer a meaningful role for old-style tort law. An analogous example at EU level is product safety. There is a framework dealing with standards and procedures involving controls by public authorities at both EC and national level (the General Product Safety Directive).[16] In addition, and performing a complementary role, there is an autonomous, harmonised, civil liability regime for damage caused by defective products (the Product Liability Directive).[17] Indeed, this approach was also adopted in the waste policy area with the Commission's 1991 Amended Proposal for a Council Directive on civil liability for damage caused by waste.[18] It includes a free standing liability regime with strict liability of waste producers for damage resulting from their waste. This is indeed a remarkably extensive liability, since not only does it encompass impairment of the environment as a whole, but it is no defence that the defendant complied with a permit or regulatory requirements. This mixed approach, it is submitted, is better suited to deal with risks that slip through the regulatory net – civil liability is then there to pick them up.[19]

Nor has the Commission had any hesitation in promoting private enforcement in other areas than environmental law. Particularly noteworthy, apart from the case of product liability already mentioned, are competition law (including unfair commer-

---

12 E.g. *Code Civil*, § 1382 and its progeny.

13 With preludes in the 19th century, public bodies having had long extensive powers of interference: see, for example, the "statutory nuisance" regime in England under the Public Health Act 1875, ss. 91 *et seq.*

14 Bergkamp (1998); cf. Cane (2002-1).

15 Stallworthy (2003); Arcuri (2001); see also, from 41 *Washburn Law Review* 2002, Spring issue: Abraham, Anderson, Hylton and Kanner.

16 Directive 2001/95/EC of the European Parliament and the Council of 3 December 2001 on general product safety, *OJ* 2002 L 11/4.

17 Council Directive 85/374/EEC of 25 July 1985 on the approximation of the laws, regulations and administrative provisions of the Member States concerning liability for defective products, *OJ* 1985 L 210/29 as amended by Directive 1999/34/EC of the European Parliament and of the Council of 10 May 1999 amending Council Directive 85/374/EEC on the approximation of the laws, regulations and administrative provisions of the Member States concerning liability for defective products, *OJ* 1999 L 141 /20; a consolidated version is available on the EUR-LEX Website, URL: europa.eu.int/ eur-lex/en/consleg/index1.html.

18 *OJ* 1991 C 192/6.

19 See Abraham (2002), at 397.

cial practices) and intellectual property.[20] As for IP, the current draft Directive focuses exactly on this very topic: it concerns solely the harmonisation of sanctions and in particular private enforcement. A need for equal effectiveness of IP rights throughout the Community is identified; "disparities between the systems of the Member States for enforcing intellectual property rights are prejudicial to the proper functioning of the Internal Market and make it impossible to ensure that intellectual property rights enjoy an equivalent level of protection throughout the Community;[21] "current disparities also lead to a weakening of the substantive law on intellectual property and to a fragmentation of the Internal Market in this field";[22] therefore, effective enforcement of the substantive IP *acquis communautaire* "must be ensured by specific action at Community level".[23] Can the same argument not be made for environmental protection? Before further analyzing the case for private enforcement from an empirical, international and judicial perspective, the next Section surveys the state of the legislative art *Anno Domini* 2003.

2 Council Common Position on Draft Environmental Liability Directive

As already mentioned, the draft Directive has shifted from a primarily private law to a predominantly public law regime. The basic features of the Proposal are retained in the Common Position of the Council.[24] Space does not permit a comprehensive analysis of the Common Position. It is sufficient to outline the main features and to represent these in a Table below. Potentially liable persons covered by the draft Directive are "operators" (as defined in the Proposal). The scope of the Directive in terms of recoverable heads of damages is restricted to "environmental damage" (as defined, see Table below); property damage as such, personal injury and pure economic loss suffered by private parties are not included. The central liability provision (Art. 8) stipulates that operators "shall bear the costs for the preventive and remedial actions taken ..." (if they had not already executed them themselves). The Directive contains two forms of this operator liability: strict liability where environmental damage was caused by dangerous, occupational, activities,[25] and fault liability for any

---

20　See Commission White Paper on modernisation of the rules implementing Articles 85 and 86 of the EC Treaty, *OJ* 1999 C 132/1, Council Regulation (EC) No. 1/2003 of 16 December 2002 on the implementation of the rules on competition laid down in Articles 81 and 82 of the Treaty, *OJ* 2003 L 1/1; Proposal for a Directive of the European Parliament and of the Council concerning unfair business-to-consumer commercial practices in the internal market and amending Directives 84/450/EC, 97/7/EC and 98/27/EC (the Unfair Commercial Practices Directive), COM(2003) 356 of 18 June 2003; and Proposal for a Directive on measures and procedures to ensure the enforcement of intellectual property rights, Brussels, 31/1/03, COM(2003) 46.

21　Preamble, recital 8, COM(2003) 46 at p. 29.

22　Preamble, recital 9, *ibid*.

23　*Ibid*.

24　Brussels, 20 June 2003; text as agreed by Coreper; No. 10700/03, http://ue.eu.int/en/summ.htm. The Directive has been adopted on 21 April 2004, see Directive 2004/35, *OJ* 2004 L 143/56.

25　I.e. activities covered by existing EC environmental law and listed in Annex III of the Common Position.

other, non-dangerous, activities but only insofar as damage to protected species and natural habitats are concerned. The Community legislature leaves it up to the Member States whether or not operators, who must prove that they have not been negligent, may invoke compliance with an authorisation as a defence. It is likewise with the so-called State of the Art defence. The Directive provides that Member States may allow the operators not to bear the costs for remedying damage regarding "an emission or activity or any manner of using a product in the course of an activity which the operator demonstrates was not considered likely to cause environmental damage according to the state of scientific and technical knowledge at the time when the emission was released or the activity took place" (Art. 8(4)b). The approach taken to state of the art echoes that of the Product Liability Directive which likewise left this up to the Member States.[26]

Unlike the latter, however, the Environmental Liability Directive also allows for the regulatory compliance defence. The inclusion of this option is important in terms of the matter of the occupied field of harmonisation that the Directive in issue covers.[27] The delineation between these two instruments (once both are in force) will thus become a matter of great importance.[28] Member States are not allowed, even if they so wish, to introduce the regulatory compliance defence in their domestic strict product liability regimes (i.e. within the occupied field of the Directive); they are so allowed under the draft Environmental Liability Directive. The above may be summarised as follows:

Tables: Scope, Covered activities, Covered types of loss, Types of liability

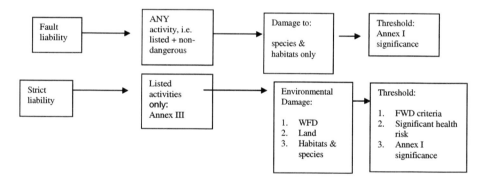

---

26 See Article 15(1)b of Directive 85/374/EEC, *OJ* 1985 L 210/29.
27 See in particular, on the Product Liability Directive, the ECJ judgments of 25 April 2002 in: Case C-52/00 *Commission* v. *France* [2002] *ECR* I-3827; Case C-154/00 *Commission* v. *Greece* [2002] *ECR* I-3879; Case C-183/00 *González Sánchez* [2002] *ECR* I-3901.
28 Cf. for a similar exercise within the Dutch Civil Code Nieuwenhuis (1997).

Put differently:

Nature of liability	*Activity*	Environmental Damage	Habitat-damage	Threshold
Strict	Annex III (dangerous) activities	X	X	Significant
Fault	All activities, incl. non-dangerous		X	Significant

"Habitat damage" is listed separately – despite it already being included in one of the three categories of "environmental damage" – because the fault liability is only relevant to that type of loss (next table):

Type of damage	Nature of liability	Activities	Damage where?	Threshold
Traditional damage[29]				
Habitat/species-damage	Strict & fault	All activities	Annex I species and habitats	Annex I significance
"Water-damage"	Strict	Annex IIII activities	FWD waters	FWD criteria
"Land-damage"	Strict	Annex III activities	Everywhere	Significant risk to human health

Although the above confirms the primarily public law nature of the proposed Directive (despite its name), two aspects do have an impact on private (international) law. As mentioned, these are the demarcation with liability of producers under the Product Liability Directive and the explicit recognition of potential claims by public authorities against operators based outside their territory (art. 15(3)). In the absence of a comprehensive system of recognition and enforcement of foreign public law acts, it would seem to follow that such claims will have to be brought under Member States' private laws and, if they also constitute a civil and commercial matter, will then benefit from the regime of the so-called Brussels I Regulation[30] to obtain effect throughout the EU.[31]

---

29 I.e. property damage, personal injury, pure economic loss.
30 Council Regulation (EC) No. 44/2001 on jurisdiction and the recognition and enforcement of judgments in civil and commercial matters, *OJ* 2001 L 12/1; the so-called Brussels I Convention remains relevant for Denmark, see generally Briggs (2002), pp. 52 *et seq.*
31 See for more details Bernasconi & Betlem (2003).

3 Deterrent Effect of Tort Law

There is anecdotal evidence in a recent Dutch article highlighting the ineffectiveness of public enforcement regimes, in particular judicial review. The authors advocate the use of civil remedies as a more effective enforcement tool.[32] Is there any further, more systematic, empirical proof for this belief in tort law as a tool of enforcement? Schwartz has carried out extensive empirical research on the deterrent effect of tort.[33] He investigated industrial injury,[34] motorist liability, medical malpractice, product liability, non-profit and governmental agencies, occupiers' liability and has made a special study of the unique accident compensation scheme operating in New Zealand. The main aim of his work was to examine the view defended by many Law and Economics scholars that tort law was such a strong deterrent that no regulation at all was needed. He concluded that tort makes a significant contribution to risk prevention/minimisation as a supplement to (or alongside) command and control systems of regulation. For example, worker compensation claims compared to an alternative of no employers liability had reduced workplace deaths by 33%;[35] a before-and-after study on the abolition of tort for car accidents in Quebec indicated an increase in fatalities, with similar results from New Zealand's complete exclusion of civil liability for all accidents; "[t]he general threat of liability clearly affects the behaviour of doctors;"[36] and finally, the abolition of immunity from suit of certain non-profit organisations in the US had spurred the introduction of risk management systems. More generally speaking, the latter point is important: it was only because of the threat of liability that risk managers were able to persuade managers of their companies to invest in risk prevention measures. It follows that empirical proof exists of the useful role tort plays as a deterrent to harmful conduct either independent of or in conjunction with regulation.

4 The Aarhus Convention

Together with all the Member States, the European Community signed the Aarhus Convention in 1998.[37] To date, however, it has not ratified, approved or adopted the Convention.[38] Of the three main components of the Convention – access to information, public participation in decision-making and access to justice – only the first two have been covered fully by Community legislation.[39] The Aarhus access to justice

---

32 Hazewindus & Van der Wilt (2003).
33 Schwartz (1994).
34 See also, for an English case study, Pontin (1998).
35 Schwartz, at p. 393.
36 *Ibid.*, at p. 401.
37 Convention on Access to Information, Public Participation in Decision-Making and Access to Justice in Environmental Matters, Aarhus, 25 June 1998, (1999) 38 I.L.M. 517. In force since 30/10/01, see http://unece.org/env/pp/.
38 Website Aarhus Convention | Status of ratification, www.unece.org/env/pp/ (visited 22/7/03). Of the Member States, the Convention is binding upon Belgium, Denmark, France, Italy and Portugal. On 24/10/03 the Commission adopted a package of proposals to fully implement Aarhus.
39 Directive 2003/4/EC of the European Parliament and of the Council of 28 January 2003 on public access to environmental information and repealing Council Directive 90/313/EEC, *OJ* 2003 L 41/26.

pillar, has, to date, been given effect in Community law only as amendments to the IPPC and EIA Directives.[40] Notably this means that, as a matter of Community law, the Convention's provision on access to civil remedies forms no part of the EC legal order. But as a signatory, the EC is loosing political credibility if it is not prepared to make Aarhus binding on itself.

Importantly, the third pillar of Aarhus – access to justice – is not limited to public law. On the contrary, in addition to ensuring access of the public to legal mechanisms – mainly in the form of judicial review – in the event of non-compliance with the Convention's first and second pillars, i.e. the provisions on access to information and public participation, access to the courts must be made available to combat violations of domestic environmental law by both private persons and public authorities, Art. 9(3).[41] Moreover, the Convention requires parties to make available effective remedies, including injunctive relief, which are fair, equitable, timely and not prohibitively expensive, Art. 9(4). Finally, the Convention requires States to "consider the establishment of appropriate assistance mechanisms to remove or reduce financial and other barriers to access to justice" Art. 9(5).

It follows that Aarhus, at least as regards those States that have ratified it, includes obligations upon States to ensure that their legal system includes effective civil remedies for the public (as defined in the Convention) against any person or entity breaching environmental protection law.[42] Although Aarhus explicitly talks only of violations of States' "*national* law relating to the environment" (Art. 9(3), emphasis added), in the context of EC law "national" must be construed as including Community law, in particular directives and regulations within the meaning of Art. 249 EC containing substantive environmental law. This issue will arise even without ratification of Aarhus by the EC/EU because some Member States are already bound by the Convention and, of course, most of their *national* environmental law is nothing other than transposed *Community* law. Accordingly, private enforcement of EC environmental law is therefore already legally required in some EU Member States.[43]

Although highly significant in terms of the harmonisation, as a matter of international – not EC – law, of domestic tort law for the purpose of enforcement of national

---

40 Directive 2003/35/EC of the European Parliament and of the Council of 26 May 2003 providing for public participation in respect of the drawing up of certain plans and programmes relating to the environment and amending with regard to public participation and access to justice Council Directives 85/337/EEC and 96/61/EC, *OJ* 2003 L 156/17.

41 Article 9(3) Access to Justice: "In addition and without prejudice to the review procedures referred to in paragraphs 1 and 2 above, each Party shall ensure that, where they meet the criteria, if any, laid down in its national law, members of the public have access to administrative or judicial procedures to challenge acts and omissions by private persons and public authorities which contravene provisions of its national law relating to the environment."

42 See also Stephen Stec *et al.*, *The Aarhus Convention: an Implementation Guide*, UN Doc. ECE/CEP/ 72, New York and Geneva 2002, pp. 123-125, available at http://unece.org/env/pp/, at pp. 130-136. It is true that the Convention requires access to a court of law *and/or* another body, but the latter must be an independent and impartial body established by law. Normally, only civil courts will be competent to deal with disputes between private actors. Contra Rodenhoff (2002), at p. 349. Lee & Abbot think it is debatable whether a "citizen suit" is required by this provision: Lee & Abbot (2003), at p. 105.

43 As mentioned, they are: Belgium, Denmark, France, Italy and Portugal. And, after enlargment: Cyprus, Estonia, Hungary, Latvia, Lithuania, Malta and Poland.

environmental law, the Aarhus Convention does no more than concretise, in the context of environmental law, the more general obligation of States to provide effective remedies arising under provisions such as Article 6 and 13 of the European Convention of Human Rights.[44] In the next section, it will be seen that a parallel obligation to make available private enforcement mechanisms arises under EC law as a result of a seminal judgment of the European Court of Justice.

5 Private Enforcement and the ECJ's *Muñoz* Judgment

It is well known that lack of action by the Community legislature does not necessarily mean that Community law does not develop in parallel. Indeed, the ECJ, within the remit of its jurisdiction can, and has, made significant contributions to the development of EC law.[45] Most notable in the present context is the consistent law on the role of private enforcement mechanisms in addition to the provisions of the Treaties (and secondary Community law) on a public law enforcement scheme. The latest step in this connection is the 2002 *Muñoz* case.[46] At issue was not environmental law as such but an analogous point – the right of a trader to seek enforcement of food quality standards against a competitor in civil proceedings. The ECJ ruled that the relevant Regulations "are to be interpreted as meaning that compliance with [the quality standards] must be capable of enforcement by means of civil proceedings instituted by a trader against a competitor" (operative part). This judgment has wider implications than for the field of EC food law alone; indeed, in my view, the *ratio decidendi* of this landmark ruling covers all usage of tort law as a tool for enforcing EC public law standards before national civil courts. Tort law of the Member States must, as a matter of Community law, be made available as an effective private enforcement instrument. If necessary, restrictive requirements barring this are to be modified or removed. Let us therefore examine the case in more detail.

5.1 *Muñoz* – Facts and Legal Framework

Community law lays down quality standards for varieties of table grapes in two Regulations.[47] Briefly summarised they provide that these products may not be marketed in any other manner within the Community than in compliance with these standards. Checks must be made by the competent authorities of the Member States to

---

44 Specifically in the environment sector, the same point has been made by the Global Judges Symposium meeting during the Johannesburg World Summit on Sustainable Development, which adopted the "Johannesburg Principles on the Role of law and sustainable Development," 18-20 August 2002, available at the UNEP Website (www.unep.org/documents/) and the WSSD Website (www.dfa.gov.za/docs/wssd288g.htm, visited 15/04/03); reprinted in (2003) 15 *Journal of Environmental Law* 107.

45 See e.g. Van Erp (2001).

46 Case C-253/00 *Muñoz and Superior Fruiticola* [2002] *ECR* I-7289; [2002] 3 C.M.L.R. 26; [2003] 3 W.L.R. 58; [2003] All E.R. (EC) 56.

47 Regulation (EEC) No. 1035/72 of the Council of 18 May 1972 on the common organisation of the market in fruit and vegetables, *OJ* 1972 L 118/1 and Council Regulation (EC) No. 2200/96 of 28 October 1996 on the common organisation of the market in fruit and vegetables, O.J 1996 L 297/1.

ensure that goods do indeed comply with those standards. Specifically regarding table grapes, the regime prescribes an exhaustive system of marking and labelling. That is to say that a variety such as "Superior Seedless" may not be named anything other than "Superior Seedless." In the UK, the body entrusted with enforcement of these rules is the Horticultural Marketing Inspectorate (HMI). The applicable UK legislation imposes penalties for breach of the Community standards. The Spanish company Muñoz holds exclusive rights to grow these grapes. Competitors marketed their grapes in breach of these exclusive rights. The HMI took no action in response to complaints about mislabelling. Muñoz then sued them before the High Court seeking an injunction as well as damages.[48] The English court held that the Regulations at issue here did not give the claimants a right of action in civil proceedings. The action therefore failed. On appeal, the Court of Appeal acknowledged that the question of a civil remedy for breach of the regulations was one of general importance in Community law and accordingly made a reference for a preliminary ruling to the ECJ.[49]

5.2 *Muñoz* – The Judgment of the ECJ

The sole issue before the ECJ was whether the relevant food quality standards regulations give rise to an obligation for traders in fruit and vegetables to comply with those standards, enforceable by means of civil proceedings instituted by a competitor. In other words, do product standards laid down by Community (public) law entail, as a matter of EC law, a right of action under national tort law? In a few considerations, the ECJ answered in the affirmative. It started its reasoning by referring to the normative force of EC regulations under Article 249 EC and their place in the hierarchy of sources of Community law: they are of general application, directly applicable and "owing to their very nature ... operate to confer rights on individuals which the national courts have a duty to protect" (para. 27). Secondly, the ECJ reaffirmed that those courts must ensure the full effectiveness of those Community rules (the classic *effet utile* requirement; para. 28).

Thirdly, the ECJ focused on the regulations in hand. It deduced from its preamble and its scheme that the purpose of the common quality standards for fruit and vegetables is threefold: (i) to exclude unsatisfactory products from the market, (ii) to guide traders as to consumer requirements and (iii) to facilitate fair competition between traders. Accordingly, the ECJ held that the noted *effet utile* and more specifically the practical effect of the traders' duty to comply with the standards[50] "imply that it must be possible to enforce that obligation by means of civil proceedings instituted by a trader against a competitor" (para. 30). Finally, the Court underlined that the availability of tort claims strengthens the *effect utile* of the quality standards. It supplements enforcement by public authorities with a view to discouraging "practices, often difficult to detect, which distort competition" (para. 31). Indeed, the ECJ

---

48 See English High Court 26 March 1999 *Muñoz* v. *Frumar* [1999] 3 C.M.L.R. 684 (Laddie J.).

49 Judgment of 10 May 2000, unreported, see Lexis.

50 I.e. Article 3(1) of both Reg. 1035/72 and 2200/09, which reads, as far as relevant here: "The holder of products covered by the quality standards adopted may not display such products or offer them for sale, or deliver or market them in any other manner within the Community than in conformity with those standards. The holder shall be responsible for observing such conformity. ...."

considers civil actions by competitors "particularly suited to contributing substantially to ensuring fair trading and transparency of markets in the Community" (*ibid*). It follows that the ECJ's reply to the question referred is that the relevant Regulations, properly construed, include obligations imposed upon traders enforceable by civil action at the behest of other traders.

Three aspects of the judgment merit more detailed consideration in the context of this contribution: (i) enforcement of Regulations, (ii) enforcement of Directives and other EC law instruments, and (iii) impact on the tort of breach of statutory duty.

5.3 Private Enforcement of Regulations

Firstly, under precisely which conditions should a tort claim be made available to enforce norms laid down in a Regulation? The answer is not clearly given in *Muñoz* because there are some differences between the ECJ's judgment and the Advocate General's Opinion. In a word, the ECJ applied a wider, broad-brush, approach to the interaction between the violated norm and the civil action than the more precise and more circumscribed approach of A-G Geelhoed. As pointed out above, the ECJ requires that national law makes available a civil enforcement action to competitors as a matter of interpretation of Regulations 1035/72 and 2200/96 (operative part and para. 32). It does not say explicitly that only directly effective provisions of the Regulations give rise to a civil action.

However, if read in conjunction with para. 27, this does seem to be the case because in that consideration it is said in essence that all Regulations automatically have direct effect.[51] Without entering into the long standing debate as to the equivalence or otherwise of "directly applicable" and "directly effective," it is submitted that it is somewhat misleading to regard each and every provision of a Regulation as being directly effective by virtue of its nature. Most provisions will but some do not; for instance the duty to adopt sanctions or to designate competent authorities require further action by Member States.[52] Accordingly, one would need to establish first and foremost whether a particular provision of a Regulation has direct effect and then to enquire whether it entails civil enforcement opportunities.

This is exactly what A-G Geelhoed did. According to the Advocate General, the fundamental issue before the court is the availability of civil enforcement to a person where the designated public law enforcement body declined to take action (this important aspect of public-private interaction is returned to below). Mr Geelhoed reformulated the preliminary question as consisting of three components: does a Regulation give a person a right to compliance by another person?; secondly, if so, does EC law require that that right can be enforced?; thirdly, to what extent does EC law require the national legal order to provide for a civil action? (Opinion, No. 22). After the A-G had established that the Regulations in hand seek to promote fair trading – i.e. its protective scope thus includes competitors – he examined its direct effect in a horizontal situation (trader versus trader). Applying well-established case law, there

---

51 Citing an earlier authority on this point: Case 34/73 *Vaiola* [1973] *ECR* 981.

52 Hartley (2003) at p. 204. And see e.g. Article 36 of Council Regulation (EEC) No. 259/93 of 1 February 1993 on the supervision and control of shipments of waste within, into and out of the European Community, *OJ* 1993 L 30/1 (as amended).

was no doubt that the crucial obligation in question had horizontal direct effect; i.e. the addressee's duty not to market products in any other manner within the Community than in conformity with the standards; under the Regulations, holders of products are responsible for observing such conformity.

Does this directly effective provision also confer rights on individuals? The fundamental criterion proposed by Mr Geelhoed is a linkage between the protective scope of the violated norms and the harmed interests (Nos. 46-49). In essence this test is nothing other than the well-known *Schutznorm* issue – does the scope of protection of the infringed norm include the harmed interests of the claimant? – of both EC liability law under Article 288 EC and domestic tort law.[53] In the light of the examined scope of protection, it was said that non-compliance by Frumar could result in an unlawful act with an adverse impact on Muñoz; the latter then has a right to compliance by the former under Community law. The ECJ presumably has implicitly agreed with its Advocate General on this *Schutznorm* point in that it also underlined the aims and objectives of the Regulation albeit that its operative part can be read more widely.

Secondly, does EC law require the Member States to enable private enforcement? The most important aspect of *Muñoz* (both the judgment and the Opinion) is the obligation for national law to make available civil enforcement by competitors as a supplement to the public enforcement regime. A-G Geelhoed points out that the regulations require a public law enforcement system. Crucially, this does not mean that it therefore excludes a private enforcement regime. Put differently, "the Regulation grants no monopoly in regard to enforcement" (Opinion, No. 55). Like the ECJ, Mr. Geelhoed considers civil actions by competitors a useful and necessary adjunct to public enforcement by supervisory authorities. A parallel is drawn with competition law where it is Community policy to actively encourage private enforcement. The civil courts' powers stand alongside the enforcement functions of both the European Commission and the national competition authorities (Nos. 58-62).[54]

The complementary role of public and private enforcement mechanisms as reaffirmed by the ECJ in *Muñoz* is certainly not a novel or freak strand in the Court's jurisprudence. On the contrary, it goes back to one of its earliest, and most important cases, *Van Gend & Loos*. Of course this case is most famous for the introduction of the concepts of direct effect and the new, autonomous, legal order of Community law, but it also laid down the dual system of enforcement of EC law obligations by explicitly rejecting the argument by various Member States that the centralised, public, enforcement mechanism of infringement actions of the Treaty, Articles 226-228 EC, are exclusive. It held that:

---

53 See for EC law Hartley (2003) at p. 468; Craig & De Burca (2003) at p. 549; the leading cases are: Joined Cases 5, 7 and 13-24/66 *Kampffmeyer and Others* v *Commission* [1967] *ECR* 245 and Case C-282/90 *Vreugdenhil II* [1992] *ECR* I-1937. See for Dutch, English and German law: Asser-Hartkamp 4-III (2002), No. 197.

54 See the Commission White Paper on modernisation of the rules implementing Articles 85 and 86 of the EC Treaty, *OJ* 1999 C 132/1; Council Regulation (EC) No. 1/2003 of 16 December 2002 on the implementation of the rules on competition laid down in Articles 81 and 82 of the Treaty, *OJ* 2003 L 1/1; the ECJ's Case C-453/99 *Courage v. Crehan* [2001] *ECR* I-6297, [2001] 5 C.M.L.R. 28 and Kominos (2002).

A restriction of the guarantees against an infringement of Article 12 [now Art. 25 EC] by Member States to the procedures under Article 169 and 170 [now 226 and 227 EC] would remove all direct legal protection of the individual rights of their nationals. There is the risk that recourse to the procedure under these Articles would be ineffective if it were to occur after the implementation of a national decision taken contrary to the provisions of the Treaty. The vigilance of individuals concerned to protect their rights amounts to an effective supervision *in addition to* the supervision entrusted by Articles [226] and [227] to the diligence of the Commission and of the Member States.[55]

It follows that right from the beginnings of Community law as a shared legal order within the Member States the ECJ acknowledged the relevance of private enforcement in Community law, and, more particularly, its complementary role to the public enforcement mechanism explicitly contained in the Treaty.[56] The three "pillars" of the argument have since then been consistently confirmed and applied – (i) legal protection of individuals, (ii) dual enforcement mechanism and (iii) *effet utile* – perhaps most notably in the Court's landmark *Francovich* judgment on State liability for infringements of Community law.[57]

5.4   Private Enforcement of Directives

The above analysis dealt with the exact situation of *Muñoz* itself – civil enforcement of obligations addressed to individuals laid down in a EC Regulation. The second question in assessing the *ratio decidendi* of *Muñoz* is: does the same apply when the relevant EC norm is contained not in a directly applicable Regulation but in a Directive? Strictly speaking, there is also a question about Treaty rules (as they were not in issue in *Muñoz*). It is obvious, however, that Treaty provisions can qualify for civil enforcement in the wake of *Muñoz* as the very horizontal effect of Regulations was equated to the horizontal direct effect of relevant Treaty provisions in A-G Geelhoed's Opinion.[58] No further examination is required. But what about directives? Most EC environmental law consists of directives, so this question is particularly pertinent in the context of environmental liability.[59] Of course directives lack exactly this *horizontal* direct effect;[60] They can, however, nevertheless be decisive in disputes between two private parties either under the doctrine of consistent interpretation of national law or by way of so-called incidental effect following *CIA Security* and *Unilever Italia*.[61]

Despite this, it can be argued that since the ECJ underlined the directly effective nature of regulations, *a contrario* they must be distinguished from directives, which therefore do not qualify for "*Muñoz*-enforcement."[62] This is not in my view, how-

---

55 Case 26/62, [1963] *ECR* 1 at p. 13 (emphasis added).
56 Craig & De Burca (2003) at p. 404.
57 Joined Cases C-6 and 9/90 *Francovich* [1991] *ECR* I-5357 at paras. 32, 33.
58 See Nos. 43-45 referring to Case C-281/98 *Angonese* [2000] *ECR* I-4139.
59 Jans (2000), Chapter 8.
60 Case C-91/92 *Faccini Dori* [1994] *ECR* I-3325.
61 C-194/94 *CIA Security* [1996] *ECR* I-2201; Case C-443/98 *Unilever Italia* v. *Centralfood* [2000] *ECR* I-7535; see also C-77/97 *Österreichische Unilever* [1999] *ECR* I-431 and Case C-159/00 *Sapod Audic* [2002] *ECR* I-5031. See generally Craig & de Burca (2003) at 211-227 and Betlem (2002).
62 Para. 27 of *Muñoz*; Opinion A-G Geelhoed, Nos. 33-45; see also the head notes in [2003] 3 C.M.L.R. 26.

ever, the correct approach. The better view is to focus on the analogy between State liability and the liability of private persons for breach of Community law. After all, we are not talking about the use of EC law before a national court – either as a shield or as a sword – to displace or modify the application of some rule of Member State law deemed to be incompatible with Community law. At issue is only one point (exactly the question for preliminary ruling as formulated by the English Court of Appeal): the civil liability, under domestic tort law, of a private person *vis-à-vis* another private person for non-compliance with obligations under EC law.

Accordingly, what guidance does the analogy with State liability under *Francovich* principles give us? There is no ECJ case on Community liability of individuals for breach of EC law. The only direct precedent is the Opinion of Advocate General Van Gerven in *Banks*.[63] He contended that individuals are liable – just like Member States – as a matter of Community law, for breaches of directly effective provisions of EC law, such as Articles 81 and 82 EC on competition law (as the rule at issue of the ECSC Treaty was held not to produce any direct effect by the ECJ, the latter did not rule on the matter). In line with this conclusion, based on the scope of the *Francovich* liability and its place in the system of EC law, it is submitted that even in the absence of a horizontal direct effect of directives, civil enforcement à la *Muñoz* must be made available for non-compliance with obligations laid down in a Directive (after, of course, expiry of the transposition date), because it is no requirement of the *Francovich* liability that the infringed norm produces direct effect.[64] Crucially, this was the case in *Francovich* itself.[65] Indeed, as has been well-settled in the post-*Francovich* case law, the decisive criterion is the conferral of rights on individuals.[66] It follows that at least for directives that address rights and obligations of individuals, "*Muñoz*-enforcement" must be made available.[67] There is also support for this view in para. 27 of *Muñoz* where the ECJ talks about "confer[ing] rights on individuals which the national courts have a duty to protect". So, even if the provision has no direct effect but as long as rights are conferred on individuals, they can enforce these rights via civil remedies before national courts against other individuals.

Is it not, however, the case that many environmental law provisions concern the public at large, imposing obligations on (primarily or even exclusively) public authorities? It is true that that may be so but that still does not prevent it from conferring rights on individuals as they can be derived from obligations imposed on the State and/or other individuals.[68] This matter has already been addressed in previous case law both in the environmental context and in the State liability context. As for the former, the Directives on air pollution, drinking water, shell fish water and on

---

63 Case C-128/92, [1994] *ECR* I-1209.
64 See also Van Gerven (2000) at 895; Prechal (1995) at 329 and 331.
65 Para. 26 of the judgment.
66 See most recently Opinion A-G Léger in Case C-224/01 *Köbler* of 8 April 2003, No. 123, which, incidentally, itself concerns an application of the *Francovich* liability to a new situation, i.e. State liability for breach of Community law by a supreme court.
67 See for an in-depth analysis of this distinction Opinion of AG Jacobs in Case C316/93 *Vaneetveld* [1994] *ECR* I763 and Opinion of A-G Lenz in Case C-91/92 *Faccini Dori* [1994] *ECR* I-3325.
68 This reasoning echoes Case 26/62 *Van Gend en Loos* [1962] *ECR* 1 at p. 12; see also para. 31 of *Francovich*.

groundwater protection were held to be capable of creating individual rights.[69] Whereas in the latter sphere, the ECJ's judgment in *Dillenkofer* leaves no doubt that the directive in question does not explicitly have to contain individual rights as such, they can be inferred from obligations imposed on the addressee of the norm.[70] This is because the relevant directive – the Package Travel Directive[71] – provided only that operators must provide sufficient evidence of security for the refund of money paid and for the repatriation of the consumer in the event of insolvency. According to the ECJ, this amounts to a conferral of rights on consumers mainly because of the aims and objectives of the Directive, namely consumer protection.[72] Thus, the requirement of granting rights by a norm of EC law, even if laid down in a directive which leaves considerable discretion to Member States about its transposition, will generally be satisfied in EC (environmental) law. Finally, according to the English Court of Appeal, the notion of "granting rights" for the purpose of a civil action also plays a significant part in ensuring compliance with the standards of Community public (environmental) law.[73]

5.5 Towards a European Breach of Statutory Duty

Third and finally in assessing *Muñoz*, one should ask what impact does it have on domestic tort law and in particular on "breach of statutory duty?" Put differently, has it achieved any harmonisation of national tort law? In modern societies, tort law functions in a regulatory context (as seen above). Undoubtedly, all EU Member States' legal systems recognise non-contractual liability for violations of written, both public and private law, obligations in some form or other (either literally as a "breach of statutory duty" (England, Germany: § 823-III BGB) or as part of a more general tort formula (France, the Netherlands).[74] One of the major elements of this tort is the issue of the protective scope. Generally speaking, the liability for a violation of a written norm is circumscribed by a *Schutznorm* approach (as noted above). That is to say, only those persons are entitled to a civil remedy who belong to a class of protected persons, while they suffer loss of a kind or are harmed in interests of a type included in the protective scope of the violated norm: in shorthand: the *Schutznorm* doctrine.[75] This applies both to domestic tort law and to Community liability (both EC and Member State liability).[76]

---

69 See Jans (2000) at p. 213; Prechal (1995) at p. 137; the cases are all *Commission v. Germany*: C-131/88, [1991] *ECR* I-825 (groundwater), Case C-58/89, [1991] *ECR* I-4983 (drinking water), Case C-59/89, [1991] *ECR* I-2607 (air); Opinion A-G Jacobs in Case C-237/90, [1992] *ECR* I-5973, No. 15 (drinking water); Case C-298/95, [1996] *ECR* I-6747 (shellfish water).

70 Joined Cases C-178/94, C-179/94, C-188/94, C-189/94 and C-190/94, [1996] *ECR* I-4845.

71 Council Directive 90/314/EEC of 13 June 1990 on package travel, package holidays and package tours, *OJ* 1990 L 158/59.

72 Paras. 30-42 of the judgment; see also Van Gerven (2000) at 929.

73 *Bowden* v. *Southwest Services Ltd.* [1999] 3 C.M.L.R. 180, para. 14 (C.A.).

74 Markesinis & Deakin (1999) at 336; Markesinis & Unberath (2002) at 885; Asser-Hartkamp 4-III (2002), No. 34; Van Gerven (2000), p. 305.

75 The term is presumably a kind of "euro-German" as the "real" legal German seems to be: *Schutzgesetzverletzung* (Markesinis & Unberath, *ibid.*, at 885) or *Normzwecklehre* (Asser-Hartkamp 4-III, *ibid.*, at No. 97).

76 Van Gerven (2000), p. 894.

Obviously, even though the protective scope question features as the most important legal "agenda point" in this context across all these legal systems, subtle differences as well as differing applications by different courts do occur. For example, regarding which type of norms may be relevant as violated norms in order to constitute unlawfulness – in other words what is the meaning of "statute" for this purpose – the systems vary. Dutch law includes not only "real" statutes, i.e. Acts of Parliament, secondary legislation etc., but also the conditions of a licence issued under a statute, international conventions and even, in transnational situations, foreign laws.[77] German law, on the other hand, seems to be limited to domestic primary and secondary legislation. But, like Dutch law, provided the norm is a *Schutznorm*, a breach of a statute will always entail tortious liability.[78] By contrast, the starting point under English law is more or less the opposite: whenever the statute in question provides for a criminal sanction, a civil sanction would be excluded but for two exceptions: (i) the statute intends to protect a particular class of persons; (ii) the statute created a public right and a particular member of the public suffers particular, special (i.e. different from the rest of the public), loss.[79] A French equivalent of the Dutch, German and English "breach of statutory duty" does not as such exist, as the component of violation of a norm is subsumed under the notion of fault.[80] Having said that, any breach of the criminal law in general automatically constitutes a civil fault, giving rise to non-contractual liability. In addition, breach of any other statute or statutory instrument (in French: a *lois* or *règlement*) likewise constitutes a tort within the meaning of the *Code Civil* provisions. Finally on French law, and most pertinently in the *Muñoz* context, an offence relating to anti-competitive practices entitles a victim suffering loss caused by it to recover damages.[81]

In the light of this brief *tour d'horizon*, it would seem to follow that the clearest impact of *Muñoz*'s civil enforcement requirements is on English law. In particular the complementary nature of private and public (including criminal) enforcement means a fundamental re-assessment of the approach of the English courts to "breach of statutory duty." A less restrictive approach to granting civil remedies is necessary. No great upheaval in the English law of torts will ensue, however, as legal doctrine in England already thought this was needed and, in the exact context of liability – under English not Community law – for the directly effective Treaty provisions on competition law, the House of Lords had already acknowledged liability in damages for breach of Articles 81, 82 EC. It held that those provisions not only promoted general economic prosperity in the Common Market but also purported to protect private individuals suffering loss as a result of a violation of them; the relevant tort under English law being "breach of statutory duty". [82]

As for German law, in the post-*Muñoz* era, breach of a Regulation will have to be included in the notion of "statute/*Gesetz*" within the meaning of § 823-III BGB. The

---

77 Asser-Hartkamp 4-III (2002), No. 34; HR 24 November 1989, NJ 1992 404 (the *Interlas* case), see for discussions in English: Betlem (1993) at 122 ff., and Betlem (1995), pp. 184-229; available online at www.ex.ac.uk/law/staff/betlem/index.html.
78 Markesinis & Unberath (2002), pp. 885, 886.
79 Markesinis & Deakin (1999), p. 343; Opinion A-G Geelhoed in *Muñoz*, No. 55.
80 Bell (1998), pp. 355, 359. Zweigert & Kötz (1998), p. 619; Youngs (1998), p. 219.
81 Bell, *ibid.*, at pp. 359-360; 361-364; Van Gerven (2000), p. 305.
82 Markesinis & Deakin (1999), p. 353: citing *Garden Cottage Foods* v. *Milk Marketing Board* [1984] A.C. 130.

same can be said for Dutch law but that had already been held to be the case in any event. By the same token, it would seem that the ECJ's approach in *Muñoz* was the established law in French tort law. Accordingly, like in particular *Brasserie du Pêcheur & Factortame III* on State liability,[83] *Muñoz* constitutes yet another example of the harmonising effects on Member States' law of non-contractual liability by judgments of the ECJ. The judgment is an important contribution to enhancing the effectiveness of food quality standards as well as other regulatory standards of Community law.

6 Conclusions

The years 2000-2003 have produced two developments in the Communitarisation of (environmental) liability law, a legislative one more notable for what it does not include rather than for what it does, and a judicial one: a landmark ECJ judgment on the obligatory availability of civil actions for the purposes of enforcement of Community law. The Proposal for a Directive on environmental liability does not include private rights of action against polluters. It will therefore fail to secure effective enforcement of substantive EC environmental law. Particularly ineffective is the protection against harm caused by GMOs. This is out of step with the EU's international obligations (Aarhus) and with developments in ECJ case law as well as (future) national (case) law. It is also out of step with developments in other policy areas, notably intellectual property, where the Commission seeks to minimise the disparities between the Member States' laws on remedies to ensure effective and uniform enforcement of the *acquis communautaire* in those fields. However, after the ECJ's *Muñoz* judgment, EU-wide availability of private enforcement is required. A new genuinely European tort is emerging, to wit breach of "EC-statutory" duty.

BIBLIOGRAPHY: Kenneth S. Abraham, "The Relation Between Civil Liability and Environmental Regulation: An Analytical Overview," 41 Washburn L.J. 379 (2002); Michael Anderson, "Transnational Corporations and Environmental Damage: Is Tort law the Answer?," 41 Washburn L.J. 399 (2002); Alessandra Arcuri, "Controlling environmental risk in Europe: the complementary role of an EC environmental liability regime", TMA 2001, 37; *Asser-Hartkamp 4-III*: C. Asser's Handleiding tot de beoefening van het Nederlands burgerlijk recht, Verbintenissenrecht, Deel III, De verbintenis uit de wet, by A.S. Hartkamp, 11th ed. (2002); John Bell et al., *Principles of French Law* (1998); L. Bergkamp, *De vervuiler betaalt dubbel* (1998); Christoph Bernasconi & Gerrit Betlem, "Licences, Liability and Cross-Border Pollution," [2003] *Environmental Liability* 83-89; Gerrit Betlem, "The Doctrine of Consistent Interpretation – Managing Legal Uncertainty," 22 OJLS (2002), p. 397; Gerrit Betlem & Edward Brans, 'The Future Role of Civil liability for Environmental Damage in the EU,' in Han Somsen et al. (eds.), 2 *Yearbook of European Environmental Law* 183-221 (2002); Gerrit Betlem, "Being 'Directly and Individually Concerned," The *Schutznorm* Doctrine and *Francovich* Liability", in: Hans-W. Micklitz & Norbert Reich (eds.), *Public Interest Litigation before European Courts*, p. 319-341 (1996); Gerrit Betlem, "Transboundary Enforcement: Free Movement of Injunctions", in: Sven Deimann & Bernard Dyssli eds., *Environmental Rights* – Law, Litigation & Access to Justice (1995), p. 184-229; available online at

---

83 Joined Cases C-46 & 48/93, [1996] *ECR* I-1029; Van Gerven (2000), p. 951.

<www.ex.ac.uk/law/staff/betlem/index.html>; Gerrit Betlem, *Civil Liability for Transfrontier Pollution* – Dutch Environmental Tort Law in International Cases in the light of Community Law (1993); Adrian Briggs, *The Conflict of Laws* (2002); P. Cane, "Using Tort Law to Enforce Environmental Regulations?" (2002) 41 Washburn L.J. 427; P. Cane, "Tort as Regulation" (2002) 31 C.L.W.R. 305; Paul Craig & Gráinne de Burca, *EU Law – Text, Cases and Materials* (2003); Sjef van Erp, "European Union Case Law as a Source of European Private Law: A Comparison with American Federal Common Law," Vol. 5.4 *Electronic Journal of Comparative Law*, (December 2001), <http://www.ejcl.org/ejcl/54/art54-1.html>; Walter van Gerven *et al.*, *Tort Law* (2000: Common Law of Europe Casebooks); T..C. Hartley, *The Foundations of European Community Law* (2003); W.G.A. Hazewindus & C.J. van der Wilt, "Rechtsbescherming tegen milieuoverlast. Een pleidooi voor de civiele rechtsgang," NJB 2003, 322; Keith N. Hylton, "When Should We Prefer Tort Law to Environmental Regulation?," 41 Washburn L.J. 515 (2002); Jan H. Jans, *European Environmental Law* (2000); Allan Kanner, "Toxic Tort Litigation in a Regulatory World," 41 Washburn L.J. 535 (2002); Kominos, "New Prospects for Private Enforcement of EC Competition law: *Courage v. Crehan* and the Community Right to damages, 39 CMLRev. 447 (2002); R.G. Lee, "EU Proposals on Environmental Liability: From a Private to a Public Law Framework" [2003] J.B.L. 180; Maria Lee & Carolyn Abbot, "The Usual Suspects? Public Participation Under the Aarhus Convention" (2003) 66 M.L.R. 80; B.S. Markesinis & S.F. Deakin, *Tort Law*, 4th ed. (1999); Basil S. Markesinis & Hannes Unberath, *The German Law of Torts – A Comparative Treatise*, 4th ed. (2002); J.H. Nieuwenhuis, *De ramp op het Pikmeer: bezwaren tegen de geest van het post-moderne aansprakelijkheidsrecht* (1997); Ben Pontin, "Tort Law and Victorian Government Growth: the Historiographical Significance of Tort in the Shadow of Chemical Pollution and Factory Safety Regulation," 18 OJLS 661 (1998); Sacha Prechal, *Directives in European Community Law* (1995); Vera Rodenhoff, "The Aarhus Convention and its Implications for the 'Institutions' of the European Community," 11 RECIEL 343 (2002); Gary T. Schwartz, "Reality in the Economic Analysis of Tort Law: Does Tort Law Really Deter?," [1994] *UCLA Law Review* 377; Mark Stallworthy, "Environmental Liability and the Impact of Statutory Authority," 15 JEL 3 (2003); Peter v. Wilmowsky and Gerhard Roller, *Civil Liability for Waste* (Frankfurt am Main etc.: Peter Lang, 1992), Studies of the Environmental Law Network International, Vol. 2; R. Youngs, *English, French and German Comparative* Law (1998); K. Zweigert & H. Kötz (T. Weir transl.), *Introduction to Comparative Law* (1998)

ABBREVIATIONS

A.C.	Appeal Cases (Law Reports)
All E.R	All England Law Reports
C.L.W.R.	Common Law World Law Review
C.M.L.R.	Common Market Law Reports
CMLRev.	Common Market Law Review
ECJ	Court of Justice of the European Communities
ECR	European Court Reports
I.L.M.	International Legal Materials
JBL	Journal of Business Law
JEL	Journal of Environmental Law
MLR	Modern Law Review
O.J.	Official Journal of the European Communities
OJLS	Oxford Journal of Legal Studies
RECIEL	Review of European Community and International Environmental Law
TMA	Tijdschrift voor Milieu Aansprakelijkheid/Environmental Liability Law Review
W.L.R.	Weekly Law Reports

CHAPTER 38

The Frontier between Contractual and Tortious Liability in Europe: Insights from the Case of Compensation for Pure Economic Loss

Mauro Bussani* & Vernon Valentine Palmer**

1 Introduction

Pure economic loss is one of the most discussed topics in today's tort law scholar-ship. Fascination with the subject has developed into a wealth of literature.[1] The rea-son is that recoverability of pure economic loss stands at the cutting edge of many crucial questions, such as: To what extent should tort rules be compatible with the market orientation of the legal system?[2] Or, as some may phrase it, how far can tort liability expand without imposing excessive burdens upon individual activity? As a matter of policy should the recovery of pure economic loss be the domain principally of the law of contract?

---

*   Professor of Law at the University of Trieste Law School.
** Professor at Tulane Law School.
1   The literature is overwhelmingly weighted to those countries where the concept is well-recognised by practitioners, judge and scholars. See, e multis, R. Bernstein, *Economic Loss*, 2nd ed., (1998); S. Banakas (ed.), *Civil Liability for Pure Economic Loss* (1996); B. Feldthusen, *Economic Negligence: The Recovery of Pure Economic Loss* (1989); J. Kleineman, *Ren förmögenhetsskada* (1987); J.M. Barendrecht, Pure Economic Loss in the Netherlands, in: E.H. Hondius (ed.), *Netherlands Reports to the Fifteenth International Congress of Comparative Law* (1998), pp. 115 ff.; B. Markesinis, *The German Law of Torts*, 4th ed., (2002), pp. 52 ff.; J. Spier (ed.), *The Limits of Liability: Keeping the Floodgates Shut* (1996) (discussion of eight "Tilburg Hypotheticals" – four of which concern pure economic loss); J.M. Thomson, Delictual Liability for Pure Economic Loss: Recent Developments, *SLT*, 1995, p. 139; H. Kötz, Economic Loss in Tort and Contract, 58(3) *RabelsZ* 1994, p. 423; P. Cane, Economic Loss in Tort and Contract, 58(3) *RabelsZ* 1994, p. 430; Ch. von Bar, Liability for Information and Opinions Causing Pure Economic Loss to Third Parties: A Comparison of English and German Case Law, in: B. Markesinis (ed.), *The Gradual Convergence* (1994), pp. 99 ff. See also J. Herbots, Le Duty of Care et le dommage purement financier en droit comparé, 62 *Rev. dr. int. dr. comp.* 1985, pp. 7-33; L. Khoury, The Liability of Auditors Beyond Their Clients : A Comparative Study, 46 *McGill Law Journal* 2001, p. 413.
2   P. Benson, The Basis for Excluding Liability for Economic Loss in Tort Law, in: D.G. Owen, *The Philosophical Foundations of Tort Law* (1995), pp. 427, 431. The same author, articulating a well known tòpos among tort lawyers (see e.g., G. Viney, Pour ou contre un principe général de responsabilité pour faute?, 49 *Osaka Univ. Law R.* 2002, pp. 33, 37 ff.; P.G. Monateri, La responsabilità civile, in: R. Sacco (ed.), *Tratt. dir. civ.* (1998), pp. 8 ff. writes: "[T]he fact that every individual is somewhere and is making use of some external objects, with the result that he or his property is put into relation with them and is subject to being affected by conduct that affects them, is an inevitable incident of being active in the world … as beings who exist in space and time and who are inescapably active and purposive, persons are necessarily and always connected in manifold ways with other things which they can affect and which in turn can affect them as part of a causal sequence." *Ibidem*, at 443 (emphasis and footnotes omitted). See also D. Howarth, Three Forms of Responsibility: On the Relationships Between Torn Law and the Welfare State, 60 *C.L.J.* 2001, p. 553).

This paper pursues the modest goal of sketching possible answers to these questions.[3] Thus, we will first (cc. 2-4) outline the notion and the factual situations where this loss is likely to occur. Then, we will discuss the broad spectrum of differing approaches to this kind of damage in Europe (cc. 5-7) as well as the basic arguments for an exclusionary rule (c. 8). We will come (c. 9) to the question whether, in methodological and substantive terms, a common core of agreement exists in Europe on this issue. Finally, we will try to set the scene for the recoverability of pure economic loss in the European Civil Code stage (c. 10).

2 The Distinction Between Pure and Consequential Economic Loss

There has never been a universally accepted definition of "pure economic loss."[4] What is universally clear instead is the negative cast and the patrimonial character of that loss.

In countries where the term is well recognised its meaning is essentially explained in a negative way. It is loss without antecedent harm to plaintiff's person or property. Here the word "pure" plays a central role, for if there is economic loss that is connected to the slightest damage to person or property of the plaintiff (provided that all other conditions of liability are met) then the latter is called *consequential* economic loss and the whole set of damages may be recovered without question.[5] *Consequential* economic loss (sometimes also termed parasitic loss[6]) is recoverable because it presupposes the existence of physical injuries, whereas pure economic loss strikes the victim's wallet and nothing else.[7]

Thus, before going any further it will be useful to give some specific examples of the factual situations usually subsumed under the label 'pure economic loss'.

---

3   The following pages are based on a research conducted over the last five years by the authors. See M. Bussani & V.V. Palmer (eds.), *Pure Economic Loss in Europe* (2003). The research – developed within "The Common Core of European Private Law" Project (M. Bussani & U. Mattei, General Eds.) – covers thirteen jurisdictions: Austria, Belgium, England, Finland, France, Germany, Greece, Italy, the Netherlands, Portugal, Scotland, Spain, Sweden.

4   Gary Schwartz refers to "the general economic loss no liability doctrine" in his essay "The Economic Loss Doctrine in American Tort Law: Assessing the Recent Experience", in: Banakas (ed.), *supra* note 1, at pp. 103-130.

5   Perhaps another way to describe pure economic loss is to say it does not arise as a consequence of some earlier physical loss, and it is not a court's substituted valuation of physical loss.

6   For this usage, see W. Keeton, *Prosser and Keeton on the Law of Torts*, 5th ed. (1984), sec. 43, at 291.

7   In Sweden, where the legislator says that only victims of crimes may recover for pure economic loss, the Tort Law Act, §2, defines the notion exactly in these terms: "In the present act, 'pure economic loss' (ren formögenhat-sskanda) means such economic loss as arises without connection to personal injury or property damage to anyone." See van Gerven *et al.* (eds), *Tort Law – Scope of Protection*, (1998), p. 44.
    A similar definition seems to prevail in England and Germany. See Lord Denning's statement that "… it is better to disallow economic loss altogether at any rate when it stands alone, independent of any physical damage." *Spartan Steel & Alloys Ltd.* v. *Martin & Co. Ltd.* (1973) *Q.B.* 27, (1972) 3 *All E.R.* 557. Regarding reiner vermögensschaden, W. van Gerven, J. Lever and P. Larouche, *Tort Law* (2000), at p. 68, speak of a "worsening of one's overall economic position (loss of profit,

3   The Standard Cases: A Taxonomy

Broadly speaking, pure economic loss arises out of the interdependence of relationships and interests. These relationships are sometimes two-dimensional and other times three-dimensional. Our aim is to draw up a taxonomy of the principal ways in which this loss arises within such relationships. This list will surely not exhaust all the conceivable ways in which such damage may arise. Our real interest lies in tracing the most recurrent and typical patterns which we simply call the "standard cases."[8] With these provisos in mind, we venture to set forth four categories that seem to be functionally and relationally distinct.[9]

3.1   "Ricochet loss"

Ricochet loss classically arises when physical damage is done to the property or person of one party and that loss in turn causes the impairment of a plaintiff's right – certain authors call this situation "relational economic loss."[10] A direct victim sustains physical damage of some kind, while plaintiff is a secondary victim who incurs only economic harm.

To illustrate, A has a contract to tow B's ship. C's negligent act of sinking the ship makes it impossible for A to perform his contract and thus deprives him of expected profits. A's financial loss is the ricochet effect of C's negligence toward B. The loss is purely economic since no property interest of A's has been impaired.[11]

Ricochet loss can also arise from the impairment of an employment contract. For instance, B is a key employee in A's business or sporting team. C's negligent driving leads to B's death or incapacity, thus causing A's team or business to lose profits and revenues. Here B's injury is physical, but A's loss is purely financial.[12]

---

diminution in the value of property, etc.) that is not directly consequential upon injury to the person or damage to a particular piece of property." (emphasis in original)

8   Although we have sometimes borrowed and other times given new names to these standard situations, we will not attempt to explain or employ all of the descriptive labels and tags that writers and judges use. These diverse and contradictory ideas showed are not always compatible with the results of the study we mentioned above (note 3) and would serve no purpose here.

9   For a longer taxonomic list consisting of eight categories (in which we think there is considerable overlap), see W. Bishop and J. Sutton, Efficiency and Justice in Tort Damages: The Shortcomings of the Pecuniary Loss Rule, 15 *J. of Legal Studies* 1986, pp. 347, 360-61. Benson's taxonomy consists of five situations, two of which he calls "exclusionary situations." His three other situations are called "non-exclusionary." P. Benson, *supra* note 2, at pp. 427-430.

10   See this terminology and analysis in R. Bernstein, *Economic Loss*, 2nd ed. (1998), pp. 163 ff. and Bruce Feldthusen, *Economic Negligence* (1989), pp. 199 ff.

11   The example closely follows *La Société Anonyme de Remorquage à Helice* v. *Bennets* [1911] 1 *KB* 243.

12   The Meroni Case (*Torino Calcio SPA* v. *Romero*, Cass. Civ., SU 26.1.1971, n. 174, *GI*, 1971, I, 1, 681) and certain other hypotheticals dealt with in our general study (above note 3) are also variations of ricochet harm. See the "Cable Cases" and authorities such as *Spartan Steel and Alloys* v. *Martin & Co.* [1973] *QB* 27. Concern about the indeterminate number and size of the claims for losses is often associated with cases falling within this category.

3.2 "Transferred loss"

Here C causes physical damage to B's property or person, but a contract between A and B (or the law itself) transfers a loss that would ordinarily be B's onto A.

Thus a loss *ordinarily falling on the primary victim* is passed on to a secondary victim. The transfer of the loss from its "natural" to an "accidental" bearer differentiates this from a case of ricochet loss where the damage in question is not transferred but is a distinct damage to the interests of the secondary victim.[13] These transfers frequently result either by operation of law or from leases, sales, insurance agreements and other contracts that separate property rights from rights of use or specifically reallocate risk bearing.

To illustrate, A is time charterer of a ship owned by B. The day before the time charter is to go into effect and while the ship is in B's possession, C negligently damages the ship's propeller, thus necessitating repairs and a two week delay, which causes A to lose all use of the ship. Here B suffers property damage and ordinarily B as owner would recover for the consequential loss of the ship's use, but the right of use – and the risks related to it – were transferred to A by the boat charter. So A's loss is purely pecuniary because he has no antecedent property loss.[14]

A similar effect can result under a sales contract which reserves title in B (seller) while the goods are in shipment but places the risk of loss in transit upon the buyer A. If the goods (still technically owned by B)[15] are damaged in transit by the carrier's negligence, then a loss normally incurred by the owner has been transferred to A. A's loss is purely financial since he has no property interest in the goods.[16]

An equivalent result is reached when the transfer occurs by operation of law. For instance B, A's employee, may be injured by the negligent driving of C and thus find himself unable to work for three months. Nevertheless a statute requires A to continue to pay B's salary, even though no work is received in return. Thus what ordinarily would have been B's loss is statutorily transferred to A as a combined result of C's negligence and the effects of the pay continuation statute.[17]

---

13 This category receives extensive consideration in Ch. von Bar, *The Common European Law of Torts*, vol. I (1998), pp. 507-512.

14 The illustration is based upon *Robins Dry Dock* v. *Flint*, 13 F2d 3 (2d Cir. 1926), 275 US 303 (1927) and a case ('The Canceled Cruise') in our general study's (see supra note 3) Questionnaire.

15 As is well known, who should be called the "owner" of goods in shipment depends on the law applicable to the transfer of ownership, and above all on the validity and extent of the principle of transfer of possession. See Ch. von Bar, above note 13, at p. 509, fn. 499.

16 This illustration is based upon The Aliakmon, [1985] 2 AER 44.

17 Transferred loss cases are liability neutral from the perspective of the tortfeasor and should allay fears of indeterminate liability. An additional argument in favour of an award of compensation is that the tortfeasor who is clearly liable to the primary victim should not benefit from the accidental operation of rules which by pure chance exclude him from liability. According to von Bar, the concept of transferred loss is intended "to prevent someone appealing to rules whose purpose is not to protect that person, but to protect others": *The Common European Law of Torts*, vol I (1998), pp. 510-511.

3.3 Closures of Public Markets, Transportation Corridors and Public Infrastructures

Here economic loss arises without a previous injury to anyone's property or person. There may be physical damage, but it is to "unowned resources" that lie in the public domain.[18] A single negligent act may necessitate the closure of markets, highways and shipping lanes which no person owns, yet the closure inflicts economic loss directly on individuals whose livelihoods closely depend upon the use of these facilities.[19]

To illustrate, C negligently spills chemicals into the river, and all traffic on the waterway is suspended for two weeks during a cleanup effort. As a result shippers must take more expensive overland routes, and marinas, boat suppliers, hotel operators, and commercial fishermen in the area suffer severe economic loss.[20]

A similar chain of loss may arise when C negligently allows infected cattle to escape from his premises, and the government must order all cattle and meat markets to close. As a result broad classes of plaintiffs will suffer pure economic loss, including cattle raisers who are unable to sell or deliver their stock to butchers who are unable to obtain supplies.[21]

3.4 Reliance upon Flawed Data, Advice or Professional Services

Those who furnish advice, prepare data or render services concerning financial matters often understand that the information will be furnished to a client and then relied upon by third persons with whom they have no contractual relation. If the advice, data or services are carelessly compiled or executed, this may not only breach the provider's contract with his/her client but cause a relying third party to sustain pure pecuniary loss.

For instance, C, an accountant, carelessly conducts an audit of B, a publicly traded company, and vastly overstates the company's net financial worth. Relying upon the accuracy of the audit, investor A buys shares in B at twice their actual value. Here A's loss arises not in consequence of physical damage to B, but on the basis of misplaced reliance.[22] Similarly, erroneous information about a client's solvency may

---

18 V. Goldberg, Recovery For Economic Loss Following the Exxon Valdez Oil Spill, 23 *J. Legal Studies* 1994, pp. 1, 37.

19 This category raises the greatest concern about liability to an indeterminate class in an indeterminate amount.

20 This illustration resembles Louisiana ex rel. *Guste* v. *M/V Testbank* (The Testbank), 752 F2d 1019 (1985).

21 See *Weller* v. *Foot & Mouth Disease Research Inst.* [1966] 1 *QB* 569.

22 According to Tony Honoré, economic losses based upon someone's "reliance" pose a causation issue which is different in kind than causation in the context of physical damage. His discussion seems pertinent to the concern of some that this category of pure economic loss opens the floodgates of liability. When a person is said to "rely" on another's statement, he or she often has two or more (typically many more) reasons or motives for reaching a decision and acting on it. The question whether A's statement "caused" B's response is highly indeterminate. A potential investor in Eldorado Mines, for instance, may be influenced by a false statement in a prospectus as well as by advice from his stockbroker, by his own review of the company books, and so forth. How are we to say that from among all these reasons that the false statement in the prospectus "caused" his financial

lead to financial losses. Thus A, before extending credit to B, takes the precaution of asking C (the merchant bank where B kept its account) for an assessment of B's creditworthiness. C carelessly replies that B is "good for its ordinary engagements" (when in fact B would soon go into liquidation) and thereby influences A to advance credit and to lose a large sum.[23] Here A's loss is purely financial, not because it ricochets off or is transferred from someone else's physical damage, but because it arises directly from A's reliance.

Professional services for a client may cause pecuniary loss to a non-client. B, an elderly man, asks C, his lawyer, to prepare a will in which he will leave €100,000 to A. C takes no action for six months, whereupon B dies intestate and A thereby receives nothing.[24] A's loss is purely economic.

4 Present v. Future Wealth

To the above taxonomy let us add an impotant distinction.

Examples given so far would suggest that patrimonial injury may take two distinguishable forms. It may relate to the existing as opposed to the anticipated wealth of the victim. In the first sense, plaintiff's present wealth may be simply depleted by poor financial advice, or by wasting time and petrol taking overland routes because of the closure of a waterway. In the second sense, plaintiff may instead lose that which s/he expected to acquire, such as a testamentary legacy lost because of a defectively drawn instrument, or a sport club's reduced gate receipts due to the accidental death of the club's star player. Sometimes, when an expectation is destroyed *in utero* (and proof that it would have materialised is difficult, for instance: a commission unlawfully rejects a candidate's application for a job or a fellowship[25]), it is called the loss of a chance.[26]

As between these types of wealth, it is the loss of expected wealth – unrealised profits, canceled legacies, loss of chances – which presents the sharpest question for tort systems to deal with. The difficulty is not simply that the demand for proof is more exigent – by definition expectancies explore a future that only might have occurred. The difficulty also concerns the appropriateness of affording protection in tort. For when an economic expectation receives legal protection in tort, as in principle it does under French law, plaintiff may end up being compensated to the same

---

loss? See T. Honoré, Necessary and Sufficient Conditions in Tort Law, in: D.G. Owen (ed.), *Philosophical Foundation of Tort Law* (1995), pp. 382-383.

23 These facts are taken from the well-known case of *Hedley Byrne & Co. v. Heller & Partners Ltd.,* [1964] *AC* 465 (HL).

24 See *White v. Jones,* [1995] 2 *AC* 207 (HL); *Lucas v. Hamm,* 11 *Cal. Rept.* 727 (1967); *Ross v. Caunters* [1980] *Ch.* 297.

25 See e.g. Conseil d'Etat, 12.11.1965, in *Rec. Lebon,* 1965, 613: « le réquérant, évincé d'un concours auquel il se serait présenté avec des chances sérieuses de succès en raison de ses titres et travaux, a subi un préjudice ».

26 As to the debate, see G. Viney & P. Jourdain, Les conditions de la responsabilité, 2e éd., in: J. Ghestin (ed.), *Traité dr. civ.* (1998), pp. 71 ff.; N. Jansen, The Idea of a Lost Chance, 19 *Oxford J. Leg. St.* 1999, pp. 271 ff. (discussing German and English experience); P.G. Monateri, La responsabilità civile, in: R. Sacco (ed.), *Tratt. dir. civ.* (1998), pp. 283 ff., 583 ff.

extent *as if* he or she were protected by a contract with the tortfeasor.[27] In countries where the recovery of pure economic loss is barred by an exclusionary rule of tort law, there is a tendency to say that wealth expectancies should be protected in contract.[28] For instance German courts are generally unable to approach the question through tort, but at the same time they unreluctantly stretch contractual concepts to make defendant liable to plaintiff, though there is no actual contract between the parties.[29]

From a comparative point of view, whenever legal systems show these attitudes it becomes difficult to tell where tort ends and contract begins. In all these circumstances we seem to be once more at the frontier where functions meet and merge, for though it has been theorised that contract creates wealth whereas tort only protects that which we already have,[30] the notion of pure economic loss presents a challenge to traditional views about the relationship between the two concepts.

---

27 See G. Viney & P. Jourdain, Les conditions de la responsabilité, 2e éd., in: J. Ghestin (ed.), *Traité dr. civ.* (1998), pp. 71 ff., 195 ff.; G. Viney, Introduction a la responsabilité, 2e éd., in: J. Ghestin (ed.), *Traité dr. civ.* (1995), pp. 360 ff. See also our comparative Comments to Case 18 ('Wrongful Job Reference') of the volume cited above (note 3), regarding the distinction to be made between cases in which the lost chance is to be understood as a distinct loss in itself (an autonomous loss), as distinguished from the case where the concept is invoked as an equitable means of proving a loss.

28 Note for example the tense unease in the following statement from a British judge: "I do not consider that damages for loss of an expectation are excluded in cases of negligence arising under the principle in Hedley Byrne, simply because the cause of action is classified as tortious. Such damages may in principle be recoverable in cases of contractual negligence; and I cannot see that, for present purposes, any relevant distinction can be drawn between the two forms of action...." Per Lord Goff of Chieveley in *White* v. *Jones*, [1995] *AC* 207. On this subject see also J. Stapleton, The Normal Expectancies Measure in Tort Damages, 113 *L. Q. Rev.* 1997, p. 257; H. Reece, Loss of Chances in the Law, 59 *MLR* 1996, p. 188.

29 Most of these 'stretches' have now been given official sanction in Germany through the reform of many BGB provisions carried out by the Act on the Modernisation of the Law of Obligations [Gesetz zur Modernisierung des Schuldrechts] – in *BGBl*, November 29, 2001, I, Nr. 61, pp. 3138 ff. This Act, effective as from January 1, 2002, has deeply affected the portion of legal landscape which concerns our topic. It establishes, for instance, new terms for the prescription of tort (up to 30 yeas) and contract (up to 10 years) actions, and codifies both the principles of culpa in contrahendo (see § 311 sec. 2 and sec. 3 as well as § 241 sec. 1 BGB) and of the "contract with protective effects for third parties" (see § 311, sec. 3 BGB). For a general discussion of the reform, see H.-P. Mansel, Die Neuregelung des Verjährungsrecht, 55 *NJW* 2002, pp. 89 ff.; W. Däubler, Neues Schuldrecht – ein erster Überblick, 54 *NJW* 2001, pp. 3729 ff.; M. Schwab, Das neue Schuldrecht im Überblick, *JuS*, 1, 2002, pp. 1 ff. See also R. Zimmermann, Breach of Contract and Remedies under the New German Law of Obligations, in: Centro Studi e ricerche di diritto comparato e straniero (ed.), 48 *Saggi, conferenze e seminari* 2002; C.-W. Canaris (ed.), *Schuldrechtsmodernisierung* (2002); B. Dauner-Lieb, Th. Heidel, M. Lepa, G. Ring (eds.), *Das neue Schuldrecht – ein Lehrbuch* (2002); S. Lorenz and Th. Riehm, *Lehrbuch zum neuen Schuldrecht* (2002); P. Huber and F. Faust, *Schuldrechtsmodernisierung: Einführung in das neue Recht* (2002); G. Wagner, Das Zweite Schadensersatzrechtsänderungsgesetz, 55 *NJW* 2002, 29, pp. 2049 ff.; D. Zimmer, Das neue Recht der Leistungsstörungen, 55 *NJW* 2002, 1, pp. 1 ff.; H. Otto, Die Grundstrukturen des neuen Leistungsstörungsrecht, *Jura* 2002, pp. 1 ff.; R. Schwarze, Unmöglichkeit, Unvermögen und änliche Leistungshindernisse im neuen Leistungsstörungsrecht, *Jura* 2002, pp. 73 ff.; S. Meier, Neues Leistungsstörungsrecht, *Jura* 2002, pp. 118 ff.; For a commentary, rule by rule, see B. Dauner-Lieb, Th. Heidel, M. Lepa, G. Ring (eds.), *Anwaltkommentar Schuldrecht, Erläuterungen der Neuregelungen zum Verjährungsrecht, Schuldrecht, Schadensersatzrecht und Mietrecht* (2002).

30 T. Weir, Complex Liabilities, XI *International Encyclopedia of Comparative Law* (1976), n. 6, p. 5. ("Contract is productive, tort law protective.")

5 Irrelevance of Legal Families

The question of the recoverability of pure economic loss is a generic question for all European legal systems. Comparative law research shows that it is not just a civil law versus common law issue. Civil law countries are themselves divided, not *from* the common law, but between themselves and the common law. An important question is how to understand the various differences and similarities between these systems, but this will have little to do with the « legal families » in which they happen to be placed. Instead, as indicated in the next section, there is a broad spectrum of approaches, methods and policies at work in Europe.

6 Liberal, Pragmatic and Conservative Approaches

Our study reveals that five countries – France, Belgium, Italy, Greece and Spain – take a liberal stance toward pure economic loss. A leading characteristic of their tort systems is the presence of a unitary general clause which does not, *a priori,* screen out pure economic loss. Another characteristic is that cases of this kind are resolved almost exclusively on the basis of extracontractual liability and not by crossing over to contract principles. These systems are liberal in appearance and liberal in the recoveries allowed. France permits (in principle) recoveries in delict in seventeen of the twenty cases in our study – Belgium in fourteen cases – whereas in more conservative systems like Portugal and Austria, the number of delictual recoveries is but five and seven respectively.

England, Scotland and the Netherlands display a pragmatic attitude. It is true that the judges of the Netherlands appear to be considerably more receptive to this form of loss than the judges of the United Kingdom, but it is the similarity in their reasoning, their technique and their candor which prompts us to group these three together. These systems are characterised by a cautious case-by-case approach which carefully studies the concrete socio-economic implications before granting or denying recovery for pure economic loss. Solutions are not driven by the dictates of wide tort principle, nor on the other hand by a checklist of absolute rights. The judges perform the role of gatekeeper, and their method of screening recoveries is through the "duty of care" concept.

The tort law of Germany, Austria, Portugal, Sweden and Finland is distinctly more conservative toward the issue. A striking characteristic in the first three is that pure economic loss is not among the so-called "absolute rights" which are protected by their tort law.[31] Recovery in tort, therefore, must be excluded as a general rule, and a remedy, if any exists, must be found elsewhere in the system, either on the basis of more specific tort provision or by an expansive application of contract principles. The latter is not infrequently the answer. There is an extensive resort to the law of contracts (also special statutes) as a corrective for the narrowness of tort. Nevertheless,

---

31 The exclusion in § sec. 823, sec.1 BGB, is well known, but as developments in Austria and Portugal amply show, the influence of German doctrine has resulted in a philosophy of absolute rights superimposed upon those countries' general clauses. See our study, above note 3.

even with the lateral support of contract, recoveries are substantially fewer than in the liberal regimes.

Our spectrum of systems indicates that, contrary to what one distinguished writer has asserted,[32] there is no "true Continental Divide" on this issue in Europe. If any split is to be recognised, in our view it lies between those countries which have an overt system of protected interests in tort (such as Germany and Austria) and those like France and Belgium which do not. It is this criterion (along with vigorous policy debate in the background) which seems to underlie differences within the civilan camp and makes English law seem conceptually closer to German law.

7   Awareness of the Time Factor

Any general assessment of common tendencies must take into account the factor of time. One can easily notice that legal attitudes toward pure economic loss are not always stable. Indeed some recent developments should serve as a warning that we could be describing a "provisional" landscape in which some positions are still evolving and changing.

Just in the past forty years Italy in effect changed its stripes from a system of "protected interests" to a general clause system. Within that same period England and Scotland admitted as many as five exceptions to the rule of no recovery. If we take an even longer view we may note that France abandoned in the 20th century a more restrictive attitude that had been current throughout the previous century (grounded on a praeter legem resort to the unlawfulness conception) in order to match more closely its codistic liberal façade. Moving along an opposite path, Austrian history reveals a sharp departure from the liberal appearances of the ABGB in the second half of the 19th century, and since then its legal system has been accepting bodily German doctrinal thought on pure economic loss together with the usual justifications for its control.

Our point is simply that legal positions have not stood still and some have abruptly changed and may change again. Old, and even current, snapshots of the law, therefore, may be of limited utility if one is willing to determine once for ever the existence or non-existence of a common core as to the recoverability of pure economic loss.

8   Basic Arguments for the Exclusionary Rule

Before discussing the possible existence of a 'common core' agreement across the legal systems about the recoverability of pure economic loss, we wish to consider the fundamental arguments which are usually presented in support of an exclusionary rule. These arguments are usually developed by jurists in legal systems which take the position that such losses should not be generally recoverable in tort, except in de-

---

32 Jan van Dunné, "Liability for Pure Economic Loss: Rule or Exception? A Comparatist's View of the Civil Law-Common Law Split on Compensation of Non-Physical Damage in Tort Law," 4 European Review of Private Law 397, 399 (1999).

fined and limited circumstances. The experience of other countries, however, may suggest certain counterarguments. These viewpoints are worth considering in presenting a full picture of the recoverability of pure economic loss and in approaching any harmonisation effort of European tort law.

8.1 The Floodgates

This is the most important of the three arguments we will discuss. It is not only pervasive but has proved persuasive. It usually links up with and reinforces the other arguments. Though not always noticed, there are actually three distinct strands to the floodgates argument, and it is helpful to separate them.

The *first* strand is the belief that to permit recovery of pure economic loss in some cases would unleash an infinity of actions that would burden if not overwhelm the courts. If defendant's negligence necessitates the closure of trading markets or shuts down all commerce traveling a busy motorway, there may be hundreds, perhaps thousand of persons who would be financially damaged. Assuming a large number of these cases reach the courts, there would be administrative overload. The justice system could not cope with the sheer numbers of claims.

The *second* strand is the fear is that widespread liability would place an excessive burden upon the defendant who, for purposes of the argument, is treated as the living proxy of human initiative and enterprise. Von Ihering's statement "Where would it all lead if everyone could be sued...!"[33] is a famous rendition of the argument. The potentially staggering liability would be out of all proportion to the degree to which defendant was negligent. It is also said that it is manifestly impossible for defendant to predict in advance how many relational economic loss claims he might face when, for example, he injures the property of a primary victim. Whether there is a small or large class of secondary loss sufferers depends, fortuitously, upon the number of parties with economic interests linked to the exploitation of the property.[34]

The danger of disproportionate consequences resulting from minor blameworthiness is of course an issue of fairness no matter what kind of damages have been caused[35] but some scholars believe that the danger is far greater in pure financial loss cases. Financial harm is assumed to have a greater propensity to travel far and wide. It has often been pointed out that the laws of Newton do not apply on the road to financial ruin.[36] Physical damage has at least a final resting point, but patrimonial harm is not slowed down by gravity and friction.[37] The harm has often been compared to

---

33 R. von Jhering, Culpa in contrahendo oder Schadensersatz bei nichtigen oder nicht zur Perfektion gelangten Verträgen, 4 *Jherings Jahrbücher* (1861), pp. 12-13.

34 The rationales of predictability and practicality are discussed in R. Bernstein, *Economic Loss*, 2nd ed. (1998), pp. 201-203.

35 See, J. Waldron, Moments of Carelessness and Massive Loss, in: D. Owen, *Philosophical Foundations of Tort Law* (1995) at p. 387.

36 T. Weir, supra note 30, at n. 14(d). This was also the view of Fleming James who stated that the "physical consequences of negligence usually have been limited, but the indirect economic repercussions of negligence may be far wider, indeed virtually open-ended.": Limitations on Liability for Economic Loss Caused by Negligence: A Pragmatic Appraisal, 25 *Vand. L. Rev.* 1972, pp. 43, 45.

37 See, however, J. Stapleton, Legal Cause: Cause-in-Fact and the Scope of Liability for Consequences, 54 *Vand. L. Rev.* 2001, p. 941, at 974: "The reference to the laws of physics reflects a long-standing

the recovery of damages for nervous shock, since there too the loss can be "pure" as opposed to consequential, and there too the danger of reverberating impacts is commonly given as a reason for restrictive rules.[38]

The *third* strand of the argument maintains that pure economic loss is simply part of a broad modern trend toward greater and greater tort liability, a trend that must be kept under control. Allowing exceptions to the exclusionary rule is a slippery slope that may lead to reversal of the rule and may also encourage the development of other types of tort liability.[39]

In assessing the cumulative weight of the argument, there are in our view a number of considerations to bear in mind.

To begin with, it should be remembered that the floodgates argument has never purported to be a scientific claim nor a claim based upon comparative law research. It is not very easy to test whether the dire prophecy of the "nightmare scenario" is dream or reality. Is it founded on blind conservatism or does it have a rational basis?[40] For instance, the central assertion that physical damage is different than

---

fallacy in traditional running down cases that control of liability for consequences can be achieved by some 'billiard ball' notion of the laws of physics. That is, this reference rests upon the faulty notion that "claims for physical damage, whether to person or property, are inherently limited by the laws of physics which teach that physical forces will ultimately come to rest. After I have run you over and broken your leg, we have "come to rest" in a crude sense. Yet if you later suffer negligent treatment at a hospital that damages your other leg, the law may well say this injury is within the appropriate scope of my liability for consequences. What is doing the work in this judgment is not some inherent limit on my liability set by the law of physics but a judgment about the appropriate scope of liability for consequences in light of, among other things, the perceived purpose underlying the recognition of the obligation in the first place."

38 The analogy, however, must not be pressed too far. Courts in emotional shock cases have been troubled by a number of rather different concerns, particularly the difficulty of defining the threshold harm (what degree of shock should be cognizable? what manifestation of the harm should be required?) and the difficulty of detecting false or fraudulent claims. In the case of pure economic loss, however, the problem of defining the threshold of the harm is minimal, (the threshold of financial damage always begins at zero); the factual existence of loss is objectively demonstrable and its measurement and proof are not easy but perhaps less problematic. The characteristic uncertainty of financial loss does not consist in defining or verifying the harm but in establishing the causal link between it and defendant's conduct. The threat of fraud is also of less concern because such loss is free of the danger that claimants may simulate its symptoms. Accordingly economic loss is less easily feigned than the manifestations of nervous shock. We therefore suggest that the most important similarity between the two areas centers upon judicial concern about expanding liability in favour of an indeterminate number of plaintiffs, for indeterminate amounts of damages. Cp. Ch. von Bar, *The Common European Law of Torts*, vol. II (2000), pp. 76-84. For a discussion in American law, see R.L. Rabin, Tort Liability For Negligently Inflicted Economic Loss: A Reassessment, 37 *Stan. L. Rev.* 1985, p. 1513, at pp. 1524-1525.

39 The Tilburg Group, for example, argues that the floodgates must be kept shut in order "to dam crushing liability" and to resist the general trend toward expansion of liability. Six of eight hypotheticals chosen for comparative study by the Tilburg Group deal with the subject of pure economic loss. The floodgates metaphor plays a central role in their orientation. See J. Spier (ed.), *The Limits of Liability* (1996) and also J. Spier, *The Limits of Expanding Liability* (1998). Their view may mean that the exclusionary rule should be invoked even in factual instances where there is no danger of a flood of claims or of disproportionate recovery. No compensation should be made for fear of establishing an exception that erodes the rule or any exception that may receive analogical extension in the future.

40 For example, in 1939 the eminent American torts scholar, William Prosser, forcefully argued: 'It is

financial damage because it is more contained and judicially manageable seems increasingly difficult to understand in view of today's mass torts which sometimes involve innumerable physically injured victims asserting claims sometimes amounting to billions of dollars.[41] These disasters range from single-event catastrophes like the Exxon Valdez oil spill and the Bhopal gas leak, to multiple-event injuries like the asbestos and DES tragedies which extend over a wide geographic area, producing literally thousands of actual claims that stretched judicial resources to their limits.[42] The Exxon Valdez oil spill by itself produced more than 30,000 litigated claims.[43] The recent outbreak of foot and mouth disease in Europe which spreads physical and/or financial loss by the same prevailing wind may prove to be a bigger disaster.

These examples would suggest that the law is normally content to impose liability even though the potential plaintiff class is large.[44] It would sound very odd if the defendant could argue that s/he should not owe a duty because s/he would have injured too many victims.[45] For many scholars, therefore, the justification for a no-recovery rule based upon a supposed difference in ripple effect or in the sheer size of the plaintiff class is hard to reconcile with the recovery of extremely large economic losses resulting from negligently caused physical injury.[46]

---

the business of the law to remedy wrongs that deserve it, even at the expense of a "flood of claims"; and it is a pitiful confession of incompetence on the part of any court of justice to deny relief upon the ground that it will give the courts too much work to do': Intentional Infliction of Mental Suffering: a New Tort, 37 *Mich LR* 1939, p. 874 at 877.

41 The point is repeatedly emphasised by H. Bernstein, Civil Liability for Economic Loss, 46 *AJCL* 1998, p. 111, at pp. 126-128.

42 For a summary of the American scene, see C.H. Peterson and J. Zekoll, Mass Torts, 42 *AJCL* 1994, p. 79. For a valuable analysis of the doctrine of pure economic loss in relation to the Valdez and Amoco Cadiz oil spills, see V. Goldberg, Recovery for Economic Loss Following The Exxon Valdez Oil Spill, 23 *J. of Leg. Studies* 1994, p. 1. On its facts the Exxon Valdez accident caused enormous physical damage to the environment, that is, to things in the public domain such as shoreline, waters and wildlife. The individual litigants were directly affected as fishermen, tour operators, hotel owners. Their claims were viewed as a specie of pure economic loss. Such accidents, however, could just as well occur in places where thousands of private owners would suffer property losses and consequential economic losses. The threat of an avalanche of claims, therefore, is hardly reduced by the metaphysical nature of the damage, and it is questionable that the law can construct a sensible rule based upon such a distinction.

43 V.P. Goldberg, Recovery For Economic Loss Following the Exxon Valdez Oil Spill, 23 *J. Legal Studies* 1994, p. 1.

44 As Professor Jane Stapleton wrote in a private communication to the authors of these pages: "we should not forget that modern procedural reforms, such as statutory provisions facilitating class actions, reflect society's concern to address the barriers to justice that might otherwise face the mass of victims that can result in today's complex society from a single piece of wrongdoing. They are a way of addressing, by lowering, the 'costs of mass litigation' concern."

45 The judgement of *Griffiths* v. *British Coal Corporation* (January 23rd 1998, *Q.B.D.*) upheld the largest personal injury claim in British history which led to a record settlement of £2 billion being agreed for the benefit of 100,000 ex-miners suffering from a range of chest illnesses, a sum considerably more than government received from the privatisation of the coal industry: see J. Stapleton, Legal Cause: Cause-in-Fact and the Scope of Liability for Consequences, 54 *Vand. L. Rev.* 2001, 941 ff., 962, fn. 53.

46 See J. Stapleton, Duty of Care Factors: a Selection from the Judicial Menus, in: P. Cane and J. Stapleton (eds.), *The Law of Obligations: Essays in Celebration of John Fleming* (1998), p. 59. The author, at 65-6, argues that "Concern that, in a particular context, imposition of a duty of care might

The geographical distribution of the floodgates argument is another interesting facet of its development. While a perennial in some soils and climates, the argument has failed to take root in others. We have no clear explanation why this occurs. One might say that the theme resonates better in particular legal cultures, but what makes one culture or legal infrastructure more receptive than another? The answer is not clear. Until research is available, the question is open to speculation and to discussion of interesting clues. For instance, litigation rates in Europe are known to be very variable, and it appears that some of the more litigious countries adhere to the no-recovery rule.

Is it coincidence that both the exclusionary rule and floodgates argument flourish in Germany and Austria where the rates are among the highest in Europe? Does this factor explain why in neighbouring The Netherlands, where rates are remarkably low, there is no categorical rule against recovery, nor even – so far as an outside observer can judge – any particular fear of docket inundation?[47] Consider England and Scotland where the floodgates argument has enjoyed significant success. Should we be surprised that an historically small, close-knit coterie of judges may be sensitive to the question of administrative overload? Does institutional structure and conditioning play a role in this question?

Another relevant issue may be to investigate the way in which broad arguments of this kind circulate in international channels. The ruling ideas of influential exporting legal cultures (not merely substantive law ideas, but "soft" formants such as the conventional wisdom and dominant policy arguments) clearly have extra-territorial scope and impact. It does not seem accidental that in countries where English and German legal cultures have a decisive sphere of influence (e.g. English influence in Commonwealth countries and the United States; Germanic influence in Austria and Portugal) the floodgates argument has been received almost unquestioned.

It is interesting that in countries where French leadership is acknowledged, one vainly searches for any trace or mention of floodgates anxiety. As stated earlier this discussion is purely speculative. The subject merits deeper investigation, to be carried out through a multidisciplinary approach.

8.2 In the Scale of Human Values

A second argument is cast in terms of philosophical values. It maintains that intangible wealth is not and should not be treated on the same level as protecting bodily

---

expose defendants to a large volume of claims (as opposed to an indeterminate number of claims – see below) are unconvincing given that the law is content elsewhere to impose liability where the potential plaintiff class is large. Indeed, it would be very odd if a defendant could argue in favour of his argument that he should not owe a duty that he had many victims!".

47 For relevant figures see E. Blankenburg, Civil Litigation Rates as Indicators of Legal Culture, in: D. Nelkin (ed.), *Comparing Legal Cultures* (1997), at pp. 41 ff. where the author discusses the thesis that differences in legal culture may account for the disparities in civil litigation rates between neighbouring countries with very similar legal traditions and socio-economic conditions. For further comparisons, see A.A.S. Zuckerman (ed.), *Civil Justice in Crisis. Comparative Perspectives of Civil Procedure* (1999), *passim*; B.S. Markesinis, Litigation-mania in England, Germany and the USA; Are We So Very Different? 49 *CLJ* 1990, p. 133; P. Atiyah, Tort Law and the Alternatives: Some Anglo-American Comparisons, *Duke L.J.* 1987, p. 1002.

integrity or even physical property. People are more important than things, and things are more important than money.[48] Our legal interest in liberty, bodily integrity, land, possessions, reputation, wealth, privacy and dignity are all good interests, "but they are not equally good." The law protects the better interests better. And so "a legal system which is concerned with human values (and the law is supposed to reflect the proper values of society) would be right to give greater protection to tangible property than to intangible wealth."[49]

The exclusionary rule is then a reflection of the lower value ascribed to unreified wealth.[50] It is important to notice that this view has a silent premise: these interests must be ranked because the law *cannot* simultaneously protect all interests fully.

Even if one accepts, for sake of argument, that wealth is less important than other values, still there would be no justification for a rule restricting its recovery unless we had to do so in order to protect other, more meritorious interests. Thus the philosophical point is persuasive to the extent that (1) there is indeed a finite limit to the law's ability to protect interests and (2) giving full protection to pure patrimonial wealth would clearly exceed that capacity and therefore impinge on other protections or the interests of third persons.

The first point may be less controversial than the second. No one doubts that resources are finite: Judicial resources are not unlimited; tort liability cannot be extended indefinitely without stifling human initiative; and responsible defendants can be bankrupted by financial claims that leave claims for bodily injury unsatisfied.

It may be argued, therefore, that if pure economic loss were freely protected and allowed to compete on an equal footing with other, worthier claims for limited resources, the effect might be to crowd out "better" interests and leave them unsatisfied. That conclusion depends, however, on the answer to the second point, namely whether those limits would be surpassed by a presumption of recoverability. The answer to this question again seems to be conjectural since it ultimately depends to some extent upon the same unverified assumptions inherent in the floodgates rationale.

It also raises the question how countries like France and Belgium, which follow a rule of presumptive recovery of economic loss, have managed to avoid what the floodgates argument predicts. Is their experience proof that the argument is a gross exaggeration of the consequences, or does their experience tend to prove that these countries are simply using hidden and indirect means of controlling those consequences? There is an additional question.

The exclusionary rule is associated with the negligence standard. All systems, however, permit recovery when pure financial loss is inflicted intentionally. Thus the exclusionary rule cannot be seen simply as an abstract ordering of interests but it is

---

48 The argument has been made in England that "The philosophy of the market place presumes that it is lawful to gain profit by causing others economic loss, ... Certainly there seems to have developed an understanding that economic loss at the hands of others is something we have to accept without legal redress, unless caused by some specifically outlawed conduct such as fraud or duress" The Aliakmon, [1985] 2 *AER* 44, at p. 73 (per Ld. Goff).

49 T. Weir, *A Casebook on Tort*, 9th ed. (2000), p. 6.

50 But shouldn't one care about memories, sentiments, pains, personal well-being and all the other values-conveying occurrences that most of the time represent the real and only wealth of a person and, probably, her/his closest link to the notion of 'human values'?.

also a rule tied to the gradations of blame. It would be difficult to say whether the nature of the interest or the nature of the fault is the more important factor in the equation.

Indeed we think it would be essentially misguided to assign such priorities, because the rule, when it is applied and to the extent that it is a rule, is really the outcome of many other interacting factors as well.[51] Not the least of these are many metalegal considerations, such as the size of the plaintiff class, the potential scope of the damages, public policy toward professional standards and so forth, which have varying degrees of cogency in actual context. Only through study of these factors in their liability context will we understand why the alleged rule operates selectively and situationally, never mechanically, and indeed leaves untouched a number of defined situations where one may even speak (as we will see below) of a limited core of protection for pure economic loss.

8.3 In Historical Perspective

Some scholars assert as an historical matter that pure economic loss has traditionally been left unprotected by the law. If the assertion were generally true, it may have important normative implications for the present and the future. Professor Kötz deduces a teleological point in the evolution of tort law: The primary *purpose* of the law in England and Germany, he maintains, has "always been" to provide protection against personal injuries and harm to physical property. Pure economic loss seems left out of historical development, at least in those two countries.[52]

Another writer argues that the rules of tort based on foreseeability were developed for physical damage and are not workable outside of the context for which they were developed. The straightforward application of the foreseeability test to claims of pure financial loss would lead to ruinous levels of liability.[53] Because they are products of history, tort rules today are ill-adapted to the problem of pure economic loss.

Whether these views do justice to the past, however, is open to question. James Gordley's essay, which explores the history of pure economic loss in some detail, notes that many early civilians said that plaintiff could recover if he suffered "damage" and damage meant simply a diminution of his *patrimonium*. They did not distinguish between loss of a physical asset and other kinds of loss. They occasionally put cases in which the plaintiff would recover what we today would regard as pure economic loss, though he cautions that they did not know or use this term and did not recognise an autonomous category by that name.[54]

---

51 For a nuanced attempt to use various factors in a sliding scale to explain the lesser protection given to pure economic loss, see H. Koziol (ed.), *Unification of Tort Law: Wrongfulness* (1998), pp. 29-30.

52 H. Kötz, Economic Loss in Tort and Contract, 58(3) *RabelsZ* 1994, 423, 428.

53 B. Feldthusen, *Economic Negligence*, 2nd ed. (1989), pp. 10-11. The author asserts that the "remoteness" of the damage from the initial conduct of the defendant is the characteristic and endemic issue which distinguishes pure economic loss, as a practical matter, from cases involving physical damage.

54 The Rule Against Recovery in Negligence for Pure Economic Loss: An Historical Accident, in: M. Bussani & V.V. Palmer (eds.), above, note 3, and *ibidem* the citations to the views of Durandis, Baldus, Brunnemann, Lauterbach and Grotius.

For instance there was the dependent's action for loss of support due to wrongful death, which clearly existed on the continent in Grotius' time. This was in effect an action for the recovery of pure economic loss sustained by wife and children, but it was not referred to in those terms. Evidence of this kind would suggest that there was no *per se* rule against compensation for pure economic harm in the civilian tradition.[55] Indeed, Gordley's account characterises the rise of the exclusionary rule both in England and Germany as a late development of the 19th century[56] and the peculiar outgrowth of analytical thinking. He concludes that the rule is an "accident" of legal history, not a pervasive feature of it.

9   In Search of a Common Core

It is time to appraise to what extent arguments and counterarguments about the recoverability of pure economic loss helped shape the actual rules of legal systems. Although a full review of the research we mentioned before is beyond the scope of this paper, the results of the study may be briefly summarised in methodological and substantive terms.

9.1   Absence of Methodological Common Core

Methodologically speaking, the tort scene strikes us as diverse and unsettled. Comparative research reveals that four principal methodologies dominate the European landscape. Though some countries resort to more than one of these methods (thus adding to the complexity) generally each has one characteristic means of dealing with the issue of pure economic loss.

Thus the compensation issue may be left to

(1)   flexible causal determinations (the characteristic method found in Spanish, Italian and French regimes)

(2)   preliminary judicial screening using a "duty of care" analysis (the approach particularly prominent in England, Scotland)

(3)   rigid causation techniques aiming straightforwardly to exclude 'third party loss" (Sweden and Finland) and

---

55   See R. Zimmermann, *The Law of Obligations:Roman Foundation of the Civilian Tradition* (1996), pp. 1024-25; V.V. Palmer, The Fate of the General Clause in a Cross-Cultural Setting: The Tort Experience of Louisiana, 46 *Loyola L.Rev.* 2000, p. 535, at p. 551; V.V. Palmer, The Lousiana *Civilian Experience: Critiques of Codification in a Mixed Jurisdiction*, ch. 6 (2004).

56   Insurance practices tend also to show the late development of the rule. Development of business interruption insurance, often called "consequential loss insurance," belongs to the late nineteenth century, and even now the availability of such insurance is still rather limited. A prevalent restriction is that interruption insurance is essentially "follow-on" coverage to another insured peril, such as fire. Under the wording of standard fire policies, there is no compensation for interruption unless it results from a fire. This is not really compensation for pure economic loss, however, but rather compensation for parasitic loss. See, e.g., G.J.R. Hickmott, *Principles and Practice of Interruption Insurance* (1982), pp. 3-4; D.C. Jess, *The Insurance of Commercial Risks, Law and Practice* (1986), pp. 244-251; Ch. Lowstein, Pure Economic Loss and Liability Insurance, in: W.H. van Boom, H. Koziol, Ch.A. Witting (eds.), Pure Economic Loss (2003), pp. 162-166.

(4)   a scheme of absolute rights that, by deliberate omission, leaves this interest unprotected (the approach of Germany, Austria and Portugal).

Perhaps a simpler way to summarise the position is to say that some regimes rely
upon general clauses and start from an inclusive position, but others impose a limited
listing of protected interests and start from an exclusionary position. The first group
allows recovery *in* principle, the second denies it *on* principle. The first grants recoveries through tort actions, the second must deny relief in tort if it cannot find an
exception, and failing that, it must turn to paracontractual actions like *culpa in
contrahendo* or contracts with protective effects for third parties. Indeed the resort to
contractual actions as a means of overcoming the narrowness of tort protection reveals *still another* methodological split: Some countries deal with this issue solely in
tort while others rely heavily on flexible contractual devices to palliate the sternness
of their tort approach. It is therefore fair to conclude that there is no methodological
common care that can be suggested by this picture.

9.2   A Limited Substantive Common Core

Whether there is a substantive common core of principles governing pure economic
loss could depend to a large extent upon our unconscious reformulation of the question driven by our national traditions and cultures. Yet comparative law, if it teaches
anything, teaches us to resist this.

Culture and tradition have summary ways of telling us to which field this question
belongs (tort or contract ?) and thus may project a prejudice about its proper resolution and the coherence or incoherence of national solutions. To those who believe
that pure economic loss is the natural preserve of tort, there may be little common
core. But to those who would say that it is the natural preserve of contract we think
there will appear to be even less common core.

Our comparative and fact-based approach to the question makes us skeptical of
these labels. The issue is situated at the frontier of the law of obligations where there
is both tort and contract, or where tort behaves like contract and contract behaves like
tort. We believe that the existence of a common core can only be discussed in factual
terms.

To place the matter in perspective, let us first isolate four areas: (a) consequential
economic loss, (b) statutorily protected interests; (c) negligently inflicted economic
loss, and (d) intentionally caused economic loss. Out of these will emerge the contours of a 'limited common core' on the recoverability of pure economic loss.

(a) Consequential economic loss is in principle recoverable in every system –
whether the source of the loss is intentional or negligent conduct, or an activity
subject to strict liability. Here is an area of common ground that is worth noting.
(b) The recovery of pure economic loss is not regarded as doubtful when such loss
stems from the infringement of statutorily protected interests,[57] such as those protected by antitrust, copyright and patent laws, as well as by State liability laws.[58]

---

57 Cp. Ch. von Bar, *The Common European Law of Torts*, vol. II (2000), pp. 54-56.
58 The same could be said as to some other fields, particularly the field of 'business torts'. Although

(c) As to negligently inflicted economic loss, we can sort out three areas of agreement.

Pure economic loss turns out to be a head of damage that faces no problem across European countries when plaintiff's loss is due to negligently performed *professional services*.[59] There is widespread agreement that careless notaries, the negligent auditors or negligent credit rating institutes will be responsible for the economic losses of some persons (beyond their clients) with whom they had no contractual tie. Although there may be specific requirements that must be met in some systems that others do not clearly impose (for example, German and English emphasis upon showing the "reliance" of the third party) still it seems fair to say that in many situations (provided indeterminate and excessive liability is excluded) plaintiffs may recover losses caused by negligent professionals regardless of the general features and traditions of a given legal system. This seems to reflect the collective view that a high standard of professional services can and ought to be maintained.[60]

---

legal systems such as France, the Netherlands, the UK and Portugal handle these problems with the help of the general law of obligations (the 6th book of the Dutch civil code devotes an entire chapter to unfair advertising), these subjects were not dealt with in our general study. Since rules in these areas largely depend on policy factors which are only partially common to our field and would deserve detailed investigation, reasons of space compelled the editors to place limits on the research. For a general survey, Ch. von Bar, *The Common European Law of Torts*, vol. II (2000), pp. 4-200, 245-249 and, more closely related to our issue, 52-56; W. van Gerven, J. Lever, P. Larouche, *Tort Law* (2000), pp. 208-248, 358-394.

59 Discussed above, c. 3, sec. d.

60 A breach of European Community law may entail liability for pure economic loss. The liability of the Community institutions and its servants in the performance of their duties finds its source in art. 288 (2) EC Treaty. The liability of a member State has its origins in the case law of the European Court of Justice, particularly the preliminary rulings pursuant to art. 234 EC Treaty. It is true that under these provisions plaintiffs can recover only when s/he falls into a group of persons which the infringed provision was designed to protect, but no 'in principle' restriction is made regarding the interests that are protected. Indeed, since Community law is primarily concerned with economic matters, breaches of Community law will typically result in economic or purely economic losses. The compensability of these losses when caused by Community institutions has been clearly set forth in ECJ, 19 May 1992, *Mulder* v. *Council*, Case C-104/89 [1992] *ECR* I-3061. With regard to the member States, their liability has been clearly endorsed by ECJ 5 March 1996, *Brasserie du Pêcheur* v. *Germany*, r. v. Secretary of State for Transport, ex pa. Factortame, Case C-46/93 [1996] *ECR* I-1029 (wherein the ECJ explicitly rejects the use of German and English national rules which would have prevented individuals from benefitting from the use of Community law to impose liability on Member States). The rejection was particularly important in the case of the English rule requiring proof akin to abuse of power to establish the tort of misfeasance in public office, and in the case of the German hierarchy of protected interests under BGB 823. For a comparative survey, see W. van Gerven, J. Lever, P. Larouche, *Tort Law* (2000) at pp. 889 ff; see *passim*, T. Heukels & A. McDonnell (eds.), *The Action for Damages in Community Law* (1997); P. Craig, Once More Unto the Breach: The Community, the State and Damages Liability, 113 *L. Q. Rev.* 1997, 67 ff. See also B.S. Markesinis, *The German Law of Torts*, 4th ed. (2002), pp. 833 ff.

It is a different, and still open issue, whether individuals are entitled to compensation under national law when other individuals infringe Community law and thereby cause economic loss. Under the laws of the Member States a right to recovery is generally acknowledged in cases of breach of a Community law provision which imposes direct obligations upon individuals – such as arts. 81 and 82 EC Treaty, or other provisions having the so called 'horizontal' direct effect: see W. van Gerven, Bridging the Unbridgeable: Communityh and National Tort Laws after Francovich and Brasserie, 45

A second area of common core lies in the field of "transferred" economic loss.[61] Jurists in both liberal and conservative systems have recognised that transferred loss is liability neutral from a tortfeasor perspective and the legal questions regarding recovery are mainly technical rather than prudential. This may explain why nine countries, including three conservative regimes which, as we know, do not generally protect pure economic loss in tort, permit recovery of the losses sustained by the lessee of a cruise ship when the voyage must be canceled for repairs due to defendant's negligent act. Here the lessee essentially claims the loss of profits that might have equally been lost by the ship's owner had he or she seen fit to operate the boat in the cruise business instead of leasing it for that purpose.

The third area of substantive agreement involves cases in which defendant's act negligently interferes with the operation of a business or trade, such as when a truck blocks the entrance to business premises, or a mistakenly issued job reference prejudices plaintiff's employment. As many as ten countries, which include tort regimes across the spectrum, permit recoveries in such cases. We believe that these results are surely influenced by the absence of the spectre of indeterminate or widespread liability.

(d) All systems agree that intentionally inflicted pure economic loss is recoverable where the conduct in question is regarded as culpable, immoral or contrary to public policy. The significance of this point is of more practical importance than may appear at first sight. Its range of application may be somewhat greater than the narrow liability which the words "intentionally inflicted" harm suggests. In some systems a broad, flexible meaning is given to the "intention" element.[62]

Besides, it is interesting to observe from the comparative point of view that the shift to higher degrees of culpability tends to broaden the scope of recovery in all systems. This suggests to us that the exclusionary rule should not be conceived as a simple rule based solely on the nature of plaintiff's damage. The nonmaterial nature of the damage is no more than one element in a complex balancing which decides where and when limits will be imposed in tort. To set up reasonable limits to the recovery, judges, scholars and legislators must consider other important factors as well, including the actor's state of mind.[63]

These are the contours of an area of substantive agreement on the protection of pure economic loss. While financial interests are not as comprehensively protected as

---

ICLQ 1996, pp. 507 ff. and, recently, upholding 'horizontal' direct effect of arts. 81 and 82 EC Treaty, Courage Ltd v Bernard Crehan and Bernard Crehan v Courage Ltd and Others: ECJ, Judgment of 20 September 2001 – reference for a preliminary ruling: Court of Appeal (England and Wales) (Civil Division)-United Kingdom -. Case C-453/99 [2001] *ECR* I-6297.

61 Discussed above in c. 3, sec. b

62 See, e.g., C. von Bar, in B. Markesinis, Gradual Convergence, at 104.

63 The existence of a balancing process is not so apparent in open, liberal systems such as the French which appear to make little use of the distinction between intentional and careless fault, but the complex interaction of scienter with other factors clearly surfaces in the English and German systems. In those systems, where harm is intentionally inflicted, restrictions on the recoverability of the type of harm are dropped, and in addition, concepts of remoteness of causation are relaxed. As David Howarth correctly notes, the overall result is that intentionality removes restrictions on liability that do not exist in the first place in other jurisdictions. "The General Conditions of Unlawfulness," in A. Hartkamp *et al.* (eds.), *Towards a European Civil Code*, 2nd ed. (1998) at p. 411.

other interests, there is indeed a considerable core frame of European protection. Should one judge by developments of the past forty years, when this frame has been increasing, one could guess it is likely to continue to grow.

10 The Recoverability of Pure Economic Loss within the Perspective of a European Codification

In tune with present European times, one may wonder how the above remarks and results might be of any use to the would-be codifiers of a European Civil Code.

To be sure, any codification attempt should be seasoned with – and this applies not simply to tort law but to all subjects – a certain amount of constructive scepticism. Yet, leaving aside any positive or negative bias *vis-à-vis* the very idea of the Code, as well as the many reasons put forward to deny, support or simply postpone its feasibility, the point is that the inquiry into 'pure economic loss' confirms how deeply conscious the code-drafters will need to be about the overall implications of remoulding the law of tort.

10.1 Pure Economic Loss Astride Private Law Frontiers

The kind of awareness that is required in legal debate can be shortly illustrated by consideration of the following.

Throughout our study we have seen the conceptual dependency which exists between underlying contract and property ideas and the law of tort. Suffice it to recall, for instance, the problems raised by the notion itself of pure economic loss, the flexible boundaries that comparative analysis enabled us to draw as to the so called "consequential" economic loss, as well as, in certain regimes, the great reliance upon contract rules to handle the issue.

Even more strikingly than in other domains, any attempt at codification concerning pure economic loss will therefore be closely dependent on the solutions which the same Code intends to offer in the other fields of private law, mainly with regard to contract and property.

To give further evidence of what we are referring to, we can return to some examples taken from our study. They concern the actual impact on our issue of the choices any legal system can make about the place and use of a series of legal tools, such as (a) possession, (b) property rights, (c) contract law devices, and (d) rules governing transfer of ownership.

(a) If possession is included in the framework of property rights, or if it is at any rate protected by proprietary remedies, any infringement of possession will permit recovery of the economic loss, regardless that it is called consequential or pure. If possession is not included in the property framework, however, or if the power of control over the thing is not sufficient in and of itself for the holder to be deemed a possessor, then the recoverability of the economic loss caused to the holder (by interference with the thing itself) becomes an issue to be settled.[64]

---

64 Cp. Ch. von Bar, *The Common European Law of Torts*, vol. II (2000), p. 55.

(b) If the right to electricity (but the same could apply to hertzian or other electro-magnetic waves[65]) is deemed a right in rem whose transfer from the supplier to the user is completed as of the date of the agreement, any damage to the system supplying that energy (such as the cutting of power cables) will be considered an infringement of property rights and therefore will raise no problems in any of the European legal systems.

(c) If the manner in which Germany and Austria apply the notions of 'culpa in contrahendo' or the 'contract with protective effect to third parties',[66] is adopted as a model for a European Code, it is beyond doubt that many of the issues raised in pure economic loss cases will be settled by contract principles, with little need to resort to tort law rules.[67]

(d) The Code's infrastructure regarding transfer of ownership would clearly have manifold effects in any 'Double Sale' case (where the seller transfers the title over a property to two different persons). Indeed, the right of the first buyer (*solo consensu*) to obtain compensation depends on a variety of factors, the role of which is actually to define who has the property right in the thing. These factors include the presence of good or bad faith, the completion of delivery (for movables), compliance with formalities like registration and recordation (for immovables) and the effects assigned to the registration itself.

10.2 A Destiny to be Interpreted

All this, once more, shows nothing but what is the real and general problem to cope with, no matter the 'façade' of the Code, no matter the purposes of the debate.

Based on our research we agree with a leading comparative law scholar's remark that whether pure economic loss is placed on the stage of tort or contract "is a point of legal technique and not of substance".[68] But precisely under the technical point of view the problem consists in the setting of systematically and socially acceptable boundaries to the shifting of losses incurred by the victim onto another party.[69] Whenever this shifting is governed neither by property law nor by contract law,[70] it is

---

65 For the debate on the legal nature of these entities, see U. Mattei, *Basic Principles of Property Law. A Comparative Legal and Economic Introduction* (2000), pp. 76 ff., 153 ff.

66 The same could be said for notions such as the French concept 'chaîne de contrats'. This refers to a series of contracts which, though distinct in law, form part of an economic complex. An example can be found in the chain which links a site owner to the contractor, the contractor to the sub-contractor and the latter to the supplier of the building materials. See H. Kötz & A. Flessner, *European Contract Law*, I, transl. by T. Weir (1997), pp. 255 ff.; H. Beale, A. Hartkamp, H. Kötz, D. Tallon (eds.), *Contract Law* (2002), pp. 47 ff. As to this technical notion and its actual impact on the recovery of pure economic losses, see G. Viney, *Introduction à la responsabilité* (1995), pp. 338 ff.

67 Nevertheless, different technical rules could still exist in each liability regime of liability concerning e.g., prescriptive periods or rules on the burden of proof.

68 H. Kötz, Economic Loss in Tort and Contract, 58(3) *RabelsZ* 1994, p. 423, at 428 ff.; see also P. Cane, Economic Loss in Tort and Contract, 58(3) *RabelsZ* 1994, pp. 430, 437.

69 For a comparative survey of the boundaries between the law of unjust enrichment and tort law, see Ch. von Bar, *The Common European Law of Torts*, vol. I (1998), pp. 525 ff.; P. Gallo, Unjust Enrichment. A Comparative Analysis, 40 *AJCL* 1992, pp. 431 ff.

70 Especially when victims lack the bargaining power to obtain adequate contractual protection. See F.

up to tort law to provide the solution. Thus – and in spite of the positivistic approach some may take –, the question of whether or not to award compensation to the victim falls to the interpreter charged with making the choice, that is, the judge and the scholar.[71]

Both of these actors have crucial tasks to perform. The scholar has primarily the role of uncovering whatever specific factors in each individual case are crucial to determining the liability. Whilst it may be acceptable for a judge to make conclusionary statements, at least in some systems, no scholar may merely assert that the plaintiff's damage was proximate, that a duty was justified because the parties were in a 'special relationship' or entered into a contract with protective effect to third parties, or that the plaintiff had reasonably relied on the defendant or merely that it was 'just, fair and reasonable' to impose the liability. Unless given substantive content, these are just labels. Scholars in their role of decision-inspirers are bound to focus explicitly on why and whether that particular damage was proximate, the relation was special, the reliance was reasonable, and so on.

The judge too, of course, brings his or her own legal culture to bear.

S/he has admired or criticised the judicial precedents, and s/he has learnt the opinions of the given authorities at law school. S/he has both an attitude of self-restraint and a reservoir of legal notions, 'reactions' and answers stemming from the legal tradition of the country in which s/he lives.[72]

This repertoire may also include the role that the judiciary plays in the given legal framework: a role entailing a variable degree of respect paid to scholarly opinions, to superior court rulings, to the legislature's prospective or actual choices. Hence, it is no surprise to find that decisions end up being grounded on the balance between the various circumstances of the given case, as qualified, i.e. sized, in legal terms through the overall interpretative culture of the decision maker.

All of this is possibly true of many fields of law. But within private law, at the frontier between contract and tort law in particular, it does seem to be the appropriate way to appraise what the making of law entails. Some might prefer to rephrase the same concept by saying that along this legal frontier there are policy factors which frame the technical outcomes according to changes in social demands.[73] For our purposes, however, the choice of how to phrase the concept is neutral, insofar as the legal notions of change[74] and tradition are essential to our issue too.

Werro, Tort Law at the beginning of the New Millenium. A Tribute to John G. Fleming's Legacy, 49 *AJCL* 2001, pp. 147, 153; P. Cane, Economic Loss in Tort and Contract, 58(3) *RabelsZ* 1994, p. 430, at p. 434.

71 Cp. Ch. von Bar, above note 13, at pp. 464 ff.

72 From the comparative 'law and economics' point of view, see M. Bussani & U. Mattei, Making the Other Path Efficient. Economic Analysis and Tort Law in Less Developed Countries, in: E. Buscaglia, W. Ratliff and R. Cooter (eds.), *The Law and Economics of Development* (1997), pp. 149 ff.

73 Cp. the point made by J. Stapleton, Tort, Insurance and Ideology, 58 *MLR* 1995, p. 820. See also J. Stapleton, Comparative Economic Loss: Lessons from Case-Law-Focused "Middle Theory, 50 UCLA L. Rev. 2002, 53 ff. S. Banakas, Liability for Incorrect financial Information: Theory and Practice in a General Clause System and in a Protected Interests System, 7 *ERPL* 1999, pp. 261, 265, 284.

74 "Sans variations, nous n'aurions pas de progrès, car le progrès est la variation. Si nous voulons le progrès, nous voulons la variation; et si nous acceptons la variation, nous acceptons la diversité": R.

The point is that the real life of the law constantly reveals its interpretative fate, its interpretative mode of existence. As we have seen, the issue of recoverability of pure economic loss does not escape this fate.

BIBLIOGRAPHY: P. Atiyah, Tort Law and the Alternatives: Some Anglo-American Comparisons, *Duke L.J.* 1987, 1002; S. Banakas (ed.), *Civil Liability for Pure Economic Loss* (1996); S. Banakas, Liability for Incorrect financial Information: Theory and Practice in a General Clause System and in a Protected Interests System, 7 *ERPL* 1999, 261; J.M. Barendrecht, Pure Economic Loss in the Netherlands, in: E.H. Hondius (ed.) *Netherlands Reports to the Fifteenth International Congress of Comparative Law* (1998), 115; H. Beale, A. Hartkamp, H. Kötz, D. Tallon (eds.), *Contract Law* (2002); P. Benson, The Basis for Excluding Liability for Economic Loss in Tort Law, in: D.G. Owen, *The Philosophical Foundations of Tort Law* (1995), 427; H. Bernstein, Civil Liability for Economic Loss, 46 *AJCL* 1998, 111; R. Bernstein, *Economic Loss*, 2nd ed. (1998); W. Bishop and J. Sutton, Efficiency and Justice in Tort Damages: The Shortcomings of the Pecuniary Loss Rule, 15 *J. of Legal Studies* 1986, 347; E. Blankenburg, Civil Litigation Rates as Indicators of Legal Culture, in: D. Nelkin (ed.), *Comparing Legal Cultures* (1997), 41; M. Bussani & U. Mattei, Making the Other Path Efficient. Economic Analysis and Tort Law in Less Developed Countries, in: E. Buscaglia, W. Ratliff and R. Cooter (eds.), *The Law and Economics of Development* (1997), 149; M. Bussani & V.V. Palmer (eds.), *Pure Economic Loss in Europe* (2003); M. Bussani, V.V. Palmer, F. Parisi, Liability for Pure Financial Loss in Europe: An Economic Restatement, in 51 *Am. J. Comp. L.* 2003, 113; in G. De Geest & R. Van den Bergh (eds.), *Comparative Law and Economics* (2004), 270; M. Bussani, The Contract Law Codification Process in Europe: Policies, Targets and Time Dimensions, in: S. Grundmann & Stuyck (eds.), *An Academic Green Paper on European Contract Law* (2002); C.-W. Canaris (ed.), *Schuldrechtsmodernisierung* (2002); P. Cane, Economic Loss in Tort and Contract, 58(3) *RabelsZ* 1994, 430; A. Chamboredon, The Debate on a European Civil Code: For an "Open Texture", in: M. van Hoecke & F. Ost (eds.), *The Harmonisation of European Private Law* (2000), 63; M. Coestez and B.S. Markesinis, Liability of Financial Exploits in German and American Law, 51 Rev. J. Comp. L. 2003, 275; P. Craig, Once More Unto the Breach: The Community, the State and Damages Liability, 113 *LQR* 1997, 67; W. Däubler, Neues Schuldrecht – ein erster Überblick, in 54 *NJW* 2001, 3729; B. Dauner-Lieb, Th. Heidel, M. Lepa, G. Ring (eds.), *Anwaltkommentar Schuldrecht, Erläuterungen der Neuregelungen zum Verjährungsrecht, Schuldrecht, Schadensersatzrecht und Mietrecht* (2002); B. Dauner-Lieb, Th. Heidel, M. Lepa, G. Ring (eds.), *Das neue Schuldrecht – ein Lehrbuch* (2002); B. Feldthusen, *Economic Negligence: The Recovery of Pure Economic Loss* (1989); P. Gallo, Unjust Enrichment. A Comparative Analysis, 40 *AJCL* 1992, 431; P. Giliker, A Role for Tort in Pre-Contractual Negotiations? An Examination of English, French and Canadian Law, 52 I.C.L.Q. 2003, 969; H.P. Glenn, *Legal Traditions of*

Sacco, La diversité des droits, in: R. Ruedin (ed.), *Mélanges en l'honneur de C.A. Cannata* (1999), pp. 411 *et seq.* See also R. Sacco, Diversity and Uniformity in the Law, 49 *AJCL* 2001, p. 171. On the same tune, A. T. von Mehren, The US Legal System: Between the Common Law and Civil Law Traditions, in: 40 *Centro di studi e ricerche di diritto comparato e straniero. Saggi e conferenze* (2000); M. Bussani, The Contract Law Codification Process in Europe: Policies, Targets and Time Dimensions, in: S. Grundmann & Stuyck (eds.), *An Academic Green Paper on European Contract Law* (2002). Cp. A. Chamboredon, The Debate on a European Civil Code: For an "Open Texture", in: M. van Hoecke & F. Ost (eds.), *The Harmonisation of European Private Law* (2000), pp. 63, 68 *et seq.* and *ibidem* further references; «change *is* the tradition»: H.P. Glenn, *Legal Traditions of the World: Sustainable Diversity in Law* (2001), at p. 117 (emphasis in original); M. van Hoecke, The Harmonisation of Private Law in Europe: Some Misunderstandings, in: M. van Hoecke & F. Ost (eds.), *The Harmonisation of European Private Law*, pp. 1, 5 *et seq.*; B.S. Markesinis, Comparative Law in the Courtroom and in the Classroom (2003), pp. 55 *et seq.*

the World: Sustainable Diversity in Law (2001); V.P. Goldberg, Recovery For Economic Loss Following the Exxon Valdez Oil Spill, 23 J. Legal Studies 1994, 1; J. Gordley, The Rule Against Recovery in Negligence for Pure Economic Loss: An Historical Accident, in: M. Bussani & V.V. Palmer (eds.), Pure Economic Loss in Europe (forthcoming 2003); J. Herbots, Le Duty of Care et le dommage purement financier en droit comparé, in 62 Rev. dr. int. dr. comp., 1985, 7; T. Heukels & A. McDonnell (eds.), The Action for Damages in Community Law (1997); G.J.R. Hickmott, Principles and Practice of Interruption Insurance (1982); T. Honoré, Necessary and Sufficient Conditions in Tort Law, in: D.G. Owen (ed.), Philosophical Foundation of Tort Law (1995), 382; D. Howarth, Three Forms of Responsibility: On the Relationships Betweeen Tort Law and the Welfare State, 60 C.L.J. 2001, 553; D. Howarth, The General Conditions of Unlawfulness, in: A. Hartkamp et al. (eds.), Towards a European Civil Code, 2nd ed. (1998), 411; P. Huber and F. Faust, Schuldrechtsmodernisierung: Einführung in das neue Recht (2002); N. Jansen, The Idea of a Lost Chance, in 19 Oxford J. Leg. St. 1999, 271; D.C. Jess, The Insurance of Commercial Risks, Law and Practice (1986); L. Khoury, The Liability of Auditors Beyond Their Clients: A Comparative Study, 46 McGill Law Journal 2001, 413; J. Kleineman, Ren förmögenhetsskada (1987); H. Kötz & A. Flessner, European Contract Law, I, transl. by T. Weir (1997); H. Kötz, Economic Loss in Tort and Contract, 58(3) RabelsZ 1994, 423; H. Koziol (ed.), Unification of Tort Law: Wrongfulness (1998); S. Lorenz and Th. Riehm, Lehrbuch zum neuen Schuldrecht (2002); H.-P. Mansel, Die Neuregelung des Verjährungsrecht, in 55 NJW 2002, 89; B.S. Markesinis, The German Law of Torts, 4th ed. (2002); B.S. Markesinis, Litigation-mania in England, Germany and the USA; Are We So Very Different? 49 CLJ 1990, 133; U. Mattei, Basic Principles of Property Law. A Comparative Legal and Economic Introduction (2000); S. Meier, Neues Leistungsstörungsrecht, in Jura 2002, 118; P.G. Monateri, La responsabilità civile, in: R. Sacco (ed.), Tratt. dir. civ. (1998); H. Otto, Die Grundstrukturen des neuen Leistungsstörungsrecht, Jura 2002, 1; V.V. Palmer, The Fate of the General Clause in a Cross-Cultural Setting: The Tort Experience of Louisiana, 46 Loyola L. Rev. 2000, 535; V.V. Palmer, The Louisiana Civilian Experience: Critique of Codification in a Mixed Jurisdiction (2004); C.H. Peterson and J. Zekoll, Mass Torts, 42 AJCL 1994, 79; Prosser and Keeton on the Law of Torts, 5th ed., (1984); W. Prosser, Intentional Infliction of Mental Suffering: a New Tort, 37 Mich LR 1939, 874; R.L. Rabin, Tort Liability For Negligently Inflicted Economic Loss: A Reassessment, 37 Stan. L. Rev. 1985, 1513; H. Reece, Loss of Chances in the Law, 59 MLR 1996, 188; R. Sacco, La diversité des droits, in: R. Ruedin (ed.), Mélanges en l'honneur de C.A. Cannata (1999), 411; R. Sacco, Diversity and Uniformity in the Law, 49 AJCL 2001, 171; H.-B. Schafer, Liability of Exports and the Boundary between Tort and Contract Theoretical Inq. L. 2002, 453; M. Schwab, Das neue Schuldrecht im Überblick, JuS, 1, 2002, 1; G. Schwartz, The Economic Loss Doctrine in American Tort Law: Assessing the Recent Experience, in: S. Banakas (ed.), Civil Liability for Pure Economic Loss (1996), 103; R. Schwarze, Unmöglichkeit, Unvermögen und änliche Leistungshindernisse im neuen Leistungsstörungsrecht, Jura 2002, 73; J. Spier (ed.), The Limits of Liability: Keeping the Floodgates Shut (1996); J. Spier, The Limits of Expanding Liability (1998); J. Stapleton, Comparative Economic Loss: Lessons from Case-Law-Focused "Middle Theory", 50 UCLA L. Rev.' 2002, 531; J. Stapleton, Legal Cause: Cause-in-Fact and the Scope of Liability for Consequences, 54 Vand. L. Rev. 2001, 941; J. Stapleton, Duty of Care Factors: a Selection from the Judicial Menus, in: P. Cane and J. Stapleton (eds.), The Law of Obligations: Essays in Celebration of John Fleming (1998), 59; J. Stapleton, The Normal Expectancies Measure in Tort Damages, 113 Law Q. Rev. 1997, 257; J. Stapleton, Tort, Insurance and Ideology, 58 M.L.R. 1995, 820; J.M. Thomson, Delictual Liability for Pure Economic Loss: Recent Developments, SLT 1995, 139; W.H. van Boom, H. Kozial, Ch.A. Witting (eds.), Pure Economic Loss (2003). J.M. van Dunné; Liability for Pure Economic Loss: Rule or Exception? 4 ERPL 1999, 397; W. van Gerven et alii (eds.), Tort Law – Scope of Protection (1998); W. van Gerven, J. Lever and P. Larouche – Tort Law (2000); W. van Gerven, Bridging the Unbridgeable: Communityh and National Tort Laws after Francovich and Brasserie, 45 *ICLQ* 1996, 507; M. van Hoecke, The Harmonisation of Private Law in Europe: Some Misunderstandings, in: M. van Hoecke & F. Ost (eds.), *The Harmonisation of European Private Law* (2000), 1; G. Viney & P. Jourdain, Les conditions de la responsabilité, 2e éd., in: J. Ghestin (ed.), *Traité dr. civ.*, (1998), 71; G. Viney, Pour ou contre un principe général de responsabilité pour faute?, 49 *Osaka Univ. Law R.* 2002, 33; G. Viney, Introduction a la responsabilité, 2e éd., in: J. Ghestin (ed.), *Traité dr. civ.* (1995); Ch. von Bar, Liability for Information and Opinions Causing Pure Economic Loss to Third Parties: A Comparison of English and German Case Law, in: B. Markesinis (ed.), *The Gradual Convergence* (1994), 99; Ch. von Bar, *The Common European Law of Torts*, vol. I (1998), vol. II (2000); R. von Jhering, Culpa in contrahendo oder Schadensersatz bei nichtigen oder nicht zur Perfektion gelangten Verträgen, 4 *Jherings Jahrbücher* (1861); A.T. von Mehren, The US. Legal System: Between the Common Law and Civil Law Traditions, in: 40 *Centro di studi e ricerche di diritto comparato e straniero. Saggi e conferenze* (2000); G. Wagner, Das Zweite Schadensersatzrechtsänderungsgesetz, 55 *NJW* 2002, 29, 2049; J.Waldron, Moments of Carelessness and Massive Loss, in: D. Owen, *Philosophical Foundations of Tort Law* (1995), 387; T. Weir, Complex Liabilities, n. 6, XI *International Encyclopedia of Comparative Law* (1976); T. Weir, *A Casebook on Tort*, 9th ed., (2000); T. Weir, Limitations on Liability for Economic Loss Caused by Negligence: A Pragmatic Appraisal, 25 *Vand. L. Rev.* 1972, 43; F. Werro, Tort Law at the Beginning of the New Millenium. A Tribute to John G. Fleming's Legacy, 49 *AJCL* 2001, 147; D. Zimmer, Das neue Recht der Leistungsstörungen, 55 *NJW* 2002, 1, 1; R. Zimmermann, Breach of Contract and Remedies under the New German Law of Obligations, in: Centro Studi e ricerche di diritto comparato e straniero (ed.), 48 *Saggi, conferenze e seminari* (2002); R. Zimmermann, *The Law of Obligations:Roman Foundation of the Civilian Tradition* (1996); A.A.S. Zuckerman (ed.), *Civil Justice in Crisis. Comparative Perspectives of Civil Procedure* (1999).

F – Property

CHAPTER 39

Transfer of Property

Ulrich Drobnig*

1 Introductory Remarks

In the context of the present book, the topic must be limited to contractual transfers of property, thus excluding statutory transfers (such as succession). The economic importance and legal complexity of the contractual transfer of property are obvious: it usually (although not always) signifies a change of attribution of an economic asset from one person or enterprise to another. Market economies depend upon such changes of attribution to facilitate the optimal use of assets by citizens and professional market participants.

It is the specific aspect of a market economy that such transfers are effectuated voluntarily by both parties to the transaction; legally speaking, they are based upon a contract. Contractual transfers of property, therefore, are located at the cross-roads of contract and property, and this feature creates, as we will see, one of the major obstacles for legal regulation.

A lawyer familiar only with the legal system of his home country may regard the contractual transfer of property as a relatively straight forward, if not simplistic topic; its central rules must be mastered by any first-year law student. A comparative survey, however, quickly reveals unanticipated difficulties: Not only do the basic rules differ profoundly between the various European countries, but it also becomes apparent that a considerable number of subsidiary rules have to be taken into account in order to obtain a true and complete picture.

These legal complexities justify one further limitation of this study: It will be restricted to the transfer of property in corporeal movables, thus excluding transfers of immovables as well as transfers of intangibles, such as the assignment of monetary claims (or debts). While in these areas essentially the same issues arise, the answers differ due to the different subject matters involved.

2 Three Issues

A brief comparative survey of the basic rules on the transfer of property reveals a disquieting variety of diverging basic principles. The weight and practical relevance of the different principles is best exposed if they are examined in the light of the three basic issues involved in the transfer of property.[1]

The first and most basic dichotomy exists as to the fundamental requirements that must be fulfilled in order to transfer property. Does property pass from the transferor

---

* Former director at the Max-Planck-Institute for Foreign Private and Private International Law; Hamburg and Professor at the Faculty of Law, University of Hamburg.
1 A similar exposition of the issues is offered by Sacco (1981), pp. 252, 258.

to the transferee by mere consent of the parties; or is, in addition to such consent, delivery of the object of the transfer required? These basic alternatives are usually reduced to a choice between two basic legal principles, that of consent and that of delivery. Many authors regard this dichotomy as the only issue in the field.[2] However, the dichotomy is neither correctly stated nor is it exhaustive.

The second issue is whether the necessary consent resides in, or is to be derived from, the primary contractual relationship between the parties, for example a contract of sale. The alternative is an additional, or secondary, agreement between the parties for the sole purpose of determining whether a delivery transfers title or merely possession (or any other limited right) to the transferee. The first solution may be called the principle of unity, the second the principle of separation. Since the requirement of an additional agreement relates to proprietary aspects of the transaction, it may be called a 'real agreement'.[3] Whether such an additional agreement is required, depends upon the applicable law. This may provide that a contract of sale *ex lege* transfers property to the buyer. Conversely, it may merely establish an obligation of the seller to transfer property. If this is the case, a second agreement is necessary to ensure the performance of the seller's obligation.

A third issue arises in the countries which separate the underlying contract and the transfer of property: What is the relationship between the two contracts? In particular, does the invalidity of the underlying contract automatically invalidate the agreement to transfer property? Or does the latter, in general, stand on its own feet? The first solution is called for by the principle of causality, while the second rests on the principle of abstraction.

It would be treacherous and misleading if comparison was confined only to the exposition, juxtaposition and evaluation of these lofty principles. Rather, a sober analysis and appreciation of the basic three principles requires that for each of them a certain number of subsidiary and complementary rules be taken into account.

3   Consent or Consent and Delivery

3.1   The Principle of Consent

3.1.1   The Principle

According to the principle of consent, property passes from the transferor to the transferee by virtue of any contract between those parties implying such transfer of property.

This solution originates in the French Civil Code of 1804. Here it is spelt out consistently in the texts of various provisions, both in the law of property (Art. 711 *Code civil*: 'La propriété des biens s'acquiert et se transmet ... par l'effet des obligations') and in the law of contracts: for contracts to give in general (Art. 1138 *Code civil)*[4] as

---

2   Cf., e.g., Waelbroeck (1961), p. 15; the Swiss thesis by Röthlisberger (1982) is expressly devoted to a discussion of these two principles.

3   *Dingliche Einigung* in German.

4   'L'obligation de livrer la chose est parfaite par le seul consentement des parties contractantes. – Elle rend le créancier propriétaire et.... encore que la tradition n'en ait point été faite, ...'

well as for contracts of sale (Art. 1583 *Code civil*)[5] and an accepted promise of a gift (Art. 938 *Code civil*).[6] These last three provisions expressly state that the passing of property occurs even if the asset has not been delivered.

Belgium and Luxembourg, having preserved the French Civil Code, retain the French solution. Italy also follows the same approach (Art. 1376 Italian Civil Code).

The codification of sales in English law has taken the same course, although in a more differentiated way. The English Sale of Goods Act of 1979[7] distinguishes between absolute and conditional contracts of sale (s. 2 (3)). An absolute contract of sale is a 'sale' 'by which the seller transfers ... the property in goods to the buyer' (s. 2 (4) and (1)). A conditional contract of sale is an agreement to sell by which the seller 'agrees to transfer the property in goods to the buyer' at a future time or subject to some condition.[8] It is remarkable to note how strongly the time of passing of property influences the classification of the contract of sale! The decisive criterion is the intention of the parties (s. 17). Where the intention of the parties is lacking a number of presumptions fill the gap. The most important is that laid down in section 18 Rule 1 under which, in an unconditional contract, the property passes at the time the contract is made![9]

3.1.2   Refinements

The English and Italian provisions, enacted much later than the French Civil Code, contain three useful refinements of the basic principle which are worthy of note. These three refinements are also implicit in the original French rule. All of them have therefore been accepted in each of the major countries adhering to the principle of consent.

1. Both the English and the Italian provisions state that the general rule applies only to the transfer of property in specific goods.[10] Moreover, the inner logic of the rule presupposes that the goods must be in existence at the time of the contract[11] and must be owned by the seller.[12]

---

5   'Elle est parfaite entre les parties, et la propriété est acquise de droit à l'acheteur à l'égard du vendeur, dès qu'on est convenu de la chose et du prix, quoique la chose n'ait pas encore été livrée ni le prix payé.'

6   'La donation dûment acceptée sera parfaite par le seul consentement des parties; et la propriété des objets données sera transférée au donataire, sans qu'il soit besoin d'autre tradition.'

7   Statutes 1979 c. 54, as amended by Amendment Acts of 1994 (c. 32) and 1995 (c. 28).

8   Sale of Goods Act 1979 s. 2 (3), (5) and (1).

9   'Where there is an unconditional contract for the sale of specific goods, in a deliverable state, the property in the goods passes to the buyer when the contract is made, and it is immaterial whether the time of payment or the time of delivery, or both, be postponed.'

10 Sale of Goods Act 1979 s. 18 Rule 1 (quoted *supra* n. 9); Art. 1376 Italian Civil Code; France: Ghestin/Desché (1990), no. 544: *un objet immédiatement identifiable.*

11 Sale of Goods Act 1979 s. 18 Rule 1 (quoted *supra* n. 9) requires that the good must be 'in a deliverable state', i.e. present; France: Ghestin/Desché, preceding note. As to future goods, cf. *infra* 3.1.3, a, *in fine.*

12 France has drawn the radical consequence of declaring the contract of sale of an asset not owned by the seller to be void, Art. 1599 Cc! However, the courts regard this as a 'relative' nullity which may only be invoked by the buyer (Cass.civ. 16 April 1973, *Bull.civ.* 1973 Ill no. 303) and which will be

2. The English provision emphasizes the primary importance of the intention of the parties with respect to the transfer of property.[13] One particularly important application of this rule is the contract of sale with reservation of ownership where property does not pass to the buyer until he has paid the purchase price (or other debts). However, this topic will not be pursued here since it reaches – in fact if not in law – into the broad field of security rights.[14]

3. The Italian provision expressly demands the validity of the parties' consent.[15]

3.1.3 Qualifications

The transfer of property *solo consensu* is subject to a number of restrictions and qualifications. These must be taken into account in assessing the true scope of the principle of consent.

a   Generic and Future Goods

As mentioned before, transfer of property by consent is effective only with respect to specific, presently existing goods.[16] Property in generic goods passes to the transferee only after they have been appropriated to the contract.[17] Where in contracts of sale the goods are transported to the buyer by an independent carrier, appropriation usually takes place upon delivery to the carrier;[18] this is usually regarded as delivery of possession to the buyer. Similar rules have been developed for the transfer of property in future goods.[19]

b   Effects Inter Partes

The transfer of property by mere consent has full effects between the parties. This is clearly stated for French sales law[20] and results indirectly from the text of the English SGA 1979.[21] However, the situation is quite different with respect to third parties.

c   Effects *vis-à-vis* Third Persons

The provisions and rules which govern the transfer of property by mere consent and without delivery in the relationship between seller and buyer[22] obviously imply that

---

cured if, before the buyer has avoided, the seller obtains ownership (Ghestin/Desché (1990), no. 372; Cass.com. 2 July 1979, *Bull.civ.* 1979 IV no. 224).

13 Sale of Goods Act 1979 s. 17 and s. 18 Rule 1, quoted *supra* n. 9. For France cf. Ghestin/Desché (1990), pp. 622-713.

14 *Infra* ch. 40, sub 3.5.1.

15 Art. 1376 Italian Civil Code. In other countries, this rule is implied in the principle of consent, but rarely expressed; cf. in England Benjamin (Guest) (1997), no. 7-025.

16 *Supra* 3.1.2 at n. 10-11.

17 Elaborate provisions in English Sale of Goods Act 1979 s. 16 and 18 Rule 5; Art. 1378 first sentence Italian Civil Code. For France, Ghestin/Desché (1990), no. 544.

18 English Sale of Goods Act 1979 s. 18 Rule 5 (2) and Italian Civil Code Art. 1378 sent. 2. For France, see Ghestin/Desché (1990), no. 547.

19 Benjamin (Guest) (1997), no. 5-030; Ghestin/Desché (1990), no. 550; cf. Art. 1472 Italian Civil Code.

20 Art. 1583 Cc, quoted *supra* n. 5. Cf. Ghestin/Desché (1990), no. 530-531.

21 Sale of Goods Act ss. 16-20 are placed under the title 'Transfer of Property as between Seller and Buyer'.

22 *Supra* 3.1.1-3.1.3, b.

such transfer of property may not have to be fully effective *vis-à-vis* third persons. And this indeed is the case, as will be demonstrated. Today, all French writers distinguish between the effects of the transfer of property between the parties and its effects *(opposabilité) vis-à-vis* third persons.[23] We shall discuss seriatim dispositions by the seller in possession of sold goods and by the non-possessing buyer as well as the effects of the transfer of property in the event of the seller's or the buyer's insolvency.

1   Dispositions by Seller in Possession
Both in England and in France dispositions by the seller in possession to a second buyer are under certain circumstances regarded as effective although the seller is no longer the owner. The second buyer prevails if two conditions are met: firstly, the asset must have been delivered to him, and secondly, he must have been 'in good faith and without notice of the previous sale'.[24] The same rule prevails in Italy.[25]

2   Dispositions by Non-Possessing Buyer
The non-possessing buyer disposes as owner and can therefore transfer property to his sub-buyer but, of course, not possession. Consequently, the original seller's rights *vis-à-vis* the first buyer remain effective also *vis-à-vis* the second buyer. The original seller remains entitled to possession according to the terms of the original contract.

In addition, both English and French law grant to an unpaid seller a right of retention – a lien – and a right of stoppage.[26] These rights are not affected by the first buyer's dispositions.[27] In England, the seller may in the exercise of his rights resell the goods; the second buyer will acquire 'a good title to them as against the original buyer.'[28]

3   Seller's Insolvency
Both in England and France, the non-possessing buyer, as the owner, may claim his purchased goods in the seller's insolvency.[29] However, if the seller is still unpaid at the time of insolvency, his right of retention prevails.[30]

4   Buyer's Insolvency
English and French sales law again agree. Against a buyer's claim for delivery of goods, based upon his ownership, an unpaid seller in possession may invoke his lien

---

23   Cf. Ghestin/Desché (1990), no. 530-542; references in no. 531 n. 21.
24   For sales English Sale of Goods Act 1979 s. 24; the provision explains the result by a fictitious authorisation of the seller 'by the owner of the goods'. In France the general rule of Art. 1141 Cc applies; cf. for a clarifying interpretation Ghestin/Desché (1990), no. 540.
25   Art. 1155 Italian Civil code.
26   English Sale of Goods Act 1979 s. 39-44. In France, the seller in possession has, until payment, a right to retain the goods sold, Art. 1612 Cc.
27   Sale of Goods Act 1979 s. 47 (1).
28   Sale of Goods Act 1979 s. 48 (2).
29   England: Atiyah/Adams/MacQueen (2001), p. 311; Benjamin (Guest) (1997), no. 5-005. France: Derruppé (1988), no. 251-323. This rule is in keeping with the rule set out *supra* no. 1.
30   The holder of a lien is a 'secured creditor', see Insolvency Act 1986 (c. 45), s. 383 (2).

or right of retention and even resell the goods. The second buyer will acquire property in them, even as against the first buyer.[31]

3.1.4 Summary

The non-possessing buyer's position is inferior in case of dispositions by a possessing seller, unless the second buyer is mala fide. In the seller's insolvency the buyer cannot claim the goods if he has not yet paid the seller; the latter may then effectively sell the unpaid asset to a second buyer. The same is true if the buyer disposes of his property to a sub-buyer. In the buyer's insolvency, the unpaid seller may resist a claim for delivery by invoking his right of retention and effectively transfer the buyer's goods to a second buyer.

The buyer's position is markedly improved only after the goods are delivered to him. Effective dispositions by the seller/transferor are then precluded, so that the buyer/transferee is no longer subject to lose his property by such transactions.

In essence, under the principle of consent, transfer of property takes place in two stages: by mere consent, without delivery, a right of property with limited effects *vis-à-vis* third persons is transferred. This diminished right of property becomes fully effective only upon delivery of the assets to the transferee.

English and French authors have criticised this two-step system on theoretical grounds since the idea of mere *inter-partes* effects of property contravenes the basic general notion of property as being effective against everybody.[32] In its practical operation it is rather complicated in contrast to the simpler Roman law system of consent and delivery.[33] In France, but not in England, the parties' consent is of relatively small importance.[34] In fact, property passes *ex lege,* not *ex contractu;* in this respect, the principle of consent is a misnomer (cf. *infra* 4). Probably the most devastating criticism has been expressed by a leading Belgian author; De Page summarizes his critique in the recommendation: 'On renoncera à l'effet translatif des contrats, qui n'est qu'un non-sens, un nid à difficultés, et que la plupart des législations contemporaines eurent la sagesse de ne pas emprunter au Code civil français.'[35]

3.2 The Principle of Delivery and Consent

3.2.1 The Principle

The second main principle for transferring property seems to build upon the principle of consent by adding a second requirement, that of delivery or transfer of possession. In fact, however, the principle of delivery emphasizes delivery of the asset to the transferee which must be accompanied by consent of the parties as to the transfer of property.

---

31 England: Sale of Goods Act 1979 s. 41 (1) (c) and 48 (2) ; cf. Benjamin (Guest) (1997), no. 5-005 and Atiyah/Adams/MacQueen (2001), p. 310; France: cf. Law no. 85-98 on reorganisation and judicial liquidation of enterprises (Loi *no. 85-98 relative au redressement et à la liquidation judiciaire des entreprises)* of 25 January 1985 (JO 26 January, p. 1097) Arts. 116, 118-119.
32 Atiyah/Adams/MacQueen (2001), p. 309.
33 Ghestin/Desché (1990), no. 542.
34 Dalhuisen 404-405; for France Ghestin/Desché (1990), no. 542.
35 De Page (1942), p. 86. References supporting the three main objections are omitted.

This principle originates from Roman law which demanded titulus and modus. Several European countries still follow this system, especially Germany and Greece,[36] the Netherlands,[37] Spain[38] and Scotland.[39] In the first three countries the codified provisions are in very similar terms. They all mention first delivery (or transfer) to the transferee and only thereafter some of them deal with consent of the parties as to the passing of property.

This sequence is not accidental. Delivery has indeed primary importance. But delivery (or transfer of possession) is in itself ambiguous since the parties may pursue varying purposes; in particular, it may or may not coincide with an intention of the parties to transfer property. Recourse to the intention of the parties therefore is necessary to determine the purpose of a delivery.

3.2.2 Refinements and Qualifications

The principle of delivery and consent is, like its antipode, subject to certain exceptions and qualifications regarding the requirement of delivery. Some of these are more in the nature of refinements, others are genuine qualifications.

a   Brevi Manu Traditio

A refinement is involved where the asset to be delivered is already held by the transferee. Since in this case delivery is superfluous all codes agree that the parties' consent as to the passing of property suffices.[40]

b   Asset Held by Third Person

Somewhat more complicated rules have been developed for situations in which the asset to be transferred is in the custody of a third person, e.g. a warehouseman. Formally, two different techniques are used, either an assignment of the transferor's claim for return of the asset or an agreement between transferor and transferee.

German law takes recourse to assignment: the transferor must assign his claim against the third party possessor for return of the asset.[41] The claim to be assigned is the contractual claim for return of the asset which arises from the contractual relationshiop between the transferor and, for example, his warehouseman.[42]

---

36 § 929 sent. 1 BGB provides: 'The transfer of property in a movable thing requires that the owner transfers the thing to the transferee and that both agree that property is to pass.' Art. 1034 Greek Civil Code adopts this German provision almost literally.

37 In the Dutch New Civil Code book 3 which entered into force on 1 January 1992, Art. 3:84 par. 1 consecrates the principle of delivery as follows: 'Transfer of property of an asset requires delivery pursuant to a valid title by the person who has the right to dispose of the asset.' The term 'asset' (*goed*) comprises both things and patrimonial rights (Art. 3:1). Cf. also Art. 3:90.

38 Cf. Spanish Civil Code art. 1473 par. 1

39 Walker (1989), pp. 418 ff. Scots law basically still follows Roman law, except insofar as English statutes are applicable. This exception is true with respect to sales law since the English Sale of Goods Acts extend to Scotland.

40 § 929 sent. 2 BGB; Art. 976 sent. 2 Greek Civil Code; Art. 3:115 lett. b Dutch Civil Code.

41 § 931 BGB.

42 Baur/Stürner (1999), p. 584-586. A somewhat different solution results where the present holder of the asset is unknown, e.g. upon theft, *ibidem* at pp. 585-586.

Dutch law adopts a different approach. In the Netherlands, transferor and transferee must agree that the holder of the asset shall henceforth hold it for the transferee and the holder must be notified accordingly or, alternatively, he must acknowledge the transfer.[43]

In essence, the two solutions coincide. An agreement between transferor and transferee that the third person shall henceforth hold the asset for the transferee would in Germany be regarded as an implied assignment.[44] In Germany the validity of an assignment does not depend upon notification of the debtor.[45] Notification is, however, advisable for the protection of the transferee since otherwise the holder may be discharged by returning the assets to the transferor.

c   Seller in Possession

Frequently, the seller remains the holder of the assets even though he has transferred property in them; this is especially so if a security transfer of property is involved.[46]

Germany and the Netherlands essentially agree that in this situation physical delivery should be replaced by a legal act, i.e. an agreement between transferor and transferee (*constitutum possessorium*). However, the contents of this agreement is in dispute. Germany and Greece require that the transferor's continued holding of the assets must be based upon a specific legal relationship.[47] In practice, usually a gratutious loan for use is concluded.[48] However, it must be acknowledged that this requirement has degenerated into an empty formality. Therefore, the Dutch solution requiring merely a contractual clause acknowledging that the transferor holds in future for the transferee[49] is a sensible improvement.

'Constructive' delivery by agreement between a seller remaining in possession (or becoming a holder) and the non-possessing buyer creates a situation which resembles that existing under the system of consent when the seller remains in possession:[50] Property and possession (or retention) of the assets are separated, the buyer being a 'naked' owner and the seller still holding the assets.

Both Germany and the Netherlands restrict the protection of the buyer's property. In the first place, a third person to whom the seller transfers may acquire property, provided factual delivery has been made to the third person and the latter, in good faith, regards his transferor as the owner.[51] This corresponds to the rule laid down for the same situation by the countries following the principle of consent.[52] A similar rule applies in the Netherlands to a double transfer of future assets.[53]

---

43 Art. 3:115 litt. c Dutch Civil Code.
44 Baur/Stürner (1999), p. 586.
45 § 398 BGB, Art. 455 Greek Civil Code.
46 Cf. *infra* ch. 40 sub 3.5.2. Art. 3:84 par. 3 Dutch Civil Code now expressly declares such security transfers to be invalid. In the present context, the security aspects of such transfers are not discussed.
47 § 930 BGB, Art. 977 Greek Civil Code.
48 Cf. Baur/Stürner (1999), pp. 576, 67.
49 Art. 3:115 litt. a Dutch Civil Code.
50 See *supra* 3.1.3.
51 §§ 930, 933 BGB; Arts. 3:86 par. 1, 3:90 par. 2 Dutch Civil Code.
52 Cf. *supra* 3.1.3, c, 1.
53 Art. 3:97 par. 2 Dutch Civil Code.

3.3 Evaluation

Having presented the two competing principles of transfer of property by mere agreement on the one hand, and by delivery plus agreement on the other, an evaluation of, and choice between them remains to be made. This evaluation can be short since the merits and demerits of both principles have already become reasonably clear.

1. A first major disadvantage of the principle of consent is that it cannot be directly applied to the greater part of modern commercial transactions involving transfer of property. Subsidiary rules are needed to apply the principle to transfers of generic goods and of future goods.[54]
2. Its limited effects create a second major disadvantage. Primarily, the principle of consent governs the legal situation between transferor and transferee. *Inter partes*, however, the terms of their underlying contract and the supplementary general rules of contract law provide the relevant regulation.
   By contrast, the relationship *vis-à-vis* third persons, be they transferees from, or creditors of one of the parties, is influenced by several rules which negate the transfer of property effected by virtue of the contract. In this respect, the principle of consent is a treacherous rule since it 'promises' more than it can fulfill.
3. From a dogmatic point of view, to differentiate between a contract's proprietary effects *inter partes* and as against third persons is not only complicated, it also conflicts with the basic principle of property law that real rights have effects *erga omnes*.
4. The scepticism against the principle of consent is confirmed by highly critical voices from countries that have adopted this system and have worked with it.
5. On all the foregoing three substantive aspects, the competing principle of delivery and consent furnishes solutions which can be derived directly from the principle, except where substitute forms of delivery are being used. The principle of delivery is therefore, on the whole, clearer and much less subject to exceptions. It maintains the unitary concept of property since it need not distinguish between the effects of a transfer of property *inter partes* and *erga omnes*.
6. For these practical and theoretical reasons, a European Civil Code should make the transfer of property subject to delivery of the asset to the transferee and to an accompanying agreement of the parties on the passing of property.[55]
7. If a uniform provision on passing of property upon delivery and consent would be adopted, the countries currently applying the principle of consent will have to examine whether adaptations of subsidiary rules which are based upon the consent principle become necessary.[56]

---

54 This objection is regarded as decisive by von Caemmerer (1938/39), pp. 689-693.
55 The same conclusion was reached earlier by Waelbroeck (1961), pp. 166-172; and more recently by Ferrari (1993), pp. 77, 78.
56 Some considerations in Waelbroeck (1961), pp. 172-181.

4 A Special Agreement on the Transfer of Property?

The second aspect of transfer of property by virtue of or according to a contract is also controversial between the European countries. In some countries, the law itself expressly provides for the passing of property upon the conclusion of a contract implying such transfer, such as a contract of sale, for work or of gift, etc. Other countries demand an additional term or agreement providing for the transfer of property, i.e. a 'real' agreement.[57] The alternative approaches may be epitomised by the catchwords of unitary or double consent.

This issue seems to be closely related to the preceding dichotomy with respect to the transfer of property by mere consent or by delivery accompanied by consent (*supra* 3). This link provides a convenient scheme for the following survey.

4.1 Delivery and Consent

Germany and the Netherlands, the two major representatives of the principle of delivery plus consent, clearly separate the contractual agreement providing for the transfer of property from the 'real agreement' which is necessary (in addition to delivery) to effectuate the transfer. The major reason behind this separation lies in the fact that under neither of the two legal systems does a contract of sale ex *lege* pass property to the buyer – as under Anglo-French law – not even upon delivery of the purchased goods. Rather, the seller is expressly obliged to transfer property[58] and he must act in order to fulfil this obligation.

In Germany, the 'real agreement' of the parties is required for any disposition of proprietary rights and is therefore regulated in Book 3 of the Civil Code governing property.[59] The required content of the 'real agreement' for the transfer of property in movables is fixed by § 929 BGB (first sentence): The transferor as owner must agree with the transferee 'that property is to pass'. This agreement is regarded by the relevant rules as an appendix to the necessary delivery. In fact, the 'real agreement' must exist at the time of delivery.[60]

Notionally, the 'real agreement' is separate from the underlying contract of the parties which provides for transfer of property, although in fact it may be contained in one of the terms of that contract. But the contract as such (merely) creates obligations of the parties; insofar as the transferor obliges himself to transfer property to the transferee, this promise must be performed by delivering the promised asset with the intention of transferring property to the transferee and the latter must accept this intention.

Three elements of the 'real agreement' clearly indicate that it is distinct from the parties' underlying contractual agreement. Firstly, the Civil Code differentiates between the terms 'real agreement' *(Einigung)* and contract *(Vertrag)*. Secondly, the 'real agreement' is regulated in Book 3 on property. Thirdly, until delivery the 'real

---

57 On this term, cf. *supra* 2 at n. 3.
58 § 433 par. 1 BGB; Art. 7:9 par. 1 first sentence Dutch Civil Code.
59 §§ 873, 877 BGB in general, § 925 BGB for transfer of property in immovables, § 929 BGB for that in movables; cf. also § 398 BGB for assignment of claims and other rights.
60 Baur/Stürner (1999), pp. 571.

agreement' is revocable by either party.[61] An illustration: the courts have held and most writers agree, that a seller who has contracted to sell and transfer property unconditionally may upon delivery reserve his property, that is to say that he may make his transfer of property to the buyer subject to the condition of being paid by the latter. [62]

Dutch law is much less explicit than the German Civil Code. The Dutch New Civil Code merely requires 'delivery pursuant to a valid title' (Art. 3:84 par. 1 BW). 'Title' is understood as being the legal ground for a delivery which is usually an obligation of the transferor.[63] Although not expressly mentioned in the New Civil Code, important writers regard a 'real agreement' as the central element of 'delivery'.[64] However, there are also strong opponents to this idea.[65]

4.2 'Consent' Only

In England and France, the idea of a special 'real agreement' is virtually unknown;[66] this is easily explicable. Both countries expressly provide that, as a rule and unless otherwise agreed, property passes to the buyer by virtue of the conclusion of a contract of sale.[67] An additional 'real agreement', therefore, is usually unnecessary. Nor is, in this context, the consent which has been raised to the rank of a principle specifically directed at the passing of property. It merely refers in a general way to the underlying contract of sale.

Within that Anglo-French approach, agreements of the parties as to the passing of property are, however, necessary if the parties wish to deviate from the legal scheme. The most important situation is, of course, to defer the transfer of property until payment of the purchase price (or other claims of the seller). The English Sale of Goods Act 1979 distinguishes between present sales and conditional contracts of sale where the seller 'agrees to transfer the property in goods to the buyer' at a future time or subject to a condition.[68] In substance, such clauses could be regarded as 'real agreements'.

---

61 Baur/Stürner (1999), pp. 46, 571.
62 BGH 9 July 1975, *BGHZ* 64, 395, 397 with references; cf. also BGH 14 November 1977, NJW 1978, 696. The courts demand, however, an unambiguous declaration at the latest at the time of delivery; in the two cases these requirements were not met.
63 Asser(-Mijnssen/de Haan) (2001), no. 239.
64 See, *inter alia*, Asser (-Mijnssen/de Haan) (2001), nos. 206-207 and Snijders/Rank-Berenschot (1994) nos. 325-327, both with extensive discussion of other views; Hartkamp (1990), no. 91 who reasons that the necessity of separate delivery implies that of a 'real agreement'.
65 See especially Vriesendorp (1985), pp. 9-31; Den Dulk (1979); Pitlo (Reehuis/Heisterkamp) (1994), nos. 131-134.
66 Atiyah/Adams/MacQueen (2001), p. 35 remark on a sale, invoking English Sale of Goods Act 1979 s. 2 (1), that the contract suffices to transfer the property in the goods, i.e. it may 'operate both as a conveyance and a contract'. But this observation is not further pursued.
67 Cf. *supra* 3.1.1.
68 Sale of Goods Act s. 2 (4) and (1) on the one hand and s. 2 (3), (5) and (1) on the other; cf. *supra* 3.1.1 *in fine*.

4.3 Preliminary Conclusion

This brief comparative overview shows primarily that the 'real' agreement is recognised in those countries which, in addition to consent, require delivery for the passing of property (*supra* 4.1). While normally the 'real' agreement accompanies and specifies delivery, it may replace the latter where, exceptionally, physical transfer is not required (*supra* 3.2.2). Conversely, in those countries in which property passes by mere consent the latter is found exclusively in the underlying contract (*supra* 4.2). While this fully explains the present sale of specific goods, the contractual basis for appropriating generic and future goods to the contract is open. A final and difficult point is the relationship between the 'real' agreement and the underlying contract (*infra* 5).

5 Relationship Between Contract and 'Real Agreement'

5.1 The Issue

For those countries which – like Germany and the Netherlands – distinguish between the underlying (e.g., sales) contract and an additional 'real agreement' transferring property to the buyer, a further issue arises: what is the relationship between the underlying contract and the 'real agreement'? In particular: Does any initial or subsequent invalidity of one of the agreements also affect the other?

The answer is obvious for an invalidity which affects the 'real agreement' only. Such a defect prevents the purported performance of the seller's obligation to pass property to the buyer. But his obligation as such arising from the underlying contract of sale is not affected. The seller remains obliged to perform the contract and must make a new attempt at transferring property or else he will be charged with the consequences of his non-performance.

The matter is quite controversial in the reverse situation where only the underlying contract is affected by an initial or a subsequent invalidity. Does such an invalidity extend to the 'real agreement' which, after all, is but a collateral contract? On this point, Dutch and German law adopt two opposite solutions. Under the first, the 'real' agreement is made dependent upon the legal fate of the underlying contract as its causa (doctrine of causality); under the second, the validity of the 'real agreement' is determined independently (doctrine of abstraction).

5.2 The 'Causal' Real Agreement

In the Netherlands, the validity of the transfer and therefore also of the 'real agreement' accompanying it, depends upon the validity of the underlying contract. That is clearly spelt out by the relevant provision which demands 'delivery pursuant to a valid title'.[69] This 'causal' nature of the 'real' agreement is also unanimously accepted in Dutch literature.

---

69 *Levering krachtens geldige titel*, Art. 3:4 par. 1 BW. Full quotation of English version *supra* n. 37.

The 'real' agreement has mainly a supplementary function. It is meant to execute that term of the underlying contract which fixes the proprietary effects agreed upon, e.g. whether a transfer of property should be unconditional or subject to a specific condition. It only differs as to its effects, since these are proprietary and not contractual. While the 'real' agreement is usually implied, except where the Civil Code expressly provides for it,[70] deviations are possible, although they will be rare.[71]

5.3 The 'Abstract' Real Agreement

In contrast, the German 'real agreement' is, in principle, independent of the underlying contract. Its existence and validity, and therefore also the validity of the transfer to the transferee, do not depend upon the prior or continuing existence of an underlying contract or its validity. This is not expressly spelt out by the Civil Code but is implied and is the unanimous view of both writers and the courts.[72]

The principle of abstraction may well be regarded as a general feature of German law since it permeates several fields of law. It applies to all transfers of full or limited rights in things, claims and rights. Also, the rules on representation clearly separate an agent's authority *vis-à-vis* third persons from the contract of agency which determines his relationship with the principal. The general idea which inspires all rules distinguishing between two related legal relationships and insulating one from the other is the desire to protect third persons from the impact of possible defects existing in an underlying primary relationship.

This purpose of the idea of abstraction can be discerned from its historical development. The German *jus commune* adopted the old Roman law principle of *Nemo dat quod non habet*. In order to mitigate the negative effects of this rule on legal transactions involving the transfer of goods, the theory of the 'real' agreement was developed by von Savigny in the middle of the 19th century.

Its function was to insulate the transfer of a proprietary right to the transferee from possible defects (such as illegality, avoidance for mistake or non-observance of a formal requirement) affecting the underlying transaction. True, as between the parties the transferee would be obliged to re-transfer the asset received since he was unjustly enriched. But with respect to third persons (especially sub-transferees and creditors) the first transferee retained the property until re-transfer to the original transferor. Consequently, he was able to pass good title to a sub-transferee and his creditors could satisfy themselves from these assets.

On the other hand, the protection of the interest of transferees and sub-transferees is unavoidably at the expense of the transferor. Therefore, in order to achieve a proper balancing of the interests of all parties involved, certain rules were developed in practice which in effect limit the scope of the principle of abstraction. Firstly, a defect (an illegality or immorality, a deceit or threat) may affect not only the underlying contract but also its performance; secondly, the parties may make the validity of the proprietary transfer dependent upon the validity of the underlying contract; or

---

70 Thus, immovables are transferred by a notarial deed of the parties aiming at transfer which must be registered, Art. 3:89 par. 1 BW.

71 On the practical relevance, cf. Snijders/Rank-Berenschot (1994), no. 328.

72 Baur/Stürner (1999), pp. 47-53 with many references.

perhaps thirdly, the invalidity of the underlying contract may indirectly affect the proprietary transfer if the latter cannot survive separately.[73] These three doctrines are, however, applied with circumspection since the principle of abstraction must not be overturned.

5.4 Equivalent Protection Against Contractual Defects?

How do legal systems that do not have a counterpart to the German 'abstract' real agreement protect transferees from defects of a contractual transfer of property? This issue arises not only for the Netherlands which expressly demand 'delivery pursuant to a *valid* title' (*supra* 5.2) but also for France and England where transfer of property is based solely upon consent (*supra* 3.1) which also implies valid consent.

In all three countries, the most important remedy is the protection granted to good faith transferees. However, the details of this protection differ very considerably. Only the more important traits can be mentioned in the present context.

Strangely, England has embraced the Roman law principle of *Nemo dat quod non habet* more strictly than most of the Continental countries.[74] Apart from consent of or estoppel by the owner with respect to a sale conducted by another person, only sales by a mercantile agent acting for the owner convey a good title.[75]

The French Civil Code's art. 2279 (1) establishes a very broad general principle: 'For movables, possessionn means title.'[76] Case law understands this provision as meaning that a person who is full possessor must have believed in good faith to have acquired these assets from the true owner.[77] Both the English and the French provision apply only to tangible movables since the transferor's possession of the sold goods justifies the good faith belief of the transferor being the owner.

The Dutch rules are most recent, far-reaching and differentiated. They apply primarily to tangible assets if these have been acquired for consideration; if the assets had been lost or stolen, the owner may in general reclaim the goods during three years.[78] Another provision extends protection of good faith acquisition to some other tangible assets and even claims.[79]

If one compares these various provisions on the protection of the good faith transferee with the German abstract 'real' agreement, it is obvious that the protection afforded by the latter goes further: First, since the abstract 'real' agreement protects sub-transferees even in the absence of good faith. Secondly, the abstract 'real' contract in effect provides general protection to the transferee's (and the sub-transferee's) creditors – an advantage not available under the general rules.[80] On the other

---

73 Baur/Stürner (1999), pp. 50-52 with examples from case law.
74 Sale of Goods Act 1979 s. 21 (1).
75 For details, cf. Atiyah/Adams/MacQueen (2001), pp. 368-414.
76 En fait de meubles, possession vaut titre.
77 Cass.civ. 23 March 1965, *Bull.civ.* 1965 part I no. 206; Cass.civ. 4 Jan. 1972, *ibidem* 1972 part I no. 4.
78 Dutch Civil Code art. 3:86; the goods cannot be reclaimed from a consumer who had purchased the goods in business premises.
79 Dutch Civil Code art. 3:88.
80 See especially Kegel (1977), pp. 57-86, cf. also Ferrari (1993), pp. 65-66.

hand, the abstract 'real' agreement is subject to certain exceptions, the precise contours of which are not yet entirely clear.[81] Some prominent German writers conclude that the abstract 'real' agreement should be abandoned as a general principle of property law.[82] On the other hand, a recent comparative monography has strongly defended the principle of abstraction.[83]

5.5 Conclusions

1. Most European countries do not know the intricate institution of an 'abstract' real agreement. Undoubtedly, however this 'institution' fulfils the useful practical function of insulating a disposition of property rights from defects of the underlying contractual relationship. It is true that this protection of the transferee (and of subsequent transferors and transferees) is achieved at the expense of the original transferor. However, in the context of a European internal market the transferor must be regarded as the person who generally is, or at least ought to be, more familiar with the legal situation and risks of a disposition over his assets than the transferee. Moreover, the basic idea of insulating certain transactions, such as negotiable instruments, from objections derived from an underlying contract, is familiar to all European legal systems. Therefore, serious consideration should be given to adopting the idea of insulating the validity of proprietary dispositions from defects of the underlying contractual relationship between transferor and transferee, unless the parties otherwise agree or a defect affects also the proprietary disposition.

2. An alternative avenue would be recourse to the familiar institution of protecting acquisitions made in good faith, as demonstrated by the rules prevailing in England, France and the Netherlands. However, these rules, in their present form, would only partially be equivalent to the more general protection achieved by the principle of abstraction. First, the scope of application of these rules varies considerably. It is very narrow in England, though broader in France; in both countries, however, it is limited to dispositions over tangible property. Broader and more sophisticated are the Dutch provisions of 1992; in particular, they extend to dispositions over accounts receivables, an asset of growing commercial importance for which a high degree of negotiability is desirable.

3. In the light of the preceding considerations it does not yet seem to be possible to submit a definitive proposal for a rule to be adopted by a future European Civil Code. In the light of the presently existing national provisions and rules, the present author has a preference for the solution sketched sub 1) since it most effectively protects the first transferee and successive transferors and transferees.

---

81 *Supra* 5.3 at n. 73.
82 Kegel (1977), pp. 85-86; Larenz (1986), pp. 20-121. For similar considerations of the Dutch legislator cf. *Parlententaire Geschiedenis van het Nieuwe Burgerlijk Wetboek. Boek 3: Vermogensrecht in het algemeen* (1981) p. 317.
83 Stadler (1996), especially the conclusions at pp. 717-740.

6 Final Conclusions

For the contractual transfer of property in corporeal movables, a future European Civil Code should be guided by the following two rules:

1. The transfer of property in tangible assets should, unless otherwise agreed, be subject to delivery and agreement about transfer of property to the transferee.

2. The validity of the transfer of property should , unless otherwise agreed, be insulated from defects of the underlying contractual relationship between transferor and transferee, except if the defect affects also the proprietary disposition.

These two rules would reverse the existing legal situation in the countries of the consent principle (such as England and France) on the one hand. The second rule would affect also the legal situation in the Netherlands. Both groups of countries will have to investigate any undesired indirect effects which may result from the new uniform rules on the transfer of property.

BIBLIOGRAPHY: C. Asser (F.H.J. Mijnssen/P. de Haan), Handleiding tot de Beoefening van het Nederlands Burgerlijk Recht vol. 3/I Goederenrecht. Algemeen Goederenrecht (ed. 14 2001); P.S.Atiyah/J.N. Adams/H. MacQueen, *The Sale of Goods* (ed. 10 2001); F. Baur/D. Baur/R. Stürner, *Lehrbuch des Sachenrechts* (ed. 17 1999); Benjamin (Guest), *Benjamin's Sale of Goods* (ed.5 1997); E. von Caemmerer, Rechtsvergleichung und Reform der Fahrnisübereignung, *Zeitschrift füir ausländisches und internationales Privatrecht* 12 (1938/39), pp. 675-713; Dalhuisen, *On International Commercial, Financial and Trade Law* (2000); Den Dulk, *De zakelijke overeenkomst* (1979); F. Derruppé, Modifications des droits acquis, in: *Dalloz, Répertoire de Droit Commercial III*, s.v. Faillite – Redressement Judiciaire (Phase de traitement – Les créanciers) (1988); F. Ferrari, Vom Abstraktionsprinzip und Konsensualprinzip zum Traditionsprinzip, *ZEuP* (1993), pp. 52-78; J. Ghestin/B. Desché, *Traité des Contrats*.I: *La Vente* (1990); G. Kegel, Verpflichtung und Verfügung – Sollen Verfügungen abstrakt oder kausal sein?, in: Flume a.o., ed., *Festschrift F.A. Mann* (1977), pp. 57-86; K. Larenz, *Lehrbuch des Schuldrechts* II 1 (ed. 13 1986); Mijnssen/Schut, *Bezit, levering en overdracht* (ed. 3 1991); De Page, *Traité élémentaire de droit civil belge* VI (1942); A. Pitlo (Reehuis/Heisterkamp), *Het Nederlands burgerliik recht III, Goederenrecht* (ed. 10 1994); Röthlisberger, Traditionsprinzip und Konsensprinzip bei der Mobiliarübereignung *(Schweizer Studien zum internationalen Recht* 28) (1982); R. Sacco, Le transfert de la propriété des choses mobilières determinées par acte entre vifs, in: Petéri and Lamm, ed., *General Reports to the 10th International Congress of Comparative Law* (1981), pp. 247-268; Snijders/Rank-Berenschot, *Goederenrecht* (1994); A. Stadler, *Gestaltungsfreiheit und Verkehrsschutz durch Abstraktion* (1996); Vriesendorp, *Het eigendomsvorbehoud* (1985); Waelbroeck, *Le transfert de la propriété dans la vente d'objets mobiliers corporels en droit comparé* (1961); Walker, *Principles of Scottish Private Law* III (ed. 4 1989).

CHAPTER 40

Security Rights in Movables

Ulrich Drobnig*

1 Introduction

Economies in contemporary developed countries largely depend upon credits for their financing. Credits, however, in most cases are granted only against security, be it upon real estate (immovables), or upon movables. Since the volume and value of movables increases and these are much more widely available to both individuals and enterprises, the role of security rights in movables has correspondingly and steadily increased since the last quarter of the nineteenth century up to current times.

Legal regulation has, however, generally speaking, not kept pace with the increasing economic demand for security in movable assets. It is true that there are well-established and widely accepted rules for one specific branch of security in movables, namely for possessory pledges. Due to modem economic demands, however, this particular branch has lost much of its earlier economic relevance. In our times, non-possessory security in movables has become of overwhelming importance. Ironically, however, this branch is legally least developed and in this area legal development has been most varied between the various countries.

The present contribution is limited to security rights created by contract. Non-contractual security rights, which may be created by statute or the law (liens) or also by judicial decision, are of much lesser importance.

We will first deal with corporeal security. This may be possessory (*infra* 2) or non-possessory (*infra* 3). A separate part will discuss incorporeal security, especially in accounts and other rights (*infra* 4). The conclusion will be devoted to recommendations concerning the treatment of the topic in a future European Civil Code (*infra* 5).

2 Possessory Security – the Pledge

The pledge – without qualification – is the classical form of possessory security. 'Possessory' indicates that the pledged corporeal items are not held by the debtor but by the secured creditor or, otherwise, by a third person.

2.1 Economic Function

The decisive legal and economic criterion for distinguishing a (possessory) pledge from a non-possessory pledge is that under the former the debtor must be dispossessed of the pledged items (*infra* 2.3). This strict criterion determines the economic

---

* Former director at the Max-Planck-Institute for Foreign Private and Private International Law; Hamburg and Professor at the Faculty of Law, University of Hamburg.

functions of pledges. Pledges primarily make sense only for goods which the debtor does not immediately need for industrial or trade purposes but which are dispensable for the time being, such as securities, precious metals, luxury goods, jewellery etc. A small business branch which specialises in granting small-scale credits against the pledging of household goods are pawnshops. Since their customers typically are consumers, they are everywhere subject to special regulation. Exceptionally, merchandise or supplies held by the debtor may be pledged, provided the debtor transfers to the creditor a document of title issued for those items since such a document incorporates the rights existing in those items.

2.2 Historical Roots and Contemporary Legal Regime

The pledge is probably the oldest security device and was well known to Roman law (*pignus*). This Roman institution has spread over Europe and has been incorporated into all Continental Civil Codes. Due to the common historical root these code provisions are in substance quite similar to each other. Even the uncodified English common law of pledge is, generally speaking, in accord with the general European pattern, with minor deviations.

2.3 Creation

The characteristic feature of the pledge as a possessory security is clearly expressed by the method of its creation. The debtor must be dispossessed of the pledged goods, either by transferring possession to the secured creditor himself or to a (mutually agreed) third person.[1] The debtor's dispossession of the pledged goods is an essential and therefore permanent requirement which must be fulfilled until termination of the pledge.[2] The debtor's dispossession fulfills two major functions: it makes it more difficult for the debtor to dispose of the pledged goods to a third person; and the debtor can no longer create the misleading impression in the minds of his other creditors of owning the pledged goods which might be available for the satisfaction of their claims.

In addition to transfer of possession by the debtor, many Romanic countries demand that certain pledge contracts comply with a certain formality. In France, 'civil' pledges, but not commercial ones, are effective *vis-à-vis* third persons only if the pledge contract is in an authenticated form or, if in a private form, is duly registered with the tax authority.[3] In Italy, a document with a 'certain date' is necessary, except if the creditor is a credit institution.[4]

---

1   Arts. 2071, 2076 of the French *Code civil*; § 1205, 1206 of the German BGB; Art. 2786 of the Italian Civil Code; Art. 3:236 of the Dutch Civil Code; England: Bell (1989), p. 144.
2   Expressly Art. 2076 of the French *Code* civil and Art. 2787 s. 2 of the Italian Civil Code; this requirement is established in all other countries as well; cf. for England Bell (1989), p. 143 ss.
3   Art. 2074 of the French *Code civil* on the one hand, Art. L521-1 s. 1 of the *Code de commerce* on the other.
4   Art. 2787 ss. 3-4 of the Italian Civil Code.

2.4 Relationship Between the Parties

Since the debtor has only dispossessed himself of the pledged goods, he remains their owner, while the secured creditor merely becomes their holder. Such a relationship is qualified as a bailment in English law,[5] while on the Continent the Romanic countries regard this as detention, the Germanic countries as possession. In spite of these different concepts, the relevant rules are in close harmony. The secured creditor, as the depositee,[6] is responsible, at the debtor's expense, for the preservation and upkeep of the pledged goods.[7] Breach of this duty exposes him to a claim for damages.[8]

2.5 Protection Against Third Persons

That the secured creditor enjoys a preferential position over unsecured creditors is the main purpose of any security. This rule is generally recognised unless certain specific claims are 'reinforced' by a privilege which sometimes prevails even over a pledge which had been created earlier.

The rank between several secured creditors is, as a rule, determined by the time of creation: *prior tempore, potior jure.*[9] This time-honoured principle not only applies between several creditors with contractual, or with contractual and statutory, security rights but also *vis-à-vis* execution creditors.

The debtor's insolvency traditionally did not affect the pledgee's rights, including his right of enforcement.[10] In some Continental countries, the insolvency administrator is, however, entitled to acquire the pledged good against payment of the outstanding (part of the) secured claim.[11] The administrator may also, after a certain time has passed without action by the secured creditor, demand delivery of the pledged good and is then entitled to enforcement.[12] In France the administrator, and not the creditor, has the primary right to enforce the pledge; but this may pass to the pledgee.[13] It is generally agreed that, if the proceeds of enforcement do not suffice to cover the secured claim, the deficit can be claimed from the estate but merely as a dividend;[14] whereas a surplus must be paid over to the administrator.

2.6 Enforcement by Secured Creditor

The interests of debtor and secured creditor clash sharply after the debtor has defaulted on his primary obligation to pay and the creditor seeks to enforce his propri-

---

5   Bell (1989), p. 150.
6   Expressly Art. 2079 French *Code civil*, § 1215 German BGB and Art. 2790 s. 1 Italian Civil Code.
7   Art. 2080 s. 2 French *Code civil*; Art. 2790 s. 2 Italian Civil Code; Art. 3:243 s. 2 Dutch Civil Code.
8   Art. 2080 s. 1 French *Code civil*; Art. 2790 s. 1 Italian Civil Code; England: Crossley Vaines (1973), pp. 85 ff.; for Germany, cf. § 823 s. 1 BGB.
9   Expressly § 1209 German BGB. Cf. For England Bell (1989), p. 516.
10 Generally Art. 57 s. 1 of the Dutch Bankruptcy Act *(Faillissementswet)*. For pledges see the new German Insolvency Act of 1999 § 166 s. 1, § 173 s. 1.
11 Art. L622-21 s. 1 French *Code de commerce*; Art. 58 par. 2 Dutch Bankruptcy Act.
12 The new German Insolvency Act of 1999 § 173 s. 2; Art. 58 s. 1 Dutch Bankruptcy Act.
13 Art. L622-21 s. 2, Art. L622-23 s. 1 French *Code de Commerce*.
14 The new German Insolvency Act of 1999 §§ 52, 190 s. 1, 192; Arts. 59, 132 of the Dutch Bankruptcy Act.

etary right of satisfaction against the pledged goods. Legal systems have evolved quite differing solutions for this conflict.

It is broadly agreed that a contractual forfeiture clause under which upon the debtor's default title to the pledged goods would automatically pass to the creditor is void (*lex commissoria*).[15]

On the Continent, enforcement by the creditor is more or less strictly regulated – on the assumption that the creditor is not sufficiently motivated to achieve an optimal price for the pledged good beyond the amount of his own claim (for capital, interest and expenses). Usually a public auction is prescribed. In France, the auctioning of a civil pledge must be authorised by the judge[16] in order to ascertain the debtor's default; in the Netherlands, the parties may agree that enforcement be subject to judicial ascertainment of such default.[17] The debtor must be notified of the auction[18] which must usually be conducted by an official, a notary or an appointed auctioneer.[19] Exceptionally, if the pledged good has a more or less official market price, sale by a broker is allowed.[20]

Alternatively, in France and the Netherlands, the secured creditor may apply for judicial attribution of the pledged goods. With the aid of an expert the court fixes the value of the attributed goods;[21] the secured claim is then reduced by this amount.

After maturity, the parties can everywhere freely agree on any method of enforcement.[22]

The most liberal regime is that which obtains in England: the secured creditor may sell the pledged goods after the debtor's default. It is merely required that the sale be 'a reasonable one'.[23]

Everywhere, any surplus of the proceeds of sale remaining after paying the creditor's claims and his expenses must be paid over to the debtor. In the reverse situation, any deficiency can be claimed from him.[24]

3   Non-Possessory Security

Non-possessory is a comprehensive label for all those forms of security where the charged corporeal movable assets are not delivered to the creditor or else to a third person (therefore non-possessory), but remain in the debtor's hands.

---

15 Art. 2078 s. 2 of the French *Code civil;* Art. L521-3 s. 4 French *Code de commerce;* § 1229 German BGB; Art. 3:235 of the Dutch Civil Code.

16 Art. 2078 s. 1 of the French *Code civil*

17 Art. 3:248 s. 2 of die Dutch Civil Code.

18 An informal notification suffices in Gerniany (§ 1237 BGB) and for commercial pledges in France (Art. L521-3 s. 1 *Code de commerce*).

19 § 1235 s. 1 and § 383 s. 3 of the German BGB.

20 §§ 1235 s. 1, 1295, 1221 German BGB; Art. 3:250 Dutch Civil Code; Art. L521-3 s. 2 and 3 French *Code de commerce* for commercial pledges.

21 Art. 2078 s. 1 French *Code civil;* Art. 3:251 s. 1 Dutch Civil Code.

22 §§ 1229, 1245 German BGB; Art. 3:251 s. 2 Dutch Civil Code. In France, a forfeiture clause may already be agreed upon after the creation of the pledge since the debtor is then thought to be no longer subject to economic pressure, cf. Cabrillac/Mouly (1997), no. 907; Mestre/Putman/Billiau (1996) II no. 856.

23 Crossley Vaines (1973), p. 461; Bell (1989), p. 147 specifies that the sale must not be under value.

24 These two rules are so basic that they are hardly laid down by legislation; cf. however Art. 3:253 s. 1, second sentence of the Dutch Civil Code.

As was indicated above (*supra* 1), although economically of overwhelming importance in our time, the legal regulation of non-possessory security is neglected in many countries and, in addition, varies considerably from country to country, even within the European Union.

3.1 Economic Function

The economic function of non-possessory security can easily be derived from the description of the disadvantages of possessory security (*supra* 2.1) the validity of which depends upon the debtor's dispossession of the pledged goods.

The decisive advantage of non-possessory security therefore is that the debtor may retain the charged goods (collateral): A consumer may use collateral consisting of durable household goods. An industrialist may use machinery and other equipment; he may process raw material or semi-finished goods; a merchant may sell merchandise. The use, refinement or sale of these items of collateral will enable the debtor producer or merchant to earn the money with which to repay the credit secured by the above-mentioned items of collateral.

3.2 Contemporary Legal Regime

Contrary to the very long tradition of the possessory pledge (*supra* 2.2), the historical roots of non-possessory security are very weak. In particular, it was almost nonexistent in the 19th century, and does not therefore appear in the Civil Codes of that or the 20th century, except in the last decade.

However, in order to cope with the increasing economic needs for non-possessory security, a few, usually very specific statutes were enacted in the 19th century and a growing number in the 20th century. In addition, in some countries the courts over many years constructed a more or less liberal legal regime on the basis of provisions and rules which had been designed for other purposes. The result of this uncoordinated development is that in almost all member countries of the European Union the present regime of non-possessory security is haphazard, sometimes even contradictory. There is even less harmony between the various countries.

One noteworthy exception is the new Dutch Civil Code. Its relevant Book 3, which entered into force in 1992, offers a consistent, although not quite exhaustive regulation of non-possessory security in movables.

3.3 Basic Models

In view of the extremely diverse sources and forms of non-possessory security and also the limited space available, it would be impossible to offer here a detailed survey of the various national regimes of non-possessory security. It is more fruitful to ask whether the great variety of legislative, judicial and doctrinal solutions and proposals which have been developed in order to cope with pressing contemporary needs can be reduced to a few basic models. Such models could help to detect common denominators which would be an intellectual key for understanding past developments, present diversities and possibly even to forecast future trends.

In my view, there are two basic models which underlie the great number of highly diverse legal instruments which are everywhere being used in order to achieve security in assets. These models are the pledge (or charge) and ownership of (or full title to) an asset. The first is especially designed to serve the functions of security in assets, although some specific features may have become disfunctional for present economic requirements. The second is the broadest proprietary right that exists and is not designed for purposes of security. Since it may convey too many powers to the creditor, it may be necessary to impose restrictions in order to reach adequate results.

I propose to demonstrate the utilisation of these two models, their respective advantages and disadvantages as well as their modifications and adaptations, by analysing the four legal systems to be investigated. None of them relies on only one of the models. All combine both models, but each does so in different ways.

3.4 Non-Possessory Pledge

3.4.1 Terminology

The term pledge as used in the present context has, of course, a broader meaning than that of 'possessory security' (*supra* 2). It comprises non-possessory security, but apart from this important distinction it is closely patterned upon the traditional legal regulation of the possessory pledge. This extension of the meaning of the original pledge is clearly reflected in most Civil Law countries (including France and Germany) in the titles of statutes regulating specific forms of non-possessory security; they all use pledge terminology.[25] This is even more true in the Netherlands where Book 3 of the Civil Code contains a unified general regime for the non-possessory pledge which is integrated with the possessory pledge.[26]

By contrast, in English common law the pledge is narrowly limited to possessory security. Its non-possessory sibling is the charge;[27] the rules governing it are akin to but not consciously derived from the possessory pledge.

3.4.2 Creation

In one crucial respect the requirements for the creation of a non-possessory pledge everywhere differ from those of a possessory pledge: the debtor need not dispossess himself of the collateral. In order to make up for the loss of the functions of that dispossession (*supra* 2.3), all legislators have introduced some more or less effective

---

25 France has a dozen special statutes or regulations. The more important ones regulate the *nantissement du fond de commerce* and the *nantissement de l'outillage et du matériel d'équipement,* governed by statutes of 1909 and 1951, respectively; and the *gage automobile,* created by a statute of 1934. For details cf. Mestre/Putman/Billiau (1996) II nos. 871-1016. Germany has three special statutes of minimal practical importance on agricultural tenants' inventories, on agricultural fruits and on overseas cables of 1951, 1949 and 1925, respectively. For details see Drobnig (1974), pp. 187-191, 192.

26 Arts. 3:236-3:259 of the Dutch Civil Code; these provisions are preceded by general rules applicable to both pledges and *hypothecs,* cf. Arts. 3:227-3:235.

27 Cf. Goode (1995), p. 646 who defines the (equitable) charge as an encumbrance.

substitute for publicity so as to inform interested persons about the existence of charges upon certain assets of their (potential) debtor. Usually, the observation of these requirements is a condition for the effectiveness of the non-possessory security *vis-à-vis* third persons.

The most popular and effective means of substitute publicity is registration of the security agreement. This is required in France for all three forms of security considered here[28] and in England for charges over parts or all of an incorporated company's assets.[29] The French legislator encourages the secured creditor to reinforce publicity of a non-possessory security in equipment by affixing a small plaque with details of the registration on an essential part of the charged equipment.[30]

Other countries replace registration by less demanding requirements. For a German security in an agricultural tenant's inventory, merely the deposit of the security agreement at the local court at the location of the farm is demanded.[31] And the Netherlands is content with requiring a strict form for the security agreement which must be in a public or a registered private document;[32] this serves primarily as proof of the date of the agreement.

The special character of non-possessory pledges is for certain types underlined by limitations upon the nature of the secured claims. France restricts two types to securing credits for the acquisition of the collateral;[33] and Germany even restricts the class of creditors that are allowed to secure their loans upon agricultural tenants' inventories.[34]

3.4.3 Funds as Collateral

It is one of the virtues of non-possessory security to facilitate the creation of a security in a fund, i.e. in a mass of assets with changing elements. This technique is especially important for securing credits used as working capital (as distinct from investment credits). The English floating charge, the French enterprise (*fonds de commerce*) pledge and the German pledge on an agricultural tenant's inventory exemplify this idea.

3.4.4 Protection Against Third Persons

The protection of the non-possessory secured creditor against third persons is, generally speaking, the same as that of the possessory creditor (*supra* 2.5). However, he will be affected by certain procedural disadvantages in insolvency proceedings over the debtor's property, especially with respect to the enforcement of the security, since the insolvency administrator holds the collateral.

---

28 Cf. Mestre/Putman/Billiau (1996) II nos. 880-882, 895-897, 968-971.
29 Companies Act 1985 (8 Statutes 104) s. 396 (1).
30 Mestre/Putman/Billiau (1996) (1996) II no. 897 for equipment.
31 Cf. Drobnig (1974), p. 189.
32 Art. 3:237 s. 1 of the Dutch Civil Code.
33 Mestre/Putman/Billiau (1996) II nos. 878, 893.
34 Drobnig (1974), p. 188.

Another issue of protection arises if the debtor without the creditor's permission disposes of the collateral. Does the broad Civil Law principle of good-faith acquisition protect the purchaser (especially a buyer or – another – secured creditor) if the security had been duly registered (provided this was feasible, *supra* 3.4.2)? Can the secured creditor therefore reclaim the collateral from the purchaser (*droit de suite* in French)? The answers differ and are often uncertain. For the French pledge on the debtor's equipment a negative answer is implied since the legislator provides for additional, but optional publicity by means of a sign to be affixed to the collateral (*supra* 3.4.2). For the French pledge on automobiles the courts tend to take seriously the creditor's fictive possession of the collateral (*supra* 3.4.2) as excluding the purchaser's good faith.[35] In England it has been said by a leading author that 'registration fixes a party with notice ... if and only if the dealing between him and the debtor with respect to the asset is of such a kind that it would be reasonable to expect the party in question to search'.[36]

3.4.5 Enforcement by Secured Creditor

The enforcement of non-possessory pledges is in general governed by the same rules that apply to the enforcement of possessory security (*supra* 2.6). Two of the special French statutes refer expressly to the relevant provision of the Commercial Code.[37] The new Dutch Civil Code even has a unified set of rules for both types of pledges.[38]

Two special features deserve mention. First, the secured creditor cannot begin to enforce his security until he has obtained the collateral held by the debtor. He is therefore entitled to request its surrender to him.[39]

Secondly, the enforcement of an enterprise pledge deviates in certain respects from that of a pledge over specific assets. Until recently, the holder of an English floating charge was entitled to appoint a receiver who took over the administration of the collateral in order to secure an optimal return from it.[40] In France, a provisional administrator of the enterprise may be appointed by the court; by contrast, a judicial attribution of the charged enterprise to the creditor is expressly excluded.[41]

3.5 Ownership (title)

Full ownership of things is an unspecific basis for obtaining security. Since it confers upon the creditor/owner more rights than are necessary for purposes of security, it may be made subject to limitations, at least in certain respects. Since even within any specific country, a creditor's ownership may be treated differently depending upon

---

35 Mestre/Putman/Billiau (1996) II no. 886.
36 Goode (1995), p. 719.
37 Cf. Mestre/Putman/Billiau (1996) II no. 887 and no. 897, pp. 333-334.
38 Arts. 3:248-3.253 of the Dutch Civil Code.
39 Expressly Art. 3:237 s. 3 of the Dutch Civil Code. French Cass.civ. 24 November 1993, Bull.civ. 1993 I no. 348.
40 Goode (1995), pp. 737-738. This right was abolished in 2002.
41 Art. L143-1 s. 1 and Art. L142-1 s. 2 *Code de Commerce*.

the nature of the secured claim, we must follow this differentiation as well and distinguish between reservations of ownership (title) and security transfers of ownership (*infra* 3.5.1 and 3.5.2).

3.5.1 Reservation of Ownership (title)

The reservation of ownership is the typical and widely used security of sellers who grant (trade) credit to their purchasers with respect to payment of the purchase price. Legal treatment differs depending upon the nature and extent of the secured debt(s).

a Simple Reservation of Ownership (title)

'Simple' is a reservation of ownership (title) if it is limited to securing the seller's claim for the purchase price. This form of reservation of ownership is today fully valid in all the four countries here investigated. In particular, since 1980 even France regards it as effective in the buyer's bankruptcy.

1 Creation

England, Germany and the Netherlands have no specific provisions so that even an informal agreement suffices to deviate from the seller's normal duty under a contract of sale of immediately transferring ownership.[42] The relevant French provision makes the effect of a reservation in the buyer's insolvency dependent upon a written clause which must be established at the latest upon delivery of the sold goods to the buyer.[43]

2 Effects as against third persons

The seller's position as the owner is respected even in the two most critical situations, i.e. as against the execution and the insolvency creditors of the buyer. The seller may object against an execution affecting his goods and he may reclaim them in the buyer's insolvency.[44]

3 Community-wide recognition

A rather hidden provision, Art. 4 of the Directive on late payments of 2000,[45] obliges the member States to give effect, according to the (national) rules of private international law, to a (simple) reservation of ownership expressly agreed upon by the buyer and the seller before the goods are delivered. The provision seems to cover both "internal" reservations of title as well as those agreed upon in one member State when the goods are later imported from that State into another Member State.[46]

---

42 § 455 s. 1 of the German BGB and Art. 3:92 s. 1 of the Dutch Civil Code specify that normally a retention clause makes the transfer of ownership subject to the suspensive condition of full payment of the purchase price. For English law cf. McCormack (1990), pp. 100-104.

43 Art. L621-122 s. 2 of the French *Code de Commerce*.

44 Cf. for England, s. 251 Insolvency Act 1986; for France Mestre/Putman/Billiau (1996) I no. 495; for Germany, Bülow (1999), nos. 721, 725 and Drobnig (1974), p. 194 sub c; for the Netherlands, Polak/Polak (1995), p. 130.

45 Directive 2000/35/EC of 29 June 2000 on combating late payments in commercial transactions (*OJ* 2000 L 200, p. 35).

46 For details cf. especially McCormack (2001).

b   Extended Reservations of Ownership (title)

Extensions of a reservation of ownership may relate either to the secured debts (*infra* 1) or to substitutes of the original collateral (*infra* 2).

1   Coverage of additional debts

The general Dutch provision and the specific French insolvency rule limit coverage of a reservation to the claim for the purchase price.[47] By contrast, English and German courts allow the parties to extend the reservation of ownership to secure other debts owed to the seller that are unrelated to the purchase of the specific goods; even a so-called 'all claims'-clause is given effect.[48] However, the degree of effectiveness varies. While English courts give full effect to the clause,[49] German courts have restricted it. It deploys full effects – like a simple reservation (*supra* a) – only so long as the purchase price for the 'reserved' goods is still open. As soon as it has been paid, the reservation of ownership is reduced to the lower status of a mere security transfer of ownership (*infra* 3.5.2) since it now secures indebtedness other than the purchase price. The owner is treated like[50] a pledgee; he can no longer reclaim the 'reserved' goods in the buyer's insolvency, but is still entitled to preferred satisfaction.

2   Coverage of substituted assets

The original goods may be replaced either by the proceeds of a sub-sale if the first buyer, being a trader, had been authorised to sell them; or by products if the buyer, being a producer, had been authorised to process them. In both cases, the first seller may wish to extend his reservation of ownership to the proceeds or to the product (or to the proceeds of sale of the product); or by replacements after resale by the buyer.

French insolvency law does not honour the first two extensions since it demands that the sold good must still be present in the insolvent estate *en nature*.[51] Dutch and English general law come to the same result on the ground that such extensions create a (non-possessory) security interest which requires the observation of the special formalities mentioned above (*supra* 3.4.2).[52] Along the same line of thinking, in Germany such extensions, while valid in civil law, are treated like security transfers of ownership in the critical case of a conflict with the debtor's insolvency creditors.[53] With respect to replacements, however, the French legislator opened the door in 1994 by extending the reservation of title to fungible goods of the same description as those sold under reservation of title and then resold.[54]

---

47   *Supra* n. 44; Art. 3:92 s. 2 of the Dutch Civil Code adds claims for damages for breach of the contract of sale.
48   However, debts of third parties may in Germany no longer be validly covered, § 455 s. 2 BGB, effective as of 1 January 1999.
49   *Armour* v. *Thyssen Edelstahlwerke AG*, [1991] 2 AC 339 (HL).
50   Serick (1990), pp. 134-136, 72-74; Drobnig (1974), n. 120.
51   *Supra* n. 43.
52   Goode (1995), pp. 654-656; Asser/Mijnssen (1994), no. 425.
53   Serick (1990), pp. 114-116, 85-88. Cf. *infra* 3.5.2.
54   Art. L621-122 s. 3 second sentence *Code de Commerce*.

3.5.2   Security Transfer of Ownership

This institution is a peculiarity of German law which has been developed in court practice. Until 1992 it also existed in Dutch court practice but it has now been invalidated (new Civil Code Art. 3:84 s. 3) and replaced by the non-possessory pledge (*supra* 3.4). The legal structure is akin to an English (chattel) mortgage. This mortgage, however, has been regarded with great distrust as being an instrument of defrauding creditors. Mortgages created by individuals and small companies have therefore been subjected to an extremely strict regime by legislation on bills of sale;[55] they are of very limited importance and will therefore not be considered here.

By contrast, for German lenders of money the security transfer of ownership is the most important form of non-possessory security, in many, but not all respects comparable to a reservation of ownership. Externally, the security transfer of ownership is in most respects indistinguishable from an ordinary transfer of ownership.

a   Creation

The general rules on the transfer of ownership[56] apply, although the parties' economic motive is to transfer certain assets of the debtor merely as security for his indebtedness to the creditor. While it is possible to make that transfer subject to the resolutory condition of full payment by the debtor, usually the transfer is unconditional. Upon payment the creditor is merely obliged to retransfer the assets to the debtor.

Just as the reservation of ownership, a security transfer may either be in simple form, securing only one specific debt by transferring one specific asset to the creditor. Or it may be extended in the same way as a reservation of ownership, into other debts or into substitutes of the original collateral, be they proceeds of a sale or products or the proceeds of the sale of a product (*supra* 3.5.1, b).

b   Effects

Contrary to the split regime of the effects of a reservation of ownership – depending upon whether it is simple or extended (*supra* 3.5.1, a and 3.5.1, b) – the effects of the German security transfer of ownership are uniform, whatever form is used. The effects are the same as those of an extended reservation of ownership (which is itself regarded as a security transfer, cf. *supra* 3.5.1, b). In other words, the security owner, if he competes with his debtor's insolvency creditors, is treated like a pledgee. He cannot reclaim the transferred assets, but is merely entitled to preferred satisfaction from their proceeds.[57]

---

55 Bills of Sale Act 1878 and Amending Act of 1882, reproduced in McCormack (1990), pp. 231-247.
56 Cf. *supra*. ch. 39.
57 Serick (1990), *supra* n. 51. Expressly the new Insolvency Act (effective 1 January 1999) § 51 no. 1.

4   Monetary Claims as Security

Intangibles, such as intellectual property rights and especially monetary claims (debts) have multiplied in our times and have become of growing economic importance. Consequently, they are being increasingly used as collateral for securing credits.

4.1   Basic Models

The basic legal instruments for utilising monetary claims as security are the same as for corporeal assets (comp. *supra* 3.3), namely either a pledge or a full transfer to the creditor, i.e. an assignment. Also the basic legal issue is identical: by assignment of a claim the creditor obtains more rights than are needed for the purposes of security so that here also the question arises whether and how these powers must be restricted in certain circumstances. Since the issues and also the solutions are in most respects identical, the following survey can be limited to the special features of the use of intangibles as collateral.

4.2   Pledge

4.2.1   Pledge with Notification of the Account Debtor

a   Civil Law countries

The pledging of monetary claims is governed by the general rules on pledges (*supra* 2). However, under the narrow 'possessory' conception of the pledge that obtained in the 19th century (*supra* 2.2), the requisite of dispossessing the debtor/pledgor of an intangible poses difficulties. The Civil Codes require notification of the debtor of the pledged claim (account debtor).[58] The French Supreme Court has held that that formal notification 'sufficiently realises' the transfer of possession demanded by Article 2076 *Code civil*.[59]

The required notification of the account debtor is desirable in order to assure that he will pay his debt to the pledgee and not to the pledgor. On the other hand, in many cases the necessity of notifying the account debtor may commercially be inconvenient: if there are a great number of such debtors owing modest amounts; since the pledgor's reputation will suffer; and since it is in many cases more convenient to leave the collection of the pledged claims to the pledgor on behalf of the pledgee to whom the former must account and pay over.

b   England and Wales

English law has never extended its narrow conception of the possessory pledge to intangibles.

---

58   Art. 2075 of the French *Code civil;* § 1280 of the German BGB. For the Netherlands, this results from Arts. 3:236 s. 2 and 3:94 s. 1 Civil Code.

59   Cass.civ. 10 May 1983, D. 1984, 433 with note Légier.

4.2.2   Pledge without Notification of the Account Debtor

a   The Netherlands

The new Dutch Civil Code has introduced, in addition to the pledge with notification (*supra* 4.2.1 under a), one without notification. This corresponds closely to the non-possessory pledge of tangibles (*supra* 3.4). As the latter, it must be established by a public or registered private document.[60]

If the pledgor does not perform his obligations *vis-à-vis* the pledgee or the latter has reason to be afraid of such breach, the pledgee may notify the account debtor.[61] Before such notification, the pledgor is entitled to deal with the account debtor and to receive payment; after notification, these rights are exercised by the pledgee.[62]

b   England and Wales

Monetary claims may be made subject to an (equitable) charge without notification of the debtor. Such charges, however, must be registered.[63] The charge may be fixed or floating (i.e., comprise a changing fund of debts).[64]

4.3   Assignment

4.3.1   Assignment for Security

A more flexible alternative to a pledge of monetary claims with notification of the account debtor is their full-scale transfer to the creditor by way of assignment. This is an equivalent of the security transfer of ownership (*supra* 3.5.2). However, it is useful for the parties only if it does not itself require notification, as does the general French and also the new Dutch law,[65] but not German law.[66] Also the former Dutch law did not require this so that assignment was widely used for security purposes. The new Civil Code, however, no longer recognises a transfer of assets for security (art. 3:84 s. 3) and has instead made available a pledge without notification (*supra* 4.2.2 under a).

In Germany the assignment for security is governed by the general rules on assignment. As far as the right to collect assigned claims is concerned, the Dutch rules established for pledges of claims without notification (*supra* 4.2.2, under a) correspond to German law.[67] The effects of an ordinary assignment are, however, restricted in the most critical situation, namely in the assignor's insolvency: The creditor as the assignee is no longer entitled to separate the assigned claim(s) from the assignor's insolvency estate but is reduced to the status of a pledgee; he has merely the right of preferential satisfaction from the proceeds of the debt.[68]

---

60 Art. 3:239 s. 1 of the Dutch Civil Code.
61 *Ibidem* s. 3.
62 Art. 3:246 s. 1 of the Dutch Civil Code.
63 Cf. Companies Act 1989 (c. 40) ss. 395, 396(1)(c (iii) (reproduced in McCormack (1990), p. 269).
64 Goode (1995), pp. 656-657, 800-802.
65 Art. 1690 French *Code civil*, as generally understood. Art. 3:94 s. 1 of the Dutch Civil Code.
66 § 398 BGB.
67 Cf. Serick (1990), pp. 102-106.
68 See the new Insolvency Act of 1999 § 51 no. 1.

4.3.2   Assignment for Sale

In England and Wales, an outright sale of monetary claims to the creditor is not regarded as a charge and is therefore not subject to registration (*supra* 4.1.2, under b)
and other restrictions.[69]

5   Conclusions

The complex nature of the subject, the limited number of legal systems considered
and the limitations of space preclude a detailed exposition of proposals for a future
European Civil Code. But two major suggestions can be derived from the preceding
survey.

5.1   A Unified Regime Based on the Idea of the Pledge/Charge

A future Code should integrate the two heterogeneous regimes which have grown up
in most countries (i.e. the pledge and ownership/title) into a modernised pledge law.
Today the basic model should be the non-possessory pledge (which also fits monetary claims as collateral). Extended reservations and security transfers of ownership
– where allowed at all – have at least in the debtor's insolvency already been reduced
to the effects of a pledge. By contrast, the simple reservation of ownership is everywhere granted the effects of full ownership; this should be preserved but converted
into a privileged regime for pledges securing claims for purchase money.

This general approach has to a considerable degree been adopted by the Dutch legislator; but it goes further – following the American model – by including also the
reservation of ownership.

5.2   Registration

On the issue of registration, the legal systems are divided. While some – France and
the United Kingdom – require it, although with considerable exceptions, Germany
and the Netherlands do without it. The modern legal trend favours registration and
technical progress facilitates it. In particular, the exemption of reservations of title
should be abandoned under a unified substantive regime (*supra* 5.1). On the other
hand, exemption from registration for small and short-term security rights should be
envisaged. Insofar as registration is required, formal requirements for the security
agreement – especially the "certain date" – can be abandoned.

BIBLIOGRAPHY: Asser/Mijnssen, *Handleiding tot de Beoefening van het Nederlands Burgerlijk
Recht III/3, Zakenrecht, Zekerheidsrechten,* 12th ed. (Zwolle 1994); Bell, *Modern Law of Personal Property in England and Ireland* (1989); Bülow, *Recht der Kreditsicherheiten,*5th ed.
(1999); Cabrillac/Mouly, *Droit des Sûretés,* 4th ed. (1997); Crossley Vaines, *Personal Property,* 5th ed. (1973); Drobnig, Security over Corporeal Movables in Germany, in: Sauveplanne

---

69   Goode (1995), pp. 800-802.

(ed.), *Security over Corporeal Movables* (1974), pp. 181-205; Ghestin (ed.), *Traité de Droit civil.* Mestre/Putman/Billiau, *Droit commun des sûretés réelles. Droit spécial des sûretés réelles*, two vol. (Paris 1996); Goode, *Commercial Law,* 2nd ed. (Penguin Books 1995); Kieninger, *Mobiliarsicherheiten im Europäischen Binnenmarkt* (1995); McCormack, *Reservation of Title* (1990); *idem*, Retention of Title and the Late Payment Directive, in *Journal of Corporate Law Studies* vol. 1 (2001) 501-518; Polak/Polak, *Faillissementsrecht,* 6th ed. (1995); Rutgers, *International Reservation of Title Clauses* (Thesis 1998); Serick, *Securities in Movables in German Law. An Outline* (1990); Woods, *Comparative Law of Security and Guarantees* (1995).

CHAPTER 41

The Cape Town Convention on International Interests in Mobile Equipment*

Roy Goode**

1 Introduction

On 16 November 2001 there were concluded at Cape Town under the joint auspices of UNIDROIT and ICAO[1] two international instruments which are likely to prove among the most significant and innovative ever to be made in the field of commercial law. The Convention on International Interests in Mobile Equipment is designed to facilitate the acquisition and financing of economically important items of mobile equipment – aircraft objects, railway rolling stock and space assets – by providing for the creation of an international interest that will be recognised and enforced in all Contracting States and the perfection of such interest in an international registry, and by prescribing rules for the priority of competing interests and legal protection against the debtor's insolvency.

Why were these instruments necessary? In the ordinary way, the effect of a movement of equipment subject to a security interest from one jurisdiction to another is resolved through the conflict of laws. The almost universal approach is to apply the law of the place where the equipment is situated at the time of the last dealing or event. In conflict of laws terms this usually works well enough where the equipment is normally used in one place but it is less useful for equipment which by its nature is constantly moving from one jurisdiction to another in the ordinary course of business. For aircraft and ships this problem is resolved by application of the law of the State of nationality registration of the aircraft or ship. But there is no such international system for railway rolling stock or satellites. Moreover, a uniform conflicts rule does not address the real problem, which is the insecurity created by differences in national laws and the fact that while some jurisdictions have a liberal attitude towards the creation and enforcement of security and title-retention interests, and a developed

---

* This paper provides a general introduction to the Cape Town Convention and Aircraft Equipment Protocol. For a full analysis, see the author's Official Commentary on the Convention and Protocol, published by UNIDROIT in 2002 and available from UNIDROIT. For earlier discussions, see Roy Goode, 'The Cape Town Convention on International Interests in Mobile Equipment: A Driving Force for International Asset-Based Financing', 2002-1 Uniform Law Rev. 3, and for a more detailed examination of the instruments when in draft 'Transcending the Boundaries of Earth and Space: The Preliminary Draft UNIDROIT Convention on International Interests in Mobile Equipment', 1998-1 Uniform Law Rev. 52. See also Jeffrey Wool, 'Rethinking the Notion of Uniformity in the Drafting of International Commercial Law; A Preliminary Proposals for the Development of a Policy-based Unification Model', 1997-1 Uniform Law Rev. 46, and the collection of papers published in 1999-2 Uniform L. Rev. 242, an issue devoted entirely to the Convention and Protocol while still in draft.
** Norton Rose Professor of English Law at St John's, Oxford
1 UNIDROIT: the International Institute for the Unification of Private Law; ICAO: the International Civil Aviation Organization.

set of priority rules underpinned by national registration systems, others do not. What the financier of an expensive item such as an aircraft, a fleet of railway wagons or a satellite needs when lending on the security of such an item or supplying it under a title reservation or leasing agreement, is, first, the assurance of adequate remedies (including speedy interim relief) in the event of default, secondly a single, international registration system for the perfection of its interest and thirdly a set of workable priority rules and protection of its interest if the debtor becomes insolvent.

The importance attached to a sound international legal regime for international interests in mobile equipment is apparent from the fact that a study commissioned by the Aircraft Protocol Group and conducted under the auspices of INSEAD and the New York University Salomon Center[2] concluded that such a regime could reduce borrowing costs by several billion US dollars a year, while more recently the Export-Import Bank of the United States, the official US export credit agency, has announced that buyers of large US commercial aircraft in foreign countries that ratify the Cape Town Convention will qualify for a reduction of one-third in Ex-Im Bank's exposure fee.[3]

2 Innovative Techniques

The Convention and Protocol embody a number of innovations, both in what they create and in their structure and flexibility.

2.1 The International Interest

In contrast to earlier conventions, particularly in the field of transport law, which are based on the recognition and priority of interests derived from national law, the Cape Town Convention establishes a wholly new legal construct, an international interest, which is the creation of the Convention itself and which is protected by registration in an international registry. An interest which satisfies the requirements of Articles 2 and 7 of the Convention[4] constitutes an international interest whether or not it would be recognised as such by national law. The international interest does not displace interests created under national law – usually the two will exist concurrently – but when registered it will have priority over a domestic interest.[5]

---

2 Anthony Saunders and Ingo Walter, *Proposed Unidroit Convention on International Interests in Mobile Equipment as Applicable to Aircraft Equipment Through the Aircraft Equipment Protocol: Economic Impact Assessment*, September 1998.

3 News release 31 January 2003.

4 These require that the interest (1) relate to an object of a category specified by the Convention as indicated above and designated in and identifiable in accordance with the Protocol and (2) be embodied in an agreement in writing which is a security agreement, a title reservation agreement or a leasing agreement and relates to an object of which the chargor, conditional seller or lessor has power to dispose and, in the case of a security agreement, enables the secured obligation to be determined.

5 There is an exception for national interests arising under internal transactions the subject of a declaration by a Contracting State, which can be protected by registration of notice of a national interest, and for non-consensual rights or interests covered by a declaration under Article 39.

2.2 The International Registry

The second innovation is the creation of an International Registry to record the grant of international interests and dealings in such interests, as well as certain other matters. The registry, when set up, will be wholly electronic, enabling registrations to be effected and search results supplied without human intervention. No comparable registry currently exists.

2.3 The Facility to Register Non-Consensual Rights or Interests

National registration systems do not normally provide for the registration of non-consensual interests, if only because it can rarely be determined in advance when these will arise. However, Article 40 of the Convention allows a Contracting State to make a declaration listing the categories of non-consensual right or interest which are to be registrable under the Convention as if they were international interests. Any non-consensual right or interest so registered has priority as from the time of registration in accordance with the priority rules. The type of non-consensual right or interest envisaged by Article 40 is one which is susceptible to a first-to-file rule, such as attachment of the object by way of execution of a judgment debt and the rights of a creditor under a lien for repair given by law.[6]

2.4 The Two-Instrument Approach

As stated above, the Convention applies to three different categories of equipment, namely airframes, aircraft engines and helicopters;[7] railway rolling stock; and space assets,[8] with the possibility of other categories being added later.[9] It will be obvious that while many provisions would be common to all three categories, there are various points on which the rules must be equipment-specific, because the factual background and practices of the three industry sectors concerned vary widely from one to another. There were three possible ways of dealing with this. One would have been to have a single instrument covering all the required provisions, but this would have been extremely long, complex and cluttered up with definitional detail. Another would have been to have a separate, free-standing Convention for each category of object. That was seriously mooted and only finally rejected on the opening day of the Diplomatic Conference, by which time the disadvantages had become apparent, in particular, the duplication of effort and the risk that drafting of the various conventions by different hands would undermine the unity of the provisions that were not in principle equipment-specific, thus precluding interpretative rulings concerning one

---

6　Art. 39 provides a separate rule by which a Contracting State may make a declaration specifying the non-consensual rights or interests (whether secured or unsecured) which under its law would have priority over an interest equivalent to that of the holder of a registered international interest and are to have priority over a registered international interest. Possible examples are non-consensual liens for unpaid air navigation charges and claims for unpaid taxes or wages in the debtor's insolvency.

7　Referred to collectively in the Aircraft Equipment Protocol as aircraft objects.

8　Art. 2(3).

9　Art. 51.

category from being applied to a different category. It was thus decided to have a single Convention containing provisions that were not equipment-specific and to supplement this with a series of equipment-specific protocols that would meet the particular needs of the industry sector affected. One unusual consequence of this approach is the paramountcy of a Protocol over the Convention as regards objects of a category within the Protocol. As regards any such category the Convention takes effect only as from the time of entry into force of the Protocol and subject to its terms, and only as between States parties to both the Convention and the Protocol.[10]

2.5 The Declaration System

The Convention and Protocol contain an elaborate system of declarations by which certain provisions that Contracting State might find unacceptable as contrary to their basic legal philosophy are dependent on an opt-in or alternatively can be disapplied by an opt-out. For example, a Contracting State may make a declaration that would allow certain types of non-consensual interest to be registered in the International Registry as if they were international interests,[11] and in the Aircraft Equipment Protocol the remedies given to a creditor on the debtor's insolvency are dependent on an opt-in,[12] while Contracting States whose laws do not permit self-help may by declaration require a court order for the exercise of what would otherwise be a self-help remedy.[13] It is, of course, true that the availability of opt-ins and opt-outs to some extends weakens the uniformity which the Convention and Protocol are designed to achieve, but that is a price which was considered worth paying to secure agreement, given the great advantages of the remaining provisions of the two instruments.

3 Creation, Enforcement, Perfection and Priority

3.1 Creation and Registration of the Interest

An international interest is created as soon as the conditions specified in Articles 2 and 7 are satisfied provided that at the time of conclusion of the agreement the debtor is situated in a Contracting State.[14] Registration is not necessary for the creation of an interest, its function being to give notice of the existence of the interest to third parties. Chapters IV and V of the Convention provide for the establishment of the International Registry and prescribe what is registrable[15] and the registration requirements. A very useful facility is the registration of a prospective international interest, that is, one which is intended to be granted in an identified object but is not yet in existence, e.g. because the parties are still negotiating terms. A search certificate is required to state that the creditor named has acquired or intends to acquire an interna-

---

10 Art. 49(1).
11 Art. 39.
12 Protocol, arts. XI and XXX(3).
13 Art. 55.
14 Art. 3.
15 See art. 16.

tional interest but must not indicate whether the interest is existing or prospective.[16] This enables the interest, when coming existence, to rank for priority as from the time of registration as a prospective interest without need of any further registration.[17] A third party making a search is expected to ascertain the facts by enquiry of the creditor.

3.2 Enforcement of the International Interest

Chapter 3 provides a set of basic default remedies, which can for the most part be expanded or restricted by agreement. These vary according to whether the creditor is a chargee on the one hand or a conditional seller or lessor on the other. The default remedies of a chargee are: to take possession or control of any object; to sell or grant a lease of any such object; to collect or receive any income or profits from the management or use of an object;[18] and, with the agreement of the debtor and all other interested persons or by order of the court, to have ownership vested in the chargee in total or partial satisfaction of the debt,[19] though the court may make an order only if the amount of the secured obligations to be satisfied by the vesting is commensurate with the value of the object.[20] The provisions relating to the default remedies of the conditional seller or lessor are much simpler, the remedies being simply termination of the agreement and the taking of possession or control.[21] No other remedies were considered necessary, because the creditor is the owner and can do as it wishes with its own property.

In general, remedies may be exercised by self-help or by court order, but recourse to the court is necessary for (a) exercise of the default remedies in Article 8 to which the debtor has not agreed and (b) the vesting of ownership if there is a failure to procure the agreement of all interested persons. In addition, a Contracting State may make a declaration barring self-help.[22] Finally, there is a useful provision in Article 13 for speedy relief for the creditor pending final determination of a claim on its merits where the creditor adduces evidence of default, safeguards being provided if the creditor fails to perform its obligations to the debtor under the Convention or Protocol or fails to establish its claim on the final determination of that claim.

3.3 The Priority Rules

The Convention eschews the subtleties and complexities of priority rules found in national legal systems and goes for simplicity. Hence, remarkably, all the Convention priority rules are gathered together in a single article, Article 29. There are in fact very few rules. The main rule is that a registered interest has priority over any other

---

16 Art. 22(3).
17 Art. 19(4).
18 Art. 8.
19 Art. 9(1),(2).
20 Art. 9(3).
21 Art. 10.
22 Art. 54(2).

interest subsequently registered and over an unregistered interest.[23] In principle unregistered interests are subordinated even if they are of a kind not capable of registration[24] and even if the registering creditor has knowledge of them.[25] There are three exceptions. First, an outright buyer takes free from an interest not registered at the time of his purchase.[26] The reason for this is that the outright buyer does not have a registrable interest,[27] and outright purchases are so common that it was considered essential to exempt them from the general rule. The second exception relates to a conditional buyer or lessee, who can shelter under the registration of his conditional seller or lessor and obtain priority over another claimant whose own interest was registered after that of the conditional seller or lessor.[28] The third exception relates to non-consensual rights or interests covered by the declaration of a Contracting State under Article 39.[29]

The priority of competing interests may be varied by agreement.[30] Any priority given by Article 29 to an interest in an object extends to proceeds.[31] Finally, Article 29(7) embodies a rule to preserve rights given by the applicable law in an item other than an object[32] despite its installation on an object or created by the applicable law in an installed object after its removal.

And that is the sum total of the Convention's priority rules governing a registered interest[33] – a convincing demonstration of the clarity and simplicity that can be achieved by concentration on essentials.

4   The Impact of the Debtor's Insolvency

4.1   Effectiveness of a Pre-Insolvency Registered Interest

Article 30(1) provides that in insolvency proceedings against the debtor an international interest is effective if registered in conformity with the Convention prior to the opening of insolvency proceedings or if otherwise effective under the applicable law.

---

23 It will be recalled that under art. 19(4) when a prospective international interest becomes an international interest it is considered to have been registered as from the time of registration of the prospective international interest.

24 See the definition of 'unregistered interest' in art. 1(mm). An exception is a non-consensual interest not covered by a declaration under Article 39, as to which see below.

25 Art. 29(2)(a). This is a good example of the robust nature of the priority rules and is designed to avoid factual disputes as to whether a person did or did not have knowledge. Similarly the creditor who is first on the register has priority even as to future advances made with knowledge of a subsequent interest, whether or not registered.

26 Art. 29(3).

27 The position is otherwise under the Aircraft Equipment Protocol. See below.

28 Art. 29(4)(b).

29 See n. 7 above.

30 Art. 29(5).

31 Art. 29(6). But note the restricted meaning of 'proceeds' in Art. 1(w)

32 That is, an item which is not an aircraft object, an item of railway rolling stock or space property.

33 The Convention does not regulate priorities between unregistered interests; that is left to the applicable law. The only other priority rules in the Convention are those relating to successive assignments of associated rights. See below.

By 'effective' is meant that the international interest will be recognised as proprietary in character and, as a starting point, will rank ahead of the claims of unsecured creditors.

4.2 Preservation of Certain Rules of Insolvency Law

Article 30(3) makes two qualifications. First, this provision does not affect rules of insolvency law relating to the avoidance of a transaction as a preference or a transfer in fraud of creditors. Secondly, it does not affect any rules of procedure relating to the enforcement of rights to property which is under the control or supervision of the insolvency administrator. The purpose of this latter provision is to preserve the efficacy of rules restricting the enforcement of rights in an insolvency proceeding designed to facilitate corporate rescue and reorganisation,[34] for example, by imposing an automatic stay on such enforcement. Article 30 reflects the general approach of national insolvency laws, which is to respect pre-insolvency proprietary entitlements validly perfected under the applicable law but to subject these to avoidance or modification to reflect the policies of insolvency law. However, the limited scope of Article 30(3) should be noted. The only rules of insolvency law that are allowed to disturb a pre-insolvency registered international interest are those relating to the unfair preference of one creditor at the expense of the general body of creditors (typically by a payment or transfer made at a time when the debtor is already insolvent or on the verge of insolvency) and to transactions made to defraud creditors by removing from the estate assets which would otherwise have been available to the general body of creditors. Other rules, such as those relating to the ranking of claims, which in certain jurisdictions allow preferential debts (e.g. for unpaid taxes or wages) to trump even secured debts, cannot be invoked to impeach a registered international interest.[35]

5 Subordinations

5.1 Subordinations

It has been mentioned above that the priority rules embodied in Article 29 may be varied by agreement between the holders of the competing interests. Article 16(e) allows for the registration of subordinations, a necessary step if the assignee of the subordinated interest is to be bound by the subordination,[36] of which he might otherwise have no knowledge.[37]

---

34 As opposed to a winding-up.

35 In this respect Article 30(3) differs from Article 8 of the 2002 Hague Convention on the law applicable to certain rights in respect of securities held with an intermediary, which, though inspired by Article 30 of the Cape Town Convention, preserves the application of all substantive and procedural insolvency rules, including those relating to the ranking of categories of claim.

36 Art. 29(5).

37 But in line with the policy to preserve the integrity of the registration system and avoid factual disputes as to whether a person did or did not have knowledge, the fact that the assignee knew of the unregistered subordination is irrelevant.

6 Assignments

6.1 Associated Rights and Assignments

Chapter 9 deals with the assignment of associated rights and international interests, 'associated rights' being defined as 'all rights to payment or other performance by a debtor under an agreement which are secured by or associated with the object.'[38]

Except as otherwise agreed an assignment of the associated rights made in conformity with the Convention[39] also transfers to the assignee the related international interest and all the interests and priorities of the assignor under the Convention.[40] It may seem slightly odd that a Convention dealing with international interests and their assignment, not with the assignment of receivables as such, should focus on the assignment of associated rights and then provide for these to transfer the related international interest. Indeed, an earlier draft had done it the other way round and stated that the assignment of an international interest should transfer the associated rights, which in a sense was more logical, given the scope of the Convention. But the view prevailed that this would be contrary to the near-universal rule that security interests do not exist in the abstract but are accessory to the rights secured. Hence the reference to the assignment of associated rights as the starting point and the consequential need for a rule that the assignment of such rights in isolation from an international interest, though permitted, is outside the scope of the Convention.[41]

6.2 Priority of Competing Assignments

Article 35 deals with two forms of competition between successive assignments of associated rights of which at least one includes the related international interest.[42] The first is the competition between the assignee of associated rights related to a registered interest and the assignee of associated rights under a subsequently registered or unregistered interest. Here the rule is that each assignee takes the priority of its assignor, so that an assignee of the first registered interest has priority over the assignee of a later registered interest or a unregistered interest. The second is the competition between competing assignees of associated rights related to the same international interest. In this case the starting position is that the assignees rank in order of registration of their respective assignments. However, the priority given by this

---

38 Art. 1(c). Rights are 'secured by' a security agreement and 'associated with' a title reservation or leasing agreement. Only rights to performance by the debtor under such an agreement fall within the definition of associated rights and they are associated rights only in relation to the particular agreement under which they arise. Rights against the debtor under another agreement or under a promissory note and rights against a third party, such as a guarantor, are not associated rights under the first agreement unless (a) the debtor also undertakes in that agreement to perform the obligations under the other agreement or note and (b) such undertaking is secured on or associated with the object.

39 See art. 32. As to the debtor's duty to the assignee, see art. 33; as to the assignee's default remedies under an assignment by way of security, art. 34.

40 Art. 31(1).

41 Art. 32(3).

42 If neither includes a related international interest the Convention does not apply (art. 32(3)).

rule is cut down by Article 36, which requires that the contract under which the asso-ciated rights arise states that they are secured by or associated with the object,[43] and restricts the priority to associated rights that are object-related in the sense that they consist of rights to payment or performance that are related to the acquisition of an object or its rental.[44]

7 Jurisdiction

As regards any claim brought under the Convention the courts of a Contracting State chosen by the parties have jurisdiction, and subject to Articles 43 and 44 such juris-diction is exclusive unless the parties otherwise agree.[45] Article 43 is confined to claims for relief under Article 13 and confers concurrent jurisdiction on courts of the Contracting State on the territory of which the object is located to grant relief under Article 13(1)(a), (b) and (c) and on courts of the Contracting State on the territory of which the debtor is situated to grant relief under Article 13(1)(d),[46] though the relief must by the terms of the order be enforceable only in such territory. Under Article 44 orders can be made against the Registrar of the International Registry only by the courts of the place in which the Registrar has its centre of administration. This is be-cause to allow national courts to make orders against the Registrar would be incom-patible with its international functions and could lead to conflicting decisions by different courts.

8 Entry into Force

The Convention enters into force after three months from deposit of the third instru-ment of ratification, but so far as it relates to a category of objects to which the Proto-col applies, only as from the time of entry into force of the Protocol and subject to its terms.[47] The Aircraft Equipment Protocol requires eight ratifications.

9 The Aircraft Equipment Protocol

Space does not allow more than a brief mention of the key features of the Aircraft Equipment Protocol, which, it will be recalled, overrides or modifies the Convention

---

43 It might not do so where there is a prior registered agreement between the same parties which secures the debtor's obligations both under that agreement and under subsequent agreements between the same parties, in which case it would not be necessary for the subsequent loan agreement to state that the rights under it were secured (this being already provided by the earlier agreement) and another assignee of the loan agreement would not be able to ascertain from its terms that the loan was secured.

44 For a more detailed explanation of arts. 35 and 36 with illustrations, see the Official Commentary, pp. 19-22, 126-134.

45 Art. 42.

46 Which relates to the lease or management of the object and the income from it.

47 Art. 49. The Convention entered into force on 1 April 2004.

so far as inconsistent with it. Article III of the Protocol extends the registration provisions of the Convention and its priority rules to outright sales of aircraft objects, pursuant to Article 41 of the Convention. The Convention's provisions on default remedies do not, of course, apply, since the transferor is not retaining title. Article IV provides in relation to aircraft objects an alternative connecting factor to that of the debtor's situation, namely the State of registration of the relevant aircraft where this is a Contracting State of the State of registry.[48] Where a Contracting State has made a declaration to apply Article VIII, this confers on the parties the power to choose the law to govern their agreement, and in a Contracting State this choice cannot be disregarded by the forum, which otherwise could have applied its own conflict of laws restrictions on choice of law. Two additional default remedies are provided, namely de-registration of the aircraft object and its export.[49]

Of particular interest are the provisions of Article XI on insolvency of the debtor, which apply only where a Contracting State has made a declaration to that effect and which allow the declaring State a choice between the so-called 'hard' option (Alternative A) and the softer option (Alternative B). Where Alternative A is selected, the insolvency administrator[50] must either give up possession within a waiting period specified in the declaration (or by such earlier date as that on which the creditor would be entitled to take possession) or cure all defaults other than the default constituted by the opening of insolvency proceedings and agree to perform all future obligations under the agreement. Alternative B requires the insolvency administrator to state within the period specified by the declaring State's declaration whether it will cure all defaults, etc., or give the creditor an opportunity to take possession. If the insolvency administrator fails to give this statement or fails to give up possession when it has agreed to do so, it is for the court to decide whether to permit the creditor to take possession. A Contracting State may elect to make no declaration under Article XI, in which case its domestic insolvency law will continue to apply.

Finally, there are certain modifications of the priority and assignment provisions, as well as provisions for protection of the debtor's possession, which will not be discussed here.[51]

10 Conclusions

It is anticipated that the Cape Town Convention will be widely adopted, because of the substantially increased security given the international legal regime it establishes and the consequent reduction in risk, borrowing costs and exposure fees on credit insurance. The Supervisory Authority is not yet in place[52] and the International Regis-

---

48 As defined by art. I(2)(p).
49 Art. IX.
50 Alternatively the debtor in cases where the insolvency-related event is not the commencement of insolvency proceedings but the declared intention to suspend payment where the creditor's right to institute insolvency proceedings is prevented or suspended. See art. I(2)(m).
51 See arts. XIV–XVI and the Official Commentary, pp. 37-38, 206-210.
52 Resolution No. 2 of the Diplomatic Conference resolved to invite ICAO to fulfil this role. ICAO has not yet formally signified its acceptance.

try has yet to be established and the Registrar designated, but it is envisaged that these matters will be resolved in the near future. What augurs well for the future of the Convention and Protocols[53] is the great volume of industry expertise contributed from an early stage right through to the end of the Diplomatic Conference which helped to ensure that the rules adopted were responsive to legitimate market needs and practices, while governments, assisted by independent experts, exercised a controlling influence to secure a fair balance of competing interests and respect for differing legal traditions and philosophies.

---

53 The Aircraft Equipment Protocol was the only one ready for consideration at the Diplomatic Conference. The draft Rail Protocol has been examined at three successive joint meetings of UNIDROIT and the Intergovernmental Organisation for International Carriage by Rail (OTIF) and is expected to come before a Diplomatic Conference by June 2005. The draft Space Protocol was examined at a first meeting of governmental experts in December 2003.

CHAPTER 42

Real Security regarding Immovable Objects – Reflections on a Euro-Mortgage

Hans G. Wehrens*

1 Introduction

In a future European Civil Code statutory provisions on *real securities regarding immoveable property* will be indispensable, irrespective of whether corresponding regulations or directives of the European Union (EU) will already exist at the time of codification or not. In both cases the preparatory work in this sector which has been carried out under the provisional title *Euro-mortgage, (Eurohypothek, Eurohypothèque)* can serve as a basis.

What does 'Euro-mortgage' mean and where does this new legal term come from?[1] The Member States of the European Union have already grown so closely together in the economic sector that cross-border mortgage credits are becoming increasingly frequent. For this reason the occupational groups mainly dealing with this topic – the mortgage banks and the notaries – have for a couple of years especially raised the following questions:[2]

- Is it possible to simplify and unify the very different statutory provisions in existing legislation on mortgage within the particular EU Member States by means of contractual agreements?
- Will it be of any use, if the objective cannot be reached in this way, to introduce a new uniform right in rem within the EU, i.e. the Euro-mortgage?
- To what extent should this new European regulation include uniform provisions for all EU Member States and in how far should existing domestic peculiarities be preserved?

---

* The author would like to thank Dirk Voß for his translation of this chapter.
Vice-President of the Commission for European Union affairs – International Union of Latin Notariat.

1 Up to now, the term 'Euro-mortgage' has mainly been used in the following publications and the publications mentioned in the bibliography.
2 Cf. the CAUE/UINL reports mentioned in the bibliography and in addition:
EC Mortgage Federation: *L 'Hypothèque sur soi-même*, Brussels 1972.
EC Mortgage Federation: *Examen de droit comparé des procédures de saisie. Crédit transfrontalier au logement – Les incompatibilités*, Brussels 1983.
EC Mortgage Federation: *Ordre des privilèges et hypothèques*, Brussels 1984.
EC Mortgage Federation: *Les conditions minimales des hypothèques conventionnelles*, Brussels 1985.
EC Mortgage Federation: *Hypothèques libellées en monnaie étrangère*, Brussels 1985.
EC Mortgage Federation: *Variability of interest rates on mortgage loans in the EC*, Brussels 1989 (also available in other languages).
EC Mortgage Federation: *Mortgage credit in the European Community*, 2nd ed. 1990, Domus-Verlag Bonn (also available in French and German).

The clarification of these questions lies in the interest of the persons who have to apply the law or in that of the 'consumers' who will no longer have to accept avoidable disadvantages in the future. A uniform regulation would also increase the importance and the volume of *cross-border mortgage credits,* since immoveable property is, due to its stability, the most common security for loans and will retain its position within the European internal market.

The endeavours to reach a simplification of cross-border operation of mortgage credits up until now can be summarised as follows:

a. The *Segré Report* of 1966[3] considered it to be of primary importance to approximate and harmonise the different types of land charges within the EC; at the same time the authors advocated the introduction of a uniform type of land charge as a contribution to the integration of the capital markets.
b. Since its foundation the *European Community Mortgage Federation* in Brussels has tried to show the obstacles existing on the national level to a Europeanisation of the mortgage credit and to create the conditions necessary for them to be overcome.[4]
c. In 1967, a commission composed of civil law notaries and solicitors of the EC states was established on the European level within the *International Union of the Latin Notariat,* dealing with legal questions within the framework of community law (Commission des Affaires de l'Union Européenne –CAUE/UINL). It bears a French name since French was agreed on as the main working language. In 1983 this commission set up a special committee dealing with the legal possibilities for a uniform European mortgage.[5]
d. The *EU Commission* has further[6] reaffirmed the necessity for the short-term creation of a specific regulation on the operation of mortgage credits. In this context the Commission referred to the amended proposal for a Council directive on the freedom of establishment and the free supply of services in the field of mortgage credit. This proposal acknowledges the differences in the conditions for the operation of mortgage credits in the various Member States. Nevertheless it does not provide for a complete harmonisation of these conditions which would be a very laborious and lengthy task, but for a mutual recognition of the financing techniques.

The EU Commission and the EU Member States have not yet finished the discussion on whether the amended proposal for a directive on mortgage credit should be taken up again or whether the liberalisation of mortgage credit[7] could be reached by other

---

3 Report of an expert committee set up by the EC-Commission on the topic: 'The building of a European Capital Market', Brussels November 1966; due to its chairman Prof. Claudio Segré it is generally called the 'Segré-Report'.
4 Cf. the works of the European Mortgage Federation mentioned in footnote 2.
5 The works of the CAUE/UINL on the Euro-mortgage are listed in the bibliography.
6 *OJ* C 47/8.
7 The proposal amended several times for this EC-Directive on the free supply of services in the field of mortgage credit provides in Art. 3 that credit institutions may grant mortgage credit secured by mortgages on real property situated in another Member State. The original proposal of 18 February 1985 can be found in *OJ* C 42 and the amended proposal in *OJ* C 161.

means; moreover they wanted to wait and see what effects the two banking directives have on the markets for mortgage credits of the Member States.[8]

2 Survey of the Existing Laws of Mortgage within the EU

Whereas the greatest obstacles for activities abroad of business banks have been removed since the First and Second Banking Directive of the EC came into force,[9] the operation of mortgage credits across the border of a EU Member State still faces considerable – legal and practical – difficulties, since the Member States of the EU have very different systems regarding the law of mortgage as well as the law of land registration. These systems can only be presented briefly at this place.[10]

In all states the mortgage entitles the creditor to enforce his claim, if necessary, by realising the charged real property with priority to other creditors and he can do so no matter whether the initial debtor is still the owner of this property or not.

In most states, the legal regulations up to now only provide for a mortgage strictly accessory to the underlying debt meaning that its coming into being, its size and discharge depend on the existence and respective actual size of the debt. The advantages of a land charge independent of the underlying debt like the Swiss *Schuldbrief/cédule hypothécaire* or the German *Grundschuld* are still quite unknown in most of the Member States. The same is true for the advantages of a *Hypothekenbrief* (an officially issued transferable mortgage certificate) or of an owner's charge or owner's mortgage.

The principle of *accessoriness* of mortgage and debt as derived from older codifications influenced by Napoleonic legislation has nevertheless been abandoned in practice by several auxiliary arrangements. There are already more or less far reaching exceptions mainly in Belgium, the Netherlands and in Denmark. Thus, the mortgage can exist at least for a certain period without an exactly determined underlying debt; moreover, it can serve as security for a debt, the size of which varies permanently, e.g. as security for an overdraft.

Considerable differences can be observed in regard to the time at which the mortgage starts to exist. In France, Belgium, and Luxembourg, the mortgage already comes into existence at the moment of the recording by the notary whereas the subsequent entry into the *Hypothec Register* (Mortgage Register) gives the mortgage legal

---

8 This can be gathered from the address of Martin Bangemann held on the annual meeting of the European Mortgage Federation in Brussels on 22 June 1990.

9 1st Directive of 17 December 1988, *OJ* L 322/30, and 2nd Directive of 15 December 1989, *OJ* L 386/1.

10 More details can be found in the brochure *Mortgage credit in the European Community,* edited by the European Mortgage Federation in Brussels (footnote 2). Cf. moreover the series *Recht der Kreditsicherheiten in europäischen Ländern,* vol. I – VII, edited by the *Institut für internationales Recht des Spar-, Giro- and Kreditwesens* at the University of Mainz (Verlag Duncker & Humbolt, Berlin 1976 until 1988). Moreover Jackson, *Die Grundpfandrechte in den Rechtsordnungen Dänemarks, Irlands sowie des Vereinigten Königreichs von Großbritannien und Nordirland;* expertise of 1976 for the EC Commission – Directorate General Internal Market – and the corresponding expertise of the Max-Planck-Institute in Hamburg, *Die Grundpfandrechte in Recht der Mitgliedstaaten der EG,* Hamburg 1971.

effect in regard to third parties and determines the specific rank of the mortgage in relation to other charges, on the other hand, the mortgage does not exist before registration in Germany, Austria, Switzerland, the Netherlands, Italy, Greece or Spain.

In most countries it is sufficient if only the owner of the charged property who is at the same time the personal debtor signs the mortgage deed since there exist no particular format requirements regarding the consent of the mortgage creditor according to substantive law. However, in France, the Netherlands and Belgium the creditor has to participate in the creation of the mortgage.

There are basically two different procedures for the entry of the mortgage into the Land Register or into the Hypothec (Mortgage) Register respectively[11]

a. According to the *Grundbuchsystem* (a system of comprehensive land registration providing for a complete recording of the particulars of all real property e.g. ownership and charges in rem on it, established in Germany, Switzerland, Austria, in a modified form also Spain, Alsace-Lorraine and South Tyrol[12]) the applicant or the notary has to file an original or an authenticated copy of the mortgage deed with the Land Registry together with the application for registration of the mortgage according to its intended specific rank. Before registration is effected, application and enclosures are examined in regard to formal and substantive requirements by an official of the Land Registry with legal training (a judicial officer or Land Registry judge). The official of the Land Registry formulates the intended text of the registration on his own as an abridged version of the filed mortgage deed. The registration itself is effected – handwritten, typed or computer aided – by 'writing in'. Afterwards, creditor, debtor and notary each receive a copy of the effected registration; on request they can also receive a complete abstract from the Land Register revealing all entries effected up to now including the specific rank of the mortgage in relation to other charges.

b. According to the *Publication System (Publikationssystem:* France, Belgium, Luxembourg, the Netherlands,[13] Italy etc.) not only does the applicant have to file the mortgage deed with the Hypothec Registry but he must also file two signed certificates of entry. One of them is handed back to the applicant bearing a confirmation of the performance of the entry; it serves as proof of the right. The examination of the application is limited to the fulfilment of the formal requirements; in France, the examining officer does not even belong to the judiciary but to the fiscal administration. The registration itself is in some countries not performed by a 'writing in' but the submitted documents and the second certificate of entry are merely filed away.

---

11 Fundamental: Hoffmann, *Das Recht Des Grundstückkaufs,* Tübingen 1982, pp. 27 ff. Cf. also Burseau, L'organisation de la publicité foncière et l'hypothèque conventionelle dans divers pays de l'Europe occidentale, *Juris-Classeur Périodique* 1968 No. 2174-Doctrine.

12 In their comparative study *Das moderne Grundbuch,* the Austrian writers Herbert Hofmeister and Helmut Auer call this system the *mitteleuropäisches Grundbuchsystem* [central European system of land registration], No. 58 of the Schriftenreihe des Bundesministeriums für Justiz, Wien 1992.

13 In the Netherlands, the former system based on two certificates of entry has been replaced by a new registration system on the basis of two authenticated copies of the contracts since the entering into force of the new Civil Code (1 January 1992).

Finally, divergent regulations can be found regarding the question of whether the amount of mortgage debt and interest rates may only be stated in the national currency or in a foreign currency as well. At present, only the national currency (euro) is permitted in Spain and France, whereas for example in Belgium, Italy, Greece, the Netherlands and Denmark a foreign currency can also be chosen. Further peculiarities have to be observed in regard to the language used in the mortgage deed. Only the national language may be used in France, Italy, Greece and Spain, whereas in Belgium all three national languages and in Luxembourg French and German are permitted. On the other hand, in Germany, the United Kingdom, Ireland and the Netherlands foreign languages can be used as well on the condition of a corresponding knowledge of the respective language; an authenticated translation into the national language has nevertheless to be added for the Land or Hypothec Registry.

3 A Uniform Mortgage for Cross-border Credits

For the above-mentioned reasons the following considerations have been made by the CAUE:

Instead of a harmonisation of the mortgage laws of all EU Member States, which is neither practicable nor desirable, this field of law should – at least where it concerns the cross-border operation of credits – be simplified in such a way that it will be possible to provide mortgage credits across the borders according to uniform legal provisions.

For banks and borrowers, a uniform Euro-mortgage should be optionally available besides the different types of mortgage already existing in the several Member States. When required it should also be possible to use it for domestic credits.

This uniform Euro-mortgage could largely be shaped according to the model of the Swiss *Schuldbrief*[14] since this Swiss type of land charge is even more suitable for this purpose than the German *Grundschuld*.[15] Moreover, it could partially be based on the trilingual legal regulation of the *Schuldbrief* in the Swiss Civil Code.[16]

In this way a negotiable and versatile type of mortgage would be offered to banks and borrowers as an alternative to the types of mortgage already existing within the various Member States. Doing this could avoid difficulties and complications arising from the observance of the different mortgage laws in the various Member States.

In this way, the legal, economic and practical disadvantages of the conventional hypothec depending strictly on the underlying debt could be avoided as well. At the moment land charges not depending on the underlying debt do not exist in the EU Member States except for Germany and Switzerland, but only types of mortgage

---

14 By the *Schuldbrief* or *cédule hypothécaire* the debtor agrees to pay a certain amount of money including interest rates for which he accepts personal liability. This personal claim is secured at the same time by a land charge (the *Schuldbrief*, Art. 842 of the Swiss *Zivilgesetzbuch*).

15 The *Grundschuld* is a land charge according to which a certain amount of money including interest and other additional performances have to be paid to the creditor, the charged real property being liable for this obligation while this liability is in principle independent of the existence of an underlying debt (§ 1191 BGB).

16 For more details see Wehrens (1988) and Soergel/Stöcker (2002).

which are – apart from the very few legal makeshifts developed in practice (e.g. adaptation of the interest rate in the case of inflation or other amendments of the credit conditions) – closely linked to the personal claim.

For the operation of mortgage credits across the borders of two adjoining states like France and Germany, for example, the Euro-mortgage would not strictly be worth the trouble of lengthy preparatory work. But since the method suggested for the mortgage credit could be operated in a uniform way in all Member States, the efforts towards achieving a Euro-mortgage are worthwhile.

Difficulties can mainly arise from the fact that states with a 'Napoleonic' hypothec law can only slowly be convinced of the advantages of a mortgage independent of an underlying claim and will have difficulties in accepting the 'security contract' as a substitute for the close connection to the claim. If the Anglo-Saxon states should insist on preserving their existing system this would not cause complications due to the optional character of the Euro-mortgage.

Shaping the Euro-mortgage largely according to the Swiss model would be relatively simple; in contrast, the uniform shaping of the execution of the real estate will be very difficult. Therefore a way should be found in which the execution can be carried out according to existing domestic law while approximating only terms and costs.

The members of the working group of the CAUE all agreed that the term 'Euro-mortgage' is preferable to the other expressions suggested so far, for example *Hypothèque sur soi-même, Engagement foncier, Hypothèque indépendante du crédit* or *Dette foncière.*

Searching for an appropriate expression the working group of the CAUE started out by observing that the term indicating the new mortgage, uniformly valid within the entire EU, must not give rise to confusion with types of mortgage already existing. The name should be generally understandable in all Member States; this requires that it should be short but significant, impressive and easy to translate. But it must also fit within the abbreviations already used within the EU. For these reasons the working group of the CAUE decided in favour of the term 'Euro-mortgage' (*'Eurohypothek', 'Eurohypothèque'*) which is meanwhile commonly used.

The following objections have mainly been put forward to the other expressions used in the initial stages:

The term 'Hypothèque sur soi-même' means 'owner's mortgage', 'mortgage for the property owner's own benefit' or 'mortgage on the own real property', but the Euro-mortgage comprises much more than the function of an *Eigentümerhypothek* or an *Eigentümergrundschuld* (land charges for the owner's own benefit in German law). Moreover, in German law this expression could lead to confusions with the corresponding subject of §§ 1163 and 1177 BGB. The final objection was that, from 1795 there existed a 'hypothèque sur soi-même' in French law which was not satisfactory in practice and was therefore abolished soon afterwards.

The suggestion 'Engagement foncier' was not convincing either. The occasionally used term 'dette foncière' is not suitable because in the German translation it can be confused with the *Grundschuld* and in the other EU-Member States this expression is not meaningful enough.

4   Shaping the Euro-Mortgage as a Right *in rem*

The suggested Euro-mortgage will not exclude the different types of mortgage already existing in the various Member States but be added to the existing regulations as an additional possibility. In this the Euro-mortgage is primarily meant to be used for securing cross-border credits. However, if required and as far as it is wanted, it can, after a transitional period, also be used for domestic credits besides the conventional types of mortgage.

The introduction of the Euro-mortgage by a future European Civil Code requires that if one voluntarily chooses the Euro-mortgage instead of one's usual national type of mortgage one has to observe provisions regarding the particulars of the Euro-mortgage and its existence from its creation until its discharge which have to be codified at the same time. Therefore a short but sufficient minimum regulation should be incorporated into the new Civil Code uniformly for the entire EU. It could be comparable, for example, to the clear regulation of the Swiss *Schuldbrief.* The success of this new type of mortgage will depend not so much on coping with the legal and technical problems as on its economic advantages. The development in Switzerland and in Germany can be presented as an example for the success of a mortgage separated from the underlying personal claim. During the last 40 years, legal practice in both states switched for economic considerations from the *Hypothek* which is strictly connected to the underlying credit, to the more flexible *Schuldbrief* (Switzerland) and to the more economic *Grundschuld* (Germany).

The Euro-mortgage can be defined as a land charge which is independent of the existence of a concrete personal claim; and as the creation of the Euro-mortgage also includes an abstract acknowledgment of indebtedness it allows access to the charged real property (real liability) as well as to the personal property of the debtor (personal liability).

According to its purpose, the creation of the Euro-mortgage will depend on the composition of the respective national system of land registration. In states having a *Grundbuchsystem,* the Euro-mortgage will be created by notarial recording of the mortgage contract, entry of the mortgage into the land charge register and handing over of the mortgage certificate connected with a notarial declaration of enforceability. In states having either only a *Grundstücksregister* (a system of real estate registration) or only a system of *Hypothec Registration* the creation of the Euro-mortgage will be achieved by the notarial deed connected with the notarial declaration of enforceability. If a *Hypothekenbrief* for the Euro-mortgage should be provided for, it would moreover be necessary to legally regulate whether the notary or the registry is in charge of issuing this certificate.

Finally, in those EU countries not having the institution of the Latin notariat, it has to be legally determined that the Euro-mortgage comes into existence with the minimum content prescribed as soon as it is created according to the conventional procedures of those states and the mortgage deed has been handed over; as until now, the advantages of the notarial declaration of enforceability could not be enjoyed in these states.

In order to simplify the description, the peculiarities of the EU Member States

775

having common law systems will be left out of consideration in the following remarks.[17] Land registration will hereafter include Hypothec Registration.

The Euro-mortgage can already be created before the granting of the credit or to a higher amount than that of the actual debt. Accordingly, the interest rates could, for the purpose of registration, be fixed at a higher level than that of the real interest rates usual at the time of creation.

It could be registered in reserve in order to be immediately available on a later occasion if required.

It could be created as security for an overdraft or for a credit ceiling.

It could serve as security in cases where the credit is not granted to the property owner but to a third party but where nevertheless the property owner is prepared to give his land as real security. The owner's liability is then limited to the land and this does not affect his residual property, whereas the borrower is liable towards the creditor with his entire assets. The same applies if it is to serve as security for the liabilities of several debtors.

The Euro-mortgage is an appropriate means to secure a cross-border credit operation against currency fluctuations if the total amount entered into the Land Registry is fixed at a high enough level. This is important in cases where the mortgage can only be registered in the currency of the state in which the charged land is situated but the credit secured is to be paid out in another currency.

After the total redemption of a credit, it can be used for the securing of a new credit granted by the same creditor, even if many years have passed in between, since an automatic discharge of the Euro-mortgage as a result of time expiry does not exist according to the system suggested.

If in the case just mentioned another creditor grants the new credit, the old creditor has to assign the Euro-mortgage to the new creditor. This assignment is to be performed by a corresponding declaration of the old creditor, for reasons of security preferably recorded by a notary, and the handing over of the *Hypothekenbrief (cédule hypothécaire)* at the same time. The assignment should be entered into the Land Registry (deviating from the Swiss model).

Even in the case of an alienation of the property charged with the Euro-mortgage this mortgage can continue to exist, if the new creditor agrees, and subsequently be used by the property owner being the new debtor.

It is also possible to create and register the Euro-mortgage initially for the property owner's own benefit thus enabling him, if required, to assign the Euro-mortgage which is already entered into the Land Register to a creditor of his choice by handing over the transferable mortgage deed *(Hypothekenbrief)*.

The *Hypothekenbrief* (officially issued transferable mortgage certificate) shows some features of a negotiable instrument (marketability and easy transferability). As far as this is not desired one has to deviate from the Swiss model.

For the practice of credit operation, the Euro-mortgage delivers a reliable and at the same time comfortable form of security. It is safe in its creation (independent of the initial debt), secured in its continued existence (in case of an alteration of the ini-

---

17 Reference can be made to the publication of the European Community Mortgage Federation on the mortgage credit within the EC (Footnote 2), pp. 423 ff.

tial debt), and finally secured in its transferability and thus easy to re-finance.

The Euro-mortgage is an ideal legal institute for the borrower (consumer) as well, especially if permanently changing interest rates have to be secured or if after the redemption of the first credit a second one is to be secured by the same Euro-mortgage or if the creditor changes. The considerable additional costs for annulment and deletion of the old mortgage and the creation of a new one could be avoided. The same is true for the other financing techniques to which some banks have resorted, e.g. absolute guarantees, pledging of movables, assignments of financial claims or claims against insurances. These securities, which can in some individual cases perhaps be comfortable for the borrower, hold considerable risks for the consumer and his guarantor. These disadvantages could largely be avoided by the creation of the Euro-mortgage. When shaped in the right way it satisfies the interests of the creditor as well as the interests of the borrower, especially since the consumer is in the first place interested in a security which is both economical and contains the minimum of risk to his property.

5   The Obligatory Contract[18] Creating tbe Security

In the suggested Euro-mortgage the legal relationship between the creditor on the one side and the borrower as well as the owner of the real property on the other side consists of three elements:

The basic legal relationship is the *loan contract* between creditor and borrower, thus without participation of the owner of the real property if he is not identical to the borrower. To the essentials of this loan contract belong provisions concerning the volume of the credit, interest rates and redemption as well as a description of the securities which the borrower has to provide.

The second element is the Euro-mortgage created for the creditor allowing access to the charged real property (real liability) and, by the abstract acknowledgment of indebtedness connected to it, to the personal property of the respective debtor (personal liability).

Of special importance is the obligatory security contract concluded between creditor and borrower; the property owner should advisably participate in this conclusion if he is not identical to the borrower.

While the loan contract needs no further explanation in this context and the content of the Euro-mortgage has already been outlined, the importance and main content of the 'security contract' will be described right now.

The 'security contract' (*Sicherungsvertrag*)[19] contains the obligatory relations between creditor and borrower as far as they are covered neither by the loan contract nor by the Euro-mortgage or the abstract acknowledgment of indebtedness connected to it; these are especially the obligation of the borrower to create the Euro-mortgage and the obligation of the creditor to use this security only under the conditions agreed to in the contract. In this way the accessoriness between the Euro-mortgage on the

---

18 In this context the term 'obligatory' means the right in personam (contract *in personam*).
19 For details see Stöcker (1992), pp. 218 ff. and 222.

one hand and the debt in its real size on the other is restored on the obligatory level, since for the reasons mentioned above it would have been a hindrance to realise it on the level of a right *in rem* (as content of the Euro-mortgage). The security contract contains the *causa* of the Euro-mortgage; therefore one could also call it a *pactum de hypothecando*. The security contract makes it possible that the creditor enjoys the un-limited position of a Euro-mortgage in his external relations whereas he is bound by the particular of this legal shaping; the Euro-mortgage should as far as possible be limited to the securing of credits granted by institutional creditors (banks, savings banks, building societies, insurances and state creditors).

Normally, the content of the security contract will contain provisions regarding the creation of the Euro-mortgage, the determination of its purpose, the possibilities of a refinancing or an assignment of the Euro-mortgage as well as the obligation of the creditor to reassign the Euro-mortgage to the property owner or to agree to the can-cellation of its entry (waiver). Moreover, it can be provided that the Euro-mortgage may secure only one particular personal debt and therefore must not be assigned, or that the rights arising out of the Euro-mortgage may not be enforced before the matu-rity (or the paying out) of the credit. Finally, special provisions are required if the borrower and the property owner are not the same person.

Because of the far-reaching importance of the security contract it seems to be ad-visable that the minimum content or the basic conditions of a typical security contract should be determined by law; this would create a softened accessoriness which sup-plies the property owner with sufficient protection against the initial creditor as well as against later assignees.[20] Under no circumstances may the shaping of the security contract be left totally to the discretion of the persons involved or to national legisla-tion.[21] In the continental European states entrusting the certification of the Euro-mortgage to the impartial notary, it could be legally prescribed at the same time that either the security contract has to be recorded as well or that it has at least to be pre-sented on the occasion of the recording of the Euro-mortgage in order to facilitate the control of its compliance with the minimum content determined by law. Furthermore, one could ensure in this way the necessary instruction of the parties about the legal consequences of Euro-mortgage and security contract.

6   Important Questions Regarding Details

Parallel to a legal regulation of a future Euro-mortgage, important questions regard-ing details need to be solved. These details include the question of which way the valid creation of the Euro-mortgage, its specific rank and its later assignment can be made known to the public in states without a system of land registration. But it com-prises also the difficult decision of which peripheral legal fields need to be regulated in a uniform way and which particulars can still be treated according to provisions of national law.

Because of the differing systems of land and land charge registration it will be ad-

---

20 Cf. the succinct formulation of Stümer (1992), p. 388.
21 Stürner (1992).

visable in the interest of legal certainty to introduce an official confirmation of the proper registration of the Euro-mortgage and of its specific rank in relation to other charges on the respective land (*lettre de confirmation uniforme*). The uniform text of this certificate of registration and specific rank should be formulated so broadly that it fits within the legal relations in all EU Member States. The certificate could include declarations on the valid creation according to the *lex loci actus,* on the validity of the declaration of enforceability connected to the mortgage certificate, on the valid registration of the Euro-mortgage according to the *lex loci actus* and on the resulting specific rank of the Euro-mortgage in relation to other land charges. Moreover, it could contain peculiarities of the individual case, e.g. references to the creation of a transferable mortgage document and to the person to whom it has been handed over. Such a certificate could indicate which assignments have taken place or which amendments to the original content of the Euro-mortgage have been effected.

Such certificates will advisably be issued by those persons, authorities or institutions which are generally in charge of the certification of the Euro-mortgage according to the respective domestic law. The *Publizitätswirkung* (in how far can it be treated as notice to the whole world?) and *öffentlicher Glaube* (public reliance) of this certificate should be regulated by law as well; the same applies to the legal consequences of a divergence between the contents of the certificate and actual legal position.

In practice, it will also be of considerable importance, whether the Euro-mortgage – as an alternative to the conventional kinds of land charge in the respective states – may only be created for or assigned to institutional creditors in the widest sense and not for or to private persons. A further problem is caused by the much-discussed question of whether it should be permitted to create the Euro-mortgage initially as an owner's mortgage in order to facilitate an assignment to the final creditor on a later occasion. Practising lawyers seem to agree that each assignment should be subject to the same formal requirements as the creation of the Euro-mortgage itself. It will be incompatible with the future Euro-mortgage to subject this land charge to a time limitation set by law as applied at present to inter alia mortgages according to French law.

7   Results and Prospect

The problems facing the practice of credit operation in regard to the cross-border securing of credits by immoveable property cannot be solved by contemporary Private International Law.

The principle of mutual recognition does not bring about a breakthrough to the European International Market in the field of land charges; mainly in France and Spain numerous difficulties arise from the cumbersome nature of the accessoriness of the mortgage to the underlying debt.[22]

For these reasons, all possible efforts should be made to introduce – besides the

---

22 This has been made clear by the thesis of Stöcker (1992).

national kinds of land charge which continue in existence – a Euro-mortgage being uniformly in force within the EU. Not only economic considerations but also the principles of a well-understood consumer protection count in favour thereof. The Euro-mortgage could be shaped according to the Swiss *Schuldbrief,* embody a personal as well as a real title, be independent of an underlying debt and transferable. Moreover, the specific rank of the Euro-mortgage revealed by the Land Register should not be substantially interfered with by legal privileges and prerogatives not being registered.[23]

On the basis of the experiences of the practice of credit operation in Europe it can be recommended to introduce the Euro-mortgage in addition to the national kinds of mortgage continuing in force. In this way it can prove its value in free competition with the traditional kinds of land charge of domestic law.

The Euro-mortgage will experience this test at first in regard to the cross-border operation of credits secured by immoveable property which soon will be very common in the European Internal Market. The disadvantages of the mortgage accessory to the debt which have already been demonstrated in relation to domestic mortgage credits will be multiplied in relation to cross-border financing, not least as a result of the different laws applicable according to Private International Law.

The time remaining should be used to discuss and to develop the suggestions at hand and perhaps also to add further alternatives. Those competent to do this are in the first place the European law institutes of the universities. Co-operation with the *Fédération Hypothécaire* [European Mortgage Federation] in Brussels and the *Commission des Affaires de l'Union Européenne* within the framework of the International Union of the Latin Notariat (CAUE/UINL) would be advisable.

The importance of the Euro-mortgage is underestimated by those who argue that the introduction of a uniform mortgage in Europe is unrealistic, would undermine the current systems of mortgage credit in the various Member States and would cause insolvable conflict-of-law problems. Therefore, it is argued, one should not continue the project for the creation of a Euro-mortgage, but one should be content with the more limited aim of harmonisation of the various national mortgages.[24] Advocates of this point of view can be accused of unwillingness to develop the project further, although all objections which they put forward may possibly be solved.

As many opponents to the further development of the Euro-mortgage can be found in France,[25] it could be argued that the actual motive for the rejected position could be that the French system of mortgages as contained in the *Code civil* is gradually becoming obsolete and is no longer able to adapt itself to the – also in France – very

---

23 Discussed in detail by Stöcker (1992), pp. 84 ff. and Mortgage credit in the European Community (footnote 2) pp. 222 ff.

24 This is the conclusion which is reached by the French Bank Association *(Association française des Banques* (AFB)) in the 10th International Cadastre Conference *(Congrès international de la publicité foncière* (CINDER)) which was held from 5-8 September 1994 in Paris. Comp. Guy Chauvin: Les techniques juridiques modernes de garantie et la pratique notariale, Rapports officiels du Notariat français pour le Congrès de l'UINL in Berlin 1995, pp. 391 ff.

25 A favourable exception is the Report of the Association of French Land Mortgage Registrars *(Association des Conservateurs des Hypothèques français* (AMC)) for the 10th International Land Register Conference in Paris 1994, pp. 391 ff.

progressive credit market. For it has been established that the amount of mortgages in France is considerably lower than in other comparable Member States with more modern and advantageous mortgage systems. Through the introduction of the Euro-mortgage as an alternative to the *Code civil* mortgage, the influence of the latter could significantly diminish. However, this kind of motive cannot have any place in a scientific debate, as it is based on egoistic, and not on professional arguments.[26]

Looking back, it is amazing to ascertain the diversity of the ideas and proposed legislation in Eastern and Western Europe that have been based on the Euro-mortgage project as well as on the established system of the abstract German *Grundschuld* and the debt-independent Swiss *Schuldbrief* since 1987, when the CAUE first developed the idea of the Euro-mortgage project.

In *Estonia*, it was decided as far back as 1993 to incorporate the abstract *Grundschuld* as sole real right (*hüpoteek*) in its new Law of Property Act, namely in the form of a non-certificated land charge which is created through entry in the land register.[27]

In *Hungary*, there has for some years now been an accessorial hypothec (*jelzálogjog*) alongside a non-accessorial "independent pledge"(*önálló zálogjog*), which can be applied to movables as well as immovables.[28]

---

26 Professional arguments and receptive scientific statements on the other hand, can be found in the Netherlands: e.g. G.R. de Groot & S. Bartels, Goederenrecht in de Europese Unie; Comparative Law, *Ars Aequi* 1994, p. 323; J.B. Vegter, Over het rechtskarakter van de Eurohypotheek, *WPNR* 1993, pp. 55 ff.; A.A. van Velten, Enkele opmerkingen over een nieuwe maatvoering in het goederenrecht, *NJB* 1996, pp. 1042 Cf. For Germany, one could refer to R. Stürner, Dienstbarkeit heute, *AcP* 1994, Band 194, p. 278 Cf. Because of its specific significance for the scientific debate on the Euro-mortgage, part of Stürner's article is cited here: 'Die streng akzessorische französische Hypothek als einziges Grundpfandrecht mit ihrem Streben nach inhaltlicher Gerechtigkeit kommt nur mit mühsamen Korrekturen in Richtung Abstraktion über die Runden. Die englische mortgage kann noch heute ihre sicherungsvertragliche Herkunft (Lease, conveyance) nicht verbergen und ist verglichen mit kontinentalen Grundpfandrechten am wenigsten im Sinne einer Rechtsklarheit und leichten Verkehrsfähigkeit typisiert. In der europäischen Reformdiskussion spielt ein grundschuldähnliches Briefgrundpfandrecht die zentrale Rolle, wenn man sich an bisherigen Vorschlägen zur Europäisierung des Kreditmarktes durch Einführung eines zusätzlichen Eurogrundpfandrechtes orientiert. Die Wahl fiele damit auf eine Typisierung zugunsten der Rechtsklarheit; der individuelle Intressenausgleich wäre in das System nationaler Vertragsrechte verbannt; nationale Typen mit dem Zweck inhaltlicher Kreditkontrolle wären verdrängt. Der weithin wertneutrale und abstrakte Baustein, wie ihn das an Rechtsklarheit und Verkehrsfähigkeit orientierte beschränkte dingliche Recht darstellt, zeigt hier eine Überlegenheit, die allen zu denken geben müßte, die das Abstraktionsprinzip mit allzu leichter Hand wegwischen und sich dabei ... auf das Recht des Kaufs beweglicher Sachen verengen, ohne die weitere Bedeutung des Themas zu erfassen.'
See also: Stöcker (1992), pp. 77 Cf, 89 Cf. 217 Cf.; Stürner (1992), pp. 377Cf. and 386 Cf; Baur/Stürner, *Lehrbuch des Sachenrechts*, 16th edition (München 1992), § 36 VIII; A. Stadler, *Gestaltungsfreiheit und Verkehrsschutz durch Abstraktion – Eine rechtsvergleichende Studie zur abstrakten und kausalen Gestaltung rechtsgeschäftlicher Zuwendungen anhand des deutschen, schweizerischen, österreichischen, französischen und US-amerikanischen Rechts,* Habilitation an der Universität Konstanz (Verlag Mohr, Tübingen 1995), pp. 516 Cf, 606 Cf. and 611-617.
27 §§ 325 ff. of the Law of Property Act of 9 June 1993 (Estonia).
28 Details in Jójárt/Györfi – Tóth: *Immobiliar-Sachenrecht in Ungarn.* Published by the Forschungsinstitut für Mittel- und Osteuropäisches Wirtschaftsrecht, 2nd edition, Vienna 2001. Also Layos Vékás: *Ungarn.* In: Christian von Bahr (publisher): *Sachenrecht in Europa – systematische Einführung und Gesetzestexte.* Band 2, Osnabrück 2000.

On 1 January 2003, *Slovenia*'s new Code of Property Law (SPZ) came into effect, resulting in the introduction of the abstract land charge (*zemliski dolg*), fundamentally as a certificated land charge (*zemliski pismo*), alongside the accessorial hypothec (*hipoteka*).[29]

In *Poland*, the final negotiations in preparation for the introduction of an abstract land charge are currently being conducted.

In *Switzerland*, where the law on immovable property is being partly revised, the Federal Justice Ministry has commissioned a report for the preparation of a hypothec under Swiss law as a paperless pledge subject to registration. In this report,[30] the authors advocate the introduction of an abstract pledge on property entered in the land register without the certification required until now, so in Swiss terminology a *"papierloser Register–Schuldbrief"*. This new arrangement is intended as a modern, more economic alternative alongside the Swiss *Schuldbrief* (with certificate), which will continue to exist. In giving their reasons, the authors refer inter alia to the project of a future Euro-mortgage and quote the second edition of Towards a European Civil Code, pages 551 ff., with its comprehensive bibliography.

BIBLIOGRAPHY: Graf van Bernstorff, Das Hypothekenrecht in den EU-Staaten, *Recht der internationalen Wirtschaft (RIW)* 1997, p. 181; CAUE/UINL, *La Cédule hypothécaire suisse et la dette foncière allemande – Etude comparative, base d'une future Euro-hypothèque.* Published by Stichting tot bevordering der notariële wetenschap (French/German), Amsterdam 1988; CACE/UINL, L 'Eurohypothèque; Rapport de la 'Commission des Affaires de la Communauté Européenne' au sein de l 'Union Internationale du Notariat Latin (CAUE/UINL).* Published by Stichting tot bevordering der notariële wetenschap (French/German), Amsterdam 1992; S. van Erp, NTBR 2003/2 Kronieken; Maria Elena Sánchez Jordán, Antonio Gambaro (red.), *Land Law in Comparative Perspective*, The Hague, Kluwer Law International, 2002 ; Gresser, L 'Eurohypothèque, *Revue Suisse du Notariat et du registre foncier* 1993, p. 337; Habersack, Die Akzessorietät -Strukturprinzip der europäischen Zivilrechte und eines künftigen europäischen Grundpfandrechts, *Juristen-Zeitung* 1997, p. 857; Hamou, L'hypothèque marocaine sur soi-même et l'eurohypothèque, *La Semaine Juridique* 1989, p. 241; Hofmeister, Das Liegenschaftsrecht im Zeichen der Annäherung Österreichs an die Europäische Gemeinschaft, *Österreichische Notariats-Zeitung* 1991, p. 282; Kaindl, Die Eurohypothek, *Österreichische Notariats-Zeitung* 1993, p. 277; Kremer, *De Zwitserse Schuldbrief*, Bachiene-reeks nr. 1, Amsterdam 1997 ; Licini, L'Euroipoteca Cartolare (a proposito di un instituto giuridico che non esiste ancora), *Quadrimestre – Rivista di Diritto Privato* 1993, p. 765; Uwe H. Schneider, Europäische und internationale Harmonisierung des Bankvertragsrechts – Zugleich ein Beitrag zur Angleichung des Privatrechts in der Europäischen Gemeinschaft, *NJW* 1991, p. 1985; Soergel/Stöcker, Elargissement de la Communauté européenne aux pays de l'Est et questions dogmatiques soulevées par le droit immobilier – causalité, droit accessoire et objet du contract de garantie, *Not. Int'l Vol. 7* 2002/3+4; Stadler, *Gestaltungsfreiheit und Verkehrsschutz durch Abstraktion – Eine rechtsvergleichende Studie zur abstrakten und kausalen Gestaltung rechtsgeschäftlicher Zuwendungen anhand des deutschen,*

---

29 Text of the law and notes to the text on the home page www.hypverband.de or www.pfandbrief.org – "Europe + G7" – "Publications" – "Slovenia".

30 Wolfgang Wiegand/Christoph Brunner, *Vorschläge zur Ausgestaltung des Schuldbriefs als papierloses Registerpfand.* Bibliothek zur Zeitschrift für Schweizerisches Recht/Beiheft 39. Helbing & Lichtenhahn, Basel 2003. Prof. Dr. iur. Wolfgang Wiegand teaches at the University of Bern and Dr. iur. Christoph Brunner, LL.M. practises law in Bern and Geneva.

schweizerischen, österreichischen, französischen und US-amerikanischen Rechts, Habilitation, Konstanz 1995, pp. 561 ff., 576 ff., 606 fr. 611 ff., Stöcker, *Die 'Eurohypothek' – Zur Bedeutung eines einheitlichen nicht-akzessorischen Grundpfandrechts für den Aufbau eines 'Europäischen Binnenmarktes für den Hypothekarkredit',* doctoral thesis of the Universität Würzburg, Verlag Duncker & Humblot, Berlin 1992; Stürner, *Das Grundpfandrecht zwischen Akzessorietät und Abstraktheit und die europäische Zukunft,* Festschrift für Rudolf Serick, Heidelberg 1992, p. 377; Stürner, Dienstbarkeit heute, *AcP* 1994, p. 278; Vegter, Over het rechtskarakter van de Eurohypotheek, *WPNR* (6077), 1993, p. 55; Van Velten, Hypotheek en Europese Gemeenschap, *WPNR* (6001), 1991, p. 241; Van Velten, Enkele opmerkingen over een nieuwe maatvoering in het goederenrecht *NJB* 1996, p. 1042; Van Velten, Asser *Goederenrecht* 3-III (Kluwer Deventer 2003) nr. 214; Wachter, La garantie de crédit transfrontalier sur les immeubles au sein de l'Union européenne, L'Eurohypothèque, *Not. Int'l Vol. 4* (1999), pp. 174 ff.; Wehrens, Der schweizer Schuldbrief und die deutsche Briefgrundschuld – Ein Rechtsvergleich als Basis für eine zukünftige Eurohypothek, *Österreichische Notariats-Zeitung* 1988, p. 181; Wehrens, Das Projekt einer Europhypothek –, Rückblick und Ausblick, *WPNR* (6126), 1994, p. 170; van Wilmowsky, *Europäisches Kreditsicherungsrecht – Sachenrecht und Insolvenzrecht unter dem EG- Vertrag,* Tübingen 1996, pp. 80 ff., 154 ff.

G – Trust

CHAPTER 43

Trust and *Fiducie*

Michel Grimaldi* & François Barrière**

While the trust is well known in common law countries,[1] it has often been presented as an unknown institution in civil law countries. The source of civil law is – generally speaking – Roman law. An English writer has stated that "we shall not find the trust, as a general institution, in Roman Law".[2] If the trust institution is unknown in civil law countries, is it because there would be no interest in adopting such an institution? Or, is it because the institution itself has not yet been or cannot be accepted in a civil law system? In other words: is it desirable and feasible to expand the trust institution throughout Europe, as the November 15, 2001 European Parliament resolution on the approximation of the civil and commercial law of the Member States seems to suggest?[3]

Different kinds of trusts exist: some arise out of a voluntary decision (express trusts) and some are construed by judges after an interpretation of facts, or imposed by legislators (these are known as implied, constructive, or resulting trusts). In this chapter, we will focus on the common law express trust and on the civil law *fiducie* (which is often considered as the trust's civil law equivalent), since time does not allow a thorough study of the other kinds of trust.

The Roman *fiducia* has sometimes been presented as the ancestor of the trust. Without debating the precise origin of the trust, there is at least one interesting comparison, namely the primary development of the *fiducia* and the trust. A striking parallel can be drawn between the two.[4] At the beginning, the transfer of property made to one for the benefit of another was sanctioned neither by the *fiducia* nor the trust. In each case, recourse was made to remedies to modify this situation, and these remedies were provided by a body of law: the Praetor in Roman law, the Chancellor in

---

* Professor of Law at the University Panthéon-Assas (Paris II); General Secretary of the *Association Henri Capitant*.
** University Panthéon- Assas (Paris II).

1 Maitland (1957), p. 129: "If we were asked what is the greatest and most distinctive achievement performed by Englishmen in the field of jurisprudence, I cannot think that we should have any better answer to give than this, namely the development from century to century of the trust idea". Hayton (1998), p. 1: "Trusts play a vital role in British society".

2 Buckland (1911), pp. 14-15; *see also*: Johnston (1988), p. 1.

3 Official Journal of the European Communities, June 13, 2002, C140E/541. This Resolution was drafted in both English and French; it proposes, *inter alia*, a cooperation to find common legal concepts and solutions and a common legal terminology of the legal systems of the Member States in various fields. One of these fields is the law on trusts, pursuant to the English version (No.14.a). A discrepancy exists, however, with the French version which refers to "*droit des ententes*", i.e. anti-trust law (which is a branch of economic law, rather than civil and commercial laws). This example shows the risks associated with any enterprise aiming to unify laws of jurisdictions that do not use the same language, as well as the necessity to use the official languages of all, or at least most, Member States for an harmonisation of laws to be efficient.

4 For the regime of the various *fiducies* in Roman law, *see* Monier (1947), at pp. 110 *et seq.*

English law. The *fiducia* disappeared as Roman law invented other legal tools which were more flexible and offered more efficient remedies. Mechanisms similar to the *fiducia* reappeared and modern *fiducies* exist in some European countries.[5] The *fiducie*, like the express trust,[6] involves three actors who embark upon a triangular relationship. The course of events can schematically be described as follows: the first actor, the *constituant* (settlor), transfers some or all of his assets to a *fiduciaire* (trustee), who will then hold them, for a particular purpose, for the benefit of one or more *bénéficiaires* (cestuis que trust).

First of all, we will try to demonstrate that it is desirable that the trust, or its civil law equivalent, expands throughout Europe. Secondly, we will examine the feasibility of expanding a trust device throughout Europe.

1 Desirability of a Trust Throughout Europe

The trust first appeared in the Middle Ages in England. In European countries, an equivalent institution to the trust has often been either adopted or considered for adoption. Historically, we should question why European countries other than England have felt, or currently feel, the need to incorporate a similar institution to the English trust into their legal system. At least one main reason is apparent, it being the interdependency between countries, which can be illustrated by economic competition and duplications of conventions between countries.

1.1 Economic Competition

The 20th century has seen dynamic change; economically this has principally been represented by increasing competition between countries. Economic barriers have, step by step, been lowered, and consequently economic exchange between countries has increased.

1.1.1 Legal Systems

One of the elements influencing economic competition is the legal system of each country. A business decision cannot be made without taking into account the legal means that can be used in order to achieve its aim. Legal means have a cost.[7] There-

---

5   *See*, for reports on *fiducies* exising in different European countries, *La fiducie en droit moderne* (1937); Seel-Viandon (1979); *Les opérations fiduciaires* (1985); *La fiducie ou le trust dans les droits occidentaux francophones* (1990); *La fiducie et ses applications dans plusieurs pays européens* (1991); *Principles of European Trust Law* (1999). *See also* Wulf (1965); *La fiducie face au* trust *dans les rapports d'affaires* (1999). For French *fiducies, see* especially Witz (1981); Grimaldi (1991); Barrière (2001).

6   Trust comes from the Danish *trost* (confidence), *troster* (faith). *Fiducie* comes from the Latin *fiducia* (confidence), *fides* (faith). For the requirements of an express trust, *see* Edwards and Stockwell (2002), pp. 79 *et seq.*

7   Notwithstanding the fact that legal tools are too often chosen for tax reasons. May we remind our legislators that competition would improve if legal tools were chosen for their own characteristics rather than for simple tax savings.

fore, companies, as well as individuals, usually take into account the various characteristics of the tools before choosing one. If they are unable to find an appropriate tool within their national legal system, they will more often try to find it elsewhere. In this way, some major French companies have decided to make use of the common law trust because the French system does not offer a similar institution.

1.1.2 Reaction of the French government

The French government could not continue to tolerate the use of foreign tools in such cases, due solely to a loop-hole in the French civil law. In an attempt to incorporate a device analogous to the common law trust into the French system,[8] the French government presented a draft to Parliament to introduce the *fiducie* on February 20, 1992. Practitioners such as bankers[9] and notaries[10] requested that the *fiducie* should become an integral part of the French system. This draft has not been adopted by the French Parliament (mainly due to tax concerns), since it has not yet been debated[11] nor even discussed.[12] The draft Act is ambitious in that it is without doubt the most comprehensive proposal to create a complete and general regime of *fiducie* in a European country.[13] We will go on to describe some of its potential practical uses, but before doing that, we shall just remind the reader that mechanisms corresponding to the *fiducie* do already exist in French law but under other names.[14] In addition, it should be noted that in 1996, a new draft was prepared by the French government. To resolve the tax issue, i.e. the risk that transfers of ownership be made by individuals to *fiduciaires* in favour of third parties, with the sole purpose of evading inheritance taxes, this new draft (which has not been submitted to the French Parliament) proposed that only legal entities be entitled to set up a *fiducie*, i.e. to become settlor. Representatives of the current French government recently confirmed that a new draft on *fiducie* might be prepared and could be submitted to the French Parliament in the future.

---

8   When an institution has proved to be useful, it has a tendency to seep into other legal systems; *see* Schwartz (1952). See also Oppetit (1990). Larroumet (1990), #4: *"A l'évidence l'avant-projet de loi sur le contrat de fiducie est inspiré du* trust"; Barrière (2001).

9   *See* Cerles (1990).

10 *See* Charlin (1985); Travaux du 86è Congrès des Notaires de France (1990), pp. 56 *et seq.*

11 Much has already been written on the issue. *See, inter alia*: Barrière (2001) ; Bénabent (1993); Berger (1993); Cantin Cumyn (1992); Chapelle and Guillenschmidt (1992); Denoix de Saint Marc and Guillenschmidt (1992); Grimaldi (1991); Guillenschmidt (1990)(1991); Larroumet (1990-1)(1990-2)(1991); Le Gall (1992); Pézard (1990)(1991); Pisani (1990); Witz (1990)(1991)(1993); *Communiqué de la Chancellerie, Projet de loi relatif à la fiducie* (1992); *La fiducie ou du* trust *dans les droits occidentaux francophones* (1990); *La fiduce pour quoi faire?* (1990); *La fiducie, contribution à l'avant-projet de loi* (1990); *La fiducie et ses applications dans plusieurs pays européens* (1991); *La fiducie, une révolution sous notre droit* (1990); *La transmission des entreprises, vaincre l'obstacle* (1990); *Spécial fiducie* (1990); Trust *et fiducie: projet français et pratique internationale* (1991).

12 Technically, this draft proposal no longer exists since the French government has not presented it to Parliament since the end of the 1992 parliamentary year.

13 On the other side of the Atlantic Ocean, in Quebec, the new Civil Code of Quebec, which has been in effect since January 1, 1994, also proposes a general regime of *fiducie*. Prior to that the *Code civil du Bas-Canada* only proposed a very limited number of applications for the *fiducie*.

14 These *fiducies* are unnamed. This has been developed at length by Witz (1981), by Schmidt, Witz and Bismuth (1985), pp. 305 *et seq.*, and by Grimaldi (1991), #3.

1.1.3   Possible Practical Uses

The trust has a very wide range of practical applications. The *fiducie* could also have numerous applications in civil law countries. However, trusts have a far wider scope of use than the *fiducie* will have. This is because the French system and other civil law systems already have various different institutions which play a role equivalent to that of the trust.[15]

a   Legal Environment

The trust has been developed since the Middle Ages and has been used to achieve various goals. When the trust first appeared, the English legal system was not very sophisticated and was still in the early stages of development. The use, the ancestor of the trust, was itself used at the beginning because the English system did not offer enough flexibility nor adequate legal tools.[16] For example, the use and the trust were used by knights leaving for the Crusades where a knight who was leaving for a long period, whose wife and children were not entitled to hold the family land, would transfer the land to someone he could trust so that the latter could hold it on behalf of his wife and children.

However, most civil law systems at present have a series of institutions which largely duplicate the role fulfilled by the trust today. For this reason, if other institutions already offer a means of achieving the same result, a civil law *fiducie* may not present as much interest as the common law trust. Moreover, a device which is imported into an already existing legal system has to respect the foundations of that system, therefore a new device can only be accepted if it respects the principles of that system. Public policy rules, which may differ between countries, may limit the scope of a device, since the device must respect mandatory rules and cannot depart from them. In this way, a *fiducie* device has to respect such rules and as a result may be less flexible in some countries than in others.

Practical applications of the trust can be divided into two categories, being, management and securities interests. There follows a description of how the trust device operates in each of these categories.

b   Trust as a management device

The English trust is used to manage property in various cases, especially because of its flexibility. It can be created in order to simplify business structures when there are frequent changes in beneficial ownership of property, or in order to create financial empires. A trust may also be used to limit the use of certain characteristics of ownership, such as the power to transfer assets.[17] Trusts are also used to manage chattels in the broadest sense of the term, including the transfer of chattels themselves from one

---

15 Lepaulle (1932), at p. 114: the trust is *"l'ange gardien de l'anglo-saxon"*, *"il le suit partout, impassible depuis son berceau jusqu'à sa tombe"*.

16 It is true that the English use also arose as a means of escaping feudal taxes.

17 For practical examples of the English trust used as a management device, *see* Elland-Goldsmith (1991), pp. 73 *et seq.*

person to another, as well as estate plans. Charitable foundations are also usually a form of trust.[18]

In Germany, the *Treuhand* is the device most similar to the English trust. The German version of the management trust is called the '*Verwaltungstreuhand*'. The *Verwaltungstreuhand* is a concept which corresponds to various management environments as diverse as Euro-market operations by banks for individuals and stockholder relationships with companies, where the *Verwaltungstreuhand* can be used as a tool to simplify procedures.[19] The Netherlands have a management trust device;[20] the new Civil Code proposal planned to bring in a new device, the *bewind*, to replace it. The proposal to introduce the *bewind* has, however, not been enacted.[21] The *bewind*, if in effect, would not have transferred ownership, only the powers of management would have been transferred. Although the *bewind* could serve the same purpose as the trust, in the absence of a transfer of property, it would be a very poor cousin of the trust device, which can award the trustee property rights. The French proposal to introduce the *fiducie* in the French system could be used to facilitate both management of chattels and business, and also transfers, particularly of family businesses.[22]

The few examples of practical management applications of the trust device in different countries show that a trust can represent a real interest, even if its use may differ, depending on the other existing devices in each country.

c   Trust as a security interest device

The English trust is used in the creation and enforcement of security interests.[23] However, the trust will also create rights of a real nature in favor of the cestuis que trust of the trust.[24] In Germany, the *Treuhand* security interest, the *Sicherungstreuhand*,[25] is highly developed; it is often used as a security interest for movables. It can represent a property transfer of either chattels or capital, where its success is partially due to the fact that it does not share the drawbacks of possession.[26] The Netherlands used to have a transfer of property device used as a security interest. However, the new Civil Code of the Netherlands did not maintain this, preferring non-possessory liens to the trust device. In France, the use of property as a security interest has developed in the past decade. Property has been used in two ways. First of all, reservations of title

---

18 For a presentation of the modern functional uses of the trust device, *see* Dyer and van Loon (1984), pp. 40 *et seq.* and Edwards and Stockwell (2002), pp. 53 *et seq.*

19 For more details, *see* Blaurock (1985), at pp. 224 *et seq.* and Jahn (1991) and pp. 61 *et seq. See* also Kötz (1999-4), p. 55.

20 Kortmann and Verhagen (1999), pp. 196 *et seq.* For the Dutch regime prior to the new Civil Code, *see* Meinertzhagen-Limpens (1985).

21 For a discussion on the *bewind's* legislative process, and the final decision of the Dutch legislator to refuse trusts to be created under Dutch law, *see* Koppenol-Laforce and Kottenhagen (1999), p. 293.

22 Guillenschmidt (1990).

23 *See* Tettenborn (1999), pp. 57 *et seq.*

24 A heated debate exists in the Anglo-American legal community as to the precise nature of the *cestui que* trust's rights. *See* Waters (1967). It is not the purpose of this chapter neither to present the debate nor to take any position.

25 *See* H. Kötz (1999-2), p. 89.

26 For examples of the practical uses of the *Sicherungstreuhand*, *see* Jahn (1991), pp. 62 *et seq. See* also: Kötz (1999-1), No. 5.

have been used for security purposes. Reservation of title is an agreement in which the seller retains the property of the chattel until complete payment. Secondly, transfers of title for security purposes also developed in France. This is a kind of trust device since property is dedicated to a special purpose as it guarantees payment. The transfer of property as a security interest has enjoyed large success with professionals who use this kind of unnamed *fiducie*.[27] If the *fiducie* were to be generally introduced, it could also often be used as a useful and powerful security interest. Property proved to be the most efficient protection against the insolvency of the debtor. More and more non-possessory security devices are desired and the trust device can be one of these.

The flexibility of the trust device allowed it to be used for numerous purposes. Countries may have other devices to fulfil some of these purposes but the trust's versatility often means that it is the most attractive option. The introduction of a trust device throughout Europe should be, to a varying extent, desirable.

1.2 Desirability due to the impact of International Conventions

1.2.1 The Hague Trust Convention

The Hague Convention on the Law Applicable to Trusts and on their Recognition (the 'Hague Trust Convention'), dated July 1, 1985, resulted from a process of research and negotiation over a period of several years. Civil law countries have faced increasing complications due to the extensive use of the trust in international affairs. This has been due mainly to the growing use of trusts by economic actors in transnational business, but also the mobility of individuals themselves. Foreigners from common law countries tried to import the trust into civil law countries; individuals from civil law countries sometimes became involved in trust relationships during their stay in common law countries. Civil law courts were faced with difficult situations and difficult choices when having to deal with trusts, since trusts did not exist in their country. Civil law courts could (i) decide to ignore the trust, (ii) draw an analogy between the trust and a civil law category, or (iii) consider the trust as a completely independent institution and treat it as such. French courts have given different responses throughout the 20th century. These can be divided into two principal groups.

Initially, French courts tried to assimilate the English trust into an existing French institution.[28] In this way, the trust was sometimes qualified into a form of legal representation of the settlor.[29] The English trust has also been analysed as being a form of the old French *fiducie*.[30] Later, French courts tried to respect the originality of the trust device.[31] French courts have also tried to respect the finality of the trust itself.

---

27 The January 2, 1981 Act (as modified by the January 24, 1984 Act) organises the transfer of professional claims used as security interests, in other words, dedicated to a specific purpose.
28 *See* Panhard (1987), at p. 28.
29 Trib. Seine, 10 December, 1880, Clunet 1881. 435; Trib. Seine, 26 December, 1894, Clunet 1895. 587; Trib. civ. Seine, 28 June, 1901, Clunet 1901. 812; Gaz. Pal. 1901-2. 71; D. 1902-2. 36; Paris 27 January, 1904, D.P. 1905. 2. 356.
30 *See* Trib. civ. Seine, 19 December, 1916, Clunet 1917. 1069.
31 Paris, 18 February, 1909, Clunet 1910. 1144 stated that the trust had no equivalent in France.

These judgements also had to qualify the trust as a civil law institution already known to the French legal system. Most of the qualifications then made were intended to respect the effects of the trusts.[32] Nevertheless, the French courts were still not able to fully accept the trust as an original institution as the trust could not be easily incorporated into civil law categories and had to be translated into them.[33]

The Hague Trust Convention will (once it is ratified) allow the effects of trusts to be recognised in France. This Convention has been analysed in depth by many legal scholars.[34] We will limit our presentation to the objective of the Hague Trust Convention and the means used to achieve this objective.

The main objective of the Hague Trust Convention is to provide automatic and complete recognition of trusts, or, more precisely, of express trusts.[35] So as to fulfil this objective, the Hague Trust Convention had to enable civil law courts to determine what constituted a trust. For this purpose, Article 2 of the Hague Trust Convention lays down the characteristics of the trust. No reference is made to equity or equitable ownership; otherwise, legal systems which do not have equity as one of their legal branches would have encountered difficulties. The main characteristics which are laid down are that (i) the assets constitute a separate fund, (ii) the title stands in the trustee's name, and (iii) the trustee must respect the terms of the trust. The trust will then be governed by the law chosen by the settlor or, if no law has been designated, the law which is the most closely connected will apply.[36]

It is true that the Hague Trust Convention is not intended to, and will not, incorporate the trust device into the legal system of countries which did not previously have this institution. Once the Hague Trust Convention is in full effect, countries which have ratified it will be able to (i) recognise trusts established under a foreign law and (ii) give them full effect. To allow foreign trusts to have effect in a country whose legal system cannot allow the creation of the same device would create a serious situation of unfair competition where on the one hand, a foreign trust would have legal consequences and, on the other hand, local actors could not establish the same effects for the sole reason that this legal system did not permit such a device to be created.

1.2.2 Other International Conventions

In addition to the Hague Trust Convention, other conventions also advocate the introduction of the trust device in European countries which have not yet incorporated it in their legal systems. That is because some conventions make reference to the trust, either to exclude it from their scope or to expressly include it in their scope.

---

32 Trib. Civ. Pau, 3 July, 1956, Gaz. Pal. 1956, 2, 339; Paris, 10 January, 1970, D. 1972. 122, comment Malaurie; RCDIP 1971. 518, comment Droz; Gaz. Pal., 1970. I. 313, comment R.S.; Clunet 1973, 207, comment Loussouarn; TGI Bayonne, 28 April, 1975, RCDIP 1976. 331, comment Necker; JCP 1975. II. 18168, comment R.B.; Rép. Commaille 1976. 463, comment Droz.

33 For a recent analysis, *see* Barrière (2001), #157 *et seq* ; Lequette (1996), especially #19 and 20.

34 For an analysis in French, *see* Gaillard and Trautman (1985); Jauffret-Spinosi (1987); Revillard (1986); Gaillard (1990); Reymond (1991). For an analysis in English, *see* Gaillard and Trautman (1987); Dyer (1993); Underhill and Hayton (1995) at pp. 939 *et seq.*; Kötz (1999-3).

35 The scope of the Hague Trust Convention is limited to express trusts.

36 Article 7 of the Hague Trust Convention lays down a series of criteria which will be used to ascertain the law with which a trust is most closely connected.

The Rome Convention relating to the applicable law of contractual obligations, dated June 19, 1980, for example, excludes from its scope of application, in its Article 1, Paragraph 3, under 8, both the creation of trusts and the relationships arising from existing trusts.

The Brussels Convention, dated September 27, 1968, aims to expand a system of automatic recognition of judgments. Article 5, under 6, of this Convention provides that a defendant can defend an action brought against him as settlor, trustee or *cestui que* trust, before the national courts of the country where the trust is based.

Is it not abnormal that judges should have to determine whether or not a device is a trust (in order to establish whether or not a convention applies), even though the judges may not know the definition of such trusts? Of course, judges could always use foreign law to determine what constitutes a trust. However, one of the aims of international conventions is to simplify international relationships, the reason being that if in order to determine whether a convention applies a judge has to refer to foreign law regarding a specific device, then at the end of the day the mechanism will not have been adequately simplified.

If trust devices could be implemented in countries which do not include them in their legal systems, various advantages would result such as, for example, it would enable actors to use similar tools and therefore increase fair competition between corporations and legal devices that could be used by individuals; and it would also simplify transnational transactions.

2   Feasibility of a European Trust

The English trust has often been analysed as having a unique structure. Nonetheless, is the trust device so tied by its structure that other national legal systems could not adapt it?

2.1   Structure of the Trust

2.1.1   Historical Development

History is always a very useful tool as the analysis of historical developments allows a better understanding of present phenomena.

Before the trust, the English use existed.[37] Its mechanism was as follows: a feoffor transferred to a feoffee the right to use the legal ownership of some – or all – of what he owed, and the feoffee undertook to use the property for the benefit of the *cestui que* use.

The use first existed as early as the 12th century.[38] The common law courts did not, however, offer adequate protection to the *cestui que* use if the feoffee misapplied the property. As per the *cestui que* use request, the English Chancellor recognised an enforceable right in equity in favor of the *cestui que* use. However, the use was too often used to escape feudal tax obligations.

---

37 For an historical outline, *see* Hanbury & Martin (2001), pp. 5 *et seq*.
38 Fratcher, p. 9; Lepaulle (1964), at p. 227: "The 'use' appears as born in a complete legal vacuum".

For this reason, the 16th century English legislation tried to stop the use of uses. However, it was already too late since the use was much too helpful; it could not be allowed to disappear without being replaced. Therefore, the statute's prohibition was not respected and the former use reappeared under a new name and was called the trust. The equity jurisdiction continued to recognise the interests of the *cestui que* trust in the trust.

The common law trust is influenced by the duality of titles which are held by the trustee-legal title, and by the *cestui que* trust-equitable title. This duality of titles was created by the equity courts. Such a duality of proprietary titles does not exist in the civil law systems. *Prima facie*, the common law trust is a pure product of Equity, which is unknown in the civil law system.

It is also for historical reasons that the express trust was created by a unilateral declaration of the settlor, as opposed to a contract between the settlor and the trustee.[39] The common law did not enable co-contractors to stipulate for the benefit of third parties.[40] The *fiducie* usually may take the form of a contract. The distinction between the creation of the device – unilateral declaration vs. contract – does not necessarily imply that the two devices are different, in light of the fact that it is the substance that will result from the modes of creation of the device that it is important, and that will characterize whether the two institutions are similar (or even identical) or not.

Finally, it is true that, historically, the English trust was created by day-to-day uses, without any legislation providing for it, and that its validity and enforceability have been decided by Courts, without any statute providing for a trust regime. Here again, this historical characteristic – the absence of trust law – does not mean that the equivalent to the trust could not be created by specific legislation if needed. Provided that the essential characteristics of the trust are met by the legislation, then the reception of the trust could be achieved. Furthermore, it should be noted that the absence of statute law on trusts in England is no longer true . It is still correct that there is no English Act providing for all of the parts of the regime of trusts; a number of statutes, however, have specific provisions on various aspects of trusts, including, recently, the Trustee Act of 2000, which, *inter alia*, makes a number of provisions on trustees' duties of care.[41]

2.1.2   Obstacles to a Trust Device in Civil Law

Two main obstacles have been presented as reasons for not permitting the introduction of a trust device in civil law namely the unity of patrimonium and the civil law concept of ownership. Neither of the two arguments is convincing.

---

39 For a recent analysis of the contractarian basis of the trust, *see* Langbein (1995).
40 The English Third Party Beneficiary Act (1999) modified this privity of contract rule, and permits third party to benefit from contracts.
41 Among these provisions, one of them permits a trustee to be bound by duties of care of a lesser degree, which may seem surprising in light of the fact that the fiduciaries duties of the trustees have for a long time been one of the main asset of the device.

a   Concept of Ownership

Civil law systems will not be able to create a duality of ownership. The *fiducie* does not require such a duality of property to be created. However, the Hague Trust Convention did not specify the duality of ownership as a fundamental characteristic of the trust device as the mere fact that the *fiducie* does not create a duality of ownership is not enough to consider the *fiducie* as a non-trust device.

The *fiducie* will result in a transfer of property to a *fiduciaire*. The *fiduciaire* will be the only one to have any property rights in the assets put in *fiducie*. The *fiducie* has been presented as contrary to civil law principles because it would create an unauthorised dismemberment of ownership. While it is true that the *fiduciaire* may not have as many powers as the previous owners, nevertheless the *fiduciaire* will be in sole control of the property. Therefore, absolutely no dismemberment of property is created by a *fiducie* and no criticism can be made in this respect. Other criticisms have been made concerning the property which was going to be the *fiduciaire*'s. It has been alleged that this property would be of a different nature than usual civil law property. In this respect it is true that the *fiduciaire* will be unable to use the property as a normal owner would. The *fiduciaire* will, for example, not be permitted to use the property so as to benefit from it nor will he be able to transfer it to another, under any condition. Nevertheless, this special property is not the first to be reduced from the usual scope of common property. Property acquired under a clause binding the acquiror not to resell is a perfect precedent, having a different scope than traditional property; and no criticism has been made in this regard, precisely because the 'new' property arrangement could be incorporated into civil law. Property transferred to the *fiduciaire* will be a special ownership arrangement, and it should also be able to be integrated into civil law. This property will be a fiduciary property, property not to be used personally by the *fiduciaire* but to be used according to the end to which it is devoted and in respect of the confidence given to the *fiduciaire*. The civil law concept of ownership is, therefore, not an obstacle to the introduction of *fiducies* in civil law countries.

b   Unity of Patrimony

It has often been considered in civil law countries that 'each person has a patrimony, each person only has one patrimony'. This construction is essentially due to the reading by some French authors of some provisions of the French Civil Code. The French proposal aiming to introduce the *fiducie*, if it is enacted, will make the *fiduciaire* have two patrimonies namely his personal patrimony and that of the *fiducie*. Would this dual patrimony be contrary to civil law principles?

Instances of multiple patrimonies have been increasing incessantly. For example, French law offers the possibility for one person to create a legal entity all by himself, in other words to create a second patrimony. Thus the *fiducie* would represent merely one further exception to the principle of the unity of patrimony. In any case, it is not so much the *fiduciaire*'s patrimonium which is divided as that of the settlor since the settlor puts aside some assets whereas the *fiduciaire* does not receive in his personal patrimony assets which are appropriated for a special purpose.

In order for the *fiducie* to be as efficient as the trust, it must also protect the interests of the *bénéficiaire*. The trust assets are part of a trust fund which separates them from the trustee's personal assets. The *fiducie* assets also have to be separated from the *fiduciare*'s personal assets. The separation of the different kinds of assets is a very efficient means of ensuring protection of their appropriation, and of the interests of the *bénéficiaires* and the cestuis que trust. If the trust and the *fiducie* have a different structure, essentially due to the existence or absence of an equity jurisdiction, is it nevertheless possible to obtain a device similar to the trust concept throughout Europe?

2.2 Concept of the trust device

2.2.1 Similarity of characteristics

The basic idea of the common law trust and of the civil law *fiducie* is very similar in that the assets are going to be transferred so as to be used only for a certain purpose,[42] an appropriation; the assets being devoted to a specific end.

We will try to illustrate the characteristics of the *fiducie* and of the trust, appropriation for a purpose and confidence in the actor who has to carry out that purpose, and compare the effects of these two regimes, which should not be too dissimilar, since the same characteristics underlie both institutions.

The French government draft provides that the *fiduciaire* will have only those powers to manage and to dispose which have been contractually laid down. Therefore, it is not necessary to give every power of an owner to the *fiduciaire*. The *constituant* can decide that only some powers of ownership should be given to the *fiduciaire*. The *constituant* can of course decide to transfer every power he has. Such appropriated transfers will create a property which will be a tool to achieve the contractual objective. The *fiduciaire* is entrusted with the management of the assets whereas the *bénéficiaires* will be entitled to the profits of those assets. Such a dissociation seems to make the *fiducie* similar in effect to the common law trust. The trustee – the holder of the legal interest[43] – has the powers of management and the title to the assets, whereas the *cestui que* trust – the holder of the beneficial interest[44] – is the party entitled to the benefits of the trust. In both systems, the beneficial enjoyment of the property is separated from its management. Like the trustee (legal owner), the *fiduciaire* is also an owner, he can have the powers of an owner, and he is not allowed to exercise his powers in his personal interest.

These two dualities of ownership, legal interest and *propriété juridique* (property which is not amputated from the fructus) on the one hand, beneficial interest and *propriété économique* (which gives the benefit to the cestuis que trust and *bénéficiaires*) on the other, have indeed very similar effects. The assets are owned in

---

42 *See* Guinchard (1976), at p. 15: "*Affecter, c'est à la fois choisir un but et le réaliser par des techniques appropriées*".
   Lepaulle (1933), at p. 20, defined a patrimony by appropriation: "Every individual, every legal entity has a patrimonium. Now the *res* of a trust presents this extremely striking feature that it is a patrimonium which of being crystallised around an individual or legal entity, owes its unity to the end to which it is devoted, i.e., to its appropriation".

43 This is a mere short-hand term; a trustee can hold a beneficial title if a beneficial interest was passed.

44 Comp. Maitland (1936), at p. 17: "Equity did not say that the *cestui que* trust was the owner of the land, it said that the trustee was the owner of the land, but added that he was bound to hold the land for the *cestui que* trust".

both cases by the trustee-*fiduciaire*, but the proprietary interest will be used and the assets managed to achieve the purpose of the transfer of assets.[45] In both systems, neither the *fiduciaire* nor the trustee have a simple management objective; they both also have to achieve the appropriation of the assets, to achieve the objective which is its purpose. In both the trust and the *fiducie*, the title to the assets stands in the name of the trustee and the *fiduciaire* and the latter has the power and duty to manage them.

This devotion to an end, this appropriation, is very clearly demonstrated by the fact that, in both systems, there exists a criminal sanction for the principal actor, trustee or *fiduciaire*, using the appropriated property, trust fund or *fiducie*, which is his property (holder of the legal title or of *droits*). A 'normal' owner would never be sanctioned criminally for his use of his property! The autonomy of the assets is therefore incomplete as the autonomy is limited by the devotion to the end, the appropriation, which is why the assets left the first actor (settlor or *constituant*) in the first place.

The English courts constructed the trust so that the trust assets do not form part of the trustee's own estate in order to protect the interests of the cestuis que trust. The French proposal to introduce the *fiducie* takes this necessity into account with the autonomous fund it proposes. To a lesser extent, German judges also protect the beneficiary of the *Treuhand* by creating an appropriated fund with similar effects, but only for some categories of assets.

Perhaps the major difference between the two regimes is that common law courts have a wider range of matters in which they may intervene. Not only do the courts intervene if the objective has become too difficult to accomplish, they also do so when their advice is sought by a trustee who is not sure of his powers. A trustee can ask the court for advice and can seek the direction of the court on any question concerning the management of the trust property. The role of the courts has led one author to say:

'*le trust vit à l'ombre du Palais de Justice qui lui apporte à la fois le conseil et le contrôle. Ce rôle de conseiller, un peu étonnant de prime abord pour un juriste français, est constant*'.[46]

The court's power to enlarge the management or administrative powers of the trustee over the trust property is extensive. The court has the right to override a direction despite a contrary provision in the deed.[47] A court's decision is considered to be a discharge of the trustee's responsibility in the matter. However, while the courts will advise on whether a trustee may take certain action, they have consistently refused to exercise a discretion for the trustee.[48] Principally, the courts seem to intervene if the

---

45 The proprietary interest is in principle never managed for the sole benefit of the trustee or *fiduciaire*. It is also true that, in common law, a trustee can never also be the *cestui que* trust (except if other persons are also *cestui que* trust). The French proposal to introduce the *fiducie* would allow one exception, which would be a *fiduciaire* could receive property as a security interest for his sole benefit.

46 Lepaulle (1932), at p. 207.

47 Re O'Brien (1958), 15 D.L.R. (2nd) 484 (N.S.).

48 *See*, for example, Re Warden (1928), 34 O.W.N. 146 where the courts refused to advise whether certain stock should be sold.

cestuis que trust are, for any reason, incapacitated. Under the French proposal, the *fiduciaire* will be allowed to ask the Court to modify his objective if it has become too difficult to accomplish. The same regime as that of the *'révision des charges'* will apply.[49] This is a significant proposal, for the *fiduciaire*'s powers are established by contract and the French system does not normally allow courts to interfere with contracts, which are supposed to be the sole field of the parties. However, French law has already witnessed a continual increase in the powers of judges to intervene in the field of contracts. Initially, the legislation gave more and more power to judges to control the content of contractual provisions. Secondly, judges themselves have developed such a power. Judges have principally used two tools to achieve this, namely they controlled abuses in the use of rights[50] and also checked that the parties performed their obligations in good faith.[51] Such a possibility has to be approved.[52] Yet, the situation will frequently arise, especially when a *fiducie* is supposed to last for many years, that new circumstances prevent the *fiduciaire* from performing his role. For this reason, the transfer of assets will best be achieved if the fiduciary has the necessary powers. In our view, a trust should not be modified if the modification would prevent the original purpose of the trust from being achieved; this would permit the appropriation to be fully respected. The ends to which they are devoted should allow such modifications of powers as are necessary for the fulfillment of the purpose or objective of either one of the institutions allowing for the purpose of the *fiducie* or of the trust to be respected in the fullest way possible.

2.2.2 Method to be Used to Incorporate the Trust Device

a Transferring Ipso Facto the Trust

A method that could be envisaged to incorporate the trust device throughout Europe would be to transfer the common law trust, in its entirety, into the civil law systems.

However, this method does not seem to be feasible. As we have seen, the structure of the trust is profoundly linked to the development of equity jurisdiction in England and the duality of ownerships which resulted from it. Civil law countries do not know such duality of jurisdictions, since they never developed an equity jurisdiction. The

---

49 For the regime of the *révision des charges*, (Articles 900-2 to 900-8 C. civ.) see, especially, Witz (1985) and Boulanger (1985).

50 *See*, already, Req., 3 August, 1915, D. 1917. I. 19.

51 *See* especially the recent following cases which are of fundamental practical importance and extended the power of judges to control good faith performance in the price fixing of long-term contracts: Civ. 1, 29 November, 1994, *Alcatel*, Bull. civ. 1994, I, #348; JCP éd. G., 1995. II. 22371, comment Ghestin; D. 1995. 122, comment Aynès; RTD civ. 1995. 358, comment Mestre; JCP éd. E., 1995. II. 662, comment Leveneur; Contrats, conc, consom, February 1995, #24, comment Leveneur; Déf. 1994. 335, comment Delebecque; and C. Cass, Ass. Plein., 1 December, 1995, Bull. civ. 1995, #7, 8, 9; Bull. Inf. C. cass., 15 January, 1996, p. 10, comment Fossereau; Gaz. Pal., 9 December, 1995, comment Fontbressin; Quot. jur., December 12, 1995, p. 3; BRDA, 15 December, 1995, p. 16; D. 1996. 13, comment Aynès; JCP éd. G., 1996. II. 22565, comment Ghestin; Déf. 1996. 747, comment Delebecque; RTD civ. 1996. 153, comment Mestre; JCP éd. N, 1996. I. 493, comment Boulanger; D. Aff. 1996. 3, comment Laude.

52 Even though a *fiducie* takes the form of a contract and, in principle, *"les conventions légalement formées tiennent lieu de loi à ceux qui les ont faites"*. (Art. 1134 par. 1 C. civ.)

structure of the trust can only be successfully imported in a system which has an analogous structure to the English one. Therefore, another method has to be envisaged.

2.2.3 Creating an Analogous Institution: The *Fiducie*

Civil law countries can obtain a similar device to the common law trust in their own country by creating a device whose similar characteristics to the trust will produce effects similar to the Anglo-American trust.[53]

The French proposal to introduce the *fiducie* presents striking features because all of the main trust characteristics are present. A separate patrimonium from the personal patrimonium of the *fiduciaire* will enable respect for the *fiducie*'s own interests. A *fiduciaire* will have powers which will enable him to benefit from the appropriation of the *fiducie*'s assets. He will also have duties as the *fiduciaire*'s liability will be very strict. The most interesting feature of this proposal is that if it was enacted, it would be the first proposal to offer such a general scope for a trust device in a civil law country.

The trust device developed in Germany as a result of judicial acceptance of the concept. Complete recognition of the device was, however, never obtained. Practical enactment may in fact be a way of obtaining full recognition of the device. Enactment may also be the only means of lessening the resonance of some legal principles that are currently awarded too much importance, such as the unity of patrimony. However, enactment will have to take into account the particularities of the legal background of each country, including mandatory rules and already existing devices which may be fulfilling the same means in a perfectly satisfactory way.

3   Conclusion

In conclusion, throughout the above, we have observed that the *fiducie* and the trust can share many similarities, even though they are destined to live in two different legal worlds. The *fiduciaire* and the trustee will play the main roles in each scenario, and these roles will be very similar.

These similarities can principally be explained by the identical characteristics of the two institutional frameworks. In both cases, assets are transferred to a fiduciary, because the transferor has confidence in that individual, so that the assets will be devoted to a specific end, in other words to their appropriation.

A trust device can therefore expand throughout Europe and it is our hope that it does; and maybe one day the statement that "the English trust has everywhere planted itself like a cuckoo in the nest of the civil law"[54] will be true.

---

53   The *Principles of European Trust Law* (1999), pp. 13 *et seq.* suggest a number of provisions that aim to constitute a trust, and that could be a source of inspirations for legislators considering implementing a trust device in their jurisdiction. *See* also Hayton (1999-3).
54   Amos (1937), at p. 1263.

BIBLIOGRAPHY: M.S. Amos, *The Common Law and the Civil Law in the British Commonwealth of Nations*, (1937) 50 Harvard L.R. 1236; F. Barrière, *La réception du* trust *au travers de la fiducie*, th. Paris II, 2001; A. Bénabent, *La fiducie (analyse d'un projet de loi lacunaire)*, JCP éd. N, 1993. I. 275 ; P. Berger, *Fiducie et transmission d'entreprise*, Banque et Droit 1991. 3; G. Blanluet, *Essai sur la notion de propriété économique en droit privé français. Recherches au confluent du droit fiscal et du droit civil*, LGDJ, préf. P. Catala and M. Cozian (1999); U. Blaurock, *Les opérations fiduciaires en droit allemand*, in Les opérations fiduciaires, Colloque de Luxembourg, Cl. Witz (ed.), preface of B. Oppetit, Feduci-LGDJ (1985), p. 223; F. Boulanger, *La loi du 4 juillet 1984 sur la révision des charges dans les libéralités*, JCP éd G, 1985. I. 3177; W.W. Buckland, *Equity in Roman Law*, London, University of London Press (1911); S. Camara Lapuente, *La fiducia sucesoria secreta*, Dykinson (1996); M. Cantin Cumyn, *L'avant-projet de loi relatif à la fiducie, un point de vue de civiliste d'outre-atlantique*, D. 1992. 117; A. Chapelle and J. de Guillenschmidt, Trusts, business trusts, *et fiducie*, Les Petites Affiches, 1992, #76, p. 4; V. Denoix de Saint Marc and J. de Guillenschmidt, *De quelques exemples de fiducies en Europe occidentale*, Les Petites Affiches, 1992, #58, p. 85; J. Derrupé, *De la fiducie au crédit-bail*, in Mélanges Ellul, PUF, 1983, p. 449; J.A. Dominguez Martinez, *El fideicomiso*, Porrua-Mexico (1994-1); J.A. Dominguez Martinez, *Dos aspectos de la esencia del fideicomiso mexicana*, Porrua-Mexico (1994-2); Ph. Dunand, *Le transfert fiduciaire: «donner pour reprendre».* Mancipio dare ut remancipetur. *Analyse historique et comparatiste de la fiducie-gestion*, Helbing (2000); A. Dyer, *The Hague Trust Convention and its Importance for Panama*, in El Fideicomiso en el Derecho Comparado (1993), Imprenta Universitaria – Panama; A. Dyer and H. van Loon, *Report on Trusts and Analogous Institutions*, in Proceeding of the 15th session of the Hague Confeence of Private International Laws, Nethterlands Printing Office (1984); E. Edwards and N. Stockwell, *Trusts & Equity*, Pitman Pub., 5th. ed. (2002); M. Elland-Goldsmith, *Le trust: ses emplois bancaires et financiers*, in La fiducie et ses applications dans plusieurs pays européens, Cl. Witz (ed.), Bull. Joly, 1991 #4 bis; W.F. Fratcher, *Property and Trust*, in International Encyclopedia of Comparative Law, vol. 6., International Association of Legal Science, J.C.B. Mohr; E. Gaillard, *Les enseignements de la Convention de la Haye du 1° juillet 1985 relative à la loi applicable au trust et à sa reconnaissance*, in La fiducie ou du trust dans les droits occidentaux francophones, Rev. jur. pol. indépendance et coopération 1990. 304; E. Gaillard and D. Trautman, *La Convention de la Haye du 1° juillet 1985 relative à la loi applicable au trust et à sa reconnaissance*, RCDIP 1985; E. Gaillard and D. Trautman, *Trusts in Non-Trust Countries: Conflicts of Laws and the Hague Convention on Trusts*, (1987) Am. Jo. Comp. Law 307; A. Gambaro, *Trust in Continental Europe*, in Aequitas and Equity: Equity in Civil Law and Mixed Jurisdictions, s. la dir. d'A. Rabello, Hamaccabi Press, 1997, pp. 777 *et seq*; J. Garton, *Trustee Act 2000*, (2001) 15 Trusts Law International 34; J.L. Gretton, *Trusts Without Equity*, (2000) 49 ICLQ 599; M. Grimaldi, *La fiducie: réflexions sur l'institution et sur l'avant-projet de loi qui la consacre*, Déf. 1991. a. 35085 and a. 35094; M. Grimaldi & F. Barrière, *La fiducie en droit français*, in La fiducie face au trust *dans les rapports d'affaires*, M. Cantin Cumyn (ed.), Bruylant, 1999, pp. 237 *et seq*; J. de Guillenschmidt, *La fiducie pour quoi faire? Présentation de l'avant-projet de loi relatif à la fiducie*, Rev. dr. Bcaire 1990. 105; J. de Guillenschmidt, *La France sans la fiducie*, R. J. com 1991. 49; S. Guinchard, *L'affectation en droit privé français*, LGDJ (1976); Hanbury & Martin, *Modern Equity*, 16th. ed. by J.E. Martin, Sweet & Maxwell (2001); H. Hansmann and U. Mattei, The Functions of Trust Law: a Comparative Legal and Economic Analysis, (1998) 73 N.Y. Univ. L.R. 434; H. Hansmann and U. Mattei, Trust Law in the United States: a Basic Study to its Special Contribution, (1998) 46 (suppl.) Am. Jo. of Comp. Law 133; D.J. Hayton, *The Law of Trusts*, Sweet & Maxwell, 3rd. ed. (1998); D.J. Hayton, *Principles of European Trust Law*, in Modern International Development in Trust Law, Kluwer Law International, 1999, pp. 19 *et seq*; D.J. Hayton, Developing the Obligation Characteristics of the Trust, (2001) 117 LQR 96; U. Jahn,

La treuhand *dans la pratique bancaire*, in La fiducie et ses applications dans plusieurs pays européens, Bull. Joly 1991, #4 bis, p. 61; C. Jauffret-Spinosi, *La Convention de La Haye relative à la loi applicable et à sa reconnaissance (1° juillet 1985)*, Clunet 1987. 23; C. Jauffret-Spinosi, Trust *et fiducie*, in Et. Sayag, Litec, 1997, pp. 332 *et seq*; J.L. Jeghers, *Du* trust *à la fiducie*, in *Relations familiales internationales*, M. Verwilghen and R. de Valkeneer (eds.) , Bruylant, 1993, pp. 431 *et seq*; D. Johnston, *The Roman Law of Trusts*, Oxford, Clarendon Press (1988); M.E. Koppenol-Laforce and R.J.P. Kottenhagen, *The Institution of the Trust and Dutch Law*, in *La fiducie face au* trust *dans les rapports d'affaires*, M. Cantin Cumyn (ed.), Bruylant, 1999, pp. 289 *et seq*; S.C.J.J. Kortmann and H.L.E. Verhagen, *National Report for the Netherlands*, in *Principles of European Trust Law*, D.J. Hayton, S.C.J.J. Kortmann, and H.L.E. Verhagen (eds.), Kluwer Law International, 1999, pp. 195 *et seq*; H. Kötz, *Trusts in Germany*, in *La fiducie face au* trust *dans les rapports d'affaires*, M. Cantin Cumyn (ed.), Bruylant, 1999, pp. 175 *et seq*. (1999-1); H. Kötz, *National Report for Germany*, in *Principles of European Trust Law*, D.J. Hayton, S.C.J.J. Kortmann, and H.L.E. Verhagen (eds.), Kluwer Law International, 1999, pp. 85 *et seq*. (1999-2); H. Kötz, *The Hague Convention on the Law Applicable to Trusts and their Recognition*, D.J. Hayton (ed.), *Modern International Development in Trust Law*, Kluwer Law International, 1999, pp. 37 *et seq*. (1999-3); H. Kötz, *The Modern Development of Trust Law in Germany*, D.J. Hayton (ed.), *Modern International Development in Trust Law*, Kluwer Law International, 1999, pp. 49 *et seq*. (1999-4); H. Kötz, *The Uses of Trusts in the Commercial Context*, D.J. Hayton (ed.), *Modern International Development in Trust Law*, Kluwer Law International, 1999, pp. 145 *et seq*. (1999-5); J.H. Langbein, *The Contractarian Basis of the Law of Trusts*, (1995) 107 Yale L.J. 625; J.H. Langbein, The Secret Life of the Trust: the Trust as an Instrument of Commerce, (1997) 109 Yale L.J. 625; Ch. Larroumet, *La fiducie inspirée du* trust, D. 1990. 119 (1990-1); Ch. Larroumet, *Introduction*, and *Conclusion*, in La Fiducie, une révolution sous notre droit, Banque et Droit, 1990. 239 and 1991. 9 (1990-2); Ch. Larroumet, *Sur la réalisation d'une defeasance en droit français*, in Mélanges Breton-Derrida, Dalloz, p. 193 (1991); J.P. Le Gall, *Première réflexion sur les dispositions fiscales de l'avant-projet de loi relatif à la fiducie*, JCP éd. C.I., 1991. I. 40. ; J.P. Le Gall, *Le concept de fiducie dans le projet de loi sur la fiducie*, Gaz. Pal. 1992. 507; P. Lepaulle, *Traité théorique et pratique du* trust *en droit interne, droit fiscal, et en droit international privé*, Rousseau (1932); P. Lepaulle, *Trust and the Civil Law*, (1933) 15 JCL 18; P. Lepaulle, *The Strange Destiny of Trusts*, in Perspectives of Law, Essays for A.W. Scott, Little Brown (1964); Y. Lequette, *De l'ordre des réductions des libéralités réalisées au moyen d'un* trust *entre vifs (à propos d'un arrêt rendu par la première Chambre civile de la Cour de cassation, le 20 février 1996)*, D. 1996. 231; M. Lupoi, The Civil Law Trust, (1999) 32 Vanderbilt Jo. of Trnasnational Law 967; M. Lupoi, Trusts: a Comparative Study, Cambridge Univ. Press (2000); F.W. Maitland, *Equity*, 2nd ed. (1936); F.W. Maitland, *Selected Essays*, Univ. Press (1957); U. Mattei, *Comparative Law and Economics*, Univ. of Michigan Press (1998); A. Meinertzhagen-Limpens, *Les opérations fiduciaires en droit néerlandais*, in Les opérations fiduciaires, Colloque de Luxembourg, Cl. Witz (ed.), Feduci-LGDJ, 1985, p. 391; R. Monier, *Manuel élémentaire de droit romain*, t.2, 6th. ed., Domat (1947); U. Morello, *Fiducia e* Trust: *due esperienz a confronto*, Giuffre-Italia (1991); B. Oppetit, *Les tendances régressives du droit contemporain*, in Mélanges Holleaux, Litec, p. 317 (1990); R. Panhard, *Le traitement des* trusts *en droit français*, JCP éd. N, 1987. I. 27; A. Pézard, *Les diverses applications de la fiducie dans la vie des affaires*, Rev. dr. bcaire 1990. 108; A. Pézard, *La fiducie, un instrument juridique utile*, Les Petites Affiches, May 27, 1991, #64, p. 18; C. Pisani, *La fiducie*, Déf. 1990. 535; P.J. Reed and R.C. Wilson, *The Statutory Duty of Care*, (2001) 25 Trusts & Estates L.J. 14; Ph. Rémy, *National Report for France*, in *Principles of European Trust Law*, D.J. Hayton, S.C.J.J. Kortmann, and H.L.E. Verhagen (eds.), Kluwer Law International, 1999, pp. 131 *et seq*; Cl. Reymond, *Réflexions de droit comparé sur la Convention de La Haye sur le* trust, Rev. dt. int. et dt. comp. 1991. 7; Cl. Reymond, *Vers une autre fiducie?*, in Mél. P. Van Ommeslaghe, Bruylant, 2000, pp. 659 *et seq*; M. Revillard, *La Convention de la Haye du 1° juillet 1985 sur la loi applicable au* trust *et à sa reconnaissance*, Déf. 1986 art. 33731; K.W. Ryan, The Reception of the Trust in the Civil Law, th. Cambridge (1959); K.W. Ryan, The Reception of the Trust, (1961) 10 ICQL 265; D. Schmidt, Cl. Witz, and J-L. Bismuth, *Les opérations fiduciaires en droit français*, in Les opérations fiduciaires, Colloque de Luxembourg, Cl. Witz (ed.), preface of B. Oppetit, Feduci-LGDJ (1985), p. 305; R. Schwartz, *La réception et l'administration des droits étrangers*, 1952 R. du B. 510. ; E. Seel-Viandon, *La fiducie en droit comparé et en droit international privé*, th. Paris II (1979); A. Tettenborn, The Trust in Business: Property and Obligation in England, in *La fiducie face au* trust *dans les rapports d'affaires*, M. Cantin Cumyn (ed.), Bruylant, 1999, pp. 35 *et seq*; L. Thévenoz, *La fiducie, cendrillon du droit suisse. Proposition pour une réforme*, Rev. dt. suisse 1995. 253; Underhill and Hayton, *Law relating to Trusts and Trustees*, 15th. ed. by D.J. Hayton, Butterworths (1995); D.W.M. Waters, *The Nature of the Trust Beneficiary's Interest,* (1967) 45 Can. Bar Rev. 219; D.W.M. Waters, The Institution of the Trust in Civil Law and Common Law, *Recueil de cours de l'Académie de droit international de La Haye*, 1995, pp. 113 *et seq*; Cl. Witz, *La fiducie en droit privé français*, preface of D. Schmidt, Economica (1981); Cl. Witz, *La fiducie-sûreté en droit français*, R.J. Com 1982. 67; Cl. Witz, *La révision des charges et conditions en matière de libéralites après la loi du 4 juillet 1984*, D. 1985. 125. ; Cl. Witz, *Synthèse*, Rev. dr. bcaire 1990.120; Cl. Witz, *L'avant-projet de loi français relatif à la fiducie à la lumière des expériences étrangères (rapport de clôture)*, Banque et Droit, 1991. 225; Cl. Witz, *Réflexions sur la fiducie-sûreté*, JCP éd. E, 1993.I. 244; Cl. Witz, *La fiducie en Europe: France, Suisse, Luxembourg, Allemagne, Liechtenstein. Analyse des lois existantes et des projets en cours*, in Le trust *et la fiducie – implications pratiques*, J. Herbots and D. Philippe, Bruylant (1997); C. de Wulf, *The Trust and Corresponding Institutions in the Civil Law*, Bruylant (1965); *La fiducie en droit moderne*, in Rapports préparatoires à la Semaine Internationale du droit, Sirey (1937); *Trusts and Trusts-Like Devices,* W.A. Wilson (ed.), United Kingdom Comparative Law Series, vol. 5 (1981); *Les opérations fiduciaires*, Colloque de Luxembourg, Cl. Witz (ed.), Feduci-LGDJ (1985); *La fiducie ou du trust dans les droits occidentaux francophones*, Rev. jur. pol. indépendance et coopération, 1990, #2; *La fiducie pour quoi faire?*, Rev. dr. bcaire. 1990. 105 and 1990. 176; *La fiducie, contribution à l'avant-projet de loi*, Rev. dr. bcaire. 1990. 176; *La transmission des entreprises, vaincre l'obstacle,* Travaux du 86° Congrès des Notaires de France (1990); *La fiducie, une révolution sous notre droit*, Banque et Droit, 1990, #14, 1991, #15; *Spécial fiducie*, Rev. dr. bcaire 1990, #19; *La fiducie et ses applications dans plusieurs pays européens*, Bull. Joly, 1991, # 4 bis; *Trust et fiducie: projet français et pratique internationale*, Les Petites Affiches, 1991, #83, p. 16; *Communiqué de la Chancellerie, Projet de loi relatif à la fiducie*, JCP éd. E, 1992. bloc note 11; *The Trust, Bridge or Abyss Between Common Law and Civil Law Jurisdictions?*, F. Sonnevelld and H. van Mens, Kluwer Law International (1992); *El fideicomiso en el derecho comparado*, Imprenta Universiataria-Panama (1993); *Trends in Contemporary Trust Law*, A.J. Oakley (ed.), Clarendon Press (1996); *Le* trust *et la fiducie – implications pratiques*, J. Herbots and D. Philippe, Bruylant (1997); *Itinare Fiduciae, Trust and Treuhand in an Historical Perspective,* R. Helmolz and R. Zimmermann, Duncker & Humblot (1998); *Fondation et* trust *dans la protection du patrimoine*, Cornu & Fromageau (eds.), L'Harmattan (1999); *La fiducie face au* trust *dans les rapports d'affaires,* M. Cantin Cumyn (ed.), Bruylant (1999); *Principles of European Trust Law*, D.J. Hayton, S.C.J.J. Kortmann, and H.L.E. Verhagen (eds.), Kluwer Law International (1999); *Modern International Development in Trust Law*, D.J. Hayton (ed.), Kluwer Law International (1999); *The Chinese Trust Law – Materials on the Drafting Process*, FEC of the National People's Congress, Z. Shaoping & I. Gebhardt (eds.), Publishing House of the Supreme Chinese Procuratorate (2001)

H – Company Law

CHAPTER 44

Corporate and Business Law in the European Union: Status and Perspectives 2004

Peter Hommelhoff*, Christoph Teichmann** & Carl-Heinz Witt***

1 Introduction

The status of corporate and business law harmonisation within the European Union gives rise to more optimism than it did half a decade ago.[1] Admittedly, there has not been much action relating to corporate law within the Union during the last five years, and, indeed, there has been failure. But the small amount of action must be regarded as significant, particularly the adoption of the *Societas Europaea* (SE) statute in October 2001 followed only recently by the statute for the European Co-operative (SCE). The up-coming creation of these supranational organisation forms at Union-level is a historic break-through which should, combined with promising approaches and tendencies, be able to shake the Union-influenced corporate law out of its longstanding stagnation. In May 2003, the European Commission published in its "Plan to Move Forward"[2] the first conclusions from the recommendations for a more flexible and modern EU company law which were made by the High Level Group of Company Law Experts on November 4, 2002.[3] And even with regard to takeover law where the harmonisation efforts had temporarily been unsuccessful, the recently found compromise has brought a certain degree of harmonisation although the EU Commission did not prevail with its far-reaching ambitions. However, the mere fact that an agreement could finally be reached is of eminent importance because the regulation of takeover bids is a crucial part of a secure and transparent environment for cross-border restructuring and a key element of the EU's goal to create an integrated capital market for financial services in the Union by 2005.[4] With this ambitious goal in mind the EU Commission has proceeded at a remarkable pace. Should it succeed in standing this pace it may well be that in days to come the first years of the new century will be remembered as the period of a wilful and courageous promotion

---

* Professor of Law at the University of Heidelberg.
** *Institut für Deutsches und Europäisches Gesellschafts- und Wirtschaftsrecht*, University of Heidelberg.
*** *Institut für Deutsches und Europäisches Gesellschafts- und Wirtschaftsrecht*, University of Heidelberg.
1 See Hommelhoff (1998), pp. 585 *et seq.*
2 Modernizing Company Law and Enhancing Corporate Governance in the European Union – A Plan to Move Forward, COM (2003) 284 final, retrievable at www.europa.eu.int/eur-lex.
3 The report of the High Level Expert Group is retrievable at the website of the European Commission: http://europa.eu.int/comm/internal_market/en/company/company/index.htm
4 Cf. the Action Plan "Financial Services: Implementing the Framework for Financial Markets" adopted by the EU Commission on May 11, 1999 (COM (1999) 232) and the Commission's later reports on progress on the Plan of June 20, 2002 and of June 3, 2003.

of the European corporate and business law. Even though this piece is focussing on harmonisation of corporate and business law within the European Union, it should be noted that an assessment to what extent further harmonisation may be necessary is highly influenced by the interpretation of the freedom of establishment given by the European Court of Justice. In this respect, the recent decisions in the cases *Centros*, *Überseering* and *Inspire Art* will be taken into account where it seems necessary to assess the necessity or desirability of further harmonisation. Having said this the construction of this piece will be as follows.

First of all, we would like to present a short overview of harmonisation attempts and their status within the Union (Section 2). Afterwards, we shall go into the EC Commission's approach to establish a secure and transparent environment for cross-border restructuring focusing on takeover law (Section 3), and then address the SE (Section 4). This piece will end with some words on the increased need for a EU regulation with regard to small and medium-sized companies (Section 5).

2 The Status of the Harmonisation Attempts

Compared to other areas of law, the harmonisation of the Member States' national laws is most advanced[5] in corporate and business law. This is certainly founded in the increasing growing-together of national economies within the Union, and in the connections between companies and groups. Corporate lawyers should therefore (with all due modesty) be entitled to make the following statement: corporate and capital market law, accompanied by accounting and bank contract law, have for many years been the motor for the harmonisation of the European civil law. In the meantime, however, labour[6] and particularly consumer protection law[7] have significantly gained in importance. However, we should nevertheless be a step further with European corporate and business law: in the meanwhile such a magnitude of norms has been created that it is now time to begin to search for systematic overall connections and legal principals.[8]

2.1 Passed Harmonisation Projects

The corporate and business law harmonisation projects already passed by the EC shall be mentioned only briefly: beginning with the 1st Directive on Publicity of 1968[9] to the 3rd Directive on Domestic Mergers[10] and to the 4th,[11] 7th[12] and 8th[13]

---

5 Cf. the overviews by Lutter (1996), pp. 45 *et seq.*; Wiesner (2000), pp. 1792 *et seq.* (in table from); regarding the adoption instruments see Oppermann (1999), lit. 1208 *et seq.*

6 Survey of the harmonisation in the area of labour law by Wiesner (2000), pp. 1798, 1807 *et seq.* (in table form).

7 On the ruling concepts for an EU consumer protection Goyens (1992), pp. 72 *et seq.*; Heiss (1996), pp. 626 *et seq.*; Hommelhoff (1996), pp. 4 *et seq.*, 44 *et seq.*; Müller-Graff (1993), pp. 20 *et seq.*; Reich (1996), pp. 27 *et seq.*, 119 *et seq.*, 324 *et seq.*; Tonner (1996), pp. 537 *et seq.*; very critical on the entire development Dreher (1997), p. 167.

8 See the systematisation by Lutter (1996), pp. 36 *et seq.*; Werlauff (2003-I), passim.

9 *OJ* 1968 L 65/8; reproduced in Lutter (1996), pp. 104 *et seq.*; in Habersack (2003), lit. 133; recently amended by a new directive (*OJ* 2003 L 221/13).

10 *OJ* 1978 L 295/36; in its latest version reproduced in Lutter (1996), pp. 131 *et seq.*; in Habersack (2003), lit. 258.

Directives on Accounting of the years 1978 to 1984, the line of increasing harmonisation extends via the 6th Directive on Divisions of 1982,[14] the 11th Directive on Branches of 1989[15] and the 12th Directive on the Single-Member Private Limited-Liability of 1989[16] to the Middle Class and GmbH & Co. Directive passed in 1990.[17] All these projects were successfully launched by the EU Commission, and were – or presently are being – transformed to national laws by the Member States. What is more, with the amending of the 2nd Capital Directive[18] in 1992[19] even a European change in corporate law was achieved. And last but not least the SE Statute and the additional Directive on Employees' Participation in the SE have been passed in 2001,[20] and so has the 13th Directive on Takeover Bids in 2003.[21]

But we find another area in which there has recently been a lot of progress. The EU Council of Ministers and the Commission have taken two important steps forward towards achieving the objective of guaranteeing uniform accounting for stock corporations. First of all, the EU Regulation on the application of international accounting standards was passed in July 2002.[22] Under this Regulation stock-exchange-listed companies are obliged to draw up consolidated annual statements in accordance with the IAS (International Accounting Standards; in future: IFRS – International Financial Reporting Standards) provisions as far as the business year begins on or after January 1, 2005.[23] This is to ensure that the accounting information given by the companies has a high degree of transparency and comparability which is supposed to be useful for the capital market's efficiency. In order to improve the application of IAS/IFRS in the Union, the Regulation provides for the setting up of a newly created Accounting Regulatory Committee. On the other hand, those companies to which the new Regulation does not apply and which, therefore, continue to

---

11 *OJ* 1978 L 222/11; reproduced in Lutter (1996), pp. 147 *et seq.*; in Habersack (2003), lit. 315.

12 *OJ* 1983 L 193/1; reproduced in Lutter (1996), pp. 211 *et seq.*; in Habersack (2003), lit. 316.

13 *OJ* 1984 L 126/20; in its latest version reproduced in Lutter (1996), pp. 232 *et seq.*; in Habersack (2003), lit. 317.

14 *OJ* 1982 L 378/47; in its latest version reproduced in Lutter (1996), pp. 199 *et seq.*; in Habersack (2003), lit. 259.

15 *OJ* 1989 L 395/36; in its latest version reproduced in Lutter (1996), pp. 269 *et seq.*; in Habersack (2003), lit. 134.

16 *OJ* 1989 L 395/40; in its latest version reproduced in Lutter (1996), pp. 278 *et seq.*; in Habersack (2003), lit. 338.

17 *OJ* 1990 L 317/57; 317/60; on this also Niessen (1991), pp. 195 *et seq.*; Biener (1993), pp. 707 *et seq.*; Lutter (1996), pp. 143 *et seq.*

18 *OJ* 1976 L 26/1; in its latest version reproduced in Lutter (1996), pp. 114 *et seq.*; in Habersack (2003), lit. 206.

19 *OJ* 1998 L 347/64; on this amendment which was about restricting the purchase of a corporation's own shares by a subsidiary, Lutter (1996), p. 110; Neye (1995), p. 195.

20 *OJ* 2001 L 294/1; 294/22; cf. below at 4. The break-through of the SE paved the way for the second supranational legal form, the European Co-operative the statute of which was adopted in July 2003 (*OJ* 2003 L 207/1).

21 At 3.4.

22 *OJ* 2002 L 243/1; reproduced in NZG 2002, pp. 1095 *et seq.*; in Habersack (2003), lit. 317a. See also the Commission's Regulation of September 2003 (*OJ* 2003 L 261/1).

23 The single Member States are given the option of deferring application of the Regulation until 2007 as far as companies are concerned which up to now have drawn up annual statements in accordance with other internationally accepted accounting regulations, particularly US-GAAP.

draw up their annual statements according to the 4th and 7th Directives[24] shall also be given the opportunity to draw up statements comparable to IAS. Consequently, the Commission presented a directive proposal amending both of the said directives in May 2002.[25] This directive was passed in June 2003;[26] it has to be transformed into Member States law by January 1, 2005. Divergences which had existed between the EU directives on accounting on the one hand and IAS on the other were removed; in order to achieve that object, one inserted extensive option rights in both directives which enable the Member States to adjust their national accounting regulations to IAS as circumstances may require.

In the light of this harmonisation process, something else becomes obvious, too: at the European Union's level, corporate law may not be seen from a strictly secluded and isolated viewpoint. Its functional connections with capital market[27], tax[28] and merger control law,[29] both under legal-dogmatic and practical aspects, illustrate this. In regard to the legal instruments for the protection of shareholders and investors, corporate and capital market law are to a large extent interchangeable, to the extent aimed at the shareholders of stock-exchange-listed companies.[30] This becomes obvious particularly from the project on implementing a directive on takeover bids. For this reason it seems appropriate to use a legal category of "business law" at European level. This term should be understood in a much broader meaning than in Germany, where "business law" (*Unternehmensrecht*) is commonly perceived[31] as corporate law and co-determination only.

2.2 Up-Coming Harmonisation Projects

In connection with the Commission's goal to create a secure and transparent environment for cross-border restructuring, the recently passed Directive on Takeover Bids, although it doesn't fulfil all harmonisation expectations, is an important milestone. And it doesn't have to be the last for there is also justified hope that it might opportune to bring forward the 10th as well as the 14th directives in the foreseeable future. We will go into this more closely below.[32]

2.3 "Pending" Harmonisation Projects

Notwithstanding the above harmonisation feats in corporate and capital market law, there are still a number of other important harmonisation projects which have in the meantime developed into "continual pending projects".

---

24 See above notes 11 and 12.
25 *OJ* 2002 C 227E/07/336. On the proposal Niehus (2002), pp. 1385 *et seq.*; Busse von Colbe (2002), pp. 1530 *et seq.*
26 *OJ* 2003 L 178/16.
27 See Lutter (1996), p. 76; for German law: Möllers (1997), p. 338.
28 Lutter (1996), pp. 69 *et seq.*; Werlauff (2003-I), pp. 91 *et seq.*
29 Lutter (1996), pp. 71 *et seq.*
30 On the corporate group law dimension of such directive: Hommelhoff (1993-II), p. 445.
31 For example Duden (1993), pp. 309 *et seq.*; cf. also K. Schmidt (2002), pp. 483 *et seq.*
32 At 3.4.

a. First of all, the amended suggestions on a Union-wide harmonisation on corporate group law,[33] which have not at all been convincing, must be mentioned:[34] in this area the harmonisation efforts did not even mature to a formal directive proposal by the Commission;[35] this has had the result that up to now the Council of Ministers never had to deal with corporate group law. And as far as the organisation of stock corporations is concerned, the first proposal of a 5th directive (structure directive) was submitted back in 1972 and amended in 1991.[36] The need for further harmonisation on the management structure of public limited-liability companies, however, is doubtful since the European Company statute adopted the optional model whereby the company itself in its statutes chooses between the one-tier and the two-tier system.[37] The report of the High Level Group of Company Law Experts recommended the same approach for national legislation; at least listed companies should have the choice to opt for either of the systems.[38]

b. With regard to the organisation of stock corporations, the main problem always was and, indeed, still is, co-determination and its rules within the Union.[39] While most other Member States are – if not generally, then at least with regard to its German form – opposed to co-determination, the German trade unions, the business associations and even almost all politicians (from whatever political party) keep fighting against any cutting-back on parity co-determination in an unusually unisono way, and furthermore fear a co-determinational "Delaware-effect", i.e. the retreat of German companies to co-determination-free or -weaker countries.

From a legal-political point of view, the question of co-determination at Union level cannot even be attacked in small steps, much less can it be solved entirely. Only if they do not even raise the question of co-determination,[40] will any short- or medium-term projects relating to European corporate and business law have chance of success. The EC Commission's proposal to reduce co-determination to information and consultation processes,[41] based on the rough model of the German Company Constitution Code (*Betriebsverfassungsgesetz*) and oriented towards the Euro Works Council Directive,[42] appeared more than doubtful for several reasons[43] and, consequently, did not succeed at all. However, there might be reason to hope that the per-

---

33 Printed in ZGR 1985, pp. 446 *et seq.*, and in Lutter (1996), pp. 244 *et seq.*; see Hommelhoff (1988), pp. 125 *et seq.*
34 Wiesner (1996), p. 395, makes the following matter-of-fact statement: "no imaginable subject of consensus".
35 On feasible other steps: Hommelhoff (1992), pp. 422 *et seq.*
36 *OJ* 1991 C 321/9; reproduced in Lutter (1996), pp. 176 *et seq.*
37 See Hommelhoff (2001).
38 Chapter III, sub 4.1. (for reference see note 3).
39 More detailed on this: Behrens (1996), pp. 833 *et seq.*; Westermann (1984), p. 123; specifically on the Structure Directive: Kolvenbach (1983), p. 2235.
40 Cf. for the European Economic Interest Grouping (EEIG) the limit of 500 employees (Art. 3 ss. 2c EEIG Regulation, *OJ* 1985 L 199/1, reproduced in Lutter (1996), pp. 751 *et seq.*) which helps to avoid from the very beginning on the question of a "one third-parity" co-determination of German kind.
41 Doc. DE/05/95/67860.100.P00 (FR).
42 *OJ* 1994 L 254/64; reproduced in Lutter (1996), pp. 685 *et seq.*
43 Correct therefore Behrens (1996), pp. 834 *et seq.*

petual brake block co-determination can be overcome: the compromise that has been found with regard to employees' participation, particularly co-determination, in the SE: "priority to negotiations"[44] could be ground-breaking. As a matter of fact, it already has been useful as a blueprint for another supranational entity, the European Co-operative, and for the new proposal on cross-border mergers.[45]

c. The last experts' draft on corporate group law[46] was generally, and also in significant details, oriented toward the provisions contained in paras. 291 *et seq.* of the German Stock Corporation Act (*Aktiengesetz*), particularly its distinction between contractual and factual corporate groups, so that it was – except for Portugal[47] – not acceptable to the other Member States: "Too severe, too clumsy and too perfectionistic; in a word: too German".[48] And even in German jurisprudence and politics this draft did not really receive any attention; so the discussions on corporate group law issues in the European Union need to be started from scratch. What seems inevitable, is a totally new approach, one that is not oriented towards the ruling concept of one single Member State but, instead, in regard to the "corporate group" falls back upon the legal situation that has in the meantime evolved in a number of Member States. Admittedly, there are considerable differences in the company laws applicable to corporate groups. These differences not only apply to the question of whether at least a partially systematic regulation of the matter exists in the 15 (in future: 25) legal systems of the EU – partial regulation exists in many instances, a systematic partial regulation, however, only in Germany and Portugal – but rather to the question of the legal attitude to and the evaluation of the "corporate group" concept. The other 13 Member States, therefore, have not imposed legal regulation in this area, not through neglect but rather by choice; doubt is expressed both as to the necessity of legal regulation and as to the amenability of the disparate circumstances which arise in company law to entire sectors of this area in force in the 13 Member States;[49] and in almost all EU Member States there is a rich and varied case law on the legal questions arising from the "corporate group" concept.[50]

This way a collection of more or less functionally identical ruling approaches has developed in the Member States, in order to cope with the legal problems relating to corporate groups. This finding could be a fertile ground for a very careful legal harmonisation; for example, one should think about whether the Union should not harmonise specific elements and instruments of the national laws in a group-specific way. Very detailed proposals have been made by the Thyssen-work group "Corporate

---

44 See below at 3.

45 On this proposal see below at 3.4

46 Above note 33.

47 On the Portuguese law on corporate groups Lutter/Overath (1994), p. 229.

48 So the concise finding by Hopt (1992), p. 273. The last draft had been preceded by the first attempt in 1974/75 with the idea of an "organic corporate group structure", printed in Lutter (1984), pp. 187 *et seq.* On the critical objections for example: Schilling (1978), pp. 415 *et seq.*; Rittner (1990), pp. 214 *et seq.*

49 For example, France has a special corporate group Labour Law, Italy a special Insolvency Law, and all the Member States supervise their banks and insurance companies on a consolidated group basis etc.; see the references in Forum Europaeum Konzernrecht (1998), notes 13 to 15.

50 See the references in Forum Europaeum Konzernrecht (1998), note 16.

Group Law for Europe" in 1998.[51] Certainly – this would be the (at least a temporary) departure from its own conceptionally complete corporate group law in the European Union; but that would not do any harm: by such only selective harmonisation, the national corporate laws would be harmonised at least to an extent, which though not the extent required, would, at least, be very helpful for trans-border group-connections within a common market without legal borders. For the German corporate group law such harmonisation programme might mean giving up some of the traditional legal elements. However, for the sake of Union-wide accepted rules on corporate group law, such loss would probably be tolerable.[52] It must be remembered: without any doubt, this is the only way in which Union-wide acceptance might be possible.

3 The Takeover Directive – Failure and the Aftermath

Never has corporate and business law harmonisation within the European Union made the headlines as much as during the last years as it happened with regard to the proposed 13th directive on takeover bids and its preliminary failure.[53] But this failure caused the Commission to generate even more activity: It is true, the compromise that finally could be achieved did not lead to the degree of harmonisation one had aimed at. But nevertheless, the passed directive, combined with the fact that the European Court of Justice in the meantime has removed some stumbling blocks, expresses a certain progress on the thorny way towards a secure and transparent environment for cross-border restructuring.

3.1 The Directive's Preliminary Failure in 2001

For many years, the EU Commission had made efforts to harmonise the law relating to takeover bids in the Member States,[54] and in the course of time it had presented no less than four proposals for a 13th directive.[55] After the project had been hotly debated among the Member States for a very long time, the Council of Ministers finally reached an agreement and passed a common position on June 19, 2000.[56] However,

---

51 Forum Europaeum Konzernrecht, ZGR 1998, pp. 672 *et seq.* (in English: EBOR 2000, pp. 203 *et seq.*; in French: Rev. Soc. 1999, pp. 43 *et seq.*; in Spanish: Revista de Derecho Mercantil 1999, pp. 445 *et seq.*); reactions by Blaurock (2000), pp. 79 *et seq.*; Windbichler (2000), pp. 265 *et seq.*; Halbhuber (2002), pp. 236 *et seq.*

52 On this already: Hommelhoff (1993-I), pp. 304 *et seq.*

53 For the first time in EU history, a directive proposal adopted by the Council of Ministers was thwarted by the Parliament's opposition.

54 On history of the proposals for a EU takeover directive see Assmann/Bozenhardt, in: Assmann/Basaldua/Bozenhardt/Peltzer (1990), pp. 33 *et seq.*; Basaldua, ibid., pp. 158 *et seq.*; Peltzer, ibid., pp. 179 *et seq.*

55 The four official directive proposals dated January 19, 1989, *OJ* 1989 C 64/8; September 10, 1990, *OJ* 1990 C 240/7; February 7, 1996, *OJ* 1996 C 162/5; and November 11, 1997, *OJ* 1997 C 378/10; on the official proposals' chronology Witt (1998), pp. 319 *et seq.* There was an additional, but unofficial proposal dated June 21, 1999, Document No. 9482/99, printed in AG 2000, pp. 296 *et seq.*

56 Common position on the adoption of a directive of the European Parliament and of the Council on company law concerning takeover bids, *OJ* 2001 C 23/1; reproduced in Pötzsch/Möller (2000), pp. 32

the European Parliament voted to amend the common position, but the Council opposed the amendments; so the matter went to a Conciliation Committee.[57] In that committee a joint text was found on June 6, 2001 by a bare majority.[58] But this compromise – and, consequently, the entire directive – finally failed in Parliament where it came to a tie.[59]

The takeover directive's preliminary failure should not obscure the fact that, on the large scale, unanimity had been reached in the Council as well as in Parliament. This refers not only to key elements of the takeover procedure, but also to another substantial part of takeover law: the mandatory bid to be launched by anyone holding shares of a stock-exchange-listed company which give him a specified percentage of voting rights conferring on him the control of that company.[60] Such mandatory bid rule had particularly been opposed by German voices for a very long time,[61] and this opposition had again and again been based on the argument that the group existence protection, as it exists in German law, would be sufficient and an (additional) group entrance protection would not be necessary or at least not sufficient by itself.[62] But finally the opposition against a mandatory bid rule was abandoned because of the realisation that for the sake of the status of Germany as a financial location and its attractiveness for investors from abroad, international standards should be accepted. And even more can be reported: despite the takeover directive's failure, a mandatory bid rule was embodied in German law as of January 1, 2002; such a bid has to be

---

et seq.; on this Neye (2000), pp. 289 *et seq.*; Pötzsch/Möller (2000), pp. 4 *et seq.*; van Hulle (2000), p. 524.

57 On the legislative way to the directive the extremely complicated parliamentary co-decision procedure pursuant to Art. 251 EC (former Art. 189b) must be complied with.

58 Joint text of a directive of the European Parliament and of the Council on company law concerning takeover bids approved by the Conciliation Committee provided for in Art. 251 ss. 4 EC, Document No. C5-0221/2001 of June 6, 2001; reproduced in ZIP 2001, pp. 1123 *et seq.*; on the conciliation procedure: Neye (2001), pp. 1121 *et seq.*

59 The vote on July 4, 2001 was 273 ayes versus 273 nays with 22 abstentions (EP-Document No. A5-237/2001). On the preliminary failure of the 13th directive see Hommelhoff/Witt (2001), pp. 561 *et seq.*; Pluskat (2001-I) pp. 1937 *et seq.*

60 Art. 5 ss. 1 of the joint text (above note 58). It was intended to leave it to the individual Member State in which the company has its registered office to define the percentage of voting rights which confers control and the method of its calculation (Art. 5 ss. 5 of the joint text). And nothing else applies under the 13th Directive on Takeover Bids as it has been passed in the meantime (Art. 5 ss. 1 and 3 of the directive). – With the political agreement on a mandatory bid rule in the EU, harmonisation was tangible on one of the fields where it had been notified by the Forum Europaeum (cf. above at 2.3. c).

61 In the directive proposals of 1996 and 1997 it was provided that the individual Member State should not be forced to embody a mandatory bid to be launched by someone gaining control if the national law provided for other appropriate and at least evenly-matched precautions for the protection of the company's minority shareholders; on this in great detail (and propagating a "cumulative concept"): Hommelhoff (1998), pp. 598 *et seq.*

62 See Assmann/Bozenhardt (1990), pp. 49 *et seq.*; Mertens (1990), pp. 256 *et seq.*; Sandberger (1993), pp. 325 *et seq.*; Assmann (1995), p. 570; Altmeppen (2001), pp. 1080 *et seq.*; Pluskat (2001-I), pp. 1941 *et seq.*; see also Hommelhoff (1998), pp. 598 *et seq.*; disapproving of a mandatory bid rule prescribed by EU law formerly also Hommelhoff/Kleindiek (1990), pp. 108 *et seq.* (facing a future harmonized corporate group law).

launched by any shareholder who reaches 30% or more of a stock-listed corporation's voting rights.[63]

The only reason for the 13th directive's preliminary failure was disagreement about the extent and limits of a potential passivity commitment to which the target's management would be subjected.[64] We use the term "passivity", not "neutrality" commitment, intentionally. This is to make clear that a transaction's potential hindering or even its prevention is at stake, not the fact that in the dispute about a takeover bid, the target's management should be prevented from giving a statement, whether to the corporation's shareholders, or the general public.[65] For a long time there had been unanimity on the view that the target's management (in Germany: the board of management [*Vorstand*] and the supervisory board [*Aufsichtsrat*]) should not be entitled to frustrate a takeover bid; on the contrary, there was a general agreement that a passivity commitment should be imposed on it.[66]

But in 2001, the German Federal Government, influential circles of German business and the trade unions – a fatal alliance – underwent a complete, politically motivated conversion and turned to damming the target's management's passivity commitment as an inappropriate restriction. It was claimed that other EU Member States' corporate law, as well as US capital market law, on a large scale enable the corporations there to torpedo takeover bids; at the same time it was claimed that conversely companies from abroad should not be given unimpeded access to German *Aktiengesellschaften*. So from that time forth, one insisted on the admissibility of "on-hand resolutions": the shareholders' meeting should be entitled to authorise management to fend off future takeover bids. Consequently, the takeover directive (which did not provide the admissibility of such resolutions) was brought down in Parliament at the very last moment, and the admissibility of "on-hand resolutions" was embodied in German law.[67] Unfortunately, this wasn't the end: literally at the last minute[68] the

---

63 Paras. 35 *et seq*. German Takeover Act (*Wertpapiererwerbs- und Übernahmegesetz* – WpÜG); on WpÜG in general Zschocke (2002), pp. 79 *et seq*.; Zinser (2002), pp. 15 *et seq*.; Krause (2002-I), pp. 705 *et seq*.; particularly on the mandatory bid rule Harbarth (2002), pp. 321 *et seq*.; Letzel (2002), pp. 293 *et seq*.; Vetter (2002), pp. 1999 *et seq*.; Wymeersch (2002), pp. 520 *et seq*.; Kiesewetter (2003), pp. 1638 *et seq*.

64 In the limelight of a lot of pieces on takeover law was the question, whether and, if so, which defensive measures against hostile takeovers would be admissible and promising in Germany before the Takeover Act (WpÜG) came into force and how a legal provision could and should look; see only Hahn (1992), pp. 163 *et seq*.; Ebenroth/Rapp (1991), pp. 2 *et seq*.; Harrer/Grabowski (1992), pp. 1326 *et seq*.; Herkenroth (1994), pp. 92 *et seq*.; Michalski (1997), pp. 154 *et seq*.; Klein (1997), pp. 2086 *et seq*.; Kirchner (1999), pp. 481 *et seq*.; Weisner (2000), pp. 520 *et seq*.; Baudisch/Götz (2001), pp. 251 *et seq*.; Wiese/Demisch (2001), pp. 849 *et seq*.; Grunewald (2001), pp. 288 *et seq*.; Schneider/Burgard (2001), pp. 967 *et seq*.

65 On the contrary: pursuant to Art. 9 ss. 1 lit. d of the joint text (above note 58) it was intended to impose on the target's management the right and the obligation to comment on a takeover bid, a rule that has been retained in 13th Directive on Takeover Bids as it has been passed in the meantime (Art. 9 ss. 5 of the directive). And nothing else applies to *Vorstand* and *Aufsichtsrat* under para. 27 German Takeover Act (WpÜG).

66 Cf. Art 9 ss. 1 lit. a to c and ss. 2 of the joint text (above note 58).

67 Para. 33 German Takeover Act (WpÜG); on this Winter/Harbarth (2002), pp. 1 *et seq*.; Krause (2002-II), pp. 1053 *et seq*.

68 Namely during the negotiations in the Legal Committee of the German parliament; cf. this committee's recommendation and report, Parliamentary Printed Materials BT-Drucks (14/7477).

same fatal alliance pushed through the provision that defensive measures against takeover bids by the *Vorstand* are admissible even without a resolution by the shareholders' meeting (*Hauptversammlung*), if only the (co-determined) *Aufsichtsrat* gives its consent. In other words: the *Vorstand* can block every unwanted takeover bid, if it has the support of all the *Aufsichtsrat* members representing the employees and one additional member.

3.2 The Report of the High Level Expert Group and the ECJ's Holdings on "Golden Shares"

After all, the takeover directive's preliminary failure was not due to disagreement on takeover procedure, but on a deficit of harmonisation in the area of company law. Bearing this in mind, the EU Commission set up a High Level Group of Company Law Experts (*Winter* Group) in September 2001 and instructed this Group to advise the Commission with regard to the adoption of EU law on takeover bids in the first place and afterwards with regard to the priorities for a modernisation of company law in the EU.

The Group submitted its first report to the EU Commission on January 10, 2002 and presented it to the public at the same time. In this report, the Group claimed that any European company law regulation aimed at creating a level playing field for takeover bids should be guided by two guiding principles which are *shareholder decision-making* and *proportionality between risk-bearing capital and control*: that means on the one hand that in the event of a takeover bid, the shareholders should always be the ones to ultimately decide whether to tender their shares to a bidder and for what price; in the Group's opinion, it is not for the board of a company to decide whether a takeover bid for the shares in the company should be successful or not. On the other hand, the Group believes that share capital which has an unlimited right to participate in the profits of the company or in the residue on liquidation (the so-called risk-bearing capital), and only such share capital, should normally carry control rights, in proportion to the risk carried.

On the basis of these guiding principles the Group submitted – inter alia – the following recommendations:

- The target board should be permitted to take actions frustrating a takeover bid only on the basis of a shareholders' meeting authorisation taken after the bid has actually been announced; "on-hand resolutions" should be unlawful.
- After announcement of the bid, any authorisation by the shareholders' meeting to take actions frustrating the bid should be given by a majority of votes exercised by the holders of the proportionate majority of the risk-bearing capital of the company. The bidder should also be allowed to vote in such meeting to the extent he already holds risk-bearing capital in the company.
- A rule should be introduced which allows the bidder who, after completion of a takeover bid holds a certain share of risk-bearing capital, to break-through mechanisms and structures which may prevent him from exercising control, as defined in the Articles of Association and other constitutional documents. The bidder should be able to vote his shares in the shareholders' meeting in accordance with his share of risk-bearing capital and to determine the make-up of the company's

board as well as the managerial policy. The threshold for exercising the break-through right should not be set at a percentage higher than 75% of the risk-bearing capital of the company on the date of completion of the bid.
- The break-through should also apply to so-called golden shares, i.e. shares which are held by states and entail specific control rights.[69] As far as such golden shares are admissible under community law, Member States refusing to give up control of a company should pass an appropriate legislative provision.

A substantial step on the way towards a level playing field for takeover bids can be seen in three judgments by the European Court of Justice dated June 4, 2002[70] and in another two ECJ judgments dated May 13, 2003[71] which, to a great extent, eliminated "golden shares". The ECJ ruled that specific provisions in Portuguese and in French as well as in Spanish and in British law guaranteeing the state influence on privatised companies constitute a restriction on the movement of capital between Member States and on the freedom of establishment[72] and, therefore, must be repealed;[73] on the other hand, the Court entitled Belgium to sustain its special provision concerning the natural gas economy. A statute granting golden shares may only be maintained, the ECJ held, with regard to companies which are active in fields involving the provision of services in the public interest or strategic services; for instance, this is the case if the legislation is justified by the objective of guaranteeing energy supplies in the event of a crisis. However, such a scheme must be based on objective, non-discriminatory criteria which are known in advance to the companies concerned, and all persons affected by a restrictive measure of that type must have a legal remedy available to them. And additionally, the Court continued, such a scheme must be proportionate to the aim pursued, inasmuch as the same objective could not be attained by less restrictive measures. General financial interests of a Member State cannot constitute adequate justification.

To what extent the ECJ's judgement on "golden shares" may effect the so-called VW Act which grants crucial influence on the car manufacturer *Volkswagen* to the German State of Lower Saxony and which has been a thorn in the EU Commission's side for a long time,[74] cannot be foreseen; it is likewise uncertain, whether the voting right restrictions which in Sweden guarantee the extensive holdings of the influential *Wallenberg* family, can be sustained. Anyway, relying on the ECJ's judgements the

---

69 On golden shares: Wackerbarth (2001), pp. 1747 *et seq.*
70 Cases C-367/98 (Commission v. Portuguese Republic), C-483/99 (Commission v. French Republic), C-503/99 (Commission v. Kingdom of Belgium); printed in BB 2002, pp. 1282 *et seq.* The three enforcement proceedings had been brought by the Commission in 1998 and 1999. On the "golden shares" judgments of June 4, 2002 Ebke/Traub (2002), pp. 335 *et seq.*; Ruge (2002), pp. 421 *et seq.*; Krause (2000-III), pp. 2747 *et seq.*; Grundmann/Möslein (2002), pp. 758 *et seq.*; Grundmann/Möslein (2003), pp. 289 *et seq.*
71 Cases C-463/00 (Commission v. Kingdom of Spain), C-98/01 (Commission v. United Kingdom); printed in ZIP 2003, pp. 991 *et seq.* On the "golden shares" judgments of May 13, 2003 Kilian (2003), pp. 2653 *et seq.*; Spindler (2003), pp. 850 *et seq.*
72 Arts. 43 and 56 EC (former Arts. 52 and 73b).
73 In autumn 2002 the state of France gave up its specific rights in Total-Fina-Elf S.A., those "golden shares" the ECJ case C-483/99 had been about.
74 Cf. Krause (2000-III), pp. 2748 *et seq.*; on VW Act also Wellige (2003), pp. 427 *et seq.*

Commission has taken uncompromising action against state takeover obstacles in the meantime: so Italy and France have been served with an ultimatum to open their public power supply industry to investors from abroad; not surprisingly at all, the Commission initiated enforcement proceedings under Art. 226 EC (former Art. 169) against Germany with regard to VW Act in March 2003 and formally ordered Germany to amend the Act in March 2004; the case will probably be taken to the ECJ.

3.3 The 13th Directive's Final Adoption

On October 2, 2002 the EU Commission presented a new proposal for a 13th directive on takeover bids.[75] In this proposal, the rule that the target's board must obtain the shareholders' authorisation before launching defensive measures was retained (Art. 9 ss. 2 to 4 of the proposed directive). At the same time, rules aiming at establishing a "level playing field" were introduced. In particular, the recommendations of the High Level Expert Group on increased transparency concerning the capital and control structure of companies and defensive measures were adopted: listed companies would be required to disclose all of this in the annual report, and, in addition, the proposal would require the board to submit these structures and defensive measures to scrutiny by the shareholders' meeting at least every other year (Art. 10 of the proposed directive).

On the other hand, the proposed directive would introduce a "mini-break-through" provision putting an end to a number of measures currently used to restrict takeover bids even when the bids may be in the shareholders' interests, i.e. restrictions on the transfer of securities, voting right restrictions and restrictions on the power to appoint or to remove board members (Art. 11 of the proposed directive). However, this was not the complete "break-through" solution proposed by the High Level Expert Group which suggested that, after the announcement of the bid, any authorisation by the shareholders' meeting to take actions frustrating the bid should be given by a majority of votes exercised by the holders of the proportionate majority of the risk-bearing capital of the company. The Commission did not follow the Group's advice that all corporate law-based special provisions, particularly voting caps, multiple voting shares and ownership restrictions, should become inoperative in takeover cases. It argued, i. a., that a complete "break-through" solution would lead to many complex legal problems which would include the definition of risk-bearing capital which does not exist in any Member State and the fixing of the threshold for triggering the break-through; the dilution of the rights of ordinary shareholders that would result from giving voting rights to non-voting shares and constitutional problems resulting from the suppression of multiple voting rights were mentioned, too. The issue of "golden shares" was not regulated, either; as far as that goes the Commission referred, i.a., to the above-mentioned judgments of the European Court of Justice.

Although the VW Act was not affected by the new proposal which would not invalidate the voting right restrictions contained in that Act, the proposed directive did

---

75 *OJ* 2003 C 45E/1; reproduced in ZIP 2002, pp. 1863 *et seq.* and in NZG 2002, pp. 1146 *et seq.*; on the new proposal Krause (2002-IV), pp. 2341 *et seq.*; Seibt/Heiser (2002), pp. 2193 *et seq.*; Neye (2002-II), pp. 1144 *et seq.*; Zinser (2003), pp. 10 *et seq.*

meet strong resistance in Berlin where a strict principle "one share, one vote" was demanded. But there were other EU Member States also reacting guardedly or disapproving. Consequently, the proposed directive was discussed intensively in the Council, but also with the Commission and with Parliament. However, one could not come to an agreement because a "big solution" which would have removed all company law defensive measures and, consequently, allowed a perfect level playing field did not find a majority, and neither did a "small solution" which would leave all barriers in the EU Member States untouched and would just have focussed on the harmonisation of proceeding rules and a better protection of minority shareholders.

A compromise solution for a takeover directive seemed to be receded into a dim distance when the Portuguese government presented a new proposal in spring 2003 granting the Member States and, in the second place, the companies the right to make its choice whether to apply takeover obstacles as defensive measures in case of a takeover bid. While there was general scepticism towards this proposal at the beginning Parliament sent out positive signals after a while. This encouraged the Italian presidency in the EU Council to follow up such option model and to present its own proposal. In November 2003 the Council approved this proposal unanimously (with only Spain abstaining) and adopted the directive against the opposing Commission which disapproved of any such compromise. Parliament approved December 2003, and the Council formally adopted the directive in March 2004; so the 13th Directive on Takeover Bids came into force on May 20, 2004.[76]

Compared to the Commission's proposal Art. 9 of the directive was left unchanged while the transparency rule of Art. 10 was even extended; pursuant to Art. 10 ss. 3 of the directive Member States shall ensure that, in the case of stock-listed companies, the board must every year present an explanatory report to the shareholders' meeting on the disclosed matters. In Art. 11 of the directive a complete "break-through" rule was adopted with a threshold for exercising the break-through set at the percentage of 75% of the capital carrying voting rights; this is true for the first shareholders' meeting following closure of the bid, called by the bidder in order to amend the Articles of Association or to remove or appoint board members.

The general rule is that the target board should keep passivity in case of a takeover bid and multiple voting rights as well as voting right restrictions should be suspended. But pursuant to Art. 12 of the directive Member States may deviate from this rule and retain its respective law. The companies in those Member States that made use of its right to opt out may, nevertheless, opt in which means decide for the European rule to apply. This decision of the company must be taken by the shareholders' meeting in accordance with the rules applicable to amendments of the respective company's Articles of Association.

The compromise achieved did not lead to the degree of harmonisation the Commission had aimed at initially. But there might grow an interesting and fertile competition between those companies that waive defensive measures hoping for better valuation and those that do not and may, therefore, have to face a worse image and backwardations on the exchange; this competition could result in an indirect process

---

76 *OJ* 2004 L 142/12; on this directive Krause (2004), pp. 113 *et seq.*; Kindler/Horstmann (2004), pp. 866 et seq.

of harmonisation. From a German point it is of particular interest that the Takeover Act (*WpÜG*) which has been in force since the beginning of 2002 can be left unchanged, if Germany makes use of its right to opt out.

3.4 Looking Ahead: The 10th and 14th Directives – Get Going?

For a long time, the 10th directive on cross-border mergers and the 14th directive on cross-border transfer of registered office were among the "pending" harmonisation projects. But in the meantime there is reason to hope that these two projects which are important stages on the thorny way towards a secure and transparent environment for cross-border restructuring, will get going.

As far as the 10th directive on cross-border mergers is concerned, the EU Commission presented a proposal in 1985.[77] But from the beginning, this proposal has not been at all convincing; as with regard to the organisation of stock corporations, the main problem is co-determination. This resulted in the fact that up to now the Council of Ministers never dealt with the regulation of international mergers. But things have changed: the Commission presented a revised proposal in November 2003.[78] Compared to the 1985 proposal two main features should be mentioned: Firstly, the scope of the proposal is no longer restricted to public limited-liability companies but includes all Community companies with share capital. Secondly and concerning employees' participation, the proposal reflects the solution already adopted in the European Company statute.[79] There is, however, a particular innovation in this regard: The rules on employee participation only apply where at least one of the merging companies is operating under an employee participation system *and* where the national law applicable to the company created by the merger does not impose compulsory employee participation. Hence, a German company merging with a Dutch or Scandinavian company into a new company located in the Netherlands or Scandinavia would have to give up the German-style co-determination and to accept the system of employee participation known in the other countries. It remains to be seen whether this flexible approach can be upheld in the negotiations on the proposal.

As regards the 14th directive on cross-border transfer of registered office, the situation is as it is in the area of corporate group law: harmonisation efforts did not even mature to a formal directive proposal by the Commission.[80] But such a proposal is announced for the near future in the Commission's Plan to Move Forward;[81] the proposal is expected to adopt similar provisions on the transfer of seat as the European Company statute. Since the ECJ's judgment in *Überseering*, however, there seem to be other ways to achieve the cross-border transfer of registered or head office. The background of the judgment is as follows: At all times the German Federal Court of Justice (*Bundesgerichtshof*) supported the so-called real seat theory according to

---

77 *OJ* 1985 C 23/11; reproduced in Lutter (1996), pp. 261 *et seq.*

78 Proposal for a directive on cross-border mergers of companies with share capital, COM (2003) 703 final; on this proposal Maul/Teichmann/Wenz (2003), pp. 2633 *et seq.* Pluskat (2004). pp. 1 *et seq.*).

79 Cf. below at 4.

80 In 1997 only a draft on a directive on cross-border transfer of seat was presented; printed in ZGR 1999, pp. 157 *et seq.*; see Di Marco (1999), pp. 3 *et seq.*; Neye (1999), pp. 13 *et seq.*; K. Schmidt (1999), pp. 20 *et seq.*; Priester (1999), pp. 36 *et seq.*

81 See above note 2.

which a legal entity formed in accordance with the law of another state when moving its centre of administration to a domestic place would be subject to German company law. Since the company moving into Germany has not been formed in accordance with German company law it would loose its legal capacity, i. e. could no longer enjoy rights or be the subject of obligations. But then the ECJ's ruling in *Centros*[82] encouraged the *Bundesgerichtshof* to refer to the ECJ for a preliminary ruling under Art. 234 EC two questions on the interpretation of Arts. 43 and 48 EC.[83] In *Überseering*[84] the ECJ ruled: Where a company formed in accordance with the law of a Member State (A) in which it has its registered office is deemed, under the law of another Member State(B), to have moved its actual centre of administration to Member State B, Arts. 43 and 48 EC preclude Member State B from denying the company legal capacity. And secondly the court held: Where a company formed in accordance with the law of a Member State (A) in which it has its registered office exercises its freedom of establishment in another Member State (B), Arts. 43 and 48 EC require Member State B to recognise the legal capacity which the company enjoys under the law of its State of incorporation.[85]

It follows that under the freedom of establishment a company may transfer its centre of administration to another Member State without being denied its legal capacity. On the other hand, many questions remain unsolved as to what legal rules will be applicable to this company in the course of its further business. Liability of directors, rights and duties of shareholders, contracts with employees and customers and many other legal issues will have to be dealt with. Neither can they be treated exclusively by the legal rules of the company's home state nor exclusively by the rules of the state where it transferred its head office. The recent *Inspire Art* judgment[86] clarified, however, that Member States may not restrict the freedom of establishment by imposing on "pseudo-foreign companies" the provisions (e.g. a minimum capital requirement) provided for the formation of national companies. It remains to be seen where the line is to be drawn between unjustified restrictions of the freedom of establishment and the legitimate application of provisions for the protection of third parties (in particular the creditors). For the time being, a company which is transferring its seat based on *Überseering* has to face a high level of legal uncertainty. Therefore, the directives on the transfer of seat and the international merger are still of particular interest.

---

82 Case C-212/97 of March 9, 1999; printed in NJW 1999, 2027 *et seq.* The case *Daily Mail* (Case 81/87 of September 27, 1988, printed in NJW 1989, 2186 *et seq.*) did not yet seem to threaten the real seat theory.

83 BGH ZIP 2000, 967, 968 *et seq.*

84 Case C-208/00 of November 5, 2002; printed in ZIP 2002, 2037 *et seq.* On the *Überseering* judgment Eidenmüller (2002), pp. 2233 *et seq.*; Zimmer (2003), pp. 1 *et seq.*; Lutter (2003), pp. 7 *et seq.*

85 It should be noted that the English term "recognize" is misleading since the French and the German version use a somewhat weaker expression ("achten" / "respecter").

86 Case C-167/01 of September 30, 2003, printed in ZIP 2003, 1885 *et seq.*

4   Finally: The European Company (Societas Europaea)

From the time of the draft founding document of the Council of Europe in 1949[87] the European Company has been debated for half a century; the unexpected happened at the Nice Summit Meeting of the Council of Heads of States and Governments. The Member States overcame their manifold reservations and approved the European Company (SE), the favourite of company law academics in Europe.[88] The political breakthrough in Nice was implemented in two legal acts under EU law: firstly, the Council Regulation (EC) No 2157/2001 of October 8, 2001, on the Statute for a European Company (SE)[89] and, secondly, the Council Directive 2001/86/EC of October 8, 2001, supplementing the Statute for a European Company with regard to the involvement of employees.[90]

A dispute raged in the foreground since the European Parliament claimed a right of co-determination under Art. 251 EC.[91] In its view, the legal acts to be passed by the Council represented measures towards the harmonisation of legal and administration regulations of the Member States, under Art. 95 ss. 1 EC. Both the Commission and Council did, however, base the legal acts on Art. 308, with the consequence that they hold that they were subject only to hearings[92] and possibly an expression of opinion of the European Parliament. Even though the Legal Affairs Committee wanted Parliament to challenge the Councils' decision on the European Company, the President of the European Parliament wisely decided not to interfere with the coming into force of the legal acts which had already lingered about for so many years.[93]

4.1   Formation of the European Company

Arts. 2 and 3 ss. 2 of the Regulation set out five basic ways of forming a European Company,

- Merger SE created from at least 2 national public limited-liability companies (Art. 2 ss. 1 together with Annex I, Art. 17-31),
- Holding SE created from at least 2 national public or private limited-liability companies (Art. 2 ss. 2 together with Annex II, Art. 32-34),
- Subsidiary SE (Arts. 2 ss. 3 and 35 et seq.) created from at least 2 national companies according to Art. 48, ss. 2 EC or other public or private legal persons of Member States,

---

87 See Schwarz (2000), pp. 25; cf. ibid., p. 643 et seq. for history of the SE.

88 For legal literature cf. references in Schwarz (2000), p. 640.

89 OJ 2001 L 294/1. See the commentaries of Blanquet (2001), Colombani/Favero (2002), Esteban Velasco (2001), Hirte (2002), Hommelhoff (2001), Hommelhoff/Teichmann (2002), Lutter (2002), Menjucq (2002), Teichmann (2002-I).

90 OJ 2001 L 294/22.

91 See Neye (2002-I).

92 On the various procedures, hearings, co-operation, co-determination or agreement; Oppermann (1999), pp. 112 et seq.

93 See Neye (2002-I). The same dispute arose, however, with regard to the statute of the European Co-operative and has not yet been settled.

– Transformation SE from one national public limited-liability company (Arts. 2 ss. 4, 37),[94]

In addition to these four forms of direct creation of an SE, there is one secondary form mentioned,

– Subsidiary SE, created by separation from a parent SE (Art. 3 ss. 2).

These five forms correspond to those of the revised draft Statute of 1991:[95] in that draft, the Transformation SE was newly introduced. Many public limited-liability companies in the Member States of the EU will examine this form first to see whether they should become transformed from national companies to the new supra-national legal form under EU law.[96] This opportunity of companies to change their legal form will encourage legal advisors to intensively engage with the detailed regulations on the SE. Even more, the law faculties and law schools must adjust to this development.

Seen from the point of view of freedom to found companies under company law, the five possible forms, which are based on a numerus clausus principle, must be regarded as restrictive of this freedom. This is clear from two exclusions: firstly, a natural person cannot be a sole founder of a SE – whether that person is professionally independent, in trade or a private investor; such a person may, at best, join an SE founded by certain companies or legal persons. Secondly, the forms of SE provided are not equally open to all companies, but are specific to individual company forms: while private limited-liability companies may join in the foundation of a Holding SE (Art. 2 ss. 2 of the Regulation), and in the Subsidiary SE (Art. 2 ss. 3 of the Regulation together with Art. 48 ss. 2 of the EU-Treaty), the Merger SE and the Transformation SE are restricted to the public limited-liability company.

The requirement of a cross-border element is likewise an inhibition. Apart from establishing an SE as a subsidiary under Art. 3 s. 2 of the Regulation, all formations of an SE must affect at least two Member States. Even the transformation of a national public limited liability company into the supranational form of an SE requires that the public limited liability company has participated in a subsidiary in another Member State for at least two years (Art. 2 ss. 4 of the Regulation). The imposition of this minimum time requirement apparently has the purpose of preventing the formation now of companies in another state in order to circumvent the requirement.

The Regulation requires a certain minimum organisational basis – whether by means of the formation of an SE over several states, a subsidiary or branch in another state. The Commission and Council therefore rejected the suggestion made some time ago that the cross-border element be defined commercially by certain minimum turnover in several Member States.[97] However, business will, in practice, find that it is possible to live with the fact that the cross-border requirement be satisfied by an organisational structure. This belief is reinforced by the generous provision that com-

---

94 It may be assumed that Appendix I to the Regulation applies also to this form.
95 Reproduced, *inter alia*, in Lutter (1996) p. 724.
96 On the characteristics of a supranational company, see Hommelhoff (1997), p. 2104.
97 Hommelhoff (1990), p. 423.

panies with their registered office in one Member State but their management head-quarters outside the Community find in Art. 2 ss. 5 of the Regulation; each Member State is free to treat such companies as Member State companies, if they have a real and continuous link with a Member State's economy.[98]

4.2 Organisation

Under Art. 38 b) of the Regulation, the founders have the choice between the one-tier system with one administrative organ, on the one hand, and the two-tier system with management organ and supervisory organ, on the other hand. This choice is available irrespective of whether the SE is subject to co-determination or not. The German leg-islature and each company which wishes to establish a single management, control and supervisory system will have to deal with the problem – which is both theoreti-cally challenging and of immense practical importance – of incorporating co-determi-nation in the monistic corporate constitution in such a way that management decision-making will not be rendered so difficult that the capacity of the SE to act and react in competitive markets is threatened.[99] The necessary steps can be provided for by the German legislature by means of the power to make regulations under Art. 43 ss. 4 of the Regulation.

4.2.1 One-Tier System

The one-tier system is well known from the British and many continental legal sys-tems such as France, Italy or Spain. The Regulation contains only a few detailed points with regard to internal structures within the one-tier system. According to Art. 43 ss. 1 of the Regulation, within a single administrative organ, one or more managing directors may be responsible for the day-to-day business of the company, provided that the company law of the Member State permits this, and the Member State in addition extends this autonomy to the managing directors of an SE. Art. 48 ss. 1 also imposes an obligation to specify the transactions which require an express decision by the administrative organ. It is left to the Member States to specify the competences which are to be mandatorily reserved to such full board decision (Art. 48 ss. 2 of the Regulation). While, by means of these few rules, a more or less practical and flexible internal structure for the SE is established, it is also noticeable that a central assumption in the preamble has not been taken into the text for the one-tier system: the clear distinction between the respective responsibilities of the persons

---

98 The wording of the Regulation speaks of one Member State, so that a commercial connection to a third state appears to suffice. However, this cannot be, because the founding state alone can hardly make a decision on whether a company founded under its law is to be treated as a Member State company and thereby privileged, if this privilege is based on a commercial connection with a third state. The other Member State must participate in this decision. As this is evidently not intended, one must assume that a company having its management headquarters outside the EU can be treated as a Member State company if its commercial connection is to the founding state. On the European Company having the same head office and registered office, cf. Art. 7 of the Regulation.

99 It is for this reason that, in the dual system, co-determination is situated in the supervisory board and not the management board. For the plans of the German legislature see Teichmann (2002-I), pp. 441 *et seq.* and Teichmann (2002-II).

who manage the company, and the others who are charged with supervision (recital 14 of the preamble). Nevertheless, the national legislatures may feel encouraged by recital 14 to introduce such distinction in their national rules implementing the one-tier system.[100]

4.2.2   Two-Tier System

The provisions of the SE Articles on the two-tier system are taken to a considerable extent from German and Austrian company law. The provisions on the dual SE system begin in Art. 39 ss. 1 s. 1 of the Regulation by giving the management organs the clear and unmistakable instruction to conduct the business of the SE on their own responsibility. This management autonomy is founded on the security of tenure of the members of the organs: they are appointed for a period fixed in the Articles (Art. 46 ss. 1 of the Regulation) and cannot be freely removed prematurely. The maximum period of office of six years seems remarkable from the point of view of German law, but is still acceptable. This applies also to the maximum six year period of office of supervisory board members. However, they cannot be removed prematurely, either (Art. 46 ss. 1 of the Regulation); this strengthens their position vis-à-vis the management organs in the exercise of their supervisory functions (Art. 40 ss. 1 of the Regulation). The latter functions are – thankfully – no longer referred to as "control", and furthermore, are distinguished clearly (Art. 40 ss. 1 s. 2 of the Regulation) from management functions. "Co-determination qua consent" is provided for in Art. 48 ss. 1 of the Regulation – with welcome flexibility as to the choice of law, in remarkable contrast to the stark catalogue of items requiring consent in Art. 72 of the Regulation 1991.

Two matters are particularly worthy of mention from the viewpoint of German corporate law. Firstly, the possibility for members of the company organs not to be appointed and removed by the supervisory board, but by the shareholders' meeting. This possibility is available at the choice of each Member State (Art. 39 ss. 2 s. 2 of the Regulation). This could be significant for an SE which is a group member – which most of the SE probably will be due to the fact that formation is only open to existing legal entities (above II. 2).

Secondly, the SE's articles may provide that companies or other legal persons may be members of the management and supervisory organs of an SE (Art. 47 ss. 1 s. 1 of the Regulation). In some jurisdictions, for example, France, this is already possible.[101] Providing this possibility remains reserved to each Member State.

4.2.3   Liability of the Company Organs

The Regulation refers the question of the liability of members of the organs of the SE to national law (Art. 51 of the Regulation). By so doing the Council avoids creating a special regime for the SE and at the same time does not include the mandatory joint

---

100 For Germany see the discussion draft on the act of the implementation of the SE (printed in AG 2003, pp. 204 et seq.), commented by Neye/Teichmann (2003); especially on the one-tier system (with further references to the discussion in Germany): Teichmann (2004).

101 See Guyon (2001), pp. 325 et seq.

liability of all organ members for their own misconduct and that of others which was contained in the 1991 draft. By referring to the liability provisions of the Member States, the possibility is provided at least in Germany, to distribute tasks and responsibilities sensibly according to function and specialities and to attribute liability only to the organ member for his own misconduct. The same applies to members of the monistic administrative organ.

4.3 Legal Sources

In contrast to the first draft the present Regulation with 70 articles is concise and confined, because it does not itself regulate many issues, but refers them to the national law of each Member State in which an SE is registered. This applies, for example, to the law on capital contributions and maintenance of capital (Art. 5 of the Regulation), and to accountancy and publicity (Art. 61 f. of the Regulation). The influence of this referral is made clear by the fact that Art. 5 of the Regulation at the same time transfers responsibility completely to the Member States for the entire law on capital increases and reductions, though the second EEC Capital Directive was a precursor on this point. Moreover, European law leaves to the Member States a certain degree of discretion in implementing the SE: Not only needs the directive to be transformed by its very legal nature, but also does the regulation – which in principle is directly applicable – contain several options and instructions which may be transformed differently by each Member State.[102] Individual SE, therefore, will have as a legal basis, a sophisticated pyramid of legal layers made up of community law, national law and company specific Articles of Association. Logically, therefore, as pointed out emphatically a decade ago, there is no community wide uniform SE Articles of Association, but rather different Articles of Association from Member State to Member State.

Such a mixture of legal sources has its disadvantages. A shareholder in a foreign SE will have the same difficulty in ascertaining which law applies to the SE as a shareholder in any foreign company would have, and indeed greater difficulty, because the different national laws must be integrated with the SE Articles of Association. This will result in considerable demand for the services of expensive specialists who are versed in the law of the European Company as well as in the national company laws of at least the most important Member States, from an economic and taxation point of view. Such consultancy services are required not only for the formation of an SE, but also for its day to day business operations. A certain degree of uncertainty in the interpretation and application of the law to the actual circumstances of any SE is bound to be caused due to the variety of legal sources, national and community. This uncertainty will also be accompanied by difficult demarcation issues between the European Courts and national courts. Which is the competent court to definitively interpret a provision of company law, if it is closely interwoven with a provision in the Regulation – the national court or the ECJ?

---

102 For a state-by-state account see the collection of articles edited by Oplustil/Teichmann (2004).

4.4 Involvement of Employees

In addition to the Regulation on the company law aspects of the European Company, the European council passed a Directive on employee participation.[103] This reflects the fact that agreement on a unified model of employee involvement was not possible over many decades of negotiation. Recourse was taken to the position that it is best when the participants themselves agree upon their own model. This results in the principle of the "Primacy of Negotiation". Prior to the formation of an SE, the employer and employees must consult and agree on employee participation. If they do so successfully, the agreement applies – nothing else applies, not even the German co-determination provisions. If, however, they do not reach agreement, standard rules apply which follow the "before and after" principle. Where there was co-determination before, there will continue to be co-determination, and without affecting the level of co-determination.

In the case of a German company, this could result in the entire SE being subject to co-determination, although this applied only to the German company beforehand. The German economy is very unhappy with this solution. German companies are going around as if they had an infectious disease. It is feared that they will, therefore, have particular difficulties in forming SE with foreign partners.[104] We are much more optimistic in this respect. German companies will soon realise that negotiating co-determination is not a bad thing. There are good reasons why social partners should engage in serious negotiations. A flexible co-determination structure tailored to the individual companies could serve the interests of both sides more efficiently than the straightjacket of the existing German statutory provisions. The existing mandatory provisions left no room for negotiation. Now there is a clear field for creative solutions and we can be quite confident that German employers and trade unions will be able to make the best of it.

4.5 The Open Flank: Tax Law

The tax implications will be absolutely crucial for the acceptance of the European Company in the business world.[105] Less favourable treatment in the Member States as compared with that of national companies will result in no take-up. On the other hand, if the choice of the European Company is advantageous, a dangerous (at least in the view of some Member States) rush to the SE would result. The political line must therefore be that the tax treatment is the same for national legal forms as for the SE in the state where it is registered. The question of equal tax treatment arises in four separate areas: on the formation of the SE; in the course of its operations; on the transfer of its registered office to another state (Art. 8 of the Regulation); and on the winding up of this supranational legal form. The core tax problems are the hidden reserves, their compulsory release and consequent taxation.

The Regulation does not cover taxation matters. Consequently, the provisions of the Member States' law are applicable with regard to tax issues. There are, however,

---

103 See Heinze (2002) and Esteban Velasco (2002).
104 See Nagel (2001) on agreements to reduce the level of participation.
105 See Klapdor (2001) and Schulz/Petersen (2002).

a few provisions on the European level that try to avoid double taxation and the exposure of hidden reserves: the Parent Subsidiary Directive of 1990 applies to distributions of profit received by parent companies which come from their subsidiaries in other Member States.[106] The state of the parent company shall either exempt such profits or tax them subject to a deduction of the tax paid by the subsidiary. Moreover, the Directive on mergers, divisions, transfer of assets and exchange of shares of 1990 tries to introduce a common system of taxation for cross-border restructuring operations.[107] Each Member State shall apply the Directive to those transactions in which companies from two or more Member States are involved. The hidden reserves will not have to be exposed if a permanent establishment remains in the state where the company taking part in the restructuring operations was resident for tax purposes. Meanwhile, the European Company is mentioned in the Annex defining the scope of the Directive. However, some states, like Germany, did not yet transform the Tax Merger Directive for the simple reason that such cross-border restructuring operations were not possible under national company law. With the coming into force of the SE-Regulation this will fundamentally change, consequently such Member States will be obliged to implement the Directive.

5 The Next Step: The European Private Company

5.1 On the Application of the SE to Small and Medium-Sized Enterprises (SME)

Now that the SE Regulation is about to come into force, the question must again be asked whether the European Company is suitable as an organisational form for small and medium sized enterprises.[108] The position of the Commission and the Council is clear. By specifying, in the Regulation (Art. 4), a minimum capital of 120,000 Euro, these bodies have stated an amount which they believe make it possible for small and medium sized businesses to form a European Company (recital 13 s. 2 of the preamble). In the EU Member States, however, the minimum limit of liability prescribed for the second company form, which is that usually favoured by small and medium-sized enterprises (in Germany: the GmbH), is not more than 30,000 Euro. That the SE provides for a multiple of this figure by four can lead only to the conclusion that the European Company is intended to be fit for a stock exchange quotation, i.e. its statute is directed towards the capital markets.

Other factors also apply: as is the case with the German *Aktiengesellschaft* (para. 23 ss. 5 Stock Corporation Act (*Aktiengesetz*)), the European Company's contractual freedom is considerably reduced. This follows for all companies in each Member State from the provisions of Art. 9 ss. 1 b, of the Regulation, according to which the SE is subject to the provisions of its Articles of Association, in so far as the Regula-

---

106 *OJ* 1990 L 225/6; recently amended by the directive of December 22, 2003 (*OJ* 2004 L 7/41); on the amendments Brokelind (2003), pp. 451 *et seq.*

107 *OJ* 1990 L 225/1. See also the recent proposal for amendments, COM (2003) 0613 final; on this proposal Haritz/Wisniewski (2004), p. 28 *et seq.*

108 See Hommelhoff (1997), p. 2102.

tion expressly so provides which it rarely does. For European Companies having their registered offices in Germany, this general rule will be strengthened by the fact that Art. 9 ss. 1 c (iii) of the Regulation extends the provisions of para. 23 ss. 5 *Aktiengesetz* to SE resident in Germany. This wide application deprives small and medium businesses in Germany and elsewhere in the community of the possibility of adjusting their Articles of Association precisely to their own situations, their activities, their financial requirements and their shareholder composition.

In addition, the expense of obtaining the advice necessary for the SE as an organisational form will present difficulty for small and medium sized businesses, as well as the legal uncertainties which are of greater significance for small and medium sized businesses than for major companies and groups precisely because they concern issues which relate to the core activities of small and medium businesses and not merely to marginal activities.

5.2 The European Private Company: A Flexible Legal Form for SME in Europe

It follows from the above that medium sized enterprises – just as the global players – require a supranational legal form, tailored to their needs, to enable them to participate in the internal market on the way to a currency and economic union, and that means that it be characterised by structural freedom. After the SE, there must now be energetic concentration on the preparatory work for the European Private Company (EPC),[109] even on the grounds of competitive equality. The draft statute drafted by a group of practitioners and academics from several European countries provides the following advantages for SME: it is an organisational form based exclusively on European law and leaves the most freedom possible to the Articles of Association drafted by the partners of the company. It thereby allows uniform structures and even hierarchies for SME with Europe-wide activities. The uniformity of the legal form enables a uniform steering and controlling of all subsidiaries in a corporate group. Moreover, the EPC is capable of creating a particular supranational corporate identity and thereby can help to break down prejudices among employees, customers and particularly local authorities. In addition, the EPC provides particular advantages for the legal design of joint-ventures since one does not have to fall back on the different national laws. Instead the parties to the joint venture are free to design their own company by way of agreeing on tailor-made Articles of Association.

If, at the level of the community and the Member States, only the European Company project was completed, without creating also a European Private Company, a legal structural advantage would be created in favour of major companies and groups and the international capital demand in the internal market and later in the economic union, as against smaller and medium-range businesses. This would prejudice the latter, although such businesses contribute the overwhelming proportion of gross national product in all Member States.[110] While the creation of the European Company

---

109 See CREDA (1997), Boucourechliev/Hommelhoff (1999), Drury (2001), Helms (1998), Hommelhoff/Helms (2001).

110 See the imposing figures in Drury/Hicks in Boucourechliev/Hommelhoff (1999), p. 90 note 81. In addition, for some EU Member States, the SE is of little significance because of the limited size of

significantly simplifies access for major companies and groups to the entire internal market, the smaller and medium-sized businesses will continue to be confronted by the immaterial restrictions on establishment which the unfamiliar legal forms in other states present for them.

In April 1999 the then EU commissioner responsible, *Mario Monti*, stated in Paris "I think that the European Private Company can be a solution, which should be implemented, not in the place of the European Company..., but at its side, so that all businesses in the Union – and not only the public limited-liability companies – obtain the means they require to develop in the economic and currency union". The High Level Group of Company Law Experts set up by the European Commission in September 2001 conducted a consultation process on questions of European Company Law, including the European Private Company which received wide response. The report of the High Level Expert Group was issued on November 4, 2002. The Group acknowledges that the desire to have an EPC statute to serve the needs of SME in Europe has been clearly and repeatedly expressed. Respondents to the consultation document raised the cost argument, in particular. The costs for legal advice when setting up a subsidiary operation in various Member States would be greatly reduced if the legal form of the subsidiaries in all Member States were the same. The Group therefore recommended that the European Commission carry out a feasibility study in order to assess the additional practical need for – and problems related to – the introduction of an EPC statute. The EU Commission in its Plan to Move Forward[111] listed the feasibility studies within the measures to be performed in the short term period until 2005.

BIBLIOGRAPHY: *Altmeppen*, ZIP 2001, *p. 1073; Assmann*, AG 1995, *p. 563; Assmann/ Basaldua/Bozenhardt/Peltzer*, Übernahmeangebote, *1990; Blanquet*, Revue du Droit de l'Union Européenne 2001, *p. 65; Baudisch/Götz*, AG 2001, *p. 251; Behrens*, in: *Immenga/ Möschel/Reuter (eds.)*, Festschrift Mestmäcker, *1996, p. 831; Biener*, WPg 1993, *p. 707; Blaurock*, in: *Berger/Ebke/Elsing/Großfeld/Kühne (eds.)*, Festschrift Sandrock, *2000, p. 79; Boucourechliev/Hommelhoff*, Vorschläge für eine Europäische Privatgesellschaft, *1999 (in French:* CREDA, Propositions pour une société fermée européenne, *1997); Brokelind*, European Taxation 2003, *p. 451; Busse von Colbe*, DB 2002, *p. 1530; Colombani/Favero*, Societas Europaea – La société européenne, *2002; Dreher*, JZ 1997, *p. 167; Drury*, in: *Neville/ Sørensen*, The Internationalisation of Companies and Company Law, *2001, p. 53; Duden*, in: *Fischer/Hefermehl (eds.)*, Festschrift Schilling, *1973, p. 309; Ebenroth/Rapp*, DWiR 1991, *p. 2; Ebke/Traub*, EWS 2002, *p. 335; Eidenmüller*, ZIP 2002, *p. 2233; Forum Europaeum Konzernrecht*, ZGR 1998, *p. 672 (in English:* EBOR 2000 *p. 203; in French:* Rev. Soc. 1999, *p. 43; in Spanish:* Revista de Derecho Mercantil 1999, *p. 445); Esteban Velasco*, Rev. de derecho de sociedades 2001, *p. 141; Esteban Velasco* in: Derecho de sociedades, *Libro Homenaje al Profesor Fernando Sánchez Calero, 2002, p. 1677; Goyens*, CMLR 1992, *p. 71; Grundmann/Möslein*, BKR 2002, *p. 758; Grundmann/Möslein*, ZVglRWiss 2003, *p. 289; Grunewald*, AG 2001, *p. 288; Guyon*, Droit des Affaires, *11th ed., 2001; Habersack*, Europäisches Gesellschaftsrecht, *2nd ed., 2003; Hahn*, Die feindliche Übernahme von Aktiengesellschaften, *1992; Halbhuber*, ZEuP 2002, *p. 236; Harbarth*, ZIP 2002, *p. 321;*

---

their companies, while the significance for other states with many major companies active throughout Europe and world-wide, is much greater. Paulina Dejmek/Lund has thankfully referred to this discrepancy.

111 See above note 2.

Haritz/Wisniewski, GmbHR 2004, *p. 28; Harrer/Grabowski*, DStR 1992, *p. 1326; Heinze*, ZGR 2002, *p. 66; Heiss*, ZEuP 1996, *p. 625; Helms*, Die Europäische Privatgesellschaft, *1998; Herkenroth*, Konzernierungsprozesse im Schnittfeld von Konzernrecht und Übernahmerecht, *1994; Hirte*, NZG 2002, *p. 1; Hommelhoff, in: Goerdeler/Hommelhoff/ Lutter/Wiedemann (eds.)*, Festschrift Fleck, *1988, p. 125; Hommelhoff*, ZGR 1992, *p. 422; Hommelhoff, in: Müller-Graff (ed.)*, Gemeinsames Privatrecht in der Europäischen Gemeinschaft, *1993, p. 287 (cited as: Hommelhoff (1993-I)); Hommelhoff, in: Bierich/ Hommelhoff/Kropff (eds.)*, Festschrift Semler, *1993, p. 455 (cited as: Hommelhoff (1993-II)); Hommelhoff*, Verbraucherschutz im System des deutschen und europäischen Privatrechts, *1996; Hommelhoff*, WM 1997, *p. 2101; Hommelhoff, in: Hartkamp/Heeselink/Hondius/ Joustra/Perron (eds.)*, Towards a European Civil Code, 2nd ed., *1998; Hommelhoff*, AG 2001, *p. 279; Hommelhoff/Helms*, Neue Wege in die Europäische Privatgesellschaft, *2001; Hommelhoff/Kleindiek*, AG 1990, *p. 106; Hommelhoff/Teichmann*, SZW/RSDA 2002, *p. 1; Hommelhoff/Witt*, RIW 2001, *p. 561; Hopt*, ZGR 1992, *p. 265; van Hulle*, EWS 2000, *p. 521; Kiesewetter*, ZIP 2003, *p. 1638; Kilian*, NJW 2003, *p. 2653; Kindler/Horstmann*, DStR 2004, *p. 866; Kirchner*, AG 1999, *p. 481; Klapdor*, EuZW 2001, *p. 677; Klein*, NJW 1997, *p. 2085; Kolvenbach*, DB 1983, *p. 2235; Krause*, NJW 2002, *p. 705 (cited as: Krause (2002-I)); Krause*, BB 2002, *p. 1053 (cited as: Krause (2002-II)); Krause*, NJW 2002, *p. 2747 (cited as: Krause (2002-III)); Krause*, BB 2002, *p. 2341 (cited as: Krause (2002-IV)); Krause*, BB 2004, *p. 113; Letzel*, BKR 2002, *p. 293; Lutter*, Europäisches Unternehmensrecht, 2nd ed., *1984*, 4th ed., *1996; Lutter*, BB 2002, *p. 1; Lutter*, BB 2003, *p. 7; Lutter/Overath, in: Lutter (ed.)*, Konzernrecht im Ausland, *1994, p. 229; Di Marco*, ZGR 1999, *p. 3; Maul/Teichmann/Wenz*, BB 2003, *p. 2633; Menjucq*, Rev. Soc. 2002, *p. 225; Mertens*, AG 1990, *p. 252; Michalski*, AG 1997, *p. 152; Möllers*, ZGR 1997, *p. 334; Müller-Graff, in: id. (ed.)*, Gemeinsames Privatrecht in der Europäischen Gemeinschaft, *1993, p. 7; Nagel*, AuR 2001, *p. 406; Neye*, ZGR 1995, *p. 191; Neye*, ZGR 1999, *p. 13; Neye*, AG 2000, *p. 289; Neye*, ZIP 2001, *p. 1120; Neye*, ZGR 2002, *p. 377 (cited as: Neye (2002-I); Neye*, NZG 2002, *p. 1144 (cited as: Neye (2002-II)); Neye/Teichmann*, AG 2003, *p. 169; Niehus*, DB 2002, *p. 1385; Niessen*, WPg 1991, *p. 193; Oppermann*, Europarecht, 2nd ed., *1999; Oplustil/Teichmann*, The European Company – all over Europe, *2004; Pluskat*, WM 2001, *p. 1937 (cited as: Pluskat (2001-I)); Pluskat*, DStR 2001, *1483 (cited as: Pluskat (2001-II)); Pluskat*, EWS 2004, *p. 1; Pötzsch/ Möller*, WM Sonderbeilage No. 2/2000, *p. 1; Priester*, ZGR 1999, *p. 36; Reich*, Europäisches Verbraucherrecht, 3rd ed., *1996; Rittner*, ZGR 1990, *p. 203; Ruge*, EuZW 2002, *p. 421; Sandberger*, DZWiR 1993, *p. 319; Schilling*, ZGR 1978, *p. 415; K. Schmidt*, ZGR 1999, *p. 20; K. Schmidt*, Gesellschaftsrecht, 4th ed., *2002; Schneider/Burgard*, DB 2001, *p. 963; Schulz/Petersen*, DStR 2002, *p. 1508; Schwarz*, Europäisches Gesellschaftsrecht, *2000; Seibt/ Heiser*, ZIP 2002, *p. 2193; Spindler*, RIW 2003, *p. 850; Teichmann*, ZGR 2002, *p. 383 (cited as: Teichmann (2002-I)); Teichmann*, ZIP 2002, *p. 1109 (cited as: Teichmann (2002-II)); Teichmann*, BB 2004, *p. 53; Tonner*, JZ 1996, *p. 533; Vetter* WM 2002, *p. 1999; Wacker- barth*, WM 2001, *p. 1741; Weisner*, ZRP 2000, *p. 520; Wellige*, EuZW 2003, *p. 427; Wer- lauff*, EU Company Law, 2nd ed., *2003 (cited as: Werlauff (2003-I)); Werlauff*, SE – The Law of the European Company, *2003 (cited as: Werlauff (2003-II)); Westermann*, RabelsZ 1984, *p. 123; Wiese/Demisch*, DB 2001, *p. 849; Wiesner*, AG 1996, *p. 390; Wiesner*, ZIP 2000, *p. 1793; Windbichler*, EBOR 2000, *p. 265; Winter/Harbarth*, ZIP 2002, *p. 1; Witt*, EWS 1998, *p. 318; Wymeersch*, ZGR 2002, *p. 520; Zimmer*, BB 2003, *p. 1; Zinser*, NZG 2000, *p. 573; Zinser*, WM 2002, *p. 15; Zinser*, EuZW 2003, *p. 10; Zschocke*, DB 2002, *p. 79.*

Index

About the Authors

François Barrière

FIELD OF SPECIALISATION: French Private Law and Comparative Law. CORRESPONDENCE ADDRESS: Université Panthéon-Assas (Paris II) 92, rue d'Assas, 75006 Paris, France. E-mail: F. Barriere@wanadoo.fr

Jürgen Basedow

FIELD OF SPECIALISATION: International Private Law, European Private Competition, Transportation and Insurance Law. CORRESPONDENCE ADDRESS: Max-Planck-Institut für ausländisches und internationals Privatrecht, Mittelweg 187, D-20148 Hamburg, Germany. E-mail: professor Basedow <fuente@mpipriv-hh.mpg.de>

Klaus Berger

FIELD OF SPECIALISATION: Contract Law, Private International Law, International Commercial Arbitration Law, Banking Law, Comparative Law. CORRESPONDENCE ADDRESS: Banking Law Institute, Center for Transnational Law (CENTRAL), Universität Köln, Albertus-Magnus-Platz 1, D-50923 Köln, Germany. E-mail: kp.berger@uni-koeln.de

Gerrit Betlem

FIELD OF SPECIALISATION: European private (international) law. CORRESPONDENCE ADDRESS: University of Exeter, School of Law, Amory bld., Rennes Drive, Exeter EX4 4RJ, United Kingdom. E-mail: G.Betlem@exeter.ac.uk

Michael Joachim Bonell

FIELD OF SPECIALISATION: Comparative Law; Uniform Law; International Trade Law. CORRESPONDENCE ADDRESS: University of Rome I "La Sapienza"; Unidroit, Via Panisperna 28, Roma, I-00184 Italy. E-mail: mj.bonell@unidroit.org

Mauro Bussani

FIELD OF SPECIALISATION: Comparative Law – Private Law. CORRESPONDENCE ADDRESS: Facoltà di Giurisprudenza, Università di Trieste, Piazzale Europa, 1, 34100, Trieste. E-mail: bussanim@units.it

Claus-Wilhelm Canaris

FIELD OF SPECIALISATION: Private Law, Commercial Law, Banking Law, Labour and Employment Law and Philosophy of Law. CORRESPONDENCE ADDRESS: Institut für Privatrecht und Zivilverfahrensrecht der Universität München, Prof.-Huber-Platz 2, D-80539 München, Germany.

Eric Clive

FIELD OF SPECIALISATION: Private Law; Legislative Drafting. CORRESPONDENCE ADDRESS: The University of Edinburgh, Law School, Old College, South Bridge, Edinburgh, EH8 9YL, United Kingdom. E-mail: eric.clive@ed.ac.uk

Ulrich Drobnig

FIELD OF SPECIALISATION: Comparative Law, European Private Law, Private International Law. CORRESPONDENCE ADDRESS: Max-Planck-Institut fürausländisches und internationales Privatrecht, Mittelweg 187D-20148 Hamburg, Germany. E-mail: professor Drobnig <gross@MPIPriv-HH.mpg.de>

Sjef Erp, van

FIELD OF SPECIALISATION: Comparative and European Private Law and Comparison of the American federal experience with European integration. CORRESPONDENCE ADDRESS: Faculty of Law, Postbus 616, 6200 MD, Maastricht, the Netherlands. E-mail: S.vanErp@PR.unimaas.nl

Muriel Fabre-Magnan

FIELD OF SPECIALISATION: Contracts, Torts. CORRESPONDENCE ADDRESS: Maison des Sciences de l'Homme, 21, Boulevard Gaston Doumergue, Nantes Cedex 2, BP 76235-44262 France. E-mail: Muriel Fabre-Magnan <muriel.fabre-magnan@ wanadoo.fr>

Michael Faure

FIELD OF SPECIALISATION: Comparative Law and Private International Law. CORRESPONDENCE ADDRESS: University of Maastricht, METRO, Postbus 616, 6200 MB Maastricht, the Netherlands. E-mail: Michael.Faure@FACBURFDR.unimaas.nl

Walter Gerven, van

FIELD OF SPECIALISATION: Private Law (Contract and Torts) and European Community Law. CORRESPONDENCE ADDRESS: K.U. Leuven, Faculty of Law, Tiensestraat 41, B-3000 Leuven, Belgium. E-mail: walter.vangerven@law.kuleuven.ac.be

Roy Goode

FIELD OF SPECIALISATION: Corporate and Commercial Law International Commercial Arbitration. CORRESPONDENCE ADDRESS: The Faculty of Law, University of Oxford, St Cross Building, St Cross Road, Oxford, OX1 3UL, United Kingdom. E-mail: roy.goode@st-johns.oxford.ac.uk

James Gordley

FIELD OF SPECIALISATION: Comparative Law, Private Law, Legal History. CORRESPONDENCE ADDRESS: University of California at Berkeley, School of Law, 798 Boalt, Berkeley, CA 94720-7200, USA. E-mail: James Gordley <gordleyj@law.berkeley. edu>

Hans Christoph Grigoleit

FIELD OF SPECIALISATION: Chair of Private Law, Commercial and Corporate Law, European Private Law, University of Regensburg. CORRESPONDENCE ADDRESS: Universitätsstr. 31, D-93053 Regensburg, Germany. E-mail: christoph.grigoleit@jura. uni-regensburg.de

Michel Grimaldi

FIELD OF SPECIALISATION: Private Law. CORRESPONDENCE ADDRESS: Université Panthéon-Assas (Paris II), 12 Place du Panthéon, F-75231 Paris Cedex 05, France.

Arthur Hartkamp

FIELD OF SPECIALISATION: Dutch Private Law and Comparative Law. CORRESPONDENCE ADDRESS: De Hoge Raad der Nederlanden, P.O. Box 20303, NL-2500 EH The Hague, the Netherlands. E-mail: a.hartkamp@hogeraad.nl

Martijn Hesselink

FIELD OF SPECIALISATION: Law of Obligations, European Private Law. CORRESPONDENCE ADDRESS: Amsterdams Instituut voor Privaatrecht, Postbus 1030, 1000 BA Amsterdam, the Netherlands. E-mail: hesselink@jur.uva.nl

Viola Heutger

FIELD OF SPECIALISATION: European Private Law. CORRESPONDENCE ADDRESS: Centre for European Private Law, Molengraaff Institute, Nobelstraat 2a, NL-3512 EN Utrecht, the Netherlands. E-mail: v.heutger@law.uu.nl

Peter Hommelhoff

FIELD OF SPECIALISATION: Company Law. CORRESPONDENCE ADDRESS: Ruprecht-Karls-Universität Heidelberg, Institut für Deutsches und Europäisches Gesellschafts- und Wirtschaftsrecht, Friedrich-Ebert-Platz 2, D-69117 Heidelberg, Germany. E-mail: peter.hommelhoff@urz.uni-heidelberg.de

Ewoud Hondius

FIELD OF SPECIALISATION: Consumer Protection; Contract Law; Tort Law. CORRESPONDENCE ADDRESS: Centre for European Private Law, Molengraaff Institute, Nobelstraat 2a, NL-3512 EN Utrecht, the Netherlands. E-mail: e.hondius@law.uu.nl

David Howarth

FIELD OF SPECIALISATION: Tort, Comparative Law, Economic Analysis of Law, Sociology of Law, Environmental Law. CORRESPONDENCE ADDRESS: Clare College, Trinity Lane, GB-Cambridge CB2 1TL, United Kingdom. E-mail: David Howarth <drh20@cam.ac.uk>

Geraint Howells

FIELD OF SPECIALISATION: Consumer Law, Private Law, Comparative Law. CORRESPONDENCE ADDRESS: The University of Sheffield, Department of Law, Crookesmoor Building, Conduit Road, GB-Sheffield S10 1 FL, United Kingdom. E-mail: G.Howells@Sheffield.ac.uk

Richard Hyland

FIELD OF SPECIALISATION: Contract Law, Commercial Law, Comparative Law. CORRESPONDENCE ADDRESS: School of Law, Rutgers University, 217 N. Fifth St., Camden NJ 08102 USA. E-mail: hyland@camden.rutgers.edu

Christoph Jeloschek

FIELD OF SPECIALISATION: European Private Law. CORRESPONDENCE ADDRESS: Centre for European Private Law, Molengraaff Institute, Nobelstraat 2a, NL-3512 EN Utrecht, the Netherlands. E-mail: c.jeloschek@law.uu.nl

Christian Joerges

FIELD OF SPECIALISATION: European Economic and Private Law, Private International Law, Transnational and European Governance, Compliance, Risk Regulation and Standardisation, History of Integration Concepts. CORRESPONDENCE ADDRESS: European University Institute, Law Department, Via Boccaccio 121, I-50133 Firenze, Italy. E-mail: Christian Joerges <christian.joerges@iue.it>

Konstantinos Kerameus

FIELD OF SPECIALISATION: Civil Procedure, Private International and Foreign Law. CORRESPONDENCE ADDRESS: Hellenic Institute of International and Foreign Law, Solonos St. 73, GR-10679 Athens, Greece. E-mail: hiifl@ath.forthnet.gr

Ole Lando

FIELD OF SPECIALISATION: Comparative Law and Conflicts of Law. CORRESPONDENCE ADDRESS: Skovlodden 26, DK 2840 Holte, Denmark. E-mail: Ole Lando <ol.jur@cbs.dk>

Pierre Legrand

FIELD OF SPECIALISATION: Comparative Law. CORRESPONDENCE ADDRESS: 10 bis, rue Vavin, 75006 Paris, France. E-mail: Legrand <P.Legrand295@wanadoo.fr>

Yves-Henri Leleu

FIELD OF SPECIALISATION: Family Law, Family Property Law, Comparative Law, Notarial Law, Bioethics and Medical Law. CORRESPONDENCE ADDRESS: Université de Liège, Faculté de Droit, 7 Boulevard du Rectorat Bâtiment B31, Sart Tilman, B-4000 Liège, Belgium. E-mail: yh.leleu@ulg.ac.be

Marco Loos

FIELD OF SPECIALISATION: European Private Law, Consumer Law, Services. CORRESPONDENCE ADDRESS: Universiteit van Amsterdam, Faculteit der Rechtsgeleerdheid, Postbus 1030, 1000 BA, Amsterdam. E-mail: loos@jur.uva.nl

Brigitta Lurger

FIELD OF SPECIALISATION: Comparative Law, Law of Contract, Consumer Protection Law, Property Rights in Movables, European Private Law, EC-Competition and - Antitrust Law, Conflict of Laws. CORRESPONDENCE ADDRESS: Institut für Zivilrecht, Ausländisches und Internationales Privatrecht, Rechtswissenschaftliche Fakultät Karl-Franzens-Universität Graz, Universitätsstraße 15 D4, A-8010 Graz, Austria. E-mail: brigitta.lurger@uni-graz.at

Hector MacQueen

FIELD OF SPECIALISATION: Scottish Legal History, Intellectual Property and Technology, Contract, Delict, Unjustified Enrichment. CORRESPONDENCE ADDRESS: Edinburgh Law School, University of Edinburgh, "Law School, Old College South Bridge", Edinburgh EH8 9YL, United Kingdom. E-mail: Hector MacQueen <eusl07 @srv0.law.ed.ac.uk>

Dieter Martiny

FIELD OF SPECIALISATION: German Civil Law, Comparative Law; Private International Law. CORRESPONDENCE ADDRESS: Europa-Unversitaet Viadrana, Grosse Scharrnstr. 59, 15230 Frankfurt (Oder), Germany. E-mail: Prof. Dieter Martiny <martiny@euv-frankfurt-o.de>

Ugo Mattei

FIELD OF SPECIALISATION: Comparative Law, Economics and Law, European Community Law. CORRESPONDENCE ADDRESS: University of California, Hastings College of Law, San Francisco, California 94102-4978, USA. E-mail: umattei@cisi.unito.it

Horatia Muir Watt

FIELD OF SPECIALISATION: International Private Law, Comparative Law, Law of Obligations. CORRESPONDENCE ADDRESS: Université Panthéon-Sorbonne (Paris I) 12, Place du Panthéon, 75005 Paris, France. E-mail: HMUIRWATT@aol.com

Peter-Christian Müller-Graff

FIELD OF SPECIALISATION: Private Law, Commercial and Economic Law, Law of the European Communities and the European Union, Comparative Law. CORRESPONDENCE ADDRESS: Ruprecht-Karls-Universität Heidelberg, Institut für Gesellschafts- und Wirtschaftsrecht, Friedrich-Ebert-Platz 2, D-69117, Heidelberg, Germany. E-mail: p.mueller-graff@urz.uni-heidelberg.de

Vernon V. Palmer

FIELD OF SPECIALISATION: Comparative Law, Civil Law, French Law, Obligations, Delict, European Legal Studies. CORRESPONDENCE ADDRESS: Tulane Law School, 6329 Freret St. New Orleans, La. 70118, USA. E-mail: vpalmer@law.tulane.edu

Christina Ramberg

FIELD OF SPECIALISATION: Private Law, Commercial contract law, Sales, Export Law, Electronic Commerce. CORRESPONDENCE ADDRESS: Göteborg University, Handelshögskolan, P.O. Box 650, Göteborg, SE-405 30 Sweden. E-mail: christina.ramberg@ law.gu.se

Rodolfo Sacco

FIELD OF SPECIALISATION: Contract Law. CORRESPONDENCE ADDRESS: Università degli studi di Torino, Via Sant'Ottavio, 20, I-Torino 10124, Italy. E-mail: professor Sacco <benepiolacaselli@yahoo.com>

Ruth Sefton-Green

FIELD OF SPECIALISATION: Comparative Law, Private Law. CORRESPONDENCE ADDRESS: Département de Droit Comparé, Université Paris I, Panthéon-Sorbonne, 12 Place du Panthéon, 75005 Paris, France.

Denis Tallon

FIELD OF SPECIALISATION: French Civil Law, Comparative Law. CORRESPONDENCE ADDRESS: Université Panthéon-Assas (Paris II), 12 Place du Panthéon, F-75231 Paris Cedex 05, France.

Christoph Teichmann

FIELD OF SPECIALISATION: German and European Company and Economic Law. CORRESPONDENCE ADDRESS: Ruprecht-Karls-Universität, Institut für Deutsches and Europäisches Gesellschafts- und Wirtschaftsrecht, Friedrich-Ebert-Platz 2, D-69117 Heidelberg, Germany. E-mail: christoph.teichmann@urz.uni-heidelberg.de

Noah Vardi

FIELD OF SPECIALISATION: Comparative Law, European Private Law. CORRESPONDENCE ADDRESS: University of Rome, Dipartimento di studi giuridici, Via Ostiense 161, Roma 00154, Italy.

Alain Verbeke

FIELD OF SPECIALISATION: Contracts, Family Property Law, Notary Law, Conflict of Laws, Comparative Law. CORRESPONDENCE ADDRESS: University of Leuven, Law Faculty, Institute for Contract Law, Tiensestraat 41, B-3000 Leuven/ Universiteit van Tilburg, Faculteit der Rechtsgeleerdheid, Postbus 90153, 5000 LE Tilburg. E-mail: alain.verbeke@law.kuleuven.ac.be

Hans Georg Wehrens

FIELD OF SPECIALISATION: European Civil Law, German Private Law. CORRESPONDENCE ADDRESS: Wilhelm-Dürr-Strasse 31, D-79117, Freiburg, Germany. E-mail: HWehrens@t-online.de

Thomas Wilhelmsson

FIELD OF SPECIALISATION: Contract Law, Tort Law, Consumer Law, European Private Law. CORRESPONDENCE ADDRESS: Department of Private Law, P.O. Box 4, 00014 University of Helsinki, Finland. E-mail: thomas.wilhelmsson@helsinki.fi

Carl-Heinz Witt

FIELD OF SPECIALISATION: German and European Company and Economic Law. CORRESPONDENCE ADDRESS: Ruprecht-Karls-Universität, Institut für Deutsches and Europäisches Gesellschafts- und Wirtschaftsrecht, Friedrich-Ebert-Platz 2, D-69117 Heidelberg, Germany. E-mail: Carl-Heinz Witt <Carl-Heinz.Witt@urz. uni-heidelberg. de>

Vincenzo Zeno-Zencovich

FIELD OF SPECIALISATION: Comparative Law, European Private Law, ITC Law, Tort Law. CORRESPONDENCE ADDRESS: University of Roma Tre, Facoltà di Giurisprudenza, Via Ostiense 161, Roma 00154, Italy. E-mail: zeno-zencovich@giur.uniroma3.it

Reinhard Zimmermann

FIELD OF SPECIALISATION: Law of Obligations in Historical and Comparative Perspective; German Private Law; History of European Private Law; Mixed Legal Systems. CORRESPONDENCE ADDRESS: Max-Planck-Institut für ausländisches und internationales privatrecht, Mittelweg 187, D-20148 Hamburg, Germany. E-mail: r.zimmermann@mpipriv-hh.mpg.de

847